DESIGN FOR

UNDERSTANDING
MUSIC

by A. VERNE WILSON

To Billie, Arthur,
Terry Jean,
Jim and Bob

Contents

Illustrations

Literature

Preface

During the present decade two potent forces coming together have served as the inspiration for writing *Design for Understanding Music*. The first of these has been the need to provide challenging educational experiences for the intellectually gifted, and a general consensus that our national survival may well depend upon the kind of college education we are able to provide for our youth. A corollary has been the re-evaluation of the kinds of high school educational experiences being provided for college-bound students.

The second of these forces has been the increased attention which music educators have given to providing music experiences in depth for high school students not participating in performing groups but desiring an opportunity to develop some knowledge, understanding and appreciation of music. A typical example of this latter concern is to be found in the experience of the Portland, Oregon, Public Schools.

During the 1957-1958 school year, the Portland School Board initiated a project designed to evaluate high school subjects being taken by college-bound students. The Portland School District entered into a cooperative arrangement with the seven liberal arts colleges in the state: Fifty-four college professors of liberal arts subjects were to spend the entire year observing the content and the effectiveness of the curriculum for college-bound students. These professors spent their time visiting classes; having conferences with students, teachers and administrators; and conducting their own weekly conferences during which they discussed what had been observed. At the end of the year this group presented a report of their findings with recommendations. Three significant items appeared in this report—one of a general nature and the other two referring to music:

1. Since many Portland high school graduates do not attend college because of financial rather than intellectual limitations, the study should be directed to college-capable students—roughly the upper 50 percent of the high school population.
2. The fifty-four college professors stated in their report that "Music and art should be considered significant in the preparation and education of the college-capable student."
3. The report stated that the Portland high school band, orchestra and choral programs were providing a definitive contact with music and were doing an effective job of music education for students who had the musical talent and interest necessary for these courses. They pointed out, however, that there was no music available for college-capable students wishing to know something about music but who were unable to experience it through membership in a performing group. The recommendation was that a music course be provided for this group. The recommendation was approved by the administration and the school board.

The task was to develop a course in music for the intellectually capable student—roughly the upper 50 percent of the high school population—which would give him a way of entering into sympathy with the full range of Western art and music and encourage him to become a devotee. It was hoped that the student's taste would be cultivated and that his powers of discrimination would be enhanced by (a) presenting examples of the most interesting and valuable kinds of music, (b) equipping students with a basic minimum literacy in music, and (c) showing how music is constructed through listening, examining, and sounding it.

The task was accomplished through the efforts of a committee of three high school music teachers, E. Bruce Johnson, George W. Bell and Eugene J. Kaza, and Edmund A. Cykler, professor of music at the University of Oregon. The author acted as consultant to the committee. This committee worked together for two years developing the course, UNDERSTANDING MUSIC. It proposed that musical compositions of intrinsic value be heard in recordings and live performance and be examined and discussed in relation to other art forms. The course would exercise the intellect; it assumed that education is not a diversion and that a high school student who can learn physics, German, and trigonometry successfully can understand some of the intricacies of musical form and analysis and so can make more intelligent value judgments. The major goal of the course was to help the student at all times to understand better the role of music as an important member of the fine arts. The course consisted of eight units the first of which, "How We Listen," was the basic unit. Each of the succeeding units was based on the knowledge and understandings acquired in Unit One. Since there was no existing single text which met the needs of the course, it was necessary to turn to a number of supplementary reference sources.

The present book brings together in one publication the recommended literature, art and music examples deemed necessary for study in developing a basic understanding of music. It makes the same basic assumptions which the course does on the ability of the college-capable student to understand and enjoy great works of music. It too is constructed in units and Unit One is the basic unit. After completing Unit One the reader may follow his own particular interest as he meets the many and varied types of music representing the creative efforts of great composers from the Middle Ages to contemporary times.

The author wishes to make special acknowledgment of his deep gratitude to E. Bruce Johnson, George W. Bell, Eugene J. Kaza and Edmund A. Cykler for their invaluable help and suggestions in the preparation of the manuscript. Their original research and work in preparing the course made the task of writing infinitely easier.

Special acknowledgment should also be made to the following:

School District No. 1, Portland, Oregon, for permission to reproduce certain sections of copyright material from the Teachers' Manual for the course, UNDERSTANDING MUSIC.

Dr. Norman Hamilton, Assistant Superintendent of Schools, Portland, Oregon, for his friendly and helpful cooperation and advice in the development of the course, UNDERSTANDING MUSIC, and the preparation of the manuscript for this book.

Sue Parr for her invaluable help in the preparation and typing of the manuscript.

Margaret Smutz for permission to use her translations of "Christ lag in Todesbanden" and "Die Fledermaus."

A.V.W.

Acknowledgments

Credit and appreciation are due these sources for permission to use wholly or in part the following:

ART REPRODUCTIONS

Albright-Knox Art Gallery, Buffalo: *Peasants in the Field*, gift of A. Conger Goodyear.

Anderson, Beckwith and Haible and Paul Rudolph, Associated Architects, and Clemens Kalischer, Photographer: *Blue Cross-Blue Shield Building*, Boston.

The Art Institute of Chicago: *Open Window in Nice*, the Joseph Winterbotham Collection.

Art Reference Bureau, Inc., Ancram, New York: *Ceiling Fresco*, Sistine Chapel.

Boston Museum of Fine Arts: *Dance at Bougival*.

Cleveland Museum of Art: *Death on a Pale Horse*, gift of J. H. Wade.

Mrs. Jon Corbino and International Business Machines Corporation Gallery: *Harvest Festival*.

Trustees, Courtauld Institute of Art, London: *Cap d'Antibes*.

European Art Color, New York: *The Married Couple* and *Statue of Moses*, photos by Peter Adelberg.

French Government Tourist Office, Chicago, Illinois: *Basilica of Sacré Coeur, Notre Dame* and *Paintings on the Wall of a Lascaux Cave*.

Galerie Stangl, Munich: *The Red Deer*.

Hackley Art Gallery, Muskegon, Michigan: *Tornado Over Kansas*.

Henry E. Huntington Library and Art Gallery, San Marino, California, copyright owner: *The Blue Boy* (Master Jonathan Buttall).

Keystone Press Agency, Inc., New York: *Stained Glass Window*, U. S. Memorial Chapel, St. Paul's Cathedral, London.

The Metropolitan Museum of Art, New York: *Beethoven*, the Rogers Fund, 1926; *Chalice*, the Cloisters Collection, purchase 1950; *Spanish XVth Century Retable and Altar*, the Cloisters Collection, gift of J. Pierpont Morgan, 1909, purchase by Rogers Fund, 1914, and gift of Emile Pares, 1916.

Trustees, The National Gallery of Art, London: *The Nativity* and *The Virgin and Child*.

National Gallery of Art, Washington, D. C.: *The Dancing Couple*, the Widener Collection; *The Adoration of the Magi*, Andrew Mellon Collection.

New York Graphic Society, Greenwich, Connecticut: *Dancer—Study No. 1*.

The Phillips Collection, Washington, D. C.: *Maine Islands*.

Portland Art Museum, Portland, Oregon: *Chief's Headdress* from Alaskan Eskimos; *Mask Tsoneqoa* from Kwakiutl, British Columbia; *Spirit of Dead Man* and *Woman Who Told Lies*, masks from the Tlingit Tribe, Alaska.

Stedelijk Museum, Amsterdam: *Town Hall at Auvers*.

Swedish Information Service, New York: *Orpheus Fountain*.

Three Lions, Inc., New York: *American Gothic, The Crucifixion with the Virgin and Saint John, The Dancer, A Helping Hand, The Orchard, The Wedding Dance* and *Zapatistas*.

Tourist Division, New Mexico Department of Development: *Navajo Rug-Weaving, Navajo Silversmith* and *Two Gray Hills*, Navajo Indian blanket.

LITERATURE

Prologue to Canterbury Tales from *Chief British Poets of the Fourteenth and Fifteenth Century* by W. A. Neilson and K. G. T. Webster. Copyright © 1916 by Houghton Mifflin Company.

Casey Jones. Copyright © 1909 by Newton and Seibert, renewed and assigned to Shapiro, Bernstein and Company, Inc. Used by permission of Shapiro, Bernstein and Company, Inc., and Francis, Day and Hunter, Ltd.

Children and Their Art by Charles D. Gaitskell. Copyright © 1958 by Harcourt, Brace and Company.

The Congo from *Collected Poems* by Vachel Lindsay. Copyright © 1914 by The Macmillan Company, renewed 1942 by Elizabeth C. Lindsay.

Eclogue by Stéphane Mallarmé, paraphrased by Edmund Gosse, from *The Collected Essays of Edmund Gosse*, Volume VI. Used by permission of William Heinemann, Ltd.

How we listen

chapter 1

Music About Us

Music is found in all civilizations; it is a natural, spontaneous expression of peoples of all times and in all places. Music is and always has been used to enhance our most cherished, ceremonial and festive occasions—for example, marriage, commencement, religious rites, love of country, war... While music systems may differ, the fact is that all cultures employ music in this manner. A comparison of the various cultures will reveal certain common elements. A feeling of tenderness and affection inspires the lullaby whether it is sung by an American Indian or the wife of a Javanese farmer, or is composed by, say, Johannes Brahms. In the same way, love of homeland is found in the music of Russia, China, France, England, the United States and other countries.

Each generation inherits the ever-increasing accumulation of musical works from the past, and no period in the past has had a body of works as large and as varied as the present. And never before have these works been so readily and widely available. Before this century, people's experience in music was much more confined by geographical proximity, limited distribution of the printed score, and the fact that radio, television and recordings were still things of the future. These limitations, however, made for a more intensive familiarity with the music that was met. Although in the past the number of people who came into contact with art music was much smaller than now, that contact was generally based upon participation and musical literacy.

Today we are literally surrounded by music—music which is good, bad and not so bad. It is, in fact, difficult to escape from music. A traveler upon entering the air terminal is met with the strains of a Broadway musical being played over the public address system. He is even quite apt to hear this same kind of music inside the airplane while the passengers are boarding. At the supermarket strains of Drigo's "Serenade" played by a lush string orchestra

3

furnish a musical backdrop while we purchase our breakfast cereal, vegetables and the other staples of life. Because of this music we may be enticed into purchasing more than we originally planned.

Dramatic performances seen and heard in the movies, on television and on radio make copious use of music for background and for establishing emotional states. Then too, we recognize certain radio and television programs because they are introduced and have become familiar through the use of a musical signature. In this sense music might be said to be the vehicle for entertainment. Musical shows such as the Gilbert and Sullivan operas, the Broadway musical, and the operetta presented by your school are examples of this particular use of music. In this instance, a dramatic production is clothed in musical vestments in order to enhance the total effect and value of the performance.

Churches also make use of music as a means of enriching and deepening the act of worship. Music as used in the church may range from a complete and complex musical liturgy, involving a highly trained choir, to simple hymn singing by the congregation. It may be a combination of these.

A dance without some form of music, whether it is a simple rhythm played on a primitive drum or the sophisticated playing of a name orchestra, would almost be a physical impossibility. It is music which gives the beat and puts life, sparkle and spontaneity into the movements of the dance. It is music that helps define the kind of dance we are dancing or viewing. From the music we identify the dance as being a tango, a schottische, a waltz or a polka. Because the dance is a physical expression of music, our reaction to the music of the dance, as we shall see later on, is largely physical, and in this instance we literally "listen with our feet."

As we shall also see later, music is a means of expressing emotion. It is small wonder then that man has turned to music to express patriotic fervor. Through music of this type man has long been able to make known his feelings of loyalty and love of country. The patriotic songs of a country in a very real sense give us a picture of the hopes and aspirations of its people. Patriotic songs sing not only a paean of praise for the native land but also recount the exciting history of the trials and the successes that were a part of the development of the country. In our land, for example, we immediately associate the song "Yankee Doodle" with the Revolutionary War, or the "Battle Hymn of the Republic" with the Civil War period. On the other hand, songs such as our national anthem, "The Star-Spangled Banner," or songs such as "America," "America the Beautiful" and "Columbia, the Gem of the Ocean" stir our hearts with pride of country and thus reinforce the lessons of patriotism learned from other sources.

The uses of music discussed so far have been uses which have extra-musical values. That is, music is used as a vehicle or background for something else. Music can also have value for its own sake. Much of the music we hear in the concert hall is representative of this particular use of music.

It is in the concert hall that one is able to listen to the most sublime musical utterances of man—a symphony by Brahms, an opera by Wagner or a choral work such as *Belshazzar's Feast* by Walton. It is to this type of music that we wish to direct our attention in the forthcoming pages of this book.

In the concert hall we can truly make the distinction between *hearing* and *listening to* music. Our pleasure and our sensitivity to music will be enhanced if we are able to bring understanding of music to the listening process. Listening with understanding requires listening with concentration and receptivity. It implies a knowledge of the composer's intent, the elements of composition which he used to realize this purpose, and a recognition of how well the performer or performing group is able to carry out this intention.

1. Make a comprehensive list of the many ways that music is being used in your community.
2. What do you think is the role of music in our society?
3. How many ways can music be used besides for concert performance?
4. One of the characteristics of folk music is that it is a spontaneous expression of a people. Does one find such spontaneous expression today in the music of our society? If your answer is yes, give an example.
5. *a.* Do you know anyone who truly dislikes to sing, play or listen to music? *b.* What do the psychologist and psychiatrist say about the person who lacks a response to any form of beauty?
6. It has been said that a person who has played football is able to understand and enjoy the game more than a person who has not played the game. Compare this point of view with listening to a piece of music.
7. In how many ways can man contact music?

1. Chapter 1. "The Pleasures of Music," from *Copland on Music.*
2. Chapter 1. "Music All Around Us," from *Invitation to Music.* Elie Siegmeister.
3. "Introduction" to *The Joy of Music.* Leonard Bernstein.
4. Chapter 1. "Bull Session in the Rockies," from *The Joy of Music.* Leonard Bernstein.
5. Chapter 1. "The Humanism of the Arts," from *An Introduction to Music and Art.* Milo Wold and Edmund Cykler.

1. Carnival of the Animals....................Camille Saint-Saëns (1835-1921)
2. Ma Mère l'Oye................................Maurice Ravel (1875-1937)
3. Selections from *Carousel*.................Richard Rodgers & Oscar Hammerstein
4. March, "Fairest of the Fair" or "Sabre and Spurs"..John Philip Sousa (1854-1932)
5. A Mighty Fortress Is Our God.............Johann Sebastian Bach (1685-1750)
6. Clair de Lune.................................Claude Debussy (1862-1918)
7. Hoe Down from *Rodeo*.......................Aaron Copland (1900——)
8. Dave Brubeck Plays Brubeck.................Dave Brubeck (1920——)

5

6

DANCE AT BOUGIVAL, Pierre Auguste Renoir

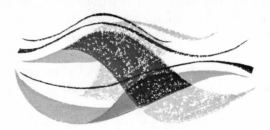

chapter 2

Man's Response to Music

Man contacts music in three ways: he performs it, he listens to it, or he creates it. No matter which way he contacts music, certain responses are elicited. In general these responses are referred to as being physical, emotional or intellectual. The ideal response is one that involves all three working together to realize all of the emotional and communicative facets of the music to which one is listening. In fact, it is rather difficult to separate man's reaction into only one or even two of these reaction elements. One reaction has a way of involving all of the other responses. But for purposes of making clear the possibilities in each type of response, let us consider each one separately and concentrate upon the particular response we are studying.

Physical Response

When man reacts physically to music he is reacting to the rhythm. In this there is little or no involvement of the emotions or the mind. It is a reaction at the most primitive level. When participating in a social dance we are more aware of the steady rhythmic beat of the dance band than we are of the melodic or harmonic elements. Someone has said that this is "listening with our feet." As we shall see later on, the rhythmic aspect of music ranges from very simple, unsophisticated rhythms to highly complex polyrhythms. We shall also see that complex rhythmic structure is not peculiar to Occidental music of the twentieth century, but can also be found in Oriental as well as ancient and primitive music.

Rhythm and response to rhythm are not peculiar to music. Rhythm is used and is reacted to in all of the fine arts. One might preface an inquiry into the use of rhythm in the arts by noting the importance, even the necessity, of rhythm in nature. Our existence is dependent upon the rhythm of nature: the coming and going of day and night, the ebb and flow of the tides, our heartbeat, our breathing—even in the act of walking rhythm is necessary.

Before we examine examples of rhythmic response to music, let us look briefly at two of the other fine arts to study the use of rhythm in each of them and see how this use affects our reaction. Often one sees the expression, "the music of poetry." One of the principal reasons why poetry is linked with music in this context is the rhythmic element inherent in poetry. Rhythm in poetry, or in any good writing, is the regular rise and fall of sound which results from an arrangement of accented and unaccented syllables. Poetry, like music, makes use of *meter*, which is defined as a regular recurrence of accented and unaccented syllables. Children may enjoy hearing poetry which they do not understand precisely because of its strong rhythm.

As a prime example of responding to the rhythm in poetry, read the following delightful poem by Lewis Carroll. Note the effect the rhythm of the nonsense syllables has on our enjoyment and reaction to this poetic bit:

Jabberwocky from
Alice in Wonderland

'Twas brillig, and the slithy toves
  Did gyre and gimble in the wabe:
All mimsy were the borogoves,
  And the mome raths outgrabe.

"Beware the Jabberwock, my son!
  The jaws that bite, the claws that catch!
Beware the Jubjub bird, and shun
  The frumious Bandersnatch!"

He took his vorpal sword in hand;
  Long time the manxome foe he sought—
So rested he by the Tumtum tree,
  And stood awhile in thought.

And, as in uffish thought he stood,
  The Jabberwock, with eyes of flame,
Came whiffling through the tulgey wood,
  And burbled as it came!

One, two! One, two! And through and through
  The vorpal blade went snicker-snack!
He left it dead, and with its head
  He went galumphing back.

"And has thou slain the Jabberwock?
  Come to my arms, my beamish boy!
O frabjous day! Callooh, Callay!"
  He chortled in his joy.

'Twas brillig, and the slithy toves
  Did gyre and gimble in the wabe:
All mimsy were the borogoves,
  And the mome raths outgrabe.   —Lewis Carroll

Also read the following fragment, noting how the strength of the poetry seems to stem from the strong rhythm of the words, rather than from the sense of the words.

The Congo

The cake-walk royalty then began
To walk for a cake that was tall as a man
To the tune of "Boomlay, boomlay, boom,"
While the witch-man laughed, with a sinister air,
And sang with the scalawags prancing there:—
"Walk with care, walk with care,
Or Mumbo-Jumbo, God of the Congo
And all of the other Gods of the Congo,
Mumbo-Jumbo will hoo-doo you.
Beware, beware, walk with care,
Boomlay, boomlay, boomlay, boom.
Boomlay, boomlay, boomlay, boom.
Boomlay, boomlay, boomlay, boom.
Boomlay, boomlay, boomlay,
Boom."
                              —Vachel Lindsay

The poetry of the first major English poet, Geoffrey Chaucer (c. 1340-1400), provides us with yet another example of responding to strong rhythm.

Prologue to
Canterbury Tales

Whan that Aprille with his shoures sote
The droghte of Marche hath perced to the rote,
And bathed every veyne in swich licour,
Of which vertu engendred is the flour;
Whan Zephirus eek with his swete breeth
Inspired hath in every holt and heeth
The tendre croppes, and the yonge sonne
Hath in the Ram his halfe cours y-ronne,
And smale fowles maken melodye,
That slepen al the night with open yë,
(So priketh hem nature in hir corages);

9

Than longen folk to goon on pilgrimages
(And palmers for to seken straunge strondes)
To ferne halwes, couthe in sondry londes;
And specially, from every shires ende
Of Engelond, to Caunterbury they wende,
The holy blisful martir for to seke,
That hem hath holpen, whan that they were seke.

—Geoffrey Chaucer

In the graphic arts we also find that man may react strongly to the rhythm of the work. The recurring use of accented and unaccented lines, curves and arcs, and color takes immediate hold of our attention and provides the basis for an immediate response which may be on a very elementary or even primitive level. Study the picture "The Nativity" by Piero della Francesca (c. 1420-1492) and identify the rhythmic factors which the artist used to help convey the message of the picture.

THE NATIVITY,
Piero della Francesca

10

Note that the repeated forms of the heads of the angels form a rhythm not unlike the scalloped edge of a piece of embroidery. The repetition of the identical shapes of the two lutes held in identical manner is also a means of depicting visual rhythm. Other evidences of rhythm are seen in the vertical folds of the robes which are repeated in opposition to the foil found in the repeated horizontal lines of the roof and brick walls of the shelter. As one studies this picture, the other visual rhythms become increasingly apparent. And here we have one means for looking at and reacting to art.

Another good example of rhythm in painting (with its attendant response) is the painting "American Gothic" by the American artist, Grant Wood (1892-1942). Again, let us examine and study it carefully to identify some of its rhythmic elements.

AMERICAN GOTHIC,
Grant Wood

First of all, note the pitchfork and its design. How many times can you find this design repeated? For example, look at the bib of the overalls, and the second floor window. Note the repetition of the circle and the dot found in the dress. How many times is the circle repeated? Note also the repeated use of horizontal lines with a foil consisting of vertical lines. Study the painting carefully and identify as many of these rhythmic elements as possible.

11

In examining the following music, listen carefully to the beat or the rhythm of the music. Focus your attention upon this one element. Because reacting to the rhythm of music implies physical response or movement, try to duplicate the rhythm of the music by either tapping your foot or softly clapping the rhythm with your hands. Listen for the pattern of accented and unaccented beats in the music, and express these accented and unaccented beats as you clap the rhythms. Also try to determine if the music swings in two, in three, in four, or in six.

1. Washington Post March......................John Philip Sousa (1854-1932)
2. Chit-Chat Polka................................Johann Strauss (1825-1899)
3. African Tribal Music and Dances...........................Sonar Senghor
4. Gold and Silver Waltz............................Franz Lehar (1870-1948)

TOPICS FOR DISCUSSION

1. How do poetry, painting and music use the element of rhythm?
2. How do we react to rhythm as expressed in poetry? In painting? In music?
3. How is the element of rhythm handled in drama? In architecture? In sculpture? In the dance?
4. One hears the statement that "a good golfer must have rhythm in his swing." Is this an accurate statement?

a. If your answer is yes, how is the use of rhythm in the golf swing analogous to the use of rhythm in music or one of the other fine arts?
b. If your answer is no, what term would you use to describe the trait listed as necessary for a good golf swing?

Emotional Response

If all of the arts have the same characteristic—expressing emotion—these emotions will be crystalized and expressed through the medium used by the creator of the work of art. In the case of the composer, it is music. In turn, the consumer, whether he is a listener or a viewer, must let the work of art involve him emotionally. In reacting emotionally to a work of art, we feel more than we think.

The consumer, reacting to the emotional impact of a work of art, may feel that it represents any one of many emotional states. It may be merry, playful, serene, tender, noble. Or it may have overtones of charm, religious fervor, nostalgia, love, humor ... While no two people may have the same exact emotional reaction, it is doubtful that their reactions to the same stimulus would be diametrically opposed to one another. For example, it is rather doubtful that one person would feel the mood of the Scherzo from Beethoven's *Seventh Symphony* was happy while another person would classify its mood as sad. While they might use different words to describe the mood, there would be a relationship to the emotional state being expressed.

In poetry, emotional climate is often established by the imagery created by certain emotionally charged words. Read the following poem and describe the mood or emotion evoked:

12

Lost

Desolate and lone
All night long on the lake
Where fog trails and mist creeps,
The whistle of a boat
Calls and cries unendingly,
Like some lost child
In tears and trouble
Hunting the harbor's breast
And the harbor's eyes.

—Carl Sandburg
(1878———)

There may be some who will feel that the mood of this poetry is one of sadness. Others may feel loneliness as the emotion. Still others may be moved by the desolation and bleakness of the poetry. There is little chance that anyone would feel that the mood was one of happiness. Note how the author used certain emotionally charged words to heighten the feeling of loneliness—words such as "desolate," "all night long," "fog trails," "lost child."

Let us look at another poem and attempt to discover the mood which the author is communicating.

O Captain! My Captain!

O Captain! my Captain! our fearful trip is done,
The ship has weather'd every rack, the prize we sought is won,
The port is near, the bells I hear, the people all exulting,
While follow eyes the steady keel, the vessel grim and daring;
  But O heart! heart! heart!
  O the bleeding drops of red,
  Where on the deck my Captain lies,
  Fallen cold and dead.

O Captain! my Captain! rise up and hear the bells;
Rise up—for you the flag is flung—for you the bugle trills,
For you bouquets and ribbon'd wreaths—for you the shores
        a-crowding,
For you they call, the swaying mass, their eager faces turning;
  Here Captain! dear father!
  The arm beneath your head!
  It is some dream that on the deck,
  You've fallen cold and dead.

13

My Captain does not answer, his lips are pale and still,
My father does not feel my arm, he has no pulse nor will,
The ship is anchor'd safe and sound, its voyage closed and done,
From fearful trip the victor ship comes in with object won:
    Exult O shores and ring O bells!
    But I with mournful tread,
    Walk the deck my Captain lies,
    Fallen cold and dead.

                    —Walt Whitman
                     (1819-1892)

What is the mood of this poem? What is the story back of it? What are some of the key words which help to convey the mood?

Here is a poem completely different from the two poems we have just studied. The emotional reaction we have to it will be definitely different from the emotional reaction we have had to the two poems above. Read it and determine its mood.

The Society
Upon the Stanislaus

I reside at Table Mountain, and my name is
    Truthful James;
I am not up to small deceit, or any sinful games;
And I'll tell in simple language what I know about the
    row
That broke up our Society upon the Stanislow.

But first I would remark, that it is not a proper plan
For any scientific gent to whale his fellow-man,
And, if a member don't agree with his peculiar whim,
To lay for that same member for to "put a head" on
    him.

Now nothing could be finer or more beautiful to see
Than the first six months' proceedings of that same
    Society,
Till Brown of Calaveras brought a lot of fossil bones
That he found within a tunnel near the tenement of
    Jones.

14

Then Brown he read a paper, and he reconstructed
    there,
From those same bones, an animal that was extremely
    rare;
And Jones then asked the Chair for a suspension of the
    rules,
Till he could prove that those same bones was one
    of his lost mules.

Then Brown he smiled a bitter smile, and said he was
    at fault,—
It seemed he had been trespassing on Jones's family
    vault:
He was a most sarcastic man, this quiet Mr. Brown,
And on several occasions he had cleaned out the town.

Now I hold it is not decent for a scientific gent
To say another is an ass,—at least, to all intent;
Nor should the individual who happens to be meant
Reply by heaving rocks at him, to any great extent.

Then Abner Dean of Angel's raised a point of order—
    when
A chunk of old red sandstone took him in the abdomen,
And he smiled a kind of sickly smile, and curled up
    on the floor,
And the subsequent proceedings interested him no more.

For, in less time than I write it, every member did
    engage
In a warfare with the remnants of a palaeozoic age;
And the way they heaved those fossils in their anger
    was a sin,
Till the skull of an old mammoth caved the head of
    Thompson in.

And this is all I have to say of these improper games,
For I live at Table Mountain, and my name is Truthful
    James;
And I've told in simple language what I know about
    the row
That broke up our Society upon the Stanislow.

—*Francis Brett Harte (1836-1902)*   15

We see, therefore, that poetry may range from moods of desolation and sadness to moods of gay good humor. And all ranges of human emotion between these two extremes can be portrayed.

This same quality may also be found in painting. It is possible when viewing a work of art to sense just what the artist is trying to say to us.

How does the artist communicate emotion to the viewer? Or more properly, how do we receive an emotional impact in viewing a painting? One way might be from the subject matter, suggestive of a strong emotion. In the painting "The Wedding Dance" by Pieter Brueghel (1520-1569), one finds an excellent example of mood—one in which the mood is first suggested by the subject matter of the painting. The artist used several devices to help convey mood, such as rhythm, shapes, the arrangement of the dancers into a circle, and bright colors to convey a feeling of gaiety and happiness. However, the subject matter of the painting itself provides us with a confident starting point in determining the mood of this particular painting.

THE WEDDING
DANCE,
Pieter Brueghel,
The Elder

Now examine the painting of the American painter, John Steuart Curry (1897-1946), entitled "Tornado Over Kansas." Note its mood of violence and terror. Observe also how the tornado funnel and the figure of the big, red-headed father seem to dominate the composition.

16

TORNADO OVER KANSAS, John Steuart Curry

For a feeling of the mysterious and the unearthly let us turn our attention to the painting "Death on a Pale Horse" by Albert Pinkham Ryder (1847-1917). The dark and shadowy forms, the somber colors and the absence of living things combine to suggest that we may be glimpsing a scene in the underworld.

DEATH ON A PALE HORSE, Albert Pinkham Ryder

Music, too, has the power to project and communicate mood. While the painting "Death on a Pale Horse" is fresh in our mind let us listen to a musical composition which might be said to have a similar mood value. It is "Danse Macabre" by Camille Saint-Saëns (1835-1921). Again, the subject matter is death, more specifically the rite which occurs on All Saints' Eve when skeletons and ghosts get together for a dance. The composition begins with the clock striking twelve; then death tunes his fiddle. There follows the dance which lasts to the crow of the cock—the signal for all to return to the grave for another year. Note the "gruesome" strain which furnishes the musical basis for the dance. Compare also the poem of Henri Cazalis (1840-1909) which was the inspiration for Saint-Saëns' "Danse Macabre."

18

Danse Macabre

On a sounding stone,
With a blanched thigh-bone,
The bone of a saint, I fear,
Death strikes the hour
Of his wizard power,
And the specters haste to appear.

From their tombs they rise
In sepulchral guise,
Obeying the summons dread,
And gathering round
With obeisance profound,
They salute the King of the Dead.

Then he stands in the middle
And tunes up his fiddle,
And plays them a gruesome strain.
And each gibbering wight
In the moon's pale light
Must dance to that wild refrain.

Now the fiddle tells,
As the music swells,
Of the charnal's ghastly pleasures;
And they clatter their bones
As with hideous groans
They reel to those maddening measures.

The churchyard quakes
And the old abbey shakes
To the tread of that midnight host,
And the sod turns black
On each circling track,
Where a skeleton whirls with a ghost.

The night wind moans
In shuddering tones
Through the gloom of the cypress tree,
While the mad rout raves
Over yawning graves
And the fiddle bow leaps with glee.

So the swift hours fly
Till the reddening sky
Gives warning of daylight near.
Then the first cock crow
Sends them huddling below
To sleep for another year.   —*Henri Cazalis*

19

Does the music of Saint-Saëns catch the mood of this poetry? Is the music a literal translation of the poem?

The music of Dmitri Shostakovich (1906———) provides us with a wonderful example of wit and humor in music. Listen to "Polka" from his *Golden Age Ballet* and see if you can keep from smiling as the composer pulls his musical "jokes." One must be careful not to laugh too long or too loud for fear of missing the next one.

Pathos, despair, melancholy and grief are the moods communicated to us in the fourth movement of the *Symphony Pathétique* (No. 6 in B minor) by Peter Ilyich Tchaikovsky (1840-1893). We sense a feeling of utter dejection and a tortured soul crying for release in the downward pouring of the poignant melody around which the movement is constructed. It would seem that this music plumbs the dark depths of despair.

TOPICS FOR DISCUSSION

1. What is mood?
2. What are some of the moods which may be expressed in fiction? In essays? In poetry?
3. What are some of the moods which may be expressed in painting? In sculpture?
4. Is it possible to react emotionally to architecture?
5. What are some of the moods which may be expressed in music?

ADDITIONAL CLASS ACTIVITIES

1. Read several of the following examples from literature and discuss the mood of each.

Fog ....Carl Sandburg (1878———)
The Pit and the Pendulum......................Edgar Allan Poe (1809-1849)
A Dissertation on Roast Pig......................Charles Lamb (1775-1834)
Much Ado About Nothing...................William Shakespeare (1564-1616)
Tale of Two Cities.............................Charles Dickens (1812-1870)
How Do I Love Thee?......................Elizabeth Browning (1806-1861)

2. Examine several of the following paintings and discuss the mood of each.

Liberty Leading the People.....................Eugène Delacroix (1799-1863)
Arab Rider Attacked by Lion.............................Eugène Delacroix
In the Meadow..........................Pierre Auguste Renoir (1841-1919)
The Tempest................................Oskar Kokoschka (1886———)
Third Class Carriage.........................Honoré Daumier (1808-1879)
The Angelus.............................Jean François Millet (1814-1875)
The Peaceable Kingdom........................Edward Hicks (1780-1849)
Landscape With Ploughed Fields..............Vincent van Gogh (1853-1890)

3. Listen to several of the following examples of music and discuss the mood of each.

Overture to *Romeo and Juliet*............Peter Ilyich Tchaikovsky (1840-1893)
Valse Triste.....................................Jean Sibelius (1865-1957)
Toccata and Fugue in D Minor............Johann Sebastian Bach (1685-1750)
Revolutionary Etude...........................Frédéric Chopin (1810-1849)
Fingal's Cave Overture......................Felix Mendelssohn (1809-1847)
Golliwog's Cake-Walk from *Children's Corner Suite*...Claude Debussy (1862-1918)
The Sorcerer's Apprentice.........................Paul Dukas (1865-1935)

Intellectual Response

In responding to a work of art, there comes a time when there is a need to involve the consumer's intellectual faculties. He may be moved by the insistent pulse of the rhythm of the composition or he may feel deeply the emotional message of the art work. But he may also respond to certain intellectual aspects which help to strengthen the communicative force of words, mass, paint or music. The artist's use of line, shape, color, scale, texture or form; the writer's use of words, rhythm, imagery, phrase or form; and the composer's use of rhythm, melody, harmony, timbre or form are all keys to the way in which the intellect is involved in reacting intellectually to a work of art. A work of art will have a content of its own which is unique and individual and which can be revealed through an analysis of the materials which its creator used. Simply stated, observing and studying these elements constitute the process of responding intellectually.

While there are no absolute analogies between the arts, there are strong similarities. If we are able to see and understand the process in one art, this understanding can be helpful in developing an understanding in another medium. So it is with the intellectual response. If we understand the implications of the intellectual response in one art, we are in a better position to understand the role of the intellect in another art. Before we turn to music, let us turn to literature and painting and examine some of the elements to consider when using our intellectual powers in responding to an aesthetic experience.

In analyzing literature, in addition to determining the meaning which connotes emotional response, one should also be able to analyze in rather precise terms the formal and technical structure used by the writer to strengthen his communicative powers. One looks at the various devices which the author has used to achieve unity, coherence and variety. It is also possible to determine how the writer develops words, phrases, sentences and paragraphs into extended form. In prose, the total action may be strengthened through a wise division of the work into significant sections called chapters. In drama it is possible to compare scene for scene, act for act. To react intellectually to a drama, a person analyzes the total work into the elements of the *exposition* or the introduction of the situation and the attendant characters; the section on the rising action or the *complication*; the arrival at the *climax*, sometimes referred to as the crisis; and finally the resolving of the crisis through the falling action which has the term *dénouement*—the French word meaning "untying." When responding intellectually to poetry, we may examine the rhyme scheme, the meter, the number of feet in a line, the form, the precise meaning of words, and myriad other elements which the poet may bring to bear to express himself better. From this it can be seen that man may react intellectually to a given work of art through an examination of the technical structure.

Let us examine carefully the following stanza, a fragment from a larger work, to learn just how the poet achieved his purpose.

Childe Harold

There is a pleasure in the pathless woods,   *(a)*
There is a rapture on the lonely shore,   *(b)*
There is society, where none intrudes,   *(a)*
By the deep sea, and music in its roar;   *(b)*
I love not man the less, but nature more,   *(b)*
From these our interviews, in which I steal   *(c)*
From all I may be, or have been before,   *(b)*
To mingle with the universe, and feel   *(c)*
What I can ne'er express, yet cannot all conceal.   *(c)*

—Lord Byron
(1788-1824)

In terms of meaning, Lord Byron seems to be saying that there is a universal truth in nature which is apart from society. There is also the thought that an affinity for nature cannot be expressed in words but is something which is felt.

But what about the formal structure? A close examination will reveal several interesting facts. We note that there are nine lines with a rhyme scheme of a b a b b c b c c. An examination of the meter reveals that the first eight lines are iambic pentameter, because each line consists of five feet of an unaccented syllable followed by an accented syllable. Thus:

$$u \quad / \quad u \quad / \quad u \quad / \quad u \quad / \quad u \quad /$$
There is / a plea / sure in / the path / less woods /

The ninth line is iambic hexameter, because the line consists of six feet of an unaccented syllable followed by an accented syllable. Thus:

$$u \quad / \quad u \quad / \quad u \quad / \quad u \quad / \quad u \quad / \quad u \quad /$$
What I / can ne'er / express, / yet can / not all / conceal. /

Technically this particular structure is known as the Spenserian stanza.

Examine once again the poem "Lost" (page 13) by Carl Sandburg. While it is also a nine-line stanza it is immediately possible to distinguish considerable difference between "Lost" and the fragment from "Childe Harold." One of the first differences to be observed is the absence of a rhyme scheme. Also, in trying to determine the meter and number of feet in each line we run into trouble and become confused. The answer to this perplexing problem, of course, is that one characteristic of this poem is its lack of rhyme scheme and formal meter. We say, instead, that it is in cadence and that it is free verse. So we see that it is possible to form certain intellectual judgments about poetry, whether it is highly structured as in the case of the poetry of Lord Byron or is in the free verse of Carl Sandburg.

In analyzing a painting, a print, an engraving or a piece of sculpture, it is possible to pinpoint the elements and the manner in which the artist uses them to enhance his power of emotional expression. We may see that the work has either strong or restrained emotional expression because of the particular way in which the artist manipulates these elements. In an intellectual reaction to art we are concerned with the way the artist handles the problem of achieving unity and variety, the way he uses line, mass or shape, color, balance, perspective, and the skill with which he combines these elements into a living organic whole.

THE ADORATION OF THE MAGI, Sandro Botticelli
National Gallery of Art, Washington, D.C. (Andrew Mellon Collection)

With the foregoing in mind, examine the painting "The Adoration of the Magi" by Sandro Botticelli (c. 1444-1510) with the idea of isolating some of the elements and determining the manner in which they were used by the artist. We note rather quickly that while there are intense emotional overtones conveyed by the painting, they are still conventional and restrained statements. In the division of space observe the symmetrical balance achieved by the central structure with the principal figure in the center. Note also how the balance is obtained by having figures on both sides of the central structure looking at the central figure. The architectural detail is also symmetrical and suggests a revival of the classic style. One finds that the picture suggests the Renaissance because the background shows the artist's concern with the natural world around him. Line is symmetrical and is used to achieve rhythm and perspective.

The artist has achieved perspective and the division of space by having an obvious foreground, a middleground, and a background which seems to stretch almost to infinity. The scale and masses are used tellingly to show perspective and emphasis. We note that the detail is representational and pictorial.

What about the artist's use of color? Several facts strike us immediately. The use of strong colors in the foreground with grayed colors in the background is a technic used to impart a sense of depth. We see, also, that there is a symbolic use of color in the royal red, blue and gold robes of the Magi. Carrying the eye from those adoring to the Adored to the adoring (left to right) is another interesting use of color. And color is used to establish the proper balance between restful and busy areas.

How did the artist achieve unity? An inspection of the painting reveals that he achieved this through his manipulation of shape and color. Strangely enough, he used the same technic to achieve variety. As one studies the painting he becomes aware that through changing shapes and colors Botticelli was also able to bring the relief of variety to this exciting work.

Where the Botticelli is conventional and restrained in its emotional expression, the work of Vincent van Gogh (1853-1890) in "The Orchard" demonstrates strong emotional expression. While different in technic from "The Adoration of the Magi" it can nevertheless be analyzed in much the same terms. Look first at the artist's division of space. This division is simple but compelling because of the strong lines which carry the eye from left to right and back to left. The balance is asymmetrical and is achieved by the use of strong color against a restful color. It is also achieved by the use of both large and small areas of color.

Perspective and depth seem to be shallow. Van Gogh used two elements to suggest depth. First, he used size of shape to convey the idea of foreground or background. He also used color to suggest the idea of nearness and distance—for example, the use of dark blue for the mountains seems to give them a faraway quality. This picture is pictorial and representational.

THE ORCHARD, Vincent van Gogh

A dominant characteristic of the van Gogh painting is the strong use of color. Strong colors are used on and against strong colors. There is little of neutral color—it is a strong statement throughout. Color is used to carry the eye into the picture—for example, the use of the color red along the road. The brush strokes are short and strong. Observe this particular brush technic in his treatment of the sky and clouds or the roadway. It is important to see that "The Orchard" has a strong rhythm which is expressed by the artist's use of line, brush stroke and color.

As in "The Adoration of the Magi" the artist achieved unity through the repetition of colors and shapes. At the same time, by using different colors (strong colors and grayed colors) and by using different shapes (large areas and small areas), van Gogh was able to satisfy the need for variety and thus give to us a work which has aesthetic significance.

25

In reacting intellectually to a musical composition we focus on the elements used by the composer, and on the manner, the technic and the skill with which he makes use of these elements. The expressive quality of the music, indeed the total emotional impact of the music, depends on the skill with which the composer handles these elements. The elements of music composition which we will study in depth are rhythm, melody, harmony, timbre and form. For our brief orientation to what it means to react intellectually to a musical work we are going to listen to the "Fugue in G Minor," known as the "Little Fugue," by Johann Sebastian Bach.

The fugue takes its name from the Latin word "fuga" meaning flight. It seemed to early musicians that the first voices in the composition were fleeing through the piece with the others in close pursuit. This kind of writing is also called polyphonic music, which means that the composer uses two or more separate and independent melodies which, when sounded together, form harmony. The listener has to be able to hear the separate melodies sung or played by separate voices or instruments instead of hearing all parts together as they might appear at a given moment. It is being aware of the horizontal music line:

rather than the vertical relationship which we call harmony.

All of us have sung rounds from early childhood. A round is a form of polyphonic music and a relative of the fugue. The emphasis is on the separate melodic line rather than on the up-and-down relationship. Technically, the round is known as a *canon*. Here voice follows voice in exact repetition of the first voice.

Before going any further, take a familiar round and sing it, first all singing the melody together and then as a three-part round. As you sing it as a round, try to hear the other two voices as they make their way independently of each other and of the part you are singing.

Row, Row, Row Your Boat

Traditional Round

The fugue as a form furnishes the composer with one way to take a musical idea and extend it into a larger work. Through this extension he is able at the same time to achieve unity of structure and variety of means. Unlike the round, the repetition of the second and succeeding voices does not have to be an exact duplication of the first voice but may appear above or below the original statement. The fugue consists of a single melody called the *subject* which is announced by a single voice. After the melody or subject is established, a second voice enters with the same theme either five steps higher or four steps lower. At this point the first subject continues with new melodic material which is called the *countersubject*—a kind of accompaniment to the subject. In turn, new voices take up the subject until all are heard. While there may be from two to eight voices taking part in a fugue, there is only one subject.

The fugue also has a larger structure through which the composer is able to find the means for giving breadth and meaning to his expression. The first large section is called the *exposition,* which is the introduction of the subject and countersubject in all voices. The second section is the *development* or the working out of the subject. This is accomplished in a variety of ways; for example, writing the subject in different keys, or if it is in minor giving it in major, turning the music upside down by writing the subject below the countersubject, by inverting the subject, by writing the subject so that it will be performed twice as fast (called diminution), or twice as slow (called augmentation), and so forth. Normally a third section utilizing a series of entries based on the material which has appeared in the first section brings the fugue to its brilliant climactic close. From time to time, to keep the music from becoming monotonous, new bits of melodic material are added. These are called *episodes.* One is impressed with the almost mathematical exactness with which the composer handles his musical material, both the fugal material in each division or part of the fugue and the fugue as a large form. Every note must be exactly in place and must be sounded at the precise moment the score calls for. Despite its mathematical structure, the greatness of the fugue is its expressive power—a result of its structural perfection.

The "G Minor Fugue" is a four-voice fugue beginning with a vigorous theme which is considered to be rather masculine. It is in the key of G minor. First listen to the subject played on the piano and then sing it using the syllable "loo."

Six measures later the second entrance of the subject appears four notes lower, this time in the key of D minor. The first voice continues with a countersubject which is an accompaniment to the second statement of the subject.

Eight measures later the subject is again announced, this time five notes below the second subject or once again in the key of G minor. The second voice plays the accompanying countersubject.

Six measures later the final statement of the subject occurs. It is announced by the bass voice and is four notes below the third statement of the subject, once more being in the key of D minor. To this point (which completes the *exposition*), the subject has been stated either in the tonic (G minor) or in its dominant relationship (D minor).

The *exposition* is connected to the *development* section by means of new material which is fresh and delightful and which is known as the *episode*. This material will occur several times during the course of the composition.

A short *stretto* section returns the subject (sounded with greater emphasis) back to the original key and brings the work to a close—one which at first hearing may shock us, but which is often found in this kind of writing. This is the changing of the last chord from the expected minor sound to the unexpected sound of major. This is known as the *tierce de Picardie*.

1. What is it in music that gives us pleasure and satisfaction?
2. Can one receive pleasure in music if he responds only to the rhythm? Only to the mood? Only to the intellectual aspect?
3. What is it that music communicates?
4. What does a technically fine performance have to do with our enjoyment and understanding of music?
5. Is it possible that too much knowledge about music might get in the way of our complete enjoyment of music? Draw an analogy to watching a sport such as football or hockey.

1. Read several of the following examples of literature and discuss the various elements used by the writers, such as rhythm, rhyme, use of words, use of phrases, use of sentences, form, imagery, symbolism.

As You Like It............................William Shakespeare (1564-1616)
Our Town.................................Thornton Wilder (1897———)
After Apple-Picking.............................Robert Frost (1874-1963)
To Autumn....................................John Keats (1795-1821)
To a Skylark.............................Percy Bysshe Shelley (1792-1822)
Elegy...Thomas Gray (1716-1771)

2. Examine several of the following examples of painting and discuss the artist's use of art elements such as line, form, color, shape, texture.

Rain in the Jungle...........................Henri Rousseau (1844-1910)
Boulevard des Anglais..............................Raoul Dufy (1877-1953)
Still Life: The Table...........................Georges Braque (1882———)
Landscape: Mont Sainte-Victoire....................Paul Cézanne (1839-1906)
Tower of Babel.....................Pieter Brueghel, the Elder (c. 1520-1569)
Italian Woman...........................Amedeo Modigliani (1884-1920)
The Isle of the Grand Jatte......................Georges Seurat (1859-1891)
The City....................................Fernand Léger (1881-1955)

3. Play several of the recordings listed below and discuss the elements of music used by the composer, such as rhythm, melody, harmony, form and timbre.

Minuet from the *G Minor Symphony* (K. 550).......Wolfgang Amadeus Mozart
(1756-1791)
Andante, *Surprise Symphony*.................Franz Joseph Haydn (1732-1809)
Twenty-Fourth Caprice.......................Niccolò Paganini (1782-1840)
First Movement, *String Quartet No. 1, Op. 7*...........Béla Bartók (1881-1945)
Prelude to the Afternoon of a Faun...............Claude Debussy (1862-1918)
Toccata and Fugue in D Minor.............Johann Sebastian Bach (1685-1750)
First Movement, *String Quartet in C Major* (K. 465)...Wolfgang Amadeus Mozart
(1756-1791)
First Movement, *Classical Symphony*...............Serge Prokofiev (1891-1953)

30

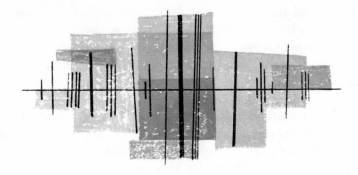

The Composer's Tools

In speaking of the intellectual response to the "Fugue in G Minor" by Johann Sebastian Bach it was necessary to use rather technical terms about the way this music was constructed. It became apparent that the expressive power of this music was not the result of happenstance, but rather was entirely dependent on the masterful way in which Bach was able to manipulate the elements with which he worked. If our concern is only with responding to the rhythm of music, or if all we wish to receive from a performance of music is to sense the mood, then we can probably react to either aspect without having any awareness of how music is put together. If, on the other hand, our concern is with developing an understanding of music based on an intelligent and literate response to music, we must use our intellectual faculties and analyze the music more deeply, so that we may discover the full impact of the composer's particular mode of communication.

When man speaks and makes use of his mother tongue he makes use of certain symbols which are aural sounds. In writing his language man again uses symbols—this time printed symbols. These symbols make for ease and validity of communication. Because music is a means of communication, it depends on certain symbols to make this communication manageable and effective. These symbols called notes, rests, staffs, key signatures, and so forth, are used by the composer to record his musical ideas and thoughts and are again used by him in re-creating these same ideas and thoughts.

The composer must not only learn the basic vocabulary of musical symbols, he must also learn how to manipulate skillfully the various elements of musical composition. These elements—rhythm, melody, harmony, timbre and form—might be termed the tools of the composer. In order to have a clear understanding of what is to come, we first need a clear definition of each of these elements.

31

Rhythm

Of the various elements of music rhythm is probably the most fundamental and most easily understood. It is the element which literally surrounds man and his every activity. The very essence of life is rhythmic—the beating of the heart, the breathing in and out of life-giving oxygen, day following night following day, the coming and going of the seasons, and the ebb and flow of the tides are all evidences of the important role rhythm plays in our daily life. Even the simple act of walking or running down the street would be an impossibility if the element of rhythm were lacking. The physical and psychological makeup of man also reflects a certain rhythmic pattern as seen in the rhythmic change of high and low moods, a period of depression followed by a period of exhilaration, or a period of sadness followed by a period of happiness. One has but to look at life about us to find countless examples of rhythm as it applies to nature and to life itself.

In Chapter Two, rhythm in poetry was defined as the regular rise and fall of sound which results from an arrangement of accented and unaccented syllables. We saw that poetry makes use of meter which comes from a regular recurring of accented and unaccented syllables. In poetry, the rhythmic pattern may vary according to the number of feet in a line (called a verse), a foot having two or more syllables and having a particular arrangement of accented and unaccented syllables. The most commonly used feet are:

			u /
Iambic	*short-long*	*u /*	*Forlorn*
			u u /
Anapestic	*short-short-long*	*u u /*	*Unadorned*
			/ u
Trochaic	*long-short*	*/ u*	*Robin*
			/ u u
Dactylic	*long-short-short*	*/ u u*	*Likeable*

A verse is constructed by using one or more feet and is named according to the type and number of feet. These are:

monometer	*1 foot in a line*
dimeter	*2 feet in a line*
trimeter	*3 feet in a line*
tetrameter	*4 feet in a line*
pentameter	*5 feet in a line*
hexameter	*6 feet in a line*

If we mark the rhythm of the following stanza by indicating the accented and unaccented syllables and by dividing each verse into the proper number of feet, we see that each line has four feet of iambic rhythm.

```
u  /   u   /  u /  u   /
I hear/the noise/about/thy keel;
u  /  u   /   u   /  u     /
I hear/the bell/struck in/the night;
u  /  u  /  u  /  u      /
I see/the ca/bin-win/dow bright;
u  /  u  /  u  /  u    /
I see/the sail/or at/the wheel.¹
```

This stanza would be classified rhythmically as having four lines of iambic tetrameter.

An example of another kind of foot can be found in the first two stanzas of a poem by William Blake (1757-1827).

The Tiger

```
/  u   /  u   /  u    /
Tiger,/Tiger,/burning/bright          (trochaic tetrameter)
/  u   /  u  /  u   /
In the/forests/of the/night,          (trochaic tetrameter)
  /  u  /  u   /  u   /
What im/mortal/hand or/eye            (trochaic tetrameter)
 u    /   u   /  u   /   u   /
Could/frame thy/fearful/symme/try?    (trochaic tetrameter)

/   u  /  u   /   u   /
In what/distant/deeps or/skies        (trochaic tetrameter)
 /   u  /u  /  u    /
Burnt the/fire/of thine/eyes?         (trochaic tetrameter)
 /   u   /   u   /  u   /
On what/wings dare/he as/pire?        (trochaic tetrameter)
 /   u   /   u   /  u   /
What the/hand dare/seize the/fire?    (trochaic tetrameter)
```

The stress falling on the first of two syllables indicates that the rhythm is trochaic. There are four feet in a verse, so each verse would be analyzed as being trochaic tetrameter.

The painter, the architect, the sculptor also must contend with the element of rhythm in order to strengthen the communicative power of the design. One writer has said that "as we study a recognized masterpiece we become fascinated by the numerous pathways of its design. A line may ripple in one direction, then change to an undulation in another direction.

This movement may be momentarily halted by an obstruction of a highly colored mass before it darts away elsewhere along a pathway formed by areas of light and shade. The controlled movements which are found in all good design are called rhythms. Rhythm is a device used by designers to give orderly movement to the manner in which our eyes move over a work of art and to control the pace at which they travel."[2]

How does the artist indicate the element of rhythm? He may do so by placing the forms so that they recur. He may also make use of recurring shapes. Repeating lines, masses, and colors are additional ways in which the artist may express rhythm. Areas of light and shade are capable of expressing rhythmic movement.

Examine the painting "Zapatistas" by the artist José Clemente Orozco (1883-1949) and observe the exciting way in which the element of rhythm has been used.

ZAPATISTAS, José Clemente Orozco

To help isolate the rhythms, note the diagram of some of the rhythms created by repeated lines which are to be found in *Zapatistas*.

Notice also that the artist has made copious use of overlapping planes which seem to limit the spatial depth. By tilting the planes to the left the artist was able to create the feeling of marching. The rhythmic use of sharply contrasting dark and light areas lends an atmosphere of drama to the painting.

Another graphic example of the power of the rhythmic aspect as used in painting is to be found in the painting "The Red Deer" by Franz Marc (1880-1916).

35

THE RED DEER, Franz Marc

A diagram of some of the rhythms reveals a concern with the repetition of curved lines—which are both repeated and used as foils for other curved lines.

36

The contrast of strong, dominant colors as well as the use of dark and light areas of color also helps to define the rhythmic structure.

In music, rhythm is characterized by the arrangement of long and short sounds which, as in the case of poetry, are organized into a pattern of accented and unaccented pulses. Rhythm is completely separate from the elements of melody and harmony and can be notated on a single line without reference to pitch. Rhythm has been defined as the skeleton of music. It is easy to determine the rhythm of a musical composition by clapping the long and short sounds. As an example, try to recognize the following songs by clapping their rhythms:

If the arrangement of long and short sounds is disturbed, it becomes almost impossible to make musical sense out of a composition. Recognition of the tune may be well-nigh impossible. The following melodies are well known but have had the rhythmic element removed. Play, or have someone play, each one on the piano and try to identify the name of each composition (four counts to each note):

Rhythmic design may be organized in a variety of different ways. One organization might be termed the question and answer. For example:

The teacher may clap:.......

And the student may answer:

or

Teacher:.... ......

Student:...........

If we wish to become a little more involved and sophisticated we may have the teacher and student do something like this:

Teacher:

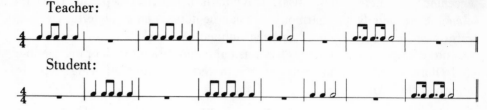

Student:

Clap the following rhythms and observe that the rhythmic structure may be organized into phrases:

Sometimes rhythms are combined. One simple way is to add a second rhythm pattern to a simple rhythmic *ostinato*—which in this case means a continuous and repeated figure.

or

Rhythmic patterns can also be arranged into rhythmic canons. A canon is a musical form in two or more parts using imitation in its strictest sense (page 26). Clap the following rhythmic canons:

Aaron Copland, in speaking of the lack of rhythmic invention in the European music of the late nineteenth century, states that Stravinsky was able to apply a "rhythmic hypodermic" to Western music.[3] What he means by this is that Stravinsky in his creative efforts made new and exciting uses of rhythm. One of these devices is known as *polyrhythm*, which is simply defined as the performing of one rhythm against a different rhythm. For example, clap the following rhythms together. Note that one score is marked 2/4 meter and the second score is marked 3/4 meter. When they are performed together the result is one example of polyrhythm. Note that the first beats in both meters always come together. To accomplish this performance of three-against-two, it is necessary that the part in 3/4 meter be clapped at a slightly faster speed or tempo than the part in 2/4 meter.

The use of rhythm in music, as in poetry, results in dividing the accented and unaccented pulses into equal units of time known as measures. The number of units in a measure gives the basic metrical structure for the composition.

There are musical works also written in meters such as 5/4, 6/4, 7/8, 9/8, 12/8, and so forth. Although in most of these metrical structures there are an uneven number of beats to a measure, one usually finds that there is a regular pattern of two followed by three or three followed by two.

For the most part, accented and unaccented pulses are arranged in regular order:

In 4/4 meter, there is a primary accent on the first beat of the measure and a secondary accent on the third beat of the measure, thus: $\frac{4}{4}$ ♩ ♩ ♩ ♩ | ♩ ♩ ♩ ♩ | ♩ ♩ ♩ ♩ | ♩ ♩ | . In 6/8 meter, the primary accent falls on the first beat of the measure and the secondary accent falls on the

fourth beat of the measure $\frac{6}{8}$ ♪♫♪♫ | ♫♪♫♪ | ♪♫♪♫ | ♩. ♩. | .
Sometimes a 6/8 composition is performed in a fast tempo and is counted
in two beats to the measure ♫♪♫♪ | ♪♫♪♫ | . In this case the primary
accent falls on one and the secondary accent falls on two.

A composer may choose, however, to accent a beat other than the beat
normally accented. For example, instead of this ♩ ♩ ♩ ♩ | ♩ ♩ ♩ ♩ | ♩ ♩ ♩ ♩ | ♩
he might write ♩ ♩ ♩ ♩ | ♩ ♩ ♩ ♩ | ♩ ♩ ♩ ♩ | ♩ or he might write
♩ ♩ ♩ ♩ | ♩ ♩ ♩ ♩ | ♩ ♩ ♩ ♩ | ♩ . Clap each of these examples and note the
effect of the changed accent. In the final analysis, where the accent is to fall
is determined by the expressive intent of the composer.

1. Emperor Waltz . . . . Johann Strauss (1825-1899)
This composition has an introduction in
4/4 meter followed by four separate
waltzes in 3/4 meter. The work is
brought to its conclusion by the addition of a coda also in 3/4 meter. After
becoming acquainted with the music
through listening, play the recording
again and softly clap the rhythm, noting the change from 4/4 to 3/4 meter,
the arrangement of accented and unaccented pulses, and the arrangement
of long and short sounds.

2. Capriccio Espagnol . . . . Nicolas Rimsky-Korsakov (1844-1908)
One associates music of the dance with
Spain because the Spanish music is so
essentially rhythmic. It is characterized
by the use of sharp accents, use of percussion instruments such as tambourine
and castanet, an ever-present syncopation, changing moods, and changing
tempos. It is interesting to note that
some of the best-composed Spanish
music has been written by French and
Russian composers. The "Capriccio Espagnol" is typical of this kind of composed Spanish music and reflects the
common bond of temperament to be
found between the Spanish and Russian
people. (Both Spanish and Russian people express themselves through exciting
rhythms, grace of form, love of savage
color.) Listen to this composition several times to become acquainted with
it. Play the recording again and softly
clap the rhythm noting the changes of
rhythm, changes of tempo, and changes
of mood. It begins with a sprightly little
tune in 2/4 with an accompaniment
figure of ♩ ♫ | ♩ ♫ | . A rhythmic
change to 3/8 changes the mood. A
feeling of excitement follows because of
the shift in meter to 6/8. A return to
3/4 is then followed by a return to the
original 2/4 out of which the composer
fashions a brilliant ending.

3. Allegro con grazia (second movement)
from *Symphony No. 6* . . . . Peter Ilyich Tchaikovsky (1840-1893)
For a musical experience with an irreg-
ular rhythm listen to the second movement of *Symphony No. 6 in B Minor*
know as the "Pathétique." It is a famous example of the use of 5/4 meter.
This irregular rhythm, however, has a
regular pattern of two followed by
three. After becoming acquainted with
the music through listening, play the
recording again and softly clap the
rhythm. Try counting the number of
beats in each measure. Also count the
composition by the pattern: one, two,
one, two, three; then one, two, three,
one, two. Which method of counting is
easier?

41

4. Other listening experiences

Listen to and observe the rhythmic structure of the following music. Compare some of the rhythms found in the album of African rhythms with the rhythms heard in the above listed music as well as the compositions listed below.

Clap the rhythm and note the arrangement of accented and unaccented pulses, the number of beats to a measure, and the arrangement of long and short sounds.

African Tribal Music and Dances...........................Sonar Senghor
Le Sacre du Printemps...........................Igor Stravinsky (1882——)
Chit-Chat Polka.............................Johann Strauss (1825-1899)
Ritual Fire Dance...........................Manuel de Falla (1876-1946)
Mikrokosmos...............................Béla Bartók (1881-1945)
Création du Monde...........................Darius Milhaud (1892——)

TOPICS FOR DISCUSSION

1. What is rhythm in music?
2. Contrast rhythm in music with rhythm in poetry. In sculpture. In painting.
3. What is a measure in music? What is a beat?
4. What is syncopation in rhythm?
5. What is the rhythm of the gavotte? The waltz? The march?

ADDITIONAL CLASS ACTIVITIES

1. Examine several of the following examples of poetry and analyze the rhythmic structure of each:
   The Tiger.....................................William Blake (1757-1827)
   Patterns.....................................Amy Lowell (1874-1925)
   Ode to Evening...............................William Collins (1721-1759)
   Crossing the Bar........................Alfred, Lord Tennyson (1809-1892)
2. Examine several of the following paintings and analyze the rhythmic structure of each:
   Rain in the Jungle............................Henri Rousseau (1844-1910)
   Ecole de Danse...................Hilaire Germain Edgar Degas (1834-1917)
   Versailles.......................................Raoul Dufy (1877-1953)
   Mont Sainte-Victoire...........................Paul Cézanne (1839-1906)
   The Starry Night...........................Vincent van Gogh (1853-1890)
   The Yellow Violin...............................Raoul Dufy (1877-1953)

ANSWERS

Page 37

1. Caisson Song
2. America
3. Deck the Halls
4. Home on the Range
5. Jingle Bells

Page 37

1. I've Been Working on the Railroad
2. Battle Hymn of the Republic
3. A Mighty Fortress Is Our God

Page 39

Canon No. 1 ... Come Follow—Hilton

Page 39

Canon No. 2 ... The Bell Doth Toll

Melody

The dictionary defines melody as musical sounds in an agreeable succession or arrangement. One might also say that the meaningful arrangement of these sounds into a "tune" gives sense to a musical composition. In other words, there is a certain logic to the arrangement of sounds in melody.

In our language the arrangement of letters into words, the arrangement of words into phrases, and the arrangement of phrases into sentences fulfill this same purpose. The arrangement of letters and words in the following sentence has no meaning to us and appears at first glance to be no more than a jumble of letters placed in meaningless groupings:

Diwe kys ratsry dan nedur het
Varge dan gid hte eil etl em.

If the letters in each of the words are rearranged, the words take on individual meanings but do not seem to have any relationship to one another and the grouping of words still has little or no meaning to the reader.

Wide sky starry and under the
Grave and dig the lie let me.

But when the words are then rearranged the meaning becomes apparent and the reader recognizes that

Under the wide and starry sky
Dig the grave and let me lie.

are the opening lines of "Requiem" by Robert Louis Stevenson (1850-1894). Not only is the meaning of each individual word clear but the meaning and logic of all of the words used in combination also become clear. Sense is given to the combination of letters, words and sounds. The meaningful arrangement of symbols which in this instance are letters and words makes valid the writer's communication.

This logical and meaningful arrangement of letters and words makes it possible for the writer to reveal to the reader the theme or central idea of his creation. Through the use of a theme the writer is able to "keep on the subject" and bring unity to his work. To the casual reader this theme may be obscure and sometimes difficult to recognize because it may be subtly interwoven into the fabrics of plot and counterplot, each overlaid with passages of rich descriptive content. In *The Red Badge of Courage* by Stephen Crane (1871-1900) the brilliant description of one of the major battles of the Civil War might make it appear that the theme of this novelette is an extremely accurate account of battle conditions during the Civil War. The thoughtful reader, however, will soon realize that this is really a countermelody or theme which helps the real theme stand out in bold relief. He sees that the real theme is the self-conflict which went on in the life of the youthful soldier—a conflict more internal than external in its manifestation. Through this central idea we are permitted the insight that the youth was not only resisting change, he was also resisting spiritual growth.

In reading poetry one of the first steps in developing an understanding of it is looking for the central idea. Here again the theme, once recognized, will serve to illuminate the work with meaning; this in turn will result in added appreciation and pleasure on the part of the reader.

It is in this sense that in literature the theme or central idea might be considered analogous to melody in music.

Line for the artist, likewise, fulfills the function of making the meaning of his work clear. "Line . . . is a revealing of action, letting us know what its creator thinks and feels, and helping us to respond to whatever he had in mind."[4]

What does line, like melody for music, do for the expressive character of art whether it be graphic, sculpture or architecture? Line is an element which gives definition to a work of art. It consists of considerably more than the sketch of a projected painting. In fact, some drawings are complete aesthetic experiences in themselves. In a painting, a piece of sculpture, or architecture, line will describe the edges and will outline form. Line also is used to complete a shape. In this instance, the line may be drawn or implied. For example, the following dots at first glance may not appear to have

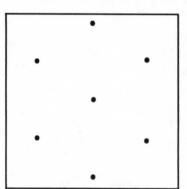

any relationship to each other. But a closer look will reveal that each dot is but the corner of a cube, and an implied line will carry the eye from one dot to another. As a result, we are able to visualize the cube.

Line also suggests movement. It carries the eye from one point to another. The use of line in the painting "Zapatistas" by Orozco (page 34) gives the feeling that the group is marching.

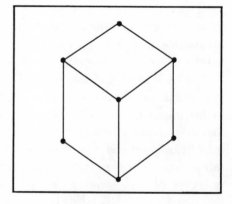

Line can be expressive. If an artist wishes to communicate anger, for example, the lines may appear to be angular, slashing and abrupt. Beauty might be expressed by flowing, rippling or undulating line. Line may also express strength and vigor. Certainly line can help the viewer focus on what is essential.

Examine closely the painting "A Helping Hand" by Émile Renouf (1845-1894) and notice the different ways in which line is used to help the painter express his thoughts and feelings.

44

A HELPING HAND, Émile Renouf

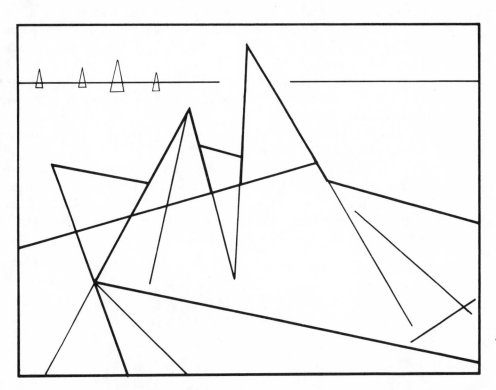

45

A schematic presentation of the painting reveals that line is used to form an outline or sketch of the total work. To this outline the artist added color. We note the long horizontal line (the horizon) which runs from the left to the right side of the picture and which acts to stabilize the picture. It also acts to cast the central shape in the proper perspective. A closer examination of the oar and the mast leads to the discovery that an implied line extends from each one to the edge of the picture, and that these lines oppose one another, and therefore tend to keep the eye centered upon the focal point of interest. One also notices the small lines which are lines of detail, so important in giving total meaning to the work. Lines delineating the fingers, the ribs of the boat, and the sailboats in the distance are representative examples of this latter use of line.

As one inspects the use of line in painting, one sees that the element of rhythm is and must be present in the expressive use of line. And finally, if the element of line is to have strength and vigor it must have sense and logic. It cannot have either if the arrangement comes as a result of happenstance or without thought as to its meaning.

In music the element of melody furnishes a common meeting ground for the composer, the performer and the consumer. Through the use of a melody or tune the composer is able to express his musical idea or ideas. The performer is then able to give his interpretation of these expressive ideas. Finally, the consumer by attending to the melodic element is able to follow and understand what it is the composer is saying.

Melody is more than a pleasing sequence of sounds. It is a meaningful arrangement of sounds which involves rhythmic arrangement of accented and unaccented as well as long and short sounds. Melody plays a two-fold role in musical composition. First of all, it is the means of arousing an emotional response in the consumer or listener. It is also the thread which ties the musical composition together. Stated differently, it is the means by which the listener is able to follow a musical composition from its beginning to its conclusion.

In our system of notation, the musical alphabet is broken up into units of eight notes called *octaves:* A B C D E F G, A B C D E F G, A B C and so forth. If we examine the piano keyboard we see that each of these members of the musical alphabet may be raised or lowered by a half step, thus giving us twelve tones out of which we might fashion a melody. A half step is the distance between a white and black key, a black and white key, or between B and C as well as E and F on the piano.

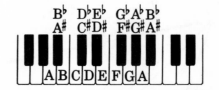

Generally speaking, melodies are written within a scale system which is a given arrangement of notes based on a given pattern. Much of occidental music makes use of the major scale which has this pattern:

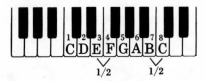

There are half steps between the third and fourth and the seventh and eighth steps of the scale. This can be seen quite easily if we refer again to the piano keyboard and play eight ascending tones beginning on C.

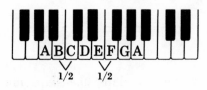

Similar sounding scales can be constructed on any other white or black key as long as this pattern is maintained.

Another scale used in occidental music is called minor. While there are three forms of the minor scale, for the purpose of this discussion we will confine our attention to just one form—the natural minor. Here the half-step pattern falls between steps two and three and steps five and six.

Another scale, the chromatic, is also found in much of Western music. Here all twelve members of the octave become available to the composer. On the piano keyboard each white and black key is used in succession.

A characteristic of the music of the French composer Claude Debussy (1862-1918) is the use of what is known as the whole-tone (step) scale, or a scale that does not make use of the half step.

Melodic movement has three tendencies. First, a melody may move upward,

All in — a — wood there grew a tree,

it may move down,

Joy to the world, the Lord is come,

or it may move straight across.

Now the day is o - ver,

Second, when moving up or down the melody may move by steps or by skips.

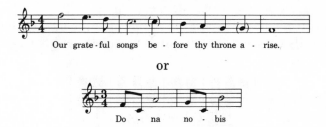

Our grate-ful songs be - fore thy throne a - rise.

or

Do - na no - bis

Third, if the melody moves by skips, the skips may be large, small or medium.

Lul-la - by and good - night,

A - mer - i - ca! A - mer - i - ca!

Twin-kle, twin-kle, lit - tle star

What so proud - ly we hail'd

Do - na no - bis

To identify and remember a melody requires great concentration. One must be aware not only of pitch differences but also the direction the melody or tune moves. One must also be aware of the rhythmic arrangement of the notes, because pitch alone may not give enough information to the listener to enable him to identify the tune.

Have someone play the following notes on the piano and try to identify the melodies from which the excerpts are taken:

48

The pitches without the rhythm do not tell the listener much. Neither will the rhythm without the different pitches give the listener very much help.

But if the different pitches are used in combination with rhythm, the listener is in a favorable position to identify and remember the melody.

An examination of the foregoing melodies indicates that a good melody has several characteristics:

1. The melody is expressive of the thoughts and the feelings which the composer is trying to communicate.
2. The arrangement of the notes is such that the melody or tune is easily remembered.
3. The melody has high as well as low points of interest.
4. The melody has interesting rhythmic as well as pitch arrangement.
5. If the melody is intended for singing it will neither go too high nor too low.
6. The intervals or the distance between pitches is not extremely large or awkward.
7. It is a graceful and broad-flowing musical expression.

49

The following songs are considered examples of good melody writing. Sing each one and then analyze it in terms of:

1. The seven characteristics of good melody.
2. The direction of the melody—up, down or straight across.
3. The use of steps or skips. If skips, are they large, small or medium?

America

With dignity

Traditional Tune (Words by Samuel Francis Smith)

My coun-try, 'tis of thee, Sweet land of lib-er-ty,

Of thee I sing; Land where my fa-thers died, Land of the

pil-grims' pride, From ev-'ry __ moun-tain-side, Let __ free-dom ring!

Jingle Bells

Brightly

J. Pierpont

Dash-ing thro' the snow In a one-horse o-pen sleigh; O'er the fields we

go, Laugh-ing all the way. Bells on bob-tail ring, Mak-ing spir-its

bright, What fun it is to ride and sing A sleigh-ing song to-night!

CHORUS

Jin-gle bells! Jin-gle bells! Jin-gle all the way! Oh, what fun it is to ride

In a one-horse o-pen sleigh. Oh! is to ride In a one-horse o-pen sleigh!

Sweet and Low

Smoothly

Joseph Barnby (1838-1896) (Words by Alfred Lord Tennyson, 1809-1892)

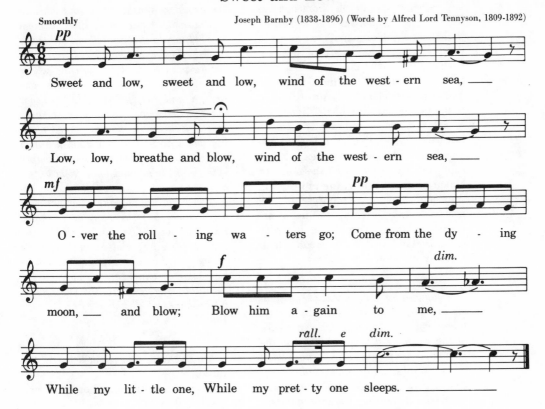

Sweet and low, sweet and low, wind of the west - ern sea, ___

Low, low, breathe and blow, wind of the west - ern sea, ___

O - ver the roll - ing wa - ters go; Come from the dy - ing

moon, ___ and blow; Blow him a - gain to me, ___

While my lit - tle one, While my pret - ty one sleeps. ___

Listen to the following recordings and analyze the melody of each:

LISTENING ACTIVITIES

1. Morning from *Peer Gynt Suite No. 1* . . . . Edvard Grieg (1843-1907)

   a. Does the melody conform to the seven characteristics of good melody?

   b. Do you think the melody is expressive of the mood? Why?

   c. In general, what direction or directions does the melody take?

   d. In general, does the melody move by steps or skips?

2. Air from *Suite No. 3 in D Major* . . . . Johann Sebastian Bach (1685-1750)

   a. How many melodies are used in this composition?

   b. Is this a singable melody or is it

   essentially an instrumental melody? Why?

   c. Indicate the high points of interest as they occur in this composition.

3. Prelude to the Afternoon of a Faun . . . . Claude Debussy (1862-1918)

   Debussy was inspired to write this music after having read the poem "Eclogue" by Stéphane Mallarmé (1842-1898). Mallarmé was a member of a group of French poets whose reactions against the abuses and excesses of Romanticism led to the formation of a new and dif-

   ferent kind of poetry. Known as *Symbolists* these poets used words to suggest rather than define. For the Symbolist, words became symbols for suggesting as well as evoking subconscious thoughts and emotions. The end result of their writing was often candidly sensuous,

51

always graceful and more often than not, rather unintelligible. Someone has said of the Symbolists that according to their credo the thoughts expressed in the lines themselves were of less importance than what the reader was able to read between the lines. Stéphane Mallarmé's "Eclogue" is no exception to the unintelligibility of the Symbolist school. It has been said to defy an accurate and intelligible translation. Edmund Gosse, however, has succeeded in capturing the essence and the mood of Mallarmé's original writing in his beautiful and moving paraphrase of the poetry. Before listening to the music read this famous paraphrase in order to understand better the mood which Debussy attempted to portray.

A faun—a simple, sensuous, passionate being—wakens in the forest at daybreak and tries to recall his experience of the previous afternoon. Was he the fortunate recipient of an actual visit from nymphs, white and golden goddesses, divinely tender and indulgent? Or is the memory he seems to retain nothing but the shadows of a vision, no more substantial than the arid rain of notes from his own flute? He cannot tell. Yet surely there was, surely there is, an animal whiteness among the brown reeds of the lake that shines out yonder? Were they, are they, swans? No! But Naiads plunging? Perhaps!

Vaguer and vaguer grows the im-

pression of this delicious experience. He would resign his woodland godship to retain it. A garden of lilies, golden-headed, white-stalked, behind the trellis of red roses? Ah! the effort is too great for his poor brain. Perhaps if he selects one lily from the garth of lilies, one benign and beneficent yielder of her cup to thirsty lips, the memory, the ever receding memory, may be forced back. So, when he has glutted upon a bunch of grapes, he is wont to toss the empty skins into the air and blow them out in a visionary greediness. But no, the delicious hour grows vaguer; experience or dreams, he will now never know which it was. The sun is warm, the grasses yielding; and he curls himself up again, after worshipping the efficacious star of wine, that he may pursue the dubious ecstasy into the more hopeful boskages of sleep.[5]

After reading the poem listen to the music.
a. Is this an instrumental or vocal melody? Why?
b. Do you think that the melody is expressive of the paraphrase of the poetry?
c. This composition is an excellent example of the use of the whole-tone scale. Are you able to detect the difference between the scale used in this composition and the one used by Grieg in his "Morning"?

ADDITIONAL CLASS ACTIVITIES

1. Examine several of the following examples of painting and analyze the artist's use of line in a manner analogous to the composer's use of melody. Note how he uses vertical, horizontal, and diagonal lines. Are curves and circles a significant part of the expressive possibilities of line?

Saint Francis Receiving the Stigmata...............Jan van Eyck (1370-1440)
Spring Landscape ....Grant Wood (1892-1942)
Thanksgiving ....Doris Lee (1905——)
Autumn Oaks..George Inness (1825-1894)
Company for Supper...............................Dale Nichols (1904——)
The Bridge..Vincent van Gogh (1853-1890)
Suburban Street...................................Maurice Utrillo (1883-1955)

52

2. Play several of the recordings listed below and observe the manner in which the composer has used the element of melody.
   a. The Flight of the Bumble Bee
      The Song of India from *Sadko*.........Nicolas Rimsky-Korsakov (1844-1908)
      Melodies based on the chromatic scale.
   b. Lullaby from the *Gayane Suite*.............Aram Khachaturian (1903——)
   c. Variations for Orchestra....................Arnold Schönberg (1874-1951)
      A new kind of melody.
   d. First Movement, *Quartet No. 1*...................Béla Bartók (1881-1945)
   e. Elegie for Cello and Orchestra.................Gabriel Fauré (1845-1924)
   f. Water Music Suite....................George Frideric Handel (1685-1759)

1. Chapter 5, "Melody" from *What to Listen for in Music* by Aaron Copland, New York: McGraw-Hill Company, Inc., 1939.
2. Pages 14-16 in *Listening to Music Cre-* *atively* by Edwin John Stringham, New York: Prentice-Hall, Inc., 1946.
3. Pages 13-26 in *Invitation to Music* by Elie Siegmeister, Irvington-on-Hudson: Harvey House, Inc., 1961.

Harmony

When one considers the word "harmony," several synonyms immediately come to mind. Interestingly enough, no matter which word we select, it will have a connotation similar to the other possible synonyms we might have selected. We sense that one function of harmony is to enrich the product, whether it is a work of art or human life itself. On the one hand, words such as order, regularity, symmetry, proportion and balance may be used to define harmony; on the other hand, words such as agreement, accord, concord, consonance, peacefulness, friendliness, friendship, neighborliness or brotherliness may also be helpful in establishing a frame of reference for a better understanding of the role of harmony.

In the realm of human living there is certainly the implication of getting along together, with one phase of life enriching another. For example, if a community is examined from this point of view one finds that even though it is made up of individuals there are also certain aspects of grouping and working together which result in the common good for all. Life is ordered so that what one individual does may serve to complement what someone else may do. In this sense, what one individual contributes to society is repaid by the contribution made by another individual. It is no longer practical or even possible for the individual to be so self-sufficient that he need not depend on others.

A brief look at the organization of our country will serve to give another example of harmonious arrangements of separate parts. We have seen how the life of the individual fits into that of the community. In the same way the community plays a role in terms of its integration into the county, which in turn is a part of the state. And finally, the state becomes a separate but distinct part of the national organization. Each unit makes its own unique contribution to the other parts and in return receives the benefits of the contributions of the other members. Because of this harmonious relationship each is able to work with the others for the welfare of all without loss of individual identity.

In literature this element, while not called harmony, may be found to be present in all good writing. The writer, to strengthen his power of communication, strives to achieve a harmonious arrangement of words and parts so that each complements the other. And certainly a further use of this element is the providing of a means for the reinforcement and enrichment of the central theme.

What technics does the writer use to apply this element to his writing? In considering this question three technics are immediately suggested. Each one contributes to achieving a harmonious arrangement of words and parts, to developing symmetry or proportion in the work, and finally, to reinforcing the central theme. These three technics which will be examined briefly are: use of symbolism, use of figures of speech, use of counterpoint.

Refer once again to the poem "O Captain! My Captain!" by Walt Whitman.

O Captain! My Captain!

O Captain! my Captain! our fearful trip is done,
The ship has weather'd every rack, the prize we sought is won,
The port is near, the bells I hear, the people all exulting,
While follow eyes the steady keel, the vessel grim and daring;
     But O heart! heart! heart!
     O the bleeding drops of red,
       Where on the deck my Captain lies,
         Fallen cold and dead.

O Captain! my Captain! rise up and hear the bells;
Rise up—for you the flag is flung—for you the bugle trills,
For you bouquets and ribbon'd wreaths—for you the shores
                         a-crowding,
For you they call, the swaying mass, their eager faces turning;
     Here Captain! dear father!
     The arm beneath your head!
     It is some dream that on the deck,
     You've fallen cold and dead.

My Captain does not answer, his lips are pale and still,
My father does not feel my arm, he has no pulse nor will,
The ship is anchor'd safe and sound, its voyage closed and done,
From fearful trip the victor ship comes in with object won:

Exult O shores and ring O bells!
But I with mournful tread,
Walk the deck my Captain lies,
Fallen cold and dead.   —Walt Whitman (1819-1892)

The central theme or idea is the grief which the poet feels upon learning of the assassination of President Lincoln. He might have expressed this grief in very direct terms, such as:

O President, my President, the war is over; the nation
has been saved from every danger. The ideal of a united
country seems close to being realized and the people are
extremely happy. All observe the steadfast purpose of
the nation. But while all of this is transpiring you, my
President, lie dead in the Capitol.

While the details are clearly expressed, the passage is a mere description of fact and is completely barren of feeling. Referring back to the poem, note that the poet communicates the great depth of his feelings through the addition of rich symbolism to reinforce his central idea. Note the beauty of symbolic expressions such as: "our fearful trip is done" referring to the recently completed Civil War; the reference to the nation as a "ship"; and President Lincoln being represented as the "Captain." Reread the entire poem to identify the other uses of symbolism which are present.

In this particular instance, the use of symbolism may provide a euphemism for a frightening or at least an unpleasant thought. What happens when man's life is finished is a question which has occupied the thinking of philosophers, theologians, scientists, writers—in fact, all people since time immemorial. Not only have accounts of the life hereafter sprung into being because of religious beliefs, but there have also been theories about the next life which were developed by man as he sat around his fire and attempted to find his own answer to the mystery of death. Many of these latter attempts to explain the next life resulted in folk legends, told in symbolic terms, which were passed along from one generation to the next. Yet another source of material on life after death comes from imaginative writers who create idealized accounts of what life in the next world may be like. With this in mind, read the play *Outward Bound* and observe how the author, Sutton Vane, employs symbolism to strengthen and support his central theme. Also observe how, at the same time, this symbolism embellishes and heightens the dramatic effect. The symbol of the ship for ferrying the dead from this life to the next has been used by many writers; in this instance it provides an ideal medium for the author to communicate his ideas. The following excerpts from *Outward Bound* demonstrate the way in which the author made use of this element.

Outward Bound *

Act 1

The curtain rises on a room which suggests rather than represents the smoke-room of a small ocean liner. There is a bar on the right with the usual array of glasses and bottles on the counter and on the shelves behind it. On the extreme left is a small writing table, and the rest of the furniture consists of the usual small round tables and swivel armchairs that are found in the smoke-room on most liners. Around the room at the back is a red cushioned wallseat. The carpet is of warm neutral tone. There are three doors: one behind the bar, another leading off left and a third, center, opening on to the deck. This center door is wide open, and behind it can be seen the liner railings. The color of the sky at the back arrests the attention at once. It is a curious color—vague and almost nondescript. There are four portholes in the back wall, fitted up with small curtains which are now drawn. Three large lights hang from the ceiling, and some small lamp brackets on the walls.

The sun is shining, and it is a clear still morning. Behind the bar stands Scrubby, busy polishing the glasses—preparatory to the boat sailing. He is dressed in the usual uniform of a ship's steward. His manner is always calm and reposeful, and his voice gentle and kindly. He is an elderly man, typically English.

Ann is seen to pass along the deck, and she comes through the center door into the room. She is wearing a hat and coat, underneath which is a simple but very smart clinging frock of green. She is young, but one sees at once that she is terribly nervous. She pauses and looks around in a frightened manner. Then Scrubby clinks a glass and she turns and sees him.

Ann.	Oh, I beg your pardon—good morning.
Scrubby.	Good morning, madam.
Ann.	I'm sorry to bother you, but I'm afraid we've lost our way.
Scrubby.	Where do you want to get to, madam?
Ann.	The cabins, of course.
Scrubby.	Cabins?
Ann.	Yes! Where we sleep. I'm afraid I'm awfully stupid. I've never been on the sea before.
Scrubby.	The old ship will be highly flattered. You'll find all the berths right forward (*points to the left*) down there.
Ann.	Thank you very much. (*She goes up to the center and speaks to someone outside.*) Henry, come along, dear, I was quite right, this is the way. (*Henry enters from the deck. He is wearing a well-cut lounge suit and a dark soft hat. He is an ardent young man, about thirty years old. He is good looking, quietly emotional, serious and sincere. He is rather mystic in manner, and behaves like a dazed man who has recently received a severe shock.*)
Henry.	Sorry, I was looking at the sea. What did you say?
Ann.	This *is* the way, dear.
Henry.	Oh, good! We'll probably find all of our stuff in the cabin already. How did you find out?

Ann.	He told me. (*Indicating Scrubby.*)
Henry.	Oh!—good morning!
Scrubby.	Good morning, sir.

(*Ann moves down to left.*)

Henry.	Bit confusing these boats, aren't they?
Scrubby.	Yes sir, to begin with.
Ann.	Come along, dear.
Henry.	I say, I'm feeling awfully tired.
Ann.	Do you wonder?—after what you've been through?
Henry.	No, I suppose I don't. I can't quite focus it all even now, you know. By jove, we'll have a gorgeous trip though, won't we?
Ann.	Yes, dear.
Henry.	The rest—the peace and—and—
Ann.	Don't worry so, dear.
Henry.	And the forgetfulness—
Ann.	Of course, dear, don't worry.
Henry.	No, I won't, I won't! (*To Scrubby*) Thanks for telling my—my wife the way.
Ann.	Give me your hand.
Henry.	What's that?
Ann.	Give me your hand, dear.
Henry.	Oh you treat me like a child! I am quite all right really.
Ann.	Give me your hand. (*He goes to her, and takes her hand.*) There!
Henry.	Thanks for the hand.
Ann.	Come along.

(Later on in Act 1)

Henry.	(*As he exits*) We'll see you later. We've sailed you know.

(*Scrubby appears behind the bar.*)

Tom.	Yes, I am right. (*Comes to the bar*) Scrubby!
Scrubby.	Yes, sir?
Tom.	I am right, aren't I, Scrubby?
Scrubby.	Right, sir, in the head, do you mean?
Tom.	You know what I mean.
Scrubby.	Right about what, sir?
Tom.	You—I—all of us on this boat.
Scrubby.	What about all of us on this boat, sir?
Tom.	(*Trembling with apprehension*) We are—now answer me truthfully—we are all *dead*, aren't we?
Scrubby.	(*After a pause. Very quietly with firm conviction.*) Yes, sir, we are all dead. Quite dead. They don't find out so soon as you have as a rule.
Tom.	(*Pause*) Queer! (*Sits left of table.*)
Scrubby.	Not when you get used to it, sir.
Tom.	How long have you been—you been—oh, you know?
Scrubby.	Me, sir? Oh, I was lost young.
Tom.	You were what?
Scrubby.	Lost young, sir.
Tom.	I don't understand.
Scrubby.	No, sir, you wouldn't, not yet. But you'll get to know lots of things as the voyage goes on.
Tom.	Tell me—tell me one thing—*now*.
Scrubby.	Anything I can, sir.
Tom.	(*Terrified.*) Where—where are we sailing for?
Scrubby.	Heaven, sir. (*Pause.*) And hell, too. (*Pause.*) It's the same place, you see.

The second technic is that of using figures of speech rich in meaning to relieve the starkness of direct and matter-of-fact statements. Enriching the bare statement enhances the entire communicative and artistic facets of the writing.

Edith Wharton (1862-1937) makes effective use of similes and metaphors in *Ethan Frome* to paint vividly the scene of the barrenness of life in the provincial community in Massachusetts—the setting for this novelette. The stark and poverty-bound life of Ethan Frome is clearly delineated in the statement:

> *The Frome farm was always 'bout as*
> *bare's a milkpan when the cat's*
> *been around.*

Ethan's problem with sickness, first of all with his parents, and then the sickness, pettiness and malice of his wife, Zenobia, is expressed with telling effect by Harmon Gow in:

> *Sickness and trouble: that's what Ethan's had his plate*
> *full up with, ever since the first helping.*

The sparseness of the Frome farm is described by:

> *About a mile further ... we came to an orchard of*
> *starved apple-trees writhing over a hillside among out-*
> *croppings of slate that nuzzled up through the snow like*
> *animals pushing out their noses to breathe.*

In trying to understand the contrast between the vitality of the climate and the deadness of the community, the narrator of the story is led to say:

> *When I had been there a little longer, and had seen this*
> *phase of crystal clearness followed by long stretches of*
> *sunless cold; when the storms of February had pitched*
> *their white tents about the devoted village and the wild*
> *cavalry of March winds had charged down to their*
> *support; I began to understand why Starkfield emerged*
> *from its six months' siege like a starved garrison capi-*
> *tulating without quarter.*

Read the entire novelette *Ethan Frome*, noting the numerous uses of similes and metaphors. Note how their use adds in a very real way to the strength of the story.

In music, when one melody is added to another melody and the two melodies are performed together, the technic is known as counterpoint. While these two or more melodies are being sounded simultaneously and the movement is in a horizontal direction, there is also a vertical relationship which is a harmonious arrangement of two or more tones sounding together—harmony.

This technic can also be used in writing. Thornton Wilder (1897——) in his *Our Town*, has made effective use of counterpoint in his kindly, warm-hearted yet nostalgic picture of the wholesome atmosphere of life in the small town of Grover's Corners, Massachusetts in the early years of the twentieth century. In the play the action takes place on a stage completely devoid of scenery and there is little in the way of conventional stage props. Each member of the audience is, therefore, free to exercise his imagination and to supply mentally the scenery and props according to his own background and understanding. The action of the play starts with Dr. Gibbs returning home at dawn from a maternity case. While he chats (center stage) with the paper boy and the milk-delivery man, first Mrs. Gibbs enters her kitchen (right stage) and starts breakfast, then Mrs. Webb enters her kitchen (left stage) and also begins to prepare breakfast. Mrs. Gibbs calls her children to eat; Mrs. Webb calls her children. We hear bits of breakfast-table conversation first at the Gibbses', and then at the Webbs'. While in musical counterpoint the voices would be playing simultaneously, in the play the audience merely realizes that these bits of action occur simultaneously. Later on in Act One, a third voice is added. While the action goes on in the Gibbses' house (right stage) there is also action at the Webbs' house (left stage) and, in addition, we see and hear the choir rehearsal which takes place in the orchestra pit.

Read the entire play *Our Town* and note the continuous use of the element of counterpoint by Thornton Wilder in his delineation of life in Grover's Corners. In the working out of this drama the lives of the Gibbses and the Webbs appear to us as two melodies played together. Note the method used by the author for shifting the action from one family to the other while at the same time keeping both families moving forward.

Color for the artist is similar to harmony for the musician in that it not only enriches but it also adds to the order, regularity, and symmetry of the artist's expression. Color, like harmony, may not be as essential as other elements used by the artist to express his ideas and feelings; nevertheless, both color and harmony add to the strength and appeal of a work of art. Negatively speaking, the misuse of color can be as damaging to a painting, a room or a design as the misuse of harmony can be to a melody or an extended work of music. Color and harmony are both known to have great power to intensify the emotional impact of what we see and hear. Man responds immediately ,and strongly to color. Because color gives intensity to a work it might be said to give life to a painting.

Through the years color has developed certain symbolic meanings. The color blue, for example, is thought of as being cool and remote. One immediately associates it with the color of the sky or sometimes the color of the sea.

OPEN WINDOW
IN NICE,
Raoul Dufy
(1877-1953)

Red is associated with fire and suggests violence and change. Red, however, can also denote dignity and stateliness when applied to ceremonial occasions. Black has emotional overtones of mournfulness and often even brutality. Death and bereavement are often described in terms of black. By contrast, black can also be descriptive of elegance, particularly as seen in the silk and satin dresses of ladies of high fashion. Black is also used to set off other colors more vividly. Similar meanings and reactions may be read into the various other colors which are at the disposal of the artist. Because color is so rich in association, it naturally follows that vivid color can deeply affect our emotional reaction to its use.

The repetition of color may be used to bring about proportion and harmonious relationship to a painting. A picture has two aspects known as positive and negative space. Stated in its simplest terms, positive space is that space in the picture created by the use of shapes or mass or objects. The space in the area remaining is known as negative space. Color aids in the delineation of positive and negative space. A work of art may truly come alive if the scale and proportion, form and mass are aided through the proper use of color.

If a picture is to be effective, if it is to be vivid and forceful, this effectiveness may well depend on the use of color.

In this picture by Frans Hals (c. 1580-1666) one can observe how the artist utilizes color to implement and to complement his design. We note that the big shape or mass (which consists of the couple and the tree) is expressed in dark colors, forming the positive space; the remaining space, the negative space, is expressed in light colors.

60

THE MARRIED
COUPLE,
Frans Hals

While the scene in one sense has a feeling of informality, elegance is also suggested through the black velvet and silk clothes worn by the couple. The white pleated ruff worn by the woman, the white lace neckpiece worn by the man, and the white lace gauntlets worn by both are further evidence of this feeling. The green of the grass and leaves suggests that the scene might be taking place in the summer. The serene blue sky competes for attention with massive white cumulus clouds, all of which add interest, meaning and richness to the total composition.

In a picture of contrasting style, the artist has given us a scene which has a general feeling of luminosity and clarity of tones. The colors are alive and vibrant. The technic used by the artist, known as broken color or *pointillism,* uses alternating dabs of color so that the eye mixes the color rather than the painter mixing it on his palette.

CAP D'ANTIBES,
Claude Monet
(1840-1926)

61

One is immediately struck by the sun-drenched sky which seems almost alive. While a close observation of the sky would reveal that almost every color of the spectrum has been used, there is a general impression of blue. The water appears to have a combination of blue and green tones. The majestic mountains in the distance highlighted with a tinge of pink give the effect of sunlight being reflected from them. Immediately above the mountains one sees a halo of yellow haze which acts to define the depth and distance.

The tree comes alive for us because of the green leaves and the green vegetation at the base of the tree. The highlights of yellow to be found among the leaves of the tree strongly suggest reflected sun. The splash of yellow in the water serves to accent the scene.

Color has also served in the arrangement of positive and negative space. In general, the blue and blue-green areas of sky and water form the negative space. The mountains, tree, and the brief glimpse of the shore form the positive space.

Edwin Stringham, present-day American composer and musicologist, has stated in *Listening to Music Creatively* that "as in painting, the background harmonizes with and brings out the figures, sometimes even revealing them in new light, so harmony colors and enriches the melody." He also refers to rhythm as being "the heartbeat of music," melody as "the soul of music," and harmony as "the body of music."

Another view of these elements might be in terms of visual design in a painting. In this instance, we might take a given painting and examine it in terms of three analogies to their musical counterparts. The rhythmic aspect might be likened to the skeleton of the figure.

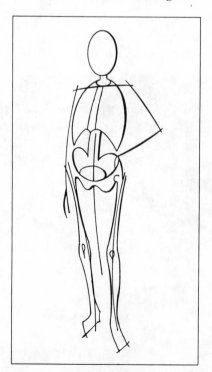

62

Melody would then be comparable to the line or outline which more fully describes the picture.

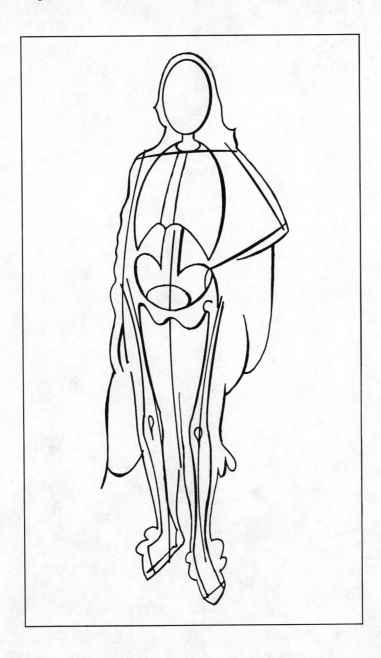

And finally, harmony would be evidenced by the use of color and the description of the background which not only provides for the rich coloring and clothing for the figure but also completes the visual experience for the viewer.

THE BLUE BOY (Master Jonathan Buttall), Sir Thomas Gainsborough, R. A. (1727-1788)

To help understand the role or function of harmony in music, it is necessary to look briefly into history to see how the concept of harmony came into being and how it has since developed. In the beginning of music history and continuing until approximately the ninth century, music consisted of a single line; this type of writing was known as *monody*. In essence, it was a simple, unadorned, unencumbered single melody. Toward the end of the ninth century a second voice or part was added to the single line by duplicating the melody at an interval of either a fifth above or a fourth below. The intervals of the fourth and fifth, as well as the unison and octave, were considered to be perfect and to have acceptable consonance. If both parts of the following arrangement of "America" are sung together, one has a rough approximation of this style which is known as *organum* (or'ga-num). Organum is characterized by the parallel movement of the voices.

My coun - try, 'tis of thee, Sweet land of lib - er - ty,

Of thee I sing; Land where my fa - thers died, Land of the

pil - grims' pride, From ev - 'ry __ moun - tain-side, Let __ free - dom ring!

The next step in the development of harmony came in the eleventh or twelfth century when the principle of organum was extended by breaking down the rule requiring parallel movement. Although still limited to the use of

65

intervals of the octave, fourth and fifth, ingenious composers found ways to use these same intervals but at the same time to inject a beginning of independence of parts—also more musical expressiveness. In general, three devices were used. In one, instead of keeping the distance between the two parts constant, the distance could be changed by changing to one of the other intervals. The movement in general, however, was parallel. In the example given below, note that in one instance the interval of the third is used, but at this time the interval of the third was still considered to be a discord. (Note use of tenor clef.)

Alleluia

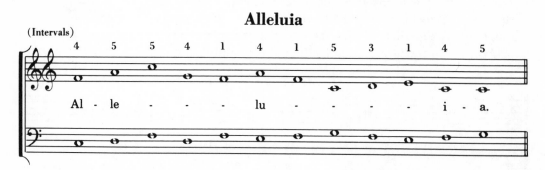

The second type introduced writing in contrary motion—that is, when one part moved up the other part moved down. This was a further step from the strict parallel motion we observed in organum. The writer was again limited to the perfect intervals which were considered to be the unison, octave, fourth and fifth. In the example below, the movement can be visualized as well as heard. We note that once again there is an occasional use of the "imperfect" interval of the third.

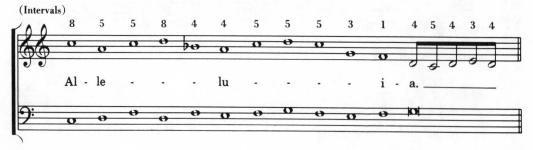

The third method of writing involved the repetition of notes in one part while the other part moved. This sometimes resulted in the sounding of intervals other than the generally accepted and approved intervals. In the example below one finds not only intervals of the third but also intervals of the sixth. Note the appearance of the interval of the second which even in the present day is classed as a dissonance.

Ut tuo propitiatus

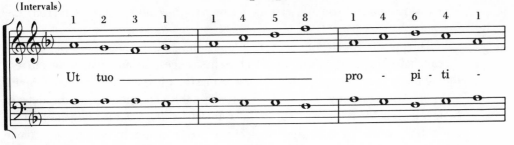

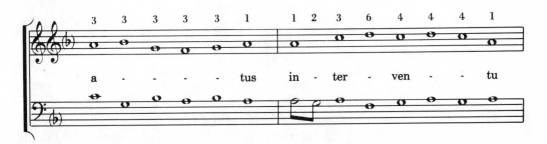

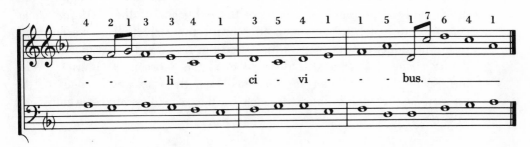

67

This style or method of writing was known as *discant* or measured music. The contrapuntal form of writing harmony grew and developed from the discant.

During the fourteenth century, Pope John XXII issued a decree against discant and forbade its use in all church services, in an attempt to correct the abuses that were becoming characteristic of the church music being written. The harmony was to be limited to the consonances of the octave, fifth and fourth. Although not countenanced by the decree, the interval of the third, which by this time was considered consonant, began to appear between the melody and other voices.

With the interval of the third being accepted as consonant, it soon followed that the sixth also became considered a consonant interval. Much of the music we know today is harmonized with chords made possible by the acceptance and use of the intervals of the unison, third, fourth, fifth, sixth and octave. The following harmonization of "America" consists of only these intervals. Because of the absence of seconds and sevenths, some of the chords may sound strange to ears accustomed to the pungent sounds of seconds and sevenths in these chords.

In the seventeenth century, some daring composer discovered that the harmonic possibilities might be increased immeasurably through the addition of the interval of the seventh:

As might have been expected, this innovation was resisted with great intensity. Composers such as Monteverdi and Gesualdo who used this interval were roundly criticized for utilizing the seventh in their writing. As late as the end of the eighteenth century the publisher of the *C Major String Quartet* returned it to its composer, Mozart, for correction of the harmony in the introduction—harmony which used the seventh. To this day this particular string quartet is still referred to as the "Dissonant Quartet." With the use of the seventh an accomplished fact, the way was opened for the ultimate use of other intervals such as the second, ninth, eleventh, and so forth.

Until the twentieth century the harmonic chords were built upon the interval of the third, thus:

With the twentieth century came new harmonic developments. The expressive demands of the new writing made imperative new scales and new harmonic sounds. New chords came into being—chords based upon intervals other than the third. Contemporary composers, especially Arnold Schönberg (1874-1951) began to make use of the *dodecuple* scale or twelve-tone scale— a scale having the same notes as the chromatic scale but with all twelve tones conceived as having equal status. In contrast, the chromatic scale considers the beginning tone as the tonic of the diatonic scale colored by the addition of the twelve chromatic semitones.

Arnold Schönberg in his "Pelléas and Mélisande" and also in his "Kammersymphonie" made use of chords based upon the interval of the perfect fourth rather than the conventional third:

Other twentieth century composers such as Erik Satie (1866-1925), Darius Milhaud (1892——), Paul Hindemith (1895-1963) and Gustav Holst (1874-1934) also used chords based upon the interval of the perfect fourth in their writing. Alexander Nicolai Scriabin (1872-1915) used a variation of chords based upon intervals of the perfect fourth by building chords using intervals of the fourth other than perfect fourths: He called this combination of fourths the "mystic chord."

With the development of the dodecuple scale and the new harmonic combinations the harmonic emphasis began to shift from that of "tonality" or a feeling for a key center to that of complete lack of tonality. The resulting harmony, known as *atonality*, rather than having one keystone center, in reality used twelve independent centers each with its own tonal and chordal relationships.

Another new tonal and harmonic device which came into general use during this time is known as polytonality. The organum of the ninth century was a precursor of the polytonality of the twentieth century, but it remained to the twentieth-century composer to bring it to its present state of acceptance and popularity. In essence polytonality means two or more strands of melody proceeding together in two or more keys or tonalities. The following example is but one example of the use of polytonality in music:

69

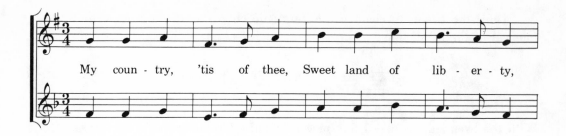

My coun - try, 'tis of thee, Sweet land of lib - er - ty,

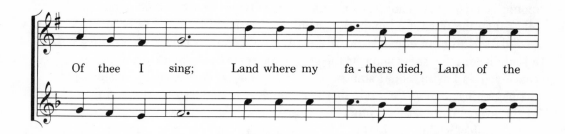

Of thee I sing; Land where my fa - thers died, Land of the

pil - grims' pride, From ev - 'ry __ moun - tain-side, Let __ free - dom ring!

Whatever one's reaction to the sound of contemporary harmonic schemes, it seems obvious that present-day harmony is a valid method of musical communication. One can say with considerable certainty that these sounds do not mark the ultimate realization of harmonic possibilities, and that tomorrow will find new devices which will compare to atonality as atonality compares to the harmony of the seventeenth century.

A reference to harmony may be in terms of either chords (vertical relationship of tones) or in terms of counterpoint (when there is also a vertical relationship present which comes from the combining of melodies).

SINGING EXPERIENCES

1. Sing the various examples which have been used to show the development of harmony.
2. While some of the world's greatest musical utterances have involved the use of counterpoint—for example, the great fugues written by Johann Sebastian Bach—it is possible to find examples in very simple musical experiences such as rounds. To develop a feel for this style of harmonization, sing the following rounds and note the effect of one melody sounding against another.

Are You Sleeping?

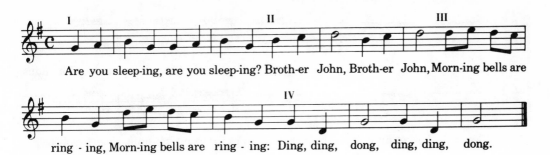

Are you sleep-ing, are you sleep-ing? Broth-er John, Broth-er John, Morn-ing bells are ring - ing, Morn-ing bells are ring - ing: Ding, ding, dong, ding, ding, dong.

Dona nobis pacem

Do - na no - bis pa - cem, pa-cem; do - na _ no - bis pa - cem.

Do - na no - bis pa - cem; do - na no - bis pa - cem.

Do - na no - bis _ pa - cem; do - na no - bis pa - cem.

Niño Querido
(Darling Child)

Spanish

Ni - ño Que - ri - do rest in my arms, Moth-er will guard you and
(Neen'yoh kay - ree' doh)

keep you from harm, Sing you to sleep all co - zy and warm.

3. Another example of counterpoint, or one melody set against a second melody, is found by combining two familiar songs:

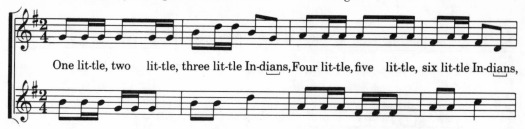

One lit-tle, two   lit-tle, three lit-tle In-dians, Four lit-tle, five   lit-tle, six lit-tle In-dians,

Flies in the but-ter-milk, shoo, fly, shoo!   Flies in the but-ter-milk, shoo, fly, shoo!

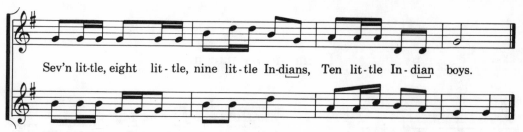

Sev'n lit-tle, eight   lit - tle, nine lit - tle In-dians, Ten lit-tle In - dian   boys.

Flies in the but-ter-milk, shoo, fly, shoo!   Skip to my Lou, my   dar - lin'.

4. The concept of chordal harmony can be best understood if a person can contribute to the harmonization of a tone by performing and at the same time by listening and observing the effect of each new tone added to the chord. Divide the class into four different parts and sing the following, observing how the addition of each part adds to the richness of the sound.

Hel - lo

Hel - lo

Hel - lo

Hel - lo

Hel - lo

Hel - lo

Hel - lo

Hel - lo

5. Another experience in singing harmony is to be found in the following arrangement of the southern folksong "Down in the Valley." The teacher or some student may sing the melody while the remainder of the group sings the harmony, using the syllable "loo," according to this pattern:

Loo,   loo,   loo.

I   V₇   I

Down in the Valley

Kentucky Mountain Song

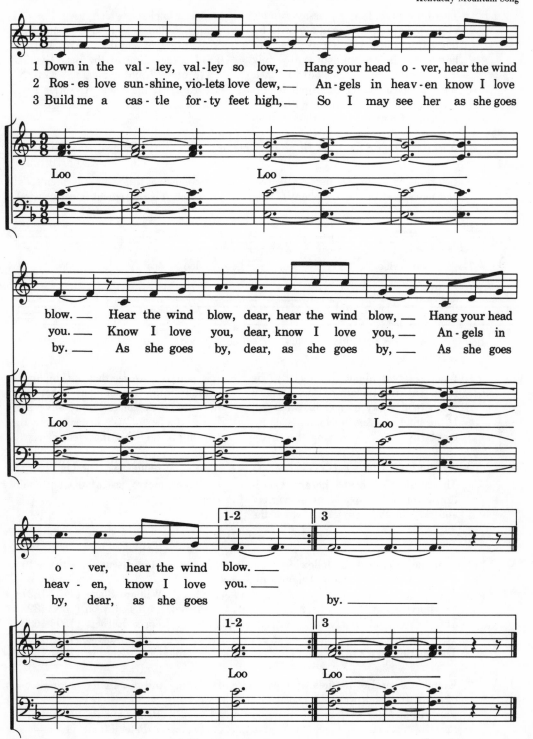

1 Down in the val-ley, val-ley so low, __ Hang your head o-ver, hear the wind
2 Ros-es love sun-shine, vio-lets love dew, __ An-gels in heav-en know I love
3 Build me a cas-tle for-ty feet high, __ So I may see her as she goes

Loo   Loo

blow. __ Hear the wind blow, dear, hear the wind blow, __ Hang your head
you. __ Know I love you, dear, know I love you, __ An-gels in
by. __ As she goes by, dear, as she goes by, __ As she goes

Loo   Loo

1-2   **3**

o - ver, hear the wind blow. __
heav - en, know I love you. __
by, dear, as she goes   by. __

Loo   Loo

73

1. Prelude in C Major from *The Well-Tempered Clavier*......Johann Sebastian Bach
(1685-1750)

This little prelude is a classic example of a composition which derives its interest from the perfection of the use of harmony. The broken chords give only a faint suggestion of melody. In fact, some 150 years after this prelude was composed the French composer Charles François Gounod (1818-1893) com-posed a melody which used this "C Major Prelude" as its accompaniment. This work is entitled "Ave Maria." Find a recording of the Bach-Gounod "Ave Maria" and compare it with the recording of the Bach "C Major Prelude."

2. Allegretto from *Symphony No. 7 in A Major*............Ludwig van Beethoven
(1770-1827)

Before listening to this music (the second movement of the symphony), sing the following fragment—the theme out of which this movement is constructed.

Loo loo loo loo loo, Loo loo loo loo loo,

Loo loo loo loo loo, Loo loo loo loo.

What is great about this melody? Is it an exciting melody? Does it have much in the way of melodic interest? If the interest is not melodic, is its interest rhythmic? Analyzing the rhythmic patterns, we see that the rhythm is actually rather monotonous. What then does make the music come alive and have interest for us? Listen to the recording to see what this element is.

3. Adagio for Strings............................Samuel Barber (1910——)

This music by a contemporary American composer displays great variety and skill in the manner in which the composer makes use of the harmonic element.

1. Examine several of the following examples of literature and discuss how the writer made use of symbolism and figures of speech.
The Tiger.....................................William Blake (1757-1827)
Crossing the Bar.........................Alfred, Lord Tennyson (1809-1892)
The Pulley...................................George Herbert (1593-1633)
The Pilgrim's Progress............................John Bunyan (1628-1688)
The Scarlet Letter........................Nathaniel Hawthorne (1804-1864)

2. Examine several of the following examples of painting and discuss the painter's use of color. In which ways does color enrich the work?
The Vision After the Sermon......................Paul Gauguin (1848-1903)
Parade...Peter Blume (1906——)

The Church at Cagnes....................Pierre Auguste Renoir (1841-1919)
Mont Sainte-Victoire..........................Paul Cézanne (1839-1906)
Lady in Blue..................................Henri Matisse (1869-1954)
Landscape with Viaduct.........................Paul Cézanne (1839-1906)
Rain in the Jungle............................Henri Rousseau (1844-1910)

3. Play several of the recordings listed below and observe the manner in which the composer has used the element of harmony.
Excerpts from *The Messiah*................George Frideric Handel (1685-1759)
Water Music Suite......................George Frideric Handel (1685-1759)
The Last Spring/Heart-Wounds (Two Elegiac Melodies)...........Edvard Grieg (1843-1907)
First Movement from *Symphony No. 1 in F*......Dmitri Shostakovich (1906——)
Variations for Orchestra.....................Arnold Schönberg (1874-1951)

Timbre

The medium with which the writer, painter, sculptor or composer works determines to a considerable extent the individuality of the work. Each work of art has a characteristic and distinctive flavor which comes from the specific instrument chosen by its creator because he feels that it best expresses his ideas and feelings.

Consider for a moment the several different vehicles of expression available to the writer desiring to communicate a certain message. He may cast his writing in any one of several molds such as a poem, an essay, a letter, a biography, a novel, a play. One may be quite certain that whichever medium he chooses it will be the one most appropriate for his artistic communication—in fact, it may be the only one which will express in precise terms what the author is trying to say. To use one of the other ways of writing might seriously limit his powers of communication. This explains in great measure why dramatic adaptions of great fiction or biographical material often fail to measure up in power of expression to the original writing.

The reader, in meeting the work of a writer, immediately recognizes the particular medium which the author uses in his writing. It is highly unlikely that a literate person could read the Walt Whitman poem "O Captain! My Captain!" and classify it as a play, although there is certainly a dramatic element present in the poem. Similarly, there is little likelihood that a reader would confuse the monumental biography of Abraham Lincoln by Carl Sandburg with fiction, although there are numerous incidents in the biography which are as exciting as any fiction could be.

To make these distinctions abundantly clear, it might be well to consider, identify and contrast the following literary excerpts in order to distinguish the medium used by each author.

The Uncommon Man
HERBERT HOOVER

*"The true test of civilization is, not the census,
nor the size of the cities, not the crops—
no, but the kind of man the country turns out."*

—*Ralph Waldo Emerson*

In my opinion, there has been too much talk about the Common Man. It has been dinned into us that this is the Century of the Common Man. The idea seems to be that the Common Man has come into his own at last.

Thus we are in danger of developing a cult of the Common Man, which means a cult of mediocrity. But there is at least one hopeful sign: I have never been able to find out who this Common Man is. In fact, most Americans, and especially women, will get mad and fight if you try calling them common.

This is hopeful because it shows that most people are holding fast to an essential fact in American life. We believe in equal opportunity for all, but we know that this includes the opportunity to rise to leadership—in other words, to be uncommon.

Let us remember that the great human advances have not been brought about by mediocre men and women. They were brought about by distinctly uncommon people with vital sparks of leadership. Many of the great leaders were, it is true, of humble origin, but that alone was not their greatness.

It is a curious fact that when you get sick you want an uncommon doctor; if your car breaks down you want an uncommonly good mechanic; when we get into war we want dreadfully an uncommon admiral and an uncommon general.

I have never met a father and mother who did not want their children to grow up to be uncommon men and women. May it always be so. For the future of America rests not in mediocrity, but in the constant renewal of leadership in every phase of our national life.

A Penny from Heaven
MAX WINKLER

I walked back to the house. I put my fiddle back in the case. I sat down and took off my hat. I was dead tired and unhappy beyond description. But there was something sticking in the brim of my hat. Almost mechanically I pulled it out. It was a penny, dark and flat with age. I polished it carefully and put it in a pocket close to my heart. Suddenly I felt myself smile in confidence. Suddenly I knew that I was still going to lick that city and that somewhere there was going to be a place for me. I felt happy, strong, and sure.

As I left the house a little later, friend Wolf was sitting on the stoop.

"Come on," he said when he saw me come down the stairs, "Come on, I'll buy you a soda."

"I am sorry." I smiled. "I don't think I can afford it today."

Wolf took it good-heartedly.

"Sit down here with me," he said, "What's your hurry?"

What really was my hurry? Pennies were raining down on me out of the open sky. I had no reason in the world to worry. I sat down in the sunshine.

"So you are playing the fiddle," Wolf took up the talk. "A fiddler, hm, a musician."

He unfolded the *Staatszeitung*. "Here is something for you, Maestro. What about trying, *wunderkind*?"

I took the paper. It said that a music publishing house was looking for a boy and to apply in writing to Box 65, *Staatszeitung*.

I walked over to the candy store and took out my penny. "You'll bring me luck," I heard myself say. "I know it, you'll bring me luck." The woman behind the counter looked at me queerly. I handed her the penny.

"Give me a stamp—I have to write a letter."

"You can't write a letter for a penny," she said.

Then she must have seen my sagging, disappointed face. "Here—I give you a postcard for your penny."

I took it and walked over to the little marble table. I thought for a long time. Then I put down the best words I knew, beginning with a solemn *Sir* and ending *Respectfully yours* and in between trying to explain that I played a violin and was a musician and would take any, underlined, any job. I addressed it carefully. Box 65. No waiting in line this time. No boss picking the next man because you were too tall or too young or too old. Box 65. A shiny office somewhere, a music publisher surrounded by stacks of music: "here is an application from a young man who plays the violin, a musician, just the man we need. Miss Crawford, take a letter to Max Winkler, Fifth Floor, 115 St. Mark's Place—Dear Sir, we are in receipt of and we will be delighted to . . ."

I walked over to the corner and slowly saw the postcard slide down in the mailbox. Then I went home. I didn't go out for the rest of the day. For the first time since I had come to America I just lay on my bed dreaming and thinking and smiling. When Dave came home he found me stretched out there, fully dressed and sleeping peacefully.

Three days passed. Three days of waiting for the mailman, of seeing him pass the house on his dreary rounds and disappear around the corner towards Avenue A. I couldn't get myself to leave the house in a paralyzing fear that a message might arrive, and that I might miss the appointed hour to meet my unknown boss—the man who began to take on in my excited mind the appearance of a mystical benefactor. I could see him, looking like the good Lord I had once seen on an early picture of the Creation —a long beard, a benevolent smile—a fatherly protector who would take me out of my misery and make me a useful citizen of my new country.

Dave began to get irritated when he came home at night and saw me loafing around the house. Aunt Minnie didn't say anything. She still fed me on credit, but it wasn't difficult to feel that she began to wonder just how long this big lug was still going to sit on her pocket.

But I didn't move. Ever since I had mailed that postcard I was filled with a childish confidence that here, here alone was going to be my salvation. I read for hours in my little dictionary. In Aunt Minnie's meagre library I found a little booklet, "How to Become an American Citizen." Here I made my first acquaintance with the great principles of the American creed. I read the Constitution of the United States and its amendments. I read and tried to memorize the words of "The Star-Spangled Banner." I explored the basic facts of history and philosophy of my new country—and began, for the first time, fully to understand what it meant to be an American. It would be five more years before I would be eligible to be a citizen, I read—and it looked like a very long time. But then as I kept on reading about the government of the people, by the people, for the people, as I began to understand the fundamental thoughts of the Constitution and the tremendous accomplishments of the history of this country, I was filled with a deep and ever-growing conviction that only the Lord could have done a better job than the framers of these laws and that a five-year probation period wasn't too long for anybody to prove himself worthy of the privileges of citizenship and the final and unreserved admittance to the land of freedom, justice, and liberty.

I don't know how many times I read the little book over and over during these days of voluntary house arrest. When I got tired I just lay on my bed, staring at the ceiling and waiting for the next round of the postman which would find me sitting on the stoop, looking down the street till I would see the already familiar figure approach —and pass. Once in a while, to kill the time, I took out my little black book. There, right on the first page and framed with large red pencil—the intense color of love—was the name of Hulda and the American address of her people—46 Avenue B. It was only a few blocks from where Aunt Minnie lived. My heart went out to her; but when I looked at the appearance of my pants and shoes and counted the contents of my pockets —no contents at all—I decided that Hulda, as everything else in my life, just had to wait for the arrival of that letter. I put the little black book back in my pocket and Hulda's picture out of my mind and went down to take my observation post on the stoop. Wolf was there. He joined me in silent watch.

And then the mailman came and the mailman stopped and the mailman came up the stairs.

"Does a Max Winkler live here?" the mailman said. That was all. No flags, no cannon firing a salute, no drums and trumpets and fanfares. Just a mailman asking whether Max Winkler was living here. And a mailman handing me a letter. The flags were in my heart and the whole street was echoing with drums of victory and the trumpet of redemption.

You Can't Take It With You
GEORGE S. KAUFMAN and MOSS HART

(The following scene is taken from the latter part of Act II. Tony's parents, the Kirbys, have arrived for dinner with the parents of his fiancée, Alice Sycamore, on the wrong night. One near disaster has piled on another near disaster and the Kirbys are now taking their leave.)

Kirby *(to Alice)*.   I'm sorry, my dear—very sorry...
                    Are you ready, Miriam?
Mrs. Kirby *(with enormous dignity)*. Yes, Anthony.
Kirby.   It's been very nice to have met you all...
                    Are you coming, Anthony?
Tony.   No, Father. I'm not.
Kirby.   I see...Your mother and I will be waiting for you at home...Good night. *(With Mrs. Kirby on his arm, he sweeps toward the outer door.)*

(Before the Kirbys can take more than a step toward the door, however, a new figure looms up in the archway. It is a quiet and competent-looking individual with a steely eye, and two more just like him loom up behind him.)

The Man *(very quietly)*. Stay right where you are, everybody. *(There is a little scream from Mrs. Kirby, an exclamation from Penny.)* Don't move.
Penny.   Oh, good heavens!
Kirby.   How dare you? Why, what does this mean?
Grandpa.   What *is* all this?
Kirby.   I demand an explanation!
The Man.   Keep your mouth shut, you! *(He advances slowly into the room, looking the group over. Then he turns to one of his men.)* Which one is it?

Another Man *(goes over and puts a hand on Ed's shoulder)*.

                        This is him.

Essie.	Ed!
Ed *(terrified)*.	Why, what do you mean?
Alice.	Grandpa, what is it?
Kirby.	This is an outrage!
The Man.	Shut up! *(He turns to Ed)* What's your name?
Ed.	Edward—Carmichael. I haven't done anything.
The Man.	You haven't, huh?

Grandpa *(not at all scared)*. This seems rather highhanded to me. What's it all about?

The Man.	Department of Justice.
Penny.	Oh, my goodness! J-men!
Essie.	Ed, what have you done?
Ed.	I haven't done anything.
Grandpa.	What's the boy done, Officer?
Alice.	What is it? What's it all about?

The Man *(taking his time, and surveying the room)*.

                        That door lead to the cellar?

Penny.	Yes, it does.
Paul.	Yes.

The Man *(ordering a man to investigate)*. Mac…

                        (Mac goes into the cellar) …Jim!

Jim.	Yes, sir!
The Man.	Take a look upstairs and see what you find.
Jim.	Okay. *(Jim goes upstairs)*
Ed *(panicky)*.	I haven't done anything!
The Man.	Come here, you! *(He takes some slips of paper out of his pocket)* Ever see these before?
Ed *(gulping)*.	They're my—circulars.
The Man.	You print this stuff, huh?
Ed.	Yes, sir.
The Man.	And you put 'em into boxes of candy to get 'em into people's homes.
Essie.	The Love Dreams!
Ed.	But I didn't mean anything!
The Man.	You didn't, huh? *(He reads the circulars)* "Dynamite the Capitol!" "Dynamite the White House!" "Dynamite the Supreme Court!" "God is the State; the State is God!"
Ed.	But I didn't mean that. I just like to print. Don't I, Grandpa?

(Donald returns with the eggs at this point, and stands quietly watching the proceedings.)

Grandpa.	Now, officer, the government's in no danger from Ed. Printing is just his hobby, that's all. He prints anything.
The Man.	He does, eh?
Penny.	I never heard of such nonsense.
Kirby.	I refuse to stay here and—

(Mr. De Pinna, at this point is shoved through the cellar door by Mac, protesting as he comes.)

De Pinna.	Hey, let me get my pipe, will you? Let me get my pipe!
Mac.	Shut up, you!…We were right, Chief. They've got enough gunpowder down there to blow up the whole city.

Paul.	But we only use that—
The Man.	Keep still!...Everybody in this house is under arrest.
Kirby.	What's that?
Mrs. Kirby.	Oh, good heavens!
Grandpa.	Now look here, Officer—this is all nonsense.
De Pinna.	You'd better let me get my pipe. I left it—
The Man.	Shut up, all of you!
Kolenkhov.	It seems to me, Officer—
The Man.	Shut up!

(From the stairs comes the sound of drunken singing—"There was a young lady," etc. Gay Wellington, wrapped in Penny's negligee, is being carried down the stairway by a somewhat bewildered G-Man.)

The G-Man. Keep still, you! Stop that! Stop it!
The Leader *(after Gay has been persuaded to quiet down)*. Who's that?
Grandpa *(pretty tired of the whole business)*. That—is my mother.

(And then, suddenly, we hear from the cellar. Mr. De Pinna seems to have been right about his pipe, to judge from the sounds below. It is a whole year's supply of fireworks—bombs, big crackers, little crackers, skyrockets, pin wheels, everything. The house is fairly rocked by the explosion.)

(In the room, of course, pandemonium reigns. Mrs. Kirby screams; the G-Man drops Gay right where he stands and dashes for the cellar, closely followed by Mr. De Pinna and Paul; Penny dashes for her manuscripts and Ed rushes to save his xylophone. Kolenkhov waves his arms wildly and dashes in all directions at once; everyone is rushing this way and that.)

(All except one. The exception, of course, is Grandpa, who takes all things as they come. Grandpa just says "Well, well, well"—and sits down. If a lot of people weren't in the way, in fact, you feel he'd like to throw a few darts.)

Curtain

In considering each of the above examples the reader should ask himself, first of all, what medium the writer chose for expressing his feelings and ideas. He should determine if the central idea is best expressed in the medium chosen by the writer. Finally, he should try to decide if the work would have been as effective if the author had chosen one of the other media for his vehicle of expression. Each example has its own distinctive and characteristic individuality which easily makes it possible for the reader to determine immediately whether the author is writing an essay, a biography, a novel or in some other form. For one hoping to grow in understanding and appreciation of literature, a necessary step in this development is the recognition of the various media used by the writer for the precise communication of his thoughts and feelings. In this context, the use of media by the writer is analogous to the use of timbre by the composer.

The artist also has different media, such as drawing, oil, water color, ceramics, sculpture, at his disposal. Each one has its own special kind of individuality and is easily identifiable by the viewer. The abstract design created by the arrangement of three-dimensional materials which may be odds and ends found around the house or studio, and which may have smooth, rough, opaque or transparent qualities upon a two-dimensional surface, is known as a collage. After once having been introduced to a collage it is doubtful if the viewer would ever thereafter confuse a collage with an oil painting or a piece of sculpture.

An examination limited to three of the various media used by the artist will serve to make this distinction clear. For this purpose the study of drawing, sculpture and painting will suffice.

In drawing the artist uses an element which the architect, sculptor and painter share in common with him—line. His use of expressive line, however, results in a totality of expression which gives the drawing its communicative as well as aesthetic impact. Some drawings give the impression of being a sketch or an outline for a planned painting—for example, this study of a dancer by Degas (1834-1917).

DANCER—STUDY No. 1, H. G. E. Degas

In this drawing one has the feeling that the artist was experimenting and jotting down an impression of the dancer which he hoped to capture later in a more elaborate setting. Nevertheless, the response of the viewer is one of completeness and satisfaction with the drawing itself. No detail seems to have been neglected.

Other drawings may be complete artistic entities by themselves. There seems to be no need for further adornment. Such a work is the "Town Hall at Auvers" by Vincent van Gogh (1853-1890). The power of expression in this drawing comes from the working out of the gross features of the scene. One feels the artist's concentration upon the essentials. The viewer does not feel the lack of color and is able to enjoy and appreciate the drawing for itself.

TOWN HALL AT AUVERS: Black crayon, Vincent van Gogh

The characteristics of a drawing may be influenced by the particular tool used by the artist. The effect of a work may be different if, for example, the artist uses pen instead of charcoal. To draw an analogy in music, a melody may be played by one instrument or some other instrument—the problem for the composer is to choose the one which will best express the idea he wishes to communicate. The commonly used tools employed by the artist in drawing are pencil, pen, charcoal, conté crayon or brush. Each one makes its own distinctive and effective contribution to the design of the artist.

The sculptor also uses line in his artistic creation, but in this instance it is a carved line. A finished piece of sculpture might be said to be a drawing made by a cutting tool. One of the distinguishing qualities of a piece of sculpture is that it is three-dimensional. It is observed as an object in space whether it is the type known as bas-relief or is a sculpture-in-the-round. Because it is an object in space it will have innumerable profiles, and to be completely enjoyed one view or profile is not enough—it must be observed from many different profiles or views, with each new profile providing the viewer with new meanings.

Sculpture does not need to rely on other factors such as color, background or ornamentation for its power of expression. It is a strong statement in itself and does not try to create illusion. Its strength comes from the strong verticals and horizontals.

A sculpture may range in size from the small ivory carving by an Alaskan Eskimo to massive works weighing countless tons. In this sculpture by Antoine Bourdelle (1861-1929) entitled "Beethoven" the sculptor reveals to us the strength of character and soul of Beethoven through the twisted features and roughness of surface.

BEETHOVEN,
Antoine Bourdelle

83

The rough handling of the clay by the sculptor serves to deepen the feeling of strength, intensity and forcefulness. An examination of the sculpture reveals flickering highlights stemming from the modeling of the surface of the head with its many hills and hollows. If we could walk around this work, each new view would reveal a new profile, a new feeling and new highlights.

For contrast, a sculpture of heroic proportions, the "Statue of Moses" by Michelangelo (1475-1564), offers an opportunity to study strength of character which the sculptor is able to portray in his work. This work reveals both physical strength and vigor. As the viewer looks at the statue he is struck by the vigor and intensity expressed. While there is an over-all smoothness of effect created by the polished surfaces, there are also highlights reflected from the uneven surfaces representing the hair, beard and draped robe of the figure.

STATUE OF
MOSES,
Michelangelo

84

The sculptor must express himself in material which is tough, solid, rigid, hard and unpliable such as wood, stone, metal, ivory and clay which must be chiseled, molded, bent or welded.

For the painter many choices of media are available to express his ideas and feelings. We have already considered how color fulfills the same function in painting that harmony does in music. We saw that color harmonized and brought out the figures, that it implemented and complemented the design, that it delineated positive and negative space, and, in general, enriched the artistic expression of the painter.

Color may also be compared to timbre in music. As the ear is trained to recognize and distinguish the sound of the violin, the soprano voice, the oboe, the trombone, so is the eye capable of being trained to recognize and distinguish different color values such as red, green, yellow, black. The traditional color chart with its different hues might be likened to the different instruments available to the composer. Further, each color is capable of being modified by being blended with another color, resulting in a new color which is also recognizable to the viewer. Thus one problem for the painter to solve is the choice of the exact color to express with integrity what he is trying to communicate.

TRADITIONAL COLOR CHART

85

The problem does not end here but is further complicated by the kind of paint which the artist will use. He may choose to use oil, water color, casein, pastel or tempera paint. Each kind of paint having its own individuality will have its own individual effect and will influence the reaction of both the artist and the viewer to a given painting. A picture using oil paint will be expressive in a different way from a picture in which the artist has used water color.

PEASANTS IN
THE FIELD,
Camille Pissarro
(1830-1903)

In the painting above the viewer is conscious of the roughness of surface characteristic of oil paint, which tends to make the colors appear heavy. At the same time, this very roughness tends to give a feeling of ruggedness and strength to the scene. One notes the daubs of color which stand out from the surface. One is also aware of the alternating use of two contrasting colors, side by side, a technic the artist used in which the eye of the viewer is asked to mix the exact color rather than have the painter mix it on his palette. We see the paint as a definite substance as we study the picture and we note that it is the paint which builds up the surface.

The medium used by John Marin (1870-1953) in the water color below offers striking contrast to the foregoing oil painting.

MAINE ISLANDS, John Marin

There is an overall smoothness to this painting which gives the colors an appearance of lightness. There is a feeling of fresh transparency which comes, in part, from the viewer being able to see the paper. The eye is struck

87

by patches of color as opposed to the individual daubs of color found in the oil. The drawing and coloring seem to have been achieved in one operation, thus giving the picture a feeling of spontaneity. Because this paint is, in the final analysis, water with color added to it, the blending of colors has a characteristic quality. The blending is accomplished while the painting is wet.

The kind of tool used by the artist in applying the paint further determines the individuality of the medium. Brushes come in a variety of different sizes and shapes, each one capable of contributing a different effect. When the artist applies paint with his palette knife, the resulting character of the paint shows clearly that it has been applied in that way. The viewer is not apt to be misled into seeing it as brush-applied paint. Some present-day artists are finding new and interesting ways of applying paint, such as dribbling it on the canvas or using an implement such as an oil can to squirt the color on the work. Here again, the method of applying the paint leaves its individual mark on the finished product. This in turn gives the work its individuality, which can be recognized by both the artist and the viewer.

Up to this point we have been concerned with the effect of the kind of paint and the way it is applied. One other circumstance influences our final reaction to a painting: the material upon which it is placed. There are numerous surfaces which may be used, each having an individuality of its own and each suitable for the particular purpose which the artist may have in mind. Consider a few of the surfaces which artists use in their painting. Probably the most common and practical surface used by painters is linen (or cotton) canvas. Some of the greatest pictures of all time have been painted on this surface. In renaissance times, artists developed a method of painting with water colors on plaster while it was still wet and fresh—this painting on wet plaster is known as *fresco*. An artist desiring an especially rough surface may substitute burlap for canvas. Another painter may use wood panels—the wood surface ranging from rough to smooth according to the artist's desire and need. And, of course, some artists prefer to work on paper. Here again there may be different degrees of roughness or smoothness depending on what the artist wishes to say.

We have seen how the medium used by the painter, the tool by which the medium is applied, and finally the surface on which the paint is applied all work together to make a work of art say exactly what it was its creator intended it to say. Using a different medium would have limited the artist's power of expression and might have resulted in an ineffectual statement of his ideas and feelings.

For the musician the term *timbre* means the distinctive quality of a tone which makes it possible for the listener to identify the human voice or the various instruments. In the foregoing discussion of color we pointed out that most people learn to distinguish between colors when they see them—for example, red and black. Most people can also learn to identify a *sound* as being that of the bass voice, the violin, the trombone or the clarinet. While there may be minute differences in quality from one violin to another, in the final analysis, the similarities are so great that one will not confuse the typical sound of a violin with that of some other instrument, such as a cornet. Complete understanding of music depends on being able to recognize the typical sound of any voice or instrument, not just the ones that are commonly known.

What is it that gives the oboe its characteristic sound? The viola? The trombone? For an answer it is necessary to examine briefly the concept of the fundamental tone and its system of overtones. If a certain tone is sounded it will have a given number of vibrations per second and we ascribe a certain pitch to it. The string which produces middle C on the piano vibrates at a rate of 256 vibrations per second when struck, and gives us the fundamental pitch which we identify as being middle C. In addition to its fundamental pitch this note has another attribute: quality. Quality is determined by the number and arrangement of overtones present in the sound in addition to the fundamental. While the overtone series can be built on any fundamental tone, for convenience we will take the C one octave below middle C and chart the overtone series. The picture will look like this:

*out of tune to our ears

Eleven overtones which are a part of the fundamental are shown. The octave above the fundamental is the first overtone which is indicated by its 2:1 ratio. The interval above this (G) provides the second overtone, the octave above middle C is the third overtone, and so on until the G one octave above the staff is reached. Thus when the fundamental C is sounded (one octave below middle C) these overtones are also present in varying degrees. To prove this, go to the piano and depress the middle C key without letting it sound. While holding it down strike the octave C below sharply and briefly. The middle C will be heard sounding. Do this to each member of the overtone series for C and determine how many are present in the typical sound of the C used as the fundamental. The answer, therefore, to the question of what gives an instrument its typical sound is the number and arrangement of overtones present when the fundamental is sounded. This is referred to as the harmonic series.

Exactly what is it that determines the arrangement of the harmonic series? This arrangement is determined by the acoustical properties of the different instruments and voices. The instruments are divided into four types or families:

1. The strings (violin, viola, violoncello, string bass) are bowed or plucked. Normally the sound is produced by rubbing a bow across the strings which are stretched over a wood bridge resting on a resonating body of wood. Sound may also be produced by plucking the string. The individual tone color of a string instrument depends on the size of the resonating chamber and the diameter and length of the string.

2. The woodwinds (flute, oboe, clarinet, bassoon) are blown, and with the exception of the flute make use of a reed. The reed is made to vibrate by blowing on it, with the vibration being transmitted into and through the instrument which is the resonating body. The flute is a closed pipe and does not use a reed. The performer blows across a blowhole, setting air vibrations into motion which are transmitted into the tube or resonating body. This method of producing a tone is the same as blowing across the opening of a bottle. The clarinet makes use of a single reed which vibrates against the mouthpiece. The oboe and bassoon make use of double reeds which are made to vibrate against each other. The characteristic tone of the woodwind family is determined by the length and size of the pipe, whether the tube is an open or shut pipe, whether the bore of the tube is cylindrical or conical, and whether the instrument uses a single reed, a double reed or no reed at all.

3. The brass (cornet, trumpet, French horn, baritone horn, trombone, tuba) are blown through the use of a cup mouthpiece. In playing a brass instrument the lips of the player fulfill the same function the reed does for the woodwind instrument. The lips are "buzzed" or set to vibrating against the lip of the mouthpiece. These vibrations are then carried through the tubing or the resonating chamber of the instrument. The characteristic tone color of the brass family is determined by the length and size of the tubing including the mouthpiece, and the bore of the tubing—that is, whether it is conical or cylindrical.

4. Percussion (drums, rattles, timpani, xylophone, claves, and so forth) are struck by sticks, mallets, fingers, hands or each other to produce the characteristic sound. Some of the percussion instruments have bodies or shells of different sizes with animal-hide heads stretched over the top and often the bottom of the shell. The instruments of the xylophone family have tuned bars of wood or metal which are struck by mallets. Instruments such as the castanet and claves are made of two pieces of wood which are sounded by striking each other. The characteristic sound of this family of instruments is exactly what the name implies—percussive or banging. For this reason we might say that the function of this family of instruments is essentially rhythmic.

The human voice is divided into four classifications. The woman's high voice is known as the soprano while the woman's low voice is called alto. In the same way the man's high voice is referred to as tenor and the man's low voice is called bass. Within each broad classification there are subtle differences which are further defined—such as the coloratura soprano which is a very high and light soprano or the mezzo-soprano which has a range and quality somewhere between the soprano and alto voices.

We have indicated that the literate listener will be able to recognize and identify by their individual and characteristic sound each member of the vocal family and each member of the instrumental family. Not only must the listener recognize and identify the individual sound but he must also be able to recognize the sound in combination. Combination sound in this instance might be homogeneous where the ensemble would consist of instruments of the same family, such as a string quartet or a woodwind quintet, or it might refer to a heterogeneous arrangement of instruments, as in an orchestra. In either instance the educated listener must be able to separate the sound and classify it into terms of individual instruments, instrument family or the total voice of the orchestra.

For the composer the musical character of a particular passage dictates the character of sound needed, and this in turn determines the voice or instrument to give life to this musical thought. For example, it would be difficult to imagine the opening passage in the "Bacchanale" from *Samson and Dalila* by Camille Saint-Saëns (1835-1921) being played by any instrument other than the oboe:

Certainly the sound of another instrument—for example, the trumpet—would not have been as happy a choice as the oboe for creating the vivid oriental atmosphere which is so much a part of this piece of music.

Selecting the proper instrument or instruments for a particular passage may pose certain problems for the composer because of limitations inherent in any instrument or voice. In the first place there is the problem of the range of an instrument—that is, the distance from the lowest note to the highest note on an instrument. While an instrument may have an actual range of x number of notes, the technical difficulties involved in producing the extreme upper and/or lower pitches may result in a practical range of considerably less spread. Consider once again the opening passage from the "Bacchanale." No matter how much the composer, Camille Saint-Saëns, might have wanted to use the bassoon for this passage, he could not have used it because even with an artist performer the highest note on the bassoon is four notes below the highest note required here. So the composer must concern himself not only with the problem of selecting the characteristic sound demanded by the writing but he must also select an instrument with sufficient range to accomplish the passage. The ranges of the commonly used orchestra instruments are given below to help the reader understand better this problem confronting the composer.

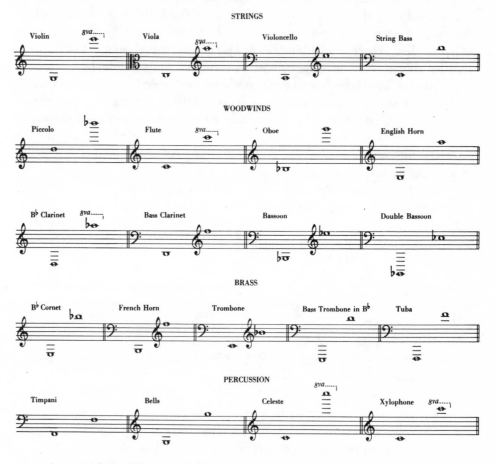

A second problem confronting the composer when selecting an instrumental color for a particular passage is the limitation placed on the instrument by certain construction problems. On the clarinet, for example, an awkward shifting of fingers is required for the performer to change from

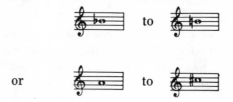

Passages such as this  written for the clarinet
would be technically impossible to perform and so would not realize the
composer's intent if he did try to write it. Because each instrument has its
own limitations, the wise composer informs himself on what these limitations
are and takes them into account when deciding on the musical timbre
necessary to express his musical ideas and feelings.

A third consideration in determining what instrument to use to play a
particular passage is the dynamic limitation of the instrument. Some instruments by their very nature are much louder than others. If an instrument
having a somewhat limited dynamic range is used to carry a solo line and
this instrument is accompanied by instruments of unlimited dynamic range
playing at the loudest possible level, the effect the composer is seeking may
be completely lost. If in "Morning" from the *Peer Gynt Suite No. 1*, Edvard
Grieg (1843-1908) had accompanied the theme given to the flute and oboe

by the driving sound of the full brass choir playing *fortissimo*, not only
would the voices of the flute and oboe have been lost but the magic musical
spell of dawn breaking over the desert would also have been lost. The effect,
then, of the proper use of musical timbre is a precise communication of
the musical ideas and feelings of the composer.

1. Have each member of the class read
aloud by himself the following lines:
Sleep, my child, and peace attend thee
All through the night;
Guardian angels God will send thee,
All through the night.
From the sound of the spoken voice
classify each member of the class as
soprano, alto, tenor or bass. During
this classification note the difference in
quality in each basic group as well as
the similarities.

2. When the class has been divided into
the four basic groups, have each group
sing the following melody by itself.

93

All Through the Night

Welsh

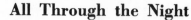

1 Sleep, my child, and peace at-tend thee All through the night;
2 While the moon her watch is keep-ing All through the night;

Guard-ian an-gels God will send thee, All through the night;
While the wea-ry world is sleep-ing All through the night;

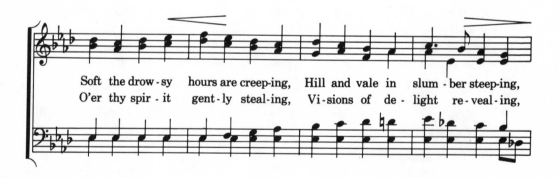

Soft the drow-sy hours are creep-ing, Hill and vale in slum-ber steep-ing,
O'er thy spir-it gent-ly steal-ing, Vi-sions of de-light re-veal-ing,

I my lov-ing vig-il keep-ing, All through the night.
Breathes a pure and ho-ly feel-ing, All through the night.

94

As each group sings, compare the quality of sound it produces with the sound of the other groups. Explain the reason for this difference in quality of sound.

3. Repeat the harmonic experiment on page 72 by:
   a. Dividing all of the girls into the four parts.
   b. Dividing all of the boys into the four parts.
   c. Dividing the class into soprano, alto, tenor and bass.

   Note how the individual quality of the vocal grouping influences the sound of the chord.

Repeat the harmonic experiment on page 72

LISTENING ACTIVITIES

1. Instruments of the Orchestra
   Study the example of each instrument presented, keeping in mind the way in which its basic construction, method of playing and construction problems determine the characteristic sound or timbre of the instrument.
2. Adagio for Strings.............................Samuel Barber (1910———)
   The sound of each of the string instruments by itself and in combination with the other members of the string family.
3. Fanfare for the Common Man....................Aaron Copland (1900———)
4. Trois Pièces brèves..............................Jacques Ibert (1890———)
5. Toccata for Percussion...........................Carlos Chavez (1899———)
6. Sketches for Woodwind Quintet..................Darius Milhaud (1892———)
7. The following films have excellent demonstrations of instrumental timbre:
   a. Instruments of the Orchestra.........................Contemporary, 1947
      The film setting of Benjamin Britten's famous "Young Person's Guide to the Orchestra."
   b. Hearing the Orchestra..............................McGraw-Hill, 1952
      How sound is produced and how humans hear sound.
   c. Exploring the Instruments...........................McGraw-Hill, 1952
      The acoustical properties of tone produced by orchestral instruments. The overtone series is explained.
   d. Looking at Sounds..................................McGraw-Hill, 1952
      Demonstrates the visual dimensions of sound.

ADDITIONAL CLASS ACTIVITIES

1. Examine several of the following examples of literature and analyze the medium used by the writer to communicate his ideas and feelings.
   Much Ado About Nothing...................William Shakespeare (1564-1616)
   The Misanthrope.......................................Molière (1622-1673)
   Self-Reliance..........................Ralph Waldo Emerson (1803-1882)
   On His Blindness...............................John Milton (1608-1674)
   Fog..Carl Sandburg (1878———)
   The Rustic at the Play........................George Santayana (1863-1952)
   Of Studies..Francis Bacon (1561-1626)
2. Examine several of the following works of art and analyze the artist's use of medium, color, type of tool and the surface on which he worked.
   The Drawbridge at Arles.....................Vincent van Gogh (1853-1890)
   Morning Scene: Sea and Ledges.....................John Marin (1870-1953)
   Any United States Coin
   The Discus Thrower.............................Fifth Century B.C., Greece
   The Great Sphinx.................................Egypt (2780-2250 B.C.)
   Brother and Sister.............................Auguste Rodin (1840-1917)
   The Three Musicians............................Pablo Picasso (1881———)
   Any sculpture that is to be found in your community.

3. Play several of the recordings listed below and analyze the instrumental timbre used in each composition.

Nocturne from *Quartet No. 2 in D* . . . . Alexander Borodin (1833-1887)
Façade Suite . . . . William Walton (1902———)
Fantasia on a Theme by Tallis . . . . Ralph Vaughan Williams (1872-1958)
March to the Scaffold from *Symphonie Fantastique* . . . . Hector Berlioz (1803-1869)
Nocturnes . . . . Claude Debussy (1862-1918)

Form

Form might be defined as the plan of organization as well as the shape and structure of anything. For the writer, artist and musician it is the rational organization and arrangement of the creator's material to bring about the successful communication of his ideas. When thinking of form in the arts we are concerned with the formal structure or design used by the artist. It is the very heart of any work of art. Form is an ordering by man's physical, intellectual and emotional means—an ordering of nature as expressed in a painter's landscape, an ordering of space and materials as expressed in an architect's building, an ordering of thoughts and feelings as expressed in a composer's symphony. Form might be considered the mold into which the creative artist casts his ideas. While formal structure is important to small or miniature expression, it becomes of the greatest importance to the creative artist when he attempts to find expression for more extended ideas.

Nature furnishes man with graphic examples of the importance, even necessity, of form and structure. Consider, for example, a leaf from a tree. It has its own individuality which is easily identifiable from its size, shape and configuration. One observes the symmetry of the sides of the leaf which gives us the outline of the shape. The backbone and veins also contribute to its formal organization. Because of this organization it is possible to identify one species from another by close observation of the formal structure. We are able to see that the maple leaf is completely different from that of the willow or the oak.

Taken as a whole, design helps man meet some of his most basic needs: physical, through the design of his cities, houses, clothes and tools; psychological, through these same designs, their accompanying embellishments and designs of art objects; spiritual, through designs of churches, objects of worship and related art. In handling the elements of design, the creator selects, modifies and accentuates in order to make a statement of his own. Whether his thoughts and feelings will be communicated depends greatly on his design. And design sparks a response in the consumer, involving him physically, emotionally and intellectually.

Good design always depends on three principles—unity, coherence and variety. Unity requires keeping on the subject or central theme. If a work has unity the consumer is able to follow the plot or the melodic theme to its ultimate conclusion. If a work has coherence it will have a logical and coherent arrangement of ideas and connectives furnishing the thread which holds the work together. Variety is the addition of new and supplementary material from time to time, to highlight and lend a certain emphasis to the central theme.

Form or design begins with a small or even a single unit and, through repetition, addition of new material, and extension of this material, larger units become available for the extended communication of ideas. This can be seen quite clearly if one compares the units in language and music which the writer and musician use in their creative efforts.

Language	Music
Letter	Note
Word	Figure
Phrase	Phrase
Sentence	Period

The writer, by the addition of new letters, words, phrases and sentences, is able to extend his work into paragraphs, paragraphs into chapters, chapters into books. For the dramatist the extension of sentences into scenes, scenes into acts, acts into a complete drama is a further example of the extension of the basic elements of form. For the poet the extension of these units may result in extended works ranging from the simple two-part form of the couplet to the sonnet and on to epic poetry of truly heroic proportions.

The musician by putting two periods together achieves a larger form, the two-part primary form (A B), and with an additional part, three-part primary form (A B A). Through the development and extension of his material the composer is ultimately able to realize the larger forms such as the sonata allegro, fugue, passacaglia, and so forth.

A consideration of a few of the elements of form which the poet uses in casting his ideas may prove to be helpful in understanding ultimately the function of form in music. As we have already seen, the smallest unit with which he works is the letter—the basic unit for the construction of words full of individual meaning. This, when placed in juxtaposition with other words, helps fashion a sentence which completes the thought. In poetry, however, it may take several lines of words to accomplish the effect of the sentence in prose. A line of poetry is referred to as a *verse:*

The curfew tolls the knell of parting day,[6]

When the poet combines two rhyming lines or verses the resulting stanza is known as a *couplet:*

I went to turn the grass once after one
Who mowed it in the dew before the sun.[7]

While not commonly used, there are times when the poet may choose to use a stanza of three rhyming lines. This form of the stanza is known as the *triplet*:

> *O Galuppi, Baldassare, this is very sad to find!*
> *I can hardly misconceive you; it would prove me deaf and blind;*
> *But although I take your meaning, 'tis with such a heavy mind![8]*

The *quatrain* may be defined as a stanza containing four lines. The rhyme scheme may assume any one of several different patterns such as: a b a b, a b b a, a a b b.

> *White in the moon the long road lies,*
> *The moon stands blank above;*
> *White in the moon the long road lies*
> *That leads me from my love.[9]*

Stanzas may also be organized with five, six, seven, eight or nine lines, depending on the design selected and what is needed by the writer for the expression, through language, of his ideas and feelings.

The *sonnet* furnishes an example of a further extension of form in poetry. In general, the sonnet is a stanza containing fourteen iambic pentameter lines. Sonnets vary in that there are two styles, the Italian and the English. The Italian sonnet usually consists of an arrangement of two parts; the first eight lines called the octave have a rhyme scheme of a b b a, a b b a, and the last six lines called the sestet have a rhyme scheme of c d e, c d e. The Italian sonnet concerns itself with a single thought or feeling. The English sonnet, on the other hand, differs from the Italian sonnet in that its fourteen lines are divided into three quatrains and one couplet with the rhyme scheme being a b a b, c d c d, e f e f, g g. One does not find the severe organization in the English sonnet that is a characteristic of the Italian sonnet. The following sonnet is a fine example of the English sonnet:

Sonnet XXIX

> *When in disgrace with fortune and men's eyes*
> *I all alone beweep my outcast state,*
> *And trouble deaf heaven with my bootless cries,*
> *And look upon myself, and curse my fate,*
> *Wishing me like to one more rich in hope,*
> *Featur'd like him, like him with friends possess'd,*
> *Desiring this man's art, and that man's scope,*
> *With what I most enjoy contented least:*

Yet in these thoughts myself almost despising,
Happy I think on thee,—and then my state,
Like to the lark at break of day arising
From sullen earth, sings hymns at heaven's gate;
For thy sweet love remember'd such wealth brings
That then I scorn to change my state with kings.

—William Shakespeare
(1564-1616)

As the poet's need grows for more extended means or forms of expression, he adds to the communicative power of his writing by writing longer poems—constructing additional stanzas according to the basic designs outlined above. In the poem "White in the Moon the Long Road Lies" by A. E. Housman of which we read the first stanza, the poet requires three additional stanzas of quatrain design to fulfill the expressive principle of his writing.

White in the Moon the Long Road Lies

White in the moon the long road lies,
The moon stands blank above;
White in the moon the long road lies
That leads me from my love.

Still hangs the hedge without a gust,
Still, still the shadows stay:
My feet upon the moonlit dust
Pursue the ceaseless way.

The world is round, so travellers tell,
And straight though reach the track,
Trudge on, trudge on, 'twill all be well,
The way will guide one back.

But ere the circle homeward hies
Far, far must it remove:
White in the moon the long road lies
That leads me from my love.

—A. E. Housman
(1859-1936)

There are times when the poet has so much material to use that it is impractical for him to string these stanzas into one long series. In this case it is
necessary for him to organize his work into large sections or parts, with
each section contributing to the on-going dramatic force of the poetry. In
analyzing these divisions the reader sees that each large section makes use
of smaller units organized according to a definite design. In "The Rime of
the Ancient Mariner," the author, Samuel Taylor Coleridge (1772-1834),
extends the communicative possibility of his writing by dividing the poem
into seven large sections, each section containing stanzas of four, five and
six lines in length.

The Rime of the Ancient Mariner

PART I

It is an ancient Mariner,
And he stoppeth one of three.
"By thy long gray beard and glittering eye,
Now wherefore stopp'st thou me?

The Bridegroom's doors are opened wide,
And I am next of kin;
The guests are met, the feast is set:
May'st hear the merry din."

He holds him with his skinny hand,
"There was a ship," quoth he.
"Hold off! unhand me, gray-beard loon!"
Eftsoons his hand dropt he.

He holds him with his glittering eye—
The Wedding-Guest stood still,
And listens like a three year's child:
The Mariner hath his will.

The Wedding-Guest sat on a stone:
He cannot choose but hear;
And thus spake on that ancient man,
The bright-eyed Mariner.

"The ship was cheered, the harbor cleared,
Merrily did we drop
Below the kirk, below the hill,
Below the lighthouse top.

The sun came up upon the left,
Out of the sea came he!
And he shone bright, and on the right
Went down into the sea.

Higher and higher every day,
Till over the mast at noon—"
The Wedding-Guest here beat his breast,
For he heard the loud bassoon.

The bride hath paced into the hall,
Red as a rose is she;
Nodding their heads before her goes
The merry minstrelsy.

The Wedding-Guest he beat his breast,
Yet he cannot choose but hear;
And thus spake on that ancient man,
The bright-eyed Mariner.

"And now the storm-blast came, and he
Was tyrannous and strong:
He struck with his o'ertaking wings,
And chased us south along.

With sloping masts and dipping prow,
As who pursued with yell and blow
Still treads the shadow of his foe
And forward bends his head,
The ship drove fast, loud roared the blast,
And southward aye we fled.

And now there came both mist and snow,
And it grew wondrous cold:
And ice, mast-high, came floating by,
As green as emerald.

And through the drifts the snowy clifts
Did send a dismal sheen:
Nor shapes of men nor beasts we ken—
The ice was all between.

The ice was here, the ice was there,
The ice was all around:
It cracked and growled, and roared and howled,
Like noises in a swound!

At length did cross an Albatross,
Through the fog it came;
As if it had been a Christian soul,
We hailed it in God's name.

It ate the food it ne'er had eat,
And round and round it flew.
The ice did split with a thunder-fit;
The helmsman steered us through!

And a good south wind sprung up behind;
The Albatross did follow,
And every day, for food or play,
Came to the mariners' hollo!

In mist or cloud, on mast or shroud,
It perched for vespers nine:
Whiles all the night, through fog-smoke white,
Glimmered the white moon-shine."

"God save thee, ancient Mariner!
From the fiends, that plague thee thus!—
Why look'st thou so?"—"With my cross-bow
I shot the Albatross!"

PART II

"The sun now rose upon the right:
Out of the sea came he,
Still hid in mist, and on the left
Went down into the sea.

And the good south wind still blew behind,
But no sweet bird did follow,
Nor any day for food or play
Came to the mariners' hollo!

And I had done a hellish thing,
And it would work 'em woe:
For all averred, I had killed the bird
That made the breeze to blow.
'Ah wretch!' said they, 'the bird to slay,
That made the breeze to blow!'

Nor dim nor red, like God's own head,
The glorious Sun uprist:
Then all averred, I had killed the bird
That brought the fog and mist.
''Twas right,' said they, 'such birds to slay,
That bring the fog and mist.'

The fair breeze blew, the white foam flew,
The furrow followed free;
We were the first that ever burst
Into that silent sea.

Down dropt the breeze, the sails dropt down,
'Twas sad as sad could be;
And we did speak only to break
The silence of the sea!

All in a hot and copper sky,
The bloody Sun, at noon,
Right up above the mast did stand,
No bigger than the Moon.

Day after day, day after day,
We stuck, nor breath nor motion;
As idle as a painted ship
Upon a painted ocean.

Water, water, everywhere,
And all the boards did shrink;
Water, water, everywhere,
Nor any drop to drink.

The very deep did rot: O Christ!
That ever this should be!
Yea, slimy things did crawl with legs
Upon the slimy sea.

About, about, in reel and rout
The death-fires danced at night;
The water, like a witch's oils,
Burnt green, and blue, and white.

And some in dreams assured were
Of the Spirit that plagued us so;
Nine fathom deep he had followed us
From the land of mist and snow.

And every tongue, through utter drought,
Was withered at the root;
We could not speak, no more than if
We had been choked with soot.

Ah! well-a-day! what evil looks
Had I from old and young!
Instead of the cross, the Albatross
About my neck was hung."

PART III

"There passed a weary time. Each throat
Was parched, and glazed each eye.
A weary time! a weary time!
How glazed each weary eye,
When looking westward, I beheld
A something in the sky.

At first it seemed a little speck,
And then it seemed a mist;
It moved and moved, and took at last
A certain shape, I wist.

A speck, a mist, a shape, I wist!
And still it neared and neared:
As if it dodged a water-sprite,
It plunged and tacked and veered.

With throats unslaked, with black lips baked,
We could not laugh nor wail;
Through utter drought all dumb we stood!
I bit my arm, I sucked the blood,
And cried, 'A sail! a sail!'

With throats unslaked, with black lips baked.
Agape they heard me call:
Gramercy! they for joy did grin,
And all at once their breath drew in,
As they were drinking all.

'See! see!' I cried, 'she tacks no more!
Hither to work us weal;
Without a breeze, without a tide,
She steadies with upright keel!'

The western wave was all a-flame.
The day was well nigh done!
Almost upon the western wave
Rested the broad bright Sun;
When that strange shape drove suddenly
Betwixt us and the Sun.

And straight the Sun was flecked with bars,
(Heaven's Mother send us grace!)
As if through a dungeon-grate he peered
With broad and burning face.

Alas! (thought I, and my heart beat loud)
How fast she nears and nears!
Are those her sails that glance in the Sun,
Like restless gossameres?

Are those her ribs through which the Sun
Did peer, as through a grate?
And is that Woman all her crew?
Is that a Death? and are there two?
Is Death that woman's mate?

Her lips were red, her looks were free,
Her locks were yellow as gold:
Her skin was as white as leprosy,
The Nightmare Life-in-Death, was she,
Who thicks man's blood with cold.

The naked hulk alongside came,
And the twain were casting dice;
'The game is done! I've won! I've won!'
Quoth she, and whistles thrice.

The Sun's rim dips; the stars rush out:
At one stride comes the dark;
With far-heard whisper o'er the sea,
Off shot the spectre-bark.

We listened and looked sideways up!
Fear at my heart, as at a cup,
My life-blood seemed to sip!
The stars were dim, and thick the night,
The steersman's face by his lamp gleamed white;
From the sails the dew did drip—
Till clomb above the eastern bar
The horned Moon, with one bright star
Within the nether tip.

One after one, by the star-dogged Moon,
Too quick for groan or sigh,
Each turned his face with a ghastly pang,
And cursed me with his eye.

Four times fifty living men,
(And I heard nor sigh nor groan)
With heavy thump, a lifeless lump,
They dropped down one by one.

The souls did from their bodies fly,—
They fled to bliss or woe!
And every soul, it passed me by,
Like the whizz of my cross-bow!"

PART IV

"I fear thee, ancient Mariner!
I fear thy skinny hand!
And thou art long, and lank, and brown,
As in the ribbed sea-sand.

I fear thee and thy glittering eye,
And thy skinny hand, so brown."—
"Fear not, fear not, thou Wedding-Guest!
This body dropt not down.

Alone, alone, all, all alone,
Alone, on a wide, wide sea!
And never a saint took pity on
My soul in agony.

106

The many men, so beautiful!
And they all dead did lie:
And a thousand thousand slimy things
Lived on; and so did I.

I looked upon the rotting sea,
And drew my eyes away;
I looked upon the rotting deck,
And there the dead men lay.

I looked to heaven, and tried to pray;
But or ever a prayer had gusht,
A wicked whisper came and made
My heart as dry as dust.

I closed my lids, and kept them close,
And the balls like pulses beat;
For the sky and the sea, and the sea and the sky
Lay like a load on my weary eye,
And the dead were at my feet.

The cold sweat melted from their limbs,
Nor rot nor reek did they:
The look with which they looked on me
Had never passed away.

An orphan's curse would drag to hell
A spirit from on high;
But oh! more horrible than that
Is the curse in a dead man's eye!
Seven days, seven nights, I saw that curse,
And yet I could not die.

The moving moon went up the sky,
And nowhere did abide:
Softly she was going up,
And a star or two beside—

Her beams bemocked the sultry main,
Like April hoar-frost spread;
But where the ship's huge shadow lay,
The charmed water burnt away
A still and awful red.

Beyond the shadow of the ship,
I watched the water-snakes:
They moved in tracks of shining white,
And when they reared, the elfish light
Fell off in hoary flakes.

Within the shadow of the ship
I watched their rich attire:
Blue, glossy green, and velvet black
They coiled and swam; and every track
Was a flash of golden fire.

O happy living things! no tongue
Their beauty might declare:
A spring of love gushed from my heart,
And I blessed them unaware:
Sure my kind saint took pity on me,
And I blessed them unaware.

The self-same moment I could pray;
And from my neck so free
The Albatross fell off, and sank
Like lead into the sea."

PART V

"Oh sleep! it is a gentle thing,
Beloved from pole to pole!
To Mary Queen the praise be given!
She sent the gentle sleep from Heaven,
That slid into my soul!

The silly buckets on the deck,
That had so long remained,
I dreamt that they were filled with dew;
And when I awoke, it rained.

My lips were wet, my throat was cold,
My garments all were dank;
Sure I had drunken in my dreams,
And still my body drank.

I moved, and could not feel my limbs:
I was so light—almost
I thought that I had died in sleep,
And was a blessed ghost.

108

And soon I heard a roaring wind:
It did not come anear;
But with its sound it shook the sails,
That were so thin and sere.

The upper air burst into life!
And a hundred fire-flags sheen,
To and fro they were hurried about!
And to and fro, and in and out,
The wan stars danced between.

And the coming wind did roar more loud,
And the sails did sigh like sedge;
And the rain poured down from one black cloud;
The Moon was at its edge.

The thick black cloud was cleft, and still
The Moon was at its side:
Like water shot from some high crag,
The lightning fell with never a jag,
A river steep and wide.

The loud wind never reached the ship,
Yet now the ship moved on!
Beneath the lightning and the Moon
The dead men gave a groan.

They groaned, they stirred, they all uprose,
Nor spake, nor moved their eyes;
It had been strange, even in a dream,
To have seen those dead men rise.

The helmsman steered, the ship moved on;
Yet never a breeze up-blew;
The mariners all 'gan work the ropes,
Where they were wont to do;
They raised their limbs like lifeless tools—
We were a ghastly crew.

The body of my brother's son
Stood by me, knee to knee:
The body and I pulled at one rope,
But he said nought to me."—

"I fear thee, ancient Mariner!"
"Be calm, thou Wedding-Guest!
'Twas not those souls that fled in pain,
Which to their corses came again,
But a troop of spirits blest:

For when it dawned—they dropped their arms,
And clustered round the mast;
Sweet sounds rose slowly through their mouths,
And from their bodies passed.

Around, around, flew each sweet sound,
Then darted to the Sun;
Slowly the sounds came back again,
Now mixed, now one by one.

Sometimes a-dropping from the sky
I heard the skylark sing;
Sometimes all little birds that are,
How they seemed to fill the sea and air
With their sweet jargoning!

And now 'twas like all instruments,
Now like a lonely flute;
And now it is an angel's song,
That makes the heavens be mute.

It ceased; yet still the sails made on
A pleasant noise till noon,
A noise like of a hidden brook
In the leafy month of June,
That to the sleeping woods all night
Singeth a quiet tune.

Till noon we quietly sailed on,
Yet never a breeze did breathe:
Slowly and smoothly went the ship,
Moved onward from beneath.

Under the keel nine fathom deep,
From the land of mist and snow,
The Spirit slid: and it was he
That made the ship to go.
The sails at noon left off their tune,
And the ship stood still also.

The Sun, right up above the mast,
Had fixed her to the ocean:
But in a minute she 'gan stir,
With a short uneasy motion—
Backwards and forwards half her length
With a short uneasy motion.

Then like a pawing horse let go,
She made a sudden bound:
It flung the blood into my head,
And I fell down in a swound.

How long in that same fit I lay,
I have not to declare;
But ere my living life returned,
I heard and in my soul discerned
Two voices in the air.

'Is it he?' quoth one, 'Is this the man?
By Him who died on cross,
With his cruel bow he laid full low
The harmless Albatross.

The Spirit who bideth by himself
In the land of mist and snow,
He loved the bird that loved the man
Who shot him with his bow.'

The other was a softer voice,
As soft as honey-dew:
Quoth he, 'The man hath penance done,
And penance more will do.' "

PART VI FIRST VOICE

" 'But tell me, tell me! speak again,
Thy soft response renewing—
What makes that ship drive on so fast?
What is the ocean doing?'

111

'Still as a slave before his lord,
The ocean hath no blast;
His great bright eye most silently
Up to the moon is cast—

If he may know which way to go;
For she guides him smooth or grim.
See, brother, see! how graciously
She looketh down on him.'

FIRST VOICE

'But why drives on that ship so fast,
Without or wave or wind?'

SECOND VOICE

'The air is cut away before,
And closes from behind.

Fly, brother, fly! more high, more high!
Or we shall be belated:
For slow and slow that ship will go,
When the Mariner's trance is abated.'

I woke, and we were sailing on
As in a gentle weather:
'Twas night, calm night, the moon was high;
The dead men stood together.

All stood together on the deck,
For a charnel-dungeon fitter:
All fixed on me their stony eyes,
That in the Moon did glitter.

The pang, the curse, with which they died,
Had never passed away:
I could not draw my eyes from theirs,
Nor turn them up to pray.

And now this spell was snapt: once more
I viewed the ocean green,
And looked far forth, yet little saw
Of what had else been seen—

Like one, that on a lonesome road
Doth walk in fear and dread,
And having once turned round walks on,
And turns no more his head;
Because he knows, a frightful fiend
Doth close behind him tread.

But soon there breathed a wind on me,
Nor sound nor motion made:
Its path was not upon the sea,
In ripple or in shade.

It raised my hair, it fanned my cheek
Like a meadow-gale of spring—
It mingled strangely with my fears,
Yet it felt like a welcoming.

Swiftly, swiftly flew the ship,
Yet she sailed softly too:
Sweetly, sweetly blew the breeze—
On me alone it blew.

Oh! dream of joy! is this indeed
The light-house top I see?
Is this the hill? Is this the kirk?
Is this mine own countree?

We drifted o'er the harbor-bar,
And I with sobs did pray—
O let me be awake, my God!
Or let me sleep alway.

The harbor-bay was clear as glass,
So smoothly it was strewn!
And on the bay the moonlight lay,
And the shadow of the Moon.

The rock shone bright, the kirk no less,
That stands above the rock:
The moonlight steeped in silentness
The steady weathercock.

And the bay was white with silent light,
Till rising from the same,
Full many shapes, that shadows were,
In crimson colors came.

A little distance from the prow
Those crimson shadows were:
I turned my eyes upon the deck—
Oh, Christ! what saw I there!

Each corse lay flat, lifeless and flat,
And, by the holy rood
A man all light, a seraph-man
On every corse there stood.

This seraph-band, each waved his hand:
It was a heavenly sight!
They stood as signals to the land,
Each one a lovely light;

This seraph-band, each waved his hand,
No voice did they impart—
No voice; but oh! the silence sank
Like music on my heart.

But soon I heard the dash of oars,
I heard the Pilot's cheer;
My head was turned perforce away
And I saw a boat appear.

The Pilot and the Pilot's boy,
I heard them coming fast:
Dear Lord in Heaven! It was a joy
The dead men could not blast.

I saw a third—I heard his voice:
It is the Hermit good!
He singeth loud his godly hymns
That he makes in the wood.
He'll shrieve my soul, he'll wash away
The Albatross's blood."

PART VII

"This Hermit good lives in that wood
Which slopes down to the sea.
How loudly his sweet voice he rears!
He loves to talk with marineres
That come from a far countree.

He kneels at morn, and noon, and eve—
He hath a cushion plump:
It is the moss that wholly hides
The rotted old oak-stump.

The skiff-boat neared: I heard them talk,
'Why this is strange, I trow!
Where are those lights so many and fair,
That signal made but now?'

'Strange, by my faith!' the Hermit said—
'And they answered not our cheer!
The planks look warped! and see those sails,
How thin they are and sere!
I never saw aught like to them,
Unless perchance it were

Brown skeletons of leaves that lag
My forest-brook along;
When the ivy-tod is heavy with snow,
And the owlet whoops to the wolf below,
That eats the she-wolf's young.'

'Dear Lord! it hath a fiendish look'—
(The Pilot made reply)
'I am a-feared'—'Push on, push on!'
Said the Hermit cheerily.

115

The boat came closer to the ship,
But I nor spake nor stirred;
The boat came close beneath the ship,
And straight a sound was heard.

Under the water it rumbled on,
Still louder and more dread:
It reached the ship, it split the bay;
The ship went down like lead.

Stunned by that loud and dreadful sound,
Which sky and ocean smote,
Like one that hath been seven days drowned
My body lay afloat;
But swift as dreams, myself I found
Within the Pilot's boat.

Upon the whirl, where sank the ship,
The boat spun round and round;
And all was still, save that the hill
Was telling of the sound.

I moved my lips—the Pilot shrieked
And fell down in a fit;
The holy Hermit raised his eyes,
And prayed where he did sit.

I took the oars: the Pilot's boy,
Who now doth crazy go,
Laughed loud and long, and all the while
His eyes went to and fro.
'Ha! ha!' quoth he, 'full plain I see,
The Devil knows how to row.'

And now, all in my own countree,
I stood on the firm land!
The Hermit stepped forth from the boat,
And scarcely he could stand.

'Oh shrieve me, shrieve me, holy man!'
The Hermit crossed his brow.
'Say quick', quoth he, 'I bid thee say—
What manner of man art thou?'

Forthwith this frame of mine was wrenched
With a woeful agony,
Which forced me to begin my tale;
And then it left me free.

Since then, at an uncertain hour,
That agony returns:
And till my ghastly tale is told,
This heart within me burns.

I pass, like night, from land to land;
I have strange power of speech;
That moment that his face I see,
I know the man that must hear me:
To him my tale I teach.

What loud uproar bursts from that door!
The wedding-guests are there:
But in the garden-bower the bride
And bride-maids singing are:
And hark the little vesper bell,
Which biddeth me to prayer!

O Wedding-Guest! this soul hath been
Alone on a wide, wide sea:
So lonely 'twas, that God himself
Scarce seemed there to be.

O sweeter than the marriage-feast,
'Tis sweeter far to me,
To walk together to the kirk
With a goodly company!—

To walk together to the kirk,
And all together pray,
While each to his great Father bends,
Old men, and babes, and loving friends
And youths and maidens gay!

Farewell, farewell! but this I tell
To thee, thou Wedding-Guest!
He prayeth well, who loveth well
Both man and bird and beast.

He prayeth best, who loveth best
All things both great and small;
For the dear God who loveth us
He made and loveth all."

The Mariner, whose eye is bright,
Whose beard with age is hoar,
Is gone: and now the Wedding-Guest
Turned from the bridegroom's door.

He went like one that hath been stunned,
And is of sense forlorn:
A sadder and a wiser man,
He rose the morrow morn.

—Samuel Taylor Coleridge

While there are other ways of organizing poetry for extended expression, it can be seen from this discussion that for the greatest power of expression poetry must conform to a plan or design. As one reads poetry he becomes aware that the principles of unity, coherence and variety demand some form of reasoned design, and that strong statements of ideas and feeling result only if the writer casts his work in some kind of planned design.

For the artist composition, form and design are synonymous terms which are used to describe his plan of organization. This organization is apparent in the creative efforts of all artists, whether the area of concentration is painting, architecture, sculpture, ceramics or any of the other areas in which artists create. It is through this organization that the artist is able to breathe meaning and definition into his creation. We might say that through composition the artist is striving to bring organization and significance to his work. Without this organization the artist's choice of the elements of line, rhythm, color and choice of media will come to nought.

As the viewer looks at a work of art he sees that the artist has a number of ways in which he achieves his composition or design. One of his first steps in developing his design is the division of space or work area. He divides the space in order to project and emphasize the main idea. In the painting "The Dancer," Renoir (1841-1919), by placing the figure of the dancer in the center of the canvas with little space at top, bottom or sides, conveys to the viewer the importance of the subject by having the figure stand out. In other words, the position of the shape or shapes in relation to the borders has considerable bearing on the composition of the picture. Space is also divided by adding detail and lesser figures which contribute to the main idea.

The distinctive costume of the ballerina further identifies and emphasizes the main thought. The viewer can almost feel the laciness of the ballerina's skirt. Splashes of color seen in the shoulder bows, sash, shoes, neck ribbon and hair ribbon give further definition. Also, the artist's choice of a flat background, with little or no depth, serves to highlight the figure by not relating it to time or environment.

The artist's use of line, tone and color in creating shapes is another key to identifying the compositional aspects of a work of graphic art. Refer again to the painting "The Dancer" and note that Renoir's selection of light tones of color to delineate the dancer against the darker tones of the background gives accent to the figure and a feeling of balance to the entire work.

THE DANCER,
Pierre Auguste Renoir

119

We have suggested, by implication, the importance of the size and values of shapes to composition. Shapes that are too large or small for the space to which they are assigned will upset design or composition. This can be readily seen if one will cut out the three basic shapes of nature—the square, the circle and the triangle—in a given size and then experiment by arranging them within frames of different sizes. In many pictures the viewer will be able to analyze the composition of the total work in terms of these three basic shapes. Study the center panel of the triptych "Crucifixion With Saints" by Pietro Perugino (1446-1523). The head of Christ is the focal point of the painting and thus the apex of the triangle. His head is bent and he is looking downward to the Madonna, establishing a strong line which might be considered to be the left side of the triangle.

THE CRUCIFIXION
WITH THE VIRGIN
AND SAINT JOHN,
Pietro Perugino

The Madonna is also looking down, thus reinforcing and completing the feeling of line no less real than if it had actually been drawn. On the right-hand side of the cross the figure of St. John, in the same way, creates the line for the right side of the triangle by looking upward to the head of Christ. The base of the triangle is created by the line running from the feet of the Madonna to the base of the cross to the feet of the Saint. As a foil to this major triangle the artist worked into his design lesser triangles, usually inverted, which can be found in the landscape at either side of the cross and in the folds of the robes worn by each figure.

Shapes contribute to composition through their tension or activity. The direction in which shapes carry the eye fulfills a twofold function. First, the tension or activity of the shape directs the eye to the artist's choice of climax. This directing of the eye to the climax can readily be seen in the painting above. A secondary function of the activity of shapes is the control of the speed of movement. This is necessary if the eye is to have time to grasp the significant details on its way to discover the climax.

For the artist, then, the communication of his ideas and feelings depends largely on his ability to solve his problem of design or composition. Works with poor composition will tend to have little or no communicative value. Works with well-achieved and forceful design will demonstrate great expressive power through which the viewer will be able to share with the artist a particular idea or feeling.

Since music exists in time and not in space—that is, once the tone or chord is produced the sound is immediately gone—the organization of the musical structure is of the utmost importance. Because music exists in time the listener must use all of his powers of concentration and memory to follow the course of a musical performance. Unless music is arranged in some sort of coherent order, man's ear and mind will not be able to attend nor remember the orderless scramble of sounds. For the composer, form in music is more than a means by which he extends his musical ideas from miniatures to the larger forms such as the symphony, the sonata, the fugue. It is also the means for ensuring that his musical statement achieves coherence, unity and variety. Form is necessary for making significant the smallest musical statement and giving the consumer the means for identifying such statements.

We have pointed out that the smallest unit of musical form is the note which is analogous to the letter in language. This is the raw material out of which all music is fashioned. If a person should sit down at a piano and strike a white or black key, the resulting sound would be a tone or note. These random and disconnected sounds are notes:

In language the smallest grouping of letters which conveys a definite meaning is called a word. In music the smallest group of notes conveying a definite idea is called a figure. The genius of Ludwig van Beethoven was such that he was able to construct the entire first movement of his *Fifth Symphony in C Minor* out of a figure using these four notes:

In the song "Sweet Genevieve" the composer has constructed an entire song from a series of short melodic figures strung together like a string of beads.

Sing each separate figure and then compare each figure with the other figures. A study of the figures from "Sweet Genevieve" will reveal that they have at least three traits which help to identify them as figures. First of all, the end of the figure is indicated by a longer tone. Second, the figures have a similarity of formation achieved through the melodic and rhythmic direction. Third, each figure has a similarity of metric grouping.

Figures are combined to make musical phrases which fulfill the same function in music that the phrase does in language. Generally speaking, a phrase is four measures in length, although there are many compositions in which the composer has used phrases of different lengths such as two measures, three measures, five measures, six measures. The four-measure phrase, however, is most widely used; because of this it is known as a "regular" phrase while phrases of other lengths are referred to as "irregular."

The phrase is the smallest musical unit which expresses a complete idea; it is also the smallest musical unit to be terminated by a *cadence*. A cadence is a point of repose which brings about a breaking of the phrase. In general the cadence is created by the use of two or more chords such as, IV-I; IV-V or V_7; V_7-I; IV-V_7-I. The "Amen" which is sung at the end of hymns represents one type of cadence. This is known as a *plagal* cadence.

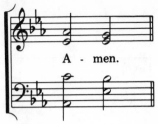

A - men.

Knowledge of two other types of cadence is necessary before one can recognize and analyze the phrase. The first of these is the *authentic* cadence which involves the chordal progression of V or V₇ to I. There are two versions of the authentic cadence. The first, called the *perfect* authentic cadence, is achieved by having the root of the I chord in both outside voices (the soprano and bass).

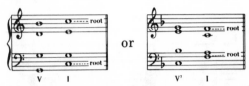

The other form of the authentic cadence is the *imperfect* in which the third or fifth of the I chord is found in the soprano. In rare instances the third of the I chord is found in the bass.

The other type of cadence which is necessary for analyzing phrases is the *half cadence*. It is usually the progression of any chord into the V or V₇.

With this brief background of the cadence we are ready to examine the phrase. The phrase, while it expresses a complete idea, does not necessarily express a musical idea that is completely finished. Normally it depends on an additional phrase or phrases to complete its function. The phrase should be long enough so that a sense of tonality is established. There should also be a feeling of beginning, flow and ending.

We have seen how the composer of "Sweet Genevieve" made use of a series of figures to express his musical ideas and feelings. Let us examine this song again with the idea of seeing how these self-same figures when used together result in musical phrases.

123

Sweet Genevieve

Moderately

Henry Tucker

Oh, Gen-e-vieve, I'd give the world To live a-gain the love-ly past;
D.S. Gen-e-vieve, sweet Gen-e-vieve, The days may come, the days may go,

The rose of youth was dew-im-pearled, But now it with-ers in the blast.
But still the hands of mem-'ry weave The bliss-ful dreams of long a-go.

I see thy face in ev-'ry dream, My wak-ing tho'ts are full of thee

Thy glance is in the star-ry beam That falls a-long the sum-mer sea, Oh,

124

We note that the phrases are four measures in length and thus are regular. At the end of each phrase there is a feeling of repose resulting from the use of a cadence. We also note that the music phrase follows quite naturally the word or text phrase.

Mark the phrases in the following songs. After the phrases have been indicated, sing each of them noting the effect of the phrase. Pay particular attention to the way in which each phrase begins, how it is developed, and how it is concluded.

God of Our Fathers

George W. Warren (Words by Daniel C. Roberts)

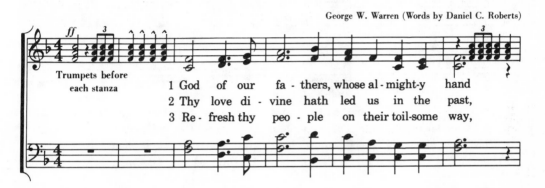

Trumpets before
each stanza

1 God of our fa - thers, whose al - might-y hand
2 Thy love di - vine hath led us in the past,
3 Re - fresh thy peo - ple on their toil-some way,

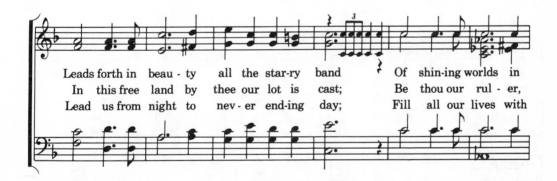

Leads forth in beau - ty all the star-ry band   Of shin-ing worlds in
In this free land by thee our lot is cast;   Be thou our rul - er,
Lead us from night to nev - er end-ing day;   Fill all our lives with

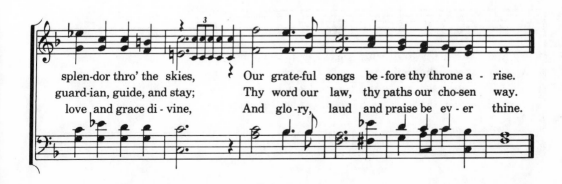

splen-dor thro' the skies,   Our grate-ful songs be -fore thy throne a - rise.
guard-ian, guide, and stay;   Thy word our law, thy paths our cho-sen way.
love and grace di - vine,   And glo-ry, laud and praise be ev - er thine.

125

America, the Beautiful

Samuel A. Ward (Words by Katharine Lee Bates)

1 O beau - ti - ful for spa - cious skies, For am - ber waves of grain, ____
2 O beau - ti - ful for pil - grim feet Whose stern im - pas - sioned stress ____
3 O beau - ti - ful for he - roes proved In lib - er - at - ing strife, ____
4 O beau - ti - ful for pa - triot dream That sees be - yond the years ____

For pur - ple moun - tain maj - es - ties A - bove the fruit - ed plain. ____
A thor - ough-fare for free - dom beat A - cross the wil - der - ness. ____
Who more than self their coun - try loved, And mer - cy more than life. ____
Thine al - a - bas - ter cit - ies gleam Un - dimmed by hu - man tears. ____

A - mer - i - ca! A - mer - i - ca! God shed his grace on thee, ____
A - mer - i - ca! A - mer - i - ca! God mend thine ev - 'ry flaw, ____
A - mer - i - ca! A - mer - i - ca! May God thy gold re - fine ____
A - mer - i - ca! A - mer - i - ca! God shed his grace on thee, ____

And crown thy good with broth - er - hood From sea to shin - ing sea.
Con - firm thy soul in self - con - trol, Thy lib - er - ty in law.
Till all suc - cess be no - ble - ness And ev - 'ry gain di - vine.
And crown thy good with broth - er - hood From sea to shin - ing sea.

Form is further extended when two phrases are added together. The resulting union of two musical phrases is called a *period*. In a musical period the first phrase is known as the *antecedent* phrase or the phrase that asks a question. The second phrase is known as the *consequent* phrase or the phrase that answers the question. In the period the antecedent phrase usually ends with a half cadence or an imperfect authentic cadence while the consequent phrase usually ends with a perfect authentic cadence. For an example of a period refer once again to the song "Sweet Genevieve" and observe the first two phrases.

Sweet Genevieve

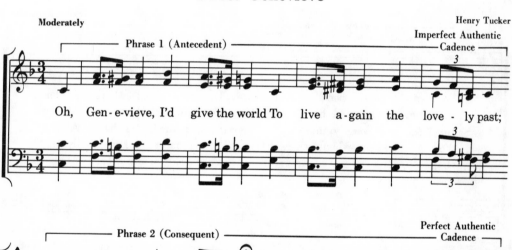

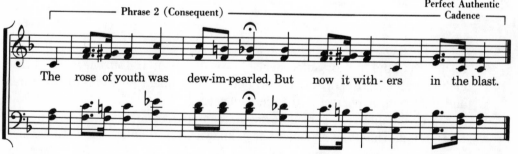

Another example of the period is found in the old Scottish folk song "Barbara Allen."

Barbara Allen

Scottish Folk Song

In this song the first or antecedent phrase is a regular four-measure phrase ending with a half cadence. The second or consequent phrase is also regular and ends with a perfect authentic cadence.

In extending the period form the composer sometimes adds a period to a period. This type of extension is known as a *double period*. In essence it makes possible a composition which is double the length of a period, or sixteen measures in length if the phrases are regular and not extended. The double period contains four coherent phrases and usually the perfect cadence is avoided at the end of the first period. In the first period of the "Crusader's Hymn" the consequent phrase ends with a half cadence. In both periods, the antecedent phrase ends with an imperfect authentic cadence while in the second period, the consequent phrase ends with a perfect authentic cadence.

128

Note the phrases, periods and cadences in this composition. Sing the song noting the effect of the four coherent phrases and the use of the half cadence for punctuating the musical thought.

Crusader's Hymn

From the German, 17th century

1 Fair-est Lord Je - sus, Rul-er of all na - ture, O thou of
2 Fair are the mead - ows, Fair-er still the wood - lands, Robed in the
3 Fair is the sun - shine, Fair-er still the moon - light, And all the

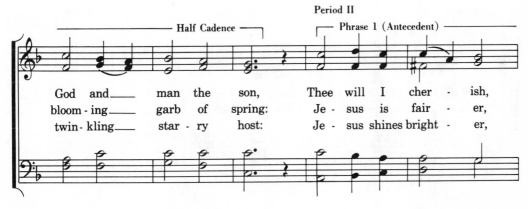

God and___ man the son, Thee will I cher - ish,
bloom-ing___ garb of spring: Je - sus is fair - er,
twin-kling___ star - ry host: Je - sus shines bright - er,

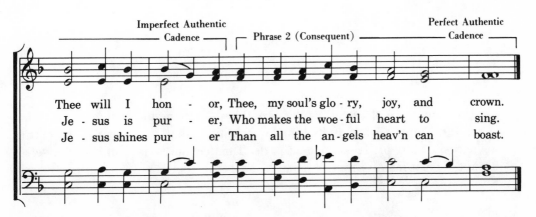

Thee will I hon - or, Thee, my soul's glo - ry, joy, and crown.
Je - sus is pur - er, Who makes the woe-ful heart to sing.
Je - sus shines pur - er Than all the an - gels heav'n can boast.

129

Analyze the following song by marking the phrases, periods and cadences.

Poetry

Arthur S. Sullivan (1842-1900)

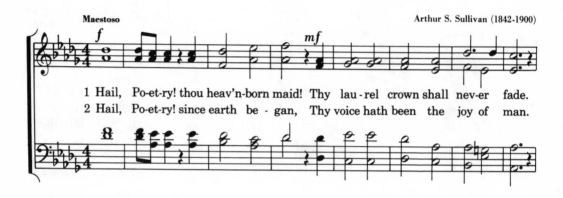

1 Hail, Po-et-ry! thou heav'n-born maid! Thy lau-rel crown shall nev-er fade.
2 Hail, Po-et-ry! since earth be - gan, Thy voice hath been the joy of man.

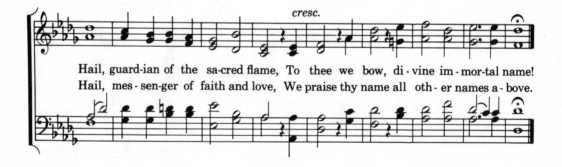

Hail, guard-ian of the sa-cred flame, To thee we bow, di - vine im - mor-tal name!
Hail, mes - sen-ger of faith and love, We praise thy name all oth - er names a - bove.

There are ways of extending the period besides using the double period. One of the simplest ways is by simple repetition—that is, repeating the entire period or any of its component parts. This technic is used in both the verse and the chorus of "Santa Lucia."

Santa Lucia

Neapolitan Boat Song

Andantino

1. Now 'neath the sil-ver moon o - cean is glow - ing, O'er the calm bil - low
   Here balm - y breez-es blow, pure joys in - vite __ us, And as we gent-ly row,
2. When o'er thy wa - ters light winds are play - ing, Thy spell can soothe __ us,
   To thee, sweet Na-po-li, what charms are giv - en, Where smiles cre - a - tion,

soft winds are blow-ing;   light us.   Hark, how the sail-or's cry Joy-ous-ly
all things de -   light us.   Home of fair Po-e - sy, Realm of pure
all care al - lay - ing;
toil blest by   heav - en.

ech-oes nigh: San - ta Lu - ci - a! San-ta Lu - ci - a!
har-mo-ny, San - ta Lu - ci - a!   Santa Lu - ci - a!

Another method of extending the period is to increase its size from two phrases to three phrases. An imperfect authentic cadence will occur at the end of the first phrase and a half cadence at the end of the second phrase. The perfect authentic cadence will then come at the end of the third phrase.

131

The Silver Fountain

French Canadian Folk Song

Phrase 1 — Imperfect Authentic Cadence

1 Here, by the spar-kling foun-tain, slow - ly I wend my way,
2 I rest be - neath an oak tree, dry ___ in the leaf - y vale.
3 Sing bird, keep up your war-bling, you ___ with your songs so gay.
4 Now I have lost my la - dy, fate ___ that was most un - fair,
5 I would the rose were turn - ing back ___ to a bud once more,

Phrase 2 — Half Cadence

Seek - ing the cool - ing wa - ter, where I may dip to - day. ___
Far on the high - est branch-es there sings a night - in - gale. ___
You have the heart for laugh-ter; I, though, could weep all day. ___
All for some love - ly ros - es, which I re - fused to share. ___
While I and my fair la - dy loved, as we loved be - fore. ___

Phrase 3 — Perfect Authentic Cadence

1-5 She, now for years my be-lov - ed, al - ways in my heart shall stay.

The method of extension by phrase groups of three is different from extend-ing a period by repeating either the antecedent or consequent phrase. In this latter instance the composer is still dealing with only two phrases.

For the Beauty of the Earth

Arr. from Conrad Kocher (Words by Folliot S. Pierpont)

The use of these devices for enlarging form still limits the composer to small expressions or miniatures. If the composer is to be able to write in larger and more extended forms he must use other methods for incorporating more material. One common way is to divide the work into parts, each part consisting of a combination of the smaller divisions just discussed. These resulting forms are known as either *simple two-part song form* (A B) or *simple three-part song form* (A B A). In simple two-part song form the parts are as follows:

$$\text{Part I Consisting of} \begin{cases} \text{a period, or} \\ \text{a double period, or} \\ \text{a phrase group} \end{cases} \qquad \text{Part II Consisting of} \begin{cases} \text{a period, or} \\ \text{a double period, or} \\ \text{a phrase group} \end{cases}$$

The well-known song "America" furnishes an excellent example of simple two-part song form.

America

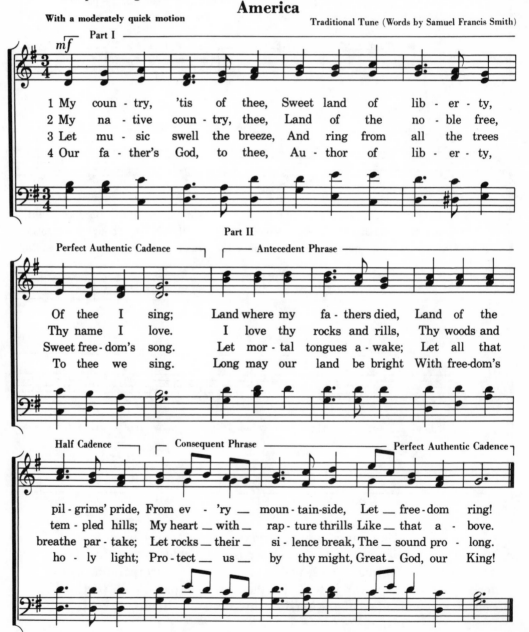

Part I consists of an irregular phrase six measures in length which concludes with a perfect authentic cadence. Part II is a contrasting period; the antecedent phrase is regular and ends with a half cadence, while the consequent phrase, also a regular four-measure phrase, ends with a perfect authentic cadence.

Another example of simple two-part song form is found in the song "Robin Adair."

Robin Adair

Scottish Air (Words by Caroline Keppel)

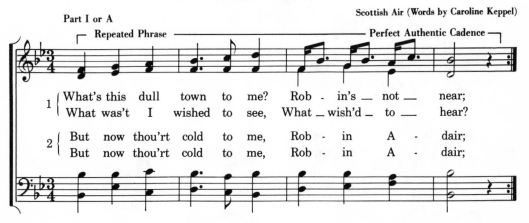

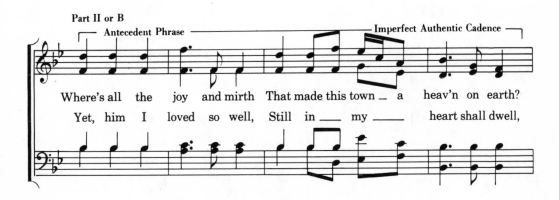

135

Part I consists of a regular four-measure phrase which is repeated and which ends on a perfect authentic cadence. Part II is a contrasting period with a regular antecedent phrase four measures in length ending with an imperfect authentic cadence. The consequent phrase is also regular and ends with a perfect authentic cadence. Note that the material for this consequent phrase is derived from the material in Part I.

In two-part song form, Part I is the statement of the main or principal idea while Part II is the statement of a contrasting idea. In this manner the composer is able to avoid the monotony of exact repetition and achieves variety through the use of contrast.

In three-part song form the composer reemphasizes the main or principal idea by repeating the material in Part I. By this means the composer is able to add unity as well as variety to his composition. If this form were outlined it would look like this:

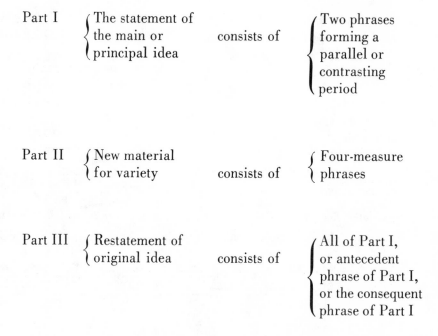

Part I	The statement of the main or principal idea	consists of	Two phrases forming a parallel or contrasting period
Part II	New material for variety	consists of	Four-measure phrases
Part III	Restatement of original idea	consists of	All of Part I, or antecedent phrase of Part I, or the consequent phrase of Part I

An excellent example of simple three-part song form is to be found in the song "The Old Oaken Bucket." Part I or A is a double period consisting of an exact repetition of the eight-measure period. Contrast and variety are achieved in Part II or B by a double period, the exact repetition of an eight-measure period. Part III or the return of A is an exact repetition of the period out of which Part I or A was constructed. Sing through this song noting how each of the parts is constructed and how each part complements the other parts.

The Old Oaken Bucket

G. Kiallmark (Words by Samuel Woodworth)

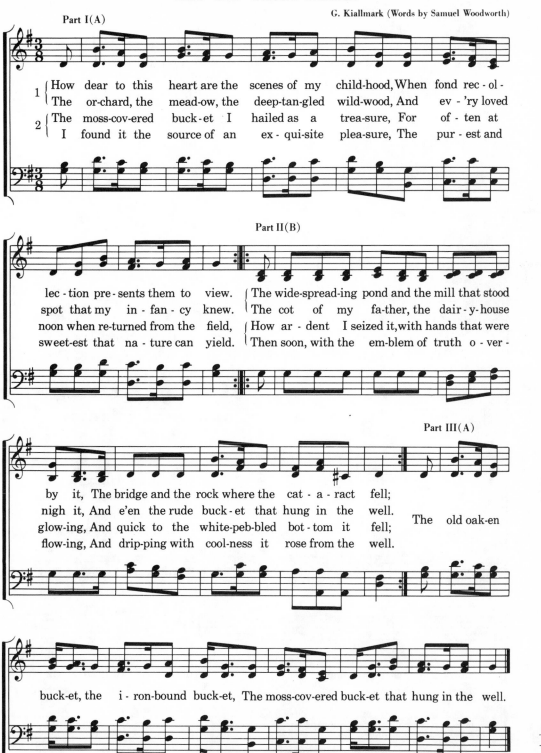

If we refer once again to the song "Sweet Genevieve" (page 124), we see that simple three-part song form is the design of this old musical friend. Analyze and mark each of the parts.

One more example of simple three-part song form should suffice. Analyze and mark the phrases and the three large divisions. What is the form of Part I or A? What is the form of Part II or B? What is the form of Part III or the final A? From where did this material come?

Long, Long Ago

T. H. Bayly

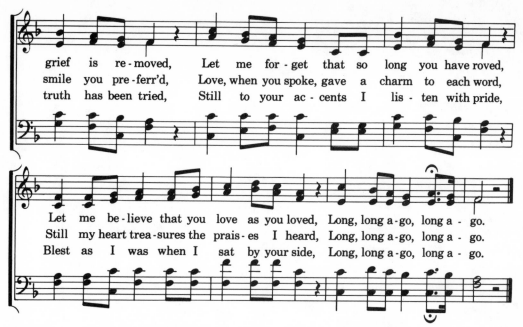

grief is re-moved, Let me for-get that so long you have roved,
smile you pre-ferr'd, Love, when you spoke, gave a charm to each word,
truth has been tried, Still to your ac-cents I lis-ten with pride,

Let me be-lieve that you love as you loved, Long, long a-go, long a-go.
Still my heart trea-sures the prais-es I heard, Long, long a-go, long a-go.
Blest as I was when I sat by your side, Long, long a-go, long a-go.

So far we have seen how the composer is able to extend his musical ideas from the note to the figure, to the phrase, to the period, and on to the simple two- or three-part song form. The possibility of extending the musical form does not end here. The composer may extend form through the use of enlarged three-part song form (A B A), or five-part song form (A B A B′ A), or he may feel the need to add an introduction to the main body and a short concluding section known as a *coda* (Introduction A B A Coda). In succeeding units other extended forms, such as the minuet-trio or song form with trio, the variation, the rondo, the sonata allegro, the fugue will be discussed. Thus these extensions of form may be studied and understood as ways in which the composer uses his material to achieve larger works.

1. Either use recordings or have someone play the following compositions on the piano. As they are being played analyze them according to their component parts—that is, the figure, phrase, period, double period, phrase group, two- or three-part song form. If it is simple song form, identify the parts.

LISTENING ACTIVITIES

    a. Album for the Young......................Robert Schumann (1810-1856)

        No. 4 A Hymn
        No. 2 Soldiers' March
        No. 7 Hunting Song
        No. 8 The Wild Horseman
        No. 10 The Merry Farmer's Return from Work
        No. 16 First Loss

    b. Songs Without Words.....................Felix Mendelssohn (1809-1847)

        Op. 19, No. 4 Confidence
        Op. 53, No. 4 Sadness of Soul
        Op. 62, No. 1 May Breezes
        Op. 67, No. 1 Meditation

Music of the people

HARVEST FESTIVAL, Jon Corbino (1905-1964)

Folk Music

From time immemorial, music, dance, art and the ballad have been an integral part of the lives of people. Through their music, art and dance, people were able to express their emotions and the events of their lives in primitive, untrained ways. Stated differently, all folk art was of the people and by the people and told of their lives and work. This rather spontaneous art product thrived long before composers, notation, artists, writers and writing were known. They were the outpourings of a simple, unlettered people and were passed along "mouth to mouth." Some scholars believe that originally a folk song came into being when one person created a song or tune and passed it along to friends and family. They in turn, if they liked it, sang it over and over and passed it along to others. In time these art statements came to be considered traditional. In a sense folk songs and folk ballads served the function of newspapers in the earlier times. Wandering minstrels chronicled the latest adventures, the choicest bits of gossip, and the latest battles in verse and song as they traveled from hamlet to hamlet. All of the folk arts share the common characteristic of being a valid communication of the cultures which produced them—a communication which is both vital and expressive.

Backgrounds in Art and Ballads

The explorations of archaeologists reveal that long before recorded history man was recording the events of his life, his ideas and his feelings in carvings, primitive drawings, paintings and decorative ornaments such as jewelry and pottery. Examples of this early art may be found in the bone carvings

143

of the Eskimos, the rock portraits of the Australian aborigines, and the drawn or painted pictures of animals found on the walls of the caves which served as homes for the prehistoric cavemen.

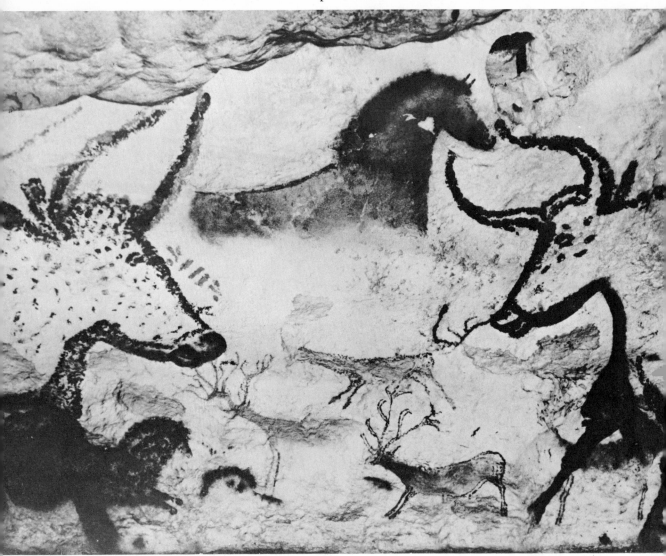

PAINTINGS ON THE WALL OF A LASCAUX CAVE

Religious motivation rather than aesthetic considerations often provided the spur for these earliest works of art. But present-day art critics praise the aesthetic properties of these works as having supreme quality. Through his ceremonial masks, icons, fetishes, totem poles and statues of his gods, early man revealed his concern for the supernatural. These early examples of folk art attest to the great skill which early man developed in carving the hardest material into artistic forms.

144

SPIRIT OF DEAD MAN,
Mask from the Tlingit Tribe, Alaska

WOMAN WHO TOLD LIES,
Mask from the Tlingit Tribe, Alaska

MASK TSONEQOA,
from Kwakiutl, British Columbia

CHIEF'S HEADDRESS,
from Alaskan Eskimos

But despite their origins in religious beliefs, these works of art clearly demonstrate that the artistic urge is innate and is shared by all mankind.

Another common characteristic of primitive folk art is its unsophisticated quality. Because it is not taught in a formal situation but rather is passed along from one generation to another, it always has a certain "unlearned" quality. Another result of this unlearned quality is a certain freshness which seems to be always present in the folk art of a people.

In the United States one can see evidence of present-day folk art in the artistic endeavors of Alaskan Eskimos and some of our American Indians. In the southwest section of the country, for example, the beautiful rug weaving and jewelry of the Navajos reflect the native artistic impulse of the people. The technic and skill necessary for the creation of these artifacts are not formally learned in a school but are passed along from one generation to the next.

NAVAJO RUG-WEAVING

TWO GRAY HILLS, Navajo Indian blanket

NAVAJO
SILVERSMITH

147

Paralleling the growth of folk art was the development of the folk ballad which tended to be a short narrative, simple in plot and structure. The metrical arrangement most commonly used in the ballad was a stanza of four lines; normally the first and third lines, each containing four iambic feet, rhymed and the second and fourth lines, each containing three iambic feet, always rhymed. A common characteristic of many of these folk ballads is a chorus or refrain which is repeated at the end of each stanza.

In the beginning the ballads were passed along from people to people by word of mouth. They were not written down because, in general, people were unable to read or write. Because these people were unable to read or write, very often the facts of the ballad were set to a given rhyme scheme to help the narrator keep track of the particulars he might otherwise forget. It is believed that the European ballads which have survived were composed in the eleventh, twelfth and thirteenth centuries, and were finally written down sometime during the seventeenth and eighteenth centuries. There is also evidence that many of the English ballads were composed by a group or groups as they participated in their folk dances and folk festivals. It was not until people had developed the ability to read and write that it became possible for some scholar or monk to set the ballads down so that they could remain in permanent form. Despite primitive and unlettered origins, the ballads provide us with a vivid picture of the period which produced them.

Scholars have pointed out that the epic, which is one of the oldest forms of literature, seems to have derived from the fusion through many centuries of these popular folk tales. Thus such superb epics as the *Iliad*, the *Odyssey* and the *Nibelungenlied*, though composed, actually had as their ancestors the early folk ballads of an unlettered people.

Because the origin of the European ballads goes back to the days of feudalism, ballads are interesting to us today since they tell us of the days when knighthood was in flower. The daring exploits, the chivalry and the beautiful ladies all contributed to the excitement and color of those earlier times. In telling their stories the action of the ballad occurs by implication and suggestion. Communication of the idea is achieved by a technic of compression. Another characteristic of these ballads is the songlike quality each possesses. Not only the story but the images come to us in the form of song. This is accomplished through the use of much repetition and the use of a refrain to reinforce the central idea.

In classifying the subject matter of the English ballad we find that, in general, an English ballad will fall into one of seven categories:

1. Ballads which have a humorous content
2. Ballads which deal with the subject of tragic love
3. Ballads which tell of domestic tragedy
4. Ballads which chronicle historical incidents
5. Ballads which are known as border ballads

6. Ballads which concern themselves with the supernatural
7. Ballads which concern themselves with the exploits of Robin Hood and his companions.

The ballad "Sir Patrick Spens" furnishes us with a typical example of the English ballad. This ballad, while lacking in details, derives its impact from the fact that such details as are given are very clear and in the form of visual images. Understatement makes the story all the more moving. The subject matter deals with a heroic kind of bravery—the nobleman dying in the performance of his duty to his king. Yet there seems to be an undercurrent of irony as if the unknown author, who might have been a poor man, were communicating scorn rather than pity for the loss of Sir Patrick Spens and the other noblemen.

Sir Patrick Spens

> The king sits in Dumferling toune,
>   Drinking the blude-reid wine:
> O quhar will I get guid sailor,
>   To sail this schip of mine?
>
> Up and spak an eldern knicht,
>   Sat at the king's richt knee:
> Sir Patrick Spens is the best sailor,
>   That sails upon the sea.
>
> The king has written a braid letter,
>   And signed it wi' his hand;
> And sent it to Sir Patrick Spens,
>   Was walking on the sand.
>
> The first line that Sir Patrick red,
>   A loud laugh lauched he:
> The next line that Sir Patrick red,
>   The teir blinded his ee.
>
> O quhar is this has don this deid,
>   This ill deid don to me;
> To send me out this time of yeir,
>   To sail upon the sea?
>
> Make haste, make haste, my mirry men all,
>   Our good schip sails the morn.
> O say na sae, my master deir,
>   For I feir a deadlie storme.

149

Late late yestreen I saw the new moone
  Wi' the auld moone in hir arme;
And I feir, I feir, my deir master,
  That we will come to harme.

O our Scots nobles wer richt laith
  To weet their cork-heild schoone;
But lang owre a' the play were played,
  Their hats they swam aboone.

O lang, lang may the ladies stand
  Wi' their fans into their hand,
Or e'er they see Sir Patrick Spens
  Come sailing to the land.

O lang, lang may the ladies stand
  Wi' their gold kems in their hair,
Waiting for their ain deir lords,
  For they'll see them na mair.

Have owre, have owre to Aberdour,
  It's fifty fadom deip:
And thair lies guid Sir Patrick Spens,
  Wi' the Scots lords at his feit.

Often ballads were composed by using a question and answer pattern. This is found in the ballad "Lord Randal." Treachery, often the subject matter of the ballad, is the thread which strings this story together. The implication is that Lord Randal's sweetheart was treacherous and poisoned him. The repetition of the lines, "mak my bed soon, For I'm wearied wi huntin, and fain wad lie down," serves to help the memory as well as to furnish a point of emphasis. The final stanza confirms the suspicion of treachery on the part of the sweetheart and provides us with the climax to the ballad.

Lord Randal

"O where ha you been, Lord Randal, my son?
And where ha you been, my handsome young man?"
"I ha been at the greenwood; mother, mak my bed soon,
For I'm wearied wi huntin, and fain wad lie down."

"An wha met ye there, Lord Randal, my son?
An wha met you there, my handsome young man?"
"O I met wi my true-love; mother, mak my bed soon,
For I'm wearied wi huntin, and fain wad lie down."

150

"And what did she give you, Lord Randal, my son?
And what did she give you, my handsome young man?"
"Eels fried in a pan; mother, mak my bed soon,
For I'm wearied wi huntin, and fain wad lie down."

"And wha gat your leavins, Lord Randal, my son?
And wha gat your leavins, my handsome young man?"
"My hawks and my hounds; mother, mak my bed soon,
For I'm wearied wi huntin, and fain wad lie down."

"And what becam of them, Lord Randal, my son?
And what becam of them, my handsome young man?"
"They swelled and they died; mother, mak my bed soon,
For I'm wearied wi huntin, and fain wad lie down."

"O I fear you are poisoned, Lord Randal, my son!
I fear you are poisoned, my handsome young man!"
"O yes, I am poisoned; mother, mak my bed soon,
For I'm sick at the heart, and I fain wad lie down."

"What d' ye leave to your mother, Lord Randal, my son?
What d' ye leave to your mother, my handsome young man?"
"Four and twenty milk kye; mother, mak my bed soon,
For I'm sick at the heart, and I fain wad lie down."

"What d' ye leave to your sister, Lord Randal, my son?
What d' ye leave to your sister, my handsome young man?"
"My gold and my silver; mother, mak my bed soon,
For I'm sick at the heart, and I fain wad lie down."

"What d' ye leave to your brother, Lord Randal, my son?
What d' ye leave to your brother, my handsome young man?"
"My houses and my lands; mother, mak my bed soon,
For I'm sick at the heart, and I fain wad lie down."

"What d' ye leave to your true-love, Lord Randal, my son?
What d'ye leave to your true-love, my handsome young man?"
"I leave her hell and fire; mother, mak my bed soon,
For I'm sick at the heart, and I fain wad lie down."

The number of stories about Robin Hood and his band which are extant leads us to believe that there must have been a number of early English ballads dealing with the life and adventures of this outlaw hero of the poor. These ballads describe Robin Hood as being an outlawed English yeoman who robbed the nobility and the higher orders of the clergy and gave the proceeds to the poor. Robin Hood was celebrated for his courage, his sportsmanship, his kindliness and his courtesy. Typical of the Robin Hood ballads is this one which tells of his introduction to Little John.

Robin Hood and Little John

When Robin Hood was about twenty years old,
*   With a hey down down and a down*
He happened to meet Little John,
A jolly brisk blade, right fit for the trade,
For he was a lusty young man.

Tho he was called Little, his limbs they were large,
And his stature was seven foot high;
Wherever he came, they quaked at his name,
For soon he would make them to fly.

How they came acquainted, I'll tell you in brief,
If you will but listen a while;
For this very jest, among all the rest,
I think it may cause you to smile.

Bold Robin Hood said to his jolly bowmen,
"Pray tarry you here in this grove;
And see that you all observe well my call,
While through the forest I rove.

"We have had no sport for these fourteen long days,
Therefore now abroad will I go;
Now should I be beat, and cannot retreat,
My horn I will presently blow."

Then did he shake hands with his merry men all,
And bid them at present good b'w'ye;
Then, as near a brook his journey he took,
A stranger he chanced to espy.

They happened to meet on a long narrow bridge,
And neither of them would give way;
Quoth bold Robin Hood, and sturdily stood,
"I'll show you right Nottingham play."

With that from his quiver an arrow he drew,
A broad arrow with a goose-wing;
The stranger replied, "I'll liquor thy hide,
If thou offerst to touch the string."

Quoth bold Robin Hood, "Thou dost prate like an ass,
For were I to bend but my bow,
I could send a dart quite through thy proud heart,
Before thou couldst strike me one blow."

"Thou talkst like a coward," the stranger replied;
"Well armed with a long bow you stand,
To shoot at my breast, while I, I protest,
Have naught but a staff in my hand."

"The name of a coward," quoth Robin, "I scorn,
Wherefore my long bow I'll lay by;
And now for thy sake, a staff will I take,
The truth of thy manhood to try."

Then Robin Hood stepped to a thicket of trees,
And chose him a staff of ground-oak;
Now this being done, away he did run
To the stranger, and merrily spoke:

"Lo! see my staff, it is lusty and tough,
Now here on the bridge we will play;
Whoever falls in, the other shall win
The battel, and so we'll away."

"With all my whole heart," the stranger replied;
"I scorn in the least to give out."
This said, they fell to 't without more dispute,
And their staffs they did flourish about.

At first Robin he gave the stranger a bang,
So hard that it made his bones ring;
The stranger he said, "This must be repaid,
I'll give you as good as you bring.

"So long as I'm able to handle my staff,
To die in your debt, friend, I scorn."
Then to it each goes, and followed their blows,
As if they had been threshing of corn.

The stranger gave Robin a crack on the crown,
Which caused the blood to appear;
Then Robin, enraged, more fiercely engaged,
And followed his blows more severe.

So thick and so fast did he lay it on him,
With a passionate fury and ire,
At every stroke, he made him to smoke,
As if he had been all on fire.

O then into fury the stranger he grew,
And gave him a damnable look,
And with it a blow that laid him full low,
And tumbled him into the brook.

"I prithee, good fellow, O where art thou now?"
The stranger, in laughter, he cried.
Quoth bold Robin Hood, "Good faith, in the flood,
And floating along with the tide.

"I needs must acknowledge thou art a brave soul;
With thee I'll no longer contend;
For needs must I say, thou has got the day,
Our battel shall be at an end."

Then unto the bank he did presently wade,
And pulled himself out by a thorn;
Which done, at the last, he blowed a loud blast
Straightway on his fine bugle-horn.

The echo of which through the valleys did fly
At which his stout bowmen appeared,
All cloathed in green, most gay to be seen;
So up to their master they steered.

"O what's the matter?" quoth William Stutely;
"Good master, you are wet to the skin."
"No matter," quoth he; "the lad which you see,
In fighting, hath tumbled me in."

"He shall not go scot-free," the others replied;
So straight they were seizing him there,
To duck him likewise; but Robin Hood cries,
"He is a stout fellow, forbear."

"There's no one shall wrong thee, friend, be not afraid;
These bowmen upon me do wait;
There's threescore and nine; if thou wilt be mine,
Thou shalt have my livery straight.

"And other accouterments fit for a man;
Speake up, jolly blade, never fear;
I'll teach you also the use of the bow,
To shoot at the fat fallow-deer."

"O here is my hand," the stranger replied,
"I'll serve you with all my whole heart;
My name is John Little, a man of good mettle;
Ne'er doubt me, for I'll play my part."

"His name shall be altered," quoth William Stutely,
"And I will his godfather be;
Prepare then a feast, and none of the least,
For we will be merry," quoth he.

They presently fetched in a brace of fat does,
With humming strong liquor likewise;
They loved what was good; so in the greenwood,
This pretty sweet babe they baptize.

He was, I must tell you, but seven foot high,
And, maybe, an ell in the waist,
A pretty sweet lad; such feasting they had;
Bold Robin the christening graced.

With all his bowmen, which stood in a ring,
And were of the Nottingham breed;
Brave Stutely comes then with seven yeomen,
And did in this manner proceed:

"This infant was called John Little," quoth he,
"Which name shall be changed anon;
The words we'll transpose, so wherever he goes,
His name shall be called Little John."

They all with a shout made the elements ring,
So soon as the office was ore;
To feasting they went, with true merriment.
And tippled strong liquor gillore.

155

Then Robin he took the pretty sweet babe,
And clothed him from top to the toe
In garments of green, most gay to be seen,
And gave him a curious long bow.

"Thou shalt be an archer as well as the best,
And range in the greenwood with us;
Where we'll not want gold nor silver, behold,
While bishops have aught in their purse.

"We live here like squires, or lords of renown,
Without ere a foot of free land;
We feast on good cheer, with wine, ale, and beer,
And ev'rything at our command."

Then music and dancing did finish the day;
At length, when the sun waxed low,
Then all the whole train the grove did refrain,
And into their caves they did go.

And so ever after, as long as he lived,
Although he was proper and tall,
Yet nevertheless, the truth to express,
Still Little John they did him call.

One of the interesting things about ballads is the way in which certain ballads travel from one country to another and the new version becomes identified with its new home. There are few American ballads as such. Many of the ballads we attribute to America in reality had their origins in England and Scotland and were brought to this country to thrive, especially in the Southern Appalachian mountain area. In their new location these ballads were passed from one group to another and one generation to another through word of mouth. The English "Bonnie Barbara Allan" which reappears in the Appalachian region as "Barb'ry Ellen" is typical of these popular transplanted ballads which stand as eloquent testimony to the universal appeal of the ballad. "The Twa Sisters," which tells a sad and grievous tale of jealousy and crime and inevitable retribution, is another transplanted ballad which in its Kentucky version has become a favorite in this country.

American ballads, like their English and Scottish counterparts, may be classified according to their subject matter. Some of the more popular types are:

1. Ballads whose subject matter deals with outlaws and other lawless characters
2. Ballads which deal with various sections or areas of the country
3. Ballads which are identified with war, such as the Revolutionary War or the Civil War
4. Ballads which tell of racial groups or the exploits of an individual member of a racial group
5. Ballads which have as their subject matter the occupations of a pioneer people
6. Religious folk ballads which grew out of the woes of slavery.

In America as the railroads began to stretch out over the land and, as a result, the country began to grow and expand, songs and tales, sometimes humorous, sometimes telling of tragedy, sprang up to attest to the importance the people attached to their railroads. The ballad "Casey Jones" is typical of the interest in the railroads of that time. Casey Jones was not the only "brave engineer" whose death at the throttle was recounted in verse and song. Since the principle mode of passing these verses along was word of mouth, it is reasonable to expect that the version given below is only one of many versions. "Casey Jones" is also illustrative of the ballad dealing with the occupations of a primitive people.

Casey Jones

> *Come, all you rounders, if you want to hear*
> *A story 'bout a brave engineer.*
> *Casey Jones was the rounder's name*
> *On a six eight wheeler, boys, he won his fame.*
> *The caller called Casey at a half past four*
> *Kissed his wife at the station door*
> *Mounted to the cabin with his orders in his hand*
> *And he took his farewell trip to that Promised Land:*
>
> CHORUS: *Casey Jones, Mounted to the cabin*
> *Casey Jones, With his orders in his hand*
> *Casey Jones, Mounted to the cabin*
> *And he took his farewell trip to the Promised Land.*

157

Put in your water and shovel your coal
Put your head out the window, watch them drivers roll
I'll run her till she leaves the rail
'Cause I'm eight hours late with that Western mail
He looked at his watch and his watch was slow
He looked at the water and the water was low
He turned to the fireman and then he said
We're goin' to reach Frisco but we'll all be dead:

CHORUS: *Casey Jones, Goin' to reach Frisco*
Casey Jones, But we'll all be dead
Casey Jones, Goin' to reach Frisco
We're goin' to reach Frisco, but we'll all be dead.

Casey pulled up that Reno hill
He tooted for the crossing with an awful shrill
The switchman knew by the engine's moan
That the man at the throttle was Casey Jones.
He pulled up within two miles of the place
Number Four stared him right in the face
He turned to the fireman, said "Boy, you better jump
'Cause there's two locomotives that's a-goin' to bump":

CHORUS: *Casey Jones, Two locomotives*
Casey Jones, That's a-goin' to bump
Casey Jones, Two locomotives
There's two locomotives that's a-goin' to bump.

Casey said just before he died
There's two more roads that I'd like to ride
The fireman said what could that be
The Southern Pacific and the Santa Fe.
Mrs. Jones sat on her bed a sigh'n'
Just received a message that Casey was dy'n'
Said "Go to bed, children, and hush your cry'n'
'Cause you got another papa on the Salt Lake Line":

CHORUS: *Mrs. Casey Jones, Got another papa,*
Mrs. Casey Jones, On that Salt Lake Line
Mrs. Casey Jones, Got another papa
And you've got another papa on the Salt Lake Line.

A legend was born in 1776 when the English captured and executed the American, Nathan Hale, taken while on a spying mission. As is true of Casey

Jones, the story of Nathan Hale has come down to us in many versions and forms. The ballad of "Nathan Hale" is an especially good example of a ballad which tells of the Revolutionary War period. Note the use of repetition in this ballad.

Nathan Hale

The breezes went steadily through the tall pines
  A-saying "Oh! hu-ush!" a-saying "Oh! hu-ush!"
As stilly stole by a bold legion of horse,
  For Hale in the bush, for Hale in the bush.

"Keep still!" said the thrush, as she nestled her young
  In a nest by the road, in a nest by the road;
"For the tyrants are near, and with them appear
  What bodes us no good, what bodes us no good."

The brave captain heard it, and thought of his home
  In a cot by the brook, in a cot by the brook;
With mother and sister and memories dear,
  He so gaily forsook, he so gaily forsook.

Cooling shades of the night were coming apace,
  The tattoo had beat, the tattoo had beat;
The noble one sprang from his dark lurking-place
  To make his retreat, to make his retreat.

He warily trod on the dry rustling leaves
  As he passed through the wood, as he passed through the wood,
And silently gained his rude launch on the shore,
  As she played with the flood, as she played with the flood.

The guards of the camp on that dark dreary night,
  Had a murderous will, had a murderous will;
They took him and bore him afar from the shore,
  To a hut on the hill, to a hut on the hill.

No mother was there, nor a friend who could cheer,
  In that little stone cell, in that little stone cell;
But he trusted in love from his Father above—
  In his heart all was well, in his heart all was well.

159

An ominous owl with his solemn bass voice
    Sat moaning hard by, sat moaning hard by:
"The tyrant's proud minions most gladly rejoice,
    For he must soon die, for he must soon die."

The brave fellow told them, no thing he restrained—
    The cruel gen'ral; the cruel gen'ral!
His errand from camp, of the ends to be gained,
    And said that was all, and said that was all.

They took him and bound him and bore him away,
    Down the hill's grassy side, down the hill's grassy side.
'Twas there the base hirelings, in royal array,
    His cause did deride, his cause did deride.

Five minutes were given, short moments, no more,
    For him to repent, for him to repent.
He prayed for his mother—he asked not another—
    To heaven he went, to heaven he went.

The faith of a martyr the tragedy showed,
    As he trod the last stage, as he trod the last stage.
And Britons still shudder at gallant Hale's blood,
    As his words do presage, as his words do presage:

"Thou pale king of terrors, thou life's gloomy foe,
    Go frighten the slave, go frighten the slave;
Tell tyrants to you their allegiance they owe—
    No fears for the brave, no fears for the brave!"

To some it might seem strange that a young and vigorous America could evidence through its ballads an intense interest in stories about its development and the heroic exploits of great patriots who gave their lives—and at the same time be interested in the exploits of the lawless. Yet for hundreds of years tales of violence, crime, passion and tragedy have been a consuming interest of peoples. Even today we see evidence of this morbid curiosity in the large circulations of "tabloid" newspapers which seem to thrive on the misfortunes and transgressions of people. For a people who in their daily life faced danger and a rugged contest with the land, the elements, wild animals and Indians, it seems natural to expect that they might like and even prefer tales which told of violence.

Typical of this category of folk ballads is the story of Jesse James. To many people Jesse James was a fine man who, like Robin Hood in England, was concerned about the plight of the poor and down-trodden. He lived in

Missouri under the name of Thomas Howard. To the citizens of this small community he was an upstanding member of the community. There is a legend that from time to time he even served as a member of the sheriff's posse which was out looking for Jesse James. There are any number of stories which speak of his kindness to widows and other people suffering misfortunes. The following ballad, however, deals with his death which came not from the hands of the lawmen but through betrayal by one of his trusted followers.

Jesse James

Jesse James was a lad that killed a-many a man,
He robbed the Glendale train;
But the dirty little coward that shot Mister Howard,
Has laid poor Jesse in his grave.

CHORUS: *Poor Jesse had a wife to mourn for his life,*
Three children, they were brave,
But that dirty little coward that shot Mister Howard
Has laid poor Jesse in his grave.

It was Robert Ford, that dirty little coward,
I wonder how does he feel?
For he ate of Jesse's bread and he slept in Jesse's bed
And laid poor Jesse in his grave.

It was his brother, Frank, who robbed the Gailatin bank
And carried the money from the town;
It was in this very place that they had a little race
For they shot Captain Sheets to the ground.

They went to the crossing not very far from there
And there they did the same;
With the agent on his knees, he delivered up the keys
To the outlaws, Frank and Jesse James.

It was on a Wednesday night, the moon was shining bright,
They robbed the Glendale train;
The people they did say for many miles away,
It was robbed by Frank and Jesse James.

It was on a Saturday night, Jesse was at home,
Talking to his family brave,
Robert Ford came along like a thief in the night
And laid poor Jesse in his grave.

161

The people held their breath, when they heard of Jesse's death
And wondered how he ever came to die;
It was one of the gang, called little Robert Ford,
He shot poor Jesse on the sly.

Jesse went to his rest with his hand on his breast;
The devil will be on his knee.
He was born one day in the county of Clay
And came from a solitary race.

This song was made by Billy Gashade,
As soon as the news did arrive;
He said there was no man with the law in his hand,
Who could take Jesse James when alive.

We have seen how the literary ballads told of the lives and interests of the people. In the same way the folk music was expressive of the mood, the interests, and the lives of these people. There was, in fact, a natural tie-in of the music to the ballad. Through the use of the rhyme scheme and a simple melody the minstrel was helped to remember details that he might otherwise have forgotten. Because of this relationship to the ballad, folk music itself has many of the same characteristics of the ballad. Generally, the folk song is simple. One senses the untrained and primitive origins of the song. Although there may be a certain lack of refinement in the simple music of the people, we should never be misled into believing that folk music is always uncouth or that it lacks the power to be expressive to a fine degree.

Often the question is raised, why are there so many different versions of a given folk song? When one remembers how these songs were transmitted from one person to another and from one community to another, the answer seems to be quite obvious. As is true today the song which struck a responsive chord in the people became popular and there was a demand for its repetition. We have seen that in earlier times people were unlettered and untrained, and that the only means of transmitting their music was by word of mouth. This naturally led to errors in learning which were passed along to new learners. They, because it was repeated inaccurately, learned what amounted to a new version of the song. And if the new learner in turn taught the new version inaccurately another new version came into being.

New and different versions also came into being when a song was transplanted into a new location and there was a conscious altering, adapting and adding to the text and music to meet local conditions. One of the simplest adaptions was the adding to the melody of new words and verses which told of personages or events in the new locale. Sometimes in order to make the new words fit the music it was necessary to change and often add new melodic and rhythmic figures. Often, also, the locale contributed to the alteration of the original folk song through the substituting of a new and different phrasing. It seems obvious that only the best elements of a song would be able to survive the innumerable mutations and transfusions which were carried on as the song went from one person to another, one community to another, one country to another.

When we speak of folk music we often think of it in context with dance or group situations. Certainly folk music was an integral part of the gathering of people whether it was for a dance, a husking bee, a barn raising or a religious service. Certainly music served as an effective instrument in bringing people together in any sort of social situation. So we see that very often folk music called for a group situation or a group performance.

We have seen that there was a natural tie-in between music and the ballad. As a result there are any number of folk songs which tell the stories and legends found in the earlier ballads or which are, in other words, musical settings of these ballads. There are many folk songs, however, whose subject matter comes from other sources besides folk ballads. In addition to folk songs whose origins are connected with literary ballads there are folk songs whose subject matter concerns itself with:

1. Work songs. Songs which help man make his work easier, either by relieving the monotony or by helping the group to work together through the rhythm of a song. Sea chanteys are particularly good examples of this kind of folk music.
2. Songs for dancing. In much of the folk music there is a relatively short step between song and dance. In fact many folk dances began as songs while many songs had their beginnings in the dance.
3. Songs for religious ceremonies and holidays. Many of the Christmas carols commonly used today had folk beginnings with unknown authors and composers whose names have been lost in antiquity. The spirituals of the Negroes who sang to a kindly God to free them from their miseries would also fit into this category. In the Appalachian Mountains the whites were at this time also producing a type of spiritual, now called "white spirituals," which gave the people an opportunity for the spontaneous raising of their hearts in song in praise of, or petition to, the God above who ruled their lives.
4. Songs which celebrated the virtues of patriotism or commemorated certain events which took place during war.
5. Songs which told of love and marriage.
6. Songs which were the special province of children, including singing games, cradle songs and nursery rhymes.
7. Songs which had a satirical basis and were usually concerned with politics.
8. Songs about drinking and strong drink.
9. Songs which dealt with funerals and mourning.

National characteristics, conditions and even climate may affect the music of the people. For this reason the forces which apply to the lives of people, in many instances, make it possible to identify the music, upon hearing it, as being from this country or that country. The people of Spain have long been known for their love of color, gaiety and the dance. Their music is characterized in these terms—gay in mood, highly rhythmic, with beautiful and warm harmonies—an expression of the people of Spain. Their concern for the rhythmic structure is emphasized by the use of typical Spanish rhythm instruments such as the castanet and tambourine. We are not apt to confuse the vigorous Spanish music with the music of Scandinavia, much of which is plaintive and somber and tends to be mostly in the minor mode or even modal in character.

It is possible to study the folk music of any country to determine what these national characteristics are which influence the music. There are many authoritative and interesting anthologies which put into authentic form the folk music of the past and preserve these vital musical expressions of earlier peoples.

A comparison of the folk music of England and America will reveal some of the national characteristics which gave rise to the music of both countries. Because it came from the people, we say that it is folk music.

English Folk Music

As was true of the ballads of the English people, the text of English folk songs generally tells a story of people rather than of nature. The life and adventures of Robin Hood and his companions, for example, furnished a natural subject not only for the ballads but for the folk songs of this country. A further interest was found in the affairs of the lords and ladies of the time. At the other end of the social scale one finds many songs which tell of the activities of common people such as milkmaids, sailors and other workers. One even finds an interest in the ominous activities of the hangman. On the other hand, some of the world's most beautiful and appealing Christmas carols had their origin in England.

SINGING
EXPERIENCES

Scarborough Fair

With motion

```
1 "Oh,   where  are   you    go - ing?" "To   Scar - b'ro    Fair,"
2 "And   tell   her   to    make  me   a    cam - bric    shirt,"
3 "And   tell   her   to    wash  it   in   yon - der    well,"
4 __    "Tell   her   to    dry   it   on   yon - der    thorn,"
5 "Oh,   will   you   find   me ___    an   acre   of     land,"
```

164

Sa - vo - ry, sage, _____ rose - mar - y and thyme,

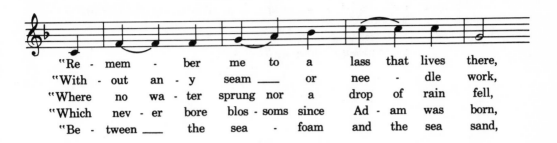

"Re - mem - ber me to a lass that lives there,
"With - out an - y seam _____ or nee - dle work,
"Where no wa - ter sprung nor a drop of rain fell,
"Which nev - er bore blos - soms since Ad - am was born,
"Be - tween _____ the sea - foam and the sea sand,

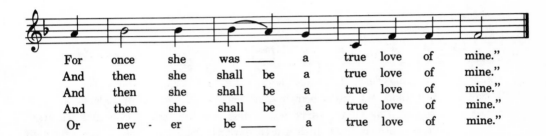

For once she was _____ a true love of mine."
And then she shall be a true love of mine."
And then she shall be a true love of mine."
And then she shall be a true love of mine."
Or nev - er be _____ a true love of mine."

"Scarborough Fair" is a good example of an old English folk song type known as a riddle song. This particular riddle song will be found to have many different versions. Note the repetition of the words, "Savory, sage, rosemary, and thyme," also "And then she shall be a true love of mine" in each verse. These serve in a limited sense the function of a chorus or refrain which, in turn, brings a certain unity to the work. There is a gay and capricious mood to this song which stems in part from the nonsense words and in part from a melody which complements the text.

RHYTHM: The song moves in three with a rolling motion. Because of its movement and motion there is a dance-like feeling to the music. The meter is given as 3/4. The note values which are used are quarter notes (♩ ♩ ♩), half notes (♩), combinations of half and quarter notes (♩ ♩), and dotted half notes (♩.) .

MELODY: The melody is in the key of F major. It has an octave range from middle C to the octave above, using every note except E. The melody is essentially conjunct or stepwise in its conception but is relieved occasionally by medium- or small-sized skips. In measures 1 and 9 the melody consists of repeated tones.

HARMONY: As is typical of folk music, this particular example has a simple harmonization. It may be harmonized by the use of three chords, the I (FAC), the IV (B♭DF), and the V₇ (CEGB♭). To prove this, use the autoharp, strumming the proper chord at the beginning of each measure. The cadences in measures 4, 8 and 12 are half cadences based on the V₇ (CEGB♭) chord while the cadence in measure 16 is a perfect authentic cadence based on the I (FAC) chord.

TIMBRE: This will depend on the voice singing this folk song as well as the kind of instrument or instruments used for the accompaniment.

165

In analyzing this folk song for form, we see that it contains four regular phrases, each being four measures in length:

Phrase 1   measures 1-4 *(with pick-up)*
Phrase 2   measures 5-8
Phrase 3   measures 9-12
(with pick-up in measure 8)

Phrase 4   measures 13-16
(with pick-up in measure 12)

Phrase 3 is an exact repetition of Phrase 1. Because of the half cadence at the end of Phrase 2, the overall form of the work can be analyzed as being *double period.*

The Turtledove

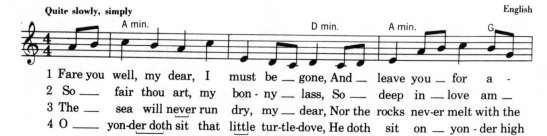

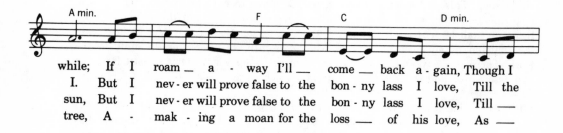

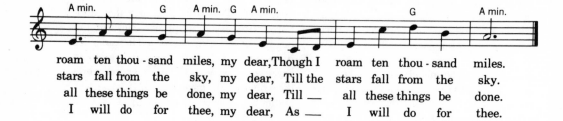

"The Turtledove" belongs to the classification of folk songs known as love songs. This particular song is known as a farewell love song. It is available to us in many different versions. One senses the mood of the song as one of sincerity and devotion.

RHYTHM: The song moves in four. The meter is given as 4/4 which means that there is the equivalent of four quarter notes in every measure. The rhythm is regular. The music moves slowly but steadily. The note values which are used are eighth (♪) notes, quarter (♩) notes, dotted half (♩.) notes, and combinations of these notes (♩ ♫ ♩ ♫) and (♫ ♫ ♩ ♫).

MELODY: If one plays a scale at the piano beginning with A, using only the white keys ending on A, the resulting scale is said to be modal, that is, it is neither major nor minor. This particular mode is known as the *Aeolian mode*. If the notes of "The Turtledove" are plotted we find that the melody falls in the *Aeolian mode*, giving it a special character which could not be found if it were written in either major or minor. The melody has a range from middle C up one octave plus one tone to D. All of the notes within this range, with the exception of F, are used. While the melody is essentially stepwise, there are a number of skips used to make the melody more expressive. In most instances, the skips are small but in three places one finds a minor sixth.

HARMONY: While more chords are used in the harmonization of this folk song than in "Scarborough Fair," the harmonization is still relatively simple. The basic tonality is established through the use of the A minor (ACE) chord. One other minor chord is used, the D minor (DFA) chord. In addition to the two minor chords there are three major chords: a G major (GBD) chord, an F major (FAC) chord, and a C major (CEG) chord which are used to furnish harmonic contrast. This song may be accompanied with the autoharp.

TIMBRE: This will depend on the voice singing this song as well as the kind of instrument or instruments used for the accompaniment.

FORM: This song contains two phrases; the first phrase, measures 1-4, is regular and ends with a perfect cadence. The second phrase, measures 5-10, is an irregular phrase six measures in length. Note that in measure 8 there is a feeling of a partial ending or pause created by the use of a cadence chord; but this does not really complete the musical sense of the phrase, making necessary the additional material found in the last two measures.

Some of the most beloved of our Christmas carols had their origins in the early folk music of England. Carols such as "We Wish You a Merry Christmas," "The Friendly Beasts," "I Saw Three Ships Come Sailing In," "God Rest Ye Merry, Gentlemen," and "What Child Is This" have become such a part of our own Christmas celebrations that we are apt to think of them as our own and overlook their humble origins in England. The English carol "The Twelve Days of Christmas" is representative of the English folk carol. It is very old and is unusual in that it uses the very successful folk song technic of the cumulative verse. This provides a type of chorus or refrain constructed through the piling up and singing back in reverse order of each successive verse. The twelve days of Christmas in the song are the days between Christmas and Epiphany.

167

The Twelve Days of Christmas

Traditional English Carol

1 On the first day of Christ-mas my true love sent to me,

A par-tridge ___ in a pear tree.

2 On the sec-ond day of Christ-mas my true love sent to me,
3 On the third ___ day of Christ-mas my true love sent to me,
4 On the fourth ___ day of Christ-mas my true love sent to me,

repeat preceding stanza

two tur-tle-doves
three French ___ hens, and a par-tridge ___ in a pear tree.
four call-ing birds,

5 On the fifth day of Christ-mas my true love sent to me,
6 On the sixth day of Christ-mas my true love sent to me,
7 On the seventh day of Christ-mas my true love sent to me,

(omit for stanza 5)

six geese a-lay-ing, five gold ___ rings, four ___ call-ing birds,
sev'n swans a-swim-ming,

three French hens, two ___ tur-tle-doves and a par-tridge ___ in a pear tree.

8 On the eighth day ... eight maids a-milking,
9 On the ninth day ... nine ladies dancing,
10 On the tenth day ... ten lords a-leaping,
11 On the eleventh day ... eleven pipers piping,
12 On the twelfth day ... twelve drummers drumming,

168

This particular folk song is gay in mood and reflects the happiness of the Christmas season.

RHYTHM: The rhythm, in general, gives a rollicking movement which carries the song from one stanza to the next. Note that the song is written in two different meters: 4/4 and 3/4, with the song basically being in 4/4 but shifting to one or two measures of 3/4 to accommodate the rhythm of the text. The note values used are eighth (♪) notes, quarter (♩) notes, half (♩) notes and dotted half (♩.) notes.

HARMONY: This folk carol may be harmonized with the use of three chords, the I (FAC or F major chord), the V₇ (CEGBb or C₇ chord) in the key of F major and the V₇ (GBDF or G₇ chord) of C major. The song, therefore, has a very simple harmonization. "The Twelve Days of Christmas" may be accompanied with the autoharp using these three chords.

TIMBRE: This will depend on the voice singing this carol, and the kind of instrument or instruments used for the accompaniment.

MELODY: The melody is written in the key of F major. The melody begins on the fifth of the scale, the C, and has a range of one octave and one note. All of the notes within this range are used. Note the altered note, B♮, in the fifth stanza which temporarily gives us a feeling of a new key, C major, but which immediately goes back into the original key of F major. The melody is a combination of small skips and ascending stepwise progressions.

FORM: The first stanza consists of a four-measure phrase ending with a perfect authentic cadence. The second phrase is an irregular phrase, five measures in length, because of the addition of the last two measures of the first stanza. Each succeeding stanza likewise becomes longer through the addition of the preceding verses until the last stanza is reached, which contains twenty-eight measures. It was in this manner that the form of the original four measures was extended. The song ends with a perfect authentic cadence.

Tam Pierce

This English folk song is also known as "Widdecombe Fair." The subject is the request of a group of Tam Pierce's cronies for the loan of his gray mare in order to attend the Widdecombe Fair and the subsequent loss of the mare. Note the repetition of the two choruses:

"All along, down along, out along lee,"
and
"Bill Brewer, Jan Strewer, Peter Gurney,
Peter Davy, Dan'l Whidder, Harry Hawke,
Old Uncle Tom Cobleigh and all. Old Uncle
Tom Cobleigh and all."

RHYTHM: The rhythm of "Tam Pierce" is in 6/8 meter, or basically a long pulse followed by a short pulse which gives the song a rollicking, skipping or galloping movement. The tempo or speed of the last verse is slower in order to convey the mood of the text. The note values which are used are quarter (♩) notes, eighth (♪) notes, sixteenth (♬) notes, dotted

169

quarter (♩.) notes and dotted eighth
(♪.) notes. Although there are six beats
to the measure there is really a feeling
of only two beats to the measure.

MELODY: The melody is written in
              the key of G major and
begins on the fifth of the scale. The
melody which begins on D above middle C has a range of one octave with
all of the notes within this range being
used. The melody is a combination of
small skips plus one large skip found
between measures 10 and 11 and descending in stepwise progressions. It
is a simple, singable melody which can
be learned easily by rote just by hearing it sung.

HARMONY: This song has a very sim-
              ple harmonization. It may
be harmonized with the use of two
chords, the I (GBD or G major) chord
and the V₇ (DF♯AC or D₇) chord.

TIMBRE: This particular version is
              sung by a male singer ac-
companied with a guitar. In the final
stanza the singer changes the vocal
quality in order to communicate the
meaning of the text.

FORM: The song consists of eight
              stanzas. Each stanza is
thirteen measures in length, which indicates that the individual phrases are
irregular in length. There are actually
only two phrases separated by the two
choruses. The form of each stanza is:

two-measure phrase *(ends on perfect
authentic cadence)*
two-measure chorus *("All along,
down along, out along lee."
Ends on a half cadence)*
two-measure phrase *(ends on a
deceptive cadence)*
seven-measure chorus *("With Bill
Brewer, Jan Strewer, Peter Gurney,"
etc. Ends on a perfect authentic
cadence)*

High Barbary

The early versions of this very old folk
song probably told of a battle between
the ships of the French and English. A
revival of the song, which took place
sometime between the years 1795 and
1815, came during a time when pirates
were taking a fearsome toll from the
ships they captured.

RHYTHM: The rhythm of "High Bar-
              bary" is in 2/4 meter and
has for the most part a long pulse followed by a short pulse. It has a vigorous movement which seems to reflect
the movement of the sea. The note
values used are quarter (♩) notes, eighth
(♪) notes and dotted quarter (♩.) notes.

MELODY: The melody is written in
              E minor and begins on the
fifth of the scale, the B below middle
C. The melody has a range of one octave. The melody for the most part is
a series of figures which ascend or
descend stepwise with small skips to
give variety to the melody. The interval
used for "blow high" is a large skip—
a skip of an octave or the B below
middle C to the B one octave above.

HARMONY: As is typical of folk music
              this song has a very sim-
ple harmonization. Two chords, the I
(EGB or E minor) chord and the V₇
(BD♯F♯A or B₇) chord, are used.

170

TIMBRE: In this version the song is sung by a male singer using a guitar for accompaniment.

FORM: The song contains four 4-measure phrases with two of the phrases being repeated choruses. The form of each verse is as follows:

Phrase 1   four measures (ends on perfect authentic cadence)

Phrase 2   four-measure chorus ("Blow high! Blow low! and so sailed we." Ends on half cadence)

Phrase 3   four measures (ends on half cadence)

Phrase 4   four-measure chorus ("A-sailing down all on the Coasts of High Barbary." Ends on a perfect authentic cadence)

John Peel

The words to "John Peel" were written by John W. Graves to honor John Peel who was a master of the hounds around the year 1820. He set the words to an old folk melody called "Bonnie Annie." It is a song which portrays the interest of the English people in the affairs of the aristocracy of the time and their love of fox hunting. While the song speaks of the death of John Peel, there is a feeling of the gaiety and color of the hunt. One can almost hear the sound of the hunting horn and see the fox and the hounds.

RHYTHM: The rhythm of "John Peel" is in 4/4 meter. It has a definite feeling of four beats to the measure. For the most part the rhythm is derived from a combination of quarter (♩) notes and eighth (♪) notes. There are occasional uses of the dotted eighth (♪.) note which makes necessary a compensating sixteenth (♪) note. The last measure of the verse and also the chorus make use of a half (♩) note.

MELODY: The melody is in the key of C major and begins on the third of the scale—the E above middle C. The melody ranges from the B below middle C to C the octave above, using all of the notes within this range. The melody for the most part consists of small skips and ascending and descending stepwise progressions. There is an octave skip upwards in measures 5 and 13.

HARMONY: "John Peel" may be harmonized with a very simple harmonization which, as we have already seen, is a characteristic of folk music. Three chords, the I (CEG or C) chord, the IV (FAC or F) chord and the V_7 (GBDF or G_7) chord are sufficient to provide a satisfactory harmonization for "John Peel."

TIMBRE: This particular version is sung by a male singer accompanied with a guitar.

FORM: "John Peel" is in simple two-part song form, Part I being the verse and Part II being the chorus. Part I is a period of eight measures consisting of two regular four-measure phrases. The first or antecedent phrase ends on a half cadence while the second or consequent phrase ends on a perfect authentic cadence. In Part II, or the chorus, the antecedent phrase ends on a half cadence and the consequent phrase ends on a perfect authentic cadence.

171

American Folk Music

Much of the folk music of America was inherited from old world sources. Songs from the old country were brought to America by the early emigrants and freely adapted to the new life. New words and phrases and even new melodic bits found their way into current use, and thus new versions of older folk material became associated with the lives of the people living in this country. In addition, songs which were native to the country also sprang into being. America has always been known as a singing country and, as one result, every section and community produced its own songs. These homemade songs which were passed along by word of mouth dealt with the common man and told of the sorrows, the occupations, the loves, the heroes and the scandals of the people. Even the escapades of the lawless found their way into the songs of a pioneer people struggling to develop this country into a strong nation.

In addition to the variety to be found in American folk music, there is also an element of informality which is easily recognized. Informality is so much a part of American people that it is readily apparent in their lives, their work and their social intercourse. One can almost recognize the social gatherings out of which came these rich folk expressions.

The favorite subjects for the folk songs of America seemed to be sea chanteys, courting songs, songs of the pioneers, folk songs of the Appalachian region, cattle herding songs, songs of railroading, songs about outlaws, Negro spirituals and the songs of the different Indian tribes. Each of them covered some phase of American life as it was then being lived, and was a definite part of the culture which produced it.

**SINGING
EXPERIENCE**

John Henry

Traditional American Ballad

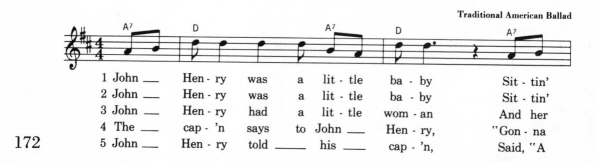

1 John __ Hen - ry was a lit - tle ba - by Sit - tin'
2 John __ Hen - ry was a lit - tle ba - by Sit - tin'
3 John __ Hen - ry had a lit - tle wom - an And her
4 The __ cap - 'n says to John __ Hen - ry, "Gon - na
5 John __ Hen - ry told __ his __ cap - 'n, Said, "A

172

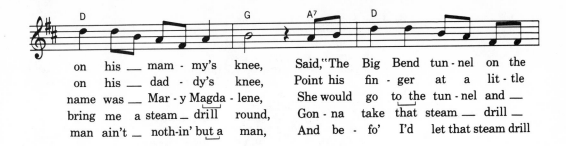

on his — mam - my's knee,   Said,"The Big Bend tun - nel on the
on his — dad - dy's knee,   Point his fin - ger at a lit - tle
name was — Mar - y Magda - lene,   She would go to the tun - nel and —
bring me a steam — drill round,   Gon - na take that steam — drill —
man ain't — noth-in' but a man,   And be - fo' I'd let that steam drill

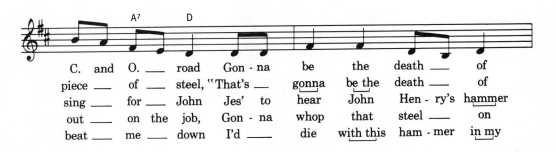

C. and O. — road Gon - na be the death — of
piece — of — steel, "That's — gonna be the death — of
sing — for — John Jes' to hear John Hen - ry's hammer
out — on the job, Gon - na whop that steel — on
beat — me — down I'd — die with this ham - mer in my

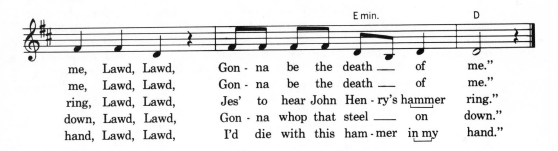

me, Lawd, Lawd, Gon - na be the death — of me."
me, Lawd, Lawd, Gon - na be the death — of me."
ring, Lawd, Lawd, Jes' to hear John Hen - ry's hammer ring."
down, Lawd, Lawd, Gon - na whop that steel — on down."
hand, Lawd, Lawd, I'd die with this ham - mer in my hand."

6 Sun were hot and burnin'
  Weren't no breeze atall,
  Sweat ran down like water down a hill,
  That day John let his hammer fall,
  Lawd, Lawd, that day John let his hammer fall.

7 White man told John Henry,
  "Nigger, damn yo' soul,
  You may beat dis steam and drill of mine,—
  When the rocks in the mountains turn to gold,
  Lawd, Lawd, when the rocks in the mountains turn to gold."

8 John Henry said to his shaker,
  "Shaker, why don't you sing?
  I'm throwin' twelve pounds from my hips on down,
  Jes' lissen to the cold steel ring,
  Lawd, Lawd, jes' lissen to the cold steel ring."

9 O the cap'n told John Henry,
  "I b'lieve this mountain's sinkin' in,"
  John Henry said to his cap'n, "O my,
  It's my hammer just a-hossin' in the wind,
  Lawd, Lawd, it's my hammer just a-hossin' in the wind."

173

10 John Henry told his shaker,
    "Shaker, you better pray,
    For if I miss this six-foot steel
    Tomorrow be yo' buryin' day,
    Lawd, Lawd, tomorrow be yo' buryin' day."

11 John Henry told his cap'n,
    "Looky yonder what I see—
    Yo' drill's done broke and yo' hole's done choke,
    An' you can't drive steel like me,
    Lawd, Lawd, an' you can't drive steel like me."

12 John Henry was hammerin' on the mountain,
    An' his hammer was striking fire,
    He drove so hard till he broke his pore heart
    An' he lied down his hammer an' he died,
    Lawd, Lawd, he lied down his hammer an' he died.

13 They took John Henry to the graveyard
    An' they buried him in the sand
    An' ev'ry locomotive come roarin' by,
    Says, "There lays a steel drivin' man,"
    Lawd, Lawd, says, "There lays a steel drivin' man."

It is interesting that one of America's greatest and most popular ballads should tell of a lowly railroad worker whose job was to drive drills into the rock to make holes for dynamite charges. John Henry is supposed to have used a ten-pound sheep-nose hammer attached to a handle four feet long. It is said that his hammer would travel like lightning over a distance of nineteen feet because he would stand back some six feet from the steel. This song tells how John Henry gave his life in a contest with a steam drill during the construction of the Big Bend tunnel on the C. and O. Railroad sometime around 1873. Although he gave his life, the song says he proved that man was better than his machines.

RHYTHM: The rhythm of "John Henry" is in 4/4 meter. It makes use of an element frequently found in this kind of music which is called syncopation. Syncopation is the shifting of an accent from its regular and expected position (♩ ♩ ♩ ♩) to an unexpected and normally weak beat (♩ ♩ ♩ ♩) . In "John Henry" the syncopation is expressed in the following rhythmic figures: ♪♩ and ♪♩. . The note values used are half (♩) notes, quarter (♩) notes, eighth (♪) notes, and dotted quarter (♩.) notes.

MELODY: The melody is written in the key of D major and begins on A or the fifth of the scale. The melody has a range from B below middle C to D an octave and one note above middle C. All of the notes within this range except middle C, G and the octave C are used in the melody. The melody is essentially constructed out of small skips which, for the most part, outline the chord of which the individual notes are members. There are occasional uses of passing tones which connect tones from the same chord.

HARMONY: The harmonization of "John Henry" is a simple harmonization based on the three primary chords in D major, the I (DF#A or D) chord, the IV (GBD or G) chord and the V_7 (AC#EG or A_7) chord. These three chords are supplemented with the use of one secondary chord, the E minor (EGB) chord found on the third beat of measure 9.

TIMBRE: This will depend on the voice or voices singing the folk song, and the kind of instrument or instruments used for the accompaniment.

174

The form of "John Henry" is a double period with two additional measures at the end called a codetta. Each phrase is two measures in length. Phrase 1 ends on a perfect authentic cadence. Phrase 2 ends on a IV chord.

Phrase 3 ends on a perfect authentic cadence. Phrase 4 ends on a I chord. The codetta ends with a II_7-I progression. This codetta serves the purpose of adding a short refrain to each stanza.

Sourwood Mountain

Appalachian Folk Song

With dancing rhythm

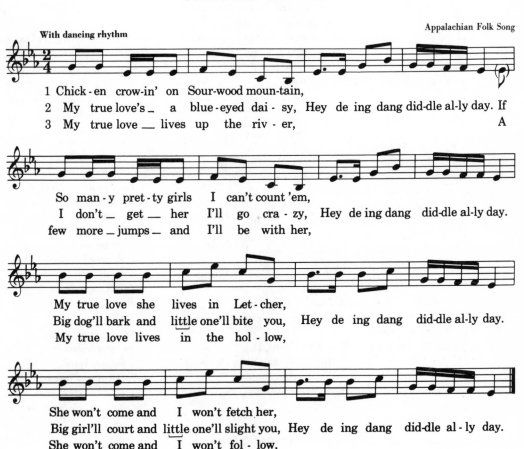

1 Chick-en crow-in' on Sour-wood moun-tain,
2 My true love's _ a blue-eyed dai-sy, Hey de ing dang did-dle al-ly day. If
3 My true love _ lives up the riv-er,   A

So man-y pret-ty girls   I can't count 'em,
I don't _ get _ her   I'll go cra-zy, Hey de ing dang   did-dle al-ly day.
few more _ jumps _ and   I'll be with her,

My true love she   lives in Let-cher,
Big dog'll bark and   little one'll bite you,   Hey de ing dang   did-dle al-ly day.
My true love lives   in the hol-low,

She won't come and   I won't fetch her,
Big girl'll court and   little one'll slight you,   Hey de ing dang   did-dle al-ly day.
She won't come and   I won't fol-low,

In the early days when settlements were few and far between and people were separated by great distances, they eagerly looked for excuses to come together for social good times. Husking bees, barn raisings, harvest festivals, weddings and dances furnished the necessary excuse for gathering the people together for work and sociability. The dance furnished the principal form of entertainment for these gatherings and the fiddle was the popular accompanying instrument for the dance. In fact, while the fiddle was an integral part of the dance, at this time it had not yet been accepted as an instrument for polite society. "Sourwood Mountain" is a typical good fiddle tune

175

and was a favorite of the dancers. Dancers would sometimes alternate with the fiddler by singing different verses and choruses as they danced. It tells a simple story of a young lover who looks across the hills to the cabin where his fair love lives and thinks about what a desirable young girl she is. He imagines that he asks her father for her hand but he finally decides he would not want her anyway.

RHYTHM: The rhythm is a dance rhythm written in 2/4 meter. It is a regular rhythm which makes it easy to put your feet down on the beat. The occasional long pulse followed by a short pulse gives rhythmic interest to the song. The note values used are quarter (♩) notes, eighth (♪) notes, sixteenth (♬) notes and dotted eighth (♪.) notes.

MELODY: This version of "Sourwood Mountain" has the melody written in the key of E♭ major. The melody begins on G, the third of the scale. The melody has a range from B♭ below middle C to E♭ on the fourth space of the staff. Within this range all of the notes of the scale except the D above middle C, the D one octave above and A♭ are used. The melody is constructed of short skips and short descending stepwise progressions.

HARMONY: "Sourwood Mountain" can be harmonized through the use of the three primary chords in the key of E♭ major. The I (E♭GB♭ or E♭) chord, the IV (A♭CE♭ or A♭) chord, and the V₇ (B♭DFA♭ or B♭₇) chord are the three necessary chords for this simple harmonization.

TIMBRE: This will depend on the voice or voices and the kind of instrument or instruments used for the accompaniment.

FORM: The two-measure refrain, "Hey de ing dang did-dle al-ly day," interrupting two-measure phrases in the verse, is typical of this kind of folk song. The form of "Sourwood Mountain" would be diagrammed as follows:

Phrase 1	Two measures *(ends on a half cadence)*
Refrain 1	Two measures *(ends on a perfect authentic cadence)*
Phrase 2	Two measures *(repeat of Phrase 1)*
Refrain 2	Two measures *(repeat of Refrain 1)*
Phrase 3	Two measures *(ends on a deceptive cadence)*
Refrain 3	Two measures *(ends on a perfect authentic cadence)*
Phrase 4	Two measures *(repeat of Phrase 3)*
Refrain 4	Two measures *(repeat of Refrain 3)*

Wayfaring Stranger

Moderately

Religious Folk Ballad, U. S. A.

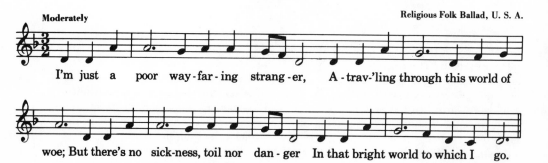

I'm just a poor way-far-ing strang-er, A-trav-'ling through this world of woe; But there's no sick-ness, toil nor dan-ger In that bright world to which I go.

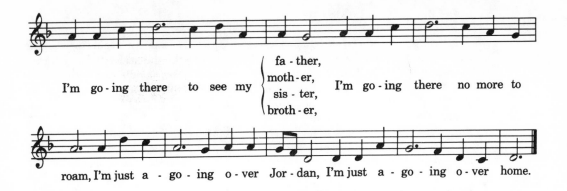

I'm go-ing there to see my { fa-ther, moth-er, sis-ter, broth-er, } I'm go-ing there no more to roam, I'm just a - go - ing o - ver Jor-dan, I'm just a - go - ing o - ver home.

"Wayfaring Stranger" is one of the most beautiful of the many spiritual folk songs of early America. While this song came from the southern mountain region, it is known and beloved by most Americans. This type of religious ballad had its beginnings back in Revolutionary times when people were fighting for both political and religious liberty. The religious struggle was revealed in the throwing out of the old psalms and the replacing of them by setting the religious songs to folk tunes which seemed to express better the religious emotions of the people.

RHYTHM: The rhythm of "Wayfaring Stranger" is in 3/2 meter, which means that there are the equivalent of three half notes in each measure. In tempo the movement is in a moderate walking time. In measures 2, 6, 10 and 14 there is a use of syncopation resulting from a short pulse on the first half of the first beat. In the other measures the first beat of the measure is longer, regular, and thus receives a heavier stress. The note values used are half (♩) notes, quarter (♩) notes, eighth (♪) notes and dotted half (♩.) notes.

MELODY: The melody is written in the key of D minor and begins on D above middle C. It has a range from middle C to the D one octave and one note above, using all of the notes within this range except E and B♭. The melody is constructed of medium-sized skips and descending stepwise two-note figures.

HARMONY: The harmonization is simple but does utilize more chords than have the folk songs thus far studied. In the first eight measures three minor chords are used: the D minor (DFA) chord, A minor (ACE) chord, and the G minor (GB♭D) chord. In the next four measures there is a feeling of major tonality and we find that three major chords will harmonize the melody: the F major (FAC) chord, the C major (CEG) chord, and the B♭ major (B♭DF) chord. In the final four measures there is a return to the use of the D minor, the A minor, and the G minor chords.

TIMBRE: This will depend on the voice or voices and the kind of instrument or instruments used for the accompaniment.

FORM: Simple two-part song form. Part I is a period consisting of two regular four-measure phrases. The antecedent phrase ends with a half cadence and the consequent phrase ends with a perfect authentic cadence. Part II is also a period with two regular four-measure phrases. The antecedent phrase ends on a half cadence while the consequent phrase ends with a perfect authentic cadence.

177

On Top of Old Smokey

This folk song comes from Kentucky but is widely known in America. Like "Down in the Valley," it is a lonesome love tune. It tells of the days when goods and produce were carried from community to community and store to store by wagons driven by devil-may-care drivers who boasted of a girl in every town.

RHYTHM: The song swings in three with a meter marking of 3/4. It moves with a moderate tempo or speed. The note values used are dotted half ($\quad$) notes, half ($\quad$) notes, quarter ($\quad$) notes and eighth ($\quad$) notes. Note the effect of tying two half notes together as in measures two and three.

MELODY: The melody is written in the key of C major and is constructed from the individual members of the three chords which harmonize the tune. As a result, in the main, the melody consists of small skips. The melody begins on C, the first note of the scale. It has a range from B below middle C to C the octave above middle C, using all of the notes in between.

HARMONY: The harmonization is simple, based on the three primary chords. These chords are the I (CEG or C) chord, the IV (FAC or F) chord and the V_7 (GBDF or G_7) chord.

TIMBRE: This particular version is sung by a male singer accompanied with a guitar.

FORM: The form is irregular in that the song contains four 3-measure phrases, each one different from any of the others. Phrase 1 ends on the IV chord, Phrase 2 ends on an imperfect cadence, Phrase 3 ends on a half cadence, and Phrase 4 ends on a perfect authentic cadence.

Peter Gray

In the middle of the eighteenth century this was a popular song of the people who lived along the Susquehanna River.

RHYTHM: The rhythm of this song is regular and swings in two with a meter of 2/4. The note values which are used are quarter ($\quad$) notes, eighth ($\quad$) notes, sixteenth ($\quad$) notes, and dotted eighth ($\quad$) notes.

MELODY: The melody is in the key of Eb minor. It begins on the fifth of the scale, the Bb below middle C, and has a range of an octave and six notes which gives it an unusually large range. All of the notes in the Eb minor scale are used except middle C and the C one octave above. Note the altered note or pitch on the last half of the second beat in measure 3. The melody is constructed with ascending and descending stepwise progressions, plus small- to medium-sized skips. In measure 15 there is a large skip, that of an octave.

HARMONY: "Peter Gray" may be harmonized with a simple harmonization. Two minor chords and one major chord suffice to give the necessary harmonic background. These three chords are the I (E♭G♭B♭ or E♭ minor) chord, the IV (A♭C♭E♭ or A♭ minor) chord and the V₇ (B♭DFA♭ or B♭₇) chord.

TIMBRE: This particular version is sung by a male singer accompanied with a guitar.

FORM: The form is simple two-part song form with Part I being the verse and Part II being the chorus. Part I is a period. The antecedent phrase is a regular four-measure phrase ending on a perfect authentic cadence. The consequent phrase is also a regular four-measure phrase ending with a perfect authentic cadence. Part II is a period. The antecedent phrase is a regular four-measure phrase ending with a perfect authentic cadence. The consequent phrase is also a regular four-measure phrase and ends with a perfect authentic cadence.

Sweet Betsy from Pike

This is another song from the period around 1850. While it tells of the trials of Sweet Betsy and her lover, Ike, on their trek to the promised land of the west, it is in reality a song about all of those hardy pioneers who endured untold hardships in order to reach California with its gold or the Oregon country with its land.

RHYTHM: There is a flowing and lilting quality to the rhythm which almost gives it the feeling of the dance. While it swings in three and is written in 3/4 meter, there is a very strong feeling of one beat to the measure with an undercurrent of three. The note values used are half (♩) notes, quarter (♩) notes and eighth (♪) notes.

MELODY: The melody is in the key of D major and begins on the first note of the scale, the D above middle C. The song has a range from this D to the D one octave above. All of the notes of the D major scale within this range are used. Small skips and repeated notes are characteristic of the melody. In measures 1 and 5, the melody is made out of the notes making up the D major chord. In measure 10, the three notes of the melody constitute the F♯ minor chord.

HARMONY: Four major chords and two minor chords are needed for the harmonization of this folk song. The three primary chords, the I (DF♯A or D major) chord, the IV (GBD or G major) chord and the V₇ (AC♯EG or A₇) chord, plus the II₇ (EG♯BD or E₇) chord, are the major chords. The minor harmonies are the B minor (BDF♯) chord found in measure 9 and the F♯ minor (F♯AC♯) chord found in measure 10.

TIMBRE: This particular version is sung by a male singer accompanied with a guitar.

FORM: The form of this folk song is simple two-part song form with Part I being the verse and Part II being the chorus. Part I is a double period containing four regular 4-measure coherent phrases. In Part I the antecedent phrase of the first period ends with a perfect authentic cadence and the consequent phrase ends with a half cadence. In the second period the antecedent phrase ends with a plagal (IV-I) cadence while the consequent phrase ends with a perfect authentic cadence. In Part II, which is a period, both the antecedent and consequent phrases end with a perfect authentic cadence.

179

ADDITIONAL CLASS ACTIVITIES

1. Examine the folk music of other European countries besides England to discover what the national characteristics may be.
2. In these other European countries what single influence affected their folk music?
3. Discuss the effect of climate upon folk music.
4. Discuss the effect of geographic location upon folk music.
5. Discuss how folk customs and folk festivals affect folk music.

ADDITIONAL READING

1. UNESCO. *Folk Songs of Europe.* London: Novello, 1956.
2. Margaret Bradford Boni. *Fireside Book of Folksongs.* New York: Simon and Schuster, 1947, 316 pp.
3. Leonhard Deutsch. *A Treasury of the World's Finest Folk Song.* New York: Howell, Siskin, 1942, 430 pp.
4. John A. Lomax and Alan Lomax. *Folk Song U.S.A.* New York: Duell, Sloan, and Pearce, 1947, 377 pp.
5. B. A. Botkin. *A Treasury of American Folklore.* New York: Crown Publishers, 1944.

chapter 5

The Composer Uses Folk Music in Extended Forms

The history of music is full of examples of composers' use of folk melodies in more extended musical works. Because the folk music of every country has its own national flavor, it is easy to understand how these folk songs could inspire the composer, and how entire folk songs or fragments of them found their way into more significant and extended forms of composition. In this instance folk music, which in essence is unsophisticated and primitive, was used as a germ for serious composition which was sophisticated and well ordered. This meant that, for the most part, when folk tunes were used by composers for their compositions these simple folk songs had to be modified and worked over, to comply with the demands of the new format. In the process of being modified, rhythmic and melodic peculiarities inherent in the folk song might be considerably altered to conform with the needs of the composer in expressing his musical feelings and ideas. A typical example of this type of modification is found in the final movement of *Symphony No. 4 in F Minor* by Peter Ilyich Tchaikovsky (1840-1893) in which

181

the composer slightly alters the old Russian folk song "The Birch Tree" and uses it as the second theme in this movement. The beautiful "Andante cantabile" from the *First String Quartet* by the same composer is also fashioned out of an old Russian folk song. This particular one is slightly foolish and ribald, and the listener wonders how Tchaikovsky could create a work of such divine beauty out of such commonplace material.

In 1880, the University of Breslau conferred on Johannes Brahms an honorary degree of Doctor of Philosophy. As a gesture of appreciation Brahms composed an extended musical work for the occasion. This work, the "Academic Festival Overture," used a number of student songs for its melodic material.

Percy Grainger (1882-1961) was another composer who made copious use of folk material in his compositions. It is said that he studied the folk songs of the entire world. He was a gentle, common man who traveled as a "commoner" riding the chair car by night rather than the sleeper. His love of hiking brought him into contact with humble people everywhere who contributed to his ever-increasing store of folk songs from the various parts of the world. His creative efforts reflect this interest in the folk expression of the people with whom he came into contact.

Another form or use of folk music is found in the musical utterances of the group of composers who were a part of the movement known as Nationalism. In the nineteenth century, as a part of the development of the romantic era in history, many composers became interested in the folk music and legends of their own countries. They saw in this material an ideal source for incorporating a national spirit into the creative musical outpouring of the time. Through the use of folk music it was possible to identify the national origin of the writing. Probably one of the most important men in this national movement was Franz Liszt (1811-1886). He not only took the old Magyar melodies and fashioned out of them new and exciting works for the piano and later on for the orchestra, but he was also one of the first to recognize the national strivings in other countries. He encouraged Glinka in forming the Russian school and recognized the important contributions being made by other Russians in the movement, such as Rimsky-Korsakov (1844-1908), Borodin (1833-1887), Balakirev (1837-1910) and Cui (1835-1918). He also befriended other national composers such as Edvard Grieg (1843-1907), César Franck (1822-1890), Camille Saint-Saëns (1835-1921) and others, by seeing that their works were performed and by helping to bring their works to the attention of publishers.

This particular use of folk music might be said to be conscious nationalism: The melody and the rhythm of the indigenous folk song is deliberately used by the composer to achieve his objective of creating a national style. Typical of the composers who have reflected the conscious use of the folk song in their compositions are Edvard Grieg (1843-1907) of Norway, Jean Sibelius (1865-1957) of Finland, Bedřich Smetana (1824-1884) of Czechoslovakia, Zoltán Kodály (1882——) of Hungary and Béla Bartók (1881-1945), also of Hungary. Many other countries have names of composers to be added to this list.

One of the prime examples of the use of folk song in an extended musical form is found in the second movement of a string quartet, the *Quartet in C Major*, known as the *Emperor Quartet*, written by Franz Joseph Haydn (1732-1809). This particular example represents a second modification of the original folk melody.

In 1797 Haydn, the composer, and Huschka, the poet, were asked to write a suitable national anthem for Austria. Haydn had a great fondness for Croatian folk songs, which stemmed from his having Croatian blood in his veins. So he chose a Croatian folk song for the melody. By rewriting some of the measures and enriching this new melody with his own beautiful harmonies, he strengthened the construction and the melody assumed new character and vigor. This improved melody is a robust melody—one which reflects great strength. It is easy to sing. One is carried along from its beginning to its powerful climax to its final moment of repose. It immediately captures one's attention so that it is also an easy song to remember. There is a feeling of dignified excitement and drama in the song—both necessary attributes of any worthy national anthem.

The hymn was first sung on February 12, 1797, and was enthusiastically received by the Austrian people. It became an instantaneous success. A success, it might be noted, that was not confined just to the Austrian people. As is the case with any fine and strong song, it also met with success with peoples in other parts of the world. The German people were soon singing it as "Deutschland, Deutschland über Alles." We all know it as one of our favorite hymns, "Glorious Things of Thee Are Spoken."

We know that the Austrian national anthem was a particular favorite of Haydn's. It is said that when the armies of Napoleon were invading Austria in 1809, and that even as the peaceful suburb in which Haydn lived was being shelled, he demonstrated his passionate patriotism by performing his beloved "Emperor's Hymn." His last performance of it took place only five days before his death.

Glorious Things of Thee Are Spoken

Glo - rious things of thee are spo - ken, Zi - on, cit - y of our God; He whose word can - not be bro - ken, Formed thee for his own a - bode; On the Rock of A - ges found - ed, What can shake thy sure re - pose? With sal - va - tion's walls sur - round - ed, Thou may'st smile at all thy foes.

184

Sing the hymn "Glorious Things of Thee Are Spoken" to become well acquainted with the melody. Remember that it is this melody out of which Haydn fashioned the second movement of his famous *String Quartet in C Major*.

RHYTHM:
1. Describe the rhythmic arrangement for this hymn.
2. What is the meter?

MELODY:
1. Is this an easy melody to sing? Why?
2. Does the melody move essentially by steps or by skips?
3. What is the key of the melody?
4. In measure 9, the melody for "Rock of" comes from what?
5. Notice the repeat of this in measure 10 with the word "founded."
6. On what note of the scale does the melody begin?
7. What is the lowest note of the melody?
8. What is the highest note of the melody?
9. Are all of the notes of this scale used between the lowest and highest note?

HARMONY:
1. First sing the song in unison and unaccompanied, then have someone accompany the song on the piano, noting the effect of harmony on the melody.
2. Analyze the harmony by finding and marking all of the I (E♭GB♭), the IV (A♭CE♭), the V (B♭DF) and V₇ (B♭DFA♭) chords.
3. What other chords are used?
4. For what reason were these additional chords used?

TIMBRE:
1. Sing the song using only the treble voices, then sing the song using only the male voices and compare the sound.
2. Sing the song using both treble and male voices and compare with the above.
3. Sing the song both with and without accompaniment and compare the sound.

FORM:
1. Mark the phrases.
2. How many phrases does the song contain?
3. How many parts does the song contain?
4. Indicate the number and kind of cadences used in this song.
5. What is the form of this composition?

Quartet No. 77 in C Major, Op. 76 No. 3 . . . . Franz Joseph Haydn (1732-1809)

Poco adagio cantabile (2nd movement)

The thematic material from this movement is derived in its entirety from the melody of the above hymn. It is easy to follow as it is subjected to the different modifications in various variations.

FORM: The form which Haydn used in this movement for the extension of his musical ideas is known as a *theme with variations*. There are two ways of extending musical form through the use of the principle of theme and variation. In the first instance the theme is simply repeated in its original form, which serves to give the composition unity while variety is achieved by providing new treatments arising from the unlimited possibilities of counterpoint.

185

Composers before the time of Haydn and Mozart used this form of theme and variations. Good examples of this kind of writing may be found in the *chaconnes* and *passacaglias* of the pre-Haydn composers. The second way of extending musical form through variation is by providing a new treatment or by recasting in a new mold the melodic material by alteration, elaboration and ornamentation. The second movement of the *C Major Quartet* by Haydn furnishes us with an excellent example of this latter way of using the theme and variations in the extension of musical form.

THEME:

This is a simple statement of the theme and is played by the first violin. The second violin, for the most part, plays a harmony part which, in the main, lies at an interval of a third or an interval of a sixth away from the melody. The viola and cello parts are in the nature of an accompaniment and serve the function of completing the harmony.

186

RHYTHM: 1. Observe and analyze the rhythm patterns used.
     2. Does the theme have the same meter as the hymn?

MELODY: 1. What did Haydn do to give additional interest to the melodic line?
     2. What is a grace note?
     3. What is an appoggiatura?
     4. Locate the use of grace notes and appoggiaturas in the melody.
     5. Why do you think Haydn made use of the *sforzando*?

HARMONY: 1. Is the harmony for the theme the same as used in "Glorious Things of Thee Are Spoken"?
      2. Why are some of the harmonies different?

TIMBRE: 1. Can you, by listening, distinguish the part that each of the four instruments plays?
     2. In terms of vocal range what part does each instrument play?

FORM: 1. Define the term *theme and variations.*
    2. How many variations are written for this movement?
    3. Does the theme have the same number of measures as the hymn?
    4. Does each variation have the same number of measures as the theme?
    5. What is a *coda* or *codetta*?
    6. How is it used in this movement?

1. What instrument plays the melody?
2. What instrument plays the other part?
3. What is the function of this second part?
4. What is meant by the term *arpeggio*?
5. In addition to being an ornamentation and an embellishment, what other functions does the arpeggio serve in this variation?
6. What is meant by the term *staccato*?
7. What is meant by the term *legato*?
8. While listening, distinguish between the use of these two styles.
9. Does Variation I have the same number of measures as the theme?

Variation II

1. What instrument plays the melody?
2. What is countermelody?
3. What instrument plays a countermelody?
4. Discuss the parts played by the other two instruments.
5. What is meant by the term *syncopation*?
6. Point out the use of syncopation in this variation. Be specific.
7. Does Variation II have the same number of measures as the theme and Variation I?

Variation III

1. What instrument plays the melody?
2. What does the cello do in the first half of the variation?
3. Is the rhythm of the countermelody played by the first violin regular? Syncopated? A combination of both?
4. Is the rhythm of the countermelody played by the second violin regular? Syncopated? A combination of both?
5. Does Variation III have the same number of measures as the theme and Variations I and II?

Variation IV

1. What instrument plays the melody?
2. Is the register in which the melody is played high, low or in the middle?
3. The other instruments play countermelodies resulting from a very effective use of counterpoint. Can you distinguish each of these three countermelodies?
4. What is a harmonic suspension? Are there any suspensions used in this variation?
5. Are there new harmonies introduced in this variation? Why?
6. Does Variation IV have the same number of measures as the theme and Variations I, II and III?
7. How many measures are there in the codetta?
8. What is the purpose of this codetta?

Greensleeves

English Song 16th century arr. by Edward Gilday (Traditional Words)

1 A - las! my love _ you do me wrong _ To cast me off _ dis - cour - teous - ly; For
2 Oh, I've been read - y at your hand _ To grant what-ev - er you would crave, I

I have lov - èd you so long _ De - light - ing in _ your com - pa - ny.
have both wag - èd life and land _ Your love _ and good _ will for to have.

Green-sleeves _ was all my joy, _____ Green - sleeves _ was my de-light, Oh,

Green-sleeves was my heart of gold, _ Ah, who but my La - dy Green-sleeves.

190

RHYTHM: 1. What is the meter of this song?
2. Does the song swing in six?
3. If not, in what does it swing?
4. Is the rhythm regular or irregular?
5. Note that rhythmically there is a feeling of a long pulse followed by a short pulse.
6. What kind of notes are used in the rhythm?

MELODY: 1. What is the key of this song?
2. On which note of the scale does the song begin?
3. What is the lowest note of the song?
4. What is the highest note of the song?
5. Are all of the notes of the scale within this range used?
6. Is the melody essentially composed of steps or skips?
7. What is the function of the occasional accidental which is found in the melody?

HARMONY: 1. Mark the I (GBbD) chord and the V or V₇ (DF♯A or DF♯AC) chord.
2. Is the IV (CEbG) chord used?
3. How many other chords are used in this harmonization?
4. This song could be harmonized with the three primary chords (I, IV, V or V₇). Why do you think these other chords are used?

FORM: 1. How many parts to this song?
2. How many phrases are contained in each part?
3. How many measures are contained in each phrase?
4. Mark the phrases and indicate the kind of cadence ending each phrase.
5. Note that the consequent phrase in Part I is almost like the antecedent phrase, differing only in the third and fourth measures. Is the consequent phrase in Part II like the antecedent phrase, almost alike, or different?

Fantasia on Greensleeves.................Ralph Vaughan Williams (1872-1958)   **LISTENING ACTIVITY**

The *fantasia* is a musical form which is free and not formal like the fugue, the theme and variation and the sonata. The word derives from a German word which means imagination. In a fantasia the composer selects a theme and using his imagination and creative skill, arranges and rearranges the thematic material and sometimes adds new bits of material until a new and stunning musical work emerges.

RHYTHM: The rhythm is the same as that used in the song "Greensleeves." It is in 6/8 meter. The time values used are the quarter (♩) note, the eighth (♪) note, the dotted eighth (♪.) note and the sixteenth (♫) note.

MELODY: The melody is essentially modal although, because of certain alterations to the melodic line, it cannot be classified as a true modal melody. The "Fantasia" follows quite faithfully the "Greensleeves" melody as we know it today. The new or added melodic material is also modal in character and effect. This new melody is also folklike in its simplicity and serves to give contrast to the "Greensleeves" melody.

191

HARMONY: In general, the harmonization is conventional, using harmonies based on primary and secondary chords. As the "Fantasia" develops we are impressed by the harmonic richness achieved by the composer's skill in contrapuntal writing.

TIMBRE: The "Fantasia" is written for flutes, harp and strings, and the tonal colors or timbre one associates with these instruments are predominant all through the work. In the introduction the flute is heard with the harp playing an arpeggiated accompaniment. This is followed by the "Greensleeves" melody played by the second violins, with the first violins playing an obbligato or countermelody in the high register, while the harp furnishes a chordal harmony and establishes a basic rhythm. This is followed by the first violins taking over and playing the melody, with the other strings furnishing the harmony. The harp adds to this with arpeggiated chords. This is then followed by the new material played first by the second violins, with the first violins playing a *tremolo* accompaniment in the high register. This is taken over by two flutes playing this new melodic ma-

terial as a duet, with the strings playing a *pizzicato* accompaniment. The section is completed by the violins playing the melody in octaves, with the counter-melody or counterpoint played by the bass instruments. As a bridge or transition the flute is heard playing a cadenza, with an arpeggiated accompaniment played by the harp which supplies the harmony. We then have a return of the "Greensleeves" melody, this time with the violas playing the melody. The violins add an ethereal effect by playing the countermelodies in a high register, with the harmony being reinforced by the harp. The final statement of the "Greensleeves" theme is given by the violins in unison, with an accompaniment of *tremolo* playing in the low strings and an arpeggiated accompaniment by the harp. The work might be said to come to an abrupt end, but this is eased somewhat by a final slowing up or retard and by a lengthening out of the *arpeggios* played by the harp.

FORM: In essence a simple three-part form with introduction.

Introduction
A (Greensleeves material)
B (New melodic material)
A (Greensleeves material)

SINGING EXPERIENCE

Sing these two folk melodies again to refresh your memory of the melody of each. Since "Down in the Valley" was not analyzed as to structure, it would be well to answer the following questions about it:

RHYTHM:
1. What is the rhythmic structure of this folk song?
2. Do you feel a basic swing of three beats to the measure with an undercurrent of three to each beat?

MELODY:
1. Out of what material is the melody constructed?
2. In what key is the melody?
3. On what note of the scale does the melody begin?
4. What is the lowest note in the song?
5. What is the highest note in the song?
6. Are all of the notes between these two extremes used?
7. Is it a melody composed of stepwise progressions or skips?
8. Do you feel that this melody is easy to sing? Why?

192

HARMONY: 1. Analyze the harmony of this folk song.
           2. How many chords are needed to harmonize this song?
           3. Sing the song, using the harmony parts found on page 72.
           4. If an autoharp is available, play the chords used for the harmonization of the melody on this instrument.
           5. This simple harmonization may also be played on the piano.

FORM: 1. How many phrases are there in this song?
           2. Mark the phrases and classify the cadences.
           3. What is the form of this folk song?

Down in the Valley.................................Kurt Weill (1900-1950)   **LISTENING
                                                                              ACTIVITY**
   This appealing folk opera was composed for five solo voices, several speaking parts, chorus and small orchestra. It is based on well-known American folk tunes including "Down in the Valley" and "Sourwood Mountain."

RHYTHM: 1. Compare the rhythmic structure of the songs "Down in the Valley" and "Sourwood Mountain" with the versions heard in this work.
           2. Are the rhythms the same or different?

MELODY: 1. In the opera how does the melodic line of "Down in the Valley" differ from that of the song?
           2. Which of the two versions is the more appealing to you? Why?
           3. Do you feel that the composer's alteration of the melody makes it express the mood of the story better?

HARMONY: 1. Harmonically are the two folk songs heard in the opera the same as the original folk songs, or has the composer changed the harmonization?
           2. If so, what did he do to the harmony?

TIMBRE: 1. Discuss the various instrumental and vocal timbres heard in this work.
           2. Contrast the speaking parts with the singing parts.

FORM: 1. What is a folk opera?
           2. Is there a difference between folk opera, grand opera, light opera, operetta and musical comedy? Explain.
           3. Is it possible to analyze this work in an overall form?

193

Music and the dance

chapter 6

Man Responds to Music of the Dance

To anyone interested in tracing the historical origins of music for the dance, it soon becomes apparent that the folk song and the folk dance are closely related. As the folk dance and the folk song are analyzed we see that both have several characteristics in common. Both stem from the people and in general were a natural outgrowth of social situations. Both had simple yet catchy tunes, simple yet vigorous rhythms and, generally, simple and regular phrase structure. We find in many instances that folk dances were sung long before they were danced and, conversely, many folk songs were danced before they were sung. Because dancing is a physical response to music, the basic response to the music of the dance might be said to be also a physical one. And yet, as we shall see later on, there are conditions when the response to music of the dance may be emotional or intellectual as well as physical.

The purpose of this unit is not to describe the history of the dance or to explain the various styles of the dance such as the primitive dance, dances of antiquity, medieval dances, folk dances or modern dances. Rather, the intent is to examine the importance of the musical background of the dance and the various responses which may be elicited.

While instrumental music as we know it today began in the sixteenth century, we know from such books as the Bible and the paintings and tapestries of early artists that the real origins of our musical instruments are lost in antiquity. For example, the harp has been in use almost from the earliest days of man's history. The lute was first used in Europe sometime around 300 A.D., while the psaltery, which was used as an accompanying instrument, came into general use in Europe sometime around the eleventh or twelfth centuries. One of the early instruments, the portative organ, dates back to the third century before Christ. During medieval and renaissance times an early ancestor of the violin, the *fiedel*, was widely used. Other instruments such as the *tromba marina* (nun's fiddle), *trumpet*, *bombarde* and *buysine* were also known before the sixteenth century.

Before the sixteenth century, instrumental music was used only as an accompaniment for vocal music or was used interchangeably with it. The first additional use of instruments was probably for the accompaniment of the court and popular dances of the medieval age. In fact, it was not until instruments began to be used as a part of the dance that instrumental music began to come into its own. Because these early instruments were quite primitive by modern standards, the music played for the medieval dances would sound strange indeed to our ears. Our reaction to it would be that it was out of tune, that the instruments were out of tune with themselves and each other, and that there seemed to be little rhyme or reason to the way they were used—they were all mixed together with little or no plan.

Around the middle of the sixteenth century the development of instrumental music took a giant step forward when a group of Italian violinists—later known as the *Vingt-quatre Violons du Roi*—traveled to France and were quickly installed as favorites of the French court in Paris. This was one of the earliest and certainly one of the most famous dance bands in history. Following the popularity of this group it became fashionable for all of the court dances to be accompanied by orchestras of bowed instruments. Beginning with this and continuing to the present time, instrumental music for both solo and ensemble has continued to develop.

One of the earliest descriptions of the dance and dance music is found in a work written in 1589. Strangely enough, this monumental work, known as the *Orchésographie*, was not written by a musician or a dancer but by a priest living and working in Langres, a small community some 175 miles southeast of Paris. Using the pseudonym Thoinet Arbeau, the priest described the steps of the various dances then popular and supplied the notation of the various tunes to which they were danced. Because the lute in the sixteenth century was the popular instrument of the time, considerable music was written for its exclusive use. Its use and the music written for it give rise to its claim to being the first really independent instrumental music. From the *Orchésographie* we learn that many of these dance tunes were played by the lute, but that some dances were accompanied by various combinations of other instruments such as strings, woodwinds and brasses.

The *basse danse*, danced by two people, was one of the popular dances of the sixteenth century and was an ancestor of the dances that survived it. The word *basse* means low. When applied to the dance it means that the dance derived its name from the graceful gliding motion of the feet, rather than from the lifting or stomping of the feet customary with some of the other popular dances of the time. The time was generally in simple duple meter, although occasionally the dance was found to be in triple meter or a combination of the two. The *tordion*, which was a contrast in character and rhythm to the *basse danse*, was a basic part of the dance. The *tordion*, characterized by leaping jumps, was added to the *basse danse*. The music was organized into three parts: (a) statement of the *basse danse*, (b) repeat of the *basse danse*, and (c) the *tordion*.

One would not suspect that the origin of our modern word "brawl" goes back to a lively circle and round dance of the sixteenth century known as the *branle*. The *branle* was of French origin and at one time was danced to the singing of the dancers as they circled first in one direction and then in the opposite direction, while the tempo of the dance gradually increased. The dance was danced to music written in duple meter, with the overall effect of the music being similar to that of the gavotte. The *branle* ultimately outgrew its rustic background and became one of the popular dances of the court of Louis XIV. It was known, however, in England before this, as both Shakespeare and Pepys refer to it in their writings.

The *pavane* and the *galliard* (or *gagliarda*) were a pair of contrasting dances which were popular at this time. The *pavane*, in simple duple meter, was slow, heavy and stately in character. The *galliard*, on the other hand, in triple meter, was rapid, light, graceful and gay in character. It featured a grouping of five steps and was sometimes referred to as the *cinque-pace*.

THE DANCING COUPLE, Jan Steen

There were many different dances in vogue during this period which are still known to us today in one guise or another. An examination of some of the more popular dances of that time will reveal a wide variety of meter, movement and mood.

Dance	Nationality	Meter	Movement
Pavane	Spanish-Italian	4/4	Slow, stately
Galliard	Italian	3/4	Rapid, gay
Sarabande	Spanish or Moorish	3/2, 3/4	Slow, stately
Courante	French-Italian	3/2, 3/4 6/4, 6/8	Fast, running
Minuet	French	3/4	Moderate, stately
Bourrée	French	¢	Fast
Gavotte	French	4/4	Moderately fast
Gigue	Italian	3/8, 6/8	Fast, gay
Allemande	German	4/4	Moderately slow

It is interesting to note the sixteenth-century practice of putting together two or more dances to achieve a contrast of fast-slow-fast-slow movements. From these humble beginnings the pre-classical sonata developed. One type of pre-classical sonata composed before 1750, known as the *sonata da camera*, consisted of a series of contrasting dances tied together by unity of key. These collections of dances are often referred to as *partitas* or *suites*. So general was the use of the *allemande, courante, sarabande* and *gigue* in the *sonata da camera* that their inclusion was almost considered a requirement, and these dances were referred to as the "four obligatory dances."

The dances of today—social, interpretive or ballet—all have a common ancestry. It began with the folk dance, continuing on through the popular rustic, as well as popular court dances of the sixteenth and seventeenth centuries, finally culminating in the various dance styles which we know today. We have seen that paralleling the growth and development of the dance was the growth and development of instrumental music. It was closely associated with the dance because of the dance's dependence on musical accompaniment.

In Chapter Two we learned that man may react in three different ways to music—physically, emotionally and intellectually. In analyzing the music of the dance we soon see that it may also be conveniently studied in terms of these same three basic reactions. Music used strictly for movement in social dancing provides us with excellent examples of reacting to the physical element in music. Attending to the music and dancing of a ballet, where our emotions are conditioned by the programmatic content of the dance, may cause us to react emotionally to what we hear and see, as well as to react physically to the rhythm. And finally, not all dance music is intended to be danced and neither is all dance music dependent on non-musical ideas to give impact to the listener. The use of idealized dances in the *sonata da camera* or *suite* illustrates the use of music of the dance where the understanding of the music depends considerably on the intellectual reaction of the listener.

Responding Physically to Music of the Dance

In studying the music of the dance it seems rather natural to begin by examining music used strictly as an accompaniment for dancing. This is, in fact, reacting to the physical aspect of the music. This kind of reaction is a natural outgrowth from folk music and the folk dance.

Gold and Silver Waltz....................................Franz Lehar (1870-1948)

LISTENING ACTIVITIES

Play this recording through several times to become familiar with the rhythm and the different melodies used in each of the sections or parts. The purpose of this composition was primarily to provide music to accompany a dance. The dance in this instance was the waltz, a dance of German or possibly Bohemian origin which maintains its popularity even today. It is a graceful, gay and gliding dance in 3/4 meter. In the waltz, the pattern described by the dancers often results in a square, so the step is often referred to as the "box waltz."

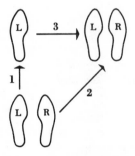

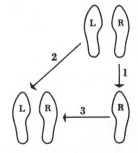

RHYTHM: A characteristic of the accompaniment to the waltz is the heavy or accented first beat played by the bass instruments, while the treble instruments rest the first beat and play the second and third beats which are unaccented.

While listening to the recording, softly clap the rhythm in order to establish the feeling of the accented first beat followed by two unaccented beats.

MELODY: Because the rhythm is expressly for a dance, there would be a certain sameness in the composition if this were the only element present. The composer, therefore, brought the elements of contrast and

201

variety to his work by introducing new melodies in new keys to maintain interest. Each new melody, gay in character, continues to express the gliding feeling which is characteristic of the waltz. For the most part the melodies are constructed of stepwise progressions and small skips. While these melodies may be sung, they are really instrumental in character because of their extended ranges and use of ornamentation.

HARMONY: The harmonization of these dances is simple. There is a strong feeling for the tonality of each separate part developed through the repetition of the I, IV and V₇ chords. Variety of the harmonic element is achieved by the occasional use of secondary chords such as the II and VI. The use of altered members of certain chords also lends harmonic interest to the composition.

TIMBRE: The four instrumental families have been used in the scoring of this waltz. As the music moves from the introduction to the first and then to the succeeding waltzes, the listener becomes aware that there is a consistent pattern in the manner in which the composer made use of the instruments. In general, note the use of first violins, cellos, first clarinet and first cornet playing the melody; the use of the string basses and bassoons playing first beat patterns while second violins, violas, horns and percussion play the second and third beat patterns—the characteristic rhythm of the waltz; and the countermelodies played by the cellos, trombones, clarinets and flutes.

FORM: The "Gold and Silver Waltz" consists of five large sections, each with two or more contrasting sections:

Introduction
Part I	4/4 meter	13 measures	
Part II	3/4 meter	47 measures	

Waltz No. 1
Part I	3/4 meter	32 measures	*(Repeated)*
Part II	3/4 meter	16 measures	*(Repeated)*

Waltz No. 2
Part I	3/4 meter	32 measures	*(Repeated)*
Part II	3/4 meter	16 measures	*(Repeated)*

Waltz No. 3
Intro.	3/4 meter	4 measures	
Part I	3/4 meter	16 measures	*(Repeated)*
Part II	3/4 meter	32 measures	*(Repeated)*

Coda
Part I	3/4 meter	25 measures	
Part II	3/4 meter	32 measures	*(From Waltz No. 1, Part I)*
Part III	3/4 meter	16 measures	*(From Waltz No. 1, Part II)*
Part IV	3/4 meter	15 measures	*(From Waltz No. 2, Part II)*
Part V	3/4 meter	38 measures	

Chit-Chat (Tritsch-Tratsch) Polka...................Johann Strauss (1825-1899)

While some people tend to associate the polka with the Scandinavian countries, the polka actually originated in Bohemia around 1830. It was not long, however, before it was popular with dancers all over Europe. It is a round dance with the music having some similarity to the *schottische*. The polka is a vigorous and strenuous dance in quick duple meter. A characteristic of the dance is a short hop which occurs on the last half of the second beat.

$\frac{2}{4}$ | ♪ | ♪ ♪ ♪ ♪ | ♪ ♪ ♪ ♪ |
| L | R L R R | L R L L |
| Hop | Step Close Step Hop | Step Close Step Hop |

The music written for the polka must therefore emphasize the lively rhythm of this dance.

Listen to the recording of the "Chit-Chat Polka" several times to become acquainted with its rhythmic structure, its melodic characteristics and the number of large divisions in the compositions. As the music is played, try to execute the dance steps given above, to experience the rhythmic character of the music.

The mood is one of gaiety but the essential impact of this composition is rhythmic, and so, our strongest response to the music will be a physical response.

RHYTHM: The introduction begins with a strongly accented second beat which immediately suggests the feeling of the hop movement, an important characteristic of the polka. This leads immediately into another characteristic of the polka—the four eighth notes to the measure:

$\frac{2}{4}$ ♩ | ♫ ♫ | ♫ ♫ |

The dance itself begins on the last half of the second beat of the last measure of the introduction:

$\frac{2}{4}$ ♪ | ♪ ♪ ♪ | ♪ ♪ ♪ |

which literally tells us to hop, step, close, step, hop, step, close, step, hop; with the rhythm for the middle steps being provided by the accompaniment.

MELODY: Because this composition is essentially an accompaniment for a dance, the emphasis is on the rhythm. The melody in this instance does not have a particularly imposing role. It serves as a thread to help tie the composition together and to complement the rhythm. Because of its non-lyric character and extended ranges, the melody is considered an instrumental melody. An examination of the music reveals that the composer used a number of devices in the construction of his melodic design. First, one finds the use of large intervallic skips—for example, the interval of the octave found at the beginning of the dance. Rapid scale-like passages are used as in measures 7, 8 and 9. In the first section of the trio each note of the melody is given an ornamentation through the use of the appoggiatura. The continued use of the grace note throughout the composition is a further example of ornamentation of melody.

HARMONY: The harmony for the entire composition is simple and consonant. Four keys, A♭ major, E♭ major, D♭ major and B♭ minor are used. In each key the basic harmony is I and V₇ with an occasional IV chord added. The composer occasionally gives harmonic interest and variety by altering individual members of the chord—for example, in measure 39 the root of the chord is raised one half step while the seventh of the chord is lowered so that we have 𝄞 instead of 𝄞 .

FORM: The "Chit-Chat Polka" is divided into three large sections to which are added a two-measure introduction and a short coda or concluding section. Each of the large sections has three or more individual parts so that the overall form consists of:

Introduction	Two measures
Part I	
A	Sixteen measures
B	Sixteen measures
C	Eight measures
Bridge passage	Eight measures
A	Sixteen measures
Part II (Trio)	
A	Sixteen measures
	(repeated—32)
B	Sixteen measures
A	Sixteen measures

Repeat of original two-measure introduction

Part III	
A	Sixteen measures
B	Sixteen measures
C	Eight measures
Bridge passage	Eight measures
A	Sixteen measures
Coda	

TIMBRE: This particular polka uses the full resources of the symphony orchestra, with all four families of the orchestra represented. The first violins, flutes, piccolo and first clarinet are responsible for playing the melody while the other woodwind, brass, lower strings and percussion are responsible for playing the secondary parts and the rhythmic accompaniment.

TOPICS FOR DISCUSSION

1. How do the rhythms of the "Gold and Silver Waltz" and the "Chit-Chat Polka" differ?
2. In general, why is each one such a good example of the dance rhythm it represents?
3. What is the purpose of the duple-meter introduction to the "Gold and Silver Waltz"?
4. Are the melodies Lehar used in this waltz easily sung? Why?
5. Examine the different melodies used in both compositions and determine if the melodies are essentially stepwise, or do they make more use of skips?
6. While both the "Gold and Silver Waltz" and the "Chit-Chat Polka" were composed for dancing, could they be used for concert material?
7. Define the following terms:
   a. Introduction
   b. Bridge passage
   c. Coda
   d. Song form with trio
   e. Appoggiatura
   f. Grace note
8. Listen to additional recordings of music written to accompany the dance and observe the rhythmic characteristics of each composition.

Responding Emotionally to Music of the Dance

While the primary response to music of the dance may be said to be physical —for example, when music is used to accompany social dancing—music of the dance may also appeal to man's emotional being. This can be easily demonstrated by turning to the forms of dancing which are highly programmatic. In this category the ballet, which is generally built around a story, provides an excellent example of music of the dance which results in a physical reaction as man reacts to the beat of the rhythm. But also, because of the appeal of the story on which the ballet is based, there is a primary appeal to the emotional self as the story and the music unfold. This inter-relationship of music, dance and drama or story as realized in the ballet had its beginning in the late middle ages. This form of dancing was included as a part of the religious spectacles of the time, and has continued in an unbroken line to the present time.

What is meant by deriving an emotional response from music of the dance? In this instance reacting with our emotional being to music of the dance stems, in part, from being conditioned by extra-musical stimuli resulting from knowledge of the program. Thus the listener is provided with a series of mental images as the music and the dance unfold. These images in turn call forth different emotional states and reactions as the music and the dance progress.

To understand better the role of programmatic material in eliciting an emotional response to music of the dance, read carefully the stories of the following two ballets before turning to the music.

Coppélia . . . . .Léo Delibes (1836-1891)

LISTENING ACTIVITIES

Coppélia is based on a tale written by the German romanticist E. T. A. Hoffmann. The action takes place in a small town in Galicia some 200 years ago. The first act is laid in the village square on which is located the shop of Coppélius who invents all sorts of things. One intriguing member of his household is a beautiful young maiden. Day by day, she sits by a second-floor window overlooking the square, and her only interest in life seems to be reading the book she holds in her hands. This is Coppélia, said to be the daughter of Coppélius, although no one has seen her on the street or has had an opportunity to talk to her.

One day late in summer, Swanilda, a high-spirited village maiden, slips out of the house and tiptoes into the square. She moves toward the shop of Coppélius, hoping to examine more closely the young lady in the window whom she suspects of being a rival for the affection of her fiancé, Frantz. Before she can complete her mission she hears Frantz approaching and has to hide. She is able to observe him in his attempts to capture the interest of Coppélia. Coppélia, with Coppélius by her side, seems to recognize Frantz. She lays down the book, nods her head, and waves with one hand. Even though her gestures are stiff and jerky, Frantz is enraptured.

The burgomaster arrives with the news that the Lord of the Manor has decided to give the town a new clock.

205

As a part of the celebration the Lord has decided to provide dowries for all worthy young couples planning to be wed on the morrow. The burgomaster asks Swanilda if she will be wed on the morrow. Looking at Frantz, she takes a sheaf of corn from one of her friends and holds it to her ear. It seems to tell her that Frantz is untrue to her. She snaps the sheaf before Frantz's eyes, a symbol that their engagement has been broken. This is followed by a gay celebration in the square, during which a brilliant series of variations are danced by the girls. These variations lead into a spirited czardas in which the girls are joined by the men. During this dance the sun goes down. One by one the crowd departs, leaving the square empty.

After dark some of the youths return and, seeing Coppélius leave his shop, decide to tease the old man. In the struggle which follows Coppélius escapes but drops the key to his shop. Swanilda reappears, finds the key and leads the way into the inventor's house.

Act II opens with Swanilda and her friends inside the workshop of Coppélius. It is cluttered with tools. Automatons in every kind of fancy dress are scattered about. Coppélia is still seated by the window but is hidden by a heavy curtain. One of the youths falls over an automaton, tripping a spring which sets it into motion. Soon all of the automatons have been wound and are in motion. Leaving the toys to her friends, Swanilda approaches her rival, Coppélia. She touches her and discovers that everyone has been deceived and that this is only another mechanical toy. Coppélius suddenly returns and is in a rage. The girls, with the exception of Swanilda, escape. Swanilda quickly changes clothes and places with Coppélia.

Frantz now appears with a ladder and enters the window. Coppélius apprehends him and demands an explanation. Frantz explains that he has broken into the shop because of his love for Coppélia. Coppélius, who believes he has completed his greatest invention—being able to bring his automatons to life—needs the services of someone such as Frantz to complete the experiment. He leads Frantz to believe that he is welcome. Coppélius gives Frantz a drink which has been drugged. It is Coppélius' plan to transfer the life matter from Frantz to Coppélia. Before the actual transfer, however, Coppélius begins to go through a mystical rite. During the incantation he sees that Coppélia is coming to life. She is, of course, Swanilda. Swanilda begins to dance a waltz which in the beginning has movements that are mechanical. As the dance progresses she becomes more and more lifelike and playful. She then dances over and tries to awaken Frantz but before she can accomplish this, Coppélius, hoping to distract her, gives her a Spanish shawl which inspires a wild Spanish dance. A gift of Scotch plaid prompts a jig. These diversions do not keep Swanilda from accomplishing her purpose. She suddenly runs wild, turning over all of the automatons and finally succeeds in awakening Frantz. Coppélius chases Frantz from the house while the unobserved Swanilda, still in Coppélia's clothes, also escapes to join Frantz.

The ballet ends as it began—in the village square. The clock has been dedicated and the young couples to be married approach to receive their dowries. In this group are Swanilda and Frantz. The ballet then closes with the great festival interpreted by both solo and group dances.

Before listening to the recording, play and sing the following melodies from *Coppélia*, to become thoroughly acquainted with each one. While listening to the recording, as each melody appears the listener will be told what part of the story is being enacted, and will also know which characters are "on stage."

Swanilda and Frantz are introduced in a short overture based on several of the melodies used later in the ballet, and concluding with this mazurka which is danced later on by the villagers and peasants.

Swanilda slips from her home into the square and dances this waltz,

to attract the attention of Coppélia, but is unable to arouse a response. Frantz appears as Swanilda hides. Frantz seems to be more successful than Swanilda in receiving an acknowledgment from Coppélia.

The burgomaster announces that the Lord of the Manor will give a dowry to every couple who will be married on the morrow. He asks Swanilda if she and Frantz will be one of the couples. Swanilda now has reason to doubt Frantz. She tells of the straw which reveals secrets. She plucks an ear of corn from one of her friends and places it to her ear. It seems to tell her that Frantz, her fiancé, has been untrue.

She then announces that their engagement is broken, by snapping the sheaf before the eyes of Frantz and the crowd.

Frantz and the men leave. Swanilda joins with the village maidens in dancing a theme and four variations.

These dances lead into an energetic czardas, in which the girls are joined by the men in the village.

While they dance the sun sets and darkness sets in over the village.

207

In the second act Swanilda, having found the key to Coppélius' workshop, has entered the shop and discovers that Coppélia is just a life-like doll. Coppélius returns before Swanilda can leave and she is forced to hide. Then Frantz returns with a ladder and is caught by Coppélius who decides to use Frantz as a guinea pig for an experiment he wishes to conduct. He supplies Frantz with so much wine that Frantz finally lays his head on the table and falls into a stupor. Meanwhile Swanilda has changed clothes with the doll. After referring to his book on magic, Coppélius begins to make mystical movements in the direction of Coppélia who, of course, is Swanilda in disguise.

Swanilda pretends that she is coming to life. She opens her eyes, looks around and begins to make a few jerky movements.

Coppélius is elated by the seeming success of his efforts. Emboldened by the success of her deception, "Coppélia" begins to dance.

208

While dancing Swanilda tries to arouse the sleeping Frantz, but Coppélius tries to divert her attention. He follows her around and around the workshop while she grows more and more lively.

To divert her attention from Frantz, Coppélius finally gives her a mantilla which inspires a vigorous Spanish dance.

At the conclusion of the Spanish dance Swanilda sees some Scottish plaid. She grabs it up and goes into a jig.

When the jig is completed, Swanilda runs wild, winding the automatons and starting them in motion. In the process several of the dolls are wrecked. She pinches and shakes the drugged Frantz until he awakens and both of them escape, leaving the shop in shambles.

The scene changes to the next day on the grounds of the Lord of the Manor. The villagers and the couples to be married are arriving. Coppélius arrives and demands payment for the damage done to his automatons and his shop. Swanilda offers him her dowry but the Lord of the Manor saves the day by throwing him a purse.

209

and

At this point the hours of the morning enter and dance for the assembled group.

and

and

These dances lead into a short vigorous dance called *Danse de Fête.*

This in turn leads into the concluding dance, a Galop-finale, in which the villagers, the newly married couples, in fact, the whole assemblage takes part in bringing the ballet to a gay conclusion.

210

Petrouchka. . . . . .Igor Stravinsky (1882———)

In many countries there are pre-Lenten celebrations which conclude with the first day of Lent. The story of *Petrouchka* takes place during such a celebration, the Shrovetide festivities in St. Petersburg in 1830. The scene is laid at a fair or carnival. There are a number of booths, each of them filled with a variety of goodies and trinkets. A crowd is milling about and everywhere there is laughing, singing and shouting.

The laughing crowd pushes and shoves toward the booths and sideshows.

Two gypsy girls and an old fortune-teller try to attract the attention of the crowd to their show.

A street dancer enters and does a vigorous dance, accompanying herself with a small metal bar. In the background we hear the sound of hand organs.

Suddenly in the midst of all this gaiety two drummers appear and beat a tattoo which serves to introduce the Charlatan, the owner of a puppet show, who is preparing to present his show.

211

The crowd shivers with excitement and expectation. The Charlatan takes a flute from his pocket and begins to play a tune which seems to have magical and mysterious portent.

He steps to the side of his booth, pulls the curtain and reveals three lifeless puppets, each lying prostrate on the floor of his own cubicle. In the first cubicle is the Moor, a large dark puppet with a malevolent expression. In the second one is the beautiful Ballerina with painted face and alluring figure. The remaining cubicle reveals Petrouchka, a sad and woebegone puppet with narrow slits for eyes.

The Charlatan then causes the three to dance.

Their dancing, at first, is stiff and puppet-like. Their dance, however, grows livelier and livelier until they finally leave the stage and join the crowd in the square. The theme of their dance is an old one—the Moor makes love to the Ballerina which enrages a jealous Petrouchka. The enraged Petrouchka attacks the Moor with a club. This is solved by the Charlatan who simply stops his playing, causing the figures to collapse and once again become lifeless puppets. Darkness falls upon the square.

The second scene is laid in the poor and miserable cell of Petrouchka, which is in reality a prison behind the puppet theater. A despondent Petrouchka is on the floor dazedly trying to rise.

Bewildered by human thoughts and emotions, he is torn between love and hatred and is tormented by his own wasted sawdust body.

Suddenly the beautiful Ballerina bursts into his cell. At first she stares at him with avid interest but is soon frightened by his savage antics. She quickly escapes. Petrouchka, in desperation, batters against the door with his fist but is unable to break it down. He then turns to the walls but is only partially successful. One wall gives way enough to bring to him the sounds of the carnival on the outside. The scene ends with a defeated Petrouchka throwing himself on the floor of his cell.

Scene Three, in contrast to the squalor of Petrouchka's cell, is laid in the cell of the Moor. The color and decoration of his cell indicate that the Moor is used to living in lavish luxury. As the scene opens, the Moor is found lying on a gorgeous couch tossing a coconut up into the air and then catching it.

Finally, letting the coconut fall to the floor he snatches his scimitar and tries to cut it in two. When he fails he attributes supernatural qualities to the coconut and genuflects to it, thinking it might be a god.

The door opens. The Ballerina enters carrying a small trumpet. She dances in a rather mechanical manner for the Moor to an unaccompanied trumpet melody.

The Moor watches her with enthusiasm which inspires her to do another dance, this time, a waltz.

Rather awkwardly the Moor joins with her in the dance.

The dance by the Ballerina and the Moor is interrupted by Petrouchka's rushing into the room in a jealous rage. The angry Moor grabs his scimitar to do battle with Petrouchka and quickly drives him from the cell. The scene ends with the Ballerina in the arms of the Moor.

Scene Four is again in the carnival square. The crowd is growing and the boisterousness is increasing.

A group of nursemaids come together and do a primitive dance to an old Russian folk tune.

To this scene is added a group of coachmen who lend more color and excitement to the festivity. A tipsy merchant enters the square and, seeing two gypsy girls, pays them to do a gypsy dance for the crowd.

The crowd draws back as a trained bear is brought into the square to entertain, but quickly forgets its fear as the bear goes through his act of walking on his hind legs and doing a clumsy dance. This is followed by a wild and frenzied dance with all of the revelers, the gypsy girls, the coachmen, the nursemaids, and even the bear taking part.

and

A party of masqueraders enter and break up the dance. They wear hideous costumes and masks.

One of them is dressed as the devil. They rush through the crowd, bringing an end to the carnival. Suddenly a wailing cry is heard, the curtains of the puppet theater are ripped asunder. Petrouchka, pursued by the Moor, rushes into the square.

The Ballerina tries in vain to stop the Moor who is determined once and for always to do away with his hated rival. They rush madly through the crowd.

The Moor finally catches Petrouchka and with one blow of his scimitar kills Petrouchka, who falls to the ground.

Someone hurries off to find the police and soon returns with not only the police but also the Charlatan. The Charlatan lifts the body of Petrouchka and shows the crowd that after all, this is only a doll made of rags and sawdust which never lived and is but a figment of the imagination. He begins to drag the ruined puppet toward the puppet theater.

A trumpet screams forth the Petrouchka theme.

Looking up, the Charlatan sees on the roof of the theater the ghost of Petrouchka swinging menacingly toward him. Petrouchka seems to say that he, at long last, is now free of his cruel master. Terrified, the Charlatan drops the bundle of rags and sawdust and rushes into the night.

215

Responding Intellectually to Music of the Dance

We have already seen that the highest form of personal involvement in listening results from an intellectual response to the music. This does not minimize the importance and impact of the physical and emotional response to music. Rather, it complements these responses by giving the listener the means for recognizing and understanding the elements of music which the composer used. An intellectual response to music is the result of intelligent listening. We need to recognize that listening to music is a difficult process because we are listening for something that is gone as soon as it is heard. If the response to music is to be literate, it is necessary to develop the ability to anticipate what is to come—and also to recognize and analyze melodic bits, rhythmic and harmonic structure, timbre and form. This analytical ability must become a part of one's musical equipment if he is to listen successfully and develop the skill to draw the maximum value from the music.

The use of the dance suite or idealized dance forms in musical composition illustrates the use of music of the dance designed to capture the spirit of the dance, rather than accompany it. In its idealized form it is not music to dance to. Neither does it depend on non-musical ideas, as the ballet does, to give its impact to the listener. Understanding this kind of music depends to a considerable extent on the intellectual response of the listener.

We have seen how the early dances were put together in a slow-fast-slow-fast arrangement. Through the use of four dances—the *allemande*, the *courante*, the *sarabande* and the *gigue* played in the same key, often referred to as the four obligatory dances—the eighteenth-century suite developed. As more and more composers began to use the form, the need for variety became apparent, with the result that composers began to substitute other dances for one or more of the obligatory dances. Later, French composers developed a slow and formal opening movement or prelude for their suites which was known by the name of French Overture. It should be noted that the term "overture," as used in connection with the classical suite, is different in form and meaning from the orchestral overture which developed later.

LISTENING ACTIVITY

Suite No. 3 in D Major . . . . Johann Sebastian Bach (1685-1750)

Bach wrote four orchestral suites using the French style of beginning with an overture. The Suite No. 3 is typical of his use of music of the dance in idealized form for the musical material for his orchestral suites.

The *Suite No. 3 in D Major* contains five movements of which only the last three are taken from the popular dances of the time. The opening movement, the overture, is characteristic of the French Overture which was in vogue during the time of Bach. It begins with a slow, rather grandiose theme which derives from a melody conceived with a broad sweep. This is followed by a Vivace or fast section which gives a feeling of contrast to the work—which in turn is followed by a return to the original tempo, with the shape of the original melody slightly altered. This slight alteration of the melody demonstrates another means for adding variety and contrast to a movement.

216

I. Overture

Johann Sebastian Bach

219

220

221

222

223

225

227

228

231

232

RHYTHM: In Part I (the Grave section) the basic rhythm has a basic four pulses to the measure, indicated by the meter marking of C (4/4). Each beat or pulse in turn has an underlying feeling of four. Two basic rhythmic patterns  and are used. There is a strong feeling of stress on the first and third beats. The tempo is slow and steady. In Part II the rhythm is still an underlying four pulses to the measure. There is more feeling of movement in this section due to a faster tempo given as *Vivace* (measure 25) and indicated also by *alla breve* marking. The gay character of the fugal melody also gives a feeling of rhythmic movement. Part III is a return to the rhythmic character and movement found in Part I (Grave).

MELODY: The melody in Part I is an imposing and dignified melody beginning with a four-note figure repeated four times in sequential form.

In the third and fourth statement of the figure the last three notes of the figure are given in inversion.

In measure 3 the melody leaps upward one octave and then descends by small skips, using the members of the chord. In measure 4 the melody again turns upward, using the members of the I chord. Out of these two melodic ideas played and repeated in different registers, Part I is constructed. The melody in Part II is basically a one-octave scale with a range of to .

This melody:

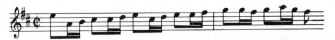

is the subject of a gay little fugue which scurries by as it is played first by one instrument and then by another. In Part III or the concluding section the melody used in Part I returns in a slightly altered shape. In Part I the melody begins on D above middle C and follows a rising line; in Part III the melody begins on the octave above and generally assumes a falling line leading to the final cadence.

HARMONY: In this "Overture" one hears a rich harmonic background resulting from the use of many different harmonies. As is to be expected from music of this period, there is a strong feeling for the tonality of D major created through the frequent repetition of the I (DF♯A), the IV (GBD) and the V or V₇ (AC♯E or AC♯EG) chords. Harmonic interest and variety are also achieved by the substitution of other harmonic structures such as the II (EGB), the III (F♯AC♯) or the VII (C♯EG) chords. The composer also enriched the harmonic background by altering the individual members of a chord—for example, in measure 6 altering the G to G♯.

233

TIMBRE: The melody is played by the first violins and doubled by the oboes. One countermelody is played by the second violins. Other countermelodies are played by violas and violoncello (and/or string bass) reinforced by three trumpets in D. The cembalo is used primarily to reinforce and project the harmonic background. Two timpani are used to give rhythmic stability to the work. (For an explanation of the instruments used in the fugue of Part II of the "Overture," refer to the following discussion of form.)

FORM: The "Overture" contains three separate sections or parts. Part I contains three phrase groups (measures 1-8, 9-16 and 17-24). Part II is in the style of the old Italian concerto grosso with a section played forte by the full ensemble called *tutti*, followed by a contrasting section played *piano* by solo instruments called *concertino*. In the initial *tutti* a spritely fugal subject is introduced by the first violins.

Following this original statement of the subject there are seven additional appearances of the subject played in order by the second violins, violas, basses, first violins, trumpets and ending with the basses. Measure 43 introduces the *concertino* section played by the first violins accompanied with light chords played by the other strings. Measure 59 marks the beginning of the middle *tutti*, followed in measure 72 with the middle *concertino* section. In measure 90 the final *tutti* begins and this in turn leads into the final section of the "Overture." Part III with its altered melodic shape is reminiscent of the opening. The form of this section is a double period.

II. Air

234

In the classical French Suite one would expect to have the overture followed by one of the dance forms. Bach, however, expressed not only his individuality but also his genius by substituting this "Air," a movement which did not have a place in the dance suite, for the expected dance movement. The emotional quality of this "Air" demonstrates that Bach was far ahead of the other writers of his period.

RHYTHM: The meter marking for the "Air" is 4/4. Its slow tempo, however, gives the movement a feeling of moving in eight. This feeling is reinforced by the eighth-note accompaniment played by the bass. This bass which is reminiscent of the pedal technic on the organ furnishes a metronomic background accompaniment for a melody which is both sublime and elegant.

235

MELODY: The melody, a fine example of the Italian *bel canto* style of writing, is played by the first violins while the rest of the strings furnish the accompaniment. The melody beginning on a high sustained F♯ has a feeling of soaring which lifts the listener with it, even though the melodic line turns in measure 2 and descends through the use of small skips and steps. In measure 4 the melody furnishes a fine example of a music sequence: it is the same as in measure 3 except that it is one note lower. The first melody is in the key of D major and ends on A, the dominant of the key of D major. The second or contrasting melody, which begins in measure 7, continues the feeling of a broadly sustained, ever rising melody. The melodic outline, however, is slightly more angular and contains larger intervallic distances—for example, the interval of the octave found in measures 7, 8 and 12. Scalewise passages and small skips in addition to the large intervals are also used in the construction of this second melody. A minimum amount of ornamentation is used for both the first and second melodies. One finds an occasional *appoggiatura* as in measure 7, a grace note as in measure 12, and a trill as in the final measure.

HARMONY: The genius of Bach was such that he not only was able to create an extraordinarily beautiful melody which can lift the listener above the mundane events of everyday living, but that he could also clothe this melody in harmonies rich, varied and complementary. The style of harmony chosen by Bach was not the static harmonic background one might expect from a composer of this period. Rather, through the use of countermelodies played by the second violins and violas, a kind of harmony is projected which actually anticipates the motion of the melody when the melody

is singing on a long tone. The skill of the composer in combining the inner voices by having voices moving against held tones

(Measure 15)

gives the movement its feeling of vibrant harmonization. We have already noted that the bass gives the underlying or basic harmonic structure through the use of broken chords—which is similar to the pedal technic used on the organ.

TIMBRE: The "Air" is essentially a movement for string orchestra. The first violin sings the melody in both Part I and Part II of the movement. Lovely countermelodies are played by the second violins and violas while the bass plays a rhythmic and harmonic accompaniment. The cembalo, used to reinforce the harmony of the movement, plays a secondary role.

FORM: The "Air" is cast in simple binary form. Part I contains a six-measure phrase which is repeated. The melody ends on the fifth of the scale and is harmonized by the V chord. Part II contains twelve measures which are repeated. These twelve measures are in turn broken into three phrase groups of four measures each: Phrase 1, measures 7-10; Phrase 2, measures 11-14; and Phrase 3, measures 15-18.

III. Gavotte

Gavotte I

237

238

Gavotte II

239

240

241

In this movement the listener meets for the first time in this suite one of the country dances out of which many of the baroque suites were fashioned. The gavotte, a wild and boisterous rural dance in 4/4 time, was refined somewhat when brought to the court at Versailles by Marie Antoinette. The characteristic steps of the gavotte are two light steps followed by one heavy step. Each phrase begins on the third beat.

Frequently the gavotte was followed by a *musette* with its characteristic drone bass which gave an element of contrast to the work. This in turn was followed by a *da capo* repetition of the gavotte. In this suite Bach used not one but two gavottes out of which he fashioned this movement. As we shall see, by his *da capo* repetition of the first gavotte he achieved the same form with its resulting unity and contrast as did other composers using the musette as the foil to the gavotte.

RHYTHM: A combination of tempo and arrangement of long and short notes gives this movement a feeling of robust gaiety. The movement is marked ¢ or *alla breve* which gives a feeling of moving forward. The characteristic gavotte steps of two light steps followed by a heavy step are represented by the rhythm ♩ ♩ | ♩ . Note the imitative effect of the light steps in the continuo part, measures 1 and 2. The rhythm in "Gavotte I" is basically ♩ ♫ | ♩ ♩ ♫ | ♩. In the second or contrasting gavotte the rhythm follows the arpeggiated melody which gives this rhythm ♫ ♩ | ♫ ♩ ♫ ♩ | ♩ .

MELODY: The melody of "Gavotte I" grows out of the rhythmic design of the dance. The melody has a range from D above middle C to B an octave and a seventh above.

Because of this extreme range and because of the large interval skips such as the octave, sixth, seventh, the melody might be said to be more instrumental than vocal in character. In the first section of "Gavotte I" the general melodic direction is down, while in the second section the melodic direction is up. In "Gavotte II" the melody has a range from A below middle C to B an octave and a seventh above middle C.

The melody is based on a two-measure arpeggiated figure followed by a contrasting two-measure conjunct (stepwise) figure. The melody, like the melody in "Gavotte I," is instrumental in character.

HARMONY: While each of the instruments plays a melodic part, the harmonic effect is one of an up-and-down chordal relationship. The basic harmonization used by Bach is simple and involves considerable use of the primary chords I, IV and V or V_7, and one finds also a liberal sprinkling of the secondary chords. Bach used four other technics to give harmonic interest and warmth as well as unity and contrast to these gavottes:

1. A close observation of the score will reveal liberal use of harmonic suspensions which serve to delay momentarily the resolution of the chord.
2. Closely related to this is the use of the passing tone which for the moment gives an alien sound as a result of not being a regular member of the chord.
3. Judicious use of seventh chords such as the I_7, V_7 or VI_7 also adds to the harmonic richness in the accompanying voices.
4. The final device—modulating to a new key—is used effectively in each of the parts of both gavottes. In this instance, Part I of the

first gavotte begins in D major, modulates into A major in measure 6, and ends in this key. Part II of the first gavotte begins in D major, goes into the key of B minor in measure 13, and returns to the key of D major in measure 24. Similarly in the second gavotte Part I begins in the key of D major and moves into A major at the cadence, while Part II begins in A major and after modulating through various keys returns to the original key of D major. Here the harmonization depends on the key being used.

TIMBRE: Both gavottes use string choir, two oboes, three trumpets in D, timpani in D and A and cembalo. In "Gavotte I" for the most part the first violin is doubled by the oboes and first trumpet in D, the second violin is doubled by the second trumpet in D, while the viola is doubled by the third trumpet in D. The timpani underscore the rhythm while the cembalo reinforces the harmonic background. In "Gavotte II" the first violin is doubled by the first oboe, the second violin is doubled by the second oboe, the arpeggiated rhythmic-melodic figure is doubled by viola and bass. This same figure is also played by the cembalo. The three trumpets in D play the melody in quarter notes, giving emphasis to the melodic movement.

FORM: The form of the complete movement is known as ternary or three-part song form. Each of the large parts or sections can be broken down into smaller units of form.

Part I	Gavotte I	Two-part song form
A	Period *(repeated)*	
	antecedent phrase	measures 1-4
	consequent phrase	measures 4-10 *(irregular)*
B	Period *(repeated)*	
	antecedent phrase	measures 10-18
	consequent phrase	measures 18-26

Part II	Gavotte II	Two-part song form
A	Double Period *(repeated)*	
	First Period	
	antecedent phrase	measures 1-4
	consequent phrase	measures 4-10
	Second Period	
	antecedent phrase	measures 10-13 *(irregular)*
	consequent phrase	measures 13-16 *(irregular)*
B	Double Period *(repeated)*	
	First Period	
	antecedent phrase	measures 16-20
	consequent phrase	measures 20-24
	Second Period	
	antecedent phrase	measures 24-28
	consequent phrase	measures 28-32

Part III	Da Capo	Repetition of Gavotte I without repeats of individual parts.

243

IV. Bourrée

245

A *bourrée*—a lively dance of French origin—is the second of the country dances used by Bach in this suite. It has a feeling of gaiety and lightness which derives largely from the light staccato style of the dance.

RHYTHM:
1. What is the rhythm of this *"Bourrée"*?
2. What is the meter of this movement?
3. How many beats are there to a measure?
4. Are the strong beats followed or preceded by light beats?
5. In each instance how many of these light beats are there?
6. What is a pickup or upbeat? Indicate on the score the composer's use of upbeats.
7. What is the purpose of the timpani part in this movement?
8. What is syncopation? This movement contains several effective uses of syncopation. Mark on the score the places where the element of syncopation was used by Bach.
9. Why does a composer use syncopation as a part of the rhythmic structure of his composition?

MELODY:
1. On what note does the melody begin? End?
2. What is the range of the melody?
3. Is the movement of the melody generally upward or downward?
4. Does the melody move by skips or steps? If by skips, are the skips large or small?
5. The melody begins in the key of D major. Does it modulate to any other key or keys?
6. Is the melody essentially instrumental or vocal? Why?
7. What are some of the devices which Bach used in this movement to achieve variety in the melodic line?

HARMONY:
1. Mark in the score the I, V and V₇ chords.
2. Indicate the various keys used in this movement.
3. Give the name for the final cadence of the movement.
4. What is the purpose of using several different keys in this movement?

TIMBRE:
1. What instrument plays the principal melodic line? Indicate where on the score.
2. What instrument or instruments double this melodic line?
3. What instruments play countermelodies? Indicate this information on the score.
4. What are the roles of the three trumpets in D in this movement?
5. What is the function of the timpani in this movement?
6. How does the cembalo contribute to the overall expressive quality of this movement?
7. Beginning in measure 11 note that while the basses are playing the melody, the other instruments are adding an ornamentation to the melody.

FORM:
1. What is the form of this movement?
2. What is the form of each of the parts?
3. Indicate the phrases in each part.

247

V. Gigue

249

250

251

The final movement of this suite also comes from an early dance. The *gigue* is often associated with the fiddle—in fact, the word derived from the Italian word *giga*, which means fiddle. Its gay, good-humored style and rhythmic vitality made it a favorite with the eighteenth-century composers for the final movement of their suites.

RHYTHM:
1. What is the meter marking for this *"Gigue"*?
2. How many pulses are there to a measure?
3. What then is the rhythm of this movement?
4. In measure 1 what instruments have the basic rhythmic pattern?
5. What are the various note values used in this movement?

MELODY:
1. What key is used for the melody?
2. What is the reason this key was used?
3. Is this melody essentially instrumental or vocal? Why?
4. Is the construction of the melody essentially stepwise or skipwise?
5. The range of the melody extends from _____ to _____.
6. In measures 18-24 which instruments play the melody? The counter-melody?
7. In measures 66-72 which instruments play the melody? The counter-melody?

HARMONY:
1. Mark the I, IV, V and V_7 chords.
2. What are some of the other chords which are used?
3. Into what other keys does this *"Gigue"* move?
4. What is the purpose of going into the new keys?
5. What is the relationship of the cadence chord in measure 24 to the beginning key?
6. At what point does the composition return to the original key?

TIMBRE:
1. Describe the use of the different instruments selected by the composer for the instrumentation of this movement.
2. What instruments are responsible for the melodic line?
3. What instruments play countermelodies?
4. Which instruments are responsible for the harmonic background?
5. What is the role of the timpani in this movement?

FORM:
1. What is the form of this *"Gigue"*?
2. How many large sections or parts are there?
3. How many parts are there in each of the large sections?
4. What is the form of each of the smaller sections?
5. In looking at the entire suite, how did the composer achieve unity? Variety? Contrast?

Music for ceremony

and ritual

The Sacred Vocal Forms

To understand more fully the role of the church as a patron of the arts, it is necessary to look back to the beginning of the Christian era to see to what extent music and the parallel arts were accepted as a part of the responsibility of the church. Even prior to the advent of Christianity music played an important role in the worship of God by the Hebrew people. Music was an integral part of the ritual of their worship. Numerous references to music are to be found in the Old Testament:

> *It shall come to pass...that thou shalt meet a company of prophets coming down from the high place with a psaltery, and a tabret, and a pipe, and a harp, before them; and they shall prophesy.*
>
> *—I Samuel, Chapter 10, Verse 5*

> *Praise him with the sound of the trumpet:*
> *praise him with the psaltery and harp.*
>
> *Praise him with the timbrel and dance:*
> *praise him with stringed instruments and organs.*
>
> *Praise him upon the loud cymbals:*
> *praise him upon the high sounding cymbals.*
>
> *—Psalm 150*

257

The texts of the Psalms could well have furnished the basis for the Jewish liturgical chants in which the priest sang or intoned the first half of each verse while the choir answered by singing the remaining portion of each verse. That music was important to the Jewish service is indicated by King David's assigning to one of the Jewish tribes the sole responsibility for providing music in the Temple. In the liturgy of the Jewish church, music was used in these ways: 1. Portions of the scriptures sung to traditional tunes but in free rhythm which give rise to melodies of highly decorated character known to us as *cantillation*. 2. The portion of the service known as the Credo or the great *Shema*. 3. Special prayers and psalms for special occasions set to music to become an integral part of the act of worship. The modes and melodies used by modern Jews in their worship are much the same as used during those early days.

Wilfred Douglas in his *Church Music in History and Practice* lists the general characteristics of this early Jewish music: 1. Music limited to a specified number of melodies, each with a musical style of great nobility, making it eminently proper for use in the liturgy of the church, as opposed to music which served a secular purpose. 2. Music which used the principle of monotonic recitation, or, as we know it, chanting. 3. Music which based its rhythm on the prose rhythm with a system of inflections and pauses corresponding to the inflections and pauses inherent in the prose. 4. Music having elaborate and brilliant ornamentations, known as *melismata*, built around certain vowels. 5. Music used by the congregation in singing the responses to the Psalms. This latter was undoubtedly the forerunner of the responsive reading and singing of Psalms and other responses in the present-day church. From the very beginning music has enjoyed a secure role in the religious worship of the Jewish people.

In contrast to this respected and important role enjoyed by music in the Jewish liturgy, music in the early Christian church was not considered acceptable. During the first three centuries A.D., Roman citizens accepted and even enjoyed the spectacle of hundreds of men and women being persecuted for their belief in a religion based on the teachings of Jesus Christ, as well as for their refusal to bow down to the pagan gods of the Romans. Despite these persecutions the movement grew and expanded until by the year 300 A.D. the Romans realized that further bloodshed was useless. In 311 A.D. the emperor Galerius decreed an end to the persecution of the Christians, and thus began an era of religious tolerance and unparalleled growth.

During this time the church had little concern for art of any kind and music in particular. By looking at the character of the early Christians one can easily see why such a state of affairs might exist. A large percentage of the early Christian converts were from the middle or lower middle classes, and were not used to any form of aesthetic expression. There was a further complication: In the minds of early Christians all art was associated with a corrupt and sinful world, a world which because of its paganism was god-less and thus doomed. Music during this time was thought to be associated with the Antichrist. Painting, however, was used to represent some of the events connected with Old Testament history.

During the years beginning with the conversion of Constantine and continuing through the coming of the Lombards, the Christian church grew, became more secure, touched more lives and became culturally mature. During this time the foundation was laid which ultimately led to its power, wealth and influence in the world. As this growth of power and wealth took place it was natural that the church began to investigate ways in which the fine arts might be brought into its service. Since the act of worship was an outward expression of man's veneration of his God, it followed that in the natural course of events man would recognize that the act of worship might be heightened by the full use of the arts. The church, therefore, became a patron of the arts, and despite many restrictive rules has been responsible for keeping the arts alive and thriving through the centuries.

The church's role in subsidizing the arts is recognized in the awe-inspiring works which are now considered to be an integral part of the religious worship. The architect's cathedrals with their Romanesque domes, vaulted arches or flying buttresses rising to the heavens testify to the artist's desire to express his artistry for the "glory of God."

NOTRE DAME IN PARIS, prime example of Gothic architecture

259

BASILICA OF SACRÉ COEUR
IN PARIS,
an outstanding example
of Byzantine architecture

A great edifice was not enough. Artists such as sculptors, painters, woodworkers and other craftsmen also made their contributions through superbly beautiful altars, statues, stained glass windows, chalices and paintings, all designed to fill a particular niche and to enhance religious worship by showing the totality of the religious experience.

SPANISH XVth CENTURY RETABLE AND ALTAR

STAINED GLASS WINDOW,
U. S. Memorial Chapel,
St. Paul's Cathedral, London

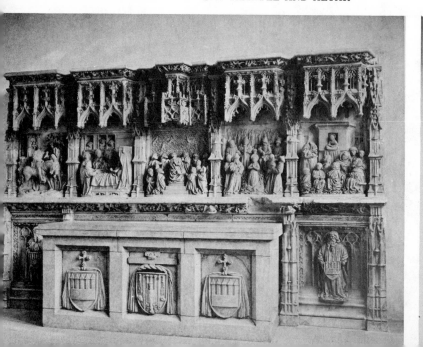

CHALICE

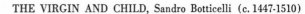

THE VIRGIN AND CHILD, Sandro Botticelli (c. 1447-1510)

Writers also contributed their creative talents to the service of the church through the setting down in language of great beauty and strength the formal ritual of the church.

Almighty God, Father of all mercies, we, thine unworthy servants, do give thee most humble and hearty thanks for all thy goodness and loving-kindness to us, and to all men. We bless thee for our creation, preservation, and all the blessings of this life; but above all, for thine inestimable love in the redemption of the world by our Lord Jesus Christ; for the means of grace, and for the hope of glory. And, we beseech thee, give us that due sense of all thy mercies, that our hearts may be unfeignedly thankful; and that we show forth thy praise, not only with our lips, but in our lives, by giving up ourselves to thy service, and by walking before thee in holiness and righteousness all our days; through Jesus Christ our Lord, to whom, with thee and the Holy Ghost, be all honour and glory, world without end. Amen.[10]

261

Other writers, although not particularly interested in writing down the prayers and order of service, nevertheless strengthened the faith of the people through their poetry, allegories and essays which dealt with this all-powerful phenomenon known as religion.

Recessional

God of our fathers, known of old,
Lord of our far-flung battle line,
Beneath whose awful Hand we hold
Dominion over palm and pine—
Lord God of Hosts, be with us yet,
Lest we forget—lest we forget!

The tumult and the shouting dies;
The Captains and the Kings depart:
Still stands Thine ancient sacrifice,
An humble and a contrite heart.
Lord God of Hosts, be with us yet,
Lest we forget—lest we forget!

Far-called, our navies melt away;
On dune and headland sinks the fire:
Lo, all our pomp of yesterday
Is one with Nineveh and Tyre!
Judge of the Nations, spare us yet,
Lest we forget—lest we forget!

If, drunk with sight of power, we loose
Wild tongues that have not Thee in awe,
Such boasting as the Gentiles use,
Or lesser breeds without the Law—
Lord God of Hosts, be with us yet,
Lest we forget—lest we forget!

For heathen heart that puts her trust
In reeking tube and iron shard,
All valiant dust that builds on dust,
And guarding calls not Thee to guard,
For frantic boast and foolish word—
Thy Mercy on Thy People, Lord! Amen.

—Rudyard Kipling
(1865-1936)

It is easy to see how music, one of the most personal and expressive of the arts, could also be called on to play an important role in the worship service of the church. From the very beginning, particularly through that period known as the Middle Ages, and continuing through to the present time, music has played an important role in the development of the church. And, conversely, the church has been of the greatest importance in the development of music.

The beginning of music in the early Christian church brought together a mixture of three influences. First, much of it was taken directly from the Jewish synagogical literature—for example, the singing of the Psalms and Canticles. A second influence stemmed from the use of some of the musical systems and traditions in vogue in Greece. Some of the early Christian chants had a strong resemblance to Greek melodies. Finally, as the early Eastern and Western congregations developed they brought their own unique philosophical and cultural contributions to bear on the musical liturgy of the church.

Gregorian Chant

As we have already seen, the earliest musical liturgy used by the Christian church came from the East. Not until the seventh century A.D., when the Roman Catholic church adopted Latin as its official language, did the Roman liturgy begin to deviate from the Grecian form and language. In the seventh century A.D. it became apparent that a musical liturgy should be developed which could effectively meet the needs of all who participated in the common service—bishop, cleric, choir or congregation. The resulting liturgy consisted of beautiful and impressive dialogues set to simple chants between the priest, acting as celebrant of the mass, and the entire congregation. There were more elaborate chants, using Psalm texts, which contained refrains that varied with the changing seasons and feasts of the church year, and which were sung by the choir. Finally, there were three parts of the liturgy, the *Kyrie eleison, Gloria in excelsis Deo* and *Sanctus,* all set to very simple chants sung by the entire congregation. The musical basis for this early liturgy was the *plainsong* which was simply a ritual melody that was monophonic or a plain melody without accompaniment or countermelody. As we shall see, the plainsong had several distinguishing characteristics.

Haec dies. . . . . .Gregorian Chant, Easter

On hearing this music for the first time the average listener is apt to react to it by feeling that it is strange and different. It is obvious that this different and strange feeling of the music stems from other factors besides the unaccompanied monophonic melody. What, then, makes this music sound strange and different?

As a starting point in our quest for an answer, we might begin by considering the rhythmic structure of chant. If the following rhythmic pattern is clapped:

it seems natural and normal to accent the first beat of each measure. In a previous unit it was shown that it is possible to shift this accent or stress to any other beat in the measure, thus

or

Now clap the rhythm to the following song and identify the title:

The rhythm fairly sings the melodic line for us, so strong is our identification with the rhythmic structure of this song, because of the strong feeling we have for accent and stress. This is often referred to as the "tyranny of the bar line."

In the Gregorian chant this regularity of accent or stress is not present.

Rather, the rhythm is free of regularly placed stress after bar lines because it conforms to the natural rhythm of the Latin phrase. This rhythm may consist of any succession of groupings of twos and threes—for example:

1-2, 1-2-3, 1-2-3, 1-2, 1-2, 1-2-3, 1-2, 1-2.

To discover the fluidity of the rhythm of the chant, count the above rhythm without stressing the one. Thus we see that one of the reasons the Gregorian chant sounds different to modern ears is the rhythmic freedom. This comes from following the rhythm of the Latin text, rather than the restricted rhythm which results when we have a rhythm dominated by the bar line.

But rhythmic freedom does not entirely explain the reason why the plainsong chant may sound strange to modern ears. It is necessary to look further and to examine rather closely the melodic line of a chant to look at the basic system used for the construction of this melodic line. It has already been pointed out that the chants were influenced by the music of the Jewish synagogue. In fact, there seems to be a strong possibility that some of the Jewish chants themselves were taken over by the early Christian church. As one means for developing an understanding of the music of the chant, one can begin by looking at and listening to the following scale which begins on E above middle C and uses only the white keys of the piano:

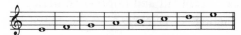

In Unit One major and minor scales were discussed. In comparing this scale with the major scale beginning on the same note,

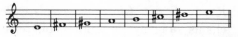

and the natural minor scale beginning on the same note,

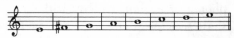

it becomes immediately apparent that this scale sounds entirely different from any of the scales so far contacted. This scale is called *modal* and had its origin in the Jewish synagogical liturgy and was later incorporated into the liturgy of the Christian church. This particular mode, beginning on E and using only the white keys to the octave E, is known as the *Phrygian mode*. Other modal scales may be constructed in like manner by beginning on any other white key of the piano and continuing for eight tones, using only the white keys. Each of these modal scales was given an identifying name and each was thought to have its own effect and mood. It was from these various modal scales that the plainsong chants of the early church were constructed.

If the whole- and half-step patterns of the *Phrygian mode* are plotted and compared with their major and minor

mode counterparts, it can be readily seen that the arrangement of whole and half steps differs considerably from either the major or minor scale. In the *Phrygian mode* the half steps fall between steps 1 and 2 and between steps 5 and 6, while in the major scale the half steps are found between steps 3 and 4 and between steps 7 and 8. In the natural minor scale given above, the pattern has the half steps occurring between the second and third steps and the fifth and sixth steps. The factor which distinguished the various modes was the arrangement of half steps rather than the beginning pitch.

As a further step in acquiring an understanding of the effect of the modal scale on music, play and listen to the melody of the following well-known song played in the *Phrygian mode* and try to identify it.

As a check and as a means of comparison, play and listen to this same melody played in its proper major tonality.

As a result of this listening experience with modal music, we can conclude that because modern ears are largely attuned to major and minor tonality, melodies based on the modal system sound strange. And since Gregorian melodies are modal, they too sound

strange. Thus we have a second reason why the Gregorian plainsong chant strikes us as being different from what our modern ears are accustomed to hearing.

If we play and listen once again to the melody of "America,"

we recognize that while the melody is complete in itself, the composition, nevertheless, is not complete. People today are so accustomed to hearing this song with its harmonic background that the ear consciously or subconsciously misses this element when it is not present.

But this is only part of the story. Play or have played the following harmonized version of "America."

With the exception of three chords, the ear rejects this harmonization as being completely unacceptable. Why should this be so? By playing and listening to the commonly accepted harmonization of this song,

we find that our ears demand not only harmony but a specific harmony. In the song "America" this accustomed harmony is so deeply instilled in all of us that we tend to consider it as the only "right" or "correct" harmonization. All of this suggests a third reason for the plainsong chant sounding strange to our ears: its complete lack of harmonic structure.

We must now consider the central function or purpose of the chant, which is to enhance the act of divine worship. Since the religious service lacks the bombast of some of the present-day movies, television presentations and musical shows which make considerable use of music, it is natural to expect that music of the chant might lack some of the excitement found in present-day music. Music of the chant has a characteristic mood of adoration and prayerfulness, marked by restraint and

a singular lack of theatrical effects. This is indicated by a rather limited dynamic range. This limited dynamic range suggests another clue to the reason why this music sounds different to ears accustomed to great differences in the dynamic spectrum.

These, then, are a few of the reasons that might affect one's initial response to music of the chant and cause him to label it as strange and different. Once, however, the listener is able to understand the music and its purpose and can begin to get inside it, he discovers that it can be music of great beauty and expressiveness. Remember that the Gregorian chant not only made an important contribution to music history in terms of its role in the growth and development of the Christian church, but it also made a vital contribution to music itself.

Kyrie eleison

12th century Plainsong

While an English translation has been substituted for the original Latin text, this *Kyrie eleison* is nonetheless an authentic example of the kind of melodic and rhythmic writing to be found in the Gregorian chant. After learning this *Kyrie* examine the music and observe the rhythmic freedom which comes from the groupings of two, three and even four, and the fluid way in which these groups are alternated. Note also the number of notes per syllable. The melody itself is calm, which results from the manner in which the melody is constructed. The melody consists essentially of stepwise progressions relieved by the interval of the minor third. The largest interval used is the interval of the perfect fourth which is only used three times in the entire melody.

Although the Gregorian chants were written according to strict rules which governed the use of the various modes, study of these early chants reveals that it was possible to achieve considerable variety in mood, character and style in the different chants. Part of the difference stemmed, of course, from the particular use to which the chant was to be put, but much of the difference could be attributed to the arrangement and number of notes given to each Latin syllable. In general, the chants may be classified into three types:

1. *Syllabic chant.* The syllabic chant uses a simple ratio of one note of music to one syllable of Latin text.
2. *Neumatic chant.* The neumatic chant uses occasional groups *(neumes)* of several notes to one syllable of Latin text. The neumatic chant falls somewhere between the simplicity of the syllabic chant and the ornateness of the melismatic chant.
3. *Melismatic chant.* Melismatic writing is ornate writing in which there may be a profusion of notes per syllable of Latin text. Another characteristic of melismatic style is often the use of extreme vocal ranges.

LISTENING ACTIVITY

Victimae paschali. . . . . .Gregorian Chant, Easter

This is a fine example of a sequence using the ratio of one note of music to one syllable of the Latin text. As defined above, *Victimae paschali* would be classified as a syllabic chant. It is in Mode I—the Dorian mode. There is refreshing originality in this chant which projects a feeling of sincerity, purity and cleanness. Note the jubilant quality in the line, "Scimus Christum surrexisse . . . we know that Christ is risen," which derives from a rising melodic line. Note also the rhythmic structure of *Victimae paschali* and try to determine how the rhythmic freedom was achieved.

Haec dies. . . . . .Gregorian Chant, Easter

This is a superb example of melismatic chant. Note the ornate melodic line which results from the use of many notes to one syllable of Latin text. The chant which tells of the day of Christ's resurrection has a quality of exultation and victory. It is written in Mode II or the Hypodorian mode. Note how the ornateness of the melodic line contributes to the expressiveness of the work by helping bring out the most important words. We also see how the extremes of range can be used to complement the ornateness of the melismatic melodic line in achieving expressive quality. One should note that the mood of this chant seems to be one of youthful exuberance and joy with overtones of religious ecstasy, all of which are derived from the text, "This is the day which the Lord has made, Let us rejoice and be glad in it." This mood is further implemented through the music. Again, examine the rhythmic scheme of this chant to see how it is an outgrowth of the rhythm of the Latin words.

268

The Mass

For many people the word "mass" suggests the religious rite of the Roman Catholic church which is the central and most solemn act of worship in its liturgy. And of course this is one of the connotations of the term. But there is a further definition of the word stemming from the fact that the composite musical form which accompanies this ceremony is also referred to as a "mass." It is to this musical definition of the term "mass" that we shall turn our attention.

A study of the music of the mass is important for a number of reasons. One reason that is immediately suggested is that the mass is and always has been extremely important in the thinking of the worshipers. Anything which can enhance and strengthen the experience of worship is immediately acceptable. One result of this attitude has been that for most of the history of the church those responsible for the development of the church and its liturgy have recognized that the mass offered a great opportunity for music and for musical participation. Thus, music became an important adjunct to the religious ceremonies of the church, and the church in turn, as a patron of a young and budding art, exerted tremendous influence on the development of music.

In Unit One we pointed out that the smaller units of form such as words, phrases, paragraphs in language, and notes, phrases, periods in music often are inadequate when attempting to express the totality of an experience. There need to be ways of writing in extended and larger forms if works of aesthetic and spiritual significance are to realize their full potential. We should not overlook the fact that music for the liturgy of the mass pointed up the need for a means of extending the writing. As a result of this need the music for the mass which, as has already been pointed out, was in its totality a composite, was the first of the larger forms to develop. This in itself makes the mass an important milestone in music history.

In the initial stages the official music of the church was the body of composition known as Gregorian chant discussed above. It is known that there are numerous Gregorian settings of the mass. Unaccompanied contrapuntal writing which began in the fourteenth century reached its zenith in the sixteenth century with the creative efforts of Palestrina (1524-1594) in Italy, Vittoria (1548-1611) in Spain, and Byrd (1543-1623) in England. These renaissance composers along with Orlando di Lasso (1532-1594) and others were strongly attracted to the form of the mass; a major part of their creative lives was devoted to liturgical composition. Officials of the church, recognizing the great value that the music of these renaissance composers might have in the liturgy, soon gave the necessary approval for the inclusion of these works as an integral part of the order of the service. Since that moment in church and music history there has been a long line of distinguished composers who have continued to use the religious impact of the mass as the inspiration for their creative efforts.

The seventeenth and eighteenth centuries witnessed continued growth and development of the music for the church. But, at the same time, music changes were taking place which were to have a great effect on the music which was to be produced for the church. Two musical developments in particular during this time had a profound effect on the music that was composed as a part of the liturgy of the mass. The first of these was the tremendous development of solo singing which led for the first time to a virtuoso school of vocal performers. Having a reservoir of artist performers provided composers with the opportunity to create choral works with very difficult solo passages which could be performed by these artist singers.

At the same time, instruments were improved and composers rapidly increased their knowledge of these instruments as well as their uses. Until men learned of the effectiveness and power of the orchestral accompaniment, there was general acceptance and satisfaction with unaccompanied musical works. With the increased use of the orchestra and its additional spectrum of sound, the unaccompanied masterpieces of the sixteenth century began to lose favor and soon were no longer in vogue. Composers such as Johann Sebastian Bach (1685-1750), Franz Joseph Haydn (1732-1809), Wolfgang Amadeus Mozart (1756-1791) were found in the mainstream of these developments and added the rich palette of orchestral tone to their choral writing for the church.

The interest of composers in music for the church has continued to the present time. Composers of the nineteenth and twentieth centuries such as Ludwig van Beethoven (1770-1827), Franz Schubert (1797-1828), Francis Poulenc (1899-1963) and Igor Stravinsky (1882———) have continued to create new musical versions of the mass. There are, however, those who believe that while the masses composed after the sixteenth century may be musically more complex and may possibly have greater musical power, they lack the religious fervor and power of the masses composed by Palestrina, Vittoria, di Lasso and the other renaissance composers.

The mass falls into two general or large segments. One part, the *ordinary*, which comes from the Latin word *ordinarium*, is the part in which the text is never changed and will appear in every service. It is in the *ordinary* that one finds the *Kyrie eleison* (Lord, have mercy), *Gloria in excelsis Deo* (Glory be to God on high), *Credo* (I believe), *Sanctus* and *Benedictus* (Holy, Holy, Holy, Lord God of Hosts—Blessed is He), and *Agnus Dei* (O Lamb of God). The texts for these musical settings remain unchanged from the days of Palestrina and Vittoria. The second segment of the mass is known as the *proper* which comes from the Latin word *proprium*. This is the flexible portion of the mass in which the text varies according to what is proper for the particular season, day or type of service. It is in the *proper* that one finds the *introits, graduals, alleluias.*

270

Kyrie eleison, Christe eleison......Gregorian Chant for Pentecost and Corpus Christi
(Kyrie III)

Kyrie eleison, Christe eleison comes from the Greek and is a plea for mercy. The words mean, "Lord, have mercy on us, Christ, have mercy on us." Many people might not expect to find the richness of sound that is present in this harmonically unadorned, unaccompanied modal melody. Yet this is a prime example of the vitality and virility to be found in the Gregorian chant. This particular *Kyrie* has a mood of calmness and restraint, yet throughout one senses a profound spirituality.

RHYTHM: The rhythm of the music is drawn from the rhythm of the text.

MELODY: The melodic line which uses Mode IV (Hypophrygian) has a rather restricted range centering around E. There is continu-

ous reference and relationship to the C below, to the third, G, above, as well as to the fourth, A, above. This *Kyrie* is representative of the melismatic chant.

HARMONY: None.

TIMBRE: The entire composition is sung by male voices. As the *Kyrie* progresses it is possible to identify and distinguish tenor and bass quality. The first *Kyrie* is sung by the cantor or leader who is joined on *eleison* by a small choir called the *schola*. There are two large choirs singing in antiphonal or double choir style.

FORM: The form is extended by the use of nine variations based on the first simple phrase.

Gloria in excelsis Deo...........................Igor Stravinsky (1882——)
from the *Mass for Mixed Chorus and Double Wind Quintet*

"Glory be to God on high. We adore thee; we praise thee." The *Gloria* is a song of praise and thanksgiving. It might be readily imagined that Stravinsky's music would be far from the *Kyrie* which was used above. Close listening, however, will reveal several striking resemblances. Note, for example, the cantorial effect of the opening phrase sung by the alto. Another point of similarity is to be heard in the antiphonal effect of soloist against choir and choir against choir.

RHYTHM: The musical rhythm is obtained from the Latin text. In the choral chant sections *Laudamus te, Benedicimus te, Adoramus te,* and so forth, the rhythmic treatment is admirably suited to the rhythm of the Latin text. Stravinsky achieved the freedom from regular stress or accent found in the Gregorian chant through

shifting the meter. The score reveals that the following meters are used in this *Gloria*: 3/4, 3/8, 2/8, 4/8, 3/8, 4/8, 3/8, 2/8, 4/8, 3/8, 4/8, 3/4, 3/8, 2/8, 3/8, 2/4, 3/4, 3/8, 2/8, 3/8, 2/8, 3/8, 2/4, 3/4, 3/8, 2/8, 3/8, 2/4, 3/4, 2/4, 3/4, 2/4, 3/4, 2/4, 3/4, 4/4. To secure consistency of forward movement, many of the 2/8 and 3/8 measures have a feeling of one to the measure. Rhythmic intensity and excitement are achieved through the use of polyrhythms—for example, in measure 7 where there is the three of the triplet in the instrumental accompaniment against the duplet or two in the vocal part.

MELODY: As has already been pointed out, this movement has a close affinity to the Gregorian chant. So there are moments when the melody has a distinct modal flavor.

271

One finds several melismatic effects in the solo line in which the singer is asked to sing an embellishment of several notes on one syllable of Latin text. The chant-like effect results also from the many repeated notes to be found in the melodic line—for example, in the soprano line in measures 19 and 20. Many perfect fourth intervals are found in the melodic line. Stepwise progressions, both ascending and descending, are used to complete the melodic movement.

HARMONY: The harmonization ranges from the simple to the complex. The harmony for the most part might be said to be atonal and not related to key. The absence of signature indicates this lack of key and also indicates that the composer can be freed of the restrictive rules governing major and minor tonalities. Thus he will have complete freedom to write each vocal and instrumental part according to his own expressive ideas. This results in much dissonance especially in the instrumental accompaniment. It is interesting to note the effect of the open perfect fifths and octaves which occur in the accompaniment. Measures 19 to 34 provide an excellent example of this style of writing. An example of one of the earliest forms of harmony is to be found in measure 44, "Domine, Fili," where the writing is that of *organum*.

TIMBRE: Stravinsky wrote this work to achieve mixed voice and wind instrument sound. While he conceived of the choir as preferably being a male choir, that is, one that uses boy sopranos and altos, many performances of this *Mass for Mixed Chorus* use women's voices for the soprano and alto parts. The accompaniment is played by two oboes, one English horn, two bassoons, two trumpets and three trombones. In terms of timbre, note the following:

1. The effect of the oboe, trumpet and English horn in measures 1-10
2. The bassoon passage in measure 10
3. The cantorial effect of the solo alto voice in measures 5-10
4. The contrast of the solo soprano voice in measures 11-17
5. The effect of the brass chords in the accompaniment in measures 19-34
6. The effect of the English horn in measures 43-47
7. The organum effect of the vocal duet between the soprano and alto in measure 44
8. The antiphonal effect of the duet-choir in measures 44-88.

FORM: Instrumental
      introduction   measures 1-4

Section 1
Alto solo—Soprano solo
                  measures 5-18
      Chorus   measures 19-34

Instrumental
      interlude   measures 35-37

Section 2 (Antiphonal)
Solo and Discanti
                  measures 38-52
      Chorus   measures 53-56
Solo and Discanti
                  measures 57-58
      Chorus   measures 59-65
Solo and Discanti
                  measures 66-67
      Chorus   measures 68-71
Solo and Discanti
                  measures 72-87
      Tutti ("Amen")
                  measure 88

272

Crucifixus and Et resurrexit . . . . Johann Sebastian Bach (1685-1750)
from the Credo of the *B Minor Mass*

The *Credo* is the longest section of the mass textually and sets forth the articles of belief of the Roman Catholic church. These two sub-sections are taken from the *Credo*. The *Crucifixus* tells of the death of Christ while the *Et resurrexit* dramatizes the subsequent resurrection. This great work of Bach is representative of the change in the harmonic basis of music which took place during the seventeenth century. During this century tonality rather than modality found its way into the creative efforts of Western composers. Music now appeared written in a new idiom—major and minor scale tonalities. The addition of the intervals of the consonant third and sixth led to triadic harmony which ultimately led to the addition of the intervals of the second and seventh. These in turn brought the seventh chord into general use.

Crucifixus. The mood is one of deepest grief. The dark coloring of a passage such as "*passus, et sepultus est*"—"he died and was buried"—contributes to this feeling of sorrow. The chromatic harmony and the descending vocal line aptly suggest suffering and grief.

RHYTHM: In contrast to the rhythmic freedom of the *Kyrie* studied above, this work of Bach offers a fine example of measured rhythm. The *Crucifixus* moves at a slow, steady pace. While it is in 3/2 meter, there is an underlying pulse of six to the measure suggested by the persistent bass figure in the accompaniment.

MELODY: Throughout the section there is a general tendency for the melody to assume a descending movement. An important characteristic of this *Crucifixus* is the imitative entrance of the vocal parts. The melody begins with a simple motive stated by the sopranos and then imitated by the other voices. This melodic bit consists of three repeated notes which then descend one half step to two repeated notes.

As the melody progresses it continues to be essentially stepwise, with a few skips to give added vitality and interest to the melodic line.

HARMONY: The *Crucifixus* is essentially in E minor, although the tonality changes to G major in the last three measures beginning with the third beat in measure 51. The vocal lines are written in contrapuntal form while the accompaniment is essentially homophonic. The harmonization consists of the basic chords to be found in E minor, but in addition there are several instances where individual members of chords have been altered to give additional harmonic richness. The result is, in effect, chromatic harmony.

TIMBRE: The *Crucifixus* is written for mixed chorus and orchestra. The vocal parts are written for soprano, alto, tenor and bass. The persistent bass figure is in the accompaniment and is played by the cellos and basses. The half-note patterns in the accompaniment are played by the strings and woodwinds. Note the sound of the flute which plays a type of descant or obbligato.

273

FORM: There is a four-measure bass ostinato consisting of a chromatically descending passage in the orchestral accompaniment.

Over this ostinato there are twelve 4-measure statements in the choral parts. There is, in addition, a four-measure instrumental introduction using this same bass ostinato.

Et resurrexit. Note the great contrast in mood from the dejection and grief of the *Crucifixus.* In the *Et resurrexit* there is a feeling of triumph and joy.

RHYTHM: While this section is marked allegro, the movement is not excessively fast but proceeds at a steady walking pace. It is in 3/4 meter. Eighth and sixteenth notes are found in profusion. Quarter notes often come at the end of the phrase and serve as a point of emphasis. One characteristic rhythmic figure is found in both the choral and instrumental parts. It is the eighth note followed by a sixteenth note triplet.

MELODY: The melodies used in this movement consist of highly ornate baroque treatments of a simple initial phrase. The melody begins in D major and moves successively through the related keys of A major and B minor. Both large and small skips as well as stepwise progressions characterize the melodic treatment of this movement. The melody is often embellished by ornate scalewise passages and by a triplet figuration.

HARMONY: The harmonic texture of this movement is essentially contrapuntal, although there are numerous instances of homophonic harmonization. The harmony is based on the triadic use of chords. The basic chords of I, IV, V or V_7 in each of the keys are used for the most part. Harmonic variety and interest are achieved by the modulations to the related keys of A major and B minor. There is an occasional altering of an individual member of a chord as in measures 29 and 30.

TIMBRE: *Et resurrexit* was written for a five-part mixed chorus using first soprano, second soprano, alto, tenor and bass. It also includes an orchestral accompaniment. The scoring includes strings, flute, oboe, trumpets in D, and timpani. The writing for the orchestra imitates the ornate baroque style of vocal writing. Notice particularly the virtuoso treatment and performance of the trumpets in D.

FORM: The movement is divided into three large sections resulting in A B A form. There are instrumental interludes to introduce B and the final A. There is a closing instrumental postlude or coda. A diagram of the form gives the following pattern:

A	D major	measures	1-34
	Instrumental		
	interlude	measures	35-49
B	A major	measures	50-65
	Instrumental		
	interlude		
	B minor	measures	67-73
	Vocal solo (bass)		
	B minor	measures	74-82
A	D major	measures	82-107
	Instrumental		
	postlude		
	or coda	measures	108-127

274

Sanctus and Benedictus from *Mass in G* . . . . Franz Schubert (1797-1828)

For this section from the *ordinary* of the mass it seems wise to turn to a mass written by a composer from the Romantic era. During this period of history creative artists were imbued with a philosophy which placed major importance on the individual and his rights. Writers, artists and musicians alike were concerned that the innate dignity of man be protected and preserved. This feeling reflected itself in all of the arts: The expression of emotion now became more important than perfection or elaborateness of design and form which was a basic tenet of the classical period. Franz Schubert, one of the Romantic composers, is known as a sublime lyricist who demonstrated his sensitive genius through fluent, beautiful melodies and rich harmonies. A thoughtful study of the *Sanctus* and *Benedictus* from his *Mass in G* will reveal the depth of emotional intensity in his writing which is in the best tradition of the Romantic movement.

The translation of the *Sanctus* is "Holy, Holy, Holy, Lord God of hosts. Heaven and earth are full of thy glory." The *Benedictus* translates "Blessed is He that cometh in the name of the Lord."

Sanctus

MOOD: Identify the mood of this *Sanctus*.

RHYTHM:
1. In what meter is the first section of this *Sanctus* written?
2. Does it move fast or slow?
3. Does this section flow in four or eight?
4. In this section what kind of notes basically are used for the vocal parts? For the accompaniment? Why should there be this difference?
5. What is the effect of the sixteenth note and the dotted sixteenth-thirty-second note figures in the accompaniment?
6. What is the meter marking of the second section of the *Sanctus*?
7. Is its movement fast or slow?
8. What kind of notes are used for the vocal parts? The instrumental parts?
9. Compare the similarity of rhythmic writing between the vocal and instrumental parts in this section with the striking difference found in the first section.

MELODY:
1. In the first section what is the key of the melody?
2. In this section which part actually sings the melody?
3. What is the range of this melody?
4. Is the movement of this melody mostly stepwise or does it employ more skips?
5. In the second section of the *Sanctus* what is the key of the melody?
6. In this section what happens to the melody in the third measure? In the sixth measure? In the ninth measure?
7. What is the range of the melody in this section?
8. Describe this melody in terms of its construction—that is, its skips and stepwise progressions.

275

HARMONY: 1. Analyze the chords used for the vocal parts in measures 2 and 3.
2. What do the altered notes in the first chords of measures 2 and 3 do to the original chords?
3. Compare the harmonization of this *Sanctus* with the harmonization of the *Crucifixus* and *Et resurrexit* from the *B Minor Mass* by Bach; with the *Gloria in excelsis Deo* from the *Mass for Mixed Chorus and Double Wind Quintet* by Stravinsky.
4. Define the harmonic texture used in the beginning of the second section of the *Sanctus*.
5. Analyze each entrance in terms of its harmonic relationship to the other parts.
6. Notice the effect of the altered chords in measures 30 and 31. Is this harmonization acceptable to the ear?

TIMBRE: 1. For what combination is this work written?
2. What vocal parts are used?
3. What instruments are used in the orchestral accompaniment?
4. Compare the use of the orchestra in the first and second sections in this *Sanctus*. In which section do the orchestra instruments double the vocal parts?
5. What does the instrumental color of this accompaniment add to the total work?

FORM: 1. How many large sections are there in this *Sanctus*?
2. Is there an instrumental introduction to this *Sanctus*?
3. What is the name of the form used in this *Sanctus*?

Benedictus

MOOD: Identify the mood of this *Benedictus*.

RHYTHM: 1. What is the meter marking for this work?
2. Does it move in six or two?
3. What kinds of notes are used in the rhythmic construction of this movement?
4. Are the rhythms sung by the trio and played by the orchestra similar or different?

MELODY: 1. In what key is the melody written?
2. What is the range of the melody? On what note does it begin?
3. What is the relationship of this beginning note to the key in which the movement is written?
4. In several instances more than one note is sung per syllable of text. Does this indicate that Schubert imitated the ornate baroque style or is it a typical example of Schubert's great ability to write a singable lyric melody?
5. Compare the melodies sung by the soprano, the tenor and the bass. Are they the same or different?

276

HARMONY: 1. What are some of the devices used by Schubert to enrich the harmonic background of this *Benedictus*?
2. Is this movement essentially homophonic or polyphonic?
3. Note the subtle harmonic effects created by the altering of individual members of chords.
4. If a score is available, mark the I_7, II_7, IV_7 and VI chords used by the composer to give harmonic coloring to this *Benedictus*.

TIMBRE: 1. Compare the sounds of the soprano, the tenor and the bass voices as each makes its appearance.
2. Discuss the difference of tonal color achieved between the solo, the duet and the trio in this work.
3. How does the instrumental accompaniment affect the emotional impact of this *Benedictus*?

FORM: 1. The soprano melody is how many measures long? The tenor melody? The bass melody?
2. Are they the same or different?
3. What is each part called?
4. What is the function of the last six measures? Note: At the end of the *Benedictus* there is a return to the second section of the *Sanctus*.

Agnus Dei II from *Missa sine nomine*..............G. P. da Palestrina (1524-1594)

For the final section of the mass we turn to the perfection and strength of sixteenth-century writing. The *Missa sine nomine* (mass without a name) by Palestrina is typical of the writing of this period. It is based on a popular folk song of the period, "Je suis desheritée." The *Agnus Dei II* from this mass is representative of the finest in Palestrina's writing. One senses the tenderness as well as the strength which Palestrina was able to bring to the writing of this movement. *Agnus Dei* translates "Lamb of God, (have mercy upon us)." *Dona nobis pacem* translates "Grant us peace."

RHYTHM: 1. What is the meter of this composition?
2. Does it swing in two or four?
3. Indicate the kinds of notes used to realize the rhythmic movement of the work.
4. Are there examples of syncopation to be found in this movement?

MELODY: 1. Compare the melodies sung by each part.
2. In general, are they alike or different?
3. In what key is this *Agnus Dei* written?
4. Indicate the range of each melody.
5. On which note does each part begin? What is its relationship to the key?
6. Note the use of skips and stepwise progressions in the construction of the different melodies.

277

1. Is the harmonization simple or complex? Why?
2. What is the harmonic texture of this composition called?
3. Note the use of suspensions and passing tones.

TIMBRE: 1. For how many voices is this *Agnus Dei* written?
2. What is the function of the second bass part?
3. Bass I is marked "Canon" while Bass II is marked "Resolutio." What is the significance of these terms?

FORM: 1. What is the form of this movement?
2. Note the elision of phrases, that is, the merging of the cadence with the beginning of the next phrase.

The Motet

Because the motet exists in several forms, it is difficult to arrive at a satisfactory all-inclusive definition of this form. As a generalization it might be said to be a short, unaccompanied, sacred work in polyphonic style. The motet was a force in the development of music for a period of over five hundred years. It had its beginnings in the thirteenth century, achieved its greatest popularity and importance during the gothic and renaissance eras, and continued its impact through the baroque period. In the initial stages of its development it was written for performance in the Roman Catholic church. In the discussion of the mass little was said of the section known as the *proper*. It was pointed out, however, that in the *proper* the texts used are not constant but vary according to the season, the day or even the service. It is in the *proper* that one would expect to find the motet. Here one might hear a motet used for a procession, during the elevation of the Host, or during the offertory. In its early form as used in the Roman Catholic church it was a musical setting of a Latin text. Later on motets began to appear with the texts written in the language of the people and ultimately found their way into the Protestant service as anthems.

Because the motet achieved its greatest importance during the renaissance period, it seems advisable first to consider some of the characteristics of the sixteenth-century motet and then to examine some examples written during this period. We now know that the sixteenth-century motet was a short choral work set to a Latin text. We have also seen that it was contrapuntal in texture. This contrapuntal or polyphonic texture was achieved by employing the usual devices for writing counterpoint, as well as using such technics as imitation and canon. In this connection renaissance composers, by having the individual parts move in different-length note values which derived from the rhythmic schemes in vogue at the time, broke away from the rhythmic rigidity of previous contrapuntal writing. Thus they achieved new and greater polyphonic freedom in their motets.

Another characteristic of the renaissance motet was that it was written for four, five, six, seven, eight or twelve voices or parts. It was meant to be sung without accompaniment. There are those, however, who believe that choirs of that day often strengthened their performance through the use of instruments doubling the voice parts. This, as will be seen later in Unit Six, was a common practice in the singing of madrigals during the same period. It is quite possible that the individual members of the recorder family were used in this fashion.

The form of the motet was divided into sections. Each of these sections was related to and suggested by a single phrase of the text. Each of these sections had its own motive. There is a direct relationship between the Gregorian chant of the middle ages and the renaissance motet: In the very early motets the motives on which these sections were based were taken from plainsong chants. This part selected from the chant was known as the *cantus firmus*. The composer then used the other choral parts for revealing his own creative individuality and technical dexterity. As the form developed, however, composers discarded the chant as the basis for the motet and created their own original melodies for the *cantus firmus*. In addition to these individual sections based on the different motives, it is also possible to analyze the sixteenth-century motet in a more extended form which divides it into two or three larger sections. These three larger divisions were known as the *Prima*, the *Secunda* and the *Tertia Pars*.

The German motet of the same period differed somewhat from the renaissance motet in that it did not develop a new motive for each new section. It differed, too, in that its text was in the vernacular rather than Latin. It also contained solo passages and included instrumental accompaniment. It might be said that the German motet led directly into the cantata.

Adoramus te.........................Giovanni P. da Palestrina (1524-1594)   **SINGING**
This exquisite miniature, the *Adoramus te* by Palestrina, provides an excellent intro-   **EXPERIENCE**
duction to the musical qualities of the motet. Inasmuch as the range of each voice is
well within the vocal limits of the average person, and because it is not musically
complex, it is recommended that *Adoramus te* be sung as a prerequisite to analyzing
the composition.

Adoramus te Christe

Giovanni Pierluigi da Palestrina

280

281

MOOD: 1. What is the mood of *Adoramus te*?

RHYTHM: 1. What is the meter marking?
             2. What can be done to minimize the feeling of stress or accent created by the bar lines?
             3. What is a fermata (⌒)?
             4. As used in this composition what effect does the fermata have on the rhythm?

MELODY: 1. Analyze the melody in terms of its range, its direction and its construction.
             2. Analyze the other parts in the same manner.
             3. Note the small decorative melodic figure which occurs at each mention of the Saviour.

HARMONY: 1. Is the harmonization simple or complex? Why?
             2. Is the texture essentially homophonic or polyphonic? Why?

TIMBRE: 1. For what kind of group was this motet composed?
             2. Would the tonal color be different if boy sopranos and altos were used instead of female sopranos and altos?
             3. Would *Adoramus te* sound different and have a different musical effect if an accompaniment were used?

FORM: 1. Indicate each of the sections of this work.
             2. Does each section have a different musical motive?
             3. Can this composition be divided into two or more large divisions?

O bone Jesu..............................Giovanni P. da Palestrina (1524-1594)

O bone Jesu in its present form has been transcribed for four voices from a motet originally written for six voices. Because it is also well within the capabilities of a group with modest vocal facility, it should be approached through singing. After it has been sung and the group has become acquainted with its devotional beauty achieved through simple harmonization, analyze it in terms of mood, rhythm, melody, timbre and form.

O bone Jesu

Giovanni P. da Palestrina

284

a - sti nos, tu re - de - mi - sti nos,

a - sti nos, tu re - de - mi - sti nos,

a - sti nos, tu re - de - mi - sti nos,

a - sti nos, tu re - de - mi - sti nos,

San - gui - ne tu - o pre - ti - o - sis - si - mo.

San - gui - ne tu - o pre - ti - o - sis - si - mo.

San - gui - ne tu - o pre - ti - o - sis - si - mo.

San - gui - ne tu - o pre - ti - o - sis - si - mo.

285

Ave Maria . . . . Tomás Luis de Vittoria (1535-1611)

MOOD: As the words suggest, this is a prayer and therefore has a deep religious feeling.

RHYTHM: Note that Vittoria achieved rhythmic freedom by following the rhythm of the Latin text, rather than by confining the rhythm of the words to the delimitative effect of measured music. If a modern transcription of this motet is available, it will be interesting to observe how this rhythmic freedom has been insured through the use of shifting meters. If, for example, the Peter J. Wilhousky transcription of this *Ave Maria* is used, the meter markings are 3/4, 2/4, 3/4, 4/4, 3/2, 2/4, 4/4, 2/4, 4/4, 3/4, 4/4, 3/4, 3/2, 4/4, 3/4 and 4/4.

MELODY: Note that after the beginning unison phrase, actually the chant phrase sung by the basses, Vittoria places the chant melody in the upper voices. The graceful melodic line of the opening phrase begins on G below middle C, skips down a perfect fourth, changes direction by moving up one step; after repeating itself it then continues upward with a skip of a perfect fifth, rises one half step and finally turns back one half step.

All of the motives have gentle curving melodic lines resulting from melodies which are essentially stepwise in their progression, with the few skips used being limited to small skips. While the various melodies move both upward and downward, there is a curious feeling that the melodies, in general, tend to move downward. The melodic writing, for the most part, is quite restrained, with only an occasional trace of ornate or melismatic writing, as in the soprano score in measure 17 on the syllable "e" in *mulieribus*, or again in measures 42-44 with the sopranos singing the syllable "nos" in the word *nostrae*.

HARMONY: The harmonization of *Ave Maria* is simple, making use for the most part of the basic chords of I, IV, V and the supplementary chords of II and VI in the key of E minor. Harmonic variety is achieved by the occasional altering of the individual members of a chord—for example, in measure 26 on the words *Sancta Maria* the chord on the third beat has the middle member or the third raised one half step, changing the I chord from E minor to E major tonality. The harmonic texture is both polyphonic as in measures 4 to 10 (*Gratia plena, gratia plena, Dominus tecum*), and homophonic as in measures 26 to 37 (*Sancta Maria, Mater Dei, Sancta Maria, Mater Dei, ora pro nobis, ora pro nobis*).

TIMBRE: This motet was written for an unaccompanied mixed chorus of four voices or parts. Note the cantorial effect of the opening three measures sung by the bass. Note also the antiphonal or echo effect of two choirs answering one another, beginning in measure 26 with the phrases *Sancta Maria, Mater Dei* and *ora pro nobis*. Notice that this effect is created not by having two choirs but through altering the dynamics or by first singing the motive *forte* and then repeating it *piano*. This *Ave Maria* by Vittoria gives the informed listener an excellent opportunity to contrast the tonal color of polyphonic writing with that of homophonic writing.

FORM: This rather short motet contains two sections. Section 1 contains two motives while Section 2 contains only one motive.

286

Section 1	Section 2
1. *Gratia plena ... Dominus tecum* measures 1-12	*Sancta Maria, Mater Dei ...* *ora pro nobis ...*
2. *Benedicta tu in mulieribus et bene-* *dictus fructus ventris tui, Jesus* *Christus.* measures 13-25	*peccatoribus nunc et in hora mortis* *nostrae.* *Amen.* measures 26-47

Hodie Christus natus est.................Jan Pieterszoon Sweelinck (1562-1621)

MOOD:
1. For what season of the church year was this motet written?
2. Should this have something to do with the mood of the composition?
3. What is the mood of this composition?
4. Name some of the technics used by the composer to achieve this feeling or mood.

RHYTHM:
1. Have the words been made to fit the rhythm or has the rhythm been made to fit the words? In other words, is the rhythmic structure more akin to the Gregorian chant or to modern measured music?
2. Is use made of shifting meters? If so, what meters are used?
3. Clap the rhythmic beats of this composition.
4. Is there a basic beat or pulse which underlies the rhythmic movement of this composition from its beginning to its end?
5. Does the speed or tempo remain constant throughout the entire motet, or does it change as the composition progresses?

MELODY:
1. Note the cantorial effect of the tenor entrance in measure 1 and how this same motive is caught up by the first soprano in measure 2.
2. How many times is this melodic phrase used in this motet?
3. In what key is this melody written?
4. Upon what note does the melody begin? What is its relationship to the key?
5. Is the melody constructed of skips? Of stepwise progressions? Of a combination of the two?
6. Does the melody have any ornate baroque characteristics or is it a simple, unadorned melodic statement?
7. Is the melody only found in the higher voices?
8. How many different melodic motives are used in the entire composition?

HARMONY:
1. Is the harmonization simple or complex?
2. Did the composer use more than one key in his composition? If so, what keys?
3. If a vocal score is available, mark the I and V chords.
4. Is the harmonic texture essentially homophonic or polyphonic?
5. Note that this particular harmonic texture makes possible the tossing of the "Noëls" from one part of the choir to another.

TIMBRE:
1. For what kind of a group was this motet written?
2. If a piano were used as an accompaniment for this motet would the effect be changed?
3. Note the use of the second soprano part. Note also that there are times when the second soprano part lies higher than that of the first soprano.
4. Indicate the places where the first soprano has an exact imitation of the second soprano part. Are there instances where the second soprano imitates the first soprano?
5. What do you feel to be the purpose of the second soprano part?

287

FORM: 1. This motet is divided into how many large sections?
         2. Is it possible to divide each of the large sections into smaller divisions?
         3. In measure 33 the second soprano part has the exact notes of the first soprano part but comes one beat later. What is this form of contrapuntal writing called?

The Chorale

Two forces came together during the renaissance period and led to a new and different kind of music for the church—the chorale. The first force which came to a head during this period, and which had implications for music, was the break from the established church, the Roman Catholic, and the formation of the Protestant movement. This was the great contribution of Germany and the German Reformation. It was not entirely the result of Martin Luther's taking issue with the authorities of the Roman Catholic church. True, there was his nailing of the ninety-five theses, accusing the Catholic church of iniquities, on a door of the University of Wittenberg. But he did not single-handedly originate the Protestant movement. Rather, there had been smouldering forces at work for many years before the arrival of Luther on the scene. Man was becoming aware of himself as an individual and was struggling to develop his own powers of self-expression. It was fortunate that a man of Luther's strength of character and great leadership ability came along at this precise time to head the revolt against the powers representing the status quo.

In our study of the music of the mass we learned that originally this service was arranged to provide an opportunity for the congregation to participate actively in the service through the singing of the *Kyrie eleison, Gloria in excelsis Deo,* and *Sanctus.* The remainder of the musical service was divided between the priest and the choir. As time passed and composers became more adept and skilled in handling the materials of music, the writing became more and more complicated. Study of the motet, which was music specifically written for choir, reveals that the writing was characterized by much contrapuntal activity where one voice or part imitated another and parts moved against parts. Renaissance composers were not satisfied with writing music for only four to eight voices but extended their writing to include individual parts for as many as forty to fifty voices. Such vocal writing ultimately became so complicated that the ordinary church-goer, and sometimes even the choir singer, untrained but devoted and willing to offer his service and what talent he had to his God, could not be expected to perform it acceptably. As the musical participation by the congregation was curtailed, more and more of the liturgical work was delegated to the special performing choir. Here, then, was the second force which ultimately led to the reform in church music.

Martin Luther (1483-1546) in his reformation took note of the lack of congregational singing and was inspired to attempt to remedy the situation. He was convinced that music had great power to stimulate and motivate

288

religious emotion, and because of this he resolved to bring music actively into the church service. One of Luther's important contributions to the cause of music was his provision for the use of hymns having simple, singable tunes for congregational singing.

To find music for the hymns or chorales which the congregation might master, and thus be able to participate actively in the service rather than passively listen to it, Luther had to look to many sources. Of these sources, three in particular were of great importance. One natural source was the music of the plainsong. Many of the early chorales were adaptions of the older plainsong melodies. Another source from which some of his chorales were taken was the music of earlier sacred folk songs. And while it may seem strange to many people, another fruitful source for the Luther chorales was the large repertoire of secular melodies of the day.

The musical construction of the Luther chorale followed one of the practices of the early motet writers in that the melody was written for the tenor. During the seventeenth century this practice was modified and ultimately the melody was moved to the soprano part as we know it today. Regular measured rhythm was not a rhythmic characteristic of the early Luther chorales. Because the melodies were borrowed from the plainsong, it was not at all unusual to find shifting meters, with one measure having two beats and another measure having three beats in order to achieve the feeling of the free rhythm of the plainsong.

Harmonically the chorale is written for four voices and is homophonic in texture. Although the chorale is harmonized for four voices, when the chorale is used for congregational singing custom dictates that it be sung in unison. In this case the harmony is supplied by the organ. An organ accompaniment has always been an integral part of chorale writing and performance. One early practice in the singing of chorales merits brief mention here. It was the usual custom for the organist to introduce the chorale by playing a rather elaborate introduction or prelude. Between each verse a variation of the chorale tune would be played. The number of these variations, which were in the form of free improvisations, varied according to the number of verses. Each interlude or variation was intended to reinforce, and be expressive of, the emotion and thought of the verse to follow. The form which grew out of this practice is known as the *chorale prelude*. The form of the chorale is generally either in two- or three-part song form. Chorales may also be constructed of phrase groups.

The chorale developed in Germany was Germany's most notable contribution to music during this era. Indeed, it was Germany's most notable contribution to renaissance art. While the chorale is found in general use today in the Protestant church, the fact remains that the "golden age" of the chorale extended from the time of Luther through the writings of Johann Sebastian Bach (1685-1750). Bach himself added only about thirty original chorales to the repertoire, but his great contribution to the chorale literature came through his reharmonization of about four hundred existing chorales.

289

A Mighty Fortress Is Our God

Martin Luther (1483-1546)

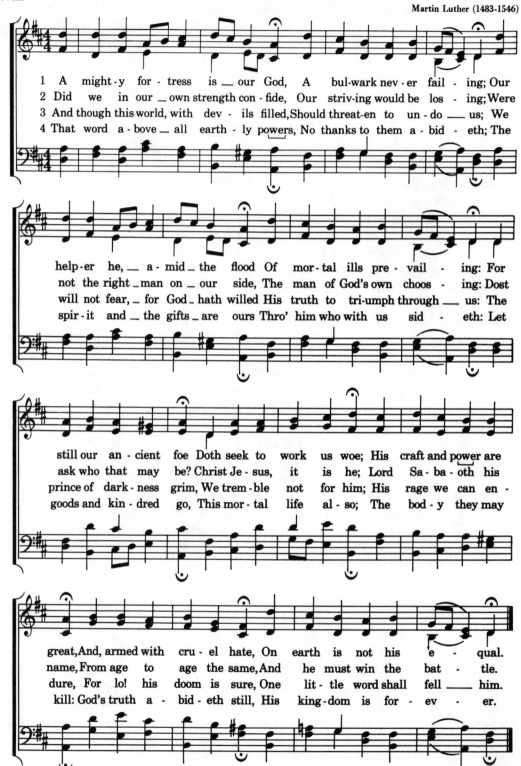

1 A might-y for-tress is __ our God, A bul-wark nev-er fail - ing; Our
2 Did we in our __ own strength con-fide, Our striv-ing would be los-ing; Were
3 And though this world, with dev-ils filled, Should threat-en to un-do __ us; We
4 That word a-bove __ all earth-ly powers, No thanks to them a-bid-eth; The

help-er he, __ a-mid __ the flood Of mor-tal ills pre-vail - ing: For
not the right __ man on __ our side, The man of God's own choos - ing: Dost
will not fear, __ for God __ hath willed His truth to tri-umph through __ us: The
spir-it and __ the gifts __ are ours Thro' him who with us sid - eth: Let

still our an-cient foe Doth seek to work us woe; His craft and power are
ask who that may be? Christ Je-sus, it is he; Lord Sa-ba-oth his
prince of dark-ness grim, We trem-ble not for him; His rage we can en-
goods and kin-dred go, This mor-tal life al-so; The bod-y they may

great, And, armed with cru-el hate, On earth is not his e - qual.
name, From age to age the same, And he must win the bat - tle.
dure, For lo! his doom is sure, One lit-tle word shall fell __ him.
kill: God's truth a-bid-eth still, His king-dom is for-ev - er.

290

In 1519, Luther was formally excommunicated from the Roman Catholic church. This act exposed him to possible danger, and to protect him his friend the Elector Frederick of Saxony kept him under virtual arrest in Wartburg for about one year. During this period he wrote a treatise on religion and completed his translation of the New Testament from the Greek into German. It is thought that during this same period of time he wrote *Ein' feste Burg ist unser Gott,* or as we know it, "A Mighty Fortress Is Our God." It soon became the musical call to arms of the Reformation. It was probably first sung when Luther and his followers made their triumphal entry into Worms. From that day until the present it has steadily grown in popularity. So great is the power and appeal of this melody that composers such as Meyerbeer (1791-1864), Mendelssohn (1809-1847), Wagner (1813-1833) and Stravinsky (1882——) have come under its spell and have freely made use of it as an integral part of one of their compositions.

MOOD: Religious fervor might be said to be the dominant mood of this chorale.

RHYTHM: "A Mighty Fortress Is Our God" is in duple rhythm having a meter marking of 4/4. Eighth and quarter notes are the only rhythmic units used in the composition. Note that the chorale begins on the fourth beat or pick-up and that it is the second note which receives the stress or accent. Each new phrase begins on a pick-up and ends on a third beat.

MELODY: The melody is derived from an old plainsong melody. It is in the key of D major and begins on the first degree of the scale, a major ninth above middle C. It is a good singable melody because its range is not extreme but extends from the D immediately above middle C to the octave D. While the melody contains many skips, particularly that of the interval of the perfect fourth, notice that the melody is essentially stepwise in its construction.

HARMONY: The harmonization is simple and is based principally on the use of the I, IV and V chords in the key of D major. The occasional use of the II and VI chords serves to provide additional harmonic richness. Note the altering of the G to G♯ in the II chord.

TIMBRE: The timbre or tone quality of this chorale will be determined by its use. Try singing it with male voices only, with female voices only, with both groups combined. Compare the quality of sound of each.

FORM: "A Mighty Fortress Is Our God" is in simple two-part song form with each part containing eight measures. The phrases are irregular. It has already been noted that the phrases begin on a fourth beat and end on a third beat. This phrase ending is indicated by a fermata (⌒).

Part I (Period repeated)
  A Antecedent phrase   measures 1-2
    Consequent phrase   measures 3-4
  A Repeated
    Antecedent phrase   measures 5-6
    Consequent phrase   measures 7-8

Part II (Phrase group)
  Phrase 1   measures 9-11
  Phrase 2   measures 12-14
  Phrase 3   measures 15-16

291

Praise to the Lord, the Almighty

Erneuertes Gesangbuch (1665) harmonized by Johann Sebastian Bach (1685-1750)

(Translation by Catherine Winkworth)

1 Praise to the Lord, the al - might-y, _ the _ king of _ cre - a - tion! O my soul,
2 Praise to the Lord, who o'er _ all things so _ won-drous-ly _ reign-eth; Who, as on
3 Praise to the Lord, O let _ all that _ is _ in me a - dore him! All that hath

praise him, for _ he is _ thy _ health and _ sal - va - tion! Join the _ full _ throng;
wings of an _ ea - gle, _ up - lift - eth, _ sus - tain - eth; Hast thou not _ seen
life and breath, come now with _ prais - es _ be - fore him! He is _ thy _ light;

wake harp and _ psal-ter _ and _ song; Sound forth in glad ad-o - ra - tion.
how thy de - sires all _ have _ been Grant - ed _ in what he or - dain - eth?
soul, keep it _ al-ways _ in _ sight; Glad - ly _ for - ev - er a - dore _ him!

Note that this is one of the early chorale melodies which was harmonized by Johann Sebastian Bach.

292

MOOD: What is the mood of this chorale?

RHYTHM: 1. What is the meter marking?
           2. What kinds of notes are used to describe the rhythm?
           3. What does the fermata do to the rhythmic movement of this chorale?

MELODY: 1. In what key is the melody written?
           2. On what note does the melody begin? What is its relationship to the key?
           3. What is the vocal range of the melody?
           4. Is this chorale more or less singable than "A Mighty Fortress Is Our God"? Defend your answer.
           5. Analyze the melodic line in terms of skips and stepwise progressions.

HARMONY: 1. Is the harmonization simple or complex?
           2. Are there any seventh chords in this harmonization?
           3. Is the harmonic texture homophonic or polyphonic?

TIMBRE: 1. Sing this chorale using male voices only.
           2. Sing this chorale using female voices only.
           3. Sing this chorale using the combined voices.
           4. Compare the effect of each combination of voices.

FORM: 1. How many large parts does this chorale have?
           2. Analyze the entire chorale in terms of its formal structure.

Andante con moto—Allegro vivace..........................Felix Mendelssohn
from *Symphony No. 5 in D Major*, "The Reformation"   (1809-1847)

The entire finale of this symphony was constructed by Mendelssohn around the superb and imposing battle song of the Reformation, *Ein' feste Burg ist unser Gott*. The use of this chorale in the final movement of the "Reformation Symphony" is said to have been Mendelssohn's tribute to Martin Luther and to the triumph of his new faith. Within this movement two other sections bear mentioning. These are the two interludes or episodes which are fugal in character. These fugal episodes also represent a tribute—in this instance to Johann Sebastian Bach, the greatest of the Lutheran composers. Note that beginning in measure 231 the composer has combined the fugal episode played by the strings with the chorale played by the brass and woodwinds. This might signify the successful joining together of Martin Luther and Johann Sebastian Bach.

MOOD: This is a triumphal hymn of praise. One senses a mood of deep religious fervor.

RHYTHM: The rhythm is duple rhythm throughout, although the meter markings change back and forth throughout the movement. It begins in 4/4 meter with the chorale being played in half and quarter notes, which gives the feeling of a definite four beats to the measure. In measure 25 the tempo changes, with the meter changed to 6/8. The strings play an arpeggiated eighth-note accompaniment figure. This section, because of its tempo change, moves in two. Measure 63 brings another tempo and meter change. Although the meter returns to 4/4, there is an underlying feeling of two to the measure. An interesting meter change in measures 147 and 258 results in one measure of 2/4 in the

293

midst of 4/4 meter. In these two measures because of the tempo or speed of the movement at this point, the measure of 2/4 in reality receives only one beat to the measure. The tempo of the final thirty-three measures is increased to the point where the rhythmic movement is in a fast two. The listener at first may feel somewhat uncertain about the rhythmic structure of the opening measures. A comparison of the rhythmic structure of the opening measures with that of the chorale on page 290 will reveal that the chorale begins on a fourth-beat quarter note and the final movement of the symphony begins on the first beat and uses a half note.

The chorale: ♩ | ♩ ♩ ♫♩ | ♫♩ ♩

The symphony: ♩ ♩ ♩ | ♩ ♩ ♩ ♩ | ♩.

When the chorale and the fugue come together beginning in measure 231 the chorale melody is given in whole and half notes. This is known as *augmentation*. In the final twenty measures the chorale melody is again given in augmentation.

MELODY: The melody upon which this movement is based is the familiar melody known as *Ein' feste Burg ist unser Gott*. Throughout the entire movement variations and modifications are found which come as a result of meeting the need for providing unity to the work. The melody for the fugal subject found in measure 92, and found again in measure 209,

repeated two times before the melody resolves itself by moving downward a major second to D.

HARMONY: The harmonization is conventional and generally follows the basic harmonization of the chorale itself. Interesting harmonic alterations of individual chords are heard from time to time. Few dissonances are heard because Mendelssohn seemingly was content to maintain the consonant sound of the chorale harmony. Mendelssohn also followed the practice of going from one key to another to achieve additional harmonic richness and variety.

TIMBRE: This movement provides the listener with a fine example of the effective use of the orchestral palette in achieving the particular expressive purpose desired by the composer. The scoring calls for two flutes, two oboes, two clarinets, two bassoons, one contrabassoon, two French horns, two trumpets, three trombones, timpani and strings. The use of these instruments ranges from solo sound, as in the flute solo in the initial measures, through duet, small ensemble, to full ensemble. The listener is aware of woodwind sound, brass sound, string sound and total sound created by combining all the instrumental families. There are several interesting uses of instrumental color which should have special mention. Notice, for example, the effect of the scoring of the woodwind family in

has a one-octave range going downward from the beginning F♯ which is the fifth of the B minor scale. After the opening note is repeated three times the melody descends scalewise down to A♯. It then skips down a major third to F♯ and then follows a large skip upward of a minor seventh to E, which is

measures 1 to 11. Compare this with the effect created by having the woodwinds giving out melodic fragments of the chorale over the rolling and arpeggiated figure played by the strings. To follow the separate entrances of the subject in the first fugal section, the listener needs to know that the instru-

294

ments enter in this order: viola, first violin, viola and cellos-string basses. In the second fugal section new instrumental color is added through the doubling of the subject material by other instruments. In this instance the entrances are: first violin-oboes, second violin-first oboe, viola and cellos-string basses. Beginning in measure 231 Mendelssohn brings together the chorale and the fugue. Note the exciting effect created here by pitting the string tone or color playing the fugue against brass and woodwind timbre playing the chorale.

FORM: In Unit Five the technic of extending music material into individual movements of the symphony will be discussed. For our purpose here let it suffice that the form for this final movement of the "Reformation Symphony" may be divided into the following five large sections:

1. Chorale
   a. Chorale   measures 1-24
   b. Variation on
      chorale   measures 25-62

2.
   a. New material   measures 63-91
   b. Fugal section   measures 93-121

3. Development
   a. From chorale   measures 121-209
   b. Fugal section   measures 209-230
   c. Chorale over
      fugue   measures 231-247

4. Restatement
   of 2 above   measures 248-294

5. Coda   measures 295-348
   The coda ends with the chorale melody being played in augmentation.

L'Histoire du Soldat (Tale of a Soldier) . . . . Igor Stravinsky (1882——)
In this interesting suite Stravinsky at one point has introduced a highly satirical version of the chorale, *Ein' feste Burg ist unser Gott*. Examine this portion of the suite and compare Stravinsky's use of the chorale with Mendelssohn's use of the same chorale.

MOOD: What are some of the devices used by Stravinsky to realize the mood?

RHYTHM: 1. Has the basic rhythm been altered in the Stravinsky version?
          2. Is the rhythm of the chorale in *L'Histoire du Soldat* more or less complex than the rhythm of the chorale as used in the final movement of the "Reformation Symphony"?

MELODY: Is the melody as used in *L'Histoire du Soldat* the same or different from the melody in the original chorale?

TIMBRE: 1. What instruments are used for this portion of the suite?
          2. What special technics were employed by Stravinsky in scoring for the instruments used in this section of the suite?

295

The Cantata

The word *cantata* derives from the Italian word *cantare*, meaning to sing, a word originally used to distinguish vocal forms from instrumental forms which were called *suonare*, meaning to sound. It was from this latter word that our modern word, sonata, was derived. The seventeenth-century form of the cantata was an extended work for solo voice and consisted of alternating sections of recitatives and arias. One, known as the *cantata da camera* or chamber cantata, had a secular text, while another, the *cantata da chiesa* or church cantata, used a sacred text.

In the eighteenth century the concept of the cantata changed from that of an extended work for solo voice to that of an extended choral work involving the use of soloists, chorus and accompaniment. Many of the cantatas included accompaniments to be played by a small or chamber orchestra. As was true of the seventeenth-century cantatas, the subject matter of these later cantatas continued to be taken from both secular and sacred sources. This concept of the cantata has continued to the present time.

The cantata has been likened to a shortened form of the oratorio or an opera given without benefit of stage sets, costumes or action. Stringham points out in *Listening to Music Creatively* that in the cantata the lyric drama or story is adapted to the music but is not intended to be acted.

As a medium of musical expression the cantata is likely to be rather more reflective than dramatic. The typical cantata is written in sections, each of which uses one of the vocal forms—chorus, duet, solo or chorale plus instrumental portions. A balanced symmetry of form and style is characteristic of the cantata. This trait is particularly observable in the cantatas written by Johann Sebastian Bach and many of his musical colleagues.

Bach, in particular, is known as a prolific composer of the cantata form. He is known to have composed over three hundred cantatas, of which some two hundred are extant. The period of 1708 to 1717, during which Bach was at Weimar as court organist and chamber musician to Duke Wilhelm Ernst, was a period of great creative activity for him, resulting in the writing of many of his finest church cantatas. In its liturgical role each cantata is designed for a specific time during the church year. During these years Bach wrote enough cantatas for the Lutheran service to provide a different cantata for each Sunday of the church year for five years without the necessity for repeating any. In addition to using the church year as the source of inspiration for his cantatas, Bach also turned to special occasions for the subject matter of his cantatas. A few of his cantatas—for example, the *Peasant Cantata*—had secular words for the text.

Cantata No. 4, Christ lag in Todesbanden......Johann Sebastian Bach (1685-1750)
    (Christ Lay in the Bonds of Death)

Bach composed this cantata of eight movements for the Easter Sunday service. The expressive intent of the score deals with the story of the resurrection. The entire cantata is actually a most compelling set of variations on a chorale tune of that name. Before listening to the entire work it would be well to become well acquainted with the chorale. The chorale is presented as the final movement. It is interesting to note that Bach used this same chorale melody in one of his organ preludes to which he gave the same title, *Christ lag in Todesbanden.* After becoming well acquainted with the entire cantata based on the chorale, *Christ lag in Todesbanden,* compare Bach's use of this chorale melody in this cantata with his use of this same melody in his organ prelude of the same name.

Because the cantata is an extended vocal form involving several different sections, it may be more helpful to the listener if a different format for analyzing *Christ lag in Todesbanden* is followed. This cantata is scored for a mixed chorus consisting of soprano, alto, tenor and bass, plus a small chamber orchestra of two violins, two violas, one cornet or trumpet, three trombones and harpsichord. The work provides for two solos or arias, one to be sung by a tenor and the other by the bass. Two duets, one using a soprano and an alto, and the other by a soprano and a tenor, are also an integral part of this cantata. The juxtaposition of chorus, solo, and duet in this particular choral work results in an interesting symmetry of media which is indicated in this bracketed diagram.

Sinfonia	Orchestral Prelude	
Chorus	Verse I	*Christ lag in Todesbanden*
Duet	Verse II	*Den Tod Niemand zwingen kunnt'*
Aria	Verse III	*Jesus Christus, Gottes Sohn*
Chorus	Verse IV	*Es war ein wunderlicher Krieg*
Aria	Verse V	*Hier ist das rechte Osterlamm*
Duet	Verse VI	*So feiern wir das hohe Fest*
Chorale	Verse VII	*Wir essen und leben wohl*

What to listen for:

Sinfonia
Observe the descending half-step motive. This descending motive with which the chorale begins is used throughout the cantata. The motive may be thought of as suggesting death—*Tod.*

Verse I
Christ lay in the bonds of death, given for our sins. He rose again and brought us life. We should praise God, be thankful to him.

Note:
a. The long, sustained chorale melody in the soprano.
b. The contrapuntal activity of the other voices and instruments.
c. The florid treatment of the melodic line for the word *fröhlich*—"joyful."
d. The healthy sound of *und singen hallelujah*—"and sing alleluia."
e. The exuberance of the final *hallelujahs.*

Verse II   *No one can force death on all mankind. Death so quickly took authority over us, Held us captive in his realm. Alleluia.*

Observe:

a. The use of the falling note motive on the words *den Tod*—"Death."
b. The chorale melody in the soprano or upper line.
c. The "walking bass" line in the accompaniment. This is a typical bass line of this period of time.
d. The *Alleluias* at the conclusion are more restrained than the *Alleluias* in the preceding verse.

Verse III   *Jesus Christ, through his death, took our sins away, and thus conquered death.*

Notice:

a. The vigorous and straightforward presentation of the chorale melody by the tenor.
b. The busy, leaping counterpoint.
c. The dramatic interruption at the word, *Tod'sgestalt*—the final vaunting of death's power.

Verse IV   *It was a battle between death and life. Life held the victory and made mockery of death.*

Note:

a. The chorale melody in the alto voice.
b. The complex fugal texture aptly portraying the struggle.
c. The interesting treatment of the word *Spott*—"mockery" in measures 35 to 37 inclusive.
d. The victory proclaiming *hallelujahs*.

Verse V   *The love and the blood of Christ high on the cross ensures that death, the murderer, can no longer harm us.*

Observe:

a. The introductory descending motive.
b. That the chorale melody is now given in triple meter.
c. The insistent repetition of the word *nicht*—"not" prior to the final *hallelujahs*.

Verse VI   *We celebrate Christ's resurrection with joyous heart and delight. The night of sins has disappeared.*

Note:

a. The canon at the fifth in the opening bars between the soprano and tenor.
b. The festive triplets first appearing in the upper voice and followed one beat later in the lower voice.
c. The exultation of the final *hallelujahs* as a result of the use of these same triplets.

Verse VII   (continues the ideas of celebration begun in Verse VI)

    Note:
      a. The telling effect of the simpler setting of the chorale after the
         more complex textures in the preceding verses.
      b. The final and convincing *"hallelujah."*

The Oratorio

The oratorio is an extended choral work of epic proportions using a sacred text. It uses the combined forces of chorus, solo voices and orchestra. As distinguished from the mass and church cantata, the oratorio is not actually an integral part of a religious service. Because of the sacred and spiritual nature of its text, one generally thinks of the performance of an oratorio as taking place in the church; however, it is equally proper for an oratorio to be performed in the concert hall.

The oratorio normally is based on a dramatic poem which chronicles an event or tells of a character of biblical history. While the subject matter and music of the oratorio may be similar to that of the opera, the oratorio is different from the opera in that, as a general rule, it is presented without the use of scenery, costumes or dramatic action. It might be characterized as a sort of reflective drama which uses the imagination of the listener in conjuring up whatever action or staging the musico-dramatic situation may suggest. Because of its religious character and dramatic style, the oratorio is exceedingly popular with church choirs and choral societies.

Because both use dramatic subject matter, it is natural that the oratorio and opera should develop from the same sources—the old medieval liturgical dramas and miracle plays. In fact, some of the very early oratorios presented by the Roman Catholic church were closely akin to opera in that the sacred texts were presented with scenic effects worked out with great care. The mid-seventeenth century, however, saw a development in the oratorio which obviated the necessity for providing scenery for the oratorio performance. This was the introduction of a narrator whose responsibility was to introduce each of the characters or personalities and to describe the action that was to take place.

The term "oratorio" derives from a seventeenth-century practice in the presentation of the oratorio form. Because the oratorio used biblical subjects for its text, it was considered quite proper to have the performance in the church itself. These performances did not take place in the nave or main church, but rather in the church oratory which was a side chapel used for private prayer. During this same time the opera which used secular themes for its subject matter was being given performances in either the theater or in the homes of members of the nobility.

The use of the orchestra is essentially the same for both the oratorio and the opera. Composers have tended to score the instrumental accompaniments for both of these large and extended vocal forms by using all of the instrumental resources available at the time. Thus, the orchestral accompaniments of the oratorio (and opera) will, in a sense, reflect the growth and development of instrumental music which coincided with the development of the oratorio.

For the past three hundred years or so the oratorio has been a popular outlet for the creative energies of many of the world's finest composers. Names such as Heinrich Schütz (1585-1672), George Frideric Handel (1685-1759), Franz Joseph Haydn (1732-1809), Felix Mendelssohn (1809-1847), Arthur Honegger (1892-1955), Paul Hindemith (1895-1963), and William Walton (1902———) have all found in the oratorio a grateful vehicle for the expression of their creative ideas.

LISTENING ACTIVITY

Belshazzar's Feast.............................William Walton (1902———)

The subject matter selected for the text of the highly dramatic oratorio *Belshazzar's Feast* was taken from the account found in the fifth chapter of the Book of Daniel. It is a dramatized version of the fulfillment of Isaiah's prophesy that because Belshazzar had been weighed in the balance and had been found wanting, he would be destroyed and his kingdom divided between the Medes and the Persians. The oratorio was composed in 1931 when the composer was twenty-nine years of age.

The libretto or text was written by Sir Osbert Sitwell, a personal friend of William Walton. To the account of Belshazzar's downfall found in the Book of Daniel, Sir Osbert added lines from Psalm 137:

By the rivers of Babylon, there we sat down, yea, we wept, when we remembered Zion.

We hanged our harps upon the willows in the midst thereof.

For there they that carried us away captive required of us a song; and they that wasted us required of us mirth, saying, Sing us one of the songs of Zion.

How shall we sing the Lord's song in a strange land?

If I forget thee, O Jerusalem, let my right hand forget her cunning.

If I do not remember thee, let my tongue cleave to the roof of my mouth; if I prefer not Jerusalem above my chief joy.

and lines from Psalm 81:

Sing aloud unto God our strength; make a joyful noise unto the God of Jacob.

Take a psalm, and bring hither the timbrel, the pleasant harp with the psaltery.

Blow up the trumpet in the new moon, in the time appointed on our solemn feast day.

It is quite possible that Sitwell conceived of the finished text as representing a continuous flow of action, but it is apparent that Walton felt the need for transition points as the narration progressed. This is indicated by the use of long pauses which serve as a bridge between the end of one idea and the beginning of the new.

300

Belshazzar's Feast is an oratorio of epic proportions. It is scored for mixed choir, baritone solo and orchestra. The choral score calls for a chorus of mixed voices, a double chorus of mixed voices, a semi-chorus of women's voices, a chorus of men's voices and a chorus of women's voices. The instrumental accompaniment calls for the resources of an enormous orchestra. In addition to the usual strings, the score calls for two flutes, one third flute and piccolo, two oboes, one clarinet in E♭, one clarinet in B♭, one bass clarinet or third clarinet, one alto saxophone, two bassoons, one contrabassoon, four French horns, three trumpets, three trombones, one tuba, timpani, cymbal, bass drum, side drum, xylophone, gong, two harps, piano, organ and two brass bands.

What to listen for:

Opening Fanfare and Prologue

NOTICE:
  a. The huge orchestra forces.
  b. The foreboding character of the tenors and basses singing, "Thus spake Isaiah: Thy sons that thou shalt beget, they shall be taken away . . ."
  c. The realistic treatment of "Howl ye."
  d. The dramatic impact of the work which is evident from the very beginning.

CHORUS: *The Jewish captives weep by the waters of Babylon. Commanded by their captors to sing, they cannot: "How shall we sing the Lord's song in a strange land?"*

NOTE:
  a. How the men's voices are joined by the women's voices.
  b. That the text at this point is taken from Psalm 137.
  c. The very effective use of the orchestral piano and percussion after the choral "wept."
  d. The use of the chorus beginning with the words, "Yea, we wept."
  e. The nostalgic touch lent by the oboe and the saxophone.
  f. The women's voices echoing the men's voices at the words, "For they that wasted us."
  g. The agitated alliteration in "sing-songs."
  h. The effectiveness of dissonant harmony on the words, "strange land."

BARITONE SOLO: *Here, the soloist speaking for the captives voices his fidelity, "If I forget thee, O Jerusalem, let my right hand forget her cunning; If I prefer not thee above my chief joy."*

NOTE:
  a. The use of the bass clarinet in the introduction to the baritone solo.
  b. That this part of the text continues to be taken from Psalm 137.
  c. The arpeggiated accompaniment played by the first and second violins and violas.
  d. How the semi-chorus answers the phrases of the soloist.
  e. The steady heavy tread of the bass instruments in the accompaniment.
  f. The effective use of the double chorus on "O Jerusalem."
  g. How the music lovingly dwells on the word "Jerusalem."

CHORUS: *At this point the chorus returns to the lamentations heard at the beginning of the oratorio and then moves on to the prophecy of the fall of Babylon. "With violence shall that great city, Babylon, be thrown down and shall be found no more at all."*

OBSERVE: a. How the harmonic treatment of "found no more" recalls the setting of "in a strange land."
b. The change of tempo at the words, "O daughters of Babylon."
c. The excitement and agitation of the accompaniment underlying this section.
d. The effect of the alto and bass singing in unison the words, "Happy shall he be that taketh thy children and dasheth them against a stone ..." while the sopranos and tenors sing a countermelody also in unison.
e. The change to a slower tempo at the words, "shall be found no more."
f. The effect of voice moving against voice on the words "no more."

BARITONE RECITATIVE: *The narrator sings "Babylon was a great city."*

NOTE: a. The irony of the text.
b. The robust quality of the recitative.
c. That this is one of the finest and most exciting recitatives ever composed.
d. This recitative is sung without accompaniment.
e. The exciting crescendo of emotional intensity between the words "gold and silver" and "the souls of men."

CHORUS. *The scene now changes to the feast of Belshazzar.*

NOTICE: a. The change of tempo and the changes of meter to suggest the anger of the Israelites.
b. The percussive effect of the piano and xylophone in the accompaniment.
c. The agitation of this entire section.
d. The use of rhythmic syncopation—for example, on the words "Belshazzar" and "tasted the wine."
e. The use of sharp accents throughout the movement.
f. The use of sudden dynamic contrasts as on the words "tasted the wine."
g. The effect of the high soprano writing in conveying the essential mood of this section.
h. The colorful melodic writing of "all kinds of music" which is melismatic in character.
i. The shock of the dissonance in "Yea! drank from the sacred vessels."

CHORUS: *This has been referred to as the "Heathen Hymn" because it is a paean of praise to the pagan gods of the people of Babylon. This chorus is without rival for sheer brilliance and power, scintillating orchestration and sweeping effect. The music is almost overpowering in its capability to exude the frightening pessimism of pagan idolatry.*

NOTE: a. How the beginning entrance of the chorus intrudes on the opening statement of the baritone soloist.
b. The colorful orchestration which assigns a specific timbre and treatment to each of the gods:
gold   mixed voices, unaccompanied
silver   female voices, flutes and piccolo, oboes, clarinets, saxophones, bassoons and glockenspiel
iron   male voices, trumpets and anvil

wood   female voices, xylophone and wood block
stone   male voices, clarinet and woodwinds
brass   mixed voices, brass bands

    c. The interplay of brass and woodwind timbre in the accompaniment at the beginning of the "praise ye" section.
    d. The accumulative effect of the "praise ye's" and the exciting use of syncopation.
    e. The power achieved by the use of the double chorus in the "praise ye" section.
    f. The melismatic effect of the vocal parts in the next to the last "praise ye."
    g. The brilliant orchestra interlude before the final "praise ye."

CHORUS: *There follows now a choral toast to the king of the Babylonians—"Thou, O King, art King of Kings. O King live forever."*

NOTE: a. How the music seems to capture the riotous mood of the pagan orgy.
    b. The almost repulsive dissonant sound of "False gods."
    c. The melismatic effect of the choral writing, "to extol the glory."
    d. The power of the dissonant harmony at the words "Thou, O King."

BARITONE SOLO: *At the very climax of this blasphemy the baritone, at first unaccompanied and then with the stark accompaniment of cymbals, gong, drum and timpani, sounds the tragic doom, "And in that same hour as they feasted came forth fingers of a man's hand; and the king saw part of the hand that wrote, And this was the writing that was written: 'Mene, Mene, Tekel Upharsin.'" The male chorus enters and inexorably translates, "Thou art weighed in the balance and found wanting." There immediately follows one of the many sensational passages in this dramatic oratorio—announcing the slaying of Belshazzar and the breakup of his kingdom.*

NOTICE: a. The recitative character of the solo line.
    b. The lugubrious effect of using cymbal, castanets, tenor drum, timpani and gong in the accompanied portion of the solo.
    c. The eerie orchestration which furnishes the background for *"Mene, Mene, Tekel Upharsin."*
    d. The effect of the male choir intoning, "Thou art weighed in the balance and found wanting."
    e. That in the announcement of the breakup of the kingdom the orchestra actually suggests the division.

CHORUS: *The final section of the oratorio is a song of thanksgiving for God's avenging his peoples. The first portion of the text is taken from Psalm 81 which proclaims, "Then sing aloud to God our strength: Make a joyful noise to the God of Jacob . . ."*

The mood changes and the small or semi-chorus sings, "While the kings of earth weep, wail, and rend their raiment. They cry, alas! alas! that great city in one hour is her judgment come. The trumpeter and pipers are silent and the harpers have ceased to harp and the light of the candle shall shine no more."

Once again the mood changes. This time the chorus gives exultant

303

voice to "Then sing aloud to God our strength: Make a joyful noise to the God of Jacob. For Babylon the great is fallen. Alleluia!"

NOTICE:

a. The downward rushing of the chorus on the word "fallen."

b. The effective use of syncopation in the rhythm.

c. The change of mood to the darker quality in the section "while the kings of the earth lament and the merchants of the earth weep . . ." gives the feeling of lost souls in limbo.

d. The moving voices in this section give the effect of voice answering voice.

e. The change of tempo which coincides with the change of mood.

f. How the orchestra drops out of the section beginning "the trumpeters and pipers are silent."

g. The strange choral effects achieved in the section beginning "candle shall shine no more, shine no more."

h. The use of the double chorus in this section.

i. The almost intemperate frenzy of the "alleluias."

j. The effective use of syncopation in this section. At times the effect of this syncopation is almost jazzy.

k. The antiphonal effect of the two choirs singing the final "alleluias."

Sacred Service (Avodath Hakodesh) . . . . Ernest Bloch (1880-1959)

It seems proper to conclude our consideration of music in religion by examining music dealing with a Hebraic text set to music rich in the Jewish idiom. The work selected is comparable to the oratorio in that it is an extended vocal form. The text for this work was selected by Ernest Bloch and was taken from various sources in the Old Testament such as the Psalms, Deuteronomy, Exodus, Isaiah, Proverbs and other sources of the Jewish spiritual heritage.

Ernest Bloch has been called the music prophet of the Hebrews. This work, the *Sacred Service*, makes plain some of the reasons why this designation is so apt. The entire composition is pregnant with an impassioned Hebraic eloquence and fervor. One is struck not only with the technical complexity and excellence of the writing but also with an emotional intensity which could only stem from the composer's deep concern and unshaken belief in the ultimate destiny of the Jewish people. Bloch, however, felt that this work was more than a Jewish service, that it had a universality of philosophy which should make it acceptable to all men.

The *Sacred Service*, like *Belshazzar's Feast*, is a work of epic proportions. It was written for baritone soloist or cantor, mixed chorus, and orchestra. The instrumental accompaniment calls for a large orchestra consisting of two flutes, one third flute and piccolo, two oboes, English horn, two bassoons, four horns, three trumpets, three trombones, tuba, harp, timpani, percussion, piano and strings.

The music is divided into five parts following the liturgy of the Jewish service. The composer intended that the work be performed in its entirety without intermission. Throughout the *Sacred Service* there are short instrumental preludes and interludes which take the place of the usual responsive readings. These interludes, in addition to providing the people with an opportunity for meditation and silent prayer, also give unity to the total work by tying together the different moods of the text. The *Sacred Service* is modal in concept with the Mixolydian mode permeating the entire work.

What to listen for:

PART I

Meditation—*Symphonic Prelude*

NOTICE:
    a. The use of the Mixolydian mode in establishing the mood of this composition.
    b. The manner in which the instruments are introduced in this opening prelude, beginning with the cellos and string basses in octaves.
    c. The elision of phrases at the beginning, which results from staggering the entrances of the different instruments—violas on the fourth beat of measure 3, second violins on the fourth beat of measure 5, first violins on the fourth beat of measure 7 and the French horn on the fourth beat of measure 9.
    d. The oriental flavor given by the oboe's playing of the triplet and duplet figurations.
    e. The change of meter in measures 13 and 17.

Mah Tovu—*Cantor and chorus*

How goodly are thy tents, Yaakov, goodly thy dwellings, Israel.
Through Thy great compassion, O Lord, I come to worship
To praise Thy name in Thy Temple;
I bow in reverence before Thee.
Adonoy, Adonoy, I love the place where Thou dwellest and the house wherein
    dwelleth Thy glory;
There I bow worshipping Thee, O Lord my God,
Power divine, Creator of life and all.
May my prayer, humbly upraised, seem good, Adonoy, in Thine eyes,
Elohim! I come in meekness.
Answer Thou,
In mercy, grant me, O Lord, Thy salvation.

NOTE:
    a. The effective use of the baritone soloist as cantor-leader, and the choral ensemble as the responding group.
    b. The woodwind accompaniment under the cantor's solo.
    c. How the composer, through the use of shifting meters involving 4/4, 2/4 and 3/4, achieved rhythmic freedom and flow.
    d. The effectiveness of dynamic contrasts.
    e. The beautiful resolution of harmony at the words "(be)-fore Thee." Note particularly that this resolution takes place in the alto line.
    f. The use of French horns, oboes and flutes in the section which begins four measures before the words "May my prayer, humbly upraised, seem good."
    g. The use of the oboe at the end of this section.

Borechu—*Cantor and chorus*
Sing His praise, sing to the Lord, praise and adore!
Sing praise to the Lord, praise and adore forevermore.

305

OBSERVE: a. The relative shortness of this section.

b. The interplay between cantor and chorus.

c. The way in which the oboe, horn, flute, strings, clarinet, third trombone and tuba are used in the introduction to this section.

d. The feeling of excitement created in the instrumental interlude which brings this section to a close—the martial sounds of the French horns and trumpets highlighted by rushing strings and woodwinds.

Shema Yisroel—*Cantor and chorus*

O hear, Israel, our God, our Creator is One!
O praised be His Name, He whose Kingdom shall never end.

NOTE: a. The tremendously powerful expression which Bloch gives to the central idea of the Jewish faith—the affirmation of the Oneness of God.

b. The change to a *misterioso* mood.

c. That this mood change is achieved by a slower tempo with a tremolo accompaniment in the strings played in the lower register.

d. That each statement of the text by the cantor is immediately repeated or restated by the chorus.

Veohavto—*Cantor, women's voices, alto solo and cantor.*

And thou shalt love Him, thy Lord God,
With all thy heart, and all thy soul, shalt love Him with all thy might.
And these words which I command thee, these words shall be on thy heart this day.
And thou shalt teach them thy children, and of them shalt speak,
When by thy hearth thou sittest, and when thou walkest on the way, and when thou liest, and when thou risest up.
Thou shalt bind a sign on thy hand, and as frontlets they shall be between thine eyes.
On the door-posts of thy house be written, also upon thy gates.

OBSERVE: a. The four-and-one-half measure introduction featuring the violins, violoncellos and harp.

b. The mood of assured tranquility which results from the recognition of the sacredness of things.

c. The almost angelic quality of the women's voices echoing "And thou shalt love Him," first sung by the cantor.

d. The poignancy of the alto solo echoing the cantor's "With all thy heart, with all thy soul, shalt love Him with all thy might."

e. The effectiveness of the violin obbligato played beneath the women's chorus and alto solo.

f. The English horn solo at "And thou shalt teach them thy children."

Mi Chomocho—*Chorus and cantor*

Who is like Thee of the mighty, O Lord?
Who is like Thee, O Lord all glorious?
Thy works we proclaim;
Thy marvels praise!
And when Thy children were shown Thy wonders, they cried, behold, this is my God!

306

NOTICE: a. The short, exciting instrumental introduction to this section played by the French horn and woodwinds, with the emphasis on the oboe and English horn over a pizzicato and tremolo accompaniment in the strings.

b. That this section, which represents the response of the people, begins with the men's voices which are then joined by the women's voices in measure 5.

c. The steady rhythmic accompaniment beneath the choral writing.

d. The exultation of the section, "And the Lord shall reign."

e. The effect of the harmonic pyramiding of chords by horns, woodwinds and strings in this section.

f. The rhythmic effect of this particular section.

g. The instrumental interlude which brings this section to a close and introduces the concluding section.

h. The use of flute and clarinet or oboe in octaves to help bring about a transition in mood.

i. The oriental character of this interlude.

Tzur Yisroel (traditional)—*Cantor and chorus*

Rock of Israel, arise to the help of Israel!
Our deliv'rer Adonoy, O bless and praise His Name,
O blessed Israel; O blest be Thou, O Lord, Redeemer of Israel.
O praise Him and His holy Name. Amen.

NOTICE: a. The mournful mood of this concluding section.

b. The florid or melismatic character of the vocal writing for the cantor's chant.

c. The contrast between this florid vocal writing and the sustained instrumental accompaniment.

d. The chant-like quality of the chorus singing, "O praise Him and His holy Name."

e. The writing for the oboes and muted trumpets in the final "Amen."

f. The use of the traditional Jewish idiom in this section.

PART II

Kedushah—*(Sanctification)*

The composer says of Part II that the music is of another world with an expressive quality which is both mysterious and suggestive of angels. Throughout Part II there is effective interplay between the cantor and the chorus which might be thought of as being representative of the people. An orchestral accompaniment rich in unusual instrumental timbres, added to frequent tempo changes, contributes to the kaleidoscopic change of moods found in this section of the *Sacred Service*. In Part II there is a continuation of the practice observed in Part I: the use of shifting meters for achieving greater rhythmic flexibility.

Nekadesh—*Cantor*

Sanctified be Thy Name evermore,
On earth as it is sanctified at Thy throne on high;
And we hallow Thy Name, as the prophets wrote,
Thy Name we glorify, proclaiming:

307

OBSERVE: a. The tranquility and assurance of this opening section of Part II.
b. The effect of the cymbal roll in measure 1.
c. The use of harp and woodwinds in the accompaniment.
d. The rhythmic movement of this section.

Kodosh—*Chorus*

Kodosh, kodosh, kodosh, Adonoy tzevoos,
Heaven and the earth are filled with His glory.

NOTE: a. That the *Kodosh* is comparable to the *Sanctus* in the mass. *Kodosh* means "holy."
b. The lifting sensation of the repeated *Kodosh*.

Adir adireinu—*Cantor and chorus*

O God, ever mighty,
Make us like unto Thee, Lord.
How glorious is Thy Name in all the earth.
We praise Thy Name, Lord our God, in Thy Dominion.

NOTICE: a. The prayerful mood of the cantor's solo.
b. The use of the harp in the accompaniment.
c. The bassoon solo under the words, "How glorious is Thy Name."
d. How the change of tempo at the words, "We praise Thy Name, Lord our God," sung by the chorus, affects the mood.

Echod hu, Eloheinu—*Cantor and chorus, cantor, alto solo, soprano solo, and chorus*

For One is the Lord our God.
He, our Father, He, our Ruler, He, our Redeemer.
And He shall answer us in His might in the sight of all men.

NOTE: a. The two-measure instrumental introduction prior to the words, "For One is the Lord our God." Why does Bloch refer to these two measures as the "cosmic motive"?
b. That the meaning of the text and music of this section might be considered as an affirmation of the unity of the world.
c. That the change of mood which occurs with the repetition of the words, "For One is the Lord our God," might be considered to represent the faith of the people in this affirmation.
d. The overlapping and movement of voices in the section, "He, our Father, He, our Ruler, He, our Redeemer."
e. The expressive quality of the short solos sung by the alto and the soprano.
f. The bassoon, French horn and cello writing following the words, "His might in the sight of all men."

Yimloch Adonoy leolom (finale)—*Chorus*

Shalt reign, Adonoy, evermore!
Zion, Zion, thy God,
From generation to generation, the Lord shall reign.
Thy God shalt reign evermore. Halleluia!

OBSERVE: a. The vigorous character of this final section.
b. The mood of exultation.
c. The instrumental introduction to this section which begins with bassoon, horn and timpani.
d. The strength of the French horn as heard in the accompaniment.
e. The contribution of the final "Halleluia" in establishing the mood of great joy with which Part II ends.

PART III

Silent devotion—*Symphonic Prelude*

OBSERVE: a. The contemplative and reverent mood of this instrumental opening to Part III.
b. The contrapuntal texture of the prelude which is cast in the form of a small fugue.
c. The entrances of the flute, bassoon and viola as each enters with its statement of the fugal subject.
d. Also the manner in which the oboe, English horn and cellos are used.

Response—*Chorus unaccompanied*

O Lord, may the words of my mouth and the meditations of my heart be acceptable before Thee, Adonoy, my Rock and Redeemer.

NOTE: a. That the choir enters very softly on the words, "O Lord, may the words of my mouth."
b. That the thought back of this passage is the purification of the heart.
c. That the appeal lies in the simplicity of utterance and sincerity of expression.
d. That the unaccompanied character of this portion of Part III complements the simplicity and sincerity of the prayer.
e. The beautiful effect created by the use of the women's voices at the beginning of the phrase, "and the meditations of my heart."
f. The use of harmonic suspensions in the final measures of this section. They will be found in the alto and tenor lines.
g. That the instrumental interlude which comes at the end of the response is taken from the musical material found in the *Silent Devotion*.
h. The effect of the melody of this interlude being played in octaves by first violins and first flute.

Seu sheorim—*Cantor and chorus*

Lift up your heads, O ye portals!
Lift ye everlasting doors!
That the King of glory may enter!
Who is this King of Glory?
Adonoy of Sabaoth, He is the King of Glory!
Selah, Selah, Selah.

309

NOTE: a. That the composer's intent in this section was to express the idea that man must cleanse himself of all hate and dark instincts which prevent him from fully realizing himself.

b. The repetition by the chorus of each of the statements of the cantor.

c. The use of strings playing pizzicato in the accompaniment after the cantor proclaims, "That the King of Glory may enter!"

d. The entrances of the voices at the words, "Who is the King of Glory?"

e. The contemplative quality of the music underlying the words, "Selah, Selah, Selah," which derives in part from the beautiful harmonization and the choice of instrumental colors in the accompaniment.

Taking the Scroll from the Ark—*Symphonic Interlude*

NOTICE: a. The finesse with which one instrument picks up the melodic line from another.

b. The composer's choice of instrumental colors for this interlude as reflected in his use of violins, flute, French horn, and oboe.

c. The buildup of emotional intensity as the music moves to the climax of the interlude.

Toroh Tzivoh—*Cantor and chorus*

The Torah, which God gave through Moses, is the Law of the house of Jacob.
O house of Jacob, Come ye, walk in the light, the light of the Lord.

NOTE: a. The feeling of divine mystery as the cantor speaks of the Torah as it is borne slowly through the people.

b. The oriental quality of the music as created by the oboe melody in the accompaniment.

c. The powerful effect created by the sopranos, tenors and basses singing in unison the words, "Torah, which God gave thro' Moses, is the Law of the house of Jacob."

d. That at this place, only the altos sing a countermelody.

e. That in this instance the "Law of the house" is defined as being the law for all men.

f. The dialogue between the cantor and the chorus (the people) which brings the section to its conclusion.

Shema Yisroel—*Cantor and chorus*

O hear, Israel, our God, our Creator, Our God is One!

NOTE: a. That this is a repetition of the Shema Yisroel of Part I.

b. The tremolo in the instrumental parts in the accompaniment.

Lecho Adonoy (Finale)—*Chorus*

And Thine, Adonoy, is the greatness and all dominion and Thine the majesty
and the glory and the pow'r,
For all things in heaven and on earth are Thine,
Adonoy, and Thine be the Kingdom,
Be Thou, Lord, exalted over all.

310

OBSERVE: a. That in the first seven measures of this section the sopranos, altos, tenors and basses are generally singing the same melody in unison.
b. That as the movement progresses to its natural conclusion the mood of great exultation becomes more and more apparent.
c. In particular, the soaring quality of the orchestral accompaniment.

PART IV

Returning the Scroll to the Ark—*Cantor*

Praise the Lord, Praise the Lord with me;
Let us exalt His Name in one voice.

NOTE: a. That here the cantor asks the people to join with him in singing praises to the Lord and to join as one voice in exalting His Name.

Hodo al Eretz—*Chorus*

Earth sees His glory, and the heavens,
And He is the strength of all His people,
The glory and praise of all the just, of Israel that came before Him, before His presence,
Halleluia!

NOTE: a. That this deals with the return of the Law to the ark.
b. The march-like quality of the music which is sung by the chorus as the Law is being returned to the ark.
c. The joyous mood of the music.
d. The reverential mood of the "Halleluias" with which this section concludes.
e. The seven-part choral writing used for these "Halleluias."
f. The change of meter from 4/4 to 2/2 to 3/2 to 3/4 in the "Halleluia" section.
g. The bassoon solo followed by muted trumpets which brings this section to its conclusion.

Toras Adonoy

The Law of the Lord is perfect,
It doth restore the soul;
His precepts are sure and enduring, and teach the simple.
The Laws giv'n by the Lord are just Laws. Rejoicing the heart.
The Law of the Lord is holy, Enduring forever.
Behold these precepts the Lord hath shown thee;
Regard them; do not forsake them.

311

OBSERVE: a. The oriental quality of the music in the instrumental introduction to this section, which results from the sound of the bassoon followed by muted trumpets playing over a background of tremolo strings and a softly played roll on the cymbals.

    b. How the cantor and chorus take turns in proclaiming the perfection and enduring qualities of the Law.

    c. That at the end of this section the cantor exhorts the people never to forsake the Law.

Etz Chayim (Song of Peace)—*Chorus, cantor, alto solo, chorus*

Tree of Life to them that shall receive it, and its preservers are happy,
For its ways are ways of beauty, and all its paths are paths of peace.
Sholom.

NOTE: a. That the key here is *Sholom*—"peace."

   b. The simplicity and sincerity of expression in this song of peace.

   c. The rich harmonization of this section.

   d. The alto solo beginning with the words, "For its ways are ways of beauty."

   e. The effect of the chromatic writing in the soprano line at the words, "and its preservers are happy."

   f. That this same chromatic writing is repeated later on the same words but in a new key.

   g. The effective orchestration under the choral writing.

   h. The mood of peaceful calm at the words, *Sholom, Sholom, Sholom.*

   i. The effect in the final seven measures of scoring the sopranos and tenors in unison on the word *Sholom*. This in turn followed by the altos and basses singing the word *Sholom* in unison.

   j. The moving melodic line of the tenor on the final *Sholom*.

PART V—Epilogue

Vaanachnu (Adoration)—*Cantor and chorus*

We adore Thee and bow the head and humble our hearts before Thee.
Before the King of Kings.
The Lord God be praised! The Lord God be adored!
Praise the Lord! Praise Him!

NOTE: a. The instrumental introduction to this section which features the bassoon and strings.

   b. That this section relates to the adoration of God.

   c. That it is also a description of the peace and solemnity of the Sabbath.

   d. The repetition by the chorus of each statement made by the cantor.

   e. The shifting of meters to achieve rhythmic flexibility.

312

Recitative—Cantor and chorus

May the time not be distant, O God, when Thy Name shall be worshipped in all the earth, when unbelief shall disappear, and error be no more.

May the day come when all men shall invoke Thy Name; when corruption and evil shall give way to purity and goodness; when superstition shall no longer enslave the mind, nor fetishism blind the eye!

O may all men recognize that they are brethren, so that one in spirit and one in fellowship, they may be forever united before Thee.

Then shall Thine Kingdom be established on earth and the word of Thine ancient seer be fulfilled. And on that day the Lord shall be One. His name be One!

And now ere we part, let us call to mind those who have finished their earthly course and have been gathered to the eternal home. Though vanished from bodily sight, they have not ceased to be, and it is well with them; they abide in the shadow of the Most High.

Let those who mourn for them be comforted. Let them submit their aching hearts to God, for He is just and wise and merciful in all His doings, though no man can comprehend His ways.

In the divine order of nature both life and death, joy and sorrow, serve beneficent ends, and in the fullness of time we shall know why we are tried and why our love brings us sorrow as well as happiness. Wait patiently all ye that mourn, and be ye of good courage, for surely your longing souls shall be satisfied.

God of Israel!
Arise to the help of Israel!
Our Redeemer, Adonoy Sabaoth, our God.

NOTE:
  a. The recitative nature of this section which is chanted by the cantor.
  b. The use of shifting meters.
  c. The woodwind color in the accompaniment under the words, "May the day come when all men shall invoke Thy Name."
  d. That this is a prayer for the arrival of the day when neither superstition nor fetishism will blind men and all men will worship one God.
  e. That in the section, "O may all men recognize they are brethren," the solo is more lyric or songlike in quality.
  f. The ethereal effect of the accompaniment played by the strings.
  g. The reiteration of the idea, "The Lord be One," by the chorus.
  h. The effect of the dissonance and its resolution in the instrumental interlude leading into, "And now ere we part, let us call to mind those who have finished their earthly course."
  i. The return to the recitative style for this section.
  j. The effective use of the strings and woodwinds in the accompaniment of this portion of the text.

k. That beginning with the words, "In the divine order of nature both life and death, joy and sorrow, serve beneficent ends," the mood changes and might be said to have elements of mournfulness.

l. The emphasis given by the bass instruments in the accompaniment which underlies this section.

m. The singing by the chorus of the return of the *Tzur Yisroel* first heard sung by the cantor in Part I.

n. The melismatic nature of the melodic line for this section.

Adon Olom—*Chorus, cantor, soprano solo, and chorus*

Eternal God, who reigned supreme,
While all was yet a formless void;
In sovereign pow'r ordained this world,
And His Name, then as King was proclaimed.
And after this, if chaos come, the Lord God will rule alone.
And One He was and One He is, and One shall be in pow'r supreme!
For He is One and One shall be.
To our God none can be compared!
He ne'er began, He ne'er will end;
To Him the might, and glory and pow'r!
He is my God, my God, my living God,
My God, my Savior,
My God, my refuge in my distress.
And He is my sign, and my refuge,
My cup of salvation, whene'er I call.
In His hand my soul shall rest when I sleep and when I wake, and with my
  soul, my body,
He is with me, I shall not fear.

NOTICE:

a. That the composer has marked this section to be sung "Like voices from another world, outside of time, outside of space."

b. How the short instrumental introduction featuring the woodwinds leads naturally into and also sets the mood for this section.

c. That the section begins with sopranos, altos, tenors and basses singing the melody in unison.

d. The beautiful countermelody played by the oboe under the words, "In sovereign pow'r ordained this world."

e. The effect of the chromatic melodic progression sung in unison by sopranos and tenors on the word "chaos."

f. The emotional tension created by the tremolo flute part in this portion of the text.

g. The use of shifting meters.

h. The chromatic triplet figure heard in the accompaniment played by the bass instruments following the words, "and One shall be in power supreme!"

i. The strength of the bass melody played by the brass bass under the words, "He ne'er will end."

j. In the instrumental introduction to the words, "He is my God," that the chromatic writing for the flutes and piccolo gives the effect of the rushing wind.

314

k. The mood of calmness with which this section ends.

l. That this section deals with the acceptance of the reality of life and death. That despite the fact that man is too limited, too bounded to understand the infinite, he must have faith and believe; he must commit himself, his soul and his body into God's hands.

Benediction—*Cantor and chorus*

Now may the Lord bless you and guard you. Amen.
And shine upon you the light of His countenance and be gracious unto you. Amen.
And lift up to you His face and give you peace.
Sholom. Amen.

OBSERVE: a. The peaceful quality of this *Benediction*.
               b. Its mood of calmness.
               c. The "Amen" of the chorus in answer to each statement of the *Benediction* by the cantor.
               d. The feeling of triumph engendered by the final "Amen."

Music for the concert hall

The Abstract Instrumental Forms

Two related problems confronted the early eighteenth-century composer wishing to create a musical work of purely instrumental character. Both had to do with the organization of the musical material—rhythm, melody, harmony and timbre—into a meaningful pattern which would successfully communicate the composer's ideas. While there were a variety of music forms in vogue during the early part of the sixteenth century, none were particularly adaptable as a means of extending form for purely instrumental writing. Before this time the role of instrumental music had largely been that of accompaniment, either for vocal writing such as the madrigal or as the accompaniment for the dance. This, then, created the first problem: the difficulty of expressing musical ideas through the pure abstract medium of instrumental sound, without reference to the accompaniment of words or movement of the dance to establish meaning. The inclusion of text or dance figures largely solved the problems of formal organization. But if the composer wished to express purely musical ideas which in no sense depended on text or movement, it was necessary to create new patterns of organization or formal structure which would give the unifying factor that words and dance movement had provided. So it was natural that composers proceeding from the known to the unknown based their first attempts to invent independent instrumental forms on the then existing vocal and dance forms.

The related problem was that of finding expression for more extended ideas. Imitation of pure dance and vocal forms as individual compositions might be satisfactory for miniature and small works, but no artist is content to restrict his creative output to miniatures. While a small work of art can be a masterpiece, almost every artist desires to create something of significance on a large scale.

Consider for the moment the enormous problem confronting a painter faced with finding a suitable structural organization for communicating such diverse ideas as these: the stories of the creation of the world, the creation of Adam and Eve, the flood, man's continued weakness as symbolized by Noah's drunkenness, and the prophecy of the coming of Christ. Yet Michelangelo during the years 1508 to 1512 undertook such an assignment, which resulted in the incomparable ceiling in the Sistine Chapel in the Vatican. In these frescos Michelangelo was able to go beyond the painting of separate miniatures. He was able to express these diverse subjects in an extended work of gigantic proportions, organically unified not only with itself but with the architecture.

CEILING FRESCO, Michelangelo

In looking for another example of the artist turning to a larger form for the expression of his ideas and feelings, we might examine sculpture. One of the finest examples of a work of art conceived in terms of extended form is found in the Orpheus fountain in Stockholm. In this sculpture by Carl

ORPHEUS FOUNTAIN,
Carl Milles

320

Milles (1875-1955), Orpheus, the central figure, is shown standing over Cerberus, the three-headed guardian of Hades. Orpheus with his lyre is attempting to lull Cerberus to sleep so that he may rescue his beloved Eurydice from the land of the dead. But this tells only part of the story. To this one subject is added more material. Eight figures are arranged around Orpheus, each one representing a listener awakened from death by the first notes of the playing by Orpheus. These figures represent such diverse characters as a deaf Beethoven shown turning his face to the music, an entranced girl reacting to the music by dropping her flower, a man quieting his bird. Each of these eight figures reveals a different reaction to the music being played by Orpheus.

One final example from the visual arts should suffice to show how the artist is able to develop his vision and style into works which encompass large conception controlled by a large formal organization. Architecture can furnish this example. Compare the simplicity of planning and construction of this small 10 foot by 6 foot toolshed with the vastly more complicated

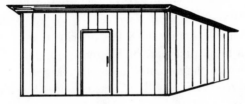

planning and construction required for the Blue Cross-Blue Shield Building in Boston which was designed by Paul Rudolph (1918———). While both enclose and cover space, it is immediately obvious that the space needs for

BLUE CROSS-BLUE SHIELD BUILDING, Boston

321

the realization of the Boston building are infinitely greater than those for the shed. One of the first problems to be solved by the architect in creating the Boston building—one shared with Michelangelo and Carl Milles in their creative efforts—was the organization of line, color, shape, texture and materials into a large and extended formal organization to realize the maximum purpose of his creative idea.

In literature one can find the application of this same principle in works such as Goethe's *Faust,* Homer's *The Iliad,* Dante's *The Divine Comedy* and Shakespeare's *Hamlet.* The epic, drama, biography, novel and history all depend on the writer's finding a more extended formal organization for the expression of his ideas.

Music has also benefited from the growth and development of the larger units of form. Without the ability to make use of the extension of musical material, composers of such great masterpieces as Beethoven's *Symphony No. 9 in D Minor,* Brahms' *Symphony No. 4 in E Minor,* Mozart's *Symphony No. 41 in C,* Prokofiev's *Classical Symphony in D* could not have brought these works into being.

While each of these geniuses—artists, writers and musicians—created exquisite works of a miniature nature, we tend to regard as the real masterpieces those works which they created using the larger forms. Even the creators themselves tend to classify as their masterpieces those works which have used these larger forms.

As we have seen, the first instrumental pieces were closely related to either existing vocal or dance forms. As instrumental music began to evolve, composers attempted to create larger works by simply composing a series of short vocal compositions or dances, joining them together loosely through key relationship and contrast of mood. Thus the earliest compositions of extended length were nothing more than collections of short pieces. Composers soon began to chafe under the limitation on depth and breadth of expression which resulted when the extension of the formal organization of their writing was restricted to stringing together a series of vocal or dance forms. They then began searching for more satisfactory ways of extending their instrumental writing. As they broke further and further away from the basic vocal and dance forms, their compositions came to be made up of fewer but larger single movements or parts. As the composer became more skillful in designing his instrumental forms he was able to extend the scope and size of his compositions. It follows that as he extended the size of the musical work, he was forced into more and more careful consideration of the problems of form which were so necessary in holding the work together and making it understandable. While it is not absolutely essential to know all of the technical intricacies of the composer's art, a recognition of the general scheme by which he has presented his musical message makes it possible for the listener to gain the fullest understanding and appreciation of such abstract instrumental music as the *fugue*, the *sonata*, the *concerto*, the *symphony*.

Rather than negating the physical and emotional responses to music, an intellectual knowledge and approach to this type of music opens infinite possibilities for enlarging and expanding all of one's responses to it. The study of the structure of absolute instrumental music is somewhat analogous to the study of the drama. The study of a play by Shakespeare should lead to an enrichment of all of one's responses to the actual play, not to a cold analysis of the technical procedures. In the same way the study of the instrumental forms or of a specific composition should result in the total enrichment of all of our responses to the performance of the work, not in acquiring mere knowledge of technical jargon and analysis. In order to know what the composer has to say we must have some understanding of how he speaks musically. Part of the clue comes from a composer's choice of organization for his musical material.

In the abstract instrumental forms the composer uses exactly the same principles that are used in the simplest vocal and dance forms. These are statement, repetition, variation and contrast. Only the materials and organization become more complex and involved as they are extended in length. Actually there are no regular set forms which a composer uses; rather there are formal principles which he uses in the construction of his musical work. Some of these principles are present in every musical composition—vocal, dance, descriptive or abstract instrumental. Some compositions are inclined to emphasize one or another of these principles, while others are the result of the balanced combination of all of them. In order to become better acquainted with these principles we will examine several typical compositions in which these principles are used.

The Fugue

In the brief introduction to the fugue found in Unit One (page 26), it was pointed out that the fugue consisted of two or more lines of melody moving against one another in accordance with certain rules for contrapuntal movement. In the fugue the composer bases the entire work on a single musical idea or melody, called the *subject*, which is announced by a single voice. After the melody or subject is established, a second voice enters with the same melody, now called the *answer*, played either five steps higher or four steps lower, placing it in a new key—the dominant key to the subject. At this point the first subject continues with new melodic material called the *countersubject*. In their proper turn other new voices take up the subject until all are heard.

While the discussion of the fugue has stressed the lateral relationship of one melody being sounded against one or more melodies, the fugue should not be thought of as lacking harmonic content. If, for example, all of the instruments should stop the forward motion and hold the third beat of the twenty-second measure of the *Little G Minor Fugue*, discussed briefly in Unit One, the result certainly would be that of vertical harmony. In polyphonic writing or contrapuntal texture, the harmonic implications derive from the horizontal movement and scoring of the individual lines of melody, rather than the up-and-down harmonization resulting from the vertical consideration of each note of the melody.

The close relationship between the fugue and the canon or round was also pointed out in Unit One. In a fugue, however, unlike the canon or round which it resembles, each line or voice is not an exact repetition of the preceding one. While the principle of repetition is the main element of design in the fugue, this element is in reality and more properly called *imitation*. We can see and hear this imitation in any fugal writing. The impression we receive from listening to fugal writing is that the two or more individual lines of melody are imitating one another, rather than being exact statements of one another. The rule that a phrase must have four measures to be considered regular does not apply to the fugal subject. In the fugue the subject may vary from one to eight measures in length. Longer fugal subjects are not unknown. In analyzing the fugue one does not consider the fugal subject as being related to either the phrase or period. To do so would imply homophonic rather than polyphonic texture.

Even the brief previous experience with the fugue revealed that there was a great deal more to its formal organization than the mere statement of a subject followed by several successive restatements of this same subject. In order to express fully his musical message in fugal form it was necessary for the composer to invent ways of extending the form. In the fugue this is accomplished by the division of the work into large sections or parts. Part I is known as the *exposition*, Part II is called the *development*. After the development section there usually follows some form of final or concluding section. Because it is freer in form after the exposition than is the first movement of a sonata, the fugue might better be called a process than a form. If there is a definite concluding section it will contain the climax of the composition. It will normally be given in the original key and will use such devices as *stretto* and *organ point* to achieve additional emphasis. If two subjects are presented sounding together in the exposition, the result is known as a *double fugue*. Similarly, if three subjects are being sounded simultaneously in the exposition, the result is known as a *triple fugue*.

In the exposition is found the introduction of the subject and countersubject in each of the voices to be used. The length of the subject has already been said to vary, normally somewhere between one and eight measures. It is the characteristic rhythmic and melodic pattern of the fugal subject which gives it its peculiar identity and enables the listener to follow its course through the complex manipulations of the several voices. The manner in which the fugal subject is introduced and then imitated by the other voices in the exposition follows a certain prescribed order. Not only the order of entrance but the key of each entrance is also subject to the rather strict rules governing fugal writing. Normally, the pattern for the entrances of the different voices in a four-voice fugue would be:

Soprano   Alto   Tenor   Bass

or sometimes

Alto   Soprano   Bass   Tenor

and of course exceptions to these general rules for the presentation of the subject may also be found. No matter what the order of voice entrances may be in the exposition, the system of key relationships remains constant according to this pattern:

Subject—*Tonic key*
Answer—*Dominant key*
Subject—*Tonic key*
Answer—*Dominant key*

This indicates that in a fugue the exposition closes in the dominant key. This is particularly true when the key of the fugue is major. If the key of the fugue is minor, however, often the final cadence of the exposition will be in the relative major.

The second large division of the fugue is known as the *development*. Here the composer sets as his task the complete exploitation of the subject material. In the exposition the composer achieved unity in his creative efforts through the use of repetition and imitation. To keep the completed composition from becoming dull and repetitious, the composer needs to introduce at this point the element of variety. This is achieved by the technic of variation. Some of the ways variation of the subject material may be accomplished are:

1. Playing the subject or fragment of the subject in different keys.

Johann Sebastian Bach
Fuga V a 4 voci
Well-Tempered Clavier, Vol. I

2. Changing the subject from major to minor or minor to major.

Fuga III a 3 voci
Well-Tempered Clavier, Vol. I

3. Inversion of the subject.

Fuga XV a 3 voci
Well-Tempered Clavier, Vol. I

4. Contrary motion.

Fuga VI a 3 voci
Well-Tempered Clavier, Vol. I

5. Augmentation of the subject through doubling the time values of the original subject, thus causing the subject to move half as fast.

Fuga VIII a 3 voci
Well-Tempered Clavier, Vol. I

6. Diminution of the subject through reducing by half each of the time values of the original subject.

August Alexander Klengel
Canon VI
Twenty-four Canons and Fugues

In this example note that the middle line is a diminution of the bass line and that the upper line is in turn a diminution of the middle line.

7. Sequence—the repetition of the subject material at higher or lower pitch.

Johann Sebastian Bach
Fuga II a 3 voci
Well-Tempered Clavier, Vol. I

The third section of the fugue may not be as well defined as is the exposition or the development. There is, nevertheless, a final or concluding section and it is in this section that the climax of the fugue occurs. Two devices used in achieving this climax deserve mention at this time.

1. *Stretto.* In the *stretto* a feeling of emotional tension, excitement and tumultuous movement to a conclusion is achieved by overlapping the subject in a second voice before it has been completed by the previous voice.

Fuga I a 4 voci
Well-Tempered Clavier, Vol. I

2. *Organ* or *pedal point.* These two synonymous terms describe a device used by the composer to achieve greater emphasis in the concluding statement. The pedal point is the scoring of a note usually derived from either the tonic or dominant harmony so that it is sustained in the bass.

Pedal point →

Fuga II a 3 voci
Well-Tempered Clavier, Vol. I

One function of the concluding section of the fugue is to bring the work back to the original key. One exception to this should be noted here. It was the consistent practice of composers in the sixteenth, seventeenth and eighteenth centuries to change the final tonic of a work written in the minor mode to major. This final major tonality in a composition written in minor tonality is known as *tierce de Picardie* or *Picardy third.* Note the example of the *tierce de Picardie* in the final chord of the example above.

LISTENING ACTIVITY

Fuga II a 3 Voci in C Minor from
   The Well-Tempered Clavier...............Johann Sebastian Bach (1685-1750)

RHYTHM: Before listening to the recording, clap the rhythm of the fugal subject.

MELODY: Before listening to the recording, sing the melody of the fugal subject using the neutral syllable *loo.*

HARMONY: By definition the fugue is a musical composition whose harmonic basis derives from its contrapuntal texture.

TIMBRE: Timbre is determined by the instrument or voice performing a work. In most recordings this fugue is performed on the piano. The timbre would be modified or changed if the performance were by an orchestra or on a pipe organ.

FORM:

Exposition

Subject (*C minor*) measures 1-3

Answer (*G minor*) measures 3-5

Countersubject (*G minor*) measures 3-5

Codetta (*note use of sequence*) measures 5-6

Second entrance of subject (*C minor*) measures 7-9

Second countersubject (*upper voices*) measures 7-9

Development

Episode I.............measures 9-13
A series of variations based on the fugal subject in the keys of F minor, Bb major, and Eb major.

Episode II.............measures 13-17
In Episode II the first countersubject is sounded in contrary motion against the second countersubject transposed to a new key. Episode II ends in the key of G minor.

Episode III...........measures 17-22
Here one finds the working over of a fragment of the fugal subject through various keys. The use of sequence is much in evidence in this episode.

Episode IV............measures 22-26
This is actually a transposition of measures 9-11 of Episode I. Episode IV ends on the V₇ of C minor and goes immediately into the concluding section.

Conclusion ....measures 26-29
The subject is given out in the bass in the key of C minor. The cadence in measure 29 brings an end to the strictly contrapuntal work.

Coda ....measures 29-31
From the strictness of contrapuntal writing Bach turned to a free style which, although based on the fugal subject, is treated in homophonic manner. Note the use of the pedal point in measures 29-31 (example on page 327). Note also the effect of the *tierce de Picardie* or *Picardy third* on the final cadence.

Pre-Classical Sonata

The term "sonata" first came into use during the sixteenth century when, as we have already seen, it was used to distinguish music that was played on instruments from music that was sung (page 296). The Latin word *sonare*, meaning "to sound," gave rise to the noun *sonata*, meaning music that is sounded or played. It would be well to remember that the term "sonata" has no real, strict definition other than the basic designation of instrumental music. It is used to designate compositions containing a single movement as well as works having a number of parts or movements.

The beginnings of instrumental music can be traced back to the growth and development of one of the vocal forms—the madrigal. As composers became more technically skilled at writing increasingly difficult music for the madrigal groups, it became customary to help the singers by using viols to double the vocal lines. As might be expected, it was not long before inventive composers began seeking ways of exploiting this instrumental resource which was being used as an adjunct to the vocal group. Vocal madrigals began to appear with pure instrumental sound being emphasized in instrumental preludes, interludes and postludes or codas. Also there were probably instances of instrumentalists playing madrigals without benefit of the singers—a practice which could be definitely pointed to as being the forerunner of our present-day instrumental music.

It is necessary, at this point, to digress momentarily to consider the kinds and quality of instruments available to the sixteenth- and seventeenth-century composer. Since composers have always had to adapt the expression of their musical ideas to the capabilities of the instrumentalists or vocalists available to them, a definite limitation was placed on these composers by the unwieldiness and raucous tone quality of early instruments. It is difficult for the present-day listener, whose ears have been attuned to the beautiful,

329

sonorous sounds possible with the instruments in use today, to realize that such has not always been the case. Indeed the sounds of some of the sixteenth-century instruments were anything but pleasant. The fiedels, viols, lutes, harps, reed instruments and trumpets of that time produced sounds that were small, flat sounding, sometimes raucous and, in general unrefined, by contemporary standards.

Many of these instruments were ungainly in size, awkward to hold, deficient in mechanical perfection and difficult to play. These limitations made it necessary for the composer to adapt his creative talent and technic to the capabilities of the existing instruments. Fortunately, however, at the time when ways were being found for exploiting instrumental sound a parallel movement was under way which resulted in the invention of new instruments and the improvement of the older ones. A group of virtuoso instrument makers and craftsmen appeared. These new and improved instruments made possible the conquering of new musical worlds by the composer. He now had at his disposal a more grateful mechanical instrument which in the hands of the performer could be relied on to express every nuance of his musical ideas and feelings. Thus, as the instruments themselves were improved, so did the technical possibilities for these instruments develop. Composers could now take advantage of the improved status of the instruments and write more and more elaborate works for instrumental combinations.

One of the earliest ensembles of which we have record is the string group, the *Vingt-quatre Violons du Roi*, which has already been mentioned (page 198). Although this group reached its heyday around 1560, it was not fully appreciated until almost half a century later. Another of the early instrumental ensembles was the group used by Monteverdi in his opera *Orpheus* in 1607.

> It consisted of the following instruments: fifteen viols of three different sizes, two violins, two large flutes, two ordinary flutes, two oboes, two cornets (the old wooden instruments), four trumpets, five trombones, a harp, two harpsichords, two small organs, and a regal (a portable reed organ). This combination of forty instruments probably made use of all of the instrumentalists available to the court composer of Mantua; but in spite of its miscellaneousness there is evident here the principle of the string choir as the foundation of the whole orchestral scheme.[11]

Thus the improvement of the older instruments and the invention of new instruments made possible new instrumental combinations which introduced a new palette of tonal colors—and made possible the complete range of an emerging system of harmony. Instrumental music, because it could now speak in a new, exciting and expressive language, at last began to come into its own.

The pre-classical sonata composed before 1750 was divided into two basic types: the *sonata da camera* or chamber sonata, and the *sonata da chiesa* or church sonata.

The Sonata da Camera

This type of the early pre-classical sonata was meant to be played in the home and for company. The *sonata da camera* was merely a series of dance forms joined together by unity of key and was often called a *partita* or *suite*. An example of this type, the *Suite in D Major* by Johann Sebastian Bach, has already been presented in Chapter Six—Music of the Dance. This type of sonata was performed on a single keyboard instrument such as the harpsichord or clavichord, by solo melodic instruments such as the violin, flute or oboe, or by chamber groups consisting of strings and woodwinds with a keyboard accompanying instrument.

Suite No. 3 in D Major......................Johann Sebastian Bach (1685-1750)

LISTENING ACTIVITY

Listen once again to the entire suite. While listening refer again to the orchestral score found on pages 217-252. Pay particular attention to the manner in which the individual movements are strung together. The point of emphasis during the rehearing of this suite should be its importance in being typical of the earliest examples of writing in an extended abstract instrumental form. Note:

1. That unity of the entire work is achieved through the use of a common key tonality (D major) throughout.

2. That variety is achieved by alternating movements of different dance forms in varying tempi.
3. That the instrumentation of this suite is for a chamber group and an accompanying keyboard instrument.
4. That this is essentially an ensemble effort rather than a composition played by a solo instrument with instrumental accompaniment.

The Sonata da Chiesa

The *sonata da chiesa* or church sonata, often merely called sonata, was an extremely popular type of instrumental composition during the seventeenth and early eighteenth centuries. As the name implies, this form of writing was originally intended for performance in the church. Next to the fugue these early sonatas were probably the most dignified and abstract musical form of expression during this period of history. The principle of contrast by the alternating use of slow, fast, slow, fast tempos for the movements was incorporated from the *sonata da camera,* but the number of movements was reduced, usually to four. At the same time the length of the movements was extended. Arcangelo Corelli (1653-1713) is generally credited with the

331

origination of the four-movement format for the *sonata da chiesa*. The movements of a Corelli sonata were based on this pattern:

Grave (*slow*)   Written in either homophonic or polyphonic style.

Allegro (*fast*)   Written in fugal form.

Andante (*slow*)   Written in homophonic style. Corelli often used triple time for this movement.

Allegro (*fast*)   Written in either homophonic or fugal style.
or Presto

Other composers used an alternating *adagio, allegro, adagio, allegro* scheme. The adagio movements were inclined to be songlike and were generally in two- or three-part homophonic form (A B or A B A). The second movement which was the first allegro was invariably an actual fugue or at least it was in fugal style. The final allegro was a dancelike movement. Dance movements were actually borrowed and freely used by Bach and others for the last movement of their church sonatas. The principle of contrast was basic in the first, third and final movements. Repetition was used in a limited manner and variation played only a small role in these movements. The form of the second movement, the fugue, was discussed in the preceding section.

Some of the most popular of the church sonatas had a trio-like character in that they were written for two high-register instruments supported by a *basso continuo*. The improvement of instruments which took place during this period has already been mentioned. Particular mention should be made of the contribution of Andrea Amati (c. 1520-c. 1577), Niccolo Amati (1596-1684), Antonio Stradivarius (1644-1737) and others who brought about the improvement and the development of the violin and the violin family. It was not long after the new and improved violins became available that they began taking over the high parts in the church sonata.

The church sonata was basically a vocal type using instruments as if they were voices. As the form evolved, the church sonata, like the chamber sonata, was played on simple keyboard instruments such as the harpsichord or clavichord, on solo melodic instruments such as the violin, flute or oboe with keyboard accompaniment (in this form they were called "solo sonatas") or by chamber music groups, the most popular of which was the trio. This last consisted of two melodic instruments such as strings or woodwinds with a keyboard accompanying instrument.

LISTENING ACTIVITY   Trio Sonata, Op. 1 No. 3 for
Two Violins and Basso Continuo.................Tomaso Albinoni (1674-1745)

This is a typical example of the trio sonata of the church sonata type. As indicated in the title, this work is for two violins playing the high melody parts, cello playing the bass line and harpsichord which, in addition to filling in the proper harmonies, helps augment the bass line. In the original composition the harmonization was indicated by a set of numbers under the bass line.

What to listen for:

Grave *(First movement)*

NOTICE: a. That the movement is marked *Grave* which is a slow and dignified tempo.
          b. That while the movement is marked 4/4, there is a feeling of eight pulses to the measure.
          c. The songlike style of the theme:

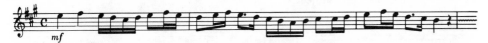

          d. That the two melodic instruments alternate in the presentation of the melody.
          e. The bass line played by the cello and harpsichord.
          f. That the form for this movement is simple A B homophonic form.
          g. That the final two measures of this movement might be considered as either an extension of the last cadence or a very short codetta.

Allegro *(Second movement)*

NOTE: a. That this is a fugue in three voices.
          b. The order of entrance of the subject in each of the three voices.
          c. That the meter is 4/4 and that the movement swings in four to the measure.
          d. That the subject begins on the second half of the first beat.
          e. The syncopation played by the first violin in measures 7-9.
          f. The melody of the subject:

          g. The beginning of the development section in measure 11.
          h. The manner in which the composer exploits the subject material in the development section.
          i. That the second violin part in measures 13-15 is an augmentation of the first violin figure found in measures 7-8.
          j. That the concluding section begins in measure 39.

Grave *(Third movement)*

NOTICE: a. That while this movement is written in 4/4 meter, there is a feeling of eight pulses to the measure.
          b. That this movement is melodically conceived and is based on this melody:

333

c. That the two melody instruments alternate in the presentation of this thematic material.

d. The chromaticism in the bass line.

e. That this movement is written in melodic minor mode.

f. That this movement ends with a major chord, because the final cadence chord is the V (C♯E♯G♯) of the key of F♯ minor, the key in which the movement is written.

Allegro *(Fourth movement)*

NOTE: a. That while the movement is marked in 3/8 meter, there is a feeling of one pulse to the measure.

b. That this movement, like the second movement, is a three-voiced fugue based on this subject:

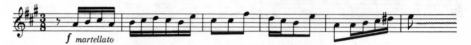

c. The three individual entrances of this subject.

d. That this subject is five measures in length.

e. The three different countersubjects:
(1) First countersubject:

(2) Second countersubject:

(3) Third countersubject:

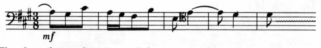

f. The three large divisions of the movement.

g. The use of the *stretto* in the concluding section to heighten the emotional effect as well as the rhythmic movement.

The Pre-Classical Concerto

With the improvement of the then-existing instruments and the invention of new instruments, the seventeenth century saw a complete metamorphosis of the role of instrumental music. The orchestra was no longer a haphazard and indiscriminate collection of instruments brought together without particular rhyme or reason to serve as a musical stepchild of vocal music. It now began to have an entity of its own. It also began to have its own character and personality and to develop the capacity for expressing its own individuality. From this there emerged an organization, personality and coloring similar to

334

what we know today as the modern symphony orchestra.

One natural outgrowth of the concern for instrumental music during this period was the considerable interest of composers in experimenting with the many possibilities of combining instruments, not only in a variety of tonal combinations but also in the use of ensembles of differing sizes. The obvious result of this experimentation was that many new instrumental combinations evolved, each one demanding a considerable amount of music literature to keep going.

Composers now had new aesthetic problems to solve. They were called upon to create music without reference to words, movement or dramatic action, but rather along purely musical lines. Another result of this experimentation with new instrumental combinations was the increasing use of the violin for solo purposes. This in turn resulted in the creation of works for solo violin with the accompaniment played by an orchestra. These works, which were a type of sonata, had multiple movements and were known by the generic term of *concerto*. Giuseppe Torelli (1658-1709) and Tommaso Albinoni (1674-1745) are credited with having written some of the first concertos for solo violin. Later composers substituted other instruments for the solo role. The form came into full fruition with Antonio Vivaldi (c. 1675-1741), a Venetian priest and violinist, whose string concertos served as models for the other composers of the time.

The concerto of the pre-classical period differed from the modern concerto as we know it in that its basic design stemmed from the antiphonal use of solo instrument and the accompanying force known as the *tutti*. The word *concerto* implies concerted effort and, as here applied, meant music made together by a group of instrumentalists. The concertos of the pre-classical period were written either for a solo instrument with orchestral accompaniment or for a small group of solo instruments which carried on a musical dialogue with the instrumental forces of a large group. The former was known as the *concerto* while the latter was known as the *concerto grosso*.

In the pre-classical concerto the principles of repetition and contrast were the main ones used. Not only were these principles achieved through rhythmic, melodic and harmonic means, but composers also took advantage of the contrasting tonal bodies of soloist or soloists and orchestra to exploit the principle of contrast through the dynamics. The pre-classical solo concerto was a three-movement work in alternating tempos of *allegro*, *adagio* and *allegro*. Principles of repetition, contrast and variation were used. The composer exploited the technical possibilities of the solo instrument in his writing so that the solo passages became the most important parts of these concertos. Variant treatment of the musical material, usually a single musical idea, was used to allow for extreme display of virtuosity on the part of the soloist. The orchestra assumed a definite accompanying role. Passages of imitative character were often present when polyphonic texture was used, as it often was.

335

Concerto in D Minor for Oboe,
   Strings and Cembalo . . . . Antonio Vivaldi (c.1675-1741)

This is an excellent example of the pre-classical solo concerto. This is one of a group by Vivaldi given the title of *Il cimento dell' armonia e dell' inventione* ("The Trial of Harmony and Invention"). There are the conventional three movements marked Allegro, Largo and Allegro. The harmonic texture of the total work is largely homophonic rather than polyphonic, a characteristic of Vivaldi's writing.

What to listen for:

Allegro moderato *(First movement)*

The first movement has two principal themes. The first principal theme is known as the orchestral theme:

The other principal theme is the solo theme:

This latter theme is played by the oboe and treated in a way that exploits all of the technical facilities of this instrument. The first movement consists mainly of a contrasting of these two themes by the orchestra and the soloist.

NOTE: a. That the movement is marked 3/4 and moves with a steady three beats to the measure.

b. The rhythmic syncopation played by the first and second violins in the opening *tutti*: ♩♩ ♩ ♩♩ ♩♩ ♩♩♩♩ ♩♩ ♩

c. The imitation of this syncopation by the solo oboe as it makes its initial entrance: ♩♩ ♩ ♩♩ ♩♩ ♩ ♩♩ ♩♩ ♩ ♩♩

d. That the harmonic texture is homophonic rather than polyphonic.

e. That the harmony is consonant rather than dissonant in character.

f. That harmonic contrast is achieved by transposing the two principal themes into other keys—for example, D minor, F major, A minor, and returning to D minor.

g. That the accompaniment is scored for first and second violins, violas, cellos, string basses and cembalo.

h. The legato playing by the first and second violins and violas of the chords in the accompaniment.

i. The running bass played by cello and string bass at this same place, which is reminiscent of the pedal technic on the organ.

j. That the cembalo reinforces the harmony by playing the basic chords.

k. The difference in timbre between solo and tutti sections.

l. That the form of this movement consists of four alternating sections of orchestral and solo themes followed by a final tutti statement of the orchestral theme.

m. That variety is achieved by rhythmic and melodic modification in the restatement of each theme, as well as through modulation to other keys.

Largo *(Second movement)*

This movement is given over entirely to the solo instrument which plays its songlike melody against an accompaniment played by the orchestra. The lyric melody of the solo instrument is in contrast to the rather strict and straightforward accompaniment played by the orchestra.

NOTE: a. That while the movement is marked 4/4 there is a feeling of eight pulses to the measure.

b. The steadiness of the rhythm. There are no accelerandos or ritardandos in the entire movement.

c. The effect created by the use of the triplet figures in measures 5 and 6.

d. The songlike quality of the melody.

e. The use of melodic sequence in the construction of the melody—for example, the melodic repetition of measures 1 and 2 a third higher in measures 3 and 4.

337

f. The other examples of sequence in the construction of the melody.

g. The simple harmonization used by the composer.

h. That the harmonic texture used by the composer is homophonic rather than polyphonic.

i. The modulation to related keys for harmonic variety and interest.

j. The use of the orchestra accompaniment as a foil to the oboe solo.

k. The use of individual instruments in the accompaniment—for example, the cellos and string basses in measures 13 and 14.

l. That the movement may be analyzed as having two divisions or parts and that each part, in turn, may also be analyzed into component parts.

Allegro *(Third movement)*

This movement is constructed in much the same form as the first movement. The solo theme is the important theme and alternates with the orchestra theme which is greatly subordinated to it and is also much shorter. Again, the virtuosity of the performer is exploited in this movement. The movement opens with the tutti or orchestra theme:

The solo theme begins on the last half of the fourth beat of the twelfth measure:

NOTICE:
a. That the rhythm has a definite feeling of four pulses to the measure.

b. The rhythmic syncopation of the solo oboe part in the fourth solo section of the movement (measures 57-64).

c. That this final movement consists of six presentations of the orchestral tutti alternating with five presentations of the solo theme played by the oboe.

d. That the solo oboe plays with the orchestra in the tutti passages.

e. That the movement begins with the orchestra theme.

f. That the orchestra theme begins on the first beat in measure 1 but in measure 2 this same rhythmic and melodic pattern begins on the third beat. What does this do to the rhythm? What happens to the accent?

338

g. That the solo theme is actually an ascending and descending D minor scale. The last three sixteenth notes in each beat of the ascending pattern are a type of ornamentation.

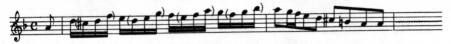

h. That the third orchestral tutti is a sequential repetition of the first orchestral tutti but a fifth higher.
i. That the fourth orchestral tutti is also a sequential repetition of the first orchestral tutti, this time a third higher.
j. The final orchestral tutti is a repetition of the final section of the first orchestral tutti.
k. The homophonic texture of the harmonization of measures 13-22, 39-52 and 66-68, while the rest of the movement uses polyphonic texture.
l. The effectiveness of the cembalo in establishing the effect of chordal harmony in the above listed measures (measures 13-22, 39-52 and 66-68).

The Concerto Grosso

The *concerto grosso*, the most important orchestral form preceding the classical symphony, reached its height of development during the late seventeenth and eighteenth centuries. The *concerto grosso* adapted elements from the chamber sonata as well as from the church sonata for the larger orchestral body, which at this time consisted mainly of string instruments. In the *concerto grosso* the composer wrote for not just one soloist but for a combination of soloists which might consist of keyboard, strings, winds or any combination of these instruments. This group of soloists was used by the composer as a contrast or foil to the larger orchestral body. In short, the composer arranged an antiphonal dialogue between the large group and the small group. The small group of soloists, usually three, was known as the *concertino* while the main body of the orchestra was called the *concerto grosso*. The main body of the orchestra was also known as the *ripieno*.

In time the form used for this particular combination of *concertino* and *ripieno* also became known as the *concerto grosso*. The form of the *concerto grosso* consisted of a series of movements contrasting in spirit, tempo and character. Movements were sometimes of dancelike character and it was not at all unusual to find minuets, gavottes or gigues inserted between movements marked *andante, allegro* or *largo*. These dances were based on the principle of contrast. The other movements, patterned after the church sonata, were usually fugal, and in this instance the main principle was that of repetition and variation.

The two instrumental bodies, the *concertino* and *ripieno*, were contrasted, one to the other, by the volume of sound possible to each group.

Another contrast, that of tonal quality, was also evident between the two groups. In later compositions a third kind of contrast evolved through the introduction of contrasting musical material for the *concertino* and the *ripieno*.

Among the finest *concerti grossi* written during the period were those composed by Arcangelo Corelli (1653-1713), George Frideric Handel (1685-1759), and Johann Sebastian Bach (1685-1750). As one studies the *concerti grossi* of Handel and the Brandenburg Concertos of Bach, it becomes apparent that in form and spirit these works are closer to the modern symphony than they are to the concerto.

LISTENING ACTIVITY

Concerto Grosso, Op. 6 No. 2
in F Major..............................George Frideric Handel (1685-1759)

In this work, representative of Handel at his greatest, the scoring is exclusively for string instruments. The soloist group, or *concertino*, consists of two violins and cello while the orchestra group, called the *concerto grosso* or *ripieno*, consists of first and second violins, violas, cellos and string basses. The form of this work is extended through the use of four contrasting movements. Each movement is based on a single theme with the exception of the final movement which utilizes two themes, one of which is treated fugally.

Each of the themes is treated alternately by the orchestral body and the solo group. In this way contrast in dynamic levels is attained. Harmonies are extremely simple and key contrast is kept at a minimum. There is no particular exploitation of technical facility for members of the *concertino*, although the use of certain ornamentations considered to be characteristic of the baroque era require a rather high degree of technical facility if the expressive purpose of the music is to be realized. It is important to remember that in this particular work the two groups are treated mainly as contrasting dynamic groups.

What to listen for:

Andante larghetto *(First movement)*

NOTE: a. The theme of this movement:

      b. That this theme is announced in unison by the first violin of the *concertino* group and the first violins of the *ripieno* group.

      c. That at this same place the second violin of the *concertino* group and the second violins of the *ripieno* play this part in unison:

      d. That while the meter of this movement is marked 4/4, there is a feeling of eight beats to the measure.

      e. The rhythmic variety in this movement.

      f. The effect of the first entrance of the *concertino* group in measure 4 and the contrast created by the entrance of the *ripieno* group in measure 6.

g. The subsequent alternation of *concertino* and *ripieno* groups.

h. That in this movement the function of the *ripieno* is not that of accompanying the *concertino* group.

i. The use of baroque ornamentation such as trills, turns and broken scale passages in this movement.

j. That the movement ends with a four-measure *adagio* section.

k. The change of key in these final four measures from F major to A major, the dominant of D minor, the key of the second movement.

Allegro *(Second movement)*

NOTICE: a. That the initial statement of the theme is given by the *concertino* group.

b. That the theme is:

c. The manner in which this theme is passed from first to second violin and from the *concertino* to the *ripieno* group.

d. That this spritely movement moves in a quick four beats to the measure.

e. The effect of the first and second violins of the *concertino* group playing the melody in thirds.

f. The effect created by having the theme played by the bass instruments as compared to the theme played by the treble instruments.

g. The ornamentation of the melodic line through the use of such devices as turns, trills and change of figuration.

h. The composer's use of rhythmic contrast in the final six measures, which changes the mood from one of rather vigorous movement to one of calmness.

i. That the movement is brought to its conclusion through the use of a two-measure *adagio*.

Largo *(Third movement)*

NOTE: a. The noble and dignified theme on which the movement is based:

b. That the movement begins with the statement of this theme played by both the *concertino* and *ripieno* groups.

c. However, that in the second, fourth and sixth measures the theme is played by only the first and second violins in the *concertino* group.

341

d. The use of dotted eighth and sixteenth notes in the rhythmic construction of the theme.

e. The change of pace and mood beginning in measure 10, a section marked *Larghetto andante e piano*.

f. That this section moves with a calmness and even flow because of the use of even eighth notes.

g. The subsequent alternating of these two contrasting sections.

h. That this movement is brought to its conclusion by the use of a two-measure *adagio* which ends in the key of C major, the dominant of the key of F major, the key of the final movement.

Allegro, ma non troppo *(Fourth movement)*

NOTICE: a. The robust character of this movement.

b. The fugal statement or subject with which the movement opens:

c. That there are three entrances of the fugal subject.

d. How the fugal subject develops into the countersubject.

e. The contrapuntal working out of the fugue.

f. The abrupt change of dynamics in measure 27 and the introduction of the second theme in measure 28, a four-note melody given in dotted half notes:

2nd Violin (Concertino)   1st Violin (Concertino)

g. That this melody is first played by the second violin of the *concertino* group and is repeated immediately a fourth higher by the first violin of the *concertino*.

h. That the harmonic texture of this section is homophonic rather than polyphonic:

i. The return of the fugal subject in measure 40 played by the cellos and string basses.

j. The return of the four-note second theme in measure 54 played by the violas and cellos.

k. In measure 66 the coming together of these two themes, the basses playing the four-note second theme while the treble instruments play the original fugue theme.

l. That following the pattern of the first three movements the fourth movement ends with a short *adagio* section.

The Classical Sonata

It is understandable that people are often confused by the term "sonata." At first glance it seems to be an all-purpose, all-inclusive term without specific reference to any one musical outlet. A pianist, in concert, performs the *Sonata in B♭ Major for Pianoforte* by Franz Schubert (1797-1828); a celebrated violinist and pianist appear together and play the *Sonata in A for Violin and Piano* by César Franck (1822-1890); a clarinetist appears with a symphony orchestra playing the *Concerto in A Major for Clarinet and Orchestra* by W. A. Mozart (1756-1791), and the program notes refer to it as being in sonata form; or an orchestra plays the *Symphony No. 5 in C Minor* by Ludwig van Beethoven (1770-1827) and again it is pointed out that the first movement of this work makes use of the sonata form. What then is a sonata? Is it a musical work for only one instrument? Is it a composition for two or more instruments? Or does the term "sonata" have something to do with the overall form of a musical composition? The answer to each of these questions is, of course, yes. The sonata is, at one and the same time, an extended musical work intended to be performed by one or more instruments, and it is a description of the formal structural organization of the first movement and sometimes other movements of this extended work. A sonata may be written for one instrument alone, for two instruments, for three instruments, for four instruments, or for any number of instruments up to and including the symphony orchestra. In each case the special title given to the sonata for the special grouping of instruments derives from the number of instruments involved—trio, quartet, concerto, symphony.

In each instance there is a common denominator. The sonata, whether solo or for a group of instruments, will be an extended musical work having several contrasting movements, generally three or four. The idea for the contrasting tempo arrangements for these movements—fast-slow-fast—actually derived from the early operatic overtures. Around the time of Franz Joseph Haydn (1732-1809), a dance, usually the minuet, was added as a fourth movement to the usual three movements found in the pre-classical concerto. The several movements of this new sonata form were then arranged somewhat in this order:

First movement	*Tempo fast*	Structure involved and intricate.
Second movement	*Tempo slow*	Usually marked *Andante* or *Adagio*. Songlike and lyric. The structure either two- or three-part song form—that is, A B or, if with a return of the first theme, A B A.

343

Third movement	*Tempo lively*	Rhythmic, lively dance. Until the time of Beethoven the usual dance was the minuet. The *scherzo* which Beethoven introduced as the third movement for his sonatas had, in addition to lively rhythmic qualities, the quality of jovial good humor.
Fourth movement	*Tempo fast*	Often marked *Allegro molto* or *Vivace.* As in the first movement the structural principle may be involved and elaborate.

The second identifying, and possibly the most important characteristic of the sonata is the structural organization of its first movement. This structural organization is sometimes also used as the basis for manipulating the musical material of the fourth movement. Basically the first movement form, to be designated as sonata allegro form, is a large A B A type of structure. The first or A section, called the *exposition*, is based on at least two thematic ideas which employ the principle of contrast to identify them. These two themes are contrasted rhythmically, melodically and harmonically. The B section, known as the *development*, uses the variation principle in that the themes originally stated in the A section are broken into fragments and are stated and restated in all possible ways. While the variation principle is used mainly in this section, the principles of repetition and contrast are also employed. In the third section, known as the *recapitulation*, there is a restatement of the A or *exposition* section which brings a final unity to the work. Because of the importance of the use of contrasting themes as a structural principle in the construction of the first movement of a sonata, melody now became pre-eminent and received the emphasis. The old practice of writing around a *basso continuo* disappeared.

There were two important developments during the late eighteenth and early nineteenth centuries which led to the ascendency of the classical sonata and to the consequent decline of the *concerto grosso* to a subordinate role. The first of these was the shift of emphasis from the vocal to the instrumental forms of expression. The classical sonata, developed in the latter part of the eighteenth century, has remained the principal vehicle for abstract instrumental writing up to and including contemporary times.

Also important, in fact necessary, in the growth and development of the sonata was the establishment of the major-minor system of tonality which formed the basis of much of the writing of the late eighteenth- and nineteenth-century composers. Intensive study of the writings of eighteenth-century composers reveals that during the entire eighteenth century there was a continuous and intense concentration on the problem of key relationships. This came to a head with the perfecting of the theory of the well-tempered scale. Even the technics of modulation and transposition were the results of what were considered to be quite daring experiments. All of these experiments culminated in the latter half of the eighteenth century in the successful crystallization of the classical sonata form which furnished the basis for so much writing of the two masters, Franz Joseph Haydn (1732-1809) and Wolfgang Amadeus Mozart (1756-1791).

Franz Joseph Haydn was particularly important in bringing the classical sonata to its ultimate development and maturity. He perfected the structural principles of the sonata—the basis for the sonata, concerto and symphony. Haydn, through this structural organization, has been a continuous influence on every succeeding composer using the sonata form for the expression of his own musical ideas. Haydn might also be said to be the father of the modern symphony orchestra. He conceived of the orchestra in terms of its different instrumental families, each with its own individual and characteristic tonal color. In Haydn's orchestra the string family became the chief protagonist or nucleus for the group. Around it the tonal, dynamic and coloristic potential of the orchestra was expanded through the addition of the brass, woodwind and percussion families. In Haydn's hands the symphony and sonata form became a harmonic and instrumental entity completely satisfying within itself. If for no other reason, Haydn will long be remembered for having brought into sharp focus the difference between chamber and orchestra music. His writing for the string quartet brought this instrumental type to a perfection recognized to this day.

Texturally the late seventeenth and early eighteenth centuries also saw a shift in harmonic design. Before this period the element of harmony was achieved largely through the polyphonic treatment of the music. In the early vocal writing, such as the mass, motet, madrigal and even in many of the oratorios, which involved singing in parts, the harmony resulted from the lateral movement of the voices, or in simpler terms, from one voice or melody moving against another one. Only in the chorale was the principle of homophony apparent. Here harmony resulted from the up-and-down arrangement of chords which served to give harmonic background for each single note of the melody. This latter form of harmonization, known as homophony, now furnished the basis for much of the sonata writing, rather than the more complex polyphony found in the earlier instrumental works. This does not mean, however, that the practice of using polyphony was completely abandoned in sonata writing. Many composers used contrapuntal devices and technics to expand the musical material in other movements besides the first.

It is now time to look more closely at the movements of the sonata and to observe in detail the structural principles involved. Subsequent listening to examples of this form will be more meaningful if a knowledge and an understanding of these structural principles can be kept in mind.

First movement—*usually in a fast tempo.*

Introduction

Optional. If included it would probably be slow to contrast with the *allegro* or fast-paced movement of the main body of the first movement.

Exposition

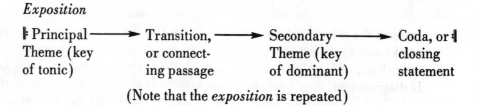

‖ Principal ⟶ Transition, ⟶ Secondary ⟶ Coda, or ‖
Theme (key   or connect-   Theme (key   closing
of tonic)   ing passage   of dominant)   statement

(Note that the *exposition* is repeated)

Development

The working over in various ways of the material found in the *exposition*. The theme may be played in its entirety, or figures taken from the theme, and then both freely modulated and transposed to other keys. Other technics such as inverting the theme may also be used. This section of the sonata is sometimes referred to as the *fantasia* section. Through the manipulation of the material in this section the composer gives free reign to his imagination. The results reveal in great measure his technical facility and even the presence of, or lack of, genius.

Recapitulation

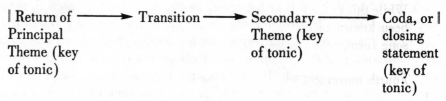

‖ Return of ⟶ Transition ⟶ Secondary ⟶ Coda, or ‖
Principal   Theme (key   closing
Theme (key   of tonic)   statement
of tonic)   (key of
                                                tonic)

(Note that the *recapitulation* is not repeated)

There is a minor variation in this pattern if the tonic key of the work is in minor. Here, the secondary theme in the *exposition* is apt to be in the relative major followed by a transition to the closing statement. In the *recapitulation* the secondary theme is in the key of the tonic but is usually followed by a connecting passage into the final closing statement.

346

Second movement—*usually a slow movement to contrast with the faster first movement.*

It has already been pointed out that this movement is lyric (songlike) in its construction. In form it often makes use of the two-part (A B) or three-part (A B A) song form. The theme with a set of variations may also be used in the handling of the musical material of the second movement. Some composers have even continued the use of the sonata allegro or first movement form for this movement.

Third movement—*lively and dancelike. Usually in the form of a minuet or scherzo.*

In form the third movement falls into three large structural units which are known as the principal song, trio, and restatement of the principal song. Each of these three large sections in turn consists of three parts. If diagrammed, third movement form would look this way:

Principal Song

‖: A ——————————————————— :‖ *(Repeated)*
‖: B —————————— A ————————— :‖ *(Repeated)*

Trio

‖: C ——————————————————— :‖ *(Repeated)*
‖: D —————————— C ————————— :‖ *(Repeated)*

Da Capo (Restatement of *Principal Song*)

‖ A ——————— B ——————— A ——————— ‖ *(Not repeated)*

While this is the form usually found for this movement, composers have been known to use other forms such as simple two-part or three-part song form, or a theme with a set of variations for the third movement.

Fourth movement—*lively, in allegro or allegro vivace tempo.*

Very often one of the *rondo* forms is used for this movement. In the *rondo* there is a principal theme which will alternate with one, two, or three secondary themes. There are several variations of *rondo* structures, each being based on the number of secondary themes used. The *first rondo* form has but two themes (A B A), the *second rondo* form has three themes (A B A C A), while the *third rondo* form has four themes (A B A C A D A).

347

Sometimes the sonata allegro or first movement form is used for this final movement, but it may be somewhat varied in structure and may not be as involved as when used in the first movement. Again, a theme with a set of variations may be the organizational structure for the fourth movement of a sonata.

Brief mention should be made of *cyclic* treatment. In cyclic treatment the composer constructs all of the movements out of the same musical material, or material which derives from the principal musical material. In this instance, even though the material may be the same, the manner of manipulating the musical material will vary from movement to movement according to the dictates of the particular movement. Well-known examples of the use of cyclic writing are to be found in the *Symphony No. 5 in C Minor* by Ludwig van Beethoven (1770-1827), *Symphony in D Minor* by César Franck (1822-1890), *Symphonie Fantastique* by Hector Berlioz (1803-1869). The use of leitmotivs is found in *Der Ring des Nibelungen* by Richard Wagner (1813-1883).

LISTENING ACTIVITY

Three examples of the sonata form are suggested—a symphony, a concerto for solo instrument and orchestra, and a sonata for two solo instruments. Particular attention should be paid to the structural organization of the first movement in each of these works, as well as the contrasting moods and technics used in the succeeding movements.

Symphony No. 94 in G Major, "The Surprise"...............Franz Joseph Haydn
(1732-1809)

Haydn is thought to have composed approximately 104 symphonies, but only twelve of them, known as the "London Symphonies," really represent Haydn at his greatest. This set of twelve symphonies received its name because all twelve were written for a series of London concerts. Before Haydn came to England for these concerts, a great deal of his orchestral writing had been for small groups consisting mostly of strings. The bulk of this music was written for and used at the lavish dinner parties given by his prince—music which today might be classed as dinner music. In England, however, he found a new experience waiting for him: a larger orchestra containing forty-one instrumentalists with flutes, oboes, bassoons, trumpets and percussion in addition to the usual strings. The *Symphony No. 94 in G Major*, or the "Surprise Symphony," is one of the better known of this set of twelve symphonies carrying the generic title of "London Symphonies." It receives its name from the sudden *fortissimo* chord played by full orchestra in the sixteenth measure of the second movement. This chord, coming in the midst of a *pianissimo* section, is said to have been Haydn's way of writing a musical joke. At the same time it would serve to waken members of the audience who made a practice of settling down to take a little nap during the playing of slow movements.

348

Symphony No. 94 in G Major

Franz Joseph Haydn (1732-1809)

350

351

352

Coda

Part I (Part III on the D. C.) A

III

Menuetto Allegro molto

B

Bassoon

A

Part II C

Trio

D

C

Men. D.C.

Part I
A Theme

IV

Finale Allegro molto

354

355

What to listen for:

Adagio cantabile—Vivace assai *(First movement)*

1. NOTICE: a. The slow introduction with which the movement begins—a characteristic of Haydn's writings.
    b. The musical dialogue between the woodwind and string groups in this introduction.
    c. That while the movement is marked 3/4, there is an underlying feeling of six beats to the measure.
    d. The change of mood in the *Vivace assai* from that in the slow, dignified introduction.
    e. That while the *Vivace assai* is marked 6/8, it moves in two beats to the measure.
    f. The three large divisions of the movement—the *exposition,* the *development* and the *recapitulation.*
    g. The principal theme of the *exposition.* Learn to sing it so that it can be easily recognized when heard.
    h. The manner in which Haydn has used ornamentation to give interest in the passage-work following the statement of the principal theme. List some of the devices used by Haydn for ornamentation.
    i. The subordinate theme of the *exposition* and the fact that it does not have the strength of the principal theme.
    j. That the subordinate theme is written in the key of D major which is the dominant of G major.
    k. The third or coda theme which is repeated with embellishments.
    l. That the *exposition* section is repeated.
    m. That the *development* is a simple, uncomplicated rehashing of the two themes of the *exposition.*
    n. The modulation to other keys in the *development.*
    o. The doubling of the first violin melody by the first oboe and the first flute.
    p. The effect of writing the melody in octaves in measures 110-114.
    q. That the restatement of the principal theme in the *recapitulation* is played by the first violins, with the first flute playing the melody one octave higher.
    r. That the restatement of the subordinate theme in the *recapitulation* is now in the key of G major rather than its original D major.
    s. That the coda is also in the key of G major.
    t. The simple harmonization of this first movement.
    u. The homophonic rather than polyphonic texture of this harmony.
    v. The use of the string family as the nucleus of the orchestra.
    w. The effective use of flutes, oboes, bassoons, trumpets and percussion in increasing the expressive potential of the orchestra.

2. Follow the one-line score as the music is being played, paying particular attention to the large structural organization of the movement.

Andante *(Second movement)*

1. NOTE: a. The charming, folklike character of this simple melody.
    b. That the "surprise" is created by a sudden contrast between *pianissimo* and *fortissimo.*

356

c. That the form of this movement is a theme with a set of four variations plus a coda. Learn to sing this theme so that it can be easily recognized when heard.

d. That the theme actually consists of two melodies—Theme A (measures 1-16) and Theme B (measures 17-32).

e. That Theme A is played in its entirety by strings with the exception of the final chord—the surprise—in measure 16 which is played by the full orchestra.

f. That the woodwinds and horns join with the strings on the repetition of the B theme.

g. That the second violins and violas play the melody in Variation I while the first violins and flute play an ornamentation around and over the theme.

h. That Variation II is in C minor, the parallel minor to the key of the original theme.

i. That Variation III returns to the major.

j. That the oboe plays the melody but in this variation plays two notes for every one in the original theme.

k. The accompaniment furnished by the strings for Variation III.

l. That trumpets and horns play the theme in Variation IV, while first violins play a running arpeggiated passage and the rest of the strings play great chords on the second half of each beat.

m. The coda and the manner in which it brings the movement to its quiet ending.

2. Follow the one-line score as the music is being played, paying particular attention to the large structural organization of the movement.

Minuetto—Allegro molto *(Third movement)*

1. NOTICE:
   a. The mood of good humor which seems to characterize this movement.
   b. That it has qualities which relate it both to the dance and to the concert hall.
   c. That the three large divisions of this movement are: the *principal song* (Part I), the *trio* (Part II), and the repeat of the *principal song* (Part III).
   d. The number of times when the first violin melody is doubled by the flute playing one octave higher.
   e. The effect in the first strain of the trio when the first violins and the bassoon play the same melody in octaves.
   f. That on the *da capo*, or the return to the *principal song*, there are no repeats of the individual sections.

2. Follow the one-line score as the music is being played, paying particular attention to the structural organization of this movement.

Finale—Allegro molto *(Fourth movement)*

1. NOTE:
   a. That the movement is written in *first rondo* form, that is, A B A.
   b. That there is no development section but rather a first and last section with a short free episode in the middle.
   c. The vivacious mood of this movement.
   d. That the first or A theme dominates the movement.
   e. The contrasting style of the B theme.

  f. The use of the woodwind family in this movement.

  g. That the horns and trumpets seem to be used to reinforce the harmonic structure.

2. Follow the one-line score as the music is being played, paying particular attention to the large structural organization of the movement.

Concerto in E Minor for Violin and Orchestra.................Felix Mendelssohn
(1809-1847)

This brilliant concerto, romantic in feeling, is undoubtedly one of the all-time favorites of the literature available for the violin. It is also considered to be one of the great examples of the concerto form. It was written in 1844 when the composer was thirty-five years of age. It is a work of great lyric beauty and vitality. The music makes considerable demands on the performer's technical virtuosity as well as his tonal powers. It is written in the regular three-movement pattern.

What to listen for:

Allegro molto appassionata *(First movement)*

NOTICE: a. That the instrumentation for the accompaniment uses two flutes, two oboes, two clarinets, two bassoons, two horns, two trumpets, timpani and strings.

  b. The very short introduction of one and one-half measures, played by strings, clarinets and bassoons, which leads into the announcement of the principal theme played by the solo violin.

  c. That the movement is divided into three large sections, the *exposition*, the *development* and the *recapitulation*.

  d. The principal theme:

  e. That underneath this melody there is an undulating accompaniment played by first violins, second violins and violas.

  f. The passage work played by the solo violin which leads into a tutti performance of this theme by the orchestra.

  g. That following the tutti there is a transitional passage played by oboes and first violins, with the remaining woodwind instruments furnishing the harmonic background:

  h. The demonstration of pyrotechnics as the soloist rushes up and down the strings.

  i. That the subordinate theme is played first by the first clarinet over a pedal tone played by the solo violin:

358

j. That after eight measures this subordinate theme is taken over by the solo violin.

k. That the *development* section is an exciting give-and-take between the solo and the orchestral accompaniment using parts of the first theme.

l. That the *development* is brought to its conclusion with a brilliant *cadenza*.

m. That a *cadenza* is an ornate passage for solo instrument or voice. It is inserted into the work to demonstrate the technical virtuosity of the performer. Normally the orchestra is silent during the playing of the *cadenza* so that the soloist, in a figurative sense, may have the center of the stage to display his artistic wares.

n. That this *cadenza* leads back into the principal theme played in unison by the first violins and first oboe and doubled by the first flute one octave higher, while the solo violin plays a series of arpeggiated ornamentations.

o. That the *recapitulation* which follows is in the same key as the principal theme.

p. The brilliant *coda* with which the movement ends.

q. The holding note played by the bassoon which joins the first and second movements together. (Generally there is a break or pause between movements.)

Andante *(Second movement)*

NOTE: a. That this movement opens with an eight-measure introduction played by the strings and woodwinds.

b. The beautiful, lyric melody on which this movement is constructed:

c. That this melody is played by the solo violin over an accompaniment played by the strings in the orchestra.

d. The effect of the 6/8 rhythm.

e. That the middle section of the movement has a feeling of restlessness—almost a feeling of foreboding.

f. That the solo violin helps to create this mood of agitation in the middle section.

g. The return of the peaceful first theme, again played by the solo violin.

h. The broken chord accompaniment written in sixteenth notes and played by the strings in this section.

i. That the overall form of this second movement is simple three-part song form or A B A.

j. The *fermata*, or hold, on the last note of the movement which serves as a means for leading directly into the last movement.

Allegretto non troppo—Allegro molto vivace *(Fourth movement)*

NOTICE: a. That the movement begins with a fourteen-measure *allegretto* which might be considered a short *interlude*.

359

b. That the melody played by the solo violin is expressive because it is lyric and songlike:

c. That there is movement but that it is a comfortable four beats to the measure and not too fast.
d. That this interlude is played by the solo violin accompanied by the strings of the orchestra.
e. That this interlude leads without break into the third movement proper which is marked *Allegro molto vivace.*
f. That the movement is fast and spirited.
g. That there is a feeling of two pulses or beats to the measure.
h. That the movement opens with a passage, played by trumpets, horns, oboes, bassoons and timpani, reminiscent of a fanfare and interrupted four times by an upward rushing figure played by the solo violin.
i. That the principal theme, an impish tune, is first announced by the solo violin over a light staccato accompaniment played by the woodwinds:

j. The pizzicato accompaniment played by the strings of the orchestra.
k. That the subordinate theme is introduced first by the entire orchestra and then eight measures later by the solo violin:

l. That while this is a contrasting theme, it still has the same sparkling, vivacious mood of the principal theme. This has been called a "cheeky" theme by Sir Donald Tovey.
m. The alternating of these two themes in the remainder of the movement.
n. That this movement has "first movement form": There is an *exposition,* a *development* and a *recapitulation.*
o. That following the *recapitulation* there is a *coda* of dazzling virtuosity, based primarily on the secondary theme, which brings the movement and the work to a close.

Sonata in A Major for Violin and Piano.........................César Franck
(1822-1890)

This sonata is not only considered to be representative of César Franck at his best but also one of the finest and most moving works ever written for the combination of violin and piano. Along with the *Symphony in D Minor,* the *String Quartet,* the *Piano Quintet in F Minor,* the oratorio *The Beatitudes* and the *Symphonic Variations for Piano and Orchestra,* the *Sonata in A* offers eloquent testimony to the musical genius of Franck. In the sonata there is more than a little suggestion of the impressionism of Claude Debussy which was yet to come.

The *Sonata in A* is a sonata written in four movements. It is somewhat different from the conventional sonata in that its most important movement is its second movement, not the first as one would normally expect. In the four movements of this sonata is to be found a prime example of the use of cyclic treatment of musical material. Careful listening and analysis will reveal that Franck made use of the same germinal musical idea in each of the four movements.

It would be helpful in developing an understanding of the structural principles used in the construction of this sonata if the listener would make use of the piano score.

What to listen for:

Allegretto ben moderato *(First movement)*

1. What is the mood of this movement?
2. What is the overall form of this movement?
3. Identify the three large divisions of the movement.
4. Identify the principal theme when played.
5. Identify the subordinate theme when played.
6. Which instrument plays each theme?
7. Is the harmonization of this movement simpler, the same or more complex than the harmonization of the first movement of the Haydn *Surprise Symphony?* Why?
8. Does the movement end with a short coda or codetta?
9. The movement is marked 9/8. How many pulses to the measure does the listener actually feel?

Allegro *(Second movement)*

1. What is the mood of this movement?
2. Why should this second movement be considered the most important movement of this sonata?
3. How many main themes are used in the construction of this movement?
4. Is the first theme heard in the piano introduction?
5. What is the overall form of this movement?
6. The final section of this movement consists of twenty-six measures. What would this section be called? What is its function?
7. What part or parts of this movement are reminiscent of the first movement, that is, make use of melodic ideas in the construction of the second movement which were found in the first movement?
8. What is the rhythm of the movement?
9. Note the use and effect of chromatic writing in the melody and in the harmony.
10. Is the harmonization of the movement simple or complex?

Recitativo-Fantasia *(Third movement)*

1. Compared to other third movements, in what way is the structure of this movement somewhat different?
2. What is the meaning of the term *recitativo?*
3. What is the meaning of the term *fantasia?*
4. How do these two terms contribute to the irregularity of form in this movement?
5. Identify the cyclic motive as it appears in this movement.

6. The movement is marked in *alla breve* time. Note, however, that during the course of the movement the number of pulses per measure seems to change. In the opening there is a definite feeling of four pulses to the measure, toward the middle of the movement the feeling changes to two pulses to the measure, while the final seven measures return to the feeling of four pulses per measure.

Allegretto poco mosso *(Fourth movement)*

1. The use of the recurring theme in this final movement identifies the overall form of the movement as being one of the *rondo* forms. As the movement is played identify each return of the rondo theme.
2. How many times does this rondo theme recur?
3. In the statement of the rondo theme the violin plays the same identical melody as the piano but two beats later. What is this form of writing called?
4. Is the same device used each time the rondo theme reappears?
5. What is the mood of this final movement?
6. Rhythmically, does this movement have a feeling of two or four pulses to the measure?
7. Identify the use of the cyclic motive in this movement.
8. Would the use of the canon in constructing the rondo theme indicate homophonic or polyphonic harmonic texture?
9. In considering the entire sonata, was the cyclic motive easy to identify and follow as it was recast in each of the movements?
10. What is one result of using cyclic writing in the construction of a sonata, concerto or symphony?

SUGGESTED RECORDINGS

Passacaglia and Fugue in C Minor............Johann Sebastian Bach (1685-1750)
Toccata and Fugue in D Minor...............Johann Sebastian Bach (1685-1750)
Fugues from *The Well-Tempered Clavier*.......Johann Sebastion Bach (1685-1750)
Polka and Fugue from *Schwanda, The Bagpiper*.....Jaromir Weinberger (1896——)
Suite No. 1 in C for Orchestra and Suite No. 2 in
    B Minor for Flute and Strings.............Johann Sebastian Bach (1685-1750)
Sonata in A for Strings........................Tommaso Albinoni (1674-1745)
Sonata for Trumpet and Strings...................Arcangelo Corelli (1653-1713)
Sonata in D for Cello and Piano.................Arcangelo Corelli (1653-1713)
Concerto in D for Violin and Strings.............Tommaso Albinoni (1674-1745)
Concerto for Violin and Orchestra...................Antonio Vivaldi (1675-1741)
Concerti Grossi, Op. 6...........................Arcangelo Corelli (1653-1713)
Concerto Grosso No. 1 for Strings and Piano............Ernest Bloch (1880-1959)
Symphony No. 40 in G Minor......................W. A. Mozart (1756-1791)
Symphony No. 5 in C Minor................Ludwig van Beethoven (1770-1827)
    (Cyclic form)
Symphony No. 1 in C Major........................Georges Bizet (1838-1875)
Symphony in D Minor.............................César Franck (1822-1890)
    (Cyclic form)
Classical Symphony in D..........................Serge Prokofiev (1891-1953)
Concerto in A Minor for Piano and Orchestra.......Robert Schumann (1810-1856)
Concerto No. 3 for Piano and Orchestra.................Béla Bartók (1881-1945)
Concerto No. 1 in A Minor for Piano and Orchestra..Edward MacDowell (1861-1908)
Sonata in C for Violin and Piano (K. 296).............W. A. Mozart (1756-1791)
Sonata in Bb for Piano...........................Franz Schubert (1797-1828)
Sonata for Cello and Piano.......................Samuel Barber (1910——)

362

unit 6

Music of the secular

vocal forms

chapter 9

The Secular Vocal Forms

Someone has said that all music is but a reflection of singing and that instruments are but artificial voices which provide for a change of timbre and give wider ranges in dynamics and pitches. We believe that song was probably the earliest form of human music. We have seen in an earlier unit the intimate connection between man and his music in the use of the folk song. We have further discussed the use of song to heighten the religious experience of man when it is incorporated into the liturgy of the church. In the preceding units there has been more than a little indication that during the first sixteen centuries of the Christian era almost the entire development of music continued along vocal lines.

It is now time to note that despite the importance attached to the development of sacred music, as seen in Unit Four, there was at the same time a parallel and equally important development of secular music. The rise of the secular music forms was, and has continued to be, of equal importance to the growth and development of sacred music.

As a starting point, it might be well to refer back to Unit Two for a short review of the role of folk music in the expression of human emotions and aspirations. We also saw that folk music sometimes acted in lieu of the newspaper or other mass communications media in chronicling the events of the day. With these types of subject matter as the basis for song, it becomes readily apparent that this subject matter is going to treat of secular subjects more often than not. It should also be remembered that this music was passed along from one generation to another by word of mouth and was not composed and set down on paper.

365

Composed music outside of the church first flourished in the days of the troubadours, the trouvères, the minnesingers and the meistersingers, who carried on their activities chiefly during the eleventh and twelfth centuries. In the twelfth century in particular, there swept across Europe a wave of romantic emotionalism that found release through the composition of poetry and music rich in emotional content. This gave great impetus to the increasing interest in secular forms of musical expression. This emotionalism seems to have been the direct result of three diverse yet interrelated developments. The first of these stemmed from the new contacts Europeans were now making with the peoples of the East and with their highly developed cultures. A second influence contributing to this wave of emotionalism was the Moorish conquest of Spain. Finally, the whole history of the various Crusades, with their high mission of liberating the Holy Land from the sinful hands of pagan conquerors, pointed in the direction of emotionalism. From these influences grew an awareness of and an interest in beauty and refinement. This in turn led to an interest in the cultivation of music and poetry as distinct entities in themselves.

Groups of men, born of both high and low estate, traveled from village to village and from country to country reading their poems and singing their songs. These were the troubadours and the trouvères in France and the minnesingers and meistersingers of Germany. These men devoted their lives and their talents to writing music which extolled the beauty of the ladies, told of the exploits of the knights and their chivalry, or told in great narrations the deeds of men and their gods. Since these men often turned to popular subjects outside of the church, and since much of the writing stemmed from a reaction against the strict discipline of church music, music which was thought to be monotonous and lacking in beauty, it is easy to see why this new music caught the popular fancy. One can also see that it would bring down the wrath of the clergy who would claim that it was "profane" writing. An important by-product of this disapproval by the clergy was that since the church largely controlled education during those times, the music that was taught was confined to the study of the then existing church music forms. This in turn forced the growth and development of secular music on the outside.

While the troubadour movement began in France, it was not long before its influence spread to include all Europe. Someone has referred to these wandering minstrels as the "beloved vagabonds of the thirteenth century" because of the manner in which they chronicled the events of the day as they passed from village to village and from country to country. In the course of their travels they shared their lot equally with those of high and low estate. Nightfall might find one of them the guest in a castle and the next night might find him in the hut of a lowly peasant. Their stage might be in the village tavern, the town hall or a nobleman's castle. They were considered so necessary that their presence was practically required at some of the more elaborate ceremonies such as the dubbing of new knights, betrothal parties, weddings and even religious rites such as baptisms and funerals.

The troubadours were, for the most part, poets. Usually they composed the melodies for the poetry they had written, and originally they even sang their own songs. As time passed, however, it became the custom for the troubadour to engage itinerant musicians who were then trained to sing the compositions written by their employers. These assistants were known as *ménestrels* or *jongleurs*.

The music of these traveling bards and musicians was strongly influenced by the popular melodies of the day. This was one result of the turning from the strict discipline of church writing. Another result was a new-found freedom of rhythmic and harmonic elements. The new-found freedom and flexibility were evidenced also in the part writing of the period. The accompaniments for this music were usually played by small orchestras of stringed instruments.

From a background of folk song and the composed songs of the troubadours, the trouvères, the minnesingers and the meistersingers grew the entire concept of secular vocal writing as we know it today.

The Art Song

Although art songs and folk songs have developed side by side, important points of difference do exist.

> *The art song is generally set to a high order of lyric poetry instead of to a simple folk rhyme. Whereas the folk song is strophic in construction—that is, the tune is repeated over and over for successive stanzas—the art song, as often as not, follows the poem throughout, interpreting each new phrase and nuance of the verse. This type of song is known as* durchkomponiert, *or "composed throughout," and it naturally captures the mood of the various stanzas more intimately than does the strophic type of song. (There are many strophic art songs too, but by and large the through-composed type has predominated, particularly since the middle of the nineteenth century.)*[12]

Just what, then, is an art song? It is a secular vocal form which consists of three equally important ingredients: the song, the words and the accompaniment. The most skillful art song composers have always kept these three in perfect balance. A few of the nineteenth-century composers whose names stand out in this type of composition are Franz Schubert (1797-1828), Robert Schumann (1810-1856), Johannes Brahms (1833-1897), Hugo Wolf (1860-1903), Peter Ilyich Tchaikovsky (1840-1893) and Edvard Grieg (1843-1907).

Who Is Sylvia?.................................Franz Schubert (1797-1828)

This beautiful example of Schubert's great lyric skill provides an excellent introduction to the art song. It is an easy song to learn to sing. The text comes from *The Two Gentlemen of Verona* by William Shakespeare. The resulting union of great poetry, beautiful melody and complementary accompaniment offers a poetic tribute to the grace and charm of the heroine.

After the song has been sung, study the structural organization to learn how Schubert handled his musical material.

Who Is Sylvia?

Franz Schubert

mend   her?
kind - ness:
cel - ling,

Ho - ly,
To   her
She   ex -

fair _____ and _____ wise   is   she; _____
eyes _____ love _____ doth   re - pair, _____
cells _____ each _____ mor - tal   thing, _____

The
To
Up -

heav'ns such grace did   lend _____ her.
help him of his   blind - ness;
on the dull earth dwell - ing,

And

369

That   a - dor - ed   she   might ___
be -   ing ___ help'd ___ in - hab - its ___
To   her ___ gar - lands   let   us ___

be, ___   That   a - dor - ed
there, ___   Be - ing   help'd   in -
bring, ___   To   her   gar - lands

she   might ___ be.
hab - its ___ there.
let   us ___ bring.

RHYTHM: Note the insistent eighth-note pulsation in the treble or right-hand accompaniment against the ♪♪ ♩ ♩ in the bass or left-hand accompaniment. A strict tempo and a delicacy in the playing of this accompaniment should be maintained throughout the song.

MELODY: The melody is lyric or songlike. It has a range from D above middle C to E a major ninth above. With the exception of two skips of an octave, the melody is confined to stepwise progressions or small skips. Notice the repeated use of the downward moving melodic line. The emphasis of the melody is on fluency and beauty of melodic line; any distortion of tempo or tone will mar the expressiveness of the melody. The melody seems to have the power to pull additional meaning from the words of the text.

HARMONY: Schubert has placed this song in the harmonic setting of the Old English ballad, with the exception that the accompaniment of repeated chords is effectively varied by his harmonic skill. Note the frequent use of the seventh chord, change of key and altered members of chords in order to achieve harmonic variety.

FORM: "Who Is Sylvia?" is an example of strophic form in that the same identical melody is used for each of the three verses. The form of the melody itself might be analyzed as A A¹ B B¹.

None But the Lonely Heart.................Peter Ilyich Tchaikovsky (1840-1893)

Pity and sorrow made up much of Tchaikovsky's life. Many of his musical utterances reflect the unhappiness which was so much a part of his life. Few songs can equal in emotional expressiveness and intensity the sadness which is inherent in this song. The Tchaikovsky setting of this song is considered to be one of the finest musical settings of the poem written by Johann Wolfgang von Goethe (1749-1832).

Nur wer die Sehnsucht kennt

Nur wer die Sehnsucht kennt,
weiss, was ich leide!
Allein und abgetrennt von
aller Freude,
Seh' ich an's Firmament nach
jener Seite.
Ach! der mich liebt und kennt
ist in der Weite.
Nur wer die Sehnsucht kennt,
weiss, was ich leide!
Allein und abgetrennt von
aller Freude,
Allein und abgetrennt von
aller Freude!
Es schwindelt mir, es brennt
mein Eingeweide,
Nur wer die Sehnsucht kennt,
weiss, was ich leide!

After the song has been sung analyze it to determine how Tchaikovsky manipulated the musical material.

371

None But the Lonely Heart

Peter Ilyich Tchaikovsky

None but the lone - ly heart Can know my sad - ness;

— A - lone, and part - ed far From joy and glad - ness.

372

Heav'ns bound-less arch I see Spread out a - bove ___ me.

Ah! What a dis - tance drear To one who loves me!

None but the lone - ly heart Can know my

sad - ness; A - lone, and part - ed far From joy and

gladness, A-lone and part-ed far

From joy and glad-ness. My sen-ses fail,

A burn-ing fire de-vours me. None but the

lone-ly heart Can know my sad-ness.

RHYTHM: The tempo marking, *Andante non tanto*, means not to exaggerate the andante tempo. The movement is marked 4/4 and there is a feeling of four pulses to the measure. From the beginning the accompaniment consists of syncopated chords which have the effect of intensifying the feeling of emotional depression.

MELODY: There seems to be no bottom to the depths of woe as painted by this melody. In the introduction the composer sounds the heavy note of grief by having the melody leap downward an interval of a minor seventh, to be followed immediately by a descending major sixth. This poignant melody is repeated by the voice as it makes its first entrance. The melody uses an unusually large range from B immediately below middle C to E a major tenth above middle C. Ascending and descending scale passages, small skips, large skips and chromatically altered tones are all used in the construction of the melodic line. Contrast the regularity of rhythm in the melodic line with the syncopation of the accompaniment.

HARMONY: Contrary to popular opinion that happy songs are written in major mode and sad songs in minor mode, "None But the Lonely Heart" is written in C major (the original was written in Db). Tchaikovsky made liberal use of seventh and ninth chords to help achieve a dark and somber harmonization of this melody. Note also the effective use of chromatically altered individual members of chords, to achieve not only harmonic variety but also a harmony more expressive of the mood.

FORM: Introduction A Interlude B A C Codetta.

LISTENING ACTIVITY

The Erlking . . . . Franz Schubert (1797-1828)

When Schubert was seventeen he was introduced to the ballad "Der Erlkönig" by Johann Wolfgang von Goethe. It is said that he was greatly excited by the tale and that he immediately sat down and with great rapidity set the ballad to music in almost the same form as it is known today. The high drama of the ballad is heightened by music which in almost realistic terms paints for us a picture of the terror of the child, the wheedling voice of the Erlking and the voice of the father trying to soothe the frightened child. The incessant galloping triplets in octaves in the accompaniment not only suggest the galloping of the horse but they also inject a feeling of urgency to the entire scene.

The Erlking

Johann Wolfgang von Goethe
(1749-1832)

Who rideth so late through night and wind?
It is the father with his child.
He has the boy so safe in his arm,
He holds him tightly, he keeps him warm.

"My son, in terror why hidest thy face?"
"Oh, father, see, the Erlking is nigh!
The Erlking dreaded, with crown and robe."
"My son, 'tis but a streak of mist."

375

"My dearest child, come go with me!
Such merry games I'll play with thee.
For many gay flowers are blooming there,
And my mother has many golden robes for thee."

"My father, my father, and hearest thou not
What the Erlking whispers so soft in my ear?"
"Be quiet, oh, be quiet, my child;
'Tis but the dead leaves stirred by the wind."

"Come, lovely boy, wilt thou go with me?
My daughters fair shall wait on thee,
There my daughters lead in the revels each night,
They'll sing and they'll dance and they'll rock you to sleep."

"My father, my father, and seest thou not
The Erlking's daughters in yon dim spot?"
"My son, my son, I see, and I know
'Twas only the olden willows so gray."

"I love thee so, thy beauty has ravished my sense;
And willing or not, I will carry thee hence."
"My father, my father, now grasps he my arm,
The Erlking has seized me, he has done me harm!"

The father shudders, he rides like the wind,
He clasps to his bosom the pale sobbing child;
He reaches home with fear and dread;
Clasped in his arms—the child was dead.

English version by Arthur Westbrook[13]

RHYTHM: The piano accompaniment suggests the flying hoofs of the horse, the storm and the supernatural setting of the story. The meter is 4/4 and there is a feeling of four pulses to the measure, with each pulse having an undercurrent of three. The tempo, marked *Allegro,* is on the fast side. While the rhythm of the accompaniment emphasizes the triplet figure, the rhythm of the melody is based principally on the use of the dotted half, half, quarter and occasional eighth notes.

MELODY: The melody is in minor. As this is an example of *durchkomponiert* or "composed throughout" art song, the melody line is constantly varied as it describes the different episodes of the story. The song begins with the melodies being written in the lower and middle registers, but at the climax when the Erlking seizes the child, the intense emotional state is helped by writing the melody in a high register. Conjunct progression, both ascending and descending, and small skips are used for the most part in the construction of the melody.

HARMONY: Harmonic variety is achieved through frequent key changes. The harmonization itself is typical of the romantic harmonization used by Schubert. An interesting use of dissonance underlies the child's scream as the Erlking takes hold of him. This dissonant harmonization by Schubert serves to give the listener a realistic insight into the terror of this frightening episode almost as clearly as if he were there.

TIMBRE: Four different voices are associated with the interpretation of this song: the terrified child, the sinister Erlking, the harried father, and the narrator who tells the story. It is all, of course, sung by one soloist who must make a change in vocal timbre as he delineates each character.

FORM: *Durchkomponiert* or "composed throughout."

The Madrigal

The madrigal is a contrapuntal composition for several voices in which the text is derived from secular sources. One might say that the madrigal is to the secular vocal forms as the motet is to the sacred vocal forms. Musicologists have subdivided madrigals into different classifications such as the *madrigal proper*, the *ayre*, and the *ballett*, according to their degree of polyphony, their "fa-la-la" endings, their function in the dance, and whether they were published in part books for separate voices or in a large book containing all the parts. But for simplicity's sake this unit will consider that these subdivisions are, in reality, only a part of the large general definition.

Madrigals, as we know them, trace their ancestry back to the fourteenth century to the *frottola* and *villanella* types of vocal music which flourished in Venice, Florence and Rome. The *frottola* was a type of folk song whose melody was given a more or less artistic treatment by a musically educated composer. Both of these types of vocal music were invented by Italians, and Italian composers achieved great fame composing in this idiom.

The *frottola* and *villanella* came into being as a protest against the strict and involved rules of contrapuntal writing in vogue in France and the Netherlands. Many of these compositions drew their inspiration from the popular dance music of the day. Often the songs were light and gay in character as they sang of affairs of the heart. The soprano was usually given the prominent melody, with the other three parts, often played by instruments, treated as a type of contrapuntal accompaniment.

But it is easy to see why there would come a time when these high-grade folk songs or low-grade madrigals would cease to satisfy the demands

377

of the musical intelligentsia of the sixteenth century and would ultimately fall into disfavor. In Italy, during the sixteenth century, literary and musical leaders did react against this form, which they considered to be uncultured, and attempted a reform. This reform was effected by having some of the foremost musicians of the time take the old forms as a base and then impose on this base a new and more complex musical writing. In fact, the delight of this music came from the manipulation of the musical material rather than from its depth of expression. This was the madrigal. It was performance-oriented and one's greatest pleasure from it derived from actually singing one of the parts. Composers began to write expressly for performance by musicians or gifted amateurs. Musically gifted noblemen and villagers alike formed groups to perform this new music. These groups eagerly searched for new material and composers were besieged for new music for weddings and other court functions which could be served by the subject matter of this new music form. This form, the madrigal, became immediately popular in court circles, took England by storm, and soon spread over all Europe.

> *From its very beginning, the form of the music was free enough as regards structure: the composer would take verses of any meter that appealed to him, usually a stanza of some five or six lines chosen from a lyric, pastoral, or amorous poem, although he sometimes set words of a grave character . . .*
>
> *The composers dealt with such words line by line, even breaking them into phrases, thus dividing their work into definite sections. The parts were usually written for four or five voices, in both harmonic and contrapuntal style, the latter often of very involved and curious workmanship. The chief distinguishing mark of the madrigal was its marvelous rhythmic freedom, no matter how complicated the weaving of the various parts. Each voice followed the meter of the verse with absolute accuracy, sometimes in slow, sometimes in quick tempo, according to the dictates of the words. The prevailing atmosphere of the poem was caught in a sort of stylized musical paraphrase, and there were often curious attempts at what may be called word painting . . . There was a good deal of imitation between the various parts, but it was hardly ever strict in the sense of the mechanical canons and devices of the earlier church music. Everything was free, yet strongly conventional; expressive, yet severely intellectual; imaginative, yet purely artificial. The madrigals were indeed a happy compromise between pure, spontaneous utterance and calculated ingenuity. Considering their restricted field, no more perfect art form has ever been devised.*[14]

The early madrigal writers believed that it was possible to use music for giving particular meaning to individual words—in short, to word-paint with music.

> *... long festoons of thirds were woven about such expressions as "chains of love"; sighs were translated by pauses and breaks in the melody; the idea of duration, of immobility, was expressed by the holding of a single voice, the others carrying their parts relentlessly. The voices rose on such words as "heaven," "heights"; they fell on the words "earth," "abyss," "hell." The notes scattered in silvery groups around the words "laughter," "joyous," "gay," etc.; tears were expressed by audacious discords and unexpected modulations.*[15]

This secular polyphonic composition for voices, usually unaccompanied, can be and is written for any number of voices. The first madrigals were written for two or three voices, with each one treated according to the strictest rules of imitation. Later madrigals used four, five, even six voices and achieved even greater perfection of technical facility in the polyphonic treatment of the voices or parts.

Thus the madrigal, which was first cultivated in Italy, then imported by England where it grew to great heights of popularity during the time of Shakespeare, finally was served up for the musical delight of all Europe and became the favorite vehicle for introducing some of the most skillful composers of the age. Men such as Adrien Willaert (c. 1480-1562), Andrea Gabrieli (c. 1520-1586), Leo Hassler (1564-1612), Jan Sweelinck (1562-1621), Claudio Monteverdi (1567-1643), Don Carlo Gesualdo (1560-1613), Orlando di Lasso (1532-1594), William Byrd (1543-1623), Thomas Morley (1557-1603), John Dowland (1563-1626) and Orlando Gibbons (1583-1625) achieved great fame due in part to the technical perfection of their madrigal writing.

Sing We and Chant It...........................Thomas Morley (1557-c. 1603)

This is but a portion of this madrigal. If the group is able to learn this much of the song quickly, and has the time and interest, it may want to obtain copies of the entire madrigal in order to complete its study of this masterpiece by Morley. "Sing We and Chant It" is similar in style to Morley's "Now Is the Month of Maying" which will be presented as a listening experience. After having learned to sing this fragment, answer the following questions about the construction of this madrigal.

Sing We and Chant It

RHYTHM: 1. What is the meter of this madrigal?
2. How many pulses to the measure?
3. Is the rhythm the same in each of the parts?
4. List the different kinds of note values used in this segment of "Sing We and Chant It."

MELODY: 1. Is any one of the five melodies more important than the others?
2. What is the vocal range used by each melody?
3. Analyze each melody in terms of its construction, that is, its step-wise progressions and skips.
4. Are the melodies easy or difficult to sing? Why?

HARMONY: 1. What is the key of the composition?
2. Is the harmonic texture homophonic or polyphonic?
3. Is the harmonization consonant or dissonant?

TIMBRE: 1. Describe the timbre which results when the entire group sings.
2. Observe the effect when each melody is sung by itself.
3. Compare the sound of each different vocal line.

FORM: 1. How many phrases are given?
2. What is this form called?
3. Mark the cadences.

The Silver Swan.............................Orlando Gibbons (1583-1625)
It would be helpful if there were a copy of the score available so that it could be followed as the recording is being played.

LISTENING
ACTIVITIES

> The silver swan, who living had no note,
> When death approached unlocked her silent throat,
> Leaning her breast against the reedy shore,
> Thus sung her first and last, and sung no more.
> Farewell, all joys,
> O death, come close mine eyes,
> More Geese than Swans now live, more fools than wise.

MOOD: 1. Read and discuss the text.
2. Does the text suggest the mood for the madrigal?

RHYTHM: 1. What is the meter marking for this madrigal?
2. Note the different time or note values used in the construction of the various melodies.
3. A fine performance of this madrigal depends on the group's ability to sing with rhythmic fluency and accuracy. Is it easy or difficult to maintain this fluency and accuracy when the tempo moves so slowly ($\downarrow$. 48)?

381

MELODY: 1. In actuality, how many melodies are there?
         2. Is any one melody more important than the rest?
         3. Someone has referred to this type of writing as "layers of melodies."
            What is meant by this statement?
         4. Note the overall vocal range of each melody.
         5. Note the use of stepwise progressions, small skips and large skips in
            the construction of each melody.

HARMONY: 1. What is the key of this composition?
          2. Is the harmonic texture homophonic or polyphonic?
          3. Does one hear many dissonances in the harmonization?

TIMBRE: 1. For what voices was this madrigal written?
         2. Would the timbre be any different if there were fifteen voices on a
            part than if there were only one voice on a part?

FORM: 1. Indicate the phrases.
       2. If a copy of the score is available mark the cadences.
       3. What is the overall form of this madrigal?

Now Is the Month of Maying....................Thomas Morley (1557-c. 1603)
Note the similarity between this madrigal and "Sing We and Chant It." Again, it
would be helpful if a copy of the score was available so that it could be followed as
the recording is being played.

Now is the month of Maying,
When merry lads are playing,
Fa la la la la la la la la,
Fa la la la la la la.
The Spring, clad all in gladness,
Doth laugh at winter's sadness.
Fa la la la la la la la la,
Fa la la la la la la.

Each with his bonnie lass,
A-dancing on the grass.
Fa la la la la,
Fa la la la la la la la la la la la.
And to the bagpipe's sound,
The nymphs tread out the ground.
Fa la la la la,
Fa la la la la la la la la la la la.

Fie, then, why sit we musing,
Youth's sweet delight refusing?
Fa la la la la la la la la,
Fa la la la la la la.

382   MOOD: 1. What is the mood of this madrigal?

RHYTHM: 1. What is the meter marking of this madrigal?
           2. Does this madrigal have two or four pulses to the measure?
           3. What are the different time or note values used?
           4. Contrast the word rhythm with the other rhythms present in this madrigal.

MELODY: 1. Is the melody of one of the parts more important than the melodies of the other parts?
           2. Describe the construction of each of the melodies in terms of step-wise progressions and skips.
           3. Which part makes the most use of skips?
           4. What is the reason more skips would be used for this part?

HARMONY: 1. What is the key of this composition?
           2. If a copy of the score is available mark the I, IV and V₇ chords in this key.
           3. Is the harmonic texture homophonic or polyphonic?
           4. What is the essential difference in harmonic texture between "Now Is the Month of Maying" and "The Silver Swan"?

TIMBRE: 1. For what voices is this madrigal written?
           2. Would the timbre be altered if a piano accompaniment were used?

FORM: 1. This madrigal may be divided into how many large sections?
           2. What would this form be called?
           3. Mark the cadences as they occur.

The Secular Cantata

A brief review of Chapter Six will serve to remind us that the term "cantata," derived from the Italian word *cantare* which means "to sing," was a term used to help distinguish between vocal and instrumental forms. As an extended vocal form its history can be traced back to the seventeenth century. Then it was a type of extended vocal composition consisting of alternating sections of recitatives and arias for solo voice only. In the eighteenth century the concept of the cantata changed from that of an extended work for solo voice to that of an extended choral work using soloists, chorus and accompaniment. The subject matter of the cantata was drawn from both sacred and secular sources.

While the subject matter of the cantata may, more often than not, be quite dramatic in content or may relate a story in quite vivid terms, it is presented without acting or action: The music and text are deemed to be entirely sufficient in communicating the central thought. The cantata has been said to be a shortened form of opera or oratorio given without benefit of stage sets, costumes or action.

We have also seen that as a medium of musical expression the cantata is more apt to be reflective than dramatic. This will become quite obvious in the example of the secular cantata to follow. The typical secular cantata, as

383

with its counterpart the sacred cantata, is written in sections, each of which uses one of the vocal forms—chorus, duet, solo or chorale—as well as instrumental portions. In the example of the secular cantata which we are to study the vocal forms are confined to baritone solo and chorus, plus the instrumental sections. Another characteristic of the cantata is the balanced symmetry of form and style. This too will be apparent in the study of the work to follow.

LISTENING
ACTIVITY

Sea Drift..................................Frederick Delius (1862-1934)

The text chosen by Delius for this work was taken from Walt Whitman's poem, "Out of the Cradle Endlessly Rocking," one of the poems in his monumental *Leaves of Grass*. The resulting marriage of text by Whitman (1819-1892) and music by Delius provides a fine example of perfect union of thought and emotion. That Delius should be attracted to the works of Whitman is understandable when the lives of both men are examined in detail. Both were nonconforming emotional personalities. During their lifetimes both Delius and Whitman suffered rejection and physical illness. It is important to remember that both believed strongly in the importance of man's place in the order of all creation as well as his affinity with nature. Each sought to express this personal conviction in his creative works.

Much of Whitman's poetry has been described in musical terms. Christopher Morley, in the introduction to one of the editions of *Leaves of Grass*, refers to the perfect music which results from the subtle exploitation and return of different sounds of one vowel.[16] At another point he says, "One of the interesting qualities of Walt's poems is that they suffer relatively little in translation into foreign language. Their validity depends on the thought more than on the exact phrase. As a matter of fact they are in a foreign tongue to begin with: the dialect of interior candor"[17]—certainly the ingredient out of which music is made. Louis Untermeyer referred to his works as having "flexible sonority, orchestral timbre, tidal rhythms, and symphonic form resulting from his piling up of details."[18] If imagery is to poetry as harmony is to music, it is easy to see why lines such as "white arms out in the breakers tirelessly tossing" and "O brown halo in the sky near the moon, drooping upon the sea" bring to Whitman's poetry the reputation for being musical.

Whitman's use of free verse is unique and often is untranslatable. It has even been described as "barbaric yawp." Yet Whitman was the poetic emancipator of his time. His major work, *Leaves of Grass*, from which the poem "Out of the Cradle Endlessly Rocking" is taken, ushered in a new era of modernism in poetry. This work also had great influence on the other literary, artistic and musical forms of the time.

Sea Drift

(Excerpt from "Out of the Cradle Endlessly Rocking")

CHORUS *Once Paumanok,*
When the lilac-scent was in the air and Fifth-month was growing,
Up this seashore in some briers,
Two feather'd guests from Alabama, two together,
And their nest, and four light green eggs spotted with brown,

SOLOIST *And every day the he-bird to and fro near at hand,*
And every day the she-bird crouch'd on her nest, silent with bright eyes,
And every day I, a curious boy, never too close, never disturbing them,
Cautiously peering, absorbing, translating.

CHORUS *Shine! shine! shine!*
Pour down your warmth, great sun!
While we bask, we two together.
Two together!
Winds blow south, or winds blow north,
Day come white, or night come black,

SOLOIST *Home, or rivers and mountains from home,*

CHORUS *Singing all time, minding no time,*
While we two keep together.
Singing all time,
Singing, singing, singing, singing.

SOLOIST *Till of a sudden,*
Maybe kill'd, unknown to her mate,
One forenoon the she-bird crouch'd not on the nest,
Nor return'd that afternoon, nor the next,
Nor ever appear'd again.
And thence forward all summer in the sound of the sea,
And at night under the full of the moon in calmer weather,
Over the hoarse surging of the sea,
Or flitting from brier to brier by day,
I saw, I heard at intervals the remaining one, the he-bird,
The solitary guest from Alabama.

CHORUS *Blow! blow! blow!*
Blow up sea-winds along Paumanok's shore;
I wait and I wait till you blow my mate to me.

SOLOIST *Yes, when the stars glisten'd,*
All night long on the prong of a moss-scallop'd stake,
Down almost amid the slapping waves,
Sat the lone singer wonderful causing tears.
He call'd on his mate,
He pour'd forth the meanings which I of all men know.
Yes, my brother I know,
The rest might not, but I have treasur'd every note,
For more than once dimly down to the beach gliding,
Silent, avoiding the moonbeams, blending myself with the shadows,
Recalling now the obscure shapes, the echoes, the
*   sounds and sights after their sorts,*
The white arms out in the breakers tirelessly tossing,
I, with bare feet, a child, the wind wafting my hair,
Listen'd long and long.
Listen'd to keep, to sing, now translating the notes,
Following you my brother.

385

CHORUS   *Soothe! soothe! soothe!*
Close on its wave soothes the wave behind.
And again another behind embracing and lapping, every one close,

SOLOIST   *But my love soothes not me, not me.*

CHORUS   *Low hangs the moon, it rose late,*
It is lagging—O I think it is heavy with love, with love.

SOLOIST   *O madly the sea pushes upon the land,*
With love, with love.
O night! do I not see my love fluttering out among the breakers?
What is that little black thing I see there in white?
Loud! loud! loud!
Loud I call to you, my love!
High and clear I shoot my voice over the waves,
Surely you must know who is here, is here,
You must know who I am, my love.

CHORUS   *O rising stars!*
Perhaps the one I want so much will rise, will rise with some of you.
O throat! O trembling throat!
Sound clearer through the atmosphere!
Pierce the woods, the earth,
Somewhere listening to catch you must be the one I want.

SOLOIST   *Shake out carols!*
Solitary here, the night's carols!
Carols of lonesome love! death's carols!
Carols under that lagging, yellow, waning moon!
O under that moon where she droops almost down into the sea!
O reckless despairing carols.
But soft! sink low!
Soft! let me just murmur,
And do you wait a moment you husky-nois'd sea.
But somewhere I believe I heard my mate responding to me,
So faint, I must be still, be still to listen,
But not altogether still, for then she might not come immediately to me.
Hither my love!
Here I am! here!
With this just-sustain'd note I announce myself to you,
This gentle call is for you my love, for you.

CHORUS   *Do not be decoy'd elsewhere,*
That is the whistle of the wind, it is not my voice,
That is the fluttering, the fluttering of spray,
Those are the shadows of leaves.
O darkness! O in vain!

386

SOLOIST   *O I am very sick and sorrowful.*
O brown halo in the sky near the moon, drooping upon the sea!
O troubled reflection in the sea!
O throat! O throbbing heart!
And I sing uselessly, uselessly all the night.
O past! O happy life! O songs of joy!
In the air, in the woods, over fields,
Loved! loved! loved! loved! loved!
But my mate no more, no more with me!
We two together no more.

While it is conceivable that composers of other eras and styles might have selected this poetry as the inspiration for one of their creative efforts, there arises a question as to the appropriateness of the music to go with this particular poetry. Is this the kind of poetry out of which a Bach, a Beethoven, a Wagner or a Mahler might have fashioned a masterpiece? What kind of music would best express the tragedy portrayed for us through the particular medium of Whitman's poetry? What kind of music should be prescribed which would best express the symbolism and imagery found in such poetry? One quickly comes to this conclusion: Neither the straight-forward musical expression of a Bach, with its emphasis on perfection of polyphonic or homophonic writing, nor the emotional excess which so often characterized the writing of the Romantic composers could best express in musical terms the deep-seated, personal impressions created in each individual by the skillful yet delicate manipulation of words and phrases found here.

The quality of the literary text seems to demand a mode of musical expression guided by the emotional demands of the poetry, rather than being limited by the straight-jacket often imposed on musical composition by the strict observance of the so-called rules governing the composition of music. This also calls for a composer skilled in extending the expressive and communicative power of his writing through a liberal application of harmonic and timbre coloring, in order to capture the some-

times vague and always changing moods of the poetry. It would seem to follow that the music which would best implement and complement this poetry would be this: Music which would not attempt to describe the scene in literal and outright terms, but rather would only suggest subtle impressions with blurred outlines—much as if we were viewing the scene through partially closed eyelids.

Frederick Delius seems to have all of the natural attributes necessary for breathing musical life into this superb poetry. In speaking of the technical procedures followed by Delius and the other impressionist composers, McKinney and Anderson point out, "[they] were primarily absorbed in the possibilities of color as an expressive medium; they looked on the communication of feeling as one of the most important elements of their music; and they were content to let the form of their work grow naturally out of its material."[19] This, in brief, might be said to be a musical description of the creative powers of Delius—except that he, probably more than any of the other impressionists, was able to make the style his own personal idiom of expression.

...the thing which makes this particularly emotional medium of Delius so effective is the spiritual nature that was back of it, a nature like that of no other in music. Delius was an ardent lover of beauty, as many a composer had been before him; but to him beauty was something that was not only connected with the

387

world about him: it was rather to be found in contemplation after an event, in regarding that which is left to man after the show of life has passed on ....It is this nostalgic longing for something that is unattainable, that has never existed, combined with a poignant tenderness that is sometimes unbearable, that makes the music of this composer [Delius] unique.[20]

In a sense *Sea Drift* might be said to be autobiographical, although it was written in 1904 and preceded by a number of years the tragedy of his blindness and the illness which ultimately led to his death in 1934. There is an otherworldliness to the music which reflects Delius' concern with the problems of both life and the infinite.

MOOD: The sea setting is obvious in the orchestral introduction and is constantly reemphasized in colors which change and vary with the changing emotions of the poem. In general two moods are most apparent, the first part being joyous, almost ec-

static in its happiness, while the mood of the second part is one of tragedy and grief.

RHYTHM: It is interesting to note that there are nine different changes of meter in *Sea Drift*:

Introduction	¢	swings in 2
at (7)	6/4	swings in 2
at (8)	c	swings in 4
at (9)	¢	swings in 2
at (11)	6/4	swings in 2

(note the motion and movement which underlie this section)

at (13)	¢	swings in 2

(note the triplet passage played in the violin obbligato)

at (14)	9/4	swings in 3
at (19)	6/4	swings in 6
at (24)	3/2	swings in 3

These nine different meter sections, combined with fourteen different changes of tempo ranging from *largamente* to *più animato*, serve to reflect the ceaseless movement of the sea. They also help to project the emotional content of the words, melody, harmony and coloring of the entire work.

MELODY: Many melodies are used in the construction of this cantata. The melodies used are in many instances irregular, with sudden leaps and difficult intervals. There are numerous instances of a melody being conditioned by its harmonic background. There are several melodic motives out of which the total work has been fashioned and which need to be recognized for maximum understanding and enjoyment of the work. The introduction begins with such a motive:

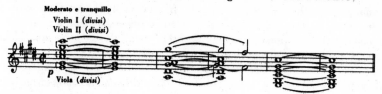

Over and above this is heard this same motive in diminution painting the movement of the waves:

Following the instrumental introduction the chorus enters with a simple narrative passage:

Once Pau - ma - nok, when the li - lac scent ____

A musical suggestion of the "feather'd guests from Alabama" is to be found in the fourteenth measure after the entrance of the chorus in a passage played by the oboe:

Shortly the happy song of the two birds as they build their nest is suggested by a solo violin, flute and the two harps:

and by the flute alone:

At the words "winds blow south or winds blow north" note that the countermelody played by the solo violin is constructed from the initial motive:

Winds blow south ____ or winds blow north

At the change of meter, the movement is intensified as the narration continues to tell of the two birds and their life together. Melodically this is done through the use of a characteristic chromatic sequence:

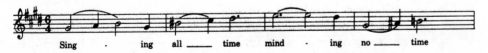

Sing - ing all ____ time mind - ing no ____ time

Notice the whirlwind of accompanying figures played underneath this melody by the strings and the woodwinds. A new section begins with the baritone soloist singing the melody:

Till of a sud - den, may - be killed,

389

which tells of the disappearance of the she-bird. A feeling of poignancy and grief is intensified in this section through the effective use of the oboe and English horn playing descending chromatically designed passages:

A new section, a section dealing with the search by the he-bird for the she-bird, begins with this melody, sung by the chorus and imitated by the horns two measures later:

Blow! ____ blow _____ up, Winds, _____ a - long _____ Pau-ma-nok's shore,

which grows and grows in intensity until this impassioned cry is heard:

I wait ____ and I wait ____ till you blow _____ my mate to me, ____

As the baritone soloist, speaking for the he-bird, sings of the lost she-bird:

Yes, my broth - er, I know, the rest might not,

the solo violin brings back the song of the happy birds heard earlier:

This, in turn, is taken up by the harps. A new section dealing with the loneliness and despair of the he-bird begins with an a cappella section based on the first motive:

Lento: Molto tranquillo

O ris - ing stars, ____ per - haps ____ the one I want so much, ____ will rise, ____

O ris - ing stars, ____ per - haps ____ the one I want so much, will rise, ____

O ris - ing stars, ____ per - haps ____ the one I want so much, ____ will rise, ____

The section reaches its climax of despair as the soloist sings:

O dark - ness! O in vain! — in vain! —

while the orchestra sobs:

A closing section, or coda, beginning with the soloist singing:

O past! O hap - py life!

is reminiscent of the first motive or melody. This coda brings the cantata to its quiet close.

HARMONY: *Sea Drift* demonstrates the extraordinary harmonic resources to be found in the writing of Delius. While it tends to chromaticism, it nevertheless maintains the stamp of individuality which is the hallmark of Delius' creative efforts. The harmonic system used by Delius is almost impossible to analyze and define. It seems to lie just within the confines of tonality without ever crossing beyond. The result is a strange and exotic harmonization which adds to but never overshadows the emotional impact of the other elements of the composition. Another characteristic of the harmonic writing of Delius is found in *Sea Drift* in the manner in which one harmony seems to dissolve into another.

TIMBRE: Delius was more interested in the effect of the total sound of a work than in the specific words of the chorus. He was, however, very skillful in his use of voices and effectively used the color of choral sound. *Sea Drift* was written for baritone solo, mixed chorus and orchestra. The score calls for a large orchestra consisting of three flutes, three oboes, English horn, three B♭ clarinets, B♭ bass clarinet, three bassoons, contrabassoon, six French horns, three C trumpets, three trombones, tuba, timpani, bass drum, two harps and the usual strings. The chorus is heard both with and without accompaniment. The soloist is heard with orchestra and against chorus and orchestra. Probably no composer can really compare with Delius in consummate skill in writing for the orchestra. He seemed to have an instinctive knack for using the resources of instruments in the best possible way to reveal the innermost sensations and emotions underlying the musical product. *Sea Drift* is a superb example of his brilliance in writing for the orchestra. There are several technical devices typical of his orchestral writing to be found in this composition. Among these devices are the use of muted brass, the effective use of the plaintive cry of the English horn, the writing of some of the woodwind parts in the low register, the use of two harps and the use of *divisi* or divided string parts.

391

FORM: Delius believed that form resulted from giving unity to one's thoughts. His own creative efforts would have been frustrated had he been restricted in the expression of his ideas to the rigid confines of some mechanical or predetermined principle of structural organization. Despite his predilection for letting the expression of his thoughts determine the final form, one finds in the formal organization of *Sea Drift* a balance of parts and writing which imparts an overall unity to the work. While there is not the simple but perfect symmetry found in the cantata *Christ lag in Todesbanden*, there is a symmetry created by the dialogue between soloist and chorus as the work progresses. The total work seems to be divided into an instrumental or orchestral introduction; a Part I which deals with the happy life of the two "feather'd visitors from Alabama"; a Part II dealing with the grief and despair of the he-bird after the loss of the she-bird; and a short coda, based on the opening motive, which brings the work to its conclusion.

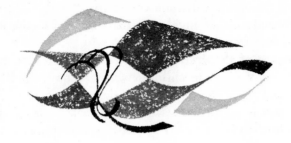

chapter 10

Music and Drama

What is meant by the term "music drama"? When the subject of music and drama is discussed, many people think only in terms of opera. It is also quite probable that within this group there are many who believe that music drama is an esoteric art form directed to, understood and enjoyed only by the musical elite. Yet, as we will shortly see, neither idea is entirely correct. We need to begin by defining just what is meant when the all-inclusive term "music drama" is used. In general, it is a play or drama set to music requiring the services of vocal soloists, chorus and orchestra throughout the entire course of action. It may or may not include parts for dancers and dance groups. It may or may not include speaking parts, depending on the kind of music drama it is. In music drama, for the most part, the characters sing their parts and their thoughts instead of speaking them.

No one doubts that the combination of music and drama as it is revealed on the stage, whether in opera, ballet, musical comedy or in any one of the many other forms of music drama, has the appearance of a highly artificial union. It is true that people in real, everyday life do not act as the persons do who are participating in an opera or ballet production. Real, everyday people do not converse musically with their fellows about the latest piece of news, or woo each other with long, ecstatic outbursts of song. It is even less likely that persons will break into dance when communicating with one another. Yet people are heard to say, "I could sing for joy," or "I could dance a jig."

Yet the musical stage in all of its forms has had a tremendously long and successful history and continues to thrive. The use of music and drama

393

in combination goes back to prerecorded history in the ritualistic exercise of primitive man. Despite the apparent artificiality of the fusion of music and drama, there seems to be a deep-felt desire to combine these arts. This is evidenced in all forms of religious ceremony, from primitive rites to the sophisticated formulation of highly civilized religions such as those of ancient Greece or our own faiths.

More evidence of the desire for the combination of music and drama is found in the play of little children who are quite undisturbed by the unreality of combining song and play (music and drama) in their childhood activities. As long as no false feeling of self-consciousness is present, the child expresses himself quite freely and effectively with actions that combine both song and play.

Strictly speaking, of course, drama itself is a very artificial form and cannot be looked upon as being any more realistic than music. Beyond that, the entire setting for dramatic presentation is purely artificial. Stage sets, scenic design, lighting and so forth are not basically attempts to be realistic, but rather attempts to create an illusion-stimulus for the imagination. An audience is not disturbed by seeing a room which contains but three walls. It accepts the fact that the fourth must be left open in order that the action may be observed. When it is viewed in this light there should be no difficulty in reconciling the fusion of music and drama. The opera and ballet are unreal only in the sense of everyday reality, but no one has proposed that they be viewed in any other light. No one has urged that Othello be regarded as a real, everyday kind of a person, neither in the play by Shakespeare nor in the opera by Verdi. But jealousy is a very real thing and the revelation of its insidious eroding of a strong man's character is portrayed effectively in the original play. And for some, at least, it is magnified and enhanced by the fusion of music with the play in the hands of Verdi and his librettist, Boito.

There are many aspects of musical dramatic production which make the combining of these two great arts difficult and sometimes embarrassing. The great difficulty is, of course, personnel. It is not always possible to find actors who can sing and singers who can act. In the more difficult and complex musical dramatic form such as the opera, the attention is more often focused on the ability to sing. This has often resulted in having such poor actors on the stage that certain periods of opera and certain operatic works scarcely made anything but vocal demands of the actors. The operatic productions of the seventeenth and most of the eighteenth centuries were mainly productions which gave opportunity for brilliant singing at the expense of dramatic sincerity. The works usually disappeared with the singers for whom they were written. There are some such operas of later date still to be found in the standard operatic repertoire—for example, *Lucia di Lammermoor*. In this opera we have a work that is still being offered almost solely because of its vocal interest. As long as the demand of an operatic work is centered on

394

the musical-vocal side, the physical appearance of the cast is not of too much importance or concern. But when there is a more even balance between music and drama, the demand for not only a reasonably good singer, but one who looks and acts the part as well, becomes apparent. It becomes embarrassing or ridiculous when a Tristan of five feet in height has to struggle with an Isolde of five feet ten inches, weighing 225 pounds.

Physical considerations extend beyond the appearance of the cast. Embarrassing moments in the use of stage properties, scenic effects, and stage machinery often tend to make a hilarious joke out of a serious incident. The inability of the mechanical swan in *Lohengrin* to traverse the stage successfully or even to appear at all has been the source of many an operatic joke. There are hundreds of such incidents, many of which appear in books that record such events on the stage. However, the real difficulty is not the reconciliation of music and drama, but rather the problem of suitably fusing word and music. The same problem exists in the simple folk song. Opera and musical dramatic works merely magnify these difficulties and expose them to a vaster audience, with all the risks involved in a stage presentation.

The delight that people derive from the musical stage is capitalized on by a number of activities in our American culture. One is the band spectacle that has grown up with and become almost an inseparable part of the interscholastic football program. In this event the dramatic element is restricted to a visual effect, but the human delight in the combination of music and movement, music and extra-musical meaning, is nevertheless there. Another activity in which music is combined with dramatic and verbal expression is the "singing commercial" on radio and television. No one, for a moment, feels that these television commercials are in any sense "real." That they are effective is only too evident by their continued use. Some of them, and some of the most effective, are those using animated cartoons, completely unrealistic characters. While the use of singing or musical commercials may be resented by a considerable part of the population, their continued use suggests that they are enjoyed by a vast majority. This should be an indication of the willingness of people not only to tolerate the combination of music and drama but to enjoy it.

In the history of music, music drama and specifically opera have played a rather important role in society. Opera early came under the patronage of the aristocracy and upper middle class. It afforded a means of entertainment and, at the same time, an opportunity for the wealthy and titled to display their wealth and importance. Opera has never entirely lost this aspect even in democratic societies. There is still something of the snobbish attitude attached to the attendance of an operatic performance. We still speak of opera gowns, opera capes and opera buffets. In European societies, however, with the exception of some gala performances, this attitude has declined almost to the point of extinction. Specific operas have often, as have dramas, become the vehicle for political and social causes or implications. *The Marriage of Figaro* was looked upon with disfavor because it was considered to be a criticism of the aristocracy of the eighteenth century. *The Magic Flute* was thought to be of political significance in its symbolism. *Wozzeck,* a twentieth-century opera, was viewed by conservative audiences as representative of a tendency toward artistic bolshevism, whatever that meant, and its performance was forbidden in certain countries during the 1920's. Later its performance was forbidden in such widely disparate societies as Nazi Germany and Communist Russia for completely different reasons. Operas have served wittingly and unwittingly as vehicles for social and political antagonisms.

Opera and ballet, however, have also served the cause of music over the past three and one-half centuries with good effect. Opera is often the first access to great music for many people in Europe where it still flourishes with undiminished popularity. Children are often introduced to the orchestra and music through ballet performance with its enchanting visual background and movement of the dancers. And while many operas are deficient in their musical value, there are many great works whose music has found an honored place not only in the opera house itself but in the concert hall. In fact, some operatic and ballet music is better known to us through its concert performances than in its original form.

Going to the opera or ballet prepared to understand that the music is only one, even though perhaps the most important one, of the several media used to convey meaning to the audience will tend to make for much greater enjoyment and appreciation. There are many devices by which composers have tried to fuse music and drama. With some it was merely the device of using the generally accepted musical gestures that gave support to the dramatic incident: a lyric, melodic line in a love scene, loud and soft dynamic values for appropriate situations, stressed regular rhythm in a military scene, the tone quality of an oboe for a pastoral effect, dissonant harmony in a tense emotional situation . . . For others the fusion of music and drama suggested such devices as those used by Richard Wagner in his great music dramas in which he employed certain musical mottoes, called *leitmotivs*, which were distinguished by special melodic, rhythmic and/or harmonic character. These mottoes were deliberately associated with persons, things or situations, and the audience is persuaded by Wagner's genius and insistence that one motto or *leitmotiv* is in reality the magic fire, or another is the person of Siegfried. The success of Wagner's persuasive power resulted in a whole school of opera composers adapting this principle, which was only an application of the principle of association used by the composers of program music. In fact, Wagner's operas are in a sense symphonic program music, originally written for dramatic production on the stage, but widely successful as purely concert pieces. The criticism of unreality or artificiality has crumbled away in the dual effectiveness of these works.

396   If the union of music and drama is to result in a meaningful art form

with strength, character and an individuality all of its own, then some of the best qualities of both music and drama must be amalgamated to produce, at the same time, good music and good theater. In looking at drama's contribution, we see there is obviously a need, first of all, for a good story or, as it is often referred to, book. The story should have a situation which is believable. Out of this good story should derive the possibility of having a colorful and distinctive setting. The story must also move in an even manner to its ultimate conclusion. Finally, if the story is to be projected in a proper manner, the characters must stand out as real and interesting individuals, whether they are a Carmen or a Mephistopheles.

If the strong features of the drama are to be complemented properly, the music itself must have certain qualities. It must, first of all, have a dramatic quality which parallels and adds to the drama inherent in the plot. It must be expressive so that it reflects the many moods expressed during the course of the action. Even though there may be a tendency to consider music of music drama as the handmaiden of the dramatic element, in reality this is not the case. The dramatic element is just as dependent on the quality of the musical effort. The same requirements for writing good music for the other music forms apply to writing good music for the musical theater. Factors such as good tunes and skillful manipulation of the other musical materials weigh heavily in the contribution which music makes to the musical theater. Poor music has ruined many a potentially strong music drama.

To understand better just how the composer is able to collaborate successfully in the production of a music drama, it is necessary to look briefly at some of the musical devices used by successful music drama composers. In general, the action and the thoughts of the characters are going to be projected through song. In music drama this is accomplished through two different kinds of vocal efforts. In the first, called *recitative,* the action is both announced to the audience and hurried along by having the singer tell of the action by using almost the natural inflection of speech, through chanting or declaiming words on one or more pitches. The accompaniment is used to punctuate the progress of the singer's monologue by playing the cadence chords in rather strict rhythm as opposed to the free rhythm used by the soloist. In the recitative the musical values and the expressive qualities of music are not of as much importance as getting across to the audience the necessary facts about the situation, the character or the action which is to follow. Consider for a moment the problem confronting the composer who desires to communicate effectively to his audience in a short interval of time the following situation: Four boon companions, interested in the arts but poverty-stricken, are faced with the problem of keeping their happy home when the landlord suddenly arrives, demanding payment of the overdue rent. How do the confreres handle this unhappy situation? Giacomo Puccini (1858-1924) handled this problem rather neatly in *La Bohème* by using the recitative form to convey the sad plight of Marcello, Schaunard,

Colline and Rodolfo, and their subsequent action which resulted in the outwitting of Benoit, the landlord.

A second type of vocal effort found in a music drama is known as the *aria*, a rather lengthy and elaborate melodic composition which often functions as a vocal showpiece for the soloist. It is in the aria that the vocalist is able to demonstrate his prowess. One should not infer from this, however, that the aria is lacking in expressiveness or that it is superficial in purpose. The aria is introspective in character and might be said to be a type of soliloquy in which the singer-actor sings his innermost thoughts. Because of the wide range of its expressive character it is possible for the aria to communicate many diverse passions. In the aria, the composer and the singer are really of more importance than the dramatist and the actor.

Musically speaking there are several ingredients which must be present if the aria is to be considered as having quality as well as appeal. First of all the melody must be lyrical and have a marked and distinctive character. Its appeal should be so great that it remains with the listener long after he hears it. It should sparkle with the composer's own personality, skill and creative gift, rather than be derivative of another composer's style. The second requirement of a good aria is that it be in character with the operatic character who gives it life in the actual performance. In the aria, "Un bel di, vedremo" ("Some Day He'll Come") from the opera *Madame Butterfly*, it seems perfectly natural to expect a passionate love song from Madame Butterfly as she sings of her faith in Pinkerton and his promise to return, because the situation and the character at this point demand this kind of aria. Music and libretto complement the character, the situation and each other. Even if the music could be made to fit the text, certainly no one could accept the aria as being in keeping if the melody had been of the flippant character of the "Habanera" ("Love Is Like a Wood-Bird") in the opera *Carmen*. A third requirement for a good aria refers to the technical aspect of writing music. The aria must be written so that it exploits the maximum coloristic potential of the voice and furnishes a vehicle for a display of vocal pyrotechnics by the singer.

Music drama should not be thought of as being limited to the vocal resources of a soloist singing either a recitative or an aria. Other combinations of vocal effort are to be found in the various types of music drama. The other uses for the voice range from duets, trios, quartets, sextets to, and including, large choruses. Each in its own way makes its own contribution to the overall effectiveness of the work. Dance groups may also contribute to the musical working out of a music drama.

Often the music drama calls for the tonal resources of a large orchestra. The orchestra's role in music drama should therefore be briefly examined. On the one hand an important function of the orchestra is to furnish an accompaniment for the various singers, vocal ensembles and dancers who appear as the action progresses. On the other hand there are other functions, any one of which may be of more importance than the accompanying function. There are times when there seems to be little or no action taking place on the stage. At these points the orchestra is most important because it can tie the action together by providing appropriate bridge passages sometimes known as "fill-in" music. But probably the orchestra's most important single contribution is the one it makes to the expressive intent of both the music and the drama. Because of the ready availability of the unlimited tonal resources of the orchestral palette, the composer has at his disposal the greatest of all instruments for expressing the various moods desired for the work.

Music dramas can and do differ in kind, intent and form. Because music drama, in all of its forms, is growing in popularity and accessibility, it seems advisable at this point to compare three of the more popular forms of music drama.

The Operetta

Since it is related to both musical comedy and to opera, one recognizes in an operetta certain elements common to both. In a sense the operetta, because of its more elaborate nature, is much closer to opera than are any of the other forms of music drama. One finds in the operetta many of the same musical devices to be found in opera. One device, for example, is having the characters carry the action and thought throughout the entire work by singing. In the operetta it is not at all uncommon to find this action and thought being carried forward by way of recitatives, arias and vocal ensembles of varying sizes and descriptions. The writing for the voice, in many instances, may closely approximate the writing of opera in the elaborate and florid manner used by the composer for the vocal line. Another favorite device found in opera and also in operetta is the revelation at the same precise time, through the use of duets, trios, quartets and other types of vocal ensembles, of the several different sentiments represented on the stage.

The operetta differs from opera in that it is not limited to the vocal forms for the projection of action. While the recitative may be used to explain and hasten the action in the operetta, more often than not, spoken dialogue is used for this function. In fact, one might say that in the operetta the action is carried forward by the use of the spoken word, and that at certain stages the action is stopped while innermost thoughts and feelings are expressed in song. Generally these songs are charming, lyrical and smooth-flowing with a slight tendency toward sentimentality.

The plot of the operetta, in most instances, treats of a country, time or situation that is highly romantic and, quite possibly, remote from the experiences of everyday people. There is probably a strong flavor of make-believe in the plot. The action of many an operetta has taken place in an imaginary kingdom. Other equally exotic settings have been used as the basis for an operetta. This kind of music drama naturally leads to some rather unconventional and, in some cases, improbable characters who may strain the credibility of the audience. The language used by these characters is not in the vernacular but tends to be high-flown. The operetta also makes more use of humor than does the opera.

Because of these factors the operetta has had and continues to have tremendous audience appeal. Some of the world's most gifted composers have turned their creative talents to the operetta field. Composers such as

Jacques Offenbach (1819-1880), Johann Strauss (1825-1899), Victor Herbert (1859-1924), Reginald De Koven (1859-1920), Rudolf Friml (1879 ——), Sigmund Romberg (1887-1951) and Jerome Kern (1885-1945) are a few who have contributed successfully to this form.

Die Fledermaus.................................Johann Strauss (1825-1899)

The Cast

Gabriel von Eisenstein ......*Tenor*
Rosalinda, his wife ......*Soprano*
Adele, their maid ....*Soprano*
Alfred, ex-admirer and
    singing teacher ....*Tenor*
Dr. Blind, Eisenstein's lawyer.*Tenor*
Dr. Falke, noted ballmaster.*Baritone*
Frank, a warden ....*Baritone*
Prince Orlofsky .....*Mezzo-soprano*
Frosch, a jailer ......*Speaking role*

Prologue

Overture

Act I

Previous to the time of the action of this story, Dr. Fritz Falke, the noted ballmaster, is the victim of a horrendous practical joke perpetrated by his friend, Eisenstein. On the way home from a party Falke, dressed as a bat (*die Fledermaus*) and having imbibed a bit too freely, passes out in the carriage of Eisenstein. Eisenstein deposits him unconscious in the middle of the public square and leaves him. When Falke regains consciousness it is nine o'clock the next morning and he is in the midst of a laughing, jeering crowd. In great embarassment he has to make his way home still costumed as a bat. Since that time people have referred to him, behind his back of course, as "Dr. Fledermaus" and he has busied himself with finding a suitable revenge for this dastardly practical joke. This revenge, carefully planned, is scheduled to come off this evening at a ball at the residence of Prince Orlofsky.

There is one slight complication. The Baron von Eisenstein has insulted some minor civic official and has been sentenced to prison for eight days. Eisenstein plans to enter the prison to serve his term this very evening. Falke, in order to carry out his plans for revenge, must persuade Eisenstein to postpone the actual arrival at the prison until the next day. Falke tells Eisenstein about the ball at Prince Orlofsky's and invites him to attend with him. Falke tempts Eisenstein by telling him there will be a number of very handsome ladies from the ballet attending. Eisenstein agrees to attend the ball with Falke but tells his wife, Rosalinda, that he is on his way to prison to begin serving his sentence.

Opens just before Falke's invitation to the ball and takes place in the apartment of Eisenstein. Just outside, Alfred, a singing teacher and former admirer of Rosalinda, is heard singing a serenade to his former sweetheart ("Täubchen, das entflattert ist, stille mein Verlangen"—"Little dove that fluttered away, still my longing"). This serenade is interrupted by Adele, who has also been invited to the ball by Falke, attempting to obtain permission to go to the ball by claiming her sister has invited her ("Was schreibt meine Schwester Ida?"—"What does my sister Ida write?"). She is denied the necessary permission by Eisenstein and Rosalinda. At the moment Eisenstein and Rosalinda are more interested in blaming Eisenstein's bumbling lawyer, Blind, for not having won the case for Eisenstein ("Nein, mit solchen Advokaten ist verkauft man und verraten"—"No, with such lawyers, one is sold and betrayed"). Dr. Falke arrives and, speaking to Eisenstein, tells of the wonderful ball being given by Prince Orlofsky. He suggests that Eisenstein post-

401

pone his reporting to the prison until the next day and that they attend the ball instead. He further suggests that Eisenstein tell his wife that he is leaving for prison as planned. Falke does not tell Eisenstein that he has also sent invitations to this same ball to Rosalinda and Adele. Rosalinda, Eisenstein and Adele then join in a trio of farewell ("O Gott, wie rührt mich dies!" —"O God, it overwhelms me!"). After this, Eisenstein leaves. He is barely out of sight when Alfred arrives ("Trinke, Liebchen, trinke schnell"—"Drink, my love, drink quickly") and proceeds to make himself at home. This is very short-lived, however, because of the arrival of Frank, the warden, who has come to escort Eisenstein to jail. He naturally mistakes Alfred for Eisenstein. Moved by Rosalinda's plea not to betray her good name, Alfred permits himself to be led away to prison as Eisenstein.

Act II

Takes place in the palatial home of Prince Orlofsky. The ball is in progress. The chorus appears, to sing of the bountiful table that has been spread and to suggest that the occasion is meant to be a merry and a gay one ("Ein Souper heut' uns winkt"—"A supper beckons us today"). Prince Orlofsky and Eisenstein appear. Orlofsky explains to Eisenstein that he derives great personal pleasure and satisfaction from people who genuinely enjoy his parties ("Ich lade gern mir Gäste ein, Man lebt bei mir recht fein" —"I invite my guests gladly, they live well at my house"). This dialogue is interrupted by the arrival of Adele who, disguised as "Olga," and thanks to all of the commotion at the Eisenstein house, has been able to slip away to attend the ball after all. Although Eisenstein has a feeling that he knows her, he is not quite able to identify her. Adele tells Eisenstein that he really needs to have his eyes examined, that

she, a lady and a blue blood, is insulted by his insinuations ("Mein Herr Marquis"—"My dear Marquis, a man like you ought to understand this better"). At this moment a masked Rosalinda arrives to observe the flirtatious Eisenstein in action. She, introduced to him as a Hungarian countess, immediately engages him in a flirtation. During the course of it she manages to extract his watch which she intends to keep as proof of his Don Juanish personality ("Dieser Anstand, so manierlich" — "This demeanor, so mannerly, this waist petite and dainty"). As Eisenstein pleads for the return of his watch, Orlofsky summons a gypsy band to launch into a czardas. Rosalinda, in character, sings of the sounds which remind her of home ("Klänge der Heimat"—"Sounds of homeland awaken my longing"). Frank, the warden, has also been invited to the ball by Falke and during this time has been spending his time courting Adele. The finale of Act II begins with a rousing drinking song as the party begins to reach its climax. The act ends with the breaking up of the party.

Act III

Takes place in the prison the next morning. Frank staggers in minus one shoe, hat perched on one side of his head and carrying a bottle. He attempts a dance, holding his cape as if it were his partner, but soon tires, drops into a chair and falls asleep. Adele chooses this precise time to arrive at the prison dressed as a peasant ("Spiel' ich die Unschuld vom Lande"—"I'm playing the innocent from the country") to see Frank. At the same time two other people arrive on the scene, each with a different purpose, Eisenstein to begin his prison term of eight days and Rosalinda to begin divorce proceedings against Eisenstein. In the confusion Eisenstein is introduced as Alfred's lawyer and learns of the reason for Alfred's incarceration during the course of the trio ("Ich stehe voll Zagen"—"I stand full of fear—what will he ask me?"). As the story unfolds, Eisenstein, finding it difficult to maintain the expected mien of a lawyer, finally gives vent to his anger by threatening to murder Rosalinda and Alfred as the penalty for their indiscretion. At the height of this confusion Falke arrives with the rest of the guests who had attended the ball. He confesses that everything that has happened has resulted from his plan for avenging the embarrassment caused him by Eisenstein's practical joke played on him a year before. His ends accomplished, he is instrumental in making the necessary arrangements for the satisfactory solution of everyone's problem except one— Eisenstein must still serve his eight days in prison ("O Fledermaus, O Fledermaus").

The Musical Comedy

Musical comedy can be, and is, pure Americana. It is a form of music drama which has had its inception and development in America during this present twentieth century. In form it lies somewhere between the extremes of the variety show on the one hand and opera on the other. A musical comedy, in fact, combines certain elements and aspects of the operetta with some of the technics characteristic of the revue. In a typical musical comedy an outstanding vocal soloist may sing alone or combine his talent with the magnificent sound of a chorus, only to have the music interrupted for a round of boisterous comedy, or for a colorful dance routine. In the musical comedy all of these activities are essential to the development of the plot. In this strictly American contribution to the music theater, the musical comedy, because of its relationship to opera, may be musically every bit as elaborate as any operetta. But because of the other factors present, it has an entity and flavor all its own.

One characteristic of the musical comedy is that it tells an American story. The plot is projected in dialogue and song with both couched in the vernacular of America. In a sense the musical comedy might be looked upon as a reflection of the life, the attitudes, the customs and even the speech of American people. For this reason the dialogue of a musical comedy may be considerably more rowdy, the humor more earthy than that found in the operetta. Musically speaking, one tends to associate soft and dreamy melodies with the operetta, while the musical comedy may employ the latest jazz idiom for the projection of its message.

While the emphasis of the opera is on the musical value and the expressive purpose of the music, the musical comedy's main purpose is pure, unadulterated entertainment. The typical musical comedy has something in it for every member of the audience. An interesting, even exciting, plot replete with romance; singing, dancing, rib-tickling comedy scenes; beautiful girls and handsome men all vie with one another to capture the

403

audience's attention. The music ranges from scintillating, toe-tapping melodies for song and dance to more serious, soulful love ballads. In general, however, there is so much briskness and verve in the musical comedy, one is left with the feeling that it has great vigor and has been presented in the lively tempo of modern living. The stage sets, the lighting and the costumes are often lavish and are calculated to enhance the general tone of the production.

No discussion of the musical comedy would be complete without mention of some of the composers who have contributed so much to its development. It has been due to the creative efforts of such composers as Jerome Kern (1885-1945), George Gershwin (1898-1937), Irving Berlin (1888———), Cole Porter (1893-1964) and Richard Rodgers (1902———) that this distinctively American form of music drama has come into being and has thrived. In the musical comedy these composers found the ideal medium for combining some of the best features of the frothy revue with those of the more sedate operetta into a unified presentation. The result is superb music theater.

LISTENING ACTIVITY

Oklahoma!....Richard Rodgers (1902———) and Oscar Hammerstein II (1895-1960)

The Cast

Aunt Eller Murphy
Curly
Laurey
Ado Annie Carnes
Will Parker
Jud Fry
Ali Hakim, the peddler
Andrew Carnes
Gertie Cummings
Boys
Girls

Time: Soon after 1900.
Place: The Indian Territory, known today as Oklahoma.

Overture

Act I—Scene 1. In front of Laurey's farmhouse.

It is a beautiful day. Aunt Eller Murphy has taken advantage of it and is sitting outside the house doing the weekly churning. From the distance, but gradually coming closer, is heard a song extolling the beauty of the day

("Oh, What a Beautiful Mornin' "). It is Curly coming to call and hopefully planning to persuade Laurey to go to the box social with him. Laurey tries to be coy and says she is not at all certain that she would be interested in going to the social with Curly, because he does not have the proper transportation for such an occasion. Curly surprises her by telling her that if they were to go to the social together there would be a proper way for taking her ("The Surrey with the Fringe on Top"). Despite the fact that Curly wants to take Laurey to the social and Laurey wants to go to the social with Curly, neither will admit his feelings toward the other, and Laurey ends the matter by flouncing into the house and slamming the door. A group of young fellows now arrives and among them is Will Parker, obviously a favorite of Aunt Eller. Will has just returned from a fair with fifty dollars which he won in a roping contest. He has stopped by for just a moment, but his real purpose is to go

404

to the home of Ado Annie Carnes to ask for her hand in marriage. He takes time, however, to tell of all of the new, interesting and strange sights he has seen while in the city ("Ev'rythin's Up to Date in Kansas City"). Aunt Eller tells Curly that while Laurey does not want to give the impression that she is interested in him, she really is, but that Curly does have a rival in Jud Fry. Jud arrives on the scene and announces that he is taking Laurey to the social. After Curly leaves, Laurey asks Aunt Eller to go with her as she is afraid to go to the social alone with Jud. She tells Aunt Eller that she only accepted Jud's invitation to make Curly jealous. While they are talking, Ado Annie arrives with Ali Hakim, the peddler. When Ado Annie learns that Will Parker is looking for her she finds herself in a bit of a dilemma. Not expecting Will to be back, she has invited the peddler to go to the social with her. She explains the reason why she is continually having these problems ("I Cain't Say No"). When Will Parker finally finds her he tells her that he has won the fifty dollars and has now come to claim her as his wife. It soon begins to look as if Gertie Cummings may be trying to capture Curly's attention. Laurey gives the impression that she is not at all concerned ("Many a New Day"). A slight complication now appears in the romance of Ado Annie and Will Parker. Will, in his happiness, has spent all of the fifty dollars on presents, and Ado Annie's father, Andrew, calls off the wedding because Will was to pay him the entire fifty dollars. The fickle Annie quickly shifts her attentions to Ali Hakim, who before he knows what hit him, finds himself engaged to Ado Annie ("It's a Scandal! It's a Outrage!"). People begin leaving for the social, leaving Laurey and Curly. Each tries to convince the other that people are saying that the other one is in love with him or her ("People Will Say We're in Love"). Curly leaves to go to the smokehouse

to see what it is about Jud that makes girls want to go to parties with him.

Scene 2. The smokehouse.

Curly finds Jud polishing a Colt .45. Curly picks up a rope and suggests that Jud might really make himself popular by hanging himself. He tells Jud that a lot of women have taken a shine to him but would never come out and show their feelings for him unless Jud died first ("Poor Jud is Daid"). At first Jud seems to be interested in the idea but when he realizes that Curly is really interested in Laurey he changes his mind in a hurry. He attempts to buy a long-bladed knife from the peddler, thinking he might be able to enforce his will over Laurey and Curly. As Curly leaves, Jud sees the smokehouse for what it really is ("Lonely Room") and decides that he must get himself a bride.

Scene 3. A grove on Laurey's farm.

Laurey has decided it is time for her to do some serious thinking. She and the girls discuss just what it is she wants ("Out of My Dreams"). She drops off to sleep and in her dreams she sees the things which are to help her make up her mind. She is awakened by Jud telling her it is time to go to the party.

Act II—Scene 1. The social at the Skidmore ranch.

The guests are making merry and dancing. Andrew Carnes stops the dancing momentarily as he asks that everybody be friendly and stick together ("The Farmer and the Cowman"). Unfortunately not all of the guests share this feeling, and the social disrupts into a brawl which is quickly ended when Aunt Eller grabs a gun from one of the men's holsters and fires it into the air. She accepts the responsibility for being the auctioneer and begins the

405

auctioning off of the box suppers. Will Parker runs into the crafty Ali Hakim who "allows" Will to sell him all of the presents for the sum of fifty dollars. Will exits looking for Ado Annie and her father. Meanwhile back at the auction all of the hampers have been sold except two. One belonging to Ado Annie is finally sold to Ali Hakim, and the other belonging to Laurey is the object of much spirited bidding by Jud, Andrew Carnes and Curly. Curly finally wins after having to sell his own saddle, horse and gun in order to have enough money. After everyone has eaten, the dancing begins anew. Will Parker and Ado Annie try to set the date for their wedding but the discussion gets slightly out of hand when Ado Annie sets the date for August 15, the date of her first kiss, only it was not Will who did the kissing ("All or Nuthin' "). Finally, however, they are able to resolve the difficulty and go ahead with the planning for the wedding.

Scene 2. The porch just off the kitchen of the Skidmore ranch house.

Jud, dancing with Laurey, dances her to this spot. They quarrel and Laurey orders Jud to leave. She sends for Curly and tells him of her fear of Jud. Curly promises to find a new farmhand for her and, in the meantime, to stay at the ranch to keep an eye on things. Laurey accepts when he asks her to marry him ("People Will Say We're in Love"). The scene closes with Ali Hakim saying goodbye to Ado Annie and Will Parker.

Scene 3. The backyard of Laurey's farmhouse.

The wedding party of Laurey and Curly is in progress. Some of the guests are discussing the advantages of living in Oklahoma, the state soon to be ("Oklahoma!"). Gertie arrives on the scene with her new husband, the hapless Ali Hakim, who was not as successful in escaping from her clutches as he was from Ado Annie. In the midst of the festivities Jud arrives and attempts to break up the party. In the fight with Curly that follows Jud falls on his own knife and is killed. Curly is not held responsible for Jud's death and everything ends happily ("Oh What a Beautiful Mornin' "—"People Will Say We're in Love").

The Opera

The acme of perfection in music drama is found in the form known as opera, sometimes referred to as "grand opera." In this form of music drama the actors project all of their thoughts and actions by singing rather than by speaking. The recitative becomes the means for describing and moving the action, while the aria is reserved for the expression of feelings. In general, opera may be said to be more serious in purpose and musical values than the other forms of music drama. In opera, or grand opera, the composer selects a serious play and sets it to music. It can be readily seen that as far as the dramatic staple is concerned, not just any plot will do—the composer must select a story which can be adapted to music and strengthened by it. The basic premise underlying the creation and performance of opera is the knowledge that the emotional potency of words can be greatly enhanced by the addition of music. Despite the popular appeal of the operetta and the musical comedy, in the final analysis it has been opera itself which has proved to be the most popular and satisfying form of music drama in our Western culture. One has only to observe the opera season in some European country to see positive proof of the strong popular attraction inherent in opera.

Successful opera depends not only on the successful union of music and drama but may involve the collaboration of other arts as well. The basic problem in the development of an opera is the fusion of all of these separate entities into a well-proportioned, symmetrical whole. In the beginning it is the author who communicates the story or theme. It is his responsibility to move the story along to its ultimate conclusion by dramatic action. It is through this dramatic action also that characters are given proper delineation and the underlying mood is created. The composer, in choosing this particular dramatic work for further exploitation through the addition of music, must in turn assume the responsibility for heightening the emotional impact and communicative power of the original work. To accomplish this he has at his disposal several musical devices and technics. He may heighten the underlying mood as well as complement and move the dramatic action forward by the use of solo voice, small ensemble, chorus or by the orchestra, depending on the needs of the scene. It might better suit his purpose at a particular point in the action to involve the resources of the ballet, which would then necessitate the close cooperation of another art form. Finally, the talents of the artist must be employed in the creation, construction and painting of the sets and in the creation of suitable costumes. All of these are necessary in adding to the communicative purpose of the opera. At the same time they must also help maintain the integrity of the original statements of the dramatist and the composer. All of these factors refer, of course, to the creation of an opera. In performance the conductor and the performers must reflect this same feeling and responsibility for proper proportion if the final production is to realize the potential power given to the work by its creators.

Because opera is a drama in which the characters sing all of their parts and their thoughts instead of speaking them, it might be well to focus again upon the vocal technics used by the composer in creating an opera. The *recitative* is used by the composer to describe and move the action. It may be little more than intensified speech taking advantage of the natural rhythm of the words. In the recitative the vocal line is punctuated from time to time by the orchestra accompaniment which serves to give added emphasis to the musical utterance.

We have already seen that the *aria*, on the other hand, is characterized by its lyric, songlike quality. It is in the aria that the singer-actor is able to express his innermost thoughts and feelings. It is to the aria that the

407

composer turns when fashioning an impassioned love song or for portraying depth of tragedy. In the early days of opera there was a concomitant use for the aria—it was a popular device for displaying the vocal skill and technic of the soloist. In this respect the aria was popular with soloist and audience alike. Modern composers, however, have considerably lessened the importance of this show aspect of the aria, or have done away with it entirely.

Another characteristic use of vocal music to be found in opera is the use of the small vocal ensemble. A given opera may well involve the vocal resources of a duet, a trio, a quartet or some other form of small vocal grouping, in addition to the singing of a large chorus. There are several good reasons for this. In the first place even with the ever-changing scene which results from the dramatic action and the solo singing of the actors, there is a need for more musical variety if the work is to hold the interest of the audience. Many worthwhile and beautiful musical effects are possible only with the use of these small vocal ensemble combinations. It would be unthinkable to limit the musical effectiveness of an opera by not including small vocal ensembles whenever necessary. There is another very practical use for the small vocal ensemble. If several of the characters were to speak at once the resulting sound would be unintelligible and the overall effect chaotic. We have also been taught from childhood that it is the height of impoliteness for everyone to talk at once. Yet there are times when it is to the advantage of a work if the audience can understand at a glance the different thoughts and sentiments being felt by the characters on the stage at a given moment. For this reason alone the use of simultaneous singing in duets, trios and the other small groupings can serve a most useful function in the communication of ideas and moods.

The structural organization of the opera has gone through many changes since the form came into existence as a musical entity. As has already been pointed out, opera's history probably goes back to the ancient Greek music dramas, although little is really known about this particular art form. It is known that another source of the opera was the church with its dramatic ceremonial masses, as well as the mystery and miracle plays of the Middle Ages. From secular sources, particularly during the feudal period, came the dance, the pantomime and the use of scenic splendor. All of these threads were brought together by Giulio Caccini (1558-1615) and Jacopo Peri (1561-1633), and by the year 1600 the art form we know today as opera had begun to take firm shape.

In the eighteenth century the Neapolitan school influenced opera through its interest in improving the existing form. From this school came the recitative and the aria. The vocal art of *bel canto* singing was fully exploited and became an integral part of the musical equipment of all singers appearing before the public. The librettos were interesting in that they dealt with classical historical subjects. These librettos were cast into a unified but strict three-act organizational structure. Composers who were particularly successful in writing operas in this form were George Frideric Handel (1685-1759), Alessandro Stradella (1642-1682) and Christoph Willibald Gluck (1714-1787).

In the mid-eighteenth century a form of comic opera known as the Italian *opera buffa* came into being. This form of opera was cast in a two-act format and departed somewhat from the rigidity of the Neapolitan school. Successful composers of opera buffa included Giovanni Battista Pergolesi (1710-1736) and Wolfgang Amadeus Mozart (1756-1791). In France at about this same time composers of opera were becoming increasingly interested in the use of the ballet. One finds in French operas of this period abundant use of ballet. The use of chorus also found its way into the French opera of this period. Musically the French opera made considerable use of short, simple songs. Instrumental music was also given a more independent role in the French opera. Jean Baptiste Lully (1632-1687), Robert Cambert (c. 1628-1677) and Jean Philippe Rameau (1683-1764) were particularly successful in developing this typically French form of the opera.

In looking at the eighteenth century and the factors which had the greatest and most lasting effects on opera as it is known today, several contributions of the era need to be mentioned. Composers such as Gluck and Mozart brought to opera new flexibility and integration of vocal and instrumental resources. This in turn led to greater flexibility in the use of the musical forms selected to project the action and meaning of the operatic work. There developed a new interest in simple plots which could be developed so that the dramatic and musical forces could achieve a degree of unity unobtainable in the older operas in which musical considerations came first. Finally, it was during this time that opera composers began to veer away from writing vocal compositions for the mere display of vocal virtuosity. The impact of this period of opera writing continued to influence succeeding composers such as Gioacchino Rossini (1792-1868), Giacomo Meyerbeer (1791-1864), Charles Gounod (1818-1893), Georges Bizet (1838-1875), Jules Massenet (1842-1912), and culminated in the inspired operas of Giuseppe Verdi (1813-1901).

One last influence on opera should be mentioned. This was the nineteenth-century German romantic opera. In this form of opera the libretto was based on one of the national legends, with the music treated in highly romantic style. Carl Maria von Weber (1786-1826) was particularly important in the creation of this distinctively national style of opera. German romantic opera culminated in the writing of Richard Wagner (1813-1883). It was Wagner's great ambition to create a new art form, one which achieved significant balance and unity between the dramatic, vocal and instrumental resources and treated them as an integrated whole. In his efforts to achieve this unity he created the musical device known as the

409

leitmotiv. This was a short but distinctive melodic bit used to identify a character, idea or situation every time it appeared in the opera. Wagner's influence has continued to be strongly felt in the twentieth century, during which opera and the other forms of music drama have continued to grow and flourish.

Carmen...Georges Bizet (1838-1875)

Opera may best be explained and understood if one of the most popular operas ever composed is examined rather closely. While *Carmen* was not an outstanding success in its premiere performance, it has become one of the staples of almost every opera house in the world. In this study the aim should be to learn the plot of the opera, to distinguish between the various characters, and to make certain judgments as to whether one is listening to solo, duet, quartet, chorus or instrumental music.

Cast

Don José, a corporal of
    dragoons ....*Tenor*
Escamillo, a toreador......*Baritone*
Zuniga, a captain...........*Bass*
El Dancairo, smuggler.....*Baritone*
El Remendado, smuggler.....*Tenor*
Morales, an officer...........*Bass*
Micaela, a peasant girl.....*Soprano*
Frasquita ....*Mezzo-soprano*
Mercedes ....*Mezzo-soprano*
Carmen, a cigarette girl
    and gypsy........*Mezzo-soprano*
Innkeeper, gypsies, friends of Carmen, guide, officers, dragoons, boys, cigarette girls and smugglers.

Time: about 1820
Place: Seville, Spain

Overture

Act I

Looking for her lover, Micaela, the country maid to whom Don José is engaged, enters a square in Seville ("Sur la place, Chacun passe"—"What a bustling"). He is not yet on duty. The relieving guard arrives (military music and Street Boys' Song), including Don José. Micaela runs away from the flirtatious soldiers before Don José's arrival, and he is told that she is seeking him and will return. Now the cigarette girls come, on their way to the factory ("Voyez-les! Regards impudents"—"Here they are! How boldly they stare"). Carmen, their leader, is asked by the soldiers to choose a lover. She sings ("Habanera"—"Love is like any woodbird") and flings the flower she wears to Don José. The factory bell rings, summoning the girls to work. The soldiers enter the guardhouse. Don José remains in the empty square. Micaela reappears. Hurriedly Don José stuffs the flower into his jacket. Micaela brings him a message from his mother urging him to marry Micaela and return home with her ("Parle-moi de ma mère!"—"Tell me, what of my mother?"). But now there is an uproar in the factory ("Que se passe-t-il donc là-bas?"—"What can be going on there?"). Carmen has stabbed another girl; Don José brings her out a prisoner ("Mon officier, c'était une querelle"—"Captain, there has been a quarrel"). While the lieutenant is writing the orders for her imprisonment Carmen sings the teasing song ("Seguidilla"—"Near to the walls of Seville, with my good friend Lillas Pastia I'll soon dance the gay Seguidilla") with the suggestion of a rendezvous at Lillas Pastia's tavern. The gypsy's sorcery so works on Don José that he undoes the cord tying her hands, and when the crowd again gathers in the square she makes her escape (Finale).

Act II

After an orchestral entr'acte on the theme of "The Dragoons of Alcala" the curtain rises on the interior of Lillas Pastia's tavern. Carmen is singing a gypsy song with two gypsy girls, Frasquita and Mercedes ("Les tringles des sistres tintaient"—"The sound of sistrum bars did greet"). General dancing and jubilation fill the scene. The bullfighter, Escamillo, enters singing his famous aria (Toreador Song). Escamillo is as captivated by Carmen as she is taken by him ("La belle, un mot"—"My fair one, a word"). She still thinks of Don José who has gone to prison for allowing her to escape and knows that he will come to the tavern when he is released. Don José does arrive after the crowd of gypsies and smugglers have dispersed ("Enfin c'est toi"—"'Tis you at last!"). Carmen dances for his pleasure ("Je vais danser en votre honneur"—"Now I shall dance in your honor"). When the bugles sound retreat Don José is torn between duty and love for Carmen; he sings an impassioned love song ("La fleur que tu m'avais jettée"—"The flower that you threw to me"). The captain of the dragoons, Zuniga, arrives and orders Don José to the barracks, but Don José refuses to obey and draws his sword on him. As Don José is about to lose the fight Carmen calls in the chief of the smugglers and Zuniga is surrounded (Finale). There is no further question of Don José's returning to the barracks. He, too, throws in his lot with the smugglers.

Act III

The smugglers, Carmen and Don José among them, are in their mountainous retreat ("Écoute, écoute, compagnon, écoute" — "Attention, attention, comrades"). Carmen is now tired of Don José and makes no secret of the fact. The image of Escamillo is now uppermost in her mind. Carmen reads her fortune in the cards and each draw tells her the same thing—death. There is the question of the customs men. Three girls promise to take care of them and the smugglers go away. The chief smuggler, having reproved Don José for his tiresome jealousy of Carmen, sends him to guard the bales of contraband. Directed by a guide, Micaela enters ("C'est des contrebandiers"—"Here is the usual place for the smugglers to gather"). She has made her way to the retreat to beg Don José to return to his dying mother and receive her forgiveness. A shot rings out. Escamillo appears ("Je suis Escamillo"—"I am Escamillo"). He has been in the highlands herding bulls. Don José fires on him as a trespasser. Now the two men face one another. Don José recognizes Escamillo and welcomes him, but when the bullfighter tells him the woman he loves is there and that she is Carmen, a duel with knives is on. The smugglers return and Carmen stays Don José's hand. Micaela reappears after having hidden during the duel. She gives Don José the message from his mother. Don José consents to go away with her but the challenge of the bullfighter rings in his ears. To Carmen he says, "Be content! I go, but we shall meet again." The curtain descends on this tableau of impending doom.

Act IV

The curtain rises on the square before the arena. It is the day of the bullfight. The bullfighter, Carmen, officials and toreros in a gala procession enter the square where the people await their idol. About to enter the ring, Escamillo bids Carmen farewell, both vowing undying love ("Si tu m'aimes, Carmen"—"If you love me, Carmen"). Carmen ignores the warnings of Frasquita and Mercedes ("Carmen, un bon conseil"—"Carmen, take my advice") who tell her that Don José may seek her here. Don José does appear ("C'est toi" —"You here"). He is the man she has morally and physically destroyed, a dramatic contrast to his triumphant

411

rival, Escamillo. Ruined, cheated and cast out because of his love, he cannot forget her. He implores Carmen to be kind to him ("J'implore, je supplie!"—"I beg you, I entreat you"). But Escamillo's name sounds in the arena amid wild applause and her thoughts are with him. She makes no secret of her pride and joy. Wrenching the ring Don José once gave her from her finger, Carmen throws it at his feet. When Escamillo's name is again thundered forth by the unseen crowd, Don José stabs her in the heart. The triumphant Escamillo steps out of the arena to see Don José throw himself on the body of Carmen crying, "O Carmen! My adored Carmen."

ADDITIONAL CLASS ACTIVITIES

1. Study the libretto of the opera *The Masked Ball* by Verdi and discuss the political overtones of the story.
2. Discuss the problem and difficulty of using English translations of opera originally written in a foreign language.
3. Discuss the vocabulary used in opera.
4. Discuss the differences between the revue, musical comedy, light opera, comic opera, operetta and opera.
5. Define overture, aria, chorus, duet and recitative.
6. Discuss the dual role of members of the chorus.
7. Discuss the variety of vocal sounds to be found in an opera.
8. Play recordings of the modernized version of the opera *Carmen* and compare it with the original version.

unit 7

Music with a program

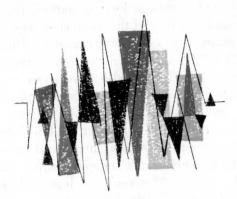

chapter 11

Extramusical Clues for Understanding Music

Music in which the composer attempts to suggest certain associations with literary, pictorial and even mental images is generally referred to as program music. Conversely, music which is created without any reference to pictorial, literary or dramatic programs is known as absolute music. In Chapter Two we saw that the poem "Danse Macabre" by Henri Cazalis (1840-1909) was the inspiration for a musical composition of the same name written by Camille Saint-Saëns (1835-1921). In the music Saint-Saëns attempted to portray in musical terms not only the mood of the poetry but also the *action*. The poem tells of the rite which occurs on All Saints' Eve when ghosts and skeletons come out of their hiding places and graves to dance the night away. In the music Saint-Saëns begins by having the harp simulate the sound of a clock striking the hour of midnight. That Death, the fiddler, is on the scene is apparent when he is heard tuning his fiddle. An eerie dance with a "gruesome" strain takes over. Ghostly wails, suggested by downward configurations of notes played by the various instruments, are a foil for the rattle of the skeletons' bones represented by the brittle sound of the xylophone. An oboe is called upon to give out with the crow of the cock—the signal that all must return to the grave for another year. In this composition the composer took the essential details of the poetry and attempted to translate them as accurately as possible into musical terms. How well he succeeded depends on the point of view of the listener.

From almost the very beginnings of music its creators have been interested in trying to give extramusical meaning to some of their musical creations. It is known, for example, that as far back as ancient Greece some anonymous composer created a musical work which he entitled "The Battle of Apollo and Marsyas." In the sixteenth century, composers began

415

to show consistent interest in creating works which attempted to imitate such everyday sights and sounds as hunting parties, the calls of birds and animals. Even the sound and fury of the storm challenged an early composer to try to express in music its awe-inspiring character. The English composer, William Byrd (1543-1623), although remembered primarily for his church music, string music and madrigals, also showed an interest in the extra-musical use of music to depict scenes and events. A composition for the spinet, "The King's Hunt," by John Bull (1563-1628) suggests in music a typical hunting scene of his time. Clément Jannequin (1485-1560), with his "Battle of Marignan" was another early composer interested in using music to portray life situations. During the seventeenth and eighteenth centuries Louis Claude Daquin (1694-1772), with his "Cuckoo" and Jean Philippe Rameau (1683-1764), who wrote "The Hen," joined the growing number of composers interested in this form of musical expression. Another of the early writers of program music was Johann Kuhnau (1660-1722), the predecessor of Bach as cantor of St. Thomas Church in Leipzig. One of his better-known sonatas, "David and Goliath's Combat," is a curious mixture of representation and suggestion as it tells of the confrontation of the pompous, boastful Goliath by David, a quiet youth of great courage and faith.

It was in the Romantic period, however, that the programmatic concept of writing music really came into full bloom. Probably one of the great contributions of the Romantic movement was the closer involvement of music with the other arts, particularly those of painting and poetry. During this period composers were no longer content with the mere act of imitating the sights and sounds of nature and the world about them. The new goal was to suggest as well as represent, to portray genuine poetic ideas and to communicate mood—certainly a more subtle and sophisticated use of music than was present in the programmatic writing of the earlier composers. The availability of great literary and art works provided an enormous impetus to the creation of program music during this period. The ready availability of great art works, plus the new political emphasis on liberty and justice, provided just the right resources and climate for a Hector Berlioz (1803-1869) and a Franz Liszt (1811-1886). They took over and nurtured the somewhat fledgling programmatic music of the previous periods and brought it to full fruition. Both Liszt and Berlioz used the technic of having short themes represent characters or ideas in their works.

Program music is written for an instrument or for a combination of instruments. It is not a musical form in the sense that sonata allegro, rondo, minuet and trio, or theme and variations are considered to be. A piece of program music may, in fact, use any one of the various formal organizational structures to tie the ideas together so that the finished product will possess both unity and variety. In short, program music is an instrumental music composition which tells a story, paints a picture or communicates a poetic idea or mood.

Program music is perhaps the easiest music for the layman to grasp. We all enjoy a good story and when this story is enhanced by music it tends to leave a more vivid impression of both. The development and recurrence of themes which represent or suggest the characters or ideas help the listener follow the continuity of the music. While there are those who tend to classify all program music as being inferior to absolute music, such a position is really quite difficult to maintain. There have been great composers of pure or absolute music who have written poor music as well as great. In a similar fashion some composers of program music have brought into being music of great worth and beauty as well as some music containing little of merit. Then too, these same great composers have been equally at home with absolute and program music, and would not want a judgment of "bad" placed on part of their music because it was program music and "good" on part of their music because it was absolute. They would want each type to be judged on its own musical merit. The point is, there is good and bad program music just as there is good and bad absolute music. The listener must be able to make the necessary value judgments as to whether the music is good or bad, whether it has intrinsic worth or is cheap and tawdry. For people whose understanding of music is not limited to a superficial response to rhythm or mood, valid as these means of communication are, knowledge of the programmatic content of a musical composition becomes another one of several avenues leading to increased enjoyment and understanding.

In writing a piece of program music the composer is restricted only in the sense that he must stay within the framework of the idea he is attempting to depict musically. The length of the composition may also depend on the subject matter selected. This results in musical compositions of varying length ranging from the relatively short "Sorcerer's Apprentice" by Paul Dukas (1865-1935) based on a story by Johann Wolfgang Goethe (1749-1832) to a five-movement expression of the dreams of an artist under the influence of opium in the *Symphonie Fantastique* by Hector Berlioz (1803-1869).

Overture-Fantasy, *Romeo and Juliet*..........Peter Ilyich Tchaikovsky (1840-1893)   **LISTENING ACTIVITY**

The idea of writing music based on Shakespeare's immortal *Romeo and Juliet* was first suggested to Tchaikovsky by his friend, Mily Balakirev (1837-1910), to whom the work is dedicated. Written in 1869, revised and republished in 1881, the work is one of the most popular staples of the orchestral repertoire. In this composition Tchaikovsky did not concern himself with a literal translation in music terms of the action of the Shakespeare drama. Rather, he contented himself with the communication of the characters and the emotional climate in which they moved. In the structural organization, Tchaikovsky chose to cast the overture in sonata allegro or first movement form.

417

The work begins with a slow introduction which with its monastic sounds and character seems to suggest Friar Lawrence and the role he is to play in the tragedy.

The main body of the overture, the *Allegro giusto*, with its abrupt change of tempo and mood, seems to describe in musical terms the anger, hatred and violence which have become so much a part of the lives of the Montague and the Capulet families.

The sound and fury of the deadly feuding between these two houses continues to build and build until at the very climax a harsh rhythmic figure played by the cymbals seems to suggest sword on sword as rival members meet in deadly duel.

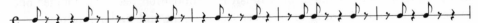

The struggle cannot last forever and from the storm of battle there emerges a change of mood which sings of the sublimity of love. This love theme, one of the most exquisite love songs ever penned, is given its initial life through the voices of the English horn and viola.

Romeo has been banished from Verona for having slain one of the Capulets in the duel. Muted strings seem to suggest the sighing of the two lovers as they take their leave from one another.

Once again the love theme returns. This time high woodwinds, sighing horns and throbbing strings add a feeling of pathos to the theme.

The middle section of the overture, the development section, is in the form of a free fantasia. Here melodic bits reminiscent of the feud and bits suggesting Friar Lawrence are worked and reworked.

The recapitulation or restatement brings about the resumption of the struggle between the two feuding families. Interwoven in the militant sounds of the combat are strains of the love theme, as well as suggestions of the ominous prophecy of Friar Lawrence. Abruptly the sounds of strife are silenced. Muffled drum beats and the doleful voices of the violins, cellos and bassoons tell of the death of Romeo and Juliet.

Fragments of the love theme rising higher and higher in the violins seem to suggest that in death Romeo and Juliet finally find peace.

Till Eulenspiegel's Merry Pranks....................Richard Strauss (1864-1949)

Till Eulenspiegel, famous legendary character, was a real-life person living in the fourteenth century. He was a vagabond shoemaker wandering all over Europe until he fell victim to the Black Death in 1350. He was a merry rogue, living by his wits and often at the expense of others. He was an inveterate practical joker whose escapades furnished the people of medieval times with subject material for countless stories. As these stories were passed along there were those who could not resist the temptation to embroider the account just a bit by adding a few fictional details of their own. These stories, because they were passed along by word of mouth, finally arrived at a place where it was difficult to separate fact from fiction. Sometime toward the end of the fifteenth century or in the early sixteenth century the many stories and legends about Till were written down by the Franciscan monk, Thomas Murner (1475-1530).

Although Till was a prankster and clown, there was also an undercurrent of sadness to his life which resulted from his being the victim of a haphazard kind of existence. Some of his mischievousness and drollery was perpetrated not so much from a malicious desire to destroy but rather as a potent weapon against the pride, vanity, dishonesty and injustice of those in positions of authority. He made himself out to be whatever the situation demanded —butcher, baker, wheelwright, joiner, monk or learned metaphysician. He seemed unable to recognize the ugliness

419

of some of his pranks or the hurt that they caused to others and even to himself.

Richard Strauss (1864-1949) who brought one kind of program music, the tone poem, to its greatest height by his ingenious use of an enlarged orchestra and his mastery of orchestration, knew every detail of the Till story. In setting down the legend of Till in music he did not attempt to follow a rigid or set program. Rather he preferred to leave the discovery of these details to the imagination of the listener.

Since the composer is asking the listener to use his imagination, the degree to which the listener responds emotionally will depend on how imaginative he is. At the same time the music can also be approached through the involvement of the intellect by examining the musical technics used by the composer in achieving the various effects. The listener who becomes conversant with these technics will better enjoy *Till Eulenspiegel's Merry Pranks.*

There are two Till themes, the first of which might be called "Till the rogue." It is impish in character, with its jumps which do not land on the expected tone.

As the work progresses this theme recurs over and over and each time the first notes, A-F-B♮-C, are always the same, despite the key to which the work has moved. This is the immature Till, impetuously moving from one escapade to another without considering the consequences. The other Till theme represents a more mature Till and is more resolute in character.

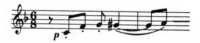

Strauss, in speaking of the work, pointed out that these two motives pervade the work "in the most manifold disguises, moods, and situations."

The composition begins with a beautiful theme which might be saying, "Once upon a time."

Seemingly nothing could be more unassuming and innocent, but already a prank is being played on the unwary listener. It is Till, the rogue, in chaste disguise.

Now comes the introduction of Till Eulenspiegel, characterized as a good-humored, likable country clown.

This theme is then taken and exploited by the various instruments, much as if to stress the importance of Till's life.

In the midst of this hubbub the clarinet gives a glimpse of the rogue, Till.

420

It is the same theme heard in the introduction but now in 6/8 meter, an insolent, flippant version which seems to picture Till in his true light.

In the development of these two themes which follows, Strauss treats first one and then the other. Changes of orchestral coloring and changes of harmony result in an ever-changing music picture of that fellow, Till Eulenspiegel. Both themes even occur in combination.

It is time for the first prank. Till has arrived in the marketplace and is riding through the stalls with wanton disregard. Pots, pans, animals and produce fly right and left. This chaotic scene is portrayed in music by the dissonances played by the oboes, the upward-rushing sixteenth-note triplets played by the clarinets, while underneath, banging cymbals and rattles all add to the seeming confusion.

To make doubly certain that no one misses the culprit, strings sound the rogue theme.

With a leap and a dash Till is away looking for the next undertaking for his dubious talents. Violas and bassoons play what seems to be a German folk song with religious connotations. As might be expected, an unrepentant Till, disguised as a monk, is found preaching to a believing people.

But Till has some fears and doubts and inwardly he is quaking over his brashness in making a mockery of religion. Muted violins, horns and trumpets take the rogue theme, and transpose it into a sniveling, almost whining version.

421

A dark, foreboding chord played by the strings seems to suggest that Till will ultimately be called to account for his actions.

But prophecy or no prophecy, the irresistible rogue in Till cannot be held in check for long,

and the gay larrikin, Till, now appears as a gay Lothario out to break the hearts of all the girls he may perchance meet. But here Till is betrayed by his own impulses—he falls in love himself. A highly sentimentalized version of the theme "Till, the man," now appears in waltz time as well as being in minor mode, as if to suggest that down deep Till is capable of experiencing some of the finer emotions of life.

Unfortunately for Till the lady of his choice refuses to be moved by his pleas and spurns his advances. To suggest Till leaving in a towering rage, Strauss takes the "Till, the man" theme, turns it upside down, and gives it to the low strings.

Mounting anger is further suggested by chromatically ascending passages played by violins and woodwinds against the rogue theme played by brasses, other woodwinds and low strings.

At the height of his rage Till, through the voice of the horns, vows vengeance on all mankind.

This mood is soon broken, however, when a solemn procession of haughty and arrogant Philistines crosses Till's path.

Till cannot resist the temptation to take advantage of the situation, and he is seen making sport of their heavy-handed ways. He seems to be very earnest as he propounds several inane questions as if expecting serious answers. The Philistines soon realize that they are being made the butt of his practical joking. In their anger they turn upon him. But Till, in glee, skips off with a lighthearted little street tune on his lips.

Bass clarinet and contrabassoon seem to foreshadow impending disaster. The rogue theme returns in an altered version as if to suggest that ominous events are in store.

A sudden drum roll signifies the beginning of the end of these mad escapades which have been a regular part of the life of Till. He is now standing at the bar of justice before a panel of wrathful judges.

Not for the world would Till want to give the impression that he might now have some doubts and that he might be concerned. To further this impression of unconcern Till whistles to himself indifferently.

But the ominous voices of the judges overpower the brave effort. A twinge of conscience disturbs Till. Violins, brass and woodwinds indicate this by playing a variant of the theme used to suggest his doubts after his having mocked religion.

But it comes too late. Bassoons and brasses, speaking for the judges, give the sentence. Till is to be hanged.

423

The sentence is being carried out. Poor Till is being marched up the steps of the gallows.

The trap is sprung; Till cries out sharply and then with trilling flutes suggesting his gasps for air and a final convulsion, the soul of Till takes flight.

An epilogue reminds us that after all, this is just a story which may or may not have happened, and if it did happen it took place long, long ago.

But the rogue, Till, really cannot be forgotten. His fiendish laughter is heard in the final few measures of the work as if to say that the memory and spirit of his mischievousness will long be remembered.

Lincoln Portrait..................................Aaron Copland (1900——)

Lincoln Portrait was one of several compositions commissioned by André Kostelanetz (1901——), who believed that music should be used as one way of expressing the spirit of our great country. It was his conviction that certain individuals and aspects of our history could be used as the subject matter for these works. Through music he wanted to be able to portray the courage, dignity, strength, simplicity and humor which are so much a part of our national spirit.

Such a work is the *Lincoln Portrait*. In Lincoln, Copland saw a man who made a noble subject for a musical portrait. Copland makes effective use of some of the speeches and letters of the great Emancipator in attempting to portray and realize in musical terms the stature of the great Lincoln. The *Lincoln Portrait* calls for the tonal resources of an enlarged orchestra and, in addition, a speaker or narrator.

Copland cast his *Lincoln Portrait* in three separate and distinct sections. In the first section the composer is trying to communicate something of the man, Lincoln, himself—the mystery and the sense of fatality attached to the man's personality, as well as his humility and gentleness. The first section opens with the first trumpet sounding the mysterious motto theme, upon which the entire work is based,

against a variant of this theme played by the first flute,

424

over an accompaniment played by the low strings.

In rapid order other variants of these two themes are played by first oboe and second trumpet, first horn and first flute, first flute, first bassoon, viola, first flute and first trumpet, and finally by the high strings. The accented entrances of the low strings furnishing the accom-

paniment to this melody are almost percussive in effect and simulate the sound of a gong.

Still another variation of this theme, played by the solo clarinet, is heard toward the end of the first section (measure 38).

Rhythmically, this first section is characterized by continuously shifting meter. The section begins in 3/2 meter and moves into 3/4, 2/2, 3/4, 3/2, 2/2, 3/2, 4/2, 3/2, 2/2, 3/2, 2/2 and ends in 3/2. These shifts of meter are particularly noticeable in the clarinet theme listed above.

Suddenly the mood changes. We might be attending a husking bee or a

barn dance. In this, the second section, Copland attempts to picture in his music something of the life and times in which Lincoln lived. The gaiety of the dancelike tune which opens this section is interrupted by a curious two-measure, songlike melody played by the violins and cellos against countermelodies played by the woodwinds.

This is followed by more agitated sections out of which are heard, from time to time, snatches of melody reminiscent of some of the popular songs of Lincoln's day. This section is mainly characterized by hustle and bustle. It is mostly in 4/4 meter played at almost *allegro* tempo. Of particular interest is the one single measure of 2/4 or 3/4 meter in between measures of 4/4. The final few measures of the second section return to a *poco largamente*, a slower and more dignified tempo, as the trumpet once again sounds the motto theme, but this time it appears in augmentation. It is in this section that Copland uses the tonal resources of the full orchestra. In addition he calls into play extra percussion such as glockenspiel, tam-tam, sleighbells, xylophone, snare drum, bass drum and cymbal,

plus harp, celesta, tuba, English horn, contrabassoon, bass clarinet and piccolo.

In the third section interest naturally focuses on the narration based on the words which Lincoln himself wrote or spoke. The listener should note, however, the manner in which music is employed in this section to give unity not only to the third section but to the total work. For example, there is the insistence of the motto theme played by the various instruments beginning with the trumpet, which serves to tie the "portrait" together. Midway in the third section (measures 214-221) note the interesting recitative effect. The section and the work closes with the first trumpet playing the melody played by the clarinet in the first section, as the speaker quotes from the "Gettysburg Address."

TOPICS FOR DISCUSSION

1. How does program music differ from music for the films or musical comedy or opera?
2. If a program were not intended by the composer but is later suggested by a critic or historian, does the composition become program music?
3. Is program music less serious, less profound than absolute music?
4. Is a song program music?
5. Write a program to a piece of absolute music that would lend itself to this kind of thing—for example, the second movement of the Bartók *Concerto for Orchestra*.
6. Create a different program for a well-known piece of program music.
7. What form of art compares with program music?
8. Show how a listener may respond rhythmically, emotionally and intellectually to a given piece of program music.

SUGGESTED RECORDINGS

1. Young Person's Guide to the Orchestra..........Benjamin Britten (1913——)
2. La Mer.......................................Claude Debussy (1862-1918)
3. Brigg Fair..................................Frederick Delius (1862-1934)
4. Sorcerer's Apprentice........................Paul Dukas (1865-1935)
5. An American in Paris......................George Gershwin (1898-1937)
6. Les Préludes................................Franz Liszt (1811-1886)
7. Pictures at an Exhibition.................Modest Moussorgsky (1839-1881)
8. A Night on Bald Mountain.................Modest Moussorgsky (1839-1881)
9. Peter and the Wolf.........................Serge Prokofiev (1891-1953)
10. The Pines of Rome.........................Ottorino Respighi (1879-1936)
11. The Fountains of Rome.....................Ottorino Respighi (1879-1936)
12. Scheherazade.....................Nicolas Rimsky-Korsakov (1844-1908)
13. Carnival of the Animals....................Camille Saint-Saëns (1835-1921)

References
Glossary
Bibliography
Sources
Index

References

Unit One, Chapter Three

1. Alfred, Lord Tennyson, "In Memoriam," *The Works of Alfred, Lord Tennyson, Poet Laureate* (New York and London: Macmillan Co., 1894), V, 66.

2. Charles D. Gaitskell, *Children and Their Art* (New York: Harcourt, Brace & Co., 1958), p. 67.

3. Aaron Copland, *Copland on Music* (New York: Doubleday & Co., 1960), p. 29.

4. Gaitskell, *op. cit.*, p. 60.

5. Edmund Gosse, "French Profiles," *The Collected Essays of Edmund Gosse* (London: William Heinemann Ltd., 1905), IV.

6. Thomas Gray, "Elegy Written in a Country Churchyard," *A Treasury of Great Poems*, ed. Louis Untermeyer (New York: Simon & Schuster, 1955), pp. 555-559.

7. Robert Frost, "The Tuft of Flowers," *Complete Poems of Robert Frost* (New York: Holt, Rinehart & Winston, Inc., 1934).

8. Robert Browning, "A Toccata of Galuppi's," *British Poets of the Nineteenth Century*, ed. Curtis Hidden Page (Chicago: Benjamin H. Sandborn & Co., 1926), p. 621.

9. A. E. Housman, "White in the Moon the Long Road Lies," *A Shropshire Lad*, in *Complete Poems* (New York: Holt, Rinehart & Winston, Inc., 1959).

Unit Four, Chapter Seven

10. "Morning Prayer — A General Thanksgiving," *The Book of Common Prayer* (Greenwich, Conn.: Seabury Press, 1953), p. 19.

Unit Five, Chapter Eight

11. Howard D. McKinney and W. R. Anderson, *Music in History* (New York: American Book Co., 1940), pp. 451-452.

Unit Six, Chapter Nine

12. Edwin John Stringham, *Listening to Music Creatively* (New York: Prentice-Hall, Inc., 1943), pp. 51-52.

13. Franz Schubert, "The Erlking," *Fifty Mastersongs*, ed. Henry T. Finck (Philadelphia: Oliver Ditson Co., 1902 and 1930).

14. McKinney and Anderson, *op. cit.*, pp. 239-241.

15. Henry Prunières, *Monteverdi, His Life and Works* (New York: E. P. Dutton & Co., Inc., 1926), pp. 28-29.

16. Walt Whitman, *Leaves of Grass*, Introd. by Christopher Morley (New York: Doubleday & Co., Inc., 1940), p. xiii.

17. *Ibid.*, p. xi.

18. *Modern American Poetry*, ed. Louis Untermeyer (New York: Harcourt, Brace & Co., 1942), p. 6.

19. McKinney and Anderson, *op. cit.*, p. 780.

20. *Ibid.*, p. 804.

Glossary

430

Rousseau, Henri (1844-1910)
roo-soh'
Rudolph, Paul (1918——)
roo'dolf
Ryder, Albert Pinkham (1847-1917)
ri'der

Seurat, Georges (1859-1891)
sir-ah'

Utrillo, Maurice (1883-1955)
oo-tree'yoh

Wood, Grant (1892-1942)

Musicians

Albinoni, Tommaso (1674-1745)
ahl-bee-noh'nee
Amati, Andrea (c. 1520-1611)
ah-mah'tee
Amati, Nicolo (1596-1684)
ah-mah'tee
Arbeau, Thoinet (1519-1595)
ar-boh'

Bach, Johann Sebastian (1685-1750)
bahk
Balakirev, Mily (1837-1910)
bah-lah'kee-ref
Barber, Samuel (1910——)
Bartók, Béla (1881-1945)
bar'tock
Bayly, T. H. (1797-1839)
Beethoven, Ludwig van (1770-1827)
bay'toh-vn
Berlin, Irving (1888——)
Berlioz, Hector (1803-1869)
bair'lyohs
Bizet, Georges (1838-1875)
bee-zay'
Bloch, Ernest (1880-1959)
block
Borodin, Alexander (1833-1887)
boh-roh-deen'
Brahms, Johannes (1833-1897)
brahmz

Britten, Benjamin (1913——)
Byrd, William (1543-1623)
bird

Caccini, Giulio (c. 1548-1618)
kaht-chee'nee
Cambert, Robert (1628-1677)
kam-bear'
Carey, Henry (c. 1690-1743)
Chávez, Carlos (1899——)
chah'vez
Chopin, Frédéric François (1810-1849)
shoh'pan
Copland, Aaron (1900——)
cope'land
Corelli, Arcangelo (1653-1713)
cor-rel'lee
Cui, César (1835-1918)
kwee

Daquin, Louis Claude (1694-1772)
dah-can'
Debussy, Claude (1862-1918)
deh-bu-see
DeKoven, Reginald (1859-1920)
dee-koh'ven
Delibes, Léo (1836-1891)
duh-leeb'
Delius, Frederick (1862-1934)
deel'yus
Dowland, John (1563-1626)
dow'land
Drigo, Riccardo (1846-1930)
dree'goh
Dukas, Paul (1865-1935)
dew'kah

Falla, Manuel de (1876-1946)
fah'yah
Fauré, Gabriel (1845-1924)
faw-ray'
Franck, César (1822-1890)
frahnk
Friml, Rudolph (1879——)
friml

Gabrieli, Andrea (c. 1520-1586)
gah-bree-ay'lee
Gabrieli, Giovanni (1557-1612)
gah-bree-ay'lee

431

Gershwin, George (1898-1937)
Gesualdo, Don Carlo (1560-1613)
jeh-zhoo-al'doh
Gibbons, Orlando (1583-1625)
Gluck, Christoph Willibald (1714-1787)
glook
Gounod, Charles François (1818-1893)
goo'noh
Grainger, Percy (1882-1961)
grain'jer
Grieg, Edvard (1843-1907)
grig

Hammerstein, Oscar II (1895-1960)
Handel, George Frideric (1685-1759)
hand'l
Hassler, Leo (1564-1612)
hass'lur
Haydn, Franz Joseph (1732-1809)
high'dn
Herbert, Victor (1859-1924)
Hindemith, Paul (1895-1963)
hin'duh-mit
Honegger, Arthur (1892-1955)
oh-nee-gair'

Ibert, Jacques (1890-1962)
ee-bair'

Jannequin, Clément (1485-1560)
jahn'neh-can

Kern, Jerome (1885-1945)
Khachaturian, Aram (1903———)
kahch-uh-toor'yun
Kiallmark, G. (c. 1850)
Klengel, August Alexander (1783-1852)
kleng'l
Kodály, Zoltán (1882———)
koh-dah'yee
Kuhnau, Johann (1660-1722)
koon'ow

Lasso, Orlando di (1532-1594)
lah'soh
Lehar, Franz (1870-1948)
lay'hahr
Liszt, Franz (1811-1886)
list

Lully, Jean Baptiste (1632-1687)
loo-lee'

MacDowell, Edward (1861-1908)
Massenet, Jules (1842-1912)
mass-en-ay'
Mendelssohn, Felix (1809-1847)
men'dl-sun
Meyerbeer, Giacomo (1791-1864)
mire'beer
Milhaud, Darius (1892———)
mee-yoh'
Monteverdi, Claudio (1567-1643)
mohn-teh-vair'dee
Morley, Thomas (1557-1603)
Mozart, Wolfgang Amadeus (1756-1791)
moh'tsart
Moussorgsky, Modeste Petrovitch
(1839-1881)
moo-sorg'skee

Offenbach, Jacques (1819-1880)
off-ehn-bahk'

Paganini, Niccolò (1782-1840)
pah-guh-nee'nee
Palestrina, Giovanni Pierluigi da
(c. 1524-1594)
pal-us-tree'nuh
Pergolesi, Giovanni Battista (1710-1736)
pair-goh-lay'se
Peri, Jacopo (1561-1633)
pair'ee
Porter, Cole (1893-1964)
Poulenc, Francis (1899-1963)
pool-ahnk'
Prokofiev, Serge (1891-1953)
proh-koff'yeff

Rameau, Jean Philippe (1683-1764)
rah-moh'
Respighi, Ottorino (1879-1936)
ray-spee'gee
Rimsky-Korsakov, Nicolas (1844-1908)
rim'ski-kor'suh-kof
Rodgers, Richard (1902———)
Romberg, Sigmund (1887-1951)
Rossini, Gioacchino (1792-1868)
roh-see'nee

432

Glossary

Terms Relating to Tempo

Largo	Very, very slowly; broadly	
Lento	Very slow but faster than Largo	
Adagio	Slow	*ah-dah'zhoh*
Andante	In walking time	*ahn-dahn'tay*
Moderato	Moderately fast	
Allegro	Fast	*ah-lay'groh*
Animato	Lively, animated	*ahn-e-mah'toh*
Vivace	Quickly, lively	*vee-vach'ay*
Presto	Very fast	
Accelerando	Gradually faster	*ah-chel-er-ahn'doh*
Stringendo	Hurrying the time	*strin-jehn'doh*
Allargando	Gradually slower	*ah-lahr-gahn'doh*
Rallentando	Gradually slower	*rahl-en-tahn'doh*
Ritardando	Gradually slower	*re-tard-ahn'doh*
Tempo	Speed	
A tempo	Resume former speed	*ah tehm'poh*
Tempo primo	Resume original speed of the movement	*pree'moh*
Meno	Less	*may'noh*
Mosso	Motion, movement	*moh'soh*
Alla breve (¢)	In duple meter when the half note is used as the unit of beat	*ah'lah brehv*

Terms Relating to Style

Cantabile	In a singing style	*cahn-tah'buh-lay*
Con brio	With spirit	*cohn bree'oh*
Dolce	Sweetly	*dohl'chay*
Glissando	To slide	*gliss-ahn'doh*
Grazioso	Gracefully	*grah-tsee-oh'soh*
Legato	Smoothly, connected	*leh-gah'toh*
Maestoso	Grandly, majestic	*my-es-toh'soh*
Marcato	Well marked	*mahr-cah'toh*
Morendo	Dying away	*more-ehn'doh*
Rubato	A means for achieving flexibility of phrasing, in that certain notes of the phrase may be shortened and others, in compensation, will be lengthened to give the phrase the necessary "flow"	*roo-bah'toh*
Slur 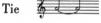	A curved line over or below a group of notes requiring the passing smoothly from one note to another	
Sostenuto	Sustained	*sos-ten-oo'toh*
Sotto voce	Subdued	*suh-toh voh'chay*
Staccato	In a short and detached manner	*stuh-cah'toh*
Tenuto	Hold a little more than the full value of the note	*ten-oo'toh*
Tie	A curved line placed over or below a note and its repetition to indicate that the combination of notes is to be played as one note	

Terms Relating to Dynamics

Pianissimo (pp)	Very soft	*pee-uh-nees'ee-moh*
Piano (p)	Soft	*pee-ah'noh*
Mezzo piano (mp)	Moderately soft	*met'zoh*
Mezzo forte (mf)	Moderately loud	
Forte (f)	Loud	*for'tay*
Fortissimo (ff)	Very loud	*for-tees'ee-moh*
Forzando (fz)	Strongly accented	*for-tsahn'doh*
Sforzando (sfz)	Very strongly accented	*tsfor-tsahn'doh*
Accent (>)	A strong and special emphasis on one note	
Calando	Diminuendo and at the same time rallentando	*cuh-lahn'doh*
Crescendo (cresc.)	Gradually louder	*creh-shen'doh*
Decrescendo (decresc.)	Gradually softer	*day-creh-shen'doh*
Diminuendo (dim.)	Gradually softer	*dih-min-you-ehn'doh*

436

Miscellaneous Terms

A cappella	Singing without accompaniment	*ah cuh-pel'luh*
Accidental (#) (♭) (♮)	The signs used to signify the temporary raising or lowering of a note by one half step	
Ad libitum	At the will of the performer	*ahd lee'bee-toom*
Arco	Bowed	
Breath mark (')	Indicates a breath	
Clef	A symbol used to denote which pitches are to be represented by the lines and spaces of the staff. (See Staff.)	
Coda	A concluding passage to a composition	*coh'duh*
Da Capo (D.C.)	Go back to the beginning	*dah cah'poh*
Dal Segno (D.S.)	Go back to the sign	*dahl sehn'yoh*
Diatonic	Melody or harmony made up predominantly from the resources of the prevailing key, with little use of notes outside its scale	
Divisi	Divide the parts	*dee-vee'see*
Fermata (⌢)	Pause or hold on a note or rest	*fair-mah'tuh*
Fine	The end of a composition	*fee'nay*
Flat (♭)	The sign for lowering the pitch of a tone by one half step	
MM	Metronome marking	
Molto	Much	
Natural (♮)	The sign for raising or lowering the pitch of a tone by one half step	
Non	Not	*nohn*
Più	More	*pew*
Pizzicato	Plucked	*pit-tsih-kah'toh*
Poco a poco	Little by little	*poh'coh ah poh'coh*
Repeat marks (⫶‖)	The sign for repeating a passage	
Sempre	Always	*sehm'pray*
Sharp (#)	The sign for raising the pitch of a tone by one half step	
Staff	A device of five lines and four spaces upon which notes are placed	
	Treble clef sign	
	Bass clef sign	
	Alto clef sign	
	Tenor clef sign	
Tutti	To be performed by the entire ensemble	*too'tee*

Bibliography

**ART
LITERATURE
MUSIC**

Art

Boswell, Payton, Jr. *Modern American Painting*. New York: Dodd, Mead & Co., 1940.
  PARADE, Peter Blume
Canaday, John. "Metropolitan Seminars in Art." New York: Metropolitan Museum of
  Art, 1960.
  Portfolio 1
  MONT SAINTE-VICTOIRE, Paul Cézanne
  THE PEACEABLE KINGDOM, Edward Hicks
  THE TEMPEST, Oskar Kokoschka
  IN THE MEADOW, Pierre Auguste Renoir
  Portfolio 2
  THE YELLOW VIOLIN, Raoul Dufy
  SAINT FRANCIS RECEIVING THE STIGMATA, Jan van Eyck
  Portfolio 3
  THE STARRY NIGHT, Vincent van Gogh
  Portfolio 5
  LADY IN BLUE, Henri Matisse
  Portfolio 7
  REHEARSAL IN THE FOYER OF THE OPERA, Hilaire Germain Edgar Degas
  TOLEDO IN A STORM, El Greco
  Portfolio 10
  BOAT OFF DEER ISLAND, John Marin
  Portfolio 11
  THE ETERNAL CITY, Peter Blume
  LIBERTY LEADING THE PEOPLE, Eugène Delacroix
  Portfolio H
  ARAB RIDER ATTACKED BY LION, Eugène Delacroix
  Portfolio I
  THIRD CLASS CARRIAGE, Honoré Daumier
  THE ANGELUS, Jean François Millet
  Portfolio K
  LANDSCAPE WITH VIADUCT, Paul Cézanne
  THE VISION AFTER THE SERMON, Paul Gauguin

438

LANDSCAPE WITH PLOUGHED FIELDS, Vincent van Gogh
RAIN IN THE JUNGLE, Henri Rousseau
THE ISLE OF THE GRAND JATTE, Georges Seurat
Portfolio L
THE CITY, Fernand Leger
ITALIAN WOMAN, Amedeo Modigliani
AMERICAN GOTHIC, Grant Wood

Janson, H. W. *History of Art.* New York: Henry N. Abrams, 1962.
THIRD CLASS CARRIAGE, Honoré Daumier
THE THREE MUSICIANS, Pablo Picasso

Janson, H. W., and Janson, Dora Jane. *The Picture History of Painting from Cave Painting to Modern Times.* New York: Harry N. Abrams, Inc., 1957.
THIRD CLASS CARRIAGE, Honoré Daumier
GIRL WITH BRAIDS, Amedeo Modigliani
A SUNDAY AFTERNOON ON THE GRAND JATTE, Georges Seurat

Myers, Bernard S. *Modern Art in the Making.* New York: McGraw-Hill Book Company, Inc., 1950.

New York Graphic Society. *Fine Art Reproductions: Old and Modern Masters.* New York: New York Graphic Society, 1951.
STILL LIFE: THE TABLE, Georges Braque
THE TOWER OF BABEL, Pieter Brueghel
THIRD CLASS CARRIAGE, Honoré Daumier
ECOLE DE DANSE, Hilaire Germain Edgar Degas
BOULEVARD DES ANGLAIS, Raoul Dufy
AUTUMN OAKS, George Inness
THANKSGIVING, Doris Lee
COMPANY FOR DINNER, Dale Nichols
BY THE SEASHORE, Pierre Auguste Renoir
THE WATERFALL, Henri Rousseau
SUBURBAN STREET, Maurice Utrillo
THE BRIDGE, Vincent van Gogh
A WALK IN THE ALYSCAMPS PARK, Vincent van Gogh
SPRING LANDSCAPE, Grant Wood

Pepper, Stephen C. *Principles of Art Appreciation.* New York: Harcourt, Brace & Co., 1949.

Robb, David M. *The Harper History of Painting.* New York: Harper & Bros., 1951.
MONT SAINTE-VICTOIRE, Paul Cézanne
TOLEDO IN A STORM, El Greco
A SUNDAY AFTERNOON ON THE GRAND JATTE, Georges Seurat

Shorewood Publishers Inc., Plainview, New York: *Catalog of Fine Art Reproductions.*

Upjohn, Everard M., and Sedgwick, John P., Jr. *Highlights: An Illustrated History of Art.* New York: Holt, Rinehart & Winston, 1963.
THE TOWER OF BABEL, Pieter Brueghel
TOLEDO IN A STORM, El Greco
MAINE ISLANDS, John Marin
WOMAN WITH A NECKLACE, Amedeo Modigliani
THE ISLE OF THE GRAND JATTE, Georges Seurat

439

Literature

Bacon, Francis. "Of Studies," *Selected Writings of Francis Bacon,* ed. Hugh G. Dick. New York: The Modern Library, 1955.

Boni, Margaret Bradford. *Fireside Book of Folksongs.* New York: Simon & Schuster, 1947.

Botkin, B. A. *A Treasury of American Folklore.* New York: Crown Publishers, 1944.

Bunyan, John. *The Pilgrim's Progress.* Mount Vernon, New York: The Peter Pauper Press.

Crane, Stephen. "The Red Badge of Courage," *Stephen Crane, An Omnibus.* Melbourne: William Heinemann, Ltd., 1959.

Dante (Alighieri). "The Divine Comedy," *The Continental Edition of World Masterpieces,* ed. Maynard Mack. New York: W. W. Norton & Co., Inc., 1962.

Deutsch, Leonard. *A Treasury of the World's Finest Folk Song.* New York: Howell, Siskin, 1942.

Emerson, Ralph Waldo. "Self-Reliance," *The Complete Essays and Other Writings of Ralph Waldo Emerson,* ed. Brooks Atkinson. New York: The Modern Library, 1950.

Hawthorne, Nathaniel. "The Scarlet Letter," *The Portable Hawthorne,* ed. Malcolm Cowley. New York: The Viking Press, 1948.

Lamb, Charles. "A Dissertation on Roast Pig," *The Essays of Elia.* New York: Heritage Press, 1943.

Lomax, John A., and Lomax, Alan. *Folk Song: U.S.A.* New York: Duell, Sloan & Pearce, 1948.

McCarthy, Agnes L., and Rodabaugh, Delmer. *Prose and Poetry of America.* Syracuse, New York: The L. W. Singer Co., 1955.

Milton, John. "On His Blindness," *The Complete Poetical Works of John Milton,* ed. Harris Francis Fletcher. Boston: Houghton-Mifflin Co., 1941.

——. "Paradise Lost," *ibid.*

Molière. "The Misanthrope," *Eight Plays by Molière.* Translated by Morris Bishop. New York: The Modern Library, 1957.

Poe, Edgar Allan. "The Pit and the Pendulum," *The Complete Tales and Poems of Edgar Allan Poe,* ed. Hervey Allen. New York: The Modern Library, 1938.

Pooley, Robert C., and others, eds. "Rondeau" by Robert Bridges, *Exploring Life Through Literature.* Chicago: Scott, Foresman & Co., 1964.

——. "The Magics in Pablo Casals" by Max Eastman, *ibid.*

——. "The Miracle Worker" by William Gibson, *ibid.*

——. "Fog" by Carl Sandburg, *Outlooks Through Literature.* Chicago: Scott, Foresman & Co., 1964.

——. "Romeo and Juliet" by William Shakespeare, *ibid.*

——. "Tale of Two Cities" by Charles Dickens, *ibid.*

Shakespeare, William, "As You Like It," *The Complete Works of William Shakespeare,* ed. W. J. Craig. London: Oxford University Press, 1962.

——. "Much Ado About Nothing," *ibid.*

——. "Romeo and Juliet," *ibid.*

UNESCO. *Folk Songs of Europe.* London: Novello, 1956.

Wilder, Thornton. "Our Town," *Three Plays by Thornton Wilder.* New York: Bantam Books, 1961.

——. "The Matchmaker," *ibid.*

——. "The Skin of Our Teeth," *ibid.*

Wright, Thomas, and Brown, Stuart Gerry, eds. "After Apple-Picking" by Robert Frost, *Reading Poems.* New York: Oxford University Press, 1941.

——. "Crossing the Bar" by Alfred, Lord Tennyson, *ibid.*

——. "Elegy" by Thomas Gray, *ibid.*

——. "Fog" by Carl Sandburg, *ibid.*

——. "How Do I Love Thee?" by Elizabeth Browning, *ibid.*

——. "Ode to Evening" by William Collins, *ibid.*

——. "Patterns" by Amy Lowell, *ibid.*

——. "The Pulley" by George Herbert, *ibid.*

——. "The Rustic at the Play" by George Santayana, *ibid.*

——. "The Tiger" by William Blake, *ibid.*

——. "To Autumn" by John Keats, *ibid.*

Music

Apel, Willi. *Harvard Dictionary of Music*. Cambridge: Harvard University Press, 1964.

Baldwin, Lillian. *A Listener's Anthology of Music*. 2 vols. Morristown, N. J.: Silver Burdett Co., 1948.

Bauer, Marion, and Peyser, Ethel R. *Music Through the Ages*. New York: G. P. Putnam's Sons, 1932.

Bernstein, Leonard. *The Joy of Music*. New York: Simon & Schuster, 1959.

Bernstein, Martin. *Introduction to Music*, 2nd ed. New York: Prentice-Hall, Inc., 1951.

Copland, Aaron. *Copland on Music*. Garden City: Doubleday & Co., 1960.

——. *What to Listen for in Music*. New York: McGraw-Hill Book Co., 1939.

Grove, Sir George. *Dictionary of Music and Musicians*, 5th ed., edited by Eric Blom. London: Macmillan & Co. Ltd., 1959-1961.

McKinney, Howard D., and Anderson, W. R. *Discovering Music*, 4th ed. New York: American Book Co., 1962.

——. *Music in History: The Evolution of an Art*. New York: American Book Co., 1940.

Rossi, Nick, and Rafferty, Sadie. *Music Through the Centuries*. Boston: Bruce Humphries, Publishers, 1963.

Scholes, Percy A. *Oxford Companion to Music*, 9th ed. London: Oxford University Press, 1955.

——. *The Concise Oxford Dictionary of Music*. London: Oxford University Press, 1952.

Siegmeister, Elie. *Invitation to Music*. Irvington-on-Hudson: Harvey House, Inc., 1961.

——. *The Music Lover's Handbook*. New York: William Morrow & Co., 1943.

Stringham, Edwin John. *Listening to Music Creatively*. New York: Prentice-Hall, Inc., 1946.

UNESCO. *Folk Songs of Europe*. London: Novello, 1956.

Wold, Milo, and Cykler, Edmund. *An Introduction to Music and Art in the Western World*. Dubuque: Wm. C. Brown Co., 1958.

Sources

16 MM Films and Recordings

Bowmar Educational Records, 10515 Burbank Blvd., North Hollywood, California. *Catalog of educational recordings.*

Capitol Records, 1750 Vine Street, Hollywood 28, California. *Catalog of educational recordings.*

Columbia Recording Corporation, 1473 Branum Avenue, Bridgeport, Connecticut. *Catalog of educational recordings.*

Decca Records, Inc., 445 Park Avenue, New York, New York 10022. *Catalog of educational recordings.*

Folkways Records, 121 W. 47th Street, New York, New York 10036. *Catalog of authentic folk music.*

Sam Goody, Inc., *The Basic Library.* 235 West 49th Street, New York, New York 10019. *Catalog of recordings sold by mail.*

R.C.A. Victor Record Division, 155 E. 24th Street, New York, New York 10010. *Catalog of educational recordings.*

The Record Hunter (Recorded masterpieces by mail), 505 Fifth Avenue, New York, New York 10017. *Catalog of recordings.*

W. Schwann, Inc., *Schwann Long Playing Record Catalog.* 137 Newbury Street, Boston, Massachusetts 02116. *Published monthly.*

Shetler, Donald J. *Film Guide for Music Educators.* Washington, D.C.: Music Educators National Conference, 1201 Sixteenth Street, Northwest, Washington, D.C. 20006. 1961, 119 pp. *Contains information regarding films on music, film distributors and a directory of 16 MM film libraries.*

Index

447

451

459

Writing
from Sources

FIFTH EDITION

Brenda Spatt

The City University of New York

BEDFORD/ST. MARTIN'S   Boston New York

For Bedford/St. Martin's

Developmental Editor: Michael Gillespie
Project Management: Books By Design, Inc.
Production Supervisor: Scott Lavelle
Marketing Manager: Karen Melton
Cover Design: Lucy Krikorian
Cover Art: © 1995 Bill Westheimer
Composition: Thompson Type
Printing and Binding: Haddon Craftsmen, an R. R. Donnelley & Sons Company

President: Charles H. Christensen
Editorial Director: Joan E. Feinberg
Editor in Chief: Nancy Perry
Director of Editing, Design, and Production: Marcia Cohen
Manager, Publishing Services: Emily Berleth

Library of Congress Catalog Card Number: 98-84409

4 3 2 1 0 9
f e d c b a

For information, write: Bedford/St. Martin's, 75 Arlington Street, Boston, MA 02116
(617-426-7440)

ISBN: 0-312-18323-2

Acknowledgments

Leach, William. Specified excerpt from pages 131–132 in *Land of Desire: Merchants, Power, and the Rise of a New American Culture.* Copyright © 1993 by William Leach. Reprinted by permission of Pantheon Books, a division of Random House, Inc.

Blank, Blanche D. "A Question of Degree." Excerpt from "Degrees: Who Needs Them?" by Blanche Blank. Autumn 1972, *AAUP Bulletin,* a publication of the American Association of University Professors. Reprinted by permission.

Paley, Grace. "Travelling" From *The New Yorker,* August 1997. Copyright © 1997 by Grace Paley. Reprinted by permission of Grace Paley. All rights reserved.

Acknowledgments and copyrights are continued at the back of the book on pages **544–546,** which constitute an extension of the copyright page.

To the Instructor

Since I first began *Writing from Sources* two decades ago, many serious issues have confronted higher education: the controversy over standards and remediation, the movement towards greater inclusiveness, the challenge of new technology, the survival of the liberal arts. During the past twenty years, instructors of composition have been able to draw upon an ever-increasing array of pedagogical choices: traditional rhetoric, expressive writing, critical thinking, collaborative learning, cultural studies, interdisciplinary writing. In this period of flux and change, *Writing from Sources* has remained committed to providing students with the basic tools for successful academic writing in college and professional writing in the workplace.

Today, there is a renewed interest in writing based on sources. Instructors are eager to have their students read and write about current topical issues; to choose interesting, yet practical topics; and to develop strong, arguable thesis statements. They want to train students to analyze the information and ideas contained in sources, distinguishing between what's important for their topic and what's not. They expect students to organize their ideas coherently, clearly, and logically, using appropriate material from sources as support within their own essays. They are determined to teach students what plagiarism is and how to avoid it; they want to imbue students with respect for sources and for responsible documentation.

Unfortunately, now as twenty years ago, many students enter college inadequately prepared for academic work. They have particular difficulty working with the abstract ideas and disparate voices typical of assignments in their general education and major courses. They often don't know how to take good lecture notes, to pinpoint and paraphrase the key ideas of a chapter in a textbook, to evaluate a group of readings, or to undertake the extended synthesis necessary for presenting research. Unaccustomed to careful reading, analysis, and synthesis, these students feel impotent and frustrated when confronted by term paper assignments and essay examinations requiring the presentation of sources.

It was for these students that *Writing from Sources* pioneered a comprehensive, step-by-step approach to the research process, including strategies for the analysis, synthesis, presentation, citation, and documentation of sources. This practical method recognizes the fundamental importance of reading: analyzing the content, structure, tone, and diction of source materials. It also provides a corresponding progression of exercises and assignments leading up to the research essay.

Writing from Sources offers a great deal of information about the technical aspects of research. It shows students how to find sources from print and electronic materials, as well as obtaining interview and field research data. But today, with most libraries computerized, locating sources has become largely a mechanical task, unlikely in itself to teach students to think or write about what they have read. Knowing how to compile an impressive bibliography through the Internet or a CD-ROM will not enable students to select appropriate materials and write about them logically and coherently. But the information and practice provided by *Writing from Sources* empowers students to choose relevant, compatible sources and incorporate them into well-organized, readable essays.

Writing from Sources is skills-centered. Instead of starting with a description of the library, the text breaks down the research process into manageable segments of progressive difficulty, so that skills are readily assimilated yet cumulatively build upon each other. In this sequential approach, each academic writing skill—paraphrase or summary or synthesis—is first considered as an end in itself, to be explained, demonstrated, and practiced, like the skills necessary for mastering a sport. Students who understand how to incorporate passages from two authors into paragraphs of their own will be able to make the transition to organizing a stack of notes into an extended essay. To make each stage of the writing process more accessible, *Writing from Sources* uses explanations and readings that students can readily understand, including essays, opinions, interview data, lists, and notes.

In response to comments from instructors who have used previous editions, there are a number of changes in the fifth edition of *Writing from Sources* that enhance its usefulness as a text, a reader, an exercise book, and a research-essay guide.

- To accommodate instructors whose curriculum focuses on persuasive writing, there is a greater emphasis on argumentation. More arguments have been included among the readings, exercises, and textual examples, creating a better balance between persuasive and informative writing.

- New sections on argumentation have also been included throughout the book. In Chapter 1, for example, the basic presentation of argumentation is more detailed, including coverage of logical fallacies. New material in subsequent chapters includes information about developing an argumentative thesis, accommodating argument within paragraphs, and organizing a persuasive research essay.

- The chapter on library research has once again been greatly revised and expanded to reflect new opportunities for online research, especially on the Internet. Students are introduced to the use of Web sites and usenet groups, as well as options for browsers and search engines.

- The discussion of evaluating sources in Chapter 6 has been strengthened by the addition of a substantial section on assessing sources obtained from the Internet, including the issue of their potential unreliability. Student interest in the Internet makes these recommendations both timely and useful.

- Appendix B has been revised to reflect new MLA and APA guidelines for documenting electronic sources.

- More specific information about revision has been included in Chapter 3 as the final stage in the discussion of writing an essay based on a single source.

- Readings throughout the text have been strengthened by the selection of more full-length, free-standing essays than in previous editions. In addition, the new casebook of readings on "Racial Perceptions in America" contained in Appendix E can provide the basis for a complete research essay or, alternatively, can be supplemented by student research.

- Through four editions, *Writing from Sources* has been known for its myriad of exercises, offering instructors great flexibility in addressing the needs of their students. While offering the same comprehensive, skills-based approach to writing from sources, the fifth edition is more user-friendly than previous editions. To make the options less overwhelming, several peripheral exercises have been deleted, and some longer exercises now contain fewer choices. To accommodate the inclusion of longer essays as well as the new material on argumentation and technology, the text itself has been slightly scaled down.

The fifth edition of *Writing from Sources* includes enough reprinted articles and essays by authors such as Robert Bork, Grace Paley, and Shelby Steele to make supplements and handouts unnecessary. The readings, drawn from a variety of disciplines ranging from anthropology and ecology to political science and sociobiology, provide an assortment of topics that should interest both students and instructors. In addition to issues of race (the subject of the casebook), topics include boxing, romantic love, television news, pornography, the environment, first amendment rights, cults, immigration, open admissions, failing grades, social promotion, covenant marriage, school uniforms, American taste in ice cream, and John Wayne as an American icon.

In preparing the fifth edition of *Writing from Sources,* I remain grateful to the hundreds of my students who first taught me how to teach the research essay and to the thousands of students who used the first four editions and who, through their instructors, have expressed their approval of the book and suggested changes to make it more useful and effective. I would like to thank the following instructors who reviewed the text: Beverly Burch, Vincennes University; Gail Caylor, Phoenix College; Kathleen Costello-Sullivan, Bentley College; Patricia Coward, Frostburg State University; Kathleen Doherty, Framingham State College; Marleen Hein-Dunne, American University; Marcia M. Lavely, University of Tennessee at Martin; David G. Miller, Mississippi College; Lyle W. Morgan, Pittsburgh State University; Steven J. Rayshich, Westmoreland County Community College; and Susan Schmeling, Vincennes University. Emily Berleth, Donna Erickson, Michael Gillespie, and Nancy Perry of Bedford/St. Martin's have been extremely helpful throughout the preparation of this edition. In addition, I am obliged to Marianne Ahokas, who provided sections on deductive and inductive logic for the fourth edition; Eve Zarin, who prepared the basis for Appendix C for the fourth edition; and Kevin Wilson, who provided information about the technical aspects of the Internet for this edition. I owe my usual debt of gratitude and affection to Richard Barsam, who is responsible for introducing me to the Internet and who can take a matchmaker's credit if the acquaintance leads to a long-term relationship.

Brenda Spatt

To the Student

Every day, as you talk, write, and work, you use sources. Most of the knowledge and many of the ideas that you express to others originate outside yourself. You have learned from your formal schooling and from observing the world around you, from reading, from watching television and movies, from the Internet, and from a multitude of other experiences. Most of the time, you do not consciously think about where you got the information; you simply go about your activities, communicating with others and making decisions based on your acquired knowledge.

In college, however, using sources becomes more concentrated and deliberate. Each course bombards you with new facts and ideas. Your academic success depends on how well you can understand what you read and hear in your courses, distinguish the more important from the less important, relate new facts or ideas to what you already have learned, and, especially, communicate your findings to others.

Most college writing is both informative and interpretive; that is, it contains material that you take from sources and ideas that are your own. Depending on the individual course and assignment, a college paper may emphasize your own conclusions supported by knowledge you have gathered, or it may emphasize that knowledge, showing that you have mastered a certain body of information. In any case it will contain something of others and something of you. If twenty students in your class are all assigned the same topic, the other nineteen papers will all be somewhat different from yours.

The main purpose of college writing assignments is to help you consolidate what you have learned and to expand your capacity for constructive thinking and clear communication. These are not merely academic skills; there are few careers in which success does not depend on these abilities. You will listen to the opinions of your boss, your colleagues, and your customers; or read the case histories of your clients or patients; or study the marketing reports of your salespeople or the product specifications of your suppliers; or perhaps even analyze the papers of your students! Whatever your job, the decisions that you make and the actions that you take will depend on your ability to understand and evaluate what your sources are saying (whether orally or in writing), to recognize any important pattern or theme, and to form conclusions. As you build on other people's ideas, you certainly will be expected to remember which facts and opinions came from which source and to give appropriate credit. Chances are that you will also be expected to draft a memo, a letter, a report, or a case history that will summarize your information and present and support your conclusions.

To help you see the connection between college and professional writing, here are some typical essay topics for various college courses, each followed by a parallel writing assignment that you might have to do on the job. Notice that all of the pairs of assignments call for much the same skills: the writer must consult a variety of sources, present what he or she has learned from those sources, and interpret that knowledge in the light of experience.

ACADEMIC ASSIGNMENT	PROFESSIONAL ASSIGNMENT	SOURCES
For a *political science* course, you choose a law presently being debated in Congress or the state legislature, and argue for its passage.	As a *lobbyist, consumer advocate,* or *public relations expert,* you prepare a pamphlet to arouse public interest in your agency's program.	debates Congressional Record editorials periodical articles your opinions
For a *health sciences* course, you summarize present knowledge about the appropriate circumstances for prescribing tranquilizers and suggest some safeguards for their use.	As a *member of a medical research team,* you draft a report summarizing present knowledge about a specific medication and suggesting likely directions for your team's research.	books journals government and pharmaceutical industry reports online abstracts
For a *psychology* course, you analyze the positive and negative effects of peer group pressure.	As a *social worker* attached to a halfway house for adolescents, you write a case history of three boys, determining whether they are to be sent to separate homes or kept in the same facility.	textbooks journals case studies interviews Web sites personal experience
For a *business management* course, you decide which department or service of your college should be eliminated if the budget were cut by 3 percent next year; you defend your choice.	As an *assistant to a management consultant,* you draft a memo recommending measures to save a manufacturing company that is in severe financial trouble.	ledgers interviews newspapers journals financial reports Dow Jones news Dialog
For a *sociology* or *history* course, you compare reactions to unemployment in the 1990s with reactions in the 1930s.	As a *staff member in the social services agency* of a small city, you prepare a report on the social consequences that would result from closing of major factory.	newspapers magazines books interviews statistics

ACADEMIC ASSIGNMENT	PROFESSIONAL ASSIGNMENT	SOURCES
For a *physical education* course, you classify the ways in which a team can react to a losing streak and recommend some ways in which coaches can maintain team morale.	As a *member of a special committee of physical-education teachers,* you help plan an action paper that will improve your district's performance in interscholastic sports.	textbooks articles observation and personal experience
For an *anthropology* course, you contrast the system of punishment used by a tribe that you have studied with the penal code used in your home or college town.	As *assistant to the head of the local correction agency,* you prepare a report comparing the success of eight minimum-security prisons around the country.	textbooks lectures articles observation and personal experience
For a *physics* course, you write a definition of "black holes" and explain why theories about them were fully developed in the second half of the twentieth century—not earlier, not later.	As a *physicist* working for a university research team, you write a grant application based on an imminent breakthrough in your field.	books journals online abstracts E-mail
For a *nutrition* course, you explain why adolescents prefer junk food.	As a *dietician* at the cafeteria of a local high school, you write a memo that accounts for the increasing waste of food and recommends changes in the lunch menu.	textbooks articles interviews observation
For an *engineering* course, you describe changes and improvements in techniques of American coal mining over the last hundred years.	As a *mining engineer,* you write a report determining whether it is cost-effective for your company to take over the derelict mine that you were sent to survey.	books articles observation and experience E-mail

Writing from Sources will help you learn the basic procedures that are common to all kinds of academic and professional writing and will provide enough practice in these skills to enable you to write from sources confidently and successfully. Here are the basic skills.

1. *Choosing a topic:* deciding what you are actually writing about; interpreting the requests of your instructor, boss, or client, and determining the scope and limits of the assignment; making the project manageable.

2. *Finding sources and acquiring information:* deciding how much supporting information you are going to need (if any) and locating it; evaluating sources and determining which are most suitable and trustworthy for

your purpose; taking notes on your sources and on your own reactions; judging when you have sufficient information.

3. *Determining your main idea:* determining the purpose of what you are writing and your probable conclusions; redefining the scope and objective in the light of what you have learned from your sources.

4. *Taking notes:* presenting your sources through summary, outline, paraphrase, and quotation; learning when each skill is most appropriate.

5. *Organizing your material:* determining what must be included and what may be eliminated; arranging your evidence in the most efficient and convincing way, so that your reader will reach the same conclusions as you; calling attention to common patterns and ideas that will reinforce your thesis; making sure that your presentation has a beginning, middle, and end, and that the stages are in logical order.

6. *Writing your assignment:* breaking down the mass of information into easily understood units or paragraphs; constructing each paragraph so that the reader will receive a general idea that will advance your main idea, as well as providing supporting examples and details that will make it convincing.

7. *Giving credit to your sources:* ensuring that your reader knows who is responsible for which idea; distinguishing between the evidence of your sources and your own interpretation and evaluation; assessing the relative reliability and usefulness of each source so that the reader can appreciate your basis for judgment.

This list of skills may seem overwhelming right now. But remember: you will be learning these procedures *gradually*. In Part I, you will learn how to get the most out of what you read and how to use the skills of summary, quotation, and paraphrase to provide accurate accounts of your sources. In Part II, you will begin to apply these skills as you prepare an essay based on a single reading and then a synthesis essay drawing on a group of sources. Finally, in Part III, you will go to the library to locate your own sources and begin the complex process of research. The gradual increase in the number of sources will make each stage of the process more complex and demanding, but not essentially different.

The best way to gain confidence and facility in writing from sources is to master each skill so thoroughly that it becomes automatic, like riding a bicycle or driving a car. To help you break the task down into workable units, each procedure will first be illustrated with a variety of models and then followed by exercises to give you as much practice as you need before going on to the next step. As you go on to write essays for other courses, you can concentrate more and more on *what* you are writing and forget about *how* to write from sources, for these methods will have become natural and automatic.

Contents

PART II
WRITING FROM SOURCES 123

PART III
WRITING THE RESEARCH ESSAY   235

5 *Finding Sources*   239

Part I

MAKING YOUR SOURCES YOUR OWN

Academic writers continually study and use the ideas of others. However good and original their own ideas may be, academic writers must explore the work of authorities in their field, to estimate its value and its relevance to their own work, and then to place the ideas and the words of others side by side with their own. We call this process *research.*

To make use of another person's ideas in developing your own work, you need to appreciate (and even temporarily share) that person's point of view. Naturally, you need to read extensively and learn to understand what you read. In Chapter 1, you will learn to distinguish the main ideas of an essay and to grasp its strategy and development. You can measure your comprehension by your ability to sum up a group of related ideas briefly, yet completely. Chapter 1 ends with some practice in presenting a source through *summary.*

In order to use what you have learned from your reading and to write about your sources in essays, you must learn two other basic methods of presenting sources. Chapter 2 will show you how to use *quotation* and *paraphrase* to represent your sources fairly. You must make it clear to your reader whether a specific idea, sentence, or group of sentences is the product of your work or that of another.

- *Quotation* shows that someone else is responsible for the precise phrasing, as well as the ideas, in the quoted sentences.
- Through *paraphrase,* you express the ideas of others in your own words and so demonstrate your understanding of the source and your ability to integrate these ideas into your own work.

Using quotation or paraphrase and including the source's name helps you to avoid the dishonest "borrowings," called *plagiarism,* that occur when the reader cannot tell who wrote what and so gives you credit for work that you did not do. Finally, whether you paraphrase or quote, you must always acknowledge your source with a clear citation of the writer's name.

Although these methods of presentation are somewhat technical, requiring a high standard of accuracy, they are used throughout the academic and professional world. You will use them again and again, until they become automatic.

▪1▪

Reading for Understanding

Before class began, I happened to walk around the room and I glanced at some of the books lying open on the desks. Not one book had a mark in it! Not one underlining! Every page was absolutely clean! These twenty-five students all owned the book, and they'd all read it. They all knew that there'd be an exam at the end of the week; and yet not one of them had had the sense to make a marginal note!

Teacher of an English honors class

Why was this teacher so horrified? The students had fulfilled their part of the college contract by reading the book and coming to class. Why write anything down, they might argue, when the ideas are already printed on the page. All you have to do is read the assignment and, later on, review by skimming it again. Sometimes it pays to underline an important point, but only in very long chapters, so that you don't have to read every word all over again. Taking notes wastes a lot of time, and anyway, there's never enough space in the margins.

Effective reading—reading that is active, not passive—requires concentration. Reading is hard work.

Responding to what you are reading and participating in a mental dialogue between yourself and an author can be challenging but difficult. But only this kind of involvement can prevent your eyes from glazing over and your thoughts from wandering off to next weekend or next summer.

As with any job, active reading seems more rewarding if you have a product to show for your labors. *In active reading, this product is notes:* the result of contact (even friction) between your mind and the author's.

Guidelines for Effective Reading

- As you read and reread, notice which ideas make you react.
- Pause frequently—not to take a break but to think about and respond to what you have read. If the reading has been difficult, these pauses will provide time for you to figure out what questions you need to ask yourself to gain full understanding.
- As you read, have a pencil in your hand so that you can make lines, checks, and comments in and around what you are reading. You may even want to use several colored pens to help you distinguish between different ideas or themes as they recur. Of course, if you don't own the book, always take notes on separate paper. If you underline or write in a library book, you are committing an act of vandalism, like writing graffiti on a wall. Others will be using the book after you and will not benefit from your notes. If the material comes from a computer screen, you will often benefit from printing it out and working with a "hard" copy.

UNDERLINING

Underlining is used for selection and emphasis. *When you underline, you are distinguishing between what is important (and worth rereading) and what you can skip on later readings.* Underlining text on a first reading is usually hard, since you don't yet know what is crucial to the work's main ideas. Underlining, then, can be a sophisticated analytical skill.

On the other hand, underlining can also be the active sign of passive reading. You can underline while you are half asleep: the brain doesn't need to work in order to make the pencil move across the page. Too often, underlining merely represents so many minutes spent on an assignment: the pencil running over the page indicates that the eyes have run over the same lines. Many pages are underlined or colored with "hi-liter" so completely that there is hardly anything left over. *Everything* has been chosen for emphasis.

Underlining means selection. Some points are worth reviewing, and some are not. Try *underlining* and also *circling* and *bracketing* words and phrases that seem worth rereading and remembering. You probably would want to underline:

- *important generalizations* and *topic sentences*
- *examples* that have helped you understand a difficult idea
- *transitional points,* where the argument changes

Or try "underlining" by using *checks in the margin.* Either way, deciding *what* to mark is the important step.

ANNOTATING

Annotation refers to the comments you write in the margins when you interpret, evaluate, or question the author's meaning, define a word or phrase, or clarify a point. You are annotating when you jot down short explanations, summaries, or definitions in the margin. You are also annotating when you note down an idea of your own: a question or counterargument, perhaps, or a point for comparison. Annotation is different from taking notes on a separate page (a procedure that will be discussed in Chapter 7). *Not every reading deserves to be annotated.* Since the process takes time and concentration, save your marginal notes for material that is especially difficult or stimulating.

Here is an example of a passage that has been annotated on the second reading. Difficult words have been defined; a few ideas have been summarized; and some problems and questions have been raised.

from LAND OF DESIRE

William Leach

why quotes?

To make customers feel welcome, merchants trained workers to treat them as "special people" and as "guests." The numbers of service workers, including those *entrust: customers are precious possessions* (entrusted) with the care of customers, rose fivefold between 1870 and 1910, at two and a half times the rate of increase of industrial workers. Among them were the restaurant and hotel employees hired to wait on tables in exchange for wages and "tips," nearly all recent immigrants, mostly poor Germans and Austrians, but also *all European* Italians, Greeks, and Swiss, who suffered nerve-wracking seven-day weeks, eleven-hour days, low wages, and the sometimes terrible heat of the kitchens. Neglected *True of all service workers?* by major unions until just before World War I, they endured (sweated) conditions equal in their misery only to those of the garment and textile workers of the day.

depends on luck, not good service

Tipping was supposed to encourage waiters and waitresses to (tolerate) these conditions in exchange for possible windfalls from customers. Tipping was an unusual practice in the United States before 1890 (although common in the luxurious *tastes and manners of the upper classes* and (aristocratic) European hotels), when the prevailing "American Plan" entailed serving meals at fixed times, no frills, no tipping, and little or no follow-up service. *meals at any time; more choice in return for higher prices* After 1900 the European system of culinary service expanded very quickly in the United States, introduced first to the (fancy) establishments and then, year by year, to the more popularly priced places. By 1913 some European tourists were even expressing "outrage" at the extent of tipping in the United States. Its effect on *why extremely?* workers was (extremely) mixed. On the one hand, it helped keep wages low, increased the frenzy and tension of waiting, and lengthened the hours. "The tipping business is a great evil," wrote an old, retired waiter in the 1940s. "It gives the *Waiter portrayed as victim* waiter an inferiority complex—makes him feel he is at the mercy of the customers all the time." On the other hand, some waiters were stirred by the "speculative excitement" of tipping, the risk and (chance) *chance = luck, not opportunity*

Margin notes (right side):

1

service grew faster than industry (same in 1980s & 90s)

Did they speak English? Who trained them?

Sweatshop = long hours/ low wages

2

barely endure

"American Plan"—based on middle-class culture

luxurious? expensive?

middle class attracted by upper class style

Hours were longer because of tipping or because of greater service?

cliché

statement
of theme
expressed
in parag. 2

all these
quotation
marks are
distracting

all an
illusion

For customers, however, tipping was intended to have only one effect—to make   3
them feel at home and in the lap of luxury. On the backs of an ever-growing sweated
workforce, it aristocratized consumption, integrating upper-class patterns of comfort into the middle-class lifestyle. Tips rewarded waiters and waitresses for making   *tipping as*
the customer "feel like 'somebody,'" as one restaurant owner put it. Such a "feel-   *a marketing*
device
ing," he wrote, "depends" on the "service of the waiter," who ushers us to "our
table" and "anticipates our every want or whim." "Courteous service is a valuable   *it's the*
asset to the restaurateur. There is a curious little twist to most of us: We enjoy the   *customer*
who has the
luxurious feeling of affluence, of being 'somebody,' of having our wishes catered to."   *inferiority*
complex

As this annotated passage demonstrates, *annotation works best as an aid to memory,* reminding you of ideas that you have thought about and understood. Some
of these notes provide no more than a shorter version of the major ideas of the
passage. However, marginal notes can also remind you of places where you disagreed with the author, looked at the ideas in a new way, or thought of fresh evidence. Your marginal notes can even suggest the topic for an essay of your own.

Finally, when you write marginal notes, *try always to use your own words* instead of copying or abbreviating a phrase from the text. You will remember
the point more easily if you have made the effort to express it yourself.

EXERCISE 1: ANNOTATING A PASSAGE

Read the following passage carefully. Then reread it, underlining and circling
key ideas and inserting annotations in the margins.

from JOHN WAYNE'S AMERICA: THE POLITICS OF CELEBRITY
Garry Wills

John Wayne is the most obvious recent embodiment of that American Adam—   1
untrammeled, unspoiled, free to roam, breathing a larger air than the cramped men
behind desks, the pygmy clerks and technicians. He is the avatar of the hero in that
genre that best combines all these mythic ideas about American exceptionalism—
contact with nature, distrust of government, dignity achieved by performance, skep-
ticism toward the claims of experts. The yearning back toward such ideals of
freedom reemerges in the oddest places. When Jim Morrison of the rock group
The Doors sang of freedom, he asked, "What have they done to the Earth? . . .
Tied her in fences and dragged her down." In Westerns, the Easterner is a dude,
comically encumbered with useless knowledge, ignorant of the basics, too crippled
with theory to act. In him, the instincts that lead to Wayne's easy responses have
been blunted, have atrophied in the stale air of commerce or technology, in the
conditioning to life on a smaller scale than the open range.

The Western popularized the sophisticates' claims for American exceptionalism
by putting them in vivid visual form—the frontier was a landscape with freely moving men and horses. The equality of opportunity was symbolized by "nature's noblemen." This ability to put so much of the American myth into such visual
immediacy made the Western what Jean-Luc Godard [sic] called "the most cinematographic genre in cinema."

ASKING QUESTIONS

As you read actively and try to understand what you read, you will find yourself asking questions about your source. Sometimes you will want to write your
answers down; sometimes answering your questions in your head is enough.

As the questions in the box below suggest, to understand what you read,
your mind has to sweep back and forth between each sentence on the page
and the larger context of the whole paragraph or essay. You can misunderstand
the author's meaning if you interpret ideas *out of context,* ignoring the way in
which they fit into the work as a whole.

Being a fast reader is not necessarily an advantage. Thorough comprehension takes time and careful reading. In fact, it is usually on the *second reading,*
when you begin to understand the overall meaning and structure of the
work, that questions begin to pop into your head and you begin to read more
carefully.

Questions to Aid Understanding

- What is the *meaning* of this word?
- How should I *understand* that phrase?
- Where do I have *difficulty understanding the text?* Why? Which pas-
  sages are *easy* for me? Why?
- What does this passage *remind me of?*
- What is the *topic sentence* of the paragraph?
- What is the *connection* between these two points?
- What is the *transitional* word telling me?
- This concept is difficult: how would I *express* it *in my own words?*
- Is this point a *digression* from the main idea, or does it fit in with
  what I've already read?
- Can the whole page be *summarized* briefly?
- Does the essay have a main idea—a *thesis?* Is the writer trying to
  make a particular point?

Annotating and Asking Questions: "A Question of Degree"

Read "A Question of Degree" once, and then go over it more slowly a second time. During your second reading, as you read each paragraph:

A. *Underline and annotate* the text, while asking yourself *comprehension questions* based on the list of questions on p. 7.

B. *Compare your annotations* with the annotated version of the first two paragraphs on p. 11.

C. *Compare your comprehension questions* with the list of sample questions starting on p. 12. (The paragraphs in the essay are numbered so that you can go back and forth from essay to list.) Think of your own response to each question, and then compare your answers with the ones that are provided in the right-hand column.

Some of the sample questions may seem very subtle to you, and you may wonder whether you would have thought of all of them yourself. But they are model questions, to show you what you *could* ask if you wanted to gain an especially thorough understanding of the essay.

A QUESTION OF DEGREE
Blanche D. Blank

Perhaps we should rethink an idea fast becoming an undisputed premise of American life: that a college degree is a necessary (and perhaps even a sufficient) precondition for success. I do not wish to quarrel with the assumptions made about the benefits of orthodox education. I want only to expose its false god: the four-year, all-purpose, degree-granting college, aimed at the so-called college-age population and by now almost universally accepted as the stepping-stone to "meaningful" and "better" jobs.   1

What is wrong with the current college/work cycle can be seen in the following anomalies: we are selling college to the youth of America as a take-off pad for the material good life. College is literally advertised and packaged as a means for getting more money through "better" jobs at the same time that Harvard graduates are taking jobs as taxi drivers. This situation is a perversion of the true spirit of a university, a perversion of a humane social ethic and, at bottom, a patent fraud. To take the last point first, the economy simply is not geared to guaranteeing these presumptive "better" jobs; the colleges are not geared to training for such jobs; and the ethical propriety of the entire enterprise is very questionable. We are by definition (rather than by analysis) establishing two kinds of work: work labeled "better" because it has a degree requirement tagged to it and nondegree work, which, through this logic, becomes automatically "low level."   2

This process is also destroying our universities. The "practical curriculum" must become paramount; the students must become prisoners; the colleges must be-   3 come servants of big business and big government. Under these conditions the university can no longer be an independent source of scientific and philosophic truth-seeking and moral criticism.

Finally, and most important, we are destroying the spirit of youth by making college compulsory at adolescence, when it may be least congruent with emotional and physical needs; and we are denying college as an optional and continuing experience later in life, when it might be most congruent with intellectual and recreational needs.

4

Let me propose an important step to reverse these trends and thus help restore freedom and dignity to both our colleges and our work-places. We should outlaw employment discrimination based on college degrees. This would simply be another facet of our "equal opportunity" policy and would add college degrees to sex, age, race, religion and ethnic group as inherently unfair bases for employment selection.

5

People would, wherever possible, demonstrate their capacities on the job. Where that proved impractical, outside tests could still serve. The medical boards, bar exams, mechanical, mathematical and verbal aptitude tests might still be used by various enterprises. The burden of proof of their legitimacy, however, would remain with the using agencies. So too would the costs. Where the colleges were best equipped to impart a necessary skill they would do so, but only where it would be natural to the main thrust of a university endeavor.

6

The need for this rethinking and for this type of legislation may best be illustrated by a case study. Joe V. is a typical liberal-arts graduate, fired by imaginative art and literature. He took a job with a large New York City bank, where he had the opportunity to enter the "assistant manager training program." The trainees rotated among different bank departments to gain technical know-how and experience and also received classroom instruction, including some sessions on "how to write a business letter." The program was virtually restricted to college graduates. At the end of the line, the trainees became assistant bank managers: a position consisting largely of giving simple advice to bank customers and a modest amount of supervision of employees. Joe searched for some connection between his job and the training program, on the one hand, and his college-whetted appetites and skills on the other. He found none.

7

In giving Joe preference for the training program, the bank had bypassed a few enthusiastic aspirants already dedicated to a banking career and daily demonstrating their competence in closely related jobs. After questioning his superiors about the system, Joe could only conclude that the "top brass" had some very diffuse and not-too-well-researched or even well-thought-out conceptions about college men. The executives admitted that a college degree did not of itself ensure the motivation or the verbal or social skills needed. Nor were they clear about what skills were most desirable for their increasingly diverse branches. Yet, they clung to the college prerequisite.

8

Business allows the colleges to act as recruiting, screening and training agencies for them because it saves money and time. Why colleges allow themselves to act as

9

servicing agents may not be as apparent. One reason may be that colleges are increasingly becoming conventional bureaucracies. It is inevitable, therefore, that they should respond to the first and unchallenged law of bureaucracy: Expand! The more that colleges can persuade outside institutions to restrict employment in favor of their clientele, the stronger is the college's hold and attraction. This rationale becomes even clearer when we understand that the budgets of public universities hang on the number of students "serviced." Seen from this perspective, then, it is perhaps easier to understand why such matters as "university independence," or "the propriety" of using the public bankroll to support enterprises that are expected to make private profits, can be dismissed. Conflict of interest is difficult to discern when the interests involved are your own. . . .

What is equally questionable is whether a college degree, as such, is proper evidence that those new skills that are truly needed will be delivered. A friend who works for the Manpower Training Program feels that there is a clear divide between actual job needs and college-degree requirements. One of her chief frustrations is the knowledge that many persons with the ability to do paraprofessional mental-health work are lost to jobs they could hold with pleasure and profit because the training program also requires a two-year associate arts degree.   10

Obviously, society can and does manipulate job status. I hope that we can manipulate it in favor of the greatest number of people. More energy should be spent in trying to upgrade the dignity of all socially useful work and to eliminate the use of human beings for any work that proves to be truly destructive of the human spirit. Outlawing the use of degrees as prerequisites for virtually every job that our media portray as "better" should carry us a long step toward a healthier society. Among other things, there is far more evidence that work can make college meaningful than that college can make work meaningful.   11

My concern about this degree/work cycle might be far less acute, however, if everyone caught up in the system were having a good time. But we seem to be generating a college population that oscillates between apathy and hostility. One of the major reasons for this joylessness in our university life is that the students see themselves as prisoners of economic necessity. They have bought the media messages about better jobs, and so they do their time. But the promised land of "better" jobs is, on the one hand, not materializing; and on the other hand the student is by now socialized to find such "better" jobs distasteful even if they were to materialize.   12

One of the major improvements that could result from the proposed legislation against degree requirements for employment would be a new stocktaking on the part of all our educational agencies. Compulsory schools, for example, would understand that the basic skills for work and family life in our society would have to be compressed into those years of schooling.   13

Colleges and universities, on the other hand, might be encouraged to be as unrestricted, as continuous and as open as possible. They would be released from the pressures of ensuring economic survival through a practical curriculum. They might best be modeled after museums. Hours would be extensive, fees minimal, and ser-   14 vices available to anyone ready to comply with course-by-course demands. Colleges under these circumstances would have a clearly understood focus, which might well be the traditional one of serving as a gathering place for those persons who want to search for philosophic and scientific "truths."

This proposal should help our universities rid themselves of some strange and gratuitous practices. For example, the university would no longer have to organize itself into hierarchical levels: B.A., M.A., Ph.D. There would simply be courses of greater and lesser complexity in each of the disciplines. In this way graduate education might be more rationally understood and accepted for what it is—more education. **15**

The new freedom might also relieve colleges of the growing practice of instituting extensive "work programs," "internships" and "independent study" programs. The very names of these enterprises are tacit admissions that the campus itself is not necessary for many genuinely educational experiences. But, along with "external degree" programs, they seem to pronounce that whatever one has learned in life by whatever diverse and interesting routes cannot be recognized as increasing one's dignity, worth, usefulness or self-enjoyment until it is converted into degree credits. **16**

The legislation I propose would offer a more rational order of priorities. It would help recapture the genuine and variegated dignity of the workplace along with the genuine and more specialized dignity of the university. It should help restore to people of all ages and inclinations a sense of their own basic worth and offer them as many roads as possible to reach Rome. **17**

"A Question of Degree": Example of Annotations

everyone believes it

Perhaps we should rethink an idea fast becoming an <u>undisputed premise</u> of American life: that a college degree is a (necessary) (and perhaps even a (sufficient)) precondition for success. I do not wish to quarrel with the assumptions made about the benefits of (orthodox) education. I want only to expose its (false god) the four-year, all-purpose, degree-granting college, aimed at the (so-called) college-age population and by now almost universally accepted as the stepping-stone to "<u>meaningful</u>" and "<u>better</u>" jobs. **1**

necessary vs. sufficient?
= false idol
18 yrs old
everyone thinks is a good education
college leads to work *B.B. doesn't agree*

What is wrong with the current (college/work cycle) can be seen in the following (anomalies) we are selling college to the youth of America as a take-off pad for the (material) good life. College is literally <u>advertised and packaged</u> as a means for getting more money through "better" jobs at the same time that Harvard graduates are taking jobs as taxi drivers. This situation is a (perversion) of the true spirit of a university, a perversion of a <u>humane social ethic</u> and, at bottom, a (patent) fraud. To take the last point first, the economy simply is not geared to guaranteeing these presumptive "better" jobs; the colleges are not geared to training for such jobs; and the (ethical propriety) of the entire enterprise is very questionable. We are by (definition) (rather than by (analysis)) establishing two kinds of work: work labeled "better" because it has a degree requirement tagged to it and nondegree work, which, through this logic, becomes automatically "low level." **2**

inconsistencies
high salary + expensive possessions
therefore, the premise is false
to reward good work
presented to the public
= corruption
= obvious
colleges can't deliver what they promise
morality definition = by saying so
analysis = by observing what's right and true
2 levels exist because of the convenience of these institutions. [But surely the "better" v.s. "low level" work existed long before colleges saw profit in the difference!]

"A Question of Degree": Questions and Answers

Paragraph One

A. What does "false god" mean?

A. A false god is an idol that does not deserve to be worshiped.

B. In what context can a college degree be a false god?

B. Colleges are worshiped by students who believe that the degree will magically ensure a good career and a better life. Blank suggests that college degrees no longer have magic powers.

C. Why does Blank put "meaningful" and "better" in quotation marks?

C. Blank uses quotation marks around "meaningful" and "better" because she doesn't believe the adjectives are applicable; she is showing disagreement, disassociating herself through the quotation marks.

Paragraph Two

D. What is an anomaly?

D. An anomaly is anything that is inconsistent with ordinary rules and standards.

E. What conclusion can be drawn from the "Harvard graduates" sentence? (Note that the obvious conclusion is not stated.)

E. If Harvard graduates are driving taxis, a degree does not ensure a high-level job.

F. What does "perversion" mean? How many perversions does Blank mention? Can you distinguish between them?

F. Perversion means distortion or corruption of what is naturally good or normally done. If degrees are regarded as vocational qualifications, the university's proper purpose will be perverted, society's conception of proper qualifications for promotion and advancement will be perverted, and, by implication, young people's belief in the reliability of rewards promised by society will be perverted.

G. In the last two sentences, what are the two types of "fraud" that are described?

G. One kind of fraud is the deception practiced on young college students who won't get the good jobs that they expect. A second type of fraud is practiced on workers without degrees whose efforts and successes are undervalued because of the division into "better" and "worse" jobs.

Paragraph Three

H. What is the "practical curriculum"?

H. "Practical curriculum" refers to courses that will train college students for specific jobs; the term is probably being contrasted with "liberal arts."

I. What is the danger to the universities? (Use your own words.)

I. The emphasis on vocational training perverts the university's traditional pursuit of knowledge for its own sake, as it makes financing and curriculum very closely connected with the economic needs of the businesses and professions for which students will be trained.

J. What groups have suffered so far as a result of "compulsory" college?

J. Blank has so far referred to three groups: students in college; workers who have never been to college; and members of universities, both staff and students, interested in a liberal-arts curriculum.

Paragraph Four

K. What new group, not mentioned before, does Blank introduce in this paragraph?

K. Blank introduces the needs of older people who might want to return to college after a working career.

Paragraph Five

L. Can you explain "'equal opportunity' policy" in your own words?

L. Equal-opportunity policy for employment means that the only prerequisite for hiring should be the applicant's ability to perform the job.

M. What is Blank's contribution to "our 'equal opportunity' policy"?

M. Blank suggests that a college degree does not indicate suitability for employment and therefore should be classed as discriminatory, along with sex, age, etc.

Paragraph Six

N. What does "legitimacy" mean in this context?

N. If certain professions choose to test the qualifications of aspirants, professional organizations should prove that examinations are necessary and that the results will measure the applicant's suitability for the job. These organizations should be responsible for the arrangements and the financing; at present, colleges serve as a "free" testing service.

Paragraphs Seven and Eight

O. What point(s) does the example of Joe help to prove?

O. Joe V.'s experience supports Blank's argument that college training is not often needed in order to perform most kinds of work. Joe V.'s expectations were also pitched too high, as Blank has suggested, while the experience of other bank employees whose place was taken by Joe exemplifies the plight of those workers without college degrees whose experience is not sufficiently valued.

Paragraph Nine

P. What are the colleges' reasons for cooperating with business? (Explain in your own words.)

P. Colleges are competing for students in order to increase their enrollment; they therefore want to be able to assure applicants that many companies prefer to hire their graduates. Having become overorganized, with many levels of authority, the bureaucratic universities regard enrollment as an end in itself.

Q. What is the conflict of interest mentioned in the last sentence, and why is it hard to discern?

Q. The interests of an institution funded by the public might be said to be in conflict with the interests of a private, profit-making company; but the conflict is not apparent now that colleges choose to strengthen their connections with business.

Paragraph Eleven

R. Can you restate the third sentence in your own words?

R. Instead of discriminating between kinds of workers and kinds of work, we should distinguish between work that benefits everyone and should therefore be considered admirable, and work that is degrading and should, if possible, not be performed by people.

S. Is Blank recommending that everyone go to work before attending college (last sentence)?

S. Although Blank is not insisting that working is preferable to or should have priority over a college education, she implies that most people gain more significant knowledge from the work than from college.

Paragraph Twelve

T. Can you explain the meaning of "prisoners of economic necessity"?

T. Young people who believe that a degree will get them better jobs have no choice but to spend a four-year term in college, whether or not they are intellectually and temperamentally suited to the experience.

Paragraph Thirteen

U. What are the "compulsory schools" and how would their role change if Blank's proposal were adopted?

U. Compulsory schools are grade and high schools, which students must attend up to a set age. If students were not automatically expected to go on to college, the lower schools would have to offer a more comprehensive and complete education than they do now.

Paragraph Fourteen

V. What role does Blank envisage for the university in a healthier society? (Try not to use "museum" in your answer.)

V. Blank sees the colleges in a role quite apart from the mainstream of life. Colleges would be storehouses of tradition, to which people could go for cultural refreshment in their spare time, rather than training centers.

Paragraph Fifteen

W. What are the "strange and gratuitous" practices of the universities? What purpose do they
serve?

W. The universities divide the process of education into a series of
clearly defined levels of attain-
ment. Blank finds these divisions
"gratuitous" or unnecessary,
perhaps because they are "hierarchical" and distinguish between those of greater or lesser
achievements and status.

Paragraph Seventeen

X. What, according to Blank, would
be a "rational order of priorities"? Does she see any connection at all between the work
experience and the educational
experience?

X. Blank's first priority is the self-
respect of the average member
of society who presently may be
disappointed and frustrated at
not being rewarded for his or
her work, whether at the job or
at college. Another priority is
restoration of the university to
its more purely intellectual role.

EXERCISE 2: UNDERSTANDING WHAT YOU READ

Read "Travelling" twice, and then answer the comprehension questions that
follow. You will notice that some of the "questions" resemble instructions, very
much like examination questions, directing you to explain, define, or in other
ways annotate the reading. *Answer in complete sentences,* and use your own
words as much as you can.

TRAVELLING

Grace Paley

My mother and sister were travelling South. The year was 1927. They had begun   1
their journey in New York. They were going to visit my brother, who was studying
at the Medical College of Virginia, in Richmond. Their bus was an express and had
stopped only in Philadelphia, Wilmington, and now Washington. Here the darker
people who had got on in Philadelphia or New York rose from their seats, put their
bags and boxes together, and moved to the back of the bus. People who boarded in
Washington knew where to seat themselves. My mother had heard that something
like this would happen. My sister had heard of it, too. They had not lived in it. This
reorganization of passengers by color happened in silence. My mother and sister
remained in their seats, which were about three-quarters of the way back.

When everyone was settled, the bus driver began to collect tickets. My sister   2
saw him coming. She pinched my mother—"Ma! Look!" Of course, my mother saw

him, too. What frightened my sister was the quietness. The white people in front, the black people in back—silent.

The driver sighed, said, "You can't sit here, ma'am. It's for them"—waving over his shoulder at the Negroes, among whom they were now sitting. "Move, please." 3

My mother said, "No." 4

He said, "You don't understand, ma'am. It's against the law. You have to move to the front." 5

My mother said, "No." 6

When I first tried to write this scene, I imagined my mother saying, "That's all right, mister. We're comfortable. I can't change my seat every minute." I read this invention to my sister. She said it was nothing like that. My mother did not try to be friendly or pretend innocence. While my sister trembled in the silence, my mother said for the third time—quietly—"No." 7

Somehow, finally, they were in Richmond. There was my brother, in school among so many American boys. After hugs and my mother's anxious looks at her young son, my sister said, "Vic, you know what Mama did?" 8

My brother remembers thinking, What? Oh! She wouldn't move? He had a class-mate, a Jewish boy like him, but from Virginia, who had had a public confrontation with a Negro man. He had punched that man hard, knocked him down. My brother couldn't believe it. He was stunned. He couldn't imagine a Jewish boy wanting to knock anyone down. He had never wanted to. But he thought, looking back, that he had been set down to work and study in a nearly foreign place, and had had to get used to it. Then he told me about the Second World War, when the disgrace of black soldiers forced to sit behind white German P.O.W.s shook him. Shamed him. 9

About fifteen years later, in 1943, in early summer, I rode the bus for about three days from New York to Miami Beach, where my husband and hundreds of other boys in sweaty fatigues were trudging up and down the streets and beaches to pre-pare themselves for war. 10

By late afternoon of the second long day, we were well into the South, beyond Richmond, maybe in South Carolina or Georgia. My excitement about travel in the wide world was damaged a little by a sudden fear that I might not recognize Jess, or he me. We hadn't seen each other for two months. I took a photograph out of my pocket; yes, I would know him. 11

I had been sleeping, waking, reading, writing, dozing, waking. So many hours, the movement of the passengers was like a tide that sometimes ebbed and now seemed to be noisily rising. I opened my eyes to the sound of people brushing past my aisle seat. And looked up to see a colored woman holding a large sleeping baby, who, with the heaviness of sleep, his arms tight around her neck, seemed to be pulling her head down. I looked around and noticed that I was in the last white row. The press of new travellers had made it impossible for her to move farther back. She seemed so tired, and I had been sitting and sitting for a day and a half at least. Not thinking, or maybe refusing to think, I offered her my seat. 12

She looked to the right and left as well as she could. Softly, she said, "Oh, no." I became fully awake. A white man was standing right beside her, but on the other 13 side of the invisible absolute racial border. Of course, she couldn't accept my seat. Her sleeping child hung mercilessly from her neck. She shifted a little to balance the burden. She whispered to herself, "Oh, I just don't know." So I said, "Well, at least give me the baby." First, she turned, barely looking at the man beside her. He made no move. Then, to my surprise, but obviously out of sheer exhaustion, she disengaged the child from her body and placed him on my lap. He was deep in child-sleep. He stirred, but not enough to bother himself or me. I liked holding him, aligning him along my twenty-year-old young woman's shape. I thought ahead to that holding, that breathing together that would happen in my life if this war would ever end. I was so comfortable under his nice weight. I closed my eyes for a couple of minutes but suddenly opened them to look up into the face of a white man talking. In a loud voice, he addressed me: "Lady, I wouldn't of touched that thing with a meat hook."

I thought, Oh, this world will end in ice. I could do nothing but look straight into his eyes. I did not look away from him. Then I held that little boy a little tighter, kissed his curly head, pressed him even closer, so that he began to squirm. So sleepy, he reshaped himself inside my arms. His mother tried to narrow herself away from that dangerous border, too frightened at first to move at all. After a couple of minutes, she leaned forward a little, placed her hand on the baby's head, and held it there until the next stop. I couldn't look up into her mother face.   14

I write this remembrance more than fifty years later. I look back at that mother and child. I see how young she is. Her hand on his head is quite small, though she tries by spreading her fingers wide to hide him from the white man. But the child I'm holding, his little face as he turns toward me, is the dark-brown face of my *own* grandson, my daughter's boy, the open mouth of the sleeper, the full lips, the thick little body of a child who runs wildly from one end of the yard to the other, leaps from dangerous heights with experienced caution, muscling his body, his mind, for coming realities.   15

Of course, when my mother and sister returned from Charlottesville the family at home wanted to know: How was Vic doing in school among all those Gentiles? Was the long bus ride hard? Was the anti-Semitism really bad or just normal? What happened on the bus? I was probably present at that supper, the attentive listener and total forgetter of information that immediately started to form me.   16

Then, last year, my sister, casting the net of old age (through which recent experience easily slips), brought up that old story. First, I was angry. How come you never told me about your bus ride with Mama? I mean, really, so many years ago.   17

I don't know, she said. Anyway, you were only about four years old and, besides, maybe I did.   18

I asked my brother why we'd never talked about that day. He said he thought now that it had had a great effect on him; he had tried unravelling its meaning for years—then life, family, work happened. So I imagined him, a youngster, really, a kid from the Bronx in Virginia in 1927—why, he was a stranger there himself.   19

In the next couple of weeks, we continued to talk about our mother, the way she was principled, adamant, and at the same time so shy. What else could we remember . . . Well, I said, I have a story about those buses, too. Then I told them: 20 how it happened on just such a journey, when I was still quite young, that I first knew my grandson, first held him close but could protect him for only about twenty minutes fifty years ago.

Paragraph One

A. Why does Paley begin with a series of facts, expressed in short sentences?

B. Why does Paley use the adjective "darker" (rather than "black" or—in the vocabulary of 1927—"Negro") to describe the people who move to the back of the bus?

C. What summarizes the paragraph?

D. Why does Paley include separate sentences for the mother's and sister's anticipation of what was happening?

Paragraph Two

E. In the first two paragraphs, is the reader supposed to understand that the mother and sister are white?

F. Why is the silence frightening?

Paragraphs Three through Six

G. Why does the driver sigh? What creates tension in the dialogue between the mother and the driver? Do we know why she refuses to move?

Paragraph Seven

H. What is the effect of the intrusion of Grace Paley's voice and thoughts into the narrative? Why does she interrupt the story?

I. Compare what did happen with Paley's "invention."

Paragraph Eight

J. Why does Paley omit the reaction to her mother's third "no"? Is "somehow" an adequate substitute? Do we need to know the driver's reaction? the reaction of the black travellers? the white?

K. What is the significance of Vic's being "in school among so many American boys"?

Paragraph Nine

L. There are four different points in time incorporated into this paragraph. Distinguish between the four, and suggest Paley's reasons for juxtaposing them in such a short space.

M. What do the two new examples of prejudice in this paragraph add to our understanding of the bus incident?

Paragraph Ten

N. The description of the troops in Miami Beach is more detailed than any scene so far in the essay. Why does Paley use words like "sweaty" and "trudging"?

Paragraph Eleven

O. What does Paley's description of her fears (about not recognizing her husband) add to our understanding of the story?

Paragraph Twelve

P. Contrast the image of the passengers as a "tide" with the "reorganization" in Paragraph One.

Q. What is the difference between "not thinking" and "refusing to think"?

R. Contrast the four situations described thus far.

Paragraphs Thirteen and Fourteen

S. Had a white man not been standing there, could the colored woman have accepted Paley's seat?

T. Consider the adjectives used to describe the baby and holding the baby. What do they tell us about the young Paley and the old Paley?

U. Explain the difference between "if this war would ever end" and "this world will end in ice."

V. Why can Paley stare at the loud man, but not look at the baby's mother?

Paragraph Fifteen

W. What is Paley telling us when she merges the baby on the bus with her grandson? The images she uses to describe her grandson are different from the flat narrative of the essay. What is the effect of these more abstract phrases?

Paragraph Sixteen

X. Why does Paley return to family reactions in 1927? In what way are the references to anti-Semitism a counter-theme?

Y. How does Paley's description of her youngest self—"the attentive listener and total forgetter of information that immediately started to form me"—serve as the key to the essay?

Paragraphs Seventeen to Nineteen

Z. Why is memory—and the frailty of memory—so important to this essay?

Paragraph Nineteen

AA. How does the description of her brother apply to Paley herself in her experience on the bus?

BB. Describe the interplay between public issues and private concerns in this essay.

Paragraph Twenty

CC. Explain the significance of the title. Could this story have been told in strict chronological order? What would be the difference in effect?

LOGIC AND ARGUMENTATION

Drawing Inferences

When you are actively reading and annotating a text, you may sometimes find yourself projecting your own thoughts and assumptions into what you are reading. While you may intend to make a statement supported by information found in your source, your generalization may not accurately reflect the factual evidence. After a while, it becomes difficult to differentiate between your own ideas, inspired by what you have read, and the evidence found in the source. Should such confusion occur, *you can easily attribute to your source ideas that are not there at all.* When you generalize from specific facts—statistics, for example—you have to be especially careful to make sure that your statement is based on a correct interpretation of the information.

There are several different ways to describe how your source uses evidence and how you form conclusions from that evidence: *proving, stating, implying,* and *inferring.* These terms will be explained and illustrated with excerpts from an article about patterns of marriage in America during the early 1980s.

Quoting a Census Bureau report, this 1984 *New York Times* article begins by *stating* that:

> More and more young Americans are putting off marriage, possibly to begin careers. . . .

At this point in the article, the *Times* is offering no specific evidence to support this conclusion. You probably accept the statement as true because you know that the *Times* is a newspaper of record, and you assume that the Census Bureau has provided statistics that justify the claim. And, in fact, several paragraphs later, we find evidence to *prove* the statement:

> The trend toward postponed marriage has been growing steadily in recent years. The study found that 74.8 percent of men aged 20 to 24 had never married, compared with 68.8 percent in 1980 and 54.7 percent in 1970. Among women aged 20 to 24, 56.9 percent were single in this year's survey, as against 50.2 percent in 1980 and 35.8 percent in 1970.

Here is an example of a statement (in italics) that is immediately followed by proof:

> *Traditional married couples continue to make up the majority of family households in the United States, but the report documents the steady erosion of this group's dominance.* The 50.1 million traditional families constitute 58.6 percent of American households, compared with 60.8 percent in 1980 and 70.5 percent in 1970.

Since the article is about postponing marriage and also refers to the increasing number of unmarried couples living together, you might jump to the conclusion that most households in the United States consist of unmarried couples or single-parent families. As the previous paragraph clearly indicates, that would be a *false conclusion.*

So far, we have been examining only what the article *explicitly states* or what it *proves.* But, in addition, most sources inform you indirectly, by *implying* obvious conclusions that are not stated in so many words. The implications of a statement can be easily found within the statement itself; they just are not directly expressed. For example, according to the Census Bureau report,

> Three-quarters of American men and more than half of American women under 25 are still single.

Although it does not say so, it *implies*—and it would be perfectly safe to conclude—that *more men than women are waiting until they are over 25 to marry.* The following paragraph also contains implication as well as statement:

> "Many of these young adults may have postponed their entry into marriage in order to further their formal education, establish careers or pursue other goals that might conflict with assuming family responsibilities," said the bureau's study of households, families, marital status and living arrangements. The report also found that Americans are once again forming new households at high rates after a decline, apparently recession-induced, last year.

In addition to several *statements* about likely reasons for postponing marriage, the paragraph also provides you with an important *implication: Economic conditions seem to be a factor in predicting how many new households are formed in the United States.*

Finally, it is perfectly acceptable to draw a conclusion that is not implicit in the source, as long as you reach that conclusion through reasoning based on sound evidence. Unlike implication, *inference* requires the analysis of information—putting 2 and 2 together—for the hidden idea to be observed. The article implies; the reader infers.

In the following brief and factual statement from the article, little of interest is *implied,* but important conclusions can be *inferred:*

> A slight increase was noted in the number of unmarried couples living together; they totaled almost two million as of March and represent about 4 percent of the couples.

From this information, as well as previous evidence provided about postponement of marriage, it would be safe to *infer* that *one reason why people are marrying later may be that they are living together as unmarried couples first.*

It is perfectly correct to draw your own inferences from the sources that you are writing about, as long as you fulfill two conditions:

1. There must be a reasonable basis within the source for your inference.
2. The inferences should be clearly identified as yours, not the source's.

When in an essay you cite a specific work as the basis of an inference, your reader should be able to go to the source, locate the evidence there, and draw a similar inference.

What inferences can you draw from the following paragraph, when you put this information together with everything else that you have read in the article?

> Though the report said that most young people are expected to marry eventually, it noted that the longer marriage was delayed the greater the chance that it would not occur. "Consequently, the percentage of today's young adults that do not ever marry may turn out to be higher than the corresponding percentage of their predecessors," the report speculated.

First, notice that the connection between delaying marriage and never marrying at all is *stated,* not *proved.* Assuming that the statement is correct, and realizing that the years of fertility are limited, it would be reasonable to *infer* that *the trend to marry later in life may be a factor in the declining birth rate.*

Because inferences are not totally rooted in the information provided by your source, they tend to be expressed in tentative terms. Both inferences cited above, for example, use "may be" to convey an appropriate degree of uncertainty. The following inference hedges in a different way: *If the trend toward later marriages continues at a steady rate, eventually there will be no more married couples in this country.* Here, the sweeping and improbable generalization— no more married couples—is put into some perspective through the conditional: "*if* this trend continues at a steady rate. . . ." However, given the variety of unpredictable influences affecting the decision to marry, the negative trend is unlikely to continue at a steady rate. In fact, this inference is absurd.

EXERCISE 3: DRAWING INFERENCES

Read "Ice Cream: Giving in to Rich Temptation." Then decide which of the sentences that follow are *stated;* which are *implied* (or suggested by the essay); which can be *inferred* from the essay; and which are *false,* according to the information in the article.

ICE CREAM: GIVING IN TO RICH TEMPTATION
Fran McCullough

Sales of the richest ice creams—what the trade calls premium and super-premium—are up 28 percent in the first six months of 1997, while sales of low-fat ice creams have dropped 5 percent from last year. The dieter's old love, frozen yogurt, first showed signs of neglect in 1995; this year, sales are down 23 percent. 1

Sales of frozen yogurt began to decline when new reduced-fat ice creams appeared in the market, said Martin Veeger, the group's director of market research. 2

But, he added, the sharper recent decline also reflects a new desire among Americans to indulge the forbidden pleasures of the table.

If steak and french fries are back on the menu, then rich ice cream is dessert.   3

Ice cream has always been the favorite American dessert; Americans ate 1.5 billion gallons of it in 1996, or about 47 pints a person, 2 percent more than the year before. That's substantially more than in any other country in the world, with Finland's 38 pints a person and Denmark's 34 pints next in line. In the United States, Portland, Oregon, and Seattle lead in annual sales of ice cream at supermarkets, with 2.87 and 2.64 gallons a person respectively; New York is 50th, at 1.45 gallons. (Perhaps people who live with more inclement weather need ice cream to cheer them up.)   4

But it is taste that is driving the $11 billion ice cream business. Even Dr. Dean Ornish, the low-fat advocate, prefers to savor a nightly spoonful of full-fat Häagen-Dazs, rather than diving into a pint of what he calls "fake-fat frozen dessert."   5

And the dissatisfaction with taste is behind the drop in low-fat ice cream sales, said Lynda Utterback, the editor of the Chicago-based National Dipper, a newsletter for retail shops. "Low-fat ice cream? It's an oxymoron," she said. "Butterfat is what makes ice cream taste so good." Häagen-Dazs low-fat vanilla has 2.5 grams of fat a serving, compared with 18 grams of fat for its regular, super-premium vanilla.   6

"We've gone about as far as we can go with the nonfat ice creams," said Bob Howe, a consultant to ice cream companies who is based in Byron, California. "The replacements for the mouth feel, good body and texture of butterfat just aren't there, so it's going to be creative flavoring that takes up the slack. With low fat, the formulations are changing all the time, so it's getting better."   7

But creative flavoring almost inevitably means more sugars and mix-ins, like candy, that may be as much of a problem for dieters as fat.   8

"No one is saying these reduced-fat ice creams are low calorie," said Betty Campbell of the Food and Drug Administration's Office of Food Labeling. While the full-fat Java Chip at Starbucks has 250 calories a serving, its low-fat Mocha Mambo still has 170 calories.   9

Ice cream labeling can be confusing. Because ice cream is sold by volume—what is defined as a serving is a miserly half cup—and not by weight, it is impossible to figure out exactly how much of the product is air that has been pumped in, what the industry calls overrun. Some air needs to be added to packaged ice cream or it would be too hard to serve easily. But the overrun percentage varies widely. Super-premiums, which cost upward of $3 a pint, are usually from 10 to 20 percent air, while some economy ice creams, which are usually under $3 for a half gallon, are half air.   10

Consumers can get a rough idea of how much overrun different brands have by comparing the weight per serving of a plain variety like vanilla, which is listed on the label. Servings of Edy's and Turkey Hill, both premiums, weigh 65 and 66 grams, respectively; super-premium Häagen-Dazs and Ben & Jerry's weigh 106 and 108 grams a serving, respectively. Almost invariably, airy ice creams are less satisfying,   11 so people tend to compensate by having larger servings. That means that the amounts of fat and calories per serving listed on the labels are less relevant.

1. Dieters who used to eat frozen yogurt are now eating low-fat ice cream.
2. Full-fat ice cream has more than seven times the fat of low-fat ice cream.
3. No other country eats as much ice cream as the United States.
4. Eating low-fat ice cream isn't much help to dieters.
5. Overrun enriches the flavor of ice cream.
6. Heavy ice cream is good ice cream.
7. Low-fat cake is likely to have lots of sugar in it.
8. Low-fat ice cream isn't as delicious as full-fat ice cream, so people eat smaller portions of it.
9. Ice cream is a big seller in cold climates.

Logical Reasoning

When making an inference, you *generalize* or *draw a specific conclusion* from the available information, drawing on personal knowledge and experience to predict a likely conclusion or next step. For instance, if you look out a window and observe that the street and sidewalk are wet and the sky is overcast, you would most likely conclude that it had rained recently. You didn't directly observe the rain, but you can generalize from past experiences with the same evidence. Although this may seem like a simpleminded illustration, it is typical of the logical reasoning we all engage in every day.

There are two types of reasoning in formal logic—*deductive* reasoning and *inductive* reasoning, each a distinct process for arriving at defensible conclusions based on available evidence.

Deductive Reasoning

The classic format for deductive reasoning is the *syllogism*, which consists of a series of carefully limited statements, or premises, pursued to a circumscribed conclusion:

All reptiles are cold-blooded.	[premise]
Iguanas are reptiles.	[premise]
Therefore, iguanas are cold-blooded.	[conclusion]

This is a line of reasoning based on classification, that is, the creation of a generalized category based on shared traits. Members of the group we call "reptiles" have cold-bloodedness in common—in fact, cold-bloodedness is a defining trait of reptiles. Iguanas are members of the group reptiles, which means that they must also have that shared trait. Notice that the opening premise of a syllogism is a statement that the reader will be willing to grant as true without explicit proof. Deductive reasoning always begins with beliefs or knowledge that the writer and reader share, and the syllogism builds from that undisputed statement.

Deductive reasoning follows an almost mathematical rigor; provided the premises are true and the line of reasoning valid, the conclusion must necessarily be true.

Inductive Reasoning

In inductive reasoning, a conclusion or common principle is reached by generalizing from a body of evidence, as in the example of the wet street and overcast sky. The conclusions reached through inductive reasoning are always conditional to some extent—that is, there's always the possibility that some additional evidence may be introduced to suggest a different conclusion. Given the available evidence, you were perfectly justified in concluding that it had rained when you observed a wet street and overcast sky; but suppose you then turned on the radio and learned that a water main in the area had broken overnight. That overcast sky may be coincidental, and you should be prepared to revise your original conclusion based on the new information.

Inductive reasoning uses the available evidence to construct the most likely conclusion.

Logic in Argumentation

Most arguments contain elements of both inductive and deductive reasoning. In argumentation, the writer attempts to prove a claim by presenting evidence and reasoning so that the reader can recreate the writer's logic. The core of the argument is usually *deductive,* but rarely based on a classical syllogism; rather, it consists of a series of *premises* or *assumptions* that the reader shares— or can be persuaded to share—with the writer. These premises often depend on *common cultural values.* That is why arguments can lose their force over time as values change. One hundred years ago, writers could safely base arguments on the premise that heroism is defined by slaying the enemy in battle, or that engaging in sex before marriage warrants a girl's expulsion from polite society, or that whipping young children is an effective and acceptable punishment. Today, those arguments would not have wide credibility.

The point of argument is to convince your reader to view an issue as you do, to share your belief that a certain result is worth achieving, and to agree that the method you propose is the best way of achieving it. To do that, you must establish common ground between you and your reader. Don't assume that your underlying assumptions will automatically be shared. Spell them out; make them seem desirable, even inevitable.

For instance, few people would challenge you if you simply claimed that cruelty to animals is bad, but there is a wide range of opinion regarding exactly what constitutes cruelty, or whether certain specific activities (the use of animals in scientific research, for instance) are or are not cruel. Is inflicting pain, or even discomfort, "cruel" by definition? If inflicting pain serves some larger purpose, is it still cruel, or does "cruelty" refer only to *unnecessary* or *unjustifiable* pain? Before contesting the ethics of medical research practices, a persuasive argument about this issue would have to begin by establishing a premise—in this case, a definition of "cruelty"—that both the reader and the writer will find acceptable.

To be fully convincing, the argument that emerges from your premises must be *inductive* as well: it must be supported by a range of *evidence*, which you present, analyze, and interpret for your reader. Evidence usually consists of *facts*, which you verify and document by specifying the sources. If your evidence depends on *data* and *statistics*, the sources must be reliable, and the results based on an adequate and representative sample and an appropriate population. How many people took part in the survey? If percentages are cited, what was the base population? If you say that 60 percent of those surveyed want to raise the tax on cigarettes, do you mean fifty or five hundred or five thousand people? Were they smokers or nonsmokers? What was their age? their income? These and other factors have some bearing on the validity of such data as evidence.

■ *Generalizing from a representative sample*
Public opinion polls use limited evidence (the opinions of, say, 1,000 respondents) to predict the opinions of a much larger group—possibly the entire nation—by assuming that the opinions of the smaller group reflect proportionately the opinions of the larger. Here, for instance, is part of a survey on attitudes toward health care taken in 1989:

> The Harvard University School of Public Health and Louis Harris and Associates surveyed nearly 4,000 American, Canadian and British adults about their country's health care. . . . A full 89 percent of U.S. citizens feel our health-care system is fundamentally flawed. . . .

You can readily see how the writer uses the responses of the 4,000 people surveyed to make larger claims about whole national groups ("A full 89 percent of U.S. citizens feel . . .").

■ *Citing authority*
Another source of evidence is *authority:* the testimony of experts whose reputation makes them credible. You need to cite the evidence of such authorities in reasonable detail and, if possible, convey the strength of their credentials. Your argument should not depend on nameless sources such as "1,000 doctors" or "authorities in the field."

■ *Reasoning through analogies*
One other basis for argument, loosely related to deduction, is *reasoning through analogies.* A writer may compare a disputed idea or situation to some other, less controversial idea in order to reveal an inconsistency or to advocate a particular course of action. For instance, some might claim that the wide availability of foreign-made consumer products is analogous to an infection that threatens to destroy the health of the nation's

economy. What similarities in the two situations is this writer exploiting? What parallels can be drawn between them?

nation	=	person
foreign-made consumer product • produced outside the nation • invades national economy	=	**infection** • originates outside the person • invades body of individual
harmful: threatens economic health of nation • workers laid off when American-made products aren't bought	=	**harmful:** threatens physical health of person • virus or infection destroys healthy cells, or otherwise weakens person
remedy: discourage imports	=	**remedy:** prevent invasive virus or infection; destroy existing virus or infection.

In both cases, some entity (in the first case a nation, and in the second a human being) is "invaded" by something potentially harmful (such as a Japanese-made VCR or German-built car in the case of the nation, and a virus or bacterial infection in the case of the person). Having suggested these similarities, the writer can extend the analogy: The undisputed remedy in the case of sickness—destroying or preventing the cause of the sickness—suggests the remedy for the economy's illness—discouraging the importation of foreign-made consumer products.

Analogies can provide vivid and persuasive images, but they are also easily distorted when pushed too far, and an alternative analogy may suggest itself to the reader. Foreign-made consumer products may have "invaded" the United States, but considering their popularity with U.S. consumers, they have also in some sense been "invited." To U.S. auto manufacturers or workers, foreign imports probably do seem very like opportunistic microbes, but consumers preparing to buy a new car are less likely to "destroy" them than to regard them as inexpensive generic medicines designed to heal ailing pocketbooks. Careful writers recognize the limits of their analogies.

Ineffective Arguments and Logical Fallacies

Not every argument convinces us to accept the writer's conclusion. What undermines the credibility or persuasiveness of an inductive or deductive argument?

- *An argument may be based on an initial premise that is unconvincing.*
- *The line of reasoning that connects premise to premise may be flawed.*
- *The evidence itself may be misrepresented in some way.*

It's easy to accept *initial premises* uncritically because they're generally expressed with confidence in the reader's agreement—remember, the writer assumes that the reader will grant the argument's opening premises without explicit proof. As you read, you should be careful to identify the assumptions a writer uses in constructing an argument. For example, look at the following opening premise, from the second paragraph of an unsigned editorial attacking the logic of a proposed ban on tobacco products. The editorial appeared in the magazine *National Review* in 1994.

> Even though nine-tenths of smokers don't die of lung cancer, there are clearly health dangers in cigarettes, dangers so constantly warned about that smokers are clearly aware that these dangers are the price they pay for the enjoyment and relaxation they get from smoking.

The writer claims here that because the health risks connected with smoking have been widely publicized, the decision to smoke is rational—that is, based on smokers' weighing their desire for "enjoyment and relaxation" against the potential health risks. You might grant the dangers of smoking have been well documented and publicized, but does it necessarily follow that knowing the risks involved ensures a rational decision? If, as has also been widely demonstrated, cigarettes are addictive, then the decision to smoke may *not* be entirely rational—that is, the decision to smoke may *not* be freely made after a careful consideration of the available data and the possible consequences.

The writer here is committing a common logical lapse known as *begging the question*. The assumption here is false; it assumes that a crucial point is self-evident and requires no further argument. The key word here is "clearly"—"smokers are clearly aware"—which may persuade the careless reader that the point has already been proven. When a writer is begging the question, you often find language that preempts the issue and discourages scrutiny: "obviously," "everyone knows," or "it goes without saying."

Sometimes, the process of begging the question is more subtle. Here, a writer arguing against euthanasia begins with a strong statement:

> Every human being has a natural inclination to continue living. Our reflexes and responses fit us to fight attackers, flee wild animals, and dodge out of the way of trucks. In our daily lives we exercise the caution and care necessary to protect ourselves. Our bodies are similarly structured for survival right down to the molecular level. . . . Euthanasia does violence to this natural goal of survival. It is literally acting against nature because all the processes of nature are bent towards the end of bodily survival.

By limiting his view of existence to purely bodily functions, J. Gay-Williams simplifies the complex issue of euthanasia. What he omits are the key functions of the mind, will, and emotions, which, some would say, can override the force of the instinct towards "bodily survival" and make the choice to die. The key here is the first sentence: "Every human being has a natural inclination to continue living." This broad assumption allows for no exceptions. It begs the question by telling only part of the story.

Even if the premises of an argument are valid, there may be *fallacies* in the reasoning that holds the premises together. Logical fallacies are breakdowns in the reasoning that connects the premises of an argument; they occur when the writer makes *unjustifiable* generalizations like the one above or draws *unjustifiable* conclusions from the available evidence. Cause-and-effect reasoning, for example, can slide into before-and-after fallacies (known as *post hoc propter ergo hoc*—after this, therefore, before this). This fallacy assumes that any event that precedes another must somehow *cause* the second event. It is often true that one event causes a second, later event, as in the case of rain causing the wet street you observe the next morning. But if you make that reasoning a universal rule, you might, for instance, conclude that because swimsuits habitually appear in your local clothing stores in May, and summer follows in June, swimsuits somehow *cause* summer. It may be perfectly true that swimsuits appear in stores in May and that summer usually begins in June, but this argument fails to consider *alternative explanations*—in this case, that the approach of summer actually causes manufacturers to ship and retailers to display swimsuits in May, rather than the other way around; the swimsuits *anticipate*, rather than *cause*, summer.

Most fallacies result from a tendency to oversimplify issues, to take shortcuts in dealing with complex and diverse ideas. An easy fallacy to slip into is the *false dilemma*. In effect, you limit the ground for argument by proceeding as if there were only two alternatives; everything else is ignored. Here is part of the argument presented by a writer who supports euthanasia:

> Reality dictates the necessity of such laws because, for some dying patients experiencing extreme suffering, a lethal prescription is the only way to end an extended and agonizing death. Consider the terrible dilemma created when so-called passive measures fail to bring about the hoped-for death. Are we to stand helplessly by while a patient whose suicide we legally agreed to assist continues to suffer and deteriorate—perhaps even more so than before? Or do we have a moral imperative, perhaps even a legal responsibility, to not only alleviate the further suffering we have brought about but to take action to fulfill our original agreement [to withdraw life support]?

Barbara Dority has reduced the situation to a simple choice: passive doctor and patient in agony versus active doctor who brings an end to suffering, who abides by morality, and who keeps her promise. There are many possibilities for intervention between these two extremes, but, at this point in her argument, the writer does not acknowledge them. Through her language, she also loads the dice: does one identify with the doctor "stand[ing] helplessly" by or the doctor with a "moral imperative" who knows how to "take action" to "alleviate . . . suffering"?

The tendency to oversimplify, to base our claims on insufficient evidence, can result in the *hasty generalization*. A convincing generalization will be supported by strong evidence. *Avoid generalizing on the basis of one or two examples.* And when you do cite examples, make sure that they are typical ones and that they clearly support your argument. Gertrude Himmelfarb, for example, builds her argument about the decline of morality in our society by criticizing an increasing tendency to be nonjudgmental. She offers the following generalization:

> Most of us are uncomfortable with the idea of making moral judgements even in our private lives, let alone with the "intrusion," as we say, of moral judgements into public affairs.

To support her generalization, she observes that public officials, such as the president's cabinet and the Surgeon General, tend to avoid using the word "immoral." In one of her two examples, the Secretary of Health and Human Services is quoted as saying:

> I don't like to put this in moral terms, but I do believe that having children out of wedlock is just wrong.

This last quotation, in itself, hardly strengthens Professor Himmelfarb's initial point since many would consider "wrong" a judgment equivalent to "immoral." Then, on the basis of these limited examples, she reiterates her original claim:

> It is not only our political and cultural leaders who are prone to this failure of moral nerve. Everyone has been infected by it, to one degree or another.

The argument has moved around in a circle, from one hasty generalization to another.

One unpleasant kind of logical fallacy is the *ad hominem* [about the man] argument. Here, the basis for argument is a personal attack: first you point out all the bad qualities of a prominent person who opposes your views; then, without considering whether those flaws are relevant to the issue, you conclude that they must taint that person's beliefs. As you have realized, the ad hominem argument is often used in political campaigns and in other well-publicized controversies. A discussion of euthanasia, for example, will sometimes get stuck in a consideration of Dr. Jack Kevorkian's conduct and motives.

Paul McHugh, for example, spends the first half of his argument against euthanasia demonstrating why he regards Dr. Kevorkian as "'certifiably' insane," comparing him with other zealots who would do anything to advance their cause, and finally citing "the potential for horror in an overvalued idea held by a person in high authority" such as Adolf Hitler. Certainly, the comparison is strained—Dr. Kevorkian is not "in high authority." Yet, even though Professor McHugh now moves to a completely different basis for argument, the opprobrium generated by the association between Kevorkian and Hitler reverberates throughout the rest of the essay.

Yet another logical fallacy derives from reasoning through analogies: in a *false analogy,* the two ideas or circumstances being compared are not actually comparable. Here is an example of a false analogy based on statistics that is being used in an argument against euthanasia:

> Gomez calculates that euthanasia accounts for about 7 percent of all deaths in the Netherlands. If the United States had a similar rate, there would be about 140,000 cases annually. If Fumento's 9 percent figure is correct, the United States number would be 180,000. And if it is correct that half of the Dutch euthanasias are unconsented, applying that proportion here would mean that the number of physician-inflicted unconsented deaths in this country would be between 70,000 and 90,000 annually.

Even though Robert Bork is not sure which of his sources is correct, he uses their statistics to develop an analogy between what has probably happened in the Netherlands (give or take a few percentage points) and what might happen in the United States. Are the two nations comparable in this regard? Professor Bork does not explore the national character, the nature of doctor-patient relationships, the availability of palliatives like medication or hospices. The only point of distinction that he raises is the higher cost of health care in the United States, which supports the conclusion encouraged by his analogy: if it were legalized in the United States, the incentive to bring down medical costs would turn euthanasia into "a license to kill."

For another example of false analogy, let's return to the editorial on the proposed tobacco ban from the *National Review*. Here's the entire paragraph.

> Even though nine-tenths of smokers don't die of lung cancer, there are clearly health dangers in cigarettes, dangers so constantly warned about that smokers are clearly aware that these dangers are the price they pay for the enjoyment and relaxation they get from smoking. As mortals we make all kinds of trade-offs between health and living. We drive automobiles knowing that forty thousand people die in them in the U.S. each year; we cross busy streets, tolerate potentially explosive gas in our homes, swim in fast-moving rivers, use electricity though it kills thousands, and eat meat and other foods that may clog our arteries and give us heart attacks and strokes. All the . . . demagoguery about the tobacco industry killing people could be applied with similar validity to the automobile industry, the electric utilities, aircraft manufacturers, the meat business, and more.

Here, the reader is asked to compare the health risks associated with smoking with those of parallel but comparatively uncontroversial activities, such as crossing a busy street. According to the writer, the situations are comparable because both involve voluntarily engaging in activities known to be health risks, and that similarity is used to suggest that laws *prohibiting* smoking would be logically inconsistent because we don't prohibit other risky activities. If potential health risks justify regulation or even prohibition, then any number of modern activities should, by analogy, be regulated. Yet, in spite of the risks in crossing busy streets, no one ever suggests preventing people from doing so for their own good; smoking, however, is singled out for regulation and possible prohibition. The reader can further *infer* from this line of reasoning that, since we daily engage in all kinds of risky activities, individuals in all cases should be allowed to decide without government interference which risks to take.

In arguments based on false analogies, the reasoning can be attacked merely by demonstrating that the differences in the two situations are more significant than the similarities. In this case, we need to consider:

- if the decision to smoke and the decision to cross a busy street are *genuinely* comparable; and
- if there may be sound reasons for regulating smoking, and equally sound reasons for *not* regulating crossing the street.

Most people could not live a normal life without crossing a busy street, but the same cannot be said of smoking. In addition, if a minimal amount of caution is exercised in crossing busy streets, most people will not be injured; when injuries do occur, they're the result of accidents or some other unexpected or unusual set of events. The same is true of the other "hazards" described in the editorial (driving automobiles, using gas appliances, and so on): injuries result from their *misuse.* By contrast, cigarettes pose a serious health threat when used exactly as intended by their manufacturers; no amount of caution will protect you from the risks associated with cigarettes.

You might also object to this argument on grounds that go beyond the logic of the reasoning to *the ways the evidence is presented.* The writer mentions, for instance, only that 9 in 10 smokers *don't die* of lung cancer, implying not only that a 10 percent death rate is insignificant but that death or lung cancer is the only potential health risk connected to smoking worth mentioning. The writer also states that "forty thousand people die" in automobiles each year in the United States, but because that number isn't presented as a percentage of all drivers on the road over the course of the year, it doesn't really address the *comparable* level of risk—those 40,000 may represent fewer than 1 percent of all drivers, which would make driving considerably less risky than smoking. Misrepresenting the evidence in this way prods the careful reader to question the writer's trustworthiness and credibility. (For another discussion of distortion in argumentation, see Chapter 8, pp. 353–355.)

Guidelines for Assessing Arguments

1. Examine the writer's initial premises. Are you willing to grant those statements without explicit proof?

2. How is the writer assembling the evidence? How is the reasoning structured, and is it sound? Can you see acceptable alternatives to the conclusion the writer has drawn?

3. Is the writer manipulating the facts and their presentation to suit the purposes of the argument?

OUTLINING

In addition to making marginal notes and asking yourself comprehension questions, you can better understand what you have read by *outlining the author's main ideas.*

When you outline, you are identifying the main points of a chapter or an essay, leaving them in roughly the same order as the original.

Outlines are built around the major points that the author uses to support the main idea, or *thesis.* In a short essay, the major points will probably all be parallel or of the same kind: the *reasons* why x is true, or the *ways* in which y happens, or the *differences* between x and y, or the chief *characteristics* of z, and so on. In a longer, more complex essay, the author may use several different sets of major points in shifting from one argument to another, or from the description of a problem to its solution.

These major points are given the most prominent place in the outline, usually in a numbered list at the left-hand margin. Secondary material—the ideas, information, or examples being used as supporting evidence—appears directly under each major point and slightly to the right. If there are different kinds of evidence presented, or several examples, or both, each should be listed on a separate line and assigned numbers or letters of the alphabet to keep them in order.

To demonstrate the standard format, here is an outline of some of the points that have been made so far in this chapter.

I. Underlining
    A. Important for active reading
        1. select what's important
           a. key generalizations and topic sentences
           b. useful examples
           c. transitional points
    B. Works best on second reading
        1. choose from alternative methods
           a. underline
           b. highlight
           c. circle
           d. bracket
           e. marginal checks

II. Annotation
    A. Helps you to understand what you read
        1. interpret, evaluate, or question meaning
        2. define difficult words or phrases
        3. clarify confusing points
        4. introduce ideas of your own
    B. Involves participatory process
        1. read slowly
        2. write notes in the margin
        3. use your own words

For each of the two skills stated in the *first level* (I/II) this outline deals first with its purpose (in the *second level:* A) and then with ways of using the skill (in the *second level:* B). The *third level* (arabic numbers: 1/2/3) is reserved for examples, while the *fourth level* (small letters: a/b/c) contains more specific examples or explanations of points on the third level.

There is no fixed number of letters and numbers allocated for each section; whether you use only the four levels that you see in the preceding outline or include even more—the next two levels could be (1) and (a)—depends on the number and complexity of the supporting ideas that you find in your source.

The purpose of outlining is to show how the author has constructed the essay and to distinguish between main ideas and supporting material.

Multilevel numbering and lettering is not always necessary in an outline. It is possible to indicate the relationships between ideas simply by the way you place them on the page. However, the numbers and letters do provide an easy way of organizing and referring to a large number of points.

There are a few rules governing *the language used in outlining*. You may take the words of your outline directly from the original, or you may express the author's ideas in your own words. You may use complete sentences or fragmentary phrases, whichever is convenient. However, *consistency is important.* Try to make all points on the same level either fragments or complete sentences. For example, in the preceding outline, the points on the third level are consistently expressed as commands, while those on the second level are all sentence fragments.

Outlining Simple Essays

Outlining is the most effective way to record the main points of an essay whose structure is clear and straightforward. In "Must Doctors Serve Where They're Told?" for example, Harry Schwartz presents the arguments for both sides so clearly that underlining and numbering the key phrases in the essay would record its structure. (Each of the main points has been italicized in the essay.) However, since Schwartz moves back and forth from positive to negative reasons, it is helpful to outline the pairing of related arguments.

Read "Must Doctors Serve Where They're Told?" and then carefully examine the outline that follows.

MUST DOCTORS SERVE WHERE THEY'RE TOLD?
Harry Schwartz

Should young doctors be "drafted" and forced to serve some years in areas of physician shortage? Or, less dramatically, should a portion of the places in the nation's medical schools be reserved for young people who promise that in return for government financial aid they will agree to serve where the government wants them to? These and related issues have been debated in Congress . . . and are still unresolved.

Currently, it costs an estimated average of about $13,000 a year to train a medical student, but those students pay directly only about $1,000 to $6,000 in tuition. The remainder is paid by government funds, by return on endowments, by gifts and similar sources. Some lawmakers see a *compulsory service liability as a means of compensating the taxpayers for subsidizing the doctors' education.*

2

The specific proposals that have been debated in Congress have ranged from Senator Edward M. Kennedy's suggestion for a universal draft for all medical school graduates to milder schemes that would give young doctors a choice between repaying the Federal Government or serving for several years in designated areas. In New York there is already a medical training program whose students have agreed to serve two years in doctor-short areas after graduating from medical school. Those who fail to meet this "service commitment" will be required to reimburse the city and state for up to $25,000 for their free undergraduate education.

3

Some conservative economists have argued that *physician incomes, which average around $50,000, remove all excuse for government subsidy.* They would require medical students to pay the full costs, financing their way, if need be, by bank loans. Such an approach would remove the motive for any doctor draft, but many in Congress fear that this "solution" would close medical schools to children of the poor, the working class, and minorities.

4

Proponents of some service requirements for young doctors usually base their arguments on the *maldistribution of doctors in this country.* In 1973, for example, California had 265 doctors per 100,000 people, more than three times as many as South Dakota's 87 per 100,000. The actual disparities are even greater, because within each state physicians tend to congregate in metropolitan areas.

5

Opponents of forced service do not deny the existence of local shortages, but they question the wisdom of *sending new physicians into shortage areas where they will have little or no help* and consultation from older, more experienced doctors.

6

Opponents also ask *whether doctors serving in isolated areas against their will are likely to give satisfactory service.* And they ask why young doctors and dentists should be *singled out for coercion* when government helps finance the education of most professionals and there are great inequalities in the current distribution of lawyers, accountants, architects and engineers as well.

7

But more is involved in this debate than the allocation of physicians. The argument about young doctors is relevant to the broader national discussion about national economic planning and about the relative roles of government decision and market forces in directing the American economy.

8

On one side are those who emphasize the *obligation of government to use all its resources to reach desirable goals for all Americans.* If one assumes, as Mr. Kennedy and others do, that every American has a "right" to health care, then it seems reasonable for government to take whatever actions are needed to make sure that doctors and related personnel and facilities are available everywhere. If market forces do not produce the desired result, this school is prepared to use either government coercion or government financial persuasion. Moreover, this school of

9

thought wants to tailor the means to the end. Thus, instead of using government money just to expand the number of doctors in general, they want to assure that doctors are available wherever needed and available, moreover, in whatever distribution of specialities Congress or its servants decide is appropriate.

Opponents argue that such *regulation would be contrary to all American history and tradition,* except for times of war or emergency when the military draft has been in effect. The *American emphasis, these opponents hold, is primarily upon the freedom of the individual and affords no warrant for infringing one person's freedom in order to benefit someone else.* The whole structure of publicly financed education in this country, from kindergarten to M.D. and Ph.D., it is pointed out, has developed over the decades without any related service requirement or repayment of any kind whatsoever. If doctors are drafted, it will provide a precedent for drafting other categories of Americans.   10

The issue is not peculiarly American, of course, nor is the problem of physician maldistribution confined to the United States. *In the Soviet Union and its associated Communist states,* most graduates of higher educational institutions—not only physicians—are *assigned specific work locations* for the first few years after graduation.   11

Some non-Communist countries, like Mexico, have a requirement for compulsory service for a limited time by doctors before they can go into normal practice. In Israel there is a universal service obligation for all young adults. *But in most countries of Western Europe there is no draft of young doctors.*   12

Most of the other democratic countries of the world are relatively small, both in area and population . . . compared with the United States. So the advocates of a doctor draft in the United States argue that the absence of such compulsion in other countries is no conclusive argument against it here.   13

I. Obligations of young doctors: partial cost of education borne by public, which is entitled to compensation
   A. Debt to public can be repaid through service
      1. Kennedy plan
      2. New York two-year term of service
   B. Bank loan can be used for initial payment of medical school fees
      1. extremely high income will allow ultimate repayment
      2. possible difficulty in applying for initial loan

II. Needs of the public: not enough doctors to serve the country
   A. "Maldistribution" necessitates drafting: doctors tend to practice in certain populous states and cities
      1. California
      2. South Dakota
   B. Coercion would not ensure efficient service
      1. inexperienced doctors would be isolated from guidance
      2. unwilling doctors are inefficient

III. Powers of the government vs. the rights of the individual

    A. The government is empowered to satisfy everyone's right to health care

    B. Public policy shouldn't encourage coercion of individuals to benefit others; to draft doctors would be an unfortunate precedent

        1. other professions aren't subject to a draft

        2. other beneficiaries of public education aren't forced to repay costs

IV. Precedents in other countries

    A. Drafting doctors is routine in some countries

        1. Communist countries

        2. Mexico

        3. Israel

    B. Drafting doctors is not required in many countries with a democratic tradition similar to ours

        1. Western Europe

            a. these Western European countries are physically smaller than the United States and therefore have different requirements

Thesis: A decision to draft young doctors for service throughout the country will have to consider the obligations and rights of the doctors, as well as the responsibility of the government to serve the public.

This is a four-level outline, with the third and fourth levels (1,2,3/a) presenting either specific examples or more narrow statements than the broad ideas contained in the first and second levels. Notice how the language within each level remains relatively consistent: levels I through IV contain fragmentary phrases; levels A and B are written in complete sentences throughout; levels 1, 2, and 3 do vary, depending on whether the supporting material consists of examples (expressed as words or fragments) or narrow generalizations (complete sentences). The phrasing is parallel within each section; the clearest example is IV.A and IV.B, which use parallel participial constructions ("drafting doctors").

Outlining Complex Essays

Most essays are not as clearly organized as Harry Schwartz's. For example, the main ideas may not appear in the obvious place at the beginning of each paragraph. Some writers tend to put their topic sentences at the ends of paragraphs; others don't use topic sentences at all, or use them minimally.

Loosely organized essays are not bad essays or even badly constructed essays. They often deal with complex subjects, too complex to be easily contained in a tightly constructed sequence of paragraphs. Nevertheless, these essays do have a plan, a structure linking one idea with the next. And that plan means that these essays can be outlined.

Essays that deal with several main ideas simultaneously are especially difficult to outline, yet they usually require and repay careful, point-by-point outlining. Such an essay is Blanche Blank's "A Question of Degree" (see pp. 8–11).

Establishing a Thesis

The outline of Harry Schwartz's essay was followed by a statement of its *thesis*—the essay's central idea.

> *A thesis is usually a substantial generalization, written as a complete sentence, that can stand by itself as the basis of an essay's development.*

A thesis should be broad enough and arguable enough to be worth defending in a work of at least several pages. In the Schwartz essay, the thesis does no more than suggest the underlying issues, since Schwartz himself does not decisively support one side of the argument or the other.

In contrast, Blanche Blank, in "A Question of Degree," *is* attempting to convince her readers to accept a specific point of view. An adequate thesis, then, should convey some of her distaste for the excessive value placed on college degrees. But even if you fully understand Blank's position, you may still write an incomplete or an inadequate thesis. What is wrong with each of these examples?

1. According to Blanche Blank, universities need to change their outlook and curricula and return to a more traditional role.

2. Blanche Blank suggests that our present ideology about the purpose of college should be reconsidered and redefined.

3. I agree with Blanche Blank's belief that college degrees have too much importance.

4. Blanche Blank argues that employment discrimination arises from an emphasis on college degrees.

5. Blanche Blank believes that a college education isn't necessary at an early age.

Remember that *a good thesis would be a generalization broad enough to cover most of Blank's argument without being so vague as to be meaningless.* Consider the following criticisms of the five theses:

- Thesis 1 accurately presents only one—and not the chief one—of Blank's points.

- Thesis 2 is uninformative: what is "our present ideology" and what sort of redefinition is in order?
- Thesis 3 is also vague: Blank may have convinced one reader, but which of her arguments did the reader find effective?
- Thesis 4 is much too broad: Blank does not argue that degrees are the only cause of employment discrimination, nor does she suggest that employment is the only area adversely affected by the importance attached to degrees.
- Thesis 5 is inaccurate and incomplete: Blank is not urging all would-be freshmen to bypass college.

The following thesis is somewhat better than the first five: it conveys something of Blank's central idea, but it says nothing about work and the self-respect of the worker, which are ideas crucial to the essay.

6. In Blanche Blank's view, acquiring a college degree immediately after high school should not be considered the best way to achieve a better life.

A satisfactory thesis would convey more precisely the dangers of overvaluing the college degree. Thesis 7 does so:

7. The possession of a college degree cannot automatically lead to a better life and better earnings for a college graduate; the universal practice of regarding the degree as an essential for getting a "good" job can only discourage a more just and efficient system of employment.

Both parts of Thesis 7 deal with the consequences of overvaluing the college degree: the first part is concerned with the effect on the individual, whose expectations may not be fulfilled; the second is concerned with the effect on social institutions and organizations, which may value credentials at the expense of merit. It is not accidental that Thesis 7 is the longest of the group; complex ideas often require complex means of expression.

Constructing an Outline Based on Categories

Because the paragraphs of "A Question of Degree" are crowded with ideas, constructing an outline is difficult. For example, within the following single paragraph, Blank mentions most of her main points, some more than once, and in varying order. (The numbers here are keyed to the outline on pp. 41–42.)

What is wrong with the current college/work cycle can be seen in the following anomalies: we are selling college to the youth of America as a take-off pad for the material good life [I.A]. College is literally advertised and packaged as a means for getting more money through "better" jobs at the same time that Harvard graduates are taking jobs as taxi drivers [I.B]. This situation is a perversion of the true spirit of a university [III], a perversion of a humane social ethic [IV.A] and, at bottom, a patent fraud. To take the last point first, the economy simply is not geared to guaranteeing these presumptive "better" jobs [I.B]; the colleges are not geared to training for such jobs [III]; and the ethical propriety of the entire enterprise is very questionable [I and II]. We are by definition (rather than by analysis) establishing two kinds of work: work labeled "better" because it has a degree requirement tagged to it and nondegree work, which, through this logic, becomes automatically "low level" [IV.A].

When outlining a complex essay, you must look for organizing principles and categories of ideas as you read and reread it. *Experienced readers learn to watch for points that are repeated and emphasized to help them find a consistent way to organize and remember what they have read.* Earlier, you were asked about the different groups of people who are affected by the unfortunate worship of college degrees. The easiest way to break down the mass of assertions in Blanche Blank's essay is to *use those groups as a way to establish categories:*

A. Students who are in college unwillingly
B. College graduates who work at frustrating jobs
C. Workers who have not been to college and are undervalued
D. True scholars who resent the decline in the quality of university life

If you combine the first two groups (both with career expectations and both disappointed by college), you have the basis for an outline with three major entries, plus a conclusion that sums up Blanche Blank's central ideas.

Thesis: The possession of a college degree cannot automatically lead to a better

life and better earnings for a college graduate; the universal practice of regard-

ing the degree as an essential for getting a "good" job can only discourage a

more just and efficient system of employment.

I. The frustration of students with vocational expectations

    A. Whether or not they are suited to college, students believe that they must spend four years getting a degree to get a good job.

    B. Rewarding jobs are not necessarily available, even to those with degrees.

II. The frustration of working people without college degrees but with hopes for advancement

    A. Workers with experience and good qualifications are bypassed for promotion and denied their rightful status.

    B. Since college is considered the province of the young, it is unlikely that an experienced older person will seek a college education.

III. The frustration of students and teachers with traditional views of college

    A. Instead of continuing to emphasize the traditional pursuit of knowledge for its own sake, universities are trying to function as a service industry, preparing students for careers.

IV. The deterioration of human values

   A. People are encouraged to make invidious comparisons between less and more desirable kinds of work.

   B. One form of educational experience is being elevated at the expense of the others.

There are a few important points to notice about the format of this outline.

First, in some ways, this is a traditional outline: *the main ideas are given Roman numerals and the secondary ideas are lettered.* As you have learned, this enables you to refer more easily to each of the items and, in the case of the lettered supporting arguments, to separate them clearly from one another. However, because the outline conforms to Blanche Blank's organization, the number of points included under each broad category varies. (For this reason, unlike some traditional outlines, it is permissible to have only one point [A] under III.)

Next, *the presentation need not be completely consistent, as long as it is consistent within each level.* In this outline, the main ideas are all written in sentence fragments and the supporting ideas are all complete sentences.

What is more important is that *all the entries are on roughly the same level of abstraction:* the main ideas are all very broad, while the secondary ideas suggest the more specific ways in which each paragraph in the essay will be developed. In contrast, here is an excerpt from an outline in which the main entries are both broad and specific:

   I. jobs aren't available

   II. Joe V. disappointed

   III. college students feel cheated

The example of Joe V. is used in the essay only to illustrate important ideas, not as an end in itself. Entry II is *evidence* in support of entries I and III, and therefore "Joe V." belongs in a more subordinate position:

   I. jobs aren't available

   II. college students feel cheated

   A. Joe V. disappointed

All the entries in the complete Blank outline are *rewordings* of ideas taken from the essay and are *self-contained and self-explanatory.* Outlines that retain the wording of the original sometimes don't make sense taken out of context. And, even if such fragmentary phrases serve as shorthand notes that you (and you alone) understand, they won't be very helpful if you want to communicate Blank's ideas to your reader in an essay of your own. Is this group of points easy to understand at a glance?

   I. Degree-granting colleges are like false gods.

   II. The college degree is regarded as a stepping-stone to "meaningful," "better" jobs.

III. The ethical propriety of the entire system is in question.

IV. Students see themselves as prisoners of economic necessity.

How these four points relate to each other or how they serve as arguments to support the essay's thesis is not immediately clear. Nor is it any more helpful to condense sentences into brief phrases.

I. destruction of adolescents

II. vocational schools instead of universities

III. nondegree work menial

It would be impossible to understand and appreciate Blanche Blank's argument from reading an outline containing these entries.

EXERCISE 4: OUTLINING AN ESSAY

Read "What Our Education System Needs Is More F's," by Carl Singleton (pp. 135–137). Establish the essay's thesis and construct an outline of its main ideas.

WRITING A SUMMARY

When you underline and annotate a text, when you ask yourself questions about its contents, when you work out an outline of its structure, you are helping yourself to understand what you are reading. When you write a summary, you are *recording* your understanding for your own information; when you include the summary in an essay of your own, you are *reporting* your understanding to your reader.

A summary of a source is usually *a condensation of ideas or information*. It is neither necessary nor desirable to include every repetition and detail. Rather, you are to extract only those points that seem important—the main ideas, which in the original passage may have been interwoven with less important material. Thus, a summary of several pages can sometimes be as brief as one sentence.

In a brief summary, *you should add nothing new* to the material in the source, nor should you change the emphasis or provide any new interpretation or evaluation. For the sake of clarity and coherence, *you may rearrange the order of the ideas;* however, you should strive to remain in the background.

The brief summary is often used as part of a larger essay. You have probably summarized your own ideas in the topic sentence of a paragraph or in the conclusion of an essay. When you discuss another piece of writing, you generally summarize the contents briefly to establish for your reader the ideas that you intend to analyze. The writer of a research essay is especially dependent on the summary as a means of referring to source materials. Through summary, you can condense a broad range of information, and you can present and explain the relevance of a number of sources all dealing with the same subject.

Summarizing a Paragraph

Before you can begin to summarize a short reading—a paragraph, for example—you must, of course, read the passage carefully and understand the significance of each idea and the way it is linked to the other ideas. The summary should above all be *comprehensive,* conveying as much as possible the totality of thought within the passage. Sometimes, you will find a single comprehensive sentence in the text itself, to be taken out verbatim and used as a summary. But, as a rule, you will find your summary in the text only when the passage is short and contains a particularly strong and comprehensive topic sentence.

The following paragraph *can* be summarized adequately by one of its own sentences. Which one?

> It is often remarked that science has increasingly removed man from a position at the center of the universe. Once upon a time the earth was thought to be the center and the gods were thought to be in close touch with the daily actions of humans. It was not stupid to imagine the earth was at the center, because, one might think, if the earth were moving around the sun, and if you threw a ball vertically upward, it would seem the ball should come down a few feet away from you. Nevertheless, slowly, over many centuries, through the work of Copernicus, Galileo, and many others, we have mostly come to believe that we live on a typical planet orbiting a typical star in a typical galaxy, and indeed that no place in the universe is special.
>
> GORDON KANE, from "Are We the Center of the Universe?"

Both the first and last sentences are possibilities, but the first is a broader generalization and a more comprehensive summary.

Usually, even when you find a strong sentence that suggests the main idea of the paragraph, you will still need to tinker with that sentence, expanding its meaning by giving the language a more general focus. Here, for example, is a paragraph in which no one sentence is broad enough to sum up the main idea, but which contains a scattering of useful phrases:

> In a discussion [with] a class of teachers, I once said that I liked some of the kids in my class much more than others and that, without saying which ones I liked best, I had told them so. After all, this is something that children know, whatever we tell them; it is futile to lie about it. Naturally, these teachers were horrified. "What a terrible thing to say!" one said. "I love all the children in my class exactly the same." Nonsense; a teacher who says this is lying, to herself or to others, and probably doesn't like any of the children very much. Not that there is anything wrong with that; plenty of adults don't like children, and there is no reason why they should. But the trouble is that they feel they should, which makes them feel guilty, which makes them feel resentful, which in turn makes them try to work off their guilt with indulgence and their resentment with subtle cruelties—cruelties of a kind that can

be seen in many classrooms. Above all, it makes them put on the phony, syrupy, sickening voice and manner, and the fake smiles and forced, bright laughter that children see so much of in school, and rightly resent and hate.

JOHN HOLT, from *How Children Fail*

Here, you might begin by combining key phrases: "a teacher who says" that she "loves all the children" "is lying to herself, or to others," and makes herself (and probably the children) "feel guilty" and "resentful." However, this kind of summarizing sentence resembles a patchwork, with the *words and phrasing pulled straight out of the original.* Even if you acknowledged the borrowings, by using quotation marks, as above, you would still be left with a weak sentence that is neither yours nor the author's. It is far better to construct an entirely new sentence of your own, such as this one:

> In Holt's view, although it is only natural for teachers to prefer some students to others, many teachers cannot accept their failure to like all equally well and express their inadequacy and dissatisfaction in ways that are harmful to the children.

Finally, some diffuse paragraphs give you no starting point at all for the summary and force you to write an entirely new generalization. How would you summarize this paragraph?

To parents who wish to lead a quiet life, I would say: Tell your children that they are very naughty—much naughtier than most children. Point to the young people of some acquaintances as models of perfection and impress your own children with a deep sense of their own inferiority. You carry so many more guns than they do that they cannot fight you. This is called moral influence, and it will enable you to bounce them as much as you please. They think you know and they will not have yet caught you lying often enough to suspect that you are not the unworldly and scrupulously truthful person which you represent yourself to be; nor yet will they know how great a coward you are, nor how soon you will run away, if they fight you with persistency and judgment. You keep the dice and throw them both for your children and yourself. Load them then, for you can easily manage to stop your children from examining them. Tell them how singularly indulgent you are; insist on the incalculable benefit you conferred on them, firstly in bringing them into the world at all, but more particularly in bringing them into it as your children rather than anyone else's. Say that you have their highest interests at stake whenever you are out of temper and wish to make yourself unpleasant by way of balm to your soul. Harp much upon these highest interests. Feed them spiritually upon such brimstone and treacle as the late Bishop of Winchester's Sunday stories. You hold all the trump cards, or if you do not you can filch them; if you play them with anything like judgment you will find yourselves heads of happy, united God-fearing families, even as did my old friend Mr. Pontifex. True, your children will probably find out all about it some day, but not until too late to be of much service to them or inconvenience to yourself.

SAMUEL BUTLER, from *The Way of All Flesh*

Guidelines for Summarizing a Brief Passage

1. Find a summarizing sentence within the passage (and, if you are using it in your own essay, put it in quotation marks); *or*

2. Combine elements within the passage into a new summarizing sentence; *or*

3. Write your own summarizing sentence.

A summary of this paragraph would recommend that parents intimidate their children and thus put them in their place. However, although such a generalization sums up the series of examples contained in the paragraph, it does not convey the fact that, in his caricature of family life, Butler is exaggerating outrageously. *A comprehensive summary, then, would have to include not only the essence of Butler's recommendations, but also his implied point: that he does not expect anyone to follow his advice. Irony* is the term used to describe the conflict between Butler's real meaning—parents should not be monsters, but sometimes are—and the meaning apparently expressed by his words as he urges them to treat their children tyrannically. Here is one way to summarize the paragraph:

> When he ironically suggests that parents can gain tranquillity and domestic happiness by tyrannizing over their children and making them feel morally inferior, Butler seems to be urging parents to treat their children with respect and justice.

Notice that this summarizing sentence includes Butler's name. *Mentioning the author's name effectively emphasizes that what you are summarizing is not your own work.* By making it clear who is responsible for what, you are avoiding any possibility of *plagiarizing*—borrowing from your source without acknowledgment.

EXERCISE 5: SUMMARIZING A PARAGRAPH

Summarize each of the following paragraphs by doing *one* of three things:

A. Underline a sentence that will serve as a comprehensive summary; or

B. Combine existing phrases; then rewrite the sentence, based on these phrases, to create a comprehensive summary; or

C. Invent a new generalization to provide a comprehensive summary.

Be prepared to explain your summary in class discussion.

1. The neurotic individual may have had some special vulnerability as an infant. Perhaps he was ill a great deal and was given care that singled him out from other children. Perhaps he walked or talked much later—or earlier—than children were expected to, and this evoked unusual treatment. The child whose misshapen feet must be put in casts or the sickly little boy who never can play ball may get out of step with his age mates and with the expectations parents and other adults have about children. Or a child may be very unusually placed in his family. He may be the only boy with six sisters, or a tiny child born between two lusty sets of twins. Or the source of the child's difficulties may be a series of events that deeply affected his relations to people—the death of his mother at the birth of the next child or the prolonged illness or absence of his father. Or a series of coincidences—an accident to a parent, moving to a new town and a severe fright—taken together may alter the child's relationship to the world.

   MARGARET MEAD, from *Some Personal Views*

2. The generic process of Blaming the Victim is applied to almost every American problem. The miserable health care of the poor is explained away on the grounds that the victim has poor motivation and lacks health information. The problems of slum housing are traced to the characteristics of tenants who are labeled as "Southern rural migrants" not yet "acculturated" to life in the big city. The "multiproblem" poor, it is claimed, suffer the psychological effects of impoverishment, the "culture of poverty," and the deviant value system of the lower classes; consequently, though unwittingly, they cause their own troubles. From such a viewpoint, the obvious fact that poverty is primarily an absence of money is easily overlooked or set aside.

   WILLIAM RYAN, from *Blaming the Victim*

3. Americans are no closer than we were half a century ago to coming up with a sound scientific rationale for the myriad ways we regard race. Certainly, . . . different races exist—if only because we have decided that they do. We can theoretically create races at will. If Americans agreed, for instance, that people with red hair constitute a separate race, these people would be one. And if we proceeded to treat all people with red hair differently from everyone else, they would soon take on all the attributes we associate with "real" races. If, for instance, they were allowed only to do menial labor, refused an education, compelled to intermarry, forced to live in predominantly redhead communities, and told that their only real gifts were drinking and song, they would eventually develop a culture that embodied the new redhead stereotype. But all we would have proved is that human beings have the power to define (and thereby create) races—not that the classification has any value or makes any sense.

   ELLIS COSE, from *Color-Blind*

4. The crippled have become the handicapped and now the differently abled. A wheelchair-bound person has become one who *uses* a wheelchair (that language is deemed to make him or her sound less passive). AIDS victims have become People with AIDS. In one of the most extreme versions, those born deaf have altered from being hearing-impaired to "having a birthright of silence." Every bit of plain speaking offends someone these days. When I metaphorically described the dancing in the ill-fated Broadway musical *Nick and Nora* as "clubfooted" in a review in *Time,* I predicted to the copy editor involved that we would get a letter from some organization for the clubfooted, objecting that this nomenclature implied a deformity—and I was right. My review of Stephen Sondheim's *Assassins* bore a headline that spoke of the killers and would-be killers of American presidents as "loony," which the vast majority of them irrefutably were. This prompted a two-page single-spaced letter from a spokeswoman for the insane, protesting that the reference to the mental state of these deranged shooters was unfair to the crazy. More recently I was struck by a lawsuit filed on behalf of a mentally retarded eighth-grader in Dayton, Ohio, whose guardian wanted the girl to be able to attend a prom limited to high school students. Noting that her daughter was the same age as others eligible to attend and asserting that the girl could exercise comparable judgment, Thelma Sell said, "Sherrie is handicapped. She's not stupid." If she is not stupid, then what exactly does mentally retarded mean?

WILLIAM A. HENRY III, from In Defense of Elitism

5. Executives in the communications industry exercise a power that is not merely concentrated but also propagandistic. They make far-reaching choices in a way that few others in our society can. They project their images of the world out into the world—"five hundred channels at a time!" being the latest industry boast; "five hundred channels of *Lucy* reruns" being the ubiquitous retort of a jaded viewing public. The media do not merely represent; they also recreate themselves and their vision of the world as desirable, salable. What they reproduce is chosen, not random, not neutral, not without consequence. To pretend (as we all do from time to time) that film or television, for example, is a neutral vessel, or contentless, mindless, or unpersuasive, is sheer denial. The media, for better and frequently for worse, constitute one of the major forces in the shaping of our national vision, a chief architect of the modern American sense of identity.

PATRICIA J. WILLIAMS, from "Unbirthing the Nation"

Summarizing an Article

When you want to summarize an essay in a few sentences, how do you judge which points are significant and which are not? Some essays, especially newspaper articles, have rambling structures and short paragraphs, so you don't even have fully developed paragraphs in which to search for summarizing topic sentences. Are there any standard procedures to help you decide which points to summarize?

Guidelines for Summarizing an Article

1. Read the entire article more than once.
2. Ask yourself why the article was written and published.
3. Look for repetitions of and variations on the same idea.

Read "Holdup Man Tells Detectives How to Do It" from the *New York Times*, and, on the second reading, observe your own method of pinpointing the key ideas.

HOLDUP MAN TELLS DETECTIVES HOW TO DO IT
Selwyn Raab

His face hidden by a shabby tan coat, the career holdup man peeked out at his audience of detectives and then proceeded to lecture them on how easy it was to succeed at his trade in New York. 1

"I don't think there's much any individual police officer can do," the guest lecturer told 50 detectives yesterday at an unusual crime seminar sponsored by the Police Department. "Once I knew what the police officer on the beat was up to I wasn't much concerned about the cops." 2

The holdup man, who identified himself only as "Nick," is serving a prison term of 6 to 13 years. He said his most serious arrest occurred after he was shot three times by a supermarket manager—not in any encounter with the police. 3

When asked by a detective taking a course in robbery investigations what the best deterrent would be against gunmen like himself, Nick replied crisply: "stiffer sentences." 4

After being seriously wounded in his last robbery attempt, Nick said he decided it was time to retire. 5

"I'm close to 40 and not getting any younger," he explained. "I just don't want to spend any more time in jail." 6

Nick also offered the detectives some tips on how robbers pick their targets and make their getaways in the city. 7

Except for wearing a hat, Nick said he affected no disguise. "I usually picked a store in a different neighborhood or in another borough where I was unknown." 8

Leads on places to hold up usually came from other criminals or from employees. There were no elaborate plannings or "casings," he said, adding: 9

"I liked supermarkets because there's always a lot of cash around. Uniformed guards didn't deter me because they're not armed, they usually just have sticks. It's 10

better to pick a busy area rather than the suburbs. The chances of someone notic-
ing you are greater in residential or suburban areas."

The detectives, sitting at desks with notepaper in front of them, were rookies as   11
well as veterans. Besides city detectives, the audience included policemen from the
Transit Authority, the Housing Authority, the Yonkers Police Department and from
Seattle.

They listened carefully as Nick outlined how he or a confederate would inspect   12
the area for signs of uniformed or plainclothes police officers.

The retired robber said he had preferred supermarkets or stores with large win-   13
dow advertisements or displays because these materials prevented him from being
seen by passers-by on the street.

"I was always a little nervous or apprehensive before a job," he continued. "But   14
once you're inside and aware of the reaction of the people and you know the possibilities then your confidence comes back."

Nick said he always made his escape in a car and he preferred heavily trafficked   15
roads because it made the getaway vehicle less conspicuous than on little used side
streets.

In New York, cheap handguns were selling from $15 to $70, he told the detec-   16
tives. Such weapons as shotguns or automatic rifles, Nick said, could be rented for
about $100 an hour.

Nick said he had been a holdup man since the age of 20 and had committed about   17
30 "jobs," but was uncertain of the exact number. The biggest robbery he had participated in netted a total of $8,000, and overall he got about $30,000 in his criminal activities.

Asked why he went back to robbing after his first arrest, Nick said: "I wanted   18
whisky, women and big autos. Like most who rob I was not socially accepted. Big
money elevates you above the people you think are looking down on you."

Short prison sentences, for first arrests, Nick asserted, probably do little to dis-   19
courage holdup men. "I see them laying up in jail and it doesn't make any difference," he said. "They just go ahead planning the next one in a different way."

During his "on-and-off" criminal career, Nick said he had never fired any of the   20
guns he carried.

After his one-hour appearance as guest lecturer, Nick, his face still covered by his   21
coat, was escorted out of the classroom back to his cell at an undisclosed prison.

1. Read the entire article more than once.

This direction is not as simple as it sounds. Because you want to identify
main ideas, you may underline what you regard as the key sentences on first
reading, and, from then on, look only at the "boiled-down" parts. But *don't
eliminate minor facts and interesting details too soon.* They do have a function in
the article, supporting and illuminating the central ideas. For example, the fact
that Nick chose to hide his face during and after his "lecture" hardly seems

worth underlining and, in fact, would never by itself be regarded as crucial. But taken together with some of Nick's remarks, that minor fact helps you to recognize a key point of the article: The robber's reliance on *anonymity* enables him to commit a successful crime; Nick may at some point wish to resume his profession despite his "retirement." Although you should always underline your key points, remember to reread and consider every part of the article as you prepare your summary.

2. Ask yourself why the article was written and published.

What does the newspaper want its readers to learn? A news article's purpose is frequently twofold—to describe an event and to suggest the event's significance—and so it is easy for you to confuse the *facts* being recorded with the underlying *reasons* for recording them. Here are two one-sentence summaries of the article that are both off the mark because they concentrate too heavily on the event:

> Nick, a convicted retired criminal, was guest speaker at a police seminar and told detectives how robbers pick their targets and make their getaways in New York.

> Nick, after committing thirty robberies, suggested to detectives some possible methods of thwarting future robberies.

Both writers seem too concerned with Nick's colorful history and the peculiarity of his helping the police at all. They ignore the significance of what Nick was actually saying. The second summary—by emphasizing the phrase "thwarting future robberies"—is misleading and almost contradicts the point of the article; in fact, Nick is really suggesting that the police will continue to be ineffectual.

A news article can also mislead you into thinking that a headline is a summary: the headline "Holdup Man Tells Detectives How to Do It" does not summarize the material in the article, but, because it is broad and vague, it "sounds" good. What, for example, is meant by the "it" of the headline—robbery or detection? What does Nick tell the detectives?

3. Look for repetitions of and variations on the same idea.

There is one concrete point that Selwyn Raab and his readers and the police and Nick himself are all interested in: *ways of preventing criminals from committing crimes.* Not only are we told again and again about Nick's contempt for the police, but we are also given his flat statement that only fear of imprisonment ("stiffer sentences") will discourage a hardened criminal.

A brief summary of this article, then, would mention *tougher sentencing as a way of preventing crime.* But, in addition, the theme of *the criminal's need for anonymity* ought, if possible, to be incorporated into a complete summary. In

Nick's opinion, his career has been relatively successful because he has managed to appear normal and blend into the crowd. The primary and secondary ideas can be joined in a summary like this one:

> Observing with contempt that the police have rarely been able to penetrate his "anonymous" disguise, Nick, the successful robber, argues that the presence of police will not deter most experienced criminals and that only "stiffer sentences" will prevent crime.

EXERCISE 6: SUMMARIZING AN ARTICLE

Carefully read "School Uniforms Growing in Favor in California" from the *New York Times*. Determine the article's purpose and pick out the arguments that the author emphasizes; then write a comprehensive summary in two or three sentences.

SCHOOL UNIFORMS GROWING IN FAVOR IN CALIFORNIA

Surrounded by a sea of white shirts and navy blue shorts in a local department store's new section devoted to school uniforms, 7-year-old Sean Smith dangled his feet from a shopping cart and proudly puffed out his chest to display the Tasmanian devil emblazoned on his favorite T-shirt. 1

"I want to wear my own clothes," he said as his mother pulled a white shirt from the rows that lay before him. "These clothes look weird. They're ugly." 2

Sean is out of luck. His public school district here, fed up with baggy jeans, oversized T-shirts, bandanas and other trappings of gang attire, has become the nation's first urban system requiring students to wear uniforms. And the new Long Beach policy, which applies to the 57,000 children in the district's elementary and middle schools, has now led the state to enact a law that encourages the adoption of similar codes by school boards elsewhere. 3

Nationwide Influence

Further, the influence of the Long Beach model does not stop at the state line. Around the country, other urban districts are closely watching. 4

Baltimore is already experimenting with school uniform requirements, as are Los Angeles and San Diego, notes Dick Van Der Laan, spokesman for the Long Beach United School District, who adds that he has also received calls from interested principals and school boards in New York City, Miami, El Paso and Seattle. 5

"We are really the prototype for this kind of thing," Mr. Van Der Laan said. "Every large city in the U.S. has been concerned about the gangs. Their clothes really are an unofficial uniform of intimidation." 6

The movement requiring more conventional kinds of uniforms—black or navy trousers or skirts, white shirts or blouses—began here five years ago, when the 7

Long Beach district gave principals the option of adopting such requirements at individual schools. Those who did so, the district says, soon found that their students were making better grades, were better behaved and were less frequently absent than before.

So nine months ago the district decided to make uniforms mandatory, effective this fall. The requirement now applies only to the elementary and middle schools, where parents' demand for it was greatest and where the district hopes to influence its youngest students, nipping their fancy for gang attire in the bud. But if the program proves effective, it may be extended to the Long Beach high schools. 8

Action by the State

The district's initiative spurred action by the California Legislature, which in mid-August passed a measure, signed into law by Gov. Pete Wilson last week, that sets out a procedure for school boards elsewhere in the state to adopt their own codes. 9

The hope is that the new law's provisions will help immunize the boards against civil liberties challenges. One of those provisions requires a school district to consult with parents, teachers and principals before adopting a uniform code. A second requires that parents be given six months' notice before any such code takes effect. And yet another gives parents the opportunity to opt out by demonstrating to the board a good reason why their children should not be required to wear uniforms. 10

Here in Long Beach, the precise look of the uniform at any given school is left largely to the principal, although the district's code explicitly allows students of either sex to wear shorts and polo shirts (in the colors designated by the school) as an alternative to trousers and dress shirts, or skirts and blouses. The code does not generally extend to jackets or other outerwear. 11

Because some parents have told the district that they cannot afford the $30 or $40 cost of a uniform, the school system is now working with retailers and public interest groups to assist low-income families so that no child will be without one. The district is also looking into the possibility of starting up a uniform recycling center where the trousers, shirts, shorts, blouses and skirts would be passed down from older to younger students. 12

Although most parents seem enthusiastic, not everyone embraces the code. The American Civil Liberties Union says that as an effort to combat gang intimidation, the program is "meaningless." One local lawyer whose child is a student in the district has sued the school system on the ground that the code restricts freedom of expression. And a few people are even pulling their children out of the district's schools. 13

George Simmons, who works at a local gas station, said he was now sending his thirteen-year-old sister, Shamera, to a school in nearby Bellflower. "Uniforms aren't going to solve anything," he said. "The gangs are still going to be there; they'll just wear baggy uniforms." 14

And Susan Kelsey, buying a uniform for her 13-year-old daughter at the Target department store here the other day, said that if all students wore uniforms, then the well-behaved children might not be able to so easily spot the troublemakers. 15

"Is it necessarily good for a kid not to be able to know a gang member on her own campus?" Mrs. Kelsey said. "I don't think so."

But the prevalent view is that uniforms will only improve the classroom atmosphere. "Children will hate this, of course, because it takes away from their individuality," said another shopper, Melanie Valsvig, accompanied by her daughter. "But it's time that they learned that school is for schoolwork." 16

And Valentino Le Veauf, who was shopping with his two sons, said: "There are no sagging jeans in my house. And I think dress codes will also help keep the gang thing out of the schools." 17

There is some evidence, most of it anecdotal, that violent acts have fallen and grades risen in schools where uniforms have already been tried. For instance, after Newcomb Academy, an elementary and middle school in the Long Beach district, opted for uniforms last year, disciplinary problems declined, A's and B's rose by 17 percent, and F's dropped by 9 percent, said Joseph Palumbo, the school's co-director. And the school now has the highest attendance rate of any in the district. 18

A survey by the school this year found that all its teachers and 80 percent of parents supported standardized student dress. 19

Already, many parents are asking that Long Beach extend its program to the high schools. 20

"It is certainly being discussed," said Mr. Van Der Laan, the district spokesman. "We have found that the most chilling effect on a student's individuality is not in wearing a uniform; it's being surrounded by other children in gang attire. Whether it's saggy baggies or red bandannas, it's intimidating." 21

Alma Licon, a 16-year-old high school student, said she and most of her friends would not object to giving up their baggy jeans, double-sized T-shirts and high-top sneakers with the woolly laces. Pointing to her sister, Malena, who proudly wore her school uniform and was shopping for a newer model, Ms. Licon said the uniform had helped keep her sister out of trouble. 22

"I think it's good for her," Ms. Licon said, looking down at her own baggy Levis. "Sometimes people mistake me for being in a gang, and I get harassed. But that doesn't happen to her." 23

Summarizing a Complex Essay

When you are asked to summarize a reading containing a number of complex and abstract ideas, a reading that may be disorganized and therefore difficult to comprehend and condense, *the best way to prepare for your summary is to isolate each important point and note it down in a list.*

Here are some guidelines for summarizing a complex essay:

1. The summary must be comprehensive.
2. The summary must be concise.
3. The summary must be coherent.
4. The summary must be independent.

Here is an essay by Bertrand Russell, followed by a preliminary list of notes, a statement of Russell's thesis, and the final summary. (The numbers in the margin are keyed to the preliminary list of notes on pp. 57–58.) Russell's essay is difficult, so be sure to read it slowly, and more than once. If you get confused at any point, try referring to the list of notes that follows; but be sure to *go back to the essay* after you have identified and understood each numbered point.

THE SOCIAL RESPONSIBILITY OF SCIENTISTS
Bertrand Russell

Science, ever since it first existed, has had important effects in matters that lie outside the purview of pure science. Men of science have differed as to their responsibility for such effects. Some have said that the function of the scientist in society is to supply knowledge, and that he need not concern himself with the use to which this knowledge is put. I do not think that this view is tenable, especially in our age. The scientist is also a citizen; and citizens who have any special skill have a public duty to see, as far as they can, that their skill is utilized in accordance with the public interest. Historically, the functions of the scientist in public life have generally been recognized. The Royal Society was founded by Charles II as an antidote to "fanaticism" which had plunged England into a long period of civil strife. The scientists of that time did not hesitate to speak out on public issues, such as religious toleration and the folly of prosecutions for witchcraft. But although science has, in various ways at various times, favored what may be called a humanitarian outlook, it has from the first had an intimate and sinister connection with war. Archimedes sold his skill to the Tyrant of Syracuse for use against the Romans; Leonardo secured a salary from the Duke of Milan for his skill in the art of fortification; and Galileo got employment under the Grand Duke of Tuscany because he could calculate the trajectories of projectiles. In the French Revolution the scientists who were not guillotined were set to making new explosives, but Lavoisier was not spared, because he was only discovering hydrogen which, in those days, was not a weapon of war. There have been some honorable exceptions to the subservience of scientists to warmongers. During the Crimean War the British government consulted Faraday as to the feasibility of attack by poisonous gases. Faraday replied that it was entirely feasible, but that it was inhuman and he would have nothing to do with it.

Modern democracy and modern methods of publicity have made the problem of affecting public opinion quite different from what it used to be. The knowledge that the public possesses on any important issue is derived from vast and powerful organizations: the press, radio, and, above all, television. The knowledge that governments possess is more limited. They are too busy to search out the facts for themselves, and consequently they know only what their underlings think good for them unless there is such a powerful movement in a different sense that politicians cannot ignore it. Facts which ought to guide the decisions of statesmen—for instance, as to the possible lethal qualities of fallout—do not acquire their due importance if they remain buried in scientific journals. They acquire their due importance only when they become known to so many voters that they affect the course of the elections. In general, there is an opposition to widespread publicity for such facts. This opposition springs from various sources, some sinister, some comparatively respectable. At the bottom of the moral scale there is the financial interest of the various industries connected with armaments. Then there are various effects of a somewhat thoughtless patriotism, which believes in secrecy and in what is called "toughness." But perhaps more important than either of these is the unpleasantness of the facts, which makes the general public turn aside to pleasanter topics such as divorces and murders. The consequence is that what ought to be known widely throughout the general public will not be known unless great efforts are made by disinterested persons to see that the information reaches the minds and hearts of vast numbers of people. I do not think this work can be successfully accomplished except by the help of men of science. They, alone, can speak with the authority that is necessary to combat the misleading statements of those scientists who have permitted themselves to become merchants of death. If disinterested scientists do not speak out, the others will succeed in conveying a distorted impression, not only to the public but also to the politicians.

It must be admitted that there are obstacles to individual action in our age which did not exist at earlier times. Galileo could make his own telescope. But once when I was talking with a very famous astronomer he explained that the telescope upon which his work depended owed its existence to the benefaction of enormously rich men, and, if he had not stood well with them, his astronomical discoveries would have been impossible. More frequently, a scientist only acquires access to enormously expensive equipment if he stands well with the government of his country. He knows that if he adopts a rebellious attitude he and his family are likely to perish along with the rest of civilized mankind. It is a tragic dilemma, and I do not think that one should censure a man whatever his decision; but I do think—and I think men of science should realize—that unless something rather drastic is done under the leadership or through the inspiration of some part of the scientific world, the human race, like the Gadarene swine, will rush down a steep place to destruction in blind ignorance of the fate that scientific skill has prepared for it.

It is impossible in the modern world for a man of science to say with any honesty, "My business is to provide knowledge, and what use is made of the knowledge is not my responsibility." The knowledge that a man of science provides may fall into the hands of men or institutions devoted to utterly unworthy objects. I do not suggest that a man of science, or even a large body of men of science, can altogether prevent this, but they can diminish the magnitude of the evil.

There is another direction in which men of science can attempt to provide leadership. They can suggest and urge in many ways the value of those branches of science of which the important and practical uses are beneficial and not harmful.

7

8

9

10

11

Consider what might be done if the money at present spent on armaments were spent on increasing and distributing the food supply of the world and diminishing the population pressure. In a few decades, poverty and malnutrition, which now afflict more than half the population of the globe, could be ended. But at present almost all the governments of great states consider that it is better to spend money on killing foreigners than on keeping their own subjects alive. Possibilities of a hopeful sort in whatever field can best be worked out and stated authoritatively by men of science; and, since they can do this work better than others, it is part of their duty to do it.

As the world becomes more technically unified, life in an ivory tower becomes increasingly impossible. Not only so; the man who stands out against the powerful organizations which control most of human activity is apt to find himself no longer in the ivory tower, with a wide outlook over a sunny landscape, but in the dark and subterranean dungeon upon which the ivory tower was erected. To risk such a habitation demands courage. It will not be necessary to inhabit the dungeon if there are many who are willing to risk it, for everybody knows that the modern world depends upon scientists, and, if they are insistent, they must be listened to. We have it in our power to make a good world; and, therefore, with whatever labor and risk, we must make it.

12

First Stage: List of Notes and Establishing a Thesis

1. Should scientists try to influence the way their discoveries are used?

2. One point of view: the scientist's role is to make the discovery; what happens afterward is not his concern.

3. Russell's point of view: scientists are like any other knowledgeable and public-spirited people; they must make sure that the products of their knowledge work for, not against, society.

4. In the past, some scientists have made public their views on controversial issues like freedom of religion; others have been servants of the war machine.

5. The power to inform and influence the public is now controlled by the news media.

6. Government officials are too busy to be well informed; subordinates feed them only enough information to get them reelected.

7. It is in the interests of various groups, ranging from weapons makers to patriots, to limit the amount of scientific information that the public receives.

8. The public is reluctant to listen to distasteful news.

9. Since the public deserves to hear the truth, scientists, who are respected for their knowledge and who belong to no party or faction, ought to do more to provide the public with information about the potentially lethal consequences of their discoveries. By doing so, they will correct the distortions of those scientists who have allied themselves with warmongers.

10. It is very difficult for scientists to speak out since they depend on government and business interests to finance their work.

11. While scientists cannot entirely stop others from using some of their discoveries for antisocial purposes, they can support other, more constructive kinds of research.

12. Speaking out is worth the risk of incurring the displeasure of powerful people; since the work of scientists is so vital, the risk isn't too great, especially if they act together.

Russell's Thesis: Contrary to the self-interested arguments of many scientists and other groups, scientists have a social responsibility to make sure that their work is used for, not against, the benefit of humanity.

Second Stage: Summary

Some scientists, as well as other groups, consider that they need not influence the way in which their discoveries are used. However, Bertrand Russell, in "The Social Responsibility of Scientists," believes that scientists have a responsibility to make sure that their work is used for, not against, the benefit of humanity. In modern times, he argues, it has been especially difficult for concerned scientists to speak out because many powerful groups prefer to limit and distort what the public is told, because government officials are too busy to be thoroughly informed, because scientists depend on the financial support of business and government, and because the public itself is reluctant to hear distasteful news. Nevertheless, Russell maintains that scientists have the knowledge and the prestige to command public attention, and their work is too vital for their voices to be suppressed. If they act together, they can warn us if their work is likely to be used for an antisocial purpose and, at least, they can propose less destructive alternatives.

This summary of Russell's essay is not a simple compilation of phrases taken from the text, nor a collection of topic sentences, one from each paragraph.

Rather, it is a clear, coherent, and unified summary of Russell's ideas, expressed in the writer's own voice and words.

A *framework* is immediately established in the first two sentences of the summary, which present *the two alternative views of the scientist's responsibility.* The next sentence, which describes the four obstacles to scientific freedom of speech, illustrates the rearrangement of ideas that is characteristic of summary. While reviewing the list of notes, the summarizer has noticed that points 6, 7, 8, and 10 each refers to a different way in which scientific truth is often suppressed; she has therefore brought them together and lined them up in a parallel construction based on the repeated word "because." Finally, the last two sentences contain *a restatement of Russell's thesis* and point out that the obstacles to action are not as formidable as they seem.

Notice that the Russell summary excludes points 1, 4, and 5 on the list of notes: point 1 is included in the presentation of points 2 and 3; point 4 is an example, one that is not essential to an understanding of the essay; and point 5 is not directly related to Russell's argument.

In summarizing Russell's essay, it would not be acceptable to include extraneous points, such as the dangers of making scientific secrets public, for that would be arguing with Russell. Such ideas should be reserved for a full-length

Guidelines for Summarizing a Complex Essay

1. *The summary must be comprehensive.* You should review all the notes on your list, and include in your summary all those ideas that are essential to the author's development of the thesis.

2. *The summary must be concise.* Eliminate repetitions in your list, even if the author restates the same points. Your summary should be considerably shorter than the source.

3. *The summary must be coherent.* It should make sense as a paragraph in its own right; it should not be taken directly from your list of notes and sound like a list of sentences that happen to be strung together in a paragraph format.

4. *The summary must be independent.* You are not being asked to imitate or identify yourself with the author about whom you are writing. On the contrary, you are expected to maintain your own voice throughout the summary. Even as you are jotting down your list of notes, you should try to use your own words. Nevertheless, while you want to make it clear that *you* are writing the summary, you should be careful not to create any misrepresentation or distortion by introducing comments or criticisms of your own. (Such distortion is most likely to occur when you strongly disagree with the material that you are summarizing.) You must make it clear to your reader when you are summarizing directly from the text and when you are commenting on, inferring from, or explaining what is being summarized.

essay whose purpose is to develop an argument of your own, not just to summarize Russell's. Within limits, however, it is acceptable to go beyond point-by-point summary, to *suggest the author's implied intention,* and, in a sense, to *interpret the work's meaning for your reader.* You might state, for example, that ours is an age that encourages interdependence and discourages independent action. *Such an interpretation would have to be supported by evidence from the reading.* While Russell does not say so specifically, in so many words, the assertion about interdependence is certainly substantiated by the material in the last two paragraphs.

ASSIGNMENT 1: SUMMARIZING AN ESSAY

Summarize one of the following two passages. Before you begin your summary (on your second reading), underline and annotate key ideas and arguments, and make a preliminary list of points.

THE CASE AGAINST NATURE
from *A Moment on Earth*
Gregg Easterbrook

In the year 1992 a graphite tube ruptured inside a Chernobyl-type reactor vessel at the Leningradskaya nuclear plant near Saint Petersburg, releasing some radioactive gas. The leak measured about 0.2 roentgens immediately downwind of the plant, according to the International Atomic Energy Agency. This is about one-fifth the radiation of a chest X-ray. The accident was banner headline news internationally. Four months later the heads of state of the G-7 nations pledged $700 million in emergency aid to former Eastern bloc countries to improve reactor safety.

Also in 1992 a tsunami struck the Pacific coast of Nicaragua, killing an estimated 2,500 people. When the wave reached the Nicaraguan shoreline it was about 65 feet tall and possessed of enough energy to move 1,000 yards inland, obliterating everything in its path. The deaths caused were sudden and horrible. Many peasants must have died trying desperately to cling to their children as waters strong enough to shatter concrete ripped apart all shelter. In addition to the loss of human life the ecology at the impact area was essentially wiped clean. The tsunami merited a blip box in the news-update sections of newspapers. Later that year another tsunami hit Indonesia, killing an estimated 1,000 people and causing extensive environmental destruction. This event also made no impression on the world's consciousness.

There are clear reasons to worry about nuclear power plants, especially those of the ill-designed Chernobyl class. Sixteen of these plumber's nightmares continue to make power in the former Eastern bloc: Investments in their safe operation represent money well spent. It is also sad but indubitable that reactors proximate to white Europeans are of greater concern to Western leaders and editors than any force imperiling the brown masses of the developing world. But the disparity in

1

2

3

reaction to these two categories of 1992 stories—an inconsequential artificial environmental event harming no one is widely viewed as a shocking horror, while natural environmental events killing thousands and leaving behind vast swaths of devastation are greeted with a collective ho-hum—reveals much about how human beings perceive the living world.

Today environmental problems caused by people are considered a maximum-priority concern, while environmental problems caused by nature are simply acts of God. This last is a curious phrase if ever there was one. It suggests that though God declines to intercede on Earth to prevent the sufferings and injustices of the world, the Maker does regularly act to hurl disasters at the innocent. Most people who use the figure of speech "act of God" do not, of course, believe that God wills the occurrence of tidal waves and similar calamities. They believe such things happen for no reason at all. In a limited sense, that will always be the best explanation. But somehow the popular understanding has come to hold that naturally occurring damage to the ecology does not count as an environmental problem: It's just something that happens. Only men and women cause environmental problems. Which events of the year 1992 were more likely to be troubling to nature, the gas leak at Saint Petersburg or the tsunamis at Nicaragua and Indonesia?

In order to highlight the transgressions of people, in contemporary environmental thought nature is depicted as a utopia. An occasional environmental slogan is "Back to Eden." This motto implies that if only humankind ceased its meddling the living world would revert to a previous condition of unlimited abundance and general bliss. Who's kidding who? The notion that nature absent man would be an Eden doubtless appeals to the fund-raising imperatives of environmental lobbies, and to modern humankind's inner need for self-opprobrium. But it is certain nature does not see itself as an Eden.

It is not inconsistent to assert that nature is learned and inspirational and also riven with faults. In a bureaucracy as monumental as the entire living world, failings are inevitable. People or institutions can be sublime at many levels yet flawed at others. Democracy is the best known form of government, but nobody pretends it does not have maddening faults. Wine is the most wonderful beverage; it's also full of calories and causes harm ranging from headaches to chronic degenerative illness. Shakespeare was a superb writer; he also penned plays and sonnets that fell to the ground with a loud clunk. And so on.

"Nature does not know best," said René Dubos, a pioneer of modern environmental thinking. Dubos, who died in 1982, was an advocate of wetlands conservation and originated the slogan "Think globally, act locally." He composed many works fiercely critical of human ecological abuses. But Dubos was also critical of nature. Dubos thought many natural systems wasteful or plagued by shortcomings. For example, he thought species such as deer that exhibit cycles of overpopulation and die-off demonstrate nature can be just as immoderate as humanity. Dubos felt veneration of nature a foolhardy distraction.

Because Dubos was critical of nature, today many in the environmental movement speak of him as having been some kind of double agent. A custom is developing in which saints of environmentalism are reclassified as demons if they criticize nature or fail to be adequately frenetic in condemnation of people. James Lovelock, once the leading science figure to environmentalists, became persona non grata when he began to say the biosphere was so resilient not even nuclear war could destroy it. The toxicologist Bruce Ames, a hero to environmentalists in the 1970s when he proved the fire retardant Tris carcinogenic, is now intensely detested because his last 20 years of research convinced him naturally occurring food-chain substances are more dangerous than additives or pesticide residues. Richard Doll, a British epidemiologist who established the link between cigarette smoking and lung cancer, was for a time an angelic figure to environmentalists. Now he's Lucifer incarnate, because his last two decades of research weigh against the notion that synthetic toxics in the environment are a leading cancer cause. Another former environmental hero whose name has been slipped down the memory hole is the oceanographer Roger Revelle, founder of modern greenhouse science. In his book *Earth in the Balance,* Vice President Al Gore cited Revelle as the great tutor who convinced him global warming was a threat of unspeakable urgency. But Revelle himself did not describe the greenhouse effect in the apocalyptic terms favored by Gore. Before his 1991 death, Revelle cautioned against greenhouse alarmism. Gore doesn't talk about Revelle any longer.

One ecological orthodoxy that has arisen in recent years is the notion that since human involvement with nature is invariably negative, the only constructive relationship people can establish regarding the biosphere is to leave it alone. There are times and places when people ought to leave nature alone: partly to preserve, partly to acknowledge our poor understanding of how the environment operates. A principle of wisdom holds: We don't know what we don't know. Not only is human understanding of the environment rudimentary but we don't yet know enough to guess where the worst gaps in our knowledge fall. Until such time as we do, people should interfere with the environment as little as possible.   9

But if people leave parts of the environment alone, we can be sure nature will not. Nature will keep changing, not in some pointless eternal vacillation but seeking refinement. Dubos believed that nature was engaged in a long-term undertaking of self-improvement and thought human beings might be able to assist nature. Before turning to the idea of people helping nature, let's review the case against the environment. It may be summarized in these words: People should not worry that they will destroy nature. It is more likely nature will destroy us.   10

Green sentiment currently holds that nature ought to be revered because natural arrangements are metaphysically superior to their artificial counterparts. There are many reasons to love nature. This is not one of them.   11

Physically the natural world is magnificent compared to most human concoctions. But metaphysically? It is easy for humans to impute sanctity to the natural scheme, since we sit at the pinnacle of the food chain. No species preys on us, no organisms save diseases challenge us. But to those of Earth's creatures that live to be chased and eaten, it is doubtful the natural scheme suggests Eden. What does   12 an antelope experience, dying in terror and agony as it is gored by a tiger—blissful oneness with the spheres? Nature may shrug at this, considering cruel death an inevitability of a biological system. Perhaps people should respect such an order. We should not offer it blind allegiance.

Nature may be a place of transcendence, but it is also a domain of danger. Danger may take the form of large-scale natural assaults such as asteroid strikes, ice ages, and eras of global volcanism. What might be called everyday natural badness can be as distressing. Consider a representative end of life under the natural scheme. Often in subarctic regions migrating caribou drown in large groups when they ford rivers that were safe to cross the year before but now are not, the water volumes and speed of wild rivers varying unpredictably. Should you think nature absent man is utopia, try to imagine drowning in a roaring subarctic river. You are seized with panic as icy water slops into your lungs. You flail helplessly, the world falling away under your feet. This is not some peaceful end to a gentle, contented cycle of birth and renewal. This is a horror.

As the animal expert Vicky Hearne has written, "The wild is not all that frolicsome a location." Hearne has noted that among wild lion cubs of Africa, 75 percent die before reaching their second year of life. This high level of mortality is what happens to the fiercest of predators—imagine what happens lower on the food chain. A statistic of significance to the debate on human population has been cited by the zoologist Ernest Mayr: In the wild on average only two of any mammal's offspring ever themselves reproduce. To people, this figure may suggest that population stability attained by replacement fertility rates would be in keeping with balancing mechanisms of nature. To animals that may bear dozens of offspring of which but two exist long enough to reproduce, this figure suggests the extreme cruelty of the natural world. Next time you coo over a litter of domesticated puppies whose secure lives are assured, reflect that if the litter were born in the cold and hungry wild, nearly all the pups would be dead in fairly short order.

Environmentalism has not come to terms with the inherent horribleness of many natural structures, considering recognition of this point to be poor public relations. For instance the Norwegian philosopher Arne Naess, inventor of the phrase "deep ecology," in his 1989 book *Ecology, Community and Lifestyle* danced around the fact that much of the natural order is based on violent death. "The ecological viewpoint presupposes acceptance of the fact that big fish eat small," Naess wrote. Deep ecologists are supposed to believe that in moral value human beings are the same as animals: no better or worse, just another creature. So if it's okay for animals to kill each other is it okay for people to kill each other? Naess waffles: "It is against my intuition of unity to say 'I can kill you because I am more valuable,' but not against that intuition to say 'I will kill you because I am hungry.'" Then would Naess object if a poor man who was hungry killed Naess to take his wallet? Because orthodox environmentalists feel they must pretend that there is nothing—not the slightest little thing—wrong with nature, they can easily be trapped, as Naess trapped himself, into declaring that it's okey-dokey to kill to eat.

13

14

15

Deep ecology can go even further than that, at its extreme asserting people are no more valuable than rocks. For a time after its founding in the mid-1960s the American wing of the deep ecology movement, led by Bill Sessions, a professor at Humboldt State University in northern California, said it advocated "biocentrism," or the importance of life above technology. Believe it or not the term biocentrism was attacked in politically correct ecological writing, as it dares imply that living things are more important than inanimate objects. Today some deep ecologists say they endorse "ecocentrism," which purports to grant rocks and plains the same ethical significance as living things. "Let the river live!" is a phrase now found in some deep ecology tracts. | 16

So it's not only fine for a tiger to gore an antelope and a hungry robber to gun down a passerby, it's fine for all these people and animals to drown in a river since the river is only expressing its right to flow. If the question of whether it is bad to be killed confounds environmental philosophers, small wonder they have such trouble coming to grips with the practical flaws in nature. | 17

Now let's expand the indictment against the environment. Nature makes pollutants, poisons, and suffering on a scale so far unapproached by men and women except during periods of warfare. | 18

For example, if the greenhouse gas carbon dioxide is considered a pollutant, as environmentalists say it should be, then nature emits an estimated 200 billion tons of this pollutant annually, versus a human-caused emission total of about seven billion tons per year. Nature makes huge quantities of the precursor chemicals for acid rain. The 1991 eruption of Mount Pinatubo alone released an estimated 60 percent more sulfur dioxide, the primary cause of acid rain, than all United States emissions that year. Lesser eruptions, and the many volcanos that release gases without erupting, add to annual natural output of acid-rain chemicals. Natural processes, mainly the photochemistry of tree leaves, place into the air volumes of volatile organic chemicals, the same class of substances that evaporate from petroleum and help form smog. Though Ronald Reagan was wrong to say that trees cause more air pollution than cars, his concept was not entirely fallacious. Pristine forest areas often exhibit palls of natural smog caused by tree emissions interacting with sunlight. Thomas Jefferson's beloved Blue Ridge Mountains are so named because even in preindustrial times they often were shrouded in a bluish haze. | 19

Nature generates toxins, venoms, carcinogens, and other objectionable substances in far larger quantities than do people, even considering the daunting output of man's petrochemical complexes. Current research is demonstrating that a significant percentage of plants make dangerous compounds for defense against environmental competitors; and that since the living quantity of plants is substantially greater than that of fauna, plants may be the principal toxin factories of the world. Recently an important topic of public discourse has been the need to preserve rainforests, in part so that drug companies can prospect for pharmaceuticals. Rainforest preservation is a good idea. But why do pharmaceutical companies find rainforest plants of such interest? Because they are rich in natural toxins that kill living cells—what many medications, especially cancer drugs, are asked to do. | 20

In recent years researchers have begun to understand that over eons of evolu- 21
tionary time, plants have acquired sophisticated chemical defenses against being
munched by animals and insects, including in some cases active "immune responses"
that dispense toxins when competitors arrive. For instance researchers have found
that when some pines are attacked by mountain pine beetles, the trees direct to
the affected bark chemicals called terpenes that make pine beetles ill. Potatoes and
tomatoes make toxins that interfere with the digestive systems of their perennial
competitors, the caterpillar. When the coyote tobacco plant is nibbled on, its
"immune system" directs an increase in nicotine, a powerful toxin, to the affected
leaves.

The discovery that plants manufacture far more toxins than once assumed has 22
led toxicologists such as Ames and Lois Gold, both of the University of California
at Berkeley, to estimate that the typical American diet contains 10,000 times more
naturally occurring carcinogens than those of the synthetic variety. Natural toxins
comprise five to ten percent of most plants by dry weight, Ames and Gold think.
Thus natural toxins are "by far the main source of toxic chemicals ingested by humans," Ames says.

People and animals must in turn have evolved resistance to natural carcinogens or 23
their ancestors would have keeled over from consuming plants long ago. If people
and animals carry some natural resistance to toxins, this hardly means consuming
chemicals has no cost, any more than people who have natural resistance to certain diseases can be assured they will never get sick. But here the finger of badness
points at nature more than people. For example, it may eventually be shown that
natural chemicals are a leading cause of cancer. After all, if natural toxins outnumber the synthetic variety 10,000 to 1 in the typical diet, then nature is a more likely
cancer cause than synthetics. In turn, if natural carcinogens in foodstuffs are an important cancer cause, the way to get rid of them would be through genetic engineering, a technology environmentalists oppose.

Next: Which would you say causes more deaths per year, industrial accidents or 24
natural disasters? The answer is nature by a substantial margin. Theodore Glick-
man, Dominic Golding, and Emily Silverman, researchers at Resources for the Future, a Washington, D.C., think tank, compared significant natural disasters to
significant industrial deaths for the postwar period. The study concentrated on immediate deaths, not long-term health degradation. The authors found that on average natural badness kills 55,786 people per year worldwide, while industrial
accidents kill 356 people annually. Natural badness took forms such as these:
700,000 dead in a 1976 earthquake in China; perhaps 500,000 dead in a 1970 cyclone in Bangladesh; another 110,000 dead in a 1948 earthquake in the former Soviet Union; another 57,000 dead in a 1949 flood in China; at least 100,000 dead in
a 1991 cyclone in Bangladesh. Industrial accidents through this same period often
have been frightful, taking forms such as the death of about 4,100 innocents at
Bhopal in 1984 or the loss of an estimated 2,700 lives in a 1982 fuel-truck explosion in a mountain tunnel in Afghanistan. All told, nature has consistently outdone
man in generation of noncombat misfortune.

Environmental orthodoxy responds to figures like the ones above by saying that   25
if the human population were lower there would be fewer deaths in natural disasters; that far too many people live in dangerous places like the coastal plain of
Bangladesh, where the likelihood of natural badness from cyclones is high, or in the
fault zone of California, where the natural threat of earthquakes is high. Such points
contain measures of truth but are deceptive, skipping over the effects of natural
disasters on the nonhuman ecology—effects that would be awful whether people
existed or not. During cyclones and similar natural badness there is tremendous
loss of plant and animal life, plus destruction of the ecosphere generally. Environmentalists sometimes fudge this counterpoint by saying that the ecosphere usually
recovers rapidly from catastrophic "acts of God." Usually that is the case. But if the
environment routinely recovers from cyclones and tidal waves, events substantially
more destructive than human action, why is it that we are in panic mode regarding
human ecological impacts? And if there were fewer people, fewer would die in any
natural disaster. But if there were fewer snow leopards or sandhill cranes fewer of
them would die at nature's hand as well. Has anyone ever heard an environmental-
ist argue that therefore there are too many animals?

Meanwhile the occupation of dangerous areas such as the coastal plain of   26
Bangladesh usually occurs out of desperation on the part of the impoverished. That
genus *Homo* has built a society in which many millions of the impoverished have no
choice but to live in places vulnerable to disaster is an inculpation of human social
institutions, but is not out of accord with the behavior patterns of nature. Countless species populate ecological niches where exposure to natural badness is above
the norm. For instance, every plant and animal that lives near an active volcano is
crazy from a detached point of view. Nature, being flawed, puts creatures in such
places nonetheless.

WACO AND RELIGIOUS FREEDOM IN AMERICA
from *Why Waco?*

James D. Tabor and Eugene V. Gallagher

The intensity of commitment demanded by some religious groups, particularly   1
when it results in purportedly strange forms of behavior, disturbs many Americans.
We suspect that the common understanding of "cults" as dangerous to both individuals and society is indeed accurate but not for the reasons usually given. The
crucial issue is not the enormous power of a leader who exercises total control
over passive followers. Such groups are threatening because they offer, sometimes
with relentless aggressiveness, another way of seeing and being. Their very existence calls into question, as it is meant to do, what we hold most important and
what our society values above anything else. Serious belief in the imminent end of
the world, for example, challenges the prevailing secular view of time as stretching

into an indefinite future and drastically foreshortens the period in which we may forge an identity, make our place in the world, and shape our lives in conformity with a hoped-for future. Committed adoption of unconventional living arrangements similarly challenges our broad acceptance of the nuclear family as the most important and appropriate social institution for inculcating and preserving our central social values. Insistence that families are formed by affiliation and commitment, rather than by biology, introduces a disruptive and disturbing new set of connections and priorities that casts doubt on what many see as the eternal verities of the relationships between parents and children. Participation in unorthodox sexual relationships seriously tests our notions of intimacy, carnality, and passion. Accepting that a human prophet's communication represents an irresistible divine command supplants cherished notions of free will by a disturbing call to a higher obedience.

Cults are "dangerous" in American society, not merely for what they might do to an unfortunate few, but for what they actually do to an uneasy many. Cults offer alternatives, not on matters of superficial importance, but on what most intimately and ultimately concerns us. Cults explicitly endeavor to get us to examine what we care most about and to consider unsparingly whether we are satisfied with our own beliefs and commitments and with the state of the world. All the statistical evidence about membership in new and unconventional religious movements shows that they are rarely successful in inspiring many dramatic conversions. The widespread fear of cults and the diligent opposition to them, however, suggest that they are amazingly successful in raising fundamental questions about human life. Few want to confront directly any challenges to the status quo. It is easier to condemn the messenger than to take the implications of the message seriously, either on a personal or societal level. Thus the eagerness to condemn cults masks an unwillingness to confront ourselves and to question our society.

Opponents of "cults" spend much of their time keeping tabs on suspicious groups, answering queries from anxious relatives or friends, producing and disseminating literature in support of their position, and holding and attending meetings. But their efforts impinge most directly and intimately on the groups they oppose in the process of deprogramming. . . . That practice has long been passionately contested, and even when it is euphemistically labeled "exit counseling," the "cult" member is seen as under the control of external forces. According to its proponents, only intervention by skilled diagnosticians can return the victim to normality. Such attempts depend on a series of revealing assumptions that are crucial to the general anticult position. The fundamental premise is expressed most directly by David J. Bardin, the Washington counsel for both the American Family Foundation and CAN, in a pamphlet produced by the latter organization to mark the first anniversary of the fire at Mount Carmel and to answer critics of the anticult position. He voices an unshakable conviction that "mind control exists." Everything follows from that assertion. From that perspective, people are drawn into "cults" by mysterious powers that they cannot effectively resist. Their perceptions are manipulated and their actions controlled by an overwhelmingly powerful leader. They are, in effect, programmed, just as a computer is, to perform certain tasks. The only way to get them out of the group is to erase the program. Only then, proponents of deprogramming claim, will former members be able to think and act for themselves. However, its advocates consistently refuse to follow the logic of their position to its conclusion and to acknowledge that former members of "cults" will need to be *re*programmed with a different and more acceptable program in order to function successfully after leaving their group. In the anticultists' view "cults" rigorously control the formation of their members' identities at the explicit direction of the leader. But outside the group, they imagine, former members are remarkably free to fashion themselves in any way they wish. Programming is limited to the activity of "cults," and the pressures to conform that typify life within the "cult" are apparently inoperative outside it. Clearly, this approach is naive and simplistic about the controls and pressures that exist outside the "cult." None of us is completely independent; no one is free from powerful forces of influence and persuasion, whether parental, conventionally religious, or political. . . .

In the end, cultbusters send confusing messages about the dimensions of the "cult" problem, the power of the "cult" leader, and the nature of the audience for "cults." The anticult position is founded on a logical contradiction. Either the attraction of "cults" is significantly weaker than their opponents would have the American public believe, or the willpower, commitment, and purpose of the general populace is significantly stronger. The opponents of "cults" bring to their discussion of the process of affiliation a short-circuited logic that signals something else is going on just out of sight. The hyperbole and exaggeration, which are the hallmarks of their argumentative styles, lend an edge of desperation to their pleadings. "Cults" come to represent fundamental challenges to their adversaries' view of the world and way of life, mirroring the cultbusters' anxieties about loss of control and acceptance.

Anticult activists see themselves as involved in a battle for the heart and soul of America. Ironically, the groups they oppose often see themselves in the same way though they are more likely to focus on a chosen few, such as the 144,000 whom [David] Koresh believed would be initially saved. The anticultists ruefully observe a society in which beliefs are quickly abandoned in favor of a new or exotic message presented with sufficient guile and flair. In that view, whatever success "cults" achieve testifies to the inherent weaknesses of contemporary American society, rather than to the personal situations of those who are attracted to such groups. On that point as well, cultbusters and cult members agree. Cults strive to provoke us to an unsparing examination of both self and society; they anticipate that we will find both wanting; and they claim to offer remedies for our individual and social problems. Cults offer a vision of an alternative society and a plan for implementing it. The anticult activists see a nation in which the necessary social support for traditional values no longer exists, and they see new and unconventional religions capitalizing on that weakness. In this view, "cults" appear a symptom, not a cause, a lamentable indication of the deterioration of a valued way of life.

Many new and unconventional religious movements offer a similar diagnosis of life in America today. They see inattention to spiritual matters, moral laxity, a weakening of communal ties, a failure to uphold biblical standards, and any number of other problems, and they offer their own solutions. Their innovative remedies often derive from their perception that they enjoy the privilege of divine revelation; and they typically demand a strong and uncompromising response.   6

Under the surface of the anticult position there is a pervasive dissatisfaction with the prevailing ethos of contemporary American society, which has made the supposed proliferation of "cults" possible. The anticultists' vigorous defense of traditional religion, the nuclear family, personal autonomy, and other core values against the challenge of the "cults" allows them to locate the vexing problems of Americans and American society outside themselves in a dangerous and alien "other." Cults *are* alien in many ways. In some cases, they introduce foreign beliefs and practices into American society; but in others, such as the Branch Davidians, they give distinctively different interpretations to common religious elements such as the biblical book of Revelation. However, cultbusters see "cults" as alien whatever their place of origin because they manifest psychological instability, moral evil, religious error, or any combination of the three. By portraying "cults" as the "other," cultbusters absolve themselves of any complicity in the problems they discuss.   7

Since "cults" represent an invasive presence, rather than an acceptable variation from the norm, anyone who rejects the cultbusters' values by participating in a "cult" is asserted to have acted under external compulsion, rather than as a result of a careful, rational choice. Such a view contrasts markedly to the democratic ideal of our society as an arena for competing and conflicting ideas, thriving on debate, differences, and diversity. In such a society, persuasiveness is valued, and minority views are welcomed, often proving their enduring value to the majority. To admit that one may join a new or unconventional religious group for "good" reasons leaves one's own choices and decisions open to evaluation and criticism. The anticult polemicists fend off such critique by denying that anyone in his or her "right mind" would join a "cult." Moreover, because affiliation is itself evidence of aberrant behavior, cultbusters can easily dismiss the diagnoses of American society that such groups offer and the remedies that they propose. They act as if they have nothing to learn and much to fear from the intruder. Their general response to "cults" is exemplified by the unheeding responses that government officials made to Koresh's religious pronouncements during the siege at Mount Carmel. When Koresh spoke *his* truth, they heard only "Bible babble." Where the Branch Davidians saw a religious community prepared for the end of the world, the authorities saw an armed compound full of "hostages."   8

The cultbusters' opposition to new and unconventional religious groups depends not only on an image of a passive self but also on an image of a broadly *uniform society* whose values and ethical codes are commonly agreed upon. They see an American consensus and claim to speak for it. In their view, the uniformity of social values guarantees the integrity of the family, harmonious interpersonal relations, and overall   9 social stability. Despite their emphasis on common values, however, cultbusters see their society as extremely fragile and besieged from without. Cult members also see the problems and weaknesses in contemporary American society, but they do not see the remedy in espousing a vaguely defined uniform set of core values without any secure links to a specific social group. Instead, they locate the remedy in the creation of an *ideal society*, a select voluntary association founded on intense commitment to explicit religious values. Their vision is often exclusive; it offers a path toward perfection for those willing to pursue it. That exclusivity, however, allows them to sharpen their critique of American society. Cults typically offer a closed system of internally consistent doctrine, such as Koresh's biblical interpretation, that is passionately espoused by the members of the elect and contributes to their distinctive individual and social identities. The exclusivity, passion, and sheer differentness that mark cult life have the potential to create considerable friction between members of the group and those outside. The Mount Carmel community maintained a sometimes uneasy, often bemused, and generally comfortable peace with its neighbors over the course of its sixty-year history. The introduction of actors who had neither personal nor doctrinal familiarity with the Branch Davidians was a scenario that presaged conflict.

Opposition to so-called cults enables many Americans to condemn much of what they find wrong in their society by attributing it to the influence of an alien "other." That strategy allows opponents to draw clear and sharp lines between right and wrong, good and evil, and legitimate and illegitimate religion. It is based from the outset, however, on an unexamined reaction that presumes that one's own position is self-evidently true and unassailable. In that sense it represents a flight from self-examination, a refusal to think hard about one's own values and commitments, and an authoritarian willingness to impose one's views on others. It is a form of intellectual, spiritual, and social isolationism that denies the possibility of learning anything new or valuable from those significantly different from oneself. When such an attitude is adopted in defense of the fundamental values of American society, as it is by the cultbusters, it is out of tune with the demands of a democratic society, particularly one that is rapidly becoming more diverse. It provides constricting and oppressive answers to serious questions about how Americans should deal with any minority groups, however they are defined. At the same time, it raises the issue of whether those whose beliefs or way of life is unconventional should receive the same protection of the law that other minority groups enjoy. In sum, the cultbusters' appeal to a supposed consensus of values expresses a nostalgia for a homogeneous society that never existed, which can have pernicious effects.

Government action against new or unorthodox religious groups, advocated by some anticult workers, bodes ill not only for such movements but also for everyone in our society. It arrogates to the state a power that all must oppose and depends on a very restricted reading of the constitutional guarantee of free exercise of religion. New and unconventional religions provide some of the most vivid examples of nay-saying in contemporary American society. To enlist the state in an effort to con-

10

11

trol or eradicate such groups is to deprive our common life of an invigorating diversity, as well as to sanction its immense power to enforce conformity. The anticult activists' claim to support the fundamental values of American democratic society is undermined by their willingness to suppress the exercise of religious freedom and, moreover, to engage the state in that campaign. If the purpose of the First Amendment is to protect religions from the state, rather than the state from religion, there is no constitutional basis for enlisting the power of the state in the campaign against so-called cults. That does not mean that the state is impotent to punish illegal acts done in the name of religion, but that the intervention must be carried out through normal legal channels. A wholesale government crusade against "destructive cults," such as that championed after Waco, is illegitimate and unconstitutional.

Much of the polemic against "cults" in America has taken an inappropriate form based on a constricted view of human abilities of self-determination, an intolerant attitude toward differences in belief and practice, and an inflated expectation of the role of the government. Also, despite the anticultists' success in shaping the negative public attitude toward "cults," their efforts to deter individuals from pursuing their chosen religious path has been surprisingly ineffective. The efforts of cult-busters can be depreciated on the basis of their own testimony. For all the small "victories" that they can count, they admit that the enemy is far from conquered. The reasons are found both in the weakness of the anticult position and in the promise of personal and social transformation held out by new and unconventional religious groups. How often that promise has actually been fulfilled is another question. 12

The body counts alone at Jonestown and Mount Carmel should give anyone pause. In addition, there are countless atrocity stories associated with so-called cults: tales of physical and psychological suffering, wasted opportunities and squandered fortunes, exploitation, and disillusionment. Even if the anticult forces have exaggerated the prevalence and misdiagnosed the cause of such experiences, they should not be ignored. There is no doubt that some people involved with new or unconventional religions suffer harm. Yet, so do many individuals who make personal choices outside the purview of the so-called cult. The important question is whether there is something *characteristic* about a given group that can *incontrovertibly* be shown to cause harm to its members or to others. Such a finding might provide justifiable cause for concern or even appropriate legal action against an entire group. The government prosecutor's assertion that Koresh preached a "theology of death" and his likening Koresh to Hitler and Stalin was an attempt to provide such a rationale for action against the Branch Davidians. But the question of the fundamental character of the whole religious group cannot be described by such facile comparisons. 13

In most instances, we believe, the damage attributed to "destructive cults" is not only peripheral to their avowed purposes but is also almost totally subjective. Common living conditions at the Mount Carmel center were often substandard and never luxurious; meals were simple at best; some of the work was physically 14 draining, and the marathon Bible study sessions were undeniably arduous. Yet, those facts of Branch Davidian life were accepted and sometimes joyfully embraced by the faithful. Such conditions can be taken as evidence of damage done by Koresh only by ignoring his adult followers' professed commitment to their chosen way of life. Even where children are involved, our society allows a great measure of latitude and freedom to a family to follow its religious convictions, however strict or unconventional. In keeping with a proper concern over the issue of damage caused by cults, but in balance with our commitment to freedom of religion, a few simple principles of judgment are proposed.

Illegal actions should be evaluated according to the appropriate laws and pur-   15
sued accordingly. The relevant criteria are explicit, public, and sanctioned by the force of the government and the will of the people it represents. The specific religious or ideological commitments of the perpetrators should be irrelevant to the process of assessing the legal status of their actions. With behavior that breaks religious or moral conventions, however, the waters become muddy. Despite cult-busters' claims to the contrary, their particular moral standards and religious convictions are not shared by the majority of the population, nor are they written into our laws. Our pluralistic society is intentionally designed to be hospitable to a wide range of moral persuasions and religious beliefs. Moral and religious judgments about cults are necessarily situated within specific subgroups of our society. Beyond the question of the legality of certain actions, where cult members must meet the same criteria as anyone else, the problem with so-called cults can only be articulated convincingly from a very specific standpoint in defense of very particular moral and religious values. By offering an alternative vision of individuals and society, cults deliberately provoke a conflict over values. Any opposition to such groups must itself offer a compelling alternative, not merely anxious alarms and exaggerated criticisms. Whatever the specific items at issue, the most effective critique of any cult would not only condemn its errors but also offer a path that the opponent would argue is closer to the truth. In other words, cults are most effectively encountered by committed representatives of the other religious communities that set forth a comprehensive view of the world and the proper place of human beings in it, which they attempt to make convincing. In that sense, cults make a signal contribution to American life by raising questions of ultimate value, by offering paradigms of commitment, and by making principled challenges to the status quo. Their presence in our society is undeniably disruptive and intentionally so. They may fade in and out of the public view, but they will not disappear as the history of religions, and particularly those in America, makes clear. Our democratic society serves, however imperfectly, as a free marketplace of ideas. Intolerant government policies, and particularly antidemocratic and military tactics like those used at Waco, have no place in such a society. Rather than conduct a war against so-called cults, we can more profitably and pointedly ask ourselves what we believe in, how we are practicing our beliefs, and what is our level of participation in the open and ongoing exchange of ideas that our society affords.

·2·

Presenting Sources to Others

I hate quotations. Tell me what you know.

Ralph Waldo Emerson (1849)

By necessity, by proclivity, and by delight, we all quote.

Ralph Waldo Emerson (1876)

These quotations appear to be contradictory, but they merely represent the development of one writer's understanding of his craft. Like Emerson in 1849, most writers hope to rely entirely on what they know and to express their knowledge in their own words. But, as Emerson realized later, one rarely writes about ideas that no one has ever explored. Someone has usually gone part of the way before, so it makes sense to build on that person's discoveries.

Because most of your writing in college will be based directly or indirectly on what you have read, you will need a working knowledge of two more methods of presenting other people's ideas to your readers: *quotation* and *paraphrase*.

REASONS FOR QUOTING

In academic writing, presenting the words of another writer through *quotation* is the most basic way to support your own ideas. Writers who know how to quote understand the need to give credit to their sources for both borrowed ideas and borrowed words.

- *Correct quotation* tells your reader that you respect your sources, that you know how to distinguish between your own work and theirs, and that you will not *plagiarize*—make unacknowledged use of another writer's words and ideas.

- *Appropriate quotation* tells your reader that you know when to quote and that you are not allowing your sources' words to dominate your writing.

Experienced writers hold quotation marks in reserve for those times when they think it essential to present the source's exact words.

Reasons to Use Quotation

1. For support
2. To preserve vivid or technical language
3. To comment on the quotation
4. To distance yourself from the quotation

---

1. Quoting for Support

You will most often refer to another writer's work as evidence in support of one of your own points. To ensure that the evidence retains its full meaning and impact, you retain the author's original language, instead of putting the sentences in your own words. Very often, quoted material appears in an essay as an *appeal to authority*; the source being quoted is important enough or familiar enough with the subject (as in an eyewitness account) to make the original words worth quoting. For example, the only quotation in a *New York Times* article describing political and economic chaos in Bolivia presents the opinion of a government official:

> Even the Government acknowledges its shaky position. "The polity is unstable, capricious and chaotic," Adolfo Linares Arraya, Minister of Planning and Coordination, said. "The predominance of crisis situations has made the future unforeseeable."

The minister's words in themselves seem vague and glib, and therefore not especially quotable. (Indeed, they may not even be true.) But his position as representative of the government makes the minister's exact words necessary evidence for the reporter's presentation of the Bolivian crisis.

2. Quoting Vivid or Technical Language

The wording of the source material may be so ingenious that the point will be lost if you express it in your own words. *You will want to quote a sentence that is very compact or that relies on a striking image to make its point.* For example, here is a paragraph from a review of a book about Vietnamese history:

> Not many nations have had such a history of scrapping: against Mongols and Chinese seeking to dominate them from the north, and to the south against weaker and more innocent peoples who stood in the way of the Vietnamese march to the rich Mekong Delta and the underpopulated land of Cambodia. Mr. Hodgkin [the author] quotes from a poem by a medieval Vietnamese hero: "By its tradition of defending the country / the army is so powerful it can swallow the evening star."

The quotation adds authentic evidence to the reviewer's discussion and provides a memorable image for the reader.

It is also important to retain the precise terminology of a *technical or legal document*. Changing one word of the text can significantly change its meaning. Here is a sentence from the final paragraph of a Supreme Court decision upholding the civil rights of three tenth-graders who had been suspended by school officials for "spiking" the punch at a meeting of an extracurricular club:

> We hold that a school board member is not immune from liability for damages if he knew or reasonably should have known that the action he took within his sphere of official responsibility would violate the constitutional rights of the student affected, or if he took the action with the malicious intention to cause a deprivation of constitutional rights or other injury to the student.

Virtually every word of the sentence has potential impact on the way this decision will be interpreted in subsequent legal suits. Note, for example, the distinction between "knew" and "reasonably should have known" and the way in which "intention" is qualified by "malicious."

3. Quoting Another Writer to Comment on the Quotation

In your essay, you may want to analyze or comment on a statement made by another writer. Your readers should have that writer's exact words in front of them if they are to get the full benefit of your commentary; *you have to quote it in order to talk about it.* Thus, when a writer reviewing Philip Norman's biography of the Beatles wants to criticize the biographer's style, he must supply a sample quotation so that his readers can make up their own minds.

> Worst of all is the overwritten prologue, about John Lennon's death and its impact in Liverpool: "The ruined imperial city, its abandoned river, its tormented suburban plain, knew an anguish greater than the recession and unemployment which have laid Merseyside waste under bombardments more deadly than Hitler's blitz." A moment's thought should have made Norman and his publishers realize that this sort of thing, dashed off in the heat of the moment, would quickly come to seem very embarrassing indeed.

4. Gaining Distance through Quotation

Writers generally use quotation to distinguish between the writer of the essay and the writer being cited in the essay. Sometimes, however, you want to distance yourself from your own choice of language. For example, you may use quotation marks to indicate that a word or phrase is not in common or standard use. A phrase may be *obsolete*, no longer in current usage:

Many "flower children" gathered at the rock festivals of the late 1960s.

Or a phrase may be *slang,* not yet having been absorbed into standard English:

She tried to "cop out" of doing her share of the work.

In effect, you want to use the phrase and at the same time "cover" yourself by signaling your awareness that the phrase is not quite right: you are distancing yourself from your own vocabulary. *It is usually better to take full responsibility for your choice of words and to avoid using slang or obsolete vocabulary, with or without quotation marks.* But if the context requires such phrasing, you may use quotation marks to gain the necessary distance.

You can achieve a different kind of distance when you use quotation marks to suggest *irony:*

The actor was joined by his "constant companion."

The quoted phrase is a familiar *euphemism,* a bland expression substituted for a more blunt term. Again, by placing it in quotation marks, the author is both *calling attention to* and *distancing him- or herself from* the euphemism.

Quotation marks also serve as a means of *disassociation* for journalists who wish to avoid taking sides on an issue or making editorial comments.

A fire that roared through a 120-year-old hotel and took at least 11 lives was the work of a "sick arsonist," the county coroner said today. Robert Jennings, the Wayne County coroner, said that he had told county officials that the building was a "fire trap."

The author of this article did not want the responsibility of attributing the fire to a "sick arsonist" or labeling the building a "fire trap"—at any rate, not until the findings of an investigation or a trial make the terminology unquestionably true. Thus, he is careful not only to use quotation marks around certain phrases, but also to cite the precise source of the statement.

USING QUOTATIONS

The apparatus for quotation is twofold:

1. By *inserting quotation marks,* you indicate that you are borrowing certain words, as well as certain ideas, that appear in your writing.
2. By *inserting a citation* containing the source's name, you give credit for both ideas and words to the author.

Citation	*Quotation*
Theodore Roosevelt said,	"Speak softly and carry a big stick; you will go far."

Direct Quotation: Separating Quotations from Your Own Writing

The simplest way to quote is to combine the citation (written by you) with the words you are quoting (*exactly as they were said or written by your source*). This method of quotation joins together two separate statements, with punctuation—comma or colon—bridging the gap and a capital letter beginning the quoted phrase.

St. Paul declared, "It is better to marry than to burn."

In his first epistle to the Corinthians, St. Paul commented on lust: "It is better to marry than to burn."

In both these forms of direct quotation, the quoted words are *not* fully integrated into the grammatical structure of your sentence. The *comma or colon* and the *capital letter* at the beginning of the quoted sentence separate the two parts, making it clear that *two voices appear in the sentence: yours and your source's*. In general, you should choose this kind of direct quotation when you want to differentiate between yourself and the quoted words. There are many reasons for wanting to emphasize this difference; an obvious example would be your own disagreement with the quotation.

The *colon* is used less frequently than the comma. It usually follows a clause that can stand alone as a complete sentence. As such, the colon separates a complete idea of your own from a complementary or supporting idea taken from your source.

Direct Quotation: Integrating Quotations into Your Sentences

In an alternative kind of direct quotation, *only the quotation marks indicate that you are using someone else's words.*

St. Paul declared that "it is better to marry than to burn."

Alvin Toffler defined future shock as "the shattering stress and disorientation that we induce in individuals by subjecting them to too much change in too short a time."

There is no signal for the reader that separates citation from quotation—no comma or colon, no capital letter. The first word of the quoted material, in this second type of direct quotation, is *not* capitalized, even if it was capitalized in the source.

Original

Beware of all enterprises that require new clothes.

HENRY DAVID THOREAU

Quotation

Thoreau warned his readers to "beware of all enterprises that require new clothes."

The effect is very smooth, and the reader's attention is not distracted from the flow of sentences.

The Two Kinds of Direct Quotation

Separated

- Comma or colon and quotation marks separate citation and quotation.
- The first letter of the quotation is capitalized.
- You are distinguishing between your ideas and those of your source.

Integrated

- No punctuation (but quotation marks) separates citation and quotation.
- The first letter of the quotation is not capitalized.
- You are integrating your ideas with those of your source.

Because integrating the quotation tends to blur the distinction between writer and source, you must be careful to avoid confusion. Look, for example, at the various ways of quoting this first-person sentence, which was originally spoken by a motorist: "I hate all pedestrians."

Separated Quotation

The motorist said, "I hate all pedestrians."

Integrated Quotation

The motorist said that "I hate all pedestrians."

The first method, quoting with separation by punctuation, requires no alteration in the original sentence. But in the second version, quoting with integration, the original wording does not quite fit.

- The first-person "I" conflicts with the third-person "motorist" (the reader may wonder who "I" is—the motorist or the writer!).
- The present-tense "hate" conflicts with the past-tense "said," so "hate" must be turned into "hated."

But once the person [I] and the tense [hate] of the original statement have been altered for clarity and consistency, only two words—"all pedestrians"—are actually being quoted:

Direct Quotation

The motorist said that she hated "all pedestrians."

You may even prefer not to put quotations around the remaining two words taken from the original source. If so, you are not quoting anything directly; you are using indirect quotation. *In indirect quotation, you report rather than quote what has been said.*

Indirect Quotation

The motorist said that she hated all pedestrians.

However, the absence of quotation marks in the indirect quotation could be confusing. If you were collecting evidence for a legal suit, quotation marks would indicate that the motorist was responsible for the precise wording. Therefore, direct quotation, separated by punctuation, is probably the most appropriate method of presenting the motorist's opinion of pedestrians.

As a rule, the writer has the obligation to insert quotation marks when using a source's exact words, whether written or oral.

Direct Quotation

Robert Ingersoll condemned those who deny others their civil liberties: "I am the inferior of any man whose rights I trample underfoot."

Indirect Quotation

Robert Ingersoll proclaimed that he was the inferior of any man whose rights he trampled underfoot.

The indirect quotation does not indicate exactly who wrote this sentence. Even if you changed "I" to "he" and the present to the past tense, *you are still not using your own words;* the basic phrasing of the sentence remains Ingersoll's. *To imply, as this indirect quotation could, that the wording is yours, not Ingersoll's, would be plagiarism.*

For this reason, *writers should use indirect quotation with great care.* If one of the two forms of direct quotation does not seem appropriate, you should invent your own phrasing—called *paraphrase*—to express the source's original statement.

The Historical Present Tense

Certain ideas and statements remain true long after their creators have died. By convention, or general agreement, writers often refer to these statements in the present tense.

Shakespeare states, "This above all: to thine own self be true."

When you are devoting part of your own essay to a "discussion" with another writer, you may prefer to conduct the discussion on a common ground of time and use the present tense, called the *historical present*. The historical present is also useful to *place a variety of different sources on equal terms, especially when they are from different eras.* In the following example, the introductory verbs, all in the present tense, are underlined:

While Shelley <u>acknowledges</u> that poets are creators of language and music and art, he also <u>asserts</u> that they have a civic role: "They are the institutors of laws, and the founders of civil society, and the inventors of the arts of life." Writing one hundred years later, Benedetto Croce <u>affirms</u> Shelley's insistence upon the social and spiritual responsibilities of the poet. According to Croce, Shelley <u>sees</u> poetry "as the eternal source of all intellectual, moral, and civil vitality."

Finally, the historical present is almost always used when you refer to *important documents* (often written by a group of people, rather than a single author) that remain in force long after they were created. Obvious examples include the Constitution, the Declaration of Independence, the laws of Congress, Supreme Court decisions, the charter of your state government, and the bylaws governing your college or university.

The Constitution guarantees that women—and, indeed, all citizens—shall have the vote in elections; Amendment XIX states that the right to vote "shall not be denied or abridged by the United States or by any State on account of sex."

Punctuating Direct Quotations

You have already learned about punctuating *the beginning of the quotation:*

1. In a separated direct quotation, the citation is followed by a comma or a colon.
2. In an integrated direct quotation, the citation is followed by no punctuation at all.

Some writers tend to forget this second point and include an unnecessary comma:

Incorrect Quotation

Ernest Hemingway believed that, "what is moral is what you feel good after and what is immoral is what you feel bad after."

Remember that *an integrated quotation should have no barriers between citation and quotation:*

Correct Quotation

Ernest Hemingway believed that "what is moral is what you feel good after and what is immoral is what you feel bad after."

In the integrated direct quotation, note that the first letter of the quotation is not capitalized.

There is no easy way of remembering the proper sequence of punctuation for *closing a quotation.* The procedure has been determined by conventional and arbitrary agreement, originally for the convenience of printers. Although other countries abide by different conventions, in the United States the following rules apply—and *there are no exceptions.*

1. All periods and commas are placed inside the terminal quotation marks.

It does not matter whether the period belongs to your sentence or to the quoted sentence: it goes *inside* the marks. This is the most important rule and the one most often ignored. Don't resort to ambiguous devices such as placing the quotes directly over the period (").

> P. T. Barnum is reputed to have said that "there's a sucker born every minute."

> P. T. Barnum is reputed to have said that "there's a sucker born every minute," and Barnum's circuses undertook to entertain each and every one.

Notice that, in the second example, the comma at the end of the quotation really belongs to the framework sentence, not to the quotation itself; nevertheless, it goes *inside* the marks.

2. All semicolons, colons, and dashes are placed outside the terminal quotation marks.

They should be regarded as the punctuation for *your* sentence, and not for the quotation.

> George Santayana wrote that "those who cannot remember the past are condemned to repeat it"; today, we are in danger of forgetting the lessons of history.

Occasionally, when a semicolon, colon, or (most likely) a dash appears at the end of the material to be quoted, you will decide to include the punctuation in the quotation; in that case, the punctuation should be placed inside the marks. In the following example, the dash appears in Lucretia Mott's original statement, so it is placed inside the quotation marks.

> Lucretia Mott argued urgently for women's rights: "Let woman then go on—not asking favors, but claiming as a right the removal of all hindrances to her elevation in the scale of being—" so that, as a result, she might "enter profitably into the active business of man."

3. Question marks and exclamation points are sometimes placed inside the quotation marks and sometimes placed outside.

- If the quotation is itself a question or an exclamation, the mark or point goes *inside* the quotation marks.
- If your own sentence is a question or an exclamation, the mark or point goes *outside* a quotation placed at the *very end* of your sentence.

> In 1864, General Sherman signaled the arrival of his reinforcements: "Hold the fort! I am coming!"

The exclamation is General Sherman's; the exclamation point goes inside the quotation.

> Can anyone in the 1980s agree with Dumas that "woman inspires us to great things and prevents us from achieving them"?

Dumas was *not* asking a question; the question mark goes at the very end of the sentence, after the quotation marks.

> Sigmund Freud's writings occasionally reveal a remarkable lack of insight: "The great question that has never been answered, and which I have not yet been able to answer despite my thirty years of research into the feminine soul, is: What does a woman want?"

Freud himself asked this famous question; the question mark goes inside the quotation.

> Freud was demonstrating remarkably little insight when he wrote, "What does a woman want?" citing his "thirty years of research into the feminine soul"!

The exclamation is the writer's, not Freud's; the exclamation point goes outside the quotation marks.

It is possible to construct a sentence that ends logically in two question marks (or exclamation points): one for the quotation and one for your own sentence. In such cases, you need include only one—and, by convention, it should be placed *inside* the quotation marks:

> What did Freud mean when he asked, "What does a woman want?"

These rules apply only to the quotation of complete sentences or reasonably long phrases. *Whether it is a quotation or an obsolete, slang, or ironic reference, a single word or a brief phrase should be fully integrated into your sentence, without being preceded or followed by commas.*

> Winston Churchill's reference to "blood, sweat and tears" rallied the English to prepare for war.

Be careful not to quote words or phrases excessively. Even though the quotation marks make it clear that you are borrowing the words, using more than one quotation, however brief, in a sentence or quoting sentence after sentence creates the impression that you cannot express your thoughts in your own words.

Interrupting Quotations

Sometimes it is desirable to break up a long quotation or to vary the way you quote your sources by interrupting a quotation *and placing the citation in the middle.*

"I do not mind lying," wrote Samuel Butler, "but I hate inaccuracy."

Butler's statement is divided into two separate parts, and therefore you need to use *four* sets of quotation marks: two introductory and two terminal. The citation is joined to the quotation by a comma on either side. There are two danger points:

- If you forget to use the marks at the beginning of the second half of the quotation, you are failing to distinguish your words from Butler's.
- You must also put the first comma *inside* the terminal quotation marks (because terminal commas *always* go inside the quotation marks) and put the comma that concludes the citation *before* the quotation marks (because it is *your* comma, not Butler's).

Quoting inside a Quotation

Sometimes a statement that you want to quote already contains a quotation. In that case, you must use *two sets of quotation marks, double and single,* to help your reader to distinguish between the two separate sources.

- *Single quotation* marks are used for the words already quoted by your source (and this is the *only* time when it is appropriate to use single quotation marks).
- *Double quotation* marks are used around the words that you are quoting.

Goethe at times expressed a notable lack of self-confidence: "'Know thyself?' If I knew myself, I'd run away."

At the beginning of World War I, Winston Churchill observed that "the maxim of the British people is 'Business as usual.'"

The same single/double procedure is used even when there is no author's name to be cited.

A Yiddish proverb states that "'for example' is not proof."

Very occasionally, you may need to use triple quotation marks, usually to quote a source who is quoting another source who is using a quoted word or phrase. An article about the author Muriel Spark included the following statement by that novelist:

I draw the line at "forever."

Victoria Glendinning, the author of the article, quoted Spark's statement using single and double quotation marks.

Eternally inquiring and curious about places and people, "I draw the line at 'forever.'"

To quote that sentence in your essay, you would need to distinguish yourself from Victoria Glendinning and Muriel Spark.

In her recent profile, Victoria Glendinning emphasizes Muriel Spark's search for variety: "Eternally inquiring and curious about places and people, 'I draw the line at "forever."'"

Notice that you would deliberately plan the quotation marks so that the double marks are used for the framework quotation.

EXERCISE 7: QUOTING CORRECTLY

A. Correct the errors in the following sentences:

1. The *Chicago Times* asserted in 1861 that, "It is a newspaper's duty to print the news and raise hell."

2. Baron de Montesquieu, a philosopher of the eighteenth-century Enlightenment, sympathized with the needs of the masses, "The real wants of the people," he wrote, ought never to give way to the imaginary wants of the state".

3. In Proust's view, "Everybody calls "clear" those ideas which have the same degree of confusion as his own".

4. Thoreau warned his readers to, "Beware of all enterprises that require new clothes.

5. Robert F. Wagner, former mayor of New York, believed in keeping a low profile and offered this advice—"When in danger, ponder; when in trouble, delegate" when in doubt, mumble"

6. "Beggars should be abolished, said Friedrich Nietzsche. "it annoys one to give to them and it annoys one not to give to them".

7. Have you anything to declare," said the customs official? No, replied Oscar Wilde. "I have nothing to declare', he paused, 'except my genius."

8. Before the Revolutionary War, Patrick Henry made a passionate speech, "is life so dear or peace so sweet, as to be purchased at the price of chains and slavery"? "Forbid it, Almighty God"! I know not what course others may take, but as for me, give me liberty or give me death."!

B. Use quotations from the following group as directed:

- Choose one quotation and write a sentence that introduces a direct quotation with separation.

- Choose a second quotation and write a sentence that introduces a direct quotation with integration.

- Choose a third quotation and write a sentence that interrupts a quotation with a citation in the middle.

1. Early in life I had to choose between honest arrogance and hypocritical humility. I chose honest arrogance and have seen no occasion to change. (Frank Lloyd Wright)

2. I must say acting was good training for the political life which lay ahead for us. (Nancy Reagan)

3. My folks didn't come over on the *Mayflower*, but they were there to meet the boat. (Will Rogers)

4. The reason so many people showed up at his funeral was because they wanted to make sure he was dead. (Samuel Goldwyn on L. B. Mayer)

5. I hear much of people's call out to punish the guilty, but very few are concerned to clear the innocent. (Daniel Defoe)

6. This has always been a man's world, and none of the reasons hitherto brought forward in explanation of this fact has seemed adequate. (Simone de Beauvoir)

7. I have now come to the conclusion never again to think of marrying, and for this reason: I can never be satisfied with anyone who would be blockhead enough to have me. (Abraham Lincoln)

Quoting Accurately

Quoting is not a collaboration in which you try to improve on your source's writing. If you value a writer's words enough to want to quote them, you should respect the integrity of the sentence.

Unless you are applying the conventional methods of presenting quotations, don't make minor changes or carelessly leave words out, but faithfully transcribe the exact words, the exact spelling, and the exact punctuation that you find in the original.

Original

Those who corrupt the public mind are just as evil as those who steal from the public purse.

ADLAI STEVENSON

Inexact Quotation

Adlai Stevenson believed that "those who act against the public interest are just as evil as those who steal from the public purse."

Exact Quotation

Adlai Stevenson believed that "those who corrupt the public mind are just as evil as those who steal from the public purse."

Even if you notice an error (or what you regard as an error), you still must copy the original wording. For example, old-fashioned spelling should be retained, as well as regional or national dialect and spelling conventions:

One of Heywood's Proverbes tells us that "a new brome swepeth clean."

In one of his humorous stories, Colonel Davy Crockett predicted the reactions to his own death: "It war a great loss to the country and the world, and to ole Kaintuck in particklar. Thar were never known such a member of Congress as Crockett, and never will be agin. The painters and bears will miss him, for he never missed them."

You do not have to assume the blame if the material that you are quoting contains errors of syntax, punctuation, or spelling. You can use a conventional way to point out such errors and inform the reader that the mistake was made, not by you, but by the author whom you are quoting. *The Latin word sic (meaning "thus") is placed in square brackets and inserted immediately after the error.* The [sic] signals that the quotation was "thus" and that you, the writer, were aware of the error, which was not the result of your own carelessness in transcribing the quotation.

In the following example, [sic] calls attention to an error in subject-verb agreement:

Richard Farson points out that "increased understanding and concern has [sic] not been coupled with increased rights."

You may also want to use [sic] to indicate that the source used archaic spelling:

In describing Elizabeth Billington, an early nineteenth-century singer, W. Clark Russell observed that "her voice was powerful, and resembled the tone of a clarionet [sic]."

It would be tedious, however, to use [sic] to indicate each misspelling in the Davy Crockett quotation; in your essay about Crockett, you could, instead, explain his use of dialect as you discuss his life and writing.

TAILORING QUOTATIONS TO FIT YOUR WRITING

There are several ways to change quotations to fit the quoted material naturally into your own sentences. Like [sic], these devices are *conventions*, established by generally accepted agreement: *you cannot improvise; you must follow these rules.* Usually, the conventional rules require you to inform your reader that a change is being made; in other words, they make clear the distinction between your wording and the author's.

Changing Capital and Small Letters

The first way of altering quotations depends entirely on how and where the quotation fits into your sentence.

- When a quotation is *integrated* completely into your sentence (usually when your citation ends in "that"), the first letter of the quotation will be small, whether or not it is a capital in the original. (Two exceptions are the pronoun "I" and proper nouns, which are always capitalized.)
- When a quotation is *separated* from your sentence, and your citation ends in a comma or a colon, the first letter of the quotation will be a capital, whether or not it is a capital in the original.

Integrated Quotation

The poet Frost wrote that "good fences make good neighbors."

Separated Quotation

The poet Frost wrote, "Good fences make good neighbors."

As a rule, it is not necessary to indicate to your readers that you have altered the first letter of your quotation from small to capital or from capital to small.

Using Ellipses to Delete Words

It is permissible to *delete* words from a quotation, provided that you indicate to the reader that something has been omitted. Your condensed version is as accurate as the original; it is just shorter. But you must remember to insert the conventional symbol for deletion, *three spaced dots*, called an *ellipsis*. Once made aware by the three dots that your version omits part of the original, any reader who wants to see the omitted portion can consult the original source.

Original

It is not true that suffering ennobles the character; happiness does that sometimes, but suffering, for the most part, makes men petty and vindictive.

W. SOMERSET MAUGHAM

Quotation with Ellipsis

Maugham does not believe that "suffering ennobles the character; . . . suffering, for the most part, makes men petty and vindictive."

Notice that:

- The three dots are spaced equally.
- The dots *must* be three—not two or a dozen.
- The semicolon is retained, to provide terminal punctuation for the first part of the quotation.

If you wish to delete the end of a quotation, and the ellipsis coincides with the end of your sentence, you must use the three dots, plus a fourth to signify the sentence's end.

Quotation with Terminal Ellipsis

Maugham does not believe that "suffering ennobles the character; happiness does that sometimes. . . . "

Here, you'll note:

- There are four dots, three to indicate a deletion and a fourth to indicate the period at the end of the sentence.
- The first dot is placed immediately after the last letter.
- The sentence ends with quotation marks, as usual, with the marks placed *after* the dots, not before.

You can also use the three dots to link two separate quotations from the same paragraph in your source; the ellipsis will indicate the deletion of one or more sentences, but *only* if the two sentences that you are quoting are fairly near each other in the original. *An ellipsis cannot cover a gap of more than a few sentences.* When you use an ellipsis to bridge one or more sentences, use only *one* set of quotation marks. Your full quotation, with an ellipsis in the middle, is still continuous—a single quotation—even though there is a gap.

When an ellipsis is used following a quoted complete sentence, the period of the quoted sentence is retained so that a total of four dots is used, as in the following example.

Original

In one sense there is no death. The life of a soul on earth lasts beyond his departure. You will always feel that life touching yours, that voice speaking to you, that spirit looking out of other eyes, talking to you in the familiar things he touched, worked with, loved as familiar friends. He lives on in your life and in the lives of all others that knew him.

ANGELO PATRI

Quotation with Ellipsis

Patri states that "in one sense there is no death. The life of a soul on earth lasts beyond his departure. . . . He lives on in your life and in the lives of all others that knew him."

An ellipsis should be used to make a quotation fit more smoothly into your own sentence. It is especially convenient when you are working with a long passage that contains several separate points that you wish to quote. But ellipses should *not* be used to condense long, tedious quotations or to replace summary and paraphrase. If you only want to quote a brief extract from a lengthy passage, then simply quote that portion and ignore the surrounding material. An ellipsis is poorly used when it is used too often. Reading a paragraph full of dots can be very distracting.

The meaning of the original quotation must always be exactly preserved, despite the deletion represented by the ellipsis.

Original

As long as there are sovereign nations possessing great power, war is inevitable.

ALBERT EINSTEIN

Inexact Quotation

Einstein believes that " . . . war is inevitable."

It would not be accurate to suggest that Einstein believed in the inevitability of war, under all circumstances, without qualifications. *To extract only a portion of this statement with ellipsis is to oversimplify and thus to falsify the evidence.*

Using Brackets to Insert Words

Brackets have an opposite function: ellipsis signifies deletion; *brackets signify addition or alteration.* Brackets are not the same as parentheses. Parentheses would be confusing for this purpose, for the quotation might itself include a parenthetical statement, and the reader could not be sure whether the parentheses contained the author's insertion or yours. Instead, brackets, a relatively unusual form of punctuation, are used as a conventional way of informing the reader that material has been inserted. (You have already seen how to use brackets with [sic], which enables you to comment on the material that you are quoting.) You simply insert the information *inside* the quotation, placing it in square brackets.

Reasons to Use Brackets

- To explain a vague word
- To replace a confusing phrase
- To suggest an antecedent
- To correct an error in a quotation
- To adjust a quotation to fit your own writing

The most common reason for using brackets is to clarify a vague word. You may, for example, choose to quote only the last portion of a passage, omitting an important antecedent:

Original

Man lives *by* habits, indeed, but what he lives *for* is thrills and excitement.

WILLIAM JAMES

Quotation with Brackets

William James argues that "what he [man] lives for is thrills and excitement."

William James argues that "what [man] lives for is thrills and excitement."

In the second example, the vague word "he" has been deleted entirely; the brackets themselves indicate that there has been a substitution, but the reader doesn't know what was originally there. For that reason, unless the presentation of both wordings seems very awkward, *it is better to follow the first example: quote the original and also provide the clarification in brackets.* This way, you will leave your reader in no doubt about your source's words.

Brackets can also be used to complete a thought that has been obscured by the omission (often through ellipsis) of an earlier sentence:

Original

A well-trained sensible family doctor is one of the most valuable assets in a community. . . . Few men live lives of more devoted self-sacrifice.

SIR WILLIAM OSLER

Quotation with Brackets

The great surgeon Sir William Osler had enormous respect for his less famous colleagues: "Few men live lives of more devoted self-sacrifice [than good family doctors]."

Here, the quotation marks are placed *after* the brackets, even though the quoted material ends after the word "self-sacrifice." The explanatory material inside the brackets is considered part of the quotation, even though it is not in the source's own words.

Your own explanatory comments in brackets should be very brief and to the point. You might, for example, want to include an important *date* or *name* as essential background information. But whatever is inside the brackets should fit smoothly into the syntax of the quotation and should not distract the reader. For example, do not use brackets to argue with the author you are quoting. The following running dialogue with the entertainer Sophie Tucker is poorly conveyed through the use of brackets.

Confusing Use of Brackets

Sophie Tucker suggests that up to the age of eighteen "a girl needs good parents. [This is true for men, too.] From eighteen to thirty-five, she needs good looks. [Good looks aren't that essential anymore.] From thirty-five to fifty-five, she needs a good personality. [I disagree because personality is important at any age.] From fifty-five on, she needs good cash."

EXERCISE 8: USING ELLIPSES AND BRACKETS IN QUOTATIONS

A. Choose one of the following quotations. By using *ellipses*, incorporate a portion of the quotation into a sentence of your own; remember to include the author's name in the citation.

B. Choose a second quotation. Incorporate a portion of the quotation into another sentence of your own; insert words in *brackets* to clarify one or more of the quoted words.

1. Man, biologically considered, and whatever else he may be in the bargain, is simply the most formidable of all the beasts of prey, and, indeed, the only one that preys systematically on its own species. (William James)

2. I have never taken any exercise, except sleeping and resting, and I never intend to take any. Exercise is loathsome. And it cannot be any benefit when you are tired, and I am always tired. (Mark Twain)

3. I love America more than any other country in the world, and, exactly for this reason, I insist on the right to criticize her perpetually. (James Baldwin)

4. I do not believe that civilization will be wiped out in a war fought with the atomic bomb. Perhaps two-thirds of the people of the earth might be killed, but enough men capable of thinking, and enough books, would be left to start again, and civilization would be restored. (Albert Einstein)

5. Unconditional war can no longer lead to unconditional victory. It can no longer serve to settle disputes. It can no longer be of concern to great powers alone. For a nuclear disaster, spread by winds and waters and fear, could well engulf the great and the small, the rich and the poor, the committed and the uncommitted alike. (John F. Kennedy)

6. I never listen to debates. They are dreadful things indeed. The plain truth is that I am not a fair man, and don't want to hear both sides. On

> all known subjects, ranging from aviation to xylophone-playing, I have fixed and invariable ideas. They have not changed since I was four or five. (H. L. Mencken)

WRITING CITATIONS

Citing the Author's Name

The first time that you refer to a source, use the author's full name—without Mr. or Miss, Mrs., or Ms.

First Reference

John Stuart Mill writes, "The opinion which it is attempted to suppress by authority may possibly be true."

After that, should you need to cite the author again, use the *last name only*. Conventional usage discourages casual and distracting references such as "John thinks," "JSM thinks," or "Mr. Mill thinks."

Second Reference

Mill continues to point out that "all silencing of discussion is an assumption of infallibility."

When you cite the author's name:

- At first reference, you may (and usually should) include the *title* of the work from which the quotation is taken:

  In *On Liberty*, John Stuart Mill writes . . .

- If there is a long break between references to the same author, or if the names of several other authors intervene, you may wish to repeat the full name and remind your reader of the earlier citation.

  In addition to his warnings about the dangers of majority rule, which were cited earlier in the discussion of public opinion, John Stuart Mill also expresses concern about "the functions of police; how far liberty may legitimately be invaded for the prevention of crime, or of accident."

- Avoid referring to the author twice in the same citation, once by name and once by pronoun. In the following citation, we really can't be sure who "he" is:

  In John Stuart Mill's *On Liberty*, he writes . . .

- Finally, unless you genuinely do not know the author's name, use it! There is no point in being coy, even for the sake of variety:

A famous man once made an ironic observation about child-rearing: "If you strike a child, take care that you strike it in anger. . . . A blow in cold blood neither can nor should be forgiven."

Your guessing game will only irritate readers who are not aware that this famous man was George Bernard Shaw.

Choosing the Introductory Verb

The citation provides an important link between your thoughts and those of your source. The introductory verb can tell your reader something about your reasons for presenting the quotation and its context in the work that you are quoting. Will you choose "J. S. Mill says," or "J. S. Mill writes," or "J. S. Mill thinks," or "J. S. Mill feels"? Those are the most common introductory verbs—so common that they have become boring! Whenever appropriate, select less stereotyped verbs. As the senses are not directly involved in writing, avoid "feels" entirely. And, unless you are quoting someone's spoken words, substitute a more accurate verb for "says."

Here are some introductory verbs:

argues	adds	concludes
establishes	explains	agrees
emphasizes	believes	insists
finds	continues	maintains
points out	declares	disagrees
notes	observes	states
suggests	proposes	compares

Of course, once you stop using the all-purpose "says" or "writes," you have to remember that verbs are not interchangeable and that you should choose the verb that best suits your purpose.

The citation should suggest the relationship between your own ideas (in the previous sentence) and the statement that you are about to quote.

You should examine the quotation before writing the citation to define the way in which the author makes a point:

- Is it being asserted forcefully?
  Use "argues" or "declares" or "insists."
- Is the statement being offered only as a possibility?
  Use "suggests" or "proposes" or "finds."
- Does the statement immediately follow a previous reference?
  Use "continues" or "adds."

For clarity, the introductory verb may be expanded:

X is aware that . . .
X stresses the opposite view

X provides one answer to the question
X makes the same point as Y
X erroneously assumes . . .

But make sure that the antecedent for the "view" or the "question" or the "point" can be found in the previous sentences of your essay. Finally, all the examples of introductory verbs are given in the *present tense,* which is the conventional way of introducing most quotations.

Varying Your Sentence Patterns

Even if you choose a different verb for each quotation, the combination of the author's name, introductory verb, and quotation can become repetitious and tiresome. One way to vary the citations is occasionally to place the name of the source in a less prominent position, tucked into the quotation instead of calling attention to itself at the beginning.

1. You can interrupt the quotation by placing the citation in the middle.

"I made my mistakes," acknowledged Richard Nixon, "but in all my years of public service, I have never profited from public service. I have earned every cent."

The verb and the name may be placed in reverse order (instead of "Richard Nixon acknowledged") when the citation appears in the middle of the quotation. Remember to include two commas: one at the end of the first portion of the quotation (*inside* the quotation marks), one at the end of the citation.
One citation is quite enough. There is no need to inform your reader back to back, as in this repetitive example:

"The only prize much cared for by the powerful is power," states Oliver Wendell Holmes. He concludes, "The prize of the general . . . is command."

2. You can avoid the monotonous "X says that . . ." pattern by phrasing the citation as a subordinate clause or phrase.

In Henry Kissinger's opinion, "Power is 'the great aphrodisiac.'"

As John F. Kennedy declares, "Mankind must put an end to war or war will put an end to mankind."

3. In your quest for variety, avoid placing the citation after the quotation.

The author's name at the end may weaken the statement, especially if the citation is pretentiously or awkwardly phrased:

Awkward Citation

"I am the inferior of any man whose rights I trample underfoot," as quoted from the writings of Robert Ingersoll.

Clear Citation

A champion of civil liberties, Robert Ingersoll insisted, "I am the inferior of any man whose rights I trample underfoot."

Two rules should govern your choice of citation:

1. Don't be too fancy.
2. Be both precise and varied in your phrasing.

Presenting an Extended Quotation

Occasionally, you may have reason to present *an extended quotation,* a single extract from the same source that runs *more than four printed or typewritten lines.* For extended quotations, you must, by conventional rule, set off the quoted passage by *indenting the entire quotation on the left.*

- Introduce an extended quotation with a colon.

- Start each line of the quotation *10* spaces from the left-hand margin; stop each line at your normal right-hand margin.

- Some instructors prefer single-spacing within extended quotations; some prefer double-spacing. If possible, consult your instructor about the style appropriate for your course or discipline. If you are given no guidelines, use double-spacing.

- Omit quotation marks at the beginning and end of the quoted passage; the indented margin (and the introductory citation) will tell your readers that you are quoting.

Here is an example of an extended quotation:

Although he worked "hard as hell" all winter, Fitzgerald had difficulty finishing The Great Gatsby. On April 10, 1924, he wrote to Maxwell Perkins, his editor at Scribner's:

> While I have every hope & plan of finishing my novel in June . . . even [if] it takes me 10 times that long I cannot let it go unless it has the very best I'm capable of in it or even as I feel sometimes better than I'm capable of. It is only in the last four months that I've realized how much I've—well, almost deteriorated. . . . What I'm trying to say is just that . . . at last, or at least for the first time in years, I'm doing the best I can.

INTEGRATING QUOTATIONS
INTO YOUR PARAGRAPHS

You have learned how to present the words of others with accuracy and appropriate acknowledgment; now, you must learn to make the quotation serve the larger purpose of your paragraph or essay. Here are some suggestions for integrating quotations into your writing:

1. Use quotation sparingly.

If quotation seems to be your primary purpose in writing, your reader will assume that you have nothing of your own to say. *Quote only when you have a clear reason for doing so:* when you are intending to analyze a quotation, when you are sure that the wording of the quotation is essential to your argument, or when you simply cannot say it in your own words.

2. Quotations generally belong in the body of your paragraph, not at the very beginning as a replacement for the topic sentence.

The topic sentence should establish—in your own words—what you are about to explain or prove. The quotation should appear later in the paragraph, as supporting evidence.

3. Let the quotation make its point; your job is to explain or interpret its meaning, not to translate it word for word.

Once you have presented a quotation, it is usually not necessary to provide an exact repetition of the same idea in your own words, making the same point twice. Instead, follow up a quotation with an *explanation* of its relevance to your paragraph or an *interpretation* of its meaning; but make sure that your commentary does more than echo the quotation.

In the following student example, the quotation used in the development of the paragraph is no more or less important than any of the other supporting sentences. The quotation adds interest to the paragraph because of the shift in tone and the shift to a sharper, narrower focus.

Some parents insist on allowing their children to learn through experience. Once a child has actually performed a dangerous action and realized its consequences, he will always remember the circumstances and the possible ill effects. Yvonne Realle illustrates the adage that experience is the best teacher by describing a boy who was slapped just as he reached for a hot iron. The child, not realizing that he might have been burned, had no idea why he had been slapped. An observer noted that "if he had learned by experience, if he'd suffered some discomfort in the process, then he'd know enough to avoid the iron next time." In the view of parents like Yvonne Realle, letting a child experiment with his environment will result in a stronger lesson than slapping or scolding the child for trying to explore his surroundings.

EXERCISE 9: INTEGRATING QUOTATIONS INTO A PARAGRAPH

1. The following student paragraph is taken from an essay, "The Compulsive Gambler." The second passage comes from *The Psychology of Gambling* by Edmund Bergler.

   Choose one appropriate supporting quotation from the Bergler passage, decide where to place it in the student paragraph, and insert the quotation correctly and smoothly into the paragraph. Remember to lead into the quotation by citing the source.

   Student Paragraph

   One obvious reason for gambling is to make money. Because some gamblers are lucky when they play, they never want to stop. Even when quite a lot of money has been lost, they go on, assuming that they can get rich through gambling. Once a fortune is made, they will feel really powerful, free of all dependency and responsibilities. Instead, in most cases, gambling becomes a daily routine. There is no freedom, no escape.

   Source

   Every gambler gives the impression of a man who has signed a contract with Fate, stipulating that persistence must be rewarded. With that imaginary contract in his pocket, he is beyond the reach of all logical objection and argument.

   The result of this pathologic optimism is that the true gambler never stops when he is winning, for he is convinced that he must win more and more. Inevitably, he loses. He does not consider his winnings the result of chance; to him they are a down payment on that contract he has with Fate which guarantees that he will be a permanent winner. This inability to stop while fortune is still smiling is one of the strongest arguments against the earnest assumption, common to all gamblers, that one can get rich through gambling.

ASSIGNMENT 2: WRITING A PARAGRAPH THAT INCLUDES A QUOTATION

1. Choose one of the following topics. Each is a specific question that can be answered adequately in a single paragraph.
   A. Question: Should children be spanked?
   B. Question: Should single-sex high schools receive public funding?
   C. Question: What is the best way to deal with sibling rivalry?

2. Ask someone you know to comment briefly on the question you have chosen, offering a suggestion or an example. Write down any part of the comment that you think might be worth quoting, transcribe the words accurately, and show the statement to your source to confirm its accuracy. Make sure

that you have the name properly spelled. If the first person you ask does not provide you with a suitable quotation, try someone else.

3. Answer your own question in a single paragraph of four to eight sentences, limiting the paragraph to ideas that can be clearly developed in such a brief space. The paragraph as a whole should express *your* views, not those of your source. Choose a *single* quotation from your source and integrate it into the development of your paragraph, using proper punctuation, citation, and (if necessary) ellipses and brackets. If your source agrees with you, use the quotation as support. If your source disagrees, answer the objection in your own way. Try not to quote in the first or second sentence of your paragraph. Hand in both your paragraph and the sheet on which you originally wrote down the quotation.

AVOIDING PLAGIARISM

Quoting without quotation marks is called plagiarism. Even if you cite the source's name somewhere on your page, a word-for-word quotation without marks would still be considered a plagiarism.

Plagiarism is the unacknowledged use of another writer's words or ideas. The only way to acknowledge that you are using someone else's actual words is through citation and quotation marks.

Chapter 9 discusses plagiarism in detail. At this point, you should understand that:

- If you plagiarize, you will never learn to write.
- Literate people consider plagiarism to be equivalent to theft.
- Plagiarists eventually get caught!

It is easy for an experienced reader to detect plagiarism. Every writer, professional or amateur, has a characteristic style or voice that readers quickly learn to recognize. In a few paragraphs or pages, the writer's voice becomes familiar enough for the reader to notice that the style has changed and that, suddenly, there is a new, unfamiliar voice. When there are frequent acknowledged quotations, the reader simply adjusts to a series of new voices. *When there are unacknowledged quotations, the absence of quotation marks and the change of voices usually suggest to an experienced reader that the work is poorly integrated and probably plagiarized.* Plagiarized essays are often identified in this way.

Instructors are well aware of style and are trained to recognize inconsistencies and awkward transitions. A revealing clue is the patched-together, mosaic effect. The next exercise will improve your own perception of shifting voices and encourage you to rely on your own characteristic style as the dominant voice in everything that you write.

EXERCISE 10: IDENTIFYING PLAGIARISM

The following paragraphs contain several plagiarized sentences. Examine the language and tone of each sentence, as well as the continuity of the entire paragraph. Then underline the plagiarized sentences.

A.   The Beatles' music in the early years was just plain melodic. It had a nice beat to it. The Beatles were simple lads, writing simple songs simply to play to screaming fans on one-night stands. There was no deep, inner meaning to the lyrics. Their songs included many words like I, and me, and you. As the years went by, the Beatles' music became more poetic. Sergeant Pepper is a stupefying collage of music, words, background noises, cryptic utterances, orchestral effects, hallucinogenic bells, farmyard sounds, dream sequences, social observations, and apocalyptic vision, all masterfully blended together on a four-track tape machine over nine agonizing and expensive months. Their music was beginning to be more philosophical, with a deep, inner, more secret meaning. After it was known that they took drugs, references to drugs were seen in many songs. The "help" in Ringo's "A Little Help From My Friends" was said to have meant pot. The songs were poetic, mystical; they emerged from a self-contained world of bizarre carnival colors; they spoke in a language and a musical idiom all their own.

B.   Before the Civil War, minstrelsy spread quickly across America. Americans all over the country enjoyed minstrelsy because it reflected something of their own point of view. For instance, Negro plantation hands, played usually by white actors in blackface, were portrayed as devil-may-care outcasts and minstrelmen played them with an air of comic triumph, irreverent wisdom, and an underlying note of rebellion, which had a special appeal to citizens of a young country. Minstrelsy was ironically the beginning of black involvement in the American theater. The American people learned to identify with certain aspects of the black people. The Negro became a sympathetic symbol for a pioneer people who required resilience as a prime trait.

PARAPHRASING

Some passages are worth quoting for the sake of their precise or elegant style or their distinguished author. But many sources that you will use in your college essays are written in more ordinary language. Indeed, some of your sources may be written in the jargon of an academic discipline or the bureau-cratic prose of a government agency. (There are few examples of jargon in this book; however, look at Excerpt 3 on p. 114 to sample the kind of prose you probably would not want to quote.) You will gain nothing by quoting such ma-terial; rather, you have a positive duty to help your readers by providing them with a clear paraphrase.

> *Paraphrase is the point-by-point recapitulation of another person's ideas, expressed in your own words.*

Through paraphrase, you are both informing your reader and proving that you understand what you are writing about. When you paraphrase, you retain everything about the original writing but the words. The primary differences between *paraphrase* and *summary* are length and emphasis. See the box on p. 105 for a comparison of paraphrase and summary.

Using Paraphrase in Your Essays

Your paraphrased explanations help your readers to gain a detailed under-standing of sources that they may never have read and, indirectly, to accept your own thesis as valid. There are two major reasons for using paraphrase in your essays.

1. Use paraphrase to present ideas or evidence whenever there is no special reason for using a direct quotation.

Many of your sources will not have sufficient authority or a distinctive enough style to justify your quoting their words. The following illustration, taken from a *New York Times* article, paraphrases a report written by an anony-mous group of "municipal auditors" whose writing merits only paraphrase, not quotation:

A city warehouse in Middle Village, Queens, stocked with such things as snow shovels, light bulbs, sponges, waxed paper, laundry soap and tinned herring, has been found to be vastly overstocked with some items and lacking in others. Munic-ipal auditors, in a report issued yesterday, said that security was fine and that the warehouse was quicker in delivering goods to city agencies than it was when the auditors made their last check, in August, 1976. But in one corner of the ware-house, they said, nearly 59,000 paper binders, the 8½-by-11 size, are gathering dust, enough to meet the city's needs for nearly seven years. Nearby, there is a 10½-year supply of cotton coveralls.

Both the overstock and shortages cost the city money, the auditors said. They estimated that by reducing warehouse inventories, the city could save $1.4 million, plus $112,000 in interest. . . .

2. Use paraphrase to give your readers an accurate and comprehensive account of ideas taken from a source—ideas that you intend to explain, interpret, or disagree with in your essay.

The first illustration comes from a *Times* article about the data and photographs provided by *Voyager 2* as it explored the farthest reaches of the solar system. In summarizing a press conference, the article paraphrases various scientists' descriptions of what *Voyager* had achieved during its journey near Triton, one of the moons of the planet Neptune. Note the limited use of carefully selected quotations within the paraphrase.

> Out of the fissures [on Triton], roughly analogous to faults in the Earth's crust, flowed mushy ice. There was no eruption in the sense of the usual terrestrial volcanism or the geyser-like activity discovered on Io, one of Jupiter's moons. It was more of an extrusion through cracks in the surface ice.
>
> Although scientists classify such a process as volcanism, Dr. Miner said it could better be described as a "slow-flow volcanic activity." A somewhat comparable process, he said, seemed to have shaped some of the surface features of Ariel, one of the moons of Uranus.
>
> Dr. Soderblom said Triton's surface appeared to be geologically young or "millions to hundreds of millions of years old." The absence of many impact craters was the main evidence for the relatively recent resurfacing of the terrain with new ice.

The next example shows how paraphrase can be used more briefly, to present another writer's point of view as the basis for discussion. Again, the writer of this description of a conference on nuclear deterrence has reserved quotation to express the precise point of potential dispute:

> Scientists engaged in research on the effects of nuclear war may be "wasting their time" studying a phenomenon that is far less dangerous than the natural explosions that have periodically produced widespread extinctions of plant and animal life in the past, a University of Chicago scientist said last week. Joseph V. Smith, a professor of geophysical sciences, told a conference on nuclear deterrence here that such natural catastrophes as exploding volcanoes, violent earthquakes, and collisions with comets or asteroids could produce more immediate and destructive explosions than any nuclear war.

Using Paraphrase as Preparation for Reading and Writing Essays

Paraphrase is sometimes undertaken as *an end in itself*. Paraphrasing difficult passages can help you to improve your understanding of a complex essay or chapter. When you grasp an essay at first reading, when its ideas are clearly stated in familiar terms, then you can be satisfied with annotating it or writing a brief outline or summary. But when you find an essay hard to understand, writing down each sentence in your own words forces you to stop and make sense of what you have read, so that you can succeed in working out ideas that at first seem beyond your comprehension.

Paraphrase can also be *a means to an end*, a preparation for writing an essay of your own. Assume that you are taking notes for an essay based on one or more sources. If you write down nothing but exact quotations, you will not only be doing a good deal of unnecessary transcription, but you may also be tempted to quote excessively in your essay.

> *When you take notes, paraphrase; quote only when recording phrases or sentences that, in your opinion, merit quotation.*

All academic writers are expected to be scrupulously accurate in their presentation of material taken from their sources. All quotable phrases and sentences should be transcribed accurately in your notes, with quotation marks clearly separating the paraphrase from the quotation.

Comparing Paraphrase and Outline

Paraphrase

- Presents ideas in the same order as the original

- Doesn't emphasize any one point more than another (unless the original writer does so)

- Suggests the scope and reasoning of the original passage, and specifies the main ideas

- Can be as long as necessary—as long as the original text or even longer if there are complex ideas to be explained; *it is a full presentation of the text.*

Outline

- Presents ideas in the same order as the original

- Doesn't emphasize any one point more than another (unless the original writer does so)

- Lists the main ideas, but doesn't attempt to present all the reasoning leading up to them

- Can be as short and condensed as you wish, provided that you include all the main ideas; *it is a memorandum for future reference.*

Writing a Good Paraphrase

In a good paraphrase, the sentences and the vocabulary do not duplicate those of the original. *You cannot merely substitute synonyms for key words and leave the sentences otherwise unchanged; that is plagiarism in spirit, if not in fact;* nor does word-for-word substitution really demonstrate that you have understood the ideas.

The level of abstraction within your paraphrase should resemble that of the original: It should be neither more general nor more specific. If you do not understand a sentence, do not try to guess or cover it up with a vague phrase that slides over the idea. Instead:

- Look up difficult words.
- Think of what they mean and how they are used together.
- Consider how the sentences are formed and how they fit into the context of the entire paragraph.
- Then, to test your understanding, write it all out.

Remember that a good paraphrase makes sense by itself; it is coherent and readable, without requiring reference to the original essay.

Guidelines for a Successful Paraphrase

- A paraphrase must be accurate.
- A paraphrase must be complete.
- A paraphrase must be written in your own voice.
- A paraphrase must make sense by itself.

Free Paraphrase

When a paraphrase moves completely away from the words and sentence structure of the original text and presents ideas in the paraphraser's own style and idiom, then it is said to be "free." A free paraphrase is not only challenging to write but can be as interesting to read as the original—provided that the substance of the source has not been altered, disguised, or substantially condensed. Because a free paraphrase can summarize repetitious parts of the original text, it may be somewhat briefer than the original, but it will present ideas in much the same order.

Here, side by side with the original, is a free paraphrase of an excerpt from Machiavelli's *The Prince.* This passage exemplifies the kind of text—very famous, very difficult—that really benefits from a comprehensive paraphrase. *The Prince* was written in 1513. Even though the translation from the Italian used here was revised in this century, the paraphraser has to bridge a tremendous gap in time and in style to present Machiavelli in an idiom suitable for modern readers.

Original Version	*Paraphrase*
It is not, therefore, necessary for a prince to have [good faith and integrity], but it is very necessary to seem to have them. I would even be bold to say that to possess them and always to observe them is dangerous, but to appear to possess them is useful. Thus it is well to seem merciful,	It is more important for a ruler to give the impression of goodness than to be good. In fact, real goodness can be a liability, but the pretense is always very effective. It is all very well to be virtuous, but it is vital to be able to shift in the other

(continued)

Original Version (continued)

faithful, humane, sincere, religious, and also to be so; but you must have the mind so disposed that when it is needful to be otherwise you may be able to change to the opposite qualities. And it must be understood that a prince, and especially a new prince, cannot observe all those things which are considered good in men, being often obliged, in order to maintain the state, to act against faith, against charity, against humanity, and against religion. And therefore, he must have a mind disposed to adapt itself according to the wind, and as the variations of fortune dictate, and . . . not deviate from what is good, if possible, but be able to do evil if constrained.

A prince must take great care that nothing goes out of his mouth which is not full of the above-mentioned five qualities, and to see and hear him, he should seem to be all mercy, faith, integrity, humanity, and religion. . . . Everyone sees what you appear to be, few feel what you are, and those few will not dare to oppose themselves to the many, who have the majesty of the state to defend them; and in the actions of men, and especially of princes, from which there is no appeal, the end justifies the means. Let a prince therefore aim at conquering and maintaining the state, and the means will always be judged honorable and praised by every one, for the vulgar are always taken by appearances and the issue of the event; and the world consists only of the vulgar, and the few who are not vulgar are isolated when the many have a rallying point in the prince.

Paraphrase (continued)

direction whenever circumstances require it. After all, rulers, especially recently elevated ones, have a duty to perform which may absolutely require them to act against the dictates of faith and compassion and kindness. One must act as circumstances require and, while it's good to be virtuous if you can, it's better to be bad if you must.

In public, however, the ruler should appear to be entirely virtuous, and if his pretense is successful with the majority of people, then those who do see through the act will be outnumbered and impotent, especially since the ruler has the authority of government on his side. In the case of rulers, even more than for most men, "the end justifies the means." If the ruler is able to assume power and administer it successfully, his methods will always be judged proper and satisfactory; for the common people will accept the pretense of virtue and the reality of success, and the astute will find no one is listening to their warnings.

Paraphrase and Summary

To clarify the difference between paraphrase and summary, here is a paragraph that *summarizes* the excerpt from *The Prince.*

> According to Machiavelli, perpetuating power is a more important goal for a ruler than achieving personal goodness or integrity. Although he should act virtuously if he can, and always appear to do so, it is more important for him to adapt quickly to changing circumstances. The masses will be so swayed by his pretended virtue and by his success that any opposition will be ineffective. The wise ruler's maxim is that "the end justifies the means."

To make the distinction between summary and paraphrase entirely clear, here is a recapitulation of the guidelines for writing a brief summary:

1. *A summary is comprehensive.* Like the paraphrase, the summary of *The Prince* says more than "the end justifies the means." While that is probably the most important idea in the passage, it does not by itself convey Machiavelli's full meaning. For one thing, it contains no reference at all to princes and how they should rule—and that, after all, is Machiavelli's subject.

2. *A summary is concise.* It should say exactly as much as you need—and no more. The summary of *The Prince* is considerably shorter than the paraphrase.

3. *A summary is coherent.* The ideas are not presented in the same sequence as that of the original passage, as they are in the paraphrase; nor are the language and tone at all reminiscent of the original. Rather, the summary includes only the passage's most important points, linking them together in a unified paragraph.

Comparing Paraphrase and Summary

Paraphrase

- Reports your understanding to your reader
- Records a relatively short passage
- Records every point in the passage
- Records these points consecutively
- Includes no interpretation

Summary

- Reports your understanding to your reader
- Records a passage of any length
- Selects and condenses, recording only the main ideas
- Changes the order of ideas when necessary
- Explains and (if the writer wishes) interprets

4. *A summary is independent.* What is most striking about the summary, compared with the paraphrase, is the writer's attitude toward the original text. While the paraphraser has to follow closely Machiavelli's ideas and point of view, the summarizer does not. Characteristically, Machiavelli's name is cited in the summary, calling attention to the fact that it is based on another person's ideas.

Either summary or paraphrase should enable you to refer to this passage quite easily in an essay. Which you would choose to use depends on your topic, on the way you are developing your essay, and on the extent to which you wish to discuss Machiavelli.

- In an essay citing Machiavelli as only one among many political theorists, you might use the brief four-sentence summary; then you might briefly comment on Machiavelli's ideas before going on to summarize (and perhaps compare them with) another writer's theories.

- In an essay about a contemporary politician, you might analyze the way in which your subject does or does not carry out Machiavelli's strategies; then you probably would want to familiarize your readers with *The Prince* in some detail through paraphrase. You might include the full paraphrase, interspersed, perhaps, with an analysis of your present-day "prince."

Writing an Accurate Paraphrase

The basic purpose of paraphrase is to present the main ideas contained in the original text. When paraphrase fails to convey the substance of the source, there are three possible explanations:

1. *Misreading:* The writer genuinely misunderstood the text.
2. *Projecting:* The writer insisted on reading his or her own ideas into the text.
3. *Guessing:* The writer had a spark of understanding and constructed a paraphrase centered around that spark, but ignored too much of the original text.

Read Christopher Lasch's analysis of the changing role of the child in family life. Then examine each of the three paraphrases that follow, deciding whether it conveys Lasch's principal ideas and, if not, why it has gone astray. Compare your reactions with the analysis that follows each paraphrase.

Original

The family by its very nature is a means of raising children, but this fact should not blind us to the important change that occurred when child-rearing ceased to be simply one of many activities and became the central concern—one is tempted to say the central obsession—of family life. This development had to wait for the recognition of the child as a distinctive kind of person, more impressionable and hence more vulnerable than adults, to be treated in a special manner befitting his peculiar requirements. Again, we take these things for granted and find it hard to imagine anything else. Earlier, children had been clothed, fed, spoken to, and educated as little adults; more specifically, as servants, the difference between childhood and servitude having been remarkably obscure throughout much of Western history. . . . It was only in the seventeenth century in certain classes that childhood came to be seen as a special category of experience. When that happened, people recognized the enormous formative influence of family life, and the family became above all an agency for building character, for consciously and deliberately forming the child from birth to adulthood.

"Divorce and the Family in America," *Atlantic Monthly*

Paraphrase A

The average family wants to raise children with a good education and to encourage, for example, the ability to read and write well. They must be taught to practice and learn on their own. Children can be treated well without being pampered. They must be treated as adults as they get older and experience more of life. A parent must build character and the feeling of independence in a child. No longer should children be treated as kids or servants, for that can cause conflict in a family relationship.

This paraphrase has very little in common with the original passage. True, it is about child-rearing, but the writer chooses to give advice to parents, rather than present the contrast between early and modern attitudes toward children, as Lasch does. Since the only clear connection between Lasch and this paragraph is the reference to servants, the writer was probably confused by the passage, and (instead of slowing down the process and paraphrasing it sentence by sentence) guessed—mistakenly—at its meaning. There is also some projection of the writer's ideas about family life. Notice how assertive the tone is; the writer seems to be admonishing parents rather than presenting Lasch's detached analysis.

Paraphrase B

When two people get married, they usually produce a child. They get married because they want a family. Raising a family is now different from the way it used to be. The child is looked upon as a human being, with feelings and thoughts of his own. Centuries ago, children were treated like robots, little more than hired help. Now, children are seen as people who need a strong, dependable family background to grow into persons of good character. Parents are needed to get children ready to be the adults of tomorrow.

This paragraph also seems to combine guessing (beginning) and projection (end). The middle sentences do present Lasch's basic point, but the beginning and the end move so far away from the main ideas that the paraphrase as a whole does not bear much resemblance to the original text. It also includes an exaggeration: are servants "robots"?

Paraphrase C

> Though the family has always been an important institution, its child-rearing function has only in recent centuries become its most important activity. This change has resulted from the relatively new idea that children have a special, unique personality. In the past, there was little difference seen between childhood and adulthood. But today people realize the importance of family life, especially the family unit as a means of molding the personalities of children from childhood to adulthood.

Although this paraphrase is certainly the most accurate of the three, it is too brief to be a complete paraphrase. In fact, the writer seems to be summarizing, not paraphrasing. Lasch's main idea is there, but the following points are missing:

1. There is a tremendous difference between pre-seventeenth-century and twentieth-century perceptions of childhood.
2. Before the seventeenth century, it was difficult to distinguish between the status and treatment of children and that of servants.
3. Child-rearing has now become of overriding ("obsessive") importance to the family.
4. Children are different from adults in that they are less hardened and less experienced.

The author of Paraphrase C has done a thorough job of the beginning and the end of Lasch's passage, and evidently left the middle to take care of itself. But a paraphrase cannot be considered a reliable "translation" of the original text unless all the supporting ideas are given appropriate emphasis. The omission of Point 2 is particularly important.

Here is a more comprehensive paraphrase of the passage:

> Though the family has always been the institution responsible for bringing up children, only in recent times has its child-raising function become the family's overriding purpose and its reason for being. This striking shift to the child-centered family has resulted from the gradual realization that children have a special, unique personality, easy to influence and easy to hurt, and that they must be treated accordingly. Special treatment for children is the norm in our time; but hundreds of years ago, people saw little or no difference between childhood and adulthood, and, in fact, the child's role in the family resembled that of a servant. It was not until the seventeenth century that people began to regard childhood as a distinctive stage of growth. That recognition led them to understand what a powerful influence the family environment must have on the child and to define "family" as the chief instrument for molding the child's personality and moral attitudes.

EXERCISE 11: IDENTIFYING A GOOD PARAPHRASE

The next passage is followed by a group of paraphrases. Examine each one and identify those that conform to the guidelines for paraphrasing. Ask yourself whether the paraphrase contains any point that is not in the original passage and whether the key points of the original are *all* clearly presented in the paraphrase.

from MULTICULTURALISM'S SILENT PARTNER
David Rieff

One of the central tenets [of multiculturalism] is to undermine the idea of the masterpiece—of the criterion of quality—as anti-democratic. For the multicultur- alist, notions such as "quality" are tainted; their real purpose is to preserve the privileges of a dominant group: in the American context, dead white males. And the multiculturalists are in command—sort of—of a couple of truths: Western cul- ture has excluded many things; art in the traditional sense is anti-egalitarian, in that it demands that people judge a given work not only subjectively but objectively su- perior to another. It is the innately hierarchical nature of art, or even, as they used to say, art appreciation, that sets the multiculturalists' teeth on edge—they are sus- picious of hierarchy. For, as they rightly surmise, if there is hierarchy how can there be liberation?

So far, so good, radically speaking. The mistake the multiculturalists make is in imagining that their efforts are in some crucial way bound to undermine the funda- mental interests of capitalism. The contrary is surely closer to the truth: the multi- culturalist mode is what any smart businessman would prefer. For if all art is deemed as good as all other art, and, for that matter, if the point of art is not great- ness but the production of works of art that reflect the culture and aspirations of various ethnic, sexual, or racial subgroups within a society, then one is in a position to increase supply almost at will in order to meet increases in demand. Instead of being a rare and costly thing, culture becomes simultaneously a product, like a car—something that can be made new every few years—and an abundant resource, like, well, people. The result is that the consumption of culture can increasingly come to resemble the consumption of goods.

1. Multiculturalism is opposed to the creation of great works of art because they are usually created by the kind of people, like dead white males, who dominate society. In some ways, the multiculturalists are right. The old- fashioned view of art means that some works are better than others, which multiculturalists don't like since that leads to cultural oppression.

    The multicultural view of art is good for business. If one work of art is as good as the next, then they're interchangeable, and you can sell more of them. That way, we can buy and sell culture, just like anything else we buy and sell.

2. Multiculturalists have very democratic ideas about art, and they don't like the idea of high quality art, which is too exclusive for them. It is better that people look at art objectively, not subjectively, and it is better to lower standards and not rank one picture against another. Dividing culture into better or worse art isn't liberating.

   The multiculturalist point of view is opposed to capitalism, but they're wrong. A good businessman can make use of multicultural ideas. Art is all alike, whatever you produce, especially if it reflects racial or sexual segments of society. The more you make, the more you sell. So, culture becomes like anything else that's for sale.

3. Because multiculturalists believe strongly in equality and reject the authority of any single powerful group, they are opposed to applying fixed standards to judging works of art. In America, what's called a great work of art conforms to and perpetuates the standards of the ruling group of white males, not the feelings of those who look at the picture. That cultural system is based on status, with those at the top as oppressors, determining what everyone else thinks.

   In their enthusiasm, multiculturalists mistakenly conclude that cultural equality would chip away at this country's business ethic. In actuality, doing away with a single standard for distinguishing between good art and bad art and substituting art that satisfies the needs of society's various subcultures makes it possible for businesses to order pictures by the yard and to adjust inventory based on market research. Without the idea of quality, art becomes a consumable commodity like anything else.

Paraphrasing a Difficult Text

Since translating another writer's idiom into your own can be difficult, a paraphrase is often written in two stages.

- In your first version, you work out a *word-for-word substitution,* staying close to the sentence structure of the original, as if, indeed, you are writing a translation. This is the *literal paraphrase.*

- In your second version, you work from your own literal paraphrase, turning it into a *free paraphrase* by reconstructing and rephrasing the sentences to make them more natural and more characteristic of *your own writing style.*

Writing a Literal Paraphrase

To write a paraphrase that is faithful to the original text is impossible if you are uncertain of the meaning of any of the words. To write a literal paraphrase of a difficult passage:

- Use a dictionary, especially if the passage contains obsolete or archaic language.
- Write down a few possible synonyms for each difficult word, making sure that you understand the connotations of each synonym.
- Choose the substitute that best fits the context of your literal paraphrase.

Too often, the writer of a paraphrase forgets that there *is* a choice and quickly substitutes the first synonym in the dictionary. Even when appropriate synonyms have been carefully chosen, the literal paraphrase can look peculiar and sound dreadful. While the old sentence structure has been retained, the key words have been yanked out and new ones plugged in.

To illustrate the pitfalls of this process, here is a short excerpt from Francis Bacon's essay "Of Marriage and Single Life," written around 1600. Some of the phrasing and word combinations are archaic and may sound unnatural, but nothing in the passage is too difficult for modern understanding *if* the sentences are read slowly and carefully.

> He that hath wife and children hath given hostages to fortune; for they are impediments to great enterprises, either of virtue or mischief. Certainly, the best works and of greatest merit for the public have proceeded from the unmarried or childless men: which both in affection and means have endowed the public.

The passage's main idea is not too difficult to establish: *Unmarried men, without the burden of a family, can afford to contribute to the public good.* But by now you must realize that such a brief summary is not the same as a paraphrase, for it does not fully present Bacon's reasoning.

Paraphrase A

He who has a wife and children has <u>bestowed</u> <u>prisoners</u> to <u>riches</u>; for they are <u>defects</u> in huge <u>business</u> <u>organizations</u> either for <u>morality</u> or <u>damage</u>.

Paraphrase B

He who has a wife and children has <u>given</u> a <u>pledge</u> to <u>destiny</u>; for they are <u>hindrances</u> to large <u>endeavor</u>, either for <u>good</u> or for <u>ill</u>.

Neither sentence sounds very normal or very clear; but the second has potential, while the first makes no sense. Yet, in *both* cases, the inserted words *are* synonyms for the original vocabulary. In Paraphrase A the words do not fit Bacon's context; in Paraphrase B they do. For example, it is misleading to choose "business organizations" as a synonym for "enterprises," since the passage doesn't actually concern business, but refers to any sort of undertaking requiring freedom from responsibility. "Impediment" can mean either "defect" (as in speech impediment) or "hindrance" (as in impediment to learning); but—again, given the context—it is the latter meaning that Bacon has in mind. You will choose the correct connotation or nuance only if you think carefully about the synonyms and use your judgment: the process cannot be hurried.

A phrase like "hostage to fortune" offers special difficulty, since it is a powerful image expressing a highly abstract idea. No paraphraser can improve on the original wording or even find an equivalent phrase. However, expressing the idea is useful: a bargain made with life—the renunciation of future independent action in exchange for a family. Wife and children become a kind of bond ("hostage") to ensure one's future social conformity. The aptness and singularity of Bacon's original phrase are measured by the difficulty of paraphrasing three words in less than two sentences!

Writing a Free Version of the Literal Paraphrase

Correct though the synonyms may be, the passage from Bacon cannot be left as it is in Paraphrase B, for no reader could readily understand this stilted, artificial sentence. It is necessary to rephrase the paraphrase, ensuring that the meaning of the words is retained, but making the sentence sound more natural. The first attempt at "freeing up" the paraphrase stays as close as possible to the literal version, leaving everything in the same sequence, but using a more modern idiom:

Paraphrase C

Married men with children are hindered from embarking on any important undertaking, good or bad. Indeed, unmarried and childless men are the ones who have done the most for society and have dedicated their love and their money to the public good.

The second sentence (which is simpler to paraphrase than the first) has been inverted here, but the paraphrase is still a point-by-point recapitulation of Bacon. Paraphrase C is acceptable, but can be improved, both to clarify Bacon's meaning and to introduce a more personal voice. What exactly *are* these unmarried men dedicating to the public good? "Affection and means." And what is the modern equivalent of means? Money? Effort? Time? Energy?

Paraphrase D

A man with a family has obligations that prevent him from devoting himself to any activity that pleases him. On the other hand, a single man or a man without children has a greater opportunity to be a philanthropist. That's why most great contributions of energy and resources to the good of society are made by single men.

The writer of Paraphrase D has not supplied a synonym for "affection," assuming perhaps that the expenditure of energy and resources result from interest and concern; affection is almost too weak a motivation for the philanthropist as he is described here.

Paraphrase E

The responsibility of a wife and children prevents a man from taking risks with his money, time, and energy. The greatest social benefactors have been men who have adopted the public as their family.

The second sentence here is the only one of the five versions that approaches Bacon's economy of style. "Adopted the public" is not quite the same as "endowed the public" with one's "affection and means"; but nevertheless, this paraphrase is successful because it speaks for itself. It has a life and an importance of its own, independent of Bacon's original passage, yet it makes the same point that Bacon does.

Guidelines for Paraphrasing a Difficult Passage

1. Look up in a dictionary the meanings of all the words of which you are uncertain. Pay special attention to the difficult words, considering the context of the whole passage.

2. Write a literal paraphrase of each passage by substituting appropriate synonyms within the original sentence structure.

3. Revise your literal paraphrase, keeping roughly to the same length and number of sentences as the original, but using your own sentence style and phrasing throughout. You may prefer to put the original passage aside at this point, and work entirely from your own version.

4. Read your free paraphrase aloud to make sure that it makes sense.

ASSIGNMENT 3: PARAPHRASING A DIFFICULT PASSAGE

Paraphrase one of the following passages, using the guidelines in the box above. (Your instructor may assign a specific paragraph for the entire class to paraphrase; you may be asked to work together with one or more of your classmates.)

1. The death of the cowboy as a viable persona for Hollywood's A-list actors means there is no archetype left that allows latter-day Coopers, Waynes and Fondas to act with exemplary courage and yet remain regular guys. Of late, any actor wanting to be a hero has, more often than not, found himself playing second fiddle to a piece of technology in a distant precinct of space or the future. Acts of great bravery have become more and more divorced from common experience. Everyday valor, in which an average Joe armed with little more than his guts and wits does battle with an intractable foe, is in danger of becoming a thing of the past.

STEPHEN AMIDON, from "Back to the Front"

2. There used to be a social modification which, excused by the erroneous belief that men were naturally more polygamous than women, gave the sort of glancing blow that is really an approving pat to men who broke out of monogamy but seriously and cruelly disapproved of women who did. The injustice of this "double standard" is now pretty clear to everyone, and in its place we have introduced a legal modification of monogamy. Divorce is a device which makes polygamy permissible, but only nonsimultaneous polygamy. In practice, even this is modified. The law sometimes insists that a divorcée remain a man's wife economically even though she is no longer so in name or in bed. The result is, just as in Moslem countries where the number of wives a man may legally have simultaneously is often whittled down in practice to the number he can support, so in Europe and the United States, under our modified monogamy, the number of ex-wives a man may legally have simultaneously is often limited to the number of those he can support.

BRIGID BROPHY, from "Monogamy"

3. It is somewhat ironic to note that grading *systems* evolved in part because of [problems in evaluating performance]. In situations where reward and recognition often depended more on who you knew than on what you knew, and lineage was more important than ability, the cause of justice seemed to demand a method whereby the individual could demonstrate specific abilities on the basis of objective criteria. This led to the establishment of specific standards and public criteria as ways of reducing prejudicial treatment and, in cases where appropriate standards could not be specified in advance, to the normal curve system of establishing levels on the basis of group performance. The imperfect achievement of the goals of such systems in no way negates the importance of the underlying purposes.

WAYNE MOELLENBERG, from "To Grade or
Not to Grade—Is That the Question?"

4. Work is not simply a way to make a living and support one's family. It also constitutes a framework for daily behavior and patterns of interaction because it imposes disciplines and regularities. Thus, in the absence of regular employment,

a person lacks not only a place in which to work and the receipt of regular income but also a coherent organization of the present—that is, a system of concrete expectations and goals. Regular employment provides the anchor for the spatial and temporal aspects of daily life. It determines where you are going to be and when you are going to be there. In the absence of regular employment, life, including family life, becomes less coherent. Persistent unemployment and irregular employment hinder rational planning in daily life, the necessary condition of adaptation to an industrial economy.

WILLIAM JULIUS WILSON, from *When Work Disappears*

INCORPORATING PARAPHRASE INTO YOUR ESSAY

The paraphrased ideas of other writers should never take control of your essay, but should always be subordinate to *your* ideas. When you insert a paraphrased sentence or a brief paraphrased passage (rather than a quotation) into one of your paragraphs, you minimize the risk that the source material will dominate your writing.

Most academic writers rely on a combination of quotation, paraphrase, and summary to present their sources.

To illustrate the way in which these three techniques of presentation can be successfully combined, here is an extract from an article by Conor Cruise O'Brien that depends on a careful mixture of paraphrase, summary, and quotation. In "Violence—And Two Schools of Thought," O'Brien gives an account of a medical conference concerned with the origins of violence. Specifically, he undertakes to present and (at the end) comment on the ideas of two speakers at the conference.

VIOLENCE—AND TWO SCHOOLS OF THOUGHT*
Conor Cruise O'Brien

Summary   The opening speakers were fairly representative of the main   I
schools of thought which almost always declare themselves when
violence is discussed. The first school sees a propensity to aggression as biological but capable of being socially conditioned into patterns of acceptable behavior. The second sees it as essentially created by social conditions and therefore capable of being removed by benign social change.

*In its original format in *The Observer,* the article's paragraphing, in accordance with usual journalistic practice, occurs with distracting frequency; the number of paragraphs has been reduced here, without any alteration of the text.

Quotation   The first speaker held that violence was "a bio-social phenome-   2
non." He rejected the notion that human beings were blank paper
"on which the environment can write whatever it likes." He de-

Paraphrase   scribed how a puppy could be conditioned to choose a dog food it
did not like and to reject one it did like. This was the creation of
conscience in the puppy. It was done by mild punishment. If human
beings were acting more aggressively and anti-socially, despite the
advent of better social conditions and better housing, this might be
because permissiveness, in school and home, had checked the process of social conditioning, and therefore of conscience-building. He
favored the reinstatement of conscience-building, through the use

Quotation   of mild punishment and token rewards. "We cannot eliminate violence," he said, "but we can do a great deal to reduce it."

Summary   The second speaker thought that violence was the result of stress;   3
in almost all the examples he cited it was stress from overcrowding.
The behavior of apes and monkeys in zoos was "totally different" from
the way they behaved in "the completely relaxed conditions in the

Paraphase/ Quotation   wild." In crowded zoos the most aggressive males became leaders
and a general reign of terror set in; in the relaxed wild, on the other
hand, the least aggressive males ruled benevolently. Space was all: "If

Paraphase/ Quotation   we could eliminate population pressures, violence would vanish."

Summary   The student [reacting to the argument of the two speakers] pre-   4
ferred the second speaker. He [the second speaker] spoke with ebullient confidence, fast but clear, and at one point ran across the vast
platform, in a lively imitation of the behavior of a charging ape. Also,
his message was simple and hopeful. Speaker one, in contrast, looked
sad, and his message sounded faintly sinister. Such impressions,

Author's Comment   rather than the weight of argument, determine the reception of papers read in such circumstances.

Summary/ Paraphase   Nonetheless, a student queried speaker two's "relaxed wild." He   5
seemed to recall a case in which a troop of chimpanzees had com-
pletely wiped out another troop. The speaker was glad the student
had raised that question because it proved the point. You see, where
that had occurred, there had been an overcrowding in the jungle,
just as happens in zoos, and this was a response to overcrowding.
Conditions in the wild, it seems, are not always "completely relaxed." And when they attain that attributed condition—through

Author's Comment   the absence of overcrowding—this surely has to be due to the "natural controls," including the predators, whose attentions can hardly
be all that relaxing, or, indeed, all that demonstrative of the validity
of the proposition that violence is not a part of nature. Speaker two
did not allude to predators. Nonetheless, they are still around, on
two legs as well as on four.

Selecting Quotations When You Paraphrase

Although we do not have the texts of the original papers given at the conference to compare with O'Brien's description, this article seems to present a clear and comprehensive account of a complex discussion. In the first paragraph, O'Brien uses brief summaries to help us distinguish between the two speakers; next, he provides us with two separate, noncommittal descriptions of the two main points of view.

The ratio of quotation to paraphrase to summary works very effectively. O'Brien quotes for two reasons: *aptness of expression* and *the desire to distance himself from the statement.* For example, he chooses to quote the vivid image of the blank paper "on which the environment can write whatever it likes." And he also selects points for quotation that he regards as open to dispute—"totally different"; "completely relaxed"; "violence would vanish." Such strong or sweeping statements are often quoted so that writers can disassociate themselves from the implications of their source material; this way, they cannot be accused of either toning down or exaggerating the meaning in their paraphrases.

Reasons to Use Quotation

- You can find no words to convey the economy and aptness of phrasing of the original text.

- A paraphrase might alter the statement's meaning.

- A paraphrase would not clearly distinguish between your views and the author's.

Avoiding Plagiarism: Citing Your Paraphrased Sources

The one possible source of confusion in O'Brien's article occurs when he begins his own commentary. In the last two paragraphs, it is not always easy to determine where O'Brien's paraphrase of the speakers' ideas ends and his own opinions begin. In Paragraph 4, his description of the student's reactions to the two speakers appears objective. At the end of the paragraph, however, we learn that O'Brien is scornful of the criteria that the student is using to evaluate these ideas. But at first we cannot be sure whether O'Brien is describing the *student's observation* or giving *his own account* of the speaker's platform maneuvers. It would be clearer to us if the sentence began: "According to the responding student, the second speaker spoke with ebullient confidence. . . ." Similarly, the last sentence of Paragraph 4 is undoubtedly O'Brien's opinion, yet there is nothing to indicate the transition from the student to O'Brien as the source of commentary.

This *confusion of point of view* is especially deceptive in Paragraph 5 as O'Brien moves from his paraphrased and neutral account of the dialogue between student and speaker to his own opinion that certain predators influence behavior in civilization as well as in the wild. It takes two readings to notice the point at which O'Brien is no longer paraphrasing but beginning to speak in his own voice. Such confusions could have been clarified by inserting citations—the name of the source or an appropriate pronoun—in the appropriate places.

In academic writing the clear acknowledgment of the source is not merely a matter of courtesy or clarity; it is an assurance of the writer's honesty.

When you paraphrase another person's ideas, you must cite the author's name, as you do when you quote, or else risk being charged with plagiarism. Borrowing ideas is just as much theft as borrowing words.

You omit the quotation marks when you paraphrase, but you must not omit the citation. Of course, the citation of the name should be smoothly integrated into your sentence, following the guidelines used for citation of quotations. The source's name need not appear at the beginning of the sentence, but it should signal the beginning of the paraphrase:

Not everyone enjoys working, but most people would agree with Jones's belief

that work is an essential experience of life.

The writer of the essay is responsible for the declaration that "not everyone enjoys working" and that most people would agree with Jones's views; but the belief that "work is an essential experience of life" is attributed to Jones. Here, the citation is well and unobtrusively placed; there are no quotation marks, so presumably Jones used a different wording.

Here, then, are additional guidelines for the proper citation of sources:

- When you *quote*, there can never be any doubt about where the borrowed material begins and where it ends: the quotation marks provide a clear indication of the boundaries.

- When you *paraphrase*, although the citation may signal the *beginning* of the source material, your reader may not be sure exactly where the paraphrase *ends*.

There is no easy method of indicating the termination of paraphrased material. (As you will see in Chapter 9, the author's name in parentheses works well if you are using that method of documentation.) It is possible to signal the end of a paraphrase simply by starting a new paragraph. However, you may need to incorporate more than one person's ideas into a single paragraph. *When you present several points of view in succession, be careful to acknowledge the change of source by citing names.*

In some kinds of essays, it may be appropriate to signal the shift from paraphrased material to your own opinions by using the first person. Instructors' attitudes toward the first person vary, but some find it acceptable to use "I" in certain kinds of writing as long as it is not inserted excessively or monotonously. A carefully placed "I" can leave your reader in no doubt as to whose voice is being heard. Make sure, however, that using "I" is consistent with the tone and point of view of your essay. If you are presenting sources through a narrative in which you otherwise remain in the background, the sudden appearance of "I" would mean a sharp break in the overall tone and would therefore be inappropriate.

EXERCISE 12: DISTINGUISHING BETWEEN QUOTATION, PARAPHRASE, SUMMARY, AND COMMENTARY

1. Read "A Prominent Scholar's Plan for the Inner Cities Draws Fire," by Chris Shea.
2. In the margin, indicate where the author uses quotation (Q), paraphrase (P), summary (S), and commentary (C).
3. In class discussion, be prepared to evaluate the use of quotation, paraphrase, and summary, and to indicate those places in the article where, in your opinion, one of the techniques is inappropriately or unnecessarily used, or where the transition from one technique to the other is not clearly identified.

A PROMINENT SCHOLAR'S PLAN FOR
THE INNER CITIES DRAWS FIRE

Chris Shea

William Julius Wilson, one of the country's most prominent experts on the problems of America's inner cities, came in for some tough criticism at the annual meeting of the American Sociological Association here last month.   1

His latest book, *When Work Disappears: The World of the New Urban Poor*, published last fall by Alfred A. Knopf, has been widely and respectfully reviewed. It is the broadest statement yet on America's social ills by the sociologist, who spent most of his career at the University of Chicago before moving to Harvard University last year.   2

But in a debate that drew a large crowd—about 400 people in a room intended for two-thirds that number—Dr. Wilson's proposals for helping cities were blasted by Douglas S. Massey, chairman of the University of Pennsylvania's sociology department.   3

Dr. Massey did not contest Dr. Wilson's observations about rising unemployment and poverty rates in Chicago ghettos. In some of the neighborhoods he describes in his book, only one in three people over the age of 16 has a job.   4

Instead, Dr. Massey took aim at Dr. Wilson's policy proposals, which emphasize strategies to help unskilled workers of all races rather than singling out black workers.   5

For example, he has proposed a program modeled on the New Deal's Works Progress Administration, which would give unemployed people such jobs as sweeping streets and picking up garbage.   6

Dr. Wilson argues that massive interventions to desegregate cities and expand affirmative action are impractical, given Americans' resistance to race-specific policies. At   7 the meeting, he said he hoped to galvanize "progressives" across racial lines with a race-blind vision of social justice.

But Dr. Massey said Dr. Wilson was using a double standard in evaluating the feasi-   8
bility of race-based and class-based solutions.

"In essence, Wilson argues that race-based remedies are a political loser," he said.   9
But a W. P. A.–style program is no less pie-in-the-sky, Dr. Massey said, given today's conservative climate.

And Dr. Wilson is dead wrong, he added, to think he can do an end-run around the   10
charged issue of race. "It will not be possible to deal with class-based divisions with-out addressing race-based issues with equal verve," he said. "Putting race on the back burner would leave the field open to those who would undermine the class-based strategies we all think we need, by manipulating racial attitudes that are still there."

Welfare is a race-neutral program, he pointed out. But editorials about black "wel-   11
fare queens," who were said to live largely off the dole, helped turn public sentiment against it.

Cynical conservative operatives could just as easily "racialize" a W. P. A.–style pro-   12
gram by caricaturing its beneficiaries as lazy black shirkers in do-nothing jobs, he said.

No solution to the problem of urban poverty, Dr. Massey said, can escape the need   13
for a dismantling of what he called "the system of *de facto* apartheid" in many cities.

In his response, Dr. Wilson shed his usual courtly demeanor. "Massey argues that I   14
have moved away from racial-specific policies," he said, his voice rising to a near shout. "*I do not.* I want to say that categorically: *I do not.*"

He said his proposals should be paired with affirmative-action policies that take   15
both class and race into account. And he said he had called for better enforcement of federal housing-discrimination laws. In a pointed allusion to his own political influence, he also noted that the Urban League, a national black civil-rights group, had embraced many of his race-neutral policies. "Now, more than ever, we need broader solutions than we have had in the past," he said.

In the current issue of *Contemporary Sociology*, Dr. Massey offers some criticisms of   16
Dr. Wilson's research that did not come up in the debate.

He calls Dr. Wilson's massive research on Chicago ghettos, known as the "Urban   17
Poverty and Family Life Study," "rather a disappointment," arguing that "despite the in-vestment of hundreds of thousands of research dollars," few resulting articles have ap-peared in refereed social-science journals. "The U. P. F. L. has simply not affected social science in a manner commensurate with its size and scope," he writes.

In a telephone interview, Dr. Wilson said that aside from his own book, which uses   18
the data, some 20 refereed journal articles and book chapters had emerged from the project, and more books—including one from Marta Tienda, a University of Chicago sociologist—are due soon.

After the debate, Dr. Massey said, "I keep pushing Wilson on the issue of race, and he   19
keeps moving slowly and grudgingly toward accepting it, but more in person than in print."

The audience seemed to agree that frontal attacks on both racial and class issues   20
are necessary, yet pessimism was the dominant mood at the meeting.

"This is rather depressing," one graduate student told the two professors. "It sounds like you are saying we need a sea change in public attitudes for anything to happen." Neither scholar disagreed.

21

PRESENTING SOURCES: A SUMMARY OF PRELIMINARY WRITING SKILLS

1. **Annotation: underlining the text and inserting marginal comments on the page.**

   The notes can explain points that are unclear, define difficult words, emphasize key ideas, point out connections to previous or subsequent paragraphs, or suggest the reader's own reactions to what is being discussed.

2. **Outlining: constructing a systematic list of ideas that reflects the basic structure of an essay or book, with major and minor points distributed on different levels.**

   Outlining is a reductive skill that presents the bones of a work, but little of its flesh or outward appearance. Outlining is especially useful for covering a long sequence of material containing ideas whose relationship is easy to grasp. Densely written passages that rely on frequent and subtle distinctions and dexterous use of language are not easily condensed into an outline.

3. **Paraphrasing: recapitulating, point by point, using your own words.**

   A paraphrase is a faithful and complete rendition of the original, following much the same order of ideas. Although full-length paraphrase is practical only with relatively brief passages, it is the most reliable way to make sense out of a difficult text. Paraphrasing a sentence or two, together with a citation of the author's name, is the best method of presenting another person's ideas within your own essay.

4. **Quotation: including another person's exact words within your own writing.**

   Although quotation requires the least amount of invention, it is the most technical of all these skills, demanding an understanding of conventional and complex punctuation. In your notes and in your essays, quotation should be a last resort. If the phrasing is unique, if the presentation is subtle, if the point at issue is easily misunderstood or hotly debated, quotation may be appropriate. When in doubt, paraphrase.

5. **Summary: condensing a paragraph or an essay or a chapter into a relatively brief presentation of the main ideas.**

   Unlike annotation, a summary should make sense as an independent, coherent piece of writing. Unlike paraphrase, a summary includes only main ideas. However, the summary should be complete in the sense that it provides a fair representation of the work and its parts. Summary is the all-purpose skill; it is neither crude nor overly detailed.

Part II

WRITING FROM SOURCES

The previous two chapters have described some basic ways to understand another writer's ideas and present them accurately and naturally, as part of your own writing. Until now, however, you have been working with forms of writing that are brief and limited—the sentence and the paragraph. Now you can use the skills that you practiced in Part I to develop your own ideas in a full-length essay based on sources.

When you write at length from sources, you must work with *two points of view—your own* and *those of the authors you're writing about.* You therefore have a dual responsibility: You must do justice to yourself by developing your own ideas, and you must do justice to each source by fairly representing its author's ideas. But blending the ideas of two or more people within the same essay can create confusion: Who should dominate? How much of yourself should you include? How much of your source? Moreover, in academic and professional writing you may have to consider a third voice—that of your teacher or supervisor, who may assign a topic or otherwise set limits and goals for your work.

Chapter 3 discusses two approaches to writing based on a single source. Each demonstrates a way to reconcile the competing influences on your writing and blend the voices that your reader ought to hear:

- You can distinguish between your source and yourself by writing about the two separately, first the source and then yourself, and, in the process, developing an argument that supports or refutes your source's thesis.

- You can use your source as the basis for the development of your own ideas by writing an essay on a similar or related topic.

In the end, *your voice should dominate.* It is you who will choose the thesis and control the essay's structure and direction; it is your understanding and judgment that will interpret the source materials for your reader. When you and your classmates are asked to write about the same reading, your teacher hopes to receive, not an identical set of essays, but rather a series of individual interpretations with a common starting point in the same source.

Combining your own ideas with those of others inevitably becomes more difficult when you begin to work with *a group of sources* and must represent several authors. This is the subject of Chapter 4. It is more than ever vital that your own voice dominate your essay and that you do not simply summarize first one source and then the next, without any perspective of your own.

Blending together a variety of sources is usually called *synthesis*. You try to look beyond each separate assertion and, instead, develop a broad generalization that will encompass your source material. Your own generalized conclusions become the basis for your essay's thesis and organization, while the ideas of your sources serve as the evidence that supports those conclusions.

Chapter 4 emphasizes the standard methods of presenting multiple sources:

- The analysis of each source in a search for common themes.
- The establishment of common denominators or categories that cut across the separate sources and provide the structure for your essay.
- The evaluation of each source's relative significance as you decide which to emphasize.
- The citation of references from several different sources in support of a single point.

These skills are closely related to some of the most common and useful strategies for constructing an essay: *definition, classification,* and *comparison.*

▪ 3 ▪

The Single-Source Essay

When you write from a source, you must understand another writer's ideas as thoroughly as you understand your own. The first step in carrying out the strategies described in this chapter is to *read carefully through the source essay*, using the skills for comprehension that you learned about in Chapters 1 and 2: annotation, outlining, paraphrase, and summary. Once you are able to explain to your reader what the source is all about, you can begin to plan your analysis and rebuttal of the author's ideas; or you can write your own essay on a similar topic.

STRATEGY ONE:
ARGUING AGAINST YOUR SOURCE

The simplest way to argue against someone else's ideas is *complete separation between your source and yourself*. The structure of your essay breaks into two parts, with the source's views presented first, and your own reactions given equal (or greater) space immediately afterward. Instead of treating the reading as evidence in support of your point of view and blending it with your own ideas, you write an essay that *first analyzes and then refutes your source's basic themes*. Look, for example, at Roger Sipher's "So That Nobody Has to Go to School If They Don't Want To."

SO THAT NOBODY HAS TO GO TO SCHOOL
IF THEY DON'T WANT TO
Roger Sipher

A decline in standardized test scores is but the most recent indicator that Amer-   1
ican education is in trouble.

One reason for the crisis is that present mandatory-attendance laws force many   2
to attend school who have no wish to be there. Such children have little desire to
learn and are so antagonistic to school that neither they nor more highly motivated
students receive the quality education that is the birthright of every American.

The solution to this problem is simple: Abolish compulsory-attendance laws and   3
allow only those who are committed to getting an education to attend.

This will not end public education. Contrary to conventional belief, legislators en-   4
acted compulsory-attendance laws to legalize what already existed. William Landes
and Lewis Solomon, economists, found little evidence that mandatory-attendance laws
increased the number of children in school. They found, too, that school systems have
never effectively enforced such laws, usually because of the expense involved.

There is no contradiction between the assertion that compulsory attendance   5
has had little effect on the number of children attending school and the argument
that repeal would be a positive step toward improving education. Most parents
want a high school education for their children. Unfortunately, compulsory attendance hampers the ability of public school officials to enforce legitimate educational and disciplinary policies and thereby make the education a good one.

Private schools have no such problem. They can fail or dismiss students, know-   6
ing such students can attend public school. Without compulsory attendance, public
schools would be freer to oust students whose academic or personal behavior undermines the educational mission of the institution.

Has not the noble experiment of a formal education for everyone failed? While   7
we pay homage to the homily, "You can lead a horse to water but you can't make
him drink," we have pretended it is not true in education.

Ask high school teachers if recalcitrant students learn anything of value. Ask   8
teachers if these students do any homework. Quite the contrary, these students
know they will be passed from grade to grade until they are old enough to quit or
until, as is more likely, they receive a high school diploma. At the point when students could legally quit, most choose to remain since they know they are likely to
be allowed to graduate whether they do acceptable work or not.

Abolition of archaic attendance laws would produce enormous dividends.   9

First, it would alert everyone that school is a serious place where one goes to   10
learn. Schools are neither day-care centers nor indoor street corners. Young people who resist learning should stay away; indeed, an end to compulsory schooling
would require them to stay away.

Second, students opposed to learning would not be able to pollute the educa-   11
tional atmosphere for those who want to learn. Teachers could stop policing recalcitrant students and start educating.

Third, grades would show what they are supposed to: how well a student is learn-   12
ing. Parents could again read report cards and know if their children were making
progress.

Fourth, public esteem for schools would increase. People would stop regarding   13
them as way stations for adolescents and start thinking of them as institutions for
educating America's youth.

Fifth, elementary schools would change because students would find out early   14
that they had better learn something or risk flunking out later. Elementary teachers
would no longer have to pass their failures on to junior high and high school.

Sixth, the cost of enforcing compulsory education would be eliminated. Despite   15
enforcement efforts, nearly 15 percent of the school-age children in our largest
cities are almost permanently absent from school.

Communities could use these savings to support institutions to deal with young   16
people not in school. If, in the long run, these institutions prove more costly, at
least we would not confuse their mission with that of schools.

Schools should be for education. At present, they are only tangentially so. They   17
have attempted to serve an all-encompassing social function, trying to be all things
to all people. In the process they have failed miserably at what they were originally
formed to accomplish.

Presenting Your Source's Point of View

Sipher opposes compulsory attendance laws. On the other hand, suppose
that you can see advantages in imposing a very strict rule for attendance. In
order to challenge Sipher convincingly, you incorporate both his point of view
and yours within a single essay.

Since your objective is to *respond* to Sipher, you begin by *acknowledging his
ideas and presenting them to your readers*. State them as fairly as you can, without
pausing to argue with him or to offer your own point of view about mandatory attendance.

At first it may seem easiest to follow Sipher's sequence of ideas (especially
since his points are so clearly numbered). But Sipher is more likely to dominate
if you follow the structure of his essay, presenting and answering each of his
points one by one; for you will be arguing on *his* terms, according to *his* conception of the issue rather than yours. Instead, make sure that your reader understands what Sipher is actually saying, see if you can find any common
ground between your points of view, and then begin your rebuttal.

*1. Briefly summarize the issue and the reasons that prompted the
author to write the essay.*

You do this by writing a brief summary, as explained in Chapter 1. Here is a
summary of Sipher's article:

Roger Sipher argues that the presence in the classroom of unwilling
students who are indifferent to learning can explain why public school students

as a whole are learning less and less. Sipher therefore recommends that public schools discontinue the policy of mandatory attendance. Instead, students would be allowed to drop out if they wished, and faculty would be able to expel students whose behavior made it difficult for serious students to do their work. Once unwilling students were no longer forced to attend, schools would once again be able to maintain high standards of achievement; they could devote money and energy to education, rather than custodial care.

You can make such a summary more detailed by paraphrasing some of the author's arguments and, if you wish, quoting once or twice.

2. Analyze and present some of the basic principles that underlie the author's position on this issue.

In debating the issue with the author, you will need to do more than just contradict his main ideas: Sipher says mandatory attendance is bad, and you say it is good; Sipher says difficult students don't learn anything, and you say all students learn something useful; and so on. This point-by-point rebuttal shows that you disagree, but it provides no common context so that readers can decide who is right and who is wrong. You have no starting point for your counterarguments and no choice but to sound arbitrary.

Instead, *ask yourself why the author has taken this position,* one that you find so easy to reject.

- What are the foundations of his arguments?
- What larger principles do they suggest?
- What policies is he objecting to? Why?
- What values is he determined to defend?
- Can these values or principles be applied to issues other than attendance?

You are now examining Sipher's specific responses to the practical problem of attendance in order to *analyze his premises* and *infer some broad generalizations* about his philosophy of education.

Although Sipher does not specifically state such generalizations in this article, you would be safe in concluding that Sipher's views on attendance derive from a *conflict of two principles:*

1. The belief that education is a right that may not be denied under any circumstances, and

2. The belief that education is a privilege to be earned.

Sipher advocates the second position. Thus, after your summary of the article, you should analyze Sipher's implicit position in a separate paragraph.

Sipher's argument implies that there is no such thing as the right to an education. A successful education can only depend on the student's willing presence and active participation. Passive or rebellious students cannot be educated and should not be forced to stay in school. Although everyone has the right to an opportunity for education, its acquisition is actually the privilege of those who choose to work for it.

Through this analysis of Sipher's position, you have not only found out more about the issue being argued, but you have also established a common context—*eligibility for education*—within which you and he disagree. Nor is there much room for compromise here; it is hard to reconcile the belief that education should be a privilege with the concept of education as an entitlement. Provided with a clear understanding of the differences between you, your reader now has a real basis for choosing between your opposing views. At the same time, your reader is being assured that this point and no other is the essential point for debate; thus, you will be fighting on ground that *you* have chosen.

You might also note that Sipher's argument is largely *deductive:* a series of premises that derive their power from an appeal to parents' concerns that their children (who faithfully attend) will have their education compromised by the recalcitrant students (who don't). His *supporting evidence* consists of one allusion to the testimony of two economists and one statistic. Both pieces of evidence confirm the subsidiary idea that attendance laws haven't succeeded in improving attendance. His third source of support—the adage about leading a horse to water—does deal more directly with the problem of learning; but can it be regarded as serious evidence?

Presenting Your Point of View

3. *Present your reasons for disagreeing with your source.*

Once you have established your opponent's position, you may then plan your own counterarguments by writing down your reactions and pinpointing the exact reasons for your disagreement. (All the statements analyzed in this section are taken from such preliminary responses; they are *not* excerpts from finished essays.) Your reasons for disagreeing with Sipher might fit into one of three categories:

- You believe that his basic principle is not valid (Student B).
- You decide that his principle, although valid, cannot be strictly applied to the practical situation under discussion (Student C).
- You accept Sipher's principle, but you are aware of other, stronger influences that diminish its importance (Student E).

Whichever line of argument you follow, it is impossible to present your case successfully if you *wholly ignore Sipher's basic principle*, as Student A does:

Student A

Sipher's isn't a constructive solution. Without strict attendance laws, many students wouldn't come to school at all.

Nonattendance is exactly what Sipher wants: he argues that indifferent students should be permitted to stay away, that their absence would benefit everyone. Student A makes no effort to refute Sipher's point; he is, in effect, saying to his source, "You're wrong!" without explaining why.

Student B, however, tries to *establish a basis for disagreement:*

Student B

If mandatory attendance were to be abolished, how would children acquire the skills to survive in an educated society such as ours?

According to Student B, the practical uses of education have become so important that a student's very survival may one day depend on having been well educated. *Implied here is the principle, in opposition to Sipher's, that receiving an education cannot be a matter of choice or a privilege to be earned.* What children learn in school is so important to their future lives that they should be forced to attend classes, even against their will, for their own good.

But this response is still superficial. Student B is confusing the desired object—*getting an education*—with one of the means of achieving that object—*being present in the classroom;* attendance, the means, has become an end in itself. Since students who attend but do not participate will not learn, mandatory attendance cannot by itself create an educated population.

On the other hand, although attendance may not be the *only* condition for getting an education, the student's physical presence in the classroom is certainly important. In that case, should the decision about attendance, a decision likely to affect much of their future lives, be placed in the hands of those too young to understand the consequences?

Student C

The absence of attendance laws would be too tempting for students and might create a generation of semi-illiterates. Consider the marginal student who, despite general indifference and occasional bad behavior, shows some promise and capacity for learning. Without a policy of mandatory attendance, he might choose the easy way out instead of trying to develop his abilities. As a society, we owe these students, at whatever cost, a chance at a good and sound education.

Notice that Student C specifies a "chance" at education. Here is a basic accommodation between Student C's views and Sipher's. *Both agree in principle that society can provide the opportunity, but not the certainty, of being educated.* The distinction here lies in the way in which the principle is applied. With his argument based on a sweeping generalization, Sipher makes no allowances or exceptions: there are limits to the opportunities that society is obliged to provide. Student C, however, believes that society must act in the best interests of those too young to make such decisions; for their sake, the principle of education as a privilege should be less rigorously applied. Students should be exposed to the conditions for (if not the fact of) education, whether they like it or not, until they become adults, capable of choice.

Student D goes even further, suggesting that not only is society obliged to provide the student with educational opportunities, but schools are responsible for making the experience as attractive as possible.

Student D

Maybe the reason for a decrease in attendance and an unwillingness to learn is not that students do not want an education, but that the whole system of discipline and learning is ineffective. If schools concentrated on making classes more appealing, the result would be better attendance, and students would learn more.

In Student D's analysis, passive students are like consumers who need to be encouraged to take advantage of an excellent product that is not selling well. To encourage good attendance, the schools ought to consider using more attractive marketing methods. *Implicit in this view is a transferral of blame from the student to the school.* Other arguments of this sort might blame the parents, rather than the schools, for not teaching their children to understand that it is in their own best interests to get an education.

Finally, Student E accepts the validity of Sipher's view of education, but finds that the whole issue has become subordinate to a more important problem.

Student E

We already have a problem with youths roaming the street, getting into serious trouble. Just multiply the current number of unruly kids by five or ten, and you will come up with the number of potential delinquents that will be hanging around the streets if we do away with the attendance laws that keep them in school. Sipher may be right when he argues that the quality of education would improve if unwilling students were permitted to drop out, but he would be wise to remember that those remaining inside school will have to deal with those on the outside sooner or later.

In this perspective, *security becomes more important than education.* Student E implicitly accepts and gives some social value to the image (rejected by Sipher) of school as a prison, with students sentenced to mandatory confinement.

Student E also ignores Sipher's tentative suggestion (in paragraph 16) that society provide these students with their own "institution," which he describes only in terms of its potential costs. What would its curriculum be? Would they be "special schools" or junior prisons? And when these students "graduate," how will they take their place in society?

A reasonably full response, like those of Students C and E, can provide the material for a series of paragraphs that argue against Sipher's position. Here, for example, is Student E's statement analyzed into the basic topics for a four-paragraph rebuttal within the essay. (The topics are on the left.)

Student E

danger from dropouts if Sipher's plan is adopted (3)

custodial function of school (2)

concession that Sipher is right about education (1)

interests of law and order outweigh interests of education (4)

We already have a problem with youths roaming the street, getting into serious trouble. Just multiply the current number of unruly kids by five or ten, and you will come up with the number of potential delinquents that will be hanging around the streets if we do away with the attendance laws that keep them in school. Sipher may be right when he argues that the quality of education would improve if unwilling students were permitted to drop out, but he would be wise to remember that those remaining inside school will have to deal with those on the outside sooner or later.

Here are Student E's four topics, with the sequence reordered, in outline format. The student's basic agreement with Sipher has become the starting point.

I. Sipher is right about education.
   A. It is possible that the quality of education would improve if unwilling students were allowed to drop out.
II. School, however, has taken on a custodial function.
   A. It is attendance laws that keep students in school.
III. If Sipher's plan is adopted, dropouts might be a problem.
   A. Youths are already roaming the streets getting into trouble.
   B. An increase in the number of unruly kids hanging out in the streets means even greater possibility of disorder.
IV. The interests of law and order outweigh the interests of education.
   A. Educators will not be able to remain aloof from the problems that will develop outside the schools if students are permitted to drop out at will.

Student E can now write a brief essay, with a summary and analysis of Sipher's argument, followed by four full-length paragraphs explaining each point. If a longer essay is assigned, Student E should go to the library to find supporting evidence—statistics and authoritative testimony—to develop these paragraphs. A starting point might be the issue that Sipher omits: how do these nonattenders fare later on when they look for work? What methods have been successful in persuading such students to stay in school?

> ## *Guidelines for Writing a One-Source Argument*
>
> - Present your source's point of view.
>   1. Briefly summarize the issue and the reasons that prompted the author to write the essay.
>   2. Analyze and present some of the basic principles that underlie the author's position on this issue.
> - Present your point of view.
>   3. Present your reasons for disagreeing with (or, if you prefer, supporting) your source.

ASSIGNMENT 4: WRITING AN ARGUMENT BASED ON A SINGLE SOURCE

Read "What Our Education System Needs Is More F's," "The Case for Censorship," "The Museum of Clear Ideas," and "'Sex' Is Also a Dirty Word." As the starting point for an essay, select one source with which you disagree. (Or, with your instructor's permission, bring in an essay that you are certain that you disagree with, and have your instructor approve your choice.)

1. Write a two-part summary of the essay, the first part describing the author's position and explicitly stated arguments, the second analyzing the principles underlying that position.
2. Then present your own rebuttal of the author's point of view.

The length of your essay will depend on the number and complexity of the ideas that you find in the source and the number of counterarguments that you can assemble. The minimum acceptable length for the entire assignment is two printed pages (approximately 500–600 words).

WHAT OUR EDUCATION SYSTEM NEEDS IS MORE F'S

Carl Singleton

I suggest that instituting merit raises, getting back to basics, marrying the university to industry, and . . . other recommendations will not achieve measurable success [in restoring quality to American education] until something even more basic is returned to practice. The immediate need for our educational system from pre-kindergarten through post-Ph.D. is not more money or better teaching but simply a widespread giving of F's.

Before hastily dismissing the idea as banal and simplistic, think for a moment about the implications of a massive dispensing of failing grades. It would dramatically, emphatically, and immediately force into the open every major issue related to the inadequacies of American education.

Let me make it clear that I recommend giving those F's—by the dozens, hundreds, thousands, even millions—only to students who haven't learned the required material. The basic problem of our educational system is the common practice of giving credit where none has been earned, a practice that has resulted in the sundry faults delineated by all the reports and studies over recent years. Illiteracy among high-school graduates is growing because those students have been passed rather than flunked; we have low-quality teaching because of low-quality teachers who never should have been certified in the first place; college students have to take basic reading, writing, and mathematics courses because they never learned those skills in classrooms from which they never should have been granted egress. 3

School systems have contributed to massive ignorance by issuing unearned passing grades over a period of some 20 years. At first there was a tolerance of students who did not fully measure up (giving D's to students who should have received firm F's); then our grading system continued to deteriorate (D's became C's, and B became the average grade); finally we arrived at total accommodation (come to class and get your C's, laugh at my jokes and take home B's). 4

Higher salaries, more stringent certification procedures, getting back to basics will have little or no effect on the problem of quality education unless and until we insist, as a profession, on giving F's whenever students fail to master the material. 5

Sending students home with final grades of F would force most parents to deal with the realities of their children's failure while it is happening and when it is yet possible to do something about it (less time on TV, and more time on homework, perhaps?). As long as it is the practice of teachers to pass students who should not be passed, the responsibility will not go home to the parents, where, I hope, it belongs. (I am tempted to make an analogy to then Gov. Lester Maddox's statement some years ago about prison conditions in Georgia—"We'll get a better grade of prisons when we get a better grade of prisoners"—but I shall refrain.) 6

Giving an F where it is deserved would force concerned parents to get themselves away from the TV set, too, and take an active part in their children's education. I realize, of course, that some parents would not help; some cannot help. However, Johnny does not deserve to pass just because Daddy doesn't care or is ignorant. Johnny should pass only when and if he knows the required material. 7

Giving an F whenever and wherever it is the only appropriate grade would force principals, school boards, and voters to come to terms with cost as a factor in improving our educational system. As the numbers of students at various levels were increased by those not being passed, more money would have to be spent to accommodate them. We could not be accommodating them in the old sense of passing them on, but by keeping them at one level until they did in time, one way or another, learn the material. 8

Insisting on respecting the line between passing and failing would also require us to demand as much of ourselves as of our students. As every teacher knows, a failed student can be the product of a failed teacher. 9

Teaching methods, classroom presentations, and testing procedures would have 10
to be of a very high standard—we could not, after all, conscionably give F's if we
have to go home at night thinking it might somehow be our own fault.

The results of giving an F where it is deserved would be immediately evident. 11
There would be no illiterate college graduates next spring—none. The same would
be true of high-school graduates, and consequently next year's college freshmen—
all of them—would be able to read.

I don't claim that giving F's will solve all of the problems, but I do argue that un- 12
less and until we start failing those students who should be failed, other suggested
solutions will make little progress toward improving education. Students in our
schools and colleges should be permitted to pass only after they have fully met established standards; borderline cases should be retained.

The single most important requirement for solving the problems of education in 13
America today is the big fat F, written decisively in red ink millions of times in
schools and colleges across the country.

THE CASE FOR CENSORSHIP
from *Slouching Towards Gomorrah*
Robert H. Bork

. . . Sooner or later censorship is going to have to be considered as popular 1
culture continues plunging to ever more sickening lows. The alternative to censorship, legal and moral, will be a brutalized and chaotic culture, with all that that
entails for our society, economy, politics, and physical safety. It is important to be
clear about the topic. I am *not* suggesting that censorship should, or constitutionally could, be employed to counter the liberal political and cultural propagandiz-
ing of movies, television, network news, and music. They are protected, and
properly so, by the First Amendment's guarantees of freedom of speech and of
the press. I *am* suggesting that censorship be considered for the most violent and
sexually explicit material now on offer, starting with the obscene prose and pictures available on the Internet, motion pictures that are mere rhapsodies to violence, and the more degenerate lyrics of rap music. . . .

Is censorship really as unthinkable as we all seem to assume? That it is unthink- 2
able is a very recent conceit. From the earliest colonies on this continent over
300 hundred [sic] years ago, and for about 175 years of our existence as a nation, we endorsed and lived with censorship. We do not have to imagine what
censorship might be like; we know from experience. Some of it was formal, written in statutes or city ordinances; some of it was informal, as in the movie producers' agreement to abide by the rulings of the Hayes office. Some of it was
inevitably silly—the rule that the movies could not show even a husband and wife
fully dressed on a bed unless each had one foot on the floor—and some of it was

no doubt pernicious. The period of Hayes office censorship was also, perhaps not coincidentally, the golden age of the movies.

The questions to be considered are whether such material has harmful effects, whether it is constitutionally possible to censor it, and whether technology may put some of it beyond society's capacity to control it.   3

It is possible to argue for censorship, as Stanley Brubaker, a professor of political science, does, on the ground that in a republican form of government where the people rule, it is crucial that the character of the citizenry not be debased. By now we should have gotten over the liberal notion that its citizens' characters are none of the business of government. The government ought not try to impose virtue, but it can deter incitements to vice. "Liberals have always taken the position," the late Christopher Lasch wrote, "that democracy can dispense with civic virtue. According to this way of thinking, it is liberal institutions, not the character of citizens, that make democracy work." He cited India and Latin America as proof that formally democratic institutions are not enough for a workable social order, a proof that is disheartening as the conditions in parts of large American cities approach those of the Third World.   4

Lasch stressed "the degree to which liberal democracy has lived off the borrowed capital of moral and religious traditions antedating the rise of liberalism." Certainly, the great religions of the West—Christianity and Judaism—taught moral truths about respect for others, honesty, sexual fidelity, truth-speaking, the value of work, respect for the property of others, and self-restraint. With the decline of religious influence, the moral lessons attenuate as well. Morality is an essential soil for free and democratic governments. A people addicted to instant gratification through the vicarious (and sometimes not so vicarious) enjoyment of mindless violence and brutal sex is unlikely to provide such a soil. A population whose mental faculties are coarsened and blunted, whose emotions are few and simple, is unlikely to be able to make the distinctions and engage in the discourse that democratic government requires.   5

I find Brubaker and Lasch persuasive. We tend to think of virtue as a personal matter, each of us to choose which virtues to practice or not practice—the privatization of morality, or, if you will, the "pursuit of happiness," as each of us defines happiness. But only a public morality, in which trust, truth-telling, and self-control are prominent features, can long sustain a decent social order and hence a stable and just democratic order. If the social order continues to unravel, we may respond with a more authoritarian government that is capable of providing at least personal safety.   6

There is, of course, more to the case for censorship than the need to preserve a viable democracy. We need also to avoid the social devastation wrought by pornography and endless incitements to murder and mayhem. Whatever the effects upon our capacity to govern ourselves, living in a culture that saturates us with pictures of sex and violence is aesthetically ugly, emotionally flattening, and physically dangerous.   7

There are, no doubt, complex causes for illegitimacy and violence in today's society, but it seems impossible to deny that one cause is the messages popular   8 culture insistently presses on us. Asked about how to diminish illegitimacy, a woman who worked with unmarried teenage mothers replied tersely: "Shoot Madonna." That may be carrying censorship a bit far, but one sees her point. Madonna's forte is sexual incitement. We live in a sex-drenched culture. The forms of sexual entertainment rampant in our time are overwhelming to the young, who would, even without such stimulations, have difficulty enough resisting the song their hormones sing. There was a time, coinciding with the era of censorship, when most did resist.

Young males, who are more prone to violence than females or older males, witness so many gory depictions of killing that they are bound to become desensitized to it. We now have teenagers and even subteenagers who shoot if they feel they have been "dissed" (shown disrespect). Indeed, the newspapers bring us stories of murders done for simple pleasure, the killing of a stranger simply because the youth felt like killing someone, anyone. That is why, for the first time in American history, you are more likely to be murdered by a complete stranger than by someone you know. That is why our prisons contain convicted killers who show absolutely no remorse and frequently cannot even remember the names of the persons they killed.

One response of the entertainment industry to criticisms has been that Hollywood and the music business did not create violence or sexual chaos in America. Of course not. But they contribute to it. They are one of the "root causes" they want us to seek elsewhere and leave them alone. The denial that what the young see and hear has any effect on their behavior is the last line of the modern liberal defense of decadence, and it is willfully specious. Accusing Senator Dole of "pandering to the right" in his speech deploring obscene and violent entertainment, the *New York Times* argued: "There is much in the movies and in hard-core rap music that is disturbing and demeaning to many Americans. Rap music, which often reaches the top of the charts, is also the music in which women are degraded and men seem to murder each other for sport. But no one has ever dropped dead from viewing 'Natural Born Killers,' or listening to gangster rap records." To which George Will replied: "No one ever dropped dead reading 'Der Sturmer,' the Nazi anti-Semitic newspaper, but the culture it served caused six million Jews to drop dead."

Those who oppose any form of restraint, including self-restraint, on what is produced insist that there is no connection between what people watch and hear and their behavior. It is clear why people who sell gangsta rap make that claim, but it is less clear why anyone should believe them. Studies show that the evidence of the causal connection between popular culture's violence and violent behavior is overwhelming. A recent study, *Sex and the Mass Media*, asked: "Does the talk about the images of love, sex and relationships promote irresponsible sexual behavior? Do they encourage unplanned and unwanted pregnancy? Are the media responsible for teenagers having sex earlier, more frequently and outside of marriage?" The researchers concluded: "The answer to all these questions is a qualified 'yes'." The answer was qualified because not enough research has as

9

10

11

yet been done on the effects of sexual images. The authors relied in part on the analogous question of media depictions of violence and their effect on aggressive behavior, which would appear to be a parallel situation. Some of the studies found positive but relatively small effects, between 5 and 15 percent. "One of the most compelling of the naturalistic studies . . . found that the homicide rates in three countries (U.S., Canada, and South Africa) increased dramatically 10–15 years after the introduction of television." That study "estimated that exposure to television violence is a causal factor in about half of the 21,000 homicides per year in the United States and perhaps half of all rapes and assaults."

The studies confirm what seems obvious. Common sense and experience are sufficient to reach the same conclusions. Music, for example, is used everywhere to create attitudes—armies use martial music, couples listen to romantic music, churches use organs, choirs, and hymns. How can anyone suppose that music (plus the images of television, movies, and advertisements) about sex and violence has no effect? 12

Indeed, Hollywood's writers, producers, and executives think popular entertainment affects behavior. It is not merely that they sell billions of dollars of advertising on television on the premise that they can influence behavior; they also think that the content of their programs can reform society in a liberal direction. They understand that no single program will change attitudes much, but they rely upon the cumulative impact of years of television indoctrination. Why should we listen to the same people saying that their programs and music have no effect on behavior? That argument is over. The depravity sold by Hollywood and the record companies is feeding the depravity we see around us. 13

The television industry, under considerable political pressure, has agreed to a ratings system for its programs. Since assigning ratings to every program—including every episode in a series—will be much more difficult than assigning ratings to motion pictures, it is doubtful that the television rating system will add much except confusion and rancor. The movie ratings have not prevented underage children from freely seeing movies they were not meant to see. No doubt the same will be true of television ratings. The vaunted V chip will prove no solution. Aside from the fact that many parents simply will not bother with it, the V chip will likely lead to even more degrading programming by providing producers with the excuse that the chip adequately safeguards children, though it does not. And the chip certainly does nothing to prevent adults from enjoying the increasingly salacious and even perverted material that is on the way. 14

The debate about censorship, insofar as there can be said to be a debate, usually centers on the issue of keeping children away from pornography. There is, of course, a good deal of merit to that, but it makes the issue sound like one of child rearing, which most people would like the government to butt out of. Opponents say parents can protect their children by using control features offered by many services. Both sides are missing a major point. Aside from the fact that many parents will not use control features, censorship is also crucial to protect children—and the rest of us—from men encouraged to act by a steady diet of 15 computerized pedophilia, murder, rape, and sado-masochism. No one supposes that every addict of such material will act out his fantasies, but it is willfully blind to think that none will. The pleasures the viewers of such material get from watching a thousand rape scenes or child kidnappings is not worth one actual rape or kidnapping.

There are those who say that the only solution is to rebuild a stable public culture. How one does that when the institutions we have long relied on to maintain and transmit such a culture—the two-parent family, schools, churches, and popular entertainment itself—are all themselves in decline it is not easy to say. Nevertheless, there is something to the point. Determined individuals and groups may be able to revitalize some of those institutions. For much that afflicts us, that is the only acceptable course. Law cannot be the answer in all or even most areas. And there are signs not just of resistance but of positive action against the forces of decadence. For the very worst manifestations of the culture, however, more directly coercive responses may be required. Whether as a society we any longer have the will to make such responses is very much in question.   16

Arguments that society may properly set limits to what may be shown, said, and sung run directly counter to the mood of our cultural elites in general, and in particular the attitude (it is hardly more than that) of our judges, many of whom, most unfortunately, are members in good standing of that elite. As constitutional law now stands, censorship would be extremely difficult, if not impossible. In *Miller* v. *California,* the Supreme Court laid down a three-part test that must be met if sexually explicit material is to be banned. It must be shown that: (1) the average person, applying contemporary community standards, would find that the work, taken as a whole, appeals to the prurient interest; (2) the work depicts or describes, in a patently offensive way, sexual conduct specifically defined by the applicable state law; and (3) the work, taken as a whole, lacks serious literary, artistic, political, or scientific value.   17

The first two prongs of the test become increasingly difficult to satisfy as contemporary community standards decline and as fewer and fewer descriptions of sexual conduct are regarded as patently offensive. But it is the third part that poses the most difficulty. There is apparently nothing that a flummery of professors will not testify has "serious value." When Cincinnati prosecuted the museum that displayed Mapplethorpe's photographs, the jury deferred to defense witnesses who said the pictures were art and hence could not be obscene. Cincinnati was widely ridiculed and portrayed as benighted for even attempting to punish obscenity. One typical cartoon showed a furtive figure stepping out of an alley in the city to offer "feelthy pictures" to a surprised passerby. The picture was a reproduction of a Michelangelo. It is typical of our collapse of standards that Mapplethorpe's grotesqueries can be compared even in a cartoon to Michelangelo's art.   18

It is difficult to see merit in the serious value test. Serious literary, artistic, political, or scientific value can certainly be achieved without including descriptions of "patently offensive" sexual conduct. This third criterion serves merely as an   19 escape hatch for pornographers whose "experts" can overbear juries. No doubt professors of literature can be found to testify to the serious literary value of the prose found in alt.sex.stories. Some of them are said to be very well written.

Without censorship, it has proved impossible to maintain any standards of de-   20
cency. "[O]nly a deeply confused society," George Will wrote, "is more con-
cerned about protecting lungs than minds, trout than black women. We legislate against smoking in restaurants; singing 'Me So Horny' is a constitutional right. Secondary smoke is carcinogenic; celebration of torn vaginas is 'mere words.'" The massive confusion Will describes is in large measure a confusion that first enveloped the courts, which they then imposed on us.

It will be said that to propose banning anything that can be called "expression"   21
is an attempt to "take away our constitutional rights." A radio talk show host said that the proposal to censor obscenities on the Internet was a denial of the First Amendment rights of teenagers. Such reactions reveal a profound ignorance of the history of the First Amendment. Until quite recently, nobody even raised the question of that amendment in prosecutions of pornographers; it was not thought relevant even by the pornographers. As late as 1942, in the *Chaplinsky* decision, a unanimous Supreme Court could agree:

> There are certain well-defined and narrowly limited classes of speech, the preven-
> tion and punishment of which have never been thought to raise any Constitu-
> tional problem. These include the lewd and obscene, the profane, the libelous,
> and the insulting or "fighting" words—those which by their very utterance inflict
> injury or tend to incite an immediate breach of the peace. It has been well ob-
> served that such utterances are no essential part of any exposition of ideas, and
> are of such slight social value as a step to truth that any benefit that may be de-
> rived from them is clearly outweighed by the social interest in order and morality.

Under today's constitutional doctrine, it would be difficult to impossible to pro-   22
hibit or punish the lewd and obscene, or the profane. First Amendment jurispru-
dence has shifted from the protection of the exposition of ideas towards the protection of self-expression—however lewd, obscene, or profane. Time Warner, citing the authority of a 1992 statute, proposed to scramble sexually explicit programs on a New York cable channel. . . . Those who wanted the shows with strip-
pers, excerpts from pornographic movies, and advertisements for phone sex and "escort" services would have to send in cards to the cable operator. A federal dis-
trict judge in New York, disagreeing with the federal court of appeals in Washington, D.C., granted a preliminary injunction against Time Warner, saying that the statute probably violated the First Amendment. The plaintiffs who produce these shows said the scrambling would hurt their ability to reach their audience and stigmatize viewers who tune in to the shows. Both are results that would have been considered laudable rather than forbidden under the First Amendment not many years ago.

Yet it is clear that if there is something special about speech, something that   23
warrants a constitutional guarantee, it is the capacity of speech to communicate ideas. There is no other distinction between speech and other human activities

that go unprotected by the Constitution. That is the point the *Chaplinsky* Court grasped. Non-speech activities can give as much pleasure as speech, develop as many human faculties, and contribute to personal and social well-being. The only difference between speech and other behavior is speech's capacity to communicate ideas in the effort to reach varieties of truth. Celebration in song of the ripping of vaginas or forced oral sex or stories depicting the kidnapping, mutilation, raping, and murder of children do not, to anyone with a degree of common sense, qualify as ideas. And when something worthy of being called an idea is involved, there is no reason to protect its expression in lewd, obscene, or profane language. Such language adds nothing to the idea but, instead, detracts from it.

Today's Court majority would have difficulty understanding *Chaplinsky*'s state-   24
ment that an utterance could inflict an injury to morality. Morality itself has become relativized in our constitutional jurisprudence, so that the Court no longer has the vocabulary to say that something is immoral and, for that reason, may be banned by the legislature. As Walter Berns wrote:

> The Court decontrolled the arts, so to speak, and the impact of that has been profound. It not only permitted the publication of sex but it *caused* the publication of sex—or, to coin a word, the "publification" of sex. . . . The immediate and obvious consequence of [the end of censorship] is that sex is now being made into the measure of existence, and such uniquely human qualities as modesty, fidelity, abstinence, chastity, delicacy, and shame, qualities that formerly provided the constraints on sexual activity and the setting within which the erotic passion was enjoyed, discussed, and evaluated, are today ridiculed as merely arbitrary interferences "with the health of the sexual parts."

Berns wrote that in 1976, when he could have had no idea just how far the publi-   25
fication of sex would be carried. We may not know that even now. Our experience after the end of censorship suggests that there are few or no limits to depravity.

It may be too much to ask that the Supreme Court, as presently constituted, re-   26
visit and revise its First Amendment jurisprudence. Most people think of the Court as a legal institution because its pronouncements have the force of law. But the perception is flawed. The Court is also a cultural institution, one whose pronouncements are significantly guided not by the historical meaning of the Constitution but by the values of the class that is dominant in our culture. In our day, that means the cultural elite: academics, clergy, journalists, entertainers, foundation staffs, "public interest" groups, and the like. The First Amendment is central to the concerns of such folk because they are chatterers by profession, and their attitudes are relativistic and permissive. The mention of censorship, even of the most worthless and harmful materials, causes apoplexy in the members of that class.

The truth is that the judiciary's view of pornographic sex and pornographic vio-   27
lence will not change until the culture to which the Court responds changes. There is no sign that that will occur any time soon. The public debate in the area of the "arts" is not encouraging. Mapplethorpe's homoerotic photos and Serrano's "Piss Christ" were displayed with grants from the National Endowment for the Arts. So

intimidating has the culture of modern liberalism become that cultural conservatives were reduced to complaining that works like these should not be subsidized with "taxpayers' dollars," as if taxpayers should never be required to subsidize things they don't like. If that were the case, government would have to close down altogether. Both spending and taxation would be at zero. To complain about the source of the dollars involved is to cheapen a moral position. The photographs would be just as offensive if their display were financed by a scatter-brained billionaire. We seem too timid to state that Mapplethorpe's and Serrano's pictures should not be shown in public, whoever pays for them. We are going to have to overcome that timidity if our culture is not to decline still further.

Libertarians join forces with modern liberals in opposing censorship, though libertarians are far from being modern liberals in other respects. For one thing, libertarians do not like the coercion that necessarily accompanies radical egalitarianism. But because both libertarians and modern liberals are oblivious to social reality, both demand radical personal autonomy in expression. That is one reason libertarians are not to be confused, as they often are, with conservatives. They are quasi- or semiconservatives. Nor are they to be confused with classical liberals, who considered restraints on individual autonomy to be essential.   28

The nature of the liberal and libertarian errors is easily seen in discussions of pornography. The leader of the explosion of pornographic videos, described admiringly by a competitor as the Ted Turner of the business, offers the usual defenses of decadence: "Adults have a right to see [pornography] if they want to. If it offends you, don't buy it." Those statements neatly sum up both the errors and the (unintended) perniciousness of the alliance between libertarians and modern liberals with respect to popular culture.   29

Modern liberals employ the rhetoric of "rights" incessantly, not only to delegitimate the idea of restraints on individuals by communities but to prevent discussion of the topic. Once something is announced, usually flatly and stridently, to be a right—whether pornography or abortion or what have you—discussion becomes difficult to impossible. Rights inhere in the person, are claimed to be absolute, and cannot be diminished or taken away by reason; in fact, reason that suggests the non-existence of an asserted right is viewed as a moral evil by the claimant. If there is to be anything that can be called a community, rather than an agglomeration of hedonists, the case for previously unrecognized individual freedoms (as well as some that have been previously recognized) must be thought through and argued, and "rights" cannot win every time. Why there is a right for adults to enjoy pornography remains unexplained and unexplainable.   30

The second bit of advice—"If it offends you, don't buy it"—is both lulling and destructive. Whether you buy it or not, you will be greatly affected by those who do. The aesthetic and moral environment in which you and your family live will be coarsened and degraded. Economists call the effects an activity has on others "externalities"; why so many of them do not understand the externalities here is a mystery. They understand quite well that a person who decides not to run a smelter will nevertheless be seriously affected if someone else runs one nearby.   31

Free market economists are particularly vulnerable to the libertarian virus. They know that free economic exchanges usually benefit both parties to them. But they mistake that general rule for a universal rule. Benefits do not invariably result from free market exchanges. When it comes to pornography or addictive drugs, libertarians all too often confuse the idea that markets should be free with the idea that everything should be available on the market. The first of those ideas rests on the efficiency of the free market in satisfying wants. The second ignores the question of which wants it is moral to satisfy. That is a question of an entirely different nature. I have heard economists say that, as economists, they do not deal with questions of morality. Quite right. But nobody is just an economist. Economists are also fathers or mothers, husbands or wives, voters, citizens, members of communities. In these latter roles, they cannot avoid questions of morality.   32

The externalities of depictions of violence and pornography are clear. To complaints about those products being on the market, libertarians respond with something like "Just hit the remote control and change channels on your TV set." But, like the person who chooses not to run a smelter while others do, you, your family, and your neighbors will be affected by the people who do not change the channel, who do rent the pornographic videos, who do read alt.sex.stories. As film critic Michael Medved put it: "To say that if you don't like the popular culture, then turn it off, is like saying if you don't like the smog, stop breathing. . . . There are Amish kids in Pennsylvania who know about Madonna." And their parents can do nothing about it.   33

Can there be any doubt that as pornography and depictions of violence become increasingly popular and increasingly accessible, attitudes about marriage, fidelity, divorce, obligations to children, the use of force, and permissible public behavior and language will change? Or that with the changes in attitudes will come changes in conduct, both public and private? We have seen those changes already and they are continuing. Advocates of liberal arts education assure us that those studies improve character. Can it be that only uplifting reading affects character and the most degrading reading has no effects whatever? "Don't buy it" and "Change the channel," however intended, are effectively advice to accept a degenerating culture and its consequences.   34

The obstacles to censorship of pornographic and violence-filled materials are, of course, enormous. Radical individualism in such matters is now pervasive even among sedate, upper middle-class people. At a dinner I sat next to a retired Army general who was now a senior corporate executive. The subject of Robert Mapplethorpe's photographs came up. This most conventional of dinner companions said casually that people ought to be allowed to see whatever they wanted to see. It would seem to follow that others ought to be allowed to do whatever some want to see.   35

The entertainment industry will battle ferociously against restraints, one segment of it because its economic interests would be directly threatened, the rest because, to avoid thinking, they have become absolutists about First Amendment freedoms. Then there are the First Amendment voluptuaries. The ACLU is to the First Amendment what the National Rifle Association is to the Second Amendment and the right   36 to bear arms. The head of the ACLU announced in a panel discussion that the Supreme Court's failure to throw protection around nude dancing in night clubs was a terrible blow to our freedom of speech. Some years back, when I suggested to a law school audience that the courts had gone too far in preventing communities from prohibiting pornography, the then president of the organization compared me to Salazar of Portugal and the Greek colonels. Afterward he said he had called me a fascist. It is fascinating that when one calls for greater democratic control and less governance by a judicial oligarchy, one is immediately called a fascist. The ACLU seems to think democracy is tyranny and government by judges is freedom. That is a proposition that in the last half of this century our judiciary has all too readily accepted. Any serious attempt to root out the worst in our popular culture may be doomed unless the judiciary comes to understand that the First Amendment was adopted for good reasons, and those reasons did not include the furtherance of radical personal autonomy.

It is not clear how effective censorship of the Internet or of digital films on home computers can be. Perhaps it is true, as has been said, that technology is on the side of anarchy. Violence and pornography can be supplied from all over the world, and it can be wireless, further complicating the problem of barring it. We may soon be at the mercy of a combination of technology and perversion. It's enough to make one a Luddite. But there are methods of presentation that can be censored. Lyrics, motion pictures, television, and printed material are candidates.   37

What we see in popular culture, from "Big Man with a Gun" to alt.sex.stories, is the product, though not, it is to be feared, the final product, of liberalism's constant thrust. Doing anything to curb the spreading rot would violate liberalism's central tenet, John Stuart Mill's "one very simple principle." Mill himself would be horrified at what we have become; he never intended this; but he bequeathed us the principle that modern liberals embrace and that makes it possible. We have learned that the founders of liberalism were wrong. Unconstrained human nature will seek degeneracy often enough to create a disorderly, hedonistic, and dangerous society. Modern liberalism and popular culture are creating that society.   38

THE MUSEUM OF CLEAR IDEAS
from *In Defense of Elitism*
William A. Henry III

Why do people go to college? In an idealistic world, they might go to develop a capacity for critical thinking, enhance an already grounded knowledge of the sciences and world culture, learn further how to deal with other people's diversity of opinion and background, and in general become better citizens. They might go for fun, for friendship, for a network of contacts. They might go for spiritual enrichment or for pragmatic honing of skills.   1

In the real world, though, mostly they go to college to make money.   2

This reality is acknowledged in the mass media, which are forever running sto- 3
ries and charts showing how much a college degree contributes to lifetime income
(with the more sophisticated publications very occasionally noting the counterweight costs of tuition paid and income foregone during the years of full-time
study). These stories are no surprise to parents, who certainly wouldn't shell out
the same money for travel or other exercises in fulfillment that do not result in a
marketable credential. The income statistics are, similarly, no surprise to banks,
which avidly market student loans and have been known to shower new graduates
or even undergraduates with credit cards. And of course the stories are no surprise to students, who avidly follow news of where the jobs are and what starting
salaries they command.

But the equation between college and wealth is not so simple. College graduates 4
unquestionably do better on average economically than those who don't go at all.
At the extremes, those with five or more years of college earn about triple the income of those with eight or fewer years of total schooling. Taking more typical examples, one finds that those who stop their educations after earning a four-year
degree earn about one and a half times as much as those who stop at the end of
high school. These outcomes, however, reflect other things besides the impact of
the degree itself. College graduates are winners in part because colleges attract
people who are already winners—people with enough brains and drive that they
would do well in almost any generation and under almost any circumstances, with
or without formal credentialing. The harder and more meaningful question is
whether the mediocrities who have also flooded into colleges in the past couple of
generations do better than they otherwise would have. And if they do, is it because
college actually made them better employees or because it simply gave them the
requisite credential to get interviewed and hired? Does having gone to college truly
make one a better salesman of stocks or real estate or insurance? Does it enhance
the work of a secretary or nanny or hairdresser? Does it make one more adept at
running a car dealership or a catering company? Or being a messenger boy? All
these occupations are being pursued, on more than an interim basis, by college
graduates of my acquaintance. Most readers can probably think of parallel or equivalent examples. It need hardly be added that these occupations are also pursued,
often with equal success, by people who didn't go to college at all, and in generations past were pursued primarily by people who hadn't stepped onto a campus.
Indeed, the United States Labor Department's Bureau of Labor Statistics reported
in 1994 that about twenty percent of all college graduates toil in fields not requiring a degree, and this total is projected to exceed thirty percent by the year 2005.
For the individual, college may well be a credential without being a qualification, required without being requisite.

For American society, the big lie underlying higher education is akin to the . . . 5
big lie about childrearing in Garrison Keillor's Lake Wobegon: that everyone can be
above average. In the unexamined American Dream rhetoric promoting mass
higher education in the nation of my youth, the implicit vision was that one day

everyone, or at least practically everyone, would be a manager or a professional. We would use the most elitist of all means, scholarship, toward the most egalitarian of ends. We would all become chiefs; hardly anyone would be left a mere Indian. On the surface this New Jerusalem appears to have arrived. Where half a century ago the bulk of jobs were blue collar, now a majority are white or pink collar. They are performed in an office instead of on a factory floor. If they still tend to involve repetition and drudgery, at least they do not require heavy lifting.

But the wages for them are going down virtually as often as up. It has become an axiom of union lobbying that replacing a manufacturing economy with a service economy has meant exporting once-lucrative jobs to places where they can be done more cheaply. And as a great many disappointed office workers have discovered, being better educated and better dressed at the workplace does not transform one's place in the pecking order. There are still plenty more Indians than chiefs. Lately, indeed, the chiefs are becoming even fewer. If, for a generation or so, corporate America bought into the daydream of making everyone a boss, the wakeup call has come. The major focus of the "downsizing" of recent years has been eliminating layers of middle management—much of it drawn from the ranks of those lured to college a generation or two ago by the idea that a degree would transform them from mediocre to magisterial.

Yet our colleges blithely go on "educating" many more prospective managers and professionals than we are likely to need. In my own field, there are typically more students majoring in journalism at any given moment than there are journalists employed at all the daily newspapers in the United States. A few years ago there were more students enrolled in law school than there were partners in all law firms. As trends shift, there have been periodic oversupplies of M.B.A.-wielding financial analysts, of grade school and high school teachers, of computer programmers, even of engineers. Inevitably many students of limited talent spend huge amounts of time and money pursuing some brass ring occupation, only to see their dreams denied. As a society we consider it cruel not to give them every chance at success. It may be more cruel to let them go on fooling themselves.

Just when it should seem clear that we are probably already doing too much to entice people into college, Bill Clinton is suggesting we do even more. In February 1994, for example, the President asserted that America needs a greater fusion between academic and vocational training—not because too many mediocre people misplaced on the college track are failing to acquire marketable vocational and technical skills, but because too many people on the vocational track are being denied courses that will secure them admission to college. Surely what we Americans need is not a fusion of the two tracks but a sharper division between them, coupled with a forceful program for diverting intellectual also-rans out of the academic track and into the vocational one. That is where most of them are heading in life anyway. Why should they wait until they are older and must enroll in high-priced proprietary vocational programs of often dubious efficacy—frequently throwing away not only their own funds but federal loans in the process—because they

6

7

8

emerged from high school heading nowhere and knowing nothing that is useful in the marketplace?

If the massive numbers of college students reflected a national boom in love of learning and a prevalent yen for self-improvement, America's investment in the classroom might make sense. There are introspective qualities that can enrich any society in ways beyond the material. But one need look no further than the curricular wars to understand that most students are not looking to broaden their spiritual or intellectual horizons. They see themselves as consumers buying a product, and insist on applying egalitarian rules of the marketplace to what used to be an unchallenged elitism of the intellect.

9

Consider three basic trends, all of them implicit rejections of intellectual adventure, all based on seeing college in transactional terms. First, students are demanding courses that reflect and affirm their own identities in the most literal way. Rather than read a Greek dramatist of two thousand years ago and thrill to the discovery that some ideas and emotions are universal, many insist on reading writers of their own gender or ethnicity or sexual preference, ideally writers of the present or the recent past. They proclaim that they cannot (meaning, of course, *will* not) relate to heritages other than their own. Furthermore, they repudiate the idea that anyone can transcend his heritage—apparently because few if any people of their own heritage are judged to have done so, and they see the very idea of "universal values" in terms of some sort of competition that their group cannot win. This is parallel to the appalling trend in history, scathingly described in several recent essays by that brilliant traditionalist Gertrude Himmelfarb, in which all fact and analysis are dismissed as "relative" and theoretical opinion is enshrined as a liberating and morally superior form of scholarship. Historians have always known, she writes in *On Looking into the Abyss,* "what postmodernism professes to have just discovered"—that historical writing "is necessarily imperfect, tentative and partial." But previous generations did not embrace the drive to be "imaginative," "inventive," and "creative" rather than as truthful as circumstances permit.

10

Professors who pander to these students often talk in terms of liberation but they reject the most liberating of all intellectual undertakings, the journey beyond one's own place and time. For their part, many students do not want college to liberate or change them. They want it merely to reinforce them as they are, and they are in their way as unimaginative and smug as the white-bread fraternity dolts Sinclair Lewis so deftly sketched in *Elmer Gantry* and *Babbitt.* Often this self-absorption and lack of intellectual humility leads them to demand a curriculum that fails to serve even their base interests. At my own alma mater, Yale, undergraduates have been able to study Yoruba and other African tribal languages of extremely limited economic utility because these pursuits had sentimental or political appeal. But because there wasn't similar pressure for teaching Korean, they were denied the opportunity to enroll in a tongue that might actually have enabled them to get a job. San Francisco State has been offering a minor in gay studies for years, and organizations of professorial ideologues are pushing nationally for majors and even

11

graduate degrees in the field. This may lead to a self-perpetuating career stream in academe. But what happens to an unsuspecting adolescent who minors in gay studies and then has to tell a job interviewer at, say, an insurance company that during the years when he might have been acquiring economically useful knowledge he was instead enrolled in such actual courses as Gay Male Relationships and Gays in Film? I'm not just worrying about the chilling effect of homophobia here. The same caveat applies to all ideologically based and impractical studies, like the feminist dialectics in the humanities that one female Columbia professor of my acquaintance dismisses as "clit lit," or Stanford's Black Hair as Culture and History. This sort of feel-good learning epitomizes the endemic confusion of the roles of the curriculum with those of the counseling service.

The second trend, implicit in the first, is that the curriculum has shifted from be-   12
ing what professors desire to teach to being what students desire to learn. In the heydey of faculty authority, professors devised set courses based on their view of the general basis for a liberal education, the essentials in each particular field, and, frequently, their personal intellectual interests. This system clearly served the professors (and nothing wrong with that), but it also served students by giving them teachers who were motivated, even excited, by the topics under discussion. My own college education took place during the Vietnam era, a time of abundance at most colleges because of government subsidy coupled with burgeoning enrollments due to the baby boom and draft avoidance. Professors could indulge their eccentricities; my freshman calculus teacher spent the entire fall term talking about his true love, Babylonian number theory, and I am probably the better for it, if only for a sense of the eons of continuity underlying all the great branches of scholarship.

Nowadays colleges have to hustle for students by truckling trendily. If the students   13
want media studies programs so they can all fantasize about becoming TV news anchors, then media studies will abound, even though most real journalists have studied something substantive in college and that subset of TV news people who are mere personalities get by, of course, on charm and cheekbones rather than anything learned in a classroom. There are in any given year some three hundred thousand students enrolled in undergraduate communications courses. I know this because I was romanced heavily by a publishing house to write a textbook for this field. My interest dwindled when I learned that I should not expect to sustain any passage on a particular topic for even as much as a thousand words because these "future communicators" had short attention spans and didn't like to read. The idea of basing a text on what and how students *ought* to learn rather than on what and how they *wish* to learn apparently never enters the discussion. The market makes the rules, and control of the market has slipped from deservedly imperious professors to baselessly arrogant students. It is one thing to question authority, as the lapel buttons of my youth urged. It is quite another to ignore it altogether, as students often do today.

This shift of curricular power from teachers to students plainly affects what goes   14
on in the classroom. I suspect it also affects scholarship for the worse. While one hopes that professors would use scholarly writing as an avenue for highbrow concerns that they find increasingly difficult to pursue within their courses, anecdotal

evidence strongly suggests they don't. In reporting several stories for *Time* on the general topics of political correctness and multiculturalism, I discovered again and again that professors were instead writing to position themselves favorably on the ideological battlefield—or at least to exploit the marketplace for fulmination created by the culture wars.

Of even greater significance than the solipsism of students and the pusillanimity of teachers is the third trend, the sheer decline in the amount and quality of work expected in class. In an egalitarian environment the influx of mediocrities relentlessly lowers the general standard at colleges to the level the weak ones can meet. When my mother went to Trinity College in Washington in the early 1940s, at a time when it was regarded more as a finishing school for nice Catholic girls from the Northeast than as a temple of discipline, an English major there was expected to be conversant not only in English and Latin but also in Anglo-Saxon and medieval French. A course labeled "Carlisle, Ruskin, and Newman" meant, as my mother wearily recalled, "everything ever written by Carlisle, Ruskin, or Newman and also, it seemed, everything ever written *about* Carlisle, Ruskin, or Newman." A course in Shakespeare meant reading the plays, all thirty-seven of them. By the time I went to college, it was possible to get out of Yale as an honors English major without ever having read Chaucer or Spenser; I know, because I did. In today's indulgent climate, a professor friend at a fancy college told me as I was writing this chapter, taking a half semester of Shakespeare compels students to read exactly four plays. "Anything more than one a week," he explained, "is considered too heavy a load."

This probably should not be thought surprising in an era when most colleges, even prestigious ones, run some sort of remedial program for freshmen to learn the reading and writing skills they ought to have developed in junior high school—not to mention an era when many students vociferously object to being marked down for spelling or grammar. Indeed, all the media attention paid to curriculum battles at Stanford, Dartmouth, and the like obscures the even bleaker reality of American higher education. Or so argues Russell Jacoby, a sometime professor of history at various American and Canadian universities, in his compellingly cranky *Dogmatic Wisdom*. Most students, he notes, are enrolled at vastly less demanding institutions, where any substantial reading list, of whatever ethnicity, would be an improvement. Jacoby admiringly cites Clifford Adelman's *Tourists in Our Land,* based on a survey of the schooling of some twenty thousand high school students, most of them not elite. "When one looks at the archive left by an entire generation," he quotes Adelman as saying, "it should be rather obvious that Stanford is not where America goes to college. Whether Stanford freshmen read Cicero or Frantz Fanon is a matter worthy of a raree show." Well, not quite. For all its intermittent palaver about the individual, the academy is one of the national centers of copycat behavior and groupthink. If a Stanford professor makes a curricular choice, dozens if not hundreds of his would-be peers elsewhere will imitate that choice. Some of them daydream that by doing so they will one day actually teach at Stanford. Most of the rest fantasize that by aping Stanford and its ilk they make their vastly lesser institutions somehow part of the same echelon.

15

16

Perhaps it seems pettish to include community colleges and erstwhile state   17
teachers' colleges when talking about the shortcomings of higher education. Most
readers who went to more prestigious institutions think of "college" as meaning
only their alma maters and the equivalents in cachet, and many expect (perhaps secretly even welcome) deficiencies at lesser places, because those failings reaffirm
the hierarchy. But in terms of public expenditure, community colleges are probably
much more expensive per capita for the taxpayer than any serious centers of learning, precisely because they tend to be relatively cheap for the student—and unlike
private colleges, they rarely have significant endowments or other resources to offset the gap between the subsidized price and the true cost. Moreover, so long as
these schools go on labeling themselves "colleges"—the word "junior" was widely
dropped because it was demeaning, a perfect example of both euphemism and
grade inflation—and so long as their students think of themselves as having "gone
to college," their academic standards will color the public understanding of what
college is.

When Vance Packard wrote *The Status Seekers* in the 1950s, he described the   18
role of the better prep schools and colleges as grooming the next generation of
the traditional ruling class while credentialing the ablest of those not quite to the
manor born. The America he described was unprepared for the radicalism of college students in the 1960s. That political aggression was bred in part by Vietnam
and the civil rights movement, but at least as much by social class anxieties among
the burgeoning numbers of students whose parents had not gone to college and
whose toehold on privilege was either shaky or nonexistent. The current college
generation is similarly radical and dismissive of tradition for much the same reasons.

Those whose parents didn't go to college come disproportionately from ethnic   19
minorities who are demanding a rewriting of the curriculum. This, not incidentally, is
an effective means of leveling the playing field to their competitive advantage. If your
classroom competitor possesses knowledge you don't, you better your prospects if
you can get that knowledge declared irrelevant—and even more if you can get your
homeboy hairstyle studied as culture and history.

Those whose parents did go to college are not necessarily any more confident.   20
They have witnessed the economic erosion of the past couple of decades, in which
it now takes two incomes for a family to live as well as it used to on one.

Both groups are understandably insistent on keeping the number of places in   21
college as large as possible, for fear of having to drop their dreams. This form of
middle-class welfare (even college students not raised in the middle class are by definition seeking to enter it) is shamelessly indulged by state legislators who recognize it as a necessity for reelection.

Other constituencies join in pushing for the maintenance and expansion of pub-   22
lic higher education. Faculty and administrators seek to protect their jobs. Merchants and civic boosters serve their interests, both economic and sentimental, by
bolstering institutions that bear the name of their town or state. Alumni often
combine a nostalgic loyalty with a pragmatic one. They think, with some justice,

that burnishing the luster of their alma mater adds to the sheen of their own education as well, even though it was acquired years or decades ago and has nothing to do with the merits or deficiencies of the institution of today.

But none of these social pressures justifies spending one hundred fifty billion dollars a year overeducating a populace that is neither consistently eager for intellectual expansion of horizons nor consistently likely to gain the economic and professional status for which the education is undertaken. Nor can one justify such expenditures by citing the racial and ethnic pressures from those who argue that only a wide-open system of higher education will give minorities a sufficient chance. Whatever the legacy of discrimination or the inadequacies of big-city high schools, a C student is a C student and turning colleges into remedial institutions for C students (or worse) only debases the value of the degrees the schools confer.   23

Beyond the material cost of college, there are other social costs implicit in our system of mass higher education. If college is not difficult to get into, students are not as likely to be motivated in high school. If the authority of a teacher's grade or recommendation is not vital because there will always be a place open at some college somewhere, students have yet another reason for disrespecting authority and learning less efficiently. Paying for their children's college education often imposes a massive financial drain on parents during the years when they should be most intent on preparing for retirement, and leaves many of them too dependent on Social Security and other welfare programs. . . . This expenditure may make sense when the education has real value for the child being supported. But some parents are wasting their money.   24

For many adolescents who finish high school without a clear sense of direction, college is simply a holding pattern until they get on with their lives. It is understandable that they should want to extend their youth and ponder their identities (or navels) for a bit; what is rather less clear is why they should do so at public as well as parental expense. At minimum, that opportunity ought to be limited to students who have shown some predisposition to absorb a bit of learning while they are waiting to discover their identities.   25

My modest proposal is this. Let us reduce, over perhaps a five-year span, the number of high school graduates who go on to college from nearly sixty percent to a still generous thirty-three percent. This will mean closing a lot of institutions. Most of them, in my view, should be community colleges, current or former state teachers' colleges, and the like. These schools serve the academically marginal and would be better replaced by vocational training in high school and on-the-job training at work. Two standards should apply in judging which schools to shut down. First, what is the general academic level attained by the student body? That might be assessed in a rough and ready way by requiring any institution wishing to survive to give a standardized test—say, the Graduate Record Examination—to all its seniors. Those schools whose students perform below the state norm would face cutbacks or closing. Second, what community is being served? A school that serves a high percentage of disadvantaged students (this ought to be measured by family   26 finances rather than just race or ethnicity) can make a better case for receiving tax dollars than one that subsidizes the children of the prosperous, who have private alternatives. Even ardent egalitarians should recognize the injustice of taxing people who wash dishes or mop floors for a living to pay for the below-cost public higher education of the children of lawyers, so that they can go on to become lawyers too.

This reduction would have several salutary effects. The public cost of education would be sharply reduced. Competitive pressures would probably make high school students and their schools perform better. Businesses, which now depend on colleges to make their prospective employees at least minimally functional, would foot some of the bills—and doubtless would start demanding that high schools fulfill their duty of turning out literate, competent graduates. And, of course, those who devise college curricula might get the message that skills and analytical thinking are the foremost objects of learning—not sociopolitical self-fulfillment and ideological attitudinizing.   27

I would like to preserve, however, one of the few indisputably healthy trends in higher education, the opening up of the system to so-called mature students (meaning, in practice, mostly housewives). Here is where open admission makes sense. Anyone who has been out of high school for, say, seven or perhaps ten years ought to be allowed to enroll and perhaps even be offered the chance to purchase a semester of not-for-credit refresher courses. If people of that age are prepared to make the sacrifices and undertake the disciplines of being students again, they are likely to succeed—indeed, at most schools that actively solicit mature students, the older enrollees outperform the younger ones.   28

Massive cuts in total college enrollment would, of course, necessitate massive layoffs of faculty. In my educational utopia, that would be the moment to eliminate tenure and replace it with contracts of no more than five years, after which renewal should be possible but not presumed. This would allow universities to do some of the same weeding out of underproductive managers and professionals that has made American business more efficient, and would compel crackpot ideologues of whatever stripe to justify their scholarship, at least to their peers and conceivably to the broader public. The justification normally offered for tenure—the potential for a revival of McCarthyism—is so remote from present-day academic reality as not to be worthy of discussion. And just what is wrong with having to defend one's opinion anyway? A college teaching position is an opportunity to think and serve, not a professor's personal capital asset. Apart from the self-interest of professors, it is hard to concoct any other rationale for affording college teachers a tenure protection enjoyed by few other managers and professionals, save civil servants who operate under much closer supervision and scrutiny. Competing for one's job on an ongoing basis could introduce a little more healthy elitism into the professorial lifestyle. Teachers might strive to meet standards more widely held than their own ideology. The risk is that the loss of tenure could make professors even more apt to kowtow to the consumerist demands of students, so as to remain popular and employed. But that is happening anyway.   29

In truth, I don't expect any suggestion as sweeping as mine to be enacted. America is in the grip of an egalitarianism so pervasive that low grades are automatically assumed to be the failure of the school and the teacher and perhaps the community at large—anyone but the student himself. We insist on saying that pretty much everyone can learn, that it's only a matter of tapping untouched potential. While we are ready to call someone handicapped "differently abled," we are not ready to label the dull-witted as "differently smart." Even more than in my youth, we cling to the dream of a world in which everyone will be educated, affluent, technically adept, his or her own boss. There is nothing wrong with discontent at having a modest place in the scheme of things. That very discontent produced the ambition that built the culture of yesterday and today. But the discontent of those times was accompanied by discipline, willingness to work hard, and ready acceptance of a competitive society. 30

Some readers may find it paradoxical that a[n argument] for greater literacy and intellectual discipline should lead to a call for less rather than more education. Even if college students do not learn all they should, the readers' counterargument would go, surely they learn something, and that is better than their learning nothing. Maybe it is. But at what price? One hundred fifty billion dollars is awfully high for deferring the day when the idle or ungifted take individual responsibility and face up to their fate. And the price is even steeper when the egalitarian urge has turned our universities, once museums of clear ideas, into soapboxes for hazy and tribalist ones. Ultimately it is the yearning to believe that anyone can be brought up to college level that has brought colleges down to everyone's level. 31

"SEX" IS ALSO A DIRTY WORD
from *Defending Pornography*
Nadine Strossen

This culture always treats sex with suspicion. . . . Sex is presumed guilty until proven innocent.   Gayle Rubin, *anthropologist*

Although [those who] campaign against sexual speech . . . employ some differing rhetoric in their unified call for censoring sexually oriented expression, they sound many common chords, notably that sex and materials that depict or describe it inevitably degrade and endanger women. In short, the war on sexual expression is, at bottom, a war on sex itself, at least as far as women are concerned. Because the philosophy of leading antipornography, procensorship feminists reflects a deep distrust of sex for women, such feminists are, in my view and in the view of others, aptly labeled "antisex." 1

Taken together, the traditional and feminist antipornography, antisex crusaders appeal to a broad gamut of the ideological spectrum in both the government and 2 the public. They pose an unprecedented danger to sexual expression, which has always been uniquely vulnerable in the United States, as well as to the concept that the First Amendment protects such expression. Moreover, their attacks have been alarmingly successful.

We are in the midst of a full-fledged "sex panic," in which seemingly all descriptions and depictions of human sexuality are becoming embattled. Right-wing senators have attacked National Endowment for the Arts grants for art whose sexual themes—such as homoeroticism or feminism—are allegedly inconsistent with "traditional family values." At the opposite end of the political spectrum, students and faculty have attacked myriad words and images on campus as purportedly constituting sexual harassment. Any expression about sex is now seen as especially dangerous, and hence is especially endangered. The pornophobic feminists have played a very significant role in fomenting this sex panic, especially among liberals and on campuses across the county.

The fear of sexual expression has become so high-pitched lately that it even has deterred an AIDS clinic from giving out information about combating the deadly spread of the virus. In Oklahoma City, the American Civil Liberties Union (ACLU) represented a doctor who was prosecuted for displaying a safe-sex poster on the windows of his AIDS clinic, which was located in an area frequented by gay men. Yet public health experts maintain that the allegedly illegal and offensive image in the poster—a man wearing a condom—is an important instrument in the life-or-death campaign to halt the spread of HIV. Although the charges were dismissed, the city has threatened further prosecutions, thus deterring the clinic from mounting similarly explicit educational displays in the future.

Society's wariness toward sex is highlighted by contrasting it with the greater societal tolerance toward violence. This dichotomy is especially vivid in the media and mass culture, where violent depictions are far more accepted than sexual ones. The contrast was aptly capsulized by Martin Shafer, a top executive at a film production company, when he noted, "If a man touches a woman's breast in a movie, it's an R rating, but if he cuts off a limb with a chain saw, it's a PG-13."

Because the domain of sexual expression, always a difficult terrain, has lately been laced with land mines placed by diverse enemies, it has become more treacherous than ever. Not surprisingly, artists, academics, and others are increasingly deterred from entering and exploring this potentially explosive—but also rich, wonderful, and important—territory.

All over the country, artists say that they dare not pursue sexual themes for fear that their work will be perceived as too controversial to be funded or displayed. Indeed, outraged officials and citizens alike have indignantly demanded the defunding and deposing from display of art with a wide range of sexual themes; lately it seems that even a mere sexual connotation, no matter how subtle, is vulnerable.

In our current epidemic of erotophobia, even images of nude or seminude bodies in wholly nonsexual contexts have been attacked. For example, in 1993, Vermont officials hung bedsheets over a mural that artist Sam Kerson had painted in a state building's conference room. One press account described the mural, which was commissioned to mark the five-hundredth anniversary of Christopher Columbus's voyage, as "a politically correct rendition of Columbus and his men arriving in the New World, battle-axes and crucifix raised, ready to oppress the natives." But the painting was not politically correct enough for a number of female employees, who complained that its depictions of bare-breasted native women constituted sexual harassment. Because the mural could not be removed without destroying it, the state resorted to the bedsheet "solution."

In 1992, a painting of the classical seminude statue the Venus de Milo was removed 9 from a store in a Springfield, Missouri, shopping mall because mall managers considered the topless masterpiece "too shocking." The painting of the ancient Greek sculpture, which was carved about 150 B.C., and which stands in a place of honor in Paris's Louvre museum, was replaced by a painting of a woman wearing a long, frilly dress.

Another example of a famous artistic masterpiece that has been suppressed in 10 the current sex panic is *The Nude Maja,* or *Maja Desnuda,* by the celebrated Spanish painter Francisco de Goya. In 1992, Pennsylvania State University officials removed a reproduction of this acclaimed work from the front wall of a classroom following a complaint by English professor Nancy Stumhofer that it embarrassed her and made her female students "uncomfortable."

No matter that the reproduction hung, along with reproductions of other masterpieces, in a room used for art history classes. No matter that university officials 11 offered to move the painting to a less prominent position in the classroom, such as the back wall. No matter that they also offered to remove the Goya from the classroom altogether whenever Professor Stumhofer taught there, or even to relocate her classes to another classroom. No. Apparently, nothing short of extirpating the work from all campus classrooms would purge its taint, from her perspective. And the university capitulated. As writer Nat Hentoff commented, at that Penn State campus the administration defines sexual harassment as "anything that makes people uncomfortable about sexual issues."

Moving even beyond nudity or partial nudity, the sex panic has engulfed certain 12 forms of clothing that some observers might deem provocative. In a 1994 *Ms.* magazine discussion on pornography, writer Ntozake Shange described one such situation that she said was "very heavy on my heart":

> I was on the cover of *Poets & Writers* and I wore a pretty lace top. In the next two issues, there were letters asking if *Poets & Writers* is now a flesh magazine— why was I appearing in my underwear? Bare shoulders are exploitation now?

In response, Andrea Dworkin, another participant in the *Ms.* discussion, confirmed that she would indeed see Shange's photograph as exploitation: "It's very hard to look at a picture of a woman's body and not see it with the perception that her body is being exploited."

Whether the stigmatizing epithet of choice for particular protesters happens to 13 be "pornography" or "sexual harassment," the result is the same: the conclusory label intimidates campus officials and others who should defend artistic expression, so they instead suppress it. Objecting to another such suppressive incident, which occurred at Vanderbilt University in 1993 . . . Vanderbilt art professor Marilyn Murphy said, "Human sexuality has been a recurring theme in art since antiquity. Visual arts is the most misunderstood discipline on this campus and on college campuses everywhere."

Liza Mundy, a writer who has chronicled campus attacks on art with sexual themes, has concluded that "MacKinnonite ideas underlie many" such attacks, noting the irony that many of these battles "pit feminist students against feminist artists." At the University of Arizona in Tucson, students physically attacked a group of photographic self-portraits by graduate student Laurie Blakeslee, which were displayed in the student union. The alleged offense? Blakeslee had photographed herself in her underwear. In Mundy's words, "Young women and men influenced by crusading law professor Catharine MacKinnon—and these are in the ascendance on many campuses—believe that . . . sexually explicit imagery create[s] an atmosphere in which rape is tolerated and even encouraged." 14

An essential aspect of women's right to equal opportunity in employment and education is the right to be free from sexual harassment. What is troubling, though, is the spreading sense—perpetuated by the feminist antipornography movement—that *any* sexual expression about a woman, or in her presence, *necessarily* constitutes such harassment. This presumption is stated expressly as the basis for the sweeping sexual harassment codes that are becoming increasingly common on campuses. 15

Syracuse University, for example, adopted a sexual harassment code in 1993 that prohibits not only "requests for sexual relations combined with threats of adverse consequences" if refused, and assaultive acts such as "pinching or fondling," but also nonassaultive, vaguely described acts such as "leering, ogling and physical gestures conveying a sexual meaning," and loosely described expressions including "sexual innuendoes, suggestive remarks, [and] sexually derogatory jokes." What all of these seemingly disparate behaviors have in common, the code informs us, "is that they focus on men and women's sexuality, rather than on their contributions as students or employees in the University." 16

But this should not be an either-or choice, should it? Are women not—along with men—sexual beings, as well as students or employees? Is women's sexuality really incompatible with their professional roles? Is it really increasing women's autonomy, options, and full-fledged societal participation to posit such an incompatibility? Have we not learned from history, and from other cultures, that the suppression of women's sexuality tends to coincide with the suppression of women's equality? And that when women's sexuality has been banished from the public sphere, women themselves are also banished from key roles in that sphere? 17

Far from advancing women's equality, this growing tendency to equate any sexual expression with gender discrimination undermines women's equality. Women are, in effect, told that we have to choose between sexuality and equality, between sexual liberation and other aspects of "women's liberation," between sexual freedom 18 and economic, social, and political freedom. This dangerous equation of sexual expression with gender discrimination, which is at the heart of the feminist antipornography movement, is a central reason that movement is so threatening to the women's rights cause.

The misguided zeal to strip all sexual expression from workplaces and campuses, in an alleged effort to strip those places of gender-based discrimination, now has reached even to subtle interpersonal expressions, prone to subjective perceptions and interpretations, such as looks and glances. A growing number of campus policies, including the one at Syracuse University already quoted, extend the concept of harassment to "sexually suggestive looks." Likewise, a survey about the sexual harassment of female doctors by their patients, published in the prestigious *New England Journal of Medicine* in December 1993, included "suggestive looks" among the "offenses" reported. In fact, though newspaper headlines trumpeted the dramatic conclusion that 75 percent of the female doctors surveyed said that they had been sexually harassed by patients, further reading revealed that "most of the offenses involved suggestive looks and sexual remarks." 19

Are women doctors, faculty, and students to be relegated to a figurative equivalent of the purdah of traditional Hindus and Muslims, or the clothing and segregation requirements of orthodox Jews—designed to prevent men from looking at women, and to "protect" women from men's looks? While these traditional religious practices shield women from the eyes of anyone outside their domestic circles, they also imprison women within those domestic circles. The outside world cannot see women, and women cannot see the outside world. 20

To be sure, "sexual looks," as well as the other nonassaultive conduct proscribed in the Syracuse code, could constitute sexual harassment if they were sufficiently severe or pervasive—for example, if a professor repeatedly subjected a young student to such behavior. In contrast, isolated incidents where the behavior is not targeted at someone who has less authority or status should not be deemed harassment. 21

STRATEGY TWO: DEVELOPING AN ESSAY BASED ON A SOURCE

This strategy gives you the freedom to develop your own ideas and present your own point of view in an essay that is only loosely linked to the source. Reading an assigned essay helps you to generate ideas and topics and provides you with evidence or information to cite in your own essay; but *the thesis, scope, and organization of your essay are entirely your own.*

1. Finding and Narrowing a Topic

As always, you begin by studying the assigned essay carefully, establishing its thesis and main ideas. As you read, start *brainstorming: noting ideas of your own* that might be worth developing. You need not cover exactly the same material as the source essay. What you want is a *spin-off* from the original reading, not a summary.

Here is one student's preliminary list of topics for an essay based on Blanche Blank's "A Question of Degree." (Blank's essay can be found on pp. 8–11.) Notice that, initially, this student's ideas are mostly personal.

- "selling college": how do colleges recruit students? how did I choose this college? has my college experience met my expectations?

- "practical curriculum": what are my courses preparing me for? what is the connection between my courses and my future career? Why am I here?

- "college compulsory at adolescence": what were my parental expectations? teachers' expectations? did we have any choices?

- "employment discrimination based on college degrees": what kinds of jobs now require a B.A.? was it always like that? what other kinds of training are possible—for clerks? for civil servants? for teacher's aides?

- financing college: how much is tuition? are we getting what we pay for? is education something to be purchased, like a winter coat?

- "dignity of work": job experience/work environment

- "joylessness in university life": describe students' attitudes—is the experience mechanical? is the environment bureaucratic?

- "hierarchical levels": what do the different college degrees mean? should they take as long as they do? should a BA take four years?

If you read the essay a few times without thinking of a topic or if you can't see how your ideas can be developed into an essay, *test some standard strategies*, applying them to the source essay in ways that might not have occurred to the original author. Here, for example, are some strategies that generate topics for an essay based on "A Question of Degree."

Process

You might examine in detail one of the processes that Blank describes only generally. For example, you could write about your own experience to explain the ways in which teenagers are encouraged to believe that a college degree is essential, citing high school counseling and college catalogues and analyzing the unrealistic expectations that young students are encouraged to have. Or, if you have sufficient knowledge, you might describe the unjust manipulation of hiring procedures that favor college graduates or the process by which a college's liberal arts curriculum gradually becomes "practical."

Illustration

If you focused on a single discouraged employee, showing in what ways ambition for increased status and salary have been frustrated, or a single disillusioned college graduate, showing how career prospects have failed to measure up to training and expectations, your strategy would be an illustration proving one of Blank's themes.

Definition

Definition often emerges from a discussion of the background of an issue. What should the work experience be like? What is the function of a university? What is a good education? By attempting to define one of the components of Blank's theme in terms of the ideal, you are helping your reader to understand her arguments and evaluate her conclusions more rationally.

Cause and Effect

You can examine one or more of the reasons why a college degree has become a necessary credential for employment. You can also suggest a wider context for discussing Blank's views by describing the kind of society that encourages this set of values. In either case, you will be accounting for, but not necessarily justifying, the nation's obsession with degrees. Or you can predict the consequences, good or bad, that might result if Blank's suggested legislation were passed. Or you might explore some hypothetical possibilities and focus on the circumstances and causes of a situation different from the one that Blank describes. What if everyone in the United States earned a college degree? What if education after the eighth grade were abolished? By taking this approach, you are radically changing the circumstances that Blank depicts, but still sharing her concerns and exploring the principles discussed in her essay.

Problem and Solution

If Cause and Effect asks "why," then Problem and Solution explains "how." Blank raises several problems that, in her view, have harmful social consequences. What are some solutions? What changes are possible? How can we effect them? How, for example, can we change students' expectations of education and make them both more realistic and more idealistic? Note that exploring such solutions means that you are basically in agreement with Blank's thesis.

Comparison

You can alter the reader's perspective by moving the theme of Blank's essay to another time or place. Did our present obsession with education exist a hundred years ago? Is it a problem outside the United States at this moment? Will it probably continue into the twenty-first century? Or, focusing on late-twentieth-century America, how do contemporary trends in education and employment compare with trends in other areas of life—housing, finance, recreation, child-rearing, or communications? With all these approaches, you begin with a description of Blank's issue and contrast it with another set of circumstances, past or present, real or hypothetical.

Before choosing any of these speculative topics, you must first decide:

- What is practical in a brief essay
- Whether it requires research
- Whether, when fully developed, it will retain some connection with the source essay

For example, there may be some value in comparing the current emphasis on higher education with monastic education in the Middle Ages. Can you write such an essay? How much research will it require? Will a discussion of monastic education help your reader better to understand Blank's ideas? Or will you immediately move away from your starting point—and find no opportunity to return to it? Do you have a serious objective, or are you simply making the comparison "because it's there"?

2. Taking Notes and Writing a Thesis

Consider how you might develop an essay based on one of the topics suggested in the previous section. Notice that the chosen topic is expressed as a question.

Topic: What is the function of a university in the 1990s?

- After thinking about your topic, start your list of notes *before* you reread the essay, to make sure that you are not overly influenced by the author's point of view and to enable you to include some ideas of your own in your notes.
- Next, review the essay and add any relevant ideas to your list, *remembering to indicate when an idea originated with the source and not with you.*

Here is a complete list of notes for an essay defining the function of a university in the 1990s. The paragraph references, added later, indicate which points were made by Blank and where in her essay they can be found. The thesis, which follows the notes, was written after the list was complete.

WHAT THE UNIVERSITY SHOULD DO

1. to increase students' understanding of the world around them

    e.g., to become more observant and aware of natural phenomena (weather, for example) and social systems (like family relationships)

2. to help students to live more fulfilling lives

    to enable them to test their powers and know more and become more versatile; to speak with authority on topics that they didn't understand before

3. to help students live more productive lives

   to increase their working credentials and qualify for more interesting and well-paying jobs (B.B., Paragraphs 3–9)

4. to serve society by creating better informed, more rational citizens not only through college courses (like political science) but through the increased ability to observe and analyze and argue (B.B., Paragraphs 3, 14)

5. to contribute to research that will help to solve scientific and social problems (not a teaching function) (B.B., Paragraphs 3, 14)

6. to serve as a center for debate to clarify the issues of the day

   people should regard the university as a source of unbiased information and counsel; notable people should come to lecture (B.B., Paragraphs 3, 14)

7. to serve as a gathering place for great teachers

   students should be able to regard their teachers as worth emulating

8. to allow students to examine the opportunities for personal change and growth

   this includes vocational goals, e.g., career changes (B.B., Paragraph 4)

WHAT THE UNIVERSITY SHOULD NOT DO

9. it should not divide the haves from the have-nots

   college should not be considered essential; it should be possible to be successful without a college degree (B.B., Paragraphs 8, 10)

10. it should not use marketing techniques to appeal to the greatest number

    what the university teaches should be determined primarily by the faculty and to a lesser extent by the students; standards of achievement should not be determined by students who haven't learned anything yet

11. it should not ignore the needs of its students and its community by clinging to outdated courses and programs

12. it should not cooperate with business and government to the extent that it loses its autonomy (B.B., Paragraphs 6, 9)

13. it should not be an employment agency and vocational center to the exclusion of its more important functions (B.B., Paragraphs 6, 9, 16)

Thesis: As Blanche Blank points out, a university education is not a commodity to be marketed and sold; a university should be a resource center for those who want the opportunity to develop their intellectual powers and lead more productive, useful, and fulfilling lives.

3. Deciding on a Strategy

As a rule, you would consider strategies for your essay as soon as you have established your thesis. In this case, however, the choice of strategy—definition—was made earlier when you chose your topic and considered several possible strategies. *The notes, divided into what a university should and should not do, already follow a definition strategy, with its emphasis on differentiation.*

4. Constructing an Outline

Having made all the preliminary decisions, you are ready to plan the structure of your essay.

- Mark those portions of the reading that you will need to use in support of your thesis. Your essay will be based on both your own ideas and the ideas of your source.
- Check whether your notes accurately paraphrase the source, and decide how many source references you intend to make so that you can write a balanced outline.
- Double-check to make sure that you are giving the source credit for all paraphrased ideas.
- If appropriate, include some examples from your own experience.
- Organize your notes in groups or categories, each of which will be developed as a separate paragraph or sequence of related paragraphs.
- Decide the order of your categories (or paragraphs).
- Incorporate in your outline some of the points from Blanche Blank's essay that you intend to include. Cite the paragraph number of the relevant material with your outline entry. If the source paragraph contains several references that you expect to place in different parts of your outline, use a sentence number or a set of symbols or a brief quotation for differentiation.

Here is one section of the completed outline for an essay on "Defining a University for the 1990s." This outline incorporates notes 3, 13, 9, and 8 from the list on pp. 162–163.

I. The university should help students to live more productive lives, to increase their working credentials, and to qualify for more interesting and well-paying jobs. (Paragraph 6—last sentence)

A. But it should not be an employment agency and vocational center to the exclusion of its more important functions. (Paragraph 9—"servicing agents"; Paragraph 12—"joylessness in our university life"; Paragraph 16)

B. It should not divide the haves from the have-nots; success without a college degree should be possible. (Paragraph 2—"two kinds of work"; Paragraph 17)

II. The university should allow students to examine the opportunities for personal growth and change; this includes vocational goals, e.g., career changes. (Paragraph 4—"an optional and continuing experience later in life")

5. Writing the Essay

When you write from sources, you are engaged in a kind of partnership. *You strive for an appropriate balance between your own ideas and those of your source.* By reading your source carefully and using annotation, outlining, and paraphrase, you familiarize yourself with the source's main ideas and reasoning and prepare to put those ideas in your essay. But *it is your voice that should dominate the essay.* You, after all, are writing it; you are responsible for its contents and its effect on the reader. For this reason, *all the important "positions" in the structure of your essay should be filled by you.* The topic sentences, as well as the introduction, should be written in your own words and should stress your views, not those of your author. On the other hand, your reader should not be allowed to lose sight of the source essay; it should be treated as a form of evidence and cited whenever it is relevant, but always as a context in which to develop your own strategy and assert your own thesis.

Here is the completed paragraph based on Points I and IA in the outline:

To achieve certain goals, all of us have agreed to take four years out of our lives, at great expense, for higher education. What I learn here will, I hope, give me the communication skills, the range of knowledge, and the discipline to succeed in a career as a journalist. But, as Blanche Blank points out, a college education may not be the best way to prepare for every kind of job. Is it necessary to spend four years at this college to become a supermarket manager? a computer programmer? a clerk in the social security office? If colleges become no more than high-level job training or employment centers, or, in Blank's words, "servicing agents" to screen workers for business, then they lose their original purpose as centers of a higher form of learning. Blank is rightly concerned that, if a college degree becomes a mandatory credential, I and my contemporaries will regard ourselves "as prisoners of economic necessity," alienated from the rich possibilities of education by the "joylessness in our university life."

6. Revising the Essay

Your work isn't finished until you have reviewed your essay carefully to ensure that the organization is logical, the paragraphs coherent, and the sentences complete. To gain some distance and objectivity, most people put their work aside for a while before starting to revise it. You can also ask someone else to read and comment on your essay, but make sure that you have reason to trust that person's judgment and commitment to the task. It isn't helpful to be told only that "paragraph three doesn't work" or "I don't get that sentence"; your reader should be willing to spend some time and trouble to pinpoint what's wrong so that you can go back to your manuscript and make revisions. Problems usually arise in these three areas.

Overall Structure

If you follow your outline or your revised list of notes, your paragraphs should follow each other fairly well. But extraneous ideas—some of them good ones—tend to creep in as you write, and sometimes you need to make adjustments to accommodate them. As you look carefully at the sequence of paragraphs, make sure that they lead into each other. Are parallel points presented in a series or are they scattered throughout the essay? Sometimes, two paragraphs need to be reversed, or two paragraphs belong together and need to be merged. In addition, your reader should be guided through the sequence of paragraphs by the "traffic signals" provided by transitional phrases, such as "in addition" or "nevertheless" or "in fact." The transitions need not be elaborate: words like "also," "so," and "too" keep the reader on track.

Paragraph Development

The paragraphs should be of roughly comparable length, each containing a topic sentence (not necessarily placed at the beginning), explanatory sentences, details or examples provided by your source or yourself, and (possibly) quotations from your source. It's important to have this mix of general material and detail to keep your essay from being too abstract or too specific. Make sure that every sentence contributes to the point of the paragraph. Look for sentences without content, or sentences that make the same point over again. If, after such deletions, a paragraph seems overly brief or stark, consider what illustrations or details might be added to support and add interest to the topic. Check back to the source to see if there are still some points worth paraphrasing or quoting.

Sentence Style

Your writing should meet a basic acceptable standard. Are the sentences complete? Eliminate fragments or run-ons. Is the sentence style monotonous, with the same pattern repeated again and again? Look for repetitions, and consider ways to vary the style, such as starting some sentences with a phrase or

Guidelines for Writing a Single-Source Essay

1. Identify the source essay's thesis; analyze its underlying themes, if any, and its strategy; and construct a rough outline of its main ideas.

2. Decide on two or three possible essay topics based on your work in Step 1, and narrow down one of them. (Be prepared to submit your topics for your teacher's approval and, in conference, to choose the most suitable one.)

3. Write down a list of notes about your own ideas on the topic, being careful to distinguish between points that are yours and points that are derived from the source.

4. Write a thesis of your own that fairly represents your list of ideas. Mention the source in your thesis if appropriate.

5. If you have not done so already, choose a strategy that will best carry out your thesis; it need not be the same strategy as that of the source essay.

6. Mark (by brackets or underlining) those paragraphs or sentences in the source that will help to develop your topic.

7. Draw up an outline for your essay. Combine repetitious points; bring together similar and related points. Decide on the best sequence for your paragraphs.

8. Decide which parts of the reading should be cited as evidence or refuted; place paragraph or page references to the source in the appropriate sections of your outline. Then decide which sentences of the reading to quote and which to paraphrase.

9. Write the rough draft, making sure that, whenever possible, your topic sentences express your views, introduce the material that you intend to present in that paragraph, and are written in your voice. Later in the paragraph, incorporate references to the source, and link your paragraphs together with transitions. Do not be concerned about a bibliography for this single-source essay. Cite the author's full name and the exact title of the work early in your essay. (See pp. 92–95 for a review of citations.)

10. Write an introduction that contains a clear statement of your thesis, as well as a reference to the source essay and its role in the development of your ideas. You may also decide to draft a conclusion.

11. Review your first draft to note problems with organization, transitions, or language. Proofread your first draft very carefully to correct errors of grammar, style, reference, and spelling.

12. Using standard-size paper and leaving adequate margins and spacing, prepare the final draft. Proofread once again to catch careless errors in copying.

subordinate clause. Are you using the same vocabulary again and again? Are too many of your sentences built around "is" or "are"? Search for stronger verbs, and vary your choice of words, perhaps consulting the thesaurus. (But think twice about using words that are totally new to you, or you'll risk sounding awkward. Use the thesaurus to remind yourself of possible choices, not to increase your vocabulary.) Finally, consider basic grammar. Check for apostrophes, for subject-verb agreement, for quotation marks. Don't let careless errors detract from your hard work in preparing and writing this essay.

ASSIGNMENT 5: WRITING AN ESSAY BASED ON A SINGLE SOURCE

A. Read "The Other Side of Suicide," "Love as an Experience of Transcendence," and "Getting Them into the Electronic Tent." One of these three essays will serve as the starting point for an essay of your own. Assume that the essay you are planning will be approximately three pages long, or 600–900 words. Using steps 1 and 2, think of *three* possible topics for an essay of that length, and submit the most promising (or, if your teacher suggests it, all three) for approval.

B. Plan your essay by working from notes to an outline. Be prepared to submit your thesis and outline of paragraphs (with indications of relevant references to the source) to your teacher for approval.

C. Write a rough draft after deciding which parts of the essay should be cited as evidence, distributing references to the source among appropriate sections of your outline, and determining which parts of the reading should be quoted and which should be paraphrased.

D. Write a final draft of your essay.

THE OTHER SIDE OF SUICIDE
from *The Beauty of the Beastly*
Natalie Angier

Considered on its face, suicide flouts the laws of nature, slashing through the sturdy instinct that wills all beings to fight for their lives until they can fight no longer. 1

Yet by a coolheaded evolutionary accounting, suicide cannot be entirely explained as a violent aberration or a human pathology lying outside the ebbs and pulls of natural selection and adaptation. Suicide, for all its private, tangled sorrows, is surprisingly common in most countries, accounting on average for about 1 percent of all deaths. And when the number of unsuccessful suicide attempts is taken into account, the prevalence of the behavior jumps considerably. The incidence, some evolutionary geneticists say, is too great to be accounted for by standard explanations like social malaise or random cases of psychiatric disease. 2

Instead, the persistence of suicide at a high rate across most cultures of the world 3
suggests an underlying evolutionary component, a possible Darwinian rationale for
an act that too often appears starkly irrational. The inclination toward suicide could
be a concomitant of a trait or group of traits that at some point in evolutionary history conferred benefits on those who bore it.

Further bolstering the case for a genetic basis to suicide is its tendency to run in 4
families. Although suicide occurs in nearly all countries, it is far more common
among some ethnic groups than others. The Hungarians and Finns, for example,
suffer from suicide rates two to three times those in the United States and most of
Europe. Significantly, the Hungarians and Finns are thought to share genetic roots
in the distant past (as well as the linguistic roots that bind the Hungarian and Finnish
tongues and set them apart from Indo-European languages). In addition, the elevated incidence of suicide holds true not only in those nations, where socioeconomic conditions could be responsible, but also for Finns and Hungarians who have
emigrated to other countries, again hinting at a biological substrate.

Nobody argues that there is a single gene for suicide, or that suicide or mental 5
illness should be thought of as good. The lure of suicide too often beckons to the
young, who clothe it in the romantic chiffon of nobility and poetry and see it as a
reasonable option should the transition to adulthood prove too traumatic, a way of
thinking that no sane adult would condone.

Nevertheless, there may be plausible evolutionary explanations for at least some 6
self-destructive acts. A number of theorists propose that the impulse to kill oneself
may be an expression of an instinct toward self-sacrifice for the good of surviving
relatives, either because those relatives will be rescued from their own death, or
because they will benefit richly from the resources that will now accrue to them.
The surviving relatives will in turn pass on the sacrificial victim's genes. To take a
short and admittedly simplistic example, a hominid in the jungle may have enhanced
his genetic survival by sacrificing himself to a leopard that would otherwise have
slain six of his brothers or sisters. However, because we live in complex social
groups, such an impulse toward martyrdom might on occasion show itself in complex, distorted forms, tugging miserably at the psyches of even those who have no
families to benefit from their deaths or to ensure that their genetic legacies survive.

In another scenario, suicide is viewed not as heritable but as the most tragic out- 7
come of another trait that may derive from natural selection—the tendency toward depression. Some Darwinian thinkers say that extremely bleak moods are
themselves too common to be the result of pathology alone. They propose that
bouts of depression may be useful, forcing people into a kind of emotional hibernation and giving them time to reflect on their mistakes. But such a strategy, if sustained too long or repeated too often, becomes maladaptive and even fatal, showing
itself as the harrowing disease called major depression.

Reasoning that human beings invent few traits but instead display intricate versions 8
of behaviors seen elsewhere in the animal kingdom, some biologists have looked to
other species for clues to the genesis of suicide and depression. The exercise is

fraught with perils. Nonhuman animals obviously do not leave behind anything as clear as a note, nor are they likely to have sufficient awareness to do something as deliberate as jump off a cliff. Still, there are numerous examples of creatures that sacrifice themselves for their kin, including termites that explode their guts, releasing the slimy, foul contents over enemies that threaten their nest, and rodents that deliberately starve themselves to death rather than risk spreading an infection to others in their burrow. What is more compelling, many species of nonhuman primates will suffer serious depression when stressed; on falling into an episode of melancholy, the monkeys may engage in all sorts of life-threatening activities—refusing food until they die of malnutrition, or swinging from dangerous tree limbs that no normal monkey would go near. So similar is monkey depression to our own that the symptoms of the mood disorder dissipate when the primates are given an antidepressant like Prozac.

Admittedly, one must approach this theoretical terrain with enormous trepida-   9
tion, for it's all too easy to sound insensitive or glib in ascribing suicide and depression to the handiwork of natural selection. Psychiatrists have struggled long and hard to get the public to view mental illness as an organic disorder rather than a self-indulgence or character flaw, and most are reluctant to describe something like depression in anything other than the most strictly disease-oriented and condemnatory terms—as the mind's version of diabetes or cancer. Researchers know too well how easily a Darwinian explanation for complex behaviors can be overdone and oversimplified.

Certainly the affairs of animals much simpler than people have been misinter-   10
preted in the past. For example, the mention of suicide in nonhuman species invariably raises the famed case of lemmings, rodents that were long thought to kill themselves en masse by running into the sea, as though alerted by a group alarm clock that today is a good day to die. As recent research has revealed, however, the tale of the suicidal lemming is false. The tawny, thickset rodents will die by the group, but that is a result of an error in judgment. Lemmings are the locusts of mammals, and they will strip a habitat bare. They then begin migrating to find new feeding grounds, swarming over boulders, around trees, whatever stands in their way. If they run into a body of water, they try to swim across, a routine that works fine for streams and ponds. If they happen to hit a lake or an ocean, they discover too late into their paddling that they can't make it.

Often it is not clear whether a death in the wilderness is deliberate or acciden-   11
tal. Some animal behaviorists have developed models predicting that, under certain circumstances, a hatchling bird in a multichick brood does better from the perspective of its genetic legacy to let itself be killed by its siblings than to fight back. Among crested penguins, for instance, a mother always lays two eggs a season, one large, one small. Given the harshness of her arctic surroundings, she can rear only one bird to independence, and usually that lucky penguin will come from the large egg. Still, she lays the double dose as an insurance policy, in case the big egg is preyed on. Should the big and little eggs both end up hatching, the smaller offspring

in theory would do best to permit the bigger sibling to kill it off without putting up a fuss—essentially, to throw itself on its sibling's sword. After all, both birds can't possibly survive, so why divert resources from the relative with the greater chance of success?

The theory has some observational data to back it up: in encounters between sibling penguins, the little ones do appear to die off without ruffling anybody's feathers. However, critics of the scenario do not buy that the smaller contender is going gently into that good night. They point out that if your ordinary Joe were stuck in a lifeboat with Mike Tyson and a very limited quantity of food, the nonboxer would be foolish to challenge Tyson to a fight; instead, the little fellow is likely to lie low and look for a chance to push him overboard, or simply pray that Tyson gets struck by lightning. 12

In general, scientists will call a death a suicide only when the animal has much to gain and little to lose, reproductively speaking, from the act. Among this group some put cryptically colored butterflies that escape being eaten by blending into their surroundings. Once an adult is past its reproductive time, it becomes a risk to its surviving offspring, for if the elder insect is discovered by a bird, the predators will gain clues from the butterfly's pattern to discriminate prey from background; thereafter, the younger butterflies will also be in danger. As it happens, the postfertile adults are known to drop to the groundcover and begin beating their wings rapidly until they die of exhaustion. They obliterate themselves and their secrets before they get caught. 13

Other exemplars of self-sacrifice abound. In some gall midges—tiny gnatlike insects—a mother offers up her body as a meal to offspring, and they happily consume every last segmented bit of her. Among naked mole rats, hairless and blind rodents that live underground and are almost as closely related to one another as are bees in a hive, an animal that is infested with parasites knows what it must do: go off to the communal toilet area of the burrow and remain there until it dies. Once its decision is made, it won't move, and it can't be force-fed, even under laboratory conditions; the sickly mole rat will not risk infecting the whole colony. 14

In applying to human beings the idea of self-sacrifice for the good of one's kith and kin, scientists cite obvious examples: mothers who gladly die to save their children, war heroes who go down in flames for their buddies, or even the recent spate of so-called rational suicides, in which elderly or terminally ill patients request that they be allowed to die quickly to avoid being a drain on their families. Researchers are much more reluctant to use such reasoning to justify the behavior of suicidal patients who very often are mentally ill, lonely, and alienated from those who care about them. Yet psychiatrists observe that people who are contemplating suicide frequently think of it in extravagantly selfless terms, as the option that would be best for the suicide's family and friends. Those who have talked to people immediately after they made a serious suicide attempt report that the patients often have an altruistic explanation for what they did, believing the action to be the wise, clever, and thoughtful thing to do. In that sense, our own version of suicide sounds 15 remarkably similar to the response of a parasitized naked mole rat. Those who consider killing themselves feel grotesque, polluted, infected, and they may think it best to destroy the source of disease before it contaminates their loved ones.

Of course, it's true that the majority of those who attempt suicide are afflicted by a disease—a mood disorder, in most cases depression or manic-depression. Such conditions are characterized by a dramatic drop in neurotransmitters like norepinephrine or serotonin, the molecules that allow nerve cells to communicate and that help modulate emotions and aggression.   16

Studying nonhuman primates, scientists say they have witnessed many of the symptoms of serious depression in their subjects, including a disregard for self-preservation. Jane Goodall, the renowned chimpanzee champion, once observed a seven-and-a-half-year-old male chimp experience such profound despair after the death of his mother that he refused to leave her corpse even to eat. The monkey slowly withered away, lay down, and died—of a broken heart, Ms. Goodall said.   17

Monkey depression resembles our own not only behaviorally but biochemically. Working with a free-ranging colony of rhesus monkeys, behavioral scientists have learned that about 20 percent of the primates are predisposed to serious depression, roughly the same as our own lifetime risk of the disorder. The monkeys fall into their slump when they lose a relative or close partner, or suffer a drop in social status, events that likewise set off human depression. In addition, the depressed monkeys show some of the same changes in brain chemistry that have been observed in human patients, including a drop in cerebrospinal levels of norepinephrine.   18

Depression, then, is evolutionarily ancient, preceding the appearance of hominids. Its purpose could be protective, allowing people and other animals with advanced cognitive skills to assess their situations, consider how their tactics may have backfired, and figure out a way to avoid repetitions of the costly error. Alternatively, depression could be the inevitable downside of a personality that offers great payoffs when times are good. In the case of the rhesus monkey, the same animals that are susceptible to depression often rise to the top of the social hierarchy because of their heightened sensory and emotional sensitivity. They're more aware than their peers of critical changes in the environment—the sound of an approaching predator, the tentative gestures of a possible new ally. They see and hear and smell everything. They are like taut strings on a beautiful violin. If bowed too hard, the strings will snap.   19

LOVE AS AN EXPERIENCE OF TRANSCENDENCE
Charles Lindholm

George Simenon, the prolific French author who was equally active as a Don Juan, was once asked to describe the difference between sexual passion and romantic love. "Passion," Simenon said, "is a malady. It's possession, something dark. You are jealous of everything. There's no lightness, no harmony. Love, that's com-   1 pletely different. It is beautiful. Love is being two in one. It is being so close that when one opens his mouth to speak, the other says exactly what you meant to say. Love is a quiet understanding and a fusion."

The erotically experienced Simenon here disengages the imperative demands of sexual desire from romantic love, which he describes as engendering a powerful and expansive sense of self-loss through merger with the beloved other. This experience of self-transcendence, I will argue in the following pages, is the essence of romantic love; it is above all a creative act of human imagination, arising as a cultural expression of deep existential longings for an escape from the prison of the self. I shall contrast this view of love with another, more prevalent view, which understands love as contingent upon sexual desire.

2

In making my case about the nature of falling in love, I am hardly being original. Rather, the question of the nature of love has divided and puzzled Western philosophers at least from the time of the Greeks. Irving Singer, in his exhaustive study of the philosophical and literary roots of the concept of romantic love, has outlined this debate, showing that the way love has been conceptualized throughout Western history can be divided into two opposing, but necessarily intertwined, perspectives. In the first, love is based on appraisal, and those who are beloved are thought capable of satisfying our deepest appetites. In other words, we assess the other to discover if they have the attributes we long for; if they do, we love them. Broadly defined, love is a matter of calculated self-interest.

3

Self-interest, however, can take on a transcendental hue. The beloved can appeal to us as an avenue to a higher level of being. There are many versions of this way of understanding love. For instance, Plato portrays love of persons as a plateau in the soul's impassioned pursuit of the ideal good. The beloved is adulated as an earthly and imperfect expression of divine harmony and beauty. But the wise man realizes that the love of persons is shallow compared to the spiritual rewards of pure reason, and progresses through enjoyment of the flawed body of the other to meditation on the abstract realm of the ideal, where beauty is absolute and eternal. Love for a person then is a means to a higher end, much like the contemplation of a work of art.

4

A more down-to-earth stance is taken by Ovid, for whom the Platonic search for a higher love in the realm of the absolute through the body of the lover is a ludicrous subterfuge. Ovid says that what the lover wants is clear enough: sexual enjoyment. His emphasis is on the game of love, and he teaches his readers, both male and female, how the idealizing imagery of romantic passion can be used with style and grace by intelligent seducers to help them gain sexual access to those whom they desire while avoiding the attentions of others whom they find unattractive. Professions of love serve to conceal a seducer's deliberate machinations and thereby render lust more attractive.

5

Ovid's appetitive perspective on love has been a dominant view for scientific minds ever since Plato's notion of the spiritual progress of the soul lost its persuasiveness. But while Ovid's portrayal of sexual desire as the underlying source of

6

love was retained, his playful attitude toward sexuality was repudiated as morally suspect by more puritanical writers such as Jonathan Swift, who wrote that love is "a ridiculous passion which hath no being but in play-books and romances."

Anthropologists, in the little they have to say about romantic love . . . have tended   7
to fall generally within the Swiftian paradigm. Most famous and representative is Ralph Linton's statement:

> The hero of the modern American movie is always a romantic lover, just as the hero of an old Arab epic is always an epileptic. A cynic may suspect that in any ordinary population the percentage of individuals with capacity for romantic love of the Hollywood type was about as large as that of persons able to throw genuine epileptic fits. However, given a little social encouragement, either one can be adequately imitated without the performer admitting even to himself that the performance is not genuine.

Similarly, Robert Lowie argues that in all cultures "passion, of course is taken for   8
granted; affection, which many travellers vouch for, might be conceded; but Love? Well, the romantic sentiment occurs in simpler conditions, as with us—in fiction."

Romantic love, from this point of view, is nothing but a self-delusion, derived   9
from the arts, used to persuade lovers that their sexual desires are actually ethereal and transcendent. Where Ovid saw the idealizing content of romantic love as an attractive and necessary convention, it now becomes a hypocritical lie. Jean-Paul Sartre has immortalized this modern perspective in a famous section in *Being and Nothingness* (1956), where he scathingly imagines the bad faith of a young girl absently permitting her hand to be stroked by a suitor while she simultaneously imagines herself admired solely as a creature of purity and abstract intellect.

This approach has the virtue of simplicity and coherence; falling in love is always   10
a fraud, and men and women who claim to be in love are invariably hypocrites or, at best, seducers. But it does little justice to the actual self-reports of lovers, who clearly do not always fit into the categories of self-deceivers and sexual predators. A more sympathetic modern version of the "eros tradition" (as Singer has called it) is to be found in sociobiology, which takes a somewhat different tack toward understanding romantic love. The aim is to give more credit to the lovers' own inner experience while still retaining the materialistic view of romantic love as essentially an expression of sexuality.

The twist is that rather than debunking romantic sentiment as self-delusion,   11
these writers understand love as a compulsive drive toward sexual contact with a specific beloved other. This compulsion is connected to evolutionary biology by utilizing contemporary theories of genetic success. Instead of consciously manipulating one another, as enjoined by Ovid, the lovers now are themselves unconscious puppets of the deep evolutionary forces that are propelling their behaviors.

This argument was first proposed by Schopenhauer, who asserted that romantic   12
love is a trick played by the Will in order to compel human beings to reproduce and carry on the movement of the *Geist* toward the future. Thus he writes that

lovers desire a "fusion into a single being, in order then to go on living only as this being; and this longing receives its fulfillment in the child they produce"; or, put more prosaically: "If Petrarch's passion had been satisfied, his song would have been silenced from that moment, just as is that of the bird, as soon as the eggs are laid."

As reworked in modern rhetoric Schopenhauer's argument is used by socio-biologists to assert that romantic love is a genetically innate mechanism serving to offset the male's natural tendency to maximize his gene pool through promiscuity. It does this by tying him to a particular female via the emotionally charged sexual contact that is understood to be the heart of romance. The enhanced pairbonding that results serves the evolutionary purpose of increasing the overall rate of survival for human children.

From this perspective falling in love is therefore a very real experience, probably a consequence of the manufacture of powerful chemicals in the brain that incite the potent feelings of merger and ecstasy lovers report; but love is not sufficient onto itself, rather it is a means to an end—perpetuation of the species. Thus sociobiology shares with the Platonic perspective a concern with teleology. But where Plato saw love as a step in the pursuit of the ideal, now the goal of romantic love is disconcertingly mundane: evolutionary success.

Some of the cultural background that informs this argument can be illustrated in a balance sheet made up by the twenty-nine-year-old Charles Darwin, who was weighing the good points and bad points of marriage. The main good point was companionship ("a nice soft wife on a sofa" . . . "better than a dog anyhow"); children were also mentioned, as Darwin expresses his fear of being a "neuter bee." The bad points were more numerous, and included the considerable financial burden a wife and children would impose on him, the inevitable constraints a family would place on his freedom of action, the "loss of time," the "anxiety and responsibility" and the fear that marriage might end as "banishment and degradation with (an) indolent, idle fool."

In reading Darwin's lists, it seems clear that the disadvantages of marriage, which are many and concrete, appear to far outweigh the advantages, which are few and abstract. As Alan MacFarlane writes, speaking from a strictly rational perspective, marriage in England "was not sane behavior, for almost all the advantages of marriage could be bought in the market—from sex to housekeeping and friendship." But Darwin married nonetheless, persuading himself that "there is many a happy slave." Why did he act so irrationally?

MacFarlane argues that in Western history, and especially in the history of England, romantic love has been precisely the factor that has been invoked as the source of the marriage tie. In a society where arranged marriage was never pervasive, where lineages were more or less nonexistent, and where personal autonomy prevailed, love acts as a deus ex machina, overcoming the reasonable reluctance of rational self-seeking individuals to commit themselves to marriage bonds they would otherwise avoid. Furthermore, love also focuses sexuality in the open market of potential partners, "some external force of desire is needed to help the individual to make a choice. Hence passionate 'love' overwhelms and justifies and provides compulsive authority."

Although MacFarlane does not carry his argument through to claim a biological source for romance, it is perfectly plausible to reconcile his position with a concept of falling in love as an expression of a biological pressure that compels individuals toward erotic encounters with a specific other. The historian Laurence Stone states this point of view most candidly when he describes falling in love as "an urgent desire for sexual intercourse with a particular individual"; a sexual encounter that, from the sociobiological standpoint, can induce the commitment and reciprocal caring necessary for maintaining a human family unit.

Following the logic of the argument further, if romantic love is simply a strong, biologically generated, hormonally induced sexual urge for a unique other, culture becomes a variable that may have an enhancing or suppressing effect on the erotic romantic impulse, and it would make sense to argue that societies valuing choice and individualism would be most conducive to romantic love, while those valuing obligation and communalism would work to control romantic desire by cultural mechanisms, such as arranged marriage, chaperoning of youth, child betrothal, and so on. On the other hand, Western culture, which favors personal autonomy and free choice, is the location where love can take its "natural," biologically induced, course, permitting romance to replace formal bonds of kinship and alliance as the motivation for marriage.

To restate: from the standpoint of the contemporary sociobiological version of the eros tradition, falling in love is understood as a biological drive, probably deriving from hormonal secretions, that intensifies sexual desire and thereby leads to strong pairbonding. It is favorable to the reproduction and care of human children, and its transcendental consummation is the successful maximization of genetic potential. It can be assumed that some cultures will favor this compulsion while others will attempt to suppress it; nonetheless it will remain as a universal and ineradicable desire for mating with a particular other person—a desire interpreted as romantic love.

But there are problems with this perspective, and they have to do with the place romantic love fills in different cultural contexts. Although giving some reluctant credit to cultural processes, sociobiology generally assumes that millions of years of evolution outweigh a few millennia of culture. Therefore, human beings, like their simian ancestors, are portrayed as basically governed by instinct, though the instincts may have been distorted, channeled, and partially curbed by cultural conditioning. However, postulating a primary cause requires a demonstration of at least some discernible secondary effect; and if culture can completely rewrite, overturn, or cancel the supposed biological matrix of romantic love, sexuality, and reproduction, then the logic of the sociobiological argument is seriously challenged.

This challenge is most evident in the aspect of culture that has most to do with evolutionary biology; that is, the institution of marriage. In all human societies marriage serves as a ritualized way of formalizing and legitimizing the sexual relation-

18

19

20

21

22

ship between couples. Furthermore, in almost every known culture married couples produce and raise the vast majority of children. Given this basic fact, one would expect that if romantic love is linked to reproduction, then marriage should be correlated with romantic love.

In the modern West, of course, this works well enough, since romantic love, marriage, and children indeed usually *do* go together and, as we shall see, have gone together for some centuries. However, in most human cultures this is not the case, nor was it necessarily the case everywhere in Western culture in the past. For example, in the courtly society of Louis XIV in France, marriage and love were decidedly opposed, since marriage was arranged for political advantage, not for romantic attraction. In this culture courtesans were the objects of romantic attraction, not wives. Interestingly, these courtesans, who stood outside of the political structure of the society because of their base birth, were prized not so much for their sexuality as for their charm and wit. Of course, having children was something these women avoided at all costs. 23

Similarly, in Rome of the Imperial Age conjugal love between husband and wife was considered ridiculous and impossible, so much so that Seneca writes, "to love one's wife with an ardent passion is to commit adultery." Rather, noble lineages were tied together through marriage bonds based on Roman virtues of austerity and piety; virtues that were sorely tested with the vast expansion of Roman conquests and the importation of huge numbers of slaves who could serve as concubines. In these circumstances marriage came to be regarded, as Plautus notes, as "an unavoidable calamity," while love was to be found with slave prostitutes of both sexes who were outside the power struggle that pitted husband against wife. 24

As in France, the romantic relationship with the courtesan had nothing to do with children: reproduction was reserved for the far more mundane and pragmatic relationship of marriage. Eventually, elite evasion of the constraints of marriage in favor of romantic (but sterile) involvement with prostitutes became so prevalent that the birthrate of the nobility dropped precipitously, obliging Augustus to offer special privileges to men producing children in aristocratic marriages. 25

Nor is this a configuration found only in complex state societies, though many more examples from such societies could easily be cited. A similar pattern occurs in Northern Pakistan, where the patrilineal Pukhtun organized marriages to cement alliances between clans, while individual men pursued romances clandestinely. Prostitutes and adolescent boys were most often the objects of their romantic desires, and neither of these ever produced children. 26

Furthermore, if romantic love is assumed to correlate with reproductive success, one would expect that societies most favoring the cultural expression of love would have the highest birth rate. However, the converse is the case. Cultures where marriages are between strangers and are arranged for political and economic benefit by parents have generally had far higher birthrates than the West. 27

For instance, if we look at English and Germanic society prior to the advances of medical knowledge, we can see the birthrates there have long been low, and 28 population growth slow, largely because of late marriage and a cautious attitude toward having children. This pattern has persisted from at least the early middle ages, and possibly much earlier. It is associated with an Anglo-Saxon cultural milieu in which personal autonomy and maximization of individual benefits outside of the extended family circle prevailed. In this context children have been (quite realistically) viewed as a cost, whose major value is as pets or as monuments to their parents. Thus Britain and Northern Europe generally have never been home to cults of fertility, nor have bachelorhood, spinsterhood, or barrenness ever been sanctioned against.

All this is in obvious contrast to cultures where the extended family is the unit   29
of production and of political power, where more children mean more labor, wealth, and physical strength invested in the extended family, and where fertility is consequently highly valued. Given these circumstances, it is difficult to see how the sociobiological paradigm could explain the fact that the Northern European constellation of low birthrate, late marriage, nuclear families, and individual autonomy *correlates* with the most highly evolved tradition of romantic love in the world!

The premise of a "deep structure" of genetic predisposition for romantic love is   30
further undercut when we consider the relationship between romantic love and sexual desire. It is taken for granted in the eros tradition that romantic love is intertwined with sexuality and is, in fact, a consequence of the erotic impulse. Thus any disavowal of sexual desire in a romantic relationship is assumed, a priori, to be self-delusive. However, this assumption requires us to dismiss ethnographic and historical examples that point in precisely the opposite direction.

For example, consider the Southern European expressions of courtly love in the   31
Medieval period. Here, in a transformation of the cult of the virgin Mary, the courtier explicitly denied any carnal feelings for his beloved, who was worshiped as an angel above the realm of earthly lust, not to be sullied in thought or deed. These courtiers singing of *fin amor* were often married men with active sex lives and children, and the lady herself was always a married woman, with husband and children of her own. However, romantic love was not to be found in these legitimized sexual relations, but only in adulation of the lady. To assume this chaste and idealizing ideology was simply a mask disguising sexual desire is taking for granted what one wishes to prove; rather, we should take at face value the truth of the courtier's song; that is, that the lady was, *for the poet,* beloved as a creature of sanctified innocence and virtue.

Such behavior patterns and idealizations are hardly unusual, though the structure   32
of the relationship may vary considerably. For example, the Marri Baluch, another patrilineal Middle Eastern people much like the Pukhtun, have a highly elaborated romantic love complex. Men and women, married for political and economic purposes, long to participate in secret and highly dangerous illicit love affairs. These passionate relationships are hugely valued in Marri culture and are the subject of innumerable poems and songs.

According to the Marri, when lovers meet they exchange tokens of mutual affec-   33
tion and talk heart to heart, without dissimulation. In marked contrast to the ele-

vation of the lady in courtly love, and in marked contrast as well to the reality of male domination in Marri society, Marri lovers regard one another as equals. For this reason the lovers should be chaste: sexuality, culturally understood as an expression of male power, imposes an element of oppression and subordination that the cultural ideal of mutuality and respect between lovers cannot permit. How many of these relationships are indeed sexless is impossible to say, but chastity is what the Marri believe to be characteristic of the deepest forms of love between men and women; once again, to suppose that this belief is a falsehood is to do them and their culture an injustice by assuming that we know the truth behind their ideals.

The separation between sexual desire and romantic love may be especially common in societies such as the Marri, where sexual intercourse is regarded as an act of violence and domination, or in Melanesia, where sexuality is associated with pollution and spiritual danger. An example of the latter is found in Manus, described by Margaret Mead, where sex is a perilous act, and marriage itself is a distasteful and shameful business. As among the Marri, Manus men and women are drawn into extramarital liaisons, but, Mead writes: "Illicit love affairs, affairs of choice, are, significantly enough, described as situations in which people need not have sex if they do not wish to, but can simply sit and talk and laugh together. . . . The wonderful thing about lovers is that your [sic] don't have to sleep with them." 34

If these examples are too exotic, we need look no further than our own Victorian forbears. The familiar split between whore and virgin was a reality for the Victorians, and sexual desire was, as much as possible, divorced from middle-class marriage, since women of culture were assumed to be without demeaning sexual impulses. Men demanded virginal purity in the women they married, while wives appear, from their own accounts, to have often managed actually to live up to the ideal. Thus sexual contact between a husband and his beloved wife was regarded as an unfortunate necessity of marriage, to be engaged in as a duty; men overcome by sexual passion were expected to spend themselves in the company of prostitutes, whom they certainly did not love. This characteristic Victorian division between love and sexuality is a mode of feeling that must be taken on its own terms. 35

It seems, then, that the correlation between falling in love, sexual desire, and reproduction has to be reconsidered. It appears that the eros tradition in its modern guise renders biological, and therefore primary and irresistible, a peculiarly modern and Western form of relationship that does indeed unite romantic love, sexual intimacy, and reproduction—elements that may certainly have a powerful affinity, but that also may be separated, both in logic and in cultural reality. The postulated biological matrix thus does not have any provable effect. 36

However, there is another standard Western way of looking at love that I wish to put forward here as an alternative to the eros paradigm in all its guises. From this alternative perspective love is not motivated by the desire to reproduce, or lust, or the ideal of beauty; rather, the beloved other is adulated *in himself or herself* as the fountainhead of all that is beautiful, good, and desirable. As Francesco Alberoni puts it, when we fall in love "the possible opens before us and the pure 37 object of eros appears, the unambivalent object, in which duty and pleasure coincide, in which all alienation is extinguished."

However, it is crucial to note that this adulation is offered in spite of the beloved's *actual* characteristics; in other words, falling in love is an act of imagination in which the other is invested with absolute value; the beloved can even be loved for his very faults. Singer calls this idealistic form of love the "bestowal tradition" to stress the lover's creativity in manufacturing the perfection of the beloved.   38

From within this framework any overt or covert calculated appraisal of the other as a good provider, a useful ally, or even as an avenue to God is felt to be a sin against the very nature of romantic love, which is defined and experienced as spontaneous, total, and boundless in its devotion to the actual person of the other. Thus, to love "for a reason" is not to love at all. We love because we love, and not because of any advantage that the beloved other has to offer us.   39

This alternative notion of unqualified love has deep intellectual and spiritual roots in the West: its heritage includes the Jewish concept of *nomos* transformed into Christian notions of God's unconditional, unreserved, and undeserved love for humanity (agape), as expressed in the sacrifice of Jesus. This notion of God's boundless love of humanity made love itself a value in Western culture while simultaneously devaluing sexuality. Love was further humanized in the cult of Mary, and, as we have seen, afterward was secularized in the courtly love that bound the courtier to his lady. As Singer writes, "Henceforth the Christian could hold not only that God is Love but also that Love is God."   40

In this context, and over time, "the idea that love is the unmerited sanctification of the sinner degenerated into the notion that sinners become sanctified through *any* love whatsoever. God disappeared, but there remained the holiness of indiscriminate love binding one worthless person to another." Love became reciprocal and individualized, as it was secularized and institutionalized into the romantic experience that is the expected prelude to marriage in contemporary culture in the West and, increasingly, everywhere in the world.   41

It is this secularized form of romantic love that is rhapsodically portrayed in songs, poems, novels, and films as an ultimate value in itself: compelling, overwhelming, ecstatic, uniquely blissful—indeed, the most powerful emotional event of one's life. This is the love in which, as the young Hegel writes, "consciousness of a separate self disappears, and all distinction between the lovers is annulled"; it is the love apostrophized by the philosopher Roberto Unger as "the most influential mode of moral vision in our culture."   42

Is this experience of falling in love as a way of imagining and experiencing transcendence through a relationship of communion in selfless and fervent merger with an idealized other a peculiarly Western one, as Singer's philosophical approach would seem to indicate? I would say not, but it is also not universal.   43

Rather, falling in love can usefully be conceived as one possible response to the human existential condition of contingency and self-consciousness. As Andre Bataille writes, "We are discontinuous beings, individuals who perish in isolation in   44 the midst of an incomprehensible adventure, but we yearn for our lost continuity." In response to this unbearable but inescapable dilemma, human beings search for ways to escape the burden of loneliness while avoiding confrontation with a cold and indifferent cosmos. One of the ways this escape can be attained is in the experience of falling in love. To quote Bataille once more, "Only the beloved can in this world bring about what our human limitations deny, a total blending of two beings, a continuity between two discontinuous creatures." Thus, instead of resembling a biological drive, falling in love is more akin to religious revelation, but with a particular real person as the focus of devotion.

I was led to this view of romantic love because in the last few years I have been involved in cross-cultural research on charismatic movements and idealization. My studies indicated that charisma, which is experienced as a compulsive and overwhelming attraction of a follower to a leader, is in almost all respects parallel to the experience of romantic love. For example, in both instances there is an intense idealization of one particular other person; in both there is a fervent subjective perception of merger with the beloved—a merger experienced as "exaltation, ecstasy and exaggeration of the ego." 45

Furthermore, in love, as in charisma, participants feel they are capable of obliterating boundaries of convention in their quest for a state of absolute communion. Both states also are characterized by a fear of loss of the idealized other—and suicidal despair if that loss occurs—and both have a strong tendency toward rationalization (charismatic groups become bureaucracies; romantic lovers become companionate couples). In both rationalization can be offset if mystery and danger are maintained by distance and obstacles that separate follower and leader, lover and beloved (the Romeo and Juliet effect). 46

Charisma and romance also appeared to be mutually exclusive—a person involved in a charismatic group generally could not be immersed in a romantic relation, and vice versa. As Kernberg writes, following Freud, "the opposition between the couple and the group is an essential characteristic of human love life"; an insight borne out in ethnographic data. People who leave charismatic organizations often do so because they have fallen in love; conversely, people who become devotees have often been disappointed in love. This fact also indicates that both arise from the same psychological matrix. The main differences are a result of the influence of the group dynamic in the charismatic relation, which renders it less susceptible to rationalization, while making real reciprocity between the leader and the disciples impossible. 47

Given these parallels, Alberoni can reasonably write that "the experience of falling in love is the simplest form of collective movement," and Miller can argue that there is an "equivalence between leaders and lovers that brings about the same kind of elevation, idealization and incorporation that endows the leader and lover with special status and powers." Falling in love and charisma thus can be plausibly conceptualized as variations on a very deep and basic human existential search—the quest for transcendence. 48

If we accept the proposition that charisma and love are parallel attempts to es-   49
cape from contingency and solipsism, this means downplaying some of the elements
that have generally been seen as diagnostic of falling in love. For instance, romantic
love does not occur only among adolescents, nor does it *necessarily* imply equality
between the lovers, or the transformation of love into marriage, or even powerful
sexual desire.

If this perspective is accepted, then further research should be oriented toward   50
understanding what sorts of social formations and historical conditions favor various characteristic expressions of the human impulse toward self-loss in ecstatic
states of union with an idealized other. We should also compare and contrast romantic love and charisma with other apparently similar experiences such as mystical
and religious communion, possession trance, reverie, artistic inspiration, and so on.
By taking this pathway, we can avoid reducing romantic love to an instrumentality
and recognize instead that it stands on its own as a specific state of transcendence—
the one most characteristic of the modern world.

GETTING THEM INTO THE ELECTRONIC TENT
from *How to Watch TV News*
Neil Postman and Steve Powers

At carnival sideshows, the barkers used to shout intriguing things to attract an   I
audience. "Step right up. For one thin dime, see what men have died for and others
lusted after. The Dance of the Veils as only Tanya can do it." The crowd would
gather as lovely Tanya, wrapped in diaphanous garb, would wiggle a bit, and entice
grown men who should have known better to part with their money for a ticket.
Instead of seeing Tanya shed her clothes, her customers shed their money.

In television news there is no Tanya we know of but there are plenty of Sonyas,   2
Marias, Ricks, and Brads who have the job of getting you into the electronic tent.
They come on the air and try to intrigue you with come-ons to get you to watch
their show. "Step right up" becomes "Coming up at eleven o'clock." And, instead
of veils, you get a glimpse of some videotape which may intrigue you enough to
part with your time instead of a dime. It is no accident that in the television news
industry, the short blurb aimed at getting you to watch a program is called a "tease."
Sometimes it delivers what it advertises but often hooks us into the electronic tent
and keeps us there long enough that we don't remember why we were there in the
first place.

The tease is designed to be very effective, very quickly. By definition, a tease   3
lasts about ten seconds or less and the information it contains works like a headline. Its purpose is to grab your attention and keep you watching. In the blink of a
tease you are enticed to stay tuned with promises of exclusive stories and tape,
good-looking anchors, helicopters, team coverage, hidden cameras, uniform blaz-
ers, and even, yes, better journalism. It is all designed to stop you from using the

remote-control button to switch channels. But the teasing doesn't stop there. During each news program, just before each commercial, you will see what are known as "bumpers"—teases that are aimed at keeping you in the tent, keeping you from straying to another channel where other wonders are being touted. And the electronic temptations do not even cease with the end of the program. When the news show is over, you are still being pleaded with "not to turn that dial" so that you can tune in the next day for an early-morning newscast, which in turn will suggest you watch the next news program and so on. If news programmers had it their way, you would watch a steady diet of news programs, one hooking you into the next with only slight moments of relief during station breaks.

If you think you can beat the system by not watching teases, you'll need to think 4 again. We are dealing here with serious professional hucksters. The game plan, aimed at getting you to watch the news, starts even before you have seen the first tease. It starts while you're watching the entertainment shows *before* the news. Whether you know it or not, we are programmed to watch the news, by programmers. They know that most of us tend to be lazy. Even with remote controls at our fingertips, we are likely to stay tuned to the channel we have been watching. So the United Couch Potatoes of America sit and sit, and sit, and before they know it, Marsha and Rick have hooked us into their news program, promising "team coverage," no less, of today's latest disaster. In the textbook vernacular: the lead-in programs must leave a residual audience for the news shows which follow. To put it plainly, a station with a strong lineup of entertainment programs can attract a large audience to the news tent. High-rated shows such as "Oprah Winfrey," programmed just before the news, bring in a big audience and premium prices at the broadcast marketplace. This is why the best news program may not have ratings as high as a news program with a strong lead-in. It may not be fair but it is television.

Now, let us say all things are equal. Station A and station B both have excellent 5 lead-ins. What news program will you watch? Most people will say something like "I want the latest news, the best reporting with state-of-the-art technology presented by people I can trust and respect."

But while people might say they like the most experienced journalists presenting 6 the news, many news consultants claim that no matter what they *say*, the audience prefers to watch good-looking, likable people it can relate to (perhaps of the same age group, race, etc.). News organizations spend a lot of time and money building up the reputations of their anchors, sending them to high-visibility stories that they hope will convince viewers that they are watching top-level journalists. Unfortunately, in some markets the top anchors are sometimes "hat racks" who read beautifully but who can barely type a sentence or two without the aid of a producer and writer. They may know how to anchor but many are strictly lightweights. In television, looking the part is better than being the real item, a situation you would rightly reject in other contexts. Imagine going to a doctor who hadn't studied medicine, but rather looks like a doctor—authoritative, kindly, understanding, and surrounded by formidable machinery. We assume you would reject such a professional fraud especially if he or she had majored in theater arts in college. But this kind of play-acting is perfectly acceptable in the world of television news and entertainment where actors who have played lawyers on a TV series frequently are called on to give speeches at lawyers' conventions and men who have played doctors are invited to speak at gatherings of medical professionals. If you can read news convincingly on television, you can have a successful career as an anchor, no journalism experience required. This is not to say there aren't bright men and women who are knowledge-able journalists and who can and do serve as anchors. But the problem is that it is almost impossible for the viewer to figure out which anchor knows his stuff and who's faking it. A good anchor is a good actor and with the lift of an eyebrow or with studied seriousness of visage, he or she can convince you that you are seeing the real thing, that is, a concerned, solid journalist.

You may wonder at this point, what difference does it make? Even if one cannot   7
distinguish an experienced journalist from a good actor playing the part of an expe-rienced journalist, wouldn't the news be the same? Not quite. An experienced jour-nalist is likely to have a sense of what is particularly relevant about a story and insist on including certain facts and a perspective that the actor-anchor would have no knowledge of. Of course, it is true that often an experienced journalist, work-ing behind the cameras, has prepared the script for the actor-anchor. But when the anchor is himself or herself a journalist, the story is likely to be given additional di-mensions, especially if the journalist-anchor does his or her own script writing.

And there is one more point: even if there were no differences between the sto-   8
ries presented by actor-anchors and journalist-anchors, the fact that the audience is being deluded into thinking that an actor-anchor is a journalist contributes a note of fakery to the enterprise. It encourages producers and news directors to think about what they are doing as artifice, as a show in which truth-telling is less impor-tant than the appearance of truth-telling. One can hardly blame them. They know that everything depends on their winning the audience's favor, and the anchor is the key weapon in their arsenal.

If you are skeptical about the importance of the anchor in attracting the audience   9
to the electronic tent, you must ask yourself why they are paid so much. Network anchors earn over a million dollars a year. Over two million dollars a year. Do we hear three? Yes, more than three million dollars a year in the case of Dan Rather at CBS. Is he worth it? From a financial point of view, certainly. He brings people into the tent because they perceive him to be an experienced, solid reporter, who has paid his dues and knows what's going on. And an experienced newsman such as Rather starts to look like a bargain when you think of local anchors being paid as much as 750,000 to a million dollars without serious journalistic credentials. An-chors who work for network-affiliated stations in the top ten markets make an av-erage of $139,447 a year. Nationwide, the average anchor, as of this writing, makes $52,284 a year, according to the National Association of Broadcasters.

So there you are ready to watch the news presented by a high-priced anchor and   10
on comes the show, complete with a fancy opening, and music sounding as though it

was composed for a Hollywood epic. The host appears—an anchor god or goddess sculpted on Mount Arbitron, at least the best of them. But even the worst looks authoritative. Of course, the anchor has had plenty of help from plenty of crafts people in creating the illusion of calm omniscience. After all, it's not all hair spray. That glittering, well-coiffed, Commanding Presence has been placed in a setting that has been designed, built, and painted to make him or her look as wonderful as possible. Consultants have been used to make sure the lights are fine-tuned to highlight the hair and to fill in wrinkles. Color experts have complemented the star's complexion with favorable background hues. Short anchors have their seats raised to look taller, with makeup applied to create just the right look, accenting cheekbones, covering baldness, enlarging small eyes, hiding blemishes, perhaps obscuring a double chin.

And of course there is camera magic. A low camera angle can make a slight anchor look imposing. Long and medium shots, rather than close-ups, can hide bags under the eyes. The anchor-star has probably had the benefit of a clothing allowance and the best hairdressers and consultants. It is cosmetic television at its finest. 11

The music fades and the parade of stories and the people reporting them begins. Whom you see depends sometimes on professional competence and journalistic ability. But it may also depend on the results of "focus groups," where ordinary viewers are shown videotapes and are then asked which anchors and reporters they prefer to watch and why. The group gives its opinion without the benefit of observing a performer over a period of time or knowledge of the reporter's background and experience. What is wanted is an immediate, largely emotional reaction. Performers are also evaluated by a service called "TV Q," which claims to rate television performers on the basis of who the public recognizes. The company, called Marketing Evaluations/TV Q, polls about six thousand Americans by mail, then sells the results to networks, advertising agencies, and anyone else willing to spend about a thousand dollars to find out someone's Q score. 12

Some news show consultants believe in forming a television news pseudo-family to attract audiences. After the "Today" show started to slide in the ratings, NBC brought back sportscaster Joe Garagiola to try to pep up the ratings. Garagiola had been on the program from 1969 to 1973. NBC had alienated its viewers by replacing popular coanchor Jane Pauley with Deborah Norville, who was supposed to be a hot ratings-getter. She wasn't. The show nosedived. Executives realized they needed something or somebody with pizzazz. They reached for a person who, they hoped, could make the "Today" show cast a family again. Warm, affable Joe Garagiola. The return of the Prodigal Son. Exit Norville, now cast as the "other woman." 13

The "family" concept is at work at many local stations. The anchors probably will be a couple, male and female, both good-looking and in the same relative age category as husband-wife (although in our modern society with second marriages common, the male anchor may be twenty years older than his female counterpart). The other "family" members may be like Archie and Veronica to appeal to the younger set: Archie the sportscaster, who never tires of watching videotapes of highlights and bloopers, and Veronica the weather person. There is also Mr. or Ms. Breathless 14

Showbiz who always feigns being thrilled to see the heartthrob or hottest rock group of the moment.

Whatever kind of television family is presented, it always has one thing in common. It is a happy family, where everybody gets along with everyone else (at least for thirty minutes) and knows his or her place. The viewer usually gets to see the whole "family" at the "top," or beginning, of the show. They will either be featured in a taped introduction or be sitting on the set, en masse, to create a sense of cohesion and stability. Throughout the program, members of the family will come on the set and do their turn, depending on their specialty. No newscast is complete without Archie the Sportscaster rattling off a list of clichés that he believes bond him to his fans. "Yes!" "In your face!" "Let's go to the videotape!" "Swish!" 15

Theoretically, sportscasters are supposed to be reporters, not fans. But depending on what they believe to be the roots of their popularity they might decide to bask in the glorious light of sports heroes and become cheerleaders. It is, in any event, the sportscaster's job to keep the audience excited, complete with taped highlights and interviews with the top players who often have nothing more to contribute than standard-brand sports-hero remarks: "It's not important how I played, as long as I can contribute to the team" or "I might have scored a few more touchdowns, but the real credit has to go to the front line who made it all possible." Picture and cliché blend to fill the eye with a sense of action and the nose with the macho smell of the locker room. 16

No newscast would be complete without a weather report that usually starts with a review of what already happened that day. The report is supposedly made interesting by moving H's and L's and by making clouds and isobars stalk across a map. Whatever the weather, the one thing you can always count on is a commercial break *before* tomorrow's weather forecast. You can also count on the peculiar tendency of anchors to endow the weather person with God-like meteorological power as in, "Well, Veronica, I hope you'll bring us some relief from this rain." To which the reply is something like "Oh, Chuck, I'm afraid we've got some more rain coming tomorrow, but wait till you see what I've got for you this weekend." 17

If you have ever wondered why all this fuss is made about the weather, the answer is that, for reasons no one knows, weather information is of almost universal interest. This means that it usually attracts an attentive audience, which in turn means it provides a good environment for commercials. The executive producer of the "CBS This Morning" show, Eric Sorensen, has remarked that research shows weather news is the most important reason why people watch TV in the morning. The weather segments also give the anchors a chance to banter with the weather people and lighten the proceedings. A pleasing personality is almost certainly more important to a weathercaster than a degree in meteorology. How significant personality is can be gauged by what these people earn. Weather people in small markets earn an average of $21,980 a year, according to the National Association of Broadcasters. Weathercasters make an average of $86,589 in the top ten markets, with some earning half a million dollars or more. Nonetheless, it should not sur- 18 prise you to know that these people rarely prepare weather forecasts. There are staff meteorologists for that. The on-air weather person is expected to draw audiences, not weather maps.

Feature reporters usually ply their craft near the "back of the book," close by the weather. They keep the mood light, and try to leave the viewer with a smile. The subject matter of some feature vignettes is called "evergreen" because it is not supposed to wilt with the passage of time. It can be stored until needed. (Two of the best practitioners of "evergreen art" are Charles Kuralt and Andy Rooney.) Locally, you usually see "evergreen" reports on slow news days, when the editor has trouble filling the news budget (the newsworthy events of the day). But as entertaining news becomes more of a commodity, feature reports are being used more and more to attract and hold audiences through the news program.

No news "family" would be complete without a science reporter, a Doctor Wizard, who usually wears glasses, may have an advanced degree, and is certainly gray around the temples. These experts bring to the audience the latest in everything from cancer research to the designer disease of the year.

Once the family has gathered, everyone in place, each with a specific role, the show is ready to begin. The anchor reads the lead story. If you are expecting to hear the most important news to you, on any given day, you will often be disappointed. Never forget that the producer of the program is trying to grab you before you zap away to another news show. Therefore, chances are you will hear a story such as Zsa Zsa's run-in with the law, Rob Lowe's home videos, Royal Family happenings, or news of a Michael Jackson tour. Those stories have glitter and glamour in today's journalism. And if glitter and glamour won't do the job, gore will. Body bags have become an important currency of TV news and a four-bagger is a grand slam.

If viewers have stayed through the lead story, they probably will be hooked for a while because the newscast is designed to keep their attention through the commercial breaks into the next "section," when the process starts again. Taped stories from reporters are peppered throughout the show to keep interest from flagging as anchors keep the show on track "eyeballing," or reading, stories on camera. When the news stories thin out, there are sports, features, and weather to fill up the time.

All this is presented with slick lighting and production values, moving along at a crisp pace. The tempo is usually fast since some programmers believe that fast-paced news programs attract younger audiences. Older audiences, they believe, are attracted to a slower-paced, quieter presentation. No matter how fast or slow the pace of the show, there is not much time to present anything but truncated information. After we have subtracted commercial time, about twenty-two minutes of editorial time are available in a half-hour broadcast. If we subtract, further, the time used for introductions, closings, sports, and the weather, we are left with about fifteen minutes. If there are five taped stories of two minutes each, that leaves five or six minutes to cover the rest of the world's events. And if more time is

19

20

21

22

23

subtracted for "happy talk," chalk up another minute or so just for "schmoozing" on the set.

Given the limited time and objectives of a television newscast, a viewer has to realize that he or she is not getting a full meal but rather a snack. And depending on the organization presenting the news, the meal may contain plenty of empty calories.

24

·4·

The Multiple-Source Essay

Until now, most of your writing assignments have been based on information derived from a *single* source. You have learned to paraphrase, summarize, re-arrange, and unify your evidence without sacrificing accuracy or completeness.

Now, as you begin to work with *many* different sources, you will need to understand and organize a wider range of materials. You will want to present the ideas of your sources in all their variety while at the same time maintaining your own perspective, encompassing all the shades of opinion.

- How can you describe each author's ideas without taking up too much space for each one?
- How can you fit all your sources smoothly into your essay without allowing one to dominate?
- How can you transform a group of disparate sources into an essay that is yours?

Some of the informal sources that you will work with in this chapter have their equivalents in professional writing. Lawyers, doctors, engineers, social workers, and other professionals often work from notes taken at interviews to prepare case notes, case studies, legal testimony, reports, and market research.

SELECTING INFORMATION FOR A MULTIPLE-SOURCE ESSAY

In academic writing, you do not usually find the materials for an essay in a neatly assembled package. On the contrary, before beginning an essay, you

189

must find and select your materials. The first stage of a research project is tra-ditionally working in the library or on the computer with a topic to explore and questions to ask, a search for information that will later be interpreted, sifted, and synthesized into a finished essay.

To demonstrate this process, assume that you have been assigned the fol-lowing project, which calls for a *narrow range of research:*

> Read an entire newspaper or news magazine published on a day of your choice during this century (such as your birthday), and write a summary describing what life was like on that day. Your sources are the articles and advertisements in that day's paper.

Given the amount and variety of information contained in the average news-paper, you must first narrow the topic by deciding what and how much to in-clude. You would look for two kinds of evidence—major events that might have altered the fabric of most people's lives, and more ordinary happenings that might suggest how people typically spent their days. While these events may have taken place before your birth, your not having been there may give you the advantage of perspective: as an outsider, you can more easily distin-guish between stories of lasting historic importance and those that simply re-flect their era.

To begin this project, follow these steps:

1. Read rapidly through the entire newspaper. Then read the same issue again more slowly, jotting down your impressions of important *kinds* of events or *characteristics* of daily life. Search for a pattern, a thesis that sums up what you have read.

2. Review your notes, and isolate a few main ideas that seem worth devel-oping. Then read the issue a third time, making sure that there really is sufficient evidence for the points that you wish to make. Note any addi-tional information that you expect to use, and write down the page num-ber next to each reference in your notes. Remember that you are not trying to "use up" all the available information.

3. Plan a series of paragraphs, each focusing on a somewhat different theme that is either significant in itself or typical of the day that you are describ-ing. Spend some time choosing a strategy for a sequence of paragraphs that will not only introduce your reader to the world that you are describ-ing, but also make apparent the pattern of events—the thesis—that seems to characterize that day.

Drawing Conclusions from Your Information

Through your essay, you should help your readers to form conclusions about the significance of the information it contains. *The evidence should not be expected to speak for itself.* Consider the following paragraph:

Some popular books in the first week of 1945 were Brave Men by Ernie
Pyle, Forever Amber by Kathleen Winsor, and The Time for Decision by Sumner
Welles. The average price of these new, hardcover books was about three
dollars each. The price of the daily Times was three cents, and Life magazine
was ten cents.

What is probably most interesting to your reader is how little the reading material cost. This evidence would be very informative in a paragraph devoted to
the cost of living or the accessibility of information through the media. Here,
however, the emphasis is on the books. Can you tell why they were popular?
Do they seem typical of 1945's bestseller list? If you don't have sufficient
knowledge to answer questions like these, you will do better to focus on some
other aspect of daily life that the paper describes in greater detail. *Unexplained
information is of no value to your reader,* who cannot be assumed to know more
than—or even as much as—you do.

In contrast, another student, writing about a day shortly after the end of
World War II, built a paragraph around a casualty list in the *New York Times.*
What seemed significant about the list was the fact that, by the end of the war,
casualties had become so routine that they assumed a relatively minor place in
daily life. Notice that the paragraph begins with a topic sentence that establishes the context and draws its conclusion at the end.

For much of the civilian population, the worst part of the war had been
the separation from their loved ones, who had gone off to fight in Europe, Africa,
and the Pacific. Even after the end of the war, they still had to wait for the safe
arrival home of the troops. In order to inform the public, the New York Times
ran a daily list of troop arrivals. However, not everyone was destined to return,
and the Times also ran a list of casualties. On September 4, that list appeared
at the very bottom of page 2, a place where it would be easily overlooked except
by those interested in finding a particular name.

Another paragraph about May 6, 1946, informs the reader that the postwar
mid-forties were a transitional period.

The process of switching over from a wartime to a peacetime economy
was not without its pains. Then, as now, there was a high rate of unemployment. The Times featured a story about the million women production workers
who had recently lost their jobs in war industries. Returning male and female
veterans were also flooding the job market. Some working wives were waiting to
see how their husbands readjusted to postwar jobs. If their ex-GI husbands
could bring home enough money to support the family, they could return to
their roles as housewives. If their husbands chose to continue their education

or vocational training under the GI Bill, they would expect to stay on the job as long as they could.

This paragraph appears to be a straightforward account of the transition from a wartime economy, as expressed in the topic sentence; but the writer is, in fact, summarizing information taken from *several* articles in that day's newspaper. (Notice that, while the source of the information—the *Times*—is cited, the names of the reporters are not considered significant in this very general summary.) The suggestion of a personal comment—unemployment, one gathers, is a recurring problem—adds immediacy and significance to a topic that might otherwise be remote to today's readers.

Finally, it is not always necessary to present your conclusion in a topic sentence at the *beginning* of your paragraph. Here is one in which the evidence is presented first:

The July 30, 1945, issue of Newsweek lists three bills that were going before Congress. The first, the Burton-Ball-Hatch Bill, proposed that all industries institute a labor management mediation system. The second, the Kilgore Bill, proposed providing $25 a week in unemployment for a period of 26 weeks. And the third, the Mead Bill, proposed raising the minimum wage from 40 cents to 65 cents. It is obvious from these three bills that a great deal of attention was being focused on employment, or the lack of it. Here we have another clue about the lifestyle of 1945. The majority of the working class must have been greatly dissatisfied with economic conditions for their congressmen to have proposed these improvements. These bills were also in keeping with the late President Roosevelt's New Deal policy, which was primarily directed toward the improvement of economic conditions. From these bills, it is safe to assume that the cost of living may have been rising, that unemployment was still something of a problem, and that strikes by workers were becoming so prevalent that a mediation system seemed necessary.

This paragraph explicitly links together three related points, suggests their possible significance, and provides a historical context (the New Deal) in which to understand them.

EXERCISE 13: SELECTING AND PRESENTING INFORMATION

Read the following student essay, a description of life taken from the *New York Times* of September 21, 1967. Analyze each paragraph and be prepared to discuss the following questions:

1. What are the writer's reasons for building a paragraph around that piece of information? (Use your own knowledge of the contents of the average newspaper today to estimate the range of choices that the writer might have had.)

2. How clear is the presentation of the information?
3. Do the topic sentences interpret the information and suggest its significance for the reader?
4. How is the essay organized: the relationship between paragraphs; the sequence of paragraphs; the unity within each paragraph; the transitions between paragraphs?
5. What is the thesis and how well does the author characterize September 21, 1967, as typical of its era and as a contrast to her own era?

According to the New York Times, on September 21, 1967, there was considerable violence and unrest in the United States, much of it in response to the United States' involvement in the Vietnam War. The United States had increased its bombing of Vietnam in an attempt to cut off the port of Haiphong from contact with the rest of the world. As a result, a group opposed to President Johnson's Vietnam policy began an "anti-Johnson" campaign. They were a coalition of Democrats who hoped to block his reelection. Meanwhile, seventy female antiwar demonstrators were arrested outside the White House. Later, to protest their arrest, 500 members of Women Strike for Peace marched to the White House and clashed with police.

There was not only civil unrest on this day, but also a conflict between President Johnson and the House Ways and Means Committee over the president's proposed tax increase. The committee would not approve the increase without a 5 billion dollar cut in spending. The Senate proposed the following cuts: a 2 billion dollar decrease in defense spending; a 1 billion dollar decrease in "long-range research"; and a 2 billion dollar decrease in other civilian services. However, aid to the poor and to cities was not to be cut. In defense of the president's request, Secretary of Commerce Trowbridge said that a tax increase would be necessary because of inflation.

Throughout the rest of the country, there was much racial tension and violence. There had been days of fighting in Dayton, Ohio's West Side, which had a large black population. A rally took place there to protest the killing of a black Social Security Administration field-worker. There was also a supermarket fire in Dayton, which resulted in $20,000 of damage. In the end, twenty teenagers were arrested. In the Casa Central Outpost, a Puerto Rican neighborhood in Chicago, Governor Romney of Michigan, a would-be presidential candidate, was given a hostile welcome. His visit to the Outpost was blocked by its director, Luis Cuza, who handed him a two-page press release claiming that the Governor was only touring these poor neighborhoods for political gain. Governor Romney expressed outrage at the accusation and the fact that the Outpost had not informed him earlier that he would not be welcome. In the meantime, the streets of Hartford, Connecticut's North End were quiet after three days of racial violence. Civil rights demonstrators were marching against housing discrimination in the South End, a predominantly middle-class Italian neighborhood. There were 66 arrests, mainly of young blacks. To control the violence, five to ten policemen were posted at every intersection, and the mayor asked for a voluntary curfew.

On the local level, a protest against traffic conditions took place in the Bronx, at 149th Street and Courtlandt Avenue. The protesters, four clergymen and dozens of neighbors, wanted Courtlandt Avenue to be one way. Two men refused to leave after police tried to disperse the crowd.   4

There was not only racial unrest in the country on this day, but also many labor disputes and strikes. Seventeen thousand Prudential Insurance Company of America agents threatened to strike if no contract was agreed on in four days. They could not accept any of the proposals previously given to them. Also, the steelhaulers' strike in Chicago was spreading east, and had already resulted in a violent confrontation in Pittsburgh. Finally, on strike were the 59,500 New York public school teachers, whose refusal to enter the classrooms had kept more than a million students out of school for eight days. The teachers' slogan was "no contract, no work."   5

Even the weather was in turmoil. Hurricane Beulah, in Texas, had winds estimated at 80 miles per hour at the center of the storm and 120–150 miles per hour at its peak. Eighty-five percent of Port Isabel, a town at the southern tip of Texas, was destroyed, and four people were killed by the record number of twenty-seven tornadoes spawned by Beulah. All the Gulf states experienced heavy rain in Beulah's aftermath. Meanwhile, rain and thunderstorms also battered the east coast.   6

ASSIGNMENT 6: WRITING AN ESSAY FROM FACTUAL INFORMATION

Choose *one* of the following:

1. At the library, examine the issue of the *New York Times* that was published on the day that your mother or father was born. Most libraries keep complete microfilms of the *New York Times*. Ask your librarian how to locate and use these microfilms. (Alternatively, locate an issue of a news magazine that covers that week.) Select the articles that seem most interesting and typical of the period, and use them as evidence for an account of what it was like to live on that day. *This essay should not merely be a collection of facts; you should suggest the overall significance of the information that you include.* Remember

that your reader was almost certainly not born on that date, and that your job is to arouse that reader's interest. If you like, draw some parallels with the present time, but don't strain the comparison. The essay should not run much more than 1,000 words: select carefully and refer briefly to the evidence.

2. Use a newspaper or magazine published this week and try to construct a partial portrait of what it is like to live in America (or in your city or town) right now. Don't rely entirely on news stories, but, instead, draw your evidence as much as possible from advertisements and features (like TV listings, classifieds, announcements of all sorts). Try, if you can, to disregard personal knowledge; pretend you are a Martian if that will enable you to become detached from your familiar environment. Don't offer conclusions that the evidence does not substantiate, and don't try to say *everything* that could possibly be said. The essay should not run much more than 1,000 words: select carefully and refer briefly to the evidence.

GENERALIZING FROM EXAMPLES

Summarizing the contents of a newspaper can be difficult because newspaper stories often have little in common except that they all happened on the same day. By contrast, in academic writing *a common theme often links apparently dissimilar ideas or facts.* The writer has to find that common theme and make it clear to the reader through generalizations that cover several items in the sources.

Assume that you have been asked to consider and react to *seven different but related situations,* and then formulate *two generalizations.*

A. In a sentence or two, write down your probable reaction if you found yourself in each of the following situations.* Write quickly; this exercise calls for immediate, instinctive responses.

1. You are walking behind someone. You see him take out a cigarette pack, pull out the last cigarette, put the cigarette in his mouth, crumple the package, and nonchalantly toss it over his shoulder onto the sidewalk. What would you do?

2. You are sitting on a train and you notice a person (same age, sex, and type as yourself) lighting up a cigarette, despite the no smoking sign. No one in authority is around. What would you do?

3. You are pushing a shopping cart in a supermarket and you hear the thunderous crash of cans. As you round the corner, you see a two-year-old child being beaten, quite severely, by his mother, apparently for pulling out the bottom can of the pile. What would you do?

4. You see a teenager that you recognize shoplifting at the local discount store. You're concerned that she'll get into serious trouble if the store detective catches her. What would you do?

*Adapted from "Strategy 24" in Sidney B. Simon et al., *Values Clarification* (New York: Hart, 1972).

5. You're driving on a two-lane road behind another car. You notice that one of its wheels is wobbling more and more. It looks as if the lugs are coming off one by one. There's no way to pass, because cars are coming from the other direction in a steady stream. What would you do?

6. You've been waiting in line (at a supermarket or gas station) for longer than you expected and you're irritated at the delay. Suddenly, you notice that someone very much like yourself has sneaked in ahead of you in the line. There are a couple of people before you. What would you do?

7. You've raised your son not to play with guns. Your rich uncle comes for a long-awaited visit and he brings your son a .22 rifle with lots of ammunition. What would you do?

B. Read over your responses to the seven situations and try to form two general statements (in one or two sentences each), one about *the circumstances in which you would take action* and a second about *the circumstances in which you would choose to do nothing*. Do *not* simply list the incidents, one after the other, divided in two groups.

You form your generalizations by examining the group of situations in which you *do* choose to take action and determining *what they have in common*. (It is also important to examine the "leftovers," and to understand why these incidents did *not* warrant your interference.) As a first step, you might try looking at each situation in terms of either its *causes* or its *consequences*. For example, in each case there is someone to blame, someone who is responsible for creating the problem—except for number five, where fate (or poor auto maintenance) threatens to cause an accident.

As for consequences, in some of the situations (littering, for example), there is *little potential danger,* either to you or to the public. Do these circumstances discourage action? In others, however, the possible victim is oneself or a member of one's family. Does self-interest alone drive one to act? Do adults tend to intervene in defense of children—even someone else's child—since they cannot stand up for themselves? Or, instead of calculating the consequences of *not* intervening, perhaps you should imagine *the possible consequences of interference.* In which situations can you expect to receive abuse for failing to mind your own business? Would this prevent you from intervening? As always, *only by examining the evidence can you discover the basis for a generalization.*

The list of examples has two characteristics worth noting:

1. Each item is intended to illustrate a specific and very different situation. Thus, although it does not include every possible example, the list as a whole constitutes a *set* of public occasions for interfering with a stranger's conduct.

2. Since you probably would not choose to act in every situation, you cannot use the entire list as the basis for your generalization. Rather, you must *establish a boundary line,* dividing those occasions when you would intervene from those times when you would decide not to act. The ex-

act boundary between intervention and nonintervention will probably differ from person to person, as will the exact composition of the list of occasions justifying intervention. Thus, there is no one correct generalization.

This exercise results in a set of guidelines for justifiably minding other people's business. *You formulate the guidelines by applying your own standards to a sampling of possible examples.*

Broad concepts offer a great deal of room for disagreement and ambiguity and therefore allow a great many interpretations. You can clarify your ideas and opinions about any important abstract issue by inventing a set of illustrations, marking off a subgroup, and then constructing a generalization that describes what is *inside* the boundary: the common characteristics of the contents of the subgroup. Thus, in the previous problem, one person might consider the set of seven examples and then decide to intervene only in Situations 3 (the child beaten in a supermarket), 5 (the wobbly wheel), and 7 (the gift of a gun). What makes these three cases different from the others? They and they alone involve protecting some person from physical harm.

This process of *differentiation,* followed by *generalized description,* is usually called "definition"; it can serve as an essay strategy in its own right or form the basis for a comparison, classification, argumentation, or evaluation essay.

ANALYZING MULTIPLE SOURCES

When you write from sources, your object is not to establish a single "right" conclusion but rather to present a thesis statement of your own that is based on your examination of a variety of views. Some of these views may conflict with your own and with each other. Because of this diversity, organizing multiple sources is more difficult than working with a series of examples, with the contents of a newspaper, or with even a highly complex single essay.

The writing process for multiple sources begins with the *analysis of ideas.*

> *Analysis is first breaking down a mass of information into individual pieces and then examining the pieces.*

As you underline and annotate your sources, you look for similarities and distinctions in meaning, as well as the basic principles underlying what you read. Only when you have taken apart the evidence of each source to see how it works can you begin to find ways of putting everything back together again in your own essay.

To illustrate the analysis of sources, assume that you have asked five people what the word *foreign* means. You want to provide a reasonably complete definition of the word by exploring all the shades of meaning (or connotations) that the five sources suggest. If each one of the five gives you a completely different answer, then you will not have much choice in the organization of your definition. In that case, you would probably present each separate definition of *foreign* in a separate paragraph, citing a different person as the source for each one. But *responses from multiple sources almost always overlap,* as these do. Notice the common meanings in this condensed list of the five sources' responses:

John Brown: "Foreign" means unfamiliar and exotic.

Lynne Williams: "Foreign" means strange and unusual.

Bill White: "Foreign" means strange and alien (as in "foreign body").

Mary Green: "Foreign" means exciting and exotic.

Bob Friedman: "Foreign" means difficult and incomprehensible (as in "foreign language").

Planning your essay depends on finding common meanings, not writing down the names of the five sources. That is why the one-source-per-paragraph method should hardly ever be used (except on those rare occasions when all the sources completely disagree).

> *When you organize ideas taken from multiple sources, you should reject the idea of devoting one paragraph to each page of your notes, simply because all the ideas on that page happen to have come from the same source.*

If you did so, each paragraph would have a topic sentence that might read, "Then I asked John Brown for his definition," as if John Brown were the topic for discussion, instead of his views on "foreign." And if John Brown and Mary Green each get a separate paragraph, there will be some repetition because both think that one of the meanings of "foreign" is "exotic." "Exotic" should be the topic of one of your paragraphs, not the person (or people) who suggested that meaning.

Analyzing Shades of Meaning

Here is a set of notes, summarizing the ideas of four different people about the meaning of the word *individualist.* How would you analyze these notes?

Richard Becker: an "individualist" is a person who is unique and does not "fall into the common mode of doing things"; would not follow a pattern set by society. "A youngster who is not involved in the drug scene just because his friends are." A good word; it would be insulting only if it referred to a troublemaker.

Simon Jackson: doing things on your own, by yourself. "She's such an individualist that she insisted on answering the question in her own way." Sometimes the word is good, but mostly it has a bad connotation: someone who rebels against society or authority.

Lois Asher: one who doesn't "follow the flock." The word refers to someone who is very independent. "I respect Jane because she is an individualist and her own person." Usually very complimentary.

Vera Lewis: an extremely independent person. "An individualist is a person who does not want to contribute to society." Bad meaning: usually antisocial. She first heard the word in psych class, describing the characteristics of the individualist and "how he reacts to society."

At first glance, all the sources seem to say much the same thing: the individualist is different and "independent." However, it is worthwhile to examine the context in which the four sources are defining this word. First, *all the responses define the individualist in terms of other people,* either the "group," or the "flock," or "society." Oddly enough, it is not easy to describe the individualist as an individual, even though it is that person's isolation that each source is emphasizing. Whatever is "unique" about the individualist—what is described as "independent"—is defined by *the gap between that person and everyone else.* (Notice that both "unique" and "independent" are words that also suggest a larger group in the background; after all, one has to be independent *of* something!)

Having found a meaning that is common to all four sources ("independence") and, just as important, having established the context for a definition ("from the group"), you must now look for differences. Obviously, Lois Asher thinks that to be an individualist is a good thing; Vera Lewis believes that individualism is bad; and the other two suggest that both connotations are possible. But simply describing the reactions of the four sources stops short of defining the word according to those reactions.

Richard Becker and Lois Asher, two people who suggest a favorable meaning, describe the group from which the individual is set apart in similar and somewhat disapproving terms: "common"; "pattern set by society"; "follow the flock." Becker and Asher both seem to suggest *a degree of conformity or sameness which the individualist is right to reject,* as Becker's youngster rejects his friends' drugs. But Vera Lewis, who thinks that the word's connotation is bad, sees the individualist in a more benign society, with which the individual ought to identify himself and to which he ought to contribute. To be antisocial is to be an undesirable person—from the point of view of Lewis and society. Simon Jackson (who is ambivalent about the word) uses the phrases "by yourself" and "on your own," which suggest the isolation and the lack of support, as well as the admirable independence, of the individualist. In Jackson's view, the individualist's self-assertion becomes threatening to all of us in society ("antisocial") only when the person begins to rebel against authority. Probably for Jackson, and certainly for Vera Lewis, the ultimate authority should rest with society as a whole, not with the individualist. Even Richard Becker, who admires independence, draws the line at allowing the individualist complete autonomy: when reliance on one's own authority leads to "troublemaking," the term becomes an insult.

EXERCISE 14: ANALYZING SHADES OF MEANING
IN MULTIPLE SOURCES

Analyze the following set of notes for a definition of the word *clever*. Then explore some ways to organize these notes by following these steps:

A. Find the important terms or concepts that can lead to a context for defining *clever*.

B. Write two generalizations that might serve as topic sentences for a two-paragraph essay. (Do not use "favorable" and "unfavorable" as your two topics.)

Harry Barton: smart, successful, able to get what you want. A "clever" person sees how to get around obstacles. It's an inborn asset, like being handsome. "If you can't be rich, be clever."

Fred Durkin: smart to the point of being slick; likely to pull a fast one; not always reliable; looking for new ways of doing things; can get you into trouble. "She's too clever by half" or "He's a clever devil."

Anna Mercurio: a problem-solving skill; mostly used for intellectual and professional work; attracts admiration and possibly envy, but not affection. "She's always been clever at taking tests; that's why she did so well at school."

Paul Perkins: different from "intelligent"; not the same as "smart"; implies a certain speed in calculating, in sizing up a situation and thinking of a good response; not worth much unless you can use it in a situation. "He figured out a clever way to impress the client and clinch the contract."

Amy Samuels: good at finding solutions, but likely to cut corners and defeat his own purpose; calculates the odds very quickly; tends to make people around him look slow and stupid. "He may be clever at what he does, but he's not a team player."

ASSIGNMENT 7: WRITING A DEFINITION ESSAY
FROM MULTIPLE SOURCES

All the words in the following list are in common use and have either more than one usual meaning or a meaning that can be interpreted both favorably and unfavorably. Choose one word from the list as the topic for a definition essay. (Or, if your teacher asks you to do so, select a word from the dictionary or the thesaurus.)

shrewd	justice	self-interest
curiosity	ordinary	respectable
capitalism	power	conservative
bias	flamboyant	polite

progress	eccentric	obedience
habit	politician	ambition
credit	genius	duty
ladylike	failure	poverty
royalty	competition	sophisticated
masculine	peace	humility
cautious	welfare	solitude
bias	immature	spiritual
dominance	culture	sentimental
revolution	aggression	glamorous
passive	failure	self-confidence
influential	feminine	passionate
criticism	imagination	impetuous
jealousy	romantic	successful
small	workman	smooth
cheap	privilege	intrigue
fashion	enthusiast	smart
pompous	mercenary	criticize
obligation	shame	freedom
control	idealistic	artificial
ambition	ethical	perfection

1. Clarify your own definition of the word by writing down your ideas about its meaning.

2. Interview five or six people, or as many as you need, to get a variety of reactions. Your purpose is to become aware of several ways of using your word. Take careful and complete notes of each reaction that you receive.

3. Each person should be asked the following questions:

   ■ What do you think X means? Has it any other meanings that you know of?

   ■ How would you use this word in a sentence? (Pay special attention to the way in which the word is used, and note down the differences. Two people might say that a word means the same thing and yet use it differently.)

   ■ Is this a positive word or a negative word? In what situation could it possibly have a favorable or unfavorable connotation?

   In listening to the answers to these questions, do not hesitate to ask, "What do you mean?" It may be necessary to make people think hard about a word that they use casually.

4. As you note reactions, consider how the meaning of the word changes and try to identify the different circumstances and usages that cause these variations. Be alert, for example, for a difference between the *ideal* meaning of the word and its *practical* application in daily life.

5. If one person's reaction is merely an echo of something that you already have in your notes, you may summarize the second response more briefly, but keep an accurate record of who (and how many) said what.

6. Although your notes for each source may run only a few sentences, plan to use a separate sheet for each person.

7. Your notes should include not only a summary of each reaction, but also, if possible, a few quotations. If someone suggests a good definition or uses the word in an interesting way, try to record the exact words; read the quotation back to the speaker to make sure that what you have quoted is accurate; put quotation marks around the direct quotation.

8. Make sure that the names of all your sources are accurately spelled.

9. Analyze your notes and make an outline of possible meanings and contexts.

10. Write a series of paragraphs, first explaining *the most common meaning attributed to the word,* according to your sources. Be sure to cite different examples of this common usage. Then, in successive paragraphs, review the other connotations, favorable and unfavorable, always trying to trace the relationships and common contexts among the different meanings. With your overview of all the variations of meaning, you are in an excellent position to observe and explain what the worst and the best connotations of the word have in common.

There is no set length for this essay. Contents and organization are governed entirely by the kind and extent of the material in your notes. *Your notes should be handed in with your completed essay.*

SYNTHESIZING MULTIPLE SOURCES

Once you have analyzed each of your sources and discovered their similarities and differences, you then reassemble these parts into a more coherent whole. This process is called *synthesis.* Although at first you may regard analysis and synthesis as contradictory operations, *they are actually overlapping stages of a single, larger process.*

To illustrate the way in which analysis and synthesis work together, let us examine a set of answers to the question: "Would you buy a lottery ticket? Why?" First, read through these summaries of all seven responses.

Mary Smith: She thinks that lottery tickets were made for people to enjoy and win. It's fun to try your luck. She looks forward to buying her ticket, because she feels that, for one dollar, you have a chance to win a lot more. It's also fun scratching off the numbers to see what you've won. Some people don't buy tickets because they think the lottery is a big rip-off; but "a dollar can't buy that much today, so why not spend it and have a good time?"

John Jones: He would buy a lottery ticket for three reasons. The first reason is that he would love to win. The odds are like a challenge, and he likes to take a chance. The second reason is just for fun. When he has two matching tickets, he really feels happy, especially when he thinks that dollars can be multiplied into hundreds or thousands. "It's like Russian roulette." The third reason is that part of the money from the lottery goes toward his education. The only problem, he says, is that they are always sold out!

Michael Green: He has never bought a lottery ticket in his life because he doesn't want to lose money. He wants to be sure of winning. Also, he says that he isn't patient enough. The buyer of a lottery ticket has to be very patient to wait for his chance to win. He thinks that people who buy tickets all the time must enjoy "living dangerously."

Anne White: Buying a lottery ticket gives her a sense of excitement. She regards herself as a gambler. "When you win two dollars or five dollars you get a thrill of victory, and when you see that you haven't, you feel the agony of defeat." She thinks that people who don't buy tickets must be very cautious and noncompetitive, since the lottery brings "a sense of competition with you against millions of other people." She also knows that the money she spends on tickets goes toward education.

Margaret Brown: She feels that people who buy tickets are wasting their money. The dollars spent on the lottery could be in the bank, getting interest. Those people who buy tickets should expect to have thrown out their money, and should take their losses philosophically, instead of jumping up and down and screaming about their disappointment. Finally, even if she could afford the risk, the laws of her religion forbid her to participate in "any sort of game that is a form of gambling."

William Black: He would buy a lottery ticket, because he thinks it can be fun, but he wouldn't buy too many, because he thinks it's easy for people to get carried away and obsessed by the lottery. He enjoys the anticipation of wanting to win and maybe winning. "I think that you should participate, but in proportion to your budget; after all, one day you might just be a winner."

Elizabeth Watson: She wouldn't buy a lottery ticket because she considers them a rip-off. The odds are too much against you, 240,000 to 1. Also, it is much too expensive, "and I don't have the money to be throwing away on such foolishness." She thinks that people who indulge themselves with lottery tickets become gamblers, and she's against all kinds of gambling. Such people have no sense or self-control. Finally, "I'm a sore loser, so buying lottery tickets just isn't for me."

Making a Chart of Common Ideas

Since you are working with seven sources with varying opinions, you need a way to record the process of analysis. One effective way is to make a *chart of commonly held views*. To do so, follow these two steps, which should be carried out *simultaneously*:

1. Read each statement carefully, and identify each separate reason that is being cited for and against playing the lottery by writing a number above

or next to the relevant comment. When a similar comment is made by another person, use *the same number* to provide a key to the final list of common reasons. In this step, you are analyzing your sources. Here is what the first two sets of notes might look like once the topic numbers have been inserted:

Mary Smith: She thinks that lottery tickets were made for people to enjoy and win. It's fun to try your luck. She looks forward to buying her ticket, because she feels that, for one dollar, you have a chance to win a lot more. It's also fun scratching off the numbers to see what you've won. Some people don't buy tickets because they think the lottery is a big rip-off; but "a dollar can't buy that much today, so why not spend it and have a good time?"

John Jones: He would buy a lottery ticket for three reasons. The first reason is that he would love to win. The odds are like a challenge, and he likes to take a chance. The second reason is just for fun. When he has two matching tickets, he really feels happy, especially when he thinks that dollars can be multiplied into hundreds or thousands. "It's like Russian roulette." The third reason is that part of the money from the lottery goes toward his education. The only problem, he says, is that they are always sold out!

2. At the same time as you number each of your reasons, also write a list or chart of reasons on a separate sheet of paper. Each reason should be assigned *the same number* you wrote next to it in the original statement. Don't make a new entry when the same reason is repeated by a second source. Next to each entry on your chart, put the names of the people who have mentioned that reason. You are now beginning to synthesize your sources.

Here's what your completed list of reasons might look like:

Reason	Sources
1. People play the lottery because it's fun.	Smith; Jones
2. People play the lottery because they like the excitement of taking a chance and winning.	Smith; Jones; Green; White; Black
3. People don't play the lottery because they think it's a rip-off.	Smith; Watson

4. People play the lottery because they are contributing to education. Jones; White

5. People don't play the lottery because they have better things to do with their money. Green; Brown; Watson

6. People play the lottery because they like to gamble. White; Brown; Watson

7. People who play the lottery and those who refuse to play worry about the emotional reactions of the players. Green; White; Brown; Black; Watson

The process of synthesis starts as soon as you start to make your list. The list of common reasons represents the reworking of seven separate sources into a single new pattern that can serve as the basis for a new essay.

Distinguishing between Reasons

One of the biggest problems in synthesis is deciding, in cases of overlapping, whether you actually have one reason or two. Since overlapping reasons were deliberately not combined, the preceding list may be unnecessarily long.

For example, Reasons 1 and 2 reflect *the difference between the experiences of having fun and feeling the thrill of excitement*—a difference in sensation that most people would understand. You might ask yourself, "Would someone play the lottery just for fun without the anticipation of winning? Or would someone experience a thrill of excitement without any sense of fun at all?" If one sensation can exist without the other, you have sufficient reason for putting both items on your chart. Later on, the similarities, not the differences, might make you want to combine the two; but, *at the beginning, it is important to note down exactly what ideas and information are available to you.*

The distinction between the thrill of excitement (2) and the pleasure of gambling (6) is more difficult to perceive. The former is, perhaps, more innocent than the latter and does not carry with it any of the obsessive overtones of gambling.

Resenting the lottery because it is a rip-off (3) and resenting the lottery because the players are wasting their money (5) appear at first glance to be similar reactions. However, references to the rip-off tend to emphasize the "injured victim" whose money is being whisked away by a public agency. In other words, Reason 3 emphasizes *self-protection from robbery;* Reason 5 emphasizes *the personal virtue of thrift.*

Reason 7 is not really a reason at all. Some comments in the notes do not fit into a tidy list of reasons for playing, yet they provide a valuable insight into human motivation and behavior as expressed in lottery-playing. An exploration of the emotions that characterize the player and the nonplayer (always allowing for the lottery preference of the source) might be an interesting way to conclude an essay.

Deciding on a Sequence of Topics

The topics in your chart appear in the same random order as your notes. Once the chart is completed, you should decide on a more logical sequence of topics by ordering the entries in the list. You can make an indirect impact on your reader by choosing a logical sequence that supports the pattern that you discovered in analyzing your sources.

Here are two possible ways to arrange the "lottery" reasons. Which sequence do you prefer? Why?

1. fun	1. fun
2. excitement	2. rip-off
3. gambling	3. excitement and gambling
4. education	4. misuse of money
5. rip-off	5. education
6. misuse of money	6. personality of the gambler
7. personality of the gambler	

The right-hand sequence *contrasts the advantages and disadvantages* of playing the lottery. Moving back and forth between paired reasons calls attention to the relation between opposites and, through constant contrast, makes the material interesting for the reader. The left-hand sequence places all the advantages and disadvantages together, providing an opportunity to *explore positive and negative reactions to the lottery separately* without interruption, therefore encouraging more complex development. Both sequences are acceptable.

EXERCISE 15: IDENTIFYING COMMON IDEAS

This exercise is based on a set of interview notes, answering the question "Would you give money to a beggar?"

A. Read through the notes. (1) Identify distinct and different reasons by placing numbers next to the relevant sentences. (2) As you number each new reason, add an entry to the chart. (The first reason is already filled in.)

Reason   Sources

1. I can afford to give to beggars.

2.

3.

4.

5.

6.

7.

8.

9.

10.

B. Arrange the numbered reasons in a logical sequence. If it makes sense to you, combine those reasons that belong together. Be prepared to explain the logic behind your sequence of points. If you can find two possible sequences, include both, explaining the advantages of each.

Would You Give Money to a Beggar?

Jonathan Cohen: When asked for money on the street, I often apply a maxim of a friend of mine. He takes the question, "Have you got any spare change?" literally: if he has any loose change, he hands it over, without regard for his impression of what the money's for, since he doesn't think ulterior motives are any of his business. Since I can always afford the kind of contribution that's usually asked for—fifty cents or a dollar—or am at least less likely to miss it than the person asking me for it, I usually take the request as the only qualification of "need." I'm more likely to give out money if I don't have to go into my billfold for it, however, and would rather give out transit tokens or food, if I have them. But I want to be sympathetic; I often think, "There but for the grace of God go I."

Jennifer Sharone: I hate to think about what people who beg have to undergo; it makes me feel so fortunate to be well dressed and to have good food to eat and a home and a job. Begging seems kind of horrifying to me—that in this country there are people actually relying on the moods of strangers just to stay alive. I give to people who seem to have fallen on hard times, who aren't too brazen, who seem embarrassed to be asking me for money. I guess I do identify with them a lot.

Michael Aldrich: If a person meets my eye and asks plainly and forthrightly (and isn't falling-down drunk), I try to empty my pocket, or at least come up with a quarter or two. If the person has an unusually witty spiel—even if it's outlandish—I give more freely. I don't mind giving small change; it's quick and easy. I try not to think about whether or not the person really "needs" the money—how could you ever know? On some level, I think that if someone's begging, they need the money. Period. There's an old guy who stands on my corner—he's been there for years. I always give him money, if I have the change. If I don't have it, he says a smile will do. I would hate to think of him going without a meal for a long time or having to sleep out in the rain. He reminds me of my father and my uncle.

Marianne Lauro: I used to give people money, but frankly, I'm too embarrassed by the whole process. It seems to me that folks who really couldn't be all that grateful for somebody's pocket change still make an effort to appear grateful, and then I'm supposed to get to feel magnanimous when I really feel ridiculous telling them they're welcome to a couple of coins that don't even amount to carfare. So the whole transaction seems vaguely humiliating for everyone concerned. Really, the city or the state or the federal government should be doing something about this—not expecting ordinary people, going home from work, or whatever, to support people who have mental or physical impairments or addictions, especially when you're never sure what their money will be used for. But maybe I'm just rationalizing now— maybe the most "humane" thing about these kinds of transactions is the mutual embarrassment.

Donald Garder: I try, when possible, to respond to the person approaching me, by looking at them, perhaps even making eye contact, which frequently lends some dignity to the moment. But then I don't always reach into my pocket. I often give to people with visible physical handicaps, but rarely to someone who's "young and able-bodied." Sometimes I feel guilty, but I'm never sure if the person is for real or not—I've known people who swindled people out of money by pretending to be homeless, so I have a nagging doubt about whether or not a beggar is legitimate.

Darrin Johnson: I never give on the subway—I hate the feeling of entrapment, of being held hostage. The "O.K., so I have you until the next stop so I'm going to wear you down with guilt until I get the money out of you." I really resent that. I flatly refuse to give under those circumstances because it just pisses me off. I might give to somebody just sitting on the street, with a sign and a cup or something—someone who isn't making a big scene, who leaves it up to me whether I give or not. But I hate feeling coerced.

Jenny Nagel: I never give to people on the streets anymore—there are places where people who are really in need can go if they're really starving or need drug treatment or something. Someone once told me, after I'd given money to some derelict looking guy, that he'd probably buy rubbing alcohol or boot polish and melt it down for the alcohol content—that my money was just helping him kill himself. After that I never gave to anyone on the street. I'd rather make a contribution to a social agency.

Paul O'Rourke: I used to give money or if asked I'd give a cigarette. But one day a beggar let loose with a stream of obscenities after I gave him some money. A lot of these people are really messed up—the government should be looking after them, doing more to help them; if they keep getting money from people off the street, they'll just keep on begging. So now I volunteer once a month at a food shelf, and give to charitable organizations, rather than hand out money on the street.

ASSIGNMENT 8: WRITING ABOUT AN ISSUE FROM MULTIPLE SOURCES

Choose a topic from the following list; or think of a question that might stimulate a wide range of responses, and submit the question for your teacher's approval. Try to avoid political issues and very controversial subjects that may make it difficult for you to control the interview and prevent you from getting a well-balanced set of notes. You want a topic in which everyone you interview can take an interest, without becoming intensely partisan.

Suggestions for Topics

Should wives get paid for housework?

Is jealousy a healthy sign in a relationship, or is it always destructive?

Should boys play with dolls?

Is "traditional" dating still desirable today?

Is it a good idea for couples to live together before marriage?

Does it matter whether an elementary-school child has a male or female teacher?

Is there a right age to get married?

What are the ingredients for a lasting marriage?

Should children be given the same first names as their parents?

Is it better to keep a friend by not speaking your mind or risk losing a friend by honesty?

Should community service become a compulsory part of the high school curriculum?

Should English be made the official language of the United States?

Are laws requiring the wearing of seat belts an infringement of individual rights?

Is graffiti vandalism?

Should animals be used in laboratory research?

Should colleges ban drinking alcohol on campus and in fraternity houses?

How should ethics be taught in the schools?

How should the commandment "honor thy parents" be put into practice today?

What, if anything, is wrong with the nuclear family?

Are students forced to specialize too soon in their college experience?

Should schools stay in session all year round?

Should citizens have to pay a fine for not voting?

Should movies have a rating system?

Should elementary-school students be left back?

Should children's TV time be rationed?

Should parents be held legally or financially responsible for damage done by their children?

At what age is it acceptable for children to work (outside the family)?

Should high school students be tested for drug use?

Should hosts who serve alcohol be held responsible if their guests later are involved in auto accidents?

Should students have to maintain passing grades in order to participate in school athletics?

How should society deal with homeless people?

When should parents cease to be financially responsible for their children?

1. Once your topic is decided (and, if necessary, approved), interview at least six people, or as many as you need to get a variety of reactions. (Some of your sources should be students in your class.) Your purpose is to learn about several ways of looking at the topic, not to argue, but to exchange views. If you wish, use the following format for conducting each interview:

Name: (first and last: check the spelling!)

Do you think . . . . ?

Why do you think so? What are some of your reasons? (later) Are there any other reasons?

Why do you think people who take the opposite view would do so?

Do any examples come to your mind to illustrate your point?

Quotation:

2. Take careful and complete notes of the comments that you receive. (*You will be expected to hand in all your notes, in their original form, with your completed essay.*) Keep a separate sheet for each person. If one of your sources says something worth quoting, write down the exact words; read them back to make sure that what you have quoted is what the speaker meant to say; then put quotation marks around the direct quotation. Otherwise, use summary or paraphrase. Do not hesitate to ask, "What do you mean?" or "Is this what I heard you say?" or "How does that fit in with what you said just before?"

3. List the ideas from your notes and arrange the points in a sequence of your choice.

4. Write an essay that presents the full range of opinion, paraphrasing and (occasionally) quoting from representative sources. After analyzing the arguments of your sources, conclude your essay with one or two paragraphs explaining which point of view, in your opinion, has the most validity, and why.

ORGANIZING MULTIPLE SOURCES

Playing the lottery is not a subject that lends itself to lengthy or abstract discussion; therefore, charting reasons for and against playing the lottery is not difficult. The article that follows defines a social, political, and humanitarian problem and suggests two methods of dealing with it, without favoring either "solution" or the values on which each is based. The reporter's sources, quoted in the article, simply cite aspects of the problem and the hope that the courts will deal with it.

Fifteen students were asked to read the article and to offer their opinions; these are presented following the article. As you read the article and the student opinions, assume that you plan to address the issue and synthesize the opinions in an essay of your own.

CITY LAYOFFS HURT MINORITIES MOST
Francis X. Clines

City officials reported yesterday that layoffs resulting from the fiscal crisis were   1
having "devastating" effects on minority employment in government.

In the last 18 months, they disclosed, the city lost half of its Spanish-speaking   2
workers, 40 percent of the black males on the payroll and almost a third of its female workers.

"You are close to wiping out the minority work force in the City of New York,"   3
said Eleanor Holmes Norton, the chairman of the Commission on Human Rights,
after releasing the data in response to a request.

The dwindling employment, in turn, has put the city in "serious jeopardy" of los-   4
ing various kinds of Federal aid, according to Deputy Mayor Paul Gibson, Jr.

The city's fiscal failure and the resultant layoffs have worsened the situation in   5
such predominantly male, white agencies as the Police Department, where, after
some limited gains in recent years, the ranks of women police officers have been reduced by 55 percent because of the budget crisis, according to the city's latest data.

Meanwhile, a Federal appeals court declared that Civil Service seniority was not   6
immune from legal challenge by women police officers who were dismissed because of the city's fiscal crisis.

Scores of complaints alleging discrimination have been filed by laid-off workers,   7
both as class members and individuals, squeezing the city between the pressures of
the traditional primacy of union seniority protections and Federal equal-employ-
ment requirements.

Federal officials said yesterday they were processing the complaints, which could   8
result in a cut-off of funds. They added that they were hoping for guidance from
the United States Supreme Court this year on the clash between the seniority principle, which tends to protect male white workers, and the Federal minority employment guidelines of Federal law.

The data on dismissals, which had been quietly compiled by city officials in re-   9
cent weeks, were a further indication of the price the city is paying in the campaign
to balance the budget and come to grips with its huge legacy of excessive debt.

Inevitably, the requirements of the austerity drive interfere, too, with attempts   10
to soften the layoff effects on minority-group workers and women.

For example, Commissioner Norton emphasized that the levying of budget cuts   11
on an even percentage basis in city agencies was the best way to protect equal opportunity. But various fiscal experts intent on improving the city's management say
across-the-board cutting is the worst way of economizing because it ignores the
relative quality of programs.

"We had begun to make an effort," Commissioner Norton said, "But one reces-   12
sion takes it all out in an instant."

Since the budget crisis surfaced in the summer of 1974, the city payroll has been   13
reduced by 40,000 jobs—two-thirds of them reported as layoffs. This was a total

cut of 13 percent to the current level of about 255,000 workers, according to city records.

A maxim of the seniority system that the last hired should be the first dismissed is the chief factor preventing an even 13 percent sharing of the layoff burden without regard to race or sex, city officials say. 14

The austerity drive, in which the city must try to cut its spending by $1 billion in less than three years, is forcing the conflict between what Commissioner Norton describes as "two competing and legitimate interests"—seniority and equal opportunity. 15

Federal and city civil rights officials were reluctant to discuss the scope of the complaints that have been filed. Werner H. Kramarsky, the state's Commissioner of Human Rights, described the issues raised as "very thorny" and extending to such questions as whether provisional, or temporary, employees should be credited with time on the job in determining relative seniority. 16

The available public records indicate that the state commission is handling at least 35 cases, some of them class complaints, and has sent 98 cases involving former city welfare workers to Federal officials of the Equal Employment Opportunity Commission, which already has received about 160 complaints from welfare workers alone. 17

The complaints are being pressed not only by women and minority group members, but also by a group of a half dozen disabled persons who contend that they were unfairly victimized in the layoff drive, according to state records. 18

There have been various court challenges in recent years of the seniority protections, which generally have been unsuccessful. One recent ruling threw out a racial quota program for city school principals. Federal civil rights officials emphasize that the Supreme Court is considering the issue at present and the hope is that some definitive standard will be set. 19

According to Deputy Mayor Gibson, minorities represented 31 percent of the payroll, but suffered 44 percent of the cuts. Males, he said, were 70 percent of the payroll and were affected by 63 percent of the cuts. 20

Commissioner Norton said that even before the layoffs, Federal officials had warned the city from time to time that financing for various programs would be cut off because of noncompliance with equal opportunity standards. She said that Mayor Beame had signed an executive order in 1974 committing city agencies to specific improvement programs. 21

Thus far there have been no Federal threats of cutoffs during the fiscal crisis, she said, apparently because the city is on record as pledging to seek a more equitable system in the event it ever resumes full-scale hiring. 22

But Deputy Mayor Gibson feels the situation is becoming critical. "We're losing ground," he said. 23

Student Opinions

Lydia Allen: The performance of a job must be the primary focus in deciding layoffs. I feel that, as a whole, people with more seniority in a job would perform that job best. Therefore, seniority, not minority, rights must be the deciding vote.

Grace Burrows: I believe that both sides have validity. I do feel that because minorities have been held back for so long *some* concessions should be made in their favor. Minorities were just beginning to make progress and now they will be set back once again. A person who's been on the job for a number of years shouldn't be made to suffer either.

Marion J. Buskin: I believe that an individual should be dismissed according to his ability to produce. A person with more seniority should not be allowed to keep his job if someone with less time on the job is capable of performing it better.

Robert Fuhst: I believe in seniority for job protection. If seniority doesn't prevail, then your job is based on how well you are liked and your freedom to express yourself is hampered.

John Giannini: Minorities should have a say in matters of layoffs, especially when a large percentage of the minority is affected. Minorities and senior personnel should share layoffs equally.

Dorothy Humphrey: I think there should be equal employment in this country. If an individual is senior in a field and satisfactorily functioning, he should remain employed. On the other hand, if a member of a minority can function even better, why not employ him instead? Production of work is what counts, not who performs it.

Rosemary McAleer: I favor seniority in employment because it is a system that does not permit discrimination. Regardless of race, color, or creed, if you have acquired more time than another employee, your job should be secure.

Marc Page: The longer a man is yoked to a job and its connected financial position, the more severe are the effects of being sundered from it. Seniority is the overriding consideration.

Megan Phillips: I feel seniority of employment is important in the job crisis because it is the only way of ensuring good and efficient services. Second, I feel the more mature one is in a job, the more the job becomes a part of one's welfare, as opposed to a younger person or a novice in the job, who only performs the job for the money.

Alice Reich: I think seniority in employment is an important consideration for the major reason that the benefits of seniority are hard-earned over the years. It seems unjust for a person who has given perhaps seven-eighths of his working lifetime to a job to find himself "out in the cold." Worse yet, the time of life when seniority would count is the time, very often, when other employment is unobtainable.

Robert Rivera: I feel that minority groups should be protected from job cutbacks. The reason is that the minorities that were hired were hired to fulfill the employment clauses set up through government laws. This law deals with equal opportunity for sexes and minorities to hold jobs and offices. Since this law has been recently enforced (in the last five or six years), why should minorities then hired be affected so tremendously by unemployment?

Jesse Rogers: I feel that minority workers for the city government should be protected, because it does not seem fair that, after waiting so long to get in, they are so easily kicked out by the unions.

Peter Rossi: I believe the federal government should compensate the minority people who were fired because of budget cuts and lack of seniority. The compensation should be the creation of new jobs and not unemployment insurance.

John Seeback: Most jobs run on the idea that the last hired are the first fired, even if the jobs held by senior workers are costing the business millions of dollars. Also, the white majority of senior workers feels superior to the minority workers on a racial basis rather than on a performance basis. Many employers also feel the minority workers are expendable: they had to hire them because of the law; now they have a good reason to fire them.

Nancy Vitale: Men and women, after putting their time and effort (not to mention their skills) into a job for a great number of years, deserve the protection of their jobs in accordance with seniority. It is unfair to dismiss a person from a longstanding position to make a position for a minority member.

When you prepare to explore a variety of opinions about a complex and perhaps controversial subject, follow these steps:

1. *Summarize the facts of the issue.*

Write a brief, objective summary of the issue under discussion (in this case, the problem described in the article). Your summary of this article should convey both the situation and the two key ideas that are stressed. Try structuring your paragraph to contrast the conflicting opinions.

2. *Establish your own point of view.*

End your summary with a statement of your own reaction to suggest a possible direction for your essay.

This step is more important than it might at first seem. Once you begin to analyze a mass of contradictory opinion, you may find yourself being completely convinced by first one source and then another, or you may try so hard to stay neutral that you end up with no point of view of your own at all. You need to find a vantage point for yourself from which to judge the validity of the statements that you read. Of course, you can (and probably will) adjust your point of view as you become more familiar with all the arguments and evidence that your sources raise. *Do not regard your initial statement of opinion as a thesis to be proven, but rather as a hypothesis to be tested, modified, or even abandoned.*

3. Synthesize your evidence.

Label your set of opinions and establish categories. The statements following the article are all personal reactions to job layoffs and the issue of seniority protection versus equal employment opportunity. For each statement, follow these steps:

A. *Read each statement carefully and think about its exact meaning.* First, get a rough idea of what each statement says—do a mental paraphrase, if you like. You will naturally notice which "side" the author of each statement is on. There is a tendency to want to stop there, as if the authors' positions are all that one needs to know. But your object is not only to find out which side of an issue each person prefers, but also to understand *why* that side was chosen.

B. *Try to pick out the chief reason put forth by each person, or, even better, the principle that lies behind each argument.* Sum up the reasoning of each person in a word or two, a phrase—invent a label, as if for a scientific specimen.

C. When you have labeled the statements, the final stage of synthesis becomes easier. *Review your summarizing phrases to see if there is an abstract idea, used to describe several statements, that might serve as a category title.* (Some change in the wording may be necessary.) Once two or three categories become obvious, consider their relationship to each other. Are they parallel? Are they contrasting? Then attempt to see how the smaller categories fit into the pattern that is beginning to form.

How the Three Steps Work

Following is one student's exploration of the article on New York City layoffs and the fifteen student opinions.

1. **Summarizing.** Here the student identifies the article to which he and his sources are responding, summarizing the issue and the nature of the conflict.

> In the New York Times, Francis X. Clines reported that the budget crisis had substantially reduced the number of minorities—blacks, women, and Hispanics—on New York City's payroll. The minority members laid off were the employees most recently hired by the city to meet federal minority employment requirements. Eleanor Holmes Norton, who chairs the Commission on Human Rights, described the situation as a conflict between "two competing and legitimate interests"—the traditional principle of union seniority protection and equal opportunity employment.

2. **Hypothesizing** (stating your own point of view). Here the student expresses an opinion that suggests the possible direction for an essay. At

this point, the student has not studied the group of opinions that accompanies the article.

Both the competing interests are right in their claims, but there is a third principle that goes beyond both: in the name of fairness, the city should take the trouble to evaluate the performance of all its employees and dismiss those whose performance is inferior. Where a senior employee and a minority employee share the same performance rating but are competing for a single position, the city should help both employees and wait for retirements to make room for both.

3. **Labeling your set of opinions and establishing categories.** In this step, the student moves away from the article to examine the opinions of others who have read the article, determining first the position of each respondent and then the reasoning behind the position. Here, the statements of the fifteen respondents are repeated, with a summarizing label following each statement.

Lydia Allen: The performance of a job must be the primary focus in deciding layoffs. I feel that, as a whole, people with more seniority in a job would perform that job best. Therefore, seniority, not minority, rights must be the deciding vote.

Allen: seniority ensures performance

Grace Burrows: I believe that both sides have validity. I do feel that because minorities have been held back for so long *some* concessions should be made in their favor. Minorities were just beginning to make progress and now they will be set back once again. A person who's been on the job for a number of years shouldn't be made to suffer either.

Burrows: evades the issue—both approaches unfortunate

Marion J. Buskin: I believe that an individual should be dismissed according to his ability to produce. A person with more seniority should not be allowed to keep his job if someone with less time on the job is capable of performing it better.

Buskin: performance should be the only criterion

Robert Fuhst: I believe in seniority for job protection. If seniority doesn't prevail, then your job is based on how well you are liked and your freedom to express yourself is hampered.

Fuhst: seniority deserves protection (without it employment becomes a popularity contest)

John Giannini: Minorities should have a say in matters of layoffs, especially when a large percentage of the minority is affected. Minorities and senior personnel should share layoffs equally.

Giannini: minorities and senior personnel should share burden equally

Dorothy Humphrey: I think there should be equal employment in this country. If an individual is senior in a field and satisfactorily functioning, he should remain employed. On the other hand, if a member of a minority can function even better, why not employ him instead? Production of work is what counts, not who performs it.

Humphrey: performance should be the prevailing criterion

Rosemary McAleer: I favor seniority in employment because it is a system that does not permit discrimination. Regardless of race, color, or creed, if you have acquired more time than another employee, your job should be secure.

McAleer: seniority protection is fundamentally the only nondiscriminatory criterion

Marc Page: The longer a man is yoked to a job and its connected financial position, the more severe are the effects of being sundered from it. Seniority is the overriding consideration.

Page: seniority protection is the more humane policy

Megan Phillips: I feel seniority of employment is important in the job crisis because it is the only way of ensuring good and efficient services. Second, I feel the more mature one is in a job, the more the job becomes a part of one's welfare, as opposed to a younger person or a novice in the job, who performs the job only for the money.

Phillips: seniority protection leads to greater efficiency, i.e., performance

Alice Reich: I think seniority in employment is an important consideration for the major reason that the benefits of seniority are hard-earned over the years. It seems unjust for a person who has given perhaps seven-eighths of his working lifetime to a job to find himself "out in the cold." Worse yet, the time of life when seniority would count is the time, very often, when other employment is unobtainable.

Reich: seniority protection is the more humane policy (other employment often impossible for those laid off)

Robert Rivera: I feel that minority groups should be protected from job cutbacks. The reason is that the minorities that were hired were hired to fulfill the employment clauses set up through government laws. This law deals with equal opportunity for sexes and minorities to hold jobs and offices. Since this law has been recently enforced (in the last five or six years), why should minorities then hired be affected so tremendously by unemployment?

Rivera: the law requires that minorities be protected

Jesse Rogers: I feel that minority workers for the city government should be protected, because it does not seem fair that, after waiting so long to get in, they are so easily kicked out by the unions.

Rogers: minority protection is the more humane policy in the light of history

Peter Rossi: I believe the federal government should compensate the minority people who were fired because of budget cuts and lack of seniority. The compensation should be the creation of new jobs and not unemployment insurance.

Rossi: compensate laid-off minority employees with new jobs (implication that city should not lay off senior employees in order to accommodate minority employees)

John Seeback: Most jobs run on the idea that the last hired are the first fired, even if the jobs held by senior workers are costing the business millions of dollars. Also, the white majority of senior workers feels superior to the minority workers on a racial basis rather than on a performance basis. Many employers also feel the minority workers are expendable: they had to hire them because of the law; now they have a good reason to fire them.

Seeback: (implies that) minorities, as victims of union and employer prejudice, deserve protection

Nancy Vitale: Men and women, after putting their time and effort (not to mention their skills) into a job for a great number of years, deserve the protection of their jobs in accordance with seniority. It is unfair to dismiss a person from a long-standing position to make a position for a minority member.

Vitale: seniority protection is the more humane policy

From this list, the student can establish five categories that cover the range of answers. Here is the list of categories:

Category	Source	Note
1. Seniority ensures good performance.	Allen; Phillips	——

Category	Source	Note
2. Performance = vital criterion	Buskin; Humphrey	——
3. Seniority protection = vital criterion	Page	Financial and emotional hardship greatest for laid-off senior employees
	Reich; Vitale	——
	Fuhst	Employment would be popularity contest without it
	McAleer	Truly nondiscriminatory policy
4. Minority protection = vital criterion	Rivera	Legally
	Seeback	Compensation for past and present injustices
	Rogers	——
5. Each group should share the burden.	(Burrows); Giannini; Rossi	Federal gov't should hire laid-off minorities Senior employees should retain city jobs

EVALUATING SOURCES

Although you are obliged to give each of your sources serious and objective consideration and a fair presentation, synthesis also requires a certain amount of selection. Certainly, no one's statement should be immediately dismissed as trivial or crazy; include them all in your chart. But do not assume that all opinions are equally convincing and deserve equal representation in your essay.

The weight of a group of similar opinions can add authority to an idea. If most of your sources hold a similar view, you will probably give that idea appropriate prominence in your essay. However, *majority rule should not govern the structure of your essay.* Your own perspective determines the thesis of your essay, and you must use your understanding of the topic to evaluate your materials, analyze the range of arguments provided by your sources, and determine for your reader which have the greatest validity.

- Review the hypothesis that you formulated before you begin to analyze the sources. *Decide whether that hypothesis is still valid* or whether, as a result of your full exploration of the subject, you wish to change it or abandon it for another.

- Sift through all the statements and *decide which ones seem thoughtful and well-balanced, supported by convincing reasons and examples, and which seem to be thoughtless assertions that rely on stereotypes, catch phrases, and unsupported references.* Your evaluation of the sources may differ from someone else's, but you must assert your own point of view and assess each source in the context of your background, knowledge, and experience.

You owe it to your reader to evaluate the evidence that you are presenting, partly through what you choose to emphasize and partly through your explicit comments about flawed and unconvincing statements.

In synthesis, your basic task is to present the range of opinion on a complex subject. You need not draw final conclusions in your essay or provide definitive answers to the questions that have been raised. But you must have a valid thesis, an overall view of the competing arguments to present to your reader. Your original hypothesis, either confirmed or altered in the light of your increased understanding, becomes the *thesis* of your essay.

WRITING A SYNTHESIS ESSAY

Spend some time planning your sequence of ideas and considering possible arrangements and strategies. Do your topic and materials lend themselves to a cause-and-effect structure, or definition, or problem and solution, or comparison, or argument? In writing about the issue of job layoffs, you might want to use an overall *problem-solution* strategy, at the same time *arguing* for your preferred solution.

Next, before starting to write each paragraph, review your sources' statements. By now, you should be fully aware of the reasoning underlying each point of view and the pattern connecting them all. But because your reader does not know as much as you do, *you need to explain your main ideas in enough detail to make all the complex points clear.* Remember that your reader has neither made a list nor even read the original sources. It is therefore important to include some explanation in your own voice, in addition to quoting and paraphrasing specific statements.

If possible, you should present your sources by using all three methods of reference: *summary, paraphrase,* and *quotation.* (See the paragraph in Exercise 16 as an appropriate model.) Remember that, as a rule, paraphrase is far more effective than quotation. When you paraphrase someone's reaction in your own voice, you are underlining the fact that you are in charge, that the opinion you are citing is only one of a larger group, and that a full exploration of the topic will emerge from your presentation of *all* the evidence, not from any one source's quoted opinion. *The first sentence presenting any new idea (whether the topic sentence of a new paragraph or a shift of thought within a paragraph) should be written entirely in your own voice,* as a generalization, without any reference to your sources.

To summarize, your essay should include the following elements:

- *Topic sentence:* Introduce the category or theme of the paragraph, and state the idea that is the common element tying this group of opinions together.

- *Explanation:* Support or explain the topic sentence. Later in the paragraph, if you are dealing with a complex group of statements, you may need a connecting sentence or two, showing your reader how one reason is connected to the next. For example, an explanation might be needed in the middle of the "seniority protects the worker" paragraph, as the writer moves from financial and emotional hardship for laid-off senior employees to the prevention of discriminatory job conditions.

- *Paraphrase or summary:* Present specific ideas from your sources in your own words. In these cases, you must of course *acknowledge your sources* by citing names in your sentence.

- *Quotation:* Quote from your sources when the content or phrasing of the original statement justifies word-for-word inclusion. In some groups of statements, there may be several possible candidates for quotation; in others, there may be only one; often you may find no source worth quoting. For example, read the statements made by Page, Reich, and Vitale once again. Could you reasonably quote any of them? Although Reich and Vitale both take strong positions well worth presenting, there is no reason to quote them and every reason to use paraphrase. On the other hand, Page's briefer statement might be quoted, since the contrast between "yoked" and "sundered" is effective and difficult to paraphrase.

As you analyze the opinions of your sources in the body of your essay, you should remain neutral, giving a fair presentation of each point of view. It is also your responsibility to use the final paragraphs of your essay to present your own conclusions, in your own voice, about this issue—to argue for seniority or equal opportunity employment, or to recommend ways to accommodate both sides.

Guidelines for Citing Sources for Synthesis

- *Cite the source's full name,* whether you are quoting or not.
- *Try not to begin every sentence with a name,* nor should you introduce every paraphrase or quotation with "says."
- *Each sentence should do more than name a person;* don't include sentences without content: "Mary Smith agrees with this point."
- If possible, *support your general points with references from several different sources,* so that you will have more than one person's opinion or authority to cite.
- When you have several relevant comments to include within a single paragraph, *consider carefully which one should get cited first—and why.*

(continued)

(continued)

- You need not name every person who has mentioned a point (especially if you have several almost identical statements); however, *you may find it useful to sum up two people's views at the same time,* citing two sources for a single paraphrased statement:

    Mary Smith and John Jones agree that playing the lottery can be very enjoyable. She finds a particular pleasure in scratching off the numbers to see if she has won.

- *Cite only one source for a quotation,* unless both have used exactly the same wording. In the example above, the first sentence would not make sense if you *quoted* "very enjoyable."

- If an idea under discussion is frequently mentioned in your sources, *convey the relative weight of support* by citing "five people" or "several commentators." Then, after summarizing the common response, cite one or two specific opinions, with names. But try not to *begin* a paragraph with "several people"; remember that, whenever possible, the topic sentence should be a generalization of your own, without reference to the supporting evidence.

- *Discuss opposing views within a single paragraph as long as the two points of view have something in common.* Radically different ideas should, of course, be explained separately. Use transitions like "similarly" or "in contrast" to indicate the relationship between contrasting opinions.

EXERCISE 16: ANALYZING A PARAGRAPH BASED ON SYNTHESIS OF SOURCES

Read the following paragraph and decide which sentences (or parts of sentences) belong to each of the categories in the preceding list. Insert the appropriate category name in the left margin, and bracket the sentence or phrase illustrating the term. Be prepared to explain the components of the paragraph in class discussion.

Those who emphasize the upgrading of minority employment have pointed out that, since the hiring of minorities has been encouraged by governmental legislation only for the last few years, the seniority system will of necessity operate against those minorities. Thus, in the opinion of Robert Rivera, it is only fair that, during the present budget crisis, workers from minority groups be protected from cutbacks. One statement, by John Seeback, even suggests the possibility of a return to racial discrimination by white workers who have seniority and by employers, if equal opportunity laws are not enforced: "Many employers feel the minority workers are expendable: they had to hire them because of the law; now they have a good reason to fire them." In a related argument, Jesse

Rogers points out that, since minorities have waited such a long time for decent job opportunities, a certain amount of preferential treatment might serve as a concrete measure of compensation. Neither Seeback nor Rogers emphasizes the abstract principle of equal opportunity implemented by the law. Peter Rossi advocates a practical solution: the federal government should undertake "the creation of new jobs," so that, presumably, there would be enough to satisfy both groups.

ASSIGNMENT 9: WRITING AN ESSAY SYNTHESIZING MULTIPLE SOURCES

Read the following excerpt by Gene Maeroff on school promotion.

1. Write a summary of the point at issue, and then write a brief explanation of your opinion of this issue.
2. Use the statements that follow as a basis for a synthesis essay. These statements were written in response to the question: Should seventh-grade students who failed a reading test repeat the grade? Analyze each statement, label each kind of reason, and organize all the categories in a chart. Then write an essay that presents the full range of opinion, paraphrasing and, if desirable, quoting from representative sources.

from RULE TYING PUPIL PROMOTION TO READING SKILL STIRS WORRY
Gene I. Maeroff

A strict new promotion policy requires the public schools to hold back seventh-grade pupils until they pass the reading test. The difficulty will be compounded this year by a requirement that new seventh graders also pass a mathematics test. [1]

"I am frightened that we may end up losing some of these kids, creating a whole new group of dropouts who leave school at junior high," said Herbert Rahinsky, principal of Intermediate School 293, on the edge of the Carroll Gardens section of Brooklyn. [2]

Students like Larry, who is 16 years old and in the seventh grade at I.S. 293, are repeating the grade because they scored too low on the reading tests last June to be promoted. If Larry does not do well enough on the test this spring, he will remain in the seventh grade in the fall. [3]

An analysis by the Board of Education has shown that about 1,000 of the 8,871 students repeating the seventh grade are already 16 years of age or older. At least one 18-year-old is repeating the seventh grade. [4]

Normally, a seventh grader is 12 years old. [5]

When the promotion policy, which threatened to hold back students with low reading scores in the fourth and seventh grades, was implemented in 1980, it was hailed by many observers as a welcome effort to tighten standards. [6]

But as the program has continued, certain students have failed to show adequate   7
progress. These youngsters are in jeopardy of becoming "double holdovers" in the
seventh grade. Some were also held back at least once in elementary school. . . .

Authorities theorize that these youngsters form a hard core of poor readers for   8
whom improvement is slow and difficult. Such students often were not held back in
prior years because it was easier to move them along than to help them.

Educators now wonder whether repeated failure will simply lessen the likeli-   9
hood of students persisting in school long enough to get a regular diploma.

Statements

Diane Basi: If these students are pushed through the system and receive a diploma,
not being able to read beyond a seventh-grade level, we will be doing them and society a grave injustice. What good will it do to have a diploma if you cannot read or
write? In the end, the students will be hurt more if they are just promoted through
the system.

Jason Berg: A student should not be repeatedly held back on the basis of one test.
A student's overall performance—such as classwork, participation, and attitude—
should be taken into consideration. If a student is not up to par for some reason
on the day of the test, all the work and effort that was put into school during the
year goes down the drain.

Rafael Del Rey: This strict rule has unfortunate consequences. The students who
are being forced out don't comprehend what is being taught to them. Exasperated
and feeling like social outcasts and inferior beings, it is no wonder that many drop
out without skills or goals. Educators should be interested in more than just test
scores.

Anita Felice: It is extremely embarrassing to be a 16-year-old in a class of 12-year-
olds. Such poor students should be promoted to a special program with other students who have the same problems. In time, there should be some improvement in
their reading scores. Being held back will only cause frustration and eventually cause
them to drop out. Test scores should be a lot less important than they are now.

Joe Gordon: By enforcing a rigid standard, the schools are actually promoting an increased dropout rate and, by doing so, are harming the student and society.

Margaret Jenkins: After two tries, a student should be able to pass a test. It's to the
child's advantage to learn and keep learning while moving upward in school. Holding them back is for their own good.

Rachel Limburg: It isn't fair to those students who can do the work just to push
these students along. It also isn't fair to the kids who can't pass the test because
eventually they are going to have to earn a living.

Barbara Martin: It's a hard question, but I think you have to look at the cost in terms
of money, as well as frustration and embarrassment. I'm sorry for kids who are left

back, but it's only going to be a problem for everyone later when they can't get a job. Work today is increasingly technical, and everyone needs basic skills. This policy is tough love, and it's necessary.

Len McGee: This policy isn't good enough because it doesn't deal with the individual student; it deals with seventh graders as a whole. The individual's problems and motivation are not taken into consideration. Sometimes exam pressure defeats intelligence. If left back, the student is trapped in a revolving door and is likely to lose interest in school.

Tina Pearson: It's a mistake to pass students solely on the basis of the reading score. It may show they have learned to read well, but it doesn't mean they learned well in their other classes. Perhaps they worked especially hard on reading and English but just coasted along in their other subjects.

Julius Pena: Automatic promotion is a guarantee that the weak student will face future problems. Making the student repeat is for his own good. Imagine how frustrating it would be for someone who can't fill out a job application. Of course, you shouldn't just throw the student back into the class, but give as much encouragement as possible.

Mark Pullman: We must have certain standards in our educational system. This is a challenge for these students, and repeating the course may encourage them to try harder, making them smarter and better prepared to face life's challenges.

Anthony Raviggio: Strict standards are best for the student. In the long run, individuals who really want the college degree will be glad to remember the ordeal they went through in junior high. It's better to make them keep trying and succeed than to let them think it's okay to fail.

Vivian Ray: If a child has been held back in elementary and held back again in junior high school, it should become quite apparent to teachers and parents that the child has a problem. Being slow to learn is not sufficient reason to hold back a child. The child should be promoted and put in a slower class with more students like himself.

Bernice Roberts: I think there's too much concern for the feelings of the "poor" student and too little concern for the needs of society. Eighteen-year-olds who can't read are likely candidates for welfare. I don't want to have the responsibility of carrying some illiterate kid who couldn't be bothered to learn when he was in school.

Althea Simms: The tough standards are good for these students because they will be motivated to become more serious about doing well. There are kids who don't care whether or not they study for their exams since they know they're going to be promoted to the next grade anyway. Knowing that you may be held back is a strong motivator to study harder.

Patricia Sokolov: Not all students are intellectually gifted, nor is the progress of the nation solely dependent on the effort of intellectuals. Laborers and blue-collar workers have been credited throughout our history for their great contribution to the wealth and progress of our country. Educators should be more concerned with nurturing students' individual potential and less concerned with passing tests.

Matthew Warren: What's the point of promoting a student who won't be able to keep up in his new classes, much less perform his job properly when he's out in the working world? Standards should be enforced regardless of age. What's age? It's just a number.

Michael Willoughby: Educators should recognize that some students don't have the capacity, for whatever social, genetic, or psychological reasons, to fulfill the educators' traditional expectations. An alternative effort must be made, emphasizing vocational skills and also basic reading and math, that will permit students to progress at their own pace.

Betty Yando: I am concerned about the large number of dropouts and their dismal prospects. Why should a student, despite obvious learning disabilities, be forced to continue in an exasperating educational process in which he is making little or no progress? The standards by which we determine whether an individual will make a good worker and a good citizen are too high.

ASSIGNMENT 10: WRITING AN ARGUMENT FROM MULTIPLE SOURCES

Read "Marriage with No Easy Outs," and the Letters to the Editor that follow.

1. Write a brief summary of the issue raised by Amitai Etzioni, and list his arguments as well as the counterarguments in the Letters to the Editor.
2. Write an essay that explores the arguments on both sides of the issue and finally supports either Etzioni's position or that of his opponents. Make sure that you use summary, paraphrase, and quotation to represent the opinions of your sources.

MARRIAGE WITH NO EASY OUTS
Amitai Etzioni

Your local ice cream parlor, after selling only ice cream for years, suddenly starts offering frozen yogurt as well. Is this an imposition on customers, who are now "required" to make a choice? Are they being "coerced to think"?   1

This is the way some critics have characterized a new Louisiana law that, as of Friday, will allow couples to choose between the standard "no fault" marriage and a "covenant" marriage.   2

Couples choosing a covenant marriage pledge to enter matrimony only after serious deliberations. They agree to try to resolve potential marital conflicts through   3 counseling if either spouse requests it and to seek divorce only by a mutually agreed upon two-year separation or under a limited set of circumstances, like adultery, abuse, imprisonment for a felony and abandonment. The law also allows married couples to renew their vows and to recast their commitment as a covenant marriage.

Basically, the new Louisiana law provides couples with a ready-made contract that, like all contracts, becomes enforceable by the state once it is entered into freely. In effect, Louisiana is providing a new form of prenuptial agreement, focused not on what happens to assets if the couple divorces, but on how to make divorce less likely.   4

The Louisiana Legislature, which is not widely known for social innovations, has come under criticism for this imaginative act. Some critics have said that the law imposes new constraints on marrying couples because they are forced to make a choice between the old no-fault and the new covenant marriage.   5

The feminist writer Katha Pollitt has characterized the law as "forcing" couples to make a choice. Margaret Carlson of Time magazine even suggested that the choice was "theoretical" because after Friday couples would no longer dare choose what she calls Marriage Lite over Marriage Plus. If only she would accept bets.   6

Most people would agree that allowing individuals to make choices is the exact opposite of coercion. Indeed, the Louisiana legislation provides a model of how a state can foster what it considers a virtue—in this case, stronger marriages—by giving people the opportunity to be virtuous, but not penalizing them if they choose not to.   7

If this approach were extended to other areas, more teachers would allow pupils to do extra schoolwork to improve a bad grade, rather than merely telling students they should do better next time. Anti-abortion forces might stop emphasizing a ban on abortion and instead offer even more pregnant women support services and help with adoption.   8

A state may favor some types of behavior over others, but it should promote these by giving people expanded options, rather than forcing them to behave in a preordained manner. And Louisiana couples who are in a rush to marry or for any other reason refuse to deliberate their joint future will not need to elope; they will still be able to marry the old-fashioned, no-fault way.   9

We are all better off if those who tie the knot are prepared for the commitment. Yes, divorce is sometimes called for. But most divorces are damaging, painful and costly for all involved. Moreover, studies show that about 20 percent of those who avail themselves of premarital counseling decide not to marry, thus perhaps sparing themselves from a bad marriage and a messy divorce.   10

Some critics of the Louisiana law have argued that slowing down divorce is poor public policy because children are better off when feuding couples break up; they are no longer subject to incessant conflict or hostile silence.   11

Yet at issue here are not physically or psychologically abusive marriages, because these can be dissolved without undue difficulty under the new law. But for two people who have simply grown apart or are otherwise discontent, a divorce will be   12 delayed for at least two years rather than the standard six months. This time could give the couple a chance to work things out.

The issue is not whether our divorce laws should be tailored for the small per- 13 centage of marriages that are seriously abusive, but whether the legal system now makes divorce too easy or too difficult. Are there millions of couples for whom a delayed divorce would cause serious and irreparable harm? Or are millions of couples calling it quits too easily?

To put it differently, should only "disposable" marriages be available to couples— 14 or should there also be an option that encourages them to work harder at sustaining their marriages?

Far from joining with those who would abolish no-fault divorce and replace it 15 with vows that severely restrict divorce, Louisiana has left the choice completely to the couples. Do they prefer to start with the promise of an easy exit, or are they willing to slow down before they quit?

The fact that some critics object to this modest, moderate step speaks to what 16 is wrong in our divorce-prone culture.

LETTERS TO THE EDITOR

To the Editor:

Amitai Etzioni assumes that divorce occurs because it is legally easy. This as- 1 sumption is not supported by the social science data. Divorce rates were rising before—not after—no-fault divorce was implemented. A more reasonable interpretation of the data is that no-fault divorce represented the rising desire of citizens to have their divorces without finger-pointing.

Mr. Etzioni seems to believe that making divorce harder will make people work 2 harder at their marriages. Again, there are no data to support that argument. An alternative scenario is that people would remain in unhappy marriages because it is too difficult to get a divorce. That can be shown to be damaging to both children and adults in the family.

JOSEPH LEVENSTEIN

To the Editor:

The major, insuperable problem with "covenant marriage" that Amitai Etzioni en- 3 dorses is that the "covenant" is that of a particular set of religious notions found in conservative Christian circles. In other words, the state of Louisiana has passed a law that essentially enshrines religious dogma as law. Moreover, the state is being asked to do what the churches have not been able to do: keep people in marriages that fail.

This law says volumes about the inability of the churches to use moral suasion to 4 encourage their adherents to stick to their marriages, if the churches find themselves having to resort to legislation to force people to do what they would not do otherwise.

DEANA MARIE HOLMES

To the Editor:

Re "Marriage with No Easy Outs." While the "covenant" marriage is an option   5
that must be mutually agreed upon and is one that can be dissolved in instances of
abuse, the reality of family violence often defies unequivocal, free decision-making.

Emotional, financial and physical coercion and intimidation make ending a rela-   6
tionship difficult for many women now under no-fault divorce laws; by extension, it
is safe to assume that those who once freely chose to enter the more highly regarded covenant marriage, with its inextricable binds, will have an even more difficult time leaving an abusive relationship.

NICOLE MELLOW

To the Editor:

Classic liberalism would say that the law that governs best governs least. Why   7
should we assume that our laws contain the full force of our moral, ethical, emotional and psychological selves? Amitai Etzioni ("Marriage with No Easy Outs")
mistakenly assumes that only if a couple had chosen to be forced by law, as they
now can under the new Louisiana "covenant" marriage, would they wait two years
to divorce rather than doing so after six months.

The underlying problem with social conservatives is that they don't trust people's   8
moral action to exceed what the law requires. Rather than allowing individuals the
most moral options that society can tolerate, social conservatives seek to limit
these options through government intervention into the private realm.

Mr. Etzioni's comparison of marriage options to an ice cream parlor is disingenu-   9
ous. For the image to reflect more accurately his claim that Louisiana simply presents a couple with a ready-made contract that they might otherwise draft
themselves, the store would need to offer more than a choice between ice cream
and yogurt. Like Howard Johnson's, which offers 32 flavors, the state would offer
ready-made contracts for every kind of marriage people wanted, including same-
sex unions.

JOHN PULTZ

To the Editor:

Several decades ago Margaret Mead suggested that couples should not need a li-   10
cense to be married, but only to have children. This desirable but impractical suggestion may have found new life in Louisiana's two-level marriage contract: one a
"no-fault" arrangement, the other a "covenant" that allows either party to veto a
divorce except under certain circumstances.

Why not have every marriage start as a no-fault contract with an automatic con-   11
version to a covenant contract upon the conception of a child? The covenant contract would then remain for the duration of any child's life to majority.

This arrangement would make conception a new stage in the deliberations of   12
any couple: Mead's original objective. There would be a greater awareness of the
responsibilities of this stage of life during the period the marriage contract has
been converted to a "child-bearing" contract.

JAMES J. WARFIELD

To the Editor:

Amitai Etzioni suggests that couples who choose to be married under Louisiana's   13
new "covenant" law, with its restrictive provisions on divorce, will have "no easy
outs" if they later decide to divorce.

Past experience with restrictive divorce laws suggests, however, that it is only   14
the poor who will be denied an easy out. The more well-to-do will find it quite
easy to establish a technical domicile in a state with a lenient divorce law and then
to obtain a valid divorce from that state. In other words, at least for those with
some money, what Louisiana may join together, Nevada may rend asunder.

WILLIAM L. REYNOLDS

SYNTHESIS AND COMPARISON

Synthesis is a method; it is not an end in itself. Some works do not lend themselves to synthesis, which tends to emphasize similarities at the expense of interesting differences between sources.

The academic writer should be able to distinguish between material that is
appropriate for synthesis and material whose individuality should be recognized and preserved. One example of the latter is fiction; another is autobiog-
raphy. Assume that three writers are reminiscing about their first jobs: one was
a clerk in a drugstore, the second a telephone operator, and the third plowed
his father's fields. In their recollections, the reader can find several similar
themes: accepting increased responsibility; sticking to the job; learning appropriate behavior; living up to the boss's or customers' or father's expectations.
But, just as important, the three autobiographical accounts *differ* sharply in
their context and circumstances, in their point of view and style. You cannot
lump them together in the same way that you might categorize statements
about the lottery or opinions about school uniforms, for they cannot be reduced to a single common experience. The three are not *interchangeable*; rather,
they are comparable.

Since *synthesis* does not always do justice to individual works, *comparison*
can be a more effective strategy for writing about several full-length essays
with a common theme. In many ways, comparison resembles synthesis. Both
involve analyzing the ideas of several sources and searching for a single vantage point from which to view these separate sources. However, there is an important difference. *The writer of a synthesis constructs a new work out of the
materials of the old; the writer of a comparison tries to leave the sources intact throughout the organizational process, so that each retains its individuality.*

When you are assigned an essay topic, and when you assemble several
sources, you are not likely to want to *compare* the information that you have
recorded in your notes; rather, you will *synthesize* that material into a complete presentation of the topic. One of your sources may be an encyclopedia;
another a massive survey of the entire subject; a third may devote several
chapters to a scrutiny of that one small topic. In fact, these three sources are
really not comparable, nor is your primary purpose to distinguish between

them or to understand how they approach the subject differently. You are only interested in the results that you can achieve by using and building on this information. In contrast, the appropriate conditions for comparison are more specific and rare.

For comparison, you must have two or more works of similar length and complexity that deal with the same subject and that merit individual examination.

Point-to-Point Comparison

Point-to-point comparison resembles synthesis. You select certain major ideas that are discussed in all the works being compared and then, to support conclusions about these ideas, describe the full range of opinion concerning *each* point, one at a time.

Because point-to-point comparison cuts across the source essays, as synthesis does, you must work hard to avoid oversimplification. If you are focusing on one idea, trying to relate it to a comparable reaction in another essay, don't forget that the two works are separate and whole interpretations of the topic. Otherwise, you may end up emphasizing similarities just to make your point.

Here is a paragraph taken from a *point-to-point comparison* of three movie reviews:

> None of the three reviewers regards Lady and the Tramp as a first-rate product of the Walt Disney studio. Their chief object of criticism is the sugary sentimentality, so characteristic of Disney cartoons, which has been injected into Lady in excessive quantities. Both John McCarten in the New Yorker and the Time reviewer point out that, for the first time, the anthropomorphic presentation of animals does not succeed because the "human" situations are far too broadly presented. Lady and the Tramp are a "painfully arch pair," says McCarten. He finds the dialogue given to the movie's human characters even more embarrassing than the clichés exchanged by the animals. Even Bosley Crowther of the Times, who seems less dismissive of feature cartoons, finds that Lady and the Tramp lacks Disney's usual "literate originality." Crowther suggests that its oppressive sentimentality is probably made more obvious by the film's use of the wide screen. McCarten also comments on the collision between the winsome characters and the magnified production: "Obviously determined to tug all heartstrings," Disney presents the birth of Lady's puppy "while all the stereophonic loudspeakers let loose with overwhelming barrages of cooings and gurglings." All the reviewers agree that the audience for this film will be restricted to dog lovers, and lapdog lovers at that.

Whole-to-Whole Comparison

In whole-to-whole comparison, you discuss each work, one at a time. This method is more likely to give the reader a sense of each source's individual qualities. But unless your sources are fairly short and simple, this method can be far more unwieldy than point-to-point. If you compare a series of long and complex works, and if you complete your entire analysis of one before you move on to the next, the reader may get no sense of a comparison and forget that you are relating several sources to each other. *Without careful structuring, whole-to-whole comparison becomes a series of loosely related summaries,* in which readers must discover for themselves all the connections, parallels, and contrasts.

There are two ways to make the structure of whole-to-whole comparison clear to the reader:

1. **Although each work is discussed separately and presented as a whole, you should nevertheless try to present common ideas *in the same order,* an order that will carry out the development of your thesis about the works being compared.**

   Thus, whichever topic you choose as the starting point for your discussion of the first work should also be used as the starting point for your treatment of each of the others. The reader should be able to find the same general idea discussed in (roughly) the same place in each section of a whole-to-whole comparison.

2. **Remind the reader that this is a comparison by frequent *cross-cutting* to works already discussed; you should make frequent use of standard transitional phrases to establish such cross-references.**

   Initially, you have to decide which work to begin with. The best choice is usually a relatively simple work that nonetheless touches on all the major points of comparison and that enables you to begin establishing your own point of view. Beginning with the second work, you should refer back to what you have said about the first writer's ideas, showing how they differ from those of the second. This process can become extremely complex when you are analyzing a large number of essays, which is one reason that whole-to-whole comparison is rarely used to compare more than three works.

Here is the second major paragraph of a *whole-to-whole comparison* that deals with critical reaction to the film *West Side Story*:

> Like the author of the Time review, Pauline Kael criticizes West Side Story for its lack of realism and its unconvincing portrayal of social tensions. She points out that the distinction between the ethnic groups is achieved through cosmetics and hair dye, not dialogue and actions. In her view, the characters are like Munchkins, stock figures without individual identities and recognizable motives. Natalie Wood as the heroine, Maria, is unfavorably com-

pared to a mechanical robot and to the Princess telephone. Just as the Time reviewer accuses the film of oversentimentalizing its teenage characters at society's expense, so Kael condemns the movie's division of its characters into stereotypical good guys and bad guys. In fact, Kael finds it hard to account for the popularity of West Side Story's "frenzied hokum." She concludes that many may have been overwhelmed by the film's sheer size and technical achievements. The audience is persuaded to believe that bigger, louder, and faster has to be better. Her disapproval extends even to the widely praised dancing; like the rest of the movie, the choreography tries too hard to be impressive. In short, Pauline Kael agrees with the Time reviewer: West Side Story never rises above its "hyped-up, slam-bang production."

Whether you choose point-to-point or whole-to-whole comparison depends on your sources. Whichever you choose, begin planning your comparison (as you would begin synthesis) by *listing the important ideas discussed by several of your sources.*

- If you eventually choose to write a *point-to-point* essay, then your list can become the basis for your paragraph outline.
- If you decide to compare each of your essays *whole to whole,* your list can suggest what to emphasize and can help you to decide the order of topics within the discussion of each work.

These lists can never be more than primitive guidelines; but unless you establish the primary points of similarity or difference among your sources, your essay will end up as a series of unrelated comments, not a comparison.

ASSIGNMENT 11: WRITING A COMPARISON ESSAY

Write a comparison of three reviews of a film. Your first concern should be the reactions of the critics, not your own opinion of the work; you are not expected to write a review yourself, but to analyze and contrast each critic's view of the film. Try to describe the distinctive way in which each reacts to the film; each will have seen a somewhat different film and will have a different understanding of what it signifies.

For films reviewed before 1970, consult James Salem's *A Guide to Critical Reviews.* Don't commit yourself to a specific film until you have seen a sampling of reviews; if they are all very similar in their criticisms or all very short, choose a different film. If you have doubts about the reviews' suitability, let your teacher see a set of copies. *Be prepared to hand in a full set of the reviews with your completed essay.*

Part III

WRITING THE RESEARCH ESSAY

Most long essays and term papers in college courses are based on library research. Sometimes, an instructor will expect you to develop and present a topic entirely through synthesizing preassigned sources; but for many other assignments, you will be asked to formulate your own opinion and then to validate and support that opinion by citing authorities. Whether your essay is to be wholly or partly substantiated through research, you will still have to start your essay by choosing sources at the library.

Your research essay (or extended multiple-source essay) will present you with several new problems, contradictions, and decisions. On the one hand, you will probably be starting out with no sources, no thesis, and only a broad topic to work with. Yet as soon as you go to the library and start your research, you will probably find yourself with too many sources—books and articles in the library and on the Internet from which you will have to make your own selection of readings. Locating and evaluating sources are complex skills, calling for quick comprehension and rapid decision-making.

- At the *indexes* and *online computer catalogs,* you have to judge which books are worth locating.
- At the *shelves,* and on the *computer screen,* you have to skim a variety of materials rapidly to choose the ones that may be worth reading at length.
- At the *library table* and *on the Internet,* you have to decide which facts and information should go into your notes and which pages should be duplicated in their entirety.

In Chapters 5, 6, and 7, you will be given explicit guidelines for using the library, choosing sources, and taking notes.

As you have learned, in order to write a multiple-source essay, you have to establish a coherent structure that builds on your reading and blends together your ideas and those of your sources. In Chapter 8, you will find a stage-by-stage description of the best ways to organize and write an essay based on complex sources. But here, again, is a contradiction.

Even as you gather your materials and synthesize them into a unified essay, you should also keep in mind the greatest responsibility of the researcher—*accountability. From your first efforts to find sources at the library and at your computer, you must carefully keep track of the precise source of each of the ideas and facts that you may use in your essay.* You already know how to distinguish between your ideas and those of your sources and to make that distinction clear to your readers.

Now, you also have to make clear which source is responsible for which idea and on which page of which book that information can be found—without losing the shape and coherence of your own paragraphs.

To resolve this contradiction between writing a coherent essay and accounting for your sources, you will use a system that includes the familiar skills of *quotation, paraphrase,* and *citation of authors,* as well as the skills of *documentation* and *compiling a bibliography.* This system is explained in Chapter 9.

Finally, in Chapter 10, you will be able to examine the product of all these research, writing, and documenting techniques: three essays that demonstrate, respectively, how to write a successful persuasive, narrative, and analytical research essay.

▪5▪
Finding Sources

Knowing exactly what you want to write about is a great advantage when you are beginning your research. Your instructor may give you that advantage by assigning a precise topic. On the other hand, you may be asked to *narrow a broad subject* or to *develop a topic of your own choosing,* perhaps an idea that you wrote about in your single- or multiple-source essay to give you a head start.

TOPIC NARROWING

Topic narrowing should be a *practical* process. Here are some of the questions that you should ask yourself before you go to the library:

- How much time do I have?
- What resources are available to me?
- How long an essay am I being asked to write?
- How complex a project am I ready to undertake?

Choosing a good topic requires some familiarity with the subject and with the available resources, which is why topic narrowing should continue all through the early stages of your research. Even before you start your research, you should invest some time in analyzing your subject and considering your options. Here are some approaches to topic narrowing that have worked well for students starting their first research project.

> ## *Guidelines for Narrowing Your Topic*
>
> 1. Whether your instructor assigns a broad topic for your research paper or you are permitted to choose your own topic, do some *preliminary reading* to get more background information.
>
> 2. As you start your reading, begin to *break down the broad topic into its components:* try thinking about a specific point in time or the influence of a particular event or person if your topic is *historical* or *biographical;* try applying the standard strategies for planning an essay if you're going to write about a *contemporary issue;* try formulating the reasons for and against if you're going to write an argument.
>
> 3. Consider *your own perspective* and what interests you about the person, event, or issue.
>
> 4. *Formulate a few questions* that might help you to structure your reading and research.
>
> 5. Think about the possible answers to these questions as you read, especially those questions and answers that might develop into a *thesis* for your essay.

Topic Narrowing: Biographical and Historical Subjects

Biographical and historical topics have an immediate advantage: they can be defined and limited by space and time. Events and lives have clear beginnings, middles, and ends, as well as many identifiable intermediate stages. You are probably not ready to undertake the full span of a biography or a complete historical event, but you could select *a specific point in time as the focus for your essay.*

Assume, for example, that by choice or assignment your broad subject is *Franklin Delano Roosevelt,* who was president of the United States for fourteen years—an unparalleled term of office—between 1932 and 1945. You begin by reading *a brief overview of FDR's life.* An encyclopedia article of several pages might be a starting point. This should give you enough basic information to decide which events in FDR's life interest you enough to sustain you through the long process of research. You might also read a few articles about the major events that formed the background to FDR's career: the Great Depression, the New Deal, the changing role of the president.

Now, instead of tracing *all* the incidents and related events in which he participated during his sixty-three years, you might decide to describe FDR at the point when his political career was apparently ruined by polio. Your focus would be the man in 1921, and your essay might develop a thesis drawing on any or all of the following topics—his personality, his style of life, his experiences, his idea of government—at *that* point in time. Everything that happened to FDR after 1921 would be relatively unimportant to your chosen perspective. Another student might choose a different point in time and describe *the new president in 1933 against the background of the depression.* Yet another might focus on an intermediate point in FDR's presidency and construct *a profile of the man as he was in 1940, when he decided to run for an unprecedented third term in office.*

The topic might be made even more specific by focusing on *a single event and its causes.* For example, the atomic bomb was developed during FDR's presidency and was used in Japan shortly after his death:

- What was FDR's attitude toward atomic research?
- Did he advocate using the bomb?
- Did he anticipate its consequences?

Or you might want to study Roosevelt in the context of an important political tradition:

- How did he influence the Democratic party?
- How did the party influence his personal and political decisions?
- What role did Roosevelt play in the establishment of the United States as a "welfare state"?

This kind of profile attempts to describe the subject and explore his or her motives and experiences. In effect, *your overriding impression of character or intention serves as the thesis, the controlling idea of the biographical profile.* You undertake to determine whether the available evidence supports your thesis, and present that thesis—if valid—to your readers, supported by facts and details.

You can also view a *historical event* from a similar specific vantage point. Your broad subject might be the Civil War, which lasted more than four years, or the Berlin Olympics of 1936, which lasted a few weeks, or the Los Angeles riots of 1991, which lasted a few days. To cover a long span of time, you might focus on an intermediate point or stage, which can serve to illuminate and characterize the entire event. The Battle of Gettysburg, for example, is a broad topic often chosen by those interested in the even broader topic of the Civil War. Since the three-day battle, with its complex maneuvers, can hardly be described in a brief narrative, you would want to narrow the focus even more. You might describe the battlefield and the disposition of the troops, as a journalist would, at a single moment in the course of the battle. In this case, your thesis might demonstrate that the disposition of the troops at this point was typical (or atypical) of tactics used throughout the battle, or that this moment did (or did not) foreshadow the battle's conclusion. In fact, always assuming that sufficient material is available, *you will find that it makes sense to narrow your focus as much as you can.*

In writing about history, you also have to consider your own point of view. If, for example, you set out to recount an episode from the Civil War, you first need to establish your perspective: Are you describing the Union's point of view? the Confederacy's? the point of view of the politicians of either side? the generals? the civilians? industrialists? hospital workers? slaves in the South? black freedmen in the North? If you tried to deal with *all* these reactions to a chosen event, you might have difficulty in settling on a thesis and, in the long run, would only confuse and misinform your reader.

The "day in the life" approach can also be applied to *events that had no specific date.*

- When and under what circumstances were primitive guns first used in battle?
- What was the psychological effect of gunfire on the opposing troops?
- What was the reaction when the first automobile drove down a village street?

Or, rather than describe the effects of a new invention, you might focus on *a social institution that has changed radically.*

- What was it like to shop for food in Paris in 1810?
- In Chicago in 1870?
- In any large American city in 1945?

Instead of attempting to write a complete history of the circus from Rome to Ringling, try portraying *the particular experience of a single person.*

- What was it like to be an equestrian performer in Astley's Circus in eighteenth-century London?
- A chariot racer in Pompeii's Circus Maximus in 61 B.C.?

Setting a tentative target date helps you to focus your research, giving you a practical way to judge the relevance and the usefulness of each of your sources. As you narrow your topic and begin your reading, *watch for your emerging thesis—a single, clear impression of the person or event that you wish your reader to receive.* Whether you are writing about a sequence of events, like a battle or a flood, or a single event or issue affecting the life of a well-known person, you will still need both a *thesis* and a *strategy* to shape the direction of your essay. *A common strategy for biographical and historical topics is the cause-and-effect sequence*—why a certain decision was made or an event turned out one way and not another.

Finally, do not allow your historical or biographical portrait to become an exercise in creative writing. Your evidence must be derived from and supported by well-documented sources, not just your imagination. The "Napoleon might have said" or "Stalin must have thought" in some biographies and historical novels is often a theory or an educated guess that is firmly rooted in research—and the author should provide documentation and a bibliography to substantiate it.

Topic Narrowing: Contemporary Subjects

If you chose to write about the early history of the circus, you would find an assortment of books describing many traditional kinds of circus activity, from the Roman arena to the turn-of-the-century Barnum and Bailey big top. But there has been an enormous increase in the amount of information published in this half of the twentieth century; reviews and features are printed—and preserved for the researcher—every time Ringling Brothers opens in a new city. Your research for an essay about the circus today might be endless and the results unmanageable unless, quite early, you focus your approach.

If your topic cannot be defined and narrowed through the perspective of time, you can analyze its component parts and select *a single aspect* as the tentative focus of your essay. If you do a computer search for information, you will scan a large number of "descriptors" for your broad topic. Reviewing all these subtopics may help you to find a narrow focus for your topic.

You will find that many of the guides, indexes, and online databases in the reference room contain not only lists of sources but also a useful breakdown of subtopics, suggesting possibilities for the direction of your essay. You will automatically narrow your perspective if you begin to ask questions about and apply different strategies to possible topics. For example, suppose that *food* is your broad topic. Your approach might be *descriptive*, analyzing *causes and effects*: you could write about some aspect of nutrition, discussing what we ought to eat and the way in which our nutritional needs are best satisfied. Or you could deal with the production and distribution of food—or, more likely, a specific kind of food—and use *process description* as your approach. Or you could analyze a different set of *causes*: Why don't we eat what we ought to? Why do so many people have to diet, and why aren't diets effective? Or you could plan a *problem-solution* essay: What would be the best way to educate the public in proper nutrition? Within the narrower focus of *food additives*, there are numerous ways to develop the topic:

- To what degree are additives dangerous?
- What was the original purpose of the Food and Drug Act of 1906?
- Would individual rights be threatened if additives like Nutrasweet were banned?
- Can the dangers of food additives be compared with the dangers of alcohol?

On the other hand, your starting point could be *a concrete object*, rather than *an abstract idea*: you might decide to write about the Big Mac. You could describe its contents and nutritional value; or recount its origins and first appearance on the food scene; or compare it to best-selling foods of past eras; or evaluate its relative popularity in different parts of the world. All of these topics require *research*.

It is desirable to have a few possible narrow topics in mind before you begin intensive reading. Then, as you start to compile your preliminary bibliography, you can begin to distinguish between sources that are potentially useful and sources that will probably be irrelevant. What you *cannot* do at this stage is formulate a definite thesis. *Your thesis will probably answer the question that you asked at the beginning of your research.* Although, from the first, you may have your own theories about the answer, you cannot be sure that your research will confirm your hypotheses. Your thesis should remain tentative until your reading has given your essay content and direction.

Topic Narrowing: Issues for Argument

Finding a topic can be easier when you set out to write an argument. Although it is possible to do well with a topic that is new to you, most people gravitate toward issues that have some significance for them. If nothing immediately occurs to you, try *brainstorming*—jotting down possible ideas in a list. Recall conversations, news broadcasts, class discussions that have made you feel interested, even argumentative. Prepare a list of possible topics over a few days, and keep reviewing the list, looking for one that satisfies the following criteria:

- *Your topic should allow you to be objective.* Your reader expects you to present a well-balanced account of both sides of the argument. Too much emotional involvement with a highly charged issue can be a handicap. If, for example, someone close to you was killed in an incident involving a handgun, you are likely to lose your objectivity in an essay on gun control.

- *Your topic should have appropriate depth.* Don't choose an issue that is too trivial: "Disney World is better than Disneyland." For a general audience, don't choose an issue that is too specialized: "The Rolling Stones were a more influential band than the Beatles," or "*2001: A Space Odyssey* is the most technically proficient science-fiction film ever made." And don't choose an issue that is too broad or too abstract: "Technology has been the bane of the twentieth century" or "A life without God is not worth living." Your topic should be definable in terms that your reader can understand and, perhaps, share. Finally, your topic should lend itself to a clear, manageable path of research. Using the keywords "god" and "life" in a database search will produce a seemingly unending list of books and articles. Where will you begin?

- *Your topic should have appropriate scope.* Consider the terms of your instructor's assignment. Some topics can be explored in ten pages; others require more lengthy development. Some require extensive research; others can be written using only a few selected sources. Stay within the assigned guidelines.

- *Your topic should have two sides.* Some topics are nonissues: it would be hard to get anyone to disagree about them. "Everyone should have the experience of work" or "Good health is important" are topics that aren't worth arguing. (Notice that they are also far too abstract.) Whatever the issue, your opponents must have a credible case for you to attack.

- *Your topic can be historical.* There are many issues rooted in the past that are still arguable. Should President Truman have authorized dropping the atomic bomb on Japan? Were there better alternatives to ending slavery than the Civil War?

- *Your topic should be practical.* It may be tempting to argue that tuition should be free for all college students, but, in the process, you would have to recommend an alternative way to pay for the cost of education—something that state and federal governments have yet to figure out.

■ *Your topic should have sufficient evidence available to support it.* You may not know for sure whether you can adequately defend your argument until you have done some library research.

■ *Your topic should be within your range of understanding.* Don't plan an argument on "the consequences of global warming" unless you are prepared to present scientific evidence, much of which is written in highly technical language. Evidence for topics in the social sciences can be equally difficult to comprehend, for many depend on surveys that are hard for a nonprofessional to evaluate.

Many of these criteria also apply to choosing either a historical narrative or a contemporary subject. What's important in writing any essay—especially one involving a commitment to research—is that the topic interest you. If you are bored while writing your essay, your reader will probably be just as bored while reading it.

EXERCISE 17: PROPOSING A TOPIC

The following topic proposals were submitted by students who had already spent two sessions at the library focusing their topics for an eight- to ten-page research essay. Consider the scope and focus of each proposal, and decide which ones suggest *practical* topics for an essay of this length. If the proposal is too broad, be prepared to offer suggestions for narrowing the focus.

Student A

Much of the interest in World War II has been focused on the battlefield, but the war years were also a trying period for the public at home. I intend to write about civilian morale during the war, emphasizing press campaigns to increase the war effort. I will also include a description of the way people coped with brown-outs, shortages, and rationing, with a section on the victory garden.

Student B

I intend to deal with the role of women in feudal life, especially the legal rights of medieval women. I would also like to discuss the theory of chivalry and its effects on women, as well as the influence of medieval literature on society. My specific focus will be the ideal image of the medieval lady.

Student C

I have chosen the Lindbergh kidnapping case as the subject of my essay. I intend to concentrate on the kidnapping itself, rather than going into details about the lives of the Lindberghs. What interests me is the planning of the crime, including the way in which the house was designed and how the kidnapping was carried out. I also hope to include an account of the investigation and courtroom scenes. Depending on what I find, I may argue that Hauptmann was wrongly convicted.

Student D

I would like to explore methods of travel one hundred and fifty years ago, and compare the difficulties of traveling then with the conveniences of traveling now. I intend to stress the economic and social background of the average traveler. My focus will be the Grand Tour that young men used to take.

Student E

I'd like to explore quality in television programs. Specifically, I'd like to argue that popular and critically acclaimed TV shows of today are just as good as comparable programs ten and twenty years ago and that there really hasn't been a decline in popular taste. It may be necessary to restrict my topic to one kind of television show—situation comedies, for example, or coverage of sports events.

Student F

I would like to do research on several aspects of adolescent peer groups, trying to determine whether the overall effects of peer groups on adolescents are beneficial or destructive. I intend to include the following topics: the need for peer acceptance; conformity; personal and social adjustment; and peer competition. I'm not sure that I can form a conclusive argument, since most of the information available on this subject is purely descriptive; but I'll try to present an informed opinion.

EXERCISE 18: NARROWING A TOPIC

A. Here are ten different ways of approaching the broad topic of *poverty in America*. Decide which questions would make good starting points for an eight- to ten-page research essay. Consider the practicality and the clarity of each question, the probable availability of research materials, and the likelihood of being able to answer the question in approximately nine pages. Try rewriting two of the questions that seem too broad, narrowing the focus.

   1. How should the nation deal with poverty in its communities?
   2. What problems does your city or town encounter in its efforts to make sure that its citizens live above the poverty level?
   3. What are the primary causes of poverty today?
   4. Whose responsibility is it to help the poor?
   5. What effects does a life of poverty have on a family?
   6. What can be done to protect children and the aged, groups that make up the largest proportion of the poor?

    7. Does everyone have the right to freedom from fear of poverty?

    8. Which programs for alleviating poverty have been particularly successful, and why?

    9. Should all those receiving welfare funds be required to work?

    10. What nations have effectively solved the problem of poverty, and how?

B. Make up several questions that would help you to develop the broad topic of *restricting immigration to America* for an eight- to ten-page research essay.

IDENTIFYING SOURCES FOR RESEARCH

> ### *Preliminary Research in the Library: Three Overlapping Stages*
>
> 1. Discovering and locating the titles of some possible sources.
> 2. Recording basic facts about each source.
> 3. Noting each source's potential usefulness—or lack of usefulness—to your topic.

These three stages of identifying sources for resources usually form a *continuous cycle.* You probably will not be able to locate *all* your sources at once, and then record *all* your basic information, and lastly take notes about *all* your sources. Rather, you will have to move back and forth from computer terminal to stacks to reference room. Even after you begin to plan and write your essay, you will probably find yourself back at the library, checking another potentially useful source.

Because you may be looking at a great many titles and because, in any one session at the library, you may be at a different stage of research with each of several different books and articles, you should thoroughly familiarize yourself with the three steps.

The Library

Even before your research essay is assigned, you should become acquainted with your college library. Every library has a different layout, with a different online (computerized) catalog, and stacks that use various kinds of numbering systems. *Find out how your library is organized, how the online catalog works, and what it contains.* Most libraries provide guided tours for groups of interested students. Ask the reference librarian about tour schedules; in fact, the librarian will probably provide you with pamphlets about the library, a map, and almost any other information you're likely to need.

If a tour is not available, make your own exploratory visit. Ask yourself some of the following questions:

- How are the books arranged?
- Are the collections for the different disciplines housed in separate buildings?
- Do you have access to all the stacks of books?
- Is there a map of the reference room on the wall?
- How are the guides and indexes arranged in the reference room? Do you have access to these online?
- Is there a list of all the periodicals owned by the library? Is this list online?
- What kinds of sources are available on microfilm and microcards? Where are the microfilm and microcard readers, and how do you locate and sign out the cards and spools of film?
- Are there computerized databases, and how do you get access to them?
- Does your library have a consortial arrangement with neighboring libraries, and do you have access to materials at these libraries, via a delivery system (interlibrary loan) or computer printout?
- Does your library provide access to the Internet? What special research services are available?

Get these questions answered before you start your research; then you will not lose time and impetus because of interruptions later on.

Online Databases and CD-ROMs

Until recently, libraries listed all their holdings on cards—one card per book—contained in narrow drawers: the *card catalog.* Sometimes, instead of cards in drawers, libraries used a series of bound volumes, with forty or more entries per page. Now, most libraries list their holdings in searchable *databases,* including online databases (often called Online Public Access Catalogs, or OPACs) and in databases stored on CD-ROMs (compact disk, read-only memory). These computerized catalogs enable you to sit at a computer terminal and, using a menu that appears on the screen, retrieve information about a topic or an author or a book. This information can consist of

- The holdings of your library.
- The holdings of other libraries that are part of a local group or libraries across the globe.
- General and specialized indexes and bibliographies that list the names of sources—books and periodicals—some of which may be owned by your library.
- Journals that are online—that is, that you can call up and read on your computer screen—and from which you can obtain printouts of specific articles.

Your library also has databases of electronic information sources available on CD-ROM. The database is stored on a computer disk, and is periodically updated. Once the disk is inserted in the library computer, you use a menu to search for information, just as you would look for sources in an online database.

Each online database or CD-ROM database has a set of commands that students can type in order to access information on the screen. You will usually find a set of instructions posted by each terminal indicating the basic steps to follow in order to find what you are looking for. Reference librarians can also assist you in using the library's computers.

Figure 5-1 shows a sample—one screen—of what's available to students on the twenty campuses of The City University of New York (CUNY). Here, you can choose between the CUNY on-line catalog—the holdings of the libraries of the university—or various online databases containing information about articles in newspapers and periodicals.

Searching a database is, in many ways, easier and more efficient than using a traditional card catalog. To check a number of possible topics or authors in the card catalog, you would have to move from drawer to drawer, pulling one out, thumbing through the cards, making notes, returning the drawer, and moving to a different section of the catalog for your next reference. It is physically easier to remain at a terminal, locating potential sources by making choices from a menu and typing in commands so that the information you want appears on the screen. What you see on the screen probably isn't much different from what you would find in the card catalog. But the process is faster and, once you become familiar with the library's system, much less tedious.

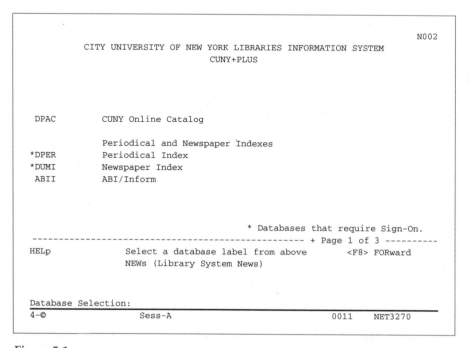

Figure 5-1

On-line databases and CD-ROMs have their limitations. Your library's on-line catalog may be restricted to its own holdings (or, if your college is part of a state university system or a consortium of universities, the combined holdings of all libraries in that system or consortium). Now, however, some online databases are linked to library databases throughout the state or even the nation. If you want to examine a range of all the possible sources on a particular topic, you will probably have to consult specialized databases that may include some titles that your library doesn't own. (See Computer Searches on pp. 254–258 for information on conducting computer searches in specialized databases.)

For decades, researchers have had access to a number of general and specialized indexes and bibliographies that they use to find articles (and sometimes books) related to their research topics. For example, *Applied Science and Technology Index* contains brief summaries of a large number of journal articles about topics in science and technology; *Human Resources Abstracts* lists articles about areas such as poverty, the workforce, and the distribution of human services. Appendix A contains an extensive list of these specialized indexes and bibliographies, the vast majority of which are now online (indicated by an asterisk).

The Internet

In addition to those resources already mentioned, the computer terminal in your library (or your dormitory room) can provide you with access to many other powerful electronic tools that will produce information of prodigious range and depth. To gain access to this information, you need access to the *Internet*—a huge worldwide network of smaller, interconnected computer networks. Currently used by 25 to 30 million people—and growing daily—the Internet is now one of the world's largest repositories of information.

Your university may provide you with free Internet access or may charge a small fee. Or your library's computers may give you access to the Internet. Or you might open an account with a local Internet service provider or subscribe to a *commercial information service*, such as America Online, CompuServe, or Microsoft Network; for a monthly fee, a subscription gives you access to the Internet and, therefore, to the kinds of services described here, as well as to other sources of information and entertainment. Whatever means of access you choose, the Internet is well worth exploring, for it has become an essential tool for anyone who engages in research.

Today, information on the Internet is accessible in three primary ways: E-mail, World Wide Web sites, and Usenet newsgroups.

E-Mail

E-mail enables people to communicate with each other and exchange information electronically all over the world, in minutes. It is as quick and easy as a telephone conversation, but expands your audience to, potentially, hundreds of thousands. Like using the postal mail ("snail-mail"), you write a message in your E-mail software, address it to one or more people, and send it through a computer network.

You can use E-mail to request assistance in exploring a research topic. If you know the E-mail address of an expert in that field, you can send the person an E-mail inquiry, asking questions or requesting specific information. (Make sure that you are courteous in making your request; some people don't have the time to answer unsolicited E-mail or may resent being asked to contribute to your "homework." Review the suggestions in Appendix C for approaching an interview subject.) Remember that any information obtained through E-mail that is subsequently used in an essay must have its source cited. (See Appendix B for the appropriate format.) E-mail also enables you to collaborate with other students on group projects by exchanging information electronically.

Another way to use E-mail is to subscribe to a *mailing list* or *list-serv* (sometimes spelled *listserve*). These are, basically, E-mail exchanges among people interested in a particular subject. When your E-mail address is added to the mailing list, you receive E-mail from members of the group and can send E-mail in return. Large mailing lists are usually automated, with a computer (or *list-serv*) receiving and distributing E-mail to and from you and the other group members. Not all list-servs are open to the public, and some are moderated: volunteers screen all E-mail to ensure that it is appropriate for distribution. You can search for mailing lists and list-servs on these web sites: www.liszt.com (Liszt) and www.tile.net (Tile.Net).

Mailing lists are potentially a source of information for research. For example, lists like TECHWR-L, TEKCOML, or TECHCOMM would provide you with opportunities for discussing technical communication. And subscribing to AAWOMLIT might help you obtain information about literature written by African-American women. Remember that material obtained through E-mail or, indeed, from the Internet in general, has not been validated for accuracy, as have works that have gone through the review and selection processes used by publishers of books and journals. See Chapter 6 for a discussion of evaluating materials on the Internet.

World Wide Web Sites

Of all the sources of information on the Internet, the fastest growing and most fluid is the World Wide Web, where files containing text, graphics, video, sound, and animation come together to form *web sites*. Web sites can vary from a text-only *web page* on a single screen to a complex, interconnected collection of web pages. Software called *web browsers* enables you to navigate the Internet and view web sites. Netscape Navigator and Microsoft Internet Explorer are web browsers that can display both text and graphics; Lynx is a web browser that displays only text.

A central concept of the Web is the *hypertext*, a system of codes that allow readers of web pages to navigate by clicking on *links* and moving to another web page, to a portion of a web page, or to another web site entirely. Clicking on a link may also allow you to see a graphic image, listen to music, or view a

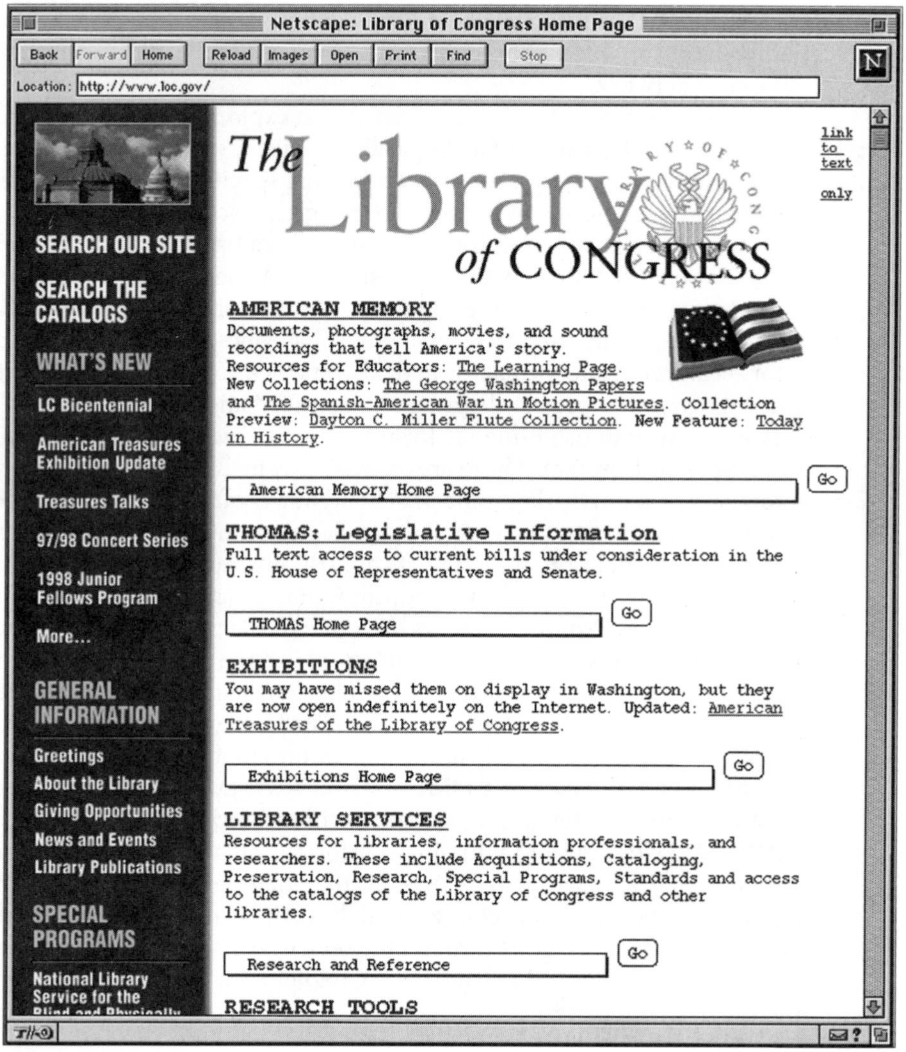

Figure 5-2

short video clip. Because links can point to anywhere on the web site or to other web sites, hypertext enables you to move through web-based documents in a nonlinear fashion. If you choose, you can read through a web-based document from beginning to end. If it isn't useful to you, at any point you can follow hypertext links to another part of the document, to another document, or to another web site. Another way to move from one web site to another is by typing in the URL (Uniform Resource Locator); the URL is the "address" of the web site you want to visit.

Web sites are created by governmental agencies, schools, businesses, non-profit organizations, and individuals (Figure 5-2 shows the home page of the

Library of Congress). Your university probably maintains a web site; some of your instructors may also have created web sites with information about their courses. You and your friends might maintain *home pages* containing information about yourselves and your interests. Web sites are clearly ideal for distributing up-to-date information to a worldwide audience cheaply and easily. (Indeed, many corporations maintain web sites, partly for purposes of advertising.) That's why you need to make sure that information for research obtained through the Internet is accurate, reliable, and objective. It may be hard to distinguish between the web site of a leading authority on the Army of the North and a Civil War buff who's done a lot of reading. Not all web sites are equally valid. Before you take notes or print out material, check credentials, cited sources, dates, and facts.

The sheer size of the World Wide Web—and the Internet in general—can complicate the process of research. With millions of web sites available, you may have to scan a great many before you can find what you need. As the amount of information stored on the Internet grew, electronic tools were developed to assist Internet users in finding and locating information. One of the first such tools was called a *gopher:* software that allows users to "burrow" from one network to another and from one database to another, using key words and phrases to search for the information. Today, gophers are almost superseded by the faster *browsers,* which navigate the Internet, and by web-based *search engines,* which obtain information on a specific subject. Web search engines are huge databases containing indexes of key words and phrases gathered from various web sites. (See Compiling a Working Bibliography on p. 254 for a description of organizing subject headings.) Methods for searching vary among search engines; before using one that is unfamiliar to you, read the help files and learn about its specific processes. Some of the more popular search engines include

www.altavista.digital.com (AltaVista)

www.infoseek.com (InfoSeek)

www.yahoo.com (Yahoo!)

www.webcrawler.com (WebCrawler)

www.lycos.com (Lycos)

www.excite.com (Excite)

www.hotbot.com (HotBot)

Usenet Groups

Usenet groups provide another means of access to information, through a worldwide network of electronic *bulletin boards,* each devoted to a particular subject. Numbering in the tens of thousands, these *newsgroups* resemble a traditional bulletin board. Using your web browser or specialized news-reading software, you can post messages to one or more newsgroups, you can read messages other people have posted, and you can reply to those messages. So, if your research topic were the Civil War, you could read the newsgroup soc.history.war.us-civil war, or you could obtain information from participants in that or other newsgroups interested in the Civil War simply by posting your questions. Here's what such a question might look like:

> I know that in the North, men born between 1818 and 1843 had to register for the draft. What about aliens? Did they have to register? If not, did they have to prove that they were not citizens? Where would I obtain records?

Before posting that request for information, you might check to see if the question has already been answered on the newsgroup's FAQ: a document, posted by volunteers, that answers frequently asked questions about the newsgroup or the newsgroup's subject. You can find a newsgroup's FAQ and Usenet messages in searchable databases, such as DejaNews (www.dejanews.com), on the World Wide Web. Or you can search Usenet from such web-based search engines as AltaVista or Yahoo! The resources available to you are vast. For example, one recent search for the phrase *home automation* turned up over 1,500 Usenet messages containing the phrase, most of them posted to alt.home. automation and comp.home.automation. Of course, sometimes the sheer number of possibilities can create problems in sorting out which documents to check first. And the same concerns about reliability and accuracy of E-mail information and web-site information apply to Usenet groups.

COMPILING A WORKING BIBLIOGRAPHY

To use virtually all online databases—OPACs, gophers, standard research indexes, and databases provided by commercial services—you have to carry out a computer search, based on the principle of *cross-referencing*. When a new source—a book, for example—is being entered into a database, it would be foolish to include a separate entry for that book under every possible subject heading; that would create an overflowing database and an unmanageable system. Instead, just as libraries have done for decades in organizing their card catalogs, most online databases today use cross-referencing. First, *a standardized set of subject headings* is created to index information in the database. Then, the newly acquired book is scanned, and an entry for that book is placed *only* under those subject headings that are relevant to its content. The most commonly used set of subject headings for cross-referencing is the three-volume *Library of Congress Subject Headings* (LCSH), containing the standard set of cross-references found in all libraries using the Library of Congress system. Or a database may have a special list of descriptors relevant to its subject that can be found in a separate "thesaurus." Libraries generally have LCSH lists or other thesauruses available online or in books near the computer terminals.

Computer Searches

Suppose that you come to the library with a broad topic in mind: you plan to write an essay about *Prohibition*, the period between 1920 and 1933 when the

Eighteenth Amendment to the U.S. Constitution prohibited the manufacture and sale of all alcoholic beverages in the United States. You want to know why Prohibition was abandoned; you wonder whether the circumstances surrounding the institution of this ban on alcohol are relevant to the increasing limitations being placed on tobacco products today. How would you determine the available sources? How would you begin your search through all these databases that contain more information than you need or want?

A computer search usually begins by consulting the LCSH or other thesaurus to identify the appropriate *key words* (called *subject headings* or *descriptors*)—that describe your topic. The object is to find a group of descriptors that you can use, separately or together, to narrow down your topic. (This process is sometimes called *Boolean searching,* a term derived from mathematics, referring to questions limited in scope by combining two descriptors—for example, greater than, less than, x *and* y, x *and not* y—in order to narrow down a topic.) Figure 5-3 shows a listing of LCSH topics that you could look up in addition to Prohibition. Be aware that a key-word search may not always turn up relevant information. Some databases are organized rigorously; others are more haphazard, with odd articles, even promotional material, included in a grab bag of information that can appear on your screen.

Many other subject headings might lead to useful information about Prohibition, yet they don't appear on the cross-referencing list. Some preliminary reading on the topic might encourage you to look up "Organized Crime," for example, or "Smuggling of Illegal Substances."

If you can't find appropriate key words in LCSH, and your online catalog has the capacity to do a Keyword or Boolean search, you would consult the menu for Keyword Searching and then type in combinations of possible key words. Figure 5-4 shows two of the Help Screens, in sequence, in the CUNY Online Catalog that give students a choice of appropriate commands to do a Keyword Search.

If you wanted to do a Keyword Search for the topic "Prohibition," using the AND search, you would choose another appropriate term ("Temperance,"

```
              PROHIBITION

                see also

          LICENSE SYSTEMS
          LIQUOR LAWS
          LIQUOR PROBLEMS
          LOCAL OPTIONS
          PROHIBITIONISTS
          TEMPERANCE
```

Figure 5-3

```
                                                        CUNY Online Catalog
                                                          Explain Keyword
      ------------------------------------------------------------------------
                          Boolean and Positional Operators

      ADJ  -- ADJACENT searches for terms in the order typed in the search and
                immediately next to each other in the same record
                  Example: k=abortion adj activists


      SAME -- searches for terms in the same group of fields in a record, but in
                any order and not necessarily next to each other
                  Example: k=car same bomb


      AND  -- searches for the terms anywhere in the same record
                  Example: k=ozone and atmosphere
                    Continued on the next screen, type for and <enter>
      --------------------------------------------------+ Page 5 of 12 ----------
      STArt over                                          <F8> FORward page
      OTHer options                                       <F7> BACk page



      NEXT COMMAND:
      _____
      4-©                  Sess-A                          0011    NET3270
```

Figure 5-4A

```
                                                        CUNY Online Catalog
                                                          Explain Keyword
      ------------------------------------------------------------------------
                       Boolean and Positional Operators - continued

      NOT  -- Searches for occurrences of the first term and will match only if
                the second term is NOT in the same record
                  Example: k=haymarket not riot


      NEAR -- Searches for the two terms next to each other, but in any order
                  Example: k=mexico near trade


      OR   -- Searches for the first term or second term or both
                  Example: k=hurricanes or typhoons


                   For information on qualifying search terms press <enter>
      --------------------------------------------------+ Page 6 of 12 ----------
      STArt over                                          <F8> FORward page
      OTHer options                                       <F7> BACk page



      NEXT COMMAND:
      _____
      4-©                  Sess-A                          0011    NET3270
```

Figure 5-4B

for example), and, at the K= prompt, you would type in: Prohibition and Temperance.

Here is the result of a computer search in the ERIC database using a combination of *three* key words: the student typed in a request for articles about PRO-HIBITION and ALCOHOL and the UNITED STATES. Only two articles fulfilled those three descriptors. Figures 5-5 and 5-6 show the summaries of those two articles that appeared on the computer screen (and could, later on, be printed).

Either of these two articles might be interesting material for an essay on Prohibition in the United States. The Rorabaugh article seems to provide general background (but note that it is only three pages long), and the last section of the Wasserman article explicitly describes the period immediately before the passage of the Eighteenth Amendment. The printout contains information about the journal, volume, and date of publication, but does not use MLA or any other standard method of documentation.

The student tried another computer search, using the same three descriptors, this time in a database called DPAC (a book catalog database). The search resulted in the titles of one book and one book review. Unlike ERIC, DPAC provides no summaries, but does include a set of additional descriptors that might prompt you to enter a different combination of commands and produce a different group of titles from the database. In Figure 5-7, the information about the Blocker book review tells you the name of the work being reviewed, suggests that the length of the review is "medium," and assures you that the review is "favorable."

```
                                                        1 of 2
                                             Marked in Search: #6

   AN ACCESSION NUMBER: EJ449332
   AU PERSONAL AUTHOR: Rorabaugh, -W.-J.
   TI TITLE: Alcohol in America.
   PY PUBLICATION YEAR: 1991
   JN JOURNAL CITATION: OAH-Magazine-of-History; v6 n2 p17-19 Fall 1991
   AB ABSTRACT: Traces the history of alcohol use in the United States from
   the colonial period to the present. Discusses changes in public attitudes
   toward drinking. Explores attempts at prohibition, alcohol preferences,
   the relationship between alcohol consumption and economic prosperity, and
   the dichotomy of alcohol as a part of a European heritage that is also a
   destructive substance. (DK)
```

Figure 5-5

```
AN ACCESSION NUMBER: EJ448301
AU PERSONAL AUTHOR: Wasserman,-Ira-M.
TI TITLE: The Impact of Epidemic, War, Prohibition and Media on Suicide:
United States, 1910-1920.
PY PUBLICATION YEAR: 1992
JN JOURNAL CITATION: Suicide-and-Life-Threatening-Behavior; v22 n2 p240-54
Sum 1992
AV AVAILABILITY: UMI
AB ABSTRACT: Estimated impact of exogenous social and political events on
suicide behavior in the United States between 1910 and 1920. Concluded that
World War I did not influence suicide; Great Influenza Epidemic caused suicide
to increase; and continuing decline in alcohol consumption from 1910 to 1920
depressed national suicide rates. (Author/NB)
```

Figure 5-6

Specialized Indexes

In addition to the larger online databases available through the Internet, a number of smaller indexes of periodicals and journals intended for research in specific disciplines are available online or through CD-ROMs that you can access yourself at a terminal. (Appendix A has a comprehensive listing.) Most library information systems have the most frequently used periodical indexes right in their online system as separate databases (usually limited to the last ten years). To continue your research on Prohibition, you might want to consult the *Social Sciences Index,* the *Readers' Guide to Periodical Literature,* or the *Times Index.*

The *Readers' Guide to Periodical Literature* is especially useful for research on contemporary issues. It contains listings of a number of popular magazines, but very few scholarly journals, so it should not be the *only* index that you consult in preparing an academic paper. For your essay on Prohibition, you would look at the *Readers' Guide* for the 1920s and early 1930s (available in bound volumes, but not online), and find titles such as "Why Repeal Will Be Coming Soon." Here is what a *Readers' Guide* entry for a 1932 article looks like:

After Prohibition, what? L. Rogers. New Repub. 73:91–99   D7 '32
[title]   [author]   [magazine]   [volume; pages]   [date]

As you can see, the title of the article comes first; then L. Rogers, the author's name, with the first name indicated only by the initial; then the title of the periodical (often abbreviated); then the volume number, followed by a colon and the

```
DPER [Periodical Database]
Sample Computer Screen entry
From search: k= prohibition and alcohol and United States

AUTHOR:       Blocker, Jack S. Jr.

ARTICLE TITLE: Book Reviews: Profits, Power, and Prohibition

SOURCE
DATE:         Journal of American History. Dec. 1990,
              v77n3, P.1010-1011

ABSTRACT:     J.S. Blocker, Jr. reviews "Profits, Power, and Prohibition:
              Alcohol Reform and the Industrializing of America,
              1800-1930," by John H. Rumbarger.

SUBJECT
DESCRIPTORS:  Nonfiction
              History
              Prohibition era
              Reforms
              United States

LENGTH:       Medium (10-30 col inches)

ARTICLE
TYPE:         Book Review Favorable

AUTHOR:       Rumbarger, John J.

TITLE:        PROFITS, POWER, AND PROHIBITION: ALCOHOL REFORM AND THE
              INDUSTRIALIZING OF AMERICA, 1800-1930.

PUBLISHER:    Albany: SUNY Press, 1989.

SUBJECTS:     Prohibition—United States—History
              Temperance—United States—History
              United States—Industries—History
```

Figure 5-7

pages (91–99) on which the article appears; then the month, day, and year (December 7, 1932) of publication. *Be aware that this citation is not the appropriate format for your bibliography.* It is merely the sequence of information used by *this* index.

Another popular source of information on contemporary life is the *Times Index*, which contains topical news articles from the *New York Times* on Prohibition, such as "Rise in Gangland Murders Linked to Bootlegging." Here is a typical *Times Index* listing for 1933:

25 Buffalo speakeasies and stills raided, S 24,   IV,   6:6
                                          [date] [section] [page: column]

The title of the article is followed by the date (24 September), the section of the newspaper (IV, indicated in Roman numerals to avoid confusion), the page (6), and the column (the sixth from left). Again, the format of this citation is peculiar to this index and is not to be used as a model for your bibliography.

Since these indexes have to cram a great deal of information into a relatively small space, they include only one entry for each book or article, and make extensive use of cross-referencing. In the *Readers' Guide* for 1932–1933, for example,

you would find four columns of articles about Prohibition, first divided into regions and then into a series of headings that include "Economic Aspects," "Enforcement," "Political Aspects," "Repeal," and "Results." But at the very
beginning of the list, the reader is referred to other subject headings to be found
elsewhere in the *Readers' Guide:*

See also
alcohol
liquor problem
liquor traffic
liquor

It is your job to check any of the other headings that seem relevant to your
topic, and include some of them in your list of key words for additional computer searches in the larger databases.

Some indexes do not provide "See also" lists. In one year's listings of the
Social Sciences Index, for example, the subject headings do not include "Prohibition," but under the broad heading of "Alcohol," you would find "Social Interaction in the Speakeasy of 1930." The Library of Congress Subject Headings
can help you to identify possible topics for checking, but you also need to use
your ingenuity and imagination to cross-reference your topic.

Using Your Library's Online Periodicals Database

Many campus libraries provide students with access to a *periodicals database*
listing all the articles in all the newspapers, magazines, and journals available
in *that* library (or group of libraries). A student searching the CUNY database—using the key word "Prohibition"—accessed the screen shown in Figure 5-8, which contains the first fourteen entries on that topic in the database.

The student wanted to know more about the first article and typed in #1 at
the prompt to get a detailed description of "Carry from Kansas Became a Nation All Unto Herself." As Figure 5-9 shows, the article (which appeared in
Smithsonian) deals with the more bizarre aspects of Carry Nation's life. Moreover, the temperance crusader died more than eight years before Prohibition
became law. Before deciding whether to read the article, you should consider
whether you are interested in exploring the historical background of the temperance movement, which was instrumental in bringing about Prohibition.
"Lessons of Prohibition" (#6) might be more relevant to a comparison with a
modern ban on tobacco.

Selecting Sources for Examination

Perhaps the most obvious source of information for an essay on Prohibition is
the online catalog of the books available for borrowing in your library system.

```
Search Request: S=PROHIBITION                    General Periodical Ind
Search Results: 52 Entries Found                          Subject Index
     PROHIBITION
  1    CARRY FROM KANSAS BECAME A NATION ALL UNTO H <1989> (RG)
  2    DRINKING IN AMERICA <1990> (RG)
  3    FISH DRY AND VOTE WET <1987> (RG)
  4    GOOD BYE WHISKEY GOOD BYE GIN <1992> (RG)
  5    LAST UNTOUCHABLE <1987> (RG)
  6    LESSONS OF PROHIBITION <1988> (RG)
  7    PROHIBITIONS FAILURE LESSONS FOR TODAY <1992> (RG)
  8    REAL ELIOT NESS <1987> (RG)
  9    REAL MCCOY <1987> (RG)
 10    REFLECTIONS ON THE DRY SEASON <1990> (RG)
 11    SHOULD WE LEGALIZE DRUGS HISTORY ANSWERS <1993> (RG)
 12    SHOULD WE LEGALIZE DRUGS HISTORY ANSWERS <1993> (RG)
 13    WANTED CONSENSUS ON ABORTION <1989> (RG)
 14    WHAT HAPPENED IN HINTON <1988> (RG)
------------------------------------------- CONTINUED on next page  ---
STArt over        Type number to display record        <F8> FORward page
HELp              GUIde
OTHer options


NEXT COMMAND:
4-©               Sess-A                        0011     NET3270
```

Figure 5-8

```
Search Request: S= PROHIBITION                   General Periodical Ind
WILSON RECORD -- 1 of 52 Entries Found                       Brief View
AUTHORS:      Day, Robert

ARTICLE TITLE: Carry from Kansas became a Nation all unto herself.

SOURCE/DATE:   20:147-8+ Apr '89 Smithsonian

SPECIAL FEATURES:
              il pors.

ABSTRACT:      Born Carry Amelia Moore in Kentucky in 1846, Carry Nation is
               remembered more for demolishing bars with hatchets than for
               her liberal beliefs on such issues as the homeless, battered
               women, smoking, and sex education. Nation had a strange
               upbringing: Her mother sometimes believed herself to be
               Queen Victoria, an aunt thought that she was a weathervane,
------------------------------------------------ + Page 1 of 3 ----------
STArt over        HOLdings            GUIde         <F8> FORward page
HELp              LONg view                         <F6> NEXt record
OTHer options     INDex
Held by library-type HOL for holdings information.

NEXT COMMAND:
4-©               Sess-A                        0011     NET3270
```

Figure 5-9

Using key words to search that catalog should be relatively simple and should turn up a list of several possible books. Figure 5-10 shows reproductions of three different computer screens accessed in response to such a subject search. How would you decide which book to examine first?

The first two titles in Figure 5-10 are both relevant to your paper topic; the third is probably not.

- *Ardent Spirits:* The topics at the bottom of the *Ardent Spirits* screen are listed in order of their importance in the book. Accordingly, Kobler's main emphasis is on Prohibition and its relation to American history; you would almost certainly find some useful information there. There is a sixteen-page bibliography.

- *Repealing National Prohibition:* Since there is only one topic listed under "Subject," *Repealing National Prohibition* is evidently concerned only with Prohibition. Judging from its title, the book focuses on the end of the period you would be concerned with. So you can conclude that its treatment of the topic will probably be more detailed than the first book's. It also has a longer bibliography—twenty pages—than *Ardent Spirits* does. However, for a broad overview of the subject, you might begin with *Ardent Spirits*.

- *Women's Suffrage and Prohibition:* If you were interested in the connection between the women's suffrage movement and the temperance movement, you might want to consult the third title. But Prohibition is not Paulson's primary subject; it is highlighted on the screen only because the book has been cross-referenced under that broad topic. Moreover, *Women's Suffrage and Prohibition* seems to consist largely of case studies; your interest would depend on what cases Paulson chooses to examine at length.

Figure 5-11 is not a reproduction of a computer screen, but a facsimile of the entry for *Ardent Spirits* found in a subject card catalog. Notice that the information about Kobler's book is almost identical to that on the computer screen and that it is organized in much the same way. Both the card and the screen provide you with a call number so that, if you wish, you can retrieve the book from the stacks. Unless your database provides you with a printout of the entire entry, remember to copy the book's call number from the screen or card, as well as other important information such as author, title, and the book's probable focus. If the stacks of your library are open to students, explore them until you find the books that you need. Otherwise, use the procedure for having the library staff find these books for you.

Using Bibliographies

Once you locate *Ardent Spirits* or *Repealing National Prohibition*, you check either book's bibliography for other books relevant to your project. This step allows you to add to your own bibliography some of the titles that these authorities used in researching their studies of Prohibition. Of course, you will

```
CALL #      HV 5089.K67  Location: 7th floor stacks   Status: not checked out
AUTHOR      Kobler, John.
TITLE       Ardent spirits : the rise and fall of prohibition / by John
               Kobler.
EDITION     1st Da Capo Press ed.
IMPRINT     New York : Da Capo Press, 1993.
DESCRIPT    386 p. : ill. ; 21 cm.
NOTE        Originally published: New York : Putnam, 1973.
            Includes bibliographical references (p. [358]-[373]) and index.
SUBJECT     Prohibition Party (U.S.)
            Prohibition--United States--History.
            Temperance--United States--History.
```

```
CALL #      HV 5089.K95  Location: 7th floor stacks   Status: not checked out
AUTHOR      Kyvig, David E.
TITLE       Repealing national prohibition / David E. Kyvig.
IMPRINT     Chicago : University of Chicago Press, 1979.
DESCRIPT    xix, 274 p. : ill. ; 24 cm.
NOTE        Bibliography: p. 245-266.
            Includes index.
SUBJECT     Prohibition--United States.
```

```
CALL #      JF 848.P3    Location: 7th floor stacks   Status: not checked out
AUTHOR      Paulson, Ross E.
TITLE       Women's suffrage and prohibition: a comparative study of
               equality and social control [by] Ross Evans Paulson.
IMPRINT     Glenview, Ill., Scott, Foresman [1973]
DESCRIPT    212 p. front. 23 cm.
NOTE        Includes bibliographical references.
SUBJECT     Woman--Suffrage--Case studies.
            Prohibition--Case studies.
            Equality--Case studies.
            Social control--Case studies.
```

Figure 5-10

subject heading
call number,
author
title, publica-
tion information
miscellany

tracings

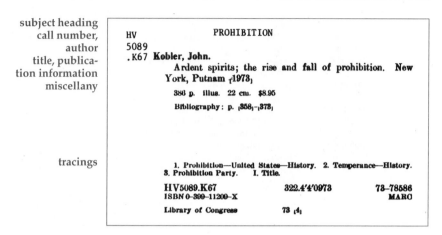

PROHIBITION

HV
5089
.K67 **Kobler, John.**
    Ardent spirits; the rise and fall of prohibition.   New
York, Putnam [1973]

386 p. illus. 22 cm. $8.95

Bibliography: p. [358]–[373]

1. Prohibition—United States—History. 2. Temperance—History.
3. Prohibition Party.   I. Title.

HV5089.K67   322.4'4'0973   73–78586
ISBN 0-399-11200-X   MARC

Library of Congress   73 [4]

Figure 5-11

have to find and examine these other titles before you can decide whether to use them. Again, check the author or title database or catalog, record their call numbers, and then find them in the stacks. (They are probably shelved together.) If your library does not own these titles, you will have to decide whether any look interesting enough to warrant a visit to another library.

If you are unable to locate a vital source in any of the local libraries, you might consult your college librarian about the possibility of an *interlibrary loan,* in which books or copies of articles are sent to your library from the library that owns the source that you need. But remember that interlibrary loans may take some time, and allow for that as you plan your research schedule. Finally, some libraries have "shared systems" that facilitate the delivery of documents. If you want a printed copy of an article in a periodical index, you press a button at your terminal and then pick up the hard copy at a central desk. There may be a charge for this service.

Focusing Your Topic

After you look in catalogs, bibliographies, and indexes, you will probably have listed and located the following *kinds* of sources for an essay on Prohibition:

- Economic and social histories for a general background of the period

- Congressional reports, political analyses, and legal studies of the Eighteenth Amendment

- Contemporary newspaper accounts, magazine articles, and memoirs describing the everyday effects of the ban on liquor

- Exposés of bootlegging and other criminal activities associated with Prohibition

- Philosophy and psychology books and articles dealing with recurring forms of Puritanism

Using Databases to Focus Your Topic

- Become familiar with your library's information system.
- Use computer searches in the databases/indexes to help you to narrow the focus of your broad topic and to identify possible sources.
- Use your library's on-line databases to get information about available books and articles that might be worth exploring; on the basis of that information, decide which ones to obtain from the library.
- Examine the bibliography at the back of each book that you obtain at the library and note down information about other titles that seem useful to your topic.
- Throughout all the stages of this process, take *complete* notes about the books and articles you may be working with (unless the system provides you with a computer printout of information about each one).
- Exploring a topic at the library is an assisted form of brainstorming. The screen or card will provide you with ideas about your topic, and that will prompt you to come up with ideas of your own. Make sure that you note down interesting directions for your research as they occur to you.

At the beginning, uncertain about the precise scope and focus of your essay, you may find it difficult to decide which of these sources will ultimately be useful to you. What are you going to write about? Will you stress:

- The reasons for the movement toward Prohibition?
- The religious influence?
- The economic background?
- Prohibition as a consequence of social changes in the era after World War I?
- The link between Prohibition and organized crime?
- The effects of Prohibition on recreation and leisure?
- The constitutionality of the Eighteenth Amendment?
- The rituals of illegal drinking?

Or will you pursue your original idea and focus on the relationship between the prohibition of alcohol in the 1920s and the restriction on the use of tobacco decades later?

To make the most efficient use of your resources, you need to estimate the *amount of material that is available* and the approximate *amount of time that you will need to spend on library research.*

1. At the beginning, if you have an hour or two to spend in the library, you should spend that time at the terminal or in the reference room, rounding

out your list of possible sources and narrowing your topic. At this stage, you should not start to read extensively (and take notes) in any single work.

2. Later, after you have compiled a working bibliography, you will begin the reading part of your research, starting with the most comprehensive source.

Certainly, you will want to find out if the most likely titles are available in the stacks and, if they are, to check them out and take them home. *But, at this point, don't spend too much time with each book.* At the most, you will want to look at a book's table of contents, index, and bibliography, or flip through an article in order to gain a rough idea of its scope and relevance.

Writing a successful research essay depends on your doing your research thoroughly and checking a reasonable number of reference works, bibliographies, indexes, and other sources. If you wonder how many is a "reasonable" number, report your progress to your instructor or a librarian, and ask for comments.

RECORDING BASIC INFORMATION
FOR YOUR BIBLIOGRAPHY

A *bibliography* is loosely defined as *a complete list of all the works that you use in preparing your essay.* In practice, however, there are really two kinds of bibliography, corresponding to the stages of your research.

Your **preliminary** or **working bibliography** consists of all the sources that you learn about and perhaps examine as you discover what material is available and as you develop your ideas about the topic.

Your **final bibliography** (sometimes called "Works Cited") consists of the material that you will actually use in the writing of your essay. (For a discussion of the final bibliography, see Chapter 9, pp. 388–392.)

You need to have very precise information for all the entries in your bibliography. If you have consistently used a computer database that has printed out lists of books or articles, then you may be able to work from those lists when you prepare your final bibliography. If you are working with a database that doesn't have a printer, or if you are relying entirely or partly on a card catalog and printed indexes from the reference room, you should, from the very beginning of your research, carefully copy down all facts that you may need later on in order to construct a complete and correct final bibliography. These notes can be written on *index cards,* in a separate section of your notebook, or in a separate file of your laptop.

It is important that your records be *accurate, readable, and reasonably consistent.* Several weeks later, when you are working on your list of "works cited" for submission with your essay, you should be able to transform your notes into the correct format without difficulty. (Some software programs, like Nota Bene, allow you to enter data about each source and then automatically prepare correct bibliographic entries in any of the standard formats.) In your early sessions at the library, even though you are at the beginning of your research and cannot be sure which sources will actually become important, *make your notes legible* and *do not abbreviate* unless you are aware of the significance of each symbol. If you cannot understand your notation, you will have to return to the library to check your references, probably when you can least spare the time.

As you work from the computer screen or the card catalog or from one of the indexes or from a bibliography, start a fresh card or a fresh line on the screen for each new item. It may help to assign a number to each new source. Since some indexes do not always provide complete information, indicate gaps in your notes that you can later fill when you are examining the article itself. If you are using a notebook page, remember to leave enough space for comments about the work's potential usefulness.

More likely than not, you will be using MLA style to document your essay. (See Chapter 9, pp. 373–381, for an explanation.) To prepare a final bibliography in MLA style, you should include the following facts in your preliminary notes:

For Books

- the author's full name
- the exact title, underlined
- the name of the editor(s) (for an anthology) or the name of the translator (for a work first written in a foreign language)
- the date and place of publication and the name of the publisher
- the original date of publication and the date of the new edition or reprint, if the book has been reissued
- the inclusive page numbers if you are planning to use only a single chapter or section of the book
- the call number, so that you will not need to return to the database/catalog if you decide to locate the book

For Articles

- the author's full name
- the title of the article, in quotation marks
- the exact title of the periodical, underlined
- the volume number and the date of the issue
- the inclusive page numbers of the article
- the call number of the periodical, so that you will not need to return to the database/catalog if you decide to locate the article

Later, when you locate the book or article itself, remember to check all these facts and supply missing information by examining the front and back of the title page of the book or the first page of the article and the title page of the periodical or newspaper. The *Readers' Guide* does not always include the author's name in its entries (especially the first name), so remember to note it down. Check the spelling of the author's name; find out if the book had an editor; find out whether the place of publication was, for example, Cambridge, Massachusetts, or Cambridge, England.

Figure 5-12 shows two sample note cards, each containing basic information about one of the works on Prohibition mentioned earlier in this chapter. Since these notes are part of a preliminary bibliography, prepared in the library under time pressure, the information is jotted down as a list, using no particular style of documentation. Notice that the first card contains a note questioning the book's relevance to the topic, and the second specifies the *Readers' Guide to Periodical Literature* as the source of the article.

To show you what information looks like when it is placed in the standard format, here is a *bibliography* for the Prohibition essay, with some of the works listed so far:

LIST OF WORKS CITED

Kobler, John. Ardent Spirits: The Rise and Fall of Prohibition. New York: Putnam, 1973.

Kyvig, David E. Repealing National Prohibition. Chicago: U of Chicago P, 1979.

Paulson, Ross E. Women's Suffrage and Prohibition: A Comparative Study of Equality and Social Control. Glenview: Scott, 1973.

Rogers, L. "After Prohibition, What?" New Republic 7 Dec. 1932: 91–99.

"25 Buffalo Speakeasies and Stills Raided." New York Times 24 Sept. 1933, sec. 4:6.

Research is open-ended. You cannot judge in advance how many sources will provide adequate documentation for your topic. *You need to include enough sources to support your thesis convincingly, yet not so many that you treat them superficially.* Your instructor may stipulate that you consult at least five authorities, or ten, or fifteen; but that is probably intended to make sure that each student in the class does a reasonable and roughly equal amount of research. Certainly, without guidelines, your preliminary list of sources could conceivably reach and exceed the dozens, even the hundreds. If you wished, you could copy whole sections of a database, or whole pages of an index, or whole rows of titles on the shelves; but you would have little knowledge of the contents or the relevance of your "Works Cited." It is not enough to have compiled the suggested number of source materials if the works on your list are minor or trivial or peripheral to the topic. An endless list of sources does not automatically demonstrate your competence in research. What is important is not quantity, but usefulness for your purpose.

A good grade for a research essay is likely to depend on the inclusion of a few crucial sources, the works of well-known authorities, whose evidence or points of view must be considered if your essay is to be thoroughly documented.

In Chapter 6, you will start learning how to distinguish those useful sources from the irrelevant ones.

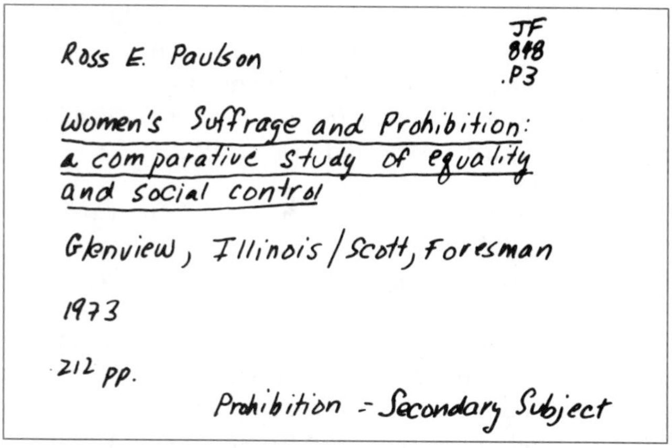

Ross E. Paulson   JF
                                         848
                                         .P3

Women's Suffrage and Prohibition:
a comparative study of equality
and social control

Glenview, Illinois / Scott, Foresman

1973

212 pp.

                    Prohibition = Secondary Subject

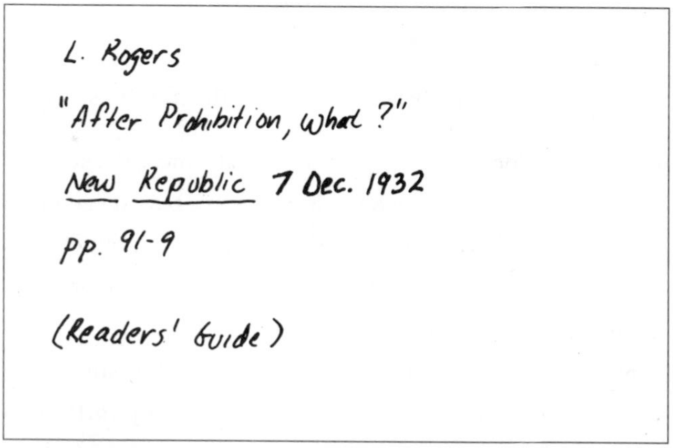

L. Rogers

"After Prohibition, what?"

New Republic 7 Dec. 1932

pp. 91-9

(Readers' Guide)

Figure 5-12

TAKING NOTES ABOUT THE USEFULNESS OF EACH SOURCE

In addition to the factual information that you will need for your bibliography, you should write down a few preliminary notes about the probable usefulness of each work. This step takes place *after* you have *located* and briefly *examined* a source. These are not notes that you will use in writing your essay, but comments indicating which sources merit closer examination and note-taking at a later stage of your research. Simply jot down your initial assessment of the work's scope and contents, strong or weak points, and possible relevance to your topic, as well as any rough impressions about the author's reliability as a source. Often, you can write down such comments just by examining the table of contents and leafing through the pages. *Don't trust your memory.* If you forget to note your reaction, weeks later you may find yourself wondering whether to return to the library to check what seems to be a likely looking title.

Your preliminary comments also enable you to review the progress of your research. You can glance through your notes after each trip to the library to decide whether your sources are going to be numerous and thorough enough to support your essay or whether you should return to the computer terminal and reference room to add a few new authors to your list.

Finally, your preliminary notes will be useful when you assemble your final bibliography, especially if you are expected to *annotate* it.

Annotation means that you insert a short comment after each item in your bibliography, describing the work's scope and specific focus and suggesting its relevance and usefulness to the development of your topic.

This is a more formal variation on annotating a text, which was the first topic in this book. The annotations in a bibliography are usually only a sentence or two, just enough to help your reader judge the importance of each source.

In the following annotated bibliography for an essay on politics and the Olympics, the notes for each entry were taken, with few changes, from the earlier working bibliography.

AN ANNOTATED LIST OF SOURCES CONSULTED

Espey, Richard. The Politics of the Olympic Games. Berkeley: U of
California P, 1979. Espey spends 8 or so pages on each of the modern Olympics up to 1976, with an emphasis on political motivation
and the shift of emphasis from the athlete to the nation.

Kieran, John, Arthur Daley, and Pat Jordan. The Story of the Olympic
Games 776 B.C.–1960. Rev. ed. Philadelphia: Lippincott, 1977.
Approximately 12 pages on each of the games up to 1976, with a
concise and interesting narrative, but little interest in politics. The
authors assume that the Olympics will always continue as they have.

Ludwig, Jack. Five Ring Circus. Toronto: Doubleday Canada, 1976. A
lengthy account of the Montreal 1976 Olympics, with anecdotes.
Most interesting on the Canadian commercial and political role in
staging the Olympics.

Mandell, Richard D. The First Modern Olympics. Berkeley: U of
California P, 1976. A detailed account of the reasons and
preparations for reviving the Olympics in Athens in 1896, with
an emphasis on Coubertin's personality and philosophy.

---. The Olympics of 1972: A Munich Diary. Chapel Hill: U of North
Carolina P, 1991. Written in the form of a literary diary, provides an
insider's views on the terrorist attacks during the 1972 Olympics.
Examines the political context and ramifications of terrorism and
sports.

"The Perseus Project." 2/21/97 HTTP://Olympics.Tufts.Edu/.10/25/97. A study, carried out at Tufts University, comparing ancient and modern Olympic games.

Shaw, Russell. "Whistling Dixie: Professionalism and Politics Lure '96 Olympics to Atlanta." Sporting News 1 Oct. 1990: 8–10. An account of Atlanta's campaign to court the International Olympic Committee in order to host the 1996 games. Analyzes Atlanta's political image.

Williams, Roger M. "Moscow '80, Playing for Political Points." Saturday Review 1 Sept. 1979: 12–16. A detailed analysis of political and nationalistic interests in the Moscow Olympics, with emphasis on Soviet motivation.

EXERCISE 19: COMPILING A WORKING BIBLIOGRAPHY

The following is a list of four different topics for a research essay dealing with the broad subject of *advertising,* followed by a bibliography of twenty articles, arranged in order of their publication dates. Each item in the bibliography is followed by a note giving a brief description of its contents.

Examine the bibliography carefully and choose a set of appropriate sources for each of the four essay topics. You are not expected to locate and read these articles; use the notes to help you make your decisions.

The bibliography is numbered to make the distribution process easier. List the numbers of the articles that you select underneath each topic. You will notice that many of the articles can be used for more than one topic.

Topics

A. What is an appropriate role for advertising in our society? What are the advertiser's responsibilities?

B. Feminists have argued that the image of women created by the advertising industry remains a false and objectionable one. Is that claim valid?

C. How do advertising agencies go about manipulating the reactions of consumers?

D. To what extent does advertising serve the public? harm the public?

1. "The Sexism Watch." *US News & World Report* 27 Mar. 1989: 12. This short but informative piece describes public reaction to sexism in advertising and the advertising industry's responses to public attitudes with regard to campaign design.

2. Eller, J. "The Era of the Big Blur." *Newsweek* 22 May 1989: 73. The author of this article presents a highly critical analysis of the increasing "blurring" of advertising and editorial content prevalent in many print media.

3. Kanner, B. "Mind Games." *New York* 8 May 1989: 34–40. This article is an overview of the psychological testing and research methods used by advertising firms to maximize the effectiveness of their campaigns.

4. Eder, Peter F. "Advertising and Mass Marketing: The Threat and the Promise." *The Futurist* May/June 1990: 38–40. This article describes alterations in mass media research techniques as advertisers employ market research to determine what consumers want. The shift considers the change from mass marketing to micro-marketing in order to better affect consumers' purchasing habits.

5. Landler, Mark. "Madison Avenue Is Getting a Lot Less Madcap." *Business Week* 29 Oct. 1990: 78+. This article examines the relationship between a decline in flamboyant advertising campaigns and shrinking marketing budgets. The new advertising style attempts to conjure links between images and values and the product in the minds of consumers.

6. Rudman, William J., and Patty Verdi. "Exploitation: Comparing Sexual and Violent Imagery of Females and Males in Advertising." *Woman & Health*. 1993: 1–14. This article attempts to trace the depiction of women in the mass media and link it to sexual violence to determine if advertising and sexual depictions can affect social interactions. The article raises the question of the responsibility of advertisers when they create images of women.

7. Madden, Patricia A. "The Frequency and Nature of Alcohol and Tobacco Advertising in Televised Sports, 1990 Through 1992." *American Journal of Public Health* Feb. 1994: 297–9. This article traces the advertising industry's attempts to link cigarettes and beer to television sports in the minds of sports viewers, so as to create an association of them with healthy activities.

8. Jolley, Reed. "The Condom War on Children." *Christianity Today* 7 Mar. 1994: 38. This article charges that the Clinton administration's public service ad campaign designed to prevent the spread of AIDS promotes casual sex between young unmarried couples, and it criticizes the manipulation of the young through advertising.

9. Ingrassia, Michele. "Going One Step Ogle the Line? (Diet Coke Ads Depict Ogling of Men by Women)." *Newsweek* 14 Mar. 1994. This article contends that gender depiction role reversal signifies a shift in the public's increasing resistance to the objectification of women.

10. Rich, Frank. "Gay Shopping Spree. (Reactions to IKEA Television Ad Featuring a Gay Male Couple; Op-Ed)." *New York Times* 3 Apr. 1994, sec. 4: 11. This article praises the first mainstream commercial featuring a gay couple, which marked a breakthrough in advertisers' depictions of society, possibly signalling a service to the audience by expanding the normal scope of images they are presented with.

11. Signorielli, Nancy. "Gender Stereotypes in MTV Commercials: The Beat Goes On." *Journal of Broadcasting & Electronic Media* Winter 1994: 91–101. This long article examines the presentation of gender roles through commercials to the typically adolescent viewer of MTV. The depiction of women as linked primarily to sexuality is also discussed.

12. Sengupta, Subir. "The Influence of Culture on Portrayals of Women in Television Commercials." *International Journal of Advertising* 1995: 314–333. This technical study compares Japanese and American television commercials and the way in which cultural influences affect the depiction of women in advertising.

13. Hitchon, Jacqueline C., and Chingching Chang. "Effects of Gender Schematic Processing on the Reception of Political Commercials for Men and Women Candidates." *Communication Research* Aug. 1995: 430–458. Another scholarly survey focusing on the appeal to gender in the marketing of commercials for political candidates.

14. Tauchi, Teresa. "Truth in Advertising." *HaasWeek Home* 30 Oct. 1995. Online. Internet. WWW.http://haas.berkeley.edu/~haasweek/issues/XXII_10/index.html. 13 Oct. 1997. A chatty little story about tasteless ads, often offensive to women, and the need for more responsible behavior on the part of advertising executives.

15. Elliott, Dorinda. "Objects of Desire." *Newsweek* 12 Feb. 1996: 41. This news story concerns the potentially big market for exotic underwear in Asia, and the ways in which advertising can sell more push-up bras to Asian women.

16. Lafky, Sue, Margaret Duffy, Mary Steinmaus, and Dan Berkowitz. "Looking through Gendered Lenses." *Journalism & Mass Communication Quarterly* Summer 1996: 379–388. Full of jargon, this article describes a study of gender-role stereotyping. High school students were given magazine ads to show how quickly they are influenced by stereotypes of gender.

17. Miller, Molly. "The Color of Money." *Mother Earth News* Feb. 1996: 78–89. The subject is environmental protection, and the false claims about their environmental policies that some companies have made in their advertisements.

18. LaTour, Michael S., Robin L. Snipes, and Sara J. Bliss. "Don't Be Afraid to Use Fear Appeals." *Journal of Advertising Research* Mar. 1996: 59–67. A video based on an appeal to the viewers' fears raised some ethical concerns; this article shows how potential criticism was avoided by trying out the video on a focus group.

19. Pratt, Charlotte A., and Cornelius B. Pratt. "Nutrition Advertisements in Consumer Magazines." *Journal of Black Studies* Mar. 1996: 504–523. The authors focus on claims made about potential benefits to health in advertisements for various foods.

20. McFadden, Daniel L., and Kenneth E. Train. "Consumers' Evaluation of New Products." *Journal of Political Economy* Aug. 1996: 683–703. This is a technical article about how people accept new products through their own or other people's experiences, and how that process can be word-of-mouth information; the authors map out a step-by-step process for evaluation that might be helpful to advertisers.

ASSIGNMENT 12: PREPARING A TOPIC PROPOSAL FOR A RESEARCH ESSAY

A. Choose a broad topic that, for the next few weeks, you will research and develop into an extended essay of eight or more pages.

- If you have a *person or an event* in mind, but do not have sufficiently detailed knowledge to decide on a focus and target date, wait until you have done some preliminary reading. Start with an encyclopedia article or an entry in a biographical dictionary; then use the online catalog and any databases and bibliographies that you find along the way. Decide whether your topic is recent enough to have been featured in available newspapers and periodicals, and consult the appropriate indexes.

- If you select a *contemporary subject or issue for argument*, examine some of the entries dealing with that topic in recent volumes of the *Readers' Guide* or the *New York Times Index*; then formulate a few questions that you might try to answer in your essay.

B. Compile a preliminary bibliography, consulting the relevant indexes and databases. At this point, you need not examine all the sources, take notes, or plan the organization of your essay. Your purpose is to assess the *amount* and, as much as possible, the *quality* of the material that is available. Whether or not your instructor asks you to hand in your preliminary bibliography, make sure that the publication information that you record is accurate and legible. Indicate which sources your library has available and which may be difficult to obtain.

C. Submit a topic proposal to your instructor, describing the probable scope and focus of your essay. (If you are considering more than one topic, suggest a few possibilities.) Be prepared to change the specifics of your proposal as you learn more about the number and availability of your sources.

▪ 6 ▪

Evaluating Sources

While compiling a preliminary bibliography, a student has located several promising sources. Her topic is *high school dropouts:* specifically, she wants to discuss the age at which adolescents should be allowed to leave school.

At the library, the student has consulted indexes and bibliographies, and has found a number of books and articles, all of which, judging by their titles, might be relevant. Some of these authors may have a better claim to being cited as authorities than others. Since all the names are unfamiliar to her, which should she read first? How can she weigh one source of evidence against another and decide whose ideas she should emphasize in her essay?

First of all, the student can try to find out something about each author's credentials. Is the writer a *teacher*? an *administrator*? an *educator*? a *journalist*, presenting secondhand information? Are the writer's qualifications appropriate for the subject? A *kindergarten teacher* may not be the best person to offer opinions about sixteen-year-olds. On the other hand, you might not think that an *economist* would be worth consulting on the topic of high school dropouts; yet, if one has made a study of the job market and the career prospects of workers without high school diplomas, then an economist's evidence and recommendations should be worth including in a research essay. Would a *social psychologist* be a useful source? That would depend on the nature of the work: a study of abnormal social behavior in adolescents might be unrelated to the problem of determining the minimum age for leaving high school; but a study of juvenile delinquency might suggest connections between teenage crime and teenage dropouts.

Chapter 3 included an article about strict attendance policies in grade school. What *are* Roger Sipher's qualifications for making such tough recommendations? Consider also "A Question of Degree" in Chapter 1. Who *is* Blanche Blank, and why should we believe her claim that we have grossly inflated the value of a college degree? Is Blank an employee denied promotion because she lacks a B.A.? Or is she a college graduate seeking a more interesting job? a homemaker eager to return to college? a college teacher who specialized in education (as, in fact, she is)? What difference would this information make to your understanding of her essay?

On the other hand, you may be asked to write about a writer or a group of writers (in an anthology, perhaps) whose names are all familiar to you. Why would you need to find out more about these authors? Would they have been chosen for inclusion in an anthology if their authority were questionable? Once again, how can information about the source help in the writing of your research essay?

LEARNING MORE ABOUT YOUR SOURCES

It is useful to know something about the mind, personality, and experience of the authors that you cite (as well as the times in which they lived), if only to provide a context for understanding their purpose and meaning. There may be some significant connection between an author's background—education, previous writings, professional interests, political leanings, life experience— and the ideas in the book or article that you may write about. Finding out about an author's credentials and background not only helps you to decide whether the source is trustworthy, but also enables you to make allowances for an individual approach to the subject and, occasionally, for bias.

In this sense, "bias" is not a bad word, nor is it quite the same thing as "prejudice." *Bias means special interest or personal angle: the line of thought that this person would be expected to pursue, which might affect his or her opinion about the subject that interests you.* Few knowledgeable people are entirely detached or objective, whether about their pet interests or about the area of learning that has been their life's work. The awareness of bias may weaken your belief in the author's credibility; it is the person who is both knowledgeable and with minimal bias whose opinions tend to carry the most weight. Nevertheless, you shouldn't discount a good idea just because you believe that the writer's ideas may reflect a special interest. Once you have identified a possible bias, you can either disregard it as harmless or adjust your judgment to allow for its influence.

Learning about an author's background does not always permit you to make assumptions about that person's probable point of view. For example, one of the authors whose writings are included in this book is a scholar whose interests are intellectual rather than popular. Yet, on the basis of that information, it would be foolish to try to trace a cause-and-effect connection between his academic background and the negative attitudes toward the media expressed in his essay. *In general, the purpose of inquiring about the author's life and work is to understand more about the wider context of the work that you are reading.*

Authors

Where do you go to find out about a writer's background? Possibly to the book itself. The *preface* may contain biographical information, and the *blurb* on the cover or jacket will probably describe the author (but frequently in such laudatory terms that you may have to discount much of the information). Periodicals may provide a *thumbnail biography* of an article's author at the bottom of its first page, or at the end of the article, or in a group of authors' biographies at the beginning or end of an issue.

What you should look for are details about the author's education, professional experience, and published works. These facts can tell you quite a bit about the writer's probable approach to the subject of your research. Look out for vague descriptions: "a freelance writer who frequently writes about this topic" can describe a recognized authority or an inexperienced amateur. You can also consult one of the many *biographical dictionaries, encyclopedias,* and *indexes.* Some of them are more informative than others. *Who's Who,* for example, provides some basic facts about positions held and works published; but you may need to know a good deal about the academic world to interpret this information, and you may not find out very much about the author's characteristic activities or interests. Good indexes to consult are *Biographical Index* and *Current Biography.*

To illustrate this evaluating process, let us look more closely at the author of one of the paragraphs in Exercise 5 on p. 46. Margaret Mead's name is very famous, yet you may have often read and heard that name without really knowing why she is famous. To find out something about her achievements and her credentials for writing about family relationships, you stop in the library and check one of the biographical reference works. (If you know where these books are shelved or you can call up the text on a computer terminal, this step can take less than ten minutes.) In the index to *Current Biography,* you find a listing for Margaret Mead's obituary in the 1978 volume; to supplement that brief paragraph, you can also look up the complete article on Mead in the 1951 volume. Here is the obituary, followed by an excerpt from the much longer 1951 article (which ends with references to twelve other sources of information about Margaret Mead).

1978 Volume

MEAD, MARGARET Dec. 16, 1901–Nov. 15, 1978. One of world's foremost anthropologists; pioneered in research methods that helped to turn social anthropology into a major science; curator emeritus (from 1969) of American Museum of Natural History, with which she had been associated since 1926; taught at Fordham, Columbia, and other universities; made many expeditions, to Samoa, New Guinea, Bali, and other parts of South Pacific; author of hundreds of articles and more than a score of books, including all-time best-seller *Coming of Age in Samoa* (1928); commented on American institutions in such books as *And Keep Your Powder Dry* (1942) and *Male and Female* (1949); promoted environmentalism, women's rights, racial harmony, and other causes; died in New York City. See *Current Biography* (May) 1951.

Obituary

NY Times A pl + N 16 '78

1951 Volume

Dr. Mead during World War II "wrote OWI pamphlets and interpreted GI's to the British" *(Saturday Review of Literature)* and also served (1942–5) as executive secretary of the committee on food habits, the National Research Council. She was a visiting lecturer at Teacher's College (1945–51) and has further served as consultant on mental health, as a member of the committee on research of the mental health division of the National Advisory Mental Health Council of the United States Public Health Service and as a member of the interim governing board of the International Mental Health Congress. . . .

What do you learn from this information?

- Margaret Mead was a *scientist,* thoroughly familiar with the rigorous methods and the complexities of scientific research; therefore, she is unlikely to be casual in her analysis of the sources of neurosis in children.

- Margaret Mead was a *social scientist,* specifically, an *anthropologist;* she was accustomed to studying the whole of a community or society, assessing its customs, its stability, its morale, its probable responses to challenges and emergencies; this training would make her acutely sensitive to and objective about the dynamics within the American family.

- Margaret Mead did not restrict her writing to anthropological studies of remote tribes; the article quoted in Exercise 5 is by no means her first comment on the American scene, and so her analysis and predictions gain the credibility that comes with *repeated observation.*

- Family relationships were among Margaret Mead's special concerns; thus, one can understand the *context* for her analysis of the neurotic child.

- Finally, the *popularity* of her best-selling scientific work suggests that her readers would be more likely to accept her conclusions than they would the ideas of an author who was less well known and whose background was exclusively academic.

On the other hand, the fact that Mead was a *popularizer*—one who takes dry and difficult ideas and makes them understandable to a wide public—helps to explain why her presentation may seem facile, with many of its assertions unsupported. In fact, the paragraph on p. 47 comes from an article written for *Redbook,* not for a scholarly journal; it can be important to consider the *audience* for which an author is writing. *The writings of Margaret Mead, the anthropologist, clearly differ from those of Margaret Mead, the social commentator.*

Finding out about your sources can enhance your understanding of what you read; however, getting this information should not dominate the research process. If your preliminary bibliography contains twenty books, and you are writing an essay in which no single source will be emphasized, don't waste your time looking up each author at length in the reference room.

But if you are building a paper around a subject for which there are clearly going to be only a few highly important sources, and if you feel uneasy about your ignorance of their qualifications, invest some time in reading a few articles about these authors and their writings.

Check the *Book Review Index* and read reviews of the books that you intend to cite, or look at articles cited in *Biographical Index*. If no other information is available, check the catalog and indexes to see what other books and articles these authors have published. In the end, however, you may have to rely on your research instincts, which will become remarkably accurate after you spend some time comparing the content and style of the sources that you find.

Dates of Publication

One indication of a work's usefulness for your purpose is its *date*. In your essay on high school dropouts, to survey past and present policy, you want to choose some representative works published over the last few decades. However, if you are focusing only on the present, using only material published in the fifties or sixties would be pointless (unless you wanted to include some predictions that might or might not have come true). An article about outdated school attendance laws or social conditions (like the draft) that have changed would be of little value in preparing an essay about contemporary dropouts. However, you may find older sources with theoretical content that is not dated, such as discussions of the role of education in the formation of personality.

Primary and Secondary Sources

To judge the usefulness of a work, you should know the difference between *primary* and *secondary sources.*

> A **primary source** *is a work that is itself the subject of your essay or (if you are writing a historical research essay) a work written during the period that you are writing about that gives you direct or primary knowledge of that period.*

"Primary source" is frequently used to describe an original document—such as the Constitution—or memoirs and diaries of historical interest, or a work of literature that, over the years, has been the subject of much written commentary.

> A **secondary source** *can be any commentary written both after and about the primary source. Thus, a history textbook is a secondary source.*

While you generally study a primary source for its own sake, the secondary source is important—often, it only exists—because of its primary source.

- If you are asked to write an essay about *Huckleberry Finn* and your instructor tells you not to use any *secondary sources,* you are to read *only* Mark Twain's novel and not consult any commentaries.

- Carl Sandburg's biography of Abraham Lincoln is a *secondary source* if you are interested in Lincoln, but a *primary source* if you are studying Sandburg.

- And if you read the *New York Times* in order to acquire information about life in America on a certain date, you are using the newspaper as a *primary source*, since it is your direct object of study; but when you look up a *Times* review of a book or a movie you want to write about, then you are locating a *secondary source* in order to learn more about your primary subject.

In the sciences and social sciences, the most recent secondary sources usually replace earlier ones. However, that rule does not always apply to secondary sources written about historical and biographical subjects. For example, Forster's biography of Charles Dickens, written in the nineteenth century, is still considered an interesting work, in part because Forster knew Dickens and could provide much firsthand information. Nevertheless, because research is always unearthing new facts about people's lives, Forster's work has been superseded by new biographies that feature the latest information. In fact, for a biographical or historical essay, you should consult some primary sources, a few secondary sources written at the time of the event or during the subject's lifetime, and the most recent and reliable secondary sources. It is the sources in the middle—written a few years after your target date, without the perspective of distance—that often lack authenticity or objectivity.

If you are in doubt about the credibility of a source, check to see whether the author has included documentation and a bibliography; *well-documented works tend to be the most reliable sources.* But the absence of documentation is not the only reason for distrusting a source. You can decide not to take a book seriously just by glancing through it. If it is written in a superficial, frivolous, or overly dramatic style, then you may be right to suspect its claim to authority.

Finally, try dividing the available sources into *three* groups: those you are sure that you will want to use, those you rejected on sight, and those you are doubtful about. *Indicate the reasons for your doubts in the notes for your bibliography.* Later in your research, you can check the qualifications of those sources with your instructor or (with the help of the reference librarian) in reference works; or you can simply annotate your bibliography to make your reader aware of your reasons for proceeding with caution.

EVALUATING SOURCES FROM THE INTERNET

No one doing research on the Internet can complain about a lack of sources. The profusion of material on every subject far exceeds the number of print articles and books listed in databases and indexes. Indeed, initially, you may feel spoiled for choice. With abundance, however, comes the need for decisions. When a random listing of over 5,000 titles appears in response to your keywords, which ones do you access and examine? Once you have a document on the screen, how can you make sure that the information is appropriate, accurate, and authoritative enough to include in your essay?

A crucial difference between publishing work on the Internet and publishing work in print is the presence or absence of a standard for publication. To get your book or article accepted by a reputable publishing house or journal, you must submit your manuscript to a lengthy process of peer review. Specialists in the field assess the quality, timeliness, and originality of your ideas, as well as the accuracy of your evidence, based on their knowledge of comparable works. The imprimatur—decision to print—means that the reader can assume that the book or article meets a reasonably high standard.

There is no comparable process for reviewing material appearing on the Internet. No one at AltaVista or Yahoo! is in charge of making choices or maintaining quality; every document listed is equal to the rest. So, you are on your own in deciding what is worth examining and what is worth using in your essay. What do you look for?

- *The author.* First, you have to locate the author's name, which can be hard to find. If it doesn't appear in the document (and there is no sponsoring organization), try doing a search, using the author's name as a keyword. Is a home page mentioned? You may need to keep on moving from one site to the next until you find out something about the author's background and credentials. Then you can check that person's claim to authority about this topic.

- *The sources cited in the document.* Are sources provided for the information contained in the document? The inclusion of appropriate documentation tells you that the author understands the basic requirements for academic scholarship and gives you some assurance that the information is reliable. You may decide to access some of those references to make sure that your author has presented them fairly. Also, check whether the information is consistent with what you have found in other sources.

- *The date of publication.* The absence of a date casts considerable doubt not only on the timeliness and currency of the information, but also on the validity of the source.

- *The writing and presentation.* Is the author's purpose clearly stated and then supported with evidence? The Internet contains a lot of self-serving material, propaganda for a cause or advertisement for a product. Is the tone of a document objective? Or is it ideological? Or frivolous?

To illustrate some of the problems of doing research on the Internet, let's continue to explore the topic *high school dropouts.* Typing those two key words in the search box of your browser results in 2,759 possible listings, with the "Top Ten List" of the best matches appearing on your screen first. Here, without access information (but with authors and sources, when they are listed), are the titles:

1. Joseph Campell [sic], cont'd: A high school dropout talks back

2. Madison's High School Dropout Rate Drops

3. High school dropout rate the lowest in two decades by Sharon Foster, Staff Writer

4. High School Dropout Gets a New Chance

5. State: Local high school dropout rate ranked second lowest in county

6. High School Dropout Rates Decline Over Two Decades Contact: Melinda Kitchell

7. Myth: The High school dropout rate is climbing

8. I'm a high school dropout! To Whom It May Concern: Chana Williford

9. Branson R-4 School District High School Dropout Rate

10. HISPANIC DROPOUT RATE HIGH. Excerpts from USA TODAY Written by HAYA EL NASSER

These ten are far from "top." A very mixed group, they appear to feature local statistics (2, 5, and 9) and human-interest stories (4 and 8), rather than issues and information useful for general research. (The grab-bag nature of Internet searching is evident in the inclusion of the "Joseph Campell" article—the noted anthropologist's name is misspelled—in the "dropout" category.) Of the four remaining articles, we access the one that has no author: "Myth: The High school dropout rate is climbing." Here is part of what appears on the screen:

Summary: Statistics by the U.S. Census show that the high school graduate rate has been increasing for many decades now, and for all sub-groups of the population. This has occurred at a time when public educators are spending more money on programs designed to keep students in school. Their success is a vindication of that policy. *Argument:* The claim that more and more American students are dropping out of high school is false. According to the U.S. Census, more young people are graduating from high school than ever before—a trend [sic] has continued for decades, and among all sub-groups of the population. In 1970, 75 percent of young people aged 25–29 had graduated from high school. By 1990, that had risen to 86 percent.

This information is followed by several tables, and the article concludes:

The above numbers refute conservative rhetoric that spending more on public education resulted in worst outcomes . . . [Public educators'] success in reducing the dropout rate would indicate that this policy is effective and conservatives have no case for arguing otherwise.

Endnotes follow, citing the U.S. Bureau of the Census as the source of the charts.

While the statistical information might be useful, you need to know who's responsible for the document before you can safely cite the text. (The statistics could be verified by checking the Census Bureau reports.) Embedded in the document is a hyperlink to another Internet document that, when accessed, produces a name—WELCOME TO STEVE KANGAS' WEB PAGE—and a title—THE LONG FAQ ON LIBERALISM—and a listing of "myths" about education, the environment, etc., that reflect Mr. Kangas' interests. Here is his introduction:

> Greetings, devils and peaceniks. I'm a college student who lives in Santa Cruz, California, a tourist/university town overlooking Monterey Bay. Besides admiring the local scenery, I'm into politics, tournament-level chess, Santa Cruz's thriving coffee shops and bookstores, writing my Great American Novel, running children's chess clubs, and movies of all types (Hollywood and foreign, young and old).

Kangas tells us that he maintains this Web site as a clearinghouse for his interests, focusing right now on liberal politics. So far, this seems a dubious prospect as a source of authoritative information about dropouts, but, just in case, we click on the listing on the Web site menu labeled "resumé," which begins:

> ABOUT ME
>
> I was born at a relatively young age in the first year of "Camelot"—no, not King Arthur's reign in the 6th Century, but President Kennedy's in 1961. You could say that I was literally a child of the 60s, but love, peace and understanding had no chance to pervert my young mind, since my family was strictly Christian conservative.

Now that you've found out something about Kangas, does he have any claim to be cited in your essay? His statistics are secondhand, and he has no demonstrable expertise in the field; moreover, he has a political agenda that may color his interpretation of facts. Kangas may be an interesting person to chat with; he appears sincere and amusing; but, as a source for a research essay, he is far from reliable.

Let's go back, then, and, still at random, choose a second "top ten" title for examination: "High School Dropout Rates Decline Over Two Decades." This turns out to be a press release (with Melinda Kitchell as contact person) describing a report released today—June 17, 1997—by the Department of Education. The summary includes quotations from Robert Riley, the Secretary of Education, mixed together with a variety of statistics. Here's an excerpt:

> "Many dropouts say they left school because they were failing or just didn't like it," Riley said as he released Dropout Rates in the United States: 1993. "Some will come back and finish, but too many find themselves unemployed or stuck in a job with no future. If we are to meet the national goal of a 90 percent high school graduation rate, we must all do more to keep our children connected to school, to teach them the value of learning, and to keep them engaged in school by making schools places where challenging courses interest and expand young minds."

The statistics correlate dropout rates with income, ethnicity, and gender, and there is a brief reference to reasons for dropping out. Since some of this information might be useful supporting evidence in your essay, it's important to verify the source. The U.S. Government Printing Office is cited as the place to obtain a copy of the report, but there is also an embedded hyperlink to access the home page of the U.S. Department of Education, which provides opportunities to find more information. This second attempt at locating a source has produced acceptable, if limited information.

It is certainly possible to carry on research in this haphazard way, following one lead after another. But the frequent digressions, characteristic of the Internet, may make it hard for you to stay on track, especially if you're not yet sure of your thesis.

Using the Internet for research becomes especially problematic if you expect to get *all* your sources from the Internet. This hit-or-miss process requires a great deal of patience; you need persistence to investigate each source, discarding many sources for every one that you can use. Persistence may not be enough: many important sources publish their work only in traditional print forms; their absence from your essay may skew the coverage of your topic, making it less complete and less objective. Another concern is length. Many Web articles are the spatial equivalent of soundbites. Their authors don't engage in the kind of complex analysis and interpretation of ideas that requires slow and careful development.

Will using the Internet exclusively make a difference to your instructor? In "How the Web Destroys the Quality of Students' Research Papers," Professor David Rothenberg says that "it's easy to spot a research paper that is based primarily on information collected from the Web," partly because no books are included in the bibliography. Most disturbing to Professor Rothenberg is the mindlessness of the research process:

> You toss a query to the machine, wait a few minutes, and suddenly a lot of possible sources of information appear on your screen. Instead of books that you have to check out of the library, read carefully, understand, synthesize and then tactfully excerpt, these sources are quips, blips, pictures, and short summaries that may be downloaded magically to the dorm-room computer screen. Fabulous! How simple! The only problem is that a paper consisting of summaries of summaries is bound to be fragmented and superficial, and to demonstrate more of a random montage than an ability to sustain an argument through 10 to 15 double-spaced pages.

There are no shortcuts to thorough research. Use the Internet as you would any tool available to you, but try to resist its facile charms.

SELECTING SOURCES THAT WORK WELL TOGETHER

In Chapter 4, when you learned how to work with multiple sources, the process was simplified to make your assignments easier: the sources were all of the same kind, homogeneous, and therefore relatively easy to synthesize. The statements in each group all came from sources with roughly the same skills and experience, whose opinions were therefore comparable. But in research at the library, the sources that you find may have nothing at all in common but their subject.

Periodicals provide a clear example, for most are published for specific audiences with well-defined interests, reading habits, and (in some cases) social and political views. Since readership varies so greatly, articles on the same subject in two different periodicals are likely to vary widely in their point of view and development. An article on dropouts in a well-known women's magazine is likely to be reassuring and helpful, filled with concrete advice to parents. It will not have the same purpose, nor cite the same kinds of evidence, nor be expressed in the same kind of vocabulary as an article of comparable length published the same year in *Psychology Today*. And that, in turn, will probably not resemble a scholarly essay on dropouts in the *Journal of the American Psychological Association* or the *American Journal of Sociology*. An equivalent article in *Newsweek* or *Time* will be shorter and livelier, filled with vivid, concrete illustrations.

Because of these differences, these periodicals will not be equally valuable as evidence for your essay:

- Newsmagazines provide factual information.
- Periodicals like *Psychology Today* popularize ideas in the social sciences, presenting them in a readable form for a wide audience.
- Scholarly journals usually contain a depth of analysis and a breadth of research that makes them comprehensive and convincing.

On the other hand, articles in scholarly journals are often written in a dense style, with a vocabulary comprehensible only to someone familiar with the discipline. Someone writing a freshman essay on a general topic may find these articles difficult to read and understand. Books can be even more difficult to synthesize since they vary so greatly in length, purpose, and presentation.

Suppose that in researching your paper on high school dropouts you have found three very different sources:

- The first is exclusively about dropouts; chapter after chapter is filled with statistical studies and case histories presented in dense detail and in an abstract language that requires concentration to absorb.
- The second book is a comprehensive study of decision-making in education; there is one lengthy chapter about the reasons why students may choose to drop out.
- The third source is a stirring speech, directed at educators and business-people, with one section devoted to the importance of making students stay in school. The issue is presented broadly and rhetorically.

Here are the excerpts from these three sources:

1. At the secondary school level the question of the impact of increased time requirements on student achievement has been examined through a series of

studies regarding the relationship between time spent on homework, a readily apprehensible form of student effort, and achievement. Coleman, Hoffer, and Kilgore, using data from the nationally representative sample of students in the High School and Beyond Survey found that differences in the time spent on homework by high school students accounted for a small but consistent part of the differences in achievement test scores between public and private sector schools. Using this same data set, Keith showed that the amount of time that students spent on homework contributed significantly and positively to their grades. A meta-analysis of 15 empirical studies of the relationship of time spent on homework to learning found a modest, positive effect of homework on learning.

EDWARD L. MCDILL, GARY NATRIELLO, and
AARON M. PALLAS, "A Population at Risk: Potential
Consequences of Tougher School Standards for Student
Dropouts," from *School Dropouts: Patterns and Policies*

2. There is indeed quite a high correlation between failure at school and the probability of dropping out. . . . (In one of the surveys analyzed here, 71 percent of the dropouts had at least one failure as opposed to an average of 44 percent over the whole sample.) There are, however, certain considerations which prevent one from concluding that dropping out is not a decision at all. First there is the fact that the correlation between repeating and dropping out is far from perfect and that more than one-quarter of those who left during high school had never been kept down. Moreover, only half of them declared that they had left as consequence of a failure.

DIEGO GAMBETTA, from *Were They Pushed or Did They Jump:
Individual Decision Mechanisms in Education*

3. In my parents' day, a child of thirteen more often than not would leave school to help support the family during the hard times of the "Great Depression." Getting a high school education ran a distant second to helping the family survive.

Today, I believe many students—and even some bitter educators—view dropping out as a viable alternative to completing school. The pressure to drop out isn't always economic any more. After all, there are many avenues of public assistance. . . .

As a citizen, I'm appalled that we'll waste the potential of so many of our young people. As a business leader, I'm shocked. We have to rely on the public schools to produce the people who will lead our businesses and our society. There are no "spare" people. Society needs us all.

ANTON J. CAMPANELLA,
from "Public Education Is Turning the Corner"

Can these three sources be integrated into the same essay? All three are relevant to the topic, and each may be interesting and useful in itself. But the difference in *depth* and *level of detail* among them is so great that it is hard to see how the three can be used together in a single essay. And, indeed, the only thing that you should not do is to plunk down excerpts from these three sources side by side, in adjoining sentences. If they are to be integrated at all, you must first recognize and then communicate to your reader that *the three sources are not equivalent or even similar.*

This does not mean that all of your sources should cover the same range of ideas, be roughly the same length, and employ the same vocabulary and depth of evidence. And certainly *you should avoid using a single book or journal as the sole source of supporting evidence for your essay.* Working with materials of the same order of difficulty may be convenient, but developing a balanced bibliography offering a variety of approaches to your topic is more important. The key is to become sensitive to the *kinds of sources* that you find in your research. As you glance through an article or a chapter in a book, ask yourself:

- Is the content primarily theoretical or practical?
- How often does the author offer evidence to support conclusions? What kind of evidence? Is it documented?
- Does the author's thesis depend on a series of broad propositions, linked together into an argument?
- What is the scope of the work?
- Is the focus narrow, with the entire work centered around one person's experience? Or does it sum up the work of others?

Finally, be alert to the kind of language that the author is using and make mental or written notes about its difficulty and your ability to understand it.

Guidelines for Choosing Sources

As you choose sources for your essay, consider the following:

- the author's background and qualifications to write on that subject;
- the date of the work, whether it is a primary or secondary source, and (if secondary) whether its information is still timely;
- the scope of the work and the extent to which it deals with your topic;
- the depth of detail, the amount and kind of evidence presented, citation and documentation of sources, and the level of analysis and theory;
- the degree to which you understand and feel comfortable with the author's language and style; and
- the way in which possible sources could be used together in your essay.

Understanding the differences among your sources will help you to determine your *research priorities*. You would not begin your research by taking notes from the book on dropouts; much of its contents would be irrelevant to your eventual thesis. Instead, you might begin with the single comprehensive chapter from the second source to give you an overview of the subject and help you to establish your own approach to the topic and your thesis. Once you have a list of specific points that you want to develop, you may not need to read every chapter of the first source; you could look up items of interest in the table of contents and the index. And don't forget the third work; the speech might provide you with a broader understanding of your topic, as well as provide you with an excellent quotation or two.

INTEGRATING YOUR SELECTED SOURCES

Once you have become familiar with your main sources, their differences, and their relative usefulness, how do you integrate them into your essay? You may simply decide to exclude those that do not mesh easily with the others. You may not want to confuse your reader by moving back and forth from extremely broad statements of policy to detailed citations of case studies or statistical evidence, especially if the different sources are expressed in a completely different vocabulary and style. The following excerpt comes from a paper in which the three sources on dropouts are lumped together through quotation. It's not clear that the writer understood the purpose of the "correlation" presented in Excerpt 1 or the relationship between higher academic standards and the decision to drop out. The writer tries to disguise this by working very hard on the transitions between quotations, leaving the reader to figure out what it all means. The transitional phrase "on the other hand" is not really contrasting anything.

> Educators find it difficult to solve the problem of dropouts. Diego Gambetta points out the "high correlation between failure at school and the probability of dropping out." On the other hand, higher standards, such as giving students more homework, can help students to achieve, not fail: "A meta-analysis of 15 empirical studies of the relationship of time spent on homework to learning found a modest, positive effect of homework on learning." It is important for efforts to be made to keep students in school because, as Anton Campanella has said, "we have to rely on the public schools to produce the people who will lead our businesses and society."

Even if you use your own style to integrate your sources through paraphrase, it would still be difficult to combine these three sources in a single paragraph. *In a short essay of less than ten pages, you would be wise to limit your sources to those that blend well together because they are of the same order of difficulty.* The writers you cite do not have to agree with each other; rather, their scope and approach should be roughly similar.

For a short essay, you would have to decide in the early stages of your research which kind of source would help develop your thesis. How sophisticated is your argument? Does it require support from complex case studies? If you intend to prove that dropouts come from a specific kind of family environment, you will probably need to cite such scholarly sources as the dropout book. On the other hand, you might want to argue that the dropout rate can be linked to a general decline in standards of education, drawing to some extent on your own high school experience. This thesis would be more "popular" in its approach to the subject and would require less rigorous sources. Remember that *a popularization is a simplification of a difficult subject; popular essays could not exist without the evidence found in longer and more complex works.* In a sense, a college research essay has to be "popular" since it is intended to be evidence of the student's understanding of the subject, rather than a contribution to scholarly knowledge.

In deciding whether or not to use the popular approach, remember to consider the level of your course. In an *introductory course,* you are expected only to grasp the broad concepts that are basic to the discipline; so your instructor will probably not expect you to go out of your depth in hunting scholarly sources for your essay. On the other hand, in an *advanced course,* you are preparing to do your own research; and so you need to demonstrate your understanding of the work of others as well as the methods that are commonly used in that field. In an advanced course, the popular approach can be regarded as superficial.

In a longer essay of ten pages or more, you should have much less trouble blending ill-assorted sources. With the opportunity for leisurely development, you can position each source in the place where it is most appropriate and where it will have the most convincing effect. Thus, for the dropout essay the quotations that you select from the speech might be placed in the introduction or conclusion of your essay; the theories relating students' decisions to drop out could be included in your preliminary presentation of your argument; and the detailed evidence of the longest source could be cited in support of your own ideas or as part of your survey of the work already done in this field. In short, these very different sources can be used together successfully, provided that you do not give your reader the impression that they are interchangeable in their usefulness. Unfortunately, a single paragraph cannot be included here to demonstrate the successful incorporation of the three excerpts on pp. 285–286 into a research essay; you would need to read the entire paper to see how each of the three sources was deployed.

Finally, in your search for a well-balanced bibliography, include only what you yourself understand. By all means, consult your instructor or librarian, or the staff of the writing center on your campus, to clarify the meaning of difficult sources that nevertheless seem important enough to include in your essay. However, *if you cite sources whose writing makes no sense to you, no matter how eminent and qualified these authorities may be, your essay will be a failure; for you will be pretending a mastery of the subject that you do not actually have.*

EXERCISE 20: CHOOSING SOURCES

Examine the following preliminary bibliography of articles for a research essay on the broad topic of *education*.

A. Make up two *narrow* topics, one focused on an issue in education that is presently being debated, the other suggesting a more historical approach that might include articles published during the last few decades. (Your instructor may ask the entire class to work on the same two topics.)

B. Carefully read the preliminary bibliography, and consider the probable contents of each article, as suggested by the *title;* the *kind of periodical* it appears in; the *length;* and the *date* of publication. What can you conclude about each article?

C. Determine your research priorities for each of your two topics by choosing a list of five articles that you believe ought to be located and consulted first. Record your two lists, and be prepared to explain your choices.

Abbott, John. "21st-Century Learning: Beyond Schools." *The Education Digest* 63 (Oct. 1997): 11–15.

Akande, B. "Six Ways to Save Our Schools." *USA Today* 122 Nov. 1993: 62–63.

"America's Schools: A Panorama of Excellence." *Today's Education* 1984–1985 Annual: 3–35.

"Are High-School Standards Too Low?" *Ladies Home Journal* Sept. 1956: 86–88.

"Are Schools Changing Too Much Too Fast?" *Changing Times* Sept. 1966: 6–10.

"Back to Basics in the Schoolhouse." *Readers Digest* Feb. 1975: 149–52.

Bailey, S. K. "Educational Planning: Purposes and Promise." *Public Administration Review* May 1971: 345–52.

Barber, B. R. "America Skips School." *Harper's* Nov. 1993: 39–46.

Bracey, G. W. "The 'Education Crisis': More Rhetoric than Reality." *The Education Digest* 57 (Fall 1992): 39–42.

Bracey, Gerald W. "75 Years of Elementary Education." *The Education Digest* 61 (Mar. 1996): 26–29.

Broudy, H. S. "Demand for Accountability: Can Society Exercise Control over Education?" *Education and Urban Society* Feb. 1977: 235–50.

Buckley, William F. "Disassembling Education." *National Review* 6 Mar. 1995: 78–79.

Burris, V. "Social and Political Consequences of Overeducation." *American Sociology Review* Aug. 1983: 454–67.

Clinchy, Evans. "Reforming American Education from the Bottom to the Top: Escaping Academic Captivity." *Phi Delta Kappan* Dec. 1996: 268–71.

Cuban, L. "Better Teaching or 'Just the Facts Ma'am'? [Flaws in Reform Agenda]." *The Education Digest* 58 (Spring 1992): 40–42.

Drucker, P. F. "How Schools Must Change." *Psychology Today* May 1989: 18–20.

Finn, Chester E., and Diane Ravitch. "Is Educational Reform a Failure?" *USA Today* 125 (Nov. 1996): 22–24.

Finnan, Christine, and Wendy Hopfenberg. "Accomplishing School Change." *Journal for a Just and Caring Education* 3.4 (Oct. 1997): 480–93.

Forbes, Steve. "Rays of Educational Sunshine." *Forbes* 13 Oct. 1997: 27–28.

Handl, J. "Educational Chances and Occupational Attitudes of Women: A Sociohistorical Analysis." *Journal of Social History* 17 (Spring 1984): 463–87.

Hechinger, Grace, and Fred M. Hechinger. "Report Card on Education." *Ladies Home Journal* Sept. 1985: 96.

Hershey, J. A. "How Schools Sabotage a Creative Work Force." *Business Week* 13 (July 1987): 16.

Hodgkinson, H. L. "Pinpointing the Failures in American Education." *The Education Digest* 57 (Fall 1992): 36–38.

Holcomb, J. H. "Can We—Should We Save the Public Schools?" *American Educator* June 1983: 34–37.

"Johnny Is Doing a Lot Better." *Life* Apr. 1961: 32.

Kirst, M. W. "How to Improve Schools without Spending Money." *Phi Delta Kappan* Sept. 1982: 6–8.

Klitgaard, R. E., and G. R. Hall. "Are There Unusually Effective Schools?" *Journal of Human Resources* 10 (Winter 1975): 90–106.

Lanier, H. B., and J. Byrne. "How High School Students View Women: The Relationship Between Perceived Attractiveness, Occupation, and Education." *Sex Roles* 7 (1981): 145–48.

Leonard, G. E. "The Great School Reform Hoax." *Esquire* Apr. 1984: 47–52.

Liazos, A. "School Alienation and Delinquency." *Crime and Delinquency* July 1978: 355–70.

Lieberman, M. "Why School Reform Isn't Working." *Fortune* 17 February 1986: 135–36.

Linton, C. D. "In Defense of a Liberal Arts Education." *Christianity Today* May 1974: 5–8.

"Low Marks for U.S. Education." *Saturday Evening Post* 20 Oct. 1962: 96.

Morris, J. P. "Principles of Education for a Free Society." *Bulletin of the National Association of Secondary School Principals* Dec. 1954: 99–100.

Petrie, M. A. "Education Without Schools." *Nation* 15 November 1971: 505–6.

Pipho, C. "Gridlock on the Road to Reform." *Phi Delta Kappan* June 1993: 750–51.

Poplin, M., and J. Weeres. "Listening at the Learner's Level: Voices from Inside the Schoolhouse." *The Education Digest* 59 (Spring 1993): 9–13.

Riesman, D. "Quixotic Ideas for Education Reform." *Society* Mar./Apr. 1993: 17–24.

Rossides, D. W. "What Is the Purpose of Education? The Worthless Debate Continues." *Change* Apr. 1984: 14–21.

Scully, M. A. "Some Hope for the Schools." *National Review* 9 March 1984: 47.

Silber, J. R. "Need for Elite Education." *Harper's* June 1977: 22–24.

Soder, Roger. "American Education: Facing Up to Unspoken Assumptions." *Daedalus* 124 (Fall 1995): 163–67.

Spock, B. "Coercion in the Classroom Won't Work." *Atlantic* Apr. 1984: 28–31.

Stafford, Tim. "Helping Johnny Be Good." *Christianity Today* Sept. 1995: 34–39.

Steller, Arthur. "Every Child, Every School: Success for All." *Educational Leadership* 55.2 (Oct. 1997): 88.

Szabo, J. C. "'Schools for the 21st Century' [G. Bush's Address on America 2000 Plan, January 1992]." *Nation's Business* 80 (Fall 1992): 22.

Tevis, C. "Why Local Schools Aren't Good Enough." *Successful Farming* Dec. 1986: 18N–18O.

Weiss, Michael J. "America's Best Elementary Schools." *Redbook* April 1995: 55–58.

"Why Our Schools Went Wrong." *Changing Times* May 1978: 25–28.

EXERCISE 21: EVALUATING SOURCES

Each of the following passages has been extracted from a longer article or book on the general subject of *boxing*. Most of these excerpts deal specifically with the dangers of the sport and the arguments for and against banning it.

A. Carefully examine the distinctive way in which each passage presents its information, noting especially:

- the amount and kind of evidence that is cited
- the expectations of the reader's knowledge and understanding
- the relative emphasis on generalizations and abstract thinking
- the characteristic tone and vocabulary
- the date of publication.

B. Take into consideration what you may already know about these publications and the audience for each. Then decide how—or whether—you would use these sources together in a single research essay exploring whether boxing should be banned.

C. Write a thesis for such an essay, and then decide which sources you would definitely use in writing your essay. Be prepared to justify your choice.

1. The action of one human striking another with the fists must date to about the time humans began to walk on two feet. Aggressive behavior is certainly a normal human trait. Defending oneself using any method available is at the top of Maslov's hierarchy, namely, survival. The use of a violent act to entertain others vicariously is also thousands of years old. Gladiatorial events, Christians being fed to lions, gunfights in the old American West, and other such events have been legendary. From time to time, however, society looks at its behavior in terms of both the effects on individual participants and the moral and ethical aspects of the events affecting society as a whole. Thus, Christians are no longer fed to lions, and gladiatorial combat, sword duels to the death, cockfights, dogfights, and gunfights have been outlawed, and, to some extent do not occur.

    Over many decades, boxing has come under public scrutiny, which has led to numerous reforms. In 1743, Broughton's rule put the testes off limits. In 1838, new rules for the London prize ring eliminated holding, butting, gouging, kicking, and the wearing of shoes with improper spikes. In 1866, the Marquis of Queensberry rules instituted gloves in all bouts and a 10-second count after a knockdown, and for the first time fighters were matched by weight. Such actions as limiting the number and length of rounds, having a referee with power, mandating medical evaluations, establishing athletic commissions, and requiring the wearing of mouthpieces have represented major efforts at reform.

On January 14, 1983, the *Journal of the American Medical Association* got the modern reform movement going with an Editorial entitled "Boxing Should Be Banned in Civilized Countries." We stated that "the principal purpose of a boxing match is for one opponent to render the other injured, defenseless, incapacitated, unconscious." We pointed out that boxing was wrong medically because of the very high frequency of brain damage being experienced by boxers and that it was wrong morally because a boxer could win by intentionally damaging the brain of an opponent. Thus, we believe that there are many excellent reasons why both professional and amateur boxing as we know them should be banned. The American Medical Association (AMA) has held a similar position since 1984, and it has been reaffirmed several times.

> GEORGE LUNDBERG, from "Blunt Force Violence in
> America—Shades of Gray or Red," *The Journal of the
> American Medical Association* (1996)

2. Ego is driving a point through to a conclusion you are obliged to reach without knowing too much about the ground you cross between. You suffer for a larger point. Every good prizefighter must have a large ego, then, because he is trying to demolish a man he doesn't know too much about, he is unfeeling—which is the ground floor of ego; and he is full of techniques—which are the wings of ego. What separates the noble ego of the prizefighters from the lesser ego of authors is that the fighter goes through experiences in the ring that are occasionally immense, incommunicable except to fighters who have been as good, or to women who have gone through every minute of an anguish-filled birth, experiences that are finally mysterious. Like men who climb mountains, it is an exercise of ego which becomes like soul—just as technology may have begun to have transcended itself when we reached to the moon. So, two great fighters in a great fight travel down subterranean rivers of exhaustion and cross mountain peaks of agony, stare at the light of their own death in the eye of the man they are fighting, travel into the crossroads of the most excruciating choice of karma as they get up from the floor against all the appeal of the sweet swooning catacombs of oblivion—it is just that we do not see them this way, because they are not primarily men of words, and this is the century of words, numbers and symbols. Enough.

> NORMAN MAILER, from "King of the Hill," *Existential
> Errands* (1975), reprinted in *Reading the Fights* (1988)

3. There were just forty seconds of the twelfth round left when the horror story started to take shape. Owen was trying to press in on Pintor near the ropes, failed to prevent that deadly space from developing again and was dropped on his knees by a short right. After rising at three and taking another mandatory count, he was moved by the action to the other side of the ring and it was there that a ferocious right hook threw him on to his back. He was unconscious before he hit the canvas and his relaxed neck muscles allowed his head to thud against the boards. Dai Gardiner and the boxer's father were in the ring long before the count could be completed and they were quickly joined by Dr. Schwartz, who called for oxygen. Perhaps the oxygen might have come rather more swiftly than it did but only if it had been on hand at the ringside. Obviously that would be a sensible precaution, just as it might be sensible to have a stretcher immediately available. It is no easy job to bring such equipment through the jostling mass of spectators at an arena like the Auditorium, where Pintor's supporters were mainly concerned about cheering its arrival as a symbol of how comprehensive their man's victory had been. The outward journey to the dressing room, with poor Johnny Owen deep in a sinister unconsciousness, was no simpler and the indifference of many among the crowd was emphasized when one of the stretcher bearers had his pocket picked.

There have been complaints in some quarters about the delay in providing an ambulance but, in the circumstances, these may be difficult to justify. Dr. Ferdie Pacheco, who was for years Muhammad Ali's doctor and is now a boxing consultant with NBC in the United States, insists that the company lay on an ambulance wherever they cover fights, but no such arrangements exist at the Auditorium and the experienced paramedics of the Los Angeles Fire Department made good time once they received the emergency call. Certainly it was grief and not blame that was occupying the sick boy's father as he stood weeping in the corridor of the California Hospital, a mile from the scene of the knockout. A few hours before, I had sat by the swimming pool at their motel in downtown Los Angeles and listened to them joke about the calls Johnny's mother had been making from Merthyr Tydfil on the telephone they had recently installed. The call that was made to Mrs. Owen from the waiting room of the California Hospital shortly before 7 A.M. Saturday, Merthyr time (11 P.M. Friday in Los Angeles) had a painfully different tone. It was made by Byron Board, a publican and close friend of the family, and he found her already in tears because she had heard that Johnny had been knocked out. The nightmare that had been threatening her for years had become reality.

She can scarcely avoid being bitter against boxing now and many who have not suffered such personal agony because of the hardest of sports will be asking once again if the game is worth the candle. Quite a few of us who have been involved with it most of our lives share the doubts. But our reactions are bound to be complicated by the knowledge that it was boxing that gave Johnny Owen his one positive means of self-expression. Outside the ring he was an inaudible and almost invisible personality. Inside, he became astonishingly positive and

1

2

3

self-assured. He seemed to be more at home there than anywhere else. It is his tragedy that he found himself articulate in such a dangerous language.

(The doctors' struggle to rescue Johnny Owen from deep coma proved to be 4 hopeless and he died in the first week of November 1980. His body was brought home to be buried in Merthyr Tydfil.)

> HUGH MCILVANNEY, from "Onward Virgin Soldier," *McIlvanney on Boxing* (1982), reprinted in *Reading the Fights* (1988)

4. Boxing's reputation is under fierce assault once more: Scottish bantamweight 1 James Murray was last night declared "clinically dead" after a title fight that ended in a riot.

The twin spectres haunting the sport—grave injury and crowd misbehavior— 2 came together in Glasgow late on Friday night, after Murray was knocked out in the 12th and final round of his title challenge to fellow Scot Drew Docherty.

While Murray was unconscious and being treated inside the ring, hooligans 3 were throwing bottles and chairs at commentators and spectators, who dived under tables or fled in terror.

The crowd violence, in the ballroom of Glasgow's Hospitality Inn hotel, where 4 the match followed a dinner, is thought to have hampered Murray's exit to the hospital, although both police and hospital authorities have denied that the rioting had worsened his condition. "As far as we are concerned, we received Mr Murray expeditely," said a spokesman for Glasgow's Southern General Hospital.

Surgeons carried out a two-hour emergency operation to remove a blood 5 clot from the brain of Murray, 25. Doctors last night told his family that he was "clinically dead," according to Murray's manager, Alex Morrison. "All I know is that there is virtually no hope," he said. . . .

The British Medical Association (BMA) has been trying since 1982 to outlaw 6 boxing. Yesterday a BMA spokeswoman asked: "How many more brain-damaged boxers do there have to be before boxing is banned?"

Yesterday one of boxing's leading figures seemed close to agreeing. The pro- 7 moter Frank Warren said it was "very difficult to justify" the sport in the light of Murray's injuries. "I could not look Jim's father and mother in the eye and say the sport should go on, but it is a very emotive subject at times like this, so we should all give it a few days," he said.

More than 500 boxers have died since the Queensberry Rules were intro- 8 duced in 1884.

> JOHN MCKIE, from "Fresh call for ban on boxing as fighter collapses," http://www.virgin.net/bv/havana/resources/ sport/athlete/features/1995101500.html (1995)

5. If boxers were boxing's only victims, railing against it wouldn't be worth the trou- 1 ble. They're big boys, after all. The real tragedy is all the inner-city teenagers who gather to watch the fights on closed-circuit TV. Many of them were born teth- ered to a values system that bodes ill for economic success, and their worship of

boxers worsens the odds. Much has been said about the unhealthy fact that so few black role models are professors and lawyers, and so many are athletes. Of all professional athletes, none are less worthy of emulation than boxers. Boxers get rich without an education. They achieve status through violence. Their victories involve no teamwork. And they indulge in ritual self-promotion. Even Tyson—fairly mild-mannered, as these guys go—declared himself "the toughest man on the planet." If there's one thing worse for poor kids than wanting to be the toughest man on the planet, it's wanting to boast about it. Violent egomania just isn't a prescription for success in a post-industrial economy. (To say nothing of the more immediate effects of emulation. According to David Phillips, a sociologist at the University of California, homicides increase appreciably after every nationally broadcast heavyweight championship fight.)

There's no denying that boxing has its up side. If the sport didn't exist, a few hardworking millionaires, like Tyson, would be spending their lives washing dishes. On the other hand, thousands of poor kids wouldn't be enticed into dropping out of school to hang around dingy gyms and get pummeled for nickels and dimes. And hundreds of thousands of young, poor blacks and Hispanics would be spared the burden of idols like James ("Bonecrusher") Smith, Hector ("Macho") Camacho, and Adilson ("Maguila Gorilla") Rodrigues.   2

The standard argument against banning boxing is libertarian: people should be allowed to do whatever they want—pay people to punch each other, get paid to get punched, etc. But even in capitalist America there are circumstances under which commerce can rightly be restrained. Boxing's apologists sound quite principled when they defend Muhammed Ali's right to get his brains scrambled, but few of them would defend a drug addict's right to do the same. The question is whether boxing is pernicious enough to join drug use, prostitution, and several other "victimless" pastimes deemed illegal. It's a tough call, but we vote yes.   3

from "Ban Boxing," Editorial. *The New Republic* (1988)

6. I have no difficulty justifying boxing as a sport because I have never thought of it as a sport.   1

There is nothing fundamentally playful about it; nothing that seems to belong to daylight, to pleasure. At its moments of greatest intensity it seems to contain so complete and so powerful an image of life—life's beauty, vulnerability, despair, incalculable and often self-destructive courage—that boxing *is* life, and hardly a mere game. During a superior boxing match (Ali-Frazier I, for instance) we are deeply moved by the body's communion with itself by way of another's intransigent flesh. The body's dialogue with its shadow-self—or Death. Baseball, football, basketball—these quintessentially American pastimes are recognizably sports because they involve play: they are games. One *plays* football, one doesn't *play* boxing.   2

Observing team sports, teams of adult men, one sees how men are children in the most felicitous sense of the word. But boxing in its elemental ferocity cannot be assimilated into childhood. (Though very young men box, even pro-   3 fessionally, and many world champions began boxing in their early or mid-teens. By the time he was sixteen Jack Dempsey, rootless and adrift in the West, was fighting for small sums of money in unrefereed saloon fights in which—in the natural course of things—he might have been killed.) Spectators at public games derive much of their pleasure from reliving the communal emotions of childhood but spectators at boxing matches relive the murderous infancy of the race. Hence, the occasional savagery of boxing crowds—the crowd, largely Hispanic, that cheered as the Welshman Johnny Owen was pounded into insensibility by the Mexican bantamweight champion Lupe Pintor, for instance—and the excitement when a man begins to seriously bleed. . . .

Considered in the abstract the boxing ring is an altar of sorts, one of those legendary spaces where the laws of a nation are suspended: inside the ropes, during an officially regulated three-minute round, a man may be killed at his opponent's hands but he cannot be legally murdered. Boxing inhabits a sacred space predating civilization; or, to use D. H. Lawrence's phrase, before God was love. If it suggests a savage ceremony or a rite of atonement it also suggests the futility of such gestures. For what possible atonement is the fight waged if it must shortly be waged again . . . and again? The boxing match is the very image, the more terrifying for being so stylized, of mankind's collective aggression; its ongoing historical madness.

4

JOYCE CAROL OATES, from On Boxing (1987)

7. Since 1950 more than 2500 studies have attempted to discover whether mass media violence triggers additional aggressive behavior (Comstock et al., 1978; Murray and Kippax, 1979; Roberts and Bachen, 1981; National Institutes of Mental Health, 1982). With few exceptions (reviewed in Phillips, 1982b), researchers have studied aggression *in the laboratory,* and there is consensus that media violence can trigger additional aggression in the laboratory setting. However, policy makers, unlike researchers, have been primarily concerned with violence *outside* the laboratory, particularly with serious, fatal violence like homicide. Studies of media effects on homicide have been extremely rare and there is no systematic evidence to date indicating that mass media violence elicits additional murders.[1] As Andison has noted (1980:564), we do not know whether "there are deaths and violence occurring in society today because of what is being shown on the TV screen."

1

This paper presents what may be the first systematic evidence suggesting that some homicides are indeed triggered by a type of mass media violence. The current study builds on earlier research (Phillips, 1974, 1977, 1978, 1979, 1980, 1982a) which showed that: (1) U.S. suicides increase after publicized suicide stories. This finding has been replicated with American (Bollen and Phillips, 1982) and Dutch (Ganzeboom and de Haan, 1982) data. (2) The more publicity given to the suicide story, the more suicides rise thereafter. (3) The rise occurs mainly in the geographic area where the suicide story is publicized. . . .

2

In reviewing the literature on media effects, Comstock (1977) concluded that violent stories with the following characteristics were most likely to elicit aggression: When the violence in the story is presented as (1) rewarded, (2) exciting, (3) real, and (4) justified; when the perpetrator of the violence is (5) not criticized for his behavior and is presented as (6) intending to injure his victim.[2]

One type of story that meets all of these criteria is the heavyweight prize fight, which is almost universally presented as highly rewarded, exciting, real, and justified. Furthermore, the participants are not criticized for their aggressive behavior and are presented as trying to injure each other.

In a well-known series of studies, Berkowitz and various associates (1963, 1966, 1967, 1973) examined the impact of a filmed prize fight in the laboratory. They found that angered laboratory subjects behaved more aggressively after seeing a filmed prize fight scene. In contrast, angered laboratory subjects exposed to a track meet film displayed a significantly lower level of aggression.

In sum, the heavyweight prize match is a promising research site because (1) it meets Comstock's criteria for stories most likely to elicit aggression, and (2) it is known to elicit aggression in the laboratory.

DAVID P. PHILLIPS, from "The Impact of Mass Media Violence on U.S. Homicides," *American Sociological Review* (1983)

8. Even as boxing exploits, it also liberates and, like most sports, it has an aesthetic quality which has intrinsic appeal to those who step into the ring. In this regard it is mistaken to view boxing as a straightforward example of exploited wage labor. Boxers take up the sport and stay involved because, first and foremost, they enjoy it as an athletic experience and, secondly, because it gives them status within the ghetto and, if they are very successful, a semblance of respectability in the wider society. Interview managers, trainers and young boxers anywhere in the world, ask them to justify boxing and, whatever the language, the message will be the same: boxing is not just a sport, it is a savior of the oppressed and a theatre of their dreams. Colin McMillan (1991), former British featherweight champion, speaks for most boxers when he claims that:

> In a world cloaked in prejudice, the ring is the one place where all men are equal . . . to us pugilists the boxing arena is a place where we can raise our self esteem; where the short can stand tall, the weak become strong, and the shy become bold. It is a place to fulfil one's dreams, aim for the stars, and better one's future.

It is possible to interpret this and the many statements like it emanating from the boxing fraternity as evidence that boxing is a site for subcultural resistance against political and economic oppression and discrimination. In the 1970s, there were a significant number of theorists who focused on subcultures as sites for reaction against an imposed social order and the dominant value system (Hall and Jefferson, 1975; Robins and Cohen, 1978; Willis, 1978; Corrigan, 1979). According to this school of thought, subcultures did not just appear and languish in the cracks of society; rather, they were produced by structured inequalities and cohered around patterns of behavior and styles which, at least at a local level, enabled members to appear to be fighting back. However, it has been pointed out that this new wave of subculture theory failed to account for the ephemeral and transient nature of most subcultures and, perhaps more significantly, underestimated the extent to which subcultures which have the appearance of resistance, like, for instance, punk rock, are incorporated into dominant cultural forms (Brake, 1980).

In this respect boxing occupies an ambivalent position. Boxing clubs do offer at least temporary sanctuary from the worst excesses of ghetto life, and a prolonged commitment to the sport often keeps "at-risk" young males on the straight and narrow. For the small minority, prolonged engagement within the subculture can lead to a successful professional career and economic, if not social, mobility. In short, it is possible to view boxing as a positively sanctioned mechanism (at least for the time being) through which young men in the ghetto, with few other opportunities, can fight back against the structures which define the poverty of their existence. It is hard for anybody who has spent time in the modern ghetto not to conclude that, given what else is on offer, boxing is an extremely positive option for the young men who have to live there.

However, a note of caution must be included. When questioned, none of the professional boxers whom I met in the course of this study were eager to have any of their children embark on a career in the ring. For them boxing was the best way to exchange their 'body capital' for a livelihood, but they wanted better futures for their children. Moreover, as we have seen, even though boxing may be interpreted by fighters themselves as a form of resistance against layers of social, political and economic disadvantage, it is, nonetheless, an extremely exploitative medium. Furthermore, while boxing draws heavily on the working-class experience for participants and followers, it is a mistake to interpret the ring as a forum for ritualized class struggle against bourgeois hegemony. If anything, given the rational and proselytizing value system which characterizes this subculture worldwide, boxing supports rather than detracts from established society.

JOHN SUGDEN, from *Boxing and Society* (1996)

EVALUATING ELEVEN SOURCES ABOUT ERNEST HEMINGWAY

Assume that you are gathering information for an essay about *Ernest Hemingway's life in Paris in 1924 and 1925*. From your introductory reading, you have already become familiar with some of the basic facts. You know that the novelist Hemingway and his wife, Hadley, traveled to Paris with their infant son,

Bumby; that the Hemingways had very little money; that they associated with many of the literary figures who lived in Paris at the time; that they took occasional trips to Spain for the bull-running and to Austria for the skiing; and that Hemingway was working on a novel called *The Sun Also Rises*. Now, through research, you intend to fill in the details that will enable you to construct a portrait of Hemingway and his Paris experiences. You have selected a preliminary bibliography of eleven sources. Here is the *annotated preliminary bibliography*; the comments are based on a rapid examination of each source and are intended for your own use in completing research and organizing the essay.

Baker, Carlos. *Hemingway: A Life Story.* New York: Scribner's, 1969. 563 pages of biography, with 100 pages of footnotes. Everything seems to be here, presented in great detail.

Donaldson, Scott. *Hemingway: By Force of Will.* New York: Viking, 1977. The material isn't organized chronologically; instead, the chapters are thematic, with titles like "Money," "Sex," and "War." Episodes from Hemingway's life are presented within each chapter. The introduction calls this "a mosaic of [Hemingway's] mind and personality." Lots of footnotes.

Griffin, Peter. *Less Than a Treason: Hemingway in Paris.* New York: Oxford UP, 1990. Part of a multivolume biography. Covers Hemingway's life from 1921–1927, exclusively. Griffin says in the preface that his goal is not to "analyze this well examined life" but "to recreate it." Reads like a novel. A little bit choppy and anecdotal, and documentation format is unwieldy. Should probably be cautious about Griffin's preoccupation with EH's stories as autobiographical/psychological documents, but could be useful for speculations on connections between personal life and work.

Gurko, Leo. *Ernest Hemingway and the Pursuit of Heroism.* New York: Crowell, 1968. This book is part of a series called "Twentieth-Century American Writers": a brief introduction to the man and his work. After fifty pages of straight biography, Gurko discusses Hemingway's writing, novel by novel. There's an index and a short bibliography, but no notes. The biographical part is clear and easy to read, but it sounds too much like a summary.

Hemingway, Ernest. *A Moveable Feast.* New York: Scribner's, 1964. This is Hemingway's own version of his life in Paris. It sounds authentic, but there's also a very strongly nostalgic tone, so I'm not sure how trustworthy it is.

Hemingway in Paris. Home page. 13 Oct. 1997 <http://204.122.127.50/WSHS/Paris/HTM/>. Three photos of the Hemingways' apartment, with brief comments.

Hemingway, Leicester. *My Brother, Ernest Hemingway.* Cleveland: World, 1962. It doesn't sound as if the family was very close. For 1924–1925, he's using information from Ernest's letters (as well as commonly known facts). The book reads like a thirdhand report, very remote; but L. H. sounds honest, not as if he were making up things that he doesn't know about.

Hotchner, A. E. *Papa Hemingway.* New York: Random House, 1955. This book is called a "personal memoir." Hotchner met Hemingway in 1948, and evidently hero-worshiped him. Hemingway rambled on about his past, and Hotchner tape-recorded much of it. The book is their dialogue (mostly Hemingway's monologue). No index or bibliography. Hotchner's adoring tone is annoying, and the material resembles that of *A Moveable Feast,* which is better written.

Meyers, Jeffrey. *Hemingway: A Biography.* New York: Harper, 1985. 572 pages of bio. Includes several maps, and two chronologies: illnesses and accidents, and travel. Book organized chronologically, with every year accounted for, according to table of contents. Well documented, and seems less gossipy than Griffin.

Reynolds, Michael. *Hemingway: The Paris Years.* Cambridge, Mass.: Blackwell, 1989. Second of three-volume biography. Includes a chronology covering December 1921–February 1926, five very basic outline maps ("Hemingway's Europe 1922–26," "France," "Switzerland," "Italy," and "Key points for Hemingway's several trips through France and Spain"). Chapters grouped into sections by single years, from "Part One: 1922," to "Part Four: 1925."

Sokoloff, Alice Hunt. *Hadley, the First Mrs. Hemingway.* New York: Dodd, 1973. This is the Paris experience from Hadley's point of view, most of it taken from her recollections and from the standard biographies. (Baker is acknowledged.) It's a very slight book—102 pages—but there's an index and footnotes, citing letters and interviews that some of the other biographers might not have been able to use.

Examining the Sources

The preliminary notes describing these eleven sources seem to be the outgrowth of two separate processes. In the first place, the student is noting basic facts about each biography—the *length* of the book, the amount of *documentation,* the potential *bias* of the writer (if it is easily recognized), and the *organization* of the material. But there are also several comments on *tone,* impressions of the way in which the information is being presented: "sounds like . . ." or "reads like. . . ." How were these impressions formed?

Let's begin with the biography, which, according to the annotations, may be the most thorough and complete of the eleven. Here is Carlos Baker's account of Ernest and Hadley Hemingway immediately after their arrival in Paris:

The first problem in Paris was to find an apartment. Ezra's pavillon in the rue Notre Dame des Champs was too cold and damp for the baby, but there was another available flat on the second floor of a building farther up the hill. It was a pleasant street sloping down from the corner of the Avenue de l'Observatoire and the Boulevard du Montparnasse, an easy stroll from the Luxembourg Gardens, where Hadley could air the baby, a stone's throw from an unspoiled café called La Closerie des Lilas, and much closer to Gertrude Stein's than the former walk-up apartment in the rue du Cardinal Lemoine. The whole neighborhood was a good deal prettier and more polite than that of the Montagne Ste.-Geneviève, though not much quieter. The Hemingways' windows at Number 113 looked down upon a sawmill and lumberyard. It was owned and operated by Pierre Chautard, who lived with his wife and a small dog on the ground floor. The whine of the circular saw, the chuff of the donkey-engine that drove it, the hollow boom of newly sawn planks being laid in piles, and the clatter of the ancient camions that carried the lumber away made such a medley that Ernest was often driven to the haven of the Closerie des Lilas to do his writing.

In the apartment itself, a dark tunnel of a hall led to a kitchen with a stone sink and a two-ring gas burner for cooking. There was a dining room, mostly filled by a large table, and a small bedroom where Ernest sometimes worked. The master bedroom held a stove and double bed, with a small dressing room large enough for the baby's crib. Hadley quickly rehired the *femme de ménage*, Madame Henri Rohrback, who had worked for her off and on before. Marie was a sturdy peasant from Mur-de-Bretagne. She and her husband, who was called Ton-Ton, lived at 10 bis, Avenue des Gobelins. Her own nickname was Marie Cocotte, from her method of calling the chickens at home on the farm in Brittany. She took at once to the child and often bore him away in a carriage lent by the Straters to see Ton-Ton, who was a retired soldier with time on his hands. Madame Chautard, the wife of the owner of the sawmill, was a plump and childless woman with brassy hair and a voice so harsh that it made the baby cry. She seemed to be envious of Hadley's motherhood. Watching the child drink his daily ration of orange juice she could only say scornfully, "*Il sera un poivrot comme sa mère.*"* Of the baby's many nicknames—Gallito, Matt, and Joe—the one that stuck was Bumby, which Hadley invented to signify his warm, plump, teddy-bearish, arm-filling solidity which both parents admired and enjoyed.

*"He'll become a lush like his mother."

CARLOS BAKER

What makes Baker's description so effective is the *impressive amount of detail.* You cannot help believing a biographer who offers so much specific information about everyone and everything with even the remotest connection to his subject. You expect to be told what Hemingway ate for dinner and, indeed, in reporting the novelist's skiing trip to Schruns, Baker writes that the cook prepared "great roasts of beef, with potatoes browned in gravy, jugged hare with wine sauce, venison chops, a special omelette soufflé, and homemade plum pudding." On the other hand, you are sometimes told more than you want to know. There's a house-that-Jack-built effect in the sentences about the Hemingways' nursemaid who was a "sturdy peasant from Mur-de-Bretagne," who had a husband named Ton-Ton, who lived in the Avenue des Gobelins, whose nickname was the result of . . . and so on. Nevertheless, Baker tells a good story and his description of the apartment is effective: notice the description of the sounds that Hemingway must have heard from his windows.

Next, in sharp contrast to all this detail, we have a comparable passage from the biography by Leo Gurko (which the bibliography described as "a summary"). *Gurko* is dealing with the same material as *Baker,* in less than one-tenth the space, and naturally offers much less detail.

> Paris in the 1920s was everyone's catalyst. It was the experimental and fermenting center of every art. It was highly sophisticated, yet broke up naturally into small intimate quartiers. Its cafés were hotbeds of intellectual and social energy, pent up during the war and now released. Young people from all over the world flocked to Paris, drawn not only by the city's intrinsic attractions but by the devaluation of the franc. 1
>
> The young Hemingways settled on the Left Bank, and since they were short of money, rented modest rooms in an ancient walkup. They moved several times, taking flats that were usually on the top floor, five or six flights up, commanding good views of the roofs of Paris. This was somehow in tune with a passion to absorb the city. Hemingway did much of his writing in cafés, where he would sit for hours over a beer or *Pernod* with paper spread before him. He took long walks through the streets and gardens, lingered over the Cézannes in the Luxembourg Museum, and let the great city permeate his senses. 2
>
> LEO GURKO

Baker was trying as much as possible to draw the reader into the scene and to share the Hemingways' own experience of Paris. In contrast, *Gurko* is outside the scene, describing what he, the observer, has seen over the distance of time. He does not hesitate to tell his reader what to think—about Paris, about its expatriate population, and about the Hemingways. Notice in this short passage how *Gurko* moves from verifiable facts to his own hypotheses:

> The Hemingways put themselves on short rations, ate, drank, and entertained as little as possible, pounced eagerly on the small checks that arrived in the mail as payment for accepted stories, and were intensely conscious of being poor. The sensation was not altogether unpleasant. Their extreme youth, the excitement of living abroad, the sense of making a fresh start, even the unexpected joy of parenthood, gave their poverty a romantic flavor.
>
> LEO GURKO

Gurko's book does not document his sources; the reader is asked to accept Gurko's assertion that being poor in Paris was "not altogether unpleasant" for

Hemingway, because of its romantic connotations. Other biographers, however, may not agree with this statement. Remember that Gurko's hypothesis is one person's opinion and is not to be confused with fact or presented as such in a research essay. Acceptance of his opinion depends on Gurko's credentials as an authority on Hemingway and on what other established authorities have to say.

Here's a final excerpt from Gurko's biography, as a starting point for a second group of comparisons. Notice his tendency to generalize and summarize and, especially, to speak for Hemingway. Then contrast *Gurko's* approach with that of *Alice Sokoloff:*

> He was becoming increasingly devoted to imaginative writing, to the point where his newspaper assignments and the need to grind out journalistic pieces were growing more and more irksome. Another threat to his work was the "arty" atmosphere of Paris. The cafés of the city, he soon recognized, were filled with aesthetes of one kind or another who wanted to be artists, talked incessantly and even knowledgeably about art, but never really produced anything. There were a hundred of these clever loafers and dilettantes for every real writer. Hemingway developed a contempt and even fear of them, perhaps because there was in him, as in most genuine artists, a feeling of uncertainty about his own talent. He drove himself to hard work and avoided the café crowd as much as he could.
>
> LEO GURKO

> It was a worldly crowd, full of intellectual and artistic ferment, some of it real, some of it bogus, some of them obsessed with their own egos, a few of them deeply and sincerely interested in Ernest's talent. The Hemingways' finances were as restricted as ever, but these people "could offer them all the amenities, could take them anywhere for gorgeous meals," could produce any kind of entertainment and diversion. Although Ernest accepted it all, Hadley thought that he resented it and always kept "a very stiff upper front to satisfy himself." He did not want "simply to sink back and take all this," but the success and admiration was heady stuff and he could not help but enjoy it.[1] Hadley used to be wryly amused when Ernest and Gertrude Stein would talk about worldly success and how it did not mean anything to them.[2] The fact that this was true for a part of him, and that he despised anything false or pretentious, was a source of inner conflict which sometimes expressed itself in malice.
>
> [1]John Dos Passos. *The Best Times* (New York: New American Library, 1966), p. 143.
> [2]Interview with Hadley Richardson Hemingway Mowrer, January 18, 1972.
>
> ALICE SOKOLOFF

Sokoloff's conclusions differ from *Gurko's*: she points to a conflict in Hemingway's reaction to his Paris acquaintances, and offers *footnotes* to support her suggestion. In another sense, Sokoloff's commentary is limited: because the subject of her biography is Hadley Hemingway, she is describing events from Hadley's point of view. On the other hand, Sokoloff's presentation makes it fairly easy to figure out where Hadley's version leaves off and the biographer's account begins, and the story is told coherently.

Leicester Hemingway's account of his brother's life is far more confusing; most of his information comes from letters, and he makes little attempt to sort out the contents into a form that the average reader can follow easily:

> Things were going very well for Ernest, with his home life as well as with his writing. Bumby was beginning to talk and Ernest was learning that a child could be more fun than fret. With wife and son he took off for Schruns in the Vorarlberg when good skiing weather set in. For months they were deep in the snow up there, working and enjoying the sports, before returning to Paris in mid-March.   1
>
> Ernest wrote the family that when they camped in the mountains, up above 2,000 meters, there had been lots of ptarmigan and foxes, too. The deer and chamois were lower down.   2
>
> He said Bumby weighed twenty-nine pounds, played in a sand pile with shovel and pail, and was always jolly. His own writing was going very well. *In Our Time* was out of print and bringing high prices, he said, while his stories were being translated into Russian and German. . . .   3
>
> Hadley added other details, thanking the family for the Christmas box which had been delayed more than two months in customs, but had arrived without damage to the fruit cake—Mother's one culinary triumph besides meat loaf. She wrote that Bumby had a wonderful nurse who had taken care of him while she and Ernest spent days at a stretch in mountain huts to be near good snow.   4
>
> LEICESTER HEMINGWAY

Ernest's writing is mixed up with Bumby's pail and shovel and fruitcakes for Christmas. This is certainly raw material. The biography offers no interpretation at all for the reader to discount or accept. The material is stitched together so crudely that one has to spend time sorting out important details from trivia. Certainly, this biography would be a poor choice for the student who was beginning research on this topic; but the details might provide interesting background once the events of 1924–1925 were made more familiar by other biographies.

Next, here are three more recent biographies of Hemingway. How do they describe the apartment near the lumberyard?

> "Hemingway had then and has always a very good instinct for finding apartments in strange but pleasant localities," wrote Gertrude Stein, "and good femmes de menage and good food." They arrived in France on January 29, 1924, and soon found a flat above a noisy sawmill, near Pound's old studio, at 113 rue Notre Dame des Champs, where the street curves parallel to the Boulevard Montparnasse.   1
>
> But the flat had more character than comfort. American friends, who were used to living well in France, were shocked by the squalor. Kitty Cannell said: "The Hemingways lived in a cold-water apartment that gave on[to] a lumber yard in the Montparnasse quarter. It had neither gas nor electric light." And the journalist Burton Rascoe wrote: "They lived, at the time, in an incredibly bare hovel, without toilet   2

or running water, and with a mattress spread on the floor for a bed; it was in the court of a lumber yard, on the second floor, to which one climbed by a flight of rickety steps."

JEFFREY MEYERS

Meyers attempts to give some idea of what the Hemingways themselves were experiencing, not by piling on physical details, but by providing a kaleidoscope of eyewitness impressions, rather like interviews in a documentary film or the accumulation of evidence at a trial. An explicit interrogation of the testimony here and the speakers might be helpful, and reminiscences aren't always reliable (the other biographers mention the lack of electricity, but no one else says there was no running water), but this passage does alert us to some of the issues of class that colored Hemingway's experience of Paris, and words like "squalor" and "hovel" offer a contrast to the romantic picture drawn by Baker.

Just before he'd left New York, Ernest had heard from Ford Madox Ford. Ford 1
had written that, since the Pounds were traveling, the Hemingways could spend a few weeks in the Pounds' flat at 70 Rue Notre Dames des Champs. But Ford had made a mistake. When Ernest arrived at Pound's apartment, he learned that, although Ezra was, as Ford said, traveling, he had left no key. Ernest, exhausted and desperate, trudged through the wet snow toward the noise of a band saw, a few buildings down the street. In a small square of black, dripping trees and narrow old wooden houses, he found Pierre Chautard, a carpenter.

When Ernest asked if the carpenter knew of a place to stay, Chautard showed 2
him a five-room flat over the sawmill. The kitchen had a slimy slate sink and a gas stove, with piles of burnt matches beneath the two burners. The place was furnished, Chautard said. But Ernest saw little more than a big bed in one room and a big table in another. Still, there was the pleasant smell of fresh-cut lumber, and windows all around. Madame Chautard, a foulmouthed, henna-haired harridan, sneered at the young couple and suggested she was doing them a favor—especially with the baby. Though he wanted to, Ernest did not haggle over the rent. For himself, his wife, and his son, nothing mattered more than a good night's sleep.

PETER GRIFFIN

Griffin's entire book is devoted to Hemingway's experiences in Paris, so we should expect a level of detail to at least rival that of Baker. Griffin acknowledges in his preface his indebtedness to Baker, and we recognize here some of the same details we learned in Baker: the slate sink, the gas stove, the big table. Baker passed over why, specifically, the Hemingways were in the Montparnasse district; Griffin gives us some sense of how professional and personal lives were entangled, with messages from Pound being relayed by another literary luminary, Ford Madox Ford. Is this additional information useful?

On February 8, after much shopping, Ernest leased a second-floor apartment at 113 rue Notre-Dame-des-Champs, a stone's throw from Ezra's studio and directly behind Montparnasse. A month's rent was 650 francs, almost three times their Cardinal Lemoine rent, but the space was better, the location closer to their friends, and with the franc fluctuating at twenty-one to the dollar, the real cost was about $30 monthly. The apartment had no electricity, and the lumberyard buzz saw in the courtyard below whined steadily during working hours, but their old *femme de menage*, Marie Rohrbach, returned to help with the baby. As February rain mixed with snow, Hadley, sick and physically worn out, watched her furniture move once more into new quarters. "We have the whole second story," she told mother-in-law Grace, "tiny kitchen, small dining room, toilet, small bedroom, medium size sitting room with stove, dining room where John Hadley sleeps and the linen and his and our bath things are kept and a very comfortable bedroom . . . you're conscious all the time from 7 A.M. to 5 P.M. of a very gentle buzzing noise. They make door and window frames and picture frames. The yard is full of dogs and workmen[,] and rammed right up against the funny front door covered with tarpaulin is the baby's buggy."

Despite the lumberyard's noise, the new apartment was an improvement over their first Paris home. Here they were only a few minutes walk from the Notre-Dame-des-Champs Metro station, the Luxembourg Gardens, Sylvia's bookshop and Gertrude Stein's place on the rue de Fleurus. The neighborhood was less working class, less down at the heels. At one end of the street stood the Clinique d'Accouchement, for which both Ernest and Hadley hoped they would have no use. (In his 1924 day book, mostly blank, Ernest was keeping careful track of Hadley's monthly periods.) Nearby, on the Boulevard Montparnasse, in good weather and bad, their American friends gathered to drink and talk at the Select, the Rotonde and the Dome where one could gossip, leave messages, borrow money, repay debts and keep generally abreast of local news.

MICHAEL REYNOLDS

Here is another full-length work devoted to the Paris years. Like *Griffin*, *Reynolds* professes his debt to Carlos Baker, and he sees the significance of the new flat in much the same light as did Baker: better, more convenient location, with the disadvantages of the apartment minimized. Like *Meyers*, Reynolds relies on eyewitness reports, in this case a letter written by Hadley, giving her own impressions of the new apartment and directly contradicting Burton Rascoe's assertion that there was no toilet (although in writing to her mother-in-law she might have minimized the "squalor").

In fact, an Internet source confirms the lack of a toilet. "Hemingway in Paris" provides three photographs: the circular stairway leading into the apartment, the window of Hemingway's room (with a plaque honoring him), and the outside of the building, including a café. The prose commentary is brief, indicating that there was no hot water and no toilet, "only a chamber pot located in a niche on each floor of the winding staircase."

Finally, here are five descriptions of Hemingway as a baby sitter, odd-job man, and scavenger, all dealing with similar experiences:

Ernest was working fairly hard. He awoke early in the spring mornings, "boiled the rubber nipples and the bottles, made the formula, finished the bottling, gave Mr. Bumby a bottle," and wrote for a time at the dining-room table before Hadley got up. Chautard had not begun his sawing at that hour, the street was quiet, and Ernest's only companions were Mr. Bumby and Mr. Feather Puss, a large cat given them by Kitty Cannell and named with one of Hadley's nicknames. But Ernest was truly domestic only in the early mornings. He took the freedom of Paris as his personal prerogative, roving as widely as he chose. There was a gymnasium in the rue Pontoise where he often went to earn ten francs a round by sparring with professional heavyweights. The job called for a nice blend of skill and forbearance, since hirelings must be polite while fighting back just enough to engage, without enraging, the emotions of the fighters. Ernest had befriended a waiter at the Closerie des Lilas and sometimes helped him weed a small vegetable garden near the Porte d'Orléans. The waiter knew that he was a writer and warned him that the boxing might jar his brains. But Ernest was glad enough to earn the extra money. He had already begun to save up to buy pesetas for another trip to Spain in July.

CARLOS BAKER

When there were the three of us instead of just the two, it was the cold and the weather that finally drove us out of Paris in the winter time. Alone there was no problem when you got used to it. I could always go to a café to write and could work all morning over a café crème while the waiters cleaned and swept out the café and it gradually grew warmer. My wife could go to work at the piano in a cold place and with enough sweaters keep warm playing and come home to nurse Bumby. It was wrong to take a baby to a café in the winter though; even a baby that never cried and watched everything that happened and was never bored. There were no baby-sitters then and Bumby would stay happy in his tall cage bed with his big, loving cat named F. Puss. There were people who said that it was dangerous to leave a cat with a baby. The most ignorant and prejudiced said that a cat would suck a baby's breath and kill him. Others said that a cat would lie on a baby and the cat's weight would smother him. F. Puss lay beside Bumby in the tall cage bed and watched the door with his big yellow eyes, and would let no one come near him when we were out and Marie, the *femme de ménage*, had to be away. There was no need for baby-sitters. F. Puss was the baby-sitter.

ERNEST HEMINGWAY

Ernest wanted me to see the neighborhood where he had first lived; we started on Rue Notre-Dame-des-Champs, where he had lived over a sawmill, and slowly worked our way past familiar restaurants, bars and stores, to the Jardin du Luxembourg and its museum, where, Ernest said, he fell in love with certain paintings that taught him how to write. "Am also fond of the Jardin," Ernest said, "because it kept us from starvation. On days when the dinner pot was absolutely devoid of content, I would put Bumby, then about a year old, into the baby carriage and wheel him over here to the Jardin. There was always a *gendarme* on duty, but I knew that around four o'clock he would go to a bar across from the park to have a glass of wine. That's when I would appear with Mr. Bumby—and a pocketful of corn for the pigeons. I would sit on a bench, in my guise of buggy-pushing pigeon-lover, casing the flock for clarity of eye and plumpness. The Luxembourg was well known for the classiness of its pigeons. Once my selection was made, it was a simple matter to entice my victim with the corn, snatch him, wring his neck, and flip his carcass under Mr. Bumby's blanket. We got a little tired of pigeon that winter, but they filled many a void. What a kid that Bumby was—played it straight—and never once put the finger on me."

A. E. HOTCHNER

. . . As he grew older (and *A Moveable Feast* was the last book he finished), Hemingway laid increasing stress on the poverty he suffered in Paris. Without question, Ernest and Hadley Hemingway lived on a relatively scant income during those years, but they were never so badly off as the writer, in retrospect, liked to believe.   1

In any case, poverty is virtually apotheosized in *A Moveable Feast*. As the title   2
hints, a gnawing hunger for food and drink symbolizes Hemingway's indigence. According to the legend constructed in this book, Hemingway worked all day in his unheated garret, too poor to buy firewood or afford lunch. At least he does not tell here the unlikely yarn that appears in A. E. Hotchner's biography: the one about Hemingway catching pigeons in the Luxembourg Gardens in order to satisfy a rumbling stomach. But poverty, and its symbolic hunger, are nonetheless celebrated. "You got very hungry when you did not eat enough in Paris," Hemingway writes, because of the good things on display in the *pâtisseries* and at the outdoor restaurants. Mostly he and Hadley survived on leeks *(poireaux)*, but at least so frugal a diet enabled one to savor, truly, the joys of eating well when an unexpected windfall made it possible for them to dine out.

SCOTT DONALDSON

In the late spring of 1925, when the cold rains that ended the winter had come and gone and the warmth of the sun increased each day, Ernest loved to take his son in the stroller, "a cheap, very light, folding carriage, down the streets to the Closerie des Lilas." They would each have brioche and cafe au lait, Ernest pouring some of the hot coffee into the saucer to cool it, and to let Bumby dip his brioche before eating. Ernest would read the papers, now and then looking up to see his son attentive to everything that passed on the boulevard. After breakfast, Ernest would wheel Bumby across the street from the cafe and past the Place de l'Observatoire. Bumby loved to see the bronze horses rearing in the fountain spray that made the June air smell so clean.

PETER GRIFFIN

Characteristically, *Baker* describes exactly how the father tended his son, pausing to explain the full name and the origins of their cat. *Griffin* pays the same attention to detail, without being so exhaustive. *Hemingway* himself, years after the event, describes much the same relationship, but with a completely different emphasis and set of details. These three passages are not in conflict; but they are not at all the same kind of writing and, in fact, they provide an excellent illustration of the difficulties of combining sources written in different modes for different kinds of audience. The Hemingway who reminisced for *A. E. Hotchner* offers a somewhat different version of the same experience, a version criticized in *Donaldson's* extract, which tries to distinguish between nostalgia and truth. Unlike *Gurko's*, *Donaldson's* presentation is detailed; unlike *Baker* and *Griffin*, he has an outsider's perspective, and the combination, backed up by documentation, is quite convincing.

In what order, then, would you consult these ten books for full-scale research? You might begin with Gurko's brief account, to establish the sequence of events, and then fill in the details by reading Baker's longer version or the more recent, comprehensive biographies by Meyers or Reynolds, which depend so much on Baker's earlier work. Donaldson gets pushed down the list to third or fourth, primarily because his biography is not chronological; gathering the scattered references to 1924 will be easier once the overall chronology has been made clear by Gurko, Baker, Meyers, or Reynolds. Now, you can also draw on the details to be found in the works by "interested" parties: wife, brother, friend, and the author himself. And, at intervals, you should stop reading and note-taking to compare these various versions of one life and determine which of the sources was in a position to know the truth—the man himself thirty years later? his correspondence at the time? records left by his wife (whom, in fact, he divorced in 1929)? his biographers, whose information is presented secondhand? a combination of all the sources?

EXERCISE 22: LEARNING ABOUT AUTHORS

Each of the following authors is represented by an essay or paragraph in this book. Choose one of the authors and:

A. Find out some information about the author's background and write a paragraph describing his or her qualifications for writing about this subject.

B. Think about the suggested research topics that accompany the references. Would you use this passage if you were writing an essay on that topic?

Bertrand Russell: "The Social Responsibility of Scientists" (Chapter 1, pp. 55–57)
   a. The arms race
   b. The power of the media

Robert Bork: "The Case for Censorship" (Chapter 3, pp. 137–146)
   a. The popularity of supermarket tabloids
   b. The decline of American culture

Shelby Steele: excerpt from "I'm Black, You're White, Who's Innocent?" (Appendix E, pp. 503–514)
   a. Are affirmative action programs justified?
   b. Should our curriculums be "politically correct"?

Margaret Mead: excerpt from *Some Personal Views* (Chapter 1, p. 47)
   a. Origins of neurosis
   b. Problems of the disabled child

EXERCISE 23: COMPARING SOURCES

In the middle of the night of November 29, 1942, a Boston nightclub called the Cocoanut Grove burned down, resulting in the deaths of at least 300 people. Read the following three accounts of this disaster, and be prepared to discuss the differences in content, organization, tone, purpose, and point of view. What is the thesis of each article? Consider how you would use the three articles in a single research essay dealing with the Cocoanut Grove disaster. Are these three variations interchangeable?

NEW YORK TIMES, 30 NOVEMBER 1942

300 KILLED BY FIRE, SMOKE AND PANIC IN BOSTON RESORT— DEAD CLOG EXITS—Terror Piles Up Victims as Flames Suddenly Engulf Nightclub—Service Men to Rescue—Many of Them Perish—Girls of Chorus Leap to Safety—150 Are Injured

BOSTON, Sunday, Nov. 29—More than 300 persons had perished early this morning in flames, smoke and panic in the Cocoanut Grove Night Club in the midtown theatre district.   1

The estimate of the dead came at 2 A.M. from William Arthur Reilly, Fire Commissioner, as firemen and riggers searched the ruins for additional bodies. It was a disaster unprecedented in this city.   2

The chief loss of life resulted from the screaming, clawing crowds that were wedged in the entrance of the club. Smoke took a terrific toll of life and scores were burned to death.   3

At the Boston City Hospital officials said there were so many bodies lined up in corridors that they would attempt no identifications before daybreak.   4

Commissioner Reilly stated that an eyewitness inside the club said the fire started when an artificial palm near the main entrance was set afire.   5

Martial law was clamped on the entire fire area at 1:35 A.M. Sailors, Coast Guardsmen, shore patrolmen and naval officers dared death time and again trying to get at bodies that were heaped six feet high by one of the entrances.   6

Firemen said that many bodies were believed to have fallen into the basement after the main floor collapsed.   7

A chorus boy, Marshall Cook, aged 19, of South Boston, led three co-workers, eight chorus girls and other floor show performers totaling thirty-five to an adjoining roof from the second-floor dressing rooms and from there they dropped to the ground from a ladder. 8

Scores of ambulances from nearby cities, the Charlestown Navy Yard and the Chelsea Naval Hospital poured into the area, but the need for ambulances became so great that even railway express trucks were pressed into service to carry away victims. At one time victims, many of them dead, lay two deep in an adjoining garage. 9

Many of the victims were soldiers, sailors, marines and Coast Guardsmen, some of them junior officers, visiting Boston for a weekend of merrymaking. In the throng were persons who had attended the Holy Cross–Boston College football game. 10

Scores of dead were piled up in the lobbies of the various hospitals as the doctors and nurses gave all their attention to the 150 injured. 11

A "flash" fire, believed to have started in the basement, spread like lightning through the dance floor area, and the panic was on. All available nurses and priests were being called into the disaster area. 12

Among the dead were a marine and one who appeared to be a fireman. Casualties were arriving at hospitals so rapidly that they were being placed in the corridors wherever a suitable place could be found. 13

It appeared probable that the greatest loss of life was in the newly opened lounge of the night club in Broadway. Here, one policeman said, burned and suffocated persons were heaped to the top of the doors, wedged in death. 14

The night club was a one-and-a-half story building with a stucco exterior. The blaze was said to have broken out in the basement kitchen at 10:17 P.M. just as the floor show performers were preparing for their next performance. Performers on the second floor were met by terrific smoke and flame as they started downstairs. Their stories were the only ones available, as those who had escaped the dance floor and tables were too hysterical to talk. 15

A temporary morgue and hospital were set up in the garage of the Film Exchange Transfer Company at the rear of the club in Shawmut Street. At least fourteen persons, suffocated and lying in grotesque positions, were lying on the garage floor at one time, while scores of injuries were cared for by garage workers and others. 16

The city's Civilian Defense Workers were called to the scene to maintain order and to give first aid to those suffering from burns and smoke inhalation. Every hospital in the area soon was loaded with the victims. 17

At least thirty-five performers and their friends were rescued by the quick actions of Marshall Cook, a South Boston boy. He was met by a blast of flame as he started down stairs, went back to the dressing room and organized those caught there. 18

He then smashed his way through a window, carrying away the casing. Through this opening he led a group to an adjoining room, where a small ladder was found. The ladder was not long enough to reach the street, but Cook and several other male performers held the top end over the roof's edge and guided the women over the side. They had to jump about 6 feet to reach the ground. 19

At the City Hospital bodies were piled on the floors, many so burned that there was no attempt to identify them immediately. Many service men were among the victims, many of whom were partly identified through their uniforms.
20

Buck Jones, the film star, was believed to be one of the victims.

Among the first at the scene was the Rev. Joseph A. Marcus of Cranwell School, Lenox, who administered the last rites for at least fifty persons. In the meantime, thirty or forty ambulances rushed to the fire, these coming from Lynn, Newton, and Brookline. Despite the hindrances caused by automobiles parked in the streets, some of the dead and injured were taken from nearby buildings, where they had been left covered only by newspapers.
21
22

Abraham Levy, a cashier at the Cocoanut Grove, said there were about 400 in the place, including many sailors.
23

Sailors saved many lives, pulling people through the doors and out of danger. A fireman said that he saw at least thirty bodies lying on the floor, and that he believed some of them were firemen.
24

Among the spectacular escapes were those of two of the eight chorus girls, who leaped from the second floor and were caught by two of the male dancers. They were Lottie Christie of Park Drive, Boston, and Claudia Boyle. They jumped into the arms of Andrew Louzan and Robert Gilbert. Louzan and Gilbert had climbed out of a window of their dressing room to an adjoining roof and then descended by ladder.
25

TIME, 7 DECEMBER 1942
CATASTROPHE: BOSTON'S WORST

Holy Cross had just beaten Boston College: downtown Boston was full of men & women eager to celebrate or console. Many of them wound up at Cocoanut Grove: they stood crowded around the dimly lighted downstairs bar, filled the tables around the dance floor upstairs. With them mingled the usual Saturday night crowd: soldiers & sailors, a wedding party, a few boys being sent off to Army camps.
1

At 10 o'clock Bridegroom John O'Neil, who had planned to take his bride to their new apartment at the stroke of the hour, lingered on a little longer. The floor show was about to start. Through the big revolving door, couples moved in & out.
2

At the downstairs bar, a 16-year-old busboy stood on a bench to replace a light bulb that a prankish customer had removed. He lit a match. It touched one of the artificial palm trees that gave the Cocoanut Grove its atmosphere; a few flames shot up. A girl named Joyce Spector sauntered toward the checkroom because she was worried about her new fur coat.
3

Panic's Start

Before Joyce Spector reached the cloakroom, the Cocoanut Grove was a screaming shambles. The fire quickly ate away the palm tree, raced along silk draperies, was sucked upstairs through the stairway, leaped along ceiling and wall. The silk hangings, turned to balloons of flame, fell on table and floor.
4

Men & women fought their way toward the revolving door; the push of bodies [5] jammed it. Nearby was another door; it was locked tight. There were other exits, but few Cocoanut Grove patrons knew about them. The lights went out. There was nothing to see now except flame, smoke and weird moving torches that were men & women with clothing and hair afire.

The 800 Cocoanut Grove patrons pushed and shoved, fell and were trampled. [6] Joyce Spector was knocked under a table, crawled on hands & knees, somehow was pushed through an open doorway into the street. A chorus boy herded a dozen people downstairs into a refrigerator. A few men & women crawled out windows; a few escaped by knocking out a glass brick wall. But most of them, including Bridegroom John O'Neil, were trapped.

Panic's Sequel

Firemen broke down the revolving door, found it blocked by bodies of the dead, [7] six deep. They tried to pull a man out through a side window; his legs were held tight by the mass of struggling people behind him. In an hour the fire was out and firemen began untangling the piles of bodies. One hard bitten fireman went in to hysterics when he picked up a body and a foot came off in his hand. They found a girl dead in a telephone booth, a bartender still standing behind his bar.

At hospitals and improvised morgues which were turned into charnel houses for [8] the night, 484 dead were counted; it was the most disastrous U.S. fire since 571 people were killed in Chicago's Iroquois Theater holocaust in 1903. One Boston newspaper ran a two-word banner line: BUSBOY BLAMED. But the busboy had not put up the Cocoanut Grove's tinderbox decorations, nor was he responsible for the fact that Boston's laws do not require nightclubs to have fireproof fixtures, sprinkler systems or exit markers.

BERNARD DEVOTO, *HARPER'S*, FEBRUARY 1943
THE EASY CHAIR

On the last Sunday morning of November, 1942, most inhabitants of greater [1] Boston learned from their newspapers that at about the time they had gone to bed the night before the most terrible fire in the history of their city had occurred. The decorations of a crowded night club had got ignited, the crowd had stampeded, the exits had jammed, and in a few minutes hundreds of people had died of burns or suffocation. Two weeks later the list of dead had reached almost exactly five hundred, and the war news was only beginning to come back to Boston front pages. While the Allied invasion of North Africa stalled, while news was released that several transports engaged in it had been sunk, while the Russians and the Germans fought monstrously west of Stalingrad and Moscow, while the Americans bombed Naples and the RAF obliterated Turin and conducted the war's most widespread raids over western Europe, while the Japs tried again in the Solomons and mowed down their attackers in New Guinea, while a grave conflict of civilian opinion over the use of Admiral Darlan developed in America and Great Britain, while the anniversary of Pearl Harbor passed almost unnoticed—while all this was going on the Boston papers reported it in stickfuls in order to devote hundreds of columns to the fire at the Cocoanut Grove. And the papers did right, for the community has experienced an angry horror surpassing anything that it can remember. For weeks few Bostonians were able to feel strongly about anything but their civic disaster.

There is irony in such preoccupation with a minute carnage. In the same fortnight thousands of men were killed in battle. Every day, doubtless, more than five hundred were burned to death, seared by powder or gasoline from bombed dumps, in buildings fired from the sky, or in blazing airplanes and sinking ships. If these are thought of as combatants meeting death in the line of duty, far more than five hundred civilians were killed by military action in Germany, Italy, France, Great Britain, Russia, China, Australia, and the islands of the Pacific. Meanwhile in two-thirds of the world civilians died of torture and disease and starvation, in prison camps and wire stockades and the rubble of their homes—they simply came to their last breath and died, by the thousand. At a moment when violent death is commonplace, when it is inevitable for hundreds of thousands, there is something grotesque in being shocked by a mere five hundred deaths which are distinguished from the day's routine only by the fact that they were not inevitable. When hundreds of towns are bombed repeatedly, when cities the size of Boston are overrun by invading armies, when many hundreds of Boston's own citizens will surely be killed in battle in the next few weeks, why should a solitary fire, a truly inconsiderable slaughter, so oppress the spirit? 2

That oppression provides perspective on our era. We have been so conditioned to horror that horror must explode in our own backyard before we can genuinely feel it. At the start of the decade our nerves responded to Hitler's murdering the German Jews with the outrage properly felt in the presence of cruelty and pain. Seven years later our nerves had been so overloaded that they felt no such outrage at the beginning of a systematic effort to exterminate an entire nation, such as Poland. By progressive steps we had come to strike a truce with the intolerable, precisely as the body develops immunity to poisons and bacteria. Since then three years of war have made the intolerable our daily bread, and every one of us has comfortably adapted to things which fifteen years ago would have driven him insane. The extinction of a nation now seems merely an integral part of the job in hand. But the needless death of five hundred people in our home town strikes through the immunity and horrifies us. 3

The fire at the Cocoanut Grove was a single, limited disaster, but it exhausted Boston's capacity to deal with an emergency. Hospital facilities were strained to the limit and somewhat beyond it. If a second emergency had had to be dealt with at the same time its victims would have had to wait some hours for transportation and a good many hours for treatment. If there had been three such fires at once, two-thirds of the victims would have got no treatment whatever in time to do them any good. Boston is an inflammable city and it has now had instruction in what to 4 expect if a dozen hostile planes should come over and succeed in dropping incendiary bombs. The civilian defense agencies which were called on justified themselves and vindicated their training. The Nurses' Aid in particular did a memorable job; within a few hours there was a trained person at the bed of every victim, many other Aids worked to exhaustion helping hospital staffs do their jobs, and in fact more were available than could be put to use. Nevertheless it was clearly demonstrated that the civilian agencies are nowhere near large enough to take care of bombings if bombings should come. There were simply not enough ambulances; Railway Express Company trucks had to be called on to take the injured to hospitals and the dead to morgues. The dead had to be stacked like cord wood in garages because the morgues could take no more; the dying had to be laid in rows in the corridors of hospitals because the emergency wards were full. The drainage of doctors into the military service had left Boston just about enough to care for as many victims as this single fire supplied. Six months from now there will be too few to handle an equal emergency; there are far too few now for one twice as serious. One planeload of incendiaries would start more fires than the fire department and its civilian assistants could put out. There would be more injured than there are even the most casually trained first-aiders to care for. Hundreds would be abandoned to the ignorant assistance of untrained persons, in streets so blocked by rubble and so jammed with military vehicles that trained crews could not reach them even when trained crews should be free. Boston has learned that it is not prepared to take care of itself. One doubts if any community in the United States is.

Deeper implications of the disaster have no direct connection with the war. An 5
outraged city has been confronting certain matters which it ordinarily disregards. As a place of entertainment the Cocoanut Grove was garish but innocuous and on the whole useful. It has been called "the poor man's Ritz"; for years people had been going there to have a good time and had got what they were looking for. With the naive shock customary in such cases, the city has now discovered that these people were not receiving the minimum protection in their pleasures to which they were entitled and which they supposed they were receiving.

The name of the night club suggests the kind of decorations that cluttered it; the 6
public supposed that the law required them to be fireproof; actually they burned like so much celluloid. The laws relating to them were ambiguous and full of loopholes; such as they were, they were not enforced. The public supposed that an adequate number of exits were required and that periodic inspections were made; they were not. There were too few exits for the customary crowds, one was concealed, another could not be opened, and panic-stricken people piled up before the rest and died there by the score. The public supposed that laws forbidding overcrowding were applied to night clubs and were enforced; on the night of the fire the place was packed so full that movement was almost impossible, and it had been just as crowded at least once a week throughout the years of its existence. The public supposed that laws requiring safe practice in electric wiring and machinery were enforced; the official investigations have shown that the wiring was installed by unlicensed

electricians, that a number of people had suspected it was faulty, and that in fact officials had notified the club that it was violating the law and had threatened to take action—but had not carried out the threat. Above all, the public supposed that an adequate building code taking into account the realities of modern architecture and modern metropolitan life established certain basic measures of protection. It has now learned that the Boston building code is a patched makeshift based on the conditions of 1907, and that though a revision which would modernize it was made in 1937, various reasons have held up the adoption of that revision for five years.

These facts have been established by five official investigations, one of them made by the Commonwealth of Massachusetts in an obvious expectation that the municipal authorities of Boston would find convincing reasons to deal gently with themselves. They have turned up other suggestive facts. The Cocoanut Grove was once owned by a local racketeer, who was murdered in the routine of business. The present owners were so expertly concealed behind a facade of legal figureheads that for twenty-four hours after the fire the authorities were not sure that they knew who even one of them was and two weeks later were not sure that they knew them all. An intimation that financial responsibility was avoided by a technically contrived bankruptcy has not yet been followed up as I write this, and other financial details are still lost in a maze of subterfuges. It is supposed that some of the club's employees had their wagescale established by terrorism. Investigators have encountered, but so far have not published, the customary free-list and lists of those entitled to discounts. Presumably such lists contemplated the usual returns in publicity and business favors; presumably also they found a use in the amenities of regulation. Names and business practices of the underworld have kept cropping up in all the investigations, and it is whispered that the reason why the national government has been conducting one of them is the presence at the club of a large amount of liquor on which the latest increase in revenue taxes ought to have been paid but somehow had not been.

In short, Boston has been reminded, hardly for the first time, that laxity in municipal responsibility can be made to pay a profit and that there can be a remunerative partnership between the amusement business and the underworld. A great many Bostonians, now writing passionate letters to their newspapers and urging on their legislators innumerable measures of reform, have gone farther than that. They conclude that one of the reasons why the modernized building code has not been adopted is the fact that there are ways of making money from the looser provisions of the old code. They suppose that one reason why gaps and loopholes in safety regulations are maintained is that they are profitable. They suppose that one reason why laws and regulations can be disregarded with impunity is that some of those charged with the duty of enforcing them make a living from not enforcing them. They suppose that some proprietors of night clubs find that buying immunity is cheaper than obeying safety regulations and that they are able to find enforcement agents who will sell it. They suppose that civil irresponsibility in Boston can be related to the fact that a lot of people make money from it.

But the responsibility cannot be shouldered off on a few small grafters and a few   9
underworld characters who have established business relations with them, and it
would be civic fatuousness to seek expiation for the murder of five hundred citizens in the passage of some more laws. The trouble is not lack of laws but public
acquiescence; the damaging alliance is not with the underworld but with a communal reverence of what is probably good for business. Five hundred deaths in a single
hour seem intolerable, but the city has never dissented at all to a working alliance
between its financial interests and its political governors—a partnership which daily
endangers not five hundred but many thousand citizens. Through Boston, as through
every other metropolis, run many chains of interests which might suffer loss if regulations for the protection of the public's health and life were rigorously enforced.
They are sound and enlightened regulations, but if they should be enforced then
retail sales, bank clearings, and investment balances might possibly fall off. The corner grocery and the downtown department store, the banks and the business
houses, the labor unions and the suburban housewife are all consenting partners in
a closely calculated disregard of public safety.

Since the system is closely calculated it usually works, it kills only a few at a time,   10
mostly it kills gradually over a period of years. Sometimes however it runs into another mathematical certainty and then it has to be paid for in blocks of five hundred lives. At such times the community experiences just such an excess of guilt as
Boston is feeling now, uncomfortably realizing that the community itself is the perpetrator of wanton murder. For the responsibility is the public's all along and the
certain safeguard—a small amount of alertness, civic courage, and willingness to
lose some money—is always in the public's hands. That means not the mayor's
hands, but yours and mine.

It is an interesting thing to hold up to the light at a moment when millions of   11
Americans are fighting to preserve, among other things, the civic responsibility of a
self-governing people. It suggests that civilians who are not engaged in the war effort, and who feel intolerably abased because they are not, could find serviceable
ways to employ their energies. They can get to work chipping rust and rot from the
mechanisms of local government. The rust and rot are increasing because people
who can profit from their increase count on our looking toward the war, not toward them. Your town may have a police force of no more than four and its amusement business may be confined to half a dozen juke joints, but some percentage of
both may have formed a partnership against your interests under cover of the war.

Certainly the town has a sewage system, a garbage dump, fire traps, a rudimen-   12
tary public health code, ordinances designed to protect life, and a number of Joe
Doakes who can make money by juggling the relationship among them. Meanwhile
the ordinary hazards of peace are multiplied by the conditions of war, carelessness
and preoccupation increase, and the inevitable war pestilence is gathering to spring.
The end-products do not look pleasant when they are seen clearly, especially when
a community realizes that it has killed five hundred people who did not need to die.

▪ 7 ▪

Taking Notes

Have copying machines and computers put an end to note-taking? Some sources, such as newspaper articles, are difficult to copy clearly; others contain only one or two useful sentences and are not worth the expense of copying. Still, there are other reasons why taking notes remains an important skill.

When you have found and copied some useful sources, what do you do with the stack of photocopied pages or the excerpts typed into your laptop computer? So far, you have only moved the raw materials from the library to your desk. How do you turn them into an essay? In order to take inventory and start working on your *essay* (as distinguished from your *research*), you must find the important points and discard the irrelevancies that surround them. Of course, you could plan the organization of your essay by cutting up each page and sorting the vital passages into separate piles; but unless you identify each source clearly on each bit of cut-up paper, you can easily lose track of its origin.

It therefore makes sense to *take notes as part of the research process* and to express as much of the information as you can *in your own words*. At the same time, you should make copies of the most important passages, so that you will have the originals to refer to if your notes let you down. *There is no substitute for good notes.*

TAKING GOOD NOTES

The following guidelines should help your note-taking:

1. **Try to complete your survey of the library's resources and work out a preliminary bibliography before you start to make copies or take notes.**

   You will get a good idea of what materials are available and the probable extent of your research, and you will also make sure that your preferred topic is a practical one. If you start taking notes before you are certain of your precise focus, you may waste a good deal of time. You may discover, for example, that there is very little documented information about the gunfight at the O.K. Corral, and decide to shift your focus to Wyatt Earp. Or the amount of technical material about Lindbergh's flight in the *Spirit of St. Louis* might overwhelm you, with the result that you switch to Lindbergh's opposition to America's entry into World War II.

2. **Use paraphrase and summary rather than quotation.**

   If you copy down sentence after sentence, word for word from your source onto index cards or a pad, or into a computer, you might as well save time and photocopy the page. Remember that using the language of the original author will make it more difficult for you to shift to your own writing style. If your first draft reads like an anthology of cannibalized quotations, then you will find it hard to make your final essay coherent and intelligible. The pasted-together sources will still be in control. Take the trouble *now* to master each new idea by putting it in your own words.

3. **Make sure that your notes make sense.**

   Remember that you will have read a vast number of similar pages by the time you begin to organize your essay and that you won't remember everything. In your notes, spell out the author's exact meaning.

4. **Include a certain number of facts to serve as your supporting evidence.**

   It is not enough to say that "X's father lost his job." What was his job? Why did he lose it? What did he do instead? Later, you may find that these details are irrelevant and will not fit into the shape of your essay; but if you do need supporting evidence, you will find it easier to look in your notes than to go back to the library.

5. **Differentiate your own ideas from those that you are paraphrasing.**

   Taking notes is often an intellectually stimulating experience, probably because it requires so much concentration and because your reading rate is slowed down. You may have plenty of comments about the source that you are paraphrasing. As you develop your own ideas and include them in your notes, be careful to separate them from those of your sources. Later, you will want to know exactly which ideas were yours and which were your source's. Using square brackets [like these] around your own ideas is a good way of making this distinction.

6. **Keep a running record of page references.**

In your essay, you will have to cite the correct page number for *each* reference, not an approximate guess. It is not enough to write "pp. 285–91" at the top of the note card or page. Three weeks later, or three hours later, how will you remember on *which* pages you found the point that you want to cite in your essay? If you are writing a lengthy set of notes that paraphrase your source, make a slash and insert a new page number to indicate exactly where you turned the page. Recording page numbers is especially important for *quotations*. Of course, it is vital that you immediately put quotation marks around all quotations.

7. **Keep a master list of the sources in your preliminary bibliography, assigning a code number or symbol to each one.**

As you take notes, use an abbreviation or code number to identify each new source. When you begin a new card or sheet, you won't have to repeat all the basic information.

Guidelines for Taking Good Notes

1. Try to complete your survey of the library's resources and work out a preliminary bibliography before you start to make copies or take notes.
2. Use paraphrase and summary rather than quotation.
3. Make sure that your notes make sense.
4. Include a certain number of facts to serve as your supporting evidence.
5. Differentiate your own ideas from those that you are paraphrasing.
6. Keep a running record of page references.
7. Keep a master list of the sources in your preliminary bibliography, assigning a code number or symbol to each one.

Using Note Cards—One Fact per Card

The traditional method of taking notes is to write *a single fact or piece of information on one three-by-five-inch index card.* These single-note cards are easily organized by topic into stacks; they can also be left at home when you go back to the library. Index cards, however, can stray from the pile and become lost. A stack of cards should be kept under control with a sturdy rubber band.

Certain topics lend themselves to note cards, topics that require the collection of small, fragmentary bits of information, like facts or brief descriptions, which fit easily on an index card. Eight-by-ten-inch cards or sheets of paper (written by hand or on the computer) may be more practical for an

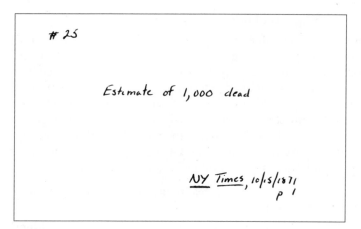

Figure 7-1. One-Fact-per-Card Method

abstract topic that depends on complex sources, with each one discussed at length. If you are typing notes into a computer, put a page break between each fact or each topic, so you can print out a separate sheet for each piece of information.

> *Whether you write on small cards or long sheets, make sure that you write on one side only. Whether you write by hand or use a computer, be careful to label each separate unit of information with its exact source and page number, using abbreviations, symbols, or numbers.*

One student, taking notes for an essay describing the 1871 fire that devastated Chicago, used the one-fact-per-card method shown in Figure 7-1. The empty space left on this card may seem wasteful, but the method enables the writer, later on, to place all the cards that refer to the category *casualties* in a single pile. If the card contained information relating to two different categories—like *casualties* and *looting*—the same card would have to be placed in two separate piles, which would defeat the purpose of the organizational system. Notice that, to keep track of all the notes, the writer has assigned a number (#25) to the card. Of course, the source *and* page number are included.

Notes Grouped by Topic

A second student used a more sophisticated system combining note-taking and preliminary organization. Early in the note-taking process, the student decided that at least one card would be devoted only to notes about *fire-fighting*. Thereafter, every time the student came across a new point about fire-fighting—no matter what the source—it was added to that card. Students who take notes using a computer can start a new file for each topic or simply establish several topics within the same file, and scroll through searching

10

fire fighting

all engines and hose carts in city come (_NYT_, 10/9, p 5)

water station on fire, with no water to put out
  small fires (Hall, p. 228)

all engines out there; fire too big to stop (_NYT_, 10/6,
                                                    p 5)

fire department "demoralized"; bad fire previous
night; men were drinking afterwards; fire
marshal "habitually drunk" (_NYT_, 10/23, p 2)

Figure 7-2. Notes Grouped by Topic

for the topic name as each new piece of information is added. Such organization depends on making a list, either written or mental, of possible categories or note topics.

Because the notes in Figure 7-2 are grouped according to topic, this student will find organizing an outline easier than will the first student. But preliminary categorizing during the note-taking stage is practical only with
relatively short items. A lengthy presentation of a theory can ruin this tidy
system by forcing the note-taker to devote card after card to a single idea
from a single source. (Notice that none of the sources on the "fire-fighting"
card seems to offer any lengthy opinions about the fire.) For this reason,
when you organize notes by topic, you may prefer to use long sheets of paper or a computer in order to be prepared for any kind of material and to
have enough space.

Notes Grouped by Source

Instead of putting one point on each card or one topic on each card, a third
student chose to use _one source per sheet_. This system, shown in Figure 7-3, "uses
up" one source at a time and produces a long sheet of notes in which the information is presented in the order of its appearance in the source.

The disadvantage of this method is that it doesn't encourage you to start categorizing. This student, however, _numbered each item_ on the sheet and also gave
each sheet _a code letter_. When the time comes to synthesize these notes into
paragraph topics, the student can establish a category dealing with, say, _food
supplies_, find the relevant references to that topic, and place the code numbers
under that heading. While writing the first draft, the writer will find H-11 under the heading _food supplies_ and have immediate access to information about
the price of bread after the fire. (For further explanation of this process, see
Chapter 8, p. 335).

Source H

NY Times, 10/15/1871, p. 1

1. city normal again
2. still martial rule; Gen. Sheridan in charge
3. citizens working at night to watch for new outbreak of fire
4. newspapers "moved" to other locations
5. estimate 1,000 dead
6. earlier reports of looting and loss of life not exaggerated
7. waterworks won't open till next day
8. two-thirds of city still using candlelight
9. suffering mostly among "humbler classes"
10. businessmen are "buoyant"
11. bread is 8¢
12. saloons are closed at 9:00 P.M. for one week

Figure 7-3. Notes Grouped by Source

TAKING NOTES FROM ABSTRACT SOURCES

As the sample notes suggest, research on the Chicago fire uncovered mostly factual information about incidents that occurred during and after the catastrophe. The notes are therefore brief, factual summaries. When the source consists of generalizations and evidence used to develop complex ideas, the note-taker must often struggle to understand and paraphrase abstract thinking.

To illustrate the difficulties, here is a brief extract from *Victorian Cities*, by Asa Briggs. Assume that the book is being consulted for an essay on "The City One Hundred Years Ago."

The industrial city was bound to be a place of problems. Economic individualism and common civic purpose were difficult to reconcile. The priority of industrial discipline in shaping all human relations was bound to make other aspects of life seem secondary. A high rate of industrial investment might mean not only a low rate of consumption and a paucity of social investment but a total indifference to social costs. Overcrowding was one problem: displacement was another. There were parts of Liverpool with a density of 1,200 persons to the acre in 1884: rebuilding might entail the kind of difficulties which were set out in a verse in *The Builder* of 1851:

> Who builds? Who builds? Alas, ye poor!
> If London day by day "improves,"
> Where shall ye find a friendly door,
> When every day a home removes?

The paragraph may seem hard to understand on first reading because Briggs is developing his image of the industrial city through *a series of abstract words combined into phrases*—"economic individualism," "common civic purpose," "industrial discipline," and "low rate of consumption."

These difficult abstractions, typical of the social sciences, are included in the paragraph as if everyone could easily understand them. Fortunately, the essential point is repeated in several different ways and supported by some straightforward facts about the density of population in Liverpool. The passage ends with quite a different kind of evidence: a verse-quotation suggesting that, earlier in the century, people were already aware of the dangers of unlimited expansion.

The figures below show attempts at note-taking based on Briggs's paragraph. In Figure 7-4, the researcher has made a point of paraphrasing, rather than copying the original phrasing, and thus has avoided the danger of quoting the author's words without acknowledgment. The researcher's brief comments in square brackets, clearly distinguished from the notes on Briggs, suggest some points for development in the research essay.

If you don't expect to refer to Briggs in any detail, making a note that summarizes his basic point more briefly would be sufficient, as in Figure 7-5.

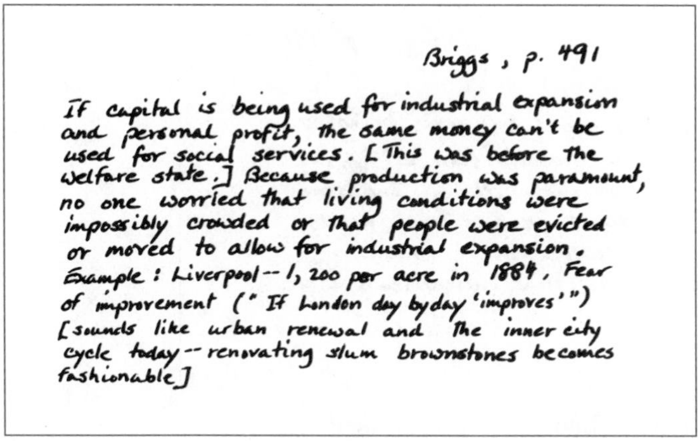
Briggs, p. 491

If capital is being used for industrial expansion and personal profit, the same money can't be used for social services. [This was before the welfare state.] Because production was paramount, no one worried that living conditions were impossibly crowded or that people were evicted or moved to allow for industrial expansion. Example: Liverpool -- 1,200 per acre in 1884. Fear of improvement ("If London day by day 'improves'") [sounds like urban renewal and the inner city cycle today -- renovating slum brownstones becomes fashionable]

Figure 7-4. Note A: Effective Summary, Using Paraphrase

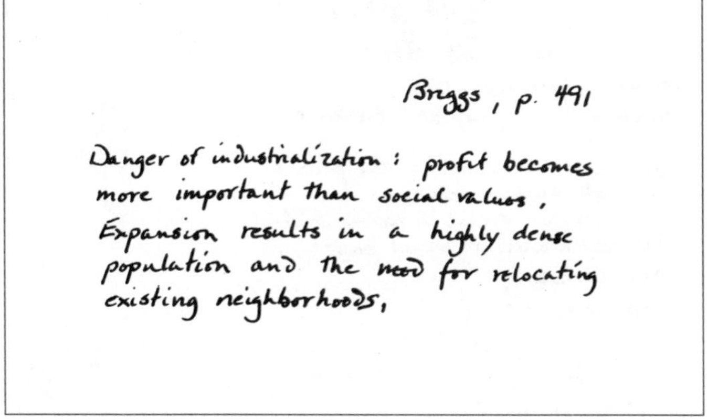
Briggs, p. 491

Danger of industrialization: profit becomes more important than social values. Expansion results in a highly dense population and the need for relocating existing neighborhoods.

Figure 7-5. Note B: Effective Short Summary

In taking good notes, everything depends on achieving a clear understanding of the author's meaning. Figure 7-6, however, suggests that the researcher did not bother to puzzle out the complexities of the paragraph and, instead, tried a few wild guesses. With the possible exception of the first sentence, none of these points can be correctly attributed to Briggs, whose meaning has been entirely distorted. On the other hand, in Figure 7-7, the attempt to play it safe by copying out the phrases verbatim is equally unsuccessful. Although this information is beautifully laid out in outline form, with quotation marks carefully inserted, there is no evidence that the researcher has understood a word of Briggs's paragraph. Moreover, the outline format makes it hard to understand the relationship among these concepts. When the time comes to include a reference to Briggs in the research essay, this student will have no idea how the phrases fit together.

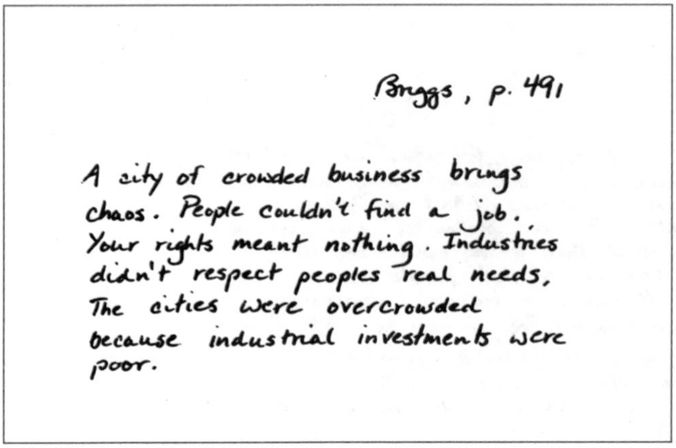

> Briggs, p. 491
>
> A city of crowded business brings chaos. People couldn't find a job. Your rights meant nothing. Industries didn't respect peoples real needs. The cities were overcrowded because industrial investments were poor.

Figure 7-6. Note C: Distortion of the Source

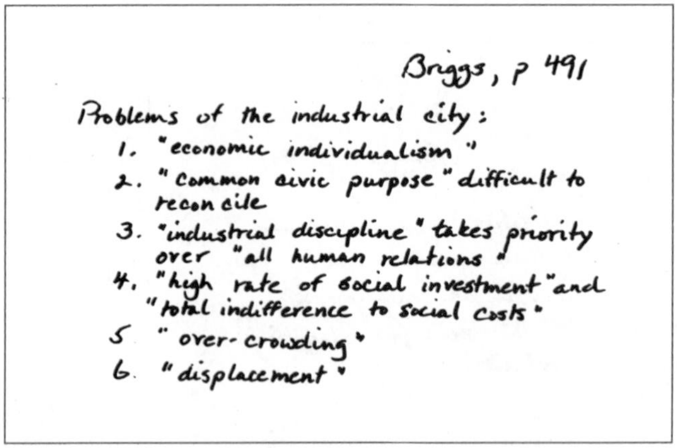

> Briggs, p 491
>
> Problems of the industrial city:
>   1. "economic individualism"
>   2. "common civic purpose" difficult to reconcile
>   3. "industrial discipline" takes priority over "all human relations"
>   4. "high rate of social investment" and "total indifference to social costs"
>   5. "over-crowding"
>   6. "displacement"

Figure 7-7. Note D: Meaningless List

Even when a reading is much less abstract and densely argued than the excerpt from Briggs, it is possible to distort the author's meaning by selecting the wrong points to emphasize in your notes. Here are two paragraphs from *Shakespeare of London,* by Marchette Chute, followed by sample notes for an essay on "Shakespeare's Education as a Playwright."

Apart from teaching him Latin, Stratford grammar school taught Shakespeare nothing at all. It did not teach him mathematics or any of the natural sciences. It did not teach him history, unless a few pieces of information about ancient events strayed in through Latin quotations. It did not teach him geography, for the first (and most inadequate) textbook on geography did not appear until the end of the century, and maps and atlases were rare even in university circles. It did not teach him modern languages, for when a second language was taught at a grammar school it was invariably Greek.

What Shakespeare learned about any of these subjects he learned for himself later, in London. London was the one great storehouse in England of living, contemporary knowledge and in that city an alert and intelligent man could find out almost anything he wanted to know. It was in London, for instance, that Shakespeare learned French; and French was taught by Frenchmen who worked in competition with each other and used oral conversational methods that were designed to get colloquial French into the student's head as quickly as possible.

In Figure 7-8, the note-taker has made the essential contrast between Stratford and London, and the generalization is clearly distinguished from the evidence that Chute cites to support it. In Figure 7-9, the focus shifts from what Shakespeare did or did not learn to the deficiencies of schools in sixteenth-century England.

What the student is missing in Note F is the contrast between an ordinary, unsophisticated school in rural England and the resources available to an

Chute, p. 17

Most of the basic knowledge that Shakespeare needed to write his plays was learned in London, not in school.

Evidence: grammar school taught no math, natural science, history, geography, modern languages

Figure 7-8. Note E: Summarizing the Main Point, with Supporting Facts

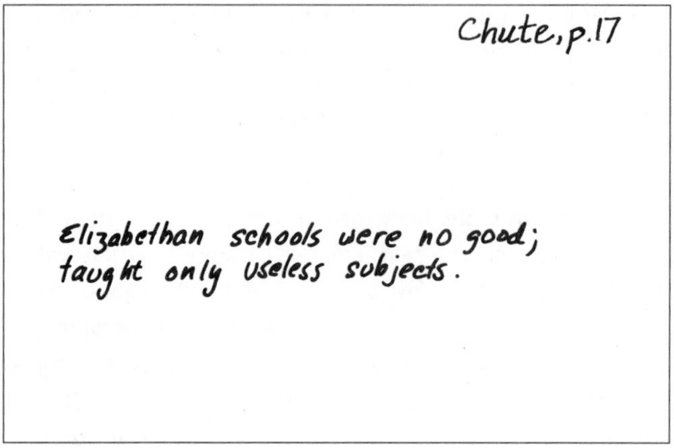

Figure 7-9. Note F: False Emphasis/Context Disregarded

inquiring young man (no longer a school boy) in the capital city. The note-taker has ignored the *context* of the two paragraphs and the material that surrounds them in the original source. Chute has previously explained the advantages that Shakespeare derived from learning Latin at school, and is now listing what he was unable to learn (partly because books and other teaching materials had not yet been developed). Chute is *not* condemning Stratford grammar school, but preparing the reader for the burst of learning that would occur when Shakespeare arrived in London. The context for the paper—Shakespeare's development—is ignored in favor of a narrower focus on the inaccurate statement that he was taught nothing at all.

EXERCISE 24: EVALUATING NOTES

In 1937, the German airship *Hindenburg* caught fire near Lakehurst, New Jersey, killing thirty-six people. Two of the many eyewitness accounts were by Leonhard Adelt and Margaret Mather, both passengers on the ship. Read these two passages (which begin on p. 329) and then evaluate the sets of notes that follow them prepared by students writing about the *Hindenburg* disaster. Consider the following criteria:

1. Does one get a good sense of the experience from reading the notes?
2. Which sets of notes are reliable? complete?
3. Do any of the notes omit anything important?
4. Which notes quote excessively?
5. Does the note-taker recognize that the two sources often confirm each other's testimony, and indicate when they agree?
6. Would the notes make sense to someone who had not read the original?
7. Which sets of notes would you prefer to work from if you were writing an essay on the *Hindenburg*?

Leonhard Adelt's Account

With my wife I was leaning out of a window on the promenade deck. Suddenly there occurred a remarkable stillness. The motors were silent, and it seemed as though the whole world was holding its breath. One heard no command, no call, no cry. The people we saw seemed suddenly stiffened. 1

I could not account for this. Then I heard a light, dull detonation from above, no louder than the sound of a beer bottle being opened. I turned my gaze toward the bow and noticed a delicate rose glow, as though the sun were about to rise. I understood immediately that the airship was aflame. There was but one chance for safety—to jump out. The distance from the ground at that moment may have been 120 feet. For a moment I thought of getting bed linen from the corridor in order to soften our leap, but in the same instant, the airship crashed to the ground with terrific force. Its impact threw us from the window to the stair corridor. The tables and chairs of the reading room crashed about and jammed us in like a barricade. 2

"Through the window!" I shouted to my fellow passengers, and dragged my wife with me to our observation window. 3

Reality ceased with one stroke, as though fate in its cruelty was yet compassionate enough to withdraw from its victims the consciousness of their horror. I do not know, and my wife does not know, how we leaped from the airship. The distance from the ground may have been 12 or 15 feet. I distinctly felt my feet touch the soft sand and grass. We collapsed to our knees, and the impenetrable darkness of black oil clouds, shot through with flames, enveloped us. We had to let go of each other's hands in order to make our way through the confusion of hot metal pieces and wires. We bent the hot metal apart with our bare hands without feeling pain. 4

We freed ourselves and ran through a sea of fire. It was like a dream. Our bodies had no weight. They floated like stars through space. 5

Margaret Mather's Account

I was leaning out of an open window in the dining saloon with many others including the young aviator, who was taking photographs. He told me that he had taken eighty during the trip. When there were mysterious sounds from the engines I glanced at him for reassurance. 1

At that moment we heard the dull muffled sound of an explosion. I saw a look of incredulous consternation on his face. Almost instantly the ship lurched and I was hurled a distance of fifteen or twenty feet against an end wall. 2

I was pinned against a projecting bench by several Germans who were thrown after me. I couldn't breathe and thought I should die suffocated, but they all jumped up. 3

Then the flames blew in, long tongues of flame, bright red and very beautiful. 4

My companions were leaping up and down amid the flames. The lurching of the ship threw them repeatedly against the furniture and the railing, where they cut their hands and faces against the metal trimmings. They were streaming with blood. I saw a number of men leap from the windows, but I sat just where I had fallen, holding the lapels of my coat across my face, feeling the flames light on my back, my 5

hat, my hair, trying to beat them out, watching the horrified faces of my companions as they leaped up and down.

Just then a man—I think the man who exclaimed "Mein Gott" as we left the   6
earth—detached himself from the leaping forms, and threw himself against a railing
(arms and legs spread wide) with a loud terrible cry of "Es ist das Ende."

I thought so too but I continued to protect my eyes. I was thinking that it was   7
like a scene from a medieval picture of hell. I was waiting for the crash landing.

Suddenly I heard a loud cry: "Come out, lady!" I looked and we were on the ground.   8

Student A

All of a sudden there was complete silence and not a sound from the
motors of the airship. Everybody in the airship "stiffened." Leonhard Adelt suddenly "heard a dull detonation from above, no louder than a beer bottle being
opened." L.A. knew that the "airship was aflame." The only way to save one's life
was to jump. This meant the jump was for 120 feet. All of a sudden, "the airship
crashed to the ground with terrific" speed. The force was so high that Margaret
Mather "was hurled a distance of fifteen to twenty feet against an end wall."

Student B

"At that moment we heard the dull and muffled sound of an explosion.
Almost suddenly the ship lurched and I was hurled a distance of 15 or 20 feet
against an end wall." This is the beginning described by two passengers that
were on the Hindenburg of 1937. After a long voyage over the Atlantic and being
so close to their destiny, this was too much of a shock for them to handle. All
the passengers had to escape death. Some were fortunate, others weren't. "I was
pinned against a projecting bench by several Germans who were thrown after
me. I couldn't breathe, and thought I should die, suffocated, but they all jumped
up." Everyone ran for their life.

Student C

Adelt: "The motors were silent"

Mather: "Dull muffled sound of an explosion"

Adelt: "I turned my gaze toward the bow and noticed a rose glow. . . ."

Mather: "The ship lurched and I was hurled a distance of fifteen or twenty feet
against an end wall."

Adelt: "Its impact threw us from the window to the stair corridor."

Mather: "Then the flames blew in"

Mather: "I saw a number of men leap from the windows."

Adelt: "We leaped from the airship."

Student D

before crash:

Adelt: "The motors were silent" "I heard a light, dull detonation from above. . . ."

"I turned my gaze toward the bow and noticed a delicate rose glow"

Mather: "Mysterious sounds from the engine" . . . "dull muffled sound of an explosion" . . . "then the flames blew in, long tongues of flame, bright red and very beautiful"

after crash:

Adelt: "'Through the window!' I shouted to my fellow passengers. . . ." ". . . how we leaped from the airship. The distance from the ground may have been 12 or 15 feet," . . . "impenetrable darkness of black oil clouds, shot through with flames" . . . "a sea of fire."

Mather: ". . . where they cut their hands and faces against the metal trimmings. They were streaming with blood."

Student E

"I turned my gaze toward the bow and noticed a delicate rose glow, as though the sun were about to rise." The blimp catches on fire: the only means of escape is jumping to the ground. Distance from the ground approximately 12 or 15 feet when couple jumped out of "airship." People "beat the hot metal apart with our bare hands without feeling pain." How mind works when in life and death situation. No pain. People had to run through fire one at a time.

Mather: "mysterious sounds from the engine." She was leaning out of the dining saloon, heard sounds of explosion. People thrown 15 or 20 feet after hearing explosion. Flames came into room after people thrown. "lurching of ship threw them repeatedly across furniture and the railings."

Student F

There was an inexplicable silence followed by a "light, dull detonation from above, no louder than the sound of a beer bottle being opened." Then it was discovered that the airship was on fire looking like "the sun were about to rise." There was the realization that the only chance for survival was to abandon the ship. By the time the decision to jump and the action itself was implemented, the ship had crashed (from 120 feet). Upon impact, everything in the ship (chairs, tables, people) was tossed about. Reality became suspended "as though fate in its cruelty was yet compassionate enough to withdraw from its victims the consciousness of their horror."

EXERCISE 25: TAKING NOTES ON TWO TOPICS

Reread the three articles dealing with the Cocoanut Grove fire of 1942 at the end of Chapter 6. Head one group of cards or one sheet of paper "The Causes of the Fire," and take a set of notes on that topic. Head another group of cards or sheet of paper "The Fire's Intensity and Speed," and take a second set of notes on the second topic. Each set of notes should make use of all three sources.

EXERCISE 26: TAKING NOTES ON THREE TOPICS

Assume that you are doing research on the Indian Wars and that you have come across the following source in the library. After doing a preliminary evaluation of the passage, take a set of notes for an essay entitled "The Native American Ideal of Honor," a second set of notes for an essay entitled "War Atrocities," and a third set of notes for an essay entitled "White Attitudes toward Native Americans."

from *KILLING CUSTER*
James Welch

Most tribal battles involved a lot of skirmishing, a lot of coup counting, with very few casualties. Indians were not out to annihilate each other, but to exact revenge or cover themselves with war honors. In most instances, it was better to humiliate the enemy than to kill him. A Blackfeet account tells of a party of horse raiders who stole into an enemy camp one night and made off with some buffalo runners. One of the raiders found a sentry sleeping at the base of a ledge near the edge of camp. The warrior pissed on the sentry from the ledge, then stole off into the darkness. This feat was talked about in the Blackfeet camps for years to come. The Blackfeet got off with the horses, and the drenched sentry had to explain to his chiefs what happened. It was almost better than counting coup. It gave the whole tribe a chuckle.

Of course, warfare was more serious than that. It was important to lift the enemy's hair, both as a warning to the enemy and as a morale-booster to the scalper, his party, and other tribesmen. Nothing delighted a waiting camp more than to see scalps on the lances of returning warriors. These scalps were passed around, talked about, laughed at, sometimes thrown into the fire or given to the dogs in disdain. Often the hair decorated a lodge or was sewn onto a war shirt. White men's hair was taken but was less desirable because it was usually short. Some of the white men were balding and weren't worth scalping. But scalping was an institution among the Plains tribes. A scalp was a trophy of war, just as it became for the whites.

Torture, and the mutilation of bodies dead and alive, was, and is, more problematic, if only because it is odious to civilized society. Throughout the years, those cultures which have "seen the light" have been horrified by the desecration of bodies committed by barbarians of other cultures. We think of the Nazis in World

War II who justified torture and mutilation of live bodies for "scientific" purposes. The communists in Russia, especially under Stalin, committed similar atrocities on ethnic groups. The Khmer Rouge beheaded and chopped the limbs from innocent people and left them by the thousands in the killing fields of Cambodia. The military did the same in El Salvador. Thousands of Moskito Indians died in such a horrible fashion. African leaders, in their beribboned military costumes and with their weapons supplied by the United States, Russia, France, and Israel, continue to kill and mutilate their tribal enemies.

European tribes beheaded their foes, posting the heads along roads or at the   4
town gates as a grisly warning to those who would oppose them. The Catholic Church in Europe, especially Spain, during the Inquisition tortured and mutilated those who it thought were possessed by the devil—or those it simply wanted to get rid of for political reasons. The Puritans in America burned, crushed, and drowned people almost gratuitously in their effort to root out witchery. Thousands, probably millions, of people have been treated in a similar fashion by the religious right of all cultures.

Soldiers who go to war commit unspeakable acts to their enemies. Homer tells   5
us that in the Trojan War, Achilles dragged Hector's mutilated body behind his chariot for twelve days. From the time of the Slaughter of the Innocents to My Lai in Vietnam, war has created a callousness toward human life to such a degree that torture and mutilation have become accepted practices. Witness the Serbs in their treatment of the Muslims, torturing and mutilating men, raping women to death— all in the name of ethnic and religious purity. Virtually all warfare has been conducted for such contrived principles as ethnic and religious purity.

On November 29, 1864, a former Methodist preacher and Civil War officer,   6
Colonel John Chivington, led two regiments of Colorado militia in a dawn attack on a sleeping camp of Southern Cheyennes at Sand Creek. This group of Indians was led by Black Kettle, who survived the attack only to be killed four years later in another dawn surprise led by General George A. Custer on the Washita River in Oklahoma.

The reason given for Chivington's attack was a familiar one. Indians had been   7
raiding, stealing horses and cattle, killing settlers. Whether the attack by Chivington's hundred-day volunteers caught the right Indians is not even debatable. They did not. It has been stated that these Colorado volunteers' enlistment was about up and they wanted some action. Because of their inefficiency in punishing Indians they were derisively called the "Bloodless" 3rd Cavalry.

Black Kettle had been given an American flag at a treaty council in 1861 by the   8
Commissioner of Indian Affairs. The chief had been told at that time that as long as the flag flew over his village his people would be safe.

It is known that some of Chivington's junior officers reminded him of this   9
promise. Evan S. Connell, in *Son of the Morning Star,* quotes the violent Chivington as replying: "I have come to kill Indians, and believe it is right and honorable to use any means under God's heaven to kill Indians!" He is reported to have added: "Scalps are what we are after. . . . I long to be wading in gore!"

And soon he was. Even after Black Kettle himself came out of his lodge waving   10
the American flag, Chivington's troopers shot men, women, and children indiscrim-
inately. There are many accounts, not only those of Indian survivors but also those
of the troopers themselves, of soldiers taking deliberate aim at fleeing children. A
Major Scott Anthony remembered the murder of a three-year-old: "I saw one man
get off his horse at a distance of about seventy-five yards and draw up his rifle and
fire. He missed the child. Another man came up and said, 'Let me try the son of a
bitch. I can hit him.' He got down off his horse, kneeled down, and fired at the little
child, but he missed him. A third man came up and made a similar remark, and
fired, and the little fellow dropped."

When the killing ended, soldiers went from body to body, scalping them, cutting   11
off ears and fingers to get at jewelry, cutting out the genitals of men, women, and
children, arranging the bodies in suggestive postures. A Lieutenant James Connor
stated in testimony that he did not find a single body that had not been mutilated.
He went on: "I also heard of numerous instances in which men had cut out the private parts of females and stretched them over the saddlebows and wore them over
their hats while riding in the ranks."

By way of justification for such acts, several men said they found scalps, which   12
they identified as belonging to whites by the color of the hair, hanging from lodge-
poles, a couple of them fresh. "The skin and flesh attached to the hair appeared to
be yet quite moist," one said. It doesn't appear that there were many of these scalps,
but by the time the militia got back to Denver the number had grown to dozens of
white scalps—as well as a blanket woven from white women's hair.

Chivington's troop's last act of heroism was to display a hundred Indian scalps on   13
the stage of a Denver theater. They were greeted by thunderous applause. The
Bloodless 3rd became celebrated as the "Bloody Thirdsters."

The Indians committed their share of atrocities, of torture and mutilation. There   14
had been many accounts in the eastern newspapers of such acts, but they were isolated, small instances, quickly forgotten in the bustle of the industrializing nation.
The frontier newspapers were more alarmed. These killings were happening too
close for comfort. In 1869, the *Helena Weekly Herald* reported: "That we are on
the verge of a general Indian outbreak no sensible man who understands the situation can deny. The pleasant and innocent amusement of butchering and scalping the
pale-faces is believed by some likely soon to begin in good earnest."

But the Plains Indians were equally outraged by the notion that an invasion force   15
of whites was seeking to conquer them, perhaps annihilate them, certainly take
their land, kill all their buffalo, and reduce them to prisoners on reservations where
they would be forced to deny their religion, their culture, their traditional methods
of supporting themselves—in short, take away their way of life as they had practiced it for centuries. They had learned at Sand Creek, the Marias, and the Washita
that the whites would stop at nothing to bend the Indians to their will. The arrogant invaders would not stop until the Indians were forced to adopt the ways of
the white man—or were executed.

▪8▪

Organizing and Writing the Research Essay

You should plan and write your research essay in exactly the same way that you would work on any other essay. Whatever the topic, you will probably start out with written notes—facts, ideas, comments, opinions—that serve as the raw materials for your synthesis. From these notes, you form a sequence of separate generalizations to be used as the focus of each of your paragraphs. These steps help you to work out the basic structure of your essay.

The difference between organizing the research essay and organizing the other essays that you have previously written comes from the unusually large quantity of *notes.* The term "notes" here refers to any of the products of your research, including your own *summaries* and *paraphrases, quotations, Xeroxed copies* of pages and articles, class *lecture notes,* and stories clipped from *newspapers,* as well as *your own ideas* about the topic.

TAKING INVENTORY AND DEVELOPING A LIST OF TOPICS

You search for ideas worth developing by reviewing all the major points that you have learned and thought about during your research. These ideas form the core of your essay.

335

You select the main ideas of your research by:

1. Carefully reading through all your notes;

2. Looking for and writing down any points that seem especially important to understanding and explaining your topic.

In other words, *you take a new set of notes from your old set.* In this way, you can reduce the accumulated mass of information to a more manageable size. The new list of generalizations can be rearranged, tried out in different versions, and eventually converted into an outline of topic sentences.

Organizing your essay involves:

- reading lists of notes,
- thinking about them,
- making new lists,
- deleting and adding items,
- rearranging the order.

You follow these steps until the list of topics—and the paragraphs of your essay—form a sequence that both makes sense and makes your point. This process is actually a more elaborate version of the synthesis that you practiced in Chapter 4.

Guidelines for Taking Inventory of Your Notes and Forming Your Paragraph Topics

1. *Do write down in any order* the important ideas that you find in your notes. At this point, the items don't have to be related to each other in sequence.

2. *Don't* try to *summarize* all your notes or even summarize each of your notes. At this point, you are working on a paragraph outline, not a summary of your research.

3. *Don't try to link* the ideas that you write down to specific sources. At this point, there is no special reason to place the names of the sources next to your new list of ideas; not every statement in your new list will be included in your essay. Later, you will decide which source to use in support of which topic sentence.

4. *Do think about your own reactions* to the information that you have collected. At this point, the many strands of your research begin to become the product of your own thinking. Now you are deciding what is worth writing about.

5. *Do use your own words.* At this point, even if you only jot down a phrase or a fragment, it should be *your* version of the source's idea. Even if the point has appeared in ten different articles (and has been noted on ten different index cards), you are now, in some sense, making it your own.

6. *Do evaluate your list* of important ideas that are worth writing about. At this point, notice which ideas are in the mainstream of your research, discussed by several of your sources, and which ones appear in only one or two sources. Consider whether you have enough evidence to support these ideas or whether you should exclude them from your master outline. Think about eliminating the ones that seem minor or remote from the topic. Remember to look for and combine similar statements. If you are developing an argument essay, make sure that each of the key points supporting your side, as well as your counterarguments to the opposition, is supported by your research.

7. *Do think about the sequence of ideas* on your final list and the possible *strategies* for organizing your essay. At this point, consider how these ideas relate to the topic with which you began your research:

- How does your list of ideas help to establish a thesis?

- Are you working with a collection of reasons? consequences? problems? dangers?

- What kind of essay are you writing: cause and effect? problem and solution? explanation of a procedure? evaluation of reasons for an argument?

If you are developing a historical or biographical topic:

- Did the event fall into distinct narrative stages?

- What aspects of the scene would an observer have noticed?

- Which of your subject's activities best reveals his or her personality?

If you are developing an argument:

- Does your issue lend itself to a cause-and-effect or a problem-and-solution essay?

- Do your main reasons require deductive or inductive support?

- Which are your most compelling arguments?

8. *Do arrange your list of topics* in a sequence that has meaning for you, carries out your strategy, and develops your thesis in a clear direction.

PLANNING A STRATEGY FOR ARGUMENT

In Chapter 1, you learned that most arguments are based on a combination of two kinds of logical reasoning:

- *deductive* reasoning: you provide a series of linked premises, based on assumptions that you and your reader share, that leads to a logical conclusion.
- *inductive* reasoning: you provide a range of evidence from which you construct a logical conclusion.

In practice, these two basic logical tools—the use of linked premises and the use of evidence—are often used to develop the most common patterns of argument: cause-and-effect and problem-and-solution.

The *cause-and-effect* essay establishes a causal linkage between two circumstances. The argumentative thesis is usually derived from answering the question "why?" Why is the high school dropout rate as high as it is today? Here are a few typical answers: because class sizes are too large; because students are poorly prepared to handle the work; because many students are foreign-born and can't speak English well; because local governments are not providing sufficient funding; because family life is breaking down, leaving students without support and discipline.

Clearly, there are many possible causes. If you try to give equal weight to every one of them, your essay will be long and unmanageable, with a thesis that pulls the reader in many contrary directions. If, however, you focus on only one cause, you run the risk of oversimplifying your argument. First, *consider whether a specific cause actually accounts for its effect and whether other circumstances also have a contributing influence.* Also consider which causes work together: the problem of class size is probably linked to—caused by—the problem of funding. Here you have a smaller cause-and-effect embedded within the larger one. It's these links that you have to point out in the deductive part of your argument.

Notice how most of the causes listed above lend themselves to *inductive support.*

You should expect to find factual evidence, including statistics, about class sizes, student preparedness, language difficulties, and diminished funding. (Whether or not that evidence supports your causal point about student dropouts will emerge from your research.) The last point on the list is more abstract; you would need to develop a series of deductive premises to make a strong causal linkage between the decline of family life and the incidence of high school dropouts.

What kinds of counterarguments would you have to anticipate and rebut? This may be a question of weight and emphasis. You believe that the poor educational environment, resulting from inadequate funding, makes it hard for students to learn so they drop out. While your research supports this thesis, you also find authorities who argue that students from strong family backgrounds perform well and stay in school even in periods of economic hardship. You must defend your preferred thesis, while acknowledging the more limited validity of your opponent's.

The *problem-and-solution* essay often incorporates the cause-and-effect essay in five stages:

1. *Establish that a problem exists.* Explain why it is a problem, and anticipate the negative consequences if nothing is done.

2. *Analyze the causes of the problem.* Here you can include a modified version of the cause-and-effect strategy: emphasize the major causes, but remind your reader that this is a complex issue, with a number of contributory influences working together. Provide some evidence, but not the full range of your research on causes.

3. *Assert the best solution.* Using the evidence of your research, demonstrate its benefits, and indicate how you would go about implementing it.

4. *Anticipate counterarguments and answer them.* Your research has turned up authorities who have recommended different solutions. What are the advantages and disadvantages of those solutions? Is your solution better? Why?

5. *Conclude in a spirit of accommodation.* Assert your solution once again, but also consider acknowledging the complexity of the problem and making room for some of your opponents' ideas. Sometimes the arguments on either side of an issue are too evenly balanced for certainty, and you need to find a solution within common ground.

As an example of such accommodation, here is the beginning of the last paragraph of Sanford Levinson's "The Court's Death Blow," a defense of assisted suicide in the context of the 1997 Supreme Court decision:

So, on balance, what should "liberals" believe in regard to assisted suicide? With fear and trembling, we should, as a political matter, support enhancing the choices available to people (including, ultimately, to us) as death begins to overtake life. But we should also recognize that people of undoubted good faith, committed no less than we are to protecting the vulnerable and to criticizing optimistic assumptions about "free markets" and "untrammeled choice," are on the other side of this issue. It is a true judgment call, balancing important autonomy interests against the possibility of exploitation.

ARRANGING THE ORDER OF TOPICS

At some point in the process of organizing your essay, your initial list of ideas becomes an outline. After you make new lists out of old ones, adding and deleting topics, you finally decide on a sequence that will correspond to the sequence of paragraphs in your essay. In a historical essay, the ordering principle is frequently time: the deployment of troops has to be described before the actual battle. In a personality portrait, dominant qualities will take precedence over minor quirks. Problems get described before solutions; causes before effects.

When you organize, you are determining priorities and prerequisites, based on the relationships between ideas. What does your reader need to know first? What information does your reader need in order to understand a second, more complex point? How does one idea lead into another?

In determining the sequence of reasons for an argument essay, first assess the degree of support that you have provided for each one through your research. At the same time, consider the strength of the arguments against each reason, as presented by your opponents. You will probably find that some points are naturally linked to others and that stronger, well-supported points take precedence over more tenuous ones. One rationale for your sequence is "most compelling" to "least compelling" reason. But a stronger rationale is "most fundamental" to "most complex" or "most peripheral." Your earlier arguments become a platform on which your later arguments can rest.

USING THE COMPUTER TO ORGANIZE YOUR ESSAY

One advantage of taking notes on a computer is that you can move the items around experimentally as you develop a new sequence of key ideas. Even if you have only a limited knowledge of word processing, you'll soon find it easy to pull a quotation or a paragraph out of your notes and add it to your outline, or to place a concrete example next to the general idea that it illustrates. A more sophisticated knowledge of "windows" and other software allows you to shift back and forth from one file to another or see two screens simultaneously, giving you even more flexibility in trying out different organizational strategies.

As you work with your notes on the computer, remember to *make a duplicate file of your notes,* keeping one file intact as a resource should you, later on, want to abandon a half-completed outline and start over or—worst case—lose your working file completely. Above all, *save your work at regular and frequent intervals*—and back up your files on a disk—or your notes and outline may suddenly dissolve into an empty screen.

The computer can make organizing, writing, and revising a research paper very easy. You can electronically manipulate notes, sentences, and paragraphs with miraculous speed. But you should apply the same thoughtfulness and care to working out your strategies for organization on the computer as you would if you were rearranging a stack of index cards and cutting and pasting a typed draft.

CROSS-REFERENCING

When you have developed a list of major topics that will roughly correspond to the paragraphs of your essay, you are ready to link your tentative outline to your research notes. Remember to:

- Leave plenty of space between the items on your outline; and
- Assign a number or a letter to each item.

Now, once again, *slowly reread all your research notes, this time keeping your list of topics in front of you.* Every time you come across a point in your notes that might be cited in support of a topic on your outline, immediately:

1. Place the number or letter of the topic in your outline next to the reference in your notes.

2. Place the source's name (and the number of the notecard, if you have used that system, or the page number of your notes) under the item on your outline.

For the system to work, you must complete both stages: notes must be keyed to the outline, and the outline must be keyed to each item in your research notes. The notes and the outline criss-cross each other; hence the term, *cross-referencing.*

To illustrate cross-referencing, here are three paragraph topics taken from an outline for an essay on the *Chicago Fire.* The outline for the essay is divided into three main sections: the *causes* of the fire, the *panic* during the fire, and *restoring order* after the fire. The three paragraph topics come from the last section of the outline. Figure 8-1 shows an excerpt from the notes for the essay. Both paragraph topics and notes have cross-references in the margins. Notice that, to avoid confusion, the paragraph topics have Roman numerals, and the notes have arabic numerals.

Paragraph Topics

IX. Feeding the homeless   G6/G7

X. Providing basic services   G4

XI. Protecting life and property   G3/G8

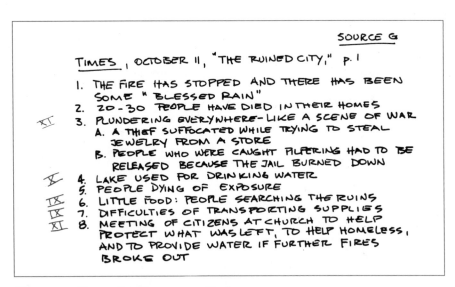

Figure 8-1. Notes: One Source per Card

Cross-referencing helps you to make full use of your notes and avoids time-consuming searches for references later on when you are writing the essay. At the end of this procedure:

- Your outline will have a list of sources to be cited for each main point, *and*

- Your research notes will have code numbers in most (but not necessarily all) of the margins.

Notice that a few items on the note card for Source G have no cross-references next to them. Some will be cross-referenced to other topics in this outline, and they have not yet been given their reference numbers. Items 2 and 5 in the notes, for example, would probably come under the heading of Casualties, in the section on panic during the fire. On the other hand, *not all the notes will necessarily be used in the essay;* some items will simply not fit into the topics chosen for the outline and will be discarded.

Figure 8-1 illustrates a method of note-taking that put all the material taken from a single source on a single card. Cross-referencing can also be used to organize *one-fact-per-card* notes, which can be sorted into piles corresponding to your topics. If you use this method, remember to put an identifying number on *each* card. In Figure 8-2, notice that:

- The code letter identifying the *source* (G) is in the upper right-hand corner.

- The code number identifying the *card* (32) is placed in the upper left-hand corner.

- The code number identifying the *outline topic* (XI) that this fact will be used to illustrate is indicated on the bottom of the card.

When you use the one-fact-per-card system, you put the relevant card number after each topic on your outline, but it is not necessary to identify the source.

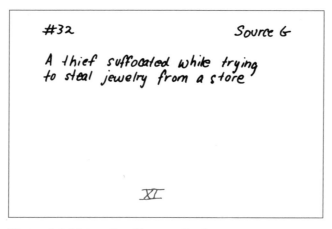

Figure 8-2. Notes: One Fact per Card

Paragraph Topics

IX. Feeding the homeless

X. Providing basic services

XI. Protecting life and property

#32, #38

The third kind of notes—*one-topic-per-card/sheet*—already incorporates the cross-referencing process by planning topics at the same time that notes are taken. Since you have already grouped your materials by topic, using a special card or sheet for each topic, you need only review your notes and shift those points (usually by cutting and pasting) that have inadvertently been placed under the wrong topic. In the next stage, as you prepare to write about each topic on your outline, you will be able to refer to the exact points in your notes that you need to cite.

Of course, if you are using a computer to organize your notes, your "cutting and pasting" will be done much more quickly on the screen. But the cross-referencing process is still important. In developing a complex research topic, it is helpful to print out your outline and your notes, to identify outline topics and sections of your notes through numbers and letters, and to match up your notes with your outline by cross-referencing using numbers and letters in the margins. When you are satisfied with your organization, and the topics in your outline are fully supported by information from your notes, then you turn to the computer and "cut and paste" on the screen.

The more notes that you have collected, the more important it is to be thorough during the preliminary organization. *Don't start to write your essay, and don't even start to sort your notes or "cut and paste" your sheets, until you have completed both your basic outline and your cross-referencing.*

EXERCISE 27: WRITING AN OUTLINE WITH CROSS-REFERENCING

Read the following set of notes, organized by source, for an argument essay on immigration.

1. Write an outline of topics for an essay to be called "The Economic and Social Consequences of Immigration in the United States Today."
2. Cross-reference the notes with your outline.

As you consider the information in these notes, remember that, if this exercise were preparation for an assigned essay, you could return to any of the sources, if you wished, and add details or examples to develop a topic that does not have enough supporting information.

Source A

Borjas, George J. "Tired, Poor, On Welfare." *National Review* 13 (Dec. 1993): 40–42.

1. It's true that immigrants contribute more in taxes to the nation's economy than they consume in welfare payments.

2. But the cost of living in this country and of using services and facilities adds an enormous amount to the cost of their support. That isn't being considered in most pro-immigration arguments. In this regard, immigrants do potentially take more than they give.

3. In 1990, a greater percentage of immigrants than natives received welfare. Immigrants comprise 8% of the population; they receive 13% of the cash benefits distributed.

4. Recent immigrants are less skilled than their counterparts 100 years ago. (B. says he's not saying that immigrants come to this country expressly to live on welfare.)

5. Whether immigrants want to work or not isn't the point; they don't have the skills, so they go on welfare.

6. B. fears creation of a new underclass of the unskilled. "A welfare state cannot afford the large-scale immigration of less-skilled persons." (42)

Source B

Brimelow, Peter. "Time to Rethink Immigration?" *National Review* 22 (June 1992): 30–46.

1. Cites large numbers of recent immigrants. Between 1951 and 1990, about one-fifth of the population of Jamaica had immigrated to the U.S.

2. 85% of legal immigrants between 1971 and 1990 were from the Third World.

3. Consequence: "The American ethnic mix *has* been upset." (31) White population of U.S. fell by 13% from 1960–90. The projection: by 2020, whites would only be 61% of population.

4. U.S. birthrate has declined since big waves of immigration at turn of century; therefore, new immigrants now have greater opportunity to dominate.

5. Major historical influence on U.S. culture has been British and German.

6. Proponents of present immigration policy are urging "Americans to abandon the bonds of a common ethnicity and instead to trust entirely to ideology to

hold together their state." (35) Historically, this bond of ideology hasn't been successful (e.g., USSR).

7. Melting pot tradition: "cultural synthesis . . . a pattern of swallowing and digestion" of immigrant groups (e.g., Irish immigrants eventually abandoned antisocial tendencies like dysfunctional families, alcoholism, disease). (36)

8. Economic argument: immigrants needed to perform jobs no one else will do. Instead, why not force unemployed Americans to work for their welfare? Or encourage a higher birth rate?

9. Cultural characteristics of each immigrant group predict whether that group will thrive or fail in new country. Cultural qualities of current major immigrant groups include unfortunate antisocial tendencies (like violence); this will have "economic consequences" for U.S.

10. Cites Borjas: welfare benefits to immigrants cost $1 billion more than they pay in taxes.

11. Hispanics in particular aren't being urged to assimilate; their tendency to support bilingualism and multiculturalism is deplorable.

Source C
Custred, Glynn. "Country Time." *National Review* 16 (June 1997): 39–40.

1. To maintain an orderly society, our country needs common cultural values, including "shared meanings, myths, and values conveyed in a common language, realized in national symbols, and supported by formal institutions, especially public education." (39)

2. Immigration can easily disturb this sense of community.

3. Earlier waves of immigration weren't a threat to national stability because those immigrants assimilated easily and willingly.

4. Immigrants in the last three decades aren't content to assimilate. They demand multiculturalism, which "drives [the nation] apart." (39) Multiculturalists attack the very concept of linguistic and cultural unity, which they regard as simply a way of oppressing ethnic and racial minorities. Custred depicts multiculturalists as whining for their rights.

5. The nation is becoming increasingly divided without any effort by our business and government leaders to prevent it.

6. The more immigrants allowed in, the more likely the newcomers will remain in their "ethnic enclaves" and this divisive multicultural attitude will grow.

7. Example: 86 languages spoken in California schools.

8. Disregard the argument that U.S. needs new workers. The danger of social tension resulting from immigration would be just as serious an economic threat.

Source D
Fukuyama, Francis. "Immigrants and Family Values." *Commentary* May 1993: 26–32.

1. "The symptoms of cultural decay are all around us, but the last people in the world we should be blaming are recent immigrants." (26)

2. Rejects Brimelow's argument that culture determines economic success for immigrants.

3. American identity doesn't derive from a specific culture; it's rooted in (a) ideals of democracy that transcend ethnicity, and (b) a consumer culture. Both are available to any immigrant group.

4. Do non-European immigrant groups threaten basic American values (e.g., nuclear family, success through hard work)? Decline of family structure and work ethic results from our declining postindustrialist society, not from values of new immigrants, who tend to have strong family loyalties (e.g., Asian immigrants: large families, economically successful).

5. Fear of immigration really directed at Hispanics: some Hispanics have had social problems, and many Americans lump together Hispanics with blacks as "a vast threatening underclass." (29)

6. F. cites diversity of Hispanics: some good, some bad. Problems really arise from poverty.

7. Reason for cultural disruption in U.S. has to do with economic and social change. Newly arrived immigrants didn't create sexual revolution, feminism, alienating workplace, single-parent households.

8. Clamor for multiculturalism comes more from leaders than from the average immigrant, for whom preserving ethnicity is not a primary goal.

9. Real issue: do we believe so strongly in our cultural heritage that we insist that all immigrants assimilate, or do we "carry respect for other cultures to the point that Americans no longer have a common voice with which to speak to one another?" (31)

Source E

Glazer, Nathan. "The Closing Door." *The New Republic* 27 Dec. 1993. Rpt. in *Arguing Immigration.* Ed. Nicolaus Mills. New York: Simon and Schuster, 1994. 37–47.

1. Some immigrants (mostly Asians) come with better education and work skills than most Americans have. Some are less qualified than Americans (mostly Hispanics and Caribbean blacks).

2. Even within these groups, ability to work and support themselves varies.

3. The economic argument isn't the crucial one. Whether we import cheap labor or not isn't the point (Japan thrives on a low immigration rate).

4. Those who use the economic argument to propose restrictions are really responding to the perceived threat of a more diverse nation. But they shouldn't be called bigots or racists. The preference for people of one's own culture is natural. "There is a difference between recognizing those who are in some sense one's own, with links to a people and a culture, and a policy based on dislike, hostility, or racial antagonism." (44)

5. Why doesn't U.S. assimilate immigrants the way it used to? "It is a different country: less self-confident, less willing to impose European and American customs and loyalty as simply the best in the world." (44)

6. G. is very tolerant of the movement to restrict immigration. "They ask why the stream of immigration should be so unrepresentative of the nation that already exists." (45)

Source F

McCarthy, Kevin. "Immigration by the Numbers." *New York Times* 15 Oct. 1997: 28.

1. McC. is a demographer who produces studies of the impact of immigrants on the California economy. Such statistics are used and sometimes distorted by proponents and opponents of present immigration policy. The issue is: does immigration have a positive effect on the national economy?

2. "No matter what ideologues on both sides say, immigration is neither absolutely good or evil."

3. On balance, California has gained more than it has lost from the availability of a low-wage immigrant work force.

4. But low-skilled workers (immigrant and native) are earning less and less.

5. Immigrants without skills aren't thriving.

6. The state is burdened by providing services to immigrants.

7. McC. suggests "modest" changes in policy: (a) scale back the number of immigrants admitted to halfway between present number and the number in the 1960s; and (b) try for a formula that favors immigrants with education and skills, rather than low-skilled immigrants who are being admitted to join family members already here.

Guidelines for Constructing Paragraphs in a Research Essay

1. *Each paragraph should possess a single main idea, usually expressed in the topic sentence.* That topic or design controls the arrangement of all the information in the paragraph. Everything that is included should develop and support that single idea, without digressions.

2. *The body of the paragraph should contain a combination of information taken from a variety of sources.* The number of different sources that you include in any one paragraph depends partly on the number of authors in your notes who have touched on its main idea and partly on the contribution each can make to the development of your topic.

3. *The topic sentence of each paragraph should support the development of your essay's thesis.*

INTEGRATING YOUR SOURCES INTO PARAGRAPHS

Writing a research essay resembles putting together a *mosaic*. Each paragraph has its basic design, determined by its topic sentence. To carry out the design, a paragraph might contain a group of reasons or examples to illustrate its main idea, *or* an extended explanation to develop that idea in greater detail, *or* a comparison between two elements introduced in the first sentence. These are the same paragraphing patterns that you use in all your writing. What makes the research essay different is the fact that the materials are assembled from many sources, *not* the way that they are organized or presented.

Imagine that the notes that you have taken from several different sources are boxes of tiles, each box containing a different color. You may find it easier to avoid mixing the colors and to work *only* with red tiles or *only* with blue, or to devote one corner of the mosaic to a red pattern and another to a blue. In the same way, you may find it both convenient and natural to work with only one source at a time and to avoid the decisions and the adjustments that must be made when you are combining different styles and ideas. But, of course, it is the design and only the design that dictates which colors should be used in creating the pattern of the mosaic, and it is the design or outline of your essay that dictates which evidence should be included in each paragraph.

When you decide to discuss a topic in a given paragraph, you must work with all the relevant information that you have gathered about that topic, whether it comes from one source or from many. Of course, you may have *too much material*; you may find it impossible to fit everything into the paragraph without overloading it with repetition. These rejected pieces may not fit into another part of the essay; instead, they will go back into their boxes as a backup or reserve fund of information.

The criteria for judging the quality of a paragraph remain the same—*clarity, coherence,* and *unity.*

- Do integrate your materials so that your reader will not be distracted by the differing sources or made aware of breaks between the various points.
- Don't integrate your materials so completely that you forget to provide appropriate acknowledgment of your sources.

Here is a paragraph from an essay about the novelist F. Scott Fitzgerald, in which four different explanations of an incident are presented, each at suitable length. Formal documentation of the sources has been omitted; but, to emphasize the variety and complexity of the research, the names of the sources and the attributing verbs and phrases have been underlined. The writer is describing an affair between Fitzgerald's wife, Zelda, and Edouard Jozan, a young Frenchman.

There is a lack of agreement about the details of the affair as well as its significance for the Fitzgeralds' marriage. According to one of Fitzgerald's biographers, Jozan and Zelda afterwards regarded it as "nothing more than a summer flirtation." But Ernest Hemingway, in his memoirs, wrote much later that Scott had told him "a truly sad story" about the affair, which he repeated many times in the course of their friendship. Gerald and Sara Murphy, who were present that summer and remembered the incident very well, told of being awakened by Scott in the middle of a September night in order to help him revive Zelda from an overdose of sleeping pills. The Murphys were sure that this incident was related to her affair with Jozan. Nancy Milford, Zelda's biographer, believes that the affair affected Zelda more than Scott, who, at that time, was very engrossed in his work. Indeed, Milford's account of the affair is the only one that suggests that Zelda was so deeply in love with Jozan that she asked Scott for a divorce. According to an interview with Jozan, the members of this triangle never engaged in a three-way confrontation; Jozan told Milford that the Fitzgeralds were "the victims of their own unsettled and a little unhealthy imagination."

This paragraph gives a brief but adequate account of what is known about the events of that summer of 1924. The writer does not try to rush through the four accounts of the affair, nor does he reduce each one to a phrase, as if he expected the reader to have prior knowledge of these people and their activities. In the context of the whole essay, the paragraph provides enough information for the reader to judge whose interpretation of the affair is closest to the truth.

ACCOMMODATING ARGUMENT IN YOUR PARAGRAPHS

When you write a paragraph based on *induction,* the topic sentence should clearly summarize the range of evidence being cited. Here is an example from Edward Tenner's *Why Things Bite Back,* a book about the dangers of technological progress:

> The startling wartime successes of penicillin created the dangerous myth of an antibiotic panacea. Even after the U.S. Food and Drug Administration began to require prescriptions in the mid-1950s, an antibiotic injection or prescription remained for many people the payoff of a medical encounter. They resisted the medical fact that antibiotics can do nothing against colds and other viral diseases. In many other countries, antibiotics are still sold legally over the counter to patients who may never get proper instructions about dosage or the importance of completing a course of treatment. Dr. Stuart B. Levy of Boston cites an Argentinian businessman who was cured of leukemia but died of an infection by the common bacterium *E. coli.* Ten years of self-medication had produced plasmids in his body that were resistant to every antibiotic used. Governments, too, have unintentionally promoted resurgence. Indonesian authorities have literally ladled out preventive doses of tetracycline to 100,000 Muslim pilgrims for a week at a time. Since the Mecca pilgrimage has historically been one of the great mixing bowls of microorganisms, it is especially disturbing to learn that half of all cholera bacilli in Africa are now resistant to tetracycline.

Paragraphs presenting inductive evidence tend to be long. Tenner makes his point about the "dangerous myth" of penicillin in the topic sentence, but he doesn't immediately cite evidence. He first explains the "danger" in the second sentence, and the "myth" in the third. Only then does he introduce his first supporting point—self-medication in countries without drug regulation—with Dr. Levy's example of the antibiotic-resistant Argentinian businessman. Signalled by the transitional word "too," Tenner's second example—the Mecca pilgrimage—increases the scale of potential danger.

In contrast to the specifics of induction, an article on "Methods of Media Manipulation" starts in a deductive mode, with a series of premises:

> We are told by people in the media industry that news bias is unavoidable. What-ever distortions and inaccuracies found in the news are caused by deadline pres-

sures, human misjudgment, budgetary restraints, and the difficulty of reducing a complex story into a concise report. Furthermore—the argument goes—no communication system can hope to report everything, selectivity is needed.

I would argue that the media's misrepresentations are not at all the result of innocent error and everyday production problems, though such problems certainly do exist. True, the press has to be selective, but what principle of selectivity is involved?

Media bias usually does not occur in random fashion; rather, it moves in the same overall direction again and again, favoring management over labor, corporations over corporate critics, affluent whites over low-income minorities, officialdom over protesters. . . . The built-in biases of the corporate mainstream media faithfully reflect the dominant ideology, seldom straying into territory that might cause discomfort to those who hold political and economic power, including those who own the media or advertise in it.

The initial presentation of Michael Parenti's argument is based on a dichotomy—contrast—between the media's view of news bias and his own. There is a disputed primary premise (bias is or is not avoidable) and a disputed secondary premise (one can't print everything vs. one prints what pleases one's corporate masters). Parenti's premises are developed in more detail, and the article goes on to support those premises through induction, by citing evidence of such manipulative tactics as "suppression by omission" and "framing."

While the opening of Parenti's article presents the opposition's argument as well as his own, the tone is grudging, even hostile. He leaves no room for accommodation between the two points of view. Yet, whenever possible, it is useful to acknowledge some merit in one's opponents or in their argument. Here are excerpts from two essays supporting opposite sides of the "wilderness preservation" issue. In the first, John Daniel is arguing that the advancement of science, if uncontrolled, can do harm to unspoiled land. He is careful, however, to distinguish between his allies and his enemies:

I don't mean to indict science in general. Many of the foremost champions of wild nature are scientists, and their work has done much to warn us of the environmental limits we are transgressing. I am arguing only against interventionist science that wants to splice genes, split atoms, or otherwise manipulate the wild—science aimed more at control than understanding, science that assumes ownership of the natural mysteries. When technological specialists come to believe that nature is answerable to their own prerogatives, they are not serving but endangering the greater community.

In William Tucker's view, society has more compelling interests, to which the wilderness movement must sometimes defer. But, before stating his argument, he pays his dues to nature:

I am not arguing against wild things, scenic beauty, pristine landscapes, and scenic preservation. What I am questioning is the argument that wilderness is a value against which every other human activity must be judged and that human beings are somehow unworthy of the landscape. The wilderness has been equated with freedom, but there are many different ideas about what constitutes freedom. . . .

Interestingly enough, Tucker then proceeds to move from his impeccably fair presentation to an argument that approaches *ad hominem*—a personal attack:

It may seem unfair to itemize the personal idiosyncrasies of people who feel comfortable only in wilderness, but it must be remembered that the environmental movement has been shaped by many people who literally spent years of their lives living in isolation.

Citing John Muir, David Brower, and Gary Snyder, leaders of the Sierra Club who spent much time alone in the mountains, Tucker continues:

There is nothing reprehensible in this, and the literature and philosophy that emerge from such experiences are often admirable. But it seems questionable to me that the ethic that comes out of this wilderness isolation—and the sense of ownership of natural landscapes that inevitably follows—can serve as the basis for a useful national philosophy.

Whatever his disclaimers, Tucker is rooting one of his key arguments against the wilderness movement in the personal preferences of three men. He does not, however, resort to using slanted, exaggerated, or dismissive language about his opponents. In contrast, here is Robert W. McChesney's attack on commercialism in the media:

The commercial blitzkrieg into every nook and cranny of U.S. culture, from schools to sport to museums to movie theaters to the Internet, has lessened traditional distinctions of public service from commercialism.

The word "blitzkrieg"—literally, lightning battle—originally referred to the German army in World War II. It immediately conjures up an image of a mechanized, pitiless army rolling over everything in its path, a reference reinforced by the domestic, vulnerable image of "nook and cranny," used to describe U.S. culture, the victim. Without even articulating his point, McChesney has created a lingering association between corporations and Nazis. This is a clever use of language, but is it a fair argument? In the next example, Leslie Savan also uses emotionally charged language to attack a similar target:

Advertising now infects just about every organ of society, and wherever advertising gains a foothold it tends to slowly take over, like a vampire or a virus.

The brutal swiftness of the blitzkrieg has been replaced by the slow insinuation of an infection, but both images are deadly and unyielding. (The allusion to a vampire must have been tempting—advertising leaves viewers bloodless and brainwashed—but it should not be placed in tandem with the insidious, slowly creeping image of infection.) Interestingly enough, McChesney and Savan are both adopting the tactics of the commercial media that they condemn: using powerful images in an attempt to force their readers into agreement.

PRESENTING ARGUMENTS FAIRLY

Perhaps the greatest disservice that you can do your sources is to distort them so that your reader is left with a false impression of what they have said or written. Such distortion is most likely to happen when you are writing an argumentative essay.

Mistakes to Avoid When Summarizing an Argument

1. Don't be one-sided; present *both* sides of an argument.
2. Don't omit crucial parts of the source's reasoning; provide a complete account of the argument.
3. Don't quote ideas out of context: make sure that you—and your reader—understand whether the source really supports the idea that you are citing.
4. Don't twist the source's ideas to fit your own purpose; provide a fair presentation.

---

1. **Present both sides of the argument.**

   One way of shading an argument to suit your own ends is to *misrepresent the strength of the opposition.* Let us assume that you are working with a number of articles, all of which are effectively presented and worth citing. Some clearly support your point of view; others are openly opposed; and a few avoid taking sides, emphasizing related but less controversial topics. If your essay cites only the favorable and neutral articles, and avoids any reference to the views of the opposition, you have presented the issue falsely. Using ostrich tactics will not convince your reader that your opinions are right; on the contrary, your unwillingness to admit the existence of opposing views suggests that your point of view has some basic flaw. A one-sided presentation will make you appear to be either biased or sloppy in your research. If the sources are available and if their views are pertinent, they should be represented and, if you wish, refuted in your essay.

2. **Provide a complete account of the argument.**

   Sometimes, distortions occur accidentally, because you have presented only a *partial* account of a source's views. In the course of an article or a book, authors sometimes examine and then reject or accept a variety of views before making it clear which are their own conclusions. Or an author may have mixed opinions about the issue and see merit in more than one point of view. If you choose to quote or paraphrase material from only one section of such a work, then you must find a way to inform your reader that these statements are not entirely representative of the writer's overall views.

3. **Make sure that you—and your reader—understand whether the source really supports the idea that you are citing.**

   Ideas can get distorted because of the researcher's misunderstanding, careless note-taking, or hasty reading. Remember to check the entire section of the article or all your notes before you attribute an opinion to your source, to make sure that you are not taking a sentence out of context or ignoring a statement in the next paragraph or on the next page that may be more typical of the writer's thinking. Writers often use an argumentative strategy that sets up a point with which they basically disagree in order to shoot it down shortly thereafter. Don't confuse a statement made for the sake of argument with a writer's real beliefs.

4. **Provide a fair presentation.**

   Occasionally, you may be so eager to uphold your point of view that you will cite any bit of material that looks like supporting evidence. To do so, however, you may have to twist the words of the source to fit your ideas. This is one of the worst kinds of intellectual dishonesty—and one of the easiest for a suspicious reader to detect: one has only to look up the source. *If you cannot find sufficient arguments and if your sources' evidence does not clearly and directly support your side, then you should seriously consider switching sides or switching topics.*

Here is a fairly clear instance of such distortion. In an essay on the need for prison reform, Garry Wills is focusing on the *deficiencies of our society's penal system;* he is not directly concerned with the arguments for or against the death penalty. But the student citing Wills in a research essay is writing specifically in support of capital punishment. To make Wills's argument fit into the scheme of this essay, the student must make some suspiciously selective references. Here is a paragraph from the research essay (on the left), side by side with the source.

Although the death penalty may seem very harsh and inhuman, is this not fair and just punishment for one who was able to administer death to another human being? A murderer's victim always receives the death penalty. Therefore, the death penalty for the murderer evens the score, or, as stated in the Bible, "an eye for an eye, and a tooth for a tooth." According to

The oldest of our culture's views on punishment is the *lex talionis*, an eye for an eye. Take a life, lose your life. It is a very basic cry—people must "pay" for their crimes, yield exact and measured recompense. No one should "get away with" any crime, like a shoplifter taking something unpaid for. The desire to make an offender suffer equivalent pain (if not compensatory excess of pain) is very

Garry Wills, "take a life, lose your life." Throughout the ages, society has demanded that man be allowed to right his wrongs. Revenge is our culture's oldest way of making sure that no one "gets away with" any crime. As Wills points out, according to this line of reasoning, the taking of the murderer's life can be seen as his payment to society for his misdeed.

deep in human nature, and rises quickly to the surface. What is lynching but an impatience with even the slightest delay in exacting this revenge? It serves our social myth to say that this impatience, if denied immediate gratification, is replaced by something entirely different—by an impersonal dedication to justice. Only lynchers want revenge, not those who wait for a verdict. That is not very likely. Look at the disappointed outcry if the verdict does not yield even delayed satisfaction of the grudge.

In the essay, the writer is citing only *part* of Wills's argument and thus makes him appear to support capital punishment. Wills is being misrepresented because (unlike the writer) he considers it fair to examine the views of the opposing side before presenting his own arguments. The ideas that the student cites are not Wills's, but Wills's presentations of commonly accepted assumptions about punishment. It is not entirely clear whether the writer of the research essay has merely been careless, failing to read past the first few sentences, or whether the misrepresentation is intentional.

INTEGRATING YOUR SOURCES: AN EXAMPLE

To illustrate the need for careful analysis of sources before you write your paragraphs, here is a group of passages, all direct quotations, which have been gathered for a research essay on college athletics. The paragraph developed from these sources must support the writer's *thesis:*

Colleges should, in the interests of both players and academic standards, outlaw the high-pressure tactics used by coaches when they recruit high school players for college teams.

The first three statements come from college coaches describing recruiting methods that they have observed and carried out; the last four are taken from books that discuss corruption in athletics.

I think in the long run, every coach must recognize this basic principle, or face the alumni firing squad. Recruiting is the crux of building a championship football team.

STEVE SLOAN, Texas Tech

Athletics is creating a monster. Recruiting is getting to be cancerous.

DALE BROWN, Louisiana State University

You don't out-coach people, you out-recruit them.

PAUL "BEAR" BRYANT, University of Alabama

It is an athletic maxim that a man with no special coaching skills can win games if he recruits well and that a tactician without talented players is a man soon without a job.

KENNETH DENLINGER

There is recruiting in various degrees in every intercollegiate sport, from crew to girls' basketball and from the Houston golf dynasty that began in the mid-50's to Southern California importing sprinters and jumpers from Jamaica.

J. ROBERT EVANS

The fundamental causes of the defects in American college athletics are too much commercialism and a negligent attitude towards the educational opportunity for which the college exists.

CARNEGIE FOUNDATION, 1929

[*Collier's* magazine, in 1905, reported that] Walter Eckersall, All-American quarterback, enrolled at Chicago three credits short of the entrance requirement and his teammate, Leo Detray, entered the school before he even graduated high school. In addition the University of Minnesota paid two players outright to play in a single game (Nebraska: 1902). A quarterback and an end also from Minnesota admitted shaving points during the 1903 Beloit game.

JOSEPH DURSO

Examining the Sources

Your paragraph will focus on *recruiting high school stars,* as opposed to developing students who enter college by the ordinary admissions procedure. Which of these ideas and observations might help to develop this paragraph? In other words, which statements should be represented by *paraphrase* or perhaps by *direct quotation*?

I think in the long run every coach must recognize this basic principle, or face the alumni firing squad. Recruiting is the crux of building a championship football team.

STEVE SLOAN

This very broad generalization seems quotable at first, largely because it sums up the topic so well; but, in fact, because it does no more than sum up the topic, it does not advance your argument any further. Therefore, you need not include it if your topic sentence makes the same point. (In general, you should write your own topic sentences rather than letting your sources write them for you.) The phrase "alumni firing squad" might be useful to quote in a later paragraph, in a discussion of the specific influence of alumni on recruiting.

Athletics is creating a monster. Recruiting is getting to be cancerous.

DALE BROWN

Coach Brown's choice of images—"cancerous" and "monster"—is certainly vivid; but the sentence as a whole is no more than a *generalized opinion about recruiting,* not an explanation of why the situation is so monstrous. To be lured into quoting Brown for the sake of two words would be a mistake.

You don't out-coach people, you out-recruit them.

PAUL "BEAR" BRYANT

This is the first statement that has advanced a specific idea: the coach may have a *choice* between building a winning team through recruiting and building a winning team through good coaching; but recruiting, not coaching, wins games. Coach Bryant, then, is not just making a rhetorical point, as the first two coaches seem to be. His seven-word sentence is succinct, if not elaborately developed, and would make a good introduction to or summation of a point that deserves full discussion.

The remaining four statements suggest a wider range of approach and style.

Walter Eckersall, All-American quarterback, enrolled at Chicago three credits short of the entrance requirement and his teammate, Leo Detray, entered the school before he even graduated high school. In addition, the University of Minnesota paid two players outright to play in a single game (Nebraska: 1902). A quarterback and an end also from Minnesota admitted shaving points during the 1903 Beloit game.

JOSEPH DURSO

This passage is as much concerned with corruption as recruiting and indicates that commercialism is nothing new in college athletics. Although the information is interesting, it is presented as a list of facts, and the language is not worth quoting. You may, however, want to summarize the example in your own words.

The fundamental causes of the defects in American college athletics are too much commercialism and a negligent attitude towards the educational opportunity for which the college exists.

CARNEGIE FOUNDATION

This extract from the 1929 Carnegie Foundation study is phrased in *abstract* language that is characteristic of foundation reports and academic writing in general. This style can be found in most textbooks (including this one) and in many of the sources that you use in college. The foundation presents its point clearly enough and raises an important idea: an athlete recruited to win games (and earn fame and fortune) is likely to ignore the primary reason for going to college—to acquire an education. Nevertheless, there is no compelling reason to *quote* this statement. *Remember that you include quotations in your essay to enhance your presentation; the quotation marks automatically prepare the reader for special words and phrasing.* But the prose here is too colorless and abstract to give the reader anything to focus on; a paraphrase is preferable.

> There is recruiting in varying degrees in every intercollegiate sport, from crew to girls' basketball and from the Houston golf dynasty that began in the mid-50's to Southern California importing sprinters and jumpers from Jamaica.
>
> J. ROBERT EVANS

This statement presents a quite different, more *detailed* level of information; it lists several sports, including some not known for their cutthroat recruiting practices. But details do not necessarily deserve quotation. Will these references be at all meaningful to the reader who is not familiar with the "Houston golf dynasty" or Jamaican track stars? To know that recruitment is not limited to cash sports, such as football, is interesting, but such specifics date quickly: in a few years, they may no longer be a useful frame of reference for most readers.

> It is an athletic maxim that a man with no special coaching skills can win games if he recruits well and that a tactician without talented players is a man soon without a job.
>
> KENNETH DENLINGER

Largely because of parallel construction, the last comment sounds both sharp and solid. In much the same way as Coach Bryant's seven words, but at greater length, Kenneth Denlinger sums up the contrast between coaching and recruiting, and suggests which one has the edge. Because the statement gives the reader something substantial to think about and because it is well phrased, Denlinger is probably worth quoting.

Should the writer include the statements by Bryant and by Denlinger, both of which say essentially the same thing? While Bryant's firsthand comment is commendably terse and certainly authoritative, Denlinger's is more complete and self-explanatory. A solution might be to include both, at different points in the paragraph, with Bryant cited at the end to sum up the idea that has been developed. Of course, the other five sources need not be excluded from the paragraph. Rather, if you wish, all five may be referred to, by paraphrase or brief reference, with their authors' names cited.

Here is *one* way of integrating this set of statements into a paragraph. (Note that, in this version, there is no documentation: none of the sources—except those quoted—is cited.)

> In college athletics, what is the best way for a school to win games? Should a strong team be gradually built up by training ordinary students from scratch, or should the process be shortened and success be assured by actively recruiting players who already know how to win? The first method may be more consistent with the traditional amateurism of college athletics, but as early as

1929, the Carnegie Foundation complained that the focus of college sports had shifted from education to the material advantages of winning. Even earlier, in 1903, there were several instances of players without academic qualifications who were "hired" to guarantee victory. And in recent years excellence of recruiting has become the most important skill for a coach to possess. Kenneth Denlinger has observed, "It is an athletic maxim that a man with no special coaching skills can win games if he recruits well and that a tactician without talented players is a man soon without a job." It follows, then, that a coach who wants to keep his job is likely to concentrate on spotting and collecting talent for his team. Coaches from LSU, Alabama, and Texas Tech all testify that good recruiting has first priority throughout college athletics. According to Bear Bryant of Alabama: "You don't out-coach people, you out-recruit them."

One problem that can arise as you are crafting your paragraph is what to do with material that casts doubt on or flatly contradicts the point you're making. (Frequently, you come across that material *after* you have worked out your thesis and structure.) Here, for example, is an excerpt from *College Sports Inc.* by Murray Sperber. How does it fit with the paragraph on recruiting to win?

Coaches who cheat do so for the same reasons that some gamblers try for an illegal advantage. They are extremely competitive, obsessed with winning, and will bend or break the rules to obtain the winning edge. They subscribe to the dictum that "winning is the only thing," that losing is not merely defeat but also a loss of self-worth. When gamblers or coaches cheat and succeed, they consider themselves "smart" and they show no remorse or inclination to stop. Only when caught do recriminations and blame—"Pressure from the school made me do it"—appear.

Richard "Digger" Phelps, head of Notre Dame's men's basketball program, has long argued that external pressure is not the main source of coaches' cheating. He says of himself and his colleagues, "You choose the job you want to take. You decide who you want to recruit—the type of person. You also decide who you want to have surround that program as far as alumni, boosters, and friends. . . ."

The coaches referred to in the earlier student paragraph about recruiting assume that winning is the point of college athletics. The author of the paragraph is focusing on the best way to win—recruiting—and the only criticism of the primacy of winning is a slight complaint by the Carnegie Foundation about the materialism of college athletics. Now, not only does Sperber denigrate the "win at all costs" philosophy, but he (and Phelps, his source) suggests that the impetus to win and cheat (and, presumably, recruit at the expense of good sportsmanship) comes from the egoism of the coaches themselves, rather than the pressure from college officials and alumni.

What do you do with this excerpt from Sperber? Should you rewrite your paragraph on recruiting to include Sperber's (and Phelps's) opinions and attempt to reconcile them with the material provided by your other sources? In this situation, do two things:

1. **Examine the new source more completely to see if the author provides a broader context for these contradictory opinions.**

   In fact, Sperber also has a good deal to say about the commercialism of college sports, pointing out that athletic departments resemble business enterprises, with program directors who are in the "entertainment business." His book indicates that the "winning is everything" philosophy derives as much from institutional (and media) expectations as from the competitive obsessions of individual coaches.

2. **If the point made by the new source is worth developing, it may be preferable to do so in a separate paragraph.**

   The "recruiting" paragraph focuses on *what* coaches do to win, not why they do it. Sperber, however, is more concerned with motivation—quite a different topic and an equally interesting one. Your essay may benefit from an exploration of this point, but to develop and support it properly, you will probably have to find more sources that deal with the pressures to compete to win. The more you read, the more new directions you are likely to find for the development of your essay.

SELECTING QUOTATIONS

Now that you are working with a great variety of sources, you may find it difficult to limit the number of quotations in your essay and to choose quotable material. If you are doubtful about when and what to quote, review the sections on quotation in Chapter 2 and Chapter 4, starting on pp. 73 and 189. As a rule, the more eminent and authoritative the source, the more reason to consider quoting it.

Are the quoted phrases in the following excerpt worth quoting? Charles Dickens is describing the house that he has rented, the Chateau des Moulineux:

Excessive Use of Quotation

Dickens rattled off a list of phrases in his attempt to describe this idyllic place. It was to become his "best doll's house," "our French watering place," and "this abode of bliss." More than anything else it would become a "happy, happy place."

Such a list of separately quoted phrases creates an awkward, disconnected effect, which, if used too often, becomes tedious to read.

Descriptions are often more difficult to paraphrase than ideas; as a result, they tend to be presented in such a sequence of quoted phrases. If your source states that the walls of the room were painted sea-green and the furniture was made out of horsehair and covered with light-brown velvet, you may find it

Guidelines for Quoting

1. *Never quote something just because it sounds impressive.* The style of the quotation—the level of difficulty, the choice of vocabulary, and the degree of abstraction—should be compatible with your own style. Don't force your reader to make a mental jump from your own characteristic voice and wording to a far more abstract, flowery, or colloquial style.

2. *Never quote something that you find very difficult to understand.* When the time comes to decide whether and what to quote, stop and observe your own reactions. Rapidly reread the quotation. If you find it difficult to understand on the first try, then either attempt to paraphrase the point or leave it out entirely. If you become distracted or confused, your reader will be, too.

3. *Primary sources are often worth quoting—if they are clear and understandable.* When you are working on a biographical or historical research essay, you may encounter special problems in deciding whether or not to quote. Primary sources often have a special claim to be quoted. For example, you would be more likely to quote one of Hemingway's own descriptions of Paris in 1925 than a comparable sentence by one of his biographers. A person who witnessed the Chicago Fire has a better claim to have his original account presented verbatim than does a historian decades later.

4. *Use single and double quotation marks to differentiate between primary and secondary sources.* When quoting primary sources, it is essential to make the exact source of the quotation clear to your reader.

next to impossible to find appropriate synonyms to paraphrase these descriptive terms. "Crin de cheval" covered with fuzzy beige fabric? Mediterranean colors decorating the walls? The result is hardly worth the effort. If the man's eyes are described as dark blue, don't alter the phrase to "piercing blue" or "deep azure" or "ocean pools." If you place "dark blue" in a sentence that is otherwise your own writing, you may omit the quotation marks.

EXERCISE 28: INCORPORATING SOURCES INTO A PARAGRAPH

The following unfinished student paragraph is followed by brief excerpts from sources.

1. Decide which excerpt contains the most appropriate sentence for quotation. (It is not necessary to quote the entire excerpt.) For the purposes of this exercise, assume that all the sources are qualified authorities.

2. Paraphrase the other excerpts.

3. Complete the paragraph by using both paraphrase and quotation, citing two *or* three sources. Maintain a consistent tone and (except for the quotation) a single voice. Do not digress too far from the topic sentence.

Student Paragraph

Today, old people are often shunted aside into nursing homes as if they were useless vegetables. Fearful of contact with those so close to death, many people avoid their company. . . .

Sources

An old person who accepts mental and physical deterioration, illness, death, and dying is closer to wisdom than one who rejects it.

ADOLF GUGGENBUHL-CRAIG

I've been called senile. Senility is a convenient peg on which to hang nonconformity. . . . A new set of faculties seems to be coming into operation. I seem to be awakening to a larger world of wonderment—to catch little glimpses of the immensity and diversity of creation. More than at any other time in my life, I seem to be aware of the beauties of our spinning planet and the sky above. I feel that old age sharpens my awareness.

FRANCES [A NURSING-HOME RESIDENT, AGED 91]

Being old is just as beautiful and holy a task as being young, learning to die and dying are just as valuable functions as any other—assuming that they are carried out with reverence toward the meaning and holiness of life.

HERMANN HESSE

It is to be assumed that if man were to live this life like a poem, he would be able to look upon the sunset of his life as his happiest period, and instead of trying to postpone the much feared old age, be able actually to look forward to it, and gradually build up to it as the best and happiest period of his existence.

LIN YUTANG

ASSIGNMENT 13: ORGANIZING AND WRITING THE RESEARCH ESSAY

1. Read through all the essays in Appendix E. (In a full-scale research project, these readings would form a substantial part, but not all, of your sources. Check with your instructor about whether you may use additional sources.) Develop a topic for a research essay using most or all of these sources.

2. Write down a tentative list of main ideas, based on these sources, that should be discussed in an essay dealing with your subject. Also include your own ideas on the subject.

3. Develop an outline based on your list of ideas, and consider possible theses for the essay and the strategy that will best fit your thesis and sources.

4. After you have compiled a substantial list of topics and developed a tentative thesis, reread the passages, cross-referencing the topics on your list with the relevant material from the essays. While you do not have to use up everything in all of the readings, you should include all relevant points.

5. Develop this outline into an eight- or ten-page essay.

▪9▪

Acknowledging Sources

When you engage in research, you continually come into contact with the ideas and the words of other writers; as a result, the opportunities to plagiarize—by accident or by intention—increase tremendously. You must therefore understand exactly what constitutes plagiarism.

Plagiarism is the unacknowledged use of another person's work, in the form of original ideas, strategies, and research, or another person's writing, in the form of sentences, phrases, and innovative terminology.

- Plagiarism is the equivalent of *theft,* but the stolen goods are intellectual rather than material.
- Like other acts of theft, plagiarism is against the law. The copyright law governing publications requires that authorship be acknowledged and (if the borrowed material is long enough) that payment be offered to the writer.
- Plagiarism violates the moral law that people should take pride in, as well as profit from, the fruits of their labor. Put yourself in the victim's place. Think about the best idea that you ever had, or the paragraph that you worked hardest on in your last paper. Now, imagine yourself finding exactly the same idea or exactly the same sentences in someone else's essay, with no mention of your name, with no quotation marks. Would you accept the theft of your property without protest?

- Plagiarists are not only robbers, but also cheats. People who bend or break the rules of authorship, who do not do their own work, will be rightly distrusted by their classmates, teachers, or future employers, who may equate a history of plagiarism with laziness, incompetence, or dishonesty. One's future rarely depends on getting a better grade on a single assignment; on the other hand, one's lifelong reputation may be damaged if one resorts to plagiarism in order to get that grade.

But plagiarism is a bad risk for a more immediate and practical reason. As you observed in Exercise 10, an experienced teacher can usually detect plagiarized work quite easily. *If you are not skilled enough to write your own essay, you are unlikely to do a good enough job of adapting someone else's work to your needs.* Anyone can learn to write well enough to make plagiarism an unnecessary risk.

Finally, you will not receive greater glory by plagiarizing. On the contrary, most instructors believe that students who understand the ideas of their sources, apply them to the topic, and put them in their own words deserve the highest grades for their mastery of the basic skills of academic writing. There are, however, occasions when your instructor may ask you not to use secondary sources. In such cases, you would be wise to do no background reading at all, so that the temptation to borrow will not arise.

ACKNOWLEDGING YOUR SOURCES

Acknowledging your sources—or *documentation*—means telling your reader that someone other than yourself is the source of ideas and words in your essay. Acknowledgment can take the form of *quotation marks* and *citation of the author's name*—techniques that are by now familiar to you—or more elaborate ways to indicate the source, which will be explained later in this chapter. There are guidelines to help you decide what can and what cannot safely be used without acknowledgment, and these guidelines mostly favor complete documentation.

DOCUMENTING INFORMATION

By conservative standards, *you should cite a source for all facts and evidence in your essay that you did not know before you started your research.* Knowing when to acknowledge the source of your knowledge or information largely depends on common sense. For example, it is not necessary to document the fact that there are fifty states in the United States or that Shakespeare wrote *Hamlet* since these facts are common knowledge. On the other hand, you may be presenting more obscure information, like facts about electric railroads, which you have known since you were a child, but which may be unfamiliar to your readers. Technically, you are not obliged to document that information; but your audience will trust you more and will be better informed if you do so. *In general, if the facts are not unusual, if they can be found in a number of standard sources, and if they do not vary from source to source or year to year, then they can be considered common knowledge, and the source need not be acknowledged.*

◆ Let's assume that you are writing an essay about *Lawrence of Arabia* for a course in film studies. The basic facts about the film—the year of release, the cast, the director, the technicians, the Academy Awards won by the film—might be regarded as common knowledge and not require documentation. But the cost of the film, the amount grossed in its first year, the location of the premiere, and the circumstances of production are relatively unfamiliar facts that you would almost certainly have to look up in a reference book. An authority on film who includes such facts in a study of epic films is expected to be familiar with this information and, in most cases, would not be expected to provide documentation. But a student writing on the same subject would be well advised to do so.

Similarly, if you are writing about the most recent World Cup and know who won a specific match because you witnessed the victory on television, then it would probably not be necessary to cite a source. Issues surrounding the World Cup—such as the use of steroids—are less clearly in the realm of common knowledge. You may remember news broadcasts about which athletes may or may not have taken steroids before a match, but the circumstances are hardly so well defined—or so memorable in their details—that you would be justified in writing about them from memory. The articles that you consult to jog your memory would have to be documented.

Documenting Ideas Found in Your Source

Your objective is both to acknowledge the source and to provide your reader with the fullest possible background. Let us assume that one of the ideas that you are writing about was firmly in your mind—the product of your own intellect—long before you started to work on your topic. Nevertheless, if you come across a version of that idea during your research, you should cite the source, *even though the idea was as much your own as the author's.* Of course, in your acknowledgment, you might state that this source is confirming *your* theories and indicate that you had thought of the point independently.

Documenting the Source of Your Own Ideas

Perhaps, while working on an essay, you develop a new idea of your own, stimulated by one of your readings. You should make a point of acknowledging the source of inspiration and, perhaps, describing how and why it affected you. (For example: "My idea for shared assignments is an extension of McKeachie's discussion of peer tutoring.") The reader should be made aware of your debt to your source as well as your independent effort.

PLAGIARISM: STEALING IDEAS

If you present another person's ideas as your own, you are plagiarizing *even if you use your own words.* To illustrate, the paragraph on the left, by Leo Gurko, is taken from a book, *Ernest Hemingway and the Pursuit of Heroism;* the paragraph on the right comes from a student essay on Hemingway. Gurko is listed in the student's bibliography and is cited as the source of several quotations elsewhere in the essay. But the student does not mention Gurko anywhere in *this* paragraph.

Source	*Student Essay*
The Hemingways put themselves on short rations, ate, drank, and entertained as little as possible, pounced eagerly on the small checks that arrived in the mail as payment for accepted stories, and were intensely conscious of being poor. The sensation was not altogether unpleasant. Their extreme youth, the excitement of living abroad, the sense of making a fresh start, even the unexpected joy of parenthood, gave their poverty a romantic flavor.	Despite all the economies that they had to make and all the pleasures that they had to do without, the Hemingways rather enjoyed the experience of being poor. They knew that this was a more romantic kind of life, unlike anything they'd known before, and the feeling that everything in Paris was fresh and new, even their new baby, made them sharply aware of the glamorous aspects of being poor.

The *language* of the student paragraph does not require quotation marks, but unless Gurko is acknowledged, the student will be guilty of plagiarism. These impressions of the Hemingways, these insights into their motivation, would not have been possible without Gurko's biography—and Gurko deserves the credit for having done the research and for having formulated the interpretations. After reading extensively about Hemingway, the student may have absorbed these biographical details so thoroughly that he feels as if he had always known them. But the knowledge is still secondhand, and the source must be acknowledged.

PLAGIARISM: STEALING WORDS

When you quote a source, remember that the quoted material will require *two* kinds of documentation:

1. *The acknowledgment of the source of the information or ideas* (through a system of documentation that provides complete publication information about the source and possibly through the citation of the author's name in your sentence), and

2. *The acknowledgment of the source of the exact wording* (through quotation marks).

It is not enough to supply the author's name in parentheses (or in a footnote) and then mix up your own language and that of your sources. The author's name tells your reader nothing at all about who is responsible for the choice of words. Equally important, borrowing language carelessly, perhaps in an effort to use paraphrase, often garbles the author's meaning.

Here is an excerpt from a student essay about Henrik Ibsen, together with the relevant passage from its source:

Source

When writing [Ibsen] was sometimes under the influence of hallucinations, and was unable to distinguish between reality and the creatures of his imagination. While working on *A Doll's House* he was nervous and retiring and lived in a world alone, which gradually became peopled with his own imaginary characters. Once he suddenly remarked to his wife: "Now I have seen Nora. She came right up to me and put her hand on my shoulder." "How was she dressed?" asked his wife. "She had a simple blue cotton dress," he replied without hesitation. . . . So intimate had Ibsen become with Nora while at work on *A Doll's House* that when John Paulsen asked him why she was called Nora, Ibsen replied in a matter-of-fact tone: "She was really called Leonora, you know, but everyone called her Nora since she was the spoilt child of the family."

P. F. D. TENNANT,
Ibsen's Dramatic Technique

Student Essay

While Ibsen was still writing *A Doll's House*, his involvement with the characters led to his experiencing hallucinations that at times completely incapacitated his ability to distinguish between reality and the creations of his imagination. He was nervous, distant, and lived in a secluded world. Gradually this world became populated with his creations. One day he had the following exchange with his wife:

Ibsen: Now I have seen Nora. She came right up to me and put her hand on my shoulder.

Wife: How was she dressed?

Ibsen: (without hesitation) She had a simple blue dress.

Ibsen's involvement with his characters was so deep that when John Paulsen asked Ibsen why the heroine was named Nora, Ibsen replied in a very nonchalant tone of voice that originally she was called Leonora, but that everyone called her Nora, the way one would address the favorite child in the family (Tennant 26).

The documentation at the end of the student's passage may refer the reader to Tennant's book, but it fails to indicate the debt that the student owes to Tennant's *phrasing* and *vocabulary*. Phrases like "distinguish between reality and the creatures of his imagination" must be placed in quotation marks, and so should the exchange between Ibsen and his wife. Arranging these sentences as dialogue is not adequate acknowledgment.

In fact, the problem here is too complex to be solved by inserting a few quotation marks. The student, who probably intended a paraphrase, has substituted some of her own words for Tennant's; however, because she keeps the original sentence structure and many of the original words, she has only succeeded in obscuring some of her source's ideas.

At times, the phrasing distorts the original idea: the student's assertion that Ibsen's hallucinations "incapacitated his ability to distinguish between reality and the creations of his imagination" is very different from "[Ibsen] was sometimes under the influence of hallucinations and was unable to distinguish between reality and the creatures of his imagination." Many of the substituted words change Tennant's meaning: "distant" does not mean "retiring"; "a secluded world" is not "a world alone"; "nonchalant" is a very different quality from "matter-of-fact." Prose like this is neither quotation nor successful paraphrase; it is doubly bad, for it both *plagiarizes* the source and *misinterprets* it.

EXERCISE 29: UNDERSTANDING WHEN
TO DOCUMENT INFORMATION

Here are some facts about the explosion of the space shuttle *Challenger*. Consider which of these facts would require documentation in a research essay—and why.

1. On January 28, 1986, the space shuttle *Challenger* exploded shortly after takeoff from Cape Canaveral.
2. It was unusually cold in Florida on the day of the launch.
3. One of the *Challenger*'s booster rockets experienced a sudden and unforeseen drop in pressure 10 seconds before the explosion.
4. The explosion was later attributed to the failure of an O-ring seal.
5. On board the *Challenger* was a $100 million communications satellite.
6. Christa McAuliffe, a high school social studies teacher in Concord, New Hampshire, was a member of the crew.
7. McAuliffe's mission duties included conducting two classroom lessons taught from the shuttle.
8. After the explosion, classes at the high school were canceled.
9. Another crew member, Judith Resnick, had a Ph.D. in electrical engineering.
10. At the time of the explosion, President Ronald Reagan was preparing to meet with network TV news correspondents to brief them on the upcoming State of the Union address.
11. The State of the Union address was postponed for a week.

EXERCISE 30: ACKNOWLEDGING SOURCES

Here are two excerpts from two books about the Industrial Revolution in England. Each excerpt is followed by a passage from a student essay that makes use of the ideas and the words of the source without any acknowledgment at all.

1. Compare the original with the plagiarized passage.
2. Insert the appropriate quotation marks.
3. Underline the paraphrases.

Source A

Materially the new factory proletariat was likely to be somewhat better off [than domestic workers who did light manufacturing work in their own homes]. On the other hand it was unfree, under the strict control and the even stricter discipline imposed by the master or his supervisors, against whom they had virtually no legal recourse and only the very beginnings of public protection. They had to work his hours or shifts, to accept his punishments and the fines with which he imposed his rules or increased his profits. In isolated areas or industries they had to buy in his shop, as often as not receiving their wages in truck (thus allowing the unscrupulous employer to swell his profits yet further), or live in the houses the master provided. No doubt the village boy might find such a life no more dependent and less impoverished than his parents'; and in Continental industries with a strong paternalist tradition, the despotism of the master was at least partly balanced by the security, education, and welfare services which he sometimes provided. But for the free man entry into the factory as a mere "hand" was entry into something little better than slavery, and all but the most famished tended to avoid it, and even when in it to resist the draconic discipline much more persistently than the women and children, whom factory owners therefore tended to prefer.

E. J. HOBSBAWM, *The Age of Revolution 1789–1848*

Student Essay

The new factory proletariat was likely to be better off materially than those who did light manufacturing in their homes, but it was unfree. There was strict control and discipline imposed by the owner and his supervisors. They had no legal recourse and only the very start of public protection. The despotism of the master was at least a little bit set off by the security, education, and welfare services that he sometimes provided. But entry into the factory as a hand wasn't much better than slavery.

Source B

Most of the work in the factories was monotonously dreary, but that was also true of much of the work done in the homes. The division of labor which caused a workman to perform over and over only one of the several processes needful for the production of any article was intensified by the mechanical inventions, but it had already gone so far in the homes that few workers experienced any longer the joy of creation. It was, indeed, more of a physical strain to tend a hand loom than a power loom. The employment of women and children in the factories finally evoked an outcry from the humanitarians, but the situation was inherited from the domestic system. In the homes, however, most of the children worked under the friendly eyes of their parents and not under the direction of an overseer. That to which the laborers themselves most objected was "the tyranny of the factory bell." For the long hours during which the power kept the machines in motion, the workers had to tend them without intermission, under the discipline established by the employer and enforced by his foreman. Many domestic laborers had to maintain equally long hours in order to earn a bare subsistence, but they were free to begin, stop and rest when they pleased. The operatives in the factories felt keenly a loss of personal independence.

W. E. LUNT, *History of England*

Student Essay

Factory work was monotonous and dreary, but that was also true of work at home. Humanitarians cried out against the employment of women and children, but that was inherited from the domestic system. What annoyed the laborers the most was the dictatorship of the factory bell. The workers had to stay at the machines without intermission, maintaining long hours to earn a bare subsistence. Those who worked in their homes were free to begin, stop, and rest whenever they felt like it. Factory workers keenly felt a loss of personal freedom.

EXERCISE 31: IDENTIFYING PLAGIARISM

In 1995, the *Chronicle of Higher Education* reported that Stanley N. Ingber, a professor of law at Drake University, had recently been accused of plagiarizing the content and language of portions of three works by Michael J. Perry, a professor of law at Northwestern University. Professor Ingber had used ten passages without attribution in two articles. Other evidence suggested that Professor Ingber might have previously plagiarized passages from an article written by Mark G. Yudof, of the University of Texas at Austin.

Here, side by side, as published in the *Chronicle,* are parallel excerpts from Perry's 1982 *The Constitution, the Courts, and Human Rights* (on the left) and Ingber's 1994 "Judging Without Judgment: Constitutional Irrelevancies and the Demise of Dialogue." Examine them and determine whether, in your opinion, Ingber has plagiarized Perry's work.

I want to emphasize that I am *not* claiming that the Court always gives right answers. Of course it does not. . . . My basic point is simply this: In the constitutional dialogue between the Court and the other agencies of government—a subtle, dialectical interplay between Court and polity—what emerges is a far more self-critical political morality than would otherwise appear. . . .	I want to emphasize that I am *not* claiming that the Court always gives right answers, because of course it does not. My basic point is simply that from the constitutional dialogue between the Court and the other agencies of government—a subtle, dialectical interplay between Court and polity—a far more self-critical political morality emerges than would otherwise appear.

USING DOCUMENTATION

In addition to using quotation marks and citing the author's name in your text, you also need to provide your reader with more detailed information about your sources. This documentation is important for two reasons:

1. By showing where you found your information, you are providing *proof that you did your research*. Including the source's *publication history* and the *specific page* on which you found the information assures your reader that you have not made up fictitious sources and quotations. The systems of documentation that are described in this chapter and in Appendix B enable your reader to distinguish your ideas from those of your sources, to know who was responsible for what, by observing the parenthetical notes or numbered notes.

2. Documentation also enables your readers to *learn more about the subject of your essay*. Methods of documentation originally developed as a way for serious scholars to share their findings with their colleagues—while making it entirely clear who had done the original research. The reader of your research essay should be given the option of going back to the library and locating the materials that you used in writing about the topic. Of course, the essay's *bibliography* can serve this purpose, but not even the most carefully annotated bibliography guides readers to the book and the precise page that will provide the information that they need. Documentation, then, provides a direct link between an interesting sentence in the paper and the source in the library that will satisfy your readers' interest.

Using Parenthetical Notes

The most widely accepted system of documentation is based on the insertion directly into your essay of the author's name and the page on which the information can be found, placed in parentheses. This style of documentation is called the Modern Language Association (MLA) style. It has replaced footnotes and endnotes as the most common form of documentation, and it will probably be the style you use in writing general research essays, especially those in the humanities. Documenting through parenthetical notes is much less cumbersome than preparing an additional page of endnotes or placing footnotes at the bottom of the page. MLA style also allows your reader to see the source's name while reading the essay, instead of having to turn to a separate page at the back. Readers who want to know more about a particular source than the author's name and the number of the page containing the information can turn to the "Works Cited" page, which provides all the necessary details of publication.

Another frequently used kind of parenthetical documentation is the one recommended by the American Psychological Association (APA) for research in the social and behavioral sciences. APA style is described on pp. 452–461 of Appendix B.

For those writing essays on a computer, many software packages (especially those, like Nota Bene, specializing in academic writing) provide documentation automatically, in a choice of styles—provided that basic information about each work cited has been entered into the computer.

MLA Format

Here is what an excerpt from a biographical essay about Ernest Hemingway would look like using MLA style. Notice that the parenthetical notes are meaningless unless the reader can refer to an accurate and complete bibliography placed at the end of the essay on a page titled "Works Cited."

Hemingway's zest for life extended to women also. His wandering heart seemed only to be exceeded by an even more appreciative eye (Hemingway 102). Hadley was aware of her husband's flirtations and of his facility with women (Sokoloff 84). Yet, she had no idea that something was going on between Hemingway and Pauline Pfeiffer, a fashion editor for Vogue magazine (Baker 159). She was also unaware that Hemingway delayed his return to Schruns from a business trip in New York, in February 1926, so that he might spend more time with this "new and strange girl" (Hemingway 210; also, Baker 165).

Works Cited

Baker, Carlos. Ernest Hemingway: A Life Story. New York: Scribner's, 1969.

Hemingway, Ernest. A Moveable Feast. New York: Scribner's, 1964.

Sokoloff, Alice Hunt. Hadley: The First Mrs. Hemingway. New York: Dodd, 1973.

Many of the basic rules for using MLA style are apparent in the previous example. Here are some points to observe.

1. **Format and Punctuation.**

   The placement of the parenthetical note within your sentence is governed by a set of very precise rules, established by conventional agreement. Like rules for quotation, these must be followed without any deviation.

   a. *The parenthetical note is intended to be a part of your sentence, which should not end until the source has been cited.* For this reason, terminal punctuation (period or question mark) should be placed *after* the parenthetical note.

   Incorrect

   Unlike most American writers of his day, Hemingway rarely came to New York; instead, he spent most of his time on his farm near Havana. (Ross 17).

Correct

Unlike most American writers of his day, Hemingway rarely came to New York; instead, he spent most of his time on his farm near Havana (Ross 17).

b. *If the parenthetical note follows a quotation, the quotation should be closed before you open the parentheses.* Remember that the note is not part of the quotation and therefore has no reason to be inside the quotation.

Incorrect

Hemingway's farm consisted of "a domestic staff of nine, fifty-two cats, sixteen dogs, a couple of hundred pigeons, and three cows (Ross 17)."

Correct

Hemingway's farm consisted of "a domestic staff of nine, fifty-two cats, sixteen dogs, a couple of hundred pigeons, and three cows" (Ross 17).

c. *Any terminal punctuation that is part of the quotation* (like a question mark or an exclamation point) *remains inside the quotation marks.* Remember also to include a period at the end of the sentence, *after* the parenthetical note.

Incorrect

One critic reports that Hemingway said of The Old Man and the Sea, "Don't you think it is a strange damn story that it should affect all of us (me especially) the way it does" (Halliday 52)?

Correct

One critic reports that Hemingway said of The Old Man and the Sea, "Don't you think it is a strange damn story that it should affect all of us (me especially) the way it does?" (Halliday 52).

d. *When you insert the parenthetical note, leave one space before it and one space after it*—unless you are ending the sentence with terminal punctuation (period, question mark), in which case you leave no space between the closing parenthesis and the punctuation, and you leave the customary one space between the end of that sentence and the beginning of the next one.

Incorrect

Given Hemingway's intense awareness of literary tradition, style, and theory, it is strange that many critics and readers have found his work primitive(Cowley 47).

Correct

Given Hemingway's intense awareness of literary tradition, style, and theory, it is strange that many critics and readers have found his work primitive (Cowley 47).

2. Placement.

The parenthetical note comes at the end of the material being documented, whether that material is quoted, paraphrased, summarized, or briefly mentioned. By convention, your reader will assume that the *parenthetical note signals the end of the material from that source.* Anything that follows is either your own idea, independently developed, or taken from a new source that will be documented by the next parenthetical note later in the text.

> One critic has remarked that it has been fashionable to deride Hemingway over the past few years (Cowley 50). However, though we may criticize him, as we can criticize most authors when we subject them to close scrutiny, we should never forget his brilliance in depicting characters having grace under the pressure of a sterile, valueless, painful world (Anderson 1036).

3. Frequency.

Each new point in your essay that requires documentation should have its own parenthetical note. Under no circumstances should you accumulate references to several different sources for several sentences and place them in a single note at the end of the paragraph. All the sources in the Hemingway paragraph cannot be covered by one parenthetical note at the end.

Incorrect

> The sources of Hemingway's fiction have been variously named. One critic has said he is driven by "personal demons." Another believes that he is occupied by a desire to truly portray reality, with all its ironies and symbols. Finally, still another has stated that Hemingway is interested only in presenting "fragments of truth" (Cowley 51; Halliday 71; Levin 85).

Correct

> The sources of Hemingway's fiction have been variously named. One critic has said he is driven by "personal demons" (Cowley 51). Another believes that he is occupied by a desire to truly portray reality, with all its ironies and symbols (Halliday 71). Finally, still another has stated that Hemingway is interested only in presenting "fragments of truth" (Levin 85).

4. Multiple Notes in a Single Sentence.

If you are using a large number of sources and documenting your essay very thoroughly, you may need to cite two or more sources at separate points in the same sentence.

> Even at this early stage of his career, Hemingway seemed to have developed a basic philosophy of writing. His ability to perceive situations

clearly and to capture the exact essence of the subject (Lawrence 93–94; O'Faolain 113) might have stemmed from a disciplined belief that each sentence had to be "true" (Hemingway 12) and that a story had to be written "as straight as you can" (Hemingway 183).

The placement of notes tells you where the writer found which information. The reference to Lawrence and O'Faolain must be inserted in mid-sentence because they are responsible only for the information about Hemingway's capacity to focus on his subject and capture its essence; Lawrence and O'Faolain are not responsible for the quoted material at the end of the sentence. The inclusion of each of the next two parenthetical notes tells you that a reference to "true" sentences can be found on page 12 of the Hemingway book and a reference to "straight" writing can be found on page 183.

5. **Multiple Sources for the Same Point.**

If you have two sources to document the same point, you can demonstrate the completeness of your research by placing both in the same parenthetical note. The inclusion of Lawrence and O'Faolain in the same note—(Lawrence 93–94; O'Faolain 113)—tells you that much the same information can be found in both sources. Should you want to cite two sources but emphasize only one, you can indicate your preference by using "also."

Hemingway's ability to perceive situations clearly and to capture the exact essence of the subject (Dos Passos 93–94; also O'Faolain 113) may be his greatest asset as a writer.

There is, of course, a limit to how many sources you can cram into a single pair of parentheses; common sense will tell you what is practical and what is distracting to the reader. Usually, one or two sources will have more complete or better documented information; those are the ones to cite. If you wish to discuss the quality of information in your various sources, then you can use an explanatory endnote to do so (see p. 384 on explanatory notes).

6. **Referring to the Source in the Text.**

In the previous examples, the writer of the Hemingway essay has chosen not to cite any sources in the text itself. That is why each parenthetical note contains a name as well as a page number. *If, however, you do refer to your source as part of your own presentation of the material, then there is no need to use the name twice; simply insert the page number in the parenthetical note.*

During the time in Paris, Hemingway became friends with the poet Ezra Pound, who told Hemingway he would teach him how to write if the younger novelist would teach him to box. Noel Stock reports what Wyndham Lewis saw when he walked in on one of their boxing sessions:

> A splendidly built young man [Hemingway] stript to the waist,
> and with a torso of dazzling white, was standing not far from me.
> He was tall, handsome, and serene, and was repelling with his
> boxing gloves—I thought without undue exertion—a hectic as-
> sault of Ezra's. (88)

Because Stock's name is cited in the text, it need not be placed in parentheses; the page number is enough. Stock's book would, of course, be
included in the list of "Works Cited." Also notice that the parenthetical
note works just as well at the end of a lengthy, *indented* quotation; but
that, because the quotation is indented, and there are no quotation marks
to signify its end, it terminates with a period placed *before* the parenthetical note, which follows separated by *two* spaces.

7. **Including the Source's Title.**

*Occasionally, your bibliography will include more than one source by the same
author or sources by different authors with the same last name. To avoid confusion and to specify your exact source, use an abbreviated title inside the parenthetical note.* Had the author of the Hemingway essay included more than
one work by Carlos Baker in the bibliography, the parenthetical note
would look like this:

> Yet, she had no idea that something was going on between Hemingway
> and Pauline Pfeiffer, a fashion editor for Vogue magazine (Baker, Life Story
> 159).

If you are working from a newspaper or periodical article that does not
cite an author, use an abbreviation of the article's title in your parenthetical note (unless you have referred to the title in your text, in which case
you need only include the page number in your note).

8. **Referring to a Whole Work.**

*Occasionally, you may refer to the overall theme of an entire work, citing the ti-
tle and the author, but no specific quotation, idea, or page. If you refer to a work
as a whole, no page numbers in parentheses are required.*

> Hemingway's The Sun Also Rises focuses on the sterility and despair per-
> vading modern culture.

9. **Referring to a Source by More Than One Author.**

*Occasionally, you will need to refer to a book that is by two, or three, or even
more authors. (If you have mentioned the authors' names in your text, just include a page reference in parentheses.) If you refer to a text by more than three
authors and you have not mentioned them in your text, it is acceptable (and saves
space) to cite the name of the first author followed by* et al., *unitalicized, and
then the page number, all within parentheses.* Et al. *is Latin for "and others."*

Two Authors

We may finally say of the writer Hemingway that he was able to depict the turbulent, often contradictory, emotions of modern man in a style as starkly realistic as that of the sixteenth century painter Caravaggio, who, art historians tell us, seems to say, "Here is actuality . . . without deception or pretence. . . . " (Janson and Cauman 221).

More than Three Authors

Hemingway did what no other writer of his time did: he captured the plight and total disenchantment of his age in vivid intensity (Spiller et al. 1300).

10. **Referring to One of Several Volumes.**

You may use a single volume from a set of several volumes. If so, refer to the specific volume by using an arabic numeral followed by a colon. In your "Works Cited," be sure to list all the volumes. (See Appendix B for proper bibliographic entry of a set of volumes.)

Perhaps Hemingway's work can be best summed up by Frederick Coppleston's comment concerning Camus: both writers prove that human greatness is not shown in escaping the absurdity of modern existence, but "in living in the consciousness of the absurd and yet revolting against it by . . . committing . . . [one]self and living in the fullest manner possible" (3:393).

11. **Referring to a Work of Literature.**

If you refer to specific passages from a well-known play, poem, or novel, then you need not cite the author; the text's name is sufficient recognition. Use arabic numerals separated by periods for divisions such as act, scene, and line in plays and for divisions like books and lines in poems. For novels, cite the page number followed by a semicolon, "ch.," and the chapter number.

Play

Hemingway wished to show reality as truly as he could, even if he found man, as did King Lear, nothing but "a poor, bare, fork'd animal . . . " (3.4.106–7).

Poem

Throughout his career as a writer, Hemingway struggled to make sense of the human condition so powerfully and metaphorically presented in The Waste Land: "Son of man/ . . . you know only/ A heap of broken images" (2.21–23).

Novel

In The Sun Also Rises, toughness is an essential for living in the modern age, but even toughness has its limits in the novel; as Jake says, "It is

awfully easy to be hard-boiled about everything in the daytime, but at
night it is another thing" (34; ch. iv).

12. **Referring to a Quotation from an Indirect Source.**

*When you quote a writer's words that you have found in a work written by
someone else, you begin the citation with the abbreviation "qtd. in." This form*
shows the reader that you are quoting from a secondhand source, not the
original.

In "Big Two-Hearted River," Hemingway metaphorically captures the
pervasive atmosphere of his time in the tersest of descriptions: "There
is no town, nothing . . . but the burned over country" (qtd. in Anderson
1027).

13. **Referring to Sources That Do Not Appear in Print.**

Sometimes you may cite information from nonprint sources such as interviews, films, or radio or television programs. If you do, be sure that
the text mentions (for an interview) the name of the interviewer and/or
the person being interviewed or (for a film) the name of the producer,
director, and/or scriptwriter; these names should also appear in your
list of "Works Cited." (For proper bibliographic form of nonprint sources,
including the Internet, see Appendix B.)

Interview

In an unpublished interview conducted by the writer of this essay, the
poet Phil Arnold said that a lean style like Hemingway's may be just as
artificial as an elaborate one.

Preparing to Document Your Essay

- Whether you take notes or use photocopies of your sources, remember always to write down the information that you will need for
  your notes and bibliography.
- Look at the front of each book or periodical and jot down the publication information.
- As you work on the first draft of your essay, include the author's
  name and the relevant page number in parentheses after every reference to one of your sources, to serve as a guide when you document your essay. Even in this early version, your essay will resemble
  the finished product, with MLA documentation.
- Finally, when the essay is ready for final typing, read through it
  again, just to make sure that each reference to a source is covered
  by a parenthetical note.

MLA Style: A Sample Page

Reference to quotation, author mentioned in text

Reference to an entire work, no page reference required

Reference to two sources in which same information can be found, emphasis on "Belkin"

Standard reference, author mentioned in note

Reference to an article with no author listed

Michelle A. Cawley defines passive euthanasia as "cooperating with the patient's dying" (959). Failing to resuscitate a patient who has suffered a massive heart attack is one example of passive euthanasia. Another is deciding not to feed a terminally ill patient who is unable to feed himself. In contrast, removing the feeding tube from a patient who is being fed that way would be considered active euthanasia. Similar to passive euthanasia is "assisted suicide," in which a doctor or other person provides a terminally ill person with the means—pills, for example—and the medical knowledge necessary to commit suicide (Orentlicher 1844). Derek Humphrey's 1991 book *Final Exit*, which describes ways to painlessly commit suicide, and the organization Compassion in Dying, which helps terminally ill patients end their lives, are both recent examples of "assisted suicide" (Belkin 50; also Elliott 27).

The professional people who care for the sick and dying think there is a great difference between active and passive euthanasia, or "assisted suicide." A recent panel of distinguished physicians declared themselves in favor, by a margin of 10 to 2, of doctor-assisted suicide for hopelessly ill patients who request it (Orentlicher 1844). In a survey taken in 1975, 73% of the nurses questioned were in favor of withholding treatment that would prolong the lives of dying patients who don't want their lives sustained in that way—in other words, passive euthanasia. But only 17% were in favor of using active means to end lives of dying patients who request euthanasia ("Taking Life" 40).

Constructing a "Works Cited" Page

None of the parenthetical notes explained above would make complete sense without a "Works Cited" page. The technical forms for bibliographic entries according to MLA style are described in Appendix B. Following is a sample "Works Cited" page for all of the parenthetical notes about Hemingway found earlier in this chapter.

Works Cited

Anderson, Charles W. Introduction. "Ernest Hemingway." American Literary
    Masters. Ed. Charles W. Anderson. New York: Holt, 1965. 1023–114.

Arnold, Philip. Telephone interview. 3 Nov. 1993.

Baker, Carlos. Ernest Hemingway: A Life Story. New York: Scribner's, 1969.

Coppleston, Frederick. Maine de Biran to Sartre. New York: Doubleday, 1974.
    Vol. 9 of A History of Philosophy. 9 vols. 1946–1974.

Cowley, Malcolm. "Nightmare and Ritual in Hemingway." Hemingway: Twentieth
    Century Perspectives. Ed. Robert P. Weeks. Englewood Cliffs: Prentice,
    1962. 40–51.

Halliday, E. M. "Hemingway's Ambiguity: Symbolism and Irony." Hemingway:
    Twentieth Century Perspectives. Ed. Robert P. Weeks. Englewood Cliffs:
    Prentice, 1962. 52–71.

Hemingway, Ernest. A Moveable Feast. New York: Scribner's, 1964.

---. The Sun Also Rises. 1926. New York: Scribner's, 1964.

Janson, H. W., and Samuel Cauman. A Basic History of Art. New York: Abrams,
    1971.

Lawrence, D. H. "In Our Time: A Review." Hemingway: Twentieth Century
    Perspectives. Ed. Robert P. Weeks. Englewood Cliffs: Prentice, 1962. 93–94.

Levin, Harry. "Observations on the Style of Ernest Hemingway." Hemingway:
    Twentieth Century Perspectives. Ed. Robert P. Weeks. Englewood Cliffs:
    Prentice, 1962. 72–85.

Ross, Lilian. "How Do You Like It Now, Gentlemen?" Hemingway: Twentieth Century
    Perspectives. Ed. Robert P. Weeks. Englewood Cliffs: Prentice, 1962. 17–39.

Shakespeare, William. King Lear. Ed. Frank Kermode. The Riverside Shakespeare.
    Boston: Houghton, 1974. 1249–305.

Spiller, Robert E., et al. Literary History of the United States. 3rd ed., rev.
    London: Macmillan, 1963.

Stock, Noel. The Life of Ezra Pound. New York: Pantheon, 1970.

Signaling the Transitions between Sources

If you go to considerable trouble to find and select the right materials to support your ideas, you will want to paraphrase and to use your sources' names in your sentences as a way of keeping them before your reader's eye. Of course, the sources' names should appear only when necessary so that the reader is not distracted by their constant appearance.

In general, the citation of the author's name signals to your reader that you are starting to use new source material; the parenthetical note signals the point of termination for that source.

If the name is not cited at the beginning, readers may not be aware that a new source has been introduced until they reach the parenthetical note. Here is a brief passage from an essay that illustrates this kind of confusion:

> The year 1946 marked the beginning of the postwar era. This meant the de-mobilization of the military, creating a higher unemployment rate because of the large number of returning soldiers. This also meant a slowdown in industry, so that layoffs also added to the rising rate of unemployment. As Cabell Phillips put it: "Motivation [for the Employment Act of 1946] came naturally from the searing experience of the Great Depression, and fresh impetus was provided by the dread prospect of a massive new wave of unemployment following demobiliza-tion" (292–3).

Here, the placement of the citation—"As Cabell Phillips put it"—creates a problem. The way in which the name is introduced into the paragraph firmly suggests that Cabell Phillips is responsible for the quotation and only the quo-tation. (The fact that the quotation is nothing more than a repetition of the first three sentences, and therefore need not have been included in the essay, may also have occurred to you.) Anyone reading the essay will assume that the ref-erence to Phillips covers only the material that starts with the name and ends with the page number. The coverage is not expected to go back any farther than the beginning of the sentence. Thus, in this passage, *the first three sentences are not documented.* Although the writer probably took all the information from Phillips, his book is not being acknowledged as the source. "Probably" is not an adequate substitute for clear documentation. Phillips's name should be cited somewhere at the beginning of the paragraph (the second sentence would be a good place); alternatively, an "umbrella" note could be used (see pp. 387–388).

You may need to insert a parenthetical note in midsentence if that single sen-tence contains references to *two* different sources. For example, you might want to place a note in midsentence to indicate exactly where the source's opinion leaves off and your own begins:

> These examples of hiring athletes to play in college games, cited by Joseph Durso (6), suggest that recruiting tactics in 1903 were not as subtle as they are today.

If the page number were put at the end of the sentence, the reader would as-sume that Durso was responsible for the comparison between 1903 and the present; but he is not. Only the examples must be documented, not the con-clusion drawn from these examples. In this case, the *absence* of a parenthetical note at the end of the sentence signals to the reader that this conclusion is the writer's own.

Here is a passage in which *the techniques of documentation have been used to their fullest extent* and *the transitions between sources are clearly indicated*. This example is taken from Jessie Bernard's "The Paradox of the Happy Marriage," an examination of the woman's role in American marriage. At this point, Bernard has just established that more wives than husbands acknowledge that their marriages are unhappy:

> These findings on the wife's marriage are especially poignant because marriage in our society is more important for women's happiness than for men's. "For almost all measures, the relation between marriage, happiness and overall well-being was stronger for women than for men," one study reports (Bradburn 150). In fact, the strength of the relationship between marital and overall happiness was so strong for women that the author wondered if "most women are equating their marital happiness with their overall happiness" (Bradburn 159). Another study based on a more intensive examination of the data on marriage from the same sample notes that "on each of the marriage adjustment measures . . . the association with overall happiness is considerably stronger for women than it is for men" (Orden and Bradburn 731). Karen Renne also found the same strong relationship between feelings of general well-being and marital happiness: those who were happy tended not to report marital dissatisfaction; those who were not, did. "In all probability the respondent's view of his marriage influences his general feeling of well-being or morale" (64); this relationship was stronger among wives than among husbands (Renne 63).[2] A strong association between reports of general happiness and reports of marital happiness was also found a generation ago (Watson).
>
> [2]Among white couples, 71 percent of the wives and 52 percent of the husbands who were "not too happy" expressed marital dissatisfaction; 22 percent of the wives and 18 percent of the husbands who were "pretty happy" expressed marital dissatisfaction; and 4 percent of the wives and 2 percent of the husbands who were "very happy" expressed marital dissatisfaction.

This paragraph contains *six parenthetical notes* to document the contents of *seven sentences*. Four different works are cited, and, where the same work is cited twice consecutively (Bradburn and Renne), the reference is to a different page. The material taken from page 64 of Renne covers a sentence and a half, from the name "Karen Renne" to the parenthetical note; the remainder of the sentence comes from page 63. Finally, there is no page reference in the note citing Watson, since Bernard is referring the reader to the entire article, not to a single part of it. Notice also that:

- Bernard quotes frequently, but she never places quotations from two different sources together in the same sentence.
- She is careful to use her own voice to provide continuity between the quotations.
- The reader is never in doubt as to the source of information.

Although Bernard does not always cite the name of the author, we are immediately told in each case that there is a source—"one study reports"; "the author wondered"; "another study based on a more intensive examination of the data on marriage from the same sample"; "Karen Renne also found." These phrases not only acknowledge the source but also provide vital transitions between these loosely related points.

EXERCISE 32: USING PARENTHETICAL NOTES

The following paragraph, taken from a research essay about the Industrial Revolution, is based on the source materials in Exercise 30 on p. 369. Compare the paragraph with its sources, and then decide where the parenthetical notes should be placed. Insert the notes, making sure that you distinguish the source material from the writer's own contributions to the paragraph.

The Industrial Revolution caused a major change in the working environment of most people in England. Historians have described the painful transition from working in the home and on the farm to working in the factory. E. J. Hobsbawm points out that most factory employees were at the mercy of the master and his foremen, who controlled their working hours with "draconic discipline." According to W. E. Lunt, those who previously did spinning and weaving in their homes had worked as long and as hard as the workers in the new textile factories, but they had been able to maintain more control over when and how they performed their tasks. It was the male workers who especially resented their loss of freedom and tended to be more resistant to discipline, and so manufacturers found it desirable to hire women and children, who were more passive and obedient. The long hours and bleak and unhealthy environment of the factories must have been particularly hard on the women and children who worked in them. Indeed, Lunt observes that it was their plight that "finally evoked an outcry from the humanitarians." Ultimately, then, an improvement in working conditions came about because of respect for the frailty of women and children, not because of respect for the rights of all workers.

Using Explanatory Notes

You will have noticed that, in the excerpt from Bernard on p. 383, following the second parenthetical reference to Renne, there is a number. This calls the reader's attention to a separate note appearing at the bottom of the paragraph. (In the actual essay, the note would appear either at the bottom of the page or, together with other notes, on a separate sheet at the end of the essay.) Jessie Bernard is using an *explanatory note* as a way of including information that does not quite fit into the text of her essay.

If your research has been thorough, you may find yourself with more material than you know what to do with. It can be tempting to use up every single point on your note cards and cram all the available information into your essay. But if you include too many extraneous points, your reader will find it hard to concentrate on the real topic of your paragraph. To illustrate this point, here are two paragraphs dealing with the domestic life of Charles Dickens: one is bulging; the other is streamlined. The first contains an analysis of Dickens's relationship with his sister-in-law; in the second, he decides to take a holiday in France.

Paragraph 1

Another good friend to Charles Dickens was his sister-in-law. Georgina had lived with the family ever since they had returned from an American tour in June 1842. She had grown attached to the children while the couple was away (Pope-Hennessy 179–80). She now functioned as an occasional secretary to Dickens, specifically when he was writing A Child's History of England, which Pope-Hennessy terms a "rather deplorable production." Dickens treated the history of his country in a very unorthodox manner (311). Dickens must have felt close to Georgina since he chose to dictate the History to her; with all his other work, Dickens always worked alone, writing and correcting it by himself (Butt and Tillotson 20–21). Perhaps a different woman would have questioned the relationship of her younger sister to her husband; yet Kate Dickens accepted this friendship for what it was. Pope-Hennessy describes the way in which Georgina used to take over the running of the household whenever Kate was indisposed. Kate was regularly too pregnant to go anywhere. She had ten children and four miscarriages in a period of fifteen years (391). Kate probably found another woman to be quite a help around the house. Pope-Hennessy suggests that Kate and her sister shared Charles Dickens between them (287).

Paragraph 2

In 1853, three of Dickens's closest friends had died (Forster 124),[5] and the writer himself, having become even more popular and busy since the publication of David Copperfield (Maurois 70), began to complain of "hypochondriacal whisperings" and also of "too many invitations to too many parties" (Forster 125). In May of that year, a kidney ailment that had plagued Dickens since his youth grew worse (Dickens, Letters 350), and, against the advice of his wife, he decided to take a holiday in Boulogne (Johnson 757).[6]

[5]The friends were Mr. Watson, Count d'Orsay, and Mrs. Macready.

[6]Tillotson, Dickens's doctor, who had been in Boulogne the previous October, was the one to encourage him to go there.

The first paragraph obviously contains too much information, most of which is unrelated to this topic. Pope-Hennessy's opinion of the history of England and the history of Kate's pregnancies are topics that may be worth discussing, but not in this paragraph. This extraneous material could be shifted to other paragraphs of the essay, placed in explanatory notes, or simply omitted. Its placement depends on the shape and structure of the entire essay.

The second, much shorter paragraph suggests that related but less important detail can usefully be put into explanatory notes where, if wanted, it is always available. Readers of the second paragraph are being given a choice: they can absorb the essential information from the paragraph alone, or they can examine the topic in greater depth by referring also to the explanatory notes.

Explanatory notes should be reserved for information that, in your view, is useful and to some degree relevant to the topic; if it is uninteresting and way off the point, simply omit it. If you indulge too often in explanatory notes, your notes may be longer than your essay. Also remember to find out whether including explanatory notes is acceptable to your instructor.

Avoiding Excessive Notes

Complex research was needed to gather the numerous details found in the biographical essays about Ernest Hemingway and Charles Dickens, and the writers of these essays use numerous parenthetical notes to document their sources. Here is a brief example:

> Dickens's regular work habits involved writing at his desk from about nine in the morning to two in the afternoon (Butt and Tillotson 19; Pope-Hennessy 248), which left a good deal of time for other activities. Some of his leisure each day was regularly spent in letter-writing, some in walking and riding in the open air (Pope-Hennessy 305, quoting Nathaniel Sharswell). Besides this regular routine, on some days he would devote time to reading manuscripts which Wills, his sub-editor on Household Words, would send to him for revision and comment (Forster 65; Johnson 702).

In this passage, three parenthetical notes are needed for three sentences because a different biographer is the source for each piece of information. To combine all the sources in a single note would confuse, rather than simplify, the acknowledgments. In addition, the writer of this essay is not only making it clear where the information came from, but is also providing the reader with a *choice of references*. The writer has come across the same information in more than one biography, has indicated the duplication of material in her notes, and has decided to demonstrate the thoroughness of her research by citing more than one reference. Since the sources are given equal status in the notes (by being placed in alphabetical order and separated by a semicolon), the reader can assume that they are equally reliable. Had the writer thought that one was more thorough or more convincing than another, she would either have omitted the secondary one or indicated its status by placing it after "also" (Johnson 702; also, Forster 65).

But an abundance of parenthetical notes does not always indicate sound research. As the following example demonstrates, excessive documentation only creates clutter.

> In contrast to the Dickenses' house in London, this setting was idyllic: the house stood in the center of a large garden complete with woods, waterfall, roses (Forster 145), and "no end of flowers" (Forster 146). For a fee, the Dickenses fed on the produce of the estate and obtained their milk fresh from the landlord's cow (Forster 146). What an asset to one's peace of mind to have such a cooperative landlord as they had (Pope-Hennessy 310; Johnson 758; Forster 147) in the portly, jolly Monsieur Beaucourt (Forster 147)!

Clearly, this entire passage is taken from three pages in Forster's biography of Dickens, and a single note could document the entire paragraph. What information is contained in the sentence leading up to the triple parenthetical note that justifies citing three sources? And what does the last note document? Is it only Forster who is aware that Monsieur Beaucourt is portly and jolly? To avoid tiring and irritating his readers, the writer here would have been well advised to ignore the supporting evidence in Pope-Hennessy and Johnson, and use a single reference to Forster. The writer was undoubtedly proud of his extensive research, but he seems more eager to show off his hours in the library than to provide a readable text for his audience.

Using Umbrella Notes

As in the previous example, sometimes the logical sequence of your ideas or information requires you to cite the same source for several sentences or even for several paragraphs at a stretch. Instead of repeating "Forster 146" again and again, you can use a single note to cover the entire sequence. These notes are sometimes called *umbrella notes,* because they cover a sequence of sentences as an umbrella might cover more than one person. Umbrella notes are generally used in essays where the sources' names are not often cited in the text, and so the reader cannot easily figure out the coverage by assuming that the name and the parenthetical note mark the beginning and ending points. An umbrella simply means that you are leaving the reader in no doubt as to how much material the note is covering.

An umbrella note consists of an explanation of how much material is being covered by a source. Such a note is too long to be put in parentheses within the text and generally takes the form of *an explanatory note placed outside the body of your essay.* Here is an example:

> [2]The information in this and the previous paragraph dealing with Dickens's relationship with Wilkie Collins is entirely derived from Hutton, Dickens-Collins Letters 41-49.

Inside your essay, the superscript number 2 referring the reader to this note would follow right after the *last* sentence that uses material from Hutton to discuss Dickens and Wilkie Collins.

Of course, umbrella notes work only when you are using a single source for a reasonably long stretch. If you use two sources, you have to distinguish between them in parenthetical notes, and the whole point of the umbrella—to cut down on the number of notes—is lost.

Umbrella notes must also be used with caution when you are quoting. Because the umbrella provides the reference for a long stretch of material, the citation usually includes several pages; but how will the reader know on which page the quotation appears? Sometimes you can add this information to the note itself:

[2]The information in this and the previous paragraph is entirely derived from Hutton, Dickens-Collins Letters 41-49. The two quotations from Dickens's letters are from pages 44 and 47, respectively.

However, if you use too many umbrella notes, or if you expect a single note to guide your reader through the intricacies of a long paragraph, you will have abused the device. Your essay will have turned into a series of summaries, with each group of paragraphs describing a single source. That is not what a research essay is supposed to be.

THE FINAL BIBLIOGRAPHY

While the bibliography is always an essential part of the research essay, it becomes especially important when you use MLA documentation, since *it is the only place where your reader can find publication information about your sources.* Which works you include in your final bibliography may depend on the wording and intention of your assignment. There is an important difference between a list of works that you have *consulted* or *examined* and a list of works that you have *cited* or actually *used in writing your essay.* Many instructors restrict the bibliography to "Works Cited," but you may be asked to submit a list of "Works Consulted." Remember that one purpose of a "Works Consulted" bibliography is to help your readers to find appropriate background information, not to overwhelm them with the magnitude of your efforts. Don't present a collection of thirty-five titles if you actually cite only five sources in your essay.

An appropriate final bibliography of "Works Consulted" for an undergraduate essay consists of all the sources that you examined (in other words, actually read) that proved to have a clear bearing on your topic, whether or not you actually used them in your essay.

If you consulted a book in the hope that it contained some relevant information, and if it provided nothing useful, should you include it in your final bibliography? You might do so to prevent your readers from repeating your unnecessary research and attempting to consult works with misleading titles in the belief that they might be useful, but only if your bibliography is *annotated* and the book's lack of usefulness can be pointed out. Finally, if you have been unable to locate a source and have thus never examined it yourself, you may not ordinarily include it in your final bibliography, however tempting the title may be.

THE ANNOTATED BIBLIOGRAPHY

Annotating your bibliography (which was described in Chapter 5, pp. 269–271) is an excellent way to demonstrate the quality of your research. But, to be of use, your brief annotations must be informative. The following phrases do not tell the reader very much: "an interesting piece"; "a good article"; "well-done"; "another source of well-documented information." What is well done? Why is it interesting? What is good about it? How much and what kind of information does it contain? A good annotated bibliography will answer some of these questions.

Examine the bibliography on p. 391 carefully, noting the way it presents the basic facts about the author, title, and publication, as well as some *evaluative information*. If the annotations were omitted, these entries would still be perfectly correct, for they conform to the standard rules for bibliographical format. Without the annotation, one would simply have to change the heading to "Works Consulted" or "Works Cited."

Guidelines for Bibliographical Entries

(Additional models can be found in Appendix B, p. 442)

1. The bibliography is always listed on a *separate sheet* at the *end* of your research essay. The title should be centered, one-half inch from the top of the page.

2. Each entry is *double-spaced*, with double spacing between entries.

3. Each bibliographical entry starts with *the author's last name at the margin;* the second line of the entry (if there is one) is indented *five spaces*. This format enables the reader's eye to move quickly down the list of names at the left-hand margin.

4. The bibliography is in *alphabetical order*, according to the last name of the author.

(continued)

(continued)

- If there are two authors, only the first has the last name placed first: "Woodward, Robert, and Carl Bernstein."
- If an author has more than one work included on your list, do not repeat the name each time: alphabetize or arrange chronologically by publication date the works by that author; place the name at the margin preceding the first work; for the remaining titles, replace the name with three hyphens, followed by a period and one space.

Freud, Sigmund. Civilization and Its Discontents. London: Hogarth,

1930.

---. Moses and Monotheism. New York: Knopf, 1939.

- A work that has no author should be alphabetized within the bibliography according to the first letter of the title (excluding "The"); the title is placed at the margin as the author's name would be.

5. A bibliographical entry for a book is read as a list of three items—author, title (underlined), and publication information—with *periods between each piece of information.* Each period is followed by *one* space. All the information should always be presented in exactly the same order that you see in the model bibliography on p. 391. Place of publication comes first; a colon separates place and name of publisher; a comma separates publisher and date.

6. A bibliographical entry for a *periodical* starts with the author's name and the article title (in quotation marks), each followed by a period and one space. Then comes the name of the periodical, followed by one space (and no punctuation at all). What comes next depends on the kind of periodical you are citing.

- For *quarterly and monthly journals,* include the volume number, followed by a space, and then the year in parentheses, followed by a colon.
- For *weekly or biweekly journals,* include only the full date—day, month, and year—followed by a colon.

All periodical entries end with the inclusive pages of the article, first page to last, followed by a period.

Tobias, Sheila, and Carol Weissbrod. "Anxiety and Mathematics: An

Update." Harvard Educational Review 50 (1980): 61-67.

Winkler, Karen J. "Issues of Justice and Individual's Rights Spur

Revolution in Political Philosophy." Chronicle of Higher Education

16 April 1986: 6-8.

7. Each entry of the bibliography ends with a period.

HEMINGWAY: AN ANNOTATED BIBLIOGRAPHY

Baker, Carlos. Hemingway: A Life Story. New York: Scribner's, 1969. 563 pages
of biography, with 100 pages of footnotes. Everything seems to be here,
presented in great detail.

Donaldson, Scott. Hemingway: By Force of Will. New York: Viking, 1977.
The material isn't organized chronologically; instead, the chapters are
thematic, with titles like "Money," "Sex," and "War." Episodes from
Hemingway's life are presented within each chapter. The introduction
calls this "a mosaic of [Hemingway's] mind and personality."

Griffin, Peter. Less Than a Treason: Hemingway in Paris. New York: Oxford UP,
1990. Part of a multivolume biography. Covers Hemingway's life from
1921–1927, exclusively. Griffin says in the preface that his goal is not
to "analyze this well examined life" but "to recreate it." Not surprisingly,
it reads like a novel, with an omniscient narrator with access to
Hemingway's emotions.

Gurko, Leo. Ernest Hemingway and the Pursuit of Heroism. New York: Crowell,
1968. This book is part of a series called "Twentieth-Century American
Writers": a brief introduction to the man and his work. After fifty pages of
straight biography, Gurko discusses Hemingway's writing, novel by novel.
There's an index and a short bibliography, but no notes. The biographical
part is clear and easy to read, but it sounds too much like summary.

Hemingway, Ernest. A Moveable Feast. New York: Scribner's, 1964. This is
Hemingway's own version of his life in Paris. It sounds authentic, but
there's also a very strongly nostalgic tone, so it may not be trustworthy.

Hemingway in Paris. Home page. 13 Oct. 1997 <http://204.122.127.50/WSHS/
Paris/HTM/>. Three photos of the Hemingways' apartment, with brief comments.

Hemingway, Leicester. My Brother, Ernest Hemingway. Cleveland: World, 1962.
For 1924–1925, L.H. uses information from Ernest's letters (as well as
commonly known facts). The book reads like a third-hand report, very
remote; but L.H. sounds honest, not as if he were making up things that
he doesn't know about.

Hotchner, A. E. Papa Hemingway. New York: Random, 1955. This book is
called a "personal memoir." Hotchner met Hemingway in 1948, evidently
hero-worshiped him, and tape-recorded his reminiscences. The book is
their dialogue (mostly Hemingway's monologue). No index or bibliography.
Hotchner's adoring tone is annoying, and the material resembles that of
A Moveable Feast, which is better written.

Meyers, Jeffrey. Hemingway: A Biography. New York: Harper, 1985. Includes several maps, and two chronologies: illnesses and accidents, and travel. Book organized chronologically, with every year accounted for, according to table of contents. Well-documented critical biography, with personal anecdotes taking a back seat to literary. Less gossipy, more circumspect in claims than Griffin.

Reynolds, Michael. Hemingway: The Paris Years. Cambridge, Mass.: Blackwell, 1989. Second of three-volume biography. Includes a chronology covering December 1921–February 1926 and five maps ("Hemingway's Europe 1922–26," "France," "Switzerland," "Italy," and "Key points for Hemingway's several trips through France and Spain").

Sokoloff, Alice Hunt. Hadley, the First Mrs. Hemingway. New York: Dodd, 1973. This is the Paris experience from Hadley's point of view, most of it taken from her recollections and from the standard biographies. (Baker is acknowledged.) It's a very slight book—102 pages—but there's an index and footnotes, citing letters and interviews that some of the other biographers might not have been able to use.

Weeks, Robert P., ed. Hemingway: Twentieth Century Perspectives. Englewood Cliffs: Prentice, 1965. Contains many important essays on Hemingway's life and art. Offers a selected annotated bibliography.

Young, Philip. Ernest Hemingway. Minneapolis: U of Minnesota P, 1959. A short psychobiography of Hemingway's life. Offers stimulating insights, but suffers from the limitations of psychoanalysis.

EXERCISE 33: PREPARING THE BIBLIOGRAPHY

Correct the errors of form in the following bibliography:

Becker, Howard S, Geer, Blanche, and Everett C. Hughes. Making the Grade: New York (1968) Wiley.

Dressel, Paul L.. College and University Curriculum, Berkeley (California): McCutcheon, 1971

(same)----Handbook of Academic Evaluation. San Francisco (California): Jossey-Bass: 1976.

J. F. Davidson, "Academic Interest Rates and Grade Inflation," Educational Record. 56, 1975, pp. 122–5

(no author). "College Grades: A Rationale and Mild Defense." AAUP Bulletin, October 1976, 320–1.

New York Times. "Job Plight of Young Blacks Tied to Despair, Skills Lack," April 19, 1983: Section A page 14.

Milton Ohmer, Howard R. Pollio and James A. Eison. GPA Tyranny, Education Digest 54 (Dec 1988): 11–14.

Leo, John. "A for Effort". Or for Showing Up. U.S. News & World Report, 18 Oct, 1993: 22.

Kennedy, Donald. What Grade Inflation? The New York Times June 13, 1994: All.

Bretz, Jr., Robert D. "College Grade Point Average as a Predictor of Adult Success: a Meta-analytical Review and Some Additional Evidence" Public Personnel Management 18 (Spring 1989): 11–22.

PRESENTING YOUR ESSAY

A well-presented research essay must conform to a few basic mechanical rules:

1. Type your essay on a computer or typewriter. Make sure that you use a letter-quality printer.
2. Double-space throughout the essay.
3. Use 8½-by-11-inch paper; leave 1½-inch margins.
4. Use only one side of the page.
5. Number each page.
6. Proofread your essay, make minor corrections, and print out the revised version. If necessary, make minor corrections in ink.
7. Do not include graphics or illustrations unless your instructor requests them.
8. Include your name, the name of the course, the date, and the title of the essay, either on a separate title page, or on the first page of the essay.

Check with your instructor for any other special rules that may apply to the assignment.

A CHECKLIST FOR REVISION

As you read and re-read your essay, keep the following questions in mind.

1. Does the essay have a single focus that is clearly established and maintained throughout?

2. Does the essay have a thesis or a consistent point of view about the events or issues being described?

3. If it is a narrative essay, does the narration have a beginning, middle, and end? If it is an argument essay, are all assumptions explained and defended, and are all obvious counterarguments accommodated or refuted?

4. Does the essay begin with an informative introduction?

5. Does the essay end on a conclusive note?

6. Does each paragraph have a clear topic sentence?

7. Does each paragraph contain one and only one topic? Should any paragraphs be merged or deleted?

8. Are the paragraphs long enough to be convincing? Is each point supported by facts and information?

9. Does the development of the essay depend entirely on a dry listing of facts and examples, or do you offer explanations and relevant commentary? Is there a good balance between generalization and detail?

10. Do you use transitions to signal the relationship between separate points?

11. Is there unnecessary repetition? Are there any sentences that lack content or add nothing to the essay?

12. Does the reader get a sense of the relative importance of the sources being used?

13. Do you use one source for very long stretches at a time?

14. Is there an appropriate number of notes rather than too many or too few?

15. Is it clear how much material is covered by each note?

16. In essays containing endnotes, do notes provide important explanatory information?

17. Are the quotations well chosen?

18. Is paraphrase properly used? Is the style of the paraphrase consistent with your style?

19. Do you use enough citations? Does the text of the essay make it clear when you are using a specific source, and who that person is?

20. Is the essay convincing? Will your reader accept your analysis, interpretation, and arguments?

▪10▪

Three Research Essays

The following three student research papers, on three very different subjects, use three different kinds of documentation.

The first writer is analyzing an issue and constructing an *argument*. In presenting some of the reasons why some people advocate and others condemn the practice of euthanasia, the writer hopes to persuade his readers that terminally ill people should have the right to choose the time of their deaths. The writer documents his sources with MLA documentation. He summarizes, paraphrases, or quotes one source at a time, which makes it practical to use brief and unobtrusive parenthetical notes at the ends of the sentences. Almost everything that the writer wants to say is said within the body of the essay, so there are only a few endnotes.

The second writer uses a *narrative* structure, with a great deal of precise detail, to describe a real event—the aftermath of a plane crash in the Andes Mountains in 1972. This essay will help you to understand why many history instructors—and also instructors in some other humanities disciplines—still prefer the traditional footnote or endnote and bibliography form of documentation. The writer frequently refers to a group of sources to support specific points; she also presents a great deal of background information that cannot be included in the body of her paper. The separate endnotes provide enough room to cite all the sources and explain some of the points that they are making.

The third writer combines *narrative and analysis* by describing the aftermath of the strange event that happened in 1908 at Lake Tunguska, Siberia, and then analyzing some of the many theories that have been used to explain that event over the last seventy years. The bibliography for this essay contains relatively few sources, which are cited less frequently than the sources are in the first two essays. The writer's purpose is to help his readers understand what might have happened at Lake Tunguska and to clarify the scientific explanations. He is not using numerous sources to reconstruct the event in complete detail, or trying to convince his readers, by citing authorities, that his conclusions are the right ones. Like many essays in the behavioral sciences, this paper uses the author-year variation of parenthetical note documentation. (This method, often called APA after the American Psychological Association, is described in Appendix B, on pp. 452–461.) Having the date, as well as the author, included within the body of the essay is especially useful when you are reading about scientific theories developed over a span of eighty years.

Jorge Catto

English 102

Spring, 1997

Euthanasia: The Right to Die

Someone you love is suffering from terminal cancer. He asks you to inject a lethal drug into him so that he can die without prolonged agony. Would you do it? Should you? Incidents such as this one, in which one person asks another for help to die, are called euthanasia. At the center of this problem is the right of a person to die with the least suffering and the most dignity and comfort. In this essay, I will consider some of the reasons why euthanasia is so vigorously opposed, and why, in spite of that opposition, we must insist on our right to decide for ourselves when to end our own lives.

Euthanasia is usually divided into two kinds: active and passive. According to Michelle Anne Cawley's definition in The American Journal of Nursing, active euthanasia involves directly causing the death of another person through an intended action (859). Administering a fatal drug to a dying person, injecting an air bubble into the bloodstream, or giving him some other means to shorten his life constitute active euthanasia. The most famous recent example of active euthanasia is Dr. Jack Kevorkian, the doctor from Michigan who helps patients to die with the help of his "suicide machine," a tank of carbon monoxide and a mask (McHugh 15–21; Belkin 50; Elliott 27).

Passive euthanasia can be described as helping someone to die by doing nothing, which, according to The Economist, "happens in hospitals all the time" ("Euthanasia War" 22). It is also called, Cawley writes, "cooperating with the patient's dying" (959). Failing to resuscitate a patient who has suffered a massive heart attack is one example of passive euthanasia. Another is deciding not to feed terminally ill patients who are unable to feed themselves. In contrast, removing the feeding tube from a patient who is being fed that way would be considered active euthanasia. Dr. David Orentlicher, in the Journal of the American Medical Association, categorizes "assisted suicide" as a form of passive euthanasia. In assisted suicide, a doctor or other person provides a terminally ill person with the means--pills, for example--and the medical knowledge necessary to commit suicide (1844). Derek Humphrey's 1991 book Final Exit, which describes ways to commit suicide painlessly, and the organization Compassion in Dying, which helps terminally ill patients to end their lives, are both recent examples of instruction in "assisted suicide" (Belkin 50; also Elliott 27).

The professional people who care for the sick and dying think that there is a great difference between active euthanasia and passive euthanasia or "assisted suicide." A panel of distinguished physicians declared themselves in favor, by a margin of 10 to 2, of doctor-assisted suicide for hopelessly ill patients who request it (Orentlicher 1844). In a 1975 survey, 73% of the nurses questioned were in favor of withholding treatment that would prolong the lives of dying patients who don't want their lives sustained in that way--in other words, passive euthanasia. But only 17% were in favor of using active means to end the lives of dying patients who request euthanasia ("Taking Life" 40).

In the past, euthanasia was not such a topic for public speculation and censure. In part, this was because death did not usually take place in a public place, and therefore no one except family members or a doctor was likely to know whether the patient was or wasn't helped to die. Also, doctors lacked the knowledge and the means to try to prolong a dying person's life. But, as Sonia Rudikoff points out in Commentary, this acceptance that death was inevitable and not to be avoided may also have been related to the idea that death was a significant and sacred event and even a welcome one, because it was the prelude to a better existence in the afterlife (62).

Today, as a result of advances in medical science, it has become both possible and, many say, desirable to try to prolong a dying person's life. Indeed, it is considered criminal not to try to do so. Twenty years ago, Peter Hammerli, a doctor in Switzerland, was arrested for "murdering" his patients. He was accused of not taking steps to prolong the lives of the terminally ill people that he was treating.[1] Thus, most controversies over euthanasia center around the issue of who, if anyone, has the right to end a sick person's life. Those concerned in this issue include the patient, the patient's family, and the doctor and nursing staff, all of whom may be affected by their differing conceptions of God or divinity or fate.

In a Gallup poll in 1975, slightly over 50% of Americans said that they do not believe that an individual has the right to end his or her own life ("Taking Life" 40). Most of these people probably share the belief that life is a gift from God and that our bodies and lives are not our private possessions, but are held in trust (Cawley 869). As Rudikoff puts it, they believe that "the breath of life in each of us is a part of a spirit or life, or a community of spirit over which we do not exert ultimate control" (63). To these people, only God has enough knowledge and power to have the right to take away life. They associate euthanasia with murder, and quote Biblical phrases such as "Thou shalt not kill" and "The Lord giveth and the Lord taketh away" as the basis for their belief (Rudikoff 66). They argue that no human being--not even the dying person--can ever be certain when death is about to happen or whether euthanasia is really necessary. So, they want to turn the matter over to God, to whom they attribute perfect objectivity and omniscience.

Advocates of euthanasia think that this argument is a way of avoiding human responsibility. The ideals of our society include the belief that we are all individuals capable of self-determination. A Catholic theologian has observed that, in this respect, man is different from the rest of living creation, because he is "the only animal who knows he is going to die and who also knows he can bring about his own death" (Maguire 57). Before becoming ill, most patients were free to choose their style of life, to decide when to eat, when to sleep, and how to take care of themselves. Why, then, should they not have the right to choose whether to live or to die? (Rudikoff 63). Writing in the New York Times about a decision he once made to end his life if his illness grew more serious, Edward M. Brecher makes the point that it is perfectly acceptable for veterinarians to put extremely sick animals out of their misery, but the same privilege is not usually extended to human beings (72). It is as if one's ability to reason and make moral choices no longer matters when someone is dying.

This issue is made even more painful by the fact that, very often, the dying person is experiencing great suffering. Peter Hammerli became a practitioner of euthanasia because he could not bear to prolong the misery of the patients whom he saw suffering ("Hammerli Affair" 1273). Similarly, a licensed practical nurse reported that she had "seen an elderly terminal patient bite through his I.V. tubing to prevent prolonging of the inevitable. I think it was horrible that we drove that man to such extremes" ("Taking Life" 40). On the other hand, such incidents may be the exceptions, and these re-actions may, to some extent, be extreme and unnecessary. According to a report made by the British Medical Association, most people, no matter how serious their illnesses are, do not die in agony, but rather peacefully and with dignity ("Against Euthanasia" 220).

The right to die with dignity is regarded as almost as important as the right to die without suffering excessive pain. In earlier times, people of all ages died at home, in a natural and familiar setting, with their loved ones about them. According to a survey in Time, 50 years ago, more than half the deaths that took place in the United States occurred at home (Tifft 68). In our time, however, four out of five Americans die in institutions ("Right to Choose" 22). Kathy Fackelmann points out in Science News that patients and their families are especially frightened by "the frantic commotion and turmoil that surround a dying patient." Those who aren't used to the new equipment and the hospital procedures intended to prolong lives think that what goes on is a form of torture inflicted on helpless victims (232).

The person making unpleasant decisions about euthanasia is often not the patient nor one of the patient's relatives, but rather the patient's doctor. The majority of doctors are strongly opposed to both passive and ac-tive euthanasia, arguing that the Hippocratic Oath, which they must swear when they receive their medical degrees, pledges them to save lives, not to end them. Few would approve of Dr. Walter W. Sackett, a general practi-tioner in Miami, who has publicly stated that he has prescribed euthanasia for hundreds of his patients during thirty years of medical practice (Maguire 64).[2] Most doctors tend to share the attitude of the British Medical Associa-tion: "No doctor or nurse should be asked to hold responsibility for deciding when euthanasia may properly be administered, or for administering it" ("Against Euthanasia" 220).

One reason that doctors frequently cite for their refusal to accept any form of euthanasia is that an error may have been made, that the case may not be hopeless, and that, as the British Medical Association puts it, "errors

Catto 5

of judgment in euthanasia cases would be irreversible" ("Against Euthanasia" 220). Some patients with symptoms that suggest a terminal illness have been known to survive for months or years. If euthanasia were an accepted practice, how could such patients be protected from a possible premature death? By prolonging life and postponing death, doctors are also buying time in the hope that a cure might soon be found for a disease that appears to be hopeless (St. John-Stevas 422; Fackelmann 233). To some extent, this concern over possible errors and possible cures may be connected to a fear of being sued. Each year, more and more lawsuits are being brought against doctors who have supposedly failed to use every possible means to ensure that the dying live as long as possible ("Right to Choose" 23). As Richard Lamm notes in his New Republic article, if it can be proven that a doctor has failed to do everything possible to prolong life, then she may be faced with a malpractice suit, and the resulting bad publicity could seriously affect her future career (21).[3]

Another strong professional objection to euthanasia is based on the special relationship that is supposed to exist between doctor and patient. Doctors have traditionally promoted and preserved human life; euthanasia may change the doctor's role, some fear, to that of a hired hand who simply caters to the whims of one person's individual idea of the good life (Callahan, "Euthanasia Debate" 15). More important, people trust doctors because they assume that a doctor's sole object is to save lives. Daniel C. Maguire makes the point that doctors are not supposed to differentiate between good death and bad death: "As medicine has developed, it is geared to promoting life under all circumstances. Death is the natural enemy of the healing science" (59). According to the British writer Norman St. John-Stevas, it is vital that patients continue to regard doctors as a force for life, not as a potential giver of death (422). This argument informs the American Medical Association's vehement opposition to the work of Dr. Jack Kevorkian, a leading practitioner of active euthanasia: "By invoking the physician-patient relationship to cloak his actions, Jack Kevorkian perverts the idea of the caring and committed physician, and weakens the public's trust in the medical profession" (Johnson, par. 1). The British Medical Association confirms that "to be a trusted physician is one thing; to appear as a potential executioner is quite another" ("Against Euthanasia" 220). But there are those who criticize this attitude, suggesting that doctors get considerable personal satisfaction from their almost godlike ability to keep people from dying.[4] Some nurses have criticized the almost proprietary attitude of doctors and other health-care professionals toward their patients:

> In a sense aren't we playing God? If God has called a patient to meet his Maker, what right does a nurse or doctor have to prolong his suffering if there is no hope?

> A patient does not belong to the nurses or to the physician.

> We saved him, if you can call it that. What it amounts to is an ego trip for us. ("Taking Life" 41)

These statements suggest that doctors and nurses may be reluctant to practice or even permit any form of euthanasia because of their own fear of failing to carry out their mission (Fackelmann 232). Conversely, conscientious physicians may find the ethical ramifications of euthanasia too disturbing to accept, for, as Leon Kass of the University of Chicago asks, "How easily will they be able to care wholeheartedly for patients when it is always possible to think of killing them as a 'therapeutic option'?" (35).

Cases of comatose or irreversibly vegetative patients, or of infants born with terminal diseases or generally fatal malformations, present additional ethical problems. In theory, these patients have little to live for, yet they are, of course, unable to request euthanasia for themselves. Who will determine whether euthanasia is appropriate in such instances? Opponents of euthanasia argue that it is impossible for anyone to determine what any individual's "likely quality of life" will be regardless of that individual's present condition (Koop 3), and that "it will be difficult--if not impossible--to develop the requisite calculus of degradation or to define the threshold necessary for ending life" (Kass 33).

One important point is that the mission of the medical profession may have changed as a result of new advances in medical science and technology. The Hippocratic Oath was relatively simple to maintain centuries, even decades ago, before drugs, equipment, and techniques were invented that could prolong the natural course of a patient's life. An article in Science

News describes "the high-tech atmosphere" existing in most hospitals today, especially in intensive care units, that supports the idea that science is stronger than death, and that encourages doctors to think of death as "an unacceptable outcome of medical therapy" (Fackelmann 232). Some hospital teams seem to regard patients as the objects of scientific experiment: Lamm cites the case of a dying woman who was resuscitated 70 times in one 24-hour period (22). Professor George J. Annas of the Boston University School of Medicine considers whether patients have the right to refuse to have their lives prolonged and concludes that "the proper role of medical technology" is at the center of the debate over euthanasia: "Is technology going to be our master or our servant? Is technology going to take on a life of its own such that we give it rights of its own? Or are we going to reassert our dominant role in controlling technology and using it for human ends?" ("Symposium").[5]

An important factor here is the high cost of these technological miracles. Maintaining a comatose patient can cost hundreds of thousands of dollars. Even if much of the financial burden is placed on health insurance agencies or the government, the gain may not be worth the cost. Noting that, in 1983, the national bill for health care was $355 billion, Lamm observes that "the time is not far off when there will be a direct conflicts [sic] between the health of the individual and the health of the society" (21). Given the limited amount of money available to pay for chronic and terminal illnesses, it may be necessary to make some unpleasant choices. Opponents of euthanasia argue that, "because death is cheaper than treatment," hospitals, concerned with costs, might be tempted to practice euthanasia without patients' consent ("Euthanasia War" 22). In contrast, those who advocate some kind of euthanasia policy point out that providing the latest medical equipment for one comatose or terminally ill patient may drain resources that might be used to pay for more nursing personnel and a more pleasant environment for other patients. There are also those who believe that available resources should be spent on preventive medicine: according to one doctor writing in The New England Journal of Medicine, "the costs of trying to preserve the life of one cirrhotic patient with bleeding esophageal varices might be used to treat and prevent alcoholism in many persons" (Lamm 21).

The final argument against euthanasia that must be given serious consideration is that it is dangerous for any society to legalize the killing of a certain class of its citizens. Daniel Callahan of the Hastings Center argues that a society that condones euthanasia condones a fundamental moral wrong, namely to give one individual

> ultimate power over another. It is to create the wrong kind of relationship between people, a community that sanctions private killings amongst its members in pursuit of their individual goals. (5)

In the Hastings Report Special Supplement, Richard Fenigsen further cautions that the line between voluntary and involuntary euthanasia--between euthanasia and "crypthanasia"--is inherently impossible to distinguish and that members of some societal groups, the elderly for instance, may submit to euthanasia against their will if they feel pressured to do so by relatives, doctors, or society at large (25). Furthermore, according to those who reject euthanasia, it is too easy to enlarge the category of people marked for euthanasia to include the handicapped, the mentally ill and retarded, those convicted of serious crimes, and other groups rejected by society. Eventually, once the barriers begin to break down, the whole attitude of a society toward its members may undergo an "ominous shift":

> Instead of the message a humane society sends to its members--"Everybody has the right to be around, we want to keep you with us, every one of you"--the society that embraces euthanasia, even the "mildest" and most "voluntary" forms of it, tells people: "We wouldn't mind getting rid of you."
> (Fenigsen 26)

In light of Washington State's 1991 Initiative 119, a narrowly defeated referendum that would have made it legal for doctors in Washington to help terminally ill patients commit suicide (Belkin 51), opponents of euthanasia believe they have even more reason to fear the "slippery slope" syndrome: once a society makes it legal to kill one patient, then what's to stop it from unfairly killing many (Elliott 26)?

Some critics of euthanasia express concern about its implications as a social policy. St. John-Stevas points to the terrible precedent of Nazi Germany and the eugenics movement, which attempted to eliminate everyone who did not meet a certain standard of social excellence and desirability (421). Rudikoff fears that we will create "euthanasia mills," which would make the termination of life a routine matter (66). It is true that, as one psychiatrist put it, euthanasia can never be "a logical decision. It is not one that you can make by a computer model" (Fackelmann 233). It is important to have some degree of personal involvement in each decision, to consider each case individually, and to assert, as Dr. Peter Hammerli did, that "I have never done anything to my patients that I would not do for my own mother and father . . . if they were in such a position" ("Hammerli Affair" 1272).

If euthanasia is going to become acceptable social policy, it is important to have some guidelines so that hospitals and nursing homes will understand when and by whom each decision will be made. Otherwise, John Ladd observes in Ethics, euthanasia will eventually take place at random: "Sometimes someone, no one knows who it is, will turn off the ventilator or will turn it on again after it has been turned off, because he thinks that one ought to let the patient die or ought not to let him die." These communication breakdowns can happen easily enough when everyone thinks it is his or her particular duty to intervene--or to stop someone else from intervening. Eventually, Ladd continues, "the patient becomes a football tossed around among those with different and competing interests and ideologies" (138).

One solution to this problem is, whenever possible, to allow individuals to assume the responsibility for deciding when they are ready to die (Modell 908). The report of the Presidential Commission in 1983 determined that a dying patient, if competent to make a decision, should be informed of all the available options and that "those who decline life-prolonging therapy should not be denied other forms of care needed to relieve pain and to maintain dignity" ("Right to Choose" 23). But doctors may not always be sure when patients are competent to make a responsible decision or whether they may have been coerced by family members for whom a lingering illness may be a continued burden (Rudikoff 66–67). For this reason, supporters of the right to euthanasia frequently recommend that each individual write a "living will" relatively early in life while still healthy and undeniably competent to make decisions (Rudikoff 64; "Hammerli Affair" 1272). Such a legal document would state that, should the person be incapable of making such a decision, he or she is establishing certain preferences among the options that

Catto 10

might be available for his or her care. Typically, such wills, which have been authorized by numerous states, instruct doctors not to start or to stop any procedures intended to sustain life if the condition is terminal (Modell 908).

Of course, a living will is no assurance that the patient would still choose euthanasia. What if the patient has changed his mind since he wrote the living will? (Fackelmann 233; Rudikoff 66). A nurse who frequently cares for the dying notes that many patients do change their minds--sometimes more than once--as death approaches: "Since the patient may be unresponsive by this time, and since hearing is the last thing to go, I have wondered if it wouldn't be a terrible thing to be laying [sic] there and each time someone came in, wondering if they were coming to kill you" ("Taking Life" 42). That is, of course, a horrifying picture. But so, too, is the picture of a patient lying there longing for death and unable to convince anyone to carry out that wish.

Today, for most of us, the dread of death is so great that we go to any lengths to avoid it for those we love, as well as for ourselves. However, death in the right circumstances is everyone's right. It may be that the right to choose euthanasia would never have become a vital issue if death were a more integral part of our lives and if the circumstances in which death took place were easier to bear. St. John-Stevas argues against euthanasia by asserting that "dying can be a vital period in a person's life, reconciling him to life and death and giving an interior peace" (422). But this kind of ideal acceptance of death is possible only if there is a lot of care and love provided by all those in charge of the patient. At present, we seem to be more concerned with keeping people alive than with the quality of the lives that are being prolonged. Until we can have some assurance of a compassionate death--without unbearable cost to others and to society--we should not be intimidated by the church, the law, or the medical profession. Just as we choose the way we live, so should we be able to choose the way we die.

Note: According to MLA guidelines, quotations more than four lines in length should start on a new line, indented either one inch or ten spaces. The first line of each note indents one-half inch or five spaces. In the "Works Cited" list, the first line of each entry should be flush left and additional lines should indent one-half inch or five spaces.

Notes

[1] When there seemed to be no hope at all of a return to consciousness for those elderly people who were being kept alive by artificial feeding, Hammerli and his staff decided against continued treatment. Defending his actions, Hammerli insisted that he did not "believe in giving extensive treatment to a patient who is hopelessly ill: sometimes it is better to allow a person to die in peace" (26).

[2] Sackett suggests that, whether they admit it or not, 75% of all doctors have acted similarly at some point in their careers.

[3] The president of a Presidential Commission on the question of euthanasia is concerned that this fear of legal action may affect doctors' medical judgment. He imagines "a future horror scene in which a dying patient looks up from his deathbed to see the doctor flipping through a thick docket of legal cases" (Fackelmann 233).

[4] Of those few (17%) nurses who favored active euthanasia, only half would allow patients themselves the means to end their own lives; the other half believe that only professionals should be allowed to make and carry out that decision ("Taking Life" 40).

[5] The case of Elizabeth Bouvia is a good illustration. A quadriplegic who is regarded as mentally competent, Bouvia has been prevented from carrying out her expressed wish to end her own life by hospital staff, who insist on force-feeding her. Ernest van den Haag compares this with force-feeding convicts who go on hunger strikes, and argues that it is acceptable to force food on convicts since they are not entitled to the same liberties that free people are. "A hospital . . . may be liable for failing to artificially feed patients who cannot eat by normal means, or are incompetent. But not a patient who will not eat. He has a perfect right to decline food, or medicine, or an operation, if he so wishes and is competent to understand the consequences" (45–46).

Works Cited

"Against Euthanasia." The Lancet 30 Jan. 1971: 220.

Belkin, Lisa. "There's No Simple Suicide." New York Times Magazine 14 Nov. 1993: 48–55+.

Brecher, Edwin. "Opting for Suicide." New York Times Magazine 18 Mar. 1979: 72–80.

Callahan, Daniel. "Can We Return Disease to Death?" Hastings Center Report Special Supplement Feb. 1989: 4–6.

---. "The Euthanasia Debate: A Problem with Self-Determination." Current Oct. 1992: 15–19.

Cawley, Michelle Anne. "Euthanasia: Should It Be a Choice?" American Journal of Nursing May 1977: 859–61.

Elliott, Carl. "Dying Rites: The Ethics of Euthanasia." New Scientist 20 June 1992: 25–27.

"The Euthanasia War." The Economist 21 June 1997: 21–24.

Fackelmann, Kathy. "A Question of Life or Death." Science News 9 Oct. 1982: 232–33.

Fenigsen, Richard. "Euthanasia: How It Works: The Dutch Experience." Hastings Center Report Special Supplement Feb. 1989: 22–30.

"The Hammerli Affair: Is Passive Euthanasia Murder?" Science 26 Dec. 1975: 1271–74.

Humphrey, Derek. Final Exit: The Practicalities of Self-Deliverance and Assisted Suicide for the Dying. Eugene: Hemlock Society, 1991.

Johnson, Kirk. "The AMA's Response to Jack Kevorkian." Ohio Right to Life. 21 Nov. 1995. 2 May 1997 <http://www.infinet.com/~life/euth/amaltr.htm>.

Kass, Leon R. "Neither for Love or for Money: Why Doctors Must Not Kill." Public Interest Winter 1989: 25–26.

Koop, C. Everett. "The Challenge of Definition." Hastings Center Report Special Supplement Feb. 1989: 2–15.

Ladd, John. "Euthanasia, Liberty, and Religion." Ethics Oct. 1982: 129–38.

Catto 13

Lamm, Richard D. "Long Time Dying." New Republic 27 Aug. 1984: 20–23.

Macguire, Daniel C. "Death By Chance, Death By Choice." Good
    Housekeeping Jan. 1975: 57–65.

McHugh, Paul R. "The Kevorkian Epidemic." *The American Scholar* Winter
    1997: 15–27.

Orentlicher, David. "Physician Participation in Assisted Suicide." Journal of
    the American Medical Association 262 6 Oct. 1989: 1844–45.

"The Right to Choose." Economist 26 March 1983: 22–23.

Rudikoff, Sonia. "The Problem of Euthanasia." Commentary Feb. 1974:
    62–68.

St. John-Stevas, Norman. "Euthanasia: A 'Pleasant Sounding Word.'"
    America 31 May 1975: 421–22.

"Symposium: When Sophisticated Medicine Does More Harm Than Good."
    New York Times 30 Mar. 1986: E6.

"Taking Life Away." Nursing 75 Oct. 1975: 4050.

Tifft, Susan. "Debate on the Boundary of Life." Time 11 Apr. 1983: 68–70.

van den Haag, Ernest. "A Right to Die?" National Review 4 May 1984: 45–46.

Walzen, Michael. "Feed the Face." *The New Republic* 9 June 1997: 29.

Smith 1

Joan Smith

History 101

December 10, 1997

The Quest for Survival in the Andes Mountains

What was meant to be a pleasure trip for forty-five people flying from
Montevideo, Uruguay, to Santiago, Chile, on October 13, 1972, turned into
the horror of instant death for some and of slow starvation in the freezing
Andes temperatures for others. The Old Christian Rugby Team and families
and friends of the team--forty-five in all--flew out of Montevideo with nothing
more on their minds than a rugby match with a Chilean team and a few
days of skiing. But a terrifying plane crash in the rugged peaks of the Andes
changed everything. What ensued for those who survived first the crash of
their plane and then a crushing avalanche a short time later was a long ordeal of hunger and cold. The events that took place during these seventy-two
days high in the icy Andes remain a fascinating story of the tenacity of the
human will to survive at almost any cost, even the cost of eating human flesh.

According to a comprehensive newspaper account, the rugby team
departed from Montevideo on October 12, 1972, in a propeller-driven Fair-
child F-227, a Uruguayan Air Force plane, and after a night in Mendoza because of bad weather, they resumed their flight on Monday, October 13, at
midday. The plane would cross an Andes mountain range that had peaks
up to 21,000 feet in a blizzard.[1] As Piers Paul Read describes it, though the
weather was inclement, everyone was assured that the flight was perfectly
safe because the plane would be able to stay above the clouds. As the plane
approached Santiago, the co-pilot Lagurara radioed Air Traffic Control at
3:35 to announce the plane's location and altitude. The controllers authorized him to lower the plane to 10,000 feet as he neared the airport of
Pudaheul. However, when he brought the plane down 3,000 feet, it began
to shake as it entered the clouds. The plane continued to jump and shake
more vigorously as it entered other cloudbanks; the passengers began to
panic and pray.[2]

Apparently, as the plane continued through clouds, it got caught in
an air pocket, sank quickly in seconds, and broke apart against the side of

Smith 2

an 11,500-foot mountain.[3] According to Benales's account, the tail section somersaulted down a mountain slope, killing those in the back of the plane immediately, while some still in their seats were swept out of the front of the plane because of the force of the air. The front section of the aircraft, or fuselage, slammed onto an area between peaks in the Hilario range of the Andes. José Luis Inciarte, one of the survivors interviewed by Benales, later described the scene as the fuselage slid over the snow: "Blood spurted all over me, people were screaming and I could smell fuel and cold air rushing in from outside, when suddenly with one big bump we came to rest."[4] Twelve of the forty-five people on board were killed in the crash.[5]

The first twenty-four hours were the worst for the survivors of the crash. Many were seriously or fatally injured, almost all were in a state of shock, and all of them froze in subfreezing temperatures of an Andes blizzard. Gustavo Zerbino, another survivor, remembers the first night as a nightmarish series of the "injured screaming, crying, dying. . . ."[6] Those who survived the first night did so by wrapping up in the ski clothes they had brought for their holiday[7] and by covering up in the seat covers they ripped from the seats of the plane. The group was almost totally exposed to the cold air, with only a makeshift barrier of seats and luggage protecting them. Worse than the cold was the hysteria.[8] It is miraculous that any survived that first night; the day after the crash, Chilean authorities said the chance for survival was "virtually nil" because those who hadn't died in the crash would die in the freezing blizzard.[9]

Suffering through the first night was the first of many trials for the sixteen who would live to tell the story. All of those who survived the crash had sustained some type of injury. In fact, three more people died during that first night. The wounded had to be attended to; fortunately, the survivors had among them an innovative medical student named Robert Canessa. Under Canessa's supervision, the survivors fought to keep their wounded alive. With the few makeshift medical tools they had, they tried several surgical operations. Cologne was the only disinfectant they had, and the harsh environment simply would not let the wounded heal properly.[10] Some would suffer from gangrene.[11] The fuselage also had to be made livable. The men of the rugby team worked tenaciously to pack the open back

Smith 3

of the plane with whatever they could find to block the wind; they continued to rip the covers off the seats for more blankets; they made hammocks for the wounded out of cable and cord and metal plates ripped from the side of the plane.[12]

And they worried about how to get food and water. For ten days after the crash, the survivors lived off the meager rations that were found on the wrecked plane. During that period, each of the twenty-seven who survived the initial ordeal lived on a daily ration of one square of chocolate, one teaspoon of jam, a bit of toothpaste, and a small mouthful of wine in a deodorant cap.[13] Thirst was a big concern. In temperatures often descending to 25°C below zero, melting snow for water was a problem. Eating snow was no substitute for drinking water, as it burned the survivors' chapped lips and gave them stomach cramps.[14] They used the metal sheets from the wreck to rig up reflectors that tediously melted the snow into bottles. This process was slow, however, and the survivors were forced to carefully ration water.[15]

Meanwhile, the survivors had hope of rescue. A transistor radio was found in the wreckage, and Carlos Rosque, the plane's mechanic and only surviving crew member, said that batteries for it could be found in the other half of the plane. Three of the strongest survivors, including Canessa and Fernando Parrado, the two who would eventually succeed in hiking out of the mountains, went in search of the lost tail. After a strenuous hike, they located it, but the batteries were too heavy to carry back to the wreck. The three returned and the next day found it easier to carry the relatively light radio back to the tail. Roy Haley, who was knowledgeable about radios, went with them, and eventually figured out a way for them to listen to Radio Spectator in Montevideo. Listening to the radio, however, may have turned out to be more tragic than hopeful. On October 21, eight days after the crash, Haley heard that the rescue mission had been called off because there was little reason to believe anyone could survive the crash and the cold.[16]

After hearing that the search had been called off, the survivors knew that they would have to discover another source of food if they were going to live. Their meager rations were quickly running out, and the men were beginning to feel the effects of starvation.[17] They considered all possible options for sustenance. No plant life that might provide food survived in the harsh weather of the Andes; they found only lichen on the exposed rocks, which was worthless as sustenance.[18] For several days, many of the men had been silently concluding that the only way they would survive was to eat the bodies of those who had died. Canessa, the medical student, finally had the courage to openly suggest the possibility of consuming human flesh. He urged that, since the rescue had been called off, the only way the group would live was by rescuing themselves, and they could only do this if they had food. Further, he admonished that they had the moral duty to stay alive, that they had been given the gift of life and were responsible for sustaining it. Though many had serious reservations about eating the flesh of their families and friends, they felt the force of Canessa's arguments.[19] Several others supported Canessa, clothing their arguments more and more in religious language. God wanted them to live, they argued; He had spared them from the crash and had given them the bodies to eat. It would be wrong to reject this gift on the grounds of squeamishness.[20]

On the tenth day after the crash and the second day after the crushing news about the cancellation of rescue efforts, after much heated discussion, Canessa, with the support of most of the twenty-six other survivors, cut into a corpse with a shard of glass and ate the flesh.[21] The group calculated that each corpse would last five days if they carefully rationed their intake.[22] Two metaphors helped them to justify their actions. The group compared their consumption of flesh to a heart transplant; just as a heart is taken from one person at death to keep another alive, so the dead bodies sustained the breath of the living. But the most powerful metaphor for the survivors, most of whom were Catholic, was the sacrament of the Holy Communion.[23] Survivor Eduardo Deigrado later said, concerning their decision, "We thought of Jesus and how in the Last Supper He had divided his body and blood to all the apostles. We understood that we had to do the same, to take His body and blood which had been reincarnated and that was an intimate communion among us. It was what helped us to subsist."[24] Catholic priests would later support the survivors' decision. Two priests said that the men had "acted justifiably" and within the bounds of religious morality; a person is permitted to eat human flesh, they said, if there is no other means for survival. They called the Communion metaphor "not unreasonable."[25]

In fact, the group's shared religious beliefs helped them through the many life-threatening difficulties they faced. As José Luis Inciarte said later, "When we got really low in spirits, we said our rosary together and we were overcome with such strong faith that it bubbled up inside of us."[26] Carlos Paez led the men in a nightly rosary throughout the ordeal.[27] But it was not only religion that kept them alive; their youthful good health, as well as the teamwork and discipline developed on the rugby field, also worked to sustain them.[28] As Claudia Dowling describes it, the survivors, all aged from nineteen to twenty-six, worked together unselfishly, making rules and organizing chores. Adolfo Staunch, Eduardo Staunch, and Daniel Fernandez, all cousins, initially took charge of apportioning labor and of the unpleasant task of flaying the bodies. Others, like Canessa and Parrado, also emerged as leaders. The men knew that to survive they must construct and follow communal rules. Their discipline and teamwork kept them from consuming too much food too quickly and encouraged them to look after each other's needs. They knew that any selfish behavior might lead to death. The fact that the men were friends from the same town definitely made their community more harmonious than it might have been in other circumstances. Inciarte remembers that when he was down to half of his body weight and barely able to move, Adolfo Staunch gave him an entire bottle of his precious water. Such unselfish behavior, generated by both religious belief and friendship, kept the men alive.[29] Dowling points out that the survivors "never degenerated into Lord of the Flies primitivism, never turned on one another. They worked together as a tribe so all might survive."[30]

Not all groups have behaved so harmoniously under the duress of cold and starvation. The comparable incident of the Donner Party, trapped in the Sierra Nevada mountains of California in the winter of 1846–47, provides a gruesome foil to the ordeal of the Uruguayan rugby team. The party, comprised of ten unrelated families and sixteen other individuals and headed by the Illinois farmer George Donner, was snowbound in the Sierra Nevadas as they were making their way west. What ensued during that winter shares with the Andes incident the same tenacious struggle to survive under similar conditions, but greed, selfishness, and possibly murder taint the story.[31] As hunger overtook the party, families with food often refused to help those with less, or charged them exorbitant prices for meager por-tions[32] and then seized their goods when they could not pay.[33] After the food ran out, the party agreed that cannibalism was the only means of sur-vival. They waited impatiently for someone to die. When a bachelor in the group accidentally caught his hand on fire, they refused to save him; he died and they ate him.[34] As one member of the party wrote in his journal, cer-tain people then began to talk freely about shooting and eating those who were probably going to die anyway.[35] Later, a woman, after eating a corpse, shot, killed, and ate the two Native Americans in the party. Finally, after some of the party had finally hiked out of the mountains and returned to rescue the others, a man named Keseberg was found alone, surrounded by several mutilated corpses and incredible filth. Though he said they had died naturally, he was frank about eating their flesh and enjoying it, and valu-ables of the dead were found on his person.[36]

Though physically taxed to the same limit as the Donner Party was, the Andes survivors maintained a sense of charity and morality. It is testi-mony to the group's fortitude that they held together in relative harmony and survived. As the days passed, their ordeal only became more dire. One week after eating their first flesh, they were struck by another tragedy. The group of twenty-seven was reduced to nineteen after an avalanche crashed into the fuselage in the middle of the night, and killed eight while wrecking the carefully arranged barrier against the cold.[37] The avalanche struck sud-denly; the men all felt a push on the plane, and then all were buried, giving themselves up to die. Again, only the strength of those lucky enough not to be fully buried prevented the number of deaths from increasing. They worked vigorously to pull others from the snow and revive them with mouth-to-mouth resuscitation.[38] Those who did survive did so miraculously. In-ciarte recalls his good fortune: "It [the avalanche] got me with my hand in front of my face, so I managed to make a little cavity and breathe a bit. I heard screaming. . . . I moved my hand about a bit but couldn't get out. I think it was the worst moment of all because I really gave myself up for lost."[39] But he was finally pulled out.

Though the group had found a way to sustain themselves and made rules for running an efficient community, the days after the avalanche

threatened their morale. Not only did the men grieve over the deaths of their
friends, but they also had to witness the slow deaths of three others due to
starvation or injuries suffered in the crash or the avalanche. Among these
was Numa Turcatti, one of the strongest and most fit of the group. During
the days after the avalanche, he had suddenly lost the will to live; he refused
food to the point that he essentially let himself die in early December.[40]
Others seemed to follow Turcatti's lead, as despair set in for the group. Strife
over cigarette rations was a constant irritation; discord started to threaten
the group's harmony.[41]

A numbing boredom made matters worse. The men were well aware
that they were miles from civilization, and that almost impassable mountains separated them from the nearest village.[42] In the face of such slim
odds for survival, the group often had bouts with apathy. Through the long
cold days and nights of November, they underwent long periods of silence.[43]
They tried various ways to invigorate their spirits. Aside from the daily routine of melting snow for water and eating their sparse meals, they engaged in
group discussions on pre-arranged topics,[44] planned what they would do
when they returned to Montevideo, listed the best restaurants in their town,
and held small birthday celebrations with red wine for the three men whose
birthdays came during their ordeal.[45]

The survivors also continued to consider how they might rescue
themselves. After several failed attempts to use the radio to call for help,
they decided that the only chance for survival lay in hiking out of the mountains.[46] Throughout their stay in the mountains, the group had been sending out small scouting parties on trial expeditions. These short excursions
allowed them to determine who the strongest of the group were and what
clothing and methods for carrying food were the most effective.[47] As December approached, the weather began to warm as spring approached in the
seasonal cycle of the Southern Hemisphere. Canessa, Parrado, and Antonio
Vizintin were selected to make the trek out of the mountains.[48] The group
began gathering food and the best clothing for the expeditioners, and tore
felt covers from the heating tubes in the aircraft to make sleeping bags for
them.[49] But the scouting trips did not provide much information on the
group's exact location. They knew Chile was to the west, and had the air-

craft compass to point them in that direction. Otherwise, the three knew they would be wandering blindly through the rugged, freezing peaks of the Andes.[50]

At the end of the first week of December, after the group had been trapped on the mountain for fifty-six days, two condors appeared and circled the sky. These were the first of several signs of spring. The weather warmed; the group heard from the radio that the search had resumed. They had planned for Canessa, Parrado, and Vizintin to leave as soon as the weather improved; the preparations for the journey were almost finished. However, the normally strong-willed Canessa began to procrastinate. As Read's account and the film based on it illustrate, strife broke out between Canessa and the others when he began finding excuses for not going on the journey. The others knew the effort would fail without him and felt that he was letting them down for the first time. Just before their greatest attempt to overcome their plight, the group seemed to be falling apart.[51]

It took another death to persuade Canessa that he must go. Turcatti finally breathed his last on December 10, reducing the number of survivors to sixteen. Canessa realized that he could wait no longer; the group's morale could stand little more. Others were on the verge of death as well.[52] Many had dropped in weight from two hundred to one hundred pounds.[53]

On December 11, the three set out, loaded with as many clothes and as much food as they could carry. On the third day of strenuous travel, during which the hunger-weakened travellers averaged only four miles a day,[54] they reached the top of a high mountain; there they saw a distant valley between the only two mountains that weren't snow-covered. They realized then that there was not enough food for the three of them to reach the valley. They decided that Vizintin must return to the plane so that Canessa and Parrado would have enough food to complete the journey.[55]

The two resumed a journey that would end seven days later. Of the many hard-fought victories over death during the ordeal, this ten-day trek was the most triumphant and the most difficult. Canessa recalls those "unending days of travel--intense cold at night, intolerable heat at midday. We rationed the water and the food and said, 'if we don't walk so far, then no food for us.'"[56] The two were near death from exhaustion and hunger when they saw a rancher's hut in Chile on December 20. The hut belonged to Sergio Catalan Martinez, a forty-four-year-old cattle hand, living in San Fernando, who at 9 p.m. heard the faint shouts of the men across the roaring Tinguiririca River. He saw what seemed to be two tramps shouting at him on the other side of the water. When he still couldn't hear them, he threw over a stone with a paper and pen attached. Parrado quickly wrote,

> I come from the plane that crashed in the mountains. I am Uruguayan. We have been walking like this for 10 days. My friend is injured [from the hike]. There are still 14 injured people in the plane. We have to get out of here quickly because we have nothing to eat. We can walk no more.[57]

He threw the rock back to Sergio, who immediately went for help; patrols reached them by 12 p.m.

Canessa and Parrado made it out just in time. By the time the men back at the plane heard the message on the radio that they would be rescued, they had almost given up hope. Each day brought the prospect of death by starvation. Christmas was approaching, and their pessimism grew each day that they heard no news of Canessa and Parrado. Only the remnants of their incredible will to stay alive kept them from sinking totally into despair like Turcatti.[58] But everything changed on the morning of December 20. As the men heard the news, euphoria spread through their camp. They abandoned their daily tasks; they made their remaining cigarettes into Havana-style cigars. Two days later, on the afternoon of December 22, most of the men were taken out by helicopter; the rest were removed the following day.[59] The seventy-two-day ordeal was over. They had survived.

The aftermath of the ordeal caused a major stir in Uruguay. As the survivors revealed their story and their methods of survival, the reaction from the media was one of admiration and sympathy. Experts were amazed that the men could walk and remain mentally lucid after such starvation.[60] People were moved by the religious metaphors the men used to describe their consumption of flesh. But the dead were not forgotten. The twenty-nine victims were given a Christian burial in a common grave near the snow-covered wreckage.[61]

The survivors' celebrity status has not waned in their home country, and now it is international in the wake of the film Alive. Dowling suggests that, while the survivors cannot forget their great victory for the force of life, they also won't forget the sacrifice and the pain. They were made soberer and wiser from the ordeal, with striking insights into what a human is capable of. Many survivors felt a religious depth on the mountain they have never again experienced.[62] As Canessa said in a recent interview about his reaction to the film Alive, "I think it's a family film because it values religion and friendship, if in a touching and different way."[63] This remark perhaps best sums up what the victory of the survivors can mean for us; life and friendship are precious and powerful gifts, and not to be taken lightly.

Notes

[1] Carlos Benales, "70 Days Battling Starvation and Freezing in the Andes: A Chronicle of Man's Unwillingness to Die," New York Times, 1 Jan. 1973: A3. This article was the first comprehensive one on the Andes story. It was issued from the South American news agency LATIN.

[2] Piers Paul Read, Alive (New York and Philadelphia: Lippincott, 1974), 36–37. Of the many books written about this Andes mountain incident, Read's is considered the most authoritative, so I have chosen to use it to elucidate certain points of the story. The survivors of the group authorized this book so that the truth could be known about the many rumors surrounding their story. The other books on the subject did not receive authorization and Frank Marshall chose Alive as the most accurate basis for his 1993 film portraying the story. The book is written in the form of a novel; it is based on actual events that Read has brought to life in more detail. Read's book contains all information that appears in this essay; I have specifically drawn on it to elucidate certain scenes that the periodical articles either did not cover or dealt with only briefly. Other unauthorized, novelistic accounts of the story may be found in Enrique Hank Lopez's The Highest Hell (New York: Pocket Books, 1973), Clay Blair Jr.'s Survive! (Berkeley: Berkeley Books, 1973), and Richard Cunningham's The Place Where the World Ends (New York: Sheed and Ward, 1973).

[3] Claudia Glenn Dowling, "Still Alive," Life, 16 Jan. 1993: 50.

[4] Benales.

[5] Several of the survivors later blamed the crash on a pilot's error. Terry Clifford, "Staying Alive," Chicago Tribune, 15 Jan. 1993: 5:3.

[6] Don Podesta, "Echoes of a Crash Unheard of: The Tales of 16 Uruguayans Are Still as Chilling as Their Survival 20 Years Ago," Washington Post, 21 Dec. 1992: C1. Benales reported that the co-pilot spent the entire night groaning for water and for his revolver.

[7] Benales.

[8] Read, 47.

[9] "Uruguayan Plane with 45 Is Missing on Andes Flight," New York Times, 14 Oct. 1972: A9.

[10] The information in this paragraph up to this point comes from "Cannibalism After Air Crash Reported," New York Times, 27 Dec. 1972: D2. Canessa extracted a steel bar, for example, from the intestines of a wounded person, who nevertheless died, as did two others who died over the next few days.

[11] Rick Miller, "A Nightmare Revisited: 20 Years Later, with the Film's Release, Andes Survivors Recall Ordeal," Boston Globe, 21 Jan. 1993: 1:2.

[12] Benales.

[13] Dowling, 50. Also, "8 Survivors of Crash Picked Up in Andes," New York Times, 24 Dec. 1972: A9.

[14] Benales.

[15] Benales; Podesta.

[16] This account of finding the batteries and listening to the radio is taken from Benales. Though official searches were called off, the parents of those on the plane continued to search throughout the ordeal. Most notably, Carlos Paez Vilaro, the father of Carlitos Paez, searched diligently for his son, plotting clairvoyants' visions of maps, hounding the authorities, and searching by means of airplanes, on a mule, and on foot. Dowling, 58.

[17] Read, 81. Read describes their hunger: "Starvation was taking its effect. They were becoming weaker and more listless. When they stood up they felt faint and found it difficult to keep their balance. They felt cold, even when the sun rose to warm them, and their skin started to grow wrinkled like that of old men."

[18] Read, 82. Benales reports that the group also tried to make a soup out of the lichens and water.

[19] Miller.

[20] Read, 84–85.

[21] Dowling, 51.

[22] Benales.

[23] "Cannibalism." Both metaphors are described in this article.

[24] "Survivors of Andes Air Crash Admit Dead Saved Their Lives," New York Times, 29 Dec. 1972: A9. Canessa also justified their actions later when he said, "I've . . . thought that if I were dying, I would be proud that a friend could use my body." Clifford, 5:3.

[25] "Two Catholic Aides Defend Cannibalism in Chilean Air Crash," New York Times, 28 Dec. 1972: A8.

[26] Benales.

[27] Podesta.

[28] Benales.

[29] Dowling, 50, 55.

[30] Dowling, 50. Dowling goes on to aptly link the men's friendship, religion, and consumption of flesh:

> At the most basic level, friendship is founded on the sharing of food; the word companion comes from the Latin "he with whom one shares bread." Sharing flesh has even more resonance. In primitive agricultural societies, the sacrifice of animals was often a sacred celebration of tribes. Jewish Passover and Christian Communion are based on such traditions.

[31] Eric Linklater, Preface, Ordeal By Hunger, by George R. Stewart (London: Jonathan Cape, 1936), p. 9. Stewart's book offers a thorough and riveting account of the Donner Pass incident.

[32] Jared Diamond, "Reliving the Donner Party," Discover 13 March 1992: 103.

[33] Patrick Breen, The Diary of Patrick Breen, One of the Donner Party, ed. Frederick J. Terrgart, Academy of Pacific Coast History Publications, Vol. 1 (Berkeley: University of California Press, 1910), p. 280. Breen's diary provides a terse day-by-day account of the ordeal; he briefly alludes to the dissension and the cannibalism.

[34] Diamond, 103.

[35] Breen, 284.

[36] Diamond, 105.

[37] Dowling, 50; Benales.

[38] "Cannibalism."

[39] Benales.

[40] Benales. Another of the group, Bobby Francois, was also reluctant to preserve himself. He refused to do his chores, and often just sat around smoking. The others told him if he didn't work, he couldn't eat. He said that sounded fair. The survivors fed him anyway, and kept him alive. Dowling 57.

[41] Read, 204–205.

[42] Podesta. The group learned how isolated they were when some men on an early scouting excursion ascended a 14,000-foot slope and saw only 100 miles of snow-covered mountains in every direction.

[43] Benales.

[44] "Cannibalism."

[45] Benales.

[46] Read, 204–208.

[47] Benales.

[48] Dowling, 51.

[49] Read, 213.

[50] Benales.

[51] All information in this paragraph comes from Read, 213–215, and the film Alive, directed by Frank Marshall (Touchstone and Paramount, 1993), which was adapted by Patrick Stanley from Read's novel. The box-office success of the film proves the story's lasting interest.

[52] Read, 218.

[53] Benales.

[54] Dowling, 51.

[55] Read, 227–228.

[56] Benales.

[57] Benales. Read, 271, reports an expanded version of the encounter with Martinez and the note.

[58] Read, 244.

[59] All information after note 58 to this point comes from Benales.

[60] Benales. Weathered mountaineers especially were amazed at the survivors' relative good health after such wear and tear on their minds and bodies.

[61] "29 Victims in Andes Crash to Receive Common Burial," New York Times 26 Dec. 1972: E12.

[62]Dowling, 58.

[63]Clifford, 5:3.

Smith 16

Bibliography

Benales, Carlos. "70 Days Battling Starvation and Freezing in the Andes: A Chronicle of Man's Unwillingness to Die." New York Times 1 Jan. 1973: A3.

Breen, Patrick. Diary of Patrick Breen, One of the Donner Party. Academy of Pacific Coast History Publications, Vol. 1. Ed. Frederick J. Terrgart. Berkeley: U of California P, 1910. 269–84.

"Cannibalism After Air Crash Reported." New York Times 27 Dec. 1972: D2.

Clifford, Terry. "Staying Alive." Chicago Tribune 15 Jan. 1993: 5:3.

Diamond, Jared. "Reliving the Donner Party." Discover 13 Mar. 1992: 100–105.

Dowling, Claudia Glenn. "Still Alive." Life Feb. 1993: 48–59.

"8 Survivors of Crash Picked Up in Andes." New York Times 24 Dec. 1972: A9.

Linklater, Eric. Preface. Ordeal By Hunger. By George R. Stewart. London: Cape, 1936.

Marshall, Frank, dir. Alive. Touchstone and Paramount, 1993.

Miller, Rick. "A Nightmare Revisited: 20 Years Later, with the Film's Release, Andes Survivors Recall Ordeal." Boston Globe 21 Jan. 1993: A2.

Podesta, Dan. "Echoes of a Crash Unheard of: The Tales of 16 Uruguayans Are Still as Chilling as Their Survival 20 Years Ago." Washington Post 21 Dec. 1992: C1.

Read, Piers Paul. Alive: The Story of the Andes Survivors. Philadelphia and New York: Lippincott, 1974.

"Survivors of Andes Air Crash Admit Dead Saved Their Lives." New York Times 29 Dec. 1972: A9.

"29 Victims in Andes Crash to Receive Common Burial." New York Times 26 Dec. 1972: E12.

"Two Catholic Aides Defend Cannibalism in Chilean Air Crash." New York Times 28 Dec. 1972: A8.

David Morgan

Natural Science I

December 15, 1998

Explaining the Tunguskan Phenomenon

The Tunguska River Valley in Siberia has always been an area of swamps and bogs, forests and frozen tundra, sparsely populated, and remote and inaccessible to most travelers. It was at dawn on June 30, 1908, that witnesses in the Tungus observed a light glaring more brightly than anything they had ever seen. This cosmic phenomenon, they said, was bluish-white in color and gradually became cigarlike in shape. Just as terrifying to the few people inhabiting that part of Siberia was the tremendous noise that accompanied the light, a noise that was reported to have been heard 1,000 kilometers from the site (Parry, 1961). Some who were in the vicinity were deafened, while others farther away apparently became speechless and displayed other symptoms of severe trauma. The Tungus community refused to go near the site or speak of the occurrence, and some even denied that it had ever happened (Crowther, 1931). The event was so frightening to these simple peasants that many believed it had been an act of divine retribution, a punishment by a god demanding vengeance (Baxter & Atkins, 1976).

Since 1921, when the first perilous expedition to the Tungus region confirmed that a remarkable event had indeed taken place, scientists have attempted to explain what it was and why it happened. Almost 80 years later, the various theories developed to explain the explosion in the Tunguska Valley have become almost as interesting a phenomenon as the original occurrence. Like doctors trying to diagnose a disease by examining the symptoms, scientists have analyzed the fragmentary evidence and published theories that supposedly account for it. However, no theory has been entirely convincing. The purpose of this essay is to provide a brief description of some of the major interpretations of the Tunguska occurrence and to suggest that, in their efforts to substantiate their theories, scientists can be fallible.

At dawn on that day in June 1908, a huge object evidently came from space into the earth's atmosphere, breaking the sound barrier, and, at

7:17 a.m., slammed into the ground in the central Siberian plateau. Moments before the collision, a thrust of energy caused people and animals to be strewn about, structures destroyed, and trees toppled. Immediately afterward, a pillar or "tongue" of fire could be seen in the sky several hundred miles away; others called it a cylindrical pipe. A thermal air current of extremely high temperature caused forest fires to ignite and spread across forty miles, melting metal objects scattered throughout the area. Several shock waves were felt for hundreds of miles around, breaking windows and tossing people, animals, and objects in the air. Finally, black rain fell from a menacing-looking cloud over a radius of 100 square miles. It is no wonder that the peasants of the Tunguska River Valley thought that this was the end of the world (Krinov, 1966; Baxter & Atkins, 1976).

For a variety of reasons, this devastating occurrence remained almost unknown outside Russia--and even outside central Siberia--for many years. The Tungus was extremely remote, even for Russia, which is such a vast country that transportation and communication between places can be slow and difficult. The few people living in the area who actually witnessed what happened were mostly peasants and nomadic tribesmen, and did not have much opportunity or inclination to talk about what they had seen. There was little publicity, and what there was was limited to local Siberian newspapers (Krinov, 1966). During that summer, there was a lot of discussion in the newspapers of the European capitals about peculiar lights and colors seen in the northern skies, unusually radiant sunsets, some magnetic disturbances, and strange dust clouds (Cowan, Atluri, & Libby, 1965). But, since news of the events at the Tungus River had hardly yet been heard even in Moscow, there was no way for scientists in other countries to see a connection between these happenings.

It was only in 1921, when Russia was relatively stable after years of war, revolution, and economic problems, that the first expedition to investigate the event at Tunguska actually took place (Crowther, 1931). That it occurred then at all was largely because an energetic Russian scientist, Leonid Kulik, had become fascinated by meteorites. He read in an old Siberian newspaper that, in 1908, a railway train had been forced to stop because a meteorite fell in its path--a story that was quite untrue. Kulik thought that he might become the discoverer of the greatest meteorite ever found on earth and determined to search for evidence that such a meteorite existed. Authorized by the Soviet Academy, Kulik led a series of expeditions to the Tungus River. In 1921, he did not even reach the site, for the route was almost impassable. In 1927, and annually for the next few years, Kulik did, indeed, explore the devastated area and was able to study the evidence of what had happened and listen to the oral accounts of the event provided by those inhabitants who were still alive and who were willing to talk to him. Finally, in 1938–39, Kulik traveled to the Tungus for the last time, for the purpose of taking aerial photographs that might confirm his meteorite theory (Baxter & Atkins, 1976).

Kulik and his fellow investigators believed that whatever had happened at the Tungus River had been caused by a meteorite. So, what they expected to find was a single, vast crater to mark the place where the meteorite had landed. Such a crater, however, was simply not there (Cowan, Atluri, & Libby, 1965). Instead, he found a vast devastated and burned area, a forest of giant trees with their tops cut off and scattered around (Crowther, 1931). In 1928, without the benefit of an aerial view of the region, Kulik concluded from his various vantage points on the ground that, around the circumference of the area where the meteorite had landed, there was a belt of upright dead trees, which he named the "telegraph pole forest." Scattered around the perimeter of the frozen swamp, which he called the "cauldron," were groups of fallen trees, with their tops all pointing away from the direction of where the blast had occurred (Cowan, Atluri, & Libby, 1965). None of this was consistent with Kulik's meteorite theory, and he could only attribute the odd pattern of upright and fallen trees to a shock wave or "hot compressed-air pockets," which had missed some trees and affected others (Baxter & Atkins, 1976). The account of his discovery in the Literary Digest of 1929 states that "each of the falling meteoric fragments must have worked, the Russian scientists imagine, like a gigantic piston," with compressed air knocking trees down like toothpicks (What a meteor, 1929, p. 34). Kulik continued to insist that the fire and the resultant effect on the trees was the result of a meteorite explosion. But the Russian scientist V. G. Fesenkov estimated that such destruction could only have been caused by an object of at least several hundred meters, and that, if anything of this size or force had hit the ground, it would have left a crater (Baxter & Atkins, 1976).

Kulik found other evidence that could not easily be explained by the meteorite theory. Although there was no trace of a single large crater (Cowan, Atluri, & Libby, 1965), there were numerous shallow cavities scattered around the frozen bog (Olivier, 1928). For several years, Kulik attempted to bore into the ground, seeking evidence that these pits and ridges were formed by lateral pressure caused by gases exploding from the meteorite's impact. Kulik described the scene as "not unlike a giant duplicate of what happens when a brick from a tall chimney-top falls into a puddle of mud. Solid ground actually must have splashed outward in every direction." In this account, the supposed meteorite became "the great swarm of meteors" that "must have traversed" the atmosphere for several hundred miles, pushing ahead of it a "giant bubble of superheated atmosphere" that was "probably responsible" for the burned countryside (What a meteor, 1929, p. 33). All the "must have's" and "probably's" make a good narrative, but are not scientifically convincing.

Similarly, Kulik endeavored to explain eyewitness accounts of the huge fireball in the sky that burned one observer's shirt off his back and threw him off his porch (Cowan, Atluri, & Libby, 1965). Such extreme heat waves had never before been known to have accompanied the fall of a meteorite, but Kulik decided that this meteorite was much larger than those previously recorded and that therefore it would have released much more energy upon impact and that would account for such radiant heat (Baxter & Atkins, 1976). So obsessed was Kulik with the idea that somewhere buried in the Tungus swamp was a phenomenal meteorite that he focused the efforts of all the expeditions to the area during his lifetime on digging beneath the frozen tundra and to some extent neglected the examination of other evidence that might have further threatened the theory that he was determined to prove (Parry, 1961). Initially, he was successful in convincing the scientific community that his theory was correct. It is most interesting to read excerpts from The American Weekly of 1929 flatly asserting that a meteorite had fallen in Siberia and that Professor Kulik had brought back photographs of the giant crater that he found, as well as small samples of meteoric materials. The article is accompanied by a photograph of Professor Kulik measuring "the main crater, where the largest mass of this celestial visitor buried itself in the earth" (Quoted in What a meteor, p. 34).

While Kulik's expeditions were still searching for evidence of a meteorite, other scientists were hypothesizing that the Tunguska explosion might have been caused by a small comet, which would account for the absence of a crater. Comets are composed of ice, frozen gases, and dust, and as they travel around the sun, they develop a long tail. Upon impact, a comet might give off a trail of gases and dust which would create a bright and colorful night sky similar to that observed after the explosion. This would not be true of a meteorite, which has no gaseous trail and thus leaves no trace in the atmosphere. It has also been suggested that the observed direction of the object's travel was more typical of a comet than a meteorite (Florensky, 1963). If the comet had blown up approximately two miles above the site, that would explain why some trees survived while others did not (Parry, 1961). On the other hand, there is no evidence that a comet had ever crashed on earth before, or caused a comparable change in magnetic and atmospheric phenomena, or even come so close without being sighted (Baxter & Atkins, 1976). Those scientists supporting the comet theory have suggested that, although it is unusual for any comet to come that close to earth without anyone sighting it, the one landing at Tunguska might have been small enough to go by unnoticed. But that idea is contradicted by Fesenkov's estimate that, to cause such destruction, the nucleus of the Tunguskan comet--if there was one--would have been only slightly smaller than those of well-documented comets that were visible at great distances (Cowan, Atluri, & Libby, 1965).

The next major explanation for the cosmic phenomenon at Tunguska could only have been formulated after World War II, when the scientific community had learned how to make atomic explosions and had become familiar with their aftermath. Aleksander Kazantsev, a Russian scientist and (equally important) science-fiction writer, had visited Hiroshima after the atom bomb explosion and had studied the data describing its impact and aftermath. Because of certain similarities in the blast effects--the burnt yet upright trees, the mushroom cloud, the black rain--Kazantsev and other

scientists concluded that the blast of 1908 was an atomic explosion estimated at a minimum of ten times the strength of the one at Hiroshima
(Parry, 1961). Witnesses had described the blinding flash and withering heat
at Hiroshima in much the same way that the Siberian peasants described
the frightening blast at Tunguska. The melting heat that Kulik found so inconsistent with his meteorite theory was more consistent with an atomic explosion (Baxter & Atkins, 1976). It is worth pointing out that scientists went
on to develop the hypothesis that a nuclear explosion had occurred at
Tunguska even though their theorizing was largely based on stories told by
ignorant peasants, believers in devils and wrathful gods, who could quite
easily have exaggerated what had actually happened to improve their stories.
Even though these eyewitness accounts were gathered twenty or more years
after the actual event, and had quite possibly entered the folklore of the
countryside (Krinov, 1966), they were still regarded as the purest evidence.

To test whether a nuclear explosion might have occurred, scientists
examined the trees for radioactivity and for any unusual increase in normal
growth patterns, shown by greater spacing between the age lines, that might
have been the result of radioactivity. What they found was that some trees at
the site grew to be four times greater than what would normally have been
expected. Similarly, scabs that appeared on the hides of local reindeer were
explained as being the result of radioactive contamination (Baxter & Atkins,
1976). This evidence, by no means conclusive (Florensky, 1963), was cited
as proof that such an atomic explosion had taken place, just as Kulik had
cited the existence of shallow pits in the terrain as proof that a meteorite
had exploded.

Assuming that what happened at Tunguska was the result of an
atomic blast, and faced with the fact that nuclear fission was not within
man's grasp before the 1940s, Kazantsev and his colleagues concluded that
the phenomenon must have involved extraterrestrial beings and that the
explosion was caused by a UFO, propelled by atomic energy, that crashed
(Parry, 1961). The pattern of devastation on the ground, as seen from the
air, suggested that the object took a zigzag path, changing its direction as it
came closer and closer to earth. Advocates of the UFO theory argue such a
change in direction would not have been possible with a natural object like a

meteorite or comet, and that the object--a spacecraft--was driven by intelligent beings who were trying to land without hitting a more densely populated area. They hypothesize that the craft had some mechanical problem that made it necessary to land but that the initial angle of its trajectory was too shallow for landing and would only have bounced the craft back into space. So the navigators tried to maneuver and correct the angle, but swerved, came down too sharply, and exploded (Baxter & Atkins, 1976). On the other hand, it seems just as possible that a natural object swerved or that debris from a nonatomic explosion was thrown in zigzag directions than that navigators from outer space ran into mechanical troubles and crash-landed. If probability is going to be disregarded in order to support one theory, then the same suspension of the natural order of things can be used to confirm an equally unlikely theory.

In the late 1950s, an exploratory team examined the Tunguska site with an advanced magnetic detector and, in 1962, scientists magnified the soil and found an array of tiny, colored, magnetic, ball-shaped particles, made of cobalt, nickel, copper, and germanium (Baxter & Atkins, 1976). According to extraterrestrial-intelligence specialists, these could have been the elements used for electrical and technical instruments, with the copper used for communication services and the germanium used in semiconductors (Parry, 1961). However, controlled experiments would be necessary to make this atomic-extraterrestrial argument convincing.

Scientists who find the UFO and extraterrestrial explanations less than credible have turned to the most recent theories of physics and astronomy to explain what might have happened in the Tungus. Some (including Kazantsev) argue that such an explosion might have been caused by debris from space colliding with the earth (Morrison & Chapman, 1990), or by anti-matter, which exploded as it came in contact with the atmosphere (Parry, 1961). Alternatively, the explosion might have been caused by a "black hole" hitting the earth in Siberia and passing through to emerge on the other side. Those opposing these theories point, again, to the absence of a crater and to the numerous eyewitness accounts that describe the shape of the object and the sound of the blast, all of which would be inconsistent with antimatter or black-hole theories (Baxter & Atkins, 1976). However, a 1973 article in

<u>Nature</u> asserts that a black hole would not, in fact, leave a crater, but would simply enter the earth at a great velocity and that a shock wave and blast might possibly accompany its entrance (Jackson & Ryan).

What is most fascinating about the Tunguska Valley phenomenon is that, despite all the advances in science over the past 80 years, investigators cannot now be any more certain of the cause of the blast than they were in 1921, when Kulik first came near the site. None of the theories presented is wholly convincing, for all of them rely to some extent on human observers, whose accounts of events are notoriously unreliable, or hypotheses based on ambiguous evidence, without the support of controlled tests and experiments. The formulation of a radically new body of scientific knowledge might provide a new theoretical context for examining the evidence and establishing a more convincing explanation. But, as it is, with the trail getting colder, finding a solution to this mystery seems to become more and more unlikely.

Examining these explanations about what did or did not land and explode in Siberia does teach us that scientific theories are sometimes based on the selective interpretation of evidence and that scientists, like everyone else, tend to believe their own theories and find the evidence that they want to find. Although the language that they use is very different, the accounts of what happened at Tunguska according to Kulik, Kazantsev, and their other scientific colleagues are not so very different from what the local peasants say that they saw. Both have a closer resemblance to science fiction than science fact.

References

Baxter, J., & Atkins, T. (1976). The fire came by: The riddle of the great Siberian explosion. Garden City, NY: Doubleday.

Cowan, C., Atluri, C. R., & Libby, W. F. (1965, May 29). Possible antimatter content of the Tunguska meteor of 1908. Nature (London), 861–865.

Crowther, J. G. (1931). More about the great Siberian meteorite. Scientific American, 144(5), 314–317.

Florensky, K. P. (1963, November). Did a comet collide with the earth in 1908? Sky and Telescope, 268–269.

Jackson, A. A., & Ryan, M. P. (1973, September 14). Was the Tungus event due to a black hole? Nature (London), 88–89.

Krinov, E. L. (1966). Giant meteorites. London: Pergamon.

Morrison, D., & Chapman, C. R. (1990). Target earth: It will happen. Sky and Telescope, 261–265.

Olivier, C. P. (1928). The great Siberian meteorite. Scientific American, 139(1), 42–44.

Parry, A. (1961). The Tungus mystery: Was it a spaceship? In Russia's Rockets and Missiles (pp. 248–267). London: Macmillan.

What a meteor did to Siberia. (1929, March 16). Literary Digest, 33–34.

Appendix A
Some Useful Reference Sources

GUIDELINES FOR USING REFERENCE WORKS

1. You can find sources for your essays by looking
   - in the library's *online database of books* or *card catalog;*
   - in the *bibliographies of standard works* on your subject;
   - in the brief bibliographies at the end of *encyclopedia articles;*
   - under the broad subject headings in *general-interest bibliographies* and *periodical indexes;* and
   - in the *indexes and abstract collections* that deal with the specific subject of your research.

2. Some reference sources are entirely bibliography: they consist of long lists of articles and (sometimes) books, each followed by the essential publication information. These indexes are usually arranged by topic. You may have to check several broad headings before you find the articles that you need. If, for example, you are doing research on educational television, you would look up "education," "television," and the names of some of the programs that you intend to write about. Most indexes are cross-referenced.

3. Some reference sources are called "abstracts" because they contain abstracts or paragraph summaries of many (but not all) of the articles published each year in that discipline. Abstracts often have two sections: the first contains a series of summaries of articles, chosen for their special in-

terest or excellence and arranged by subject; the second contains a list of all the articles published in that field in that year. (Occasionally, you will find a modified form of abstract, in which several articles are each given a one-sentence summary.) First you look up the specific subject that you are interested in and glance at the summaries. Then you get the publication information about the articles relevant to your research by looking up their *authors* in the second section of the reference work. Although abstracts give you a convenient preview, you will find that many of the articles are highly technical and may therefore be difficult to read and write about.

4. Some of the periodical articles that you want to consult may be available only on microfiche or microcards. Ask the reference librarian to help you to use the system and its apparatus.

5. Many bibliographies and indexes are available online. Ask the reference librarian to show you the commands that you need to use at the computer monitor. *Reference sources that are available online and/or on CD-ROM are asterisked.*

GENERAL ENCYCLOPEDIAS

Collier's Encyclopedia. 24 vols. with annual supplements and revisions. 1995. Easier to read and understand than the old *Britannica* or *Americana.*

Encyclopaedia Britannica. 15th ed. 24 vols. with annual supplements and periodic revisions. 1998. *Britannica Online* is constantly being updated.

Encyclopedia Americana. 30 vols. with annual supplements and revisions. 1995. Use the index volume to locate your subject within the longer encyclopedia.

New Columbia Encyclopedia. 5th ed. 1993. A single-volume encyclopedia, especially good as a starting point.

New Encyclopaedia Britannica. 15th ed. 32 vols. with annual supplements and periodic revisions. 1994.

SPECIALIZED ENCYCLOPEDIAS

Encyclopedia of American Art. New York: Dutton, 1981.

Encyclopedia of Biological Sciences. Ed. Peter Gray. 2nd ed. New York: Van Nostrand, 1981.

Encyclopedia of Computer Science and Technology. 37 vols. New York: Dekker, 1997.

The Encyclopedia of Education. Ed. Lee C. Deighton. 10 vols. New York: Macmillan, 1971.

The Encyclopedia of Human Behavior: Psychology, Psychiatry, and Mental Health. Ed. Robert M. Goldenson. 2 vols. New York: Doubleday, 1974.

Encyclopedia of Psychology. Ed. Raymond J. Corsini. 2nd ed. 4 vols. New York: Wiley, 1994.

Encyclopedia of Sociology. Ed. Edgar F. Borgatta and Marie L. Borgatta. 4 vols. New York: Macmillan, 1991.

Encyclopedia of World Art. 17 vols. New York: McGraw, 1959–87.

An Encyclopedia of World History: Ancient, Medieval, and Modern Chronologically Arranged. Ed. William L. Langer. 5th ed. Boston: Houghton, 1972.

International Encyclopedia of the Social Sciences. Ed. D. L. Sills. 17 vols. New York: Macmillan, 1977.

McGraw-Hill Encyclopedia of Physics. Ed. Sybil Parker. 2nd ed. New York: McGraw, 1993.

McGraw-Hill Encyclopedia of Science and Technology. 7th ed. 20 vols. New York: McGraw, 1996.

McGraw-Hill Encyclopedia of World Drama. 2nd ed. 5 vols. New York: McGraw, 1983.

The New Grove Dictionary of Music and Musicians. Ed. Stanley Sadie. 20 vols. New York: Macmillan, 1980.

VNR Concise Encyclopedia of Mathematics. Ed. S. Gottwald et al. 2nd ed. New York: Van Nostrand, 1989.

GENERAL INDEXES

*Book Review Digest. New York: Wilson, 1905–present. Includes excerpts from reviews as well as lists of references.

*Book Review Index. Detroit: Gale Research Co., 1965–present. Lists reviews of books on literature, art, business, economics, religion, and current affairs.

*Books in Print Plus. Lists books currently in print in the United States, with prices. Full text of book reviews is available for some titles.

*British Newspaper Index. 1990–present. Indexes major British newspapers.

*Editorials on File. New York: Facts on File, 1970–present. Selected editorials on subjects of contemporary interest, with each editorial preceded by a summary of the issue being discussed.

*Facts on File. New York: Facts on File, 1941–present. Summaries of issues and events, with selected bibliographies.

Milner, Anita Check. *Newspaper Indexes: A Location and Subject Guide for Researchers,* Metuchen, N.J., and London: Scarecrow, 1982.

*National Newspaper Index. 1990–present. Combined indexing of five major newspapers: *The New York Times, The Wall Street Journal, Christian Science Monitor, Washington Post,* and *The Los Angeles Times.*

*New York Times Full-text. Indexes the most recent years of *The New York Times,* as well as providing the text of the articles.

*New York Times Index. New York: New York Times, 1851–present.

*Periodical Abstracts Ondisc. 1986–present. Indexes and abstracts over 950 general-interest periodicals from the United States, Canada, and the United Kingdom.

Popular Periodical Index. Camden, N.J.: Popular Periodical Index, 1971–present. Includes magazines such as *New York, Playboy, Rolling Stone,* and *TV Guide.*

*Proquest Image. Indexes and abstracts articles from hundreds of news and general-interest magazines and some scholarly journals, with text for many articles.

*Readers' Guide to Periodical Literature. New York: Wilson, 1905–present. Includes listings of articles in many general-interest magazines.

Vertical File Index. New York: Wilson, 1932/1935–present. Lists pamphlets on all subjects.

BIOGRAPHICAL SOURCES

Annual Obituary. New York: St. Martin's, 1980–present. Annual collection of profiles of prominent individuals who died during the year, arranged by month of death date.

*Biography Index. New York: Wilson, 1947–present. Organized like the *Readers' Guide,* listing articles about contemporary celebrities.

Current Biography. New York: Wilson, 1940–present. Consists of full-scale articles (like encyclopedia entries) about prominent people. Use the index to find the right year for the person that you are researching.

Dictionary of American Biography. 10 vols. New York: Scribner's, 1980. Articles contain basic information about notable figures in American history. (Do not use this source for contemporary figures.)

New York Times Obituary Index 1858–1990. New York: New York Times.

SEMISPECIALIZED INDEXES AND ABSTRACTS

Humanities

*Art Index. New York: Wilson, 1929–present. Covers the literature of art and art history in periodicals, yearbooks, and museum bulletins. Subjects include architecture; archaeology; art history; fine arts; crafts and folk art; film and photography; graphic arts; industrial design.

*Humanities Index. New York: Wilson, 1974–present. Annual volumes include reviews of books and performances as well as a listing of articles on issues and new developments in all the humanities.

*MLA International Bibliography of Books and Articles in the Modern Languages and Literature. New York: MLA, 1921–present. Indexes critical documents on literature, language, linguistics, and folklore. Articles from more than 3,000 journals, serials published worldwide, conference papers and proceedings, handbooks, dictionaries, and bibliographies are indexed.

*The Music Index. Detroit: Information Coordinators, 1949–present. Includes reviews listed under composer and title.

*The Philosopher's Index. Bowling Green, Ohio: Bowling Green State U, 1967–present. Articles on philosophy and its relation to art, religion, the humanities in general, and history.

Physical and Biological Sciences

*Applied Science and Technology Index. New York: Wilson, 1958–present. Includes references to a large number of scientific and technological periodicals.

*Biological and Agricultural Index. New York: Wilson, 1964–present.

*Chemical Abstracts. Washington: Amer. Chemical Soc., 1907–present. The online and CD-ROM databases are called *CA Search.*

*Engineering Index. New York: Engineering Information, 1906–present. The online and CD-ROM databases are part of *Compendex.*

*General Science Index. New York: Wilson, 1978–present. Includes articles in 109 English-language science periodicals of general interest.

*Science Abstracts. London, Eng.: Inst. of Electrical Engineers, 1898–present. Summaries of articles about physics.

Science Citation Index. Philadelphia: Inst. for Scientific Information, 1945–present. Includes citations to the literature of science, technology, medicine, and related disciplines from 3,300 science journals worldwide. The online and CD-ROM databases are part of *SciSearch.*

Social Sciences

Almanac of American Politics. Ed. Michael Barone. Boston: Gambit, 1972–present. Lists sources for information about local and national public affairs.

America: History and Life. Santa Barbara, Calif.: ABC-Clio, 1964–present. Includes references to 2,000 publications dealing with past, recent, and present history. Part A consists of abstracts; Part B consists of one-sentence summaries of articles, grouped under topic headings.

Ethnic Newswatch. Stamford, Conn: Sofline Info. Indexes and provides full text of articles from ethnic and minority newspapers and magazines across the United States. Subjects include current events covered with a specific ethnic focus.

Guide to U.S. Government Serials and Periodicals. McLean, Va.: Documents Index, 1964–present. A cumulative index directs the user to the correct volume.

Historical Abstracts. Santa Barbara, Calif.: ABC-Clio, 1955–present. Part A deals with modern history from 1450 to 1940; Part B deals with mid-twentieth-century history. The index is in the Winter issue.

International Bibliography of Economics. Paris: UNESCO, 1952–present.

International Political Science Abstracts. Paris: International Pol. Sci. Assn., 1951–present. Summaries of articles on political science and international relations.

Psychological Abstracts. Washington: American Psychological Assn., 1927–present. Use the three-year cumulative subject and author indexes; for example, the years 1978–1980 are indexed together. The online database is called *PsycInfo,* and the CD-ROM database is called *PsycLit.*

Public Affairs Information Service Bulletin. New York: PAIS, 1915–present. Includes pamphlets and government documents and reports as well as periodical articles. Covers an unusually large number of periodicals. Emphasizes factual and statistical information.

Sage Public Administration Abstracts. Beverly Hills, Calif.: Sage, 1979–present. Summaries of books, articles, government publications, speeches, and research studies.

Social Sciences Index. New York: Wilson, 1974–present.

Sociofile. A cumulation of *Sociological Abstracts* and *Social Planning, Policy and Development Abstracts.* Indexes over 1,500 serials published worldwide in sociology and its related disciplines.

INDEXES AND ABSTRACTS FOR PROFESSIONAL STUDIES

Business

ABI/INFORM. Ann Arbor: UMI, 1971–present. Provides abstracts from more than 800 business and trade journals. Subjects include accounting and auditing, banking, data processing and information management, economics, finance, health care, human resources, labor relations, public administration, and telecommunications.

Accountants' Index. New York: Amer. Inst. of CPAs, 1944–present. Lists articles about accounting, data processing, financial management, and taxation.

*Business Periodicals Index. New York: Wilson, 1958–present. Lists articles from more than 100 periodicals dealing with new developments and methods in business management.

*Corporate Text. Current. Copies of annual reports for companies traded on the New York Stock Exchange, American Stock Exchange, and NASDAQ exchange and over the counter.

Personnel Literature. Washington: U.S. Civil Service Commission, 1969–present. Lists articles about administration, supervision, management relations, and productivity.

Education

*CIJE: Current Index to Journals in Education. Phoenix: Oryx, 1969–present. The online and CD-ROM databases are part of *ERIC.*

*Education Index. New York: Wilson, 1929–present.

*ERIC. Indexes and abstracts journal and technical literature in education and related fields, including psychology and sociology. Information is compiled from *Resources in Education* (RIE) and *Current Index to Journals in Education* (CIJE).

Law

*Index to Legal Periodicals. New York: Wilson, 1908–present. In addition to listing articles by subject and author, there is a table of cases and a group of book reviews.

Library Science

Library and Information Science Abstracts. London: The Library Assn., 1970–present. Materials about information dissemination and retrieval.

Nursing and Health

*Aidsline. Provides detailed coverage of all aspects of the AIDS crisis, focusing on clinical aspects but including health-planning implications and cancer research. Information is derived from the U.S. National Library of Medicine's *Medline, Health Planning and Administration,* and *CancerLIT* databases.

*Chem-Bank. Indexes descriptions of and toxicity information on thousands of chemical substances in the form of lists prepared by four government agencies: RTECS (Registry of Toxic Effects of Chemical Substances), from the Department of Health and Human Services; OHMTADS (Oil and Hazardous Materials Technical Assistance Data System), developed by the Environmental Protection Agency; CHRIS (Chemical Hazard Response Information System), produced by the Coast Guard; and HSDB (Hazardous Substance Databank), from the National Library of Medicine.

Cumulative Index to Nursing and Allied Health Literature. Glendale: CINAHL Information Services, 1977–present. Articles listed include health education and social services as they relate to health care. The online and CD-ROM databases are called *Nursing and Allied Health Database.*

Index Medicus. Bethesda: National Lib. of Medicine, 1960–present. Lists articles of medical interest and includes a bibliography of medical book reviews. The online and CD-ROM databases are part of *Medline.*

International Nursing Index. New York: Amer. Journal of Nursing, 1966–present.

Medline. Database of the U.S. National Library of Medicine; contains bibliographic citations and abstracts of biomedical literature. Indexes articles from approximately 3,400 journals published in more than 70 countries.

OSH-ROM. Produced by the National Institute for Occupational Safety and Health; provides citations and abstracts from journals, books, and technical reports dealing with occupational health and safety. Subjects include environmental health, toxicology, safety engineering, and industrial pollution.

Social Work

Human Resources Abstracts. Beverly Hills, Calif.: Sage, 1965–present. Covers developments in areas such as poverty, employment, and distribution of human resources.

Journal of Human Services Abstracts. Rockville, Md.: Project Share, 1976–present. Summarizes articles concerning public administration, education, psychology, environmental studies, family studies, nutrition, and health services.

Sage Family Studies Abstracts. Beverly Hills, Calif.: Sage, 1979–present.

Social Work Research and Abstracts. Albany, N.Y.: National Assn. of Social Workers, 1965–present. Selected research articles as well as abstracts of other articles in the field of social welfare. Computer database is called *Swab Plus.*

INDEXES TO STATISTICAL COMPILATIONS

American Statistics Index: A Comprehensive Guide and Index to the Statistical Publications of the U.S. Government. Washington: Congressional Information Service, 1973–present.

County and City Plus. Indexes statistical information for counties, cities, and other designated places. Subjects include population, age, race, income, labor force and unemployment, hospitals, crime, climate, and more.

Statistical Yearbook. New York: UN Dept. of Economic and Social Affairs, 1949–present. International statistics.

STATMASTER. Indexes statistical publications issued by the U.S. government, U.S. state governments, international governmental organizations, professional and trade associations, business organizations, commercial publishers, and university and independent research organizations.

Appendix B

Some Basic Forms for Documentation: MLA, APA, and Endnote

MODELS OF MLA BIBLIOGRAPHICAL ENTRIES AND PARENTHETICAL DOCUMENTATION

The following is a list of model bibliographical and parenthetical entries for MLA style. The proper bibliographical form that will appear in alphabetical order on your "Works Cited" page is followed by a sample parenthetical documentation that might appear in the text. The sample documentation in this list will always contain the author's name; but remember that in your essay you will often mention the author's name in your text, thus making necessary only the parenthetical documentation of the page(s) of your source. You can find guidelines for preparing MLA documentation in Chapter 9, on pp. 373–381. See also the list of "Works Cited" in the student essay "Euthanasia: The Right to Die" in Chapter 10.

Book by a Single Author

Veysey, Laurence R. The Emergence of the American University. Chicago: U of
     Chicago P, 1965.

(Veysey 23)

Book by Two Authors

Postman, Neil, and Charles Weingartner. Teaching as a Subversive Activity. New
York: Dell, 1969.

(Postman and Weingartner 34–36)

Book by More Than Three Authors

Spiller, Robert E., et al. Literary History of the United States. London:
Macmillan, 1946.

(Spiller et al. 67)

Edited Collection Written by Different Authors

Wheelwright, Philip, ed. The Presocratics. New York: Odyssey, 1966.

(Wheelwright 89)

Essay from a Collection Written by Different Authors

Webb, R. K. "The Victorian Reading Public." From Dickens to Hardy. Ed. Boris
Ford. Baltimore: Penguin, 1958. 205–26.

(Webb 209)

Book Published in a Reprinted Edition

Orwell, George. Animal Farm. 1946. New York: Signet, 1959.

(Orwell 100)

Book Published in a New Edition

Baugh, Albert C. A History of the English Language. 2nd ed. New York:
Appleton, 1957.

(Baugh 21)

Work in Translation

Lorenz, Konrad. On Aggression. Trans. Marjorie Kerr Wilson. 1966. New York:
Bantam, 1969.

(Lorenz 45)

Book Published in Several Volumes

Tocqueville, Alexis de. <u>Democracy in America</u>. Ed. Phillips Bradley. 2 vols. New
York: Knopf, 1945.

(Tocqueville 2: 78)

One Volume in a Set or Series

Granville-Barker, Harley. <u>Prefaces to Shakespeare</u>. Vol. 2. London: Batsford,
1963.

Gaff, Jerry G. <u>Institutional Renewal through the Improvement of Teaching</u>. New
Directions for Higher Ed. 24. San Francisco: Jossey-Bass, 1978.

(Granville-Barker 193)

(Gaff 45)

Book in an Edited Edition

Kirstein, Lincoln. <u>By With To & From</u>. Ed. Nicholas Jenkins. New York: Farrar,
1991.

Jenkins, Nicholas, ed. <u>By With To & From</u>. By Lincoln Kirstein. New York:
Farrar, 1991.

(Kirstein 190)

(Jenkins xiii)

The second entry indicates that you are citing the work of the editor (not the
author); therefore, you place the editor's name first.

Introduction, Preface, Foreword, or Afterword

Spacks, Patricia Meyer. Afterword. <u>Sense and Sensibility</u>. By Jane Austen. New
York: Bantam, 1983. 332–43.

(Spacks 338)

Article in an Encyclopedia

"American Architecture." <u>Columbia Encyclopedia</u>. 3rd ed. 1963.

("American Architecture")

Notice that no page numbers are needed for either the bibliographical entry or
the parenthetical reference when the source is an encyclopedia. If the article is

signed by an author, list the author's name at the beginning of the bibliographical entry and identify the source in your parenthetical documentation by using the author's name. If you are citing a little-known or specialized
encyclopedia, provide full publication information.

Publication of a Corporation, Foundation, or Government Agency

Carnegie Council on Policy Studies in Higher Education. Three Thousand
Futures: The Next Twenty Years for Higher Education. San Francisco:
Jossey-Bass, 1980.

United States. Bureau of the Census. Abstract of the Census of Manufactures.
Washington: GPO, 1919.

Coleman, James S., et al. Equality of Educational Opportunity. U.S. Dept. of
Health, Education, and Welfare. Washington: GPO, 1966.

(Carnegie Council 34)

(Bureau of the Census 56)

(Coleman et al. 88)

Pamphlet or Brochure

The entry should resemble the entry for a book. If the author's name is missing,
begin the entry with the title; if the date is missing, use the abbreviation *n.d.*

More, Howard V. Costa de la Luz. Turespana: Secretaria General de Turismo, n.d.

(More 6)

Classic Work

Job. The Jerusalem Bible. Reader's Edition. Ed. Alexander Jones. Garden City:
Doubleday, 1968.

Homer. The Odyssey. Trans. Robert Fitzgerald. Garden City: Doubleday, 1963.

(Job 3:7)

(Odyssey 7.1–16)

Article in a Scholarly Journal with Continuous Pagination

Shepard, David. "Authenticating Films." The Quarterly Journal of the Library of
Congress 37 (1980): 342–54.

(Shepard 350)

The four journals comprising Volume 37 are treated as a single continuous work for purposes of pagination. The first journal in Volume 38 will start again with page 1.

Article in a Scholarly Journal without Continuous Pagination

> Burnham, Christopher C. "Expressive Writing: A Heretic's Confession." Focuses
> 2.1 (1989): 5–18.
>
> (Burnham 7–8)

Article in a Monthly Periodical

> Loye, David. "TV's Impact on Adults." Psychology Today Apr. 1978: 87+.
>
> (Loye 87)

The plus sign after the page number indicates that the article is not printed on consecutive pages, but skips to later pages.

Article in a Weekly Periodical

> Meyer, Karl E. "Television's Trying Times." Saturday Review 16 Sept. 1978: 19–23.
>
> (Meyer 21)

Article in a Newspaper

> Goldin, Davidson. "In a Change of Policy, and Heart, Colleges Join Fight Against
> Inflated Grades." New York Times 4 July 1995, late ed.: 8.
>
> (Goldin)

No page number is required in a parenthetical citation of a one-page article. If the issue of the *Times* or another newspaper is divided into separate sections, the page number in both the bibliographical entry and the citation should be preceded by the section, e.g., *B6*.

Article without an Author

> "How to Get Quality Back into the Schools." US News & World Report 12 Sept.
> 1977: 31–34.
>
> ("How to Get Quality" 33)

Letter to the Editor

Kropp, Arthur J. Letter. <u>Village Voice</u> 12 Oct. 1993: 5.

(Kropp)

Editorial

"Justice Berger's Contradictions." Editorial. <u>New York Times</u> 27 June 1995, late ed.: A16.

("Justice Berger's Contradictions")

Review

Appiah, K. Anthony. "Giving Up the Perfect Diamond." Rev. of <u>The Holder of the World</u>, by Bharati Mukherjee. <u>New York Times Book Review</u> 10 Oct. 1993: 7.

(Appiah)

Personal or Published Letter

Hans, James S. Letter to the author. 18 Aug. 1991.

Keats, John. "To Benjamin Bailey." 22 Nov. 1817. <u>John Keats: Selected Poetry and Letters</u>. Ed. Richard Harter Fogle. New York: Rinehart, 1952. 300–303.

(Hans)

(Keats 302)

Unpublished Dissertation

Eastman, Elizabeth. "'Lectures on Jurisprudence': A Key to Understanding Adam Smith's Thought." Diss. Claremont Grad. School, 1993.

(Eastman 34)

Previously Printed Source Accessed from CD-ROM

Burke, Marc. "Homosexuality as Deviance: The Case of the Gay Police Officer." <u>British Journal of Criminology</u> 34.2 (1994): 192–203. <u>PsycLit</u>. CD-ROM. SilverPlatter. Nov. 1994.

(Burke 291)

Personal Interview (Conducted by the Researcher)

Nussbaumer, Doris D. Personal interview. 30 July 1988.

Albert, John J. Telephone interview. 22 Dec. 1989.

(Nussbaumer)

(Albert)

Broadcast or Published Interview

Kennedy, Joseph. Interview with Harry Smith. This Morning. CBS. WCBS, New
York. 14 Oct. 1993.

Berger, John. Interview with Nikos Papastergiadis. American Poetry Review.
July–Aug. 1993: 9–12.

(Kennedy)

(Berger 10)

Lecture

Auchincloss, Louis, Erica Jong, and Gloria Steinem. "The 18th Century Woman."
Symposium at the Metropolitan Museum of Art, New York. 29 Apr. 1982.

(Auchincloss, Jong, and Steinem)

Live Performance

Tommy. By Pete Townshend. Dir. Des McAnuff. St. James Theater, New York. 3
May 1993.

(Tommy)

Film

Dr. Strangelove. Dir. Stanley Kubrick. Columbia Pictures, 1963.

Kubrick, Stanley, dir. Dr. Strangelove. Columbia Pictures, 1963.

Put the film first if you wish to emphasize material from the film; however, if
you are emphasizing the work of the director, list that name first.

(Dr. Strangelove)

(Kubrick)

Television or Radio Program

> Serge Pavlovitch Diaghilev 1872–1929: A Portrait. Prod. Peter Adam. BBC.
>
> WNET, New York. 12 July 1982.
>
> (Diaghilev)

A radio program is entered the same way, with a listing of the program, the director or producer, the producing network, the local station and city, and the date. In citing television or radio programs, if you wish to emphasize the work of the producer or director, enter that name first.

Audio Recording

> Tchaikovsky, Piotr. The Tchaikovsky Collection. Audiocassette. CBS Special
>
> Products, 1989.
>
> (Tchaikovsky)

Videocassette

> Wuthering Heights. Dir. William Wyler. 1939. Videocassette. Embassy, 1987.
>
> (Wuthering)

Work of Art

> Brueghel, Pieter. The Beggars. Louvre, Paris.
>
> (Brueghel)

Map or Chart

> Spain, Portugal, and North Africa. Map. American Automobile Association,
>
> 1993–4.
>
> (Spain)

Cartoon

> Trudeau, Garry. "Doonesbury." Cartoon. Charlotte Observer 23 Dec. 1988: B12.
>
> (Trudeau)

MODELS OF MLA BIBLIOGRAPHICAL ENTRIES
FOR CITING INTERNET SOURCES

The models for citing sources on the World Wide Web are based on guidelines provided by the MLA. These guidelines can be found online at <www.mla.org> and in the second edition of the *MLA Style Manual and Guide to Scholarly Publishing* (1998). Using the sample below as a general guide, you should attempt to ascertain as many of the elements of citation as are appropriate to your source:

Author's last name, First name, Middle initial. "Title of Article or Chapter."

Title of Book, Periodical, or Web Site. Name of editor or translator of text.

Original print publication information if available. Date of electronic publication or most recent update. Page numbers or number of paragraphs.

Name of sponsoring institution or organization. Date of access <URL>.

Book

Skene, Felicia. Penitentiaries and Reformatories. Edinburgh: Edmonston and Douglas, 1865. Victorian Women Writers Project. Ed. Perry Willett. 10 Dec. 1996. Indiana U. 11 Mar. 1998 <http://www.indiana.edu/~letrs/vwwp/ skene/skene~reform.html>.

Poem

Yeats, W. B. "The Wild Swans at Coole." Home page. 1998. 5 Mar. 1998 <http:// www.geocities.com/Athens/5379/yeats_TheWildSwansAtCoole.html>.

Article in a Journal

Osborne, Lawrence. "A Pirate's Progress: How the Maritime Rogue Became a Multicultural Hero." Linguafranca 8.2 (March 1998): 47 pars. 17 Mar. 1998 <http://www.linguafranca.com/>.

Article in a Magazine

Cloud, John. "Harassed or Hazed?" Time 16 Mar. 1998. 19 Mar. 1998 <http://www.pathfinder.com/time/magazine/1998/dom/980316/ law.harassed_or_hazed.whll.html>.

Article in a Newspaper

Passacantado, John. "A Pothole in the Ozone Layer." Washingtonpost.com
15 Mar. 1998. 17 Mar. 1998 <http://www.washingtonpost.com/wp-srv/
WPlate/1998-03/15/130I-031598-idx.html>.

Article in a Reference Database

Staples, Brent. "Common Ground." Rev. of One Nation, After All, by Alan
Wolfe. New York Times Book Review 8 Mar. 1998. The New York
Times on the Web. 1998. The New York Times Company. 12 April 1998
<http://www.nytimes.com/books/98/03/08/reviews/
980308.08staplet.html>.

Scholarly Project

Gifts of Speech: Women's Speeches from Around the World. Mar. 1998. Sweet
Briar College. 21 Mar. 1998 <http://gos.sbc.edu/>.

E-mail or an Online Posting

Wittreich, Joseph. E-mail to the author. 12 Dec. 1997.

Porter, Don. "Inverted Pyramids." 12 Mar. 1998. Online posting. Society for
Professional Journalists. 16 Mar. 1998 <SPJL@LISTS.PSU.EDU>.

Professional Web Site

UC Berkeley Film Studies Web Page. U of California at Berkeley. 22 Jan. 1998
<http://cinemaspace.berkeley.edu/Film_Studies/index.html>.

Personal Web Site

Wong, James. Home page. 12 May 1998 <http://logic.simplenet.com/
jameswong/>.

AMERICAN PSYCHOLOGICAL ASSOCIATION (APA) PARENTHETICAL AUTHOR-YEAR DOCUMENTATION

The format for documentation recommended by the American Psychological Association is used primarily in the social and behavioral sciences, especially sociology and psychology. It is also often employed in subjects like anthropology, astronomy, business, education, linguistics, and political science.

Like MLA style, APA documentation is based on parenthetical references to author and page. The chief difference is that, in the APA system, you include the work's *date of publication* after the author's name, both within parentheses.

MLA

Primitive religious rituals may have been a means for deterring collective violence (Girard 1).

Brain Theory suggests two extremes of writing style, the appositional and the propositional (Winterowd and Williams 4).

APA

Primitive religious rituals may have been a means for deterring collective violence (Girard, 1972, p. 1).

Brain Theory suggests two extremes of writing style, the appositional and the propositional (Winterowd & Williams, 1990, p. 4).

As with MLA style, if you cite the author's name and/or the date of publication in your sentence, it is not necessary to repeat them in the parentheses.

In 1972, Girard suggested that primitive religious rituals may have been a means for deterring collective violence (p. 1).

According to Winterowd and Williams (1990), Brain Theory suggests two extremes of writing style, the appositional and the propositional (p. 4).

Here is what the bibliography for these two entries would look like in MLA style and in the style recommended by APA for student papers.

MLA

WORKS CITED

Girard, René. Violence and the Sacred. Baltimore: Johns Hopkins UP, 1972.

Winterowd, W. Ross, and James D. Williams. "Cognitive Style and Written Discourse." Focuses 3 (1990): 3–23.

APA

REFERENCES

Girard, R. (1972). Violence and the sacred. Baltimore: Johns Hopkins University
Press.

Winterowd, W. R., & Williams, J. D. (1990). Cognitive style and written
discourse. Focuses, 3, 3–23.

These are some of the ways that APA bibliographical style for student papers differs from MLA style:

- Authors' first and middle names are designated by initials. When there are multiple authors, all are listed last name first, and an ampersand (&) is used instead of *and*.

- Two or more works by the same author are listed chronologically. Instead of using a dash for repeated names (as in MLA style), you start each entry with the author's full name.

- The date of publication (in parentheses) is placed immediately after the author's name.

- In the title of a book or article, only the first word and the first word of the subtitle are capitalized.

- The title of a section of a volume (e.g., an article in a periodical or a chapter of a book) is neither underlined nor surrounded by quotation marks.

- The volume number of a journal is underlined.

Since the identification of sources greatly depends on the dates that you cite, you must be careful to clarify the dating, especially when a single author has published two or more works in the same year. Here, for example, is an excerpt from a bibliography that distinguishes among three sources published in 1972:

Carnegie Commission on Higher Education. (1972a). The campus and the city:
Maximizing assets and reducing liabilities. New York: McGraw-Hill.

Carnegie Commission on Higher Education. (1972b). The fourth revolution:
Instructional technology in higher education. New York: McGraw-Hill.

Carnegie Commission on Higher Education. (1972c). The more effective use of
resources: An imperative for higher education. New York: McGraw-Hill.

And here is how one of these sources would be documented in the essay:

In its report The More Effective Use of Resources, the Carnegie Commission
on Higher Education recommended that "colleges and universities develop a
'self-renewal' fund of 1 to 3 percent each year taken from existing allocations"
(1972c, p. 105).

For an example of the use of APA author-year documentation, look at "Explaining the Tunguskan Phenomenon," the third research essay in Chapter 10.

MODELS OF APA BIBLIOGRAPHICAL ENTRIES AND PARENTHETICAL DOCUMENTATION

The following is a brief list of model entries for APA style. Each bibliographical form that will appear in alphabetical order on the "Works Cited" page is followed by a sample parenthetical reference as it might appear in your text. Whenever there is an author, the sample parenthetical references in this list will contain the author's name; remember that, in your essay, you will often mention the author's name (and the date) in your text, with only the page of the source needed in the parenthetical reference.

Book by a Single Author

Veysey, L. R. (1965). The emergence of the American university. Chicago:
University of Chicago Press.
(Veysey, 1965, p. 45)

Book by More Than One Author

Postman, N., & Weingartner, C. (1969). Teaching as a subversive activity. New
York: Dell.
(Postman & Weingartner, 1969, p. 143)

When a source has three to five authors, name them all in the first text reference or parenthetical note; then, in all subsequent references or notes, list only the first author's name followed by "et al." For sources with six or more authors, use "et al." in the first reference or note as well. Always list all authors in bibliographical entries.

Edited Collection Written by Different Authors

Wheelwright, P. (Ed.). (1966). The presocratics. New York: Odyssey.
(Wheelwright, 1966, pp. 2–3)

Essay from a Collection Written by Different Authors

Webb, R. K. (1958). The Victorian reading public. In B. Ford (Ed.), From Dickens
to Hardy (pp. 205–226). Baltimore: Penguin.
(Webb, 1958, pp. 210–212)

Work in Translation/Work Published in a Reprinted Edition

Lorenz, K. (1969). On aggression. (M. K. Wilson, Trans.). New York: Bantam.
(Original work published 1966.)

(Lorenz, 1966/1969, p. 75)

Work Published in a New Edition

Baugh, A. C. (1957). A history of the English language. (2nd ed.). New York:
Appleton-Century-Crofts.

(Baugh, 1957, p. 288)

Book with No Author

World atlas. (1984). New York: Simon and Schuster.

(World atlas, 1984)

Article in an Encyclopedia

American architecture. (1963). Columbia encyclopedia. (3rd ed.). New York:
Columbia University Press.

(American architecture, 1963)

Publication of a Corporation, Foundation, or Government Agency

Carnegie Council on Policy Studies in Higher Education. (1980). Three thousand
futures: The next twenty years for higher education. San Francisco:
Jossey-Bass.

(Carnegie Council, 1980, p. 110)

Article in a Periodical Numbered by Volume

Plumb, J. H. (1976). Commercialization of childhood. Horizon, 18, 16–29.

(Plumb, 1976, p. 20)

Article in a Monthly Periodical

Loye, D. (1978, April). TV's impact on adults. Psychology Today, 87+.

(Loye, 1978, p. 87)

Article in a Weekly Periodical

Meyer, K. E. (1978, September 16). Television's trying times. Saturday Review, 19–23.

(Meyer, 1978, pp. 19–20)

Article in a Newspaper

Goldin, D. (1995, July 4). In a change of policy, and heart, colleges join fight against inflated grades. The New York Times, late ed., p. 8.

(Goldin, 1995)

Article without an Author

How to get quality back into the schools. (1977, September 12). US News & World Report, 31–34.

(How to get, 1977, p. 32)

Unpublished Dissertation

Eastman, E. (1993). "Lectures on jurisprudence": A key to understanding Adam Smith's thought. Unpublished doctoral dissertation, Claremont Graduate School.

(Eastman, 1993)

Film

Kubrick, S. (Director). (1963). Dr. Strangelove. [Film]. Columbia Pictures.

(Kubrick, 1963)

Material from an Electronic Information Service or Database

Belenky, M. F. (1984). The role of deafness in the moral development of hearing impaired children. In A. Areson & J. De Caro (Eds.), Teaching, learning and development. Rochester, NY: National Institute for the Deaf. (ERIC Document Reproduction Service No. ED 248 646)

(Belenky, 1984)

MODELS OF APA BIBLIOGRAPHICAL ENTRIES FOR CITING INTERNET SOURCES

Official APA citation guidelines for Internet sources are currently being developed. The citation models below are based on the guidelines provided in *Online!: A Reference Guide to Using Internet Sources,* by Andrew Harnack and Eugene Kleppinger (New York: St. Martin's Press, 1998), and are consistent with the principles of APA style. Using the sample below as a general guide, you should attempt to include as many of the elements of citation as are appropriate to your source:

Author's last name, First initial, Middle initial. (Publication date). Title of document. Title of complete work. <URL> (Date of access).

Book

Skene, F. (1865; 1996, December 10). Penitentiaries and reformatories. Victorian Women Writers Project. Ed. Perry Willett. Indiana U. <http://www.indiana.edu/~letrs/vwwp/skene/skene~reform.html> (1998, March 11).

Article in a Journal

Osborne, L. (1998). A pirate's progress: how the maritime rogue became a multicultural hero. Linguafranca, 8(2). <http://www.linguafranca.com/> (1998, March 17).

Article in a Magazine

Cloud, J. (1998, March 16). Harassed or hazed? Time. <http://www.pathfinder.com/time/magazine/1998/dom/980316/law.harassed_or_hazed.whll.html> (1998, March 18).

Professional Web Site

Cohen, A. J. (1997, January 4). Clockwork orange and the aestheticization of violence. UC Berkeley Film Studies Web Page. <http://cinemaspace.berkeley.edu/Cinema_Beyond/C_B.lectures/ClockworkOrange/Benj_CultIndustr_Clckwrk.html> (1998, April 28).

Personal Web Site

> Wong, J. Home page. <http://logic.simplenet.com/jameswong/>
> (1998, May 12).

E-mail

> Phillips, S. <sphillips@ucb.edu>. (1997, December 19). Subject line of message
> [Personal email]. (1998, January 2).

NUMBERED BIBLIOGRAPHY

In this method, used primarily in the abstract and engineering sciences, you number each entry in your bibliography. Then, each citation in your essay consists of only the number of the work that you are referring to, placed in parentheses. Remember to include the page number if you quote from your source.

> Theorem 2 of Joel, Shier, and Stein (2) is strengthened in the following theorem:

> The following would be a consequence of the conjecture of McMullen and
> Shepher (3, p. 133):

Depending on your subject, you arrange your bibliography in alphabetical order (biology or mathematics) or in the order in which you cite the sources in your essay (chemistry, engineering, or physics). Consult your instructor or a style sheet that contains the specific rules for your discipline.

ENDNOTE/FOOTNOTE DOCUMENTATION

Until about ten years ago, documentation for most research essays was provided by *footnotes* or *endnotes*. In this system, a sequence of numbers in your essay is keyed to a series of separate notes containing publication information, which appear either at the bottom of the page (footnotes) or on a separate page at the end of the essay (endnotes). It also includes a standard bibliography as part of the essay. Many authors still use footnotes or endnotes, and some of your instructors may ask you to use this system of documentation.

This brief excerpt from a biographical essay about Ernest Hemingway shows you what the endnote/footnote system looks like.

> Hemingway's zest for life extended to women also. His wandering heart seemed
> only to be exceeded by an even more appreciative eye.[6] Hadley was aware of
> her husband's flirtations and of his facility with women.[7] Yet, she had no

idea that something was going on between Hemingway and Pauline Pfeiffer, a fashion editor for Vogue magazine.[8] She was also unaware that Hemingway delayed his return to Schruns from a business trip to New York, in February 1926, so that he might spend some more time with this "new and strange girl."[9]

[6]Ernest Hemingway, A Moveable Feast (New York: Scribner's, 1964) 102.

[7]Alice Hunt Sokoloff, Hadley: The First Mrs. Hemingway (New York: Dodd, Mead, 1973) 84.

[8]Carlos Baker, Ernest Hemingway: A Life Story (New York: Scribner's, 1969) 159.

[9]Hemingway 210. Also Baker 165.

If your instructor asks you to use endnotes or footnotes, do not put parenthetical source references, as in MLA or APA style, anywhere within the text of the essay. Instead, at each place where you would insert a parenthetical reference, put a number to indicate to your reader that there is a corresponding footnote or endnote.

When *inserting the numbers,* follow these rules:

- The note number is raised slightly above the line of your essay. To do this with a typewriter, move the roller up one half-turn. Many word processing programs have provision for various styles of documentation, including inserting footnotes/endnotes. If yours does not, leave two spaces in the line and insert the number neatly by hand in the first space, slightly above the line, once the essay is finished.

- The notes are numbered consecutively: if you have twenty-six notes in your essay, the number of the last one should be 26. There is no such thing as "12a." If "12a" appears at the last moment, then it becomes "13," and the remainder of the notes should be renumbered.

- Every note should contain at least one separate piece of information. Never write a note that states only, "See footnote 3." The reader should be told enough to make it unnecessary to consult footnote 3.

- While a note may contain more than one piece of information (for example, the source reference as well as some additional explanation of the point that is being documented), the note should have only one number. Under no circumstances should two note numbers be placed together, like this: [6,7].

When you prepare the documentation for your essay, you will have two lists to make: the list of works cited, and the list of notes.

The *format of the bibliography* closely resembles the "Works Cited" format for parenthetical documentation that was described in Chapter 5 and Chapter 9: the sources are alphabetized by last name, with the second and subsequent lines of each entry indented. The entries themselves closely resemble the forms for MLA bibliographical entries listed at the beginning of this appendix.

The *format of the list of notes* resembles the bibliography in reverse: the first line of the note is indented five spaces, with the second and subsequent lines at the margin; the note begins with a raised number, corresponding to the number in the text of the essay; the author's name is in first name/last name order; author and title are separated by commas, not periods; publication information is placed in parentheses; and the note ends with the page reference and a period. Notes should be double-spaced throughout.

Here is a list of five notes, illustrating the most common forms, followed by a bibliography consisting of the same five sources:

NOTES

[1]Helen Block Lewis, Psychic War in Men and Women (New York: New York UP, 1976) 43.

[2]Gertrude Himmelfarb, "Observations on Humanism and History," in The Philosophy of the Curriculum, ed. Sidney Hook (Buffalo: Prometheus, 1975) 85.

[3]Harvey G. Cox, "Moral Reasoning and the Humanities," Liberal Education 71.3 (1985): 196.

[4]Lauro Martines, "Mastering the Matriarch," Times Literary Supplement 1 February 1985: 113.

[5]Carolyn See, "Collaboration with a Daughter: The Rewards and Cost," New York Times 19 June 1986, late ed.: C2.

WORKS CITED

Cox, Harvey G. "Moral Reasoning and the Humanities." Liberal Education 71.3 (1985): 195–204.

Himmelfarb, Gertrude. "Observations on Humanism and History." In The Philosophy of the Curriculum. Ed. Sidney Hook. Buffalo: Prometheus, 1975. 81–88.

Lewis, Helen Block. Psychic War in Men and Women. New York: New York UP, 1976.

Martines, Lauro. "Mastering the Matriarch." Times Literary Supplement 1 February 1985: 113.

See, Carolyn. "Collaboration with a Daughter: The Rewards and Cost." New York Times 19 June 1986, late ed.: C2.

Another kind of endnote or footnote, known as the *short form,* should be used when you are citing the same source more than once in your essay. The first time you cite a new source, you use the long form, as illustrated above, which contains detailed information about publication history. The second time you cite the same source, and all subsequent times, you write a separate note, with a new number, but now you use a shorter form, consisting of the author's name and a page number:

[6]Lewis 74.

The short form can be used here because there is already a long-form entry for Lewis on record in a previous note. If your bibliography contained two works by Lewis, then you would have to include an abbreviated title in the short form of the note:

[6]Lewis, Psychic War 74.

The short form makes it unnecessary to use any Latin abbreviations, like *ibid.* or *op. cit.,* in your notes.

For an example of the use of endnote documentation in a full-length essay, see "The Quest for Survival in the Andes Mountains," in Chapter 10.

NOTES PLUS PAGE NUMBERS IN THE TEXT

If you are using only one or two sources in your essay, it is a good idea to include one footnote at the first reference and, thereafter, cite the page number of the source in the text of your essay.

For example, if your essay is exclusively about Sigmund Freud's *Civilization and Its Discontents,* document your first reference to the work with a complete note, citing the edition that you are using:

[*]Sigmund Freud, Civilization and Its Discontents (Garden City: Doubleday, 1958) 72. All further citations refer to this edition.

This single note explains to your reader that you are intending to use the same edition whenever you cite this source. All subsequent references to this book will be followed by the page reference, in parentheses, usually at the end of your sentence.

Freud has asserted that "the greatest obstacle to civilization [is] the constitutional tendency in men to aggression against one another . . . " (101).

This method is most useful in essays on literary topics when you are focusing on a single author, without citing secondary sources.

Remember: The choice of documentation for your essay is not really yours. Ask your instructor which method is appropriate for your course and your paper topic.

Interviewing and Field Research

As well as the books, articles, films, videos, and other research materials available at your library, personal interviews and field research can provide worthwhile information for your research essay. A well-conducted interview with an expert in the field, if it is carefully focused on your topic, can give you information unavailable from any other source. A personal interview can also enrich your essay with details, based on actual experience, that will capture and hold your audience's interest. Similarly, your own observation of an event or environment can be a source of valuable information. Through close observation of the river flowing past a sewage treatment plant or of the behavior of people during a political demonstration, you can collect data to support your thesis, to supplement the texts you have read, and to suggest alternative interpretations of the issues and ideas developed in your essay.

As you progress through your college's general education curriculum, you will probably find that some professional fields and academic disciplines, such as literature or history, depend most on library research, while others, such as sociology or science, often call for direct observation and interviewing by the researcher. For many of the topics that you explore across the curriculum, your essays will benefit from a combination of both library and personal investigation.

INTERVIEWING

Sources for Interviews

You will want to interview experts or authorities who are both knowledgeable and appropriate sources of information about your specific topic. First, consider the faculty on your campus, not only as direct sources of information but as sources of referrals to other experts in the field at nearby colleges and universities. If your general topic is the Holocaust, for example, you may want to interview a faculty member with that specialization in your college's history, sociology, or Judaic studies department. You may, in fact, come across the names of appropriate faculty at your college in the course of your library research.

An entirely different source of direct information is a person who has had personal experience with some aspect of your essay topic. As you talk about your research on the Holocaust, one of your friends might tell you about an aunt living nearby, someone who, for example, survived the concentration camps at Auschwitz. That woman's recollections can be just as appropriate and important an addition to your essay as a professor's more theoretical comments, lending it human drama or highlighting a particular issue that interests you.

Some essays can be enhanced by interviewing several sources. For example, if you were preparing a report on an environmental issue in your town—let's say the purity of its water supply—you would want to learn about the impact of the new sewage treatment plant on the local environment. Of course, you would want to talk to the plant's manager; but you might also consult the managers of local businesses to determine some of the economic implications, and to some public health officials to learn about the kinds of health hazards the plant is intended to avoid. In this case, a single source would not cover the possible spectrum of responses.

Interviews can be time-consuming, and direct information derived from interviews will probably have to be combined with notes taken from your reading. You need to know in advance what kinds of interview will be most useful and appropriate—if any—and, thus, not waste your time and that of your source.

Planning an Interview

Whether in person or on the telephone, interviews require careful planning and preparation. First, you have to establish a courteous and professional relationship with your subject (that is what the person you are interviewing is generally called). Most potential interview subjects will be pleased to participate in your research. Your interest enhances the value of their knowledge and experience, and they are likely to enjoy being cited as authorities and having their ideas quoted and read.

You are more likely to get someone to consent to an interview if you write or phone first to make an appointment. Arrange your appointments as soon as possible once you have focused your topic and identified candidates for interviews. Since your potential subjects are likely to have busy schedules, allow enough time to make initial contact and then to wait a week or two, if necessary, until the person has enough time to speak with you at length. This way you can avoid having your initial conversation turn into an interview before you are quite prepared for it—which can be awkward if you don't have your questions ready.

When you call or write to those whom you hope to interview, politely identify yourself; then briefly describe your topic and the special focus of your essay. Ask for an interview of 20 to 30 minutes at a later time convenient for the subject. If appropriate, mention the name of the person who suggested this source, or refer to the publication in which you saw the subject's name. Your objective is to convey your own serious interest in the topic and in your subject's knowledge of the topic. Be friendly, but professional. If someone is reluctant to be interviewed, you should retreat gracefully. At the same time, don't hesitate to ask for a referral to someone else who might be in a better position to provide helpful information.

Preparing for an Interview

Because your interview, whether in person or on the phone, will probably be brief, you need to plan in advance what you intend to say and ask so that you can use the time effectively. Careful preparation is also a compliment to your interview subjects and shows respect for their expertise.

Reviewing your research notes, make a focused list of questions in writing beforehand, tailoring them to your specific paper topic and to your source's area of knowledge. If, for example, you are going to interview the manager of a sewage treatment plant on the Hudson River about the effective removal of PCBs from the water, you don't want to use up ten minutes asking about plant management. It can be helpful to prepare a questionnaire, leaving space between the questions for you to take notes. You can use the same questionnaire, with variations, for a whole series of personal interviews.

Recording Information during an Interview

During the actual interview, you will be listening intently to your subject's responses and thinking about your next question. But as a researcher, you have another challenge. You need to take away with you a comprehensive record of the interview so that you can quote your expert accurately and cite information authoritatively. Most successful interviewers use one of two techniques to record the interview, or a combination of both: tape-recording and note-taking.

Tape-recording

If you plan to use a tape-recorder, make sure you ask your subject's permission in advance; test the equipment beforehand (especially if it's borrowed for the occasion); and know how to operate it smoothly. Bring it to the interview with the tape already loaded in the machine, and be sure the batteries are fresh. (Bring along a second tape in case the first one jams or breaks, and carry extra batteries.) When the interview is about to begin, check again to see if your subject has any objection to your recording the conversation. Then, to avoid making your subject self-conscious, put the tape recorder in an unobtrusive place. After that, don't create a distraction by fiddling with the machine.

Note-taking

Even if you plan to tape-record the interview, come prepared to take careful notes; bring notebook and pens, as well as your list of questions or questionnaire. One way of preparing for detailed note-taking—the kind that will provide you with accurate direct quotations to use in your essay—is to rehearse. Pair off with a classmate who is also preparing for an interview, and practice interviewing and note-taking (including handling the tape recorder). Also review the instructions for Assignment 7 and Assignment 8 in Chapter 4 (pp. 200–202, 208–210). If your subject presents a point so well that you know you'll want to quote it, write it down rapidly but carefully, and—then and there—read it back to make sure that you have transcribed the statement correctly.

Conducting the Interview

Arrive on time (not late and not early)! Once you've been invited to sit down and your equipment is set up, *briefly* remind your subject of the essay topic and your reason for requesting the interview. Then get right down to your "script": ask each question clearly, without hurrying; be alert to recognize when the question has been fully answered (there is usually a pause); and move briskly on to the next question. Otherwise, let your subject talk freely, with minimum interruption. Remember that you are the receiver, not the provider, of information, and let your subject do almost all the talking.

Sometimes, a particular question will capture your subject's interest, and you will get a more detailed answer than you expected. Be aware of the time limit for the interview; but if you see a promising line of questioning that you didn't anticipate, and your subject seems relaxed and willing to prolong the conversation, take advantage of the opportunity and ask follow-up questions. What if your subject digresses far away from the topic of your essay? At the first opportunity, ask whether there is a time constraint. If there is, politely indicate that you have three or four more questions to ask and you hope that there will be enough time to include them.

No matter how careful your preparations, a good interview won't go exactly as you planned. You should aim to participate in a conversation, not direct an interrogation. At the end, your subject should feel that the time has passed too quickly and, ideally, offer to speak with you again, if necessary, to fill up any gaps. To maintain that good impression, be sure to send a brief note of thanks to your subject no longer than a day or two after the interview. Later on, you may want to send a copy of the completed essay.

Using Interview Sources in Your Essay

Since the purpose of the interview is to gather information (and to provide yourself with a few apt quotations), you need to have clear notes to work from as you organize your essay. If you used a tape recorder, you should transcribe the interview as soon as you can; if you took notes, you should go over them carefully, clarify confusing words, and then type a definitive version. Otherwise, you may find yourself deciphering your almost-illegible notes at a later time or searching through the entire tape to find a specific sentence that you want to quote. Transcribe the interview accurately, without embroidering or revising what your subject actually said. Keep the original notes and tapes; your instructor may want to review them along with your essay.

Working with notes from an interview is almost exactly the same as working with notes from library research. As you organize your essay (following the process described in Chapter 8), you cross-reference your notes with a list of the topics for your essay, choosing information from the interview that might be cited to support the major points in your outline. When you begin to choose quotations, you may want to review the section on "Selecting Quotations," pp. 360–361. Remember that it is the well-chosen and carefully placed source that carries authority, not the number of words quoted. Finally, document each use of material taken from your interview, whether it is ideas or words, with a parenthetical reference. (See Appendix B for the appropriate bibliographical entry.)

FIELD RESEARCH

Like interviewing, field research is a way of supplementing the material you take from texts and triggering new ideas about your topic. When you engage in field research, you are gathering information directly, acting as an observer, investigator, and evaluator within the context of an academic or professional discipline. If you are asked by your anthropology instructor to describe and analyze a family celebration as an ethnographer would, your observations of Thanksgiving dinner at home would be regarded as field research.

In many of your college courses, you will be expected to engage in field research. When, for example, the nursing program sends students to a nearby hospital for their clinical practice and asks for a weekly report on their work with patients, these students are doing field research. Other students may participate in a cooperative education program involving professional internships in preparation for potential careers; the reports these interns prepare on their work experiences are based on field research. Whatever the course, your instructor will show you how to connect your field research activities to the theories, procedures, and format characteristic of that discipline. Still, there are certain practices common to most kinds of field research that you need to know from the beginning. Let's follow that process from assignment to essay as you develop a simple topic based on field research.

Your sociology professor has suggested that, although college students like to think of themselves as unique individuals, certain patterns clearly underlie their characteristic behavior. As an example, he asserts that both male and female students prefer to work and relax with members of the opposite sex. He is asking each of you to test this hypothesis by choosing a place on campus to observe students as they go about their daily routine, keeping in mind two questions: are there patterns one can observe in these students' behavior? what might be the significance of these patterns? If you were assigned this project, your work would fall into three stages: gathering the information, analyzing that information, and writing the essay.

Gathering Information

According to your instructor's guidelines for this essay based on field research, you will need to perform at least six separate observations for 20 to 30 minutes each at a site of your choice and, later, be prepared to hand in copies of your accumulated observation notes along with your essay. So your first important decision concerns the location for gathering information about students' behavior: the cafeteria? the library? a particular class? the student union? the college bookstore? a classroom or another place on campus where students congregate? You decide to observe students gathered at the row of benches outside Johnson Hall, the busiest classroom building, extending from the bookstore on the right to the student union building on the left; these benches also face a field where gym classes meet and the baseball team practices. Since this area is an important junction on the campus, you can assume that enough students will appear to provide basic information for your field research.

Planning the Observations

To conform to your instructor's requirements and obtain all the information you need for your essay, you should prepare for your observation sessions quickly and carefully. First, establish a schedule that will fulfill the guidelines for the assignment. Since your first class in Johnson Hall is at 11 A.M., and you are free before that, you decide to schedule your observations for the half hour before class, that is, from 10:30 to 11:00 A.M. on Monday, Wednesday, and Friday, for the next two weeks.

You will need to set aside a separate notebook for recording your observations. For each session, start a fresh page, and indicate the date and the times when you begin and end your sessions. Such specific information is what establishes your authority as a field researcher. Before your first session, consider making a diagram of the site, roughly sketching in the location of the buildings, placing the seven benches correctly, and assigning each a number.

As with interviewing, a list of prepared questions will help you to spend your time profitably. This time, however, your object is not to ask for information, but to set up a framework for your observations and, possibly, a potential structure for your essay. For this assignment, you are basically trying to find out:

- How many students are spending time at this site?
- Where are they and what are they doing?
- Do they stay for the whole observation period, or do they come and go?

Engaging in Observation

Your work consists of careful observing and precise note-taking. You are not trying to write a narrative or, at this point, understand the significance of what you are seeing; you are only trying to record your subjects' activities accurately to provide notes for future reflection.

Some people may feel self-conscious to have an observer watching them closely and writing down everything they do. To avoid potential questions or confrontations, try to do your observing and note-taking unobtrusively, without staring too hard at any one person. If someone asks what you are doing, be prepared to say that you are working on an assignment for a college class, that you aren't going to identify anyone by name, and that you would be grateful for the person's cooperation. As with interview subjects, you will find that most subjects of field research are sympathetic and helpful. If someone speaks to you, take advantage of the opportunity to combine observations with a little formal interviewing, and possibly gain a useful quotation for your essay. If someone objects to being included in your study, however, you should immediately turn your attention elsewhere, or move on and try again at another time.

A portion of your notes for one session might look like that shown in Figure C-1.

After a couple of sessions, you may feel that you have a general idea of the range of students' behavior at the site, so you can begin to look specifically for repeated instances of certain activities: studying together or individually, eating, relaxing. But you will need to keep an open mind and eye about what you might observe. Again as with interviewing, your subjects' behavior may not absolutely conform to your planned questions, so you may need to add new questions as the sessions progress. For example, you may not have realized until your third session that students sitting on the benches closest to the playing field are focusing on the sports activities there; from then on, you will be looking for that behavior.

For this assignment, you would continue observing until you complete the number of observations specified; but for your own field research in a project for a course in your major field, you might conduct observations for most of a semester. As a professional researcher (like Margaret Mead when she was observing Pacific Island adolescents for her classic book *Coming of*

Monday, April 3; 10:30 am.

3 students at bench 3 -- 1 male & 2 females. Females sitting on bench. Male, between them, standing with 1 foot up on bench, smoking. They're talking quietly. About 5 minutes later, another male arrives on bike & stands, straddling bike, in front of the bench. Conversation continues, now with 4 participants. At 10:50, females get up & walk into Johnson, along with 1st male. 2nd male rides off toward library.

At benches 4 & 5, 2 people at each. At 4, 1 male reads book, stopping now and then to use a highlighter. 1 female has bunch of 3 x 5 cards, & she looks at each one for a second, then flips it, then goes to next one. At 10:35, another male comes over to her, she gets up, & they both go to bench 6, where no one is sitting. There she continues going through her cards, but now she seems to read something from each card, as male responds with a word or 2. They continue to do this for another 10 minutes.

Figure C-1

Age in Samoa), you might even live with a tribe, studying their culture for a year or more.

Analyzing Your Information

When you have all your observations recorded, you are ready to move on to the next stage: reviewing your notes to understand what you have seen, and analyzing what you have learned. You have probably noticed that this overlaps with the previous observation stage; as you watched students in front of Johnson Hall, you were already beginning to group their activities into several categories: studying, casual conversations, watching sports, eating, sleeping.

Once you establish these categories, you pull out of your notes the specific references that match the category, noting the date and time of each instance. So now you have several new pages that look like those shown in Figure C-2.

Studying

girl and guy with flash cards 4/6 10:35
group of 5 with science notes 4/8 10:30 - 10:58
   (they told me about their 11 am quiz --
   all in same class)
guy with book and highlighter 4/6
     10:30 - 10:45

Sports watching

observations 2, 4, 5, 6: groups of 2 - 5 guys at
   benches 1, 2, 3 (facing sports field).
   Groups generally talked, pointed,
   laughed, while gym classes did
   aerobics.

observations 4, 5: during baseball team
   practice, guys in small groups
   cheered, pointed; several stood up
   and walked over to edge of path
   that overlooks field.

female pairs watching sports
   during 4, 5, but no groups.

observations 1, 2: no sports scheduled
   then; few people on benches 1, 2,
   and 3.

Figure C-2

You may want to chart your observations to represent at a glance such variables as these: how many students studied, or watched sports, or socialized? Which activities were associated with males or with females? If your sessions took place during different times of the day, the hour would be another variable to record on your chart.

As you identify categories, you need to ask yourself some questions to help you characterize each one and define the differences among some of your subjects' behaviors. For example: are these differences determined by gender, as with the sports watchers, or by preferred methods of learning, like solitary or group study? As you think through the possible conclusions to be drawn from your observations, record them in your notebook, for these preliminary analyses will later become part of your essay.

Writing the Essay

An essay based on field research generally follows a format appropriate to the particular discipline. Your instructor will provide detailed guidelines and, perhaps, refer you to an article in a professional journal to use as a model. For the essay analyzing student behavior, you might present your findings according to the following outline:

Purpose: In the first section, you state the problem—the purpose of your field research—clearly indicating the question(s) you set out to investigate.

Method: Here, you explain your choice of site, the times and number of your observation sessions, and the general procedure for observation that you followed, including any exceptions to or deviations from your plan.

Observations: Next, you record the information you gathered from your observations, not as a list of random facts, but as categories or groupings that make the facts coherent to the reader. In many disciplines, this kind of information can be presented through charts, graphs, or tables.

Analysis: The heart of your essay, here is where you explain to your readers the significance of your observations. If, for example, you decided that certain activities were gender-related, you would describe the basis for that distinction. Or you could discuss your conclusion that students use the benches primarily as a meeting place to socialize. Or you might make the connection between studying as the most prevalent student activity outside Johnson Hall and the scheduling of midterms during the time of your observations.

Conclusions: At the end of your essay, you remind your readers—and the instructor who is evaluating your work—that your purpose throughout has been to answer the questions and clarify the problems posed in the first paragraph. What did you discover that can illuminate your response to your professor's assertions about students' behavior?

Using Field Research

There are several important points to remember about using field research:

1. In actual practice across the curriculum, field research is usually combined with library research. As part of your investigation, you will often be asked to include in an early section of your essay a "literature search," that is, a summary of some key articles on your topic. This summary shows that you are familiar with an appropriate range of information and, especially, the major work in the field.

2. Whether you emphasize library or field research depends on the purpose and nature of your essay. If field research is integral to your

(continued)

(continued)

topic, you will be acting as the principal investigator and interpreter of new data, and the library research will serve only as a supplement to your field research. Otherwise, you should integrate your field research into your essay as you would any other source of information.

3. For field research, careful documentation is especially important since you are asking your reader to trust the data that you yourself have gathered and upon which your speculations and conclusions are based. You can create this trust by making careful and repeated observations, recording them in detail and accurately, and presenting them in a clear and logical manner.

4. The methods of analyzing data obtained through field research are, in most cases, specific to particular disciplines. So you should indicate to your readers, by reference to authorities or models, that you are observing the conventions of the field you are working in. It is especially important that, after consultation with your instructor, you use the appropriate method of documenting both your field research and your library research, so that a reader can clearly distinguish the work of the previous investigators who are your secondary sources from your own primary contributions.

Writing Essay Examinations

Instructors give essay examinations for three reasons:

- To make sure that you have read and understood the assigned reading;
- To test your analytical skills;
- To find out if you can integrate what you have read with the ideas and information that you have learned in lectures and class discussion.

Since your instructor is usually not trying to test your memory, essay examinations are often open-book, allowing you to refer freely to the source. But in any exam, even a take-home assignment, there is likely to be some time pressure. To prepare, you should have read all the material carefully in advance and outlined, underlined, or annotated the text.

READING THE QUESTION

You determine your strategy by carefully examining the wording of the question before you begin to plan and write your essay. First, you must accept that someone else is providing the topic for your essay. The person who wrote the question wants to pinpoint a single area to be explored, and so you may have very little scope. However restrictive it may seem, you must stay within the boundaries of the question. If you are instructed to focus on only a small section of the text, summarizing the entire work from beginning to end is inappropriate. If you are asked to discuss an issue that is raised frequently throughout the work, paraphrasing a single paragraph or page is pointless. Do not include extraneous information just to demonstrate how much you know. Most teachers are more impressed with aptness and conciseness than with length.

The controlling verb of the question will usually provide you with a key. Different verbs will require different approaches. You are already familiar with the most common terms:

summarize; state; list; outline; condense; cite reasons

What is sometimes forgotten under pressure is that you are expected to carry out the instructions literally. *Summarize* means condense: the reader expects a short but complete account of the specified subject. On the other hand, *list* should result in a sequence of short entries, somewhat disconnected, but not a fully developed series of paragraphs.

Other directions may be far broader:

describe; discuss; review; explain; show; explore; determine

Verbs like these give you a wide scope. Since they do not demand a specific strategy, be careful to stay within the set topic, so that you do not explain or review more than the readers want to know about.

Still other verbs indicate a more exact method of development, perhaps one of the strategies that you have already worked with in Assignment 5 in Chapter 3:

compare and contrast; illustrate; define; show the reasons; trace the causes; trace the effects; suggest solutions; analyze

Notice that none of the verbs so far has provided an opportunity for personal comment. You have been asked to examine the text, to demonstrate your understanding of its meaning and its implications, but you have not been asked for your opinion. However, several verbs do request commentary:

evaluate; interpret; criticize; justify; prove; disagree

Although these verbs invite a personal response, they do not give you freedom to write about whatever you choose. You are still confined to the boundaries of the set subject, and you should devote as much of your essay as possible to demonstrating your understanding of what you have read. *A brilliant essay that ignores the topic rarely earns the highest grade.* If you have worked hard to prepare for the essay, you would be foolish to ignore the question. Don't reinterpret the directions in order to write about what is easiest or what would display your abilities to best advantage or what you figured out earlier would be asked. Just answer the question.

PLANNING AND DEVELOPING THE ESSAY

Even when you have worked out what you are expected to write about, you are still not ready to start writing. Your reader will also judge the way in which your essay is constructed, so organize your thoughts before you begin to write. No elaborate outline is necessary.

Guidelines for Planning and Developing Your Essay

1. *List some of the main points that come into your head, reduce the list to a manageable number, and renumber the sequence.* This process does not take very long and it can prevent unnecessary repetition, unintentional omissions, mixed-up sequences, and overemphasis.

2. *Develop each point separately.* Don't try to say everything at the same time. Consult your list, say what is necessary about each item, and then move on to the next.

3. *Develop each point adequately.* Each reason or cause or criticism deserves convincing presentation. Unless you are asked for a list, don't just write down one sentence and rush away to the next item. You will write a more effective essay by including some support for each of your points. Do not make brief, incomplete references to ideas because you assume that the reader will know all about them. It is your responsibility to explain each one so that it makes sense by itself.

4. *Refer back to the text.* Whenever possible, demonstrate that you can cite evidence or information from the assigned reading. If you think of two possible examples or facts, one from the source and one from your own experience or knowledge, and if you haven't enough time to include both, the safe choice will come from the source. However, you must always mark the transition between your own presentation of ideas and your reference to the source by citing its title, or the name of its author, or both.

ANALYZING AN ESSAY AND AN ESSAY QUESTION

Carefully read through George Stade's "Football—The Game of Aggression." Assume that you have previously read this essay and that you have between forty-five minutes and an hour to answer the following question:

Although he acknowledges that it can be violent, George Stade suggests that football may serve a constructive social function. Considering some of his descriptive comments about the sport, explain why football may not be as healthy for society as Stade implies.

FOOTBALL—THE GAME OF AGGRESSION
George Stade

There are many ways in which professional football is unique among sports, and as many others in which it is the fullest expression of what is at the heart of all sports. There is no other major sport so dependent upon raw force, nor any so dependent on a complex and delicate strategy; none so wide in the range of specialized functions demanded from its players; none so dependent upon the undifferentiated athletic *sine qua non,* a quickwitted body; none so primitive; none so futuristic; none so American.

Football is first of all a form of play, something one engages in instinctively and only for the sake of performing the activity in question. Among forms of play, football is a game, which means that it is built on communal needs, rather than on private evasions, like mountain climbing. Among games it is a sport; it requires athletic ability, unlike croquet. And among sports, it is one whose mode is violence and whose violence is its special glory.

In some sports—basketball, baseball, soccer—violence is occasional (and usually illegal); in others, like hockey, it is incidental; in others still, car racing, for example, it is accidental. Definitive violence football shares alone with boxing and bullfighting, among major sports. But in bullfighting a man is pitted not against another man, but against an animal, and boxing is a competition between individuals, not teams, and that makes a great difference. If shame is the proper and usual penalty for failures in sporting competitions between individuals, guilt is the consequence of failing not only oneself and one's fans, but also one's teammates. Failure in football, moreover, seems more related to a failure of courage, seems more unmanning than in any other sport outside of bullfighting. In other sports one loses a knack, is outsmarted, or is merely inferior in ability, but in football, on top of these, a player fails because he "lacks desire," or "can't take it anymore," or "hears footsteps," as his teammates will put it.

Many sports, especially those in which there is a goal to be defended, seem enactments of the games animals play under the stimulus of what ethologists, students of animal behavior, call *territory*—"the drive to gain, maintain, and defend the exclusive right to a piece of property," as Robert Ardrey puts it. The most striking symptom of this drive is aggressiveness, but among social animals, such as primates, it leads to "amity for the social partner, hostility for the territorial neighbor." The territorial instinct is closely related to whatever makes animals establish pecking orders; the tangible sign of one's status within the orders is the size and value of the territory one is able to command. Individuals fight over status, groups over *lebensraum*[1] and a bit more. These instincts, some ethologists have claimed, are behind patriotism and private property, and also, I would add, codes of honor, as among

[1]Literally, living space. The word is often most associated with the territory thought by the Nazis to be essential to Germany's political and economic security.

ancient Greeks, modern Sicilians, primitive hunters, teen-age gangs, soldiers, aristo-
crats, and athletes, especially football players.

The territorial basis of certain kinds of sports is closest to the surface in foot-   5
ball, whose plays are all attempts to gain and defend property through aggression.
Does this not make football *par excellence* the game of instinctual satisfactions, especially among Americans, who are notorious as violent patriots and instinctive de-
fenders of private property? . . . Even the unusual amity, if that is the word, that
exists among football players has been remarked upon. . . . And what is it that cor-
responds in football to the various feathers, furs, fins, gorgeous colors by means of
which animals puff themselves into exaggerated gestures of masculine potency?
The football player's equipment, of course. His cleats raise him an inch off the
ground. Knee and thigh pads thrust the force lines of his legs forward. His pants
are tight against his rump and the back of his thighs, portions of the body which
the requirements of the game stuff with muscle. . . . Even the tubby guard looks
slim by comparison with his shoulders, extended half a foot on each side by padding.
Finally, the helmet, which from the esthetic point of view most clearly expresses
the genius of the sport. Not only does the helmet make the player inches taller and
give his head a size proportionate to the rest of him; it makes him anonymous, in-
scrutable, more serviceable as a symbol. The football player in uniform strikes the
eye in a succession of gestalt[2] shifts; first a hooded phantom out of the paleolithic
past of the species; then a premonition of a future of spacemen.

In sum, and I am almost serious about this, football players are to America what   6
tragic actors were to ancient Athens and gladiators to Rome: models of perennially
heroic, aggressive, violent humanity, but adapted to the social realities of the times
and places that formed them.

[2]I.e., perceptual.

ANSWERING THE QUESTION

At first, you may have some difficulty determining the focus of your essay
since the question includes more than one key word to help you work out your
strategy. The main verb in this question is *explain*. You are being asked to account for something, to help your reader understand what may not be entirely
clear. *Explain* also implies persuasion: your reader must be convinced that your
explanation is valid.

- If the question asked you to explain *something that is confusing* in Stade's
  essay, your task would be to provide an interpretive summary of some
  part of the text. For example, you might have been asked to explain the
  differences, with illustrations, between violence that is occasional, incidental, and accidental, discussing the implications of these distinctions
  for sports in general.

- If the question asked you to explain *some related point that Stade omits* from his discussion, your task would be to extend his reasoning, perhaps to discuss causes or effects, or to contrast and compare. For example, you might have to explain why football lends itself to a greater degree of violence than other sports, or explain the parallel between the way football players and animals defend their territory.

- If the question asked you—as it does—to *evaluate the author's reasoning* in forming his conclusions, you would then examine Stade's "almost serious" conclusions and demonstrate—explain—the limitations of his arguments and examples; in other words, argue against his position.

The essay question raises the point that Stade may have underestimated the harmful effects of football, a sport so violent that it could undermine the social benefits that it otherwise provides. To answer the question, then, you must accept the assumption that Stade may be overenthusiastic about football, *whether or not you agree,* and proceed to point out the implications and the shortcomings of his analysis. In a sense, writing a good essay depends on your willingness to allow your views to be shaped by the examiner's, at least for the duration of the exam.

The question defines the *limits* as well as the strategy of your essay. It does not permit you to dispute Stade on grounds that are entirely of your choosing. You are firmly instructed to focus your attention on the conflict between violence and social benefit. It would be foolish to ignore these instructions and write only about the glories of football or to condemn the sport for reasons unrelated to the violence of its play.

What should you be evaluating in your essay, and how many comments are "some"? Stade makes the following points in support of his view that football can be a useful social ritual:

- It fosters individual strength and determination.

- It develops cooperation and teamwork.

- It teaches players how to acquire and defend territory and thus encourages nationalism and the patriotic defense of one's country.

- It provides players and spectators with the opportunity to act out their aggressions in a controlled and relatively harmless way.

These points should certainly be on the list of paragraph topics that you jot down as you plan your essay. Since these ideas are embedded within the paragraphs of Stade's essay, you should use your own ordering principle—least violent to most (potentially) violent might be a good choice. Each of your paragraphs should begin with a description of one characteristic of the sport as Stade presents it, followed by your own explanation of the social disadvantages or benefits that might result.

Resist the temptation to devote too much space to a single aspect of the sport. For example, if you spend too much time discussing Stade's comments about uniforms and the extent to which the football player is magnified and dehumanized by his padding and his helmet, you may not be able to develop your discussion of whether football encourages patriotism or a more divisive and dangerous nationalism. Stade's essay is based on his belief that people participate in sports as a way of expressing passions and impulses that have no place in our normal daily occupations. He implies that, if this outlet is eliminated, our instincts for violence may spill over into activities where they would be far more dangerous. This argument has often been used to justify violence as depicted on television and in the movies. While you are not expected to analyze the issue with the expertise of a trained psychologist or sociologist, your essay should reflect your awareness of and your views on Stade's conception of football as a way of controlling our aggressive instincts.

INTRODUCING YOUR TOPIC

Examination essays, like all essays, require an introduction. Before beginning to explore some of the issues inherent in George Stade's analysis, you should provide a short introduction that defines the author's topic and your own. Your later references to his ideas will need a well-established context; therefore, try to define Stade's conception of football (which might differ from someone else's) right at the outset of your essay. Although the introduction need not be longer than two or three sentences, *cite your source*—the name of the author and the name of the essay, both properly spelled—and state exactly what it is that you and your author are concerned about. To demonstrate the frustration of reading an introduction that is shrouded in mystery, look at the first paragraph from a student essay answering the question that has just been analyzed:

> The attitude of the author of this essay is highly supportive of a sport that may be the most violent in the world. It is true that players acquire a lot of skills and learn about teamwork, as well as receiving huge sums of money and becoming public idols. However, there are also risks and dangers that result, for spectators and those watching on television, as well as for those on the field wearing team uniforms, which he fails to point out in this brief essay.

"He," of course, is George Stade, and the sport under discussion is football. The student had read and understood the source essay, but is so eager to begin commenting on Stade's ideas that she fails to establish a context for her arguments. Here is a more informative introduction:

> In "Football--The Game of Aggression," George Stade presents the game of football as a necessary evil and a useful social ritual. He does not deny that the game, more than most sports, is based on a potentially lethal kind of aggression. But, contrasting football with other sports, he finds that it also encourages a sense of teamwork and an instinct for patriotism, which can be valuable both to the individual and to society. Left unclear is whether ritualizing violence through

sports does, in fact, result in a less violent society, or whether watching football players maul each other in weekly combat only encourages spectators to imitate their heroes.

PRESENTING YOUR ESSAY TO THE READER

Students often choose to divide their time into three parts. For example, if you have forty minutes during which to write an essay, try the following timetable:

- ten minutes to analyze the question and plan a strategy
- twenty minutes to write the essay
- ten minutes to proofread and correct it

During in-class examinations, students often waste vital minutes by painstakingly transcribing a new copy from their rough drafts. While *your handwriting must be legible,* it is not necessary to hand in a clean copy. Teachers expect an exam essay to have sentences crossed out and words inserted. They are used to seeing arrows used to reverse sentences and numbers used to change the sequence of paragraphs. It makes no sense to write the last word of your first draft and then, without checking what you have written, immediately take a clean sheet of paper and start transcribing a copy to hand in. Because transcription is such a mechanical task, the mind tends to wander and the pen makes errors that were not in the original draft. Take time to proofread your essay, to locate grammatical errors, and to fill in gaps in continuity. As long as your corrections and changes are fairly neat and clear, your instructor will not mind reading the first draft and will probably be pleased by your efforts to improve your writing.

Appendix E

Readings for a
Research Essay

The essays in this appendix are sources for you to work with if your instructor asks you to write a research essay based on Assignment 13 (pp. 362–363). These ten readings (including one in another part of this book) could form the entire bibliography for your research essay. Or (with your instructor's permission) you may wish to supplement these essays with additional sources of your own choosing.

Henderson, Cinqué. "Myths of the Unloved." *The New Republic* 25 Aug. 1997.

Kennedy, Randall. "My Race Problem—and Ours." *The Atlantic Monthly* May 1997.

*Paley, Grace. "Travelling." *The New Yorker* Aug. 1997.

Sleeper, Jim. "Toward an End of Blackness: An Argument for the Surrender of Race Consciousness." *Harper's* May 1997. [With three "Letters to the Editor." *Harper's* Aug. 1997.]

Steele, Shelby. "I'm Black, You're White, Who's Innocent?" *Harper's* June 1988. Rpt. in *Voices in Black and White: writings on race in America from Harper's Magazine*. Eds. Katharine Whittemore and Gerald Marzorati. New York: Franklin Square Press, 1992.

Taylor, Jared. "Middle-Class Solutions." *Paved with Good Intentions: The Failure of Race Relations in Contemporary America*. New York: Carroll & Graf, 1992.

Williams, Patricia J. "Pansy Quits." *The Rooster's Egg*. Cambridge, Mass: Harvard UP, 1995.

*See Chapter 1, pp. 16–19.

DeMott, Benjamin. "Visions of Black-White Friendship." *The Trouble with Friendship: Why Americans Can't Think Straight about Race.* New York: Atlantic Monthly Press: 1995.

Wicker, Tom. "Expanding the Center." *Tragic Failure: Racial Integration in America.* New York: Morrow, 1996.

Early, Gerald. "Whatever Happened to Integration?" Rev. of *The Trouble with Friendship* and *Tragic Failure. The Atlantic Monthly* February 1997.

MYTHS OF THE UNLOVED
Cinqué Henderson

The Ku Klux Klan owns Church's Chicken and poisons blacks with addictive, deadly ingredients. Tropical Fantasy puts chemicals in its soda to sterilize black men. The CIA runs drugs in South Central Los Angeles.   1

It is difficult to hear myths like these—myths that have gained surprisingly wide acceptance in the black community—and not realize something is dreadfully wrong with race relations in the United States. When the Kerner Commission concluded nearly thirty years ago that America was "moving towards two societies, one black, one white, separate and unequal," it failed to point out that the gross material disparities would be attended by equally vast psychological ones. In this context, Bill Clinton's national dialogue on race actually seems like a hopeful idea: What is psychology, after all, if not the therapy of curing neuroses through conversation?   2

But don't be surprised if the conversation leads off in some unexpected directions. Even though the persistence of these theories defies logic (the CIA myth, for example, has been largely disavowed by the very newspaper that started it), the "paranoid style," as Richard Hofstadter calls it, has a long, sometimes distinguished history in this country—particularly among those who, as he says, see only the consequences of power, and not the inner workings. As the historian Bernard Bailyn argued thirty years ago, the "fear of a comprehensive conspiracy against liberty throughout the English-speaking world . . . lay at the heart of the Revolutionary movement." America, in other words, was founded by conspiracy nuts.   3

The Eso Won bookstore sits in the heart of black L.A. One block west of Martin Luther King Boulevard, just south of Magic Johnson Theaters, it is California's largest black-owned bookstore. At the back of the store, next to the shelf on black health care, there is an entire shelf devoted to conspiracies, some 200 books in all. The best is Patricia Turner's *I Heard It Through the Grapevine*, which, despite some of its more questionable conclusions, provides a fascinating survey of the unlikely and sometimes bizarre beliefs that manifest themselves in the black community. As Turner notes, no myth has enjoyed more durability than the rumor of CIA drug-running in South Central Los Angeles. (Small wonder, given what crack has done to black communities.)   4

The crucial point, which she makes only glancingly, is described this way: "About 80 percent of my informants reported [belief in] what I call 'malicious intent,'" but   5 when questioned more directly, "most professed greater belief in what I call 'benign neglect.'" Maxine Waters, South Central's representative in Congress, invokes similar language when it comes to the CIA-crack theory: "It confirmed many of the suspicions about some plot or some negligence on the part of the government. . . ." Yet what an odd statement to make so offhandedly: "some plot or some negligence." Trussed together as these words are, it is easy to overlook the fact that "plot" and "negligence" describe fundamentally different things. How you get from one to the other tells a lot about being black in America.

I have a friend who believes the CIA did what everyone says it did. Her brother   6 is in jail for crack possession. He won't speak to her because she prayed for him to be arrested, and, as far as she is concerned, God heard and answered. She worries about her brother still, but knows of no decent drug rehab program in the county where she lives, so she is content to let him stay in jail. At first, she said she thought the government just didn't care about blacks and crack. She was "fed up" with the police's unwillingness to fight the drug sales where she lives. "They [crack addicts] come and go big as day, and the police just sit there." Recalling her family's attempt to get her brother into a program, she despaired, "We tried and tried. Didn't nobody lift a finger. They didn't care whether we lived or died." And then the despair turned to anger. "I believe what they say," she says, her voice rising. "I wouldn't put it past none of them. They out to get black people." Belief in the CIA myth gives my friend a measure of peace. She had considered the possibility of neglect and found the argument wanting, deciding, ultimately, that conspiracy was more plausible. This may have to do with an overestimation of the government's power, but I think the switch, as sudden and surprising as it was, was occasioned by something more powerful than reason: love.

Black Americans, despite themselves, are deeply patriotic; and the popularity of   7 conspiracy theories is, in its own odd way, a heartfelt expression of this patriotism. Strange as it sounds, black conspiracy theories remain popular precisely because so few of us are willing to believe the alternative: that our depressed stature in the American hierarchy is due in large part to America's indifference to black suffering. We contrive elaborate ways of concealing it, but the idea that this country and only this country is ours, that, at the last, there is no place for us but here, is impossible to deny.

In 1963, Maya Angelou came to this realization while in Ghana. She and a band   8 of fellow black expatriates, calling themselves the "Revolutionist Returnees," were there during the historic March on Washington, doing what most black radicals were doing: dressing like Africans, eating like Africans, calling themselves African. The Returnees had long since abandoned King's nonviolent philosophy for more radical postures. After word spread among them that W. E. B. DuBois, the great black nationalist, had died, the Returnees, in a powerful show of transatlantic solidarity, staged a march against the U.S. Embassy. When two soldiers came out the door, carrying a folded American flag, the crowd began to jeer, "This isn't Iwo Jima. . . . You haven't taken Bunker Hill, you know. This is Africa!"

The two soldiers, one black, one white, nervously fumbled the flag, and it began   9
to sag toward the ground. The black man hurriedly caught the cloth and "folded it
lovingly into the White soldier's arms." Angelou later concluded, "I shuddered to
think that while we wanted that flag dragged into the mud and sullied beyond repair we also wanted it pristine, its white stripes, summer cloud white. Watching it
wave in the breeze of a distance made us nearly choke with emotion. It lifted us up
with its promise and broke our hearts with its denial."

Glenn Loury echoed this theme in [The New Republic] after the Million Man   10
March. (See "One Man's March," November 6, 1995.) In the midst of the single
most extravagant display of black nationalism in American history, the real story,
Loury wrote, was the "young black guys . . . scrambling up the steps and lounging
between the columns of the National Gallery building . . . sharing an excited ex-
pectancy with Japanese tourists and rural whites as we all waited in line to tour the
White House . . . this is their country, too. So, embarrassed that I needed to remind myself of this fact, I wept."

Some will tell you that the persistence in the black community of speculation   11
over whether Thomas Jefferson sired black heirs is due to the fact that blacks are
less likely than whites to idolize Jefferson and therefore have no trouble facing the
truth of his paternity. But it really derives from an opposite impulse: the fact that,
quietly and mostly secretly, blacks do revere Thomas Jefferson quite as much as
whites, and they want to lay claim to the legacy of America as much as whites,
too. No less a purveyor of proper bourgeois norms than *Ebony* magazine has
heaped coverage on the issue of the Hemings-Jefferson family tree, all of whom
are reportedly tony members of black society in Virginia. So, too, conventional
wisdom holds that the switch from "black" to "African American" was occasioned
by the need to assert black peoples' African identity, but, again secretly, I think it
was to bind us, roundabout, to America. In that formulation, "African" is an adjective, "American" the supporting noun. It is the fear that America does not return
this powerful, if often concealed, devotion that drives blacks to embrace theories of
race-conspiracy.

John Edgar Wideman, commenting on his new novel canvassing four centuries of   12
black history, says "one way of visualizing African-American peoples' relationship to
America is a story of unrequited love . . . a love that has never been fully answered
or accepted." Black Americans have been engaged in a 300-year lover's quarrel with
their country; the fear that we are losing that quarrel drives us toward the madness and fevered speculations that every scorned lover knows.

Given the choice between neglect and conspiracy, black people will always   13
choose conspiracy. To be the victim of a constant, unchanging indifference is a far
greater torment than to be the object of obsession, no matter how warped. The
move from neglect to obsession is also a move from despair to rage, from a kind of
loneliness to righteous indignation. But that emotional move purchases more than
it bargains for.

And this is where the trouble starts. Anger, Aristotle argued a thousand years   14
ago, is the only passion that must be justified by speech and reason. In the anger of

the conspiracists, speech and reason take wild, unseemly, sometimes horrific, forms: outrageous theories about sun and ice people, blue-eyed evils, and big-headed scientists named Yakub; dreams of lives lived by numbers, and Egyptian miracles plundered by Greek pirates. It is a debilitating fantasy, because the anger we embrace has a chimera at its source. There are no ice people, no ravaging Greeks, no murderous Jews tainting our blood. But wrongs demand villains of equal stature—and only blue-eyed devils could conspire so wickedly against us.

This entire phenomenon rests on the acceptance of the racist assumption that   15
blacks are separate from the whole of society, even as we are part of it—a limb that may be easily amputated. As long as black people continue to accept (and white racists and black racialists continue to perpetuate) the idea that we are ancillary members of this country, that we can be ghettoized or segregated out of existence, we will forever doubt our place here. There is no "America" that exists outside of, separate and above, its citizens. Black Americans, as Ralph Ellison insisted his entire life, carry inside themselves the country's "most stringent testing and the possibility of its greatest human freedom." If America is indeed obsessed with black people, it is because it is obsessed with itself. It is not so much that "We are Americans" but, rather, "We are America."

MY RACE PROBLEM—AND OURS
Randall Kennedy

What is the proper role of race in determining how I, an American black, should   1
feel toward others? One response is that although I should not dislike people because of their race, there is nothing wrong with having a special—a *racial*—affection for other black people. Indeed, many would go further and maintain that something would be wrong with me if I did not sense and express racial pride, racial kinship, racial patriotism, racial loyalty, racial solidarity—synonyms for that amalgam of belief, intuition, and commitment that manifests itself when blacks treat blacks with more solicitude than they do those who are not black.

Some conduct animated by these sentiments has blended into the background   2
of daily routine, as when blacks who are strangers nonetheless speak to each other—"Hello," "Hey," "Yo"—or hug or give each other a soul handshake or refer to each other as "brother" or "sister." Other manifestations are more dramatic. For example, the Million Man March, which brought at least 500,000 black men to Washington, D.C., in 1995, was a demonstration predicated on the notion that blackness gives rise to racial obligation and that black people should have a special, closer, more affectionate relationship with their fellow blacks than with others in America's diverse society.

I reject this response to the question. Neither racial pride nor racial kinship of-   3
fers guidance that is intellectually, morally, or politically satisfactory.

* * *

I eschew racial pride because of my conception of what should properly be the   4
object of pride for an individual: something that he or she has accomplished. I can
feel pride in a good deed I have done or a good effort I have made. I cannot feel
pride in some state of affairs that is independent of my contribution to it. The color
of my skin, the width of my nose, the texture of my hair, and the various other signs
that prompt people to label me black constitute such a state of affairs. I did not
achieve my racial designation. It was something I inherited—like my nationality and
socio-economic starting place and sex—and therefore something I should not feel
proud of or be credited with. In taking this position I follow Frederick Douglass, the
great nineteenth-century reformer, who declared that "the only excuse for pride in
individuals . . . is in the fact of their own achievements." If the sun has created curled
hair and tanned skin, Douglass observed, "let the sun be proud of its achievement."

It is understandable why people have often made inherited group status an hon-   5
orific credential. Personal achievement is difficult to attain, and the lack of it often
leaves a vacuum that racial pride can easily fill. Thus even if a person has little to
show for himself, racial pride gives him status.

But maybe I am misconstruing what people mean by racial pride; perhaps it   6
means simply that one is unashamed of one's race. To that I have no objection. No
one should be ashamed of the labeling by which she or he is racially categorized,
because no one chooses her or his parents or the signs by which society describes
and sorts people. For this very same reason, however, no one should congratulate
herself on her race insofar as it is merely an accident of birth.

I suspect, however, that when most black people embrace the term "racial pride,"   7
they mean more than that they are unembarrassed by their race. They mean, echoing Marcus Garvey, that "to be [black] is no disgrace, but an honor." Thus when
James Brown sings "Say It Loud—I'm Black and I'm Proud," he is heard by many
blacks as expressing not just the absence of shame but delight and assertiveness in
valuing a racial designation that has long been stigmatized in America.

There is an important virtue in this assertion of the value of black life. It combats   8
something still eminently in need of challenge: the assumption that because of their
race black people are stupid, ugly, and low, and that because of their race white
people are smart, beautiful, and righteous. But within some of the forms that this
assertiveness has taken are important vices—including the belief that because of
racial kinship blacks ought to value blacks more highly than others.

* * *

I reject the notion of racial kinship. I do so in order to avoid its burdens and to   9
be free to claim what the distinguished political theorist Michael Sandel labels "the
unencumbered self." The unencumbered self is free and independent, "unencumbered by aims and attachments it does not choose for itself," Sandel writes. "Freed
from the sanctions of custom and tradition and inherited status, unbound by moral
ties antecedent to choice, the self is installed as sovereign, cast as the author of the
only obligations that constrain." Sandel believes that the unencumbered self is an
illusion and that the yearning for it is a manifestation of a shallow liberalism that

"cannot account for certain moral and political obligations that we commonly recognize, even prize"—"obligations of solidarity, religious duties, and other moral
ties that may claim us for reasons unrelated to a choice," which are "indispensable
aspects of our moral and political experience." Sandel's objection to those who,
like me, seek the unencumbered self is that they fail to appreciate loyalties and responsibilities that should be accorded moral force partly because they influence
our identity, such that living by these attachments "is inseparable from understanding ourselves as the particular persons we are—as members of this family or city
or nation or people, as bearers of that history, as citizens of this republic."

I admire Sandel's work and have learned much from it. But a major weakness in   10
it is a conflation of "is" and "ought." Sandel privileges what exists and has existed
so much that his deference to tradition lapses into historical determinism. He faults
the model of the unencumbered self because, he says, it cannot account for feelings of solidarity and loyalty that most people have not chosen to impose upon
themselves but that they cherish nonetheless. This represents a fault, however,
only if we believe that the unchosen attachments Sandel celebrates should be accorded moral weight. I am not prepared to do that simply on the basis that such
attachments exist, have long existed, and are passionately felt. Feelings of primor-
dial attachment often represent mere prejudice or superstition, a hangover of the
childhood socialization from which many people never recover.

One defense of racial kinship takes the shape of an analogy between race and   11
family. This position was strikingly advanced by the nineteenth-century black-
nationalist intellectual Alexander Crummell, who asserted that "a race *is* a family,"
that "race feeling, like the family feeling, is of divine origin," and that the extinction
of race feeling is thus—fortunately, in his view—just as impossible as the extinction
of family feeling.

Analogizing race to family is a potent rhetorical move used to challenge those   12
who, like me, are animated by a liberal, individualistic, and universalistic ethos that
is skeptical of, if not hostile to, the particularisms—national, ethnic, religious, and
racial—that seem to have grown so strong recently, even in arenas, such as major
cosmopolitan universities, where one might have expected their demise. The central point of the challenge is to suggest that the norms I embrace will, or at least
should, wobble and collapse in the face of claims on familial loyalty. Blood, as they
say, is thicker than water.

One way to deal with the race-family analogy is to question its aptness on the   13
grounds that a race is so much more populous than what is commonly thought of as
a family that race cannot give rise to the same, or even similar, feelings of loyalty.
When we think of a family, we think of a small, close-knit association of people who
grow to know one another intimately over time. A race, in contrast, is a conglom-
eration of strangers. Black men at the Million Man March assuredly called one another brothers. But if certain questions were posed ("Would you be willing to lend
a hundred dollars to this brother, or donate a kidney to that one?"), it would have
quickly become clear that many, if not most, of those "brothers" perceived one another as strangers—not so distant as whites, perhaps, but strangers nonetheless.

However, I do not want to rest my argument here. Rather, I want to accept the   14
race-family analogy in order to strengthen my attack on assumptions that privilege
status-driven loyalties (the loyalties of blood) over chosen loyalties (the loyalties of
will). In my view, many people, including legislators and judges, make far too much
of blood ties in derogation of ties created by loving effort.

A vivid illustration is provided by the following kind of child-custody decision. It   15
involves a child who has been separated from her parents and placed with adults
who assume the role of foster parents. These adults nurture her, come to love her,
and ultimately seek legally to become her new parents. If the "blood" parents of
the child do not interfere, the foster parents will have a good chance of doing this.
If, however, the blood parents say they want "their" child back, authorities in many
jurisdictions will privilege the blood connection and return the child—even if the
initial separation is mainly attributable to the fault of the blood parents, even if the
child has been with the foster parents for a long time and is prospering under their
care, even if the child views the foster parents as her parents and wants to stay
with them, and even if there is good reason to believe that the foster parents will
provide a more secure home setting than the child's blood parents. Judges make
such rulings in large part because they reflect the idolatry of "blood," which is an
ideological cousin to the racial beliefs I oppose.

Am I saying that, morally, blood ties are an insufficient, indeed bad, basis for pre-   16
ferring one's genetic relatives to others? Yes. I will rightly give the only life jacket on
the sinking ship to my mother as opposed to your mother, because I love my
mother (or at least I love her more than yours). I love my mother, however, not
because of a genetic tie but because over time she has done countless things that
make me want to love her. She took care of me when I could not take care of myself. She encouraged me. She provided for my future by taking me to the doctor
when appropriate, disciplining me, giving me advice, paying for my education. I love
her, too, because of qualities I have seen her exhibit in interactions with others—
my father, my brother, my sister, neighbors, colleagues, adversaries. The biological
connection helped to create the framework in which I have been able to see and
experience her lovable qualities. But it is deeds, not blood—doing, not being—that
is the morally appropriate basis for my preference for my mother over all other
mothers in the world.

* * *

Some contend, though, that "doing" is what lies at the foundation of black racial   17
kinship—that the reason one should feel morally compelled by virtue of one's
blackness to have and show racial solidarity toward other blacks is that preceding
generations of black people did things animated by racial loyalty which now benefit
all black people. These advocates would contend that the benefits bestowed—
for instance, *Brown v. Board of Education,* the Civil Rights Act of 1964, the Voting
Rights Act of 1965, and affirmative-action programs—impose upon blacks cor-
relative racial obligations. That is what many are getting at when they say that all

blacks, but particularly affluent ones, have a racial obligation to "give back" to the black community.

I agree that one should be grateful to those who have waged struggles for racial justice, sometimes at tremendous sacrifice. But why should my gratitude be racially bounded? Elijah Lovejoy, a white man murdered in Alton, Illinois, in 1837 for advocating the abolition of slavery, participated just as fervently in that great crusade as any person of my hue. The same could be said of scores of other white abolitionists. Coming closer to our time, not only courageous black people, such as Medgar Evers, Vernon Dahmer, and James Chaney, fought white supremacy in the shadow of death during the struggle for civil rights in the Deep South. White people like James Reeb and Viola Liuzzo were there too, as were Andrew Goodman and Michael Schwerner. Against this history I see no reason why paying homage to the struggle for racial justice and endeavoring to continue that struggle must entail any sort of racially stratified loyalty. Indeed, this history suggests the opposite.   18

* * *

Thus far I have mainly argued that a black person should not feel morally bound to experience and show racial kinship with other blacks. But what do I say to a person who is considering whether to *choose* to embrace racial kinship?   19

One person who has made this choice is Stephen L. Carter, a professor at Yale Law School and a well-known author. In a contribution to an anthology titled *Lure and Loathing: Essays on Race, Identity, and the Ambivalence of Assimilation,* Carter writes about his racial love for black people, declaring at one point that "to love one's people is to crave a kind of familyhood with them." Carter observes that this feeling of racial kinship influences his life concretely, affecting the way in which he values people's opinions of him. "The good opinions of black people . . . matter to me more," he writes, than the good opinions of white people. "That is my choice, and I cannot imagine ever making another." In *Reflections of an Affirmative Action Baby,* Carter gives another example of how racial kinship affects his life.   20

> Each December, my wife and I host a holiday dessert for the black students at the Yale Law School. . . . our hope is to provide for the students an opportunity to unwind, to escape, to renew themselves, to chat, to argue, to complain—in short, to relax. For my wife and myself, the party is a chance to get to know some of the people who will lead black America (and white America, too) into the twenty-first century. But more than that, we feel a deep emotional connection to them, through our blackness: we look at their youthful, enthusiastic faces and see ourselves. There is something affirming about the occasion—for them, we hope, but certainly for us. It is a reminder of the bright and supportive side of solidarity.

I contend that in the mind, heart, and soul of a teacher there should be no stratification of students such that a teacher feels closer to certain pupils than to others on grounds of racial kinship. No teacher should view certain students as his racial   21 "brothers and sisters" while viewing others as, well, mere students. Every student should be free of the worry that because of race, he or she will have less opportunity to benefit from what a teacher has to offer.

Friends with whom I have debated these matters object to my position, charging   22
that I pay insufficient attention to the complexity of the identities and roles that individuals assume in society, and that I thus ignore or minimize the ability of a black professor to be both a good teacher who serves all his students well *and* a good racial patriot who feels a special, racial affection for fellow blacks. These friends assert that I have no valid basis for complaint so long as the professor in his official duties is evenhanded in his treatment of students. By "official duties" they mean his conduct in the classroom, his accessibility during office hours, and his grading of students' academic performance. If these duties are met, they see no problem if the black professor, paying homage to his feelings of racial kinship, goes beyond what is officially required in his dealings with black students.

I see a variety of problems. For one thing, I find it inconceivable that there would   23
be no seepage from the personal sphere into the professional sphere. The students invited to the professor's home are surely being afforded an opportunity denied to those who are not invited—an opportunity likely to be reflected in, for instance, letters of recommendation to Judge So-and-So and Law Firm Partner Such-and-Such.

Another problem is that even in the absence of any tangible, dollars-and-cents   24
difference, the teacher's racial distinctions are likely to make a difference psychologically to the students involved. I have had the great benefit of being taught by wonderful teachers of various races, including white teachers. I never perceived a racial difference in the way that the best of these teachers treated me in comparison with my white classmates. Neither John McCune nor Sanford Levinson nor Eric Foner nor Owen Fiss ever gave me reason to believe that because of my color I took a back seat to any of my classmates when it came to having a claim on their attention. My respect for their conduct is accompanied by disappointment in others who seemed for reasons of racial kinship to invest more in white than in black students—who acted, in other words, in a way that remains unfortunately "normal" in this society.

Am I demanding that teachers make no distinctions between pupils? No. Distinc-   25
tions should be made. I am simply insisting that sentiments of racial kinship should play no role in making them.

Am I demanding that teachers be blind to race? No. It seems to me bad policy to   26
blind oneself to any potentially useful knowledge. Teachers should be aware of racial differences and differentiations in our society. They should be keenly aware, for instance, that historically and currently the dominant form of racial kinship in American life, the racial kinship that has been best organized and most destructive, is racial kinship mobilized in behalf of whites. This racial kinship has been animated by the desire to make and keep the United States "a white man's country." It is the racial kinship that politicians like Patrick Buchanan and Jesse Helms openly nurture and exploit. This is also the racial kinship that politicians take care to avoid chal-

lenging explicitly. A teacher should be aware of these and other racial facts of life in order to satisfactorily equip students with knowledge about their society.

The fact that race matters, however, does not mean that the salience and conse- 27 quences of racial distinctions are good or that race must continue to matter in the future. Nor does the brute sociological fact that race matters dictate what one's response to that fact should be.

Assuming that a teacher is aware of the different ways in which the race problem 28 bears down upon his students, how should he react? That depends on the circumstances.

Consider a case, for instance, in which white students were receiving consider- 29 able attention from teachers while black students were being widely ignored. In this case it would be morally correct for a professor, with his eyes focused on race, to reach out with special vigor to the black students. In this circumstance the black students would be more in need than the white students, whose needs for mentorship were already being abundantly met. This outreach, however, would be based not on racial kinship but on distributive justice.

* * *

The distinction is significant. For one thing, under the rationale of giving priority 30 of attention to those most in need, no racial boundary insulates professors from the obligation to attend to whatever maldistributions of mentorship they are in a position to correct. White professors are at least as morally obligated to address the problem as are black or other professors.

This is a point with ramifications that reach far beyond the university. For it is 31 said with increasing urgency by increasing numbers of people that the various social difficulties confronting black Americans are, for reasons of racial kinship, the moral responsibility of blacks, particularly those who have obtained some degree of affluence. This view should be rejected. The difficulties that disproportionately afflict black Americans are not "black problems" whose solutions are the special responsibility of black people. They are *our* problems, and their solution or amelioration is the responsibility of us all, irrespective of race. That is why it is proper to object when white politicians use the term "you people" to refer to blacks. This happened when Ross Perot addressed the NAACP annual convention during the 1992 presidential election campaign. Many of those who objected to Perot's reference to "you people," however, turned right around and referred to blacks as "our people," thereby replicating the racial boundary-setting they had denounced.

A second reason why the justification for outreach matters is that unlike an ap- 32 peal to racial kinship, an appeal to an ideal untrammeled by race enables any person or group to be the object of solicitude. No person or group is racially excluded from the possibility of assistance, and no person or group is expected to help only "our own." If a professor reaches out in response to student need, for instance, that means that whereas black students may deserve special solicitude today, Latino students or Asian-American students or white students may deserve it tomorrow. If Asian-American students have a greater need for faculty mentorship than black students, black professors as well as other professors should give them priority.

Some will argue that I ignore or minimize the fact that different groups are dif-   33
ferently situated and that it is thus justifiable to impose upon blacks and whites different standards for purposes of evaluating conduct, beliefs, and sentiments. They will maintain that it is one thing for a white teacher to prefer his white students on grounds of racial kinship and a very different thing for a black teacher to prefer his black students on grounds of racial kinship. The former, they will say, is an expression of ethnocentrism that perpetuates racist inequality, whereas the latter is a laudable expression of racial solidarity that is needed to counter white domination.

Several responses are in order.   34

First, it is a sociological fact that blacks and whites are differently situated in Amer-   35
ican polity. But, again, a brute fact does not dictate the proper human response to it. That is a matter of choice—constrained, to be sure, but a choice nonetheless. In choosing how to proceed in the face of all that they encounter, blacks should insist, as did Martin Luther King Jr., that acting with moral propriety is itself a glorious goal. In seeking to attain that goal, blacks should be attuned not only to the all too human cruelties and weaknesses of others but also to the all too human cruelties and weaknesses in themselves. A good place to start is with the recognition that unless inhibited, every person and group will tend toward beliefs and practices that are self-aggrandizing. This is certainly true of those who inherit a dominant status. But it is also true of those who inherit a subordinate status. Surely one of the most striking features of human dynamics is the alacrity with which those who have been oppressed will oppress whomever they can once the opportunity presents itself. Because this is so, it is not premature to worry about the possibility that blacks or other historically subordinated groups will abuse power to the detriment of others.

Moreover, at long last blacks have sufficient power to raise urgent concerns re-   36
garding the abuse of it. Now, in enough circumstances to make the matter worth discussing, blacks are positioned to exploit their potential racial power effectively. Hence black attorneys wonder whether they should seek to elicit the racial loyalties of black jurors or judges in behalf of clients. Black jurors and judges face the question of whether they should respond to such appeals. Black professors face the question of whether racial loyalty should shape the extent to which they make themselves available to their students. Black employers or personnel directors face the question of whether racial loyalties should shape their hiring decisions. Were blacks wholly bereft of power, as some commentators erroneously assert, these and similar questions would not arise. Thus I evaluate arguments in favor of exempting blacks from the same standards imposed upon whites and conclude that typically, though perhaps not always, such arguments amount to little more than an elaborate camouflage for self-promotion or group promotion.

A second reason I resist arguments in favor of asymmetrical standards of judg-   37
ment has to do with my sense of the requirements of reciprocity. I find it difficult

to accept that it is wrong for whites to mobilize themselves on a racial basis solely for purposes of white advancement but morally permissible for blacks to mobilize themselves on a racial basis solely for purposes of black advancement. I would propose a shoe-on-the-other-foot test for the propriety of racial sentiment. If a sentiment or practice would be judged offensive when voiced or implemented by anyone, it should be viewed as prima facie offensive generally. If we would look askance at a white professor who wrote that on grounds of racial kinship he values the opinions of whites more than those of blacks, then unless given persuasive reasons to the contrary, we should look askance at a black professor who writes that on grounds of racial kinship he values the opinions of blacks more than those of whites.

In some circumstances it is more difficult for blacks to give up the consolations of racial kinship than for whites to do so, insofar as whites typically have more resources to fall back on. But that should not matter, or at least should not matter decisively, if my underlying argument—that the sentiments and conduct of racial kinship are morally dubious—is correct. After all, it is surely more difficult for a poor person than for a rich one to give up the opportunity to steal untended merchandise. But we nevertheless rightly expect the poor person to give up that opportunity.   **38**

A third consideration is prudential. It is bad for the country if whites, blacks, or any other group engages in the politics of a racial kinship, because racial mobilization prompts racial countermobilization, further entrenching a pattern of sterile racial competition.   **39**

* * *

I anticipate that some will counter that this is what is happening, has happened, and will always happen, and that the best that blacks can expect is what they are able to exact from the white power structure through hard bargaining. In this view, racial unity, racial loyalty, racial solidarity, racial kinship—whatever one wants to call it—is absolutely essential for obtaining the best deal available. Therefore, in this view, my thesis is anathema, the most foolhardy idealism, a plan for ruination, a plea for unilateral disarmament by blacks in the face of a well-armed foe with a long history of bad intentions.   **40**

This challenge raises large issues that cannot be exhaustively dealt with here. But I should like to conclude by suggesting the beginning of a response, based on two observations.   **41**

First, it is noteworthy that those who have most ostentatiously asserted the imperatives of black racial solidarity—I think here particularly of Marcus Garvey, Elijah Muhammad, and Louis Farrakhan—are also those who have engaged in the most divisive, destructive, and merciless attacks on "brothers" and "sisters" who wished to follow a different path. My objection to the claims of racial pride and kinship stems in part from my fears of the effect on interracial relations. But it stems   **42** also in large part from my fears of the stultifying effect on intraracial relations. Racial pride and kinship seem often to stunt intellectual independence. If racial loyalty is deemed essential and morally virtuous, then a black person's adoption of positions that are deemed racially disloyal will be seen by racial loyalists as a supremely threatening sin, one warranting the harsh punishments that have historically been visited upon alleged traitors.

Second, if one looks at the most admirable efforts by activists to overcome racial   43
oppression in the United States, one finds people who yearn for justice, not merely for the advancement of a particular racial group. One finds people who do not replicate the racial alienations of the larger society but instead welcome interracial intimacy of the most profound sorts. One finds people who are not content to accept the categories of communal affiliation they have inherited but instead insist upon bringing into being new and better forms of communal affiliation, ones in which love and loyalty are unbounded by race. I think here of Wendell Phillips and certain sectors of the abolitionist movement. I also think of James Farmer and the early years of the Congress of Racial Equality, and John Lewis and the early years of the Student Nonviolent Coordinating Committee. My favorite champion of this ethos, however, is a person I quoted at the beginning of this article, a person whom the sociologist Orlando Patterson aptly describes as "undoubtedly the most articulate former slave who ever lived," a person with whose words I would like to end. Frederick Douglass literally bore on his back the stigmata of racial oppression. Speaking in June of 1863, only five months after the Emancipation Proclamation and before the complete abolition of slavery, Douglass gave a talk titled "The Present and Future of the Colored Race in America," in which he asked whether "the white and colored people of this country [can] be blended into a common nationality, and enjoy together . . . under the same flag, the inestimable blessings of life, liberty, and the pursuit of happiness, as neighborly citizens of a common country." He answered: "I believe they can."

I, too, believe we can, if we are willing to reconsider and reconstruct the basis of   44
our feelings of pride and kinship.

TOWARD AN END OF BLACKNESS: AN ARGUMENT FOR THE SURRENDER OF RACE CONSCIOUSNESS
Jim Sleeper

Last January, not long after the national furor over the decision by an Oakland   1
school board to recognize "Ebonics," I happened upon a C-SPAN telecast of the awarding of seven Congressional Medals of Honor to black World War II veterans, each of whose "gallantry and intrepidity at the risk of his life" had been ignored for more than fifty years. President Clinton strode across the East Room of the White House to present the medals to Vernon Joseph Baker, seventy-seven, the only recipient still living, and to the others' families. "History has been made whole today,"

the President told the assembly. The honorees, he said, had "helped us find a way to become a more just, more free nation . . . more worthy of them and more true to its ideals."

History has not been made whole for American blacks, of course, and yet something almost archaic in the recipients' bearing and in the ceremony itself reminded me that none of us in the younger generations can say with certainty what an American wholeness might be or, within any such presumed wholeness, what blackness and whiteness might mean. If we have trouble thinking about race, possibly it's because we no longer know how to think about America itself.

At least Second Lieutenant Baker seemed to have less trouble fifty-two years ago than we do now. In April 1945, he single-handedly wiped out two German machine-gun nests in Viareggio, Italy, drew fire on himself to permit the evacuation of wounded comrades, and led his segregated battalion's advance through enemy minefields. Asked by reporters after the East Room ceremony whether he had ever given up hope of winning the medal, he "sounded surprised . . . as if the question presumed arrogance," said one report. "I never thought about getting it," Baker said. Asked why he had joined the army in the first place, Baker responded, "I was a young black man without a job." Ah, yes, *that.* Prodded to comment on having risked his life for his country while in a segregated unit, he answered, "I was an angry young man. We were all angry. But we had a job to do, and we did it. . . . My personal thoughts were that I knew things would get better, and I'm happy I'm here to see it."

Asked what the ceremony meant to her, Arlene Fox, widow of First Lieutenant John Fox, who died in Italy in 1944, said, "I think it's more than just what it means to this family. I think it sends a message . . . that when a man does his duty, his color isn't important."

Even in the prime of their anger, Baker and Fox, as well as the black leaders and writers of their generation, such as A. Philip Randolph, Bayard Rustin, Richard Wright, and Ralph Ellison, did not urge the importance of color as much as they found color imposed on them in ways that affronted something in them that wasn't "of color" at all. Proud though they were of what blacks had endured and would overcome (as Baker "knew" they would), they believed, before most of the rest of us, that after a long dalliance with a white manifest destiny the American republic would recognize no black or white sanction from God. In Baker's black 92nd Infantry Division, in Randolph's Brotherhood of Sleeping Car Porters, and in countless churches, blacks found it within themselves to treat society torn by racism not as inherently, eternally damned but as nevertheless worth joining and redeeming. Blacks who thought and acted that way shared with whites an important belief: not, alas, a consensus that racism was wrong but a deep certainty that, despite it, they were all bound passionately to the promise of the nation.

But what was that promise? It seems a long time now since the Smothers Brothers crooned "The Lord is colorblind" to what CBS must have assumed was a reasonably receptive national audience in the late 1960s. Today many of us would think

2

3

4

5

6

such an audience naive or hypocritical, if not racist; it is almost as if any assertion that color isn't important insults what has come to be known as black pride. It is almost as if we fear that if race lost all weight in our social equations or disappeared entirely through interracial marriages and offspring, we would have nothing of value to say or give to one another. The problem is not that racism has grown stronger; it is that American civic life has become weaker—and not primarily because of racism. If we find it difficult to say that a black person's color isn't important, that is because we no longer know how to say that being an "American" is important— important enough to transcend racial identity in a classroom, in a jury room, or at the polls.

"An individual's moral character is formed by narrative and culture," writes the sociologist Alan Wolfe. "Contracts between us are not enforced by laws or economic incentives; people adhere to social contracts when they feel that behind the contract lies a credible story of who they are and why their fates are linked to those of others." But what is America's story, when Vernon Baker's and Arlene Fox's descendants can climb to the very summit of the American Mt. Parnassus only to find there Dick Morris, *Vanity Fair,* Dennis Rodman, Time Warner Inc., and a retinue of dancing pollsters? The old American story of white manifest destiny, thankfully gone, was coherent enough to give blacks enough moral footing and traction to undo its moral affronts. By comparison, our new stories (the space shuttle *Challenger? Forrest Gump?* curricular gardens of multicultural delight?) are incoherent—much like Bill Clinton, truly a man of our time. In 1963, James Baldwin wondered aloud why any black American would want "to be integrated into a burning house." Obviously, he was not proposing resegregation. What, then? How were black Americans to think about themselves? Baldwin's emigration to France left the question open. And so have we all.

For a short while twenty years ago, Alex Haley's *Roots* seemed to offer an answer. Turning on an intrepid black American's report of an astonishing encounter with his African past, it promised to weave a recovered, emblematic black story into the American national narrative, whose promise, whatever it was, would become more coherent for resolving the contradictions in its black story line. The story of Haley's story is worth retracing, because *Roots* wound up demonstrating both that blackness has no reliable myth of its own and that the summit of the American Parnassus is bare.

Published late in 1976, *Roots* became the next year's top nonfiction bestseller (selling some 1.5 million copies in one year) after a record 130 million Americans saw the twelve-hour ABC miniseries it inspired. At least 250 colleges began offering credit courses based significantly on *Roots*. Travel agencies packaged back-to-Africa "Roots" tours. Even before TV had anointed Haley, I watched him tell a rapt audience of Harvard undergraduates, many of them black, of his meeting with the *griot,* or oral historian, of a village in Gambia from which, Haley said, his ancestor Kunta Kinte had been abducted to America in 1767. When he noted, as he had in the book, that the *griot* "had no way in the world to know that [his story's particu-

7

8

9

lars] had just echoed what I had heard all through my boyhood years on my grandma's front porch in Henning, Tennessee," there were gasps, and then the packed Quincy House dining hall was awash in tears.

With this unprecedented return by a black American to the scene of the primal crime against his West African forbears—"an astonishing feat of genealogical detective work," Doubleday's original dust jacket had called it—the long, tortuous arc of black dispossession and yearning for a historic reckoning seemed, at last, to come home. *Roots* wasn't just Haley's own story; it was "a symbolic history of a people," he told a British reporter who raised doubts about its accuracy. "I, we, need a place called Eden. My people need a Pilgrim's Rock."

Indeed they did. The sudden lurch toward integration in the 1960s had disrupted old black coping strategies, scrambling the coordinates of an uneasy racial coexistence and confounding pious hopes for a smooth transition to the integration envisioned by so many of Baker and Fox's generation. Some white-ethnic Roman Catholics and Jews, who had resisted their own assimilation into Anglo-Saxon norms, now intensified the subcultural revivals of "unmeltable ethnics." Responding to these assertions and, at the same time, to the equally unsettling prospect of black dissolution into whiteness through integration, a retaliatory black parochialism surfaced in public life for the first time in decades, assailing blacks whom it deemed too accommodating and forcing even assimilationist whites to acknowledge their own hyphenated Americanism.

Appearing amid the confusion, *Roots* at first startled, then relieved, pessimists on both sides of the color line. By the grace of Haley's pilgrimage, it seemed, blacks could recover and share the true story of their dispossession. His mythopoetic triumph tugged at people's hearts, strengthening hopes for a decorous pluralism of peoples and a decent integration of persons. Americans of all colors were transfixed, even as charges emerged that Haley had taken too many folkloric and fictional liberties with material he'd claimed was historically true. (He settled out of court for $650,000 with author Harold Courlander, passages of whose novel *The African* Haley had pretty much copied.) Yet while *Roots* was denounced as a scholarly "fraud" by the historian Oscar Handlin, it was defended as an irresistible historical novel and pedagogical tool by other historians, including David Brion Davis, who told the *New York Times,* "We all need certain myths about the past, and one must remember how much in the myths about the Pilgrims or the immigrants coming here has been reversed." Haley received a "special" Pulitzer Prize and a rare "Citation of Merit" from a National Book Awards panel. ABC produced a second miniseries, *Roots: The Next Generations,* based on his new book *Search,* which chronicled his family's later tribulations and triumphs, including Haley's own work on *The Autobiography of Malcolm X.* "Now, as before," wrote Frank Rich in *Time,* "*Roots* occupies a special place in the history of our mass culture: it has the singular power to reunite all Americans, black and white, with their separate and collective pasts."

Today *Roots* is seldom mentioned. The History Channel's twentieth-anniversary broadcast in February was little remarked by viewers or print commentators. The book is still in stores—Doubleday calls it "an important title on the Dell backlist"—but it's not much read in college or high school courses. Few books on American racial matters mention Haley (who died in 1992). "*Roots?*" laughs the black religion scholar C. Eric Lincoln. "It's disappeared! Alex Haley was my friend, and I can tell you, he was a journeyman freelance writer, not a political writer or historian. He was given a status he didn't expect."

Roots's virtual disappearance can't be explained with the observation that it accomplished its mission by transforming the consciousness of a generation. Nor is it enough to say that *Roots* shortchanged women by portraying them as passive helpmates; Haley's misconstruals have been redressed by Alice Walker, Toni Morrison, Maya Angelou, and others. What drained *Roots* of its power with blacks as well as whites was a disillusionment in at least three dimensions. First, Haley idealized an Africa and a blackness that had been so overwhelmed (indeed, defined) by European invasion that they flourished only as negations of whiteness. Second, so complete was this submergence that Haley himself idealized American blacks' white abductors, if only implicitly, by telling blacks' own story in Western terms. In doing so he met his third pitfall: he tried to skirt Western mythology's tragic sense of life by telling an upbeat story for the mass market. *Roots* became the next "myth for a day," turning immense historical pain into immense profit. That was what slavery had done, and it was what *Roots* was meant to counter. But Haley's TV-friendly, docudramatic tale of black dispossession subtly reinforced the moral neutrality of classical liberalism, where markets are stronger than myths and history is not so much falsified as tamed.

In Africa, Haley depicted a precolonial Eden that hadn't existed, created his account of Kunta Kinte's youth there more out of current anthropology than history, paired all of this with the tale of his own communion with village elders in *post*-colonial Gambia, and inflated black Americans' expectations of sub-Saharan Africa, past and present. For American blacks, there was no there there: "Whatever Africans share," writes the Ghanaian intellectual Kwame Anthony Appiah, "we do not have a common traditional culture, common languages, a common religious or conceptual vocabulary. . . . [W]e do not even belong to a common race . . ." When Americans making visits inspired by Haley's epiphanies got past their African hosts, they found strangers as indifferent or hostile to them as "fellow whites" in my grandparents' native Lithuania might be to me were I to visit there now—strangers who may resemble me racially but whose religion, myths, and current interests have little in common with those of my Jewish "tribe," which they drove out or exterminated in the 1940s. American Afrocentrists (and liberal whites) seeking a romantic, Pan-African foil to a racist America found the same "ethnic cleansing" furiously under way in Nigeria, Rwanda, Zaire, and the Sudan. The very designation "black" was no more useful a moral, political, or cultural identification than is "white" in Lithuania or the Balkans. . . .

By assigning two white men to kidnap Kunta Kinte, Haley wasn't just distorting African history (in which the majority of slaves were captured and sold to whites

14

15

16

by blacks); he was juggling European archetypes, borrowing Western literary themes meant to appeal to whites as well as blacks. He formulated sub-Saharan Africa's diffuse cultural attitudes into a Western myth of "exile" or "pilgrimage" for a black American audience that had internalized such notions from the Old Testament and for other Americans who needed to understand, in both Christian and Enlightenment terms, what their own forebears had perpetrated or suborned. But the African slaves had no signs that an African god was punishing them for their sins with an exile like that of the Jews, or blessing their "errand into the wilderness" like that of the Puritans. *Roots* wasn't a product of its protagonists' own mother culture; it was the work of a thoroughly Western, Christian, *American* writer who took as much from Hebrews and Puritans as from Africans. The novel is a Western account of a monstrous Western crime—a crime only according to Western religious and political standards that triumphed later to abolish slavery, as no African authority had done and as the Sudan hasn't done yet.

The irony, of course, is that the Western Enlightenment principles that supported African colonial liberation failed to prevent colonialism in the first place. And the ghastly, bloody misadventures in Europe since 1914 remind us that Western "values" often only ratchet up the human struggle with evil into unprecedented levels of barbarity. Even the notion that skin color is destiny derives from the ignorant scientific and cultural prejudices that draped nineteenth-century European imperialist states in all their clanking, blundering glory.   17

If there *is* any glory for the West in all this, it lies not in Western power but in Western thought, which projects triumphs out of tragedies and which, for all its misuses, nourishes the capacity for rational self-contradiction that alone has put such words as "democracy," "liberation," and "human rights" into the minds and hearts of peoples on all five continents. The West's true Eden is not Haley's bucolic African village but the garden in which a serpent corrupted two human beings with the apple of knowledge. Haley's distortions—like those of countless Western writers before him—misrepresented the West as much as they did Africa. When people of any color imagine their origins as racially pure and their heroes as morally infallible, they shrink from the tragic Western truth rooted in the story of The Fall.   18

They also misunderstand that if the West has any hope of improving on its work, that hope is in America. *Roots* showed, yet could not quite proclaim, that blacks brought as slaves into the American national experiment were so thoroughly uprooted from African sources that they were obliged to accept—for lack of anything else—the transcending liberal and Christian promises of their newfound land. Blacks internalized those promises and rehearsed their implementation long before Vernon Baker joined the 92nd Infantry Division in Italy. Precisely because they had not chosen to join this society, could not dominate it, and could not leave it, they had the highest possible stakes in redeeming its oft-stated, oft-violated ideal.   19

In that sense, surely, blacks became, for better or worse, the most "American" of us all. In a nation born of fraught departures, clean breaks, and fresh starts on new frontiers, they had to construct their moral universe, . . . in the words of Glenn   20

Loury, "almost out of nothing, almost heroically, in the cauldron of slavery. Or, as my friend Nathan Huggins puts it, 'We're not an alien population, we're the alienated population We're after getting our birthright. We're the son who hasn't been acknowledged.' See, *that binds you.* You can't turn back from it. Part of what I want is an acknowledgment of my place, my legitimacy, my belonging." The special depth of this need is what makes blacks "America's metaphor," as Richard Wright called them—moral witnesses to a self-creating America, as well as the country's harshest, sometimes most nihilist, assailants.

No wonder whites at first felt relieved by the *Roots* story: it had an ending happy   21
enough to make whites as well as blacks feel better about themselves. Although Haley didn't make much of the point in the book, white Americans had responded to black fortitude and resistance not only with cross burnings and guns but with the Abolitionist crusade, the great pedagogical project that sent W. E. B. Du Bois and hundreds of New England schoolteachers South during and after Reconstruction to "uplift" freed slaves. Despite all of their cruelties, condescensions, and overweening moral self-regard, white Americans participated in a civil-rights movement that combined black Baptist communalism with a race-transcendent, New England Calvinist theology of personal responsibility and justification by a faith beyond color.

So, if there was any real nobility in Haley's effort to weave blacks more vividly   22
into the American tapestry—to make Kunta Kinte a mythic American like Paul Revere—it consisted of the tragic but potentially redemptive fact that the author had to use the abductors' language and metaphysical looms. If *Roots* hasn't helped a new generation of American blacks to fit itself into the national tapestry, we must find something else that can, for separating the black thread would harm all of us even more than hiding it deep in the weave, as we've done in the past. Even Louis Farrakhan knows this, no matter how strenuously he insists on the separatist claims of the Nation of Islam. Not for nothing did he hold his march on the Washington Mall, amid all those white monuments, rather than in the part of the Mississippi Delta that the enthusiasts of his predecessor, Elijah Muhammad, once designated as the provisional seat of the Republic of New Africa. Had Farrakhan gone there, many fewer black men would have followed.

Yet *Roots* failed to forestall the ascendancy of Farrakhan not only because Haley   23
dissembled about Africa and juggled tragic Western myths to tell a black story but also because those myths are losing their traction against the forces of a global market that employs the techniques of mass marketing to guarantee the liquidity of collective amnesia. The relentless logic of the market overwhelms not only the worst racist pretensions, white as well as black, but also the best American civic cultural traditions. Commitments to reason, individual rights, and freedom of contract aren't "Eurocentric" ruses meant to co-opt and subordinate nonwhites; they embody historic human gains, and it would be folly to abandon them for fantasies of racial destiny.

When Vernon Baker said, "I knew things would get better," surely he did not think   24
they would get "blacker" in the sense that blacks would become so protective of

blackness that whites' enthusiasm at the prospect of Colin Powell's running for president would engender marked black ambivalence about it. Nor, surely, did Baker's "better" characterize extenuated rationalizations of Ebonics, gangsta-rap celebrations of black self-immolation, or widespread black support for O. J. Simpson's acquittal and the "black" jurisprudence and epistemology invoked to excuse it.

Similarly, when Arlene Fox said, "When a man does his duty, his color isn't important," she was not applauding some recent efforts to redefine "duty" in ways that make one's skin color one's destiny all over again. Three years ago, while defending race-norming in college admissions and a dizzying array of campus "diversity" programs that transform everyone with a dark skin into a walking placard for disadvantage, Rutgers University president Francis Lawrence slid, infamously, into lingo about blacks' "genetic hereditary background." It was an all too emblematically liberal Freudian slip, born of believing that the best way to overcome racism's legacies is to create separate, remedial tracks for blacks while denying that one is doing anything of the sort by enshrining and embellishing disparities as cultural "differences." 25

On the other hand: Colin Powell could yet become president, and Oprah Winfrey could own a movie studio; black candidates keep winning in white-majority districts, and more blacks and nonblacks are marrying, which explains why many of the novels in black bookstores are about multiracial relationships. Many blacks, in fact, have anticipated and met a challenge now facing everyone else in the country; we are all being "abducted" from our ancient ethnic moorings by powerful currents we no longer control or fully comprehend. Thanks significantly to blacks, who started from "nothingness" here, other Americans have a better start on what now has become a more general problem. Europeans sometimes say that white Americans walk and talk "black." The observation fits neatly with the feeling among some Africans that black Americans are not "black" at all. America needs blacks not because it needs blackness but because it needs what they've learned on their long way out of blackness—what others of us have yet to learn on the journeys we need to take out of whiteness. 26

For all its wrong turns and dead ends, the quest by black Americans for acknowledgment and belonging in our national life is the most powerful epic of unrequited love in the history of the world. "Afrocentism," Gerald Early has written, "is a historiography of decline, like the mythic epic of the [lost, antebellum] South. The tragedy is that black people fail to see their 'Americanization' as one of the greatest human triumphs of the past 500 years." Even if every broken heart could be mended and every theft of opportunity be redressed, there would remain a black community of memory, loss, and endurance. Yet the country's special debt to blacks cannot be paid by anything less than an inclusion that brings the implosion of the identity of blackness—and, with it, of whiteness. The most that blacks can expect of the rest of us (and the most that Vernon Baker and Arlene Fox have expected) is that we will embrace and judge blacks—and let ourselves in turn be embraced and judged by them—as individual fellow participants in our common national experiment. As brothers, some used to say. 27

Letters to the Editor

I was both dismayed and offended by Jim Sleeper's essay "Toward an End of Blackness" [May], which informs us that race is a social construction, an idea that is not exactly news to black people in the United States. We happen to know that we are not stupid, that we are not lazy, and that we are not bent toward criminality. We know that we will succeed if we are given the opportunity, because, as Sleeper rightly comments, the success of the "American experiment" is founded on the presence and participation of Africans. Sleeper is absolutely right when he says that we black Americans are as American as you can get. Unfortunately, he perpetuates the racism that created "blackness" in the first place. It's not blackness that's the problem, but "whiteness."

In his writings on race and identity, James Baldwin reiterated time and again that to be "white" in America is, essentially, to be "not-black." Witness the "wigger" fad among some of America's disaffected white youths. They wear "colors" and baggy pants that fall off their hips, and speak what they perceive to be black English. And the wigger phenomenon isn't new; generations of rebellious white American youths have aspired to an image of blackness that would repel their white elders.

An unwillingness to recognize and value difference is the source of the American problem with race. And it's a problem rooted in mainstream America, not in black America.

DAVID WRIGHT
Albion, Mich.

Jim Sleeper's essay on blackness is an amazing example of white conservatives' penchant for criticizing African-American behavior. It blatantly violates one of the unwritten but well-known rules of ethnic-group etiquette: members of one ethnic community should not comment publicly on what might be called the "organic patterns" of behavior found within another ethnic community. Commentators such as Sleeper justify their effrontery to blacks by arguing that the black intelligentsia should just quiet down and defer to a newly emerging "colorblindness." This is simply another attempt to silence black dissent.

Sleeper also expends considerable energy on a critique of Alex Haley's 1976 bestseller, *Roots*. Well, *Roots* got too damn much attention in the first place. Even though other ethnic groups' quasi-mythical stories have been similarly hyped and commercialized, Sleeper's shallow understanding of the political and cultural patterns among black Americans leads him to the bizarre conclusion that *Roots* was actually the canonical text for black Americans that the media claimed it to be. His thimbleful of knowledge of black history leads him to believe that although black folks have been on American shores since the seventeenth century, they waited until the appearance of Haley's book before they could proclaim a viable understanding of their tragic history.

Sleeper and other conservatives who trash African-American reality blithely ignore the rich world of black meanings found in traditional African-American music and in the oral tales and spirituals that have been handed down from our ancestors. These deep cultural sources are the true context of black American experience and represent a massive historical counterweight to the central falsehood of Sleeper's article.

MARTIN KILSON
Committee on African Studies
Harvard University
Cambridge, Mass.

Jim Sleeper's essay is itself an ambiguous example of his thesis that black people are an integral part of the great experiment that is America. Sleeper, a non-black writing for a non-black audience, and I, a black man, are participants in his literary experiment. But I am the specimen in the petri dish, and my participation is not at the same level as that of Sleeper and his audience. Thus the writer-reader relationship excludes me, trapping me in my petri dish. I, the specimen, am helpless, as the writer pretends to capture the sentiments of my people, whose heart he does not know. He is unable to convey what my second-class American citizenship means to me; nor does he understand my need to feel connected to the elsewhere-land of my racial heritage, even if that connection is as mythical as a St. Patrick's Day parade.

Sleeper tells a story about blackness that is not true, a story that will not change the day-to-day reactions of my purported compatriots to my attempts to live my own African-American dream. Sleeper has not discovered a hidden secret to race relations in the United States. He has propagated an old lie in a clever new disguise.

D. JOSEPH WHITTEN
New York City

I'M BLACK, YOU'RE WHITE, WHO'S INNOCENT?
Shelby Steele

It is a warm, windless California evening, and the dying light that covers the red-brick patio is tinted pale orange by the day's smog. Eight of us, not close friends, sit in lawn chairs sipping chardonnay. A black engineer and I (we had never met before) integrate the group. A psychologist is also among us, and her presence encourages a surprising openness. But not until well after the lovely twilight dinner has been served, when the sky has turned to deep black and the drinks have long since changed to scotch, does the subject of race spring awkwardly upon us. Out of nowhere the engineer announces, with a coloring of accusation in his voice, that it bothers him to send his daughter to a school where she is one of only three black children. "I didn't realize my ambition to get ahead would pull me into a world where my daughter would lose touch with her blackness," he says.

Over the course of the evening we have talked about money, infidelity, past and present addictions, child abuse, even politics. Intimacies have been revealed, fears named. But this subject, race, sinks us into one of those shaming silences where eye contact terrorizes. Our host looks for something in the bottom of his glass. Two women stare into the black sky as if to locate the Big Dipper and point it out to us. Finally, the psychologist seems to gather herself for a challenge, but it is too late. "Oh, I'm sure she'll be just fine," says our hostess, rising from her chair. When she excuses herself to get the coffee, the two sky gazers offer to help.

With three of us now gone, I am surprised to see the engineer still silently hold-ing his ground. There is a willfulness in his eyes, an inner pride. He knows he has said something awkward, but he is determined not to give a damn. His unwavering eyes intimidate me. At last the host's head snaps erect. He has an idea. "The hell with coffee," he says. "How about some of the smoothest brandy you ever tasted?" An idea made exciting by the escape it offers. Gratefully we follow him back into the house, quickly drink his brandy, and say our good-byes.

An autopsy of this party might read: death induced by an abrupt and lethal injec-tion of the American race issue. An accurate if superficial assessment. Since it has been my fate to live a rather integrated life, I have often witnessed sudden deaths like this. The threat of them, if not the reality, is a part of the texture of integra-tion. In the late 1960s, when I was just out of college, I took a delinquent's delight in playing the engineer's role, and actually developed a small reputation for playing it well. Those were the days of flagellatory white guilt; it was such great fun to pin-ion some professor or housewife or, best of all, a large group of remorseful whites, with the knowledge of both their racism and their denial of it. The adolescent im-pulse to sneer at convention, to startle the middle-aged with doubt, could be indulged under the guise of racial indignation. And how could I lose? My victims—earnest liberals for the most part—could no more crawl out from under my accu-sations than Joseph K. in Kafka's *Trial* could escape the amorphous charges brought against him. At this odd moment in history the world was aligned to facilitate my immaturity.

About a year of this was enough: the guilt that follows most cheap thrills caught up to me, and I put myself in check. But the impulse to do it faded more slowly. It was one of those petty talents that is tied to vanity, and when there were ebbs in my self-esteem the impulse to use it would come alive again. In integrated situa-tions I can still feel the faint itch. But then there are many youthful impulses that still itch, and now, just inside the door of mid-life, this one is least precious to me.

In the literature classes I teach, I often see how the presence of whites all but seduces some black students into provocation. When we come to a novel by a black writer, say Toni Morrison, the white students can easily discuss the human motivations of the black characters. But, inevitably, a black student, as if by reflex, will begin to set in relief the various racial problems that are the background of these characters' lives. This student's tone will carry a reprimand: the class is afraid to confront the reality of racism. Classes cannot be allowed to die like dinner par-ties, however. My latest strategy is to thank that student for his or her moral vigi-lance, and then appoint the young man or woman as the class's official racism

3

4

5

6

monitor. But even if I get a laugh—I usually do, but sometimes the student is particularly indignant, and it gets uncomfortable—the strategy never quite works. Our racial division is suddenly drawn in neon. Overcaution spreads like spilled paint. And, in fact, the black student who started it all does become a kind of monitor. The very presence of this student imposes a new accountability on the class.

I think those who provoke this sort of awkwardness are operating out of a black identity that obliges them to badger white people about race almost on principle. Content hardly matters. (For example, it made no sense for the engineer to expect white people to sympathize with his anguish over sending his daughter to school with *white* children.) Race indeed remains a source of white shame; the goal of these provocations is to put whites, no matter how indirectly, in touch with this collective guilt. In other words, these provocations I speak of are *power* moves, little shows of power that try to freeze the "enemy" in self-consciousness. They gratify and inflate the provocateur. They are the underdog's bite. And whites, far more secure in their power, respond with a self-contained and tolerant silence that is, itself, a show of power. What greater power than that of non-response, the power to let a small enemy sizzle in his own juices, to even feel a little sad at his frustration just as one is also complimented by it. Black anger always, in a way, flatters white power. In America, to know that one is not black is to feel an extra grace, a little boost of impunity.

I think the real trouble between the races in America is that the races are not just races but competing power groups—a fact that is easily minimized perhaps because it is so obvious. What is not so obvious is that this is true quite apart from the issue of class. Even the well-situated middle-class (or wealthy) black is never completely immune to that peculiar contest of power that his skin color subjects him to. Race is a separate reality in American society, an entity that carries its own potential for power, a mark of fate that class can soften considerably but not eradicate.

The distinction of race has always been used in American life to sanction each race's pursuit of power in relation to the other. The allure of race as a human delineation is the very shallowness of the delineation it makes. Onto this shallowness—mere skin and hair—men can project a false depth, a system of dismal attributions, a series of malevolent or ignoble stereotypes that skin and hair lack the substance to contradict. These dark projections then rationalize the pursuit of power. Your difference from me makes you bad, and your badness justifies, even demands, my pursuit of power over you—the oldest formula for aggression known to man. Whenever much importance is given to race, power is the primary motive.

But the human animal almost never pursues power without first convincing himself that he is *entitled* to it. And this feeling of entitlement has its own precondition: to be entitled one must first believe in one's innocence, at least in the area where one wishes to be entitled. By innocence I mean a feeling of essential goodness in relation to others and, therefore, superiority to others. Our innocence always inflates us and deflates those we seek power over. Once inflated we are entitled; we

7

8

9

10

are in fact licensed to go after the power our innocence tells us we deserve. In this sense, *innocence is power*. Of course, innocence need not be genuine or real in any objective sense, as the Nazis demonstrated not long ago. Its only test is whether or not we can convince ourselves of it.

I think the racial struggle in America has always been primarily a struggle for in- 11
nocence. White racism from the beginning has been a claim of white innocence and, therefore, of white entitlement to subjugate blacks. And in the 1960s, as went innocence so went power. Blacks used the innocence that grew out of their long subjugation to seize more power, while whites lost some of their innocence and so lost a degree of power over blacks. Both races instinctively understand that to lose innocence is to lose power (in relation to each other). Now to be innocent some-one else must be guilty, a natural law that leads the races to forge their innocence on each other's backs. The inferiority of the black always makes the white man su-perior; the evil might of whites makes blacks good. This pattern means that both races have a hidden investment in racism and racial disharmony, despite their good intentions to the contrary. Power defines their relations, and power requires inno-cence, which, in turn, requires racism and racial division.

I believe it was this hidden investment that the engineer was protecting when he 12
made his remark—the white "evil" he saw in a white school "depriving" his daugh-ter of her black heritage confirmed his innocence. Only the logic of power ex-plained this—he bent reality to show that he was once again a victim of the white world and, as a victim, innocent. His determined eyes insisted on this. And the whites, in their silence, no doubt protected their innocence by seeing him as an un-gracious troublemaker—his bad behavior underscoring their goodness. I can only guess how he was talked about after the party. But it isn't hard to imagine that his blunder gave everyone a lift. What none of us saw was the underlying game of power and innocence we were trapped in, or how much we needed a racial im-passe to play that game.

When I was a boy of about twelve, a white friend of mine told me one day that 13
his uncle, who would be arriving the next day for a visit, was a racist. Excited by the prospect of seeing such a man, I spent the following afternoon hanging around the alley behind my friend's house, watching from a distance as this uncle worked on the engine of his Buick. Yes, here was evil and I was compelled to look upon it. And I saw evil in the sharp angle of his elbow as he pumped his wrench to tighten nuts, I saw it in the blade-sharp crease of his chinos, in the pack of Lucky Strikes that threatened to slip from his shirt pocket as he bent, and in the way his concen-tration seemed to shut out the human world. He worked neatly and efficiently, wiping his hands constantly, and I decided that evil worked like this.

I felt a compulsion to have this man look upon me so that I could see evil—so 14
that I could see the face of it. But when he noticed me standing beside his toolbox, he said only, "If you're looking for Bobby, I think he went up to the school to play baseball." He smiled nicely and went back to work. I was stunned for a moment, but then I realized that evil could be sly as well, could smile when it wanted to trick you.

Need, especially hidden need, puts a strong pressure on perception, and my need 15
to have this man embody white evil was stronger than any contravening evidence.
As a black person you always hear about racists but never meet any. And I needed
to incarnate this odious category of humanity, those people who hated Martin
Luther King, Jr., and thought blacks should "go slow" or not at all. So, in my mental
dictionary, behind the term "white racist," I inserted this man's likeness. I would
think of him and say to myself, "There is no reason for him to hate black people.
Only evil explains unmotivated hatred." And this thought soothed me; I felt innocent. If I hated white people, which I did not, at least I had a reason. His evil commanded me to assert in the world the goodness he made me confident of in myself.

In looking at this man I was *seeing for innocence*—a form of seeing that has more 16
to do with one's hidden need for innocence (and power) than with the person or
group one is looking at. It is quite possible, for example, that the man I saw that
day was not a racist. He did absolutely nothing in my presence to indicate that he
was. I invested an entire afternoon in seeing not the man but my innocence through
the man. *Seeing for innocence* is, in this way, the essence of racism—the use of others as a means to our own goodness and superiority.

The loss of innocence has always to do with guilt, Kierkegaard tells us, and it has 17
never been easy for whites to avoid guilt where blacks are concerned. For whites,
seeing for innocence means seeing themselves and blacks in ways that minimize white
guilt. Often this amounts to a kind of white revisionism, as when President Reagan
declares himself "color-blind" in matters of race. The President, like many of us, may
aspire to racial color blindness, but few would grant that he has yet reached this
sublimely guiltless state. The statement clearly revises reality, moves it forward into
some heretofore unknown America where all racial determinism will have vanished.
I do not think that Ronald Reagan is a racist, as that term is commonly used, but
neither do I think that he is capable of seeing color without making attributions,
some of which may be negative—nor am I, or anyone else I've ever met.

So why make such a statement? I think Reagan's claim of color blindness with 18
regard to race is really a claim of racial innocence and guiltlessness—the precondi-
tions for entitlement and power. This was the claim that grounded Reagan's campaign against special entitlement programs—affirmative action, racial quotas, and so
on—that black power had won in the Sixties. Color blindness was a strategic assumption of innocence that licensed Reagan's use of government power against
black power.

I do not object to Reagan's goals in this so much as the presumption of inno- 19
cence by which he rationalized them. I, too, am strained to defend racial quotas
and any affirmative action that supersedes merit. And I believe there is much that
Reagan has to offer blacks. His emphasis on traditional American values—individual
initiative, self-sufficiency, strong families—offers what I think is the most enduring
solution to the demoralization and poverty that continue to widen the gap between blacks and whites in America. Even his de-emphasis of race is reasonable in
a society where race only divides. But Reagan's posture of innocence undermines

any beneficial interaction he might have with blacks. For blacks instinctively sense that a claim of racial innocence always precedes a power move against them. Reagan's pretense of innocence makes him an adversary, and makes his quite reasonable message seem vindictive. You cannot be innocent of a man's problem and expect him to listen.

I'm convinced that the secret of Reagan's "teflon" coating, his personal popularity apart from his policies and actions, has been his ability to offer mainstream America a vision of itself as innocent and entitled (unlike Jimmy Carter, who seemed to offer only guilt and obligation). Probably his most far-reaching accomplishment has been to reverse somewhat the pattern by which innocence came to be distributed in the Sixties, when outsiders were innocent and insiders were guilty. Corporations, the middle class, entrepreneurs, the military—all villains in the Sixties—either took on a new innocence in Reagan's vision or were designated as protectors of innocence. But again, for one man to be innocent another man must be bad or guilty. Innocence imposes, *demands,* division and conflict, a right/wrong view of the world. And this, I feel, has led to the underside of Reagan's achievement. His posture of innocence draws him into a partisanship that undermines the universality of his values. He can't sell these values to blacks and others because he has made blacks into the bad guys and outsiders who justify his power. It is humiliating for a black person to like Reagan because Reagan's power is so clearly derived from a distribution of innocence that leaves a black with less of it, and the white man with more.   20

Black Americans have always had to find a way to handle white society's presumption of racial innocence whenever they have sought to enter the American mainstream. Louis Armstrong's exaggerated smile honored the presumed innocence of white society—I will not bring you your racial guilt if you will let me play my music. Ralph Ellison calls this "masking"; I call it bargaining. But whatever it's called, it points to the power of white society to enforce its innocence. I believe this power is greatly diminished today. Society has reformed and transformed—Miles Davis never smiles. Nevertheless, this power has not faded altogether; blacks must still contend with it.   21

Historically, blacks have handled white society's presumption of innocence in two ways: they have bargained with it, granting white society its innocence in exchange for entry into the mainstream; or they have challenged it, holding that innocence hostage until their demand for entry (or other concessions) was met. A bargainer says, *I already believe you are innocent (good, fair-minded) and have faith that you will prove it.* A challenger says, *If you are innocent, then prove it.* Bargainers *give* in hope of receiving; challengers *withhold* until they receive. Of course, there is risk in both approaches, but in each case the black is negotiating his own self-interest against the presumed racial innocence of the larger society.   22

Clearly the most visible black bargainer on the American scene today is Bill Cosby. His television show is a perfect formula for black bargaining in the Eighties. The remarkable Huxtable family—with its doctor/lawyer parent combination, its   23 drug-free, college-bound children, and its wise yet youthful grandparents—is a blackface version of the American dream. Cosby is a subscriber to the American identity, and his subscription confirms his belief in its fair-mindedness. His vast audience knows this, knows that Cosby will never assault their innocence with racial guilt. Racial controversy is all but banished from the show. The Huxtable family never discusses affirmative action.

The bargain Cosby offers his white viewers—I will confirm your racial innocence if you accept me—is a good deal for all concerned. Not only does it allow whites to enjoy Cosby's humor with no loss of innocence, but it actually enhances their innocence by implying that race is not the serious problem for blacks that it once was. If anything, the success of this handsome, affluent black family points to the fair-mindedness of whites who, out of their essential goodness, changed society so that black families like the Huxtables could succeed. Whites can watch *The Cosby Show* and feel complimented on a job well done.

24

The power that black bargainers wield is the power of absolution. On Thursday nights, Cosby, like a priest, absolves his white viewers, forgives and forgets the sins of the past. (Interestingly, Cosby was one of the first blacks last winter to publicly absolve Jimmy the Greek for his well-publicized faux pas about black athletes.) And for this he is rewarded with an almost sacrosanct status. Cosby benefits from what might be called a gratitude factor. His continued number-one rating may have something to do with the (white) public's gratitude at being offered a commodity so rare in our time; he tells his white viewers each week that they are okay, and that this black man is not going to challenge them.

25

When a black bargains, he may invoke the gratitude factor and find himself cherished beyond the measure of his achievement; when he challenges, he may draw the dark projections of whites and become a source of irritation to them. If he moves back and forth between these two options, as I think many blacks do today, he will likely baffle whites. It is difficult for whites to either accept or reject such blacks. It seems to me that Jesse Jackson is such a figure—many whites see Jackson as a challenger by instinct and a bargainer by political ambition. They are uneasy with him, more than a little suspicious. His powerful speech at the 1984 Democratic convention was a masterpiece of bargaining. In it he offered a Kinglike vision of what America could be, a vision that presupposed Americans had the fair-mindedness to achieve full equality—an offer in hope of a return. A few days after this speech, looking for rest and privacy at a lodge in Big Sur, he and his wife were greeted with standing ovations three times a day when they entered the dining room for meals. So much about Jackson is deeply American—his underdog striving, his irrepressible faith in himself, the daring of his ambition, and even his stubbornness. These qualities point to his underlying faith that Americans can respond to him despite his race, and this faith is a compliment to Americans, an offer of innocence.

26

But Jackson does not always stick to the terms of his bargain—he is not like Cosby on TV. When he hugs Arafat, smokes cigars with Castro, refuses to repudiate Farrakhan, threatens a boycott of major league baseball, or, more recently, talks

27

of "corporate barracudas," "pension-fund socialism," and "economic violence," he looks like a challenger in bargainer's clothing, and his positions on the issues look like familiar protests dressed in white-paper formality. At these times he appears to be revoking the innocence so much else about him seems to offer. The old activist seems to come out of hiding once again to take white innocence hostage until whites prove they deserve to have it. In his candidacy there is a suggestion of protest, a fierce insistence on his *right* to run, that sends whites a message that he may secretly see them as a good bit less than innocent. His dilemma is to appear the bargainer while his campaign itself seems to be a challenge.

There are, of course, other problems that hamper Jackson's bid for the Democratic presidential nomination. He has held no elective office, he is thought too flamboyant and opportunistic by many, there are rather loud whispers of "character" problems. As an individual he may not be the best test of a black man's chances for winning so high an office. Still, I believe it is the aura of challenge surrounding him that hurts him most. Whether it is right or wrong, fair or unfair, I think no black candidate will have a serious chance at his party's nomination, much less the presidency, until he can convince white Americans that he can be trusted to preserve *their* sense of racial innocence. Such a candidate will have to use his power of absolution; he will have to flatly forgive and forget. He will have to bargain with white innocence out of a genuine belief that it really exists. There can be no faking it. He will have to offer a vision that is passionately raceless, a vision that strongly condemns any form of racial politics. This will require the most courageous kind of leadership, leadership that asks all the people to meet a new standard.   28

Now the other side of America's racial impasse: How do blacks lay claim to their racial innocence?   29

The most obvious and unarguable source of black innocence is the victimization that blacks endured for centuries at the hands of a race that insisted on black inferiority as a means to its own innocence and power. Like all victims, what blacks lost in power they gained in innocence—innocence that, in turn, entitled them to pursue power. This was the innocence that fueled the civil rights movement of the Sixties, and that gave blacks their first real power in American life—victimization metamorphosed into power via innocence. But this formula carries a drawback that I believe is virtually as devastating to blacks today as victimization once was. It is a formula that binds the victim to his victimization by linking his power to his status as a victim. And this, I'm convinced, is the tragedy of black power in America today. It is primarily a victim's power, grounded too deeply in the entitlement derived from past injustice and in the innocence that Western/Christian tradition has always associated with poverty.   30

Whatever gains this power brings in the short run through political action, it undermines in the long run. Social victims may be collectively entitled, but they are all too often individually demoralized. Since the social victim has been oppressed by society, he comes to feel that his individual life will be improved more by changes *in* society than by his own initiative. Without realizing it, he makes society rather than himself the agent of change. The power he finds in his victimization may lead him   31 to collective action against society, but it also encourages passivity within the sphere of his personal life.

This past summer I saw a television documentary that examined life in Detroit's inner city on the twentieth anniversary of the riots there in which forty-three people were killed. A comparison of the inner city then and now showed a decline in the quality of life. Residents feel less safe than they did twenty years ago, drug trafficking is far worse, crimes by blacks against blacks are more frequent, housing remains substandard, and the teenage pregnancy rate has skyrocketed. Twenty years of decline and demoralization, even as opportunities for blacks to better themselves have increased. This paradox is not peculiar to Detroit. By many measures, the majority of blacks—those not yet in the middle class—are further behind whites today than before the victories of the civil rights movement. But there is a reluctance among blacks to examine this paradox, I think, because it suggests that racial victimization is not our real problem. If conditions have worsened for most of us as racism has receded, then much of the problem must be of our own making. But to fully admit this would cause us to lose the innocence we derive from our victimization. And we would jeopardize the entitlement we've always had to challenge society. We are in the odd and self-defeating position where taking responsibility for bettering ourselves feels like a surrender to white power. 32

So we have a hidden investment in victimization and poverty. These distressing conditions have been the source of our only real power, and there is an unconscious sort of gravitation toward them, a complaining celebration of them. One sees evidence of this in the near happiness with which certain black leaders recount the horror of Howard Beach and other recent (and I think over-celebrated) instances of racial tension. As one is saddened by these tragic events, one is also repelled at the way some black leaders—agitated to near hysteria by the scent of victim-power inherent in them—leap forward to exploit them as evidence of black innocence and white guilt. It is as though they sense the decline of black victimization as a loss of standing and dive into the middle of these incidents as if they were reservoirs of pure black innocence swollen with potential power. 33

Seeing for innocence pressures blacks to focus on racism and to neglect the individual initiative that would deliver them from poverty—the only thing that finally delivers anyone from poverty. With our eyes on innocence we see racism everywhere and miss opportunity even as we stumble over it. About 70 percent of black students at my university drop out before graduating—a flight from opportunity that racism cannot explain. It is an injustice that whites can see *for innocence* with more impunity than blacks can. The price whites pay is a certain blindness to themselves. Moreover, for whites *seeing for innocence* continues to engender the bad faith of a long-disgruntled minority. But the price blacks pay is an ever-escalating poverty that threatens to make the worst off of them a permanent underclass. Not fair, but real. 34

Challenging works best for the collective, while bargaining is more the individual's suit. From this point on, the race's advancement will come from the efforts of its individuals. True, some challenging will be necessary for a long time to come. 35

But bargaining is now—today—a way for the black individual to *join* the larger society, to make a place for himself or herself.

"Innocence is ignorance," Kierkegaard says, and if this is so, the claim of innocence amounts to an insistence on ignorance, a refusal to know. In their assertions of innocence both races carve out very functional areas of ignorance for themselves—territories of blindness that license a misguided pursuit of power. Whites gain superiority by *not* knowing blacks; blacks gain entitlement by *not* seeing their own responsibility for bettering themselves. The power each race seeks in relation to the other is grounded in a double-edged ignorance, ignorance of the self as well as the other.   36

The original sin that brought us to an impasse at the dinner party I mentioned at the outset occurred centuries ago, when it was first decided to exploit racial difference as a means to power. It was the determinism that flowed karmically from this sin that dropped over us like a net that night. What bothered me most was our helplessness. Even the engineer did not know how to go forward. His challenge hadn't worked, and he'd lost the option to bargain. The marriage of race and power depersonalized us, changed us from eight people to six whites and two blacks. The easiest thing was to let silence blanket our situation, our impasse.   37

I think the civil rights movement in its early and middle years offered the best way out of America's racial impasse: in this society, race must not be a source of advantage or disadvantage for anyone. This is fundamentally a *moral* position, one that seeks to breach the corrupt union of race and power with principles of fairness and human equality: if all men are created equal, then racial difference cannot sanction power. The civil rights movement was conceived for no other reason than to redress that corrupt union, and its guiding insight was that only a moral power based on enduring principles of justice, equality, and freedom could offset the lower impulse in man to exploit race as a means to power. Three hundred years of suffering had driven the point home, and in Montgomery, Little Rock, and Selma, racial power was the enemy and moral power the weapon.   38

An important difference between genuine and presumed innocence, I believe, is that the former must be earned through sacrifice, while the latter is unearned and only veils the quest for privilege. And there was much sacrifice in the early civil rights movement. The Gandhian principle of non-violent resistance that gave the movement a spiritual center as well as a method of protest demanded sacrifice, a passive offering of the self in the name of justice. A price was paid in terror and lost life, and from this sacrifice came a hard-earned innocence and a credible moral power.   39

Non-violent passive resistance is a bargainer's strategy. It assumes the power that is the object of the protest has the genuine innocence to morally respond, and puts the protesters at the mercy of that innocence. I think this movement won so many concessions precisely because of its belief in the capacity of whites to be moral. It did not so much demand that whites change as offer them relentlessly the opportunity to live by their own morality—to attain a true innocence based on the sacrifice of their racial privilege, rather than a false innocence based on presumed   40 racial superiority. Blacks always bargain with or challenge the larger society; but I believe that in the early civil rights years, these forms of negotiation achieved a degree of integrity and genuineness never seen before or since.

In the mid-Sixties all this changed. Suddenly a sharp *racial* consciousness emerged to compete with the moral consciousness that had defined the movement to that point. Whites were no longer welcome in the movement, and a vocal "black power" minority gained dramatic visibility. Increasingly, the movement began to seek racial as well as moral power, and thus it fell into a fundamental contradiction that plagues it to this day. Moral power precludes racial power by denouncing race as a means to power. Now suddenly the movement itself was using race as a means to power, and thereby affirming the very union of race and power it was born to redress. In the end, black power can claim no higher moral standing than white power.

It makes no sense to say this shouldn't have happened. The sacrifices that moral power demands are difficult to sustain, and it was inevitable that blacks would tire of these sacrifices and seek a more earthly power. Nevertheless, a loss of genuine innocence and moral power followed. The movement, splintered by a burst of racial militancy in the late Sixties, lost its hold on the American conscience and descended more and more to the level of secular, interest-group politics. Bargaining and challenging once again became racial rather than moral negotiations.

You hear it asked, why are there no Martin Luther Kings around today? I think one reason is that there are no black leaders willing to resist the seductions of racial power, or to make the sacrifices moral power requires. King understood that racial power subverts moral power, and he pushed the principles of fairness and equality rather than black power because he believed those principles would bring blacks their most complete liberation. He sacrificed race for morality, and his innocence was made genuine by that sacrifice. What made King the most powerful and extraordinary black leader of this century was not his race but his morality.

Black power is a challenge. It grants whites no innocence; it denies their moral capacity and then demands that they be moral. No power can long insist on itself without evoking an opposing power. Doesn't an insistence on black power call up white power? (And could this have something to do with what many are now calling a resurgence of white racism?) I believe that what divided the races at the dinner party I attended, and what divides them in the nation, can only be bridged by an adherence to those moral principles that disallow race as a source of power, privilege, status, or entitlement of any kind. In our age, principles like fairness and equality are ill-defined and all but drowned in relativity. But this is the fault of people, not principles. We keep them muddied because they are the greatest threat to our presumed innocence and our selective ignorance. Moral principles, even when somewhat ambiguous, have the power to assign responsibility and therefore to provide us with knowledge. At the dinner party we were afraid of so severe an accountability.

What both black and white Americans fear are the sacrifices and risks that true racial harmony demands. This fear is the measure of our racial chasm. And though fear always seeks a thousand justifications, none is ever good enough, and the

41

42

43

44

45

problems we run from only remain to haunt us. It would be right to suggest courage as an antidote to fear, but the glory of the word might only intimidate us into more fear. I prefer the word *effort*—relentless effort, moral effort. What I like most about this word are its connotations of everydayness, earnestness, and practical sacrifice. No matter how badly it might have gone for us that warm summer night, we should have talked. We should have made the effort.

MIDDLE-CLASS SOLUTIONS
from *Paved with Good Intentions: The Failure of Race Relations in Contemporary America*
Jared Taylor

Fortunately, despite their urgency, the problems of the underclass affect only a minority of blacks. In the other black America, what is needed is the realization that the bounty of this nation is not wrung from the reluctant, racist bosom of the white man but is won through individual responsibility and hard work. A recent book on the psychology of successful blacks includes a list of the ingredients of what the black authors call the psychology of black success. At the top of the list is personal responsibility. Another characteristic the authors found in successful blacks was that "they neither expect the Man to save them, nor blame the Man for all the problems and injustices of society."   1

Seminars on racism and mandatory college courses in ethnic studies are precisely what we do not need. Their ostensible purpose is to "sensitize" whites to the needs of minorities, but their real effect is to hammer at the old theme that whites are responsible for everything that goes wrong for blacks. This does nothing to help blacks, and whites have been so thoroughly "sensitized" that they are sick of it. College-age whites, especially, who have had no hand in shaping society, are increasingly confused and angry about constant harping on guilt they do not feel. What are they to make of the preposterous idea, propounded with the blessings of the university, that the Ivy League may be a subtle form of genocide? Ultimately, the very notion that Americans must be "sensitized" to race flies in the face of what we are presumably trying to achieve: a society in which race does not matter.   2

Moreover, there are limits to the patience with which whites will listen to appeals to a guilt they no longer feel. In the past, the best way to get whites to help blacks may have been to try to make them feel guilty. Increasingly, that will only make them angry. Blacks who seek the help and genuine goodwill of whites will not get it by dwelling on white racism and white guilt.   3

Something else that does no good is the constant proliferation of black subgroups. As soon as blacks join an organization, they band together into a racially exclusive subgroup. The doors of mainly white organizations are open to them, but their organizations are closed to whites. By any definition, this is racial discrimination.   4

There is a certain logic to this that few acknowledge. Mainly-white colleges must be integrated, but black colleges must stay black because they provide role models. Mainly-white fraternities must be integrated, but exclusively black fraternities will   5 nurture the "black identity." The Miss America contest must be open to blacks, but blacks must have their own, racially exclusive beauty contest. There is black English and a black learning style, and they must be recognized. Job preferences for blacks are a civil right, but job preferences for whites are racism. "Black pride" is healthy and necessary, but "white pride" is bigotry. Standardized tests work for other races, but they are biased against blacks. All-black interest groups must be established to fight the racism within every American organization. Blacks should patronize black-owned stores and vote for black candidates. Blacks feel closer to Africans than to white Americans. Black students must have black teachers or they will not learn properly.

One man who understands where all this leads is Louis Farrakhan, leader of the   6
Nation of Islam. The logic of black pride, black caucuses, and black role models leads straight to black nationhood. That, of course, is Mr. Farrakhan's stated objective. For him, whites are "devils" and "evil by nature." Blacks can expect nothing from them, and should carve out an independent black nation for themselves. He already has a national anthem for them. Citizens of a black nation would certainly escape the "racism" they claim to find at every turn in the United States.

Is Mr. Farrakhan's whites-are-devils theory any different from that of the equal   7
employment officer who wrote that in America all whites are racist and only whites can be racist? Is it any different from the whites-are-always-responsible theory of black failure? Is the black nation that Mr. Farrakhan would carve out for himself so very different from the black caucuses that blacks so frequently carve out for themselves?

Whether they mean to or not, when blacks set up racially exclusive groups, when   8
they demand special privileges, when they state black goals that are different from America's goals, they are widening the racial fault lines that divide this country. They cannot go on forever demanding special treatment in the name of equality, or practicing racism in the name of ethnic pride, or rebuilding segregation in the name of black identity. The "black agenda" all too often means nothing more than patronage, handouts, double standards, and open hostility to whites.

White Americans will eventually lose patience. The White Student Union at   9
Temple University, the National Association for the Advancement of White People, the popularity in Louisiana of former Klansman David Duke—these are all disquieting signs that whites are tired of double standards. Only for so long will whites watch blacks use race as a weapon before they forge racial weapons of their own.

Of course, race matters in America. It may always matter. But if we really are try-   10
ing to build a color-blind society, our methods are not merely wrong but perverse. The entire apparatus of government, industry, and education is painfully conscious of race and treats the races differently at every turn. Blacks now demand special treatment as a matter of course. In its befuddled way, society is trying to do what is right. But to favor blacks systematically and then call this sorry charade "equal opportunity" is self-delusion of the worst kind.

If anything brings down the American experiment, it will be the notion that   11
deliberate race consciousness can lead to racial harmony, that reverse racism can

eliminate racism. Affirmative action, minority set-asides, and double standards are well-meant folly. If America really were boiling with white racism and the nation's most urgent task were to stamp it out, what more insanely inflammatory policy could one invent than to discriminate against whites because of their race? When the occasional ragtag band of placard-waving Ku Kluxers is outnumbered, not only by hecklers but also by police sent to protect them from outraged citizens, can white racism really be the crippling evil it is made out to be?

Racial distinctions replace the principle of individual merit with that of group re-   12
wards. If blacks get favors simply because they are black, it encourages them to think of themselves neither as individuals nor as Americans, but as blacks. How can blacks help but think of themselves as a separate people when society, at every turn, treats them as a separate people? In turn, how can we expect whites not to respond in kind to "ethnic aggressivity"? And finally, how can blacks be expected to believe in ability and hard work when society rewards them for being black instead? They must listen to the words of Booker T. Washington, the former slave who went on to found Tuskeegee Institute:

> No greater injury can be done to any youth than to let him feel that because he belongs to this or that race he will be advanced regardless of his own merit or efforts.

Unlike the problems of the underclass, the folly of affirmative action could quickly   13
be cured. We need only to interpret the laws on our books exactly as they were written. Nothing could be clearer than a prohibition against discrimination by race, creed, color, or national origin. The layman's understanding of these laws is precisely what their authors meant. Future generations will shake their heads in wonder at the mental acrobatics of our most learned judges, who have stood justice on its head.

Of course, judges cannot, by themselves, change the way America thinks. Even if   14
all race-based preferences were thrown out tomorrow, the job would be only half done until the double standards that first justified them were discredited. For that, all Americans will have to believe that blacks can and must take hold of their own destinies. They must realize that America will cease to be America if race becomes more important than nation. Only then can we begin to heal the hidden wound.

De Tocqueville feared that white America's relations with its freed slaves would   15
be the greatest social crisis the young democracy would face. He was right. Many great Americans—Abraham Lincoln, Thomas Jefferson, James Madison, John Marshall, Henry Clay, and Daniel Webster, to name just a few—did not believe that black and white could live peaceably in the same society.

We have not yet proven that they can. But if we do, it will be because we faced   16
the truth unflinchingly. We will have to shun the shakedown artists and guiltmongers. Whites will have to turn their backs on cowardly, dishonest behavior designed solely to escape charges of "racism." They must reject wholesale, off-the-shelf accusations and search for explanations that go deeper than the sloganeering, grandstanding, and buffoonery that now control the field.

The men who founded this country and established the first modern democracy believed that in the marketplace of ideas, the truth would always prevail. It was a belief that the common man would have the courage of his convictions and that society would always honor the truth that made "the land of the free and the home of the brave" something more than an empty slogan. When whites submit to accusations they know are untrue, they are the silent accomplices of falsehood. They must have the courage to say what they know to be true. 17

Blacks have the harder but more inspiring task of shucking the old excuses and finally taking possession of their lives. They must learn, just as Asians have, that whites can thwart them only if they permit themselves to be thwarted, and that society can help them only if they are able to help themselves. They must recognize that the weapon of race consciousness, which they are so tempted to wield, is a sword that cuts in every direction. Blacks who understand this, and say so publicly, will be reviled by other blacks who are still looking for excuses and handouts. Brave, clear-sighted black men and women carry a heavy burden, for no one else can even hope to touch the desolated generations that are ravaging our cities. 18

One hundred thirty years ago, this nation very nearly tore itself apart because of race. It could do so again. Policies based on white guilt and reverse racism have failed. Policies based on the denial of individual responsibility have failed. We must have the courage to admit that they have failed, and forge new policies that will succeed. 19

PANSY QUITS
from *The Rooster's Egg*
Patricia J. Williams

> *"Help me out of these wet things, Pansy," Scarlett ordered*
> *her maid. "Hurry." Her face was ghostly pale, it made her*
> *green eyes look darker, brighter, more frightening. The young*
> *black girl was clumsy with nervousness. "Hurry, I said.*
> *If you make me miss my train, I'll take a strap to you."*
>
> *She couldn't do it, Pansy knew she couldn't do it.*
> *The slavery days were over, Miss Scarlett didn't*
> *own her, she could quit any time she wanted to.*
>
> Alexandra Ripley, *Scarlett: The Sequel to*
> *Margaret Mitchell's* Gone with the Wind

Despite the enormous social, political, and legal fluctuations of twentieth-century American life, there has been a remarkable stasis in race relations, an intractability of gender hierarchy, an entrenched power dynamic that has resisted the reorderings of the very best rhetoricians and theoreticians. When Frederick Douglass described his own escape from slavery as a "theft" of "this head" and "these arms" and "these legs," he employed the master's language of property to create the unforgettable paradox of the "owned" erupting into the category of a speaking 1 subject whose "freedom" simultaneously and inextricably marked him as a "thief." That this disruption of the bounds of normative imagining is variously perceived as dangerous as well as liberatory is a tension that has distinguished racial politics in America from the Civil War to this day. Scarcely thirty years after Martin Luther King's dream of a day when his children would be judged by the content of their character alone, the Reagan-Bush presidencies were able to reverse the metaphor of the Freedom Train into a commodity with a high-priced ticket whose fare must be earned in the marketplace.

The transformation of the rationales for enslavement or oppression from one discourse to another is perhaps a more familiar one than we in the United States would at first be comfortable acknowledging. As Walter Benn Michaels has observed:

> Imagining the slave as a buyer and seller, the contract at the same time defeu-dalizes slavery, replacing a social fact that exists independent of the desires of master or slave with a market agreement that insists on and enacts the priority of those desires . . . Hence the "new feudalism" that Progressives . . . feared . . . can never come into being not because conditions as bad as and even worse than those obtaining under "old-fashioned" slavery cease to exist but because the intervention of the market, even when it leaves these conditions intact, al-ters their meaning. In other words, the apologists for "modern slavery" defended it not by appealing to the usual paternalist ideals but by appealing to freedom, in particular freedom of contract.

Political appeals to "liberty," popular references to "freedom," and legal discussions of "equality" have always been weighted and authorized by very powerful images culled from hotly contested fields of symbolic reference. Who is really included in the notion of "national unity"? What is being negotiated when mass violence is la-beled a "war," as opposed to a revolution, a rebellion, a riot, or the hold of some cult leader over innocent followers? When did affirmative action become reverse discrimination? How did we get to the point where no one puts black bodies on the auction block anymore, only healthy white babies? Against what social backdrop is sexual harassment transformed into high-tech lynching? And how on earth did we end up in the best-selling world of *Scarlett: The Sequel,* in which ex-slaves comfort themselves, as the whip descends, with the thought that they can quit at any time?

As the civil rights movement has made claims on the civic circle of participation, those resources located in the public sphere (including not just wealth but such in-tangibles as political responsibility and general idealism) have been spirited out of reach, as in a shell game between the walnut halves of public and private; as in a shell game among a welter of legal nuts. The debate about equality has shifted to one of free speech; legal discussions involving housing, employment, and schooling have shifted from the domain of civil rights to that of the market and thus have be-come "ungovernable," mere consumption preference. It serves us well, I think, to observe the ironies as well as the consistencies, the currents of desired investment and unintended disenfranchisement that flow on and on and on beneath the surface of our finest aspirations.

It is useful to attempt to unravel the degree to which powerful negative stereotypes of race and gender play against one another, first in negotiating the subtle, sometimes nearly invisible boundaries of social life, of citizenship, and of entitlement; and then, ultimately, in dictating the very visible limits of the law itself. To study the unreflective resurrection and recirculation of the metaphors of disregard in the United States is to reveal a powerful ideological pattern, a semantic of racism that is nurtured in the hidden spaces of cognitive blind spots. As Professors Nancy Fraser and Linda Gordon have written about the genealogy of the notion of "welfare dependence," the use of overdetermined and taken-for-granted images and keywords "serve[s] to enshrine certain interpretations of social life as authoritative and to delegitimate or obscure others, generally to the advantage of dominant groups in society and to the disadvantage of subordinate ones."

The degree to which such images are influential raises the question of the degree to which they may be manipulated for better or worse ends. Thus the scope of my concern includes the rhetorical strategies by which borders are drawn and community marked, including the cultural theorist Eduardo Cadava's question of "how one's rhetoric may see its way home to the mark when the figures one uses may include, within their history, connotations that lead one's argument away from its intended end," as well as the function of the media in shaping "American" identity—in particular the currently popular configuring of "whites as victims" in the shaping of civic identity and legal outcome.

As I write, it is the fortieth anniversary of *Brown v. Board of Education,* the case that shaped my life's possibilities, the case that, like a stone monument, stands for just about all of the racial struggles with which this nation still grapples. I cite it as a watershed moment, but the *Brown* case was part of a larger story that couldn't, shouldn't be made into private property; it was an exemplary story but far from unique.

My family, like so many black families, worked in the civil rights movement, joined the NAACP, took me to march out in front of Woolworth's before I could read—not because of a great event in their lives but because of all the ordinary daily grinding little events that made life hard in the aggregate. Even though I was raised in Boston during the 1950s and 1960s, I grew up knowing the back-of-the-bus stories, the peanut gallery stories, the having-to-go-the-bathroom-in-the-woods stories, the myriad mundane nearly invisible yet monumentally important constraints that circumscribed blacks, and not only in the South. My father, who grew up in Savannah, Georgia, during the 1920s and 1930s, remembers not only the inconveniences but the dangers of being black under Jim Crow: "You had to be careful of white people, you got out of the way, or you'd get hurt, immediately. If you saw a white person coming, you got off the sidewalk. Don't make too much noise. Know which side of the street to walk on. You were always conscious of the difference. The big conversation in all 'colored' homes was just that, color. It affected everybody."

"But that's exactly why *Brown* is indeed, 'our' story," cautioned a friend of mine, who being fifteen or so years older than I was old enough to have gone on enough marches to have worn out many pairs of shoes: 8

> The civil rights movement was all about ordinary people who weren't necessarily on the road to Damascus. If some lent their names, others lent their backs, or their expertise or their lives. It was life-threatening work after all, so nobody did it to get their name up in lights; you did it because there was no alternative. Neither fame nor anonymity existed as issues per se—that's come later, as the country seems to have sorted out who it's going to remember for fifteen seconds and what it will forget. It was about group survival. You were always thinking about what would make it better for the children.

Perhaps part of the difficulty in reviewing the years since *Brown* with anything like a hopeful countenance is that we as a nation have continued to underestimate the complicated and multiple forms of prejudice at work in the United States. Segregation did not necessarily bar all forms of racial mixing; its odd, layered hierarchies of racial attitude were substantially more complicated than that. My grandfather, for example, was a doctor who owned several of the houses in the neighborhood where he lived. "Dad's tenants were white, Irish," says my father, "but I never even thought about where they went to school. We all lived kind of mixed up, but the whole system made you think so separately that to this day I don't know where they went to school." There is an old story that speaks to the profundity of these invisible norms: Three men in the 1930s South set out to go fishing in a small boat. They spent the morning in perfectly congenial and lazy conversation. At lunchtime they all opened their lunch buckets and proceeded to eat, but not before the two white men put an oar across the middle of the boat, dividing themselves from their black companion.   9

The continuing struggle for racial justice is tied up with the degree to which segregation and the outright denial of black humanity have been *naturalized* in our civilization. An aunt of mine who is very light-skinned tells of a white woman in her office who had just moved from Mississippi to Massachusetts. "The North is much more racist than the South," she confided to my aunt. "They don't give you any credit for having white blood." This unblinking racial ranking is summarized in the thoughts of James Kilpatrick, now an editor of the *National Review,* who stated the case for southern resistance in a famous and impassioned plea: 10

> For this is what our Northern friends will not comprehend: The South, agreeable as it may be to confessing some of its sins and to bewailing its more manifest wickednesses, simply does not concede that at bottom its basic attitude is "infected" or wrong. On the contrary, the Southerner rebelliously clings to what seems to him the hard core of truth in this whole controversy: Here and now, in his own communities, in the mid-60s, the Negro race, as a race, plainly is not equal to the white race, as a race; nor, for that matter, in the wider world beyond, by the accepted judgment of ten thousand years, has the Negro race, as a race, ever been the cultural or intellectual equal to the white race, as a race.

This we take to be a plain statement of fact, and if we are not amazed that our Northern antagonists do not accept it as such, we are resentful that they will not even look at the proposition, or hear of it, or inquire into it.

Dealing with the intractability of this sort of twisted social regard is what the years since *Brown* have been all about. Legal remedy after legal remedy has been challenged on the basis of assertions of not being able to "force" people to get along, assertions that "social equality" (or, these days, "market preference") is just not something that can be legally negotiated. Jack Greenberg, a Columbia University law professor and one of the attorneys who worked on the original *Brown* case, dismisses these arguments concisely: "You have to wonder how it is that *Plessy v. Ferguson,* which made segregation the law for almost seventy years, didn't come in for the same kinds of attacks, as 'social engineering.'" 11

Jerome Culp, a Duke University law professor, has observed that the litigators and activists who worked on *Brown* in the early 1950s assumed at least three things that have not come to pass: (1) that good liberals would stand by their commitment to black equality through the hard times; (2) that blacks and whites could come to some kind of agreement about what was fair and just—that there *was* a neutral agreed-upon position we could aspire to; and (3) that if you just had enough faith, if you just wished racism away hard enough, it would disappear. 12

"Growing up," says my father, "we thought we knew exactly what integration meant. We would all go to school together; it meant the city would spend the same money on you that they did on the white students. We blacks wouldn't be in some cold isolated school that overlooked the railroad yards; we wouldn't have to get the cast-off ragged books. We didn't think about the inevitability of a fight about whose version of the Civil War would be taught in that utopic integrated classroom." 13

The *Brown* decision itself acknowledged the extent to which educational opportunity depended on "intangible considerations" and relied "in large part on 'those qualities which are incapable of objective measurement but which make for greatness.'" Yet shaking the edifice sometimes brings home just how enormous the edifice really is. Moreover, the task of education in general has become vastly more complicated by the influence of television, and the task of learning racial history has been much confounded by the power of mass media. 14

"We've become a nation of sound bites," says Cheryl Brown Henderson, the daughter of the late Oliver Brown—the named plaintiff in *Brown*—and the founder of the Brown Foundation, an organization dedicated to teaching the history of the civil rights movement. 15

That millisecond of time to determine our behavior, whether it's behavior toward another individual, or behavior toward a product we might purchase, or our behavior with regard to what kind of housing or community we want to live in—I really think we allow that [millisecond] to determine far too much of our lives . . . When you take something that short and infuse it with a racial stereotype, and no other information is given, the young person looking at that—even the older person who spends most of his time watching television—that's all they know. How can you expect them to believe anything else? They're not going to pick up a book and read any history, do any research, or talk to anybody that may in fact be able to refute the stereotype.

In addition to stereotypes, perhaps the media revolution has exacerbated the very American tendency to romanticize our great moments into nostalgia-fests from which only the extremes of Pollyannaish optimism or Malthusian pessimism can be extracted. For all the biblical imagery summoned to inspire the will to go on with the civil rights struggle in this century, if the waters have parted at any given moment, perhaps it has been more attributable to all those thousands of busy people working hard to make sure Exodus occurred one way or another—just people, just working and just thinking about how it could be different, dreaming big yet surprised most by the smallest increments, the little things that stun with the realization of the profundity of what has not yet been thought about. 16

My father muses: 17

> It's funny . . . we talked about race all the time, yet at the same time you never really thought about *how* it could be different. But after *Brown* I remember it dawning on me that I *could* have gone to the University of Georgia. And people began to talk to you a little differently; I remember [the white doctor who treated my family in Boston, where I grew up] used to treat us in such a completely offhand way. But after *Brown,* he wanted to discuss it with us, he asked questions, what I thought. He wanted my opinion and I suddenly realized that no white person had ever asked what I thought about anything.

Perhaps as people like my father and the doctor have permitted those conversations to become more and more straightforward, the pain of it all, the discomfort, has been accompanied by the shutting down, the mishearing, the turning away from the euphoria of *Brown.* "It has become unexpectedly, but not unpredictably hard. The same thing will probably have to happen in South Africa," sighs my father.

Perhaps the legacy of *Brown* is as much tied up with a sense of national imagination as with the pure fact of its legal victory; it sparked our imagination, it fired our vision of what was possible. Legally it set in motion battles over inclusion, participation, and reallocation of resources that are very far from over. But in a larger sense it committed us to a conversation about race that we must move forward with, particularly in view of a new rising Global Right. 18

We must get beyond the stage of halting conversations filled with the superficialities of hurt feelings and those "my maid says blacks are happy" or "whites are devils" moments. If we could press on to a conversation that takes into account the devastating legacy of slavery that lives on as a social crisis that needs generations more of us working to repair—if we could just get to the enormity of that unhappy acknowledgement, then that alone might be the source of a genuinely revivifying, rather than a false, optimism. 19

I think that the crisis in universities over what is so snidely referred to as "political correctness" must be viewed as part of the attempt to have such a conversa- 20 tion. The much-publicized campus tensions are an unfortunate but perhaps predictable part of the institutional digestive process of the beneficiaries or demographic heirs of the civil rights movement. The battle for equal rights that is symbolized by the landmark integration of grammar schools in Topeka, Kansas, that was waged also with the integration of high schools and colleges, then professional and graduate schools, then workplaces—that battle is now just about forty years old. The generation of children who entered white schools as a result of the transformative legacy of the Supreme Court's opinion in *Brown v. Board of Education* has grown up, become middle-aged, attained the time of life when careers make their lasting mark. It is not surprising, therefore, that the bitter resistance and powerful backlash that have met every step of integrationist vision should have flowed to their current loci, those Steven Carter calls "affirmative action babies." It is not surprising, as more blacks, women, gays, Hispanics, Jews, Muslims, and wheelchair-bound people have entered the workplace, gotten tenure in universities, and risen to political office, that the new generation of fire-hosing tomato-throwers have shifted their aim and their tactics accordingly.

No longer are state troops used to block entry to schools and other public institutions—segregation's strong arm, states' rights, has found a new home in an economic gestalt that has simply privatized everything. Whites have moved to the suburbs and politicians have withdrawn funds from black to white areas in unsubtle redistricting plans. No longer is the law expressly discriminatory (as to race and ethnicity at any rate; this is not yet the case in terms of sexual orientation)—yet the phenomenon of laissez-faire exclusion has resulted in as complete a pattern of economic and residential segregation as has ever existed in this country.   21

Most of all, the moral currency of the civil rights movement's vocabulary has been under attack. "Integration" itself has been transformed in meaning, now used glowingly by former segregationists like Jesse Helms and Strom Thurmond—and rejected by many former civil rights activists—as having come to mean a form of assimilation that demands self-erasure rather than engagement of black contributions and experience.   22

This facile deflection has historical precedents in the 1950s incantations of "freedom of association" and "contract," which were used to block discussions of integration. Then, as now, civil rights activists had to respond with lawsuits focusing on substantive equality as a constitutional objective, on the premise that certain groups need not suffer unrestrained stigmatization of their humanity and of their citizenship. In today's world, such efforts have focused on harassment in the workplace, the academic freedom to include or exclude the histories of minority groups in curricula, the redefinition of citizenship to encompass the extraordinary linguistic, ethnic, religious, racial, and physical variety of those of us who are American Citizens Too.   23

While this particular battle resounds in every aspect of American life, there is no place it has been more visible than in universities; there is no fiercer entrenchment than the line drawn around the perceived property in culture. It is a battle remarkable for the persistence of prejudice: as women are still trying to overcome   24 presumptions that they really *like* getting fondled in the back office, blacks are trying to overcome presumptions that they really *deserve* to be on the bottom of the heap. It is a battle complicated not just by ignorance and denial but by disastrous yet well-intentioned experiments—such as the slavery lesson described in this news item:

> A White first-grade teacher in Atglen, Pa., who asked her only two Black pupils to pretend they were slaves during a class discussion on slavery, recently apologized to the youngsters' parents.
>
> "Teacher put us up on a table," said Ashley Dixon, 6, describing the history lesson by teacher Mary Horning. Ashley said Horning told her that, as a slave, she would be sold for about $10 as a house cleaner.
>
> Zachary Thomas, also 6, said Horning used him to demonstrate how shirtless slaves were chained to a post before flogging.
>
> Horning apologized the next day to the children's mothers and asked them to speak to her class on Black heritage. "I did not view it as racial," she said, adding, "I wanted to teach the children about prejudice. I did not do it with malice or to embarrass anyone."

Such well-meaning but thoughtless scenarios reenact and reinforce a power dynamic in which some people get to *imagine* oppression, and others spend their lives having their bodies put through its most grotesque motions. Reference to "good intentions," moreover, however blunderingly destructive their impact, tends to end all further discussion. The merest whisper of the possibility that a little education, a little history, a little forethought might improve things is too often crudely and immediately translated into electrical blizzards of fear of "fascism," "thought control," "hypersensitivity," and "lowered standards."

I can't help wondering what is implied when the suggestion of more knowledge, more history is so persistently misunderstood and devalued as unscientific unknowledge, as untruthful unhistory. In fact, the upside-downness of meaning has become a major threat to the ability to address educational inequality in a whole range of contexts. "*Inter*culturalism," said a Swarthmore undergrad firmly and disapprovingly when I used the word "multiculturalism" at a tea given in my honor not long ago. "Huh?" said I, through a mouthful of chocolate cream and crumbs. "Interculturalism," she repeated. "Multiculturalism has too much negative meaning these days."

I guess she was right. Every generation has to go through a purging of language, an invention of meaning in order to exist, in order to be seen. Renaming as fair turnaround; renaming as recapture from the stereotypes of others. Yet . . . somehow . . . it seems I am running out of words these days. I feel as if I am on a linguistic treadmill that has gradually but unmistakably increased its speed, so that no word I use to positively describe myself or my scholarly projects lasts for more than five seconds. I can no longer justify my presence in academia, for example, with words that exist in the English language. The moment I find some symbol of my presence in the rarefied halls of elite institutions, it gets stolen, co-opted, filled

25

26

with negative meaning. As integration became synonymous with assimilation into whiteness, affirmative action became synonymous with pushing out more qualified whites, and of course multiculturalism somehow became synonymous with solipsistically monocultural privilege.

While constant rejuvenation is not just good but inevitable in some general sense, the rapid obsolescence of words even as they drop from our mouths is an increasingly isolating phenomenon. In fact, it feels like a form of verbal blockbusting. I move into a large meaningful space, with great connotations on a high floor with lots of windows, and suddenly all the neighbors move out. My intellectual aerie becomes a known hangout for dealers in heresy and other soporific drugs, frequented by suspect profiles (if not actual suspects) and located on the edge of that known geological disaster area, the Slippery Slope.

The roadblock that the moral inheritance of the civil rights movement has encountered in the attack on "political correctness" strikes me as just such rhetorical robbery—it is a calculated devaluation of political property values no less than the "white flight" organized by the National Association of Realtors a few decades ago, which left us with the legacy of the "inner city." It seems to me that the ability to talk about diversity (now synonymous with balkanization) depends therefore on a constant clarification of terms, a determination to leave nothing to presupposition, and a renewed insistence upon the incorporation of multiple connotative histories into our curricula, our social lives, our politics, and our law.

I worry that while the happy universalism of assimilative "neutrality" is a fine ideal, we will never achieve it by assuming away the particularity of painful past and present inequalities. The creation of a false sense of consensus about "our common heritage" is not the same as equality. As the example of the first-grade slave auction demonstrates, the ignorant (or innocent) perpetuation of oppression, even as we purport to be challenging it, can result in situations where empowered people imagine they are learning and even end up feeling pretty good about themselves, yet the disempowered end up feeling pretty awful, bearing the burden of the lessons imparted to the more powerful while learning nothing themselves that is new or helpful. Thus powerful inequities and real social crises are ignored, are made invisible, and just get worse.

Does this mean we eliminate the topic of slavery or sexism or homophobia from our classrooms as too "dangerous" or "divisive" or "controversial"? Do we really want to avoid controversy in education? Or is that even the issue?

I am concerned that the noisy rush to discuss the legalities of censorship and the First Amendment preempts more constructive conversations about how we might reinfuse our pedagogy with dignity and tolerance for all. As I have remarked a number of times before, it is as if the First Amendment has become severed from any discussion of the actual limits and effects of political, commercial, defamatory, perjurious, or any other of the myriad classifications of speech. It is as if expressions that carry a particularly volatile payload of hate become automatically privileged as political and, moreover, get to invoke the First Amendment as a bludgeon of paradox—"I have my First Amendment right to call you a monkey, so you shut up about it." As the legal anthropologist Richard Perry observes, hatred thereby gets to cross-dress as Virtue Aggrieved.

In a much-publicized incident at Harvard University a few years ago, a white stu- 32 dent hung a Confederate flag from her dormitory window, saying that to her it symbolized the warmth and community of her happy southern home. This act produced a strong series of public denunciations from many other students, blacks in particular, who described the symbolic significance of the Confederacy as a *white* community forged against a backdrop of force, intimidation, and death for blacks. Eventually one black student hung a sheet with a swastika painted on it out her window, with the expressed hope that the university would force both her and the white student to remove such displays. The university did not, and eventually the black student removed her flag voluntarily because it was creating tension between black and Jewish students.

While the entire debate about this incident predictably focused on free speech 33 issues, what seemed strange to me was a repeated and unexamined imbalance in how the two students' acts were discussed. On the one hand, there was a ubiquitous assumption that the white student's attribution of meaning to the Confederate flag was "just hers," so no one else had any "business" complaining about it. The flag's meaning became a form of private property that she could control exclusively and despite other assertions of its symbolic power. (Those other assertions are just "their opinion"; all's fair in the competitive marketplace of meaning.)

At the same time, there was an assumption that the swastika's meaning was fixed, 34 transcendent, "universally" understood as evil. The black student's attempt to infuse it with "her" contextualized meaning (that of the translated power of what the Confederate flag meant to her) was lost in the larger social consensus on its historical meaning. This larger social consensus is not really fixed, of course, but its monopoly hold on the well-educated Harvard community's understanding is a tribute both to the swastika's overarchingly murderous yet coalescing power in the context of Aryan supremicist movements and to our having learned a great deal of specific history about it. The power of that history understandably overshadowed not only that black student's attempt at a narrower meaning but also the swastika's meaning in aboriginal American religion or in Celtic runes.

The questions remains, however, how some speech is so automatically put be- 35 yond comment, consigned to the free market of ideas, while other expressions remain invisibly regulated, even monopolized by the channels not merely of what we have learned but of what we have not learned. I do not want to be misunderstood: I do not question our consensus on the image of genocide embodied in the swastika; I wonder at the immovability of the comfy, down-home aura attending the Confederate flag—the sense that as long as it makes some people happy, the rest of us should just butt out. The limits of such reasoning might be clearer if applied to the swastika: without having to conclude anything about whether to censor it, the fact remains that we usually don't cut off discussions of Nazism with the conclusion that it was a way of creating warm and happy communities for the German bourgeoisie.

Let me be clearer still in this thorny territory: I wish neither to compare nor to   36
relativize the horrors of the Holocaust and of the legacy of slavery in the United
States. This is not an appropriate subject for competition; it is not a sweepstakes
anyone could want to win. I do worry that it is easier to condemn that which exists at a bit of cultural distance than that in which we may ourselves be implicated.
And it is easier to be clear about the nature of the evils we have seen in others an
ocean away than about those whose existence we deny or whose history we do
not know. The easy flip-flopping between "free" and "regulated" signification is a
function of knowledge; it underscores the degree to which we could all stand to
educate ourselves, perhaps most particularly about the unpleasantnesses of the
past. We should not have to rely upon the "shock" shorthand of campus crises, for
example, to bring to our public consciousness the experience of black history in
the good old days of legalized lynching. . . .

I remember when I was a little girl, in the late 1950s, two or three black families   37
moved into our neighborhood where for fifty years my mother's family had been
the only blacks. I remember the father of my best friend, Cathy, going from house
to house, warning the neighbors, like Paul Revere with Chicken Little's brain, that
the property values were falling, the values were falling. The area changed overnight.
Whites who had seen me born and baked me cookies at Halloween and grown up
with my mother now fled for their lives. ("We'd have to hold our breath all the
time because colored people smell different," said Cathy with some conviction.
Cathy, who was always a little slow about these things, had difficulty with the notion of me as "colored": "No, you're not" and then, later, "Well, you're different.")

The mass movement that turned my neighborhood into an "inner city" was part   38
of the first great backlash to the civil rights movement. I think we are now seeing
the second great backlash, disguised as a fight about reverse discrimination and
"quotas" but in truth directed against the hard-won principles of equal opportunity
in the workplace and in universities as feeders for the workplace. Universities are
pictured as "fortresses" of enlightened and universal values under "siege" by those
who are perceived to be uncivilized heathen. (Wherever 3 percent or more of us
are gathered, it's a siege, I guess.) The cry has been sounded: The standards are
falling, the standards are falling.

The story of my inner-city neighborhood would have been vastly different if   39
Cathy and her family had bothered to stick around to get to know the two nice
black families who moved in. Similarly, the future of the U.S. universities—particularly in the hoped-for global economy—could be a fascinating one if campus communities chose to take advantage of the rich multiculturalism that this society
offers. We face a quite disastrous intellectual crisis, however, if our universities
persist in the culture-baiting that has brought us the English-only movement, the
brazen assumption that any blacks on campus don't deserve to be there, and the
mounting levels of verbal and physical violence directed against anyone perceived
to be different or marginal.

This situation makes it easy to spend a lot of time being defensive. We've all   40
heard the lame retorts into which these attacks box us: "I am too qualified!" "Vote

for me but not because I'm a woman!" But they don't work. You simply can't dispel powerful cultural stereotypes by waving your degrees in people's faces. (That's precisely the premise of ultraconservative Dinesh D'Souza's much-touted book *Illiberal Education:* that an Ivy League degree just isn't worth what it used to be now that the riffraff has moved in.)

It's hard not to be defensive, of course—talking about race in any other posture   41
is extremely difficult. I recently guest-lectured in the class of a constitutional law professor who was teaching disparate impact cases (cases that consider what if any remedies might correct the racially disparate impact of rules that on their face are race-neutral). As I spoke about shifting demographics and the phenomenon of "white flight," the class grew restless, the students flipping pages of newspapers and otherwise evidencing disrespect. Afterward, the two or three black students congratulated me for speaking so straightforwardly, and for using the words "black" and "white." I later asked the professor: How is it possible to teach cases about racial discrimination without mentioning race? "I just teach the neutral principles," he replied; "I don't want to risk upsetting the black students." (And yet it was clear that those most upset were the white students.)

This tendency to neutralize is repeated throughout the law school curriculum: 42
"core" classes carve off and discard some of their most important parts, such as welfare and entitlement programs from tax policy, consumer protection law from commercial contract. And even though the civil rights movement was one of the most singularly transformative forces in the history of constitutional law, very little of it is taught in basic constitutional law classes. (When I took constitutional law, we spent almost no class time on civil rights.) Some schools—by no means all—pick up the pieces by offering such optional courses as Poverty Law, Law and Feminism, or Race and the Law. It is no wonder that the Rehnquist court has been able to cavalierly undo what took so many lives and years to build: the process of legal education mirrors the social resistance to antidiscrimination principles. Subject matter considered to be "optional" is ultimately swept away as uneconomical "special" interests—as thoughtlessly in real life as it has been in law schools.

Ironically, the smooth conceptual bulwark of "neutral principles" has been turned   43
to the task of evading the very hard work that moral reflection in any sphere requires, the constant balancing—whether we act as voters, jurors, parents, lawyers, or laypeople—of rules, precepts, principles, and context. I have always considered developing the ability to engage in such analytical thought to be the highest goal of great universities. Yet even this most traditional of educational missions is under attack. "Should [parents] be paying $20,000 a year to have their children sitting there, figuring out how they feel about what they read?" asks James Barber, founder of the neoconservative National Association of Scholars at Duke University. His question underscores the degree to which the supposed fear of balkanized campuses is in fact the authoritarian's worst nightmare of a world in which people actually think for themselves.

The necessity of thinking long and hard and aloud about the nature of prejudice   44
was exemplified for me when I was visiting Durham, North Carolina, during the

1990 senatorial race between Jesse Helms and Harvey Gantt (the first black to run for that office since Reconstruction). A friend of mine said she wanted me to see something. Without any explanation, she drove me over to Chapel Hill and dragged me to the center of the University of North Carolina campus. There, right in front of the student union, was a statue entitled *The Student Body*. It was a collection of cast bronze figures, slightly smaller than life-size. One was of an apparently white, Mr. Chips–style figure with a satchel of books on his back, pursuing his way. Another was of a young woman of ambiguous racial cast, white or maybe Asian, carrying a violin and some books and earnestly pursuing her way. A third figure was of a young white woman struggling with a load of books stretching from below her waist up to her chin. Then two white figures: a young man holding an open book with one hand; his other arm floating languidly downward, his hand coming to casual rest upon a young woman's buttocks. The young woman leaned into his embrace, her head drooping on his shoulder like a wilted gardenia. In the center of this arrangement was a depiction of an obviously black young man. He was dressed in gym shorts and balanced a basketball on one finger. The last figure was of a solemn-faced young black woman; she walked alone, a solitary book balanced on her head.

It turned out I was about the only one in the state who hadn't heard about this 45
statue. A gift from the class of 1985, it had been the topic of hot debate. Some students, particularly black and feminist students, had complained about the insensitivity of this depiction as representative of the student bod(ies). Other students said the first students were just "being sensitive" (invoked disparagingly as though numb-skulledness were a virtue). At that point the sculptor, a woman, got in on the act and explained that the black male figure was in honor of the athletic prowess of black UNC grads like Michael Jordan, and that the black female figure depicted the grace of black women. The university, meanwhile, congratulated itself publicly on how fruitfully the marketplace of ideas had been stimulated.

As I stood looking at this statue in amazement, I witnessed a piece of the 46
debate-as-education. Two white male students were arguing with a black female student.

"You need to lighten up," said one of the men. 47

"But . . ." said the black woman. 48

"Anyway, black women *are* graceful," said the other. 49

"But," said the black woman as the white men kept talking. 50

In the end the black woman walked off in tears, while the white men laughed. 51
There is a litany of questions I have heard raised about scenarios like this: Why should the university "protect" minority students against this sort of thing? Don't they have to learn to deal with it?

Let me pose some alternative questions of my own: Why should universities be 52
in the business of putting students in this sort of situation to begin with? Since when is the persistent reduction of black men and all women to their physical traits "educational" about anything? How is it that these sorts of ignorant free-for-alls are smiled upon by the same university officials who resist restructuring curricula to teach the actual histories of women and people of color?

There is a popular insistence that the solution to the struggle over campus multi- **53**
culturalism is to just talk about it, one-on-one, without institutional sanction or interference. Free speech as free enterprise zone. But this solution makes only certain
students—those who are most frequently the objects of harassment—the perpetual
teachers, not merely of their histories, but of their very right to be students. This is
an immense burden, a mountainous presumption of noninclusion that must be constantly addressed and overcome. It keeps them eternally defensive and reactive.

This denial of legitimacy is not merely an issue for students. The respect accorded   **54**
any teacher is only in small—if essential—part attributable to the knowledge inside
the teacher's head. (If that were all, we would have much more respect for street-
corner orators, the elderly, and the clear uncensored vision of children.) What
makes one a teacher is the force lent to one's words by the collective power of institutional convention. If faculty members do not treat women as colleagues, then
students will not treat women as members of the faculty.

I think that the ability to be, yes, *sensitive* to one another is what distinguishes   **55**
the joy of either multiculturalism or willing assimilation from the oppression of either groupthink or totalitarianism. Empathic relation is at the heart of diplomacy,
and a little well-deployed diplomacy can keep us from going to war with one another. But the dilemma many people of color face at this moment in the academic
and employment world is this: if we respond to or open discussion about belliger-
ent or offensive remarks—that is, if we pursue the much-touted path of responding to hate speech with "more speech"—we are called "PC" and accused of forcing
our opinions down the throats of others. If we respond with no matter what degree of clear, dignified control, we become militant "terrorists" of the meek and
moderate middle. If we follow the also-prevalent advice to "just ignore it," then we
are perceived as weak, humiliated, ineffectual doormats who ought to have told off
our harassers on the spot.

It's great to turn the other cheek in the face of fighting words; it's probably even   **56**
wise to run. But it's not a great way to maintain authority in the classroom or self-
respect in the workplace—particularly in a society that abhors "wimps" and considers "kicking ass" a patriotic duty. In such a context, "just ignoring" verbal
challenges is a good way to deliver oneself into the category of the utterly power-
less. If, moreover, all our colleagues pursue the same path (insult, embarrassed
pause, the world keeps on moving as though nothing has happened), then we have
collectively created that peculiar institutional silence known as a moral vacuum.

One of the subtlest challenges we face, if we are not to betray the hard-won   **57**
gains of the last forty years, is how to relegitimate the national discussion of racial,
ethnic, and gender tensions so that we can get past the Catch-22 in which merely
talking about it is considered an act of war, in which not talking about it is complete capitulation to the status quo, and in which not talking about it is repeatedly
covered up with a lot of high-volume substitute talk about the legalities of censorship and the First Amendment. In the long run, taking refuge in such excuses preempts more constructive conversations about how we might reinfuse our pedagogy
with dignity and tolerance for all.

The most eloquent summary of both the simplicity and the complexity of that common task remains W. E. B. Du Bois's essay "On Being Crazy": 58

> After the theatre, I sought the hotel where I had sent my baggage. The clerk scowled.
>
> "What do you want?"
>
> Rest, I said.
>
> "This is a white hotel," he said.
>
> I looked around. Such a color scheme requires a great deal of cleaning, I said, but I don't know that I object.
>
> "We object," he said.
>
> Then why, I began, but he interrupted.
>
> "We don't keep niggers here," he said, "we don't want social equality."
>
> Neither do I, I replied gently, I want a bed.

VISIONS OF BLACK-WHITE FRIENDSHIP
from *The Trouble with Friendship:*
Why Americans Can't Think Straight about Race
Benjamin DeMott

At the heart of today's thinking about race lies one relatively simple idea: the race situation in America is governed by the state of personal relations between blacks and whites. Belief in the importance of personal relations reflects traits of national character such as gregariousness, openness, down-to-earthness. It also reflects American confidence that disputes can be trusted to resolve themselves if the parties consent to sit down together in the spirit of good fellowship—break bread, talk things out, learn what makes the other side tick. 1

But there's rather more to faith in black-white friendship than off-the-rack Rotarianism. There are convictions about the underlying sameness of black and white ways of thinking and valuing, and about the fundamental causes of racial inequity and injustice, and about the reasons why the idea of addressing race problems through political or governmental moves belongs to time past. 2

One leading assumption is that blacks and whites think and feel similarly because of their common humanity. (Right responsiveness to racial otherness and full access to black experience therefore require of whites only that they listen attentively to their inner voice.) Another assumption is that differences of power and status between whites and blacks flow from personal animosity between the races—from "racism" as traditionally defined. (White friendship and sympathy for blacks therefore diminishes power differentials as well as ill feeling, helping to produce equality.) Still another assumption is that bureaucratic initiatives meant to "help" blacks merely prolong the influence of yesteryear. (The advent of good interpersonal feeling between blacks and whites, on the other hand, lessens yesteryear's dependency.) 3

Each of these closely related assumptions surfaces regularly in print media treat- 4
ment of the friendship theme—material promoting interracial amity and weaving
together concern for "the disadvantaged" and the "underclass," anecdotal evidence
of the mutual affection of blacks and whites, and implicit or explicit disparagement
of politics and politicians. And traces of the same assumptions appear in fraternal
gestures favored by campaigning political candidates.

White candidates attend services at black churches, socialize at black colleges, 5
play games with blacks (as when, during Campaign '92, Jerry Brown took gang leaders rafting). And candidates speak out in favor of black-white friendships, venturing
that such ties could be the answer to race riots. On the second day of the Los Angeles riots, Candidate Clinton declared: "White Americans are gripped by the isolation of their own experience. Too many still simply have no friends of other races
and do not know any differently."

But fantasies about black-white friendship are dramatized most compellingly for 6
large audiences in images. Movies, TV, and ads spare us abstract generalizing about
the isolation of the races. They're funny and breezy. At times, as in *Natural Born
Killers*, they deliver the news of friendship and sympathy in contexts of violence and
amorality. At times they deliver that news through happy faces, loving gestures,
memorable one-liners. Tom Hanks as Forrest Gump loses his beloved best buddy, a
black (Mykelti Williamson), in combat and thereafter devotes years to honoring a
pledge made to the departed (*Forrest Gump,* 1994). A rich white lady (Jessica Tandy)
turns to her poor black chauffeur (Morgan Freeman) and declares touchingly:
"Hoke, you're my best friend" (*Driving Miss Daisy,* 1989). Michael Jackson pours his
heart into a race-dismissing refrain: "It doan matter if you're black or white" (1991).
Scene and action hammer home the message of interracial sameness; mass audiences *see* individuals of different color behaving identically, sometimes looking alike,
almost invariably discovering, through one-on-one encounter, that they need or
delight in or love each other. . . .

A key, early contribution to the mythology of black-white friendship was that of 7
The Cosby Show. Without actually portraying blacks and whites interacting, and without preaching directly on the subject, this sitcom lent strong support to the view
that white friendship and sympathy could create sameness, equality, and interchangeability between the races. Under the show's aegis an unwritten, unspoken,
felt understanding came alive, buffering the force both of black bitterness and resentment toward whites and of white bitterness and resentment toward blacks.
*Race problems belong to the passing moment. Race problems do not involve group inter-
ests and conflicts developed over centuries. Race problems are being smoothed into nothingness, gradually, inexorably, by goodwill, affection, points of light.*

The Cosby family's cheerful at-homeness in the lives of the comfortably placed 8
middle class, together with the fond loyalty of their huge audience, confirmed
both the healing power of fellow feeling and the nation's presumably irreversible
evolution—as blacks rise from the socioeconomic bottom through the working
poor to the middle class—toward color blindness. In the years before the show,

black-white themes, in film as well as TV, had passed through several stages of development. One of a half-dozen milestones was the introduction, in *The Jeffersons,* of the first blacks to achieve middle-class affluence via entrepreneurship. Another milestone was the introduction, by adoption, of charming black children into white families—as in *Webster* and *Diff'rent Strokes.* (The "white foster parents," wrote Jannette Dates, "could then socialize the youngsters into the 'real' American way.")

And in the wake of the success of *The Cosby Show,* the eradication of race difference by friendship became an ever more familiar on-camera subject. Closeness between the races ceased to be a phenomenon registered indirectly, in surveys documenting the positive reaction of white audiences to the Huxtables; it moved to the center of mass entertainment. Everywhere in the visual media, black and white friendship in the here and now was seen erasing the color line. Interracial intimacy became a staple of mass entertainment story structures.   9

Consider *White Men Can't Jump* (1992), a movie about a white quester—a dropout eking a living on basketball courts in Los Angeles—surviving, with black help, on ghetto turf. Working first as a solitary, the young white hustles black ballplayers on their own turf, trading insults with blacks far more powerful, physically, than himself. He chides black athletes to their faces for being showboats, concerned about looking good, not about winning. He flashes rolls of bills and is never mugged. Accompanied only by his girlfriend, he walks the most dangerous ghetto streets at night, once making his way uninvited into an apartment filled with black ballplayers. He mocks black musical performers to their faces in a park, describing the hymns they sing as "shit." That an arrogant, aggressive, white wiseass can do all this and more and emerge unscathed means partly that his behavior is protected under the laws of comedy.   10

But the armor that counts more, here as in numberless black-white friendship tales, is provided by the black buddy. The acquaintance of white Billy Hoyle (Woody Harrelson) and black Sidney Deane (Wesley Snipes) begins badly: each hoaxes the other. Later they communicate through taunts. Black taunts white for incapacity to appreciate the black musicians whom white claims to admire. "Sure, you can listen to Jimi [Hendrix]. Just, you'll never hear him." Black taunts white for dreaming he can slam-dunk: "White men can't jump." Black mockingly offers technical aid to white: pumping up his Air Jordans for dream-flight. White jabs back hard, charging black with exhibitionism and sex obsession.   11

Yet the two make it as friends, form a team, work their scams in harmony. More than once the buddies save each other's tails, as when a black ballplayer whom they cheat turns violent, threatening to gun them down. (The two make a screaming getaway in the white quester's vintage ragtop.) And the movie's climax fulfills the equation—through sympathy to sameness and interchangeability. During a city-wide, high-stakes, two-on-two tournament, Billy, flying above the hoop like a stereotypical black player, scores the winning basket on an alley-oop from his black chum, whereupon the races fall into each other's arms in yelping, mutual, embracing joy. Cut to the finale that seals the theme of mutual need and interdependency;   12 black Sidney agrees to find quasi-honest work for white Billy at the floor-covering "store" that he manages:

Billy (helpless): I gotta get a job. Can you give me a job?

Sidney (affectionately teasing): Got any references?

Billy (shy grin): You.

Like many if not most mass entertainments, *White Men Can't Jump* is a vehicle of wish fulfillment. What's wished for and gained is a land where whites are unafraid of blacks, where blacks ask for and need nothing from whites (whites are the needy ones; blacks generously provide them with jobs), and where the revealed sameness of the races creates shared ecstatic highs. The precise details of the dream matter less than the force that makes it come true for both races, eliminating the constraints of objective reality and redistributing resources, status, and capabilities. That force is remote from political and economic policy and reform; it is, quite simply, personal friendship.   13

Another pop breeding ground of delusion is the story structure that pairs rich whites and poor blacks in friendship—as in *Regarding Henry* (1991), a Mike Nichols film about a white corporation lawyer and a black physical therapist. The two men meet following a holdup during which a gunman's stray bullet wounds the lawyer, Henry Turner (Harrison Ford), in the head, causing loss of speech, memory, and physical coordination. The therapist, Bradley (Bill Nunn), labors successfully at recovering Henry's faculties.   14

In outline, *Regarding Henry*—a video store hit—is a tale of moral transformation. Henry Turner is a corporate Scrooge who earns a fortune defending insurance companies against just suits brought by the injured and impecunious. Between the time of the gunshot wound and his return to his law firm, he experiences a change of heart—awakens to the meanness and corruption of his legal work and begins a movement toward personal reform. The sole influence on this transformation is Bradley, who shows the lawyer a persuasive example of selfless concern for others.   15

Bradley is called upon, subsequently, to give further guidance. Back in his luxo apartment and offices, Henry Turner, aware finally of the amoral selfishness of his professional life and of his behavior as husband and father, sags into depression—refuses to leave his bed. His wife, Sarah (Annette Bening), summons the black therapist, the only man Henry respects. Over beer in Henry's kitchen, Bradley tells his host of a crisis of his own—a football injury which, although it ended his athletic career, opened the prospect of the more rewarding life of service he now leads.   16

But does Bradley really believe, asks Henry Turner, that he's better off because of the accident? His black friend answers by citing the satisfactions of helping others, adding that, except for his football mishap, "I would never have gotten to know you."   17

The black man speaks as though fully convinced that his own turning point—his 18
unwanted second choice of life—and Henry Turner's are precisely similar. Nothing
in his voice hints at awareness either of the gap between riches and privation or of
the ridiculousness of the pretense that race and class—differences in inherited
property, competencies, beliefs, manners, advantages, burdens—don't count.
Wealthy white lawyer and humble black therapist speak and behave as though both
were Ivy League clubmen, equally knowledgeable about each other's routines,
habits, tastes. The root of Bradley's happiness as he sings his song of praise to his
white buddy is that, for Henry Turner, difference doesn't exist.

The predictable closer: a new Henry Turner launches an effort at restitution to 19
the poor whom his chicanery has cheated; black-white friendship not only makes
us one but makes us good.

When crime enters, fellow feeling should in theory exit. But visions of the force 20
of friendship challenge this rule, too. They thrust characters and audiences into
hitherto unexplored passages of self-interrogation and self-definition, obliging
whites to clarify, for themselves, the distinction between humane and racist responses to troubling black behavior. And they present the process of arriving at a
humane response—i.e., one that doesn't allow a criminal act to derail black-white
sympathy and friendship—as an act of personal reparation. . . .

Incessantly and deliberately, the world of pop is engaged in demonstrating, 21
through images, that racism has to do with private attitudes and emotions—with
personal narrowness and meanness—not with differences in rates of black and
white joblessness and poverty, or in black and white income levels, or in levels of
financing of predominantly black and white public schools. The images body forth
an America wherein some are more prosperous than others but all—blacks as well
as whites—rest firmly in the "middle income sector" (the rising black middle class
encompasses all blacks), where the free exchange of kindness should be the rule.

This America is of course remote from fact. One out of every two black chil- 22
dren lives below the poverty line (as compared with one out of seven white children). Nearly four times as many black families exist below the poverty line as
white families. Over 60 percent of African Americans have incomes below $25,000.
For the past thirty years black unemployment rates have averaged two to three
times higher than those of whites.

But in the world of pop, racism and fraternity have to do solely with the condi- 23
tions of personal feeling. Racism is unconnected with ghetto life patterns that abstractions such as income and employment numbers can't dramatize. Racism has
nothing to do with the survival strategies prudently adopted by human beings without jobs or experience of jobs or hope of jobs. It has no link with the rational rejection, by as many as half the young black men in urban America, of such dominant
culture values as ambition, industry, and respect for constituted authority. Pop
shows its audiences that racism is *nothing but* personal hatred, and that when
hatred ends, racism ends. The sweet, holiday news is that, since hatred is over, we—
black and whites together, knit close in middleness—have already overcome.

EXPANDING THE CENTER
from *Tragic Failure: Racial Integration in America*
Tom Wicker

The precipitate loss of decent jobs and decent wages was the most important factor in the explosive growth of the underclass in the 1970s and its continuing, blighting presence. To make income-earning jobs generally available to what are now inner-city residents, therefore, and to equip them to get and keep such jobs are important corollaries to the overall goal of full employment. It might even prove an effective anticrime program.

No one can pretend, however, that putting jobs into the inner city for its residents to fill would be an easy task. Quite the opposite. The frequently touted panacea of "job training" certainly is not enough. Even if in the era of technology adequate training programs for ill-educated persons could be devised, and if they could be made attractive to undisciplined ghetto youth, they would do little good if they only spewed jobless people back to the mean streets whence they came. Jobs, good jobs, have to be available at the end of the training pipeline.

If no such jobs await, the trainees are likely to believe that only a placebo has been offered in the few weeks of training—not a real remedy for a real malady. All too often, unfortunately, that has been the truth of well-intended job-training programs.

Even affluent, entrepreneurial blacks with the best will in the world can bring few jobs to the ghetto. The almost entirely white lords of the U.S. economy might—if they would. But bottom-line considerations make it unlikely that even the most public-spirited corporations actually will put major operations into the ghetto. More willing and skilled workers, at the same or lower wages, in better social and working conditions, can be found almost anywhere outside the big-city ghetto— foreign countries included. Nor would middle management and skilled technologists be likely to want to go to work every day in the dismal and dangerous South Bronx or any other inner-city neighborhood.

Substantial incentives might—or might not—lure owners and managers of job-providing enterprises to set up shop in the ghetto, finding and training their workers from among those available nearby. But such incentives are not in the political cards. President Clinton has proposed nothing of the sort. In a time of budget constraint and animosity toward racial integration, neither Congress nor any state, much less the taxpayer, seems willing to take such costly, problematical steps.

The idea of "ghetto renewal" may be illusory in any case. One who thinks so is Nicholas Lemann, the chronicler of the great post–World War II black migration out of southern cotton fields and into American cities:

> Of all the dramatic solutions to the problems of the ghettos, probably the most common and persistent for the past quarter century has been the idea that they can be "developed" into thriving ethnic enclaves. . . . Such proposals

have a powerful emotional attractiveness. They envelop the ghettos in the romanticized aura that Americans attach to small-town life.

Lemann believes, however, that "the clear lesson of experience" is that this kind 7
of "ghetto development hasn't worked." Nor does he think it *can* work: "[T]he reality is that our ghettos bear the accumulated weight of all the bad in our country's racial history, and they are now among the worst places to live in the world."

Why should blacks or anyone be expected to work or live in such areas? Le- 8
mann asks, pointing out that European immigrants of a century ago "had no intention of making the ghetto their permanent residence."

In a panel discussion at Harvard's Kennedy School of Government, Margaret 9
Weir of the Brookings Institution advocated instead a federal effort to "promote the mobility of the urban poor," in much the same way that government policies have helped whites to move out of cities into suburbs. Such mobility would increase what she called "access to prosperity" for the underclass and "help poor people as well as poor places."

That approach also presents numerous difficulties. White suburbanites as well as 10
working-class whites and middle-class blacks in better urban neighborhoods will not welcome inner-city blacks. They fear the lawlessness some might bring along, and they would resent feared newcomers being imposed on often close-knit areas by government policy.

Ghetto "dispersal," moreover, is not always a popular idea even among blacks 11
concerned about the inner city. Dispersal smacks too much of "forced removal" or, more cynically, "Negro removal." African-Americans learned to be wary of such plans from the old "slum clearance" programs that made urban land available for many a luxurious apartment building only whites could afford. And dispersal would make little allowance for the solid working-class families that somehow have remained in the inner city.

Some black elected officials would object, even if selfishly, to diminution of their 12
inner-city political bases. Other African-Americans, accustomed to doubting white motives, might believe that was the real objective: to diminish black voting strength in the cities. In some cases it might be.

If "ghetto renewal" and "ghetto dispersal" are unpromising approaches to re- 13
deeming the inner city, what's left? The range of approaches to the problems of the underclass are certainly limited. But that's not a reason for giving up, for writing off generations of African-Americans who, as things now appear, will be forever lost to productive citizenship and the good American life.

Part of the answer is that nationwide public works program—rebuilding streets, 14
highways, bridges, railways—and the business and industrial expansion it would spark. Such a renewal of the national infrastructure would symbolize, perhaps even inspire a larger national renewal.

Another vital part of the answer is improved public education, in general and in 15
the inner city. Too many of today's schoolchildren are being shortchanged by public

and taxpayer apathy; by crime- and fear-ridden schools in the inner city that teach little more than survival; by schools elsewhere that focus on driver training and sports; by shortsighted, selfish, sometimes corrupt unions; by legislative indifference and political hostility to "spending" and taxes; by an imbalance of resources favoring affluent over poor school districts.

Privatization of some public schools, competition between these and remaining public schools, vouchers to enable parents to choose more promising schools for their children—such conservative proposals deserve comprehensive testing and adoption where proved effective. They do *not* justify a precipitate turn from the public education that has been vital to the nation's development.   16

However it's done, the rejuvenation of public education is vital to the redemption of the ghetto. And for this purpose too, economic gains for the poor are all-important, tending, as they would, to improve the social and physical environment of families, upgrade student behavior and performance, and—not least—yield more political "clout" to those who now have little.   17

Perhaps more important than any specific proposal would be the fact of a new party [built by African-Americans]—the political pressure it would bring, win or lose, on the mainstream parties. Such a party would make it impossible for the Democrats to court middle-class white votes while depending on the votes of poor blacks. Republicans could no longer slight the interests of more than forty million Americans living in poverty.   18

A new party's activities and votes would focus public attention on the needs of the poor and disadvantaged, including the African-Americans for so long victimized by American society, and on the attitudes of those who no longer believe in the promise of democracy. These, rather than the supposed miseries of the relatively well-off white middle class, are the gravest threats to the national future. These are the proper objects of an enlightened politics.   19

The major parties, however, are not going to recognize that, the Republicans because their interest is in the middle class and white communities, the Democrats because they are trying to compete with the Republicans. Both parties' political pitch is to the middle class, not to an underclass that hangs like a dark cloud over the future of American cities and American life.   20

"We all know [the underclass] is the principal problem in American domestic life," Nicholas Lemann has written, "a problem that poisons not just race relations but also our attitudes toward education, law enforcement, and city life itself."   21

"We all" may *know* that; unfortunately we all—most particularly the Democratic and Republican parties—neither admit it nor want to do anything effective about it. Consequently those parties will not think, much less do anything useful, about the problems of the underclass or the unemployed or the nonvoters.   22

Only a new party, formed for that purpose, made up principally of those to be redeemed, will take up the cause of these virtually forgotten Americans. Only a new party will devote its best minds and its best efforts to their cause. And only a new party's political determination and dedicated votes can see to it that the rest of us pay attention.   23

WHATEVER HAPPENED TO INTEGRATION?
Gerald Early

In the ideological warfare between liberals and conservatives, African-Americans   1
exist as a kind of Rorschach test, an enigma to be solved in the context of their
disturbing exceptionalism in a country obsessed with its own exceptionalism. Blacks
have been in this country as long as its earliest European settlers. Why haven't they,
well, for lack of a better phrase, quite measured up? Why do they lag behind whites
and seemingly behind all the other immigrant groups to have come here? To white
liberals like Tom Wicker and Benjamin DeMott, African-Americans are incorrupt-
ible victims, sanctified by their long history of suffering at the hands of whites, and
stigmatized by the legacy of slavery and a virulent, unending white racism. As many
conservatives see it, all the problems of blacks are essentially caused by an inability
to fit in to the culture in which they live and an inability to stop seeing themselves
as victims—an attitude that white liberals encourage them to maintain.

In short, the liberal believes that whites are the problem, the conservative that   2
blacks are the problem. Any thinking black person must sit between these contesting categorizations, which have existed since antebellum days, feeling something between bemusement and contempt. Although blacks at various times, under various
circumstances, may prefer one explanation to the other (usually, though certainly
not always, the liberal's to the conservative's), the truth about blacks is to be found
not in the middle ground but, paradoxically, in both views simultaneously, and in
neither of them. The race problem is not really understood if it is seen as a white
problem or a black problem. It is an American conundrum.

Americans do not like protracted problems or problems that suggest a limit to   3
their power. Part of this is bound up with the belief of both blacks and whites in
American exceptionalism—the idea of this country as a redeemer nation, a New
Jerusalem. Americans also do not like to face the liberating possibilities of the profound historical tragedy within themselves; hence white neo-conservatism on the
one hand, Afrocentrism on the other—ideologies of tragedy avoidance or sheer
escapism.

Tom Wicker, a southerner and thus more believable as a sincere white liberal be-   4
cause he was reared amid the worst kind of racism, has in essence written a defense
of the moral and political superiority of the welfare state, apparently the only kind
of state in which blacks can thrive. (Conservatives assert that the welfare state has
been the utter ruination of blacks.) His book argues that white America has reneged
on its promise of integration and full justice and economic parity for black Americans in the 1960s and 1970s—a promise implicit in the *Brown* school-desegregation
decision of 1954 and explicit in the Civil Rights Act of 1964—as it reneged on full
citizenship and political parity for black Americans during Reconstruction. What
has happened, Wicker asserts, from the time of Richard Nixon through the time of
Ronald Reagan, has been a steady retreat on the question of civil rights and black
advancement, for reasons of expediency on the part of white politicians at best, or
of wretched cowardice on the part of white civic leadership at worst. The country

is as racist as it ever was, and the white population is still selfishly, even pathologically, venting its anger at and fashioning its scapegoats from the least among us—African-Americans. Now, this thesis is hardly new. Andrew Hacker and Derrick Bell are among the latest to sell a great number of books having anguish and outrage about the black condition as a theme. Of course, no one is very happy with race relations in the United States, the sorry state of which was supposedly revealed, according to Wicker, by the public response to the O. J. Simpson verdict. In fact, Wicker's indictment has a measure of merit and truth in it. Nonetheless, there are a great number of problems with this book.

"If racial integration is to be revived as essential to a secure future for America, an effective new political party forthrightly working for economic justice will be necessary," Wicker writes in *Tragic Failure: Racial Integration in America.* "African-Americans," he says explicitly, "must build a new political party." (Who could be more expert on the issue of economic justice or a better advocate for it than the very group that has suffered the greatest economic injustice? is, I think, Wicker's reasoning.) Then we would have the usual populist assemblage of poor whites, other racial minorities (after all, Wicker reminds us, whites themselves will be a minority come 2050), and the like—that is, people who are "likely to encounter some degree of economic and racial disadvantage."   5

Frankly, it is incomprehensible to me how black people could solve the problems of isolation and alienation they face in the political realm (Republicans and Democrats are chary about a black political agenda and even, to some degree, about the black vote itself) by forming their own political party, which would seem to do nothing more than institutionalize their isolation and alienation as a disaffected minority.   6

Tragic Failure wishes to be an accusatory book (against whites), but it is in essence a lazy book. For instance, Wicker says that "the growth of the black middle class was largely lost to view [of whites] in the lurid new visibility of the underclass remaining in the ghetto." Yet how does one explain the impact of people like Bill Cosby, Oprah Winfrey, and Michael Jordan, and of the barrage of images on television and in advertising of a seemingly happy and broad black middle class—images that have encouraged whites to believe that some blacks have indeed made it?   7

Blacks strike the white imagination in largely contradictory ways: as huge success stories and as the underclass of criminals and welfare cheats. An analysis of this contradiction is needed, but the book does not provide one. Wicker states, "It's plain now that those inner-city blacks noticed mostly when they appear on the nightly television news as perpetrators or victims of crime will be with us for years to come." But since most nightly news shows, both local and national, have black reporters and even black news anchors, why won't their images stay with "us" just as long? And if inner-city blacks are seen largely as criminal, how much have they participated in their own degradation through the marketing and commercialization of their cultural expressions, hip-hop and rap? These exploit the image of the black male as outlaw and deviant to titillate the white suburban mind and to give black culture, for the black consumers of this product, some supposedly subver-   8 sive, radical edge. Changing crime into political resistance, marginalization into a broad expression of humanity and liberation, has been a romantic preoccupation of the bourgeois intellectual since long before Foucault and the postmodern sensibility. In other words, blacks have historically been far too willing to accept distortions of themselves, because they see themselves culturally as whites see them: in intensely romantic terms.

In speaking of the connection between the black image and criminality Wicker does not mention that Danny Glover, Morgan Freeman, Whoopi Goldberg, Denzel Washington, Eddie Murphy, Martin Lawrence, Wesley Snipes, Laurence Fishburne, Jim Brown, Sidney Poitier, Paul Winfield, Yaphet Kotto, and Will Smith have all played cops or government agents in movies or on television. What impact has this had on the image of the black as criminal? If it has had none, why? 9

The book suffers greatly from this lack of consideration of the difficult contradictions in American culture. There is no serious thinking here. In a footnote Wicker suggests that although Lincoln thought that blacks should be sent back to Africa, he never suggested that whites go back to Europe. But Lincoln would have thought that sending blacks back to Africa was humane because they had been brought here against their will (unlike whites) and may very well have wanted to go back. (Of course they did not.) Also, Lincoln believed that as a recently freed people with no education and what appeared to him to be servile habits, they stood little chance of surviving in direct competition with whites. . . . 10

In speaking about sellouts, Wicker writes, "An African-American clearly would have a difficult task succeeding materially in American society (save perhaps in sports or show biz) without joining, to some extent, in the values and attitudes of that society—as a minor example, without dressing conventionally." Surely many whites, too, feel that they must "sell out," not be themselves, in order to get a job or pursue a career in the mainstream. That is what all the talk of conformity in the 1950s and surely the countercultural revolt of the 1960s was about. Selling out in order to make it is an issue that transcends race. Obviously it is even more difficult for blacks, in part because the opportunities to sell out are fewer and the demand for conformity is more charged. Dressing conventionally, Wicker suggests, is a white custom. Yet blacks have a long history of manners, etiquette, dressing well. What Ralph Ellison referred to as "elegance" is not foreign to black experience. 11

The overall problem with this book is that Wicker chose not to provide a deeply focused look at race relations and liberalism in this country. He did not interview dozens of people from various walks of life and in various locations to give their perspectives on integration and liberalism. He did not read—or at least did not provide evidence that he had read—all the books, conservative and liberal, about race and the pros and cons of integration that have come out in the past ten or fifteen years. If he had done this, *Tragic Failure* might have been an important book, instead of a sloppy, ill-considered one that says nothing new and does not condemn the failure of the national will to effect integration or defend liberalism nearly as well as the work of Jonathan Kozol and William Julius Wilson, for instance. This 12

book largely turns on the fact that a white southerner wrote it and in a rather bel-
licose way calls other whites incorrigible racists—which they may very well be, but
that does not solve much of anything. And, of course, he charitably excuses black
folk of all complicity after the fact, which is a form of rank patronization. Even the
oppressed are not immune to stupidity, opportunism, greed, demagoguery, and a
complex form of connivance in their own suffering.

Benjamin DeMott's *The Trouble With Friendship: Why Americans Can't Think Straight*   13
About Race is more interesting, in part because DeMott's concerns are largely centered in the cultural realm, where most people find the real heat and light about
race. It is also a more interestingly reasoned and argued book than Wicker's. De-
Mott's basic case is that through films, television, advertising, and other cultural
products a "friendship orthodoxy" has arisen, in which the relationship between
the races has become intensely personalized, the persistent dogma is that the races
are essentially the same, and racism is regarded as the viewpoint of a psychotic
fringe, a marginal expression that whites, once they are awakened, fight and defeat
through their good will. Racism thus has no connection to power relations, to the
purpose and coherence of American institutions, to the very sense of the nation as
a political and social entity. In these dramatizations blacks bring no brutal history of
oppression to the table and whites no sense of advantage from having had them to
oppress. Everyone is more or less innocent, and after a few rough moments a kind
of recognition of common humanity is achieved and we all go off together into that
great, gettin' up, biracial morning. As far as it goes, this thesis about the representation of race relations and racial history in American popular culture is correct.
But, alas, it does not go very far.

DeMott's marks are too easy. To condemn as fantasies most current Hollywood   14
films with major black characters misses two points. First, Hollywood films are always about fantasy human relationships, whether they deal with man against the
dark forces of society (film noir), marriage and sex (the romantic comedy, the
screwball comedy, the domestic drama), or so-called social realism (the "problem"
film, the protest film). Few American films have ever shown "power relations," "institutional influence on the formation of character," or other Marxist constructs.
The fact is that race fits in with all these other relationships and gets dramatized in
pretty much the same way. I am not sure that white America is trying to avoid anything more with race films than it is trying to avoid with films on any other subject.
What is important is how race fits into this larger overall pattern; but DeMott
simply describes the pattern, very incompletely and without the kind of historical
rigor that would have given his argument value. A consideration of the careers of
Harry Belafonte and Sidney Poitier in the 1950s alongside the careers of Hattie
McDaniel, Stepin Fetchit, Clarence Muse, Willie Best, and the cohort of black comic
actors of the 1930s and 1940s would have made his point far more powerfully and
vividly. Poitier thought what he was doing was a matter of dignity, although DeMott
would complain that his films were early versions of the black-white friendship fan-

tasy. But McDaniel thought that what she was about concerned dignity as well, which is why she said she'd rather play a maid than be one.

Second, DeMott picks films like *White Men Can't Jump* and *Regarding Henry,* which 15 are easy to analyze in the way he chooses, as friendship fantasies—but these are not expected to be anything more, politically, than, say, *The Terminator* or *Casino.* And, of course, why should they be anything more? What about a look at, for example, the blaxploitation movies of the late 1960s and early 1970s, which many blacks believe saved Hollywood financially and claimed, at times, some sort of social relevance? What about an examination of the black filmmaker in Hollywood and how he or she dealt with the "friendship orthodoxy"? Why are American films generally disposed not to deal with personal problems as having political and economic origins? Is it because of the ideology of individualism that so permeates the culture and that everyone—black and white—believes?

Another historical and cultural point DeMott misses is that, as David Riesman 16 described in his classic work, *The Lonely Crowd,* post-industrial society, in particular America after the Second World War, is other-directed—that is to say, concerned with personal relationships. The prevalence of the other-directed social character goes a long way toward explaining why the race problem is depicted as it is in our cultural products and why many blacks and whites are satisfied with that form of depiction. Why does DeMott not talk about any of this?

The racial friendship fantasy is not some recent Hollywood invention; it dates 17 back to Mark Twain's *The Adventures of Huckleberry Finn* (1884) and Harriet Beecher Stowe's *Uncle Tom's Cabin* (1852), both premised on intense friendships between people of different races. The friendship fantasy is deeply entwined with our concept of slavery itself—with one of the nation's worst political and social crimes. Herman Melville's "Benito Cereno" brilliantly explodes the idea of interracial friendship as a delusion. What lies behind the utopia of racial fusion is the horror of race war, Melville tells us. DeMott does not talk about any of this; he does not show that he is especially learned in the details of race in this culture. Those who are interested in this subject should read Melville.

Acknowledgments *(continued from copyright page)*

McCullough, Fran. "Ice Cream: Giving in to Rich Temptation." *The New York Times,* August 13, 1997, pp. C1, C6. Copyright © 1997 by The New York Times Company. Reprinted by permission.

Schwartz, Harry. "Must Doctors Serve Where They're Told?" *The New York Times,* 1942, Copyright © 1975 by The New York Times Company. Reprinted by permission.

Raab, Selwyn. "Holdup Man Tells Detectives How to Do It." *The New York Times,* March 5, 1975, p. A1+. Copyright © 1975 by The New York Times Company. Reprinted by permission.

"School Uniforms Growing in Favor in California." *The New York Times,* September 3, 1994. Copyright © 1994 by The New York Times Company. Reprinted by permission.

Russell, Bertrand. "The Social Responsibility of Scientists." Extract taken from *Fact and Fiction* by Bertrand Russell. Reproduced by the kind permission of Unwin Hyman Ltd.

Easterbrook, Gregg. "The Case Against Nature." Extract taken from pages 140–149 in *A Moment on Earth* by Gregg Easterbrook. Copyright © 1995 by Gregg Easterbrook. Used by permission of Viking Penguin, a division of Penguin Books USA Inc.

Tabor, James D. and Gallagher, Eugene V. "Waco and Religious Freedom in America." Excerpt from pages 173–186 in *Why Waco? Cults and the Battle for Religious Freedom in America* by James D. Tabor and Eugene V. Gallagher. Copyright © 1995 The Regents of the University of California. By permission of The University of California Press.

Rieff, David. "Multiculturalism's Silent Partner: Global Capitalism." Copyright © 1993 by *Harper's Magazine.* Reproduced from the August issue by special permission. All rights reserved.

O'Brien, Conor Cruise. "Violence—and Two Schools of Thought." Reprinted by permission of The Observer News Service.

Shea, Chris. "A Prominent Scholar's Plan for the Inner Cities Draws Fire." *The Chronicle of Higher Education* (September 5, 1997): A21. Copyright © 1997 The Chronicle of Higher Education. Reprinted with permission.

Sipher, Roger. "So That Nobody Has to Go to School If They Don't Want To." *The New York Times,* December 19, 1977. Copyright © 1977 by The New York Times Company. Reprinted by permission.

Singleton, Carl. "What Our Education System Needs Is More F's." *The Chronicle of Higher Education,* 1984. Reprinted by permission of the author.

Bork, Robert H. "The Case for Censorship" from Chapter 8 in *Slouching Towards Gomorrah* by Robert H. Bork. Copyright © 1996 by Robert H. Bork. Reprinted by permission of HarperCollins Publishers, Inc.

Henry III, William A. "The Museum of Clear Ideas." Extract taken from *In Defense of Elitism* by William Henry III. Copyright © 1994 by William Henry III. Used by permission of Doubleday, a division of Bantam Doubleday Dell Publishing Group, Inc.

Strossen, Nadine. "'Sex' Is also a Dirty Word." Extract from pages 19–25 in *Defending Pornography: Free Speech, Sex and the Fight for Women's Rights* by Nadine Strossen. Copyright © 1995 by Nadine Strossen. Reprinted with the permission of Scribner, a division of Simon & Schuster.

Rubin, Gayle. Quote from *Pleasure and Danger* by Carole S. Vance, editor. By permission of Routledge & Kegan Paul (1986).

Index

Instructor's Manual
to Accompany

FIFTH EDITION

Writing from Sources

BRENDA SPATT

Manufactured in the United States of America.

4   3   2   1   0   9
f   e   d   c   b   a

For information, write: Bedford/St. Martin's, 75 Arlington St., Boston, MA 02116 (617-426-7440)

ISBN: 0-312-19384-X

Pp. 18–19:   Shea, Chris. "A Prominent Scholar's Plan for the Inner Cities Draws Fire." *The Chronicle of Higher Education* (September 5, 1997):A21. Copyright © 1997 The Chronicle of Higher Education. Reprinted with permission.

CONTENTS

* in the manual text indicates an appropriate collaborative activity
# in the manual text indicates an assignment appropriate for interviewing

USING *WRITING FROM SOURCES*

The objective of this book is to teach students the analytic, organizational, and synthetic skills necessary for academic writing by breaking down the process into very small stages. Examples and exercises move gradually from the relatively simple tasks of asking and answering questions about an article to the much more complicated techniques for incorporating research into a lengthy essay. Because classes vary in their preparation for academic work and their proficiency in writing, this book provides a range of materials to suit the needs of most classes and interests of most students. It is left up to the instructor to gauge the strengths and weaknesses of each class and to determine which exercises should be assigned and which may be skipped. I taught from this book in manuscript for many years, using a different combination of exercises with each new class. I do, however, recommend that you follow the basic sequence of topics.

I strongly urge you to require that your students submit their notes with each essay, possibly before the outline stage and certainly with the final draft. Reading their notes will help you to keep your students honest and to give them guidance, as needed, at an early stage in the writing process.

Organizing Assignments

Because of its sequential structure, *Writing from Sources* has no essay-length writing assignments in Chapters 1 and 2. Opportunities for essay assignments increase thereafter. Chapter 3 presents two approaches to writing a single-source essay. In Chapter 4, Assignments 6 through 11 are all alternatives for the basic synthesis essay: you need choose only one. The final assignment is, of course, the research essay, which is discussed throughout Chapters 5 through 9.

To give you a rough idea of how the most basic and essential assignments might be scheduled, here is a timetable for a core sequence of three major essays. Built in around these assignments would be a combination of exercises and shorter essays, assigned overnight, over the weekend, or in class (individually or in groups).

Fifth week	One-source essay due
Seventh/eighth week	Multiple-source essay due
Twelfth week	First draft of research essay due
Fourteenth week	Final draft of research essay due

Students may be dismayed to wait until almost halfway through the term to receive their first important grade. I suggest that you use the normal range of letter grades, or pass/fail, to evaluate a few of the earlier assignments, such as summary or paraphrase. If, however, you prefer not to wait to assign an essay, I suggest that, after your class has completed a few exercises from Chapter 1, you choose Assignment 4 in Chapter 3 (which isn't dependent on quotation or paraphrase), and then return to Chapter 2. Another possibility is to discuss Appendix D—"Writing Essay Examinations"—and assign an in-class essay based on one of the extra "casebook" readings in Appendix E while you are working on Chapter 2.

If you want to assess your students' proficiency very early in the term, you can use the reading in Exercise 2 as the starting point for a diagnostic essay of approximately 800 words based on one of the comprehension questions. Since these essays are likely to lack structure, I suggest that you use them for diagnostic purposes only and omit grades and, possibly, comments (except for verbal comments on points of grammar and style, in conference). Instead, you might keep the essays on file in your office and use them as reference points for discussing each student's progress later in the semester.

Alternatives for Assigning the Research Essay

There are a number of practical strategies for assigning the research essay, which vary in their emphasis on "library" work. Here are the approaches that seem to me to be the most successful:

1. The class assembles *individual bibliographies* and writes individual essays on a *historical or biographical topic* of their own choice.

2. The class assembles *individual bibliographies* and writes individual essays on a *contemporary issue or argument*, developing topics of their own choosing.

3. The class works *cooperatively* to do research on a *commonly chosen subject*; students select materials from the accumulated sources and develop their own theses and essays. (For an explanation of cooperative research, see below.)

4. The class may use *only the sources provided within Appendix E*, a thematic group of readings on racial perceptions, with students developing their own theses and essays. (See Assignment 13, p. 362.)

5. The class may use *the sources provided within Appendix E, supplemented with additional sources* obtained individually or cooperatively.

Cooperative Research

Many instructors are concerned about the possibility of plagiarism if they allow students to choose individual topics for research. One solution is to use "prepackaged" sources or casebooks in order to exercise control over the research. Although *Writing from Sources* includes an appendix containing sufficient readings for the casebook approach, there are important skills to be learned from the research process, skills which the student is unlikely to be taught in any other course. Other teachers in other disciplines will require students to compile bibliographies on which their research essays will be based. The students must therefore learn how to make judgments about the titles they find in computerized databases; they must learn how to evaluate sources rapidly, to decide whether the work is authoritative and pertinent to their topic, to discriminate between relevant and irrelevant information. It is difficult to learn these skills when the sources are prepackaged and presented by the teacher. On the other hand, the assignment of a full-scale research essay not only makes a lot of work for the instructor (who must become familiar with a different group of sources for each student's essay), but also creates an unfair handicap for students with job or family responsibilities (who may not be able to devote sufficient time for research).

My solution to this problem is cooperative research leading to individual essays. Midway through the term (while working on the synthesis essay), the class begins the research essay together by choosing a broad subject (or subjects, if you have enough students), usually a contemporary issue or argument, one that can later be divided into two or three subtopics. At the next class session, you provide each student with a separate and roughly equal assignment from the *Reader's Guide* or comparable academic index. (At this point, you spend an hour or two at the library/computer parceling out assignments; the objective is to make sure that each student's list contains a half dozen or so potentially good articles.) Each student is given a page or a sequence of pages from an index and considers each entry, thinking about the title and the periodical and deciding whether the article will be useful to someone working on the topic for the class project. After eliminating any article that is clearly off the point, the student tries to locate the remaining titles, reads those that are available, and makes a copy of any article that seems interesting and pertinent enough to go into the class file. Students should be expected to hand in between three and five each. To make students accountable for their work, you may ask them to submit an annotated bibliography, in which they explain why they did or did not choose to find and read each article; if they did examine an article, they must state their reasons for copying it or rejecting it.

During the period when students are preparing their articles for submission, the class may discuss possible subtopics and theses for the research essay. At the end of the tenth week of the term, students place their articles in a file kept in your office; each article is provided with a cover sheet that contains bibliographical information and a sign-up column. Next, one class session is devoted to the selection of materials. Students examine the accumulated articles and "sign up" for the ones that they want to use in their papers. The class thus gains a second experience of the evaluation of sources, and students can tailor materials to their individual presentations of the topic. In effect, this hour with a file of readings in the classroom simulates the entire research experience (with all the time-wasting procedures removed). For optimal results, evaluation exercises in Chapter 6 should be covered before source-selection day. Most students choose between eight and ten articles. Volunteers in the class collate the choices, arrange for copying, and assess fees. By the twelfth week of the term, each student receives a package of materials and begins working on the organization, writing, and documentation of the essay.

While this kind of assignment has its disadvantages—the emphasis on issues of the day and on periodicals—the benefits are considerable. Because the instructor can become familiar with the sources, first drafts can be evaluated far more easily, and helpful and practical recommendations for revisions can be made. Ultimately cooperative research cuts down on preparation time since one does not have to examine a different set of sources for each essay or go to the library to check references. Finally, cooperative research promotes a more friendly atmosphere in the class: there is more talk about the research process, and the last weeks of the term are less likely to dissolve into individual projects, which can alienate students from each other and from the course.

CHAPTER 1: READING FOR UNDERSTANDING

This chapter encourages students to think about what they are reading, to ask themselves questions that will improve their comprehension and suggest ideas for further development, and to become aware of an essay's structure and thesis. The appropriate amount of practice in comprehension and summary will, of course, vary from class to class. For minimal coverage, I suggest assigning the comprehension exercise (2) and either the annotation exercise (1) to strengthen reading and vocabulary skills or the outlining exercise (4) to encourage your class to become more aware of organization and structure. The exercises that deal with summary (5–6) form a sequence leading up to the assignment of the brief summary at the end of the chapter.

*Exercise 1: Annotating a Passage (p. 6)

The primary objective here is to see what your students should underline, which words they have looked up in the dictionary, and which sentences they have queried, paraphrased, or explained. The passage is not especially difficult, partly because it's repetitive; but it contains some odd juxtapositions. Some of your students may never have seen a John Wayne movie or (less likely) a classic Western. In class discussion, it's worth reviewing the plot of *The Searchers* or *Red River* or *She Wore a Yellow Ribbon*. In the standard adventure mode, these films generally depict a personal mission against impossible odds. In this passage, however, Wills is interested in neither Wayne's personality nor his screen persona. He does not single out the dour strength, the isolation, the determination, the single-minded stubbornness that characterize—and humanize—Wayne and Alan Ladd and Gary Cooper in their seminal films. Wills is, rather, exploring the cultural fantasies of Wayne's audiences, fantasies associated with the American frontier and rooted in the Romantic tradition (and especially Rousseau): a return to nature, simplicity, instinct. What concerns Wills is Wayne's image as an "icon." Indeed, you might want to build a discussion around a comparison with other recent "icons" (e.g. Princess Diana) who have also satisfied societal yearnings that, prior to their appearance, had barely been recognized or understood.

Most of your students will note Wills's emphasis on the theme of freedom vs. constraint. This contrast is modified and given value by the introduction of "American exceptionalism": the qualities developed in a free environment can lift a man above the ordinary and give him a claim to superiority. Having established this moral context (about which he remains neutral), Wills pursues a series of subsidiary contrasts, including simplicity vs. refinement, instinct vs. intellect, indoors vs. outdoors, self-sufficiency vs. community (i.e. commerce), east vs. west, action vs. thought. Wills then interrupts these dichotomies with a line from the Doors' "When the Music's Over" that evokes the decadence and "stale air" of smoke-filled rooms rather than the healthy breezes of the West. As Wills acknowledges, this is an odd text, and it is an odd text for him to cite: in Western films, Earth/Nature permits the hero to be free; but for the Doors, Earth itself has become the object, chained and degraded. Nor is it clear why Wills interrupts the second paragraph—about the visual depiction of the American myth—with a provocative but undeveloped reference to "equality of opportunity." Good students will note these discontinuities.

Here are some points that might be raised in marginal notes:

1. How many different references to freedom (and its opposite) does Wills include in the first sentence? Why does Wills associate Wayne's characters with Adam? Is this a reference to the Garden of Eden? before man sinned? before there was a need for morality? What does "untrammeled" mean? What's wrong with clerks and technicians? Are they "pygmies" because they follow rules?

2. What is an "avatar"? Is an "avatar" the same thing as a symbol or an icon? How would you summarize the American myth as presented in most Westerns? Does the myth of "American exceptionalism" mean that we think we're *different* from other cultures or *better* than other cultures? What is the basis for our so-called exceptionalism? Does it depend on a rejection of authority? Why is "performance" admirable and expertise not? From the tone of the third sentence, can you tell whether Wills subscribes to the American myth he's describing?

3. Since nature is supposed to be the source of freedom, why does Wills include the reference to Earth tied up and degraded in the Doors' song? What was notable about the Doors and their music? Why does Wills think that this song is an odd place to find an allusion to freedom?

4. What's wrong with dudes? What kind of knowledge isn't "useless"? What's the effect of words like "encumbered" and "crippled" and "blunted"? Are they related to "untrammeled" in the first sentence? What does "atrophy" mean? How can an instinct atrophy? What are the characteristics of commerce or technology? Why do they take place in small rooms with "stale air"? Animals undergo conditioning; in what sense are we "conditioned" to a life of confinement? Is there any indication that Wills agrees with this contemptuous view of the "dude"?

5. Who are "the sophisticates" and what do they claim? In what sense is the Western a "popular" art form? Does popularization imply "dumbing down"? Why is a "visual form" a good way to popularize an ideal?

6. What is "equality of opportunity?" What role does it play in the American myth? What does Wills mean by "nature's noblemen"? Do they have more access to "opportunities" than dudes do? Do Western heroes need "opportunities" to prove themselves, or do they make their own opportunities? Why is the Western especially cinematographic? Who is Jean-Luc Godard? Which comes first, the Western or the myth?

Asking Questions (p. 7)

"A Question of Degree" is used several times throughout the book, and, for that reason (and also for its ability to stimulate class discussion), you may wish to spend class time discussing the comprehension questions and Blanche Blank's arguments. There's a basic similarity between this essay and Wills's that's worth pointing out: both are making statements about our need to create cultural myths as rationalizations for economic and social imperatives.

*Exercise 2: Understanding What You Read (p. 16)

This exercise works especially well as a collaborative activity. As an alternative to general class discussion, set up groups of three or four students to work on groups of answers. In a class that is unused to reading and writing academic prose, ask each student in the group to hand in his or her own version of the communally determined answers. Paley's writing is informal and anecdotal, and should be quite accessible to your students.

Paragraph 1: A) The short sentences (like stage directions) establish a setting and set the tone. Without adjectives or other evocative language, Paley's sentences are objective and dispassionate. The force of the memoir comes entirely from the tension of the situation, not the language; the reader does not feel manipulated. B) The use of the comparative ("dark*er*") assumes a continuum for skin—all people have color, some more, some less—and so suggests a common identity shared by all the people on the bus. "Black," on the other hand, suggests its opposite, while "Negro" (the special term reserved for race) serves as a brand to separate one group from the rest of humanity. C) The last two sentences summarize the paragraph: the black passengers' automatic acceptance of the need to move, and the Paley family's remaining equivocally near the back of the bus (we don't know yet if this is an active or passive decision). D) Later on, the mother and sister take on different voices in the narrative, so (to some extent) the two sentences establish them as separate characters. But the repetition also evokes the oral tradition, especially gospel preaching.

Paragraph 2: E) This question is hard to answer for someone familiar with the author. This may be a good point to discuss whether knowledge of the author can encourage bias (or, at least, preconceived ideas) in the reader. Otherwise, in the first paragraph, there is no way of knowing whether the Paleys are white; their concern at the conductor's approach in the second paragraph suggests that they are out of place in the back of the bus. F) The silence suggests total acceptance of the need to organize the bus by color. It also requires a cessation of normal conversation and noise that is unnatural and therefore frightening.

Paragraphs 3–6: G) A sigh is commonly defined as a sign of fatigue or grief. The driver may sigh because he's tired of having to make this point to passengers. He may also sigh because he believes that the law he invokes is wrong or (more likely) he understands the futility of his efforts to change the minds of passengers who don't automatically move.

5

The short sentences and separate, short paragraphs have an antistrophic effect that makes the exchange adversarial. Tension is enhanced by the repetition of "My mother said, 'No'" and by the lack of information about why she refuses to move.

Paragraph 7: H) The movement into present time distances the reader from the incident and reduces the tension. The reader is drawn away from "what happens next" and is encouraged to ponder why it happened at all. This is the first of many shifts in time as Paley moves back and forth from narrative to commentary. It also establishes Paley herself as a voice in the essay and introduces—and then apparently rejects—authorial "invention" or imagination as an influence on her account of this true story. Of course, this intrusion of the present reminds the reader that the story's truth is determined by the author's invention. I) In Paley's imagination, her mother might have found bland excuses to account for her refusal to move and might perhaps have smoothed over the situation. Paley's mother remained silent (like everyone else on the bus) perhaps because her real reasons for refusing to move were too complex to articulate in that setting, because, despite her determination, she was too frightened to speak, or (as Paley suggests) because she wouldn't stoop to "pretend innocence" with the driver.

Paragraph 8: J) Again, Paley wants to deflect our attention away from the bus story. Having established her mother's act of heroism, she wants to move quickly to the juxtaposition with her brother's response to a comparable situation in Paragraph 9. "Somehow" thus serves to dismiss the outcome of the story as not being worth our attention. It is her mother's decision that matters (as well as the manner of her action), not the reactions of her audience. K) Paley is establishing a parallel between her family and the dark people in the back of the bus: both are outside the mainstream group. Presumably, in their own minds, the Paleys aren't wholly "American." (It's not clear whether they could "pass for" Americans if they chose to.) This background information helps us to understand why Mrs. Paley refused to move.

Paragraph 9: L) 1. The present: Vic remembering; 2. The 1920s: punching the Negro; 3. The present: Vic understanding his youthful reactions; 4. The 1940s: black soldiers degraded. In a short space, Paley has introduced two more instances of discrimination against blacks, has allowed the person who observed those acts to reflect upon his reactions (specifically—in contrast to his mother—his non-intervention), and has confirmed that the Paleys are themselves outsiders—Jewish—making the impulse to intervene on behalf of those even lower in caste both natural and unwise. M) In contrast to the bus, the punching incident is not an example of organized discrimination: the fight is one-on-one, possibly impulsive. Vic seems to be reacting more to the violence than to the fact that the "victim" is a Negro. Vic also thinks it's important to assimilate into this strange world although he doesn't seem to succeed in doing so. When he encounters discrimination on a larger, more mechanized scale during the war, he has much the same horrified reaction, with an added component of shame: because it is public policy that governs the seating of the soldiers, Vic himself is implicated as a participant in discrimination.

Paragraph 10: N) This time, Paley herself is the source of the memory so she can reliably include descriptive details. This incident is the longest in the essay (comprising more than half), and Paley begins her account with what she imagined she would see (and probably did see) when at last she met her husband.

Paragraph 11: O) Again, in contrast to the first bus episode, this detail humanizes and adds to the immediacy of the story. Paley's focus is about to shift to what becomes an almost personal relationship between herself and the colored woman with the baby. In contrast with the strength shown by her mother in the Richmond bus, Paley herself seems warm and vulnerable, and her subsequent actions more difficult and complex.

Paragraph 12:   P) "Reorganization" is a mechanical process resulting from an individual or collective decision; it can be modified or reversed. A "tide" is an act of nature, inevitable, irreversible. Q) "Not thinking" means that Paley acted from instinct and feeling, innocently, passively. "Refusing to think" implies that Paley *chose* to disregard the possible consequences of her action, which assumes that (to some extent) she knew what those consequences were. R) On the bus, Mrs. Paley knowingly chose to defy a discriminatory law. At the fight, Vic was horrified yet made no protest. Observing the soldiers relegated to the back of the transport, Vic was ashamed but made no protest. Seeing the tired mother, Paley acts, possibly by instinct, possibly by choice.

Paragraphs 13–14:   S) No. The white man is only a reminder of the "invisible absolute racial border" that already exists by virtue of the organization of the seats. (Of course, the fact that Paley is sitting in the last white row makes the border slightly more permeable.) T) Initially, the words describing the baby are oppressive ones: he is "large," "heav[y]," and a "burden." He hangs "mercilessly," "pulling her head down." On the other hand, when Paley holds the child, his is a "nice weight" and, twice, she describes the way she adjusts her body to accept that weight. The older Paley, now a mother, recognizes that she was impelled by the fellow feeling—the burden and pleasure of maternity—shared by all women. U) Both phrases are fleeting references to the larger world outside the specific situation in the bus. When World War II ends (and it is worth noting that this was a war fought, in part, as a response to the oppression of a minority population), Paley and others will be able to carry on their normal lives. On the other hand, as Paley the writer knows, discrimination in the South will continue, fuelled by the racism displayed by the white man on the bus. So, her younger self's pleasure in warm maternity is compromised by the fear that the soulless mechanism of bigotry—"ice"—will persist and triumph.
V) Paley has courage enough to hold the baby and stare at her adversary, but she cannot, sensibly, do any more. She avoids the mother's eyes because she is ashamed of the need for both of them to acquiesce.

Paragraph 15:   W) Since, fifty years on, Paley can hold her own black grandson without fear, there has been some progress. (We are not, however, told whether she is doing so in public or in private.) Because of actions like her mother's refusal to move and her own earlier gesture of kindness toward the young mother, the world hasn't yet ended in ice. Paley is building a metaphor to describe the future generation: although still confined to the yard, her grandson can already move freely and so will gain confidence. Although "experienced caution" will still be necessary when this child becomes a man, he will not (unlike his grandmother, great-grandmother, and great-uncle) be restrained or cowed by prejudice.

Paragraph 16:   X) Paley is again providing a larger context for perceiving the insidious power of discrimination. Without attempting to compare the evils of racism versus anti-Semitism, she reminds us that her family was interested primarily in its own struggle with prejudice. As she describes it, this seems understandable insularity. But their awareness of and experience with anti-Semitism does help to explain the actions and nonactions of all three Paleys. Y) That sentence explains the complex layers of this essay: the shifts in time, the many parallel episodes. Paley has shown us that all experience—active or passive, immediate or at secondhand—contributes to moral growth. This is as much an essay about the character of the Paley family as it is about discrimination in the South.

Paragraphs 17–19:   Z) Paley is reminding us that so much of what we learn is secondhand, through stories, true and fictional. It doesn't matter whether we remember accurately or forget; the experience and "information" that accrues within a family "forms" our understanding of the world, whether we realize it at the time or not.

Paragraph 19:   AA) Like her brother, Paley is now, fifty years later, linking together what happened to her on the bus with the person she has become. (Note: It's not clear which incident is "that day" for Vic: the bus ride, which he only heard about, or the fight.) BB) Paley's subject is people, not issues. She uses issues to illuminate the way in which people act, learn, and grow. The acts of discrimination described on the two bus trips are trigger-points for Paley's (and, to a lesser extent, Vic's) self-realization, most of which takes place long after the actual public events.

Paragraph 20:   CC) Travelling occurs in this essay on several levels: literally, travelling on the bus; travelling through life and gaining self-knowledge and wisdom; travelling through memory and discovering what half-forgotten "information" has been influential. Because one doesn't learn and remember in a straightforward, linear way, the force of the essay would be diminished by a strictly chronological sequence. Paley makes her form express her meaning.

*Exercise 3: Drawing Inferences (p. 23)
This is an optional exercise, intended for classes that, collectively or individually, tend to jump to conclusions.

1. Implied	4. Implied	7. Inferred
2. Inferred	5. False	8. False
3. True	6. Implied	9. Inferred

*Exercise 4: Outlining an Essay (p. 43)
This essay, by Carl Singleton, is not especially complex in its thinking, but resembles Blanche Blank's in that some important points are grouped together and embedded within paragraphs, while other points are developed at length in a sequence of paragraphs. A good outline will be brief, but will extract the key points.

Thesis: Carl Singleton argues that the decline in American education can be reversed only if schools uphold standards of learning by failing those students who cannot meet those standards.

Outline

I.   Problem: recent decline in American education
    A. Possible causes
        1. teachers underpaid
        2. prospective teachers not screened
        3. basic skills need more emphasis
        4. inadequate grading standards = real cause of problem

II.   Wrong Solution: maintain present tolerant grading system: accept the fact that many students try hard but cannot meet standards; adjust grading system
    A. Consequences
        1. passing grades given even if students have learned nothing
        2. more and more high school graduates are illiterate
        3. more and more college freshmen need remediation

II.   Right Solution: maintain consistent standards by failing students who cannot do the work.
    A. Consequences
        1. parents made more responsible for improving their children's performance in school
        2. principals, school boards, voters provide financial support for programs to help students pass their courses

3. teachers encouraged to help their students learn enough to pass to the next grade
4. high school graduates will be minimally illiterate

Summary (p. 43)

Although summary, like quotation and paraphrase, is a skill used in presenting sources, I have placed it at the end of the "comprehension" chapter because it seems to be the ultimate test of the student's ability to understand a reading and to express that understanding in general terms. Most students will benefit from constructing summarizing sentences for a few of the paragraphs in Exercise 5, and from writing a brief summary for Exercise 6 or for one of the passages in Assignment 1. All of the exercises may be done in class (in groups, if you prefer) or as homework.

For Assignment 1, you can ask your students to choose their own articles for summary, but then you will have to read each one and do a rapid mental summary. Instead, you might ask each student to submit an article to you, review the topics with your class, and have them choose from the two or three that most appeal to their interests.

*Exercise 5: Summarizing a Paragraph (p. 46)

Remember that most students will try to cram an enormous number of words into the limiting structure of a single sentence and that their summaries are likely to be run-on sentences. You may want to explain why a run-on, however innocently intended, must in this context be regarded as "cheating."

1. *Mead:* (C) Here is Mead's topic sentence, deleted from the paragraph for the purposes of this exercise: "A neurotic person can be most simply described as someone who, while he was growing up, learned ways of behaving that are self-defeating in his society." Without this topic sentence, the paragraph is just a string of examples. It's worth pointing out that Mead's sentence doesn't quite cover the material she has included, for it doesn't reflect the idea that all neurotic people reached that state as a result of external circumstances, outside of their control.

2. *Ryan:* (C) The gist of the paragraph is really conveyed in the first sentence: "The generic process of Blaming the Victim is applied to almost every American problem." But since Ryan explores the plight of the poor in an extended example, the topic sentence should summarize his entire point: "Typical of the American tendency to blame the victim, we attribute the problems of the poor to their own deficiencies of character and culture." Although the summarizing sentence is in active mode, Ryan's paragraph is mostly passive: "is explained away," "is easily overlooked," "are traced"—all avoid the issue of who, actually, is doing the blaming. Note, also, the use of quotation marks to further distance Ryan from the people making these claims. Quotation marks as a distancing device are discussed in the early sections of Chapter 2.

3. *Cose:* (B) The last sentence is the nucleus of a good summary; it needs to be combined with the third sentence: "We can theoretically create races at will, choosing a distinguishing characteristic such as red hair, but all we would prove is that human beings have the power to define a race—not that the classification has any value or makes any sense." The inclusion of the example (red hair) in the summary isn't crucial (as was the example of the poor in the previous paragraph).

4. *Henry:* (C) The only abstract sentence in the paragraph—"Every bit of plain speaking offends someone these days"—isn't adequate to convey Henry's point. He is objecting not only to the devaluation of plain speaking, but also (as the title of his book suggests) to the leveling, egalitarian belief that there is no such thing as abnormality and that deficiencies do not exist. "Using euphemistic language to spare the sensitivities of the men-

tally and physically impaired removes the distinction between normal and abnormal capacity and behavior and thus distorts the truth." This paragraph should spark some intense class discussion and might serve as an alternative topic for the argument essay (Assignment 4, p. 135).

5. *Williams:* (A) The last sentence of the paragraph looks and sounds like a summarizing sentence, and—with the addition of one word—it is: "The media, for better and frequently for worse, constitute one of the major forces in the propagandistic shaping of our national vision, a chief architect of the modern American sense of identity." Unless you indicate that the media have their own message to deliver, the summary is too neutral.

Note: You may have noticed that these summaries did not include the author's name. In the context of this exercise, the summarizing sentences were really serving as topic sentences for the paragraphs, which would have made the names intrusive. If you include these suggested summaries in your discussion, by all means add "According to Ellis Cose," or "Margaret Mead describes a neurotic person as someone . . ."

Exercise 6: Summarizing an Article (p. 52)

Summary: To protect students from the gang culture symbolized by baggy and sloppy clothes, the Long Beach School District now requires all elementary and middle school students to wear conventional clothes in standard black/navy and white. While opponents argue that such uniformity stifles students' freedom of expression, the majority of parents believe that the purpose of school is to encourage learning, not the expression of individuality. Which is more important: the right to self-expression and, additionally, the right to distinguish easily between "good" students and "bad" gang members by their clothes, or the right to protection from gang members whose clothes would otherwise express an intimidating form of individuality?

This story is definitely weighted in favor of the School Board's decision to require uniforms. Most of the information is presented from the Board's point of view (which seems reasonable since that's the prevalent view). The article carefully details those provisions that anticipate and satisfy issues raised by civil liberties proponents. (Interestingly, it's not made clear what kind of "good reason" would allow a family to have the rule waived.) Since the ostensible purpose of the rule is to prevent gang intimidation, it's also worth noting that nothing is said about the diminished presence of gangs in post-uniform schools. Still, given the tenor of the article, a good summary should focus on the individuality versus uniformity argument with some stress on the latter.

ASSIGNMENT 1: Summarizing an Essay (p. 60)

For the two readings in this assignment, here is a brief list of key points that would go into the construction of a summary:

Easterbrook:

Note: This argument is very easy to follow, as Easterbrook elaborates it in small increments. The new points are clearly signalled with strong topic sentences, and the examples are crisp and not at all technical. Students with an interest in environmental issues may want to do research on this topic. Note that Point 5 is a reiteration of Point 1, this time as a thesis statement.

1. Despite the protestations of environmentalists, nature does far more harm to people and to the planet than human beings ever do. Yet we have been encouraged to regard artificially-caused disasters as alarming events to be avoided at all costs while so-called acts of God are treated as unfortunate but natural happenings that require no intervention.

2. Environmentalists believe that the Earth in its natural state, untouched by humankind, would be an ideal world, and so they condemn those who point out its flaws. But they are wrong, for the natural order is far too complex to be perfect. Plants can produce toxic substances that cause cancer; animals kill each other with ruthless savagery.

3. Because they have such an idealized view of nature, environmentalists believe that humans should do nothing at all to alter its course. While our lack of knowledge makes thoughtless interference unwise, Earth's ecology is always changing, and we may be able to encourage its evolution.

4. One belief held by environmentalists committed to "deep ecology" is that all things found in nature have equal value and importance, that humans have no ascendancy over animals or plants, and that living things have no ascendancy over inanimate forms of nature like rocks. But in a universe without a structure of moral values, humans, like animals, would be justified in killing each other for survival, and it would even be normal and appropriate for people to die in floods or avalanches or volcanic eruptions since these are expressions of nature.

5. Since the consequences of natural disasters are far more lethal (to plants and animals as well as to humans) than the consequences of human-made catastrophes, we should not be galvanized into action over a potential Bhopal or Chernobyl and yet accept as inevitable the harm to humans and nature that results yearly from phenomena like earthquakes and tidal waves.

Tabor and Gallagher:

Note: This passage is highly repetitive, and so the points for summary are few in proportion to the length of the text. Pro-cult in their arguments, the authors offer few supportive examples. Given the difficulty of this abstract prose, you may want to discuss the passage before assigning the summary and/or have your students, in groups, compare their own summaries and determine what points should be included.

1. What frightens many Americans about cults is the strong and serious commitment of members to a radically different perception of the world. Especially alarming is the aberrant style of life typical of cults, which (abandoning orthodox views of family, sex, and marriage) is based on shared affinities and commitment to the cult and its leader.

2. In fact, much of the hostility toward cults springs from fear of the unknown. However concerned they may be about the fate of individual cult members, opponents are also worried about the threat to their own complacent lives posed by the cults' insistence on self-scrutiny. That is why they tend to depict cult members as zombie-like pawns, who reject freedom of choice and "normal" behavior and are totally controlled by the will of their leader.

3. The belief that Americans have always shared a common set of moral values is a convenient fiction embraced by anticultists. Far from threatening an exemplary American way of life, cults exist and thrive only because there are significant deficiencies in our moral and social structure. Yet those hostile to cults remain defensive, unable to acknowledge our nation's problems and unwilling to believe that cults might offer new, if radical solutions.

4. Unlike their detractors, cults are not eager to force outsiders to conform to their beliefs. Self-selected, members pursue a way of life that, by their religious standards, is too pure and far too rigorous for any but the elect.

5. Of course, some cults are dangerous, and some people are harmed, materially and psychologically, by the experience. But everyone faces risks in life, whether a cult member or not.

6. The authoritarian environment opposed to cults is potentially repressive to any person or group expressing unconventional beliefs. Unless, by every standard, it's clear that a cult is engaged in illegal activity or is injurious to all its members, then those members must be allowed the freedom to choose their way of life, whether or not it challenges ours, or else the United States will have forsaken the Constitution's commitment to tolerance, diversity, and democracy.

CHAPTER 2: PRESENTING SOURCES TO OTHERS

Quoting: (p. 73)

While you may simply regard this explanation of the rules of quotation as a resource section, I recommend that you go over the more complex points with your students and ask them to do at least Exercise 7 and Exercise 9. Before assigning Exercise 7, you may wish to give your class some dictation, to find out whether they are sufficiently familiar with the rules of punctuating quotations to visualize them. Try reading aloud the following sentences, asking your class to copy them down, inserting quotation marks and appropriate punctuation and capitalization.

1. Professor Smith announced that the test would be "easy."
2. Professor Smith announced: "The test will be easy."
3. The trapeze artist shouted, "Watch out! I'm falling!"
4. "I am quite sure," my aunt declared, "that you will be the death of me."
5. Do you know who said, "Give me liberty or give me death"?

Exercise 7A: Quoting Correctly (p. 84)

1. The *Chicago Times* asserted in 1861 that "it is a newspaper's duty to print the news and raise hell."
2. Baron de Montesquieu, a philosopher of the nineteenth-century Enlightenment, sympathized with the needs of the masses: "The real wants of the people," he wrote, "ought never to give way to the imaginary wants of the state."
3. In Proust's view, "everybody calls 'clear' those ideas which have the same degree of confusion as his own."
4. Thoreau warned his readers to "beware of all enterprises that require new clothes."
5. Robert F. Wagner, former Mayor of New York, believed in keeping a low profile and offered this advice: "When in danger, ponder; when in trouble, delegate; when in doubt, mumble."
6. "Beggars should be abolished," said Friedrich Nietzsche. "It annoys one to give to them and it annoys one not to give to them."
7. "Have you anything to declare?" said the customs official. "No," replied Oscar Wilde. "I have nothing to declare," he paused, "except my genius."
8. Before the Revolutionary War, Patrick Henry made a passionate speech: "Is life so dear or peace so sweet, as to be purchased at the price of chains and slavery? Forbid it, Almighty God! I know not what course others may take, but as for me, give me liberty or give me death!"

Exercise 7B: Quoting Correctly (p. 85)

In correcting the second part of this exercise, besides looking for technical errors of punctuation and awkward phrasing, you should also check for accurate transcription of the quotation and thus begin a campaign against sloppy transcription of sentences. Also check to see whether quotations have been chosen that are appropriate for separated or integrated presentation: quotations beginning with "I" are best separated by punctuation from the citation (Sentences 1, 2, 3, and 7). In the third part of the assignment, the interrupted quotation, you will probably notice that a few students have mangled the original statement by breaking into it at the wrong place. Notice also that only Sentences 2, 6, and 7 can be effectively interrupted, and that because of parallelism, there is really no single natural break in Sentence 5. Finally—a point covered later in the chapter—the name of the source should be complete and should be properly spelled.

Exercise 8: Using Ellipses and Brackets in Quotations (p. 91)

A. Ellipses can be inserted in all the quotations:

1. "Man . . . is simply the most formidable of all the beasts of prey . . ."
2. Delete the middle sentence and/or delete the second half of the first sentence.
3. Delete "and, exactly for this reason."
4. Delete the first clause of the second sentence (and "but"), or delete the last clause of the second sentence (not a good choice).
5. Any deletion spoils Kennedy's rhetoric, but it is certainly possible to delete the second and third sentences, or the "winds and waters and fear" in the fourth.
6. The second and/or third sentences can easily be deleted (but not the last).

B. Brackets can be used in all the quotations but one:

1. "[Man] is the only [beast of prey] that preys systematically on its own species."
2. "[Exercise] can never be of any benefit when you are tired, and I am always tired."
4. "Perhaps two-thirds of the people of the earth might be killed [in an atomic war], but enough men . . ."
5. "[Unconditional war] can no longer serve to settle disputes."
6. "[Debates] are dreadful things indeed." Or "[My ideas] have not changed since I was four or five."

Note: Sentences 1 and 6 are the best choices since the substitutions won't materially interfere with the authors' style.

Exercise 9: Integrating Quotations into a Paragraph (p. 97)

This exercise simulates precisely the same kind of choices that students must make when they are preparing quotations for research essays; for that reason, it is well worth assigning. The student must first choose the appropriate quotations and then integrate them into the paragraph; both operations are equally important. You may want to ask your students to work on this exercise, individually, in class, with general discussion immediately afterward, so that the choices are fresh in their minds and your commentary will seem meaningful to them.

The most suitable sentence for quotation is the third in the second paragraph (after the semicolon), which fits into the student paragraph right after the third sentence. The idea of a "contract with Fate" is just about the only point in the source that's worth quoting; it would be very difficult for students to paraphrase. Here's how the quotation would be introduced: . . . get rich through gambling. A gambler's winnings "are a down payment. . . ." It is true that the contract with Fate is also mentioned in the first sentence of the first paragraph, but the topic there is really persistence, which is not the major issue. (The first two sentences really ought to be quoted together, if at all.) Some students may be attracted to the first sentence of the second paragraph, which deals with the "pathologic optimism" of the true gambler. You might point out that this sentence is the exact repetition of the second and third sentences of the student paragraph; nothing new is added, and there is no point in inserting a repetitive quotation.

13

#Assignment 2: Writing a Paragraph that Includes a Quotation (p. 97)

This optional assignment is useful as a test of understanding and an opportunity to develop a "real" paragraph during a long stretch of technical exercises. It can easily be begun (and completed) during class as students ask each other for suitable quotations. Most of the class will probably handle the integration of quotation adequately; but the exercise is worth doing if only because many students who understand the rules quite well will nevertheless make careless errors. It can be helpful to them to have the errors pointed out this early in the process. By all means introduce a new set of interview questions, or have your class develop their own.

Exercise 10: Identifying Plagiarism (p. 99)

Exercise 10 is an excellent way of convincing your students that the disadvantages of plagiarism outweigh the advantages. Examining one of these two paragraphs always elicits a strong and vocal reaction. Once they have assumed the teacher's role and discovered the plagiarized sentences, students rarely feel much sympathy for the plagiarizer. For this exercise to have impact, it must be done in class, unannounced, with each passage read aloud, so that students can concentrate on style and hear for themselves the shift of voices.

An obvious way of distinguishing students' segments from plagiarized, professional portions is the length of sentences: the student writing is brief and relatively plain; the professional work uses more complex sentence structure and tends to be baroque, both in structure and vocabulary. Point out that the diction of the professional writing is much more abstract. Clearly, the student authors of these paragraphs could not cope with paraphrasing the language of these generalizations, and therefore retained it verbatim. (Both essays were footnoted in their original form; neither, however, contained quotation marks.) It is the undigested quality of the plagiarized sentences which signifies that the writers haven't fully assimilated the information that they are presenting. Difficult concepts are baldly inserted without commentary or explanation. Of course, there is a stronger temptation to quote abstractions than to quote straightforward information. What your students must do at this point is to recognize the necessity of using quotation marks—or attempting to paraphrase.

First paragraph (Beatles):
plagiarized sentences are 3, 7, and 11.
Second paragraph (Minstrelsy):
plagiarized sentences are 3 and 6.

Paraphrasing: (p. 99)

Although practice in paraphrase can be tedious, I suggest that you spend part of two or three classes discussing paraphrase and working on the exercises in this section. For most students, paraphrase is the most unfamiliar of the "presentation" skills, yet academic writing calls for the ability to express someone else's ideas clearly and easily. Teaching paraphrase tends to resemble teaching a foreign language; in effect, one keeps urging the students to translate sentences that often seem to be written in a strange tongue. Because of the tendency to "translate" word for word—and to create gibberish—I have suggested a two-part process [literal and free paraphrase]. You can reinforce this lesson by reminding your students to use their own sentence structure and to avoid synonym substitution. Since comparing a paraphrase with its original text can be slow and picky work even for an experienced researcher, I suggest that you spend some time with your class going over the Machiavelli and Lasch models (pp. 103–8) before you assign Exercise 11.

*Exercise 11: Identifying a Good Paraphrase (p. 109)

This passage is difficult because it depends on several standard abstractions so loaded with meaning that they are hard to paraphrase. A good paraphrase would have to present, straightforwardly, Rieff's thoughts on egalitarianism versus hierarchy (the contrasting poles of the first paragraph) and multiculturalism harnessed to capitalism (the concept underlying the second paragraph). If the paraphraser doesn't think about what these abstractions mean and make an effort to express them (and Rieff does provide considerable assistance), then the paraphrase won't make sense. All three of these paraphrases tend to summarize, rather than paraphrase, the passage. On the other hand, Rieff's style is casual and diffuse and the prose certainly doesn't merit phrase-by-phrase preservation.

#1 has a good knack for summary: "the old-fashioned view of art means that some works are better than others" goes quite a way to capture a significant point of the first paragraph; but it doesn't convey any of the interplay between quality and equality that embellishes Rieff's idea. Key terms are hardly mentioned, let alone explained: "anti-democratic," "quality," "anti-egalitarian," "hierarchy." Similarly, the second paragraph—especially the second sentence—provides an excellent crude summary of the production of art in economic terms, as Rieff describes it, but on the capitalist level only; the paraphrase hardly mentions multiculturalism and its subversion, which (as the essay's title suggests) is crucial to Rieff's point. #1 tries to capture the essence of the passage without conveying any of its development, and that hit-or-miss technique can lapse into guessing. "The multiculturalists are in command—sort of—of a couple of truths" can hardly be boiled down to "in some ways the multiculturalists are right." The latter suggests Rieff's agreement with the multiculturalists, rather than conveying the extent to which he is distancing himself from their views. Still, this is an honest effort, with some good phrase-making, and deserves a B+.

#2 also avoids expressing abstractions. For example, the reasons for the multiculturalists' aversion to quality—which Rieff spells out—are totally ignored. Most of the time, #2 is guessing at the meaning, misunderstanding key words and rearranging them into new sentences that fail to convey Rieff's meaning: "Western art has *excluded* many things" becomes "high quality art . . . is too *exclusive*" for the multiculturalists. There is a serious misreading in the confusion over objective and subjective views of art: Rieff is not saying that it's better "to look at art objectively, not subjectively"; he is suggesting that the appreciation of art requires both. #2 hasn't really grasped the distinction between traditionalists and multiculturalists, nor does she realize that Rieff is refusing to identify with either camp. Relying on the ex cathedra "it is better," #2 projects extreme views into Rieff's relatively neutral analysis. Again, in the last sentence of Paragraph 1, #2 is pasting together words (but here we may have some sympathy for her since Rieff has tacked on "liberation" as a kind of throwaway dart aimed at the multiculturalists without really integrating it into his paragraph). In the second paragraph, #2 continues to project a judgmental tone into the paraphrase ("they're wrong"). Note how #2's "art is all alike, whatever you produce" is a debased version of #1's "if one work of art is as good as the next, then they're interchangeable." Here, #1 is more successful because he grasps the cause-and-effect (no value, so no difference) and uses the conditional to express it, while #2 sticks with the hectoring declarative. Finally, after much guessing, projecting, and misreading, #2 produces an acceptable paraphrase in the last sentence. That, however, isn't enough to merit more than a C-.

Of these three paraphrases, only #3 tackles the difficult abstractions and does her best to explain "quality," "egalitarianism," and "hierarchy." In the process, she initially abandons Rieff's objective tone and writes as if she were, indeed, a multiculturalist (which may be projecting her own views into the text or—given her neutral tone in the second paragraph—may just be simplifying a difficult text). As a result, Rieff's point about objectivity and subjectivity—traditionalists think both standards and personal reactions are needed to judge art—is reduced to the highly partisan: objectivity becomes "the standard of the ruling group of white males" which won't allow any subjectivity ("the feelings of those who look at the picture"). But at least #3 is struggling to understand what Rieff is talking about. And the paraphrase of the second paragraph is very good. The second sentence in particular covers a lot of ground accurately. Altogether, this gets an A.

Your students may observe (in this as well as the summary exercises) that successful writing from sources tends to use long, complex sentences while poor work relies on short, simple sentences with few connectives. They may ask, is longer better? A paraphrase should represent the source's complexity as completely as possible and, usually, to convey the relationship between ideas, one ends up using dependent clauses and participial phrases. But you might point out that short sentences can also convey an author's meaning—parts of paraphrase 1 attest to that—and that a "free" paraphrase doesn't have to echo the rhythms or even the sequence of the original text. #1's problem was the paucity of his sentences, not their length.

Note: This exercise and Assignment 3 make excellent group activities. Those who are slow to catch on will benefit from the informal discussion with group members who have wider vocabularies. Knowledgeable students will enjoy having a sounding board, and all will find it easier to express themselves outside formal class discussion. The collective effort and responsibility will probably produce a more thorough analysis for general class discussion later.

*Assignment 3: Paraphrasing a Difficult Passage (p. 113)

You may want to limit the choice in this section to two, rather than giving the class all four passages to choose from. Correcting paraphrases becomes much simpler when the wording is more or less in your head. In my experience, it is less tedious to grade an entire set paraphrasing the same passage than to master a group of readings in order to correct only a few versions of each one. It is also easier to have a basis for comparison when you have a dozen paraphrases to choose from. Finally, when you return the paraphrases, the class discussion will make much more sense if a substantial number of students have actually worked on the same text.

On the other hand, allowing each student to locate a passage for paraphrase would undoubtedly add to the interest for the student and for you. If you have any reason to think that prepared paraphrases of these readings may be circulating, then by all means assign some different selections by choosing a few yourself or by asking your class to submit some passages to you and making your selection from that pool. (If you decide to do this, encourage your students to come up with some primary sources that maintain the level of difficulty that they've already been working with. Or you might ask for difficult articles from recent periodicals in order to avoid receiving paraphrases that were submitted to—and corrected by—one of your colleagues.)

Finally, if you have the time, you may wish to ask your students to submit both a literal and a free paraphrase; it may be interesting to see how each student works out the difficulties, and—assuming that this is not assigned as a group activity—requiring the literal paraphrase would discourage collaboration.

1. *Amidon:* Westerns of the 30's and 40's gave male movie stars the opportunity to develop the role of the prototypical hero, who was capable of extraordinary daring yet had the common touch. Now that the day of the cowboy is over, anyone aspiring to Hollywood superstardom must demonstrate his heroic potential in science fiction films dominated by fancy high-tech equipment. The futuristic setting of films like "Star Wars"

makes it difficult for ordinary moviegoers to identify with heroes in space, however valiant they may be. Movies built around ordinary acts of bravery, pitting the brains and fortitude of a regular guy against an unassailable opponent, are now almost obsolete.

Note: This passage is relatively easy to follow. The difficulty lies in ringing the changes on basic words like "courage" and "hero." The paraphrase is slightly longer than the original (mostly because of the specificity of the third sentence, especially the introduction of the "Star Wars" example).

2. *Brophy:* Until recently, society accepted the fiction that men, unlike women, require more than one sexual partner, and it was prepared to regard men who committed adultery as naughty boys, deserving no more than a slap on the wrist, while severely punishing women who did the same. Today, we understand that assigning two levels of punishment for the same crime is unfair. Instead, by manipulating the law governing divorce, we have made it acceptable for both sexes to have multiple partners—but only one at a time—thus retaining the illusion of monogamy. In fact, under our present law, a man is even permitted to have two wives at the same time: the financially dependent former wife, receiving alimony, and the present titular wife, receiving her husband's sexual favors. In the nations of Islam, where polygamy is the law of the land, it is a man's income that determines how many wives he can have at the same time. In Western countries, where polygamy is officially forbidden but serial monogamy is encouraged, it is also a man's income that determines how many times a man can get married—and divorced.

Note: Brophy's irony makes this paraphrase difficult. The version above presents the text very cautiously, step by step, spelling out what Brophy simply glides past. For example, the comparison in the last sentence is easier to handle if Islam and the West are put into two separate sentences. The need to express concepts like "double standard" makes the paraphrase slightly longer than the original.

3. *Moellenberg:* Giving grades originated as a means of measuring achievement; it was an attempt to find a method that would not depend on the student's background or connections. To make the grading system fair and to avoid private arrangements, the student's skill would have to be judged against an impersonal standard that was established and made known to all concerned long before the testing time. If a fixed standard for achievements couldn't be decided in advance, schools could use a curve, in which the standard would be set by those who wrote the best exam. While a fixed standard for awarding grades is not always a successful one, the reasons for using it remain valid.

Note: The object of doing this paraphrase is to understand the difficulties of translating jargon and to realize that a good translation is much clearer and easier to read than the original.

4. *Wilson:* We don't work just to earn money and pay the bills for ourselves and our children; we work to establish a regular routine that orders our activities and our dealings with other people. People without steady jobs have a double disadvantage: no job and salary, and no structure to shape their lives and provide clear plans and hopes for the future. Going to work gives us a sense of our place in the world and marks the passage of time. At any given point during the work day, we can be found in the office or store or factory, doing our jobs. Without that fixed routine, even our private lives lose shape and meaning. If we work only sporadically or don't work at all, we can't prepare for the future, and careful preparation is absolutely essential for survival in an economy based on accommodating production to the uncertainties of the marketplace.

Note: This passage contains several basic words that are very hard to avoid using: work, planning, economy. The paraphrase finds some substitutes, but at least one ("careful preparation" for "planning") is weaker than the original. You might point out that, sometimes, one is forced to use the same words as the author's, for example "economy," or—the basic word of the text—"work." The language and tone of the paraphrase is far more ordinary than Wilson's more academic prose.

Exercise 12: Distinguishing between Quotation, Paraphrase, Summary, and Commentary (p. 119)

A PROMINENT SCHOLAR'S PLAN FOR THE INNER CITIES DRAWS FIRE

Chris Shea

C   William Julius Wilson, one of the country's most prominent experts on the problems of America's inner cities, came in for some tough criticism at the annual meeting of the American Sociological Association here last month.   1

C   His latest book, *When Work Disappears: The World of the New Urban Poor*, published last fall by Alfred A. Knopf, has been widely and respectfully reviewed. It is the broadest statement yet on America's social ills by the sociologist, who

S   spent most of his career at the University of Chicago before moving to Harvard University last year.   2

S   But in a debate that drew a large crowd—about 400 people in a room intend-

C   ing for two-thirds that number—Dr. Wilson's proposals for helping cities were blasted by Douglas S. Massey, chairman of the University of Pennsylvania's sociology department.   3

S   Dr. Massey did not contest Dr. Wilson's observations about rising unemployment and poverty rates in Chicago ghettos. In some of the neighborhoods he describes in his book, only one in three people over the age of 16 has a job.   4

C   Instead, Dr. Massey took aim at Dr. Wilson's policy proposals, which empha-
S   size strategies to help unskilled workers of all races rather than singling out black workers.   5

S   For example, he has proposed a program modeled on the New Deal's Works Progress Administration, which would give unemployed people such jobs as sweeping streets and picking up garbage.   6

S   Dr. Wilson argues that massive interventions to desegregate cities and expand
P/Q   affirmative action are impractical, given Americans' resistance to race-specific
P   policies. At the meeting, he said he hoped to galvanize "progressives" across racial lines with a race-blind vision of social justice.   7

S   But Dr. Massey said Dr. Wilson was using a double standard in evaluating the feasibility of race-based and class-based solutions.   8

Q   "In essence, Wilson argues that race-based remedies are a political loser," he
P   said. But a W.P.A.–style program is no less pie-in-the-sky, Dr. Massey said, given today's conservative climate.   9

p   And Dr. Wilson is dead wrong, he added, to think he can do an end-run
Q   around the charged issue of race. "It will not be possible to deal with class-based divisions without addressing race-based issues with equal verve," he said. "Putting race on the back burner would leave the field open to those who would undermine the class-based strategies we all think we need, by manipulating racial attitudes that are still there."   10

P   Welfare is a race-neutral program, he pointed out. But editorials about black
Q   "welfare queens," who were said to live large off the dole, helped turn public
P   sentiment against it.   11

P/Q   Cynical conservative operatives could just as easily "racialize" a W.P.A.–style
P   program by caricaturing its beneficiaries as lazy black shirkers in do-nothing jobs, he said.   12

P Q   No solution to the problem of urban poverty, Dr. Massey said, can escape the need for a dismantling of what he called "the system of *de facto* apartheid" in many cities.   13

C/Q   C/Q   In his response, Dr. Wilson shed his usual courtly demeanor. "Massey argues that I have moved away from racial-specific policies," he said, his voice rising to a near shout. "*I do not.* I want to say that categorically: *I do not.*"   14

P C P Q   He said his proposals should be paired with affirmative-action policies that take both class and race into account. And he said he had called for better enforcement of federal housing-discrimination laws. In a pointed allusion to his own political influence, he also noted that the Urban League, a national black civil-rights group, had embraced many of his race-neutral policies. "Now, more than ever, we need broader solutions than we have had in the past," he said.   15

C   In the current issue of *Contemporary Sociology*, Dr. Massey offers some criticisms of Dr. Wilson's research that did not come up in the debate.   16

C C Q P Q   He calls Dr. Wilson's massive research on Chicago ghettos, known as the "Urban Poverty and Family Life Study," "rather a disappointment," arguing that "despite the investment of hundreds of thousands of research dollars," few resulting articles have appeared in refereed social-science journals. "The U.P.F.L. has simply not affected social science in a manner commensurate with its size and scope," he writes.   17

P   In a telephone interview, Dr. Wilson said that aside from his own book, which uses the data, some 20 refereed journal articles and book chapters had emerged from the project, and more books—including one from Marta Tienda, a University of Chicago sociologist—are due soon.   18

Q   After the debate, Dr. Massey said, "I keep pushing Wilson on the issue of race, and he keeps moving slowly and grudgingly toward accepting it, but more in person than in print."   19

C   The audience seemed to agree that frontal attacks on both racial and class issues are necessary, yet pessimism was the dominant mood at the meeting.   20

Q C   "This is rather depressing," one graduate student told the two professors. "It sounds like you are saying we need a sea change in public attitudes for anything to happen." Neither scholar disagreed.   21

Writing in *The Chronicle of Higher Education*, Shea has singled out what must have been a highlight of the American Sociological Association's annual meeting: a debate between William Julius Wilson and Douglas S. Massey—two black scholars—over the best way to deal with inner city poverty. Shea uses summary, paraphrase, and quotation in roughly equal proportion, with most of the summary (as one would expect) placed at the beginning of the article, to establish the issues. He also provides his own comments at strategic places.

To a surprising extent (given the *Chronicle*'s reputation as the newspaper of record for higher education), Shea uses the standard tools of summary, paraphrase, and quotation to manipulate his presentation of information. As his title—"A Prominent Scholar's Plan for the Inner Cities Draws Fire"—suggests, the article is more concerned with Massey's criticism of Wilson's proposals than the proposals themselves. Of the article's 21 paragraphs, 3 (at beginning and end) provide a contextual framework, 8 deal wholly or partly with Wilson, and 10 are concerned with Massey's attack on Wilson. Since this is not a straightforward narrative of the debate, it's hard to determine how well the antagonists were matched. But the selection and arrangement of information in the article, reinforced by Shea's occasional comments, definitely puts Wilson on the defensive.

There is a striking contrast between Shea's initial presentation of Wilson as a distinguished scholar in his field and the subsequent presentation of his work exclusively in terms of Massey's attack. (Massey is described only as chair of his department; no reference is made to his reputation as a sociologist.) In order to determine whether Massey's criticism is merited, we would expect to find a substantial summary of Wilson's work, presented in neutral terms, early in the article. But the summary contained in paragraphs 3–7 is embedded in negative commentary that influences the reader's perception of the debate: "Dr. Wilson's proposals . . . were blasted by Douglas S. Massey"; "Dr. Massey did not contest Dr. Wilson's observations"; "Dr. Massey took aim at Dr. Wilson's policy proposals." Thus, it is Massey's voice that appears to control the presentation of Wilson's ideas.

The chief point at issue between the two is summarized briefly in paragraph 7: a solution to inner city problems can only emerge from the efforts of the entire community to institute programs that benefit all races, not just blacks. This is the only one of Wilson's points that Shea paraphrases (last sentence). It is unclear why Shea quotes just one word: "progressives." Since this word conveys Wilson's belief that some Americans do have a social conscience, Shea may be identifying a point that is evidently anathema to Massey.

Massey's objections are presented in a six-paragraph sequence that begins with one sentence of summary (8) and continues in a combination of paraphrase and quotation. In contrast to his cursory summary of Wilson's ideas, Shea includes three full-sentence quotations from Massey's presentation, as well as several shorter quoted phrases. It's hard to find a reason for these quotations (9, 10); the language is the jargon of the social sciences, neither clearer nor more vivid than Shea's own style of paraphrase. Shea uses quotation marks to disassociate himself from some of Massey's loaded phrases, such as "welfare queens" and "the system of *de facto* apartheid." What is notable here is that Shea offers no comment whatsoever on Massey's demeanor or the quality of his ideas. He does not, for example, point out that Massey is putting forth no proposals of his own, just chipping away at Wilson's. In contrast, he begins his presentation of Wilson's rebuttal by depicting Wilson at a loss—"Dr. Wilson shed his usual courtly demeanor"—and quoting his defensive denial—"*I do not. I want to say that categorically: I do not.*" Shea also chooses to include a comment on Wilson's "pointed allusion to his own political influence."

The second exchange between Wilson and Massey, on the effectiveness of Wilson's research, shows the same lack of balance in the tools of its presentation. Massey's doubts about Wilson's influence are paraphrased in a paragraph that includes two extended quotations (17); Wilson's telephone interview is reduced to a single paraphrased sentence (18). Similarly, Shea gives Massey the penultimate word in this debate, quoting a statement (hard to paraphrase) concerned with Wilson's character, not his ideas, that depicts him as a drudge, dim and resentful, who will one day acknowledge that he is wrong and Massey right.

And yet, by devoting his final paragraphs to the disillusionment of the spectators at this debate, Shea does put the petty squabble he has been describing back into a broader context. One is left wondering why his account was not more even-handed throughout the article.

CHAPTER 3: THE SINGLE-SOURCE ESSAY

Two approaches to writing a single-source essay are presented in this chapter. Both are useful for classes needing practice in interpreting and presenting a source's ideas. The first stresses argumentation; the second strategies for developing a topic independent of the source. Although both are followed by suggested readings, you can easily substitute selections of your own or use one of the readings in Appendix E. Throughout this chapter, as in the rest of the book, I suggest that you ask students to hand in their preliminary notes along with their final drafts so that you can see how well they have followed the recommended methods and so that you can deter would-be plagiarists.

Arguing against Your Source: (p. 127)

The discussion of Sipher's article builds on the comprehension skills that were discussed in the first section of Chapter 1. You may want immediately to remind your class of the questions that they used to gain an understanding of Blank and Paley in Chapter 1, and ask them to follow a similar approach in preparing the Singleton, Bork, Henry, or Strossen articles in this section. I would remind them to ask "Why?" as each new point arises. Students sometimes feel the temptation to agree or disagree, to approve or disapprove, without analyzing the arguments on both sides. To forestall that tendency, I would spend ten or fifteen minutes going over the five student responses to Sipher (pp. 131–34) and reinforce the text's explanation of their deficiencies. Sipher is a particularly accessible reading, and, after initially embracing attendance or nonattendance, students should find it relatively easy to appreciate both sides of the argument. It is not imperative that the student disagree with the author. Argumentation is simply the most clear-cut method of distinguishing between source and self and thus particularly suited to beginners. By all means ask your class to summarize, analyze, and then *support* one of the readings, but make it clear that "support" means supply additional arguments, not just repeat the summary.

Assignment 4: Writing an Argument Based on a Single Source (p. 135)

Singleton: This essay contains arguments that are complementary to Sipher's. Both believe that education—and the grade index and diploma, the visible tokens of education—should be reserved for those who have demonstrated their worthiness. In effect, the failing grade is a punishment for the lazy and the inept. Your students may wish to argue that many of their contemporaries, who are neither lazy nor inept, are nevertheless unable to master the work. This in turn leads to the Roger Sipher (and Blanche Blank) argument: some students are not educable and should not be forced to remain in school or college. In a way, Singleton is extending Sipher's point: If you force students to stay in school, providing no socially acceptable means of egress, and if you insist on maintaining high standards, then many students will be sentenced to an endless punishment of failing grades. The underlying question is, Whose interests is our educational system intended to serve? Society's—which would justify maintaining a high standard of excellence while effectively dooming the underachievers? Or the individual student's—which would encourage double, triple, and quadruple standards of achievement, so that all students could receive recognition for having fulfilled their potential?

Bork: The context for this justification of censorship is Judge Bork's profound distrust of democracy and, indeed, human nature. The penultimate sentence of the essay best conveys his pessimism: "unconstrained human nature will seek degeneracy often enough to create a disorderly, hedonistic, and dangerous society." Bork's overall thesis: if we are to preserve a viable social order based on democratic government, then we must limit access to extreme depictions of sexual activity (i.e. pornography) and violence in the arts and in the media. Embedded in the essay is a syllogism expressing (what Bork believes are) commonly held assumptions.

1. To be successful, democracy requires a moral society.
2. Morality is debased by exposure to uncensored sex and violence.
3. Therefore, in the interests of its survival, a democracy must censor the availability of sexual and violent material.

In his presentation of the two premises, Bork is essentially *begging the question*. He does not consider whether there have been societies where democracy flourished (or at least made progress—one thinks of eighteenth-century England) despite brutal conditions of existence for a substantial portion of the population. Nor does he look for additional reasons (other than exposure to sex and violence) that might account for a decline in morality. Finally, he ignores the emotional consequences of unlimited access to brutalizing images, limiting his concern to the debasement of the "mental faculties" essential for debating ideas. In so doing, he does not consider the many statesmen who have been as famous for their vices as for their brilliant command of rhetoric.

Through much of the essay, Bork is handicapped by his initial coupling of sex and violence. He gets far more mileage out of the latter threat, pointing with some effect to random, motiveless killings and convicted murderers who show no remorse. He cites inductive evidence, citing studies that find "positive but relatively small" correlations between media violence and actual cases of violence (11). The chief study cited concludes that the murder rate increased after TV sets became common in American homes. Here is an example of *post hoc propter ergo hoc*. If this is true (and, in recent years, the rate of crime in inner cities has markedly decreased even though time in front of the TV set has increased), are there other factors that might cause such a tendency to criminality? exposure to the wonders of commercial goods? lack of education? lack of compulsory military service? lack of exercise? Bork, and presumably his source study, beg these questions by considering only one "causal factor," seeking to "confirm what seems obvious." (11–12)

The causality that Bork tries to establish between pornography and social disorder is even more tenuous, focusing as it does on illegitimacy (8) as the resultant depravity (rather than rape, or adultery, or sexually transmitted diseases). He has no faith in self-censorship among a population so corrupted that it actually might enjoy watching pornography (14). And at no point does Bork explain how democracy can flourish in degenerate countries with liberal policies on pornography like Sweden and the Netherlands.

In his effort to demonstrate the evils fostered by a climate of sex and violence, Bork (via George Will) cites a *false analogy* with Nazi Germany, suggesting that, just as reading anti-Semitic propaganda laid the groundwork for the Holocaust, so listening to rap music will lead to comparable moral degeneration (10). Later, he uses another dubious analogy: just as a person innocently living in the neighborhood of a smelter will be harmed by the pollution, so will a decent citizen who doesn't look at pornography be harmed by his neighbors who do (31). Early in the essay, Bork uses an *appeal to authority*, citing two academic figures (as well as George Will) in support of his premises (4–6). Later, he turns to an *ad hominem* argument, alluding to "the flummery of professors," the unreliability of expert witnesses, and the malleability of libertarian courts in thrall to the permissive "chatterers" who constitute our present "cultural elite." (18–19, 26)

Throughout the latter part of the essay, Bork struggles between the imperative need to maintain a high standard of public and private decency and the right to freedom of speech (and, by extension, expression and taste) as guaranteed by the Constitution. Indeed, revealing the dangers inherent in the First Amendment seems to be Bork's real agenda. In a secondary syllogism, he declares that:

1. The First Amendment protects freedom of speech.
2. Freedom of speech can be injurious to morality.
3. The First Amendment, unless restricted, can be injurious to morality.

At the core of this essay, then, is a variation of the same question that concerns Sipher and Singleton (and also Henry): are there certain unalienable rights that a citizen can demand and society withhold? The issue is different for Sipher and Singleton since access to education has traditionally been regarded positively, as a necessary service provided by the government for the improvement of the population. We are accustomed to having an authority—teacher, principal, school board—to establish and execute standards for access and expulsion. Bork is questioning a far more tenuous right: to have access to information and artistic expression whose effect may not be salutary, may even be harmful. Who is to judge the risk? Who has the right to serve as censor? These are the questions that Bork fails to address.

Note: In the last paragraph, Bork refers to "liberalism's central tenet" as expressed by John Stuart Mill. The following passage from *On Liberty* (1859) may be useful for discussion:

> The sole end for which mankind are warranted, individually or collectively, in interfering with the liberty of action of any of their number, is self-protection ...the only purpose for which power can be rightfully exercised over any member of a civilized community, against his will, is to prevent harm to others. His own good, either physical or moral, is not a sufficient warrant. He cannot rightfully be compelled to do so, because it will make him happier, because, in the opinions of others, to do so would be wise, or even right. These are good reasons for remonstrating with him or reasoning with him, or persuading him, or entreating him but not for compelling him or visiting him with any evil in case he do otherwise. To justify that, the conduct from which it is desired to deter him, must be calculated to produce evil to someone else.

Throughout *On Liberty*, Mill considers how that calculation can be achieved and how "harm to others" may be defined; Bork does not.

Henry: A cultural critic for *Time* and two-time winner of the Pulitzer prize, William A. Henry is just as conservative and authoritarian in his beliefs as Bork, but somewhat less heavy-handed in his argument, providing more examples and less rhetoric. Like Sipher and Singleton, Henry believes that a diploma should be the reward of intellectual virtue. Henry also echoes Blanche Blank's concerns, and her thesis is his starting point: although a college degree doesn't guarantee lucrative, "high-level" employment, society has fostered the illusion that this credential is necessary for success.

One way of understanding Henry's sprawling argument is to look for three loose and interlocking syllogisms. The first is the most comprehensive:

1. The purpose of college is to gain a good education.
2. Students now go to college to make money.
3. These students are in college for the wrong reason and, therefore, subvert the purpose of higher education.

Henry *begs the question* of whether these mercenary students might seek or even (unintentionally) gain other benefits from their studies (9). Rather, he declares that they are either incapable of or indifferent to intellectual endeavor, citing, on the one hand, their egotism (causing them to insist on "relevant" curriculum) and, on the other, their basic insecurity (causing them to fear and reject universal standards) [10–11]. Here, Henry ignores the fact that "self-absorption" and "lack of intellectual humility" (11) have always been characteristic of the young, especially the intellectual young. In the examples he cites, these "baselessly arrogant" students (13) seem more motivated by political correctness than by greed.

In fact, students are not the only ones at fault. Henry believes that everyone connected with higher education is impelled by self-serving goals: faculty, administrators, alumni, even (by extension) the legislators who mandate easier access. Henry is ambivalent about the faculty's role, first calling them "deservedly imperious" (13) and suggesting that the damage began when control of the curriculum shifted from faculty to students. (Your students will no doubt appreciate his point that it is better to have courses that appeal to faculty's personal interests than to students' personal interests [12].) Later, Henry deplores the faculty's "pusillanimity" in succumbing to the prevalent idea of campus as marketplace.

Henry's second and third syllogisms focus on the unqualified students who are aspiring beyond their abilities. First, the practical consequences:

1. Unqualified students go to college for a credential that they think will ensure them a good job.

2. The credential will not help them achieve their goals.

3. These unqualified students should be refused admittance.

Here, Henry attacks the egalitarian belief that everyone has the right to aspire to a superior job (even though, by definition, not all work can be high-level) and to acquire the credential that will secure such a job. Henry quickly supports the second premise, citing studies that document the over-supply of candidates with credentials for jobs regarded as superior (4). But he is more interested in the conclusion: in his view, a large number of graduates don't deserve the credential, don't deserve the job, and should not be in college in the first place. If they are driving taxi cabs, they probably deserve their fate. There are only two kinds of students: "winners," who belong in college, and "mediocrities," who have been admitted under false pretenses (4). And the mediocrities have lowered the exalted standards of their institutions to those of the lowest common denominator.

In a lament that is familiar to readers of Bork, Henry condemns the consumerist culture that thrives by implanting fantasies in the minds of its citizens. His impatience with such illusions underlies Henry's third syllogism:

1. A consumerist society encourages the belief that everyone is entitled to a college education.

2. Unqualified students are not entitled to a college education.

3. A consumerist society is deluding these unfortunate students.

It is society's endorsement and perpetuation of this illusion—of entitlement, superiority, success, and self-esteem—that seems to infuriate Henry the most. He insists that the mediocrities be put back in their places—on the vocational track (7–8). (In the process, he takes some nasty swipes at ethnic minorities [10, 11, 19] including a disparaging remark one hopes he didn't learn at Yale.) In this respect, Henry is far more harsh than Blank (who worries about the plight of Harvard-educated taxi drivers), or Sipher (who wants to rid the system of *unwilling*, not unable, students), or even Singleton (who is willing to allow access until students have proved themselves failures). Like Bork, Henry worries that traditional values—not just intellectual standards—are eroding: automatic access to advancement discourages effort and discipline; without fear of failure, there will be no fear of authority (24).

At the end, Henry recommends implementation of a standardized test—the rough equivalent of Bork's censor—to sort out the mediocrities from the winners, restore competition and standards, and make the campus safe for the traditional curriculum. With tenure ended, even faculty will lose their egalitarian sense of entitlement and have to work for a living again (29). By admitting that his argument is in the realm of "educational utopia," Henry avoids having to tackle the lurking villain: the consumerist culture that encourages all these fantasies and delusions of grandeur, these demands for access. Or is democracy itself at fault for mandating the pursuit of happiness?

Strossen: Nadine Strossen is Professor of Law at New York University and the President of the American Civil Liberties Union. Her argument supports free expression of and access to pornography, a term which, for Strossen, includes far more than explicit sexual images. It can be read in conjunction with Bork's broader defense of censorship. (Unlike Bork's essay, which is freestanding, this passage is taken from a book, and so it has more loose ends.) Strossen provides few trappings of formal argument, but rather uses a series of examples, held together with rhetorical questions, to illustrate her point.

In Strossen's inversion of Bork's antipornography argument—unlike Bork, she separates pornography from violence—the new Puritanism emanates from an alarmist coalition of right-wing traditionalists and "pornophobic feminists." In fact, she is more interested in presenting and rebutting the feminist argument: depiction of sex "inevitably degrade and endanger women." Although she is scornful of the assumption (expressed by "inevitably") that acknowledgment of their sexuality must be demeaning to women, Strossen herself is just as sweeping in her response: "In short, a war on sexual expression is . . . a war on sex itself." Just as "inevitably" tries to bridge the lack of evidence in the feminists' argument, so does "in short" represent an enormous leap of logic. In fact, both sides are *begging the question* at the core of their arguments. Strossen makes a good point when she notes that something regarded as harmful or dangerous itself becomes endangered. That may be unfortunate or it may not. But she doesn't explain why pornography fits into the former category.

Strossen quickly moves to a series of examples that enable her to raise important issues; however, she tends to do so through rhetorical questions that don't settle anything. Is there harm in depicting sexuality? If so, what are the dangers? Does the sight of a nude woman or a woman in underwear encourage rape? If so, is the discouragement of rape a higher priority than the full expression of sexuality, especially through art? Are the pictures that so offend legislators and feminists harmful? Or are they merely offensive?

Since the whole subject of sexuality is such a hazardous one, Strossen does well to approach it through examples, asking us to consider whether specific acts of censorship were necessary, desirable, or appropriate. In an example of censorship by law, she condemns legislators for stifling artistic expression by cutting off funds for sexually explicit art, but she does not explain why these legislators should violate their own taste and principles in the service of art. Similarly, she complains abut removing the Venus de Milo from a shopping mall, without considering the businessmen's need to protect the sensibilities of their customers; otherwise, there might not be a shopping mall. That's censorship by taste. As for censorship under the guise of sexual harassment, Strossen struggles to find the appropriate response to these feminist complaints. Are the college officials within their rights in removing the Goya from the classroom? Is placing it in a more obscure part of the building the equivalent of hanging a tablecloth over it? She is annoyed at the college officials' timidity, but is it their job (or the job of the mall manager) to defend artistic expression? Although she doesn't succeed in doing so here, Strossen is very interested in defining the limits of self-expression and sexual expression. The spectrum from rape to suggestive expressions, from nudes to partially clad women, is a broad one. Which are harmful? What is acceptable?

The example of the AIDS clinic is slightly different. Is the image of a man wearing a condom more dangerous than the possibility that ignorance will result in someone contracting AIDS? Bork would say that the lewd image might be more dangerous to society than a few deaths from AIDS. Will the image actually prevent new cases? Or will it encourage lewd behavior? Does anyone know? Strossen doesn't provide these answers.

#Assignment 5: Writing an Essay Based on a Single Source (p. 168)

Assignment 5 does not especially benefit from preliminary discussion. The "Twelve Steps" are available for your students to use as guidelines, and you may also want to take them through the Blanche Blank model, emphasizing that references to the source are added to notes and outlines later. (If you don't make this point, some students will end up leading from the essay, instead of developing their own ideas, and you'll end up reading a set of interpretive summaries.) Otherwise, there's not much you can do in group discussion since, with luck, your students will be writing on a number of different topics.

Once again, to simplify the assignment, you may want to use only one reading as the starting point. (If so, I suggest that you use Lindholm or Postman and Powers; Angier's subject is a sensitive one, and some of your students may need an alternative topic.) If you want to exercise closer control over the selection of topics, instead of simply having each student submit one or more topics to you for approval, try duplicating a list of all suitable topics submitted and have everyone benefit from their classmates' inventiveness by letting them select their topics from the list. Or you can ask the class to vote on the best five, and restrict them to those five. Selecting topics through consensus tends to discourage "borrowing" old essays. No one can know in advance which topics will win the favor of the class, and different classes tend to prefer different topics. Of course, special dispensation can be made for those who genuinely want to write about arcane subjects; but I would be on the lookout for a recycled rat.

Whether you ask your students to submit an outline before writing the essay or merely request that they attach it to the final draft should depend on their previous performance and their reactions to these assignments. You can forestall some problems by having conferences with weaker students at the outline stage.

Angier: (p. 168): Natalie Angier is a journalist specializing in science who has written frequently for the *New York Times*. Angier's discussion of depression and suicide is limited to the sociobiological perspective that Lindholm finds so restrictive. She doesn't go beyond the premise that human needs and behavior are biologically determined, assuming that suicidal depression has an evolutionary purpose or is the manifestation of a disease. Angier's parallel with animals is strained. Hers is a very restricted perspective on suicidal depression, a state of mind and body that is at least as complex and variable as the romantic love that Lindholm writes about. Here are some starting points for essay topics:

1. In the controversy between "nature" and "nurture" as the primary origin of our behavior, Angier clearly supports the former. What do you think?

2. Angier touches only briefly on suicide for the dying—euthanasia. How, if at all, does euthanasia fit into her biologically determined universe?

3. Although Angier emphasizes parallels with the animal world, she acknowledges that humans live in "complex social groups." Do these social relationships make us more or less susceptible to depression and its consequences?

4. Angier refers to altruism as a possible motive for suicide, citing a parallel with the mole rat. Is the comparison credible?

5. Angier notes that a brief depression might be useful as a period of "emotional hibernation." Do you agree?

6. Consider the opposite of depressive melancholy. Are there comparable dangers in the excessively upbeat, optimistic temperament?

7. Angier cites Goodall's monkey who died of a "broken heart." How does depression resulting from loss or bereavement fit into Angier's understanding of the problem?

8. The Darwinian underpinnings of Angier's analysis assume that survival is the ultimate goal of animals and humans. Is that true in all circumstances? How does altruistic sacrifice override the instinct toward survival?

9. If depression (or even suicide) serves some sort of purpose determined by instinct, is it appropriate to intervene to prevent it, or should nature be allowed to take its course?

10. Interview a number of people who have experienced depression or who have known depressives. What, in their view, causes depression? Is the tendency congenital? To what extent is depression dependent on external circumstances or situations?

Lindholm: (p. 172): Charles Lindholm's analysis, typical of the social sciences, presents a "review of the literature" about romantic love, followed by the author's own alternative theory. He explores the nature of romantic and transcendent love by examining the received definitions, supported by various authorities in the field; dissatisfied with all of them, Lindholm hypothesizes his own, based on parallel research into the nature of charisma. In its vocabulary and its academic approach, this may be the most difficult essay in the textbook for your students to readily grasp; but the progress of Lindholm's arguments is clearly signalled, step-by-step, and the subject should certainly be attractive. Here are some starting points for essay topics:

1. What accounts for the human desire to achieve transcendent love?

2. Is romantic love necessary? desirable? possible? in an age of frank sexuality?

3. Historically, what were the motives for marriage? Why do people marry today?

4. Would romantic love exist today without the arts and the media? Which comes first, romance itself or the image of romance?

5. Can the concept of "transcendental" experience be applied to other relationships? parenthood? gratitude to a benefactor? loyalty to a leader? Can an abstraction like love of one's country or love of one's god inspire a comparable transcendence?

6. Can Lindholm's argument explain our declining birthrate?

7. How would economic concerns be factored into this explanation of romantic love?

8. Describe the status of romantic love in the United States at the millennium.

9. Analyze a few classic examples of romantic love, historical and modern, using one or more of the definitions suggested by Lindholm's essay.

10. Interview a number of sources about their experience of romantic love and determine whether their evidence confirms Lindholm's theories.

Postman and Powers: (p. 182): A specialist in media communication, Neil Postman chairs the Department of Communication Arts at New York University. This is a very accessible essay, written in a casual style, with the progression of points clearly signalled. Postman and Powers depend heavily on anecdote, stereotypes, and innuendo for their effect, and their generalizations (although probably true) are nothing if not hasty. Would an ugly, low-salaried anchor make TV news any more accurate and responsible? One can argue that the authors are employing much the same marketing tactics in their presentation of a hot topic as the broadcasters they deride. The essay is fun to read, but cynical in its perceptions, with a pervasive contempt for the suckers who watch TV (if not for those who buy their book). Good paper topics abound; here are some possibilities:

1. Discuss some examples of other "teases" that encourage people to spend time or money on a dubious product.

2. Why do people respond to the lure of "teases"?

3. Given the fact that viewers have the right to turn off the TV, what's wrong with "tease" marketing?

4. Postman and Powers insist that a news anchor should be a seasoned journalist rather than a "personality." Are their arguments valid?

5. To what extent is the "fakery"/"artifice" characteristic of broadcast news prevalent in American culture today?

6. How would you develop and market a TV news program that was honest and reliable?

7. Postman and Powers are really condemning viewers' interest in celebrities. Contrast today's celebrity-worship with obsessive devotion to entertainment figures (e.g.

Valentino, Sinatra, the Beatles) earlier in the century. Is there a difference in the nature of and reasons for this attraction to celebrities?

8. Using Postman and Powers' model, explore sports or politics as a source of entertainment that's dependent on artifice and marketing.

9. Successful marketing depends on consulting the tastes of the viewers/consumers. What's wrong with that?

10. Interview several people about their news-watching habits and form some conclusions about their motives for watching, their choice of programs, and their satisfaction with the quality of the news and its presentation.

CHAPTER 4: THE MULTIPLE-SOURCE ESSAY

At this point, the student moves from working with a single source to the type of synthesis that is the essence of the research essay. This is the pivotal chapter of the book. Without practice in synthesis, using fairly simple and uniform sources, students will later have enormous difficulties in organizing their research notes into coherent essays.

Inexperienced students should not be expected to learn both library research and synthesis within the same essay assignment. That is why Chapter 4 slows everything down to focus almost exclusively on synthesis, which is presented in such simple stages that every student will be able to master the process.

*Exercise 13: Selecting and Presenting Information (p. 192)

The model essay provides satisfactory synthesis and summary, and adheres to the theme of "turmoil" with admirable consistency. However, there is very little interpretation. Events are described without any evaluation of their significance.

Assignment 6: Writing an Essay from Factual Information (p. 194)

Although this kind of assignment requires some library work, the research is restricted to a single source; that's why this lesson is presented at the beginning of the synthesis chapter. Organizing the information is not a major problem once the student has chosen a theme and thus has a basis for selecting evidence from the newspaper. What is used here is summary, not synthesis. The assignment once again emphasizes the need for a balance between generalization and evidence. It is a good transition from the single-source to multiple-source essays, but it can only supplement, not replace, one of the full-scale synthesis assignments that are essential to this chapter. Although many students won't believe it, 6-1 is easier than 6-2.

Exercise 14: Analyzing Shades of Meaning in Multiple Sources (p. 200)

This is where the explanation of synthesis actually begins. The discussion of the five definitions of "individualist" can be difficult for students to follow because the material is so abstract; it's worth talking them through the "Analyzing Shades of Meaning" section before assigning Exercise 14.

All of the responses suggest that "cleverness" is a useful means to an end, not a quality that one would want for its own sake, like "smartness" or "intelligence." Only the first respondent is uncritically approving of the clever person, who is likely to become a rich person. The others are more dismissive, implying that clever people are different, and not very nice. None of the respondents (not even the first) associates himself or herself with being clever; rather, all five describe cleverness as a purely intellectual knack, a coldly calculating ability, almost a trick. Being clever is useful to solve problems and handle situations—but only when there's something to be gained. Even the first respondent, who sees cleverness as a natural advantage, assumes that it will be used for self-interest. Others think that cleverness enables one to take short cuts, and they resent it as an unfair advantage. One disapprovingly notes the tendency to develop unorthodox tactics, which is unfair to ordinary people who are less cunning and adaptive. The suggestion is that clever people benefit at others' expense; at the very least, they make less clever people look bad. Even if they are materially successful, clever people are hardly popular and will quite likely come to a bad end.

In their analysis, students might focus on the value—and lack of value—placed on intellect, and its association with coldness and deceit. These respondents are far from questioning material success as a desirable goal, but success based on cleverness, however enviable, is somehow tarnished, isolating, illegitimate. Your students might consider whether the element of envy may, in part, account for the hostility.

#Assignment 7: Writing a Definition Essay from Multiple Sources (p. 200)

Like the "individualist" and "lottery" models in the text, this and the next synthesis assignment (8) use interview notes as sources. Preparations for either of these two essays take slightly more time than the other essay assignments in this chapter; an extra day for interviewing should suffice. (You can assign the interviewing part of the essay *before* going over the synthesis section of the text.) Since students will each be defining different words or exploring different issues, some of the interviewing can take place in class; but, if your students are too homogenous to provide a sufficient "mix" for an interesting synthesis, then by all means ask your class to interview different types of people outside the classroom. (If yours is a residential college, remind them to get the opinions of a few older people.)

Do emphasize the importance of taking (and handing in) coherent notes. Notes are crucial to the assessment of either of these essays: the final version, even with an outline, won't give you a clear enough idea of the materials students were working from, nor will you be able to determine whether they made the most of their materials, whether their sources were responsible for the paucity of ideas, whether their synthesis of notes was askew or incomplete, or whether the ideas contained in the notes were simply ignored in the pressure of writing the essay. In some cases, you may want to glance at notes before they are converted into essays to make sure that no worthwhile angle has been omitted.

While you may occasionally decide to manipulate materials to the student's advantage, it is not a good idea to encourage the students themselves to set up or "rig" an ideal set of notes. There may be a great temptation to plan ahead for a good set of notes once students realize how important controlled variety can be to the finished essay. This assignment is, in part, intended to teach students to work with whatever materials are available; and you should offer to be interviewed yourself only in cases of genuine hardship (i.e., a run of inarticulate sources). This is another reason to have at least a few of the interviews take place in class; you'll then be sure that at least some of the sources are not mythical people who have been invented expressly for the presentation of certain desirable opinions. Do assure your classes more than once that you will make allowances for vagaries of fortune and interview subjects, and stress the importance of handing in complete notes to maximize your sympathy when you read the completed essay.

Assignment 7 is definitely the more difficult of the two, and it can only be fully effective if your students already have some awareness of nuance in definition. (For classes that know their way around a dictionary, you might try an *OED* essay, in which students synthesize the numerous definitions of their word to be found in the unabridged *Oxford English Dictionary*.)

*Exercise 15: Identifying Common Ideas (p. 206)

This is probably the most important exercise in the book. Once the class understands the cross referencing process, they can handle the organizing of the research essay, or, indeed, any kind of writing that is based on sources. You may assign this at home or do it, unannounced, at the blackboard in class. (The latter is more fun since you will probably enjoy hearing the signs of recognition—often collective—that are audible as the process becomes clear to students, one by one.) As you work on the list of common topics at the blackboard, simply read each new sentence and stop to ask, "Is this a new idea? How would you describe it?" It pays to remind the students to insert the code numbers into the statements at the appropriate points; it's hard for them to remember the "double entry" process.

Here is one chart that might emerge—although, obviously, variations will occur. (You will note that I underestimated the number of reasons and didn't provide enough slots in the text):

1. I can afford to give to beggars.	Cohen
2. I give without considering need—just asking is enough.	Cohen, Aldrich
3. I give because I identify with them and sympathize with their suffering.	Cohen, Sharone, & Aldrich
4. I give if it's convenient.	Cohen, Aldrich
5. I give even though I don't know what the money will be used for—none of my business.	Cohen, Aldrich
6. I only give to people who seem genuinely in need.	Sharone, Garder, & Nagel
7. I give to people who ask directly, respectfully, and meekly.	Sharone, Aldrich, Garder, & Johnson
8. I give to people who amuse me.	Aldrich
9. I don't give because the government should be responsible for the needs of the indigent.	Lauro, O'Rourke
10. I don't give because it's too embarrassing.	Lauro
11. I don't give because it might be some kind of con game.	Garder
12. I don't give when I feel coerced or threatened.	Johnson, O'Rourke
13. I don't give because there are social agencies to fill that need.	Nagel, O'Rourke
14. I don't give because it perpetuates the problem.	O'Rourke

Once similar ideas are combined, the ideas can be organized into a spectrum. What constitutes an effective moral response to the problems of homelessness and poverty? And, equally important, what matters to these respondents? That the poverty is real (and not a sham)? That the person is deserving? That the giver receives something in return, even if only a positive feeling?

You might reorganize the above responses into those who make their decision based on the perceived needs (or lack thereof) of the supplicant, those who project their own emotional or intellectual response on the situation, and those who decide based on theoretical principles. Another option would be to divide the comments between those that insist on a personal, one-on-one transaction with the panhandler and those that see the exchange in more abstract, almost sociological terms, either refusing or accepting responsibility for poverty without expecting to develop a relationship (however brief) with the symbolic beggar.

Assignment 8: Writing about an Issue from Multiple Sources (p. 208)

Assignment 8 is an accessible assignment for almost every student. (See the suggestions about interviewing above in the section on Assignment 7.) Urge your class to think of their own questions and to rely on the list in the text only as a last resort. A good procedure for topic selection is to ask students to submit a few possible questions the day before the session you have allotted for interviews. Then you'll be able to recommend the most promising topic and weed out the potential losers. Most of the topics on the list in the text were suggested by students and worked fairly well. As you can see, they tend to center around home and family—subjects that everyone has an opinion about. On the other hand, political issues can be really disastrous choices since they encourage sources and writers to take sides. This is not intended primarily as an argument essay but, rather, as an analysis of reasons. You might also want to encourage questions that don't just demand "yes" and "no" answers and discourage questions that are trite: "Is it better to live in the city or in the country?" As with definition, it is not usually a good idea to have two students working on the same topic. The main purpose for requiring approval of topics is your own convenience: if a weak topic forces students to switch later on, your scheduling will probably be disrupted by late papers.

Organizing Multiple Sources (p. 210)

This model may seem formidable to your students for two reasons. First, although fairly informal in style, the statements were *written* by students in response to a printed source—in contrast to the "lottery" statements which were transcriptions of *spoken* responses to an oral question. In the "layoffs" group, the ideas seem more embedded in the prose and harder to extract. Second, there simply are more statements to juggle: fifteen, rather than seven. It's difficult to keep track of so many separate reactions in one's head, but students do tend to try to retain them in their memory before consenting to the necessity for pencil and paper and making a chart.

Exercise 16: Analyzing a Paragraph Based on Synthesis of Sources (p. 221)

This exercise reviews and reinforces the skills related to the presentation of sources. Here is what Exercise 16 should look like:

topic sentence → [Those who emphasize the upgrading of minority employment have pointed out that, since the hiring of minorities has been encouraged by governmental legislation only for the last few years, the seniority system will of necessity operate against those minorities.] [Thus, in the opinion of Robert Rivera, it is only fair that, during the present budget crisis, workers from minority groups be protected from cutbacks. One statement, by John Seeback, even suggests the possibility of a return to racial discrimination by white workers who have seniority and by employers, if equal opportunity laws are not enforced:] ["Many employers feel the minority workers are expendable: they had to hire them because of the law: now they have a good reason to fire them."] [In a related argument, Jesse Rogers points out that, since minorities have waited such a long time for decent job opportunities, a certain amount of preferential treatment might serve as a concrete measure of compensation.] [Neither Seeback nor Rogers emphasizes the abstract principle of equal opportunity implemented by the law.] [Peter Rossi advocates a practical solution:] [the federal government should undertake "the creation of new jobs,"] [so that, presumably, there would be enough to satisfy both groups.]

paraphrase ... *quotation* ... *paraphrase* ... *summary* ... *explanation* ... *explanation* ... *quotation*

Assignment 9: Writing an Essay Synthesizing Multiple Sources (p. 222)

Assignments 9 and 10 are less interesting for you to read than 7 and 8 since all the students will be working with exactly the same materials. However, these two assignments bring students closer to the conditions of research, for they must interpret and weigh their information without any help other than that of the printed page. (In interviews, one can always ask for more information.)

You may not want to go through the time-consuming (but useful) process of eliciting the opinions of your own students for a "home-grown" set of statements (which is the method used in Assignment 10). In that case, use Assignment 9, which provides a brief article and twenty statements. Here is a rough chart of some of the major ideas:

1. Literacy necessary for employment; diploma meaningless without basic skills. — Basi, Limburg, Martin, Warren, & Roberts
2. Test scores not the only factor; other qualities/skills should count. — Del Rey, Felice Berg, & Sokolov
3. If left back, students feel frustrated. — Del Rey/Felice
4. Left back students drop out, harming society. — Gordon, McGee, Yando, & Del Rey
5. Give students some leeway, then fail them. — Jenkins
6. Passing poor students harms good students. — Limburg
7. Frustration/embarrassment for illiterate students seeking employment. — Martin, Pena
8. Students who fail at academic work still valuable to society. — McGee, Yando, Sokolov, & Willoughby
9. Reading not the only factor in promotion. — Pearson
10. Allow slow students to learn at own rate; offer enriched classes on separate track. — Pena, Ray, Felice, & Willoughby
11. Uphold standards. — Pullman, Warren, & Raviggio
12. Repeating a course builds character. — Pullman, Simms, & Raviggio
13. Students who fail didn't try hard enough. — Roberts, Simms
14. Student who can't pass 7th grade will have more problems in 8th grade. — Warren

Note: The list of comments is in alphabetical order, and the opinions of those at the beginning of the alphabet mostly favor promotion to the next grade. You may want to warn your students to keep an open mind as they move through the list. (If you work on this assignment in class, in groups, you may want to have some groups start at the end of the list and work backwards.) Those favoring high standards and repeating the 7th grade actually slightly outnumber the "promotion" group. Several of those inclining toward promotion recommend case-by-case consideration to avoid the stigma of automatic failure. Looking at the arguments this way, they divide into high standards and concern for society versus mitigating factors and concern for the individual.

Assignment 10: Writing an Argument from Multiple Sources (p. 226)

The arguments of Etzioni and his respondents are accessible and shouldn't need much preliminary discussion for your students to write interesting essays on the viability and desirability of covenant marriages. (Do encourage them to explore arguments not covered by this spectrum of opinion.) Etzioni's article focuses on the felicities of choice, as if this were a gift that Louisiana were giving to its citizens. Some of his respondents point out that freedom of choice is just an illusion here; they assume that the choice is to some degree forced, that there will be a social stigma, if not a legal penalty, for choosing the easier option. Levenstein and Mellow conceive of marriage as requiring a looser tie and want to ensure the availability of easy divorce. Warfield and Reynolds, in their different ways, point out that the supposedly free choice—in marriage and in divorce—depends on other factors such as availability of money and existence of children. And Pultz sees a Bork-like conservatism in Etzioni's proposal: it is unfortunate that the state doesn't trust husbands and wives to act in good faith. Louisiana may have good reasons for enacting this law, but does the state have the right to demand such a choice of couples contemplating marriage? Is divorce a right, an entitlement? Covenant marriage benefits the family and thus benefits society; does it benefit the individual spouse?

You can ask your class to write a full-length essay based only on the readings in Assignment 10, or you can make the assignment more complex by generating additional materials for synthesis from your own students. Ask your students to read the articles and letters on covenant marriage, and then write a brief response (no more than a paragraph) in class. (If you have them do the reaction-statement at home, you'll end up with a set of statements of varying lengths.) For any set of preliminary written responses, allow between ten and fifteen minutes (not counting your initial presentation of the assignment). Some students may be reluctant to commit themselves. Insist, if you can, that they come to a decision, pointing out that such choices are not eternal, that their responses on that day will not entail a lifelong commitment. A split response is acceptable as long as reasons are provided for both sides. If students seem reluctant to write down their private views, don't take refuge in the promise of anonymity. It is extremely important that the statements, when distributed, be signed, and the students accept responsibility for their views. Your class will probably understand the confusion that can result from trying to put together a number of anonymous quotations and respect the need for careful attribution and transcription when the sentences they use are signed by classmates.

Try not to let too long a time elapse between collecting the responses and duplicating and distributing the set of statements for synthesis. Before the copying, go through the entire group and discard any statements that are clearly impossible (e.g., off the topic, garbled, espousing both sides in an unbalanced way) or that duplicate a common reaction (unless there's a shade of difference in the reasoning). One can't tell in advance what the mix will be. Frequently, one point of view is taken by a large proportion of students. The need to expose students to the experience of evaluating similar statements and rejecting weak ones justifies the inclusion of most of the responses. If you include a few variations on the same point, the class will eventually be able to discuss the criteria for selecting the most effective quotations. Occasionally, when a key viewpoint is missing from the set, you may want to make up your own statement (or, after you have used the same assignment more than once, you may want to include an especially interesting response from a previous set). You will have to introduce a new name and call attention to the insertion, or use your own name and lose your position of objectivity. List the statements in random or (preferably) alphabetical order. It may be tempting, with a weak class, to do some preliminary arranging, but this would defeat the whole purpose of the assignment.

It is not even essential to start this kind of assignment with a reading. Try an unadorned question, put on the blackboard without explanation. (For example: "Does this college provide a good education?)

Another variation on the synthesis essay is the assignment based on a set of full-length essays (as opposed to brief statements). I have, for example, asked an evening class to describe their working experiences—high and low pints—in an essay of about three hundred words, duplicated a dozen examples, and then assigned the set as the source for a generalized description of the contemporary experience of working. In the assignment, the chief problem is extracting the pertinent from the masses of irrelevancy. Other possible topics: experiences of parental discipline, leading to a definition of appropriate parental authority; experiences of adolescent dating, leading to an analysis of modern-day courtship; experiences of competition and rivalry; experiences of power (healthy and unhealthy); conventional manners, leading to a definition of courtesy.

Assignment 11: Writing a Comparison Essay (p. 233)
A good way to avoid recycled essays is to assign each class a specific year from which to select a suitable film—and approve each student's choice within that year, in advance.

CHAPTER 5: FINDING SOURCES

*Exercise 17: Proposing a Topic (p. 245)
This and the next are both cautionary exercises that can be covered briefly in class. The point is made in Exercise 17 as soon as students realize that proposal B is absurdly broad. Proposals C and D seem satisfactory until the writers start to add additional objectives and thus split their focus. Proposal F obfuscates the boundaries of the topic by using jargon. Proposals A and E are satisfactory.

*Exercise 18: Narrowing a Topic (p. 246)
The most successful topics for a medium-length research essay tend to identify problems and suggest ways to solve them: 2 and 8. Some of these topics are excellent, providing an opportunity for using an argument strategy; but because they are abstract, they may be difficult to deal with in eight-to-ten pages: 4, 7, and 9. Some are too broad and need to be narrowed down: 1, 5, 6, and 10. Topics 1 and 3 are merely restatements of the general topic and provide no starting point or direction for research.

*Exercise 19: Compiling a Working Bibliography (p. 271)
This exercise focuses on the rough estimation of usefulness that is essential for compiling a preliminary bibliography. The annotated list simulates the student's skimming of a number of articles; in this way, the class can gain experience in quick decision-making. You might point out that, for good synthesis, it's preferable to list the articles next to the topics, rather than just list appropriate topics next to the articles. The articles are listed in chronological order.
  A. 6
  B. 1, 6, 9, 11, 12, 13, 14, 15, 16
  C. 1, 2, 3, 4, 5, 7, 8, 9, 13, 16, 19, 20
  D. 2, 3, 4, 6, 7, 8, 10, 13, 14, 17, 19
  Notice that a researcher would have to seek additional sources to write an essay on the "neutral" topic (A) of advertising's responsibility to society. Notice also that article 18 does not seem a likely candidate for any of the four topics.

Assignment 12: Preparing a Topic Proposal for a Research Essay (p. 274)
This is the formal assigning of the standard research essay. The next four chapters provide support for the various stages of its preparation.

CHAPTER 6: EVALUATING SOURCES

*Exercise 20: Choosing Sources (p. 290)

This exercise works best if it is begun as a class discussion, with two (or more) essay topics chosen by the class. (You may want to ask students to complete Part A and choose topics at home in preparation for class discussion; or you can begin the discussion with the selection of two or more topics.) Once topics are chosen, spend some time rapidly analyzing the suitability of the first few articles, and then let students, individually or in groups, complete bibliographies for the agreed-upon topics. The general discussion is important in the evaluation of periodical articles since students probably won't be familiar with the style and approach of all the various sources. If you ask the class to submit Part C, make sure that your task is simplified by having them write down all the information about each of the five articles that they have selected for each topic; otherwise, you'll constantly have to refer back to the bibliography in the book.

*Exercise 21: Evaluating Sources (p. 292)

This is an elaboration of the previous exercise. It requires students to evaluate not only the title and source, but also the content and style of each excerpt. The object is to make students understand that compatibility of sources is important in selecting the bibliography for their research essays. All of these sources could conceivably be cited in the same essay, but the synthesis would require some careful adjustment.

These readings (expanded for this edition to eight) provide a good spectrum for assessing the compatibility of a group of sources. The topic—boxing—also lends itself to a range of issues for class discussion. Some of the authors seem to be working in wholly different dimensions: even setting aside issues of style, it's hard to reconcile the straightforward demand that boxing be banned because of its intrinsic violence as expressed in the *JAMA* and *New Republic* editorials with the florid evocation of boxing as theater and religion in the Mailer and Oates excerpts. One could paraphrase the editorialists, but citing the latter is difficult; one would have little choice but to quote phrases like Mailer's "sweet swooning catacombs of oblivion" or Oates's "communion"/"altar"/"atonement" imagery. Yet it would be difficult to omit Oates and Mailer, given their status as elite aficionados of the sport. It's interesting to notice that Sugden, who writes in the standard prose of the social sciences, echoes the point about boxing as the "theater of dreams."

One way to approach these eight disparate views of boxing is to organize them according to the object of their interest. *JAMA* is wholly concerned with the boxers themselves and the risk of brain damage and death; its object is to save boxers from a kind of willing suicide, and, as befits a medical association, it is not concerned with their economic or social aspirations. The *New Republic* raises a second concern: the boxers are old enough to accept these risks; greater damage is done to susceptible adolescents who are seduced from more orthodox paths to power and status by the lure of the ring. Exploring the same point, Sugden is ambivalent: as well as being enjoyable, boxing is an opportunity for kids to transcend their inner-city lives; he is the only one of the eight who has dealt directly with this second group of would-be boxers, and he reluctantly concludes that it is a "positive option." The third group focuses on the spectators: for Oates, they are participating in a rite of spiritual and emotional importance; for Phillips, they are being given stimulation (if not license) to engage in their own copycat violence; in the world that McKie describes, fights always have the potential for riots.

All three concerns appear in McIlvanney's account of the death of Johnny Owen. Of all these excerpts, this evocative sports narrative is the least abstract, the most real, with a wealth of carefully chosen detail. Much in Mailer's vein, McIlvanney notes that boxing made Owen more than his ordinary self; it transfigured him. Yet at the same time, the description of his parents' response makes the reader cry out against their loss. (The fact that Owen "failed to prevent" Pintor from opening a space for his punch suggests that Owen was inadequate to the boxer's iconic role, that his death was his own fault.) And McIlvanney provides a dispassionate description of the crowd's callousness (including the detail of the pickpocketing) without condemning the sport. For him, it is up to the boxer to weigh the advantages—material and personal—against the dangers. (Your class may want to explore the link between these arguments about boxing and the "entitle-ment" issues contained in some of the essays in the earlier chapters; would a ban on box-ing interfere with the rights of aspiring young pugilists?)

Here are some other points for discussion: does boxing's role as surrogate for aggres-sion (in boxers and spectators) provide sufficient justification for sanctioning the vio-lence? Is boxing a "victimless crime"? Are aspiring boxers old enough, stable enough to make a reasoned choice? How much respect should one accord people (there *are* women boxers) who risk such severe damage and death? Should one share Mailer's view that the boxer's egomania is so compelling it gives him the right to demolish lesser opponents? Is the boxer brave or foolhardy? Why is boxing worse than other dangerous occupations? Can we admire firefighters because they save lives, sandhogs because they build tunnels, but not boxers, because they produce no material or human dividend? Why is boxing worse than race car driving? Because the instrument of death is a human fist rather than a marvel of technology? As the boxing promoter in McKie's article comments, boxing is "a very emotive subject."

Finally, the brief passage from Phillips exemplifies the kind of article that devotes more time to detailing the circumstances of the specific study being described than to provid-ing a readable interpretation of the results that emerged from the study. My point here is not that such articles are without value, but that they are useful only to those familiar with the field and should be avoided (if they can be understood at all) by students writ-ing papers for introductory courses. An article in the social sciences that begins with a "review of the literature" can be a liability for the novice. The excerpt from the Sugden book is very different. Although his approach is that of a sociologist, his prose is mostly easy to follow (exceptions occur when he is paraphrasing someone else's more jargon-rid-den work). I suggest that you spend a bit more time going over this passage with your class, demonstrating that academic writing can be accessible, useful, possibly interesting.

*Exercise 22: Learning about Authors (p. 310)

Since the first part of this optional exercise—finding out about a source's background—can be very time-consuming for students who are simultaneously engaged in research for their final essays, you may want to assign only Part B for general class discussion. Some of the essay topics are more practical than others, some are too broad, and a few are not especially suited to their sources. Try asking your students to think of one more essay topic.

Exercise 23: Comparing Sources (p. 311)

This exercise parallels Exercise 21 (boxing), providing a comparable experience in evalu-ating sources that describe a historical event. The Cocoanut Grove fire is an absorbing subject for discussion—indeed, "great disasters" make surefire research topics—and these three accounts provide a useful triple perspective. The *New York Times* article is purely informational yet unintentionally sensational. Although the *Times* tries to preserve some distance between the reader and events, the facts remain appalling. The article is extremely disorganized, written rapidly at the site of the tragedy. In contrast, the *Time* article selects and arranges the detail in order to heighten the horror; the facts are essentially the same, so what makes this account seem less reliable? The *Time* article's picture of innocent young people victimized by unknown forces is placed in the much broader context of global war in Bernard De Voto's reflective account (written some weeks after the disaster). In this article, you are supplied with more information about the night club's and the city's negligence, but De Voto ultimately accuses the public of being responsible for the deaths of five hundred people, passively accepting the need for government and business interests to ignore public safety. For De Voto's most succinct description of community indifference linked to the brutalizing effects of war, see the last three sentences of paragraph 3. You might also point out to your class that De Voto's compassion is focused on the larger implications of the fire; he finds it hard to identify with the individual patrons of the Cocoanut Grove and would never himself have entered it. His description of the nightclub—"garish but innocuous and on the whole useful" contrasts with the *Times*'s simplicity and *Time*'s heightened camera eye.

CHAPTER 7: TAKING NOTES

Exercise 24: Evaluating Notes (p. 328)
A. wrong time sequence; notes are very selective (e.g., no flames; too much quotation, not enough paraphrase)

B. very selective, with a lot of editorializing: notes aren't very reliable; too much quoting and quotations oddly chosen

C. entirely quotation; alternating structure useful for corroboration

D. good arrangement of sources and structure—double testimony; isolated quotations make the context unclear

E. good mixture of paraphrase and quotation

F. good coverage and paraphrase, but incomplete: Mather ignored; what is here is not attributed to Adelt

Exercise 25: Taking Notes on Two Topics (p. 332)
The Causes of the Fire
fire started with an artificial palm (eyewitness)
flash fire in the basement kitchen (*NYT*)
a match lit by a busboy changing a lightbulb; palm in flames
lightbulb had been removed by customer as a joke
Boston did not require Cocoanut Grove to be fireproof or to facilitate evacuation (*Time*)
inadequate exits, hidden or locked
overcrowding
unsafe wiring; electrician unlicensed
inspectors aware of violations; did not enforce the law
archaic building codes (De Voto)
The Fire's Intensity and Speed
"blast of flame" (*NYT*)
fire "ate away the palm tree, raced along silk draperies . . . leaped along ceiling and wall" (*Time*)
decorations "burned like so much celluloid" (De Voto)

Exercise 26: Taking Notes on Three Topics (p. 332)

Note the need to repeat the same information under two different categories. Material in brackets is the student's own comments.

The Native American Ideal of Honor

Object of war for Indians was to gain vengeance or glory: "cover themselves with war honors." They did not massacre their enemies; they preferred to shame them. (Pissing story/Blackfeet)

War Atrocities

Scalping was useful to threaten another tribe and to lift the spirits ("morale-booster") of one's own tribe. Afterwards, scalps were treated as symbols of triumph: touched, discussed, celebrated, and destroyed: "trophy of war." More difficult to justify torture and mangling of bodies [not always corpses!]. It's easy to feel shocked about the practices of other nations and call them "barbarians." Atrocities have occurred in every era, on every continent. (Examples: Nazis, Communists, Khmer Rouge, El Salvadorans, Africans, Europeans, Inquisition, Puritans in America) Religious fanatics in many societies have killed dissidents in gruesome and revolting ways: burning at the stake, death by drowning. Instances range from Ancient Greece, to Vietnam, to Bosnia. Sometimes, soldiers commit these acts on enemy troops; often civilians are killed in the name of righteousness ("ethnic and religious purity"). American troops during Indian War were also capable of atrocities. In Colonel John Chivington's raid (1864), Chivington (who supposedly "long[ed] to be wading in gore") led his soldiers in an attack on men, women, and children. Stories of soldiers deliberately using children as target practice; one small child targeted by three different soldiers. Later, the soldiers engaged in numerous atrocities: scalping, dismembering, cutting up bodies, cutting away genitals, displaying them lewdly. Indians were also guilty of similar atrocities, but only sporadically, a few at a time. [Does that make it more justifiable?] Welch points out that the Plains Indians were anticipating a major struggle with the white invaders, who were attempting to destroy them and appropriate their land. [Presumably this was a motive for treating white settlers as harshly as possible, to serve as a deterrent.]

White Attitudes toward Native Americans

11/29/64: Colonel John Chivington's attack on Southern Cheyennes (asleep)=reprisal for some Indians (maybe not the same ones) raiding and killing settlers. (But motive may simply have been desire to have a fight and get successful action to their credit.) Chivington broke compact that he wouldn't attack while an American flag flew over the Indian encampment. Chivington is believed to have said: ". . . it is right and honorable to use any means under God's heaven to kill Indians! . . . I long to be wading in gore!" Chivington's troops [dishonorably] ignored the efforts of the chief, Black Kettle, to prevent the slaughter by showing the flag. Soldiers killed women and children, as well as men, using them for target practice and scalping and dismembering the bodies, all this, they said, in revenge for a few scalps they had found in the camp. The scalps were later presented to audiences in a theater in Denver to great applause. Publicity in the Western newspapers abut Indian atrocities—which really amounted to only a few cases—had terrorized settlers, who feared that there would be a "general Indian outbreak," including "the pleasant and innocent amusement of butchering and scalping the pale-faces."

CHAPTER 8: ORGANIZING AND WRITING THE RESEARCH ESSAY

*Exercise 27: Writing an Outline with Cross-Referencing (p. 343)

This exercise provides excellent training for classes whose synthesis skills need reinforcement. Your students will observe that these six sources are not evenly balanced: the majority believe that, to some extent, immigration should be restricted. For a well balanced essay, one would need to find a few more sources sympathetic to the plight of recent immigrants. Here are some of the topics that should appear in students' outlines based on these notes:

I. Immigrants and the Economy
    Immigrants do/don't contribute to the economy.
        (A1, A4, B6, E1, E2)
    Immigrants do unpleasant work that Americans won't do.
        (B8, F3)
    Immigrants are poorly paid, if they work at all, and can easily become a drain on the economy.
        (A2, A3, A5, A6, B10, F4, F5, F6)
    The need for new workers is outweighed by the threat of divisiveness.
        (C8)

II. Immigrants and the Threat to a Common Culture
        (B7, C1, C8, E4)
    The strength of America is its "melting-pot" culture, which can embrace all immigrants.
        (B7, D3)
    Large numbers of non-white, non-European immigrants disturb the balance of American society.
        (B1, B2, B3, B4, B5, C2, C4, E6)
    Recent immigrants do/don't assimilate well.
        (B11, C3, C4, C6, C7, D8)
    Recent immigrants do/don't represent a particular threat because their cultures are aggressive, even violent.
        (B9, D2, D4, D5)

III. America's problems are not caused by the present influx of immigrants;
        (D4, D7, E5)
    There is a need for a non-ideological solution to the problem of immigration.
        (D1, D4, D7, D9, E3, E5, F7)

Exercise 28: Incorporating Sources into a Paragraph (p. 361)

This exercise is a more sophisticated version of Exercise 9 in Chapter 2; once again, the class must insert sources into student paragraphs. Now, however, the paragraphs are unfinished and there are several sources to be smoothly incorporated into the final version.

Old age is a difficult topic, and the high level of abstraction in the four sources only adds to the challenge. This might even be regarded as a trick exercise since the paragraph can go in two directions: one will accommodate inclusion of these sources; one will not. If you take the obvious path, you will develop the social context: "Yet old people are so interesting, so worth knowing." Unfortunately, none of the four sources is concerned with encouraging ties between young an old. Instead, you must focus on the transcendent experience of isolation as the elderly retreat from life to death. For example: "In fact, many old people retreat into themselves as they prepare for death. This acceptance of mortality deserves our greatest respect . . ." The extract from Hesse makes this point about the importance of understanding how to die well. The translation is rather awkward, so it should be paraphrased rather than quoted. The Guggenbuhl-Craig sentence sounds pithy, but doesn't really contribute much beyond the obvious; it might be omitted. The Lin Yutang is certainly germane to the paragraph and, at first glance, the imagery ("to live this life like a poem . . . to look upon the sunset of his life as his happiest period") makes quotation, rather than paraphrase, seem the preferred choice for its citation. But it's very hard to quote only a portion of this rather long, almost repetitive sentence. A possible alternative would be to paraphrase the point that is common to both Hesse and Lin—learning to die as the culminating achievement of one's life—with a dual attribution. Or paraphrase each one separately, Lin's emphasis on joyous anticipation, and Hesse's on the hallowed purpose of old age in the spectrum of life. The quotation, then, is left to Frances, and her "awakening to a larger world of wonderment."

Assignment 13: Organizing and Writing the Research Essay (p. 362)

This can be regarded as a far more elaborate version of the cross-referencing exercise (27). You may either assign the readings in Appendix E for practice in synthesis and outlining, or make this assignment the basis for the class's research essay. The time and efficiency gained by using a uniform set of sources are balanced by the disadvantage of eliminating the students' experience of locating, selecting, and evaluating sources.

CHAPTER 9: ACKNOWLEDGING SOURCES

Exercise 29: Understanding When to Document Information (p. 369)

This little exercise has been included in response to requests for more practice in distinguishing between facts that are common knowledge and facts that require acknowledgment of source. (See Documenting Information, p. 365.) With the exception of the first and possibly the sixth statements, all these facts about the explosion of the Challenger would require documentation because the information is relatively specific or technical and could not be considered common knowledge. The date of the space shuttle's explosion and the name of its civilian crew member so quickly and pervasively entered the national consciousness, however, that it hardly seems necessary to include acknowledgments for those two pieces of information.

Exercise 30: Acknowledging Sources (p. 369)

While earlier, in Chapter 2, students were asked to detect plagiarized sentences by recognizing the authors' conflicting voices, now they perform the same process by comparing sources and student essays. Through their work with sources, most students will by now have come to realize the need to acknowledge other writers' ideas and words. The purpose of this exercise is to place them once again in the teacher's role and thus to increase the distance between their perspective and that of the plagiarist. The exercise is best done in class, without announcement. I recommend that you read each source and student essay aloud, commenting only at the end of each pair. The focus of the discussion should be the points that each student has chosen to plagiarize: did they make the best use of their sources, and was their motive for plagiarism laziness or ignorance?

Exercise 31: Identifying Plagiarism (p. 371)

This exercise is intended purely for class discussion and should serve to reinforce the point that plagiarists do get caught.

Exercise 32: Using Parenthetical Notes (p. 384)

The paragraph should contain four parenthetical references—at the end of the third, fourth, fifth, and seventh sentences. Note that, in three out of four sentences, the author's name signals the starting point of the paraphrased material. You may want to remind your students that citing the author's name at the beginning of *every* sentence would establish a monotonous pattern. Having been impressed with the importance of citing the source, some of your students may insert six parenthetical references, documenting sentences two and six as well as the others. Point out to them that these sentences contain the writer's own conclusions about the sources and that no acknowledgment is necessary.

Exercise 33: Preparing the Bibliography (p. 392)

Becker, Howard S., Blanche Geer, and Everett C. Hughes. Making the Grade. New York: Wiley, 1968.

Bretz, Robert D. Jr. "College Grade Point Average as a Predictor of Adult Success: A Meta-Analytical Review and Some Additional Evidence." Public Personnel Management 18 (Spring 1989): 11–22.

"College Grades: A Rationale and Mild Defense." AAUP Bulletin Oct. 1976: 320–21.

Davidson, J. F. "Academic Interest Rates and Grade Inflation." Educational Record 56 (1975): 122–25

Dressel, Paul L. College and University Curriculum. Berkeley: McCutcheon, 1971.

---. Handbook of Academic Evaluation. San Francisco: Jossey-Bass, 1976.

"Job Plight of Young Blacks Tied to Despair, Skills Lack." New York Times 19 Apr. 1983, late ed.: A14

Kennedy, Donald. "What Grade Inflation?" New York Times 13 June 1994, late ed.: All.

Leo, John, "A for Effort. Or for Showing Up." U.S. News and World Report 18 Oct. 1993: 22.

Ohmer, Milton, Howard R. Pollio, and James A. Eison. "GPA Tyranny." Education Digest 54 (Dec. 1988): 11–14.

APPENDIX D: WRITING ESSAY EXAMINATIONS (P. 473)

In many years of preparing students to take a proficiency exam in writing that is based on reading a source, I learned that, without explicit training and instruction, even the most competent students will ignore the question on the page and write about the question in their heads. An effective way to teach students to focus on an exam topic is to have them respond to the question during class time, announcing the reading—but not the topic—in advance, and omitting all preliminary class discussion. Any of the shorter essays in the book will serve this purpose; even one as thoroughly discussed as Blanche Blank's can still provide the starting point for some questions about education, and the readings in Appendix E will also lend themselves to basic persuasive and analytical essay topics. In their first attempt at writing such an in-class essay, 75 percent of your students will probably "fail." Their essays may be well organized and well written, but, in many cases, the writers will have been unable to resist straying from the assigned focus, or summarizing the reading while omitting their own opinions, or reacting volubly to the issue and ignoring the source's ideas completely. This may be a time-consuming and perhaps ego-deflating way to make a point—but it works.

APPENDIX E: READINGS FOR A RESEARCH ESSAY (P. 481)

These nine essays, together with Paley's "Travelling" (pp. 16–19), are concerned with racial perceptions—the way whites perceive blacks, and blacks perceive whites—and the prospects for maintaining a common culture in racially divided America. The essays share many common themes, providing sufficient material for your students to write an extended essay based on sources without research. Or you can ask your students to supplement some or all of the ten by finding additional books and articles. One possible reason to do the latter is to achieve greater balance. Five of the ten authors are white; five are black. Some are angry and bitter in their perception of the problem and aggressive in their recommended solutions; others are more optimistic and conciliatory. But all of them hope for a united America, despairing, perhaps, of ever achieving the integration hoped for by civil rights workers in the 1960s, but also rejecting the movement toward racial separatism that has flourished in recent years. Your students may well wish to explore the arguments of separatists (which are represented here only in a few brief letters to the editor attached to the Sleeper essay) and weigh them against those presented in this casebook.

Six of the nine essays are presented in alphabetical order by author; the remaining three form a separate group at the end, consisting of excerpts from two recent books on race by white authors followed by a review of these two books by a black author.

Shelby Steele, who is black, is a professor of English at California State University (San José). "I'm Black, You're White, Who's Innocent?" became the first chapter in *The Content of Our Character* (1991), which won the National Book Critics Award. Steele's essay, in the form of a memoir, uses an incident at a party to establish many of the themes that were to concern the other nine authors almost a decade later. Steele hypothesizes that racial tension results from power struggles—blatant and covert—between blacks and whites, each striving to have their innocence affirmed, each hoping to prove that racial bias is someone else's fault. Whites need to affirm black inferiority in order to justify past slavery and segregation; blacks need to cling to past and present oppression in order to retain the victim's role and justify continued special treatment. No one is (or is ever likely to be) color blind, Steele concludes; the rationalization conferring a posture of innocence is too seductive to be abandoned. Blacks face a choice between "bargaining"—reassuring whites of their "innocence" in exchange for privileges like government programs—or "challenging"—demanding proof of their own innocence *and* demanding privileges. For blacks, passively clinging to the status of victim results in an avoidance of personal responsibility; to thrive would be to resemble (and acknowledge the power of) whites. It is easier to retain a sense of entitlement and at the same time challenge white society by withholding effort. Steele contends that the goals of the 1960s—justice and equality—were eroded in the 1970s and 1980s, and have been replaced by those of the Black Solidarity movement, which refuses to continue bargaining with whites and rather sets out to challenge them.

Randall Kennedy, who is black, is a professor of Law at Harvard University and author of *Race, Crime, and the Law* (1997). Although his argument is more abstract and more closely reasoned than Steele's, Kennedy's essay is also a personal reflection similarly intended for an audience of educated blacks. He is more optimistic than Steele, insisting that blacks are much the same as whites, neither better nor worse, that race should matter less and less, and that a color-blind world is possible. Like Steele, he rejects the concept of a special kinship among blacks based on race, arguing that one's race is fixed at birth, not achieved, and that pride in race cannot substitute for substantive achievement. He also deplores the tendency for the oppressed to become oppressors and to promote the interests of the group at the expense of the whole. Toward the middle of the essay, Kennedy raises the issue of faculty favoritism: can a black professor be fair to his white students while at the same time having a special relationship with black students because of the common bond of race? Citing justice as the primary criterion (as Steele does), Kennedy argues that both black and white faculty should help students based on need, not on color.

Jim Sleeper, who is white, is a former columnist for the *New York Daily News*. A version of "Toward an End of Blackness" appears in *Liberal Racism* (1997). Sleeper's approach is that of a journalist, relying on vignettes and quotations rather than reasoned argument. Taking a historical perspective, he asks why the need for Black Pride and Black Solidarity arose. Sleeper points out that civil rights leaders initially thought of themselves as Americans, wanting all races to be bound up with the future of the nation. He suggests that, with the erosion of the fabric of American life since the post-war period, racial pride (or "black parochialism") has filled the vacuum left by diminished patriotism and pride in America. In an overly long discussion of the popularity of *Roots*, Sleeper argues that, with the promise of integration unfulfilled, there was a need for a new mythic work to bind blacks into the common American myth. *Roots*, then, can be said to represent a "powerful epic of unrequited love" for blacks in their quest to belong to America. The "Letters to the Editor" written in response to Sleeper's article suggest the kind of comments black separatists might make about all these essays: the problem of racism is caused by whites, not blacks; Sleeper is trying to surpress black dissent; and Sleeper cannot possibly know anything about black history, feelings, or rejection.

Whether blacks need to belong to America is the subject of a much shorter essay by *Cinqué Henderson,* who is black and who has written for *Newsweek* and *The Boston Globe.* This feature article based on interviews and anecdotes provides testimony about the downside of the problem: blacks as an abandoned underclass, with a widening gap between those left in the inner city and those, black and white, who have ascended into the respectable working and middle classes. Like Sleeper, Henderson describes blacks as "patriotic," so eager to belong to America that they find it easier to believe in paranoid conspiracies than to accept that their country would ignore them and let them rot. For Henderson, separatism in the form of black solidarity movements is antithetical to satisfying that latent need to belong.

In the excerpt from *Paved with Good Intentions* (1992), *Jared Taylor*, who is white and a journalist, offers a practical prescription for improving the situation of individual blacks and encouraging color-blindness. In other words, he wants to show how to achieve the goals delineated by Steele, Kennedy, and Sleeper. Like Steele, Taylor believes that blacks need to rise by their own efforts, rather than continue to try to get (racist) whites to give them a hand-out. He urges blacks to avoid provoking white guilt ("challenging," as Steele puts it), and to downplay black solidarity, which is divisive—racism in reverse. Like Steele and Kennedy, he deplores "group rewards," with blacks receiving help just because they're black. Like Kennedy, he argues that the rewards should result from achievement, not from race. And like Sleeper and Henderson, he insists that the idea of a united America should transcend the claims of any individual group.

Patricia Williams, who is black, is Professor of Law at Columbia University. "Pansy Quits" is an essay in *The Rooster's Egg* (1995). The first few paragraphs of Williams's essay are written in rather opaque academic prose (phrases like "normative imagining" and "fields of symbolic reference" may be hard for your students to grasp). The essay really begins in paragraph 6, and then rambles along as a sequence of anecdotes with appended reflections. Having established the fact that integration hasn't been achieved and "laissez-faire exclusion" prevails, she supports separatist demands for legislation to ensure that blacks will gain equity and recognition at work and at school. Unless respect is institutionally enforced, blacks will never get it.

Williams is more interested in the curricular effects of black separatism than the other writers. Citing the story of the black child asked to enact a slave at auction, Williams concludes that a politically correct curriculum is justified if it prevents such humiliating blunders. Unlike Steele and Kennedy, she finds that the stick ("challenging") will work while the carrot ("bargaining") clearly has not. Challenging may be more divisive but it also confers power. Williams ponders the equivalent of Henderson's cry: "We're still rejected!" But since it is impossible to achieve "assimilative 'neutrality,'" she concludes that it is false to acknowledge any "common heritage." Black solidarity, Williams argues, is trying to beat whites at their own game.

In "Visions of Black-White Friendship" (1995), *Benjamin DeMott*, who is white and a professor of English at Amherst, uses the traditional criticism to make his point, examining black/white relationships by analyzing extended excerpts from films. DeMott rejects Williams's last resort of institutionalizing change through separatism. He points out that, in films, blacks and whites resolve their conflicts by getting together and recognizing their common beliefs and "common humanity." In the context of these films, the imbalance of power derives from personal hostility, which can be dispelled by "listening attentively." But, DeMott points out, such a view of the relations between the races is a media construct and entirely unreal.

Tom Wicker, who is white, was for many years a journalist for *The New York Times*. In this excerpt from *Tragic Failure: Racial Integration in America* (1996), Wicker focuses on race as an economic, not a cultural problem. Unlike DeMott, Wicker is strictly practical. He is concerned, as Cinqué Henderson and William Julius Wilson (see p. 119) were, with the plight of the new underclass, who, above all, need jobs. Is the ghetto really redeemable? Wicker suggests a public works program, better education, and a new political party to represent the poor of all races. In fact, Wicker is the odd man out in this group as he is really concerned with an issue of class, not race.

According to *Gerald Early* (who is black and a professor of English and African and Afro-American Studies at Washington University), both DeMott and Wicker see blacks as (in Steele's language) "innocent" victims of white racism, whose willingness to depict themselves as victims prevents their material progress in society. In fact, Early says, the fault lies with neither whites nor blacks, but with America and what it represents. Early condemns Wicker's condescending and simplistic prescription of more programs to alleviate the misery of the underclass. He points out that blacks, like whites, tend to embrace their own romantic myth, and that the need to conform—to join the prevalent culture—is true for everyone, not just blacks. As for DeMott, Early notes that he is stating the obvious since most of the media is fantasy anyway (a point that DeMott himself does make) and the "racial friendship fantasy" is nothing new. For Early, the problem lies with American culture, which prefers to conceive of problems in terms of individual relationships, not political and economic issues.

The core of these ten readings—Paley's memoir provides a literary rendering of some of these issues—comprises Steele, Kennedy, Sleeper (with his letter-writing opponents), and Williams. Most of the main themes appear in these four, and it is perfectly possible to limit your discussion and your students' essays to these four sources. Or you could assign a topic that would require assimilating all nine. For example, how would each of the other authors interpret the problem that arises at the dinner party described by Steele? Or Williams's incident with the statue or with the confederate flag? As I suggested above, some students might want to explore the arguments for separatism. Or students could choose to seek out comparable sources on racial pride and obstacles to assimilation in the context of another racial or ethnic group. Or they could extrapolate some of these arguments for issues of gender, class, sexuality, or regionalism. They might take a historical approach, writing about the Civil Rights movement, or ebonics, or the Million Man March. They might analyze the arguments for and against affirmative action or the multicultural curriculum in light of the "victimization" arguments propounded by several of these authors. Or they could explore race as it is presented in and perceived through pop culture and the media today. (There are allusions to this in Williams, DeMott, and Early.) DeMott analyzes the universality of the original Cosby show. Why have Cosby's later shows been less successful? Is it the program or the audience? A survey, published in 1998, cites evidence that adult whites and blacks don't watch the same programs. Why not? Is there a difference in content or in style, or is it simply the attraction of seeing actors of one's own race? But the same survey indicates that teenagers don't distinguish between "white" and "black" programs; their common interests blur the barriers. Is that a healthy trend? Would Kennedy approve? Would Williams?

"Racial perceptions," then, is not at all a narrow topic. There are enough possibilities here for research to accommodate a variety of classes with disparate backgrounds and interests.